HAWAII
HANDBOOK

HAWAII
HANDBOOK

BY J.D. BISIGNANI

MOON
PUBLICATIONS INC.

HAWAII HANDBOOK

Published by
Moon Publications, Inc.
722 Wall Street
Chico, California 95928, USA

Please send all comments,
corrections, additions,
amendments, and critiques to:

**J.D. BISIGNANI
MOON PUBLICATIONS, INC.
722 WALL STREET
CHICO, CA 95928, USA**

PRINTING HISTORY
First Edition—September 1987
Second Edition—July 1989
Third Edition—February 1991
Reprinted—January 1993

Printed by
Colorcraft Ltd., Hong Kong

Library of Congress Cataloging in Publication Data

Bisignani, J.D., 1947–
   Hawaii Handbook/J.D. Bisignani—3rd ed.
   p.   cm.
   Includes bibliographical references and index.
   ISBN 0-918373-48-4
   1. Hawaii—Description and travel—1981—Guidebooks.
I. Title. Hawaii Handbook.
DU622.B55   1991   90–47108
919.96904'4—dc20   CIP

Printed in Hong Kong

Cover art *Kaupo Stream* courtesy of Richard Fields Studios, Wailea, Maui.

Although the author and publisher have made every effort to ensure that the information was correct at the time of going to press, the author and publisher do not assume and hereby disclaim any liability to any party for any loss or damage caused by errors, omissions, or any potential travel disruption due to labor or financial difficulty, whether such errors or omissions result from negligence, accident, or any other cause.

WARNING: Nothing in this book is intended to be used for navigation. Mariners are advised to consult official sailing directions and nautical charts.

KAUAI-BOUND TRAVELERS, PLEASE NOTE: At press time for this printing of *Hawaii Handbook*, Kauai was still recovering from the effects of Hurricane Iniki, which hit the island on September 11th, 1992. Many of the hotels were still closed or accommodating civil defense personnel. Hotels on Kauai are expected to reopen soon, but before arriving on Kauai, travelers are advised to call one of the following numbers for current information about the island's available services. The **Kauai Hotline**, tel. toll-free (800) 262-1400 or toll-free fax (800) 637-5762, will be in service through October 1993. Or call the **Hawaii Visitor's Bureau** on Kauai, tel. (808) 245-3971.

IS THIS BOOK OUT OF DATE?

In today's world, things change so rapidly that it's impossible for one person to keep up with everything happening in any one place. This is particularly true in Hawaii, where situations are always in flux. Travel books are like automobiles: they require fine tuning and frequent overhauls to keep in shape. Help us keep this book in shape! We require input from our readers so that we can continue to provide the best, most current information available. Please write to let us know about any inaccuracies, new information, or misleading suggestions. Although we try to make our maps as accurate as possible, errors do occur. If you have any suggestions for improvement or places that should be included, please let us know about them.

We especially appreciate letters from female travelers, visiting expatriates, local residents, and hikers and outdoor enthusiasts. We also like hearing from experts in the field as well as from local hotel owners and individuals wishing to accommodate visitors from abroad.

As you travel through the islands, keep notes in the margins of this book. Notes written on the spot are always more accurate than those put down on paper later. Send us your copy after your trip, and we'll send you a fresh one as a replacement. If you take a photograph during your trip which you feel could be included in future editions, please send it to us. Send only good slide duplicates or glossy black-and-white prints. Drawings and other artwork are also appreciated. If we use your photo or drawing, you'll be mentioned in the credits and receive a free copy of the book. Keep in mind, however, that the publisher cannot return any materials unless you include a self-addressed, stamped envelope. Moon Publications will own the rights on all material submitted. Address your letters to:

J.D. Bisignani
Moon Publications
722 Wall Street
Chico, CA 95928, U.S.A.

ACKNOWLEDGEMENTS

Writing the acknowledgements for a book is supercharged with energy. It's a time when you look forward, hopefully, to a bright future for your work, and a time when you reflect on all that has gone into producing it. Mostly it's a time to say thank you. Thank you for the grace necessary to carry out the task, and thank you to all the wonderful people whose efforts have helped so much along the way. To the following people, I offer my most sincere "thank you."

Firstly, to the Moon staff, professionals every one. As time has passed, and one book has followed another, they've become amazingly adept at their work, to the point where their mastery is a marvel to watch. Mark Morris and Taran March, my editors, whose eagle eyes inspect every page, oftentimes saving me from myself, and who make the book much more presentable after they're done buffing and polishing. Christa Jorgensen, who worked in the trenches transcribing over 3,000 pages of travel information. Asha Johnson, a true dynamo, who is typesetter, computer wiz, and "positive vibe person at large." Michelle Bonzey, who actually survived an entire two months as my secretary. Nancy Kennedy who fitted all the parts of the giant jigsaw puzzle matching text with maps, illustrations, photos, graphs, charts, and itsy-bitsy weirdnesses without losing her temper even one time. Hard working Mark Voss, who did the paste-up. Louise Foote, map-maker extraordinaire, and her helper, Alex "Louise Jr." Foote who did the original maps in this book. Bob Race, who's taken over the map department and who revised each and every map, and whom we all can thank for pointing us in the right direction. Rick Johnson, who knows "where in the world" all the Moon books are, and who is chiefly responsible for keeping them on the bookstore shelves. Donna Galassi, director of sales, her assistant Bette Wells, and publicist Virginia Michaels who keep the Moon rising with every new order that they bring in the door. Cindy Fahey, bookkeeper, who, with some amazing fancy dancing, robs Peter to pay Paul and somehow makes them like it. My illustrators, Diana Lasich Harper, Louise Foote, Sue Strangio Everett, Mary Ann Abel, Debra Fau, Brian Bardwell, and Robert Race, contributing photographers David Stanley, Howard Lindeman, and R.J. Schallenberger, and cover artist Richard Fields, whose talents grace this book.

California State University at Chico professors Bob Vivian, George Benson, Ed Myles, and Ellen Walker, who provided me with quality interns from their respective departments of Journalism, Tourism, Geography, and English. The following student interns worked in the trenches transcribing, inputting, designing charts and graphs, and generally infusing my surroundings with positive energy: Caroline Schoepp, Maureen Cole, Suzanne Booth, Lee Wilkinson, Sally Price, Elena Wilkinson, Bret Lampman, Rich Zimmerman, Craig Nelson, Pat Presley, Leslie Crouch, Monica Moore, Annie Hikido, and Janeen Thomas.

I would also like to thank the following people for their special help and consideration: Dr. Greg Leo, an adventurer and environmentalist who has done remarkable field research and provided me with invaluable information about the unique flora and fauna of Hawaii; Roger Rose and Elisa Johnston of the Bishop Museum; Lee Wild, Hawaiian Mission Houses Museum; Marilyn Nicholson, State Foundation of Culture and the Arts; the Hawaii Visitors Bureau; Chris Tajeda, Tropical Car Rental; Keoni Wagner, Hawaiian Airlines; Jim and John Costello; Dr. Terry and Nancy Carolan; Sally Proctor of Aston Hotels; Renee Cochran and Will Titus, Colony Resorts; Linda Darling-Mann, Coco Palms Resort; Glenn Masutani, Hawaiian Pacific Resorts; Barbara Brundage, Dive Hawaii; Donna Jung, Judy Veirck, and Patti of Patti Cook Associates. To all of you, my deepest *aloha*.

All photos are by the author unless otherwise noted.

To Sandy B.,
who from first glance
filled my life with aloha

Love, Dad

CONTENTS

LIST OF MAPS

LIST OF CHARTS

ABBREVIATIONS

Bldg.=Building
4WD=four-wheel drive
HNL=Honolulu
HVB=Hawaii Visitors
    Bureau
mph=miles per hour

NWR=National Wildlife
    Refuge
O/W=one way
p/d=per day
p/h=per hour
P.O.=post office

p/w=per week
Rt.=Route
rm.=room
R/T=round trip
TCs=traveler's checks
YH=youth hostel

MAP SYMBOLS

MAP LEGEND

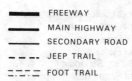 FREEWAY

MAIN HIGHWAY

SECONDARY ROAD

- - - JEEP TRAIL

·-·-·- FOOT TRAIL

(1) HIGHWAY NUMBER

WATER

+ MOUNTAIN

 LARGE TOWN OR CITY

O TOWN OR VILLAGE

o POINT OF INTEREST

● STATE OR BEACH PARK

HEIAU

▲ CAMPGROUND

All maps are oriented with north at the top of the map unless otherwise indicated.

INTRODUCTION

"No alien land in all the world
has any deep, strong charm for me,
but that one;
no other land could
so longingly and beseechingly
haunt my sleeping and waking,
through half a lifetime,
as that one has done.
Other things leave me,
but it abides."

—Mark Twain, c. 1889

The Hawaiian Islands

INTRODUCTION

The modern geological theory concerning the formation of the Hawaiian Islands is no less fanciful than the Polynesian legends sung about their origins. Science maintains that 30 million years ago Earth was little more than a mudball. While the great continents were being geologically tortured into their rudimentary shapes, the Hawaiian Islands were a mere ooze of bubbling magma 20,000 feet below the surface of the primordial sea. For millions of years this molten rock flowed up from fissures in the sea floor. Slowly, layer upon layer of lava was deposited until an island rose above the surface of the sea. The great weight then sealed the fissure, whose own colossal forces progressively crept in a southwesterly direction, then burst out again and again to build the chain. At the same time the entire Pacific plate was afloat on the giant sea of molten magma, and it slowly glided to the northwest carrying the newly formed islands with it.

In the beginning the spewing crack formed Kure and Midway islands in the extreme northwestern sector of the Hawaiian chain. Today, more than 130 islands, islets, and shoals make up the Hawaiian Islands, stretching 1,500 miles across an expanse of the North Pacific. Geologists maintain that the hotspot, now primarily under the Big Island, remains relatively stationary, and the 1,500-mile spread of the Hawaiian Archipelago is only due to a northwest drifting effect of about three to five inches per year. Still, with the center of activity under the Big Island, Mauna Loa and Kilauea volcanoes regularly add more land to the only state in the Union that is literally still growing. About 30 miles southeast of the Big Island is Loihi Seamount, waiting 3,000 feet below the waves. Frequent eruptions bring it closer and closer to the surface until one day it will emerge and become the newest Hawaiian Island.

FORCES OF NATURE

The Hawaiian Islands sit right in the middle of the North Pacific just a touch south of the Tropic of Cancer. They take up about as much room as a flower petal floating in a swimming pool. The sea makes life possible on the islands, and the Hawaiian sea is a mostly benign benefactor providing the basics: food, fresh water, and moderate climate. It is also responsible for an endless as-

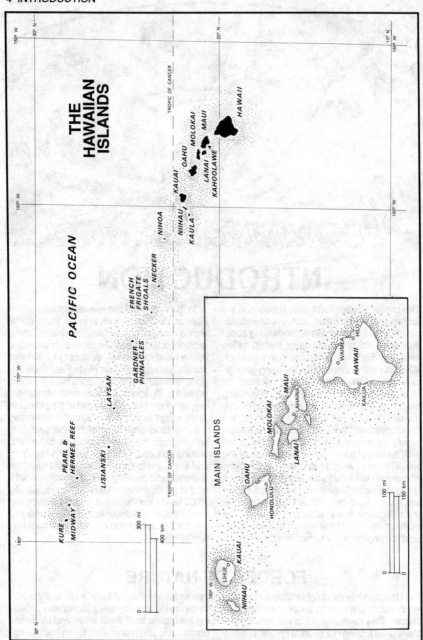

THE HAWAIIAN ISLANDS

PACIFIC OCEAN

KURE
MIDWAY

PEARL & HERMES REEF

LISIANSKI

LAYSAN

GARDNER PINNACLES

FRENCH FRIGATE SHOALS

NECKER

NIHOA

KAULA
NIIHAU
KAUAI
OAHU
MOLOKAI
LANAI
KAHOOLAWE
MAUI
HAWAII

TROPIC OF CANCER

30° N
20° N
10° N

150° W
160° W
170° W
180°

300 mi
400 km

MAIN ISLANDS

KAUAI
LIHUE
NIIHAU
OAHU
HONOLULU
MOLOKAI
LANAI
MAUI
LAHAINA
HAWAII
WAIMEA
HILO
KAILUA

100 mi
150 km

sortment of pleasure, romance, excitement, and a cultural link between Hawaii and its Polynesian counterparts. The Hawaiian Islands rise dramatically from the sea floor, not with a gradual sloping, but abruptly, like a temple pillar rising straight up from Neptune's kingdom.

Volcanism

The Hawaiian Islands are perfect examples of **shield volcanoes.** These are formed by a succession of gentle submarine eruptions which build an elongated dome much like a turtle shell. As the dome nears the surface of the sea, the eruptions combine with air and become extremely explosive due to the rapid temperature change and increased oxygen. Once above the surface they mellow again and steadily build upon themselves. As the island-mountain mushrooms, its weight seals off the spewing fissure below. Instead of forcing itself upward, the lava now finds less resistance by moving laterally. Eventually, the giant tube which carried lava to the top of the volcano sinks in upon itself and becomes a caldera. More eruptions occur periodically, but the lava is less dense and could be thought of as icing on a titanic cake. Then the relentless forces of wind and water take over to sculpt the raw lava into deep crevices and cuts that eventually become valleys. The smooth, once-single mountain is transformed into a miniature mountain range, while marinelife builds reefs around the islands, and the rising and falling of the surrounding seas during episodic ice ages combine with eroded soil to add or destroy coastal plains.

Lava

The Hawaiian Islands are huge mounds of cooled **basaltic lava** skirted by coral reefs, the skeletons of billions of polyps. The main components of Hawaiian lava are silica, iron oxide, magnesia, and lime. Lava flows in two distinct types for which the Hawaiian names have become universal geological terms: *a'a'* and *pa'hoehoe*. They are easily distinguished in appearance, but in chemical composition they are the same. Their differing appearance is due to the amount of gases contained in the flow when the lava hardens. *A'a'* lava is extremely rough and spiny, and will quickly tear up your shoes if you do much hiking over it. If you have the misfortune to fall down, you'll soon find out why it's

HAWAII VISITORS BUREAU

Lava flows on the Big Island regularly add more land to the state of Hawaii.

called *a'a'*. *Pahoehoe* is a billowy, ropy lava that looks like burned pancake batter. Not nearly as dense as *a'a'*, it can form some fantastic shapes and designs.

Lava actually forms molten rivers as it barrels down the steep slopes of the volcanoes. Sometimes these lava rivers crust over while the molten material on the inside continues to drain, until a lava tube is formed. These tubes characteristically have a domed roof and a flat floor and would make a very passable subway tunnel. Some can even measure more than 20 feet in diameter. One of the best examples is the Thurston Lava Tube at Volcanoes National Park on Hawaii. Other lava oddities are **peridots**

Engraving of Hawaii's unique pali by Barthelme Lauvergue, c. 1836.

(green gem-like stones) and clear **feldspar.** Gray lichens that cover older volcanic flows are known as **Hawaiian snow,** and volcanic glass that has been spun into hairlike strands is known as **Pele's hair,** while congealed lava droplets are known as **Pele's tears.**

Physical Features

Hawaii is the southernmost state in the Union and the most westerly except for a few far-flung islands in the Alaskan Aleutians. The Tropic of Cancer runs through the state, and it shares the same latitude as Mexico City, Havana, Calcutta, and Hong Kong. It's the fourth smallest state, larger than Rhode Island, Connecticut, and Delaware. All together its 132 shoals, reefs, islets, and islands constitute 6,450 square miles of land. The eight major islands of Hawaii account for over 99% of the total land area, and are home to 100% of the population (except for a manned military installation here and there). They cover about 400 miles of the Pacific, and from northwest to southeast include: Niihau (privately owned), Kauai, Oahu, Molokai, Maui, Lanai, Ka-

hoolawe (uninhabited), and Hawaii, the Big Island. The little-known Northwest Islands, less than one percent of the state's total land mass, are dotted through the North Pacific for over 1,100 miles running from Kure in the far north to Nihoa, about 100 miles off Kauai's north shore. The state has just over 1,000 miles of tidal shoreline, and ranges in elevation from Mauna Loa's 13,796-foot summit to Maro Reef, which is often awash.

Lakes And Rivers

Hawaii has very few natural lakes because of the porousness of the lava: water tends to seep into the ground rather than form ponds or lakes. However, *underground* deposits where water has been trapped between porous lava on top and dense subterranean layers below account for many freshwater springs throughout the islands; these are tapped as a primary source for irrigating sugar cane and pineapple. Hawaii's only large natural lakes happen to be on the private island of Niihau, and are therefore seldom seen by the outside world. **Lake Waiau,** at the 13,000-foot level on the Big Island's Mauna Kea, ranks among the highest lakes in the United States. Honolulu's **Salt Lake,** once Oahu's only natural inland body of water, was bulldozed for land reclamation. No extensive rivers are found in Hawaii except the **Waimea River** on Kauai; none are navigable except for a few miles of the Waimea. The uncountable "streams" and "rivulets" on all the main islands turn from trickles to torrents depending upon the rainfall. The greatest concern is to hikers who can find themselves threatened by a flash flood in a valley that was the height of hospitality only a few minutes before.

Tidal Waves

Tsunami, the Japanese word for "tidal wave", ranks up there in causing the worst of horror in human beings. A Hawaiian tsunami is actually a seismic sea wave generated by an earthquake that could easily have its origins thousands of miles away in South America or Alaska. Some waves have been clocked at speeds up to 500 miles per hour. The U.S. Geological Service has recently uncovered data that indicates a 1,000-foot-high wall of water crashed into the Hawaiian Islands about 100,000 years ago. They believe

LAND STATISTICS

All figures given are closest approximations

WHERE	SQ. MILES	COASTLINE	ELEVATION (FT.)
Island	6,450	1,052	
Hawaii	4,038	313	
Mauna Kea			13,796
Mauna Loa			13,677
Kilauea			4,093
Oahu	608	209	
Mt. Kaala			4,020
Tantalus			2,013
Diamond Head			760
Maui	729	149	
Haleakala			10,023
Puu Kukui			5,788
Kauai	553	110	
Kawaikini			5,243
Waialeale			5,148
Molokai	261	106	
Kamakou			4,970
Lanai	140	52	
Lanaihale			3,370
Niihau	73	50	
Paniau			1,281
Kahoolawe	45	36	
Lua Makika			1,477
Northwestern Islands (total)	32	25	
Nihoa			910
Lehua			702

a giant undersea landslide about 25 miles south of Lanai was the cause. The wave was about 15 miles wide and when it hit Lanai it stripped land more than 1,200 feet above sea level. It struck the other islands less severely, stripping land up to 800 feet above sea level. The worst tsunamis in modern times have both struck Hilo on the Big Island: the one in May 1960 claimed 61 lives. Maui also experienced a catastrophic wave that inundated the Hana coast on April 1, l946, taking lives and destroying much property. Other waves have inexplicably claimed no lives. The Big Island's Waipio Valley, for example, was a place of royalty that, according to ancient Hawaiian beliefs, was protected by the gods. A giant tsunami inundated Waipio in the 1940s,

catching hundreds of people in its watery grasp. Unbelievably not one person was hurt or injured. After the wave departed many people rushed to the valley floor to gather thousands of fish that were washed ashore. Without warning a second towering wave struck and grabbed the people again. Although giant trees and even boulders were washed out to sea not one person was harmed even the second time around. The safest place, besides high ground well away from beach areas, is out on the open ocean where even an enormous wave is perceived only as a large swell. A tidal wave is only dangerous when it is opposed by land. If you were to count up all the people in Hawaii that have been swept away by a tidal wave in the last 50 years it wouldn't come close to those killed on bicycles in a few Mainland cities in five years.

Earthquakes

Earthquakes are also a concern in Hawaii and offer a double threat because they cause tsunamis. If you ever feel a tremor and are close to a beach, evacuate as soon as possible. The Big Island, because of its active volcanoes, experiences hundreds of technical earthquakes every year, although 99% can only be felt on very delicate equipment. The last major quake occurred on the Big Island in late November 1975, reaching 7.2 on the Richter Scale and causing many millions of dollars worth of damage on the island's southern portion. The only loss of life was when a beach collapsed and two campers of a large party were drowned.

Hawaii has an elaborate warning system against natural disasters. You will notice loudspeakers high atop poles along many beaches and coastal areas; these warn of tsunamis, hurricanes, and earthquakes. They are tested at 11 a.m. on the first working day of each month. All island telephone books contain a Civil Defense warning and procedures section with which you should acquaint yourself. Note the maps showing which areas have been traditionally inundated by tsunamis and what procedures to follow in case an emergency occurs.

CLIMATE

Of the wide variety of reasons for visiting Hawaii, most people have at least one in common: the weather! Nowhere on the face of the Earth do human beings feel more physically comfortable than in Hawaii, and a happy body almost always means a happy mind and spirit too. Cooling trade winds, low humidity, high pressure, clear sunny days, negative ionization from the sea, and an almost total lack of industrial pollution combine to make Hawaii *the* most healthful spot in America.

"So Good" Weather

The ancient Hawaiians had words to describe climatic specifics such as rain, wind, fog, and even snow, but they didn't have a general word for weather. The reason is that the weather is just about the same throughout the year and depends more on where you are on any given island than on what season it is. The Hawaiians did distinguish between kau (summer, May-October) and hoo'ilo (winter, November-April), but this distinction included social, religious, and even navigational factors, far beyond a mere distinction of weather variations. The average daytime temperature throughout Hawaii is about 80°F (26° C), with the average winter (Jan.) day registering 78°, and the average summer (Aug.) day raising the thermometer only seven degrees to 85. Nighttime temperatures drop less than 10°. Altitude, however, does drop temperatures about three degrees for every 1,000 feet; if you intend to visit the mountain peaks of Haleakala, Mauna Loa, and Mauna Kea (all over 10,000 feet), expect the temperature to be at least 30° cooler than sea level. The lowest temperatures ever recorded in Hawaii were atop Haleakala in January 1961 when the mercury dropped well below freezing to a mere 11 degrees; the hottest day occurred in 1931 in the Puna District of the Big Island with a scorching (for Hawaii) 100°.

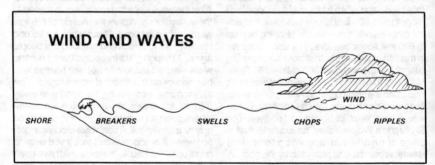

WIND AND WAVES

SHORE   BREAKERS   SWELLS   CHOPS   RIPPLES

WIND

The Trade Winds

One reason that the Hawaiian temperatures are both constant and moderate is because of the trade winds. These breezes are so prevailing that the northeast sides of the islands are always referred to as **windward,** regardless of where the wind happens to be blowing on any given day. You can count on the trades to be blowing on an average of 300 days per year: hardly missing a day during summer, and half the time in winter. They blow throughout the day, but are strong during the heat of the afternoon and weaken at night. Just when you need a cooling breeze, there they are, and when the temperature drops at night, it's as if someone turned down the giant fan. The trade winds are also a factor in keeping down the humidity. They will suddenly disappear, however, usually in winter, and might not resume for a few weeks. The Tropic of Cancer runs through the center of Hawaii, yet its famed oppressively hot and muggy weather is joyfully absent. Honolulu, on the same latitude as sweaty Hong Kong and Havana, has only a 50-60% daily humidity factor.

Kona Winds

Kona means "leeward" in Hawaiian, and when the trades stop blowing these southerly winds often take over. To anyone from Hawaii, "kona wind" is euphemistic for bad weather: bringing in hot sticky air. Luckily they are most common from October to April when they appear roughly half the time. The temperatures drop slightly during the winter so these hot winds are tolerable, and even useful for moderating the thermometer. In the summer they are awful, but luckily again they hardly ever blow during this season. A **kona storm** is another matter. These subtropical low-pressure storms develop west of the Hawaiian Islands, and as they move easterly draw winds up from the south. Usual only in winter, they can cause considerable damage to crops and real estate. There is no real pattern to kona storms—some years they come every few weeks while in other years they don't appear at all.

Rain

Hardly a day goes by where it isn't raining somewhere on *all* the main islands. If this amazes you, just consider each island to be a mini-continent:

it would virtually be the same as expecting no rain anywhere in North America on any given day. All islands have a windward (northeast, wet) and leeward (southwest, dry) side. It rains much more on the windward side, and much more often during winter than summer. (However, kona storms because they come from the south, hit the islands' leeward sides most often.) Another important rain factor are the mountains, which act like water magnets. Moist winds gather around them and eventually build rain clouds. The ancient Hawaiians used these clouds and the reflected green light on their underbellies to spot land from great distances. Precipitation mostly occurs at and below the 3,000-foot level; thus the upper slopes of taller mountains such as Haleakala are quite dry. The average annual rainfall in the seas surrounding Hawaii is only 25 inches, while a few miles inland around the windward slopes of mountains it can be 250 inches! A dramatic example of this phenomenon is seen by comparing Lahaina and Mt. Puu Kukui, only seven miles distant from each other on West Maui. Hot, arid Lahaina has an annual rainfall of only 17 inches; Puu Kukui can receive close to 40 *feet* of rainfall a year, rivaling Mt. Waialeale on Kauai as the "wettest spot on Earth." Another point to remember is where there's rain there's also an incredible explosion of colorful flowers like an overgrown natural hothouse. You'll find this effect mostly on the windward sides of the islands. Conversely, the best beach weather is on the leeward sides: Kaanapali, Waikiki, Kailua-Kona, Poipu. They all sit in the rain shadows of interior mountains, and if it happens to be raining at one leeward beach, just move down the road to the next. One more thing about Hawaiian rains—they aren't very nasty. Much of the time just a light drizzle, they hardly ever last all day. Mostly localized to a relatively small area, you can oftentimes spot them by looking for the rainbows. Rain should never spoil your outings in Hawaii. Just "hang loose, brah" and go to the sunshine.

Bad Weather

With all this talk of ideal weather it might seem like there isn't any bad. Read on. When a storm does hit an island it can be bleak and miserable. The worst storms are in the winter and often have the warped sense of humor to drop their heaviest rainfalls on areas that are normally quite dry. It's not infrequent for a storm to dump more than three inches of rain an hour; this can go as high as 10, making Hawaiian rainfalls some of the heaviest on Earth. Hawaii has also been hit with some walloping hurricanes in the last few decades. There haven't been many but they've been destructive. The vast majority of hurricanes originate far to the southeast off the coast of Mexico and Latin America. They mostly pass harmlessly south of Hawaii but some, swept along by kona winds, strike the islands. The most recent and destructive was Hurricane Iwa, which battered the islands in 1982. It had its greatest effect on Niihau, the Poipu Beach area of Kauai, and the leeward coast of Oahu. Iwa carried a destructive price tag of $200 million dollars.

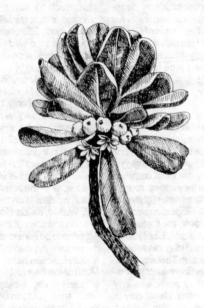

FLORA AND FAUNA

THE MYSTERY OF MIGRATION

Anyone who loves a mystery will be intrigued by the speculation about how plants and animals first came to Hawaii. Most people's idea of an island paradise includes swaying palms, dense mysterious jungles ablaze with wildflowers, and luscious fruits just waiting to be plucked. In fact, for millions of years these were raw and barren islands where no plants grew and no birds sang. Why? Because they are geological orphans that spontaneously popped up in the middle of the Pacific Ocean. The islands, more than 2,000 miles from any continental landfall, were therefore exempted from the normal ecological spread of plants and animals. Even the most tenacious travelers of the fauna and flora kingdom would be sorely tried in crossing the mighty Pacific. Those that made it by pure chance found a totally foreign ecosystem. They had to adapt or perish. The survivors evolved quickly, and many plants and birds became so specialized that they were not only limited to specific islands in the chain but to habitats that frequently encompassed a single isolated valley. It was as if after traveling so far, and finding a niche, they never budged again. Luckily, the soil of Hawaii was virgin and rich; the competition from other plants or animals was non-existent; and the climate was sufficiently varying and nearly perfect for most growing things.

The evolution of plants and animals on the isolated islands was astonishingly rapid. A tremendous change in environment, coupled with a limited gene pool, accelerated natural selection. For example, many plants lost their protective thorns and spines because there were no grazing animals or birds to destroy them. Preman Hawaii had no fruits, vegetables, palms, edible land animals, conifers, mangroves, or banyans. Flowers were relatively few. In a land where thousands of orchids now brighten every corner, there were only four native varieties, the least in any of the 50 states. Today, the preman plants and animals have the highest rate of extinction anywhere on Earth. By the beginning of this century, native plants below 1,500 feet were almost completely extinct or totally replaced by introduced species. The land and its living things have been greatly transformed by man and his agriculture. This inexorable process began when Hawaii was the domain of its original Polynesian settlers, then greatly accelerated when the land was inundated by Western man.

Plantlife Comes First

Much like the Polynesian settlers who followed, the drifters, castaways, and shanghaied of the plant and animal kingdom were first to reach Hawaii. Botanists say spores and seeds were carried aloft into the upper atmosphere by powerful winds, then made lucky landings on the islands. Some hardy seeds came with the tides and somehow managed to sprout and grow once they hit land. Others were carried on the feathers and feet of migratory birds, while some made the trip in birds' digestive tracts and were ignominiously deposited with their droppings. This chance seeding of Hawaii obviously took a very long time: scientists estimate one plant arrival and establishment occurred every 20,000-30,000 years. By latest count over 1,700 distinct species of endemic (only Hawaiian) and indigenous (other islands of Polynesia) plants had been catalogued throughout the island chain. It is reasonably certain all of these plants were introduced by only 250 original immigrants, and the 168 different Hawaiian ferns, for example, are the result of approximately 13 colonists. Most of the seeds and spores are believed to have come from Asia and Indonesia, and evidence of this spread can be seen in related plant species common to many Polynesian islands. Other endemic species such as the koa, which the Hawaiians put to great use in canoe building, have close relatives only in Australia. No other group of islands between Hawaii and Australia have such trees; the reason remains a mystery. Many plants and grasses came from North and South America and can be identified with common ancestors still there. Some species are so totally Hawaiian that relatives are found nowhere else on Earth. This last category either evolved so dramatically they can no longer be recognized, or their common ancestors have long been extinct from the original environment. An outstanding example in this category is the silversword (ahina ahina), found in numbers only atop Haleakala on Maui, with a few specimens extant on the volcanoes of the Big Island.

Insects Arrive

No one knows for sure, but it's highly probable the first animal arrivals in Hawaii were insects. Again the theory is most were blown there by ancient hurricanes or drifted there imbedded in floating logs and pieces of wood. Like the plants that preceded them, their success and rapid evolution were phenomenal. A pregnant female had to make the impossible journey, then happen upon a suitable medium in which to deposit her eggs. Here, at least, they would be free from predators and parasites with a good chance of developing to maturity. Again the gene pool was

highly restricted and the environment so foreign that amazing evolutionary changes occurred. Biologists believe only 150 original insect species are responsible for the more than 10,000 species that occur in Hawaii today. Of these 10,000, nearly 98% are found nowhere else on Earth. Many are restricted to only one island, and most are dependent on only one plant or fruit. For this reason, when Hawaiian plants become extinct, many insects disappear as well.

It's very probable there were no pests before humans arrived. The first Polynesians introduced flies, lice, and fleas. Westerners brought the indestructible cockroach, mosquito larvae in their ships' stores of water, termites, ants, and all the plant pests that could hitch a ride in the cuttings and fruits intended for planting. Today visitors often note the stringent agricultural controls at airports. Some complain about the inconvenience, but they should know that in the past 50 years over 700 new insect species have become established in Hawaii. Many are innocent enough, though others cause great problems for Hawaii's agriculture.

Land Snails

People have the tendency to ignore snails until they step on one, and then they only find them repulsive. But Hawaiian snails are some of the most remarkable and beautiful in the world. It's one thing to accept the possibility that a few insects or plant spores could have been driven to Hawaii by high winds or on birds' feet, given the

fact of their uncountable billions. But how did the snails get there? Snails, after all, aren't known for their nimbleness or speed. Most Hawaiian snails never make it much beyond the tree in which they're born. Yet over 1,000 snail varieties are found in Hawaii, and most are inexplicably found nowhere else. The Polynesians didn't bring them, sea water kills them, and it would have to be a mighty big bird that didn't notice one clinging to its foot. Biologists have puzzled over Hawaiian snails for years. One, J.T. Gulick, wrote in 1858, "These *achatinellinae* [tree snails] never came from Noah's ark." Tree snails are found on Oahu, Maui, Molokai, and Lanai, but not on Kauai. Kauai has its own land dwellers, and the Big Island has land snails that have moved into the trees. Like all the other endemic species, Hawaiian land snails now face extinction. Of the estimated 1,000 species existing when the Europeans came, 600 are now gone forever, and many others are threatened. Agriculture, the demise of native flora, and the introduction of new species add up to a bleak future for the snails.

Indigenous Land Animals

Before humans arrived, Hawaii had a paucity of higher forms of land animals. There were no amphibians, no reptiles, and except for a profusion of birdlife, insects, and snails, only two other animals were present: the **monk seal** and the **hoary bat,** both highly specialized mammals. The monk seal has close relatives in the Caribbean and Mediterranean, although the Caribbean relatives are now believed to be extinct, making the monk seal one of the only two tropical seals left on Earth. It's believed that the monk seal's ancestors entered the Pacific about 200,000 years ago when the Isthmus of Panama was submerged. When the land rose, no more seals arrived, and the monk seal became indigenous to Hawaii. The main habitat for the Hawaiian monk seal is the outer islands, from the French Frigate Atolls north to Kure Island, but infrequently a seal is spotted on the shores of one of the main islands. Though the seals' existence was known to the native Hawaiians who called them *ilio-holo-i-kauaua* ("dog running in the toughness"), they didn't seem to play much of a role in their folklore or ecosystem. Whalers and traders certainly knew of their existence, hunting them for food and

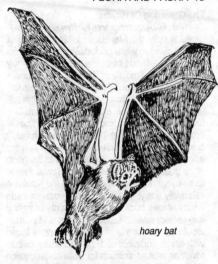

hoary bat

sometimes for skins. This kind of pressure almost wiped out the small seal population in the 18th century. Scientists were largely unaware of the monk seal until early this century. Finally, the seals were recognized as an endangered species and put under the protection of the Hawaiian Islands National Wildlife Refuge, where they remain in a touch-and-go battle against extinction. Today it's estimated that only 1,000 individuals are left.

The **hoary bat** *(pe'ape'a)* is a remarkable migratory animal that reached Hawaii from North and South America under its own power. The Hawaiian hoary bat no longer migrates, but its continental relatives still range far and wide. The Hawaiian bat has become somewhat smaller and reddish in color over the years, distinguishing it from its larger, darker brown cousins. The main population is on the Big Island, with a smaller breeding ground on Kauai. The bats normally live at altitudes below 4,000 feet, but some have been observed on Mauna Loa and Mauna Kea above 6,000 feet. Sometimes bats are spotted on the other main islands, but it remains unsure whether they inhabit the islands or simply fly there from their established colonies. The hoary bat is a solitary creature that spends the daylight hours hanging from the branches of trees. It doesn't live in caves like others of its species. Look for them over Hilo Bay on the Big Island at sunset.

The Greening Of Hawaii

The first *deliberate* migrants to Hawaii were Polynesians from the Marquesa Islands. Many of these voyages were undertaken when life on the native islands became intolerable. They were prompted mostly by defeat in war, or growing island populations that overtaxed the available food supply. Whatever the reasons, the migrations were deliberate and permanent. The first colonizers were known as "the land seekers" in the old Marquesan language—probably advance scouting parties who proved that the ancient chants which sung of a land to the north were true. Once they discovered Hawaii the return voyage to the southern homeland would be relatively easy. They had the favorable trade winds at their back, plus the certainty of sailing into familiar waters. Later both men and women would set out for the new land in canoes laden with seeds and plant cuttings necessary for survival, as well as animals for both consumption and sacrifice.

Not all the plants and animals came at once, but enough were brought to get started. The basic food plants included taro, banana, coconut, sugar cane, breadfruit, and yams. They also brought the paper mulberry from which tapa was made, and the *ti* plant necessary for cooking and making offerings at the *heiau*. Various gourds were grown to be used as bowls, containers, and even as helmets in a Hawaiian style of defensive armor. Arrowroot and turmeric were used in cooking and by the healing *kahuna* as medicines. *Awa* was brought by the high priests to be used in rituals; chewed, the resulting juice was spat into a bowl where it fermented and became a mind-altering intoxicant. Bamboo, the wonder material of natural man, was planted and used for countless purposes. The only domesticated animals taken to the new land were pigs, dogs, and chickens. Rats also made the journey but only as stowaways.

In the new land the Polynesians soon found native plants that they incorporated and put to good use. Some included: the *olona,* which made the best-known fiber cord anywhere in the world and later was eagerly accepted by sailing ships as new rigging and as a trade item; *koa,* an excellent hardwood used for the manufacture of highly prized calabashes and the hulls of magnificent seagoing canoes; *kukui* (candlenut), eaten as a tasty nut, strung to make leis, or burned as a source of light like a natural candle. For 1,000 years the distinct Hawaiian culture formed in relative isolation. When the first white men came they found a people that had become intimately entwined with their environment. The relationship between the Hawaiians and their *aina* (land) was spiritual, physical, and emotional: they were one.

BIRDLIFE

One of the great tragedies of natural history is the continuing demise of Hawaiian birdlife. Perhaps only 15 original species of birds accounted for the more than 70 native families that were established before the coming of man. Since the arrival of Capt. Cook in 1778, 23 species have become extinct, with 31 more in danger. Hawaii's endangered birds account for more than 50% of the birds listed in the U.S. Sport Fisheries and Wildlife's *Red Book* (which cites rare and endangered animals). More than four times as many birds have become extinct in Hawaii in the last 200 years than in all of North America. These figures unfortunately suggest that a full 40% of Hawaii's endemic birds no longer exist. Almost all of Oahu's native birds are gone and few indigenous Hawaiian birds can be found on any island below the 3,000-foot level.

Native birds have been reduced because of multiple factors. The original Polynesians actually helped to wipe out many species. They altered large areas for farming, and used fire to destroy patches of pristine forests. Also, bird feathers were highly prized for use in the making of lei, featherwork in capes and helmets, and for the large *kahili* fans that indicated rank among the *alii*. Introduced exotic birds and the new diseases they carried are another major reason, along with predation by the mongoose and rat—especially upon ground-nesting birds. However, the most damaging factor, by far, is the assault upon the native forests by agriculture and land developers. The vast majority of Hawaiian birds evolved into specialists. They lived in only one small area and ate only a very limited number of plants or insects, which once removed or altered soon killed the birds.

Preservation

Theodore Roosevelt established the Northwest Islands as a National Wildlife Reserve in the early 20th century, and efforts have continued since then to preserve Hawaii's unique avifauna. Many fine organizations are fighting the battle to preserve Hawaii's natural heritage, including: Hawaii Audubon Society, University of Hawaii, U.S. Fish and Wildlife Service, World Wildlife Fund, and Hawaii Department of Natural Resources. While visiting Hawaii make sure to obey all rules regarding the natural enviornment. Never disturb nesting birds or their habitat while hiking. Be careful with fire and never cut any living trees. If you spot an injured or dead bird do not pick it up but make sure to report it to the local office of the U.S. Fish and Wildlife Service. Only through a conscientious effort of all concerned does Hawaii's wildlife stand a chance of surviving.

Hawaiian Honeycreepers

A most amazing family of all the birds on the face of Earth is one known as *drepanidae,* or Hawaiian honeycreepers. There are more than 40 distinct types of honeycreepers, although many more were suspected to have become extinct before the arrival of Capt. Cook; they are all believed to have evolved from *a single* ancestral species. The honeycreepers have differing body types. Some look like finches, while others resemble warblers, thrushes, blackbirds, parrots, and even woodpeckers. Their bills range from long pointed honeysuckers to tough hooked nutcrackers. They are the most divergently evolved birds in the world. If Darwin, who studied the birds of the Galapagos Islands, had come to Hawaii, he would have found bird evolution that would make the Galapagos seem like child's play.

More Endangered Endemic Birds

Maui is the last home of the **crested honey-creeper** *(akohe'kohe).* It once lived on Molokai but no longer. Its habitat is on the windward slope of Haleakala from the 4,500 to the 6,500-foot level. A rather large bird, averaging about seven inches, it's predominantly black. Its throat and breast are tipped with gray feathers with a bright orange on its neck and underbelly. A distinctive fluff of feathers forms a crown. It primarily eats *ohia* flowers, and it's believed that the crown feathers gather pollen and help to propigate the *ohia.* The **Maui parrotbill** is another endangered bird found only on the

slopes of Haleakala above 5,000 feet. It has an olive-green back and yellow body. Its most distinctive feature is the parrot-like bill it uses to crack branches and pry out larvae. Two endangered waterbirds are the **Hawaiian stilt** *(ae'o)* and the **Hawaiian coot** *(alae ke'oke'o).* The stilt is a 16-inch, very thin wading bird. It is primarily black with a white belly. Its long stick-like legs are pink. It lives on Maui at Kanaha and Kealia ponds. The adults will pretend to be hurt, putting on an excellent performance of the "broken wing," in order to lure predators away from their nests. The Hawaiian coot is a web footed water bird that resembles a duck. Found on all the main islands but mostly on Maui and Kauai, its feathers are a dull gray with a white bill and tail feathers. It builds a large floating nest and vigorously defends its young. The **dark-rumped petrel** is slightly different than others in its family that are primarily marine birds. This petrel is found around the Visitors Center at Haleakala crater about an hour after dusk from May to October.

Hawaiian stilt

Survivors

The **amakihi** and **iiwi** are endemic birds not endangered at the moment. The *amakihi* is one of the most common native birds; yellowish green, it frequents the high branches of the *ohia, koa,* and sandalwood looking for insects, nectar, or fruit. It is less specialized than most other Hawaiian birds, the main reason for its continued existence. The *iiwi* is a bright red bird with a salmon-colored hooked bill. It's found only on Maui, Hawaii, and Kauai in the forests above 2,000 feet. It too feeds on a variety of insects and flowers. The *iiwi* is known for a harsh voice that sounds like a squeaking hinge, but is also capable of a melodious song. Other indigenous birds found throughout the islands are the wedge-tailed shearwater, white-tailed tropic bird, black noddy, American plover, and a large variety of escaped exotic birds.

The *Pueo*

This Hawaiian owl is found on all the main islands but most frequently on Maui, especially in Haleakala crater. The *pueo* is one of the oldest examples of an *amakua* (family-protecting spirits) in Hawaiian mythology, an especially benign and helpful guardian called upon in times of fear and war. Many introduced barn owls in Hawaii are easily distinguished from a *pueo* by their distinctive heart-shaped faces. The *pueo* is about 15 inches tall with a mixture of brown and white feathers. The eyes are large, round, and yellow; the legs are heavily feathered unlike a barn owl. *Pueo* chicks are a distinct yellow.

pueo

Nene

The *nene* or Hawaiian goose deserves special mention because it is Hawaii's state bird and is making a comeback from the edge of extinction. The *nene* is found only on the slopes of Mauna Loa and Mauna Kea on the Big Island, and in Haleakala Crater on Maui. It was extinct on Maui until a few birds were returned there in 1957. *Nenes* are raised at the Wildfowl Trust in Slimbridge, England, which placed the first birds at Haleakala, and at the Hawaiian Fish and Game Station at Pohakuloa on Hawaii. By the 1940s less than 50 birds lived in the wild. Now approximately 125 birds are on Haleakala and 500 on the Big Island. Although the birds can be raised successfully in captivity, their life in the wild is still in question. Some ornithologists even debate whether the *nene* ever originally lived on Maui. The *nene* is believed to be a descendant of the Canadian goose, which it resembles. Geese are migratory birds that form strong kinship ties, mating for life. It's speculated that a migrating goose became disabled and, along with its loyal mate, remained in Hawaii. The *nene* is smaller than its Canadian cousin, has lost a great deal of webbing in its feet, and is perfectly at home away from water, foraging and nesting on rugged and bleak lava flows. The *nene* is a perfect symbol for Hawaii. Let it be, and it will live.

WHALES

It is perhaps their tremendous size and graceful power, coupled with a dancer's delicacy of movement, that render whales so esthetically and emotionally captivating. In fact, many claim that they even feel a spirit-bond to these obviously intelligent mammals that at one time shared dry land with us and then re-evolved into creatures of the great seas. Experts often remark that whales exhibit behavior akin to the highest social virtues. For example, whales rely much more on learned behavior than on instinct, the sign of a highly evolved intelligence. Gentle mothers and protective "escort" males join to teach the young to survive. They display loyalty and bravery in times of distress, and innate gentleness, curiosity, and unmistakable joy for life. Their "songs," especially those of the humpbacks, fascinate scientists who consider them a form of communication unique in the animal kingdom. Hawaii, especially the shallow and warm waters around Maui, is home to migrating humpback whales every year from November to May. Here they winter, mate, give birth, nurture their young, and joyfully cavort until returning to food-rich northern waters in the spring. It's hoped that mankind can peacefully share the oceans with these magnificent giants forever. If humans can learn to love and spare the whale for the simple reason that they're beautiful creatures and deserve no less, then perhaps we will have taken the first step in saving ourselves.

Evolution And Socialization

Many millions of years ago, for an unknown reason, animals similar to cows were genetically triggered to leave the land and readapt to the sea. Known as cetaceans, this family contains about 80 species of whales, porpoises, and dolphins. Being mammals, cetaceans are warm blooded and maintain a body temperature of 96 degrees, only 2.5 degrees less than humans. After a gestation period of about one year, whales give birth to fully formed young, which usually enter the world tail first. The mother whale spins quickly to snap the umbilical cord, then places herself under the newborn and lifts it to the surface where it takes its first breath. A whale must be taught to swim or it would drown like any other air-breathing mammal. The baby whale, nourished by its mother's rich milk, becomes a member of an extended family **pod**, through which it's cared for, socialized, and protected by many "nannies."

Hawaiian Whales And Dolphins

The role of whales and dolphins in Hawaiian culture seems quite limited. Unlike fish, which were intimately known and individually named, only two generic names described them: *kohola,* ("whale"), and *palaoa* ("sperm whale"). Dolphins were all lumped together under one name, nai'a; Hawaiians were known to harvest dolphins on occasion by herding them onto a beach. Whale jewelry was worn by the *ali'i.* The most coveted ornament came from a sperm whale's tooth, called a *lei niho palaoa,* which was carved into one large curved pendant. Sperm whales have upwards of 50 teeth, ranging in size from 4 to 12 inches and weighing up to two pounds. One whale could provide numerous pendants. The most famous whale in Hawaiian waters is the humpback, (for more information see p. 364-365), but others often sighted include: the sperm, killer, false killer, pilot, Cuvier's, Blainsville, and pygmy killer. There are technically no porpoises, but dolphins include: common, bottlenose, spinner, white-sided, broad-and slender-beaked, rough-toothed, and pygmy killer. The *mahi mahi,* a favorite eating fish found on many menus, is commonly referred to as a dolphin, but is totally unrelated and is a true fish, not a cetacean.

Physiology

The best way to spot a whale is to look for its "spout," a misty spray forced from a *blowhole*—really the whale's nostrils that have moved from its snout to just behind its head. This arrange-

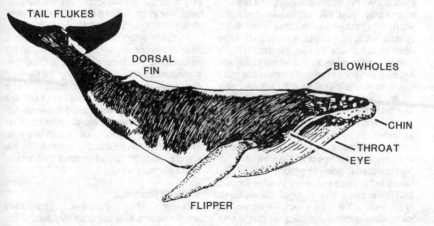

TAIL FLUKES

DORSAL FIN

BLOWHOLES

CHIN

THROAT

EYE

FLIPPER

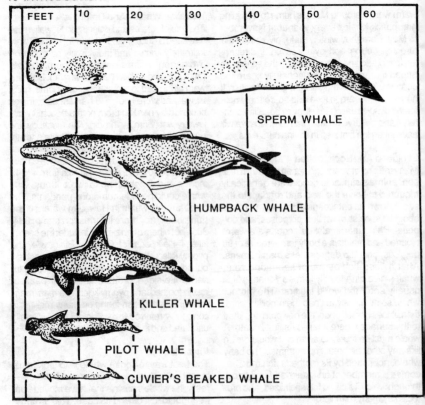

FEET | 10 | 20 | 30 | 40 | 50 | 60

SPERM WHALE

HUMPBACK WHALE

KILLER WHALE

PILOT WHALE

CUVIER'S BEAKED WHALE

ment allows the whale to surface and breathe more easily than if the nostrils remained in the snout. The spray from the spout is not water. Whales would no more take a lungful of water than would humans. Instead, the spout is highly compressed air heated by the whale's body and expelled with such force that it condenses into a fine mist. A whale's tail is called a *fluke;* unlike the vertical tail of fish, a whale's tail is horizontal. The fluke, a marvelous appendage for propelling the whale through the water, is a vestige of the pelvis. It's so powerful that a 40-ton humpback can lift itself completely out of the water with only three strokes of its fluke. Whales' flippers are used to guide it through the water. The bones in the flippers closely resemble those of the human arm and hand; small delicate bones at the ends of the flippers look like fingers and joints. On a humpback the flippers can be one-

third as long as the body, and supple enough to bend over its back, like a human reaching over the shoulder to scratch an itch.

A whale's eyes are functional but very small and not the primary sensors, since vision far beneath the sea is very limited. Instead, the whale has developed keen hearing; the ears are small holes about as big around as the lead of a pencil. There are no external ears because everything is streamlined to aid in swimming. The ears have protective wax plugs that build up over the years. Like the growth rings in a tree, the ear plugs can be counted to determine the age of a whale; its life span is about the same as that of a human being.

Types Of Whales

Although all whales, dolphins, and porpoises are cetaceans, they are arbitrarily divided according to length. Whales are all those animals longer than 30 feet; dolphins range from six to 30 feet; and porpoises are less than six feet long. There are basically two types of whales: **toothed,** which includes the sperm, killer and pilot whales, as well as porpoises and dolphins; and **baleen,** including the blue, minke, right, fin, and humpback. The humpback is also a **rorqual** whale, which means that it has a dorsal fin on its back. Toothed whales feed by capturing and tearing their prey with their teeth. The killer whale or orca is the best known of the toothed whales. With its distinctive black-and-white markings and propensity for aquabatics, it's a favorite at marine parks around the world. The orca is actually benign toward humans and hunts other cetaceans, oftentimes attacking larger whales in packs. A killer whale in the wild lives about four times as long as one in captivity, even if it is well cared for. A baleen whale eats by gliding through the water with its mouth open, sucking in marine plankton and tiny shrimplike-creatures called krill. The whale then expels the water and captures the food in row after row of a prickly, fingernail-like substance called baleen.

Whaling History

Man has undoubtedly known about whales for many thousands of years. A Minoan palace on the island of Crete depicts whales on a 5,000-year-old mural. The first whalers were probably Norwegians who used stone harpoon heads to capture their prey over 4,000 years ago. Eskimos have long engaged in whaling as a means of survival, and for centuries many peoples living along coastal waters have harpooned migrating whales that ventured close to shore. The Basques had a thriving medieval whaling industry in the 12th century centered in the Bay of Biscay, until they wiped out all the Biscayan right whales. The height of the classic whaling industry that inspired Melville's *Moby Dick* occurred from 1820 until 1860. The international capital perfectly situated in the center of the winter whaling grounds was Lahaina, Maui. At that time 900 sailing ships roamed the globe in search of whales. Of these, 700 were American, and they led the field by moving from coastal to pelagic whaling by bringing their tryworks (blubber pots) aboard ship.

Although the killing was great during these years, an unarguably romantic mystique is con-

nected with these "old salts." Also, every part of the whale was needed and used: blubber, meat, bone, teeth. Whale oil, the main product, was a superior lighting fuel and lubricant unmatched until petroleum came into general use toward the mid-19th century. Today, every single whale byproduct can be manufactured synthetically and there's absolutely no primary need to go on slaughtering whales.

During the great whaling days, the whales actually had a fighting chance. After all, they were hunted by men in wooden sailing ships that depended upon favorable winds. Once sighted by a sailor perched high in the rigging using a low-powered telescope, a small boat heaved off, and after desperate rowing and dangerous maneuvering the master harpooner threw his shaft by hand. When the whale was dead it took every able-bodied man to haul it in. Today, however, modern methods have wiped out every trace of daring and turned the hunt to technologically assisted slaughter. Low-flying aircraft radio the whales' location to huge factory-ships that track them with radar and sonar. Once the pod is spotted, super-swift launches tear into them, firing cannon-propelled harpoons with lethal exploding tips. The killer launches keep firing until every whale in the pod is dead, and the huge factory boat follows behind merely scooping up the lifeless carcasses and hauling them aboard with diesel winches.

Many pirate whalers still roam the seas. The worst example perpetrated by these vultures occurred in the Bahamas in 1971. A ship that ironically carried the name of *the* classic conservation group, the *Sierra,* succeeded in wiping out every single humpback whale that wintered in Bahamian waters. Since 1971 not one whale has been sighted in the Bahamas, and whalewatchers lament that they will never return.

A Glimmer Of Hope

A great awakening of consciousness around the world began in the mid-1960s, when people realized that we live in a finite world and our resources must be preserved and conserved. Governments could no longer ignore the mounting documentation that the great whales were disappearing at an alarming rate. Since then world opinion, coupled with benign but aggressive organizations such as Greenpeace, has labored to let the whales live. The **International Whaling Commission** (IWC), a voluntary group of 17 nations, was formed. It sets standards and passes quotas on the number and species of whales that can be killed. Over the last 18 years the blue, right, gray, bowhead, and humpback have become totally protected. Unfortunately, many great whales such as the sperm, sei, and fin are still hunted. Also, the IWC has no power of enforcement except for public opinion and possible voluntary economic sanction. It growls but it has no teeth; all it can really do is wag a finger. Fortunately, the U.S. and most other countries around the world no longer engage in whaling.

The Last Whalers

Unfortunately, two great offenders remain: Japan and the USSR. Recently the USSR has shown signs of heavily modifying its whaling industry. That leaves Japan. The Japanese technically stay within their quotas, but they hire and outfit other nationals to hunt whales for them. Their main argument is that whaling is a traditional industry upon which they rely for food and jobs. This is patently false. Hardly more than 100 years old, pelagic whaling is a new industry to the Japanese. Also, the Japanese have become meat eaters only within recent memory, and whales are meat, not fish. A vast amount of Japanese whale meat becomes pet food anyway, which is mainly exported. Besides, it's ludicrous for the third most powerful industrialized nation in the world to claim economic hardship if it had to curtail its whaling industry. Their economy is booming and there is little unemployment. The Japanese, extremely touchy on the subject, feel that they're being singled out for ridicule. The only course is to use reasonable persuasion and the affirmation that they have done no wrong or no different from many nations in the past, but that now the harvesting of the great whales must stop.

PLANTS, FLOWERS, AND TREES

Hawaii's indigenous and endemic plants, flowers, and trees are both fascinating and beautiful, but unfortunately, like everything else that was native, are quickly disappearing. The majority of flora found exotic by visitors was either introduced by the original Polynesians or later by white settlers. The Polynesians who colonized Hawaii brought foodstuffs including coconuts, bananas, taro, breadfruit, sweet potatoes, yams, and sugar cane. They also carried along gourds to use as containers, *awa* to make a basic intoxicant, and the *ti* plant to use for offerings or to string into hula skirts. Non-Hawaiian settlers over the years have brought mangoes, papaya, passionfruit, pineapples, and all the other tropical fruits and vegetables associated with the islands. Also, most of the flowers, including protea, plumeria, anthuriums, orchids, heliconia, ginger, and most hibiscus have come from every continent on Earth. Tropical America, Asia, Java, India, and China have all yielded their most beautiful and delicate blooms. Hawaii is blessed with state parks, gardens, undisturbed rainforests, private reserves, and commercial nurseries that offer an exhaustive botanical survey of Hawaii. The following is just a sampling of common, native, and introduced flora that adds the dazzling colors and exotic tastes to the landscape.

Native Trees

Koa and *ohia* are two native trees still seen on the main islands. Both have been greatly reduced by the foraging of introduced cattle and

ohia lehua

goats, and through logging and forest fires. The *koa,* a form of acacia, is Hawaii's finest native tree. It can grow to over 70 feet high and has a strong straight trunk which can measure more than 10 feet in circumference. The leaf-like foliage is sickle shaped, and produces an inconspicuous pale yellow flower. The *koa* does best in well-drained soil in deep forest areas, but scruffy specimens will grow on poorer soil. The Hawaiians used *koa* as the main log for their dugout canoes, and elaborate ceremonies were performed when a log was cut and dragged to a canoe shed. *Koa* wood was also preferred for paddles, spears, even surfboards. Today it is still considered an excellent furniture wood.

The *ohia* is a survivor, and therefore the most abundant of all the native Hawaiian trees. Coming in a variety of shapes and sizes, it grows as miniature trees in wet bogs or 100-foot giants on the cool dark slopes of higher elevations. This tree is often the first life in new lava flows. The *ohia* produces a tuft-like flower that resembles a natural pom-pom. Considered sacred to Pele, it's said that she would cause a rainstorm if you picked them without the proper prayers. The flowers are fashioned into a lei that resembles a feather boa. The strong hardwood was also used in canoe building, favored to make poi bowls and especially for temple images.

koa

Tropical Rainforests

When it comes to possessing a pure and diverse natural beauty, the U.S. is one of the finest pieces of real estate on Earth. As if purple mountain's majesty and fruited plains weren't enough, it even received a tiny living emerald of tropical rainforest. A tropical rainforest is where the Earth itself takes a breath and exhales pure sweet oxygen through its vibrant living green canopy. Located in the territories of Puerto Rico and the Virgin Islands, and in the state of Hawaii, these forests comprise only one half of one percent of the world's total, and they must be preserved. The U.S. Congress passed two bills in 1986 designed to protect the unique biological diversity of its tropical areas, but their onslaught and destruction has continued unabated. The lowland rainforests of Hawaii, populated mostly by native *ohia,* are being razed. Landowners slash, burn, and bulldoze them to create more land for cattle, agriculture, and most distressingly for wood chips to generate electricity! Introduced wild boar gouge the forest floor exposing sensitive roots, and leaving tiny fetid ponds where mosquito larvae thrive. Feral goats that roam the forests are "hoofed locusts" that strip all vegetation within reach.

Maui's Nature Conservancy Preserve in Waikamoi has managed to fence in a speck of this forest keeping it safe from these animals for the time being. Almost half of the birds classified in the U.S. as endangered are from Hawaii, and almost all of these make their home in the rainforests. For example, Maui's rainforests have yielded the *poouli,* a new species of bird discovered only in 1974. Another forest survey in 1981 rediscovered the *Bishop's o'o,* a bird thought to be extinct at the turn of the century. We can only lament the passing of the rainforests that have already fallen to ignorance, but if this ill-fated destruction continues on the global level, we will be lamenting our own passing. We must nurture the rainforests that remain, and with simple enlightenment, let them be.

NOTE: See "Flora and Fauna" in the Introductions to the various travel chapters for plants and animals specifically confined to, or more common on, those particular islands.

HISTORY

THE ROAD FROM TAHITI

Until the 1820s, when New England missionaries began a phonetic rendering of the Hawaiian language, the past was kept vividly alive only by the sonorous voices of special *kahuna* who chanted the sacred *mele*. The chants were beautiful flowing word pictures that captured the essence of every aspect of life. These *mele* praised the land *(mele aina),* royalty *(mele ali'i),* and life's tender aspects *(mele aloha).* Chants were dedicated to friendship, hardship, and to favorite children. Entire villages sometimes joined together to compose a *mele*—every word was chosen carefully, and the wise old kapuna would decide if the words were lucky or unlucky. Some mele were bawdy or funny on the surface, but contained secret meanings, often with biting sarcasm, that ridiculed an inept or cruel leader. But the most important chants took the listeners back into the dim past, even before people lived in Hawaii. From these genealogies *(ko'ihonua),* the *ali'i* derived the right to rule since these chants went back to the gods Wakea and Papa, from whom the *ali'i* were directly descended.

The Kumulipo

The great genealogies, finally compiled in the late 1800s by order of King Kalakaua, were col-lectively known as *The Kumulipo, A Hawaiian Creation Chant,* basically a Polynesian account of Genesis. Other chants related to the beginning of this world, but *The Kumulipo* sums it all up and is generally considered the best. The chant relates that after the beginning of time, there is a period of darkness. The darkness, however, mysteriously brims with spontaneous life; during this period plants and animals are born, as well as Kumulipo, the man, and Po'ele, the woman. In the eighth chant darkness gives way to light and the gods descend to Earth. Wakea is "the sky father" and Papa is "the earth mother," whose union gives birth to the islands of Hawaii. First born is Hawaii, followed by Maui, then Kahoolawe. Apparently, Papa becomes bushed after three consecutive births and decides to vacation in Tahiti. While Papa is away recovering from post-partum depression and working on her tan, Wakea gets lonely, and takes Kaula as his second wife; she bears him the island-child of Lanai. Not fully cheered up, but getting the hang of it, Wakea takes a third wife, Hina, who promptly bears the island of Molokai. Meanwhile, Papa gets wind of these shenanigans, returns from Polynesia, and retaliates by taking up with Lua, a young and virile god, and soon gives birth to the island of Oahu. Papa and Wakea finally decide that they really are meant for each other and reconcile to conceive Kauai, Niihau, Kaula, and Nihoa. These two progenitors are the source to which all the *ali'i* ultimately traced their lineage, and from which they derived their god-ordained power to rule.

Basically, there are two major genealogical families: the **Nana'ulu,** who became the royal *ali'i* of Oahu and Kauai; and the **Ulu,** who provided the royalty of Maui and Hawaii. The best sources of information on Hawaiian myth and legend are Martha Beckwith's *Hawaiian Mythology,* and the monumental three-volume opus *An Account of the Polynesian Race* compiled by Abraham Fornander from 1878 to 1885. Fornander, after settling in Hawaii, married an *ali'i* from Molokai and had an illustrious career as a newspaper man, Maui circuit judge, and finally Supreme Court justice. For years Fornander sent scribes to every corner of the kingdom to listen to the elder *kupuna.* They returned with the first-hand accounts and he dutifully recorded them.

Polynesians

Since prehistory, Polynesians have been seafaring people whose origins cannot be completely traced. They seem to have come from Southeast Asia mostly through the gateway of Indonesia, and their racial strain pulls features from all three dominant races: white, negro, and mongoloid. They learned to navigate

The Polynesians, attuned to every nuance in their environment, noticed that a migratory land bird called the golden plover arrived from the north every year. They reasoned that since the plover was not a seabird, there must be land to the north.

on tame narrow waterways along Indonesia and New Guinea, then fanned out eastward into the great Pacific. They sailed northeast to the low islands of Micronesia and southwest to Fiji, the New Hebrides (now called Vanuatu), and New Caledonia. Fiji is regarded as the "cradle of Polynesian culture"; carbon dating places humans there as early as 3,500 B.C. Many races blended on Fiji, until finally the Negroid became dominant and the Polynesians moved on. Wandering, they discovered and settled Samoa and Tonga, then ranged far east to populate Tahiti, Easter Island, and the Marquesas. Ultimately, they became the masters of the "Polynesian Triangle," which measures more than 5,000 miles on each leg, stretching across both the North and South Pacific studded with islands. The great Maori kingdom of New Zealand is the southern apex of the triangle, with Easter Island marking the point farthest east; Hawaii, farthest north, was the last to be settled.

Migrations And Explorations

Ancient legends common throughout the South Pacific speak of a great Polynesian culture that existed on the island of Raiatea about 150 miles north of Tahiti. Here a powerful priesthood held sway in an enormous *heiau* in the Opoa district called Toputapuatea. Kings from throughout Polynesia came here to worship. Human sacrifice was common, as it was believed that the essence of the spirit could be utilized and controlled in this life; therefore the mana of Toputapuatea was great. Defeated warriors and commoners were used as living rollers to drag canoes up onto the beach, while corpses were dismembered and hung in trees. The power of the priests of Opoa lasted for many generations, evoking trembling fear in even the bravest warrior just by the mention of their name. Finally, their power waned and Polynesians lost their centralized culture, but the constant coming and going from Raiatea for centuries sharpened the Polynesians' already excellent sailing skills and convinced them that the world was vast and unlimited opportunities existed to better their lot.

Now explorers, many left to look for the "heavenly homeland to the north." Samoans called it *Savai'i;* Tongans *Hawai;* Rarotongans *Avaiki;* and Society Islanders *Havai'i.* Others abandoned the small islands throughout Polynesia where population pressures exceeded the limits of natural resources, prompting famine. Furthermore, Polynesians were also very warlike among themselves; power struggles between members of a ruling family were common, as were marauders from other islands. So, driven by hunger or warfare, countless refugee Polynesians headed north. Joining them were a few who undoubtedly went for the purely human reason of wanderlust.

The Great Navigators

No one knows exactly when the first Polynesians arrived in Hawaii, but the great *deliberate migrations* from the southern islands seem to have taken place between A.D. 500 and 800, though anthropologists keep pushing the date backward in time as new evidence becomes available. Even before that, however, it's reasonable to assume that the first people to set foot on Hawaii were probably fishermen, or perhaps defeated warriors whose canoes were blown hopelessly northward into unfamiliar waters arriving by a combination of extraordinary good luck and an uncanny ability to sail and navigate by the seat of their pants. With no instruments they could navigate, using the sun by day and the moon and rising stars by night. They could feel the water and determine direction by swells, tides, and currents. The movements of fish and cloud formations were also utilized to give direction. Since their arrival was probably an accident, they were unprepared to settle on the fertile but barren lands, having no stock animals, plant cuttings, or women. Forced to return southward, undoubtedly many lost their lives at sea, but a few wild-eyed stragglers must have made it home where they told tales of a paradise to the north where land was plentiful and the sea bounteous. This is affirmed by ancient navigational chants from Tahiti, Moorea, and Bora Bora, which passing from father to son revealed how to follow the stars to the "heavenly homeland in the north." Possibly a few migrations followed, but it's known that for centuries there was no real reason for a mass exodus, so the chants alone remained and eventually became shadowy legend.

From Where They Came

It's generally agreed that the first planned migrations were from the violent cannibal islands that Spanish explorers called the Marquesas, 11 is-

The canoe hull was a log shaped by masterly stone adz work. The sides were planks that were drilled and sewn together with fiber cord.

lands in extreme eastern Polynesia. The islands themselves are harsh and inhospitable, breeding a toughness into these people which enabled them to withstand the hardships of long unsure ocean voyages and years of resettlement. Marquesans were a fiercely independent people whose chiefs could rise from the ranks because of bravery or intelligence. They must have also been a savage-looking lot. Both men and women tatooed themselves in complex blue patterns from head to foot. The warriors carried massive, intricately designed ironwood war clubs and wore carved whale teeth in slits in their earlobes which became stretched to the shoulders. They shaved the sides of their heads with sharks' teeth, tied their hair in two topknots that looked like horns, and rubbed their heavily muscled and tattooed bodies with scented coconut oils. Their cults worshiped mummified ancestors; the bodies of warriors of defeated neighboring tribes were consumed. They were masters at building great double-hulled canoes launched from huge canoe sheds. Two hulls were fastened together to form a catamaran, and a hut in the center provided shelter in bad weather. The average voyaging canoe was 60-80 feet long and could comfortably hold an extended family of about 30 people. These small family bands carried all the staples they would need in the new lands.

The New Lands

For five centuries the Marquesans settled and lived peacefully on the new land, as if Hawaii's aloha spirit overcame most of their fierceness. The tribes coexisted in relative harmony, especially since there was no competition for land. Cannibalism died out. There was much coming and going between Hawaii and Polynesia and new people came to settle for hundreds of years. Then, it appears that in the 12th century a deliberate exodus of warlike Tahitians arrived and subjugated the settled islanders. They came to conquer. This incursion had a terrific significance for the Hawaiian religious and social system. Oral tradition relates that a Tahitian priest, Paao, found the mana of the Hawaiian chiefs to be low, signifying that their gods were weak. Paao built a *heiau* at Wahaula on the Big Island, then introduced the warlike god Ku and the rigid *kapu* system through which the new rulers became dominant. Voyages between Tahiti and Hawaii continued for about 100 years and Tahitian customs, legends, and language became the Hawaiian way of life.

Then suddenly, for no recorded or apparent reason, the voyages discontinued and Hawaii returned to total isolation. It remained forgotten for almost 500 years until the indomitable English seaman, Capt. James Cook, sighted Oahu on January 18, 1778 and stepped ashore at Waimea on Kauai two days later. At that time Hawaii's isolation was so complete that even the Polynesians had forgotten about it. On an earlier voyage, Tupaia, a high priest from Raiatea, had accompanied Capt. Cook as he sailed throughout Polynesia. Tupaia's knowledge of existing archipelagos throughout the South Pacific was vast, which he demonstrated by naming over 130 islands and drawing a map that included the Tonga group, the Cook Islands, the Marquesas, even tiny Pitcairn, a rock in far eastern Polynesia, where the mutinous crew of The *Bounty* found solace. In mentioning the Marquesas Tupaia said, *"he ma'a te ka'ata,"* which equals "food is man" or simply "cannibals!" But remarkably absent from Tupaia's vast knowledge was the existence of Easter Island, New Zealand, and Hawaii. The next waves of people to Hawaii would be white men, and the Hawaiian world would be changed quickly and forever.

THE WORLD DISCOVERS HAWAII

The late 18th century was an extraordinary time in Hawaiian history. Monumental changes seemed to happen all at once. First, Capt. James Cook, a Yorkshire farm boy, fulfilling his destiny

as the all-time greatest Pacific explorer, found Hawaii for the rest of the world. For better or worse, it could no longer be an isolated Polynesian homeland. For the first time in Hawaiian history, a charismatic leader named Kamehameha emerged, and after a long civil war united all the islands into one centralized kingdom. The death of Capt. Cook in Hawaii marked the beginning of a long series of tragic misunderstandings between white man and native. When Kamehameha died, the old religious system of *kapu* came to an end, leaving the Hawaiians in a spiritual vortex. Many takers arrived to fill the void: missionaries after souls, whalers after their prey and a good time, traders and planters after profits and a home. The islands were opened and devoured like ripe fruit, as powerful nations including Russia, Great Britain, France, and the United States yearned to bring this strategic Pacific jewel under their own influence.

The 19th century brought the demise of the Hawaiian people as a dominant political force in their own land and with it the end of Hawaii as a sovereign monarchy. An almost bloodless yet bitter military coup followed by a brief period of a Hawaiian Republic ended in annexation by the United States. As the U.S. became completely entrenched politically and militarily, a new social and economic order was founded on the plantation system. Amazingly rapid population growth occurred with the importation of plantation workers from Asia and Europe, which yielded a unique cosmopolitan blend of races like nowhere else on Earth. By the dawning of the 20th century, the face of old Hawaii had been altered forever; the "sacred homeland in the north" was hurled into the modern age. The attack on Pearl Harbor saw a tremendous loss of life and brought Hawaii closer to the U.S. by a baptism of blood. Finally, on August 21, 1959, after 59 years as a "territory," Hawaii officially became the 50th state of the Union.

Captain Cook Sights Hawaii

In 1776 Captain James Cook set sail for the Pacific from Plymouth, England, on his third and final expedition into this still vastly unexplored region of the world. On a fruitless quest for the fabled Northwest Passage across the North American continent, he sailed down the coast of Africa, rounded the Cape of Good Hope, crossed the Indian Ocean, and traveled past

Capt. James Cook

New Zealand, Tasmania, the Friendly Islands (where an unsuccessful plot was hatched by the *friendly* natives to murder him), and finally spotted Hawaii. On January 18, 1778 Capt. Cook's 100-foot flagship HMS *Resolution* and its 90-foot companion HMS *Discovery* sighted Oahu. Two days later, they sighted Kauai and went ashore at the village of Waimea on January 20, 1778. Though anxious to get on with his mission, Cook decided to make a quick sortie to investigate this new land and reprovision his ships. He did, however, take time to remark in his diary about the close resemblance of these new-found people to others he had encountered as far south as New Zealand, and marveled at their widespread habitation across the Pacific.

The first trade was some brass medals for a mackerel. Cook also stated that he never before met natives so astonished by a ship, and that they had an amazing fascination for iron which they called toe, Hawaiian for "adz." There is even some conjecture that a Spanish ship under one Capt. Gaetano had landed in Hawaii as early as the 16th century, trading a few scraps of iron that the Hawaiians valued even more than the Europeans valued gold. It was also noted that the Hawaiian women gave themselves freely to the sailors with the apparent good wishes of the island men. This was actually a ploy by the *kahuna*

to test if the new whitecomers were gods or men—gods didn't need women. These sailors proved immediately mortal. Cook, who was also a physician, tried valiantly to keep the 66 men (out of 112) who had measurable cases of V.D. away from the women. The task proved impossible as women literally swarmed the ships; when Cook returned less than a year later, it was logged that signs of V.D. were already apparent on some natives' faces.

Cook was impressed with their swimming and with their well-bred manners. They had happy dispositions and sticky fingers, stealing any object made of metal, especially nails. The first item stolen was a butcher's cleaver. An unidentified native grabbed it, plunged overboard, swam to shore, and waved his booty in triumph. The Hawaiians didn't seem to care for beads and were not at all impressed with a mirror. Cook provisioned his ships by trading chisels for hogs, while common sailors gleefully traded nails for sex. Landing parties were sent inland to fill casks with fresh water. On one such excursion a Mr. Williamson, who was eventually drummed out of the Royal Navy for cowardice, unnecessarily shot and killed a native. After a brief stop on Niihau, the ships sailed away, but both groups were indelibly impressed with the memory of each other.

Cook Returns

Almost a year later, when winter weather forced Cook to return from the coast of Alaska, his discovery began to take on far-reaching significance. Cook had named Hawaii the **Sandwich Islands**, in honor of one of his patrons, John Montague, the Earl of Sandwich. On this return voyage, he spotted Maui on November 26, 1778. After eight weeks of seeking a suitable harbor it was bypassed, but not before the coastline was duly drawn by Lt. William Bligh, one of Cook's finest and most trusted officers. (Bligh would find his own drama almost 10 years later as commander of the infamous HMS *Bounty*.) The *Discovery* and *Resolution* finally found a safe anchorage at Kealakekua on the Kona Coast of the Big Island. It is very lucky for history that on board was Mr. Anderson, ship's chronicler, who left a handwritten record of the strange and tragic events that followed. Even more important were the drawings of John Webber, ship's artist, who rendered invaluable impressions in superb drawings and etchings. Other noteworthy men aboard were George Vancouver, who would himself lead the first British return to Hawaii after Cook's death and introduce many fruits, vegetables, cattle, sheep, and goats, and James Burney, who would become a longstanding leading authority on the Pacific.

The Great God Lono Returns

By all accounts Cook was a humane and just captain, greatly admired by his men. Unlike many other supremacists of that time, he was known to have a respectful attitude to any people he discovered, treating them as equals and recognizing the significance of their cultures. Not known as a violent man, he would use his superior weapons against natives only in an absolute case of self defense. His hardened crew had been at sea facing untold hardship for almost three years; returning to Hawaii was truly like re-entering paradise.

A strange series of coincidences sailed with Cook into Kealakekua Bay on January 16, 1779. It was *makahiki* time, a period of rejoicing and festivity dedicated to the fertility god of the earth, Lono. Normal *kapu* days were suspended, and willing partners freely enjoyed each other sexually, along with dancing, feasting, and the islands' version of Olympic games. It was long held in Hawaiian legend that the great god Lono would return to Earth. Lono's image was a small wooden figure perched on a tall mast-like crossbeam; hanging from the crossbeam were

long white sheets of tapa. Who else could Cook be but Lono, and what else could his ships with their masts and white sails be but his sacred floating *heiau?* This explained the Hawaiians' previous fascination with his ships, but to add to the remarkable coincidence, Kealakekua Harbor happened to be considered Lono's private sacred harbor. Natives from throughout the land prostrated themselves and paid homage to the returning god. Cook was taken ashore and brought to Lono's sacred temple where he was afforded the highest respect. The ships badly needed fresh supplies and the Hawaiians readily gave all they had, stretching their own provisions to the limit. To the sailors delight this included full measures of the aloha spirit.

The Fatal Misunderstandings

After an uproarious welcome and generous hospitality for over a month, it became obvious that the newcomers were beginning to overstay their welcome. During the interim a seaman named William Watman died, convincing the Hawaiians that the *haole* were indeed mortals, not gods. Watman was buried at Hikiau Heiau where a plaque commemorates the event to this day. Incidents of petty theft began to increase dramatically. The lesser chiefs indicated it was time to leave by "rubbing the Englishmen's bellies." Inadvertently many *kapu* were broken by the Englishmen, and once-friendly relations became strained. Finally, the ships sailed away on February 4, 1779. After plying terrible seas for only a week, the foremast on the *Resolution* was badly

"The Death of Captain Cook" by John Webber, ship's artist on Cook's third Pacific exploration, c. 1779

damaged, and Cook sailed back into Kealekekua Bay dragging the mast ashore on February 13th. The natives, now totally hostile, hurled rocks at the marines. Orders were given to load muskets with ball; firearms had previously only been loaded with shot and a light charge. Confrontations increased when some Hawaiians stole a small boat and marines set after them capturing the fleeing canoe, which held an *ali'i* named Palea. The Englishmen treated him roughly; to the Hawaiians horror, they even smacked him on the head with a paddle. The Hawaiians then furiously attacked the marines who abandoned the small boat.

Cook Goes Down

Next the Hawaiians stole a small cutter from the *Discovery* that had been moored to a buoy and partially sunk to protect it from the sun. For the first time Capt. Cook became furious. He ordered Capt. Clerk of the *Discovery* to sail to the southeast end of the bay, and to stop any canoe trying to leave Kealekakua. Cook then made a fatal error in judgment. He decided to take nine armed marines ashore in an attempt to convince the venerable King Kalaniopuu to accompany him back aboard ship where he would hold him for ransom in exchange for the cutter. The old king agreed, but his wife prevailed upon him not to trust the *haole*. Kalaniopuu sat down on the beach to think while the tension steadily grew. Meanwhile, a group of marines fired upon a canoe trying to leave the bay and a lesser chief, Nookemai, was killed. The crowd around Cook and his men reached an estimated 20,000, and warriors outraged by the killing of the chief armed themselves with clubs and protective straw-mat armor. One bold warrior advanced on Cook and struck him with his *pahoa*. In retaliation Cook drew a tiny pistol lightly loaded with shot and fired at the warrior. His bullets spent themselves on the straw armor and harmlessly fell to the ground. The Hawaiians went wild. Lt. Molesworth Phillips, in charge of the nine marines, began a withering fire; Cook himself slew two natives. Overpowered by shear numbers, the marines headed for boats standing offshore, while Lt. Phillips lay wounded. It is believed that Capt. Cook, the greatest seaman ever to enter the Pacific, stood helplessly in knee-deep water instead of making for the boats because he could not swim! Hopelessly surrounded, he was knocked on the head, then countless warriors passed a knife around and hacked and mutilated his lifeless body. A sad Lt. King lamented in his diary, "Thus fell our great and excellent commander."

The Final Chapter

Captain Clerk, now in charge, settled his men and prevailed upon the Hawaiians to return Cook's body. On the morning of February 16th a grisly piece of charred meat was brought aboard: the Hawaiians, according to their custom, had afforded Cook the highest honor by baking his body in an underground oven to remove the flesh from the bones. On the 17th a group of Hawaiians in a canoe taunted the marines by brandishing Cook's hat. The Englishmen, strained to the limit and thinking that Cook was being desecrated, finally broke. Foaming with blood-lust, they leveled their cannon and muskets on shore and shot anything that moved. It is believed that Kamehameha the Great was wounded in this flurry, along with four *ali'i* and 25 *makaainana* (commoners) killed. Finally on February 21, 1779, the bones of Capt. James Cook's hands, skull, arms, and legs were returned and tearfully buried at sea. A common seaman, one Mr. Zimmerman, summed up the feelings of all who sailed under Cook when he wrote, ". . . he was our leading star." The English sailed next morning after dropping off their Hawaiian girlfriends who were still aboard.

Captain Clerk, in bad health, carried on with the fruitless search for the Northwest Passage. He died and was buried at the Siberian village of Petropavlovisk. England was at war with upstart colonists in America, so the return of the expedition warranted little fanfare. The *Resolution* was converted into an army transport to fight the pesky Americans; the once proud *Discovery* was reduced to a convict ship ferrying inmates to Botany Bay, Australia. Mrs. Cook, the great captain's steadfast and chaste wife, lived to the age of 93, surviving all her children. She was given a stipend of 200 pounds per year, and finished her days surrounded by Cook's mementos, observing the anniversary of his death to the very end by fasting and reading from the Bible.

THE UNIFICATION OF OLD HAWAII

Hawaii was already in a state of political turmoil and civil war when Cook arrived. In the 1780s the islands were roughly divided into three kingdoms: venerable Kalaniopuu ruled Hawaii and the Hana district of Maui; wily and ruthless warrior-king Kahekili ruled Maui, Kahoolawe, Lanai, and later Oahu; and Kaeo, Kahekili's brother, ruled Kauai. War ravaged the land until a remarkable chief, Kamehameha, rose and subjugated all the islands under one rule. Kamehameha initiated a dynasty that would last for about 100 years, until the independent monarchy of Hawaii forever ceased to be. To add a zing to this brewing political stew, Westerners and their technology were beginning to come in ever-increasing numbers. In 1786, Capt. LaPerouse and his French exploration party landed in what's now LaPerouse Bay, near Lahaina, foreshadowing European attention. In 1786 two American captains, Portlock and Dixon, made landfall in Hawaii. Also, it was known that a fortune could be made on the fur trade between the great Northwest and Canton, China; stopping in Hawaii could make it all feasible. After this was reported, the fate of Hawaii was sealed.

Hawaii under Kamehameha was ready to enter its "golden age." The social order was medieval, with the *ali'i* as knights, owing their military allegiance to the king, and the serf-like *makaainana* paying tribute and working the lands. The priesthood of *kahuna* filled the posts of advisors, sorcerers, navigators, doctors, and historians. This was Polynesian Hawaii at its apex. But like the uniquely Hawaiian silversword, the old culture blossomed, and as soon as it did, it began to wither. Ever since, all that was purely Hawaiian has been supplanted by the relentless foreign influences that began bearing down upon it.

Young Kamehameha

Kamehameha was a man noticed by everyone; there was no doubt he was a force to be reckoned with. He had met Capt. Cook when the *Discovery* unsuccessfully tried to land at Hana on Maui. While aboard, he made a lasting impression, distinguishing himself from the multitude of natives swarming the ships by his royal

HAWAII STATE ARCHIVES

Kamehameha I as drawn by Louis Choris, ship's artist for the Von Kotzebue expedition, c. 1816. Supposedly the only time that Kamehameha sat to have his portrait rendered.

bearing. Lt. James King, in a diary entry, remarked that Kamehameha was a fierce-looking man, almost ugly, but that he was obviously intelligent, observant, and very good-natured. Kamehameha received his early military training from his uncle Kalaniopuu, the great king of Hawaii and Hana, who fought fierce battles against Alapai, the usurper who stole his hereditary lands. After regaining Hawaii, Kalaniopuu returned to his Hana district and turned his attention to conquering of all Maui. During this period young Kamehameha distinguished himself as a ferocious warrior and earned himself the nickname of "the hard-shelled crab," even though old Kahekili, Maui's king, almost annihilated Kalaniopuu's army at the sand hills of Wailuku.

When the old king neared death he passed on the kingdom to his son Kiwalao. He also, however, empowered Kamehameha as the keeper of the family war god Kukailimoku: Ku of the Bloody Red Mouth, Ku the Destroyer. Oddly enough, Kamehameha had been born not 500 yards from Ku's great *heiau* at Kohala, and had heard the chanting and observed the ceremonies dedicated to this fierce god from his first breath. Soon after Kalaniopuu died, Kamehameha found himself in a bitter war that he did not seek against his two cousins, Kiwalao and his brother Keoua, with the island of Hawaii at stake. The skirmishing lasted nine years until Kamehameha's armies met the two brothers at Mokuohai in an indecisive battle in which Kiwalao was killed. The result was a shaky truce with Keoua, a much embittered enemy. During this fighting, Kahekili of Maui conquered Oahu where he built a house of the skulls and bones of his adversaries as a reminder of his omnipotence. He also extended his will to Kauai by marrying his half brother to a high-ranking chieftess of that island. A new factor would be needed to resolve this stalemate of power—the coming of the *haole.*

The Olowalu Massacre
In 1790 the American merchant ship *Ella Nora,* commanded by Yankee captain Simon Metcalfe, was looking for a harbor after its long voyage from the Pacific Northwest. Following a day behind was the *Fair American,* a tiny ship manned by Metcalfe's son Thomas and a crew of five. Metcalfe, perhaps by necessity, was a stern and humorless man who would broach no interference. While anchored at Olowalu, a beach area about five miles east of Lahaina, some natives slipped close in their canoes and stole a small boat, killing a seaman in the process. Metcalfe decided to trick the Hawaiians by first negotiating a truce and then unleashing full fury upon them. Signaling he was willing to trade, he invited canoes of innocent natives to visit his ship. In the meantime, he ordered that all cannon and muskets be readied with scatter shot. When the canoes were within hailing distance, he ordered his crew to fire at will. Over 100 people were slain; the Hawaiians remembered this killing as "the day of spilled brains." Metcalfe then sailed away to Kealakekua Bay and in an unrelated incident succeeded in insulting Kameiamoku, a ruling chief, who vowed to annihilate the next *haole* ship that he saw.

Fate sent him the *Fair American* and young Thomas Metcalfe. The little ship was entirely overrun by superior forces. In the insuing battle, the mate, Isaac Davis, so distinguished himself by open acts of bravery that his life alone was spared. While harbored at Kealakekua, Metcalfe sent John Young to reconnoiter. Kamehameha, learning of the capture of the *Fair American,*

detained Young so he could not report, and Metcalfe, losing patience, marooned his own man and sailed off to Canton. (Metcalfe never learned of the fate of his son Thomas, and was later killed with another son while trading with the Indians along the Pacific coast.) Kamehameha quickly realized the significance of his two captives and the *Fair American* with its brace of small cannon. He appropriated the ship and made Davis and Young trusted advisors, eventually raising them to the rank of chief. They would all play a significant role in the unification of Hawaii.

Kamehameha The Great
Later in 1790, supported by the savvy of Davis and Young and the cannon from the *Fair American* which he mounted on carts, Kamehameha invaded Maui using Hana as his power base. The island defenders under Kalaniekupule, son of Kahekili who was lingering on Oahu, were totally demoralized, then driven back into the death-trap of Iao Valley. There, Kamehameha's forces annihilated them. No mercy was expected and none given, although mostly commoners were slain with no significant *ali'i* falling to the victors. So many were killed in this sheer-walled, inescapable valley that the battle was called *ka pani wai* which means "the damming of the waters". . . literally with dead bodies. While Kamehameha was fighting on Maui, his old nemesis Keoua was busy running amok back on Hawaii, again pillaging Kamehameha's lands. The great warrior returned home flushed with victory, but in two battles could not subdue Keoua. Finally, Kamehameha had a prophetic dream in which he was told that Ku would lead him to victory over all the lands of Hawaii if he would build a *heiau* to the war god at Kawaihae. Even before the temple was finished, old Kahekili attempted to invade Waipio, Kamehameha's stronghold. But Kamehameha summoned Davis and Young, and with the *Fair American* and an enormous fleet of war canoes defeated Kahikili at Waimanu. Kahekili had no choice but to accept the indomitable Kamehameha as the king of Maui, although he himself remained the administrative head until his death in 1794.

Now only Keoua remained in the way and he would be defeated not by war, but by the great *mana* of Ku. While Keoua's armies were crossing the desert on the southern slopes of Kilauea, the fire goddess Pele trumpeted her disapproval and sent a huge cloud of poisonous gas and mud-ash into the air. It descended upon and instantly killed the middle legions of Keoua's armies and their families. The footprints of this ill-fated army remain to this day outlined in the mud-ash as clearly as if they were deliberately encased in wet cement. Keoua's intuition told him that the victorious mana of the gods had swung to Kamehameha and that his own fate was sealed. Kamehameha sent word that he wanted Keoua to meet with him at Ku's newly dedicated temple in Kawaihae. Both knew that Keoua must die. The old nemesis came riding proudly in his canoe, gloriously outfitted in the red and gold feathered cape and helmet signifying his exalted rank. When he stepped ashore he was felled by Kamehameha's warriors and his body was ceremoniously laid upon the altar along with 11 others who were slaughtered and dedicated to Ku, of the Maggot-Dripping Mouth.

Increasing Contact
By the time Kamehameha had won the Big Island, Hawaii was becoming a regular stopover for numerous ships seeking the lucrative sandalwood trade with China. In February 1791, Capt. George Vancouver, still seeking the Northwest Passage, returned to Kealakekua where he was greeted by a throng of 30,000. The captain at once recognized Kamehameha, who was wearing a Chinese dressing gown that he had received in tribute from another chief who in turn had received it directly from the hands of Cook himself. The diary of a crewmember, Thomas Manby, relates that Kamehameha, missing his front teeth, was more fierce-looking than ever as he approached the ship in an elegant double-hulled canoe sporting 46 rowers. The king invited all to a great feast prepared for them on the beach. Kamehameha's appetite matched his tremendous size. It was noted that he ate two sizable fish, a king-size bowl of poi, a small pig, and an entire baked dog. Kamehameha personally entertained the Englishmen by putting on a mock battle in which he deftly avoided spears by rolling, tumbling, and catching them in mid-air, all the while hurling his own a great distance. The English reciprocated by firing cannon bursts into the air, creating an impromptu fireworks display. Kamehameha requested from

HAWAII STATE ARCHIVES

Capt. George Vancouver

Vancouver a full table setting with which he was provided, but his request for firearms was prudently denied. The captain did, however, leave beef cattle, fowl, and breeding stock of sheep and goats. The ship's naturalist, Archibald Menzies, was the first *haole* to climb Mauna Kea; he also introduced a large assortment of fruits and vegetables. The Hawaiians were cheerful, outgoing, and showed remorse when they indicated that the remainder of Cook's bones had been buried at a temple close to Kealakekua. John Young, by this time firmly entrenched into Hawaiian society, made no request to sail away with Vancouver. During the next two decades of Kamehameha's rule, the French, Russians, English, and Americans discovered the great whaling waters off Hawaii, and their increasing visits shook and finally tumbled the ancient religion and social order of *kapu*.

Finishing Touches
After Keoua was laid to rest it was only a matter of time till Kamehameha consolidated his power over all of Hawaii. In 1794 the old warrior Kahekili of Maui died, and gave Oahu to his son Kalanikupule, while Kauai and Niihau went to his brother Kaeo. Warring between themselves,

Kalanikupule was victorious, though he did not possess the grit of his father nor the great mana of Kamehameha. He had previously murdered a Capt. Brown who had anchored in Honolulu and seized his ship the *Jackall*. With the aid of this ship, Kalanikupule now determined to attack Kamehameha. However, while enroute, the sailors regained control of their ship and cruised to the Big Island to inform and join with Kamehameha. An army of 16,000 was raised and sailed for Maui, where they met only token resistance, destroyed Lahaina, pillaged the countryside, and vanquished Molokai in one bloody battle. The war canoes next sailed for Oahu and the final showdown. The great army landed at Waikiki, and though defenders fought bravely, giving up Oahu by the inch, they were steadily driven into the surrounding mountains. The beleaguered army made its last stand at Nuuanu Pali, a great precipice in the mountains behind present-day Honolulu. Kamehameha's warriors mercilessly drove the enemy into the great abyss. Kalanikupule, who hid in the mountains, was captured after a few months and sacrificed to Ku, The Snatcher of Lands, thereby ending the struggle for power. Kamehameha put down a revolt on Hawaii in 1796 and the king of Kauai, Kaumuali, accepting the inevitable, recognized Kamehameha as supreme ruler without suffering the hopeless ravages of a needless war. Kamehameha, for the first time in Hawaiian history, was the undisputed ruler of all the islands of "the heavenly homeland in the north."

Kamehameha's Rule

Kamehameha was as gentle in victory as he was ferocious in battle. His rule lasted until his death on May 8, 1819, under which Hawaii enjoyed a peace unlike the warring islands had ever known before. The king moved his royal court to Lahaina, where in 1803, he built the "Brick Palace," the first permanent building of Hawaii. The benevolent tyrant also enacted the "Law of the Splintered Paddle." This law, which protected the weak from the exploitation of the strong, had its origins when, many years before, a brave defender of a small overwhelmed village broke a paddle over Kamehameha's head and taught the chief—literally in one stroke—about the nobility of the common man.

However, just as Old Hawaii reached its "golden age," its demise was at hand. The relentless waves of *haole* both innocently and determinedly battered the old ways into the ground. With the foreign ships came prosperity and fanciful new goods after which the *ali'i* lusted. The *makaaina* were worked mercilessly to provide sandalwood for the China trade. This was the first "boom" economy to hit the islands, but it set the standard of exploitation that would follow. Kamehameha built an observation tower in Lahaina to watch for ships, many of which were his own, returning laden with riches from the world at large. In the last years of his life Kamehameha returned to his beloved Kona Coast where he enjoyed the excellent fishing renowned to this day. He had taken Hawaii from the darkness of warfare into the light of peace. He died true to the religious and moral *kapu* of his youth, the only ones he had ever known, and with him died a unique way of life. Two loyal retainers buried his bones after the baked flesh had been ceremoniously stripped away. A secret burial cave was chosen so that no one could desecrate the remains of the great chief, thereby absorbing his mana. The tomb's whereabouts remains unknown, and disturbing the dead remains one of the strictest *kapu* to this day. "The Lonely One's" kingdom would pass to his son, Liholiho, but true power would be in the hands of his beloved but feisty wife Kaahumanu. As Kamehameha's spirit drifted from this Earth, two forces sailing around Cape Horn would forever change Hawaii: the whalers and the missionaries.

MISSIONARIES AND WHALERS

The year 1819 is of the utmost significance in Hawaiian history. It marked the death of Kamehameha, the overthrow of the ancient *kapu* system, the arrival of the first whaler in Lahaina, and the departure of Calvinist missionaries from New England determined to convert the heathen islanders. Great changes began to rattle the old order to its foundations. With the *kapu* system and all of the ancient gods abandoned (except for the fire goddess Pele of Kilauea), a great void permeated the souls of the Hawaiians. In the coming decades Hawaii, also coveted by Russia, France, and England, was finally consumed by America. The islands had the first American school, printing press, and newspaper *(The*

the great Queen Kaahumanu, by ship's artist Louis Choris from the Otto Von Kotzebue expedition, c. 1816

HAWAII STATE ARCHIVES

Polynesian) west of the Mississippi. Lahaina, in its heyday, became the world's greatest whaling port, accommodating over 500 ships during its peak years.

The Royal Family
Maui's Hana District provided Hawaii with one of its greatest queens, Kaahumanu, born in 1768 in a cave within walking distance of Hana Harbor. At the age of 17 she became the third of Kamehameha's 21 wives and eventually the love of his life. At first she proved to be totally independent and unmanageable, and was known to openly defy her king by taking numerous lovers. Kamehameha placed a *kapu* on her body and even had her attended by horribly deformed hunchbacks to curb her carnal appetites, but she continued to flaunt his authority. Young Kaahumanu had no love for her great, lumbering, unattractive husband (even Capt. Vancouver was pressed into service as a marriage counselor), but in time she learned to love him dearly. She in turn became his favorite wife, although she remained childless throughout her life. Kamehameha's first wife was the supremely royal Keopuolani, who so outranked even him that the king himself had to approach her naked and crawling on his belly. Keopuolani produced the royal children Liholiho and Kauikeaouli, who became King Kamehameha II and III, respectively. When Kamehameha I died in 1819 he appointed Liholiho his successor, but he also had

the wisdom to make Kaahumanu the *kuhina nui* or queen regent. Initially, Liholiho was weak and became a drunkard. Later he became a good ruler, but he was always supported by his royal mother Keopuolani and by the ever-formidable Kaahumanu.

Kapu Is Pau
Kaahumanu was greatly loved and respected by the people. On public occasions, she donned Kamehameha's royal cloak and spear: so attired and infused with the king's mana, she demonstrated that she was the real leader of Hawaii. For six months after Kamehameha's death, Kaahumanu counseled Liholiho on what he must do. The wise *kuhina nui* knew that the old ways were *pau* ("finished") and Hawaii could not hope to function in a rapidly changing world under the *kapu* system. In November 1819, Kaahumanu and Keopuolani prevailed open Liholiho to break two of the oldest and most sacred *kapu:* to eat together with women and to allow women to eat previously forbidden foods, such as bananas and certain fish. Kaahumanu sat with Liholilho, heavily fortified with strong drink, and attended by other high-ranking chiefs and a handful of foreigners, they ate in public. This feast became known as *Ai Noa* ("free eating"), and as the first morsels passed her lips the ancient gods of Hawaii tumbled. Throughout the land revered *heiau* were burned and abandoned and the idols knocked to the ground. Now the

William Alexander preaching on Kauai. Drawing by A. Agate, c. 1840

HAWAII STATE ARCHIVES

people had nothing but their own weakened inner selves to rely on. Nothing and no one could answer their prayers; their spiritual lives were empty and in shambles.

Missionaries

In October 1819 the *Brig Thaddeus* left Boston carrying 14 missionaries bound for Hawaii. On April 4, 1820 they landed at Kailua on the Big Island where Liholiho had moved the royal court. The Reverends Bingham and Thurston went ashore and were granted a one-year trial missionary period by King Liholiho. They established themselves on Hawaii and Oahu and from there began the transformation of Hawaii. The missionaries were men of God, but also practical-minded Yankees. They brought education, enterprise, and most importantly, unlike the transient seafarers, a commitment to stay and build. In 1823, Rev. Richards established the first mission in Lahaina, a village of about 2,300 inhabitants.

Rapid Conversions

The year 1823 also marked the death of Keopuolani, who was given a Christian burial. Setting the standard by accepting Christianity, a number of the *ali'i* had followed the queen's lead. Liholiho had sailed off to England, where he and his wife contracted measles and died. Their bodies were returned by the British in 1825, on the HMS *Blonde* captained by Lord Byron, cousin of *the* Lord Byron. During these years, Kaahuma-

nu allied herself with Rev. Richards and together they wrote Hawaii's first code of laws based upon the Ten Commandments. Foremost was the condemnation of murder, theft, brawling, and the desecration of the Sabbath by work or play. The early missionaries had the best of intentions, but like all zealots were blinded by the singlemindedness that was also their greatest ally. The destruction of the native beliefs they felt to be abominations was not surgically selective. *Anything* native was felt to be inferior, and they set about to wipe out all traces of the old ways. In their rampage they reduced the Hawaiian culture to ashes, plucking self-will and determination from the hearts of a once-proud people. More so than the whalers, they terminated the Hawaiian way of life.

The Early Seamen

A good portion of the common seamen of the early 19th century were the dregs of the Western world. Many a whoremongering drunkard had awoken from a stupor and found himself on the pitching deck of a ship, discovering to his dismay that he had been "pressed into naval service." For the most part these sailors were a filthy, uneducated, lawless rabble. Their present situation was dim, their future hopless, and they would live to be 30 if they were lucky and didn't die from scurvy or a thousand other miserable fates. They snatched brief pleasure in every port, and jumped ship at every opportunity, especially in an easy berth like Lahaina. They displayed the worst elements of Western culture—which the Hawaiians naively mimicked. In exchange for aloha they gave drunkeness, sloth, and insidious death by disease. By the 1850s the population of native Hawaiians tumbled from the estimated 300,000 reported by Capt. Cook in 1778 to barely 60,000. Common conditions such as colds, flu, venereal disease, and sometimes smallpox and cholera decimated the Hawaiians who had no natural immunities to these foreign ailments. By the time the missionaries arrived, *hapahaole* children were common in Lahaina streets. The earliest lawless opportunists had come seeking sandalwood after first filling their holds with furs from the Pacific Northwest. Aided by *ali'i* hungry for manufactured goods and Western finery, they raped Hawaiian forests of this fragrant wood so coveted in China. Next, droves of sailors came in search of the whales. The whalers, decent men at home, left their morals back in the Atlantic and lived by the slogan "no conscience east of the Cape." The delights of Hawaii were just too tempting for most.

Two Worlds Tragically Collide

The 1820s were a time of confusion and soul-searching for the Hawaiians. When Kamehameha II died the kingdom passed to Kauikeaouli (Kamehameha III), who made his lifelong residence in Lahaina. The young king was only nine years old when the title passed to him, but his power was secure because Kaahumanu was still a vibrant *kuhina nui*. The young prince, more so than any other, was raised in the cultural confusion of the times. His childhood was spent during the very cusp of the change from old ways to new, and he was often pulled in two directions by vastly differing beliefs. Since he was royal born, according to age-old Hawaiian tradition, he must mate and produce an heir with the highest ranking *ali'i* in the kingdom. This natural mate happened to be his younger sister, the Princess Nahienaena. To the old Hawaiian advisors, this arrangement was perfectly acceptable and encouraged. To the increasingly influential missionaries, incest was an unimaginable abomination in the eyes of God. The problem was compounded by the fact that Kamehameha III and Nahienaena were drawn to each other and were deeply in love. The young king could not stand the mental pressure imposed by con-

Kamehameha III

flicting worlds. He became a teenage alcoholic too royal to be restrained by anyone in the kingdom, and his bouts of drunkenness and womanizing were both legendary and scandalous. Meanwhile, Nahienaena was even more pressured because she was a favorite of the missionaries, baptized into the church at age 12. She too vacillated between the old and the new. At times a pious Christian, at others she drank all night and took numerous lovers. As the Prince and Princess grew into their late teens, they became even more attached to each other and hardly made an attempt to keep their relationship from the missionaries. Whenever possible, they lived together in a grass house built for the Princess by her father.

In 1832, the great Kaahumanu died, leaving the king on his own. In 1833, at the age of 18, Kamehameha III announced that the "regency" was over and that all the lands in Hawaii were his, personally, and that he alone was the ultimate law. Almost immediately, however, he decreed that his half sister Kinau would be "premier," signifying that he would leave the actual running of the kingdom in her hands. Kamehameha III fell into total drunken confusion, until one night he attempted suicide. After this episode he seemed to straighten up a bit and mostly kept a low profile. In 1836, Princess Nahienaena was convinced by the missionaries to take a husband. She married Leleiohoku, a chief from the Big Island, but continued to sleep with her brother. It is uncertain who fathered the child, but Nahienaena gave birth to a baby boy in September 1836. The young prince survived for only a few hours, and Nahienaena never recovered from her convalescence. She died in December 1836, and was laid to rest in the mausoleum next to her mother, Keopuolani, on the royal island in Mokuhina Pond, still in existence in modern-day Lahaina. After the death of his sister, Kamehameha III became a sober and righteous ruler. Oftentimes seen paying his respects at the royal mausoleum, he ruled longer than any other king until his death in 1854.

The Missionaries Prevail

In 1823, the first mission was established in Lahaina under the pastorage of Rev. Richards and his wife. Within a few years, many of the notable ali'i had been, at least in appearance, converted to Christianity. By 1828 the cornerstones for Wainee Church, the first stone church on the island, were laid just behind the palace of Kamehameha III. The struggle between missionaries and whalers centered around public drunkenness and the servicing of sailors by local native girls. The normally god-fearing whalers had signed on for perilous duty that lasted up to 3 years, and when they anchored in Lahaina they demanded their pleasure. The missionaries were instrumental in placing a curfew on sailors and prohibiting native girls from boarding ships which had become customary. These measures certainly did not stop the liasons between sailor and wahine, but it did impose a modicum of social sanction and tolled the end of the wide open days. The sailors were outraged; in 1825 the crew from the Daniel attacked the home of the meddler, Rev. Richards. A year later a similar incident occurred. In 1827, confined and lonely sailors from the whaler John Palmer fired their cannon at Rev. Richards' newly built home.

Slowly the tensions eased, and by 1836 many sailors were regulars at the Seamen's Chapel, adjacent to the Baldwin Home. Unfortunately, even the missionaries couldn't stop the pesky mosquito from entering the islands through the port of Lahaina. The mosquitos arrived in 1826, from Mexico, aboard the merchant Wellington. They were inadvertently carried as larvae in the water barrels and democratically pestered everyone in the islands from that day forward regardless of race, religion, or creed.

Lahaina Becomes A Cultural Center

By 1831, Lahaina was firmly established as a seat of Western influence in Hawaii. That year marked the founding of Lahainaluna School, the first real American school west of the Rockies. Virtually a copy of a New England normal school, it attracted the best students, both native and white, from throughout the kingdom. By 1834, Lahainaluna had an operating printing press publishing the islands' first newspaper, The Torch of Hawaii, starting a lucrative printing industry centered in Lahaina that dominated not only the islands but also California for many years.

An early native student was David Malo. He was brilliant and well educated, but more importantly, he remembered the "old ways." One of the first Hawaiians to realize his native land was being swallowed up by the newcomers, Malo compiled the first history of pre-contact Hawaii and the resulting book, Hawaiian Antiquities, became a reference masterpiece which has yet to be eclipsed. David Malo insisted that the printing be done in Hawaiian, not English. Malo is buried in the mountains above Lahainaluna where, by his own request, he is "high above the tide of foreign invasion." By the 1840s, Lahaina was firmly established as the "whaling capital of the world"; the peak year 1846 saw 395 whaling ships anchored here. A census in 1846 reported that Lahaina was home to 3,445 natives, 112 permanent haole, 600 sailors, and over 500 dogs. The populace was housed in 882 grass houses, 155 adobe houses, and 59 relatively permanent stone and wooden framed structures. Lahaina would probably have remained the islands' capital, had Kamehameha III not moved the royal capital to the burgeoning port of Honolulu on the island of Oahu.

Foreign Influence

By the 1840s Honolulu was becoming the center of commerce in the islands; when Kame-

Women of many ethnic backgrounds worked the plantations at the turn of the century.

HAWAII STATE ARCHIVES

hameha III moved the royal court there from Lahaina the ascendant fate of the new capital was guaranteed. In 1843, Lord Paulet, commander of the warship *Carysfort,* forced Kamehameha III to sign a treaty ceding Hawaii to the British. London, however, repudiated this act and Hawaii's independence was restored within a few months when Queen Victoria sent Admiral Thomas as her personal agent of good intentions. The king memorialized the turn of events by a speech in which he uttered the phrase, *"Ua mau ke ea o ka aina i ka pono,"* ("The life of the land is preserved in righteousness"), now Hawaii's motto. The French used similar bullying tactics to force an unfavorable treaty on the Hawaiians in 1839; as part of these heavy handed negotiations they exacted a payment of $20,000, and the right for Catholics to enjoy religious freedom in the islands. In 1842 the U.S. recognized and guaranteed Hawaii's independence without a formal treaty, and by 1860 over 80% of the islands' trade was with America.

The Great *Mahele*

In 1840 Kamehameha III ended his autocratic rule and instituted a constitutional monarchy. This brought about the Hawaiian Bill of Rights, but the most far-reaching change was the transition to private ownership of land. Formerly, all land belonged to the ruling chief who gave wedge-shaped parcels called *ahupua'a* to lesser chiefs to be worked for him. The commoners did all the real labor, their produce heavily taxed by the *ali'i.* The fortunes of war, the death of a chief, or the mere whim of a superior could force a commoner off his land. The Hawaiians, however, could not think in terms of "owning" land. No one could *possess* land, one could only *use* land, and its *ownership* was a strange foreign concept. (As a result, naive Hawaiians gave up their lands for a song to unscrupulous traders, which remains an integral unrectified problem to this day.) In 1847 Kamehameha III and his advisors separated the lands of Hawaii into three groupings: crown land (belonging to the king), government land (belonging to the chiefs), and the people's land (the largest parcels). In 1848, 245 *ali'i* entered their land claims in the *Mahele Book,* assuring them ownership. In 1850 the commoners were given title in fee simple to the lands they cultivated and lived on as tenants, not including house lots in towns. Commoners without land could buy small *kuleana* (farms) from the government at 50 cents per acre. In 1850, foreigners were also allowed to purchase land in fee simple, and the ownership of Hawaii from that day forward slipped steadily from the hands of its indigenous people.

KING SUGAR

The sugar industry began at Hana, Maui, in 1849. A whaler named George Wilfong hauled four blubber pots ashore and set them up on a rocky hill in the middle of 60 acres he had planted in sugar. A team of oxen turned "crushing rollers" and the cane juice flowed down an open trough into the pots, under which an attending native kept a roaring fire burning. Wilfong's methods of refining were crude but the resultant high-quality sugar turned a neat profit in Lahaina. The main problem was labor. The

Hawaiians, who had made excellent whalers, were basically indentured workers. They became extremely disillusioned with their contracts, which could last up to 10 years. Most of their wages were eaten up by manufactured commodities sold at the company store, and it didn't take long for them to realize that they were little more than slaves. At every opportunity they either left the area or just refused to work.

Imported Labor

The **Masters and Servants Act of 1850,** which allowed importation of laborers under the contract system, ostensibly guaranteed an endless supply of cheap labor for the plantations. Chinese laborers were imported, but were too enterprising to remain in the fields for a meager $3 per month. They left as soon as opportunity permitted, and went into business as small merchants and retailers. In the meantime, Wilfong had sold out, releasing most of the Hawaiians previously held under contract, and his plantation fell into disuse. In 1860 two Danish brothers, August and Oscar Unna, bought land at Hana to raise sugar. They solved the labor problem by importing Japanese laborers who were extremely hard-working and easily managed. The workday lasted 10 hours, six days a week, for a salary of $20 per month with housing and medical care thrown in. Plantation life was very structured with stringent rules governing even bedtimes and lights out. A worker was fined for being late or for smoking on the job. Even the Japanese couldn't function under these circumstances, and improvements in benefits and housing were slowly gained.

Sugar Grows

The demand for "Sandwich Island Sugar" grew as California was populated during the gold rush, and increased dramatically when the American Civil War demanded a constant supply. The only sugar plantations on the Mainland were small plots confined to the Confederate states, whose products would hardly be bought by the Union and whose fields, later in the war, were destroyed. By the 1870s it was clear to the planters, still mainly New Englanders, that the U.S. was their market; they tried often to gain closer ties and favorable tariffs. The Americans also planted rumors that the British were interested in annexing Hawaii; this put pressure on the U.S. Congress to pass the long-desired **Reciprocity Act,** which would exempt sugar from import duty. It finally passed in 1875, in exchange for U.S. long-range rights to the strategic naval port of Pearl Harbor, among other concessions. These agreements gave increased political power to a small group of American planters, whose outlooks were similar to the post-Civil War South where a few powerful whites were the virtual masters of a multitude of dark-skinned laborers. Sugar was now big business and the Hana District alone exported almost 3,000 tons per year. All of Hawaii would have to reckon with the "sugar barons."

Changing Society

The sugar plantation system changed life in Hawaii physically, spiritually, politically, and economically. Now boatloads of workers came not only from Japan, but from Portugal, Germany, and even Russia. The white-skinned workers were most often the field foremen *(luna)*. With the immigrants came new religions, new animals and plants, unique cuisines, and a plantation language known as *pidgin* or better yet, *da kine*. The Orientals mainly, but also portions of all the other groups including the white plantation owners, intermarried with Hawaiian girls. A new class of people properly termed "cosmopolitan" but more familiarly and aptly known as "locals" were emerging. These were the people of multiple race backgrounds who couldn't exactly say *what* they were but it was clear to all just *who* they were. The plantation owners became the new "chiefs" of Hawaii who could carve up the land and dispense favors. The Hawaiian monarchy was soon eliminated.

A KINGDOM PASSES

The fate of Lahaina's Wainee Church through the years has been a symbol of the political and economic climate of the times. Its construction heralded the beginning of missionary dominance in 1828. It was destroyed by a tornado or "ghost wind" in 1858, just when whaling began to falter. The previously dominant missionaries began losing their control to the merchants and planters. In 1894, Wainee Church was burned to the ground by Royalists supporting the besieged Queen Liliuokalani, then was rebuilt with a grant from H.P. Baldwin in 1897 while Hawaii was a Republic ruled by the sugar planters. It wasn't until 1947 that Wainee was finally completed and remodeled.

The Beginning Of The End
Like the Hawaiian people themselves, the Kamehameha dynasty in the mid-1800s was dying from within. King Kamehameha IV (Alexander Liholiho) ruled from 1854 to 1863; his only child died in 1862. He was succeeded by his older brother Kamehameha V (Lot Kamehameha) who ruled until 1872. With his passing the Kamehameha line ended. William Lunalilo, elected king in 1873 by popular vote, was of royal, but not Kamehameha, lineage. He died after only a year in office, and being a bachelor left no heirs. He was succeeded by David Kalakaua, known far and wide as The "Merry Monarch." He made a world tour and was well received wherever he went. He built Iolani Palace in Honolulu and was personally in favor of closer ties with the U.S., helping push through the Reciprocity Act. Kalakaua died in 1891 and was replaced by his sister Lydia Liliuokalani, last of the Hawaiian monarchs.

HAWAII STATE ARCHIVES

Queen Liliuokalani

The Revolution
When Liliuokalani took office in 1891 the native population was at a low of 40,000 and she felt that the U.S. had too much influence over her homeland. She was known to personally favor the English over the Americans. She attempted to replace the liberal constitution of 1887 (adopted by her pro-American brother) with an autocratic mandate in which she would have much more political and economic control of the islands. When the McKinley Tariff of 1890 brought a decline in sugar profits, she made no attempt to improve the situation. Thus, the planters saw her as a political obstacle to their economic growth; most of Hawaii's American planters and merchants were in favor of a rebellion. She would have to go! A central spokesman and firebrand was Lorrin Thurston, a Honolulu publisher who, with a central core of about 30 men, challenged the Hawaiian monarchy. Although Liliuokalani rallied some support and had a small military potential in her personal guard, the coup was ridiculously easy—it took only one casualty. Capt. John Good shot a Hawaiian policeman in the arm and that did it. Naturally,

the conspirators could not have succeeded without some solid assurances from a secret contingent in the U.S. Congress as well as outgoing President Benjamin Harrison, who favored Hawaii's annexation. Marines from the *Boston* went ashore to "protect American lives," and on January 17, 1893, the Hawaiian monarchy came to an end.

The provisional government was headed by Sanford B. Dole who became president of the Hawaiian Republic. Liliuokalani actually surrendered not to the conspirators but to U.S. Ambassador John Stevens. She believed that the U.S. government, which had assured Hawaiian independence, would be outraged by the overthrow and would come to her aid. Actually, incoming President Grover Cleveland *was* outraged and Hawaii wasn't immediately annexed as expected. When queried about what she would do with the conspirators if she were reinstated, Liliuokalani said that they would be hung as traitors. The racist press of the times, which portrayed the Hawaiians as half-civilized bloodthirsty heathens, publicized this widely. Since

Sanford B. Dole reads the proclamation inaugurating the Hawaiian Republic on July 4, 1894.

the conspirators were the leading citizens of the land, the queen's words proved untimely. In January 1895, a small, ill-fated counterrevolution headed by Liliuokalani failed, and she was placed under house arrest in Iolani Palace. Forced to abdicate her throne, officials of the Republic insisted that she use her married name (Mrs. John Dominis) to sign the documents. She was also forced to swear allegiance to the new Republic. Liliuokalani went on to write *Hawaii's Story* and also the lyric ballad "Aloha O'e". She never forgave the conspirators and remained to the Hawaiians "queen" until her death in 1917.

Annexation

The overwhelming majority of Hawaiians opposed annexation and desired to restore the monarchy. But they were prevented from voting by the new Republic because they couldn't meet the imposed property and income qualifications—a transparent ruse by the planters to control the majority. Most *haole* were racist and believed that the "common people" could not be entrusted with the vote because they were childish and incapable of ruling themselves. The fact that the Hawaiians had existed quite well for 1,000 years before the white man even reached Hawaii was never considered. The Philippine theater of the Spanish-American War also prompted annexation. One of the strongest proponents was Alfred Mahon, a brilliant naval strategist who, with support from Theodore Roosevelt, argued that the U.S. military must have Hawaii to be a viable force in the Pacific. In addition, Japan, flushed with victory in its recent war with China, protested the American intention to annex, and in so doing prompted even moderates to support annexation in fear that the Japanese themselves coveted the prize. On July 7, 1898, President McKinley signed the annexation agreement, and this "tropical fruit" was finally put into America's basket.

MODERN TIMES

Hawaii entered the 20th century totally transformed from what it had been. The old Hawaiian language, religion, culture, and leadership were all gone. Western dress, values, education, and recreation were the norm. Native Hawaiians were now unseen citizens who lived in dwindling numbers in remote areas. The plantations, new centers of social order, had a strong Oriental flavor; more than 75% of their work force was Asian. There was a small white middle class, an all-powerful white elite, and a single political party ruled by that elite. Education, however, was always highly prized, and by the turn of the century all racial groups were encouraged to attend school. By 1900, almost 90% of Hawaiians were literate (far above the national norm) and schooling was mandatory for all children between ages 6 and 15. Intermarriage was accepted, and there was a mixing of the races like nowhere else on Earth. The military became increasingly important to Hawaii. It brought in money and jobs, dominating the island economy. The Japanese attack on Pearl Harbor, which began U.S. involvement in World War II, bound Hawaii to America forever. Once the islands had been baptized by blood, the average mainlander felt that Hawaii was American soil. A movement among Hawaiians to become part of the Union began to grow. They wanted a real voice in Washington, not merely a voteless delegate as provided under their territory status. Hawaii became the 50th state in 1959 and the jumbo jet revolution of the 1960s made it easily accessible to growing numbers of tourists from all over the world.

Military History

A few military strategists realized the importance of Hawaii early in the 19th century, but most didn't recognize the advantages until the Spanish-American War. It was clearly an unsinkable ship in the middle of the Pacific from which the U.S. could launch military operations. Troops were stationed at Camp McKinley at the foot of Diamond Head, the main military compound until it became obsolete in 1907. Pearl Harbor was first surveyed in 1872 by General Schofield. Later a military base named in his honor, Schofield Barracks, was a main military post in central Oahu. It first housed the U.S. 5th Cavalry in 1909 and was heavily bombed by the Japanese at the outset of WW II. Pearl Harbor, first dredged in 1908, was officially opened on December 11, 1911. The first warship to enter was the cruiser *California*. Ever since, the military has been a mainstay of island economy. Unfortunately, there has been long-standing bad blood between locals and military personnel. Each group has tended to look down upon the other.

Pearl Harbor Attack

On the morning of December 7, 1941, the Japanese carrier *Akagi*, flying the battle flag of the famed Admiral Togo of the Russo-Japanese War, received and broadcast over its PA system island music from Honolulu station KGMB. Deep in the bowels of the ship a radio man listened for a much different message, coming thousands of miles from the Japanese mainland. When the ironic poetic message "east wind rain" was received, the attack was launched. At the end of the day, 2,325 U.S. servicemen and 57 civilians were dead; 188 planes were destroyed; 18 major warships were sunk or heavily damaged; and the U.S. was in the war. Japanese casualties were ludicrously light and the ignited conflict would rage for four years until Japan, through Nagasaki and Hiroshima, was vaporized into total submission. At the end of hostilities, Hawaii would never again be considered separate from America (see p. 301-302 for more details).

Statehood

A number of economic and political reasons explain why the ruling elite of Hawaii desired state-

Honolulu Star-Bulletin 1st EXTRA

8 PAGES—HONOLULU, TERRITORY OF HAWAII, U.S.A., SUNDAY, DECEMBER 7, 1941—8 PAGES ✦ PRICE FIVE CENTS

(Associated Press by Transpacific Telephone)

SAN FRANCISCO, Dec. 7.—President Roosevelt announced this morning that Japanese planes had attacked Manila and Pearl Harbor.

WAR!

OAHU BOMBED BY JAPANESE PLANES

SIX KNOWN DEAD, 21 INJURED, AT EMERGENCY HOSPITAL

The Honolulu Star Bulletin banner headline announces the beginning of U.S. involvement in WW II on Sunday December 7, 1941.

hood, but simply, the vast majority of people who lived there, especially after WW II, considered themselves Americans. The first serious mention of making "The Sandwich Islands" a state was in the 1850s under President Franklin Pierce, but wasn't taken seriously until the monarchy was overthrown in the 1890s. For the next 50 years statehood proposals were made repeatedly to Congress, but there was stiff opposition, especially from the southern states. With Hawaii a territory, an import quota system beneficial to mainland producers could be enacted on produce, especially sugar. Also, there was prejudice against creating a state in a place where the majority of the populace was not white. This situation was illuminated by the infamous Massie Rape case of 1931 (see p. 66), which went down as one of the greatest miscarriages of justice in American history. During WW II, Hawaii was placed under martial law, but no serious attempt to intern the Japanese population was made, as in California. There were sim-

ply too many Japanese, who went on to gain the respect of the American people by their outstanding fighting record during the war. Hawaii's own 100th Batallion became the famous 442 Regimental Combat Team which gained notoriety by saving the Lost Texas Batallion during the Battle of the Bulge, and went on to be *the* most decorated batallion in all of WW II. When these GIs returned home, *no one* was going to tell them that they were not loyal Americans. Many of these AJAs (Americans of Japanese Ancestry) took advantage of the GI Bill and received higher education. They were from the common people, not the elite, and they rallied grass-roots support for statehood. When the vote finally occurred, approximately 132,900 voted in favor of statehood with only 7,800 votes against. Congress passed the Hawaii State Bill on March 12, 1959, and on August 21, 1959, President Eisenhower announced that Hawaii was officially the 50th state.

GOVERNMENT

Being the newest state in the Union, Hawaii has had the chance to scrutinize the others, pick their best attributes, and learn from their past mistakes. The government of the State of Hawaii is in essence no different from any other except that it is streamlined and, in theory, more efficient. There are only two levels: state and county. There are no town or city governments to deal with, and added bureaucracy is theoretically eliminated. Unfortunately, some of the state-run agencies, like the centralized Board of Education, have become "red-tape" monsters. Hawaii, in anticipation of becoming a state, drafted a constitution in 1950 and was ready to go when statehood was ratified. Politics and government are taken seriously in the "Aloha State," which consistently turns in the best national voting record per capita. For example, in the election to ratify statehood, hardly a ballot that went uncast, with 95% of the voters opting for statehood. In the first state elections that followed, 173,000 of 180,000 registered voters voted. The bill carried every island of Hawaii except for Niihau, where, coincidentally, the majority of people (total population 250, or so) are of relatively pure Hawaiian blood.

STATE GOVERNMENT

Hawaii's state legislature has 76 members, with 51 elected seats in the House of Representatvies, and 25 in the State Senate. Members serve two- and four-year terms respectively. All officials come from 76 separate electorates based on population, which sometimes makes for strange political bedfellows. For example, Maui's split 5th Senatorial District and 9th Representative District share one member from each with both Lanai and Molokai. These districts combine some of the island's richest condo and resort communities on Maui's Kaanapali coast with Lanai, where many people are Filipino field workers, and with economically depressed Molokai, where 80% of native Hawaiians live on welfare.

Oahu, which has the largest number of voters, elects 19 of 25 senators and 39.7 of 51 representatives, giving this island a majority in both houses. Maui, in comparison, elects 2.2 state

Governor
John Waihee III

Special Departments
The Department of Education is headed by a board of 13 nonpartisan representatives elected for four-year terms, 10 from Oahu and three from the other islands. The board has the right to appoint the Superintendent of Schools. Many praise the centralized board as a democratic body offering equal educational opportunity to all districts of Hawaii regardless of socio-financial status. Detractors say that the centralized board provides "equal educational mediocrity" to all. The University of Hawaii is governed by a Board of Regents appointed by the governor. They choose the president of the university.

senators and four representatives. The state is divided into four administrative counties: the **County of Kauai,** covering Kauai and Niihau; the **City and County of Honolulu,** which encompasses Oahu and includes all of the Northwestern Hawaiian Islands; the **County of Hawaii,** the Big Island, and the **County of Maui,** administering the islands of Maui, Lanai, Molokai, and uninhabited Kahoolawe, with the county seat at Wailuku on Maui.

Branches Of Government
The **State Legislature** is the collective body of the House of Representatives and the Senate. They meet during a once-yearly legislative session that begins on the third Wednesday of January and lasts for 90 working days. (These sessions are oftentimes extended and special sessions are frequently called.) The Legislature primarily focuses on taxes, new laws, and appropriations. The **Executive Branch** is headed by the governor and lieutenant governor, both elected on a statewide basis for four years with a two-term maximum. The governor has the right to appoint the heads of 20 state departments outlined in the constitution. The department appointees must be approved by the Senate, and they usually hold office as long as the appointing administration. The **Judiciary** is headed by a state Supreme Court of five justices, an appeals court, and four circuit courts. All are appointed by the governor and serve for 10 years with Senate approval. There are 27 district courts which have local jurisdiction; the judges are appointed for six-year terms by the chief justice of the Supreme Court.

Political History
The politics of Hawaii before WW II was a self-serving yet mostly benevolent oligarchy. The one real political party was Republican controlled by the Hawaiian Sugar Planters Association. The planters felt that, having made Hawaii a paradise, they should rule because they had "right on their side." The Baldwin family of Maui was the government, with such supporters as the Rice family, which controlled Kauai, and William (Doc) Hill of Hawaii. These were the preeminent families of the islands; all were represented on the boards of the Big Five corporations that ruled Hawaii economically by controlling sugar, transportation, refining, and utilities. An early native politician was Prince Jonah Kuhio Kalanianaole, a brother to Liliuokalani, who joined with the Republicans to gain perks for himself and for his own people. Nepotism and political hoopla was the order of those days. The Republicans, in coalition with the native Hawaiians, maintained a majority over the large racial groups such as the Japanese and Filipinos who, left to their own devices, would have been Democrats. The Republicans also used unfair literacy laws, land ownership qualifications, and proof of birth in Hawaii to control the large numbers of immigrant workers who could threaten their ruling position. It was even alleged that during elections a pencil was hung on a string over the Republican ballot: if a person wanted to vote Democratic he would have to pull the string to reach the other side of the voting booth. The telltale angle would give him away. He would be unemployed the next day.

The Democrats Rise To Power

The Democrats were plagued with poor leadership and internal factionalism in the early years. Their first real rise to power began in 1935 when the International Longshoremen's and Warehousemen's Union (ILWU) formed a branch in Hilo on the Big Island. In 1937, an incident known as the "Hilo Massacre" occurred when policemen fired on and wounded 25 striking stevedores, which was the catalyst needed to bind labor together. Thereafter, the ILWU, under the leadership of Jack Hall, became a major factor in the Democratic party. Their relationship was strained in later years when the ILWU was linked to Communism, but during the early days, whomever the ILWU supported in the Democratic Party won. The Democrats began to take over after WW II when returning Japanese servicemen become active in politics. The Japanese by this time were the largest ethnic group in Hawaii. A central character during the late 1940s and '50s was Jack Burns. Although a *haole*, this simple man was known to be for "the people" regardless of their ethnic background. During the war as a police captain he made his views clear that he considered the Japanese to be exemplary Americans. The Japanese community never forgot this, and were instrumental in Burns' election as governor, both in 1962 and 1966. The majority of people in the Oriental ethnic groups in Hawaii tend to remain Democrat even after they have climbed the socio-economic ladder. The first special election after statehood saw the governorship go to the previously appointed Republican Governor William Quinn, and the lieutenant governorship to another Republican, James Kealoha, of Hawaiian-Chinese ancestry. The first congressmagen elected was Japanese-American, Democrat Daniel Inouye. Since then, every governor has been a Democrat and one out of every two political offices is held by a person of Japanese extraction. The present governor, George Ariyoshi, is the first Japanese governor in the United States.

OFFICE OF HAWAIIAN AFFAIRS

In 1979, constitutional mandate created the Office of Hawaiian Affairs (OHA). This remarkable piece of legislature recognized, for the first time

The Hawaii State Seal. The translated motto reads "The life of the land is preserved in righteousness." It was uttered by Kamehameha III in July 1843 when Hawaiian sovereignty was restored by a joint declaration by France and Great Britain after a brief period in which Hawaii was under British rule.

since the fall of the monarchy in 1893, the special plight of native Hawaiians. For 75 years, no one in government was eager to face the "native question," but since 1979, OHA has opened a Pandora's box of litigation and accusation. For example, in 1983, a presidential commission investigated U.S. involvement in the overthrow of Hawaii's last queen, Liliuokalani, to decide if the federal government owed reparations to her Hawaiian people. After listening to testimony from thousands attesting to personal family loss of land and freedom, complete with old deeds documenting their claims, the commission concluded that the U.S. was guiltless and that native Hawaiians have nothing coming from Uncle Sam. Jaws dropped, and even those opposed to native Hawaiian rights couldn't believed this whitewash." Governor George Ariyoshi said in a newspaper interview, "A recent congressional study did not accurately portray what went on here at the turn of the century. . . . To say that the monarchy was not overthrown . . . is something that I cannot accept. It is not historically true."

Trouble In Paradise

OHA, as the vanguard of native political activism, has focused on gaining monies guaranteed in the state constitution as recently as 1959 for "ceded lands." They have also been instrumental in regaining disputed Hawaiian lands and have helped in the fight to save the sacred island of Kahoolawe, which is now uninhabited and has been used as a bombing target since WW II. To simply state a complex issue, native Hawaiians have been eligible for benefits from revenues accrued from ceded lands and haven't been receiving them. These lands (1.8 million acres) were crown and government lands belonging to the Hawaiian monarchy and, therefore, to its subjects. When the kingdom was overthrown, the lands passed on to the short-lived Republic, followed by the U.S. Protectorate, and then finally to the state in 1959. No one disputed that these lands belonged to *the people,* who were entitled to money collected from rents and leases. For the last 26 years, however, these tens of millions of dollars have gone into a "general fund" used by various state agencies such as the Department of Transportation and the Department of Land and Natural Resources; the state is extremely reluctant to turn these funds over to what they derisively call an "unconstitutional special interest group." A major fight is expected at the Constitutional Convention scheduled for 1988.

Native Hawaiian Rights

The question has always been, "Just what is a native Hawaiian?" The answer has always been ambiguous. The government has used the "blood quantum" as a measuring stick. This is simply the percentage of Hawaiian blood in a person's ancestry—customarily 50% qualifies a person as *Hawaiian.* The issue is compounded by the fact that no other group of people has been so racially intermarried for so many years. Even though many people have direct ancestry to pre-Republic Hawaiians, they don't have enough "Hawaiianess" to qualify. An overwhelming number of these people fall into the category of "locals": they "feel" Hawaiian, but blood-wise they're not. They suffer all of the negativity of second-class citizens and reap none of the benefits accorded Hawaiians. Those that do qualify according to blood quantum don't have the numbers or the political clout necessary to get results. In fact, many people involved with

OHA would not qualify themselves, at least not according to the blood quantum! Strong factionalism within the native Hawaiian movement itself threatens its credibility. Many people that do qualify by the blood quantum view the others as impinging on their rightful claims. The most vocal activists point out that only a coalition of people that have Hawaiian blood, combined with those who "identify" with the movement, will get results. Walter Ritte, a political firebrand and OHA trustee from Molokai, says that "anti-Hawaiian rights" lobbyists such as the tourist industry, airlines, large corporations, etc., are now stronger than the Hawaiians. Ritte advises that the only way the Hawaiian rights movement can win is to become active "political warriors" and vote for legislators that will support their cause. The rhetoric of OHA is reminiscent of the equal rights movement of the 1960s.

Obviously compromise is necessary. Perhaps certain social entitlements (such as tuition grants) could be equal for all, whereas money and land entitlements could be granted by percentages equal to the claiming person's actual "blood quantum." OHA members appeal directly to the Hawaiian people and can build political constituencies at a grassroots level. Since they are elected by the people and not appointed by the government (the case with the Hawaiian Home Lands Department and the trustees of the Bishop Estate, two other *supposedly* Hawaiian institutions), the status quo political parties of Hawaii are wary of them. Their candidates may be opposed and defeated in the future. What makes the issue even more ludicrous is that some of the state's most powerful corporate families opposed to Hawaiian rights have direct lineage to not only pre-Republic Hawaiian ancestors, but to Hawaiian royalty! They themselves would receive "entitlements" from the ceded land according to blood quantum, but socioeconomically they are the natural enemies of OHA. The problem is difficult and it is improbable that all concerned will get satisfaction. OHA maintains offices at 567 S. King Street, Honolulu 96813. They publish a newspaper entitled *Ka Wai Ola O OHA* (The Living Waters of OHA), which is available upon request.

ECONOMY

Hawaii's mid-Pacific location makes it perfect for two primary sources of income: tourism and the military. Tourists come in anticipation of endless golden days on soothing beaches, while the military is provided with the strategic position of an unsinkable battleship. Each nets Hawaii about $4 billion annually, which should keep flowing smoothly into the foreseeable future, increasing proportionally with the times. These revenues mostly remain aloof from the normal ups and downs of the mainland U.S. economy. Together they make up 60% of the islands' income, and both attract either gung-ho enthusiasts or rabidly negative detractors. The remaining 40% comes in descending proportions from manufacturing, construction, and agriculture (mainly sugar and pineapples). As long as the sun shines and the balance of global power requires a military presence, the economic stability of Hawaii is guaranteed.

TOURISM

'The earthly paradise! Don't you want to go to it? Why, of course!" This was the opening line of *The Hawaiian Guide Book* by Henry Whitney that appeared in 1875. In print for 25 years, it sold for 60 cents during a time when a round-trip sea voyage between San Francisco and Hono-

lulu cost $125. The technique is a bit dated, but the human desires remain the same: some of us seek paradise, all seek escape, some are drawn to play out a drama in a beautiful setting. Tourists have been coming to Hawaii ever since steamship service began in the 1860s. Until WW II, luxury liners carried the financial elite on exclusive voyages to the islands. By the 1920s 10,000 visitors a year were spending almost $5 million dollars—cementing the bond between Hawaii and tourism.

A $25,000 prize offered by James Dole of pineapple fame sparked a transPacific air race in 1927. The success of these aerial daredevils proved that commercial air travel to Hawaii was feasible. Two years later, **Hawaiian Air** was offering regularly scheduled flights between all of the major islands. By 1950 airplanes had captured over 50% of the transportation market, and ocean voyages were relegated to "specialty travel," catering to the elite. By 1960 the large airbuses made their debut; 300,000 tourists arrived on eight designated airlines. The Boeing 747 began operating in 1969. These enormous planes could carry hundreds of passengers at reasonable rates, so travel to Hawaii became possible for the average-income person. In 1970, two million arrived, and by 1980 close to four million passengers arrived on 22 interna-

Waikiki growing rice, c. 1920

HAWAII STATE ARCHIVES

tional air carriers. The first hotel in Honolulu was the **Hawaiian,** built in 1872. It was pre-dated by **Volcano House,** which overlooked Kilauea Crater on the Big Island, and was built in 1866. The coral-pink **Royal Hawaiian,** built in 1927, is Waikiki's graciously aging grand dame, a symbol of days gone by. As late as the 1950s it had Waikiki Beach almost to itself. Only 10,000 hotel units were available in 1960; today there are over 60,000, and thousands of condos as well.

Tourists: Who, When, And Where
Tourism-based income outstripped pineapples and sugar by the mid '60s and the boom was on. Long-time residents could even feel a physical change in air temperature: many trees were removed from Honolulu to build parking lots, and reflected sunlight made Honolulu much hotter and at times unbearable. Even the trade winds, known to moderate temperatures, were not up to that task. So many people from the outlying farming communities were attracted to work in the hotels that there was a poi famine in 1967. But for the most part, islanders knew that their economic future was tied to this "non-polluting industry." Most visitors (75%) are Americans, and the largest numbers come from the West Coast. Sun-seeking refugees from frigid Alaska, however, make up the greatest proportional number, according to population figures. The remaining arrivals are in descending order from Japan, Canada, Australia, and England. Europe, as a whole, sends proportionately less

visitors than North America or Asia, while the least amount come from South America. The Japanese market is constantly growing and by the year 1990 over a million Japanese visitors per year are expected. This is particularly beneficial to the tourist market because the average Western tourist spends about $90 per day, while his Japanese counterpart spends just over $200 per day. However, they stay only about 5 days, shorter than the typical visit. Up until very recently the Japanese traveled only in groups and primarily stayed on Oahu. Now the trend is to travel independently, or come with a group and then peel off, with a hefty percentage heading for the Neighbor Islands.

The typical visitor is slightly affluent, and about 35; 20% more women visit than men. The average age is a touch higher than most vacation areas because it reflects an inflated proportion of retirees heading for Hawaii, especially Honolulu, to fulfill a lifelong "dream" vacation. A typical stay lasts about 12 days, down from a month in the 1950s; a full 50% are repeat visitors. On any given day there are about 70,000 travelers on Oahu, 15,000 on Maui, and about 7,000 each on Kauai and Hawaii. Molokai and Lanai get so few that the figures are hardly counted. In 1964 only 10% of the islands' hotel rooms were on the Neighbor Islands, but by 1966 the figure jumped to 25%, with more than 70% of tourists opting to visit the Neighbor Islands. Today four out of 10 hotel rooms are on the Neighbor Islands and that figure should reach 50% shortly. The overwhelming number of tourists are on package tours, and the largest number of people congregate in Waikiki, which has a 74% average hotel occupancy and attracts two and a half times as many visitors as the Neighbor Islands together. Obviously, Waikiki is still most people's idea of paradise. Those seeking a more intimate experience can have it with a 20-minute flight from Oahu or a direct flight to Hilo (Hawaii) and now Maui and Kauai. Joaquin Miller, the 19th-century poet of the Sierras said, "I tell you my boy, the man who has not seen the Sandwich Islands, in this one great ocean's warm heart, has not seen the world." The times have certainly changed, but the sentiments of most visitors to Hawaii remain consistently the same.

Tourism-related Problems

Tourism is both boon and blight to Hawaii. It is the root cause of two problems: one environmental, the other socioeconomic. The environmental impact is obvious and best described in the lament of songstress Joni Mitchell: "they paved paradise and put up a parking lot." Simply, tourism can draw too many people to an area and overburden it. In the process, it stresses the very land and destroys the natural beauty that attracted people in the first place. Tourists come to Hawaii for what has been called its "ambient resource": a balanced collage of indulgent climate, invigorating waters, intoxicating scenery, and exotic people all wrapped up neatly in one area which can both soothe and excite at the same time. It is in the best interest of Hawaii to preserve this "resource."

Most point to Waikiki as a prime example of development gone mad. It is super-saturated, and amazingly enough, hotel owners themselves are now trying to keep development in check. Two prime examples of the best and the worst development can be found on Maui's south shore at Kihei and Wailea, less than five miles apart. In the late '60s Kihei experienced a development-inspired "feeding frenzy" that made the real sharks offshore seem to be about as dangerous as Winnie the Pooh. Condos were slapped up as fast as cement would dry and their architecture was as inspired as a stack of shoe boxes. They lined the coast renowned for its beauty, wiping out the view in the process. Anyone who had the bucks built, and now Kihei looks like a high-rise, low-income, federally funded housing project. You can bet those who made a killing building here don't live here. Just down the road, Wailea is a model of what development could and should be. The architecture is tasteful, low-rise, unobtrusive, and done with people and the preservation of the scenery in mind. It's obviously more exclusive, but access points to the beaches are open to everyone and the view is still there for all to enjoy. It points the way for the development of the future.

Changing Lifestyle

Like the land, humans are stressed by tourism. Local people, who once took the "Hawaiian lifestyle" for granted, become displaced and estranged in their own land. Some areas, predominantly along gorgeous beaches that were average-to low-income communities, are now overdeveloped with prices going through the roof. The locals are not only forced to move out, but often must come back as service personnel in the tourist industry and cater to the very people who displaced them. At one time the psychological blow was softened because, after all, the newcomers were merely benign tourists who would stay a short time, spend a wad of money, and leave. Today, condos are being built and a different sort of visitor is arriving. Many condo owners are in the above-average income bracket: well-educated businesspeople and professionals. The average condo owner is a mainlander who purchases one as a second or retirement home. These people are not islanders and have a tough time relating to the locals, who naturally feel resentment. Moreover, since they don't *leave* like normal tourists, they use all community facilities, find those special nooks and crannies for shopping or sunbathing that were once exclusively the domain of locals, and have a say as voters in community governments. The islanders become more and more disenfranchised. Many believe that the new order instigated by tourism is similar to what has always existed in Hawaii: a few from the privileged class being catered to by many from the working class. In a way it's an extension of the plantation system, but instead of carrying pineapples, most islanders find themselves carrying luggage, cocktails, or broiled fish. One argument, however, remains undeniable: whether it's people or pineapples, one has to make a living. The days of a little grass shack on a sunny beach aren't

*Missiles stand ready to
defend America's
unsinkable
Battleship Hawaii.*

gone, it's just that you need a wallet full of credit cards to afford one.

THE MILITARY

Hawaii is the most militarized state in the Union: all five services are represented. Oahu is the headquarters of CINPAC (Commander in Chief Pacific), which controls 70% of the Earth's surface from California to the east coast of Africa and to both poles. The U.S. military presence dates back to 1887, when Pearl Harbor was given to the Navy as part of the "Sugar Reciprocity Treaty." The sugar planters were given favorable "duty-free" treatment on their sugar, while the U.S. Navy was allowed exclusive rights to one of the best harbors in the Pacific. In 1894, when the monarchy was being overthrown by the sugar planters, the USS *Boston* sent a contingency of marines ashore to "keep order," which really amounted to a show of force, backing the revolution. The Spanish-American War saw U.S. troops billeted at Camp McKinley at the foot of Diamond Head, and Schofield Barracks opened to receive the 5th Cavalry in 1909. Pearl Harbor's flames ignited WW II and there has been no looking back since then.

About 60,000 military personnel are stationed in Hawaii with a slightly higher number of dependants. The Navy and Marines combined have the most personnel with about 36,000, followed by 17,000 Army, 6,000 Air Force, and 1,000 or so Coast Guard. Besides this, 20,000 civilian support personnel account for 65% of all federal jobs in Hawaii. The combined services are one of the largest landholders with over 242,000 acres, accounting for six percent of Hawaiian land. The two major holdings are the 100,000-acre Pohahuloa Training Area on Hawaii and 100,000 acres on Oahu, which is a full 26% of the entire island. The Army controls 71% of the military lands, followed by the Navy at 25% and the remainder goes to the Air Force and a few small installations to the Coast Guard.

The Military Has No *Aloha*

Not everyone is thrilled about the strong military presence in Hawaii. Two factions, native Hawaiians and anti-nuclear groups, are downright angry. Radical contingencies of "native Hawaiian-rights groups" actually consider Hawaii to be an independent country, besieged and "occupied" by the U.S. government. They date their loss of independence to Liliuokalani's overthrow in 1894. The vast majority of ethnic Hawaiians, though they consider themselves Americans, are concerned with loss of their rightful homelands, with no financial reparation, and a continuing destruction and disregard for their traditional religious and historical sites. A long list of grievances is cited by native Hawaiian action groups, but the best and clearest example is the controversy over the sacred island, Kahoolawe, which is used as a bombing target by the Navy. (For more information see p. 490.)

The second controversy raised by the military presence focuses on Hawaii as a nuclear target. The ultimate goal of the anti-nuclear protestors is to see the Pacific, and the entire world, free from nuclear arms. They see Hawaii as a big target that the international power merchants on the mainland use as both pawn and watchdog. There is no doubt that Hawaii is a nuclear arsenal and the anti-nuke groups say that if war breaks out the Hawaiian Islands will be reduced to cinders. The military naturally counters that a strong Hawaii is a deterrent to nuclear war and that Hawaii is not only a powerful offensive weapon, but one of the best-defended regions of the world. Unfortunately, when you are on an island there is no place to go: like a boxer in a ring, you can run, but you can't hide. Anyone interested in the nuclear controversy can contact any of the following organizations: cAtholic Action of Hawaii, 1918 University Ave., Honolulu, HI 96822; U.S. Nuclear Free Pacific Network, 942 Market St., Rm. 711, San Francisco, CA 94102; or, *Kahuliau* ("an independent newspaper focusing on Hawaii and Pacific issues"), Box 61337, Honolulu, HI 96822.

SUGAR

Sugar cane *(ko)* was brought to Hawaii by its original settlers and was known throughout Polynesia. Its cultivation was well established and duly noted by Capt. Cook when he first sighted the islands. The native Hawaiians used various strains of sugar cane for food, rituals, and medicine. It was never refined, but the stalk was chewed and juice was pressed from it. It was used as food during famine, and as an ingredient in many otherwise unpalatable medicines, and especially as a love potion. Commercial growing started with a failure on Oahu in 1825, followed by a successful venture a decade later on Kauai. This original plantation, now part of the McBryde Sugar Co., is still productive. The industry received a technological boost in 1850 when a centrifuge, engineered by David Weston of the Honolulu Iron Works, was installed at a plantation on East Maui. It was used to spin the molasses out of the cooked syrup, leaving a crude crystal.

Hawaii's biggest market has always been the mainland U.S. Demand rose dramatically during the California Gold Rush of 1849-50, and again a decade later during the American Civil War. At first Hawaiian sugar had a poor reputation that almost killed its export market, but with technological advances it became the best-quality sugar available last century.

Irrigation And Profit Politics
In 1876 the **Reciprocity Treaty** freed Hawaiian sugar from import duty. Now a real fortune could be made. One entrepreneur, **Claus Spreckles,** a sugar-beet magnate from California, became the reigning Sugar King in Hawaii. His state-of-the-art refineries on Maui employed every modern convenience, including electric lighting; he was also instrumental in building marvelous irrigation ditches necessary to grow sugar on once-barren land. The biggest hurdle to commercial sugar cane growing has always been water. One pound of sugar requires one ton of water, or about 250 gallons. A real breakthrough came when the growers reasoned that fresh water in the form of rain must seep through the lava and be stored underground. Fresh water will furthermore float atop heavier salt water and therefore be recoverable by a series of vertical wells and tunnels. By 1898, planters were tapping this underground supply of water and sugar could be produced in earnest as an export crop.

The Plantation System
Sugar cane also produced the plantation system, which was in many ways socially comparable to the pre-Civil War South. It was the main cause of the cosmopolitan mixture of races found in Hawaii today. Workers were in great demand, and the sugar growers scoured the globe looking for likely sources. Importing plantation workers started by liberalizing **The Masters and Servants Act;** this basically allowed the importation of conscripted workers. Even during its heyday, people with consciences felt that this system was no different from slavery. The first conscripts were Chinese, followed by Japanese, and then a myriad of people including other Polynesians, Germans, Norwegians, Spanish, Portuguese, Puerto Ricans, Filipinos, and even a few freed slaves from the southern U.S. (For further coverage see p. 55.) Today, grown on Oahu, Maui, Kauai, and Hawaii, yearly sugar sales reach $500 million. The state's 330 sugar cane-producing farms,

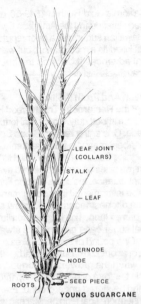

LEAF JOINT (COLLARS)

STALK

LEAF

INTERNODE

NODE

ROOTS — SEED PIECE

YOUNG SUGARCANE

and their attendant refineries, still employ a hefty amount of the islands' workforce. Newcomers, startled by what appear to be brush fires, are actually witnessing the burning of sugar cane prior to harvesting. Some sugar lands, such as those along Kaanapali on Maui, coexist side by side with a developed tourist area. Hawaii's sugar cane industry is still healthy and solvent, producing over nine million tons of cane annually. If profits remain sweet, cane as a cash crop will flourish for many years to come.

PINEAPPLES

Next to cane, the majority of Hawaii's cultivated lands (some 40,000 acres) yield pineapples. The main farms are on Oahu, the northwest tip of Maui, and central Lanai, the world's largest pineapple plantation. Pineapples were brought to the islands by **Don Francisco Marin,** an early Spanish agronomist, in the 1820s. Fresh pineapples were exported as early as 1850 to San Francisco, and a few cases of canned fruit appeared in 1876 at Hawaii's pavilion at the U.S. Centennial Exposition in Philadelphia. Old varieties of pineapples were pithier and pricklier than the modern variety. Today's large, luscious, golden fruits are the "smooth cayenne" variety from Jamaica, introduced by Capt. Kidwell in 1886.

Dole

But Hawaiian pineapple, as we know it, is synonymous with one man, **James Dole,** who actually *made* the industry at the turn of this century. Jim Dole started growing pineapples on a 60-acre homestead in Wahiawa, Oahu. He felt that America was ready to add this fruit to its diet and that "canning" would be the conveyance. By 1903, he was shipping canned fruit from his Iwilei plant and by 1920 pineapples were a familiar item in most American homes. Hawaii was at that time the largest producer in the world. In 1922, Jim Dole bought the entire island of Lanai, whose permanent residents numbered only about 100, and started the world's largest pineapple plantation. (For more information see "Lanai" p. 493). By all accounts, Jim Dole was an exemplary human being, but he could never learn to "play ball" with the economic powers that ruled Hawaii, namely "The Big Five." They ruined him by 1932 and took control of his **Hawaiian Pineapple Company**. Today, the Hawaiian pineapple industry is beleaguered by competition from Asia, Central America, and the Philippines, resulting in the abandonment of many corporate farms. Hit especially hard was Molokai, where Del Monte shut down its operations in 1982. The other plantations are still reasonably strong, bringing in about $200 million dollars annually, but employment in the pineapple industry has dropped by 25% in the last decade, and there are strong doubts that these jobs will ever return.

OTHER AGRICULTURE

Every major food crop known can be grown in Hawaii because of its amazingly varied climates and rich soil. Farming ventures through the years have produced cotton, sisal, rice, and even rubber trees. Today, Hawaii is a major producer of the Australian macadamia nut, considered by some to be the world's most useful and delicious nut. The islands' fresh exotic fruits are unsurpassed, and juices and nectars made from papaya, passion fruit, and guava are becoming well known worldwide. Dazzling flowers such as protea, carnations, orchids, and anthuriums are also commercially grown. Hawaii has a very healthy livestock industry, headed by the Big Island's quarter-million-acre Parker Ranch, the largest singly owned cattle ranch in the U.S. Also poultry, dairy, and pork are produced on many farms. The only coffee grown in the U.S. is found on the slopes of Mauna Loa in the Kona district of the Big Island. "Kona coffee" is of gourmet quality and well regarded for its aroma and rich flavor. *Pakalolo* (see "Health and Well-being") is the most lucrative cash crop, but no official economic records exist. It's grown by enterprising gardeners on all the islands.

Hawaiian waters are alive with fish, but its commercial fleet is woefully small and obsolete. Fishing revenues amount to only $25 million per year, which is ludicrous in a land where fish is the obvious natural bounty. Native Hawaiians were masters of aquaculture, routinely building fishponds and living from their harvest. Where once there were hundreds of fish ponds, only a handful are in use today. The main aquaculture is growing freshwater prawns; the state is considered the world leader although there are less than 25 prawn farms operating at a yearly value of only $1.5 million. With all of these foodstuffs, unbelievable as it may sound, Hawaii must import much of its food. Hawaii can feed *itself*, but it cannot support the four million hungry tourists that come to sample its superb and diverse cuisine every year.

ECONOMIC POWER

Until statehood, Hawaii was ruled economically by a consortium of corporations known as **The Big Five: C. Brewer and Co.,** sugar, ranching, and chemicals, founded 1826; **Theo. H. Davies & Co.,** sugar, investments, insurance, and transportation, founded 1845; **Amfac Inc.,** originally H. Hackfield Inc. (a German firm that changed its name and ownership during the anti-German sentiment of WW I to American Factors), sugar, insurance, and land develop-

ment, founded 1849; **Castle and Cooke Inc.,** (Dole) pineapple, food packing, and land development, founded 1851; and, **Alexander and Baldwin Inc.,** shipping, sugar, and pineapple, founded 1895. This economic oligarchy ruled Hawaii with a velvet glove and a steel grip.

With members on all important corporate boards, they controlled all major commerce including banking, shipping, insurance, hotel development, agriculture, utilities, and wholesale and retail merchandising. Anyone trying to buck the system was ground to dust, finding it suddenly impossible to do business in the islands. The Big Five was made up of the islands' oldest and most well-established *haole* families; all included bloodlines from Hawaii's own nobility and *ali'i*. They looked among themselves for suitable husbands and wives, so breaking in from the outside even through marriage was hardly possible. The only time they were successfully challenged prior to statehood was when Sears, Roebuck and Co. opened a store on Oahu. Closing ranks, the Big Five decreed that their steamships would not carry Sears' freight. When Sears threatened to buy its own steamship line, the Big Five relented. Actually, statehood, and more to the point, tourism, broke their oligarchy. After 1960 too much money was at stake for Mainland-based corporations to ignore. Eventually the grip of the Big Five was loosened, but they are still enormously powerful and richer than ever, though unlike before, they don't control everything. Now, their power is land. With only five other major landholders, they control 65% of all the privately held land in Hawaii.

Land Ownership

Hawaii, landwise, is a small pie. Its slices are not at all well divided. There are 6,425 square miles of land, 98% of which make up the six main inhabited islands. This figure does not include Niihau, which is privately owned by the Robinson family and inhabited by the last remaining pureblooded Hawaiians, nor does it include Kahoolawe, the uninhabited Navy bombing target just off Maui's south shore. Of the 4,045,511 acres that make up the inhabited islands 36% is owned by the state, 10% is owned by the federal government, and the remaining 54% is in private hands, but 40 owners with 5,000 or more acres

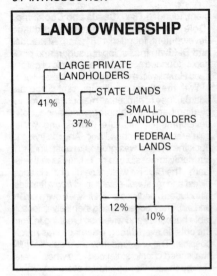

LAND OWNERSHIP

LARGE PRIVATE
LANDHOLDERS

41%

STATE LANDS

37%

SMALL
LANDHOLDERS

FEDERAL
LANDS

12%

10%

own 75% of all private lands. Moreover, only 10 private concerns own two-thirds of these lands. To be more vivid, Castle and Cooke Inc. owns 99% of Lanai, while 40-60% of Maui, Oahu, Molokai, Kauai, and Hawaii are owned by less than 12 private parties.

The largest private landowner is the Kamehameha Schools/Bishop Estate which recently lost a Supreme Court battle allowing the State of Hawaii to acquire privately owned land for "the public good." More than in any other state, Hawaiian landowners tend to lease land instead of selling it, and many private homes are on rented ground. This was the case with many homes rented from the Bishop Estate. The state acquired the land and resold it to long-term lease holders. These lands had previously earned a slow but steady profit for native Hawaiians. With land prices going up all the time, only the very rich land developers will be able to purchase long-term leases, and the "people" of Hawaii will become even more land poor.

"The land and industries of Hawaii are owned by old families and large corporations, and Hawaii is only so large."

—Jack London, c. 1916

THE PEOPLE

The people of Hawaii are no longer *in* the human race; they've already *won* it. Nowhere else on Earth can you find such a kaleidoscopic mixture of people. Every major race is accounted for, with over 50 ethnic groups adding not only their genes, but their customs, traditions, and outlooks. The modern Hawaiian is the future's "everyman": a blending of all races. Interracial marriage has been long accepted in Hawaii, and people are so mixed that it's already difficult to place them in a specific racial category. Besides the original Hawaiians, themselves a mixed race of Polynesians, people in the islands have multiple ancestor combinations from China, Japan, Korea, the Philippines, England, America, Norway, Russia, Germany, Scotland, Poland, Portugal, and Spain. There are Afro-Americans, whose forebears came just after the Civil War, Puerto Ricans, a hefty group of American Samoans, a few thousand American Indians, and recent Vietnamese refugees. Hawaii is the most racially integrated state in the Union, and although the newest, it epitomizes the time-honored American ideal of the "melting pot" society.

THE ISSUE OF RACE

This polyracial society should be a model of understanding and tolerance, and in most ways it is, but there are still racial tensions. People tend to identify with one group, and though not openly hostile, they do look disparagingly on others. Some racial barbs maintain that the Chinese are grasping, the Japanese too cold and calculating, the *haole* materialistic, Hawaiians lackadaisical, Filipinos emotional, etc. In Hawaii this labeling tendency is a bit modified because *people,* as individuals, are not usually discriminated against, but their *group* may be. Another factor is that individuals identify with a group not along strict blood lines, but more by a "feeling of identity." If a white/Japanese man married a Hawaiian/Chinese woman, they would be accepted by all groups concerned. Their children, moreover, would be what they chose to be and more to the point, what they "felt" like.

There are no ghettos as such, but there are traditional areas where people of similar racial strains live, and where outsiders are made to feel unwelcome. For example, the Wainae district of Oahu is considered a strong "Hawaiian" area where other people may meet with hostility; the Kahala area of Oahu mostly attracts upwardly mobile whites; on the plantation island of Lanai, Japanese managers don't live amongst Filipino workers. Some clubs make it difficult for non-whites to become members; certain Japanese, Chinese, and Filipino organizations attract only members from these ethnic groups; and Hawaiian *ohana* would question any person seeking to join unless they had some Hawaiian blood. Generally, however, the vast majority of people get along with each other and mix with no discernible problems.

The real catalyst responsible for most racial acceptance is the Hawaiian public school system. Education has always been highly regarded in Hawaii; the classroom has long been integrated. Thanks to a standing tradition of progressive education, democracy and individualism have always been basic maxims taught in the classroom. The racial situation in Hawaii is far from perfect, but it does point the way to the future in which all people can live side by side with respect and dignity.

Who, What, And Where
Hawaii has a population of one million, which includes 120,000 permanently stationed military personnel and their dependants. (All numbers used in this section are approximations.) It has the highest ratio of immigration to population in the U.S., and is the only state where whites are not the majority. White people are, however, the fastest growing group, due primarily to immigration from the west coast. About 60% of Hawaiian residents were born there; 25% were born on the Mainland U.S.; and 15% are foreign-born. The average age is 29, and men slightly outnumber the women. This is due to the large concentration of predominantly male military personnel, and to the substantial numbers of older bachelor plantation workers that came during the first part of this century and never found wives. The population has grown steadily in recent times, but has fluctuated wildly in the past. In 1876, it reached its lowest ebb with only 55,000 permanent residents. This was the era of large sugar plantations; their constant demand for labor was the primary cause for importing various peoples from around the world, and led to Hawaii's racially integrated society. WW II saw

the population swell from 400,000 to 900,000. These 500,000 military personnel left at war's end, but many returned to settle after getting a taste of island living. Of the one million people on the islands today, 800,000 live on Oahu, with 400,000 in the Honolulu metropolitan area. The rest are distributed as follows: 93,000 on Hawaii, with 36,000 in Hilo; 63,000 on Maui, the largest concentration around Wailuku/Kahului with 23,000; 40,000 on Kauai, including 230 pureblood Hawaiians on Niihau; Molokai with 6,000; and Lanai with just over 2,000. The overall population density is 164 people per sqare mile, equal to that of California, with Honolulu claiming more than 1,400 people per sqare mile, and Maui the second most densely populated island with only 105 people per sqare mile. City dwellers outnumber those living in the country by four to one. The average household size ranges from just over one person in Honolulu, to 3.1 persons per household throughout the remainder of the state.

THE HAWAIIANS

The drama of the native Hawaiians is a tragedy: it ends in their demise as a viable people. When Capt. Cook discovered Hawaii in 1778, an estimated 300,000 natives were living in harmony

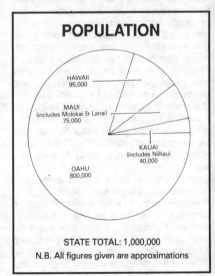

POPULATION

HAWAII
95,000

MAUI
(includes Molokai & Lanai)
75,000

KAUAI
(includes Niihau)
40,000

OAHU
800,000

STATE TOTAL: 1,000,000

N.B. All figures given are approximations

with their surroundings; within 100 years a scant 50,000 demoralized and dejected Hawaiians existed almost as wards of the state. Today, although 115,000 people claim varying degrees of Hawaiian blood, experts say that less than 1,000 can lay claim to being pure Hawaiian, and that's stretching it! A resurgence of Hawaiian ethnic pride is sweeping the islands as many people trace their roots and attempt to absorb the finer aspects of their ancestral lifestyle. It's easy to see why they could be bitter over what they've lost, since they're now strangers in their own land, much like American Indians. The overwhelming majority of Hawaiians are of mixed heritage, and the wisest take the best from all worlds. But from the Hawaiian side comes simplicity, love of the land, and acceptance of people. It is the Hawaiian legacy of aloha that remains immortal and adds that special illusive quality that "is" Hawaii.

Polynesian Roots

The Polynesians' original root stock is muddled and remains an anthropological mystery. It's believed they were nomadic wanderers who migrated from both the Indian subcontinent and South East Asia through Indonesia, where they learned to sail and navigate on protected waterways. As they migrated they honed their sailing skills until they could take on the Pacific, and absorbed other cultures and races until they coalesced into Polynesians. Abraham Fornander, still considered a major authority on the subject, wrote in his *Account of the Polynesian Race* (1885) that the Polynesians started as a white race, heavily influenced by contact with the Cushite, Chaldeo-Arabian civilization. He estimated their arrival in Hawaii at A.D. 600 based on Hawaiian genealogical chants. Modern science seems to bear this date out, but remains skeptical on his other surmises.

Thousands of years before Europeans even imagined the existence of a Pacific Ocean, Polynesians had populated the far-flung islands of the "Polynesian Triangle" stretching from New Zealand in the south, thousands of miles east to Easter Island, and finally to Hawaii, the northern apex. Similar language, gods, foods, and crafts add credibility to this theory. Other more fanciful versions are all long on conjecture and short on evidence. For example, Atlantis, the most "found" lost continent in history, pops up again,

with the Hawaiians the supposed remnants of this advanced civilization. The slim proof is that the Hawaiian *kahuna* were so well versed in the curative arts that they had to be Atlantians. In fact, they not only made it to Hawaii, but also to the Philippines where their secret powers have been passed on to the faith healers of today. That the Hawaiians are the "lost tribe of Israel" is another theory, but this too is only wild conjecture.

The "Land Seekers"

The intrepid Polynesians that actually settled Hawaii are believed to have come from the Marquesas Islands, 1,000 miles south of Hawaii and a few hundred miles east. The Marquesans were cannibals known for their tenacity and strength, two attributes that would serve them well. They left their own islands because of war and famine; these migrations went on for centuries. Ships' logs mention Marquesan seagoing canoes setting sail in search of new land as late as the mid-19th century. The first navigator-explorers, advance scouting parties, were referred to as "land seekers." They were led northward by a few terse words sung in a chant that told a general direction and promised some guiding stars (probably recounting the wild adventures of canoes blown far off course that somehow managed to return to the southern islands of Polynesia). The land seekers were familiar with the stars, currents, habits of land birds, and countless other subliminal clues that are overlooked by "civilized" man.

After finding Hawaii, they were aided in their voyage home by favorable trade winds and familiar waters. They set sail again in canoes laden with hopeful families and all the foodstuffs necessary to colonize a new land, anticipating a one-way ride with no return. Over the centuries, the fierce Marquesans mellowed into Hawaiians, and formed a new benevolent culture based on the fertility god Lono. Then, in the 12th century, a ferocious army of Tahitians invaded Hawaii and supplanted not only the ruling chiefs but also the gentler gods with their war-god Ku, who demanded human sacrifice. Abruptly, contact with Polynesia stopped. Some say the voyages, always fraught with danger, were no longer necessary. Hawaii was forgotten by the Polynesians, and the Hawaiians became the most rarified race in the world. It was to these

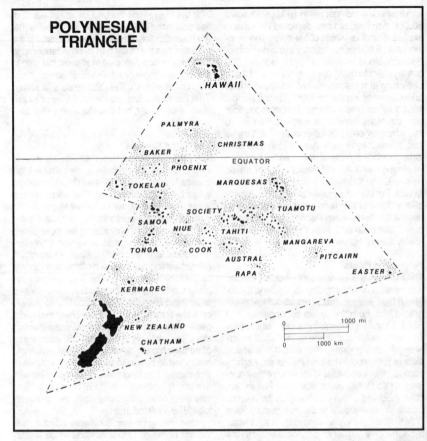

POLYNESIAN TRIANGLE

HAWAII

PALMYRA

BAKER · CHRISTMAS

PHOENIX EQUATOR

TOKELAU · MARQUESAS

SOCIETY · TUAMOTU

SAMOA

NIUE · TAHITI

TONGA · COOK · MANGAREVA

AUSTRAL · PITCAIRN

RAPA · EASTER

KERMADEC

NEW ZEALAND

CHATHAM

0   1000 mi
0   1000 km

people that Capt. Cook in 1778 brought the outside world. Finding Polynesians stretched so far and wide across the Pacific, he declared them to be "the most extensive nation upon earth."

The "Little People" Of Hawaii

The Mu, Was, Eepas, and Waos are all "little people" of Hawaii, but the most famous are the Menehune. As a group they resemble the trolls and leprechauns of Europe, but so many stories concern them that they appear to have actually existed in Hawaii at one time. Even in the late 18th century, an official census noted that King Kaumualii of Kauai had 65 Menehune, who were said to live in Wainiha Valley. Fighting

among themselves, it's held that the Menehune drove out the Mu and the Was. They also differed slightly in appearance. The Menehune are about two to three feet tall with hairy, well-muscled bodies. Their red faces have thick noses, protruding foreheads, long eyebrows, and stringy hair. They love to frolic, especially by rolling down hills into the sea, and their favorite foods are shrimp and poi. They seldom speak, but their chatter sounds like the low growling of a dog. Nocturnal creatures, Menehune are frightened of owls and dogs.

The Mu are mute, while the Was are noted for their loud blustering shouts. The Mu were thought to be black skinned and to live deep in the forest on a diet of bananas. All had their specialties, but the Menehune were stone masons par excellence. Many feats involving stonework are attributed to the Menehune. The most famous is the "Menehune Ditch" on Kauai. They finished their monumental tasks in one night, disappearing by daybreak. Even in the 1950s, masons building with stone near Diamond Head insisted that their work was disturbed at night, and a *kahuna* had to be called in to appease the Menehune. After that, all went well.

In a more scientific vein, the Tahitian word for Menehune means "commoner." Many feel that they were non-Polynesian aboriginals who somehow made it to the islands, and co-mingled with Hawaiians until their chiefs became alarmed that their little race would vanish. (Mohikia and Analike are the respective names of a Menehune prince and princess who married Hawaiians and whose names have been preserved in legend.) The Menehune assembled *en masse* and supposedly floated away on an island called "Kuaihelani" that descended from the heavens. Some say that they headed for the far-flung outer islands of Necker and Nihoa, where, oddly enough, stone gods found there are unlike any on the other Hawaiian islands. But there the trail grows cold. Today, island mothers warn their misbehaving toddlers that the Menehune will come and take them away, but in most stories they are actually pixie-like and benign.

Point Of Contact

When Capt. Cook stepped ashore on Waimea, Kauai, on the morning of Jan. 20, 1778, he discovered a population of 300,000 natives living in perfect harmony with their surroundings. Their agrarian society had flourished in the last thousand years. When they had first arrived, Hawaii was a hostile and windblown place where only a few ferns and some wild birds were fit to be eaten. Fish were plentiful, but even the coconut, mainstay of the tropics, was missing. The Polynesians brought their staples of taro and breadfruit, sweet potatos, coconuts, sugar cane, and bananas. They introduced and cultivated gourds for containers and even as armor, bamboo for a thousand uses, *ti* to wrap offerings and to fashion hula skirts, paper mulberry to produce the intricate cloth-like tapa, and arrowroot and tumeric for flavorings. They also introduced pigs, a barkless dog, and chickens that were all relished as fine food. Also, the ubiquitous rat managed to stow away on their canoes and was transported to the islands.

The Demise Of Hawaiians

The ecological system of Hawaii has always been exceptionally fragile, its people included! When the white man came he found a great people who were large, strong, and virile, but when it came to fighting even minor diseases they proved as delicate as hothouse flowers. To exacerbate the situation, the Hawaiians were totally uninhibited in sex between willing partners. Unfortunately, the white sailors were laden with syphylis, gonorrhea, and all manner of germs and common European diseases. Captain Cook tried desperately to keep the sexually diseased members of his crew away from the Hawaiian women, but it was impossible. The *hospitality* of Hawaiian women was legendary, and promises of "paradise" were actually used as a lure to get sailors for perilous cruises into the Pacific that could last for years. When Cook returned from the north in less than one year, there were already natives with telltale signs of VD.

Fatal Flaws

Hawaiian women brought VD home, and it spread like wildfire. By the time the missionaries came in 1820 and halted the widespread fornication, the native population was only 140,000, half of what it had been only 40 years after initial contact! In 1804 alone, perhaps 100,000 died from *okuu* (either typhoid or cholera). In the next 50 years measles, mumps, influenza, and tuberculosis ravaged the people. In 1853 a smallpox epidemic ate further into the doomed and weakened Hawaiian race, and leprosy ranged far and wide in the land. In addition, during the whaling years, at least 25% of all able-bodied Hawaiian men sailed away, never to return. By 1880 King Kalaukaua had only 48,000 Hawaiian subjects, a cataclysmic decrease of 82% of the original population. Wherever the king went, he would beseech his people, *"Hooulu lahui,"* ("increase the race,") but it was already too late. Nature herself had turned her back on these once-proud people. Many of their marriages were barren and in 1874 when only 1,400 children were born, a full 75% died in infancy. The final coup de grace was intermarriage. With so many inter-racial marriages, the Hawaiians literally bred themselves out of existence.

Painful Adjustments

The old paternalism inherent in the Hawaiian caste system was carried on by the ruling *haole* families of the last century. The remaining Hawaiians looked to the ruling class of whites like they had to their own *ali'i*, and for many years this attitude discouraged self help. Many Hawaiians fervently accepted the Christianity that had supplanted their own religion because it was a haven against a rapidly changing world in which they felt more and more alienated. Though Hawaiians did not make good plantation workers and were branded as lazy, they were actually hard and dedicated workers. Like all people attuned to their environment, they chose to work in the cool of the mornings and late afternoons, and could make no sense of laboring in the intense heat of the day. As fishermen they were unparalleled, and also made excellent cowboys on the ranches, preferring open ranges to the constricting plantation fields.

Hawaiians readily engaged in politics and were impressed with all the hoopla and fanfare. They would attend rallies, perform hula and songs, and in most instances sided with the whites against the Orientals. They were known to accept money for their votes and almost considered it the obligation of the leader, whom they regarded as a sort of chief, to grease their palms. Educated Hawaiians tended to become lawyers, judges, policeman, and teachers, and there are still a disproportionate number of Hawaiians, population-wise, in these fields. Hawaiians were racist toward the Japanese and Chinese. However, they would readily intermarry because, true to aloha, they accepted "people" even though they might be prejudiced toward their group. In 1910, although the native population was greatly reduced, there were still twice as many full-blooded Hawaiians as mixed bloods. By 1940 mixed-blood Hawaiians were the fastest growing group, and full bloods the fastest declining.

Hawaiians Today

Many Hawaiians moved to the cities and became more and more disenfranchised. Their folk society stressed openess and a giving nature, but downplayed the individual and the ownership of private property. These cultural traits made them easy targets for users and schemers. After repeated unfair treatment, they became either apathetic, or angry. About 116,000 people living in Hawaii have *some* Hawaiian blood. Most surveys reveal that although they number only 12% of the population, they account for almost 50% of the financially destitute families, arrests, and illegitimate births. Niihau, a privately owned island, is home to about 250 pure-blood Hawaiians, the largest concentration per capita in the islands. The Robinson family, which owns the island, restricts visitors to invited guests only. The second largest concentration is on Molokai, where 2,700 Hawaiians, living mostly on Hawaiian Homes Lands, make up 45% of the population. The ma-

Native Hawaiians lived a more and more humble existence as time passed them by.

FRITZ CRAFT, c. 1920

Many believed that the devastating Chinatown fire of 1900 was deliberately allowed to burn in order to displace the Chinese population of Honolulu.

HAWAII STATE ARCHIVES

jority, 80,000 or so, live on Oahu, where they are particularly strong in the hotel and entertainment fields. People of Hawaiian extraction are still a delight to meet, and anyone so lucky as to be befriended by one long regards this friendship as the highlight of his travels. The Hawaiians have always given their aloha freely and it is we that must accept it as a precious gift.

THE CHINESE

Next to Yankees from New England, the Chinese are the oldest migrant group in Hawaii. Since the beginning, their influence has far outshone their meager numbers. They have long been the backbone in the small, privately owned retail trade. They brought to Hawaii, along with their individuality, Confucianism, Taoism, and Buddhism. Though many became Christians, the flavor of their Oriental traditions still lingers. The Chinese population of 57,000 makes up only 6% of the state's total, and the vast majority (52,000) reside on Oahu. Their key to success has been indefatigable hard work, the shrewdness to seize a good opportunity, and above all, an almost fanatical desire to educate their children. As an ethnic group they have the least amount of crime, the highest per capita income, a disproportionate number of professionals, and remain some of Hawaii's most prominent citizens.

The First Chinese

No one knows his name, but a Chinese man is credited with being the first person in Hawaii to refine sugar. This Oriental wanderer tried his hand at crude refining on Lanai in 1802. He failed, but other Chinese were operating sugar mills by 1830. Within 20 years, the plantations desperately needed workers, and the first Chinese laborers were 195 coolies from Amoy who arrived in 1852 under the newly passed Masters and Servants Act. These conscripted laborers were contracted for three to five years, and given $3 per month plus room and board. This was for 12 hours a day, six days per week— even in 1852 absolutely miserable wages. The Chinese almost always left the plantations the minute their contracts expired. They went into business for themselves and promptly monopolized the restaurant and small shop trade.

Bad Feelings

When they left the plantations, they were universally resented, due to prejudice, Chinese xenophobia, and their success in business. The first Chinese peddler in Honolulu was mentioned as early as 1823. The Chinese hated the plantations where they were cruelly treated, and the Chinese Consul in Hawaii was very conservative and sided with the plantation owners, giving his own people no support. When leprosy became epidemic in the islands, it was blamed on the Chinese. The Hawaiians called it *pake* disease, their derisive name for Chinamen (which oddly enough was an endearment in China meaning "uncle"). Although leprosy cannot be blamed solely on the Chinese, a boatload of Chinese immigrants did bring in smallpox in 1880. At the turn of the century, a smallpox epidemic broke out again in Honolulu's Chinatown (half the residents were really Japanese), and it was promptly burnt to the ground by the authorities. Amidst all this negativity, some intrepid souls prospered. The greatest phenomenon was Chun Afong who, with little more than determination, became a millionaire by 1857, raised 16 children, and almost singlehandedly created the Chinese bourgeoisie in Hawaii. The Chinese were also responsible for making rice Hawaii's second most important crop from 1867 until 1872. It was Ah In, another Chinese entrepreneur, who brought in the first water buffalo used to cultivate rice during this period.

The Chinese Exclusion Act

Although reforms on the plantations were forthcoming, the Chinese preferred the retail trade. In 1880 half of all plantation workers were Chinese, by 1900 10%, and by 1959, only 300 Chinese worked on plantations. When the "powers that were" decided that Hawaii needed compliant laborers, not competitive businessmen, the monarchy passed the Chinese Exclusion Act in 1886, forbidding any more Chinese contract laborers from entering Hawaii. Still, 15,000 more Chinese were contracted in the next few years. In 1900 there were about 25,000 Chinese in Hawaii, but because of the Exclusion Act and other prejudices, many sold out and moved away. By 1910 their numbers were reduced to 21,000.

The Chinese Niche

Although most residents considered all the Chinese the same, they were actually quite different. The majority were two distinct ethnic groups from Kwangtung Province in southern China—the Punti made up 75% of the immigrants—and the Hakka made up the remainder. The Hakka had invaded Punti lands over 1,000 years previously and lived in the hills overlooking the Punti villages, never mixing. But in Hawaii, they mixed out of necessity. Few Chinese women came at first, so a Chinese man would gladly accept any Chinese woman as a wife, regardless of her ethnic background. The Chinese were also one of the first groups that willingly intermarried with the Hawaiians, and gained a reputation of being exceptionally caring husbands. By the 1930s, there was still resentment, but the Japanese were receiving most of

the negative scrutiny by then, and the Chinese were firmly entrenched in the merchant class. Their thrift, hard work, and family solidarity had paid off. The Chinese accepted the social order and kept a low profile. During Hawaii's turbulent labor movements of the 1930s and '40s, the Chinese community produced *not one* labor leader, radical intellectual, or left-wing politician. When Hawaii became a state, one of the two first senators was Hiram Fong, a racially mixed Chinese. Since statehood, the Chinese community has carried on business as usual, as they continue to rise even further, both economically and socially.

THE JAPANESE

Conjecture holds that a few Japanese castaways, who floated to Hawaii long before Capt. Cook, introduced iron, which the islanders seemed to be familiar with before the white men arrived. Most scholars refute this claim and say Portuguese or Spanish ships lost in the Pacific introduced iron. Nevertheless, shipwrecked Japanese did make it to the islands. The most famous episode involved Jirokichi who, lost at sea for 10 months, was rescued by Capt. Cathcart of Nantucket in 1839. Cathcart brought him to Hawaii where he boarded with prominent families. This adventure-filled episode is recounted in the Japanese classic *Ban Tan* (Stories of the Outside World) written by the scribe Yuten-sei. The first *official* arrivals were a group of ambassadors sent by the *shogun* to negotiate with the U.S. in Washington. They stopped en route at Honolulu in March 1860, only seven years after Commodore Perry and his famous "Black Ships" had roused Japan from its self-imposed 200-year slumber. A small group of Japanese plantation workers arrived in 1868, though mass migration was politically blocked for almost 20 years, and Japanese laborers didn't start coming in large numbers until 1886. King Kalakaua, among others, proposed that Japanese be brought as contract laborers in 1881; the thinking went that millions of Japanese subsistence farmers held promise as an inexhaustible supply of hardworking, uncomplaining, inexpensive, resolute workers. In 1886, when famine struck Japan, the Japanese government allowed farmers mainly from southern Honshu, Kyushu, and Okinawa to emigrate. Among these were members of Japan's little talked-about untouchable caste, called *eta* or *buraku-min* in Japan and *chorinbo* in Hawaii. They gratefully seized this opportunity to better their lot, an impossibility in their homeland.

The Japanese Arrive

The first Japanese migrants were almost all men. Under Robert Irwin, the American agent for recruiting the Japanese, almost 27,000 Japanese came, for which he received a fee of $5 per head. The contract workers received $9 plus room and board, and an additional $6 for a working wife. This pay was for a 26 working-day month at 10 hours per in the fields or 12 hours in a factory. Between 1897-1908, migration was steady with about 70% men and 30% women arriving. Afterwards, the "Gentlemen's Agreement," a euphemism for racism against the "yellow peril," halted most immigration. By 1900 over 60,000 Japanese had arrived, constituting the largest ethnic group. Until 1907 most Japanese longed to return home and faithfully sent back part of their pay to help support their families. Eventually, a full 50% did return to Japan, but the others began to consider Hawaii their home and resolved to settle . . . if they could get wives! Between 1908 and 1924, "picture brides" arrived whose marriages had been arranged *(omiai)* by family members back home. These women clung to the old ways and reinforced the Japanese ethnic identity. Excellent plantation workers, they set about making their rude camps into model villages. They felt an obligation that extended from person to family, village, and their new country. As peasants, they were imbued with a feeling of a natural social order which they readily accepted . . . if treated fairly.

Changing Attitudes

Unfortunately some plantation *luna* were brutal, and Japanese laborers were mistreated, exploited, and made to live in indecent conditions on the plantations. In unusual protest, they formed their first trade union under Yasutaro Soga in 1908 and gained better treatment and higher wages. In 1919 an unsuccessful statewide plantation strike headed by the Federation of Japanese Labor lasted seven bitter months, earning the lasting mistrust of the establishment. By the 1930s, the Japanese, frustrated at being passed over for advancement because they were non-white, began to move from the plantations and opened retail stores and small businesses. By WW II they owned 50% of retail stores and accounted for 56% of household domestics. Many became small farmers, especially in Kona, where they began to grow coffee. They also accounted for Hawaii's fledgling fishing fleet and would brave the deep waters in their small, seaworthy sampans. Like the Chinese, they were committed to bettering themselves and placed education above all else. Unlike the Chinese, they did not marry outside their own ethnic group and remained relatively racially intact.

Americans Of Japanese Ancestry (AJAs)

Parents of most Japanese children born in Hawaii before WW II were *issei* (first generation), who considered themselves apart from other Americans and clung to the notion of "We Japanese." They held traditional beliefs of unwavering family loyalty, and to propagate their values and customs they supported Japanese language schools, which 80% of their children attended before the war. This group, who were never "disloyal," were, however, "prideful" in being Japanese. Some diehards even refused to believe that Japan lost WW II and were shamed at their former homeland's unconditional surrender.

Their children, the *nissei* or second generation, were a different breed. In one generation they had become Americans through that basic melting pot called a schoolroom. They put into practice the high Japanese virtues of obligation, duty, and loyalty to the homeland—which was now, unquestionably, America. After Pearl Harbor was bombed, many people were terrified that the Hawaiian Japanese would be disloyal to America and would serve as spies and even as advance combatants for Imperial Japan. The FBI kept close tabs on the Japanese community, and the menace of the "enemy within" prompted the decision to place Hawaii under martial law for the duration of the war. Because of sheer numbers it was impossible to place the Hawaiian Japanese into concentration camps as was done in California, but prejudice and suspicion toward them, especially from Mainland military personnel, was fierce.

AJAs as GIs

Although Japanese had formed a battalion during WW I, they were insulted by being considered unacceptable as American soldiers in WW II. Those already in the armed services were relieved of any duty involving weapons. Those that knew better supported the AJAs. One was Jack Burns, a Honolulu policeman, who stated unequivocally that the AJAs were totally trustworthy. They never forgot his support, and thanks to a huge Japanese vote he was elected governor in 1963. Also, it has since been noted that not a single instance of Japanese sabotage, spying, or disloyalty was ever reported in Hawaii. Some American Japanese volunteered to serve in labor battalions, and because of their flawless work and loyalty, it was decided to put out a call for a few hundred volunteers to form a combat unit. Over 10,000 rushed to sign up!

AJAs formed two distinguished units in WW II—the 100th Infantry Battalion and, later, the 442nd Regimental Combat Team. They landed in Italy at Salerno and even fought from Guadalcanal to Okinawa. They distinguished themselves as *the* most decorated unit in American military history. They made excellent newspaper copy; their exploits hit front pages around the nation. They were immortalized as the rescuers of a Texas company pinned down during the Battle of the Bulge. These Texans became known as "The Lost Battalion" and have periodic reunions with the AJA GIs who risked and lost so much to bring them out to safety.

The AJAs Return

The AJAs returned home to a grateful country. In Hawaii, at first, they were accused of being cocky. Actually, they were refusing to revert to the pre-war status of second-class citizens and began to assert their rights as citizens who had defended their country. Many took advantage of the GI Bill and received college educations. The "Big 5 Corporations" for the first time accepted former AJA officers as executives, and the "old order" began to wobble. Many Japanese became involved with Hawaiian politics, and the first elected member to Congress was Daniel Inouye, who had lost an arm fighting in the war. Hawaii's present governor, George Ariyoshi, is the country's first Japanese American ever to reach such high office. Most Japanese, even as

The Japanese GIs returned as "our boys."

they climb the economic ladder, tend to remain Democrats.

Today, one out of every two political offices in Hawaii is held by a Japanese. In one of those weird quirks of fate, it is now the Hawaiian Japanese who are accused by other ethnic groups of engaging in unfair political practices, nepotism, and reverse discrimination. It's often heard that "if you're not Japanese, forget about getting a government job." Many of these accusations against AJAs are undoubtedly motivated by jealousy, but their record of social fairness is not without blemish, and true to their custom of family loyalty, they do stick together. There are now 240,000 people in Hawaii of Japanese ancestry, making up 25% of the state's population. Heavily into the "professions," they're committed to climbing the social ladder. The AJAs of Hawaii are now indistinguishable from "the establishment," enjoy a higher standard of living than most, and are highly motivated to get the best education possible for their children. AJA men are the least likely to marry outside of their ethnic group.

CAUCASIANS

White people have a distinction from all other ethnic groups in Hawaii—they are all lumped together as one. You can be anything from a Norwegian dock worker to a Greek shipping tycoon, but if your skin is white, you're a *haole*. What's more, you could have arrived at Waikiki from Missoula, Montana, in the last 24 hours, or your *kamaaina* family can go back five generations, but again, if you're white, you're a *haole*. The word *haole* has a floating connotation that depends upon the spirit in which it's used. It can mean everything from a derisive "honky or cracker" to nothing more than "white person." The exact Hawaiian meaning is clouded, but some say it meant "a man of no background," because white men couldn't chant a genealogical *kanaenae* telling the Hawaiians who they were. *Haole* then became euphemized into "foreign white man" and today simply "white person."

White History

Next to Hawaiians, white people have the oldest stake in Hawaii. Settlers in earnest since the missionaries of the 1820s, they were established long before any other migrant group. From last century until statehood old *haole* families owned and controlled everything, and although they were benevolent, philanthropic, and paternalistic, they were also racist. They felt (not without certain justification) that they had "made" Hawaii, and that they had the right to rule. Established *kamaaina* families, many of which made up the boards of the "Big Five" or owned huge plantations, formed an inner social circle closed to the outside except through marriage, and many managed to find mates from among close family acquaintances. Their paternalism, which they accepted with grave responsibility, at first only extended to the Hawaiians, who saw them

as replacing their own *ali'i*. Orientals were considered primarily as "instruments of production." These supremacist attitudes tended to drag on until quite recent times. Today, they're responsible for the sometimes sour relations between white and non-white people in the islands. Since the haole had the power over all the other ethnic groups for so long, they offended each group at one time or another. Today, all white people are resented to a certain degree for these past acts, although they were in no way involved.

White Plantation Workers

In the 1880s, the white landowners looked around and felt surrounded and outnumbered by Orientals. Many figured that these people would one day be a political force to be reckoned with, so they tried to import white people for plantation work. Some of the imported workers included: 600 Scandinavians in 1881; 1,400 Germans 1881-85; 400 Poles 1897-98; and 2,400 Russians 1909-12. None worked. Europeans were accustomed to much higher wages and better living conditions than provided on the plantations. Although they were workers, not considered the equals of the ruling elite, they were expected to act like a special class, and were treated preferentially, meaning higher wages for the same job performed by an Oriental. Even so, they proved troublesome, unwilling to work under Oriental conditions, and were especially resentful of Hawaiian *luna*. Most moved quickly to the Mainland, and the Poles and Russians even staged strikes after only months on the job. A contingency of Scots, who first came as mule skinners and gained a reputation for hard work and frugality, became successful plantation managers and supervisors. There were so many on the Hamakua Coast of the Big Island that it was dubbed the "Scotch Coast." The Germans and Scandinavians were well received and climbed the social ladder rapidly, becoming professionals and skilled workers. The Depression years, not as economically disastrous in Hawaii, brought more whites seeking opportunity. These new folks, many from the U.S. South and West tended to be even more racist towards brown-skinned people and Orientals than the *kamaaina haoles*. They made matters worse and competed more intensely for jobs.

The racial tension generated during this period came to a head in 1931 with the infamous **Massie Rape Case.** Thomas Massie, a naval officer, and his young wife Thalia attended a party at the Officers Club. After drinking and dancing all evening, they got into a row and Thalia rushed out in a huff. A few hours later, Thalia was at home, confused and hysterical, claiming to have been raped by some local men. On the most circumstantial evidence, Joseph Kahahawai and four friends of mixed ethnic background were accused. In a highly controversial trial rife with racial tensions, the verdict ended in a hung jury. While a new trial was being set, Kahahawai and his friends were out on bail. Seeking revenge, Thomas Massie and Grace Fortescue, Thalia's mother, kidnapped Joseph Kahawai with a plan of extracting a confession from him. They were aided by two enlisted men assigned to guard Thalia. While questioning Joseph, they killed him and attempted to dump his body in the sea but were apprehended. Another controversial trial—this time for Mrs. Fortescue, Massie, and the accomplices—followed. Clarence Darrow, the famous lawyer, sailed to Hawaii to defend them. For killing Kahahawai, these people served *one hour* of imprisonment in the judge's private chambers. The other four, acquitted with Joseph Kahahawai, maintain innocence of the rape to this day.

Later, the Massies divorced, and Thalia went on to become a depressed alcoholic who took her own life.

The Portuguese
The last time anyone looked, Portugal was still attached to the European continent, but for some anomalous reason they weren't considered *haole*. This was because they weren't part of the ruling elite, but merely workers, showing that at one time *haole* implied social standing and not just skin color. About 12,000 arrived from 1878-87 and another 6,000 came from 1906-13. They were accompanied during the latter period by 8,000 Spanish, who were considered one in the same. Most of the Portuguese were illiterate peasants from Madeira and the Azores, while the Spanish hailed from Andalucia. The majority of the Spanish and some Portuguese tended to leave for California as soon as they made passage money. Those that remained were well received because they were white but not *haole* and made a perfect "buffer" ethnic group. Unlike other Europeans, they would take any job, worked hard, and accepted authority. Committed to staying in Hawaii, they rose to be skilled workers and the *luna* class on the plantations. However, the Portuguese spent the least amount on education and became very racist toward Orientals, seeing them as a threat to job security. By 1920 27,000 Portuguese made up 11% of the population. After that they tended to blend with the other ethnic groups and weren't counted separately. Portuguese men married within their ethnic group, but a good portion of Portuguese women married other white men and became closer to the *haole* group, while another large portion chose Hawaiian mates. Although they didn't originate pidgin English (see "Language"), the unique melodious quality of their native tongue did give pidgin that certain lilt it has today. Also, the ukulele ("jumping flea") was closely patterned after a Portuguese stringed folk instrument.

The White Population
Today all white people together make up the largest racial, if not ethnic, group in the islands at 33% (about 330,000) of the population. Percentage-wise, they are spread evenly throughout Kauai, Oahu, Maui, and the Big Island, with much smaller percentages on Molokai and Lanai. Numerically, the vast majority (260,000) live on Oahu, in the more fashionable central valley and southeastern sections. Heavy white concentrations are also found on the Kihei and Kaanapali coasts of Maui and the north Kona Coast of Hawaii. The white population is also the fastest growing in the islands; most people resettling in Hawaii are white Americans predominantly from the West Coast.

FILIPINOS AND OTHERS

The Filipinos that came to Hawaii brought high hopes of making a fortune and returning home as rich heroes: for most this dream never came true. Filipinos were American nationals since the Spanish-American War of 1898, and as such weren't subject to the immigration laws that curtailed the importation of Oriental workers at the turn of the century. Fifteen families arrived in 1906, but a large number came in 1924 as strike breakers. The majority that came were illiterate

Ilocano peasants from the northern Philippines with about 10% Visayans from the central cities. The Visayans were not as hard-working or thrifty, but much more sophisticated. From the first, Filipinos were looked down upon by all the other immigrant groups, considered particularly uncouth by the Japanese. They put the least value on education of any group and, even by 1930, only half could speak rudimentary English, while the majority remained illiterate. They were billeted in the worst housing, performed the most menial jobs, and were the last hired and first fired. One big deterrent keeping Filipinos from becoming a part of mainstream society was that they had no women to marry, and they clung to the idea of returning home. In 1930 there were 30,000 men and only 360 women. This hopeless situation caused a great deal of prostitution and homosexuality, and many of these terribly lonely bachelors would feast and drink on weekends and engage in their gruesome but exciting pastime of cockfighting on Sunday. When some did manage to find wives, their mates were inevitably part Hawaiian.

Today, there are still plenty of old Filipino bachelors who never managed to get home, and the Sunday cockfight remains a way of life. Filipinos constitute 14% (140,000) of Hawaii's population, with almost 90% living on Oahu. The largest concentration, however, is on Lanai, where 1,100 Filipino pineapple workers make up 50% of that island's population. Many of these men are new arrivals with the same dream held by their countrymen for over 70 years. Many visitors to Hawaii mistake Filipinos for Hawaiians because of their dark skin. This case of mistaken identity irritates Hawaiians and Filipinos alike although some streetwise Filipinos claim to be Hawaiians because being Hawaiian is *in,* and it goes over well with tourists, especially the young women. For the most part, these people are hard-working, dependable laborers who do tough jobs for little recognition. They still remain low man on the social totem pole and have not yet organized to stand up for their rights.

Minor Groups

About 10% of Hawaii's population is made up of a conglomerate of small ethnic groups. Of these, the largest is **Korean** with 14,000 people. About 8,000 Koreans came to Hawaii from 1903-05 when their own government halted emigration. When Japan annexed their homeland in 1910, most Koreans realized that their future lay in Hawaii, and they settled in. During the same period about 6,000 **Puerto Ricans** arrived, but they have become so assimilated that only 4,000 people in Hawaii consider themselves Puerto Ricans. Two attempts were made last century to import other **Polynesians** to strengthen the dying Hawaiian race, but they were failures. In 1869, only 126 central Polynesian natives could be lured to Hawaii, and from 1878-85, 2,500 Gilbert Islanders arrived. Both groups became immediately disenchanted with Hawaii and could find no tangible reason to remain. They pined away for their own islands and departed for home as soon as possible. Today, however, 12,000 **Samoans** have resettled in Hawaii, and with more on the way are the fastest growing minority in the state. For unexplainable reasons, Samoans and native Hawaiians get along terribly, having the worst racial animosity of any groups. This is a true paradox, especially given the increased ethnic awareness of modern-day Hawaiians. The Samoans ostensibly should represent the archetypal Polynesians that the Hawaiians seek, but it doesn't work that way. Samoans are criticized by Hawaiians for their hot tempers, lingering feuds, and petty jealousies. They're clannish and are often the butt of "dumb" jokes. This racism seems especially ridiculous, but that's the way it is. Just to add a bit of exotic spice to Hawaii's people stew, there are about 10,000 **Afro-Americans,** a few thousand **American Indians,** and a smattering of **Vietnamese** refugees.

ETHNIC POPULATIONS

WHITE 33%
JAPANESE 25%
FILIPINO 14%
HAWAIIAN 12%
VARIOUS 10%
CHINESE 6%

RELIGION

The Lord saw fit to keep His island paradise secret from mankind for a few million years, but once we finally arrived we were awfully thankful. Hawaii sometimes appears like a floating tabernacle—everywhere you look there's a church, temple, shrine, or *heiau*. The islands are either very holy, or a powerful lot of sinning's going on to require so many houses of prayer. Actually, it's just America's "right to worship" concept fully employed . . . in microcosm. Everyone who came to Hawaii brought his own form of devotion. The Polynesian Hawaiians praised the primordial creators, Wakea and Papa, from whom their pantheon of animist-inspired gods sprang. Obviously, to a modern world these old gods would never do. There were simply too many, and belief in them was looked down upon as mere superstition, the folly of semi-civilized pagans. So, the famous missionaries of the 1820s brought Congregational Christianity and the "true path to heaven." Unfortunately, the Catholics, Mormons, Reformed Mormons, Adventists, Episcopalians, Unitarians, Christian Scientists, Lutherans, Baptists, Jehovah's Witnesses, the Salvation Army, and every other major and minor denomination of Christianity that followed in their wake brought their own brand of enlightenment. The Chinese and Japanese established all the major sects of Buddhism, Confucianism, Taoism, and Shintoism. Today, Allah is praised, the Torah is canted in Jewish synagogues, and nirvana is available at a variety of Hindu temples. If the spirit moves you, a Hare Krishna devotee will be glad to point you in the right direction and give you a free flower for only a dollar or two. If the world is still too much with you, you might find peace at a Church of Scientology, or meditate at a Kundalini Yoga institute, or perhaps find relief at a local assembly of Baha'i. Regardless, rejoice because in Hawaii you'll find not only paradise, you might even find salvation.

THE WATERS OF KANE

The Polynesian Hawaiians worshipped nature. They saw its forces manifested in a multiplicity of forms to which they ascribed godlike powers. Daily life was based on this animistic philosophy. Hand-picked and specially trained storytellers chanted the exploits of the gods. These ancient tales, kept alive in a special oral tradition called *moolelo,* were recited only by day. Entranced listeners encircled the chanter and, in respect for the gods and in fear of their wrath, were forbidden to move once the tale was begun. This was serious business where a man's life could be at stake; it was not like the telling of *kaao* which were simple fictions, tall tales of ancient heroes, merely related for amusement and to pass the long nights. Any object, animate or inanimate, could be a god. All could be infused with mana, especially a dead body or a respected ancestor. *Ohana* had personal family gods called *aumakua* on whom they called in times of danger or strife. Children of gods, called *kupua,* were thought to live among men, distinguished either for their beauty and strength or for their ugliness and terror. Hawaiian's believed that processions of dead *ali'i* called "Marchers of the Night" wandered through the land of the living, and unless you were properly protected it could mean death if they looked upon you. Simple ghosts known as *akua lapu* merely frightened people. Waterfalls, trees, springs, and a thousand forms of nature were the manifestations of *akua li'i* "little spirits" that could be invoked at any time for help or protection.

Behind all of these beliefs was an innate sense of natural balance and order, and the idea that everything had its opposite. The time of darkness when only the gods lived was *po.* When the great gods descended to Earth and created light, this was *ao,* and man was born. All of these *moolelo* are part of *The Kumulipo,* the great chant that records the Hawaiian version of creation. From the time that the gods descended and touched Earth at Ku Moku on Lanai, the genealogies were kept. Unlike the Bible, they included the noble families of both male and female *ali'i.*

Heiau And Idols

The basic *heiau* (temple) was a masterly built and fitted rectangular stone wall that varied in size from as large as a basketball court to the size of a football field. Once the restraining outer walls were built, the interior was backfilled with smaller stones, and the top dressing was expertly laid and then rolled, perhaps with a log, to form a pavement-like surface. All that remains of

Hawaii's many *heiau* are the stone platforms. The buildings—made from perishable wood, leaves and grass—have long disappeared. At some dreaded *heiau* humans were sacrificed. Tradition says that this barbaric custom began at Wahaula Heiau on the Big Island in the 12th century, introduced by a ferocious Tahitian priest named Paao. Other *heiau,* such as Puuhonua O Honaunau, also on the Big Island, were temples of refuge where the weak, widowed, orphaned, and vanquished could find sanctuary. Within *heiau* ceremonies were conducted by the priestly *kahuna.* Offerings of chickens, dogs, fish, fruit, and tapa were laid on the *lele,* a huge stone altar, in hopes that the gods would act favorably toward their people. Some buildings held the bones of dead *ali'i,* infused with their mana. Other structures were god houses in which idols resided, while others were oracle towers from which prophecies were made. The gods were honored by *ali'i* and *maka' ainana* alike, but the *kahuna* prayed for the *ali'i,* while the commoners represented themselves. There was a patron god for every aspect of life, especially farming and fishing, but gods could be invoked for everything from weaving to a special god who helped thieves! Men and women had their own gods, with rituals governing birth, cutting the umbilical cord, death, and sickness. Ceremonies, often lasting for many days, were conducted by *kahuna,* many of whom had highly specialized functions. Two of the most interesting were: *kahuna kilikilo,* who could see a person die in a dream and save his life through offerings of white dogs, chickens, tapa, and *awa;* and, *kahuna kaula,* semi-hermits, who could foretell the future.

All worshiped the gods in the form of idols, which were fashioned from wood, feathers, and stone. Some figures were over six feet tall, and crowned with elaborate head pieces. Figures were often pointed at the end so that they could be stuck into the ground. Until eyes, made from pearl shell, were fitted or carved, the idol was dormant. With eyes, it was alive! The hair used was often human hair, and the arms and legs were usually flexed. The mouth was either gaping or formed a figure eight on its side, usually lined with glistening dog teeth. Small figures were made of woven basketry expertly covered with red and yellow feathers taken from specific

Ku

birds by men whose only work was to roam the forests in search of them. It made no difference who or what you were in old Hawaii; the gods were ever-present, and they took a direct and active roll in your life.

GREAT GODS

Ku

The progenitors of the gods were Wakea, the "sky father," and Papa, the "earth mother," but the actual gods that were worshipped in Hawaii were Ku, Kane and Kanaloa, and Lono. Ku was a national god who represented the male aspect of nature, and Hina, the moon goddess, was his female counterpart. Ku was prayed to at sunrise and Hina at sunset. Ku's maleness was represented with pointed stones, while flat ones symbolized Hina's womanhood. Ku ruled the forest, land, mountains, farming and fishing—his benevolent side. But Ku was better known as the god of war. It was Ku that demanded human sacrifice, especially in times of calamity or in preparation for battle. At times, Ku was represented by an *ohia* log, and a human sacrifice was made in the forest where it was cut and also at the post hole that held it upright at the *heiau*. When Ku was invoked, the strict and serious ceremonies could go on for over a week. The entire *aha* (assembly) kept complete silence and sat ramrod straight with the left leg and hand crossed over the right leg and hand in an attitude called

neepu. At a precise command everyone simultaneously pointed their right hand heavenward. Anyone caught dozing or daydreaming, or who for some reason missed the command, instantly became the main course for Ku's lunch.

Kamehameha the Great carried a portable Ku into battle with him at all times, known as Kukailimoku ("the Snatcher of Lands"). It was held to be true that during battle this effigy, whose gaping mouth gleamed with canine incisors, would cry out in a loud voice and stir Kamehameha's warriors on to victory. After a battle, the slain enemies were taken to the *heiau* and placed upon Ku's altar with their arms encircling two pigs. Now Ku became Kuwahailo ("of the Dripping Maggot Mouth"). With Ku's killing nature appeased, the people would pray for good crops, good fishing, and fertile wives. The scales were balanced and life went on.

Kane And Kanaloa

Kane is the Hawaiian word for "man" or "husband," and he was the leading god of worship when the missionaries arrived. God of life, ancestor of all Hawaiians, the Hawaiian creation myth centers around Kane and the events depicted are amazingly similar to Genesis. Kane comes forward from *po* (darkness) into *ao* (light), and with the help of Ku and Lono, fashions man from clay gathered from the four cardinal points of the compass. Once the body is formed, the gods breathe (some say spit) into the mouth and nostrils and give it life. The man is placed upon a paradise island, *Kalani i hauola,* and a wife is fashioned for him out of his right side. Like Adam and Eve, these two break the law by eating from the forbidden tree and are driven from paradise by the sacred white albatross of Kane.

Kane is a forgiving god, who demands no human sacrifice, because all life is sacred to him. He is a god of a higher order, not usually rendered as an idol. Instead he was symbolized as a single upright male stone that was splashed with oil and wrapped in white tapa. Kanaloa, the antithesis of Kane, was represented as a great squid, and often likened to the Christian devil. He warred with Kane and was driven out of heaven along with his minions. Kanaloa became the ruler of the dead, and was responsible for all "black" sorcery and for all poisonous things. Oftentimes however, these two gods were linked together. For example, prayers would be offered to Kane when a canoe was built and to Kanaloa to provide favorable winds. Farmers and diviners often prayed simultaneously to Kane and Kanaloa. Both gods were intimately connected to water and the narcotic beverage *awa.*

Pele

The Hawaiian gods were toppled literally and figuratively in 1819, and began to fade from the minds of men. Two that remained prominent were Madame Pele, the fire goddess, who resides at Kilauea Volcano on Hawaii, and the demigod Maui who is like Paul Bunyan and Ulysses rolled into one. Many versions account for how Pele wound up living in Kilauea firepit, but they all follow a general outline. It seems that the beautiful young goddess, from a large family of gods, was struck by wanderlust. Tucking her young sister, who was conveniently in the form of an egg, under her armpit, she set out to see the world. Fortune had its ups and downs in store for young Pele. For one, she was ravished by a real swine, Kama pua'a the pig god. Moreover, she fought desperately with her sister, Namaka o Kahai, over the love of a handsome young chief; Pele's sister stalked her and smashed her bones on the Hana coast of Maui at a spot called *Kaiwi o Pele* (the Bones of Pele).

Pulling herself back together, Pele set out to make a love nest for her lover and herself. She chose the firepit at Kilauea Volcano and has long been held responsible for its lava flows along with anything else that deals with heat or fire. Pele can change her form from a withered old woman to a ravishing beauty; her moods can change from gentle to fiery hot. She is traditionally appeased with *ohelo* berries that were cast into her firepit, but lately she prefers juniper berries in the form of gin. Pele's myth was shattered by the Hawaiian queen Keopuolani, one of the earliest and most fervent converts to Christianity. In the 1820s this brave queen made her way to Kilauea fire pit and defiantly ate the *ohelo* berries sacred to Pele. She then cast stones into the pit and cried in a loud voice, "Jehovah is my god . . . it is my God not Pele that kindled these fires."

Still, stories abound of Pele's continuing powers. Modern-day *kahuna* are always consulted and prayers offered over construction of an *imu,* which falls under Pele's fire domain. It's said by traditional Hawaiians and educated *haole* that when Kilauea erupts, the lava miraculously stops before or circles around a homestead over which proper prayers were made to the fire goddess. In addition, the rangers at Volcanoes National Park receive hundreds of stones every year that were taken as souvenirs and then returned by shaken tourists, who claim bad luck stalked them from the day they removed Pele's sacred stones from her volcano. And, no one who has lived in the islands for any length of time will carry pork over the volcano at night, lest they offend the goddess. She's perhaps still angry with that swine, Kama pua'a.

The Strifes Of Maui

Of all the heroes and mythological figures of Polynesia, Maui is the best known. His "strifes" are like the great Greek epics, and they make excellent tales of daring that elders loved to relate to youngsters around the evening campfire. Maui was abandoned by his mother Hina of Fire, when he was an infant. She wrapped him in her hair and cast him upon the sea, where she expected him to die, but he lived and returned home to become her favorite. She knew then that he was a born hero and had strength far beyond that of mortal men. His first exploit was to "lift the sky." In those days the sky hung so low that men had to crawl around on all fours. A seductive young woman approached Maui and asked him to use his great strength to lift the sky. In fine heroic fashion this big boy agreed if the beautiful woman would, euphemistically, "give him a drink from her gourd." He then obliged her by lifting the sky.

The territory of man was small at that time, and Maui then decided that more land was needed and he conspired to "fish up islands." He descended into the land of the dead and petitioned an ancestress to fashion him a hook out of her jawbone. She obliged, and created the mythical hook *Manai ikalanai.* Maui then secured a sacred bird, the *alae* that he intended to use for bait. He bid his brothers to paddle him far out to sea, and when he arrived at the deepest spot, he lowered *Manai ikalani* baited with the sacred bird. His sister, Hina of the Sea, placed it into the mouth of "Old One Tooth" who held land fast to the bottom of the waters. Maui then exhorted his brothers to row, but warned them not to look back. They strained at the oars, and slowly a great land mass rose. One brother, overcome by curiosity, looked back, and when he did so, the land shattered into all of the islands of Polynesia.

Maui desired to serve mankind further. People were without fire and the secret was held by the sacred *alae,* who had learned it from Maui's beneficent ancestress. She had given Maui her burning fingernails, but he oafishly kept dropping them into streams until all had fizzled out, and he had totally irritated this generous relative. She pursued Maui trying to burn him to a cinder. Maui desperately chanted for rain to put out her scorching fires. When she saw her fires being quenched she hid her fire in the barks of special trees and informed common mud hens where they could be found, but first made them promise never to tell men. Maui learned of this, captured a mud hen, and threatened to wring its neck unless it gave up the secret. The bird tried trickery and told Maui first to rub together the stems of sugar cane, then banana and even taro. None worked, and Maui's determined rubbing is why these plants have hollow roots today. Finally, with Maui's hands tightening around the mud hen's neck, the bird confessed that fire could be found in the *hau* tree and also the sandalwood, which Maui named *ili aha* (fire bark). Maui then rubbed all the feathers of the mud hen's head for being so deceitful, and that's why their crown is featherless today.

Maui's greatest deed, however, was snaring the sun and exacting a promise that it would go slower across the heavens. The people had complained that there were not enough daylight hours to fish or farm. Maui's mother could not dry her tapa cloth because the sun rose and set so quickly. When she asked her son to help, Maui went to his blind grandmother for assistance. She lived on the slopes of Haleakala and was responsible for cooking the sun's bananas that he ate in passing every day. Maui kept stealing his granny's bananas until she agreed to help. She told him to personally weave 16 strong ropes and to make nooses out of his sister's hair. Some say these weavings came from her head, but other versions insist that it was no doubt Hina's pubic hair that had the power to hold "Sunny Boy." Maui positioned himself, and as each of the 16 rays of the sun came across Haleakala, he snared them until the sun was defenseless and had to bargain for his life. Maui

agreed to free him if he promised to go more slowly. The sun agreed, and Haleakala ("The House of the Sun") became his home.

Lono And The Makahiki Festival

Lono was a benevolent god of the clouds, harvest, and rain. In a fit of temper he killed his wife, whom he thought to be unfaithful. When he discovered his grave error, he roamed the countryside challenging everyone he met to a boxing match. Boxing later became an event of the Makahiki, the Harvest Festival, held in his honor. Lono decided to leave his island home, but promised one day to return on a floating island. Every year at the beginning of *ho'oilo* (winter), starting in October, the Makahiki was held. It was a jubilant time of harvest when taxes were collected and most *kapu* were lifted. It ended sometime in February, and then began the New Year. During this time great sporting events included surfing, boxing, sledding, and a form of bowling. At night, people feasted at luau to the rhythm of drums and hula. Fertility was honored, and willing partners from throughout the land coupled and husbands and wives shared their mates in the tradition of *puna'lua.* Lono's idol was an *akua loa,* a slender 15-foot

konane *board, Hawaiian checkers often played during the Makahiki Festival.*

pole with his small image perched atop. Another pole fastened at the top formed a cross. Hanging from the cross pole were long banners of white tapa and it was festooned with the feathers and skins of seabirds. To this image the *kahuna* offered red and white fish, black coconut, and immature *awa*. This image, called "Long God," proceeded in a procession clockwise around the island. It was met at every *ahuapuaa* (land division) by the chief of that region and new tapa was offered by the chieftess along with roasted taro. The *maka' ainana* came and offered their produce from sea and land and so the taxes were collected. At the end of the festival a naked man representing the god Kohoali'i ate the eyeball of a fish and one of a human victim and proclaimed the New Year.

It was just during the Makahiki that Capt. Cook sailed into Kealakekua Bay! *Kahuna* saw his great "floating islands" and proclaimed the return of Lono. Uncannily, the masts of the sailing ships draped in canvas looked remarkably like Lono's idol. Cook himself was particularly tall and white skinned, and many natives at first sight fell to their knees and worshiped him as "Lono returned."

THE CASTE (*KAPU*) SYSTEM

All was not heavenly in paradise due to horrible wars, but mostly the people lived a quiet and ordered life based on a strict caste society and the *kapu* system. Famine was contained to a regional level. The population was kept in check by herbal birth-control potions, crude abortions, and infanticide, especially of baby girls. The strict caste system was determined by birth, which there was no chance of changing. The highest rank was the *ali'i*, the chiefs and royalty. The impeccable genealogies of the *ali'i* were traced back to the gods themselves, and recorded in chants (*mo'o ali'i*) memorized and sung by professionals called *ku'auhau*. Ranking passed from both father and mother, and custom dictated that the first mating of an *ali'i* be with a person of equal rank. After a child was produced, the *ali'i* was free to mate with lesser *ali'i* or even with a commoner. The custom of **punalua,** the sharing of mates, was practiced throughout Hawaiian society. Moreover, incest was not only condoned but sanctioned among *ali'i*. To achieve an offspring of the highest rank *ni'au pi'o*

HAWAII STATE ARCHIVES

a royal woman of the Sandwich Isles as drawn by Jacques Arago, c. 1819

("coconut leaf looped back on itself"), the parents were required to be full brothers and sisters. These offspring were so sacred that they were considered an *akua* ("living god"), and people of all rank had to literally crawl on their stomachs in their presence. *Ali'i* that ran society were of lesser rank, and they were the real functionaries. The two most important were the land supervisors (*konohiki*) and caste priests (*kahuna*). The *konohiki* were in charge of the *ahua'pua*, pie-shaped land divisions running from mountain to sea. The common people came in contact with these *ali'i* who also collected taxes and ruled as judges amongst the people.

Kahuna were highly skilled people whose advice was sought before any major undertaking such as building a house, hollowing a canoe log, or even offering a prayer. The *mo'o kahuna* were the priests of Ku and Lono, in charge of praying and following rituals. These powerful *ali'i* kept strict secrets and laws concerning their various functions. The *kahuna* dedicated to *Ku* were severe: it was they that sought human sacrifice. The *kahuna* of Lono were more comforting to the people, but were of lesser rank than the Ku *kahuna*. Other *kahuna* were not *ali'i* but commoners. The two most important were the healers (*kahuna lapa'au*), and the black magicians (*kahuna ana'ana*), who could pray a person to death. The *kahuna lapa'au* had a marvelous pharmacopia of herbs and spices that could cure over 250 diseases. They employed baths, massage and used various colored stones to outline the human body and accurately pinpoint not only the organs but the internal origins of illness. The *kahuna ana ana* were given a wide berth by the people, who did everything possible to stay on their good side! The *kahuna ana ana* could be hired to cast a love spell over a person or cause his untimely death. They seldom had to send a reminder of payment!

The common people were called the **maka'-ainana,** "people of the land." They were the farmers, craftsmen, and fishermen. Their land was owned by the *ali,* but they were not bound to it. If the local *ali'i* was cruel or unfair, the *maka'ainana* had the right to leave. Very unjust *ali'i* were even put to death by their own people, with no retribution if their accusations proved true. The *maka'ainana* mostly loved their local *ali'i,* and vice versa. *Maka'ainana* who lived close to the *ali'i* and could be counted on as warriors in times of trouble were called *kanaka no lua kaua,* "a man for the heat of battle." They were treated with greater favor than those who lived in the backcountry, *kanaka no hii kua,* whose lesser standing opened them up to discrimination and cruelty. All *maka'ainana* formed extended families *(ohana)* and usually lived on the same section of land *(ahuapua'a).* Inland farmers would barter their produce with fishermen; thus all shared equally in the bounty of the land and sea.

A special group **(kauwa)** was a landless untouchable caste confined to living on reservations. Their origins were obviously Polynesian, but they appeared to be remnants of castaways that had survived and become perhaps the aboriginals of Hawaii before the main migrations. It was *kapu* for anyone to go onto *kauwa* lands; doing so meant instant death. If a *kauwa* was driven by necessity to leave his lands, he was required to cover his head with tapa cloth, with his eyes focused on the ground in a humble manner. If a human sacrifice was needed, the *kahuna* simply summoned a *kauwa* who had no recourse but to mutely comply. Through the years after discovery by Cook, the *kauwa* became obscured as a class and mingled with the remainder of the population. But even to this day, calling someone *kauwa,* which now supposedly only means servant, is still considered a fight-provoking insult.

Kapu And Daily Life

A strict division of labor existed between men and women. Only men were permitted to have anything to do with taro, a foodstuff so sacred that it had a greater *kapu* than man himself. Men pounded poi and served it to the women. Men were also the fishermen and builders of houses, canoes, irrigation ditches, and walls. Women tended gardens and were responsible for making tapa and tending to shoreline fishing. The entire family lived in the common house *(hale noa).* But certain things were *kapu* between the sexes. The primary *kapu* was that women could not enter the *mua* (men's house) nor could they eat with men. Certain foods such as pork and bananas were forbidden to women. It was *kapu* for a man to have intercourse before going fishing, engaging in battle, or attending a religious ceremony. Young boys lived with the women until they underwent circumcision *(pule ipu),* after which they were required to keep the *kapu* of men.

Ali'i could also declare a *kapu,* and often did so. Certain lands or fishing areas were temporarily made *kapu* so that they could revitalize. Even today, it is *kapu* for anyone to remove all the *opihi* (a type of limpet) from a rock. The great King Kamehameha I even placed a *kapu* on the body of his notoriously unfaithful child bride, Kaahumanu. It didn't work! The greatest *kapu* *(kapu moe)* was afforded to the highest ranking *ali'i:* anyone coming into their presence had to prostrate themselves. Lesser ranking *ali'i* were afforded the *kapu noho:* lessers had to sit or kneel in their presence. Commoners could not let their shadows fall upon an *ali'i* or enter their house except through a special door. Breaking a *kapu* meant immediate death.

Fun And Games

The native Hawaiians loved sports. A type of "Olympiad" was held each year during the Makahiki Festival. Events included boxing, swimming, diving, surfing, and running. A form of bowling used polished wheel-shaped stones that tested for distance and accuracy. Hawaiians also enjoyed a more cerebral chess-like game called *konane.* Intricately carved *konane* boards survive to this day. Hawaiians built special downhill courses for a runnered bobsled called a *holua.* They could coast over wet grasses or leaves for 200 yards. Strangely enough the

Punishment of a
kapu-breaker was
harsh and swift.

JACQUES ARAGO,
HAWAII STATE ARCHIVES

Hawaiians developed a bow and arrow but never employed it in warfare. It was merely a toy for shooting at targets or rats.

The greatest sport of all was surfing. **Surfing** originated with the Hawaiians and many old records recount this singularly exhilarating activity. The boards, made of various woods, were greatly cared for, measuring up to 15 feet long and six inches thick. James King, a lieutenant with Cook, was "altogether astonished" by surfing, and Rev. Ellis wrote in 1826 "... to see fifty or a hundred persons riding on an immense billow ... for a distance of several hundred yards together is one of the most novel and interesting sports a foreigner can witness in the islands."

Ghosts

The Hawaiians had countless superstitions and ghost legends, but two of the more interesting involve astral travel of the soul, and the "death marchers." The soul, *uhane,* was considered by Hawaiians to be totally free and independent of its body, *kino.* The soul could separate, leaving the body asleep or very drowsy. This disincorporated soul *(hihi'o)* could visit people, and was considered quite different from a *lapu,* an ordinary spirit of a dead person. A *kahuna* could immediately recognize if a person's *uhane* had left his body, and a special wreath was placed upon his head to protect them and to facilitate reentry.

If a person was confronted by an apparition, he could test to see if it was indeed dead or still alive by placing leaves of an *ape* plant upon the ground. If the leaves tore when they were walked upon, the spirit was merely human, but if they remained intact it was a ghost. Also, you could sneak up and startle the vision and if it disappeared it was a ghost, or if no reflection of the face appeared when it drank water from an offered calabash, it was also a ghost. Unfortunately, there were no instructions to follow once you had determined that you indeed had a ghost on your hands. Maybe it was better not to know! Some people would sprinkle salt and water around their houses, but this only kept away evil spirits, not ghosts.

There are also many stories of *kahuna* restoring a soul to a dead body. First they had to catch it and keep it in a gourd. They then placed beautiful tapa and fragrant flowers and herbs about the body to make it more enticing. Slowly, they would coax the soul out of the gourd, which reentered the body through the big toe.

Death Marchers

One inexplicable phenomenon that many people attest to is *ka huakai o ka po,* "Marchers of the Night." This march of the dead is fatal if you gaze upon it unless one of the marchers happens to be a friendly ancestor that will protect you. The peak time for "the march" is from 7:30 p.m. till 2 a.m. The marchers can be dead *ali'i* and warriors, the gods themselves, or the lesser *aumakua*. When the *aumakua* march there is usually chanting and music. *Ali'i* marches are more somber. The entire procession, lit by torches, oftentimes stops at the house of a relative and might even carry them away. When the gods themselves march, there is often thunder, lightning, and heavy seas. The sky is lit with torches, and they walk six abreast, three gods and three goddesses. If you get in the way of a march, remove your clothing and prostrate yourself. If the marching gods or *aumakua* happen to be ones to which you prayed, you might be spared. If it's a march of the *ali'i* you might make it if you lie face upward and feign death. If you *do* see a death march, that last thing that you'll worry about is lying naked on the ground and looking ridiculous.

MISSIONARIES ONE AND ALL

In Hawaii when you say "missionaries," it usually refers to the small determined band of Congregationalists that arrived aboard the *Brig Thaddeus* in 1820 and the "companies" or "packets" that reinforced them over the next 40 years. They were sent from Boston by the American Board of Commissioners for Foreign Missions (ABCFM), who learned of the "godless plight" of the Hawaiian people from returning sailors and from the few Hawaiians that had come to America to study. A young man named Opukahaia was instrumental in bringing the missionaries to Hawaii. An orphan befriended by a captain and taken to New England, he studied theology, and was obsessed with the desire to return home to save his people from sure damnation. His widely read accounts of life in Hawaii were the direct cause of the formation of the Pioneer Company to the Sandwich Islands Missions. Unfortunately, Opukahaia died in New England from typhus in 1819, the year before the missionaries sailed.

The missionaries first task was to Christianize and civilize. They met with extreme hostility—not from the natives, but from sailors and traders content with the open debauchery and wanton whoremongering that was the status quo in 1820s Hawaii. Many incidents of direct confrontation between these two factions even included the cannonading of missionary homes by American sea captins who were denied the customary services of island women thanks to the meddlesome "do gooders." Actually, the situation was much closer to the sentiments of James Jarves who wrote, "the missionary was a far more useful and agreeable man than his catechism would indicate; and the trader was not so bad a man as the missionary would make him out to be." The missionary's aim was conversion, but the fortuitous byproduct was education that raised the consciousness of every Hawaiian regardless of his religious affiliation.

The American Board of Missions officially ended its support in 1863, and in 40 short years Hawaii was considered a civilized nation well on the road to modernity. Some of Hawaii's finest museums and grandest architecture are part of the missionary legacy. Some of the most notable are: Mokuaikaua Church in Kona, Hawaii, the first Christian church founded in 1820; the Lyman House Museum of Hilo; Kawaiahao Church in Honolulu, founded 1821, and next door the superb Mission Houses Museum; Wainee Church, the first stone church in Hawaii, founded in Lahaina in 1828, and the Baldwin Home just down Front Street; Lahainaluna High School and Printing House, the first American school and publishing house west of the Rockies. The churches, but especially the homes and

In a sennit casket rested the bones of the dead.

museums, offer not only a glimpse of religious life, but are some of the finest "windows" into 19th century America. Their collections of artifacts, utensils, and general memorabilia put life and times of 18th C. Yankees in a setting that could hardly be more different than New England.

Bonanza For Missionaries

Although the missionaries were the first, they by no means had the field to themselves. Hot on the same religious trail came the Catholics— French Sacred Hearts led by Father Bachelot who arrived in Honolulu in July 1827 aboard the *La Comete*. Immediately Queen Kaahumanu, who had been converted by the Congregationalists, ordered them to leave. They refused. For the next 10 years the Catholic priests and their converts met with open hostility and persecution which, in true missionary fashion, only strengthened their resolve. The humiliation of a young convert, Juliana Keawahine, who was tied to a tree and scourged, became a religious rallying point, and after this incident the persecutions stopped. Honolulu's Our Lady of Peace Cathedral was completed in 1843 and Ahuimanu Catholic School, Oahu's counterpart to Lahainaluna, opened for instruction in 1846. Today, Roman Catholicism with 290,000 adherents (29% of the state's total) is the single largest religious group in Hawaii.

The Saints Come Marching In

A strange episode in Hawaii's history involved the Mormons. In 1850, the Latter-Day Saints arrived direct from missionary work in California gold fields. By 1852, George Cannon had already translated the *Book of Mormon* into Hawaiian. The five original Mormon missionaries spent every moment traveling and converting the Hawaiians. They had a grand plan of constructing a "City of Joseph" on Lanai, where they managed to gain a large tract of land. In 1858 the Mormon Wars broke out in Utah and the missionaries were called home. One of their band, Walter Murray Gibson, who stayed to manage the fledgling Mormon Church, became one of the most controversial and singularly strange fixtures in Hawaiian politics. When the Mormons returned in 1864, they found that Gibson had indeed carried on the "City of Joseph,"

but had manipulated all of the deeds and land grants into his personal possession. Furthermore, he had set himself up as an omnipotent grand patriarch and openly denounced the polygamous beliefs of the Mormons of the day. Immediately excommunicated, Gibson was abandoned to his fate and the Mormons moved to Oahu where they founded a sugar plantation and temple in Laie.

The Mormon Church now has approximately 32,000 members, the largest Protestant denomination in Hawaii. Their settlement at Laie is now home to an impressive Mormon Temple and an island branch of Brigham Young University. Close by, the Mormons also operate the Polynesian Culture Center which is one of the top five tourist attractions in all of Hawaii. As for Gibson, he was elected to the legislature in 1876 and became a private counselor to King Kalaukaua. In 1882, he worked himself into the office of "Premier," which he ran like a petty dictator. One of his more visionary suggestions was to import Japanese labor. Two of his most ridiculous were to drive all non-Hawaiians from the islands (excluding himself) and gather all Oceania into one Pacific nation with Hawaii in the lead. By 1887 he and Kalaukaua had so infuriated the sugar planters that Gibson was railroaded out of the islands and Kalaukaua was forced to sign a constitution that greatly limited his power. Gibson died in 1888 and his daughter Talulah sold the lands on Lanai for a song, after she and her husband tried but failed to grow sugar cane.

Non-Christians

By the turn of this century, Shintoism (brought by the Japanese) and Buddhism (brought by both the Japanese and Chinese) were firmly established in Hawaii. The first official Buddhist Temple was Hongpa Hongwanji, established on Oahu in 1889. Buddhist sects combined have about 170,000 parishioners (177 of the islands' religious total); there are perhaps 50,000 Shintoists. The Hindu religion has 2,000 adherents, with about the same number of Jewish people living throughout Hawaii, though only one synagogue, Temple Emanuel, is on Oahu. About 10,000 people are in new religious movements and lesser-known faiths such as Baha'i and Unitarianism. The largest number of people in Hawaii (300,000) remain unaffiliated.

LANGUAGE

Hawaii is America and people speak English there, but that's not the whole story. If you turn on the TV to catch the evening news, you'll hear "Walter Cronkite" English, unless of course you happen to tune in a Japanese-language broadcast designed for tourists from that country. You can easily pick up a Chinese-language newspaper, or groove to the music on a Filipino radio station, but let's not confuse the issue. All your needs and requests at airports, car rental agencies, restaurants, hotels, or wherever you happen to travel will be completely understood, as well as answered, in English. However, when you happen to overhear "islanders" speaking, what they're saying will sound somewhat familiar, but you won't be able to pick up all the words, and the beat and melody of the language will be noticeably different. Hawaii, like New England, the deep South, and the Midwest, has its own unmistakable linguistic regionalism. All the ethnic peoples who make up Hawaii have enriched the English spoken there with words, expressions, and subtle shades of meaning that are commonly used and understood throughout the islands. The greatest influence on English has come from the Hawaiian language itself, and words such as aloha, kapu, and muumuu are familiarly used and understood by most Americans. Other migrant peoples, especially the Chinese, Japanese, and Portuguese, influenced the local dialect to such an extent that the simplified plantation lingo that they spoke has become known as "pidgin." A fun and enriching part of the "island experience" is picking up a few words of Hawaiian and pidgin. English is the official language of the state, business, education, and perhaps even the mind; but pidgin is the language of the people, the emotions, and life, while Hawaiian remains the language of the heart and the soul.

PIDGIN

The dictionary definition of pidgin is: a simplified language with a rudimentary grammar used as a means of communication between people speaking different languages. Hawaiian pidgin is a little more complicated than that. It had its roots during the plantation days of last century when white owners and *luna* had to communicate with recently arrived Chinese, Japanese, and Portuguese laborers. It was designed as a simple language of the here and now, and was primarily concerned with the necessary functions of working, eating, and sleeping. It has an economical noun-verb-object structure (not necessarily in that order). Hawaiian words make up most of pidgin's non-English vocabulary. There is a good smattering of Chinese, Japanese, Samoan, and the distinctive rising inflection is provided by the melodious Mediterranean lilt of the Portuguese. Pidgin is not a stagnant language. It's kept alive by hip new words introduced by people who are "so radical," or especially by slang words introduced by teenagers. It's a colorful English, like "jive" or "ghettoese" spoken by Afro-Americans, and is as regionally unique as the speech of Cajuns from Louisiana's bayous. *Makaainana* of all socio-ethnic backgrounds can at least understand pidgin. Most islanders are proud of it, while some consider it a low-class jargon. The Hawaiian House of Representatives has given pidgin an official sanction, and most people feel that it adds a real local style and should be preserved.

Pidgin Lives

Pidgin is first learned at school where all students, regardless of background, are exposed to it. The pidgin spoken by young people today is "fo' real" different from that of their parents. It's no longer only plantation talk, but has moved to the streets and picked up some sophistication. At one time there was an academic movement to exterminate it, but that idea died away with the same thinking that insisted on making lefthanded people write with their right hand. It is strange, however, that pidgin has become the unofficial language of Hawaii's grass-roots movement, when it actually began as a white owners' language which was used to supplant Hawaiian and all other languages brought to the islands. Although hip young *haoles* use it all the time, it has gained some of the connotation of being the language of the non-white locals, and is part of the "us against them" way of thinking. All local people, *haole* or not, do consider pidgin their own island language, and don't really like it when it's used by *malihini* (newcomers). If you're in the islands long enough, you don't have to bother learning pidgin; it'll learn you. There's a book sold all over the islands called *Pidgin to da Max*, written by (you guessed it) a *haole* from Nebraska named Doug Simonson. You might not be able to understand what's being said by locals speaking pidgin (that's usually the idea), but you should be able to *feel* what's being meant.

CAPSULE PIDGIN

The following are a few commonly used words and expressions that should give you an idea of pidgin. It really can't be written properly, merely approximated, but for now, *"Brah, study da' kine an' bimbye you be hele on, brah! O.K.? Lesgo."*

an' den—and then? big deal; so what's next; how boring

bimbye—after a while; bye and bye. "Bimbye, you learn pidgin."

blalah—brother, but actually only refers to a large, heavyset, good-natured Hawaiian man

brah—all the bros in Hawaii are brahs; brother; pal. Used to call someone's attention. One of the most common words used even among people who are not acquainted. After a fill-up at a gas station, a person would say, "Tanks, brah."

cockaroach—steal; rip off. If you really want to find out what *cockaroach* means, just leave your camera on your beach blanket when you take a little dip.

da' kine—a catchall word of many meanings that epitomizes the essence of pidgin. *Da' kine* is easily used as a euphemism for pidgin and is substituted whenever the speaker is at a loss for a word or just wants to generalize. It can mean: you know? watchamacallit; of that type.

geev um—give it to them; give them hell; go for it. Can be used as an encouragement. If a surfer is riding a great wave, the people on the beach might yell, "Geev um, brah!"

hana ho—again. Especially after a concert the audience shouts "hana ho" (one more!).

hele on—right on! hip; with it; groovy

howzit?—as in "howzit brah?" what's happening? how is it going? The most common greeting, used in place of the more formal "How do you do?"

hu hu—angry! "You put the make on the wrong da' kine wahine brah, and you in da' kine trouble, if you get one big Hawaiian blalah plenty *hu hu*."

kapu—a Hawaiian word meaning forbidden. If *kapu* is written on a gate or posted on a tree it means "No trespassing." *Kapu*-breakers are still very unpopular in the islands.

lesgo—Let's go! Do it!

li'dis an' li'dat—like this or that; a catch-all grouping especially if you want to avoid details; like, ya' know?

lolo buggah—stupid or crazy guy (person). Words to a tropical island song go, "I want to find the lolo who stole my pakalolo."

mo' bettah—real good!; great idea. An island sentiment used to be, "mo' bettah you come Hawaii." Now it has subtly changed to, "mo' bettah you *visit* Hawaii."

ono—number one! delicious; great; groovy. "Hawaii is ono, brah!"

pakalolo—literally "crazy smoke"; marijuana; grass; reefer. "Hey, brah! Maui-wowie da' kine ono pakalolo."

pakiki head—stubborn; bull-headed

pau—a Hawaiian word meaning finished; done; over and done with. *Pau hana* means end of work or quitting time. Once used by plantation workers, now used by everyone.

stink face—basically frowning at someone; using facial expression to show displeasure. Hard looks. What you'll get if you give local people a hard time.

swell head—burned up; angry

talk story—spinning yarns; shooting the breeze; throwing the bull; a rap session. If you're lucky enough to be around to hear *kapuna* (elders) "talk story," you can hear some fantastic tales in the tradition of old Hawaii.

tita—sister, but only used to describe a fun-loving, down-to-earth country girl

waddascoops—what's the scoop? what's up? what's happening?

HAWAIIAN

The Hawaiian language sways like a palm tree in a gentle wind. Its words are as melodious as a love song. Linguists say that you can learn a lot about people through their language: when you hear Hawaiian you think of gentleness and love, and it's hard to imagine the ferocious side so evident in Hawaii's past. With many Polynesian root words that are easily traced to Indonesian and Malayan, it's evident that Hawaiian is from this same stock. The Hawaiian spoken today is very different from old Hawaiian. Its greatest metamorphosis occurred when the missionaries began to write it down in the 1820s. There is a movement to reestablish the Hawaiian language, and courses in it are offered at the University of Hawaii. Many scholars have put forth translations of Hawaiian, but there are endless, volatile disagreements in the academic sector about the real meanings of Hawaiian words. Hawaiian is no longer spoken as a language ex-

cept on Niihau, and the closest tourists will come to it is in place names, street names, and in words that have become part of common usage, such as *aloha* and *mahalo*. A few old Hawaiians still speak it at home and there are sermons in Hawaiian at some local churches. Kawaiahao Church in downtown Honolulu is the most famous of these. (See glossary for lists of commonly used Hawaiian words.)

Wiki Wiki Hawaiian

Thanks to the missionaries, the Hawaiian language is rendered phonetically using only 12 letters. They are the five vowels, a-e-i-o-u, sounded as they are in Italian, and seven consonants, h-k-l-m-n-p-w, sounded exactly as they are in English. Sometimes "w" is pronounced as "v," but this only occurs in the middle of a word and always follows a vowel. A consonant is always followed by a vowel, forming two-letter syllables, but vowels are often found in pairs or even triplets. A slight oddity about Hawaiian is the "glottal stop." This is merely an abrupt break in sound in the middle of a word such as "oh-oh" in English, and is denoted with an apostrophe ('). A good example is *ali'i* or even better, the Oahu town of **Ha'iku**, which actually means "abrupt break."

Pronunciation Key

For those unfamiliar with the sounds of Italian or other Romance languages, the vowels are sounded as follows:

A—in stressed syllables, long **a** as in **ah** (that feels good!). For example, Haleakala (**Hah** lay **ah** kah lah.) Unstressed syllables get a short **a** as in again or above." For example, Kamehameha (**Ka**meha**meha**).

E—short **e** as in pen or dent (Hale). Long **e** sounded like ay as in sway or day. For example the Hawaiian goose (**Ne ne**) is a "nay nay," not a "knee knee."

I—a long **i** as in see or we (Hawaii or pali).

O—round **o** as in no or oh (k**o**a, or **Ono**).

U—round **u** like do or stew.(ka**pu**, or **puna**).

Diphthongs

There are also eight vowel pairs known as "diphthongs" (ae-ai-ao-au-ei-eu-oi-ou). These are the sounds made by **gliding** from one vowel to another within a syllable. The stress is placed on the first vowel. In English, examples would be soil and euphoria. Common examples in Hawaiian are *lei* (lay) and *heiau*.

THE ALPHABET.

—◦‡◦—

VOWELS.		SOUND.	
Names.		Ex. in Eng.	Ex. in Hawaii.
A a ---â		as in *father*,	la—sun.
E e --- a		— *tele*,	hemo—cast off.
I i --- e		— *marine*,	marie—quiet.
O o ---o		— *over*,	ono—sweet.
U u --- oo		—*rule*,	nui—large.

CONSONANTS.	*Names.*	CONSONANTS.	*Names.*
B b	be	**N n**	nu
D d	de	**P p**	pi
H h	he	**R r**	ro
K k	ke	**T t**	ti
L l	la	**V v**	vi
M m	mu	**W w**	we

The following are used in spelling foreign words:

F f	fe	S s	se
G g	ge	Y y	yi

cover page of the first Hawaiian primer

Stress

The best way to learn which syllables are stressed in Hawaiian is just by listening closely. It becomes obvious after a while. There are also some vowel sounds that are held longer than others and these can occur at the beginning of a word such as the first "a" in *aina* or in the middle of a word like the first "a" in *lanai*. Again, it's a matter of tuning your ear and paying attention. No one is going to give you a hard time if you mispronounce a word. It's good, however, to pay close attention to the pronunciation of street and place names because many Hawaiian words sound alike and a misplaced vowel here or there could be the difference in getting to where you want to go and getting lost.

CAPSULE HAWAIIAN

The list on the following pages is merely designed to give you a "taste" of Hawaiian and to provide a basic vocabulary of words in common usage which you are likely to hear. Becoming familiar with them is not a strict necessity, but they will definitely enhance your experience and make it more congenial when talking with local people. You'll soon notice that many islanders spice their speech with certain words, especially when they're speaking "pidgin," and you too can use them just as soon as you feel comfortable. You might even discover some Hawaiian words that are so perfectly expressive that they'll become a regular part of your vocabulary. Many Hawaiian words have actually made it into the English dictionary. Place names, historical names, and descriptive terms used throughout the text may not appear in the lists below, but will be cited in the glossary at the back of the book. Also see "Pidgin," "Food," and "Getting Around" for applicable Hawaiian words and phrases in these categories. The definitions given are not exhaustive, but are generally considered the most common.

BASIC VOCABULARY

a'a—rough clinker lava. *A'a* has become the correct geological term to describe this type of lava found anywhere in the world.

ae—yes

akamai—smart; clever; wise

ali'i—a Hawaiian chief or nobleman

aloha—the most common greeting in the islands. Can mean both hello and goodbye, welcome or farewell. It also can mean romantic love, affection or best wishes.

aole—no

hale—house or building; often combined with other words to name a specific place such as Haleakala ("House of the Sun"), or Hale Pai at Lahainaluna, meaning "printing house"

hana—work; combined with *pau* means end of work or quitting time

haole—a word that at one time meant foreigner, but now means a white person or Caucasian. Many etymological definitions have been put forth, but none satisfy everyone. Some feel that it signified a person without a background, because the first white men could not chant their genealogies as was common to Hawaiians.

hapa—half, as in a mixed-blooded person being refered to as *hapa haole*

hapai—pregnant. Used by all ethnic groups when a *keiki* is on the way

heiau—a traditional Hawaiian temple. A platform made of skillfully fitted rocks, upon which structures were built and offerings made to the gods

holomuu—an ankle-length dress that is much more fitted than a muumuu, and which is often worn on formal occasions

hoolaulea—any happy event, but especially a family outing or picnic

hoomalimali—sweet talk; flattery

hu hu—angry; irritated; mad

hui—a group; meeting; society. Often used to refer to Chinese businessmen or familiy members who pool their money to get businesses started

hula—a native Hawaiian dance where the rhythm of the islands is captured in swaying hips and the stories told by lyrically moving hands

huli huli—barbecue, as in *huli huli* chicken

imu—underground oven filled with hot rocks and used for baking. The main cooking feature at a luau, used to steam-bake the pork and other succulent dishes. Traditionally the tending of the *imu* was for men only.

ipo—sweetheart; lover; girl or boyfriend

kahuna—priest; sorcerer; doctor; skillful person. *Kahuna* had tremendous power in old Hawaii which they used for both good and evil. The *kahuna ana'ana* was a feared individual because he practiced "black magic" and could pray a person to death, while a *kahuna lapa'au* was a medical practitioner bringing aid and comfort to the people.

kalua—means roasted underground in an *imu*. A favorite island food is *kalua* pork.

kamaaina—a child of the land; an old-timer; a longtime island resident of any ethnic background; a resident of Hawaii or native son. Oftentimes, hotels and air-lines offer discounts called *"kamaaina rates"* to anyone who can prove island residency.

kane—means man, but is actually used to signify a husband or boyfriend. Written on a door, it means "men's room."

kapu—forbidden; taboo; keep out; do not touch

kapuna—a grandparent or old-timer; usually means someone who has gained wisdom. The statewide school system now invites *kapuna* to talk to the children about the old ways and methods.

kaukau—slang word meaning food or chow; grub. Some of the best eating in Hawaii is from *"kaukau* wagons," which are trucks from which plate lunches and other morsels are sold.

keiki—child or children; used by all ethnic groups. "Have you hugged your *keiki* today?"

kokua—help. As in "Your *kokua* is needed to keep Hawaii free from litter."

kona wind—a muggy subtropical wind that blows from the south and hits the leeward side of the islands. It usually brings sticky hot weather, and is one of the few times when air-conditioning will be appreciated.

lanai—veranda or porch. You'll pay more for a hotel room if it has a lanai with an ocean view.

lei—a traditional garland of flowers or vines. One of Hawaii's most beautiful cus-toms. Given at any auspicious occasion, but especially when arriving or leaving Hawaii

limu—varieties of edible seaweed gathered from the shoreline. It makes an excellent salad, and is used to garnish many island dishes—a favorite at luaus.

lomilomi—traditional Hawaiian massage; also, a vinegared salad made up of raw salmon, chopped onions, and spices

lua—the toilet; the head; the bathroom

luau—a Hawaiian feast featuring poi, *imu*-baked pork and other traditional foods. A good luau provides some of the best gastronomical delights in the world.

mahalo—thanks; thank you. *Mahalo nui* means big thanks or thank you very much.

mahu—a homosexual; often used derisively like "fag" or "queer"

makai—toward the sea; used by most islanders when giving directions

malihini—what you are if you have just ar-rived: a newcomer; a tenderfoot; a recent arrival

manauahi—free; gratis; extra

manini—stingy; tight. A Hawaiianized word taken from the name of Don Francisco *Marin,* who was instrumental in bringing many fruits and plants to Hawaii. He was known for never sharing any of the bounty from his substantial gardens on Vineyard Street in Honolulu; therefore his name came to mean stingy.

mauka—toward the mountains; used by most islanders when giving directions

mauna—mountain. Often combined with other words to be more descriptive, as in Mauna Kea ("White Mountain")

moana—the ocean; the sea. Many businesses and hotels as well as place names have *moana* as part of their name.

muumuu—the garment introduced by the missionaries to cover the nakedness of the Hawaiians. A "Mother Hubbard," a long dress with a high neckline that has become fashionable attire for almost any occasion in Hawaii

ohana—a family; the fundamental social division; extended family. Now used to denote a social organization with "grass-roots," as in the "Save Kahoolawe Ohana."

okolehau—literally "iron bottom"; a traditional booze made from *ti* root; *okole* means your "rear end" and *hau* means iron, which was descriptive of the huge blubber pots that it was made in. Also, if you drink too much it'll surely knock you on your *okole*.

ono—delicious; delightful; the best. *Ono ono* means "extra or absolutely" delicious.

opu—belly; stomach

pa'hoehoe—smooth ropey lava that looks like burnt pancake batter *Pa'hoehoe* is now the correct geological term used to describe this type of lava found anywhere in the world.

pakalolo—"crazy smoke"; marijuana; grass; smoke; dope

pali—a cliff; precipice. Hawaii's geology makes them quite common. The most famous are the *pali* of Oahu where a major battle was fought.

paniolo—a Hawaiian cowboy. Derived from the Spanish *espaniola*. The first cowboys brought in during the early 19th century were Mexicans from California.

pau—finished; done; completed. Often combined into *pau hana*, which means end of work or quitting time

pilau—stink; smells bad; stench

pilikia—trouble of any kind, big or small; bad times

poi—a glutinous paste made from the pounded corm of taro which, slightly fermented, has a light sour taste. Purplish in color, it is a staple at luaus, where it is called one-, two-, or three-finger poi, depending upon its thickness.

pono—righteous or excellent

puka—a hole of any size. *Puka* is used by all island residents and can be employed when talking about a tiny *puka* in a rubber boat or a *puka* (tunnel) through a mountain.

punee—bed; narrow couch. Used by all ethnic groups. To recline on a *punee* on a breezy lanai is a true island treat.

pu pu—an appetizer; a snack; hors d'oeuvres; can be anything from cheese and crackers to sushi. Oftentimes, bars or nightclubs offer them free.

pupule—crazy; nuts; out of your mind

tapa—a traditional paper cloth made from beaten bark. Intricate designs were stamped in using beaters, and color was added with natural dyes. The tradition was lost in Hawaii, but is now making a comeback, and provides some of the most beautiful folk art in the islands.

tutu—grandmother; granny; older woman. Used by all as a term of respect and endearment

ukulele—*uku* means "flea" and *lele* means "jumping"; thus ukelele means "jumping flea," which was the way the Hawaiians perceived the quick finger movements on the banjo-type Portuguese folk instrument called a *cavaquinho*. The ukulele quickly became synonymous with the islands.

wahine—young woman; female; girl; wife. Used by all ethnic groups. When written on a door means "women's room"

wai—fresh water; drinking water

wela—hot. *Wela kahao* is a "hot time" or "making whoopee."

wiki—quickly; fast; in a hurry. Often seen as *wiki wiki* ("very fast"), as in "Wiki Wiki Messenger Service"

USEFUL PHRASES

Aloha ahiahi—Good evening.
Aloha au ia oe—I love you!
Aloha kakahiaka—Good morning.
aloha nui loa—much love; fondest regards
Hauoli la hanau—Happy Birthday.
Hauoli makahiki hau—Happy New Year.

komo mai—please come in; enter; welcome
Mele Kalikimaka—Merry Christmas.
okole maluna—bottoms up; salute; cheers; kampai

ARTS AND CRAFTS

Referring to Hawaii as "paradise" is about as hackneyed as you can get, but when you combine it into "artists' paradise" it's the absolute truth. Something about the place evokes art (or at least personal expression) from most people. The islands are like a magnet: they not only draw artists to them, but they draw art *from* the artists. The list of literary figures who have visited Hawaii and had something inspirational to say reads like a freshman survey in literature: William Henry Dana, Herman Melville, Mark Twain, Robert Louis Stevenson, Jack London, Somerset Maugham, Joaquin Miller, and of course, James Michener.

The inspiration comes from the astounding natural surroundings. The land is so beautiful yet so raw; the ocean's power and rhythm is primal and ever-present; the riotous colors of flowers and fruit leap from the deep-green jungle background. Crystal water beads and pale mists turn the mountains into mystic temples, while rainbows come riding on the crests of waves. The stunning variety of faces begging to be rendered appears as if all the world sent a local delegation to the islands. And in most cases it did! Inspiration is everywhere, as is art, good or bad.

Sometimes the artwork is overpowering in itself and in its sheer volume. Though geared to the tourist's market of cheap souvenirs, there is hardly a shop in Hawaii that doesn't sell some item that falls into the general category of "art." You can find everything from carved monkey-face coconut shells to true masterpieces. The Polynesian Hawaiians were master craftsmen, and their legacy still lives in a wide variety of woodcarvings, basketry, and weavings. The hula is art in swaying motion, and the true form is rigorously studied and taken very seriously. There is hardly a resort area that doesn't offer the "bump and grind" tourist's hula and even these revues are accompanied by proficient local musicians. Nightclubs offer "slack key" balladeers and island music made on ukuleles, and Hawaii's own steel guitars spill from many lounges.

Vibrant fabrics, which catch the spirit of the islands are rendered into muumuus and aloha shirts at countless local factories. They're almost a mandatory purchase! Pottery, heavily influenced by the Japanese, is well developed at numerous kilns. Local artisans fashion delicate jewelry from coral and olivine, while some ply the whaler's legacy of etching on ivory, called scrimshaw. There is a fine tradition of quilt making, flower art in leis, and street artists working in everything from airbrush to glass. The following is an overview; for local offerings please see "Shopping" in the travel chapters.

ARTS OF OLD HAWAII

Since everything in old Hawaii had to be fashioned by hand, almost every object was either a work of art or at least a highly refined craft. With the "civilizing" of the natives, most of the "old ways" disappeared, including the old arts and crafts. Most authentic Hawaiian art exists only in museums, but with the resurgence of Hawaiian roots, many old arts are being revitalized, and a few artists are becoming proficient.

Magnificent Canoes

The most respected artisans in old Hawaii were the canoe makers. With little more than a stone adz and a pump drill, they built canoes that could carry 200 people and last for generations—sleek, well proportioned, and infinitely seaworthy. The main hull was usually a gigantic *koa* log, and the gunwale planks were minutely drilled and sewn to the sides with sennit rope. Apprenticeships lasted for years, and a young man knew that he had graduated when one day he was nonchalantly asked to sit down and eat with the master builders. Small family-sized canoes with outriggers were used for fishing, and perhaps carried a spear rack; large oceangoing double-hulled canoes were used for migration and warfare. On these, the giant logs had been adzed to about two inches thick. A mainsail woven from pandanus was mounted on a central platform, and the boat was steered by two long paddles. The hull was dyed with plant juices and charcoal, and the entire village helped launch the canoe in a ceremony called "drinking the sea."

Carving And Weaving

Wood was a primary material, and craftsmen turned out well-proportioned and distinctive calabashes. Made mostly from *koa,* the luster and intricate grain was brought out with hand rubbing. Temple idols were a major product of woodcarving, and a variety of stone artifacts including poi pounders, mirrors, fish sinkers, and small idols were turned out.

Hawaiians became the *best* basket makers and mat weavers in all of Polynesia. *Ulana* (mats) were made from *lau hala* (pandanus) leaves. Once split, the spine was removed and the leaves stored in large rolls. When needed they were soaked, pounded, and then fashioned into various floor coverings and sleeping mats. Intricate geometrical pattterns were woven in, and the edges were rolled and well fashioned. Coconut palms were not used to make mats in old Hawaii, but a wide variety of basketry was made from the aerial root *ie'ie.* The shapes varied according to use. Some were tall and narrow, some were cones, others were flat like trays, while many were woven around gourds and calabashes.

A strong tradition of weaving and carving has survived in Hawaii, and the time-tested material of *lau hala* is still the best, although much is now made from coconut fronds. You can purchase anything from beach mats to a woven hat and all share the qualities of strength, lightness, and air flow.

Feather Work

This highly refined art was only found on the islands of Tahiti, New Zealand, and Hawaii, while the fashioning of feather helmets and idols was unique to Hawaii alone. Favorite colors were red and yellow, which came only in a very limited number on a few birds such as the *o'o, i'iwi, mamo,* and *apapane.* Professional bird hunters in old Hawaii paid their taxes to *ali'i* in prized feathers. The feathers were fastened to a woven net of *olona* cord and made into helmets, idols,

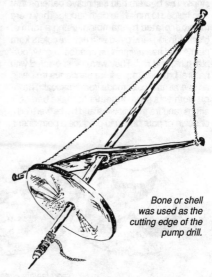

Bone or shell was used as the cutting edge of the pump drill.

fancy carved konane *board worthy of an ali'i*

and beautiful flowing capes and cloaks. These resplendent garments were made and worn only by men, especially during battle when a fine cloak became a great trophy of war. Feather-work was also employed in the making of *kahili* and leis which were highly prized by the noble *ali'i* women.

Tapa Cloth

Tapa, cloth made from tree bark, was common throughout Polynesia, and was a woman's art. A few trees such as the *wauke* and *mamaki* produced the best cloth, but a variety of other barks could be utilized. First the raw bark was pounded into a felt-like pulp and beaten together to form strips. The beaters had distinctive patterns that also helped to make the cloth supple. They were then decorated by stamping, using a form of block printing, and dyed with natural colors from plants and sea animals, in shades of gray, purple, pink, and red. They were even painted with natural brushes made from pandanus fruit, with an overall gray color made from charcoal. The tapa cloth was sewn together to make bed coverings, and fragrant flowers and herbs were either sewn or pounded in to produce a permanent fragrance. Tapa cloth is still available today, but the Hawaiian methods have been lost, and most comes from other areas of Polynesia.

First Western Artists

When Capt. Cook made first contact in 1778, the ship's artists immediately began recording things Hawaiian. John Webber and James Clevely made etchings and pen-and-ink drawings of Hawaiian people, structures, *heiau* and everyday occurrences that struck them as noteworthy or peculiar. William Ellis, ship's surgeon, also a fair hand at etching, was attracted to portraying native architecture. These three left a priceless and faithful record of what Hawaii was like at the moment of contact. Louis Choris, ship's artist with Otto Von Kotzebue in 1816, painted early portraits of King Kamehameha and Queen Kaahumanu, the two grandest figures in Hawaii's history. Jacques Arago, aboard the *Uranie* with the French Captain de Freycinet in 1819, recorded some gruesome customs of punishment of *kapu* breakers, and made many drawings of island people. Robert Dampier, who sailed on the *Blonde,* the ship that returned King Liholiho's body from England, recorded one of the earliest landscapes of Honolulu, a site which has continued to be depicted on film by more tourists than almost any other city on Earth. These early artists merely set a trend that continues unabated to this day; artists endeavour to "capture" Hawaii, and they do so with every artistic medium avilable.

Modern Masters

Countless artists working at all levels of accomplishment try to match their skills to the vigor and beauty of the islands. Some have set the standards, and their names have become synonymous with Hawaiian art. Heading this list of lumi-

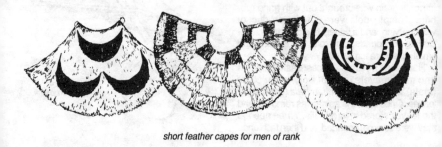

short feather capes for men of rank

naries are Huc Luquiens, Madge Tennent, Tadashi Sato, Jean Charlot, and John Kelly. Madge Tennent (1889-1972) was an Englishwoman who came to Hawaii via Samoa after spending years in South Africa and New Zealand. She worked in oils that she applied liberally and in bold strokes. Enamored with the people of Hawaii, her portraits are of a race striking in appearance and noble in character. Her works, along with those of other island artists, are displayed at the Tennent Art Foundation, on the slopes of Punchbowl on Oahu.

Huc Luquiens, former chairman of the Art Department at the University of Hawaii, was a master at etching, and was especially accomplished in dry point. His works, mainly island landscapes, are displayed in the Hawaiiana Collection of the Honolulu Academy of Arts. Maui-born Tadashi Sato, a superbly accomplished muralist, has produced such famous mosaics as the 30-foot *Aquarius* at the State Capitol in Honolulu, and the 60- foot *Portals of Immortality* at the Maui Memorial Gymnasium in Lahaina.

Frenchman Jean Charlot perfected his mural art in Mexico before coming to Hawaii in 1949. He is renowned for his frescoes and became a well-known art critic and the grand old man of Hawaiian art. He died in 1979 at the ripe old age of 90. John M. Kelly was in love with Hawaiian women; his etchings of them are both inspired and technically flawless. Kelly was infinitely patient, rendering his subjects in the minutest detail.

These artists are the "Big Five of Hawaiian Art"; their accomplishments should seen as an "artistic gauge" of what Hawaii can inspire in an artist. By observing their works you can get an instant "art course" and a comparative view of the state of the arts in Hawaii.

Contemporary Artists

The crop of new artists making their mark always seems to be bounteous and their works, heavily influenced by the "feeling of Hawaii," continue to be superb. Every island has art galleries, co-ops, or unofficial art centers. One of the finest groups of island artists can be found at the **Sunday Art Mart**, which recently changed its official name to **Artists of Oahu, Sunday Exhibit**. It's located along the "fence" of the Honolulu Zoo fronting Kapiolani Park. These artists, along with others around the islands, will be discussed in their respective travel chapters, so check. The following list of artists, with a short description of their work, is by no means exhaustive. It merely shows the wide range of artwork available.

Richard Fields, a former Californian, now lives on Maui. The fascinating beauty of the *aina* is his inspiration that he depicts in his supra-realistic paintings of birds, mountains, clouds, flowers, and waterfalls. Richard creates his rich renditions using a mixed media of airbrush, acrylic, india ink, and stencils. His works are as striking and as inspiring as the ever-changing beauty of the islands.

Robert Nelson is a Maui artist who superbly transmits the integrated mystical life of land and sea. His watercolors are often diffused with the strange filtered light found beneath the waves. A conservationist, he has often depicted the gentle frolicking life of the whales that visit Hawaiian waters.

Bill Christian is a master of scrimshaw, which he renders on slate. He also produces fine oil paintings of the sea and old salts. A world-class artist, his works are displayed at art galleries on Maui as well as in the Smithsonian, and the New Bedford Massachusetts Whaling Museum.

Pegge Hopper is often compared with Madge Tennent. She works in bold colors and strokes. Her subject matter is islanders, especially the delicacy and inner strength of women. Her works are displayed at various galleries, especially on Maui and Oahu, and are often available in limited-edition serigraphs.

John Costello, an Oahu artist, specializes in pointalism to capture the waves, women, and flora of Hawaii in a sensitive and mystical way. He co-owns and operates Kaala Art and Rainbow Island T's with his brother Jim in Haleiwa on North Shore Oahu. John's work as well as local artists is showcased in their small shop.

Alapai Hanapi is a traditionalist sculptor who tries to recreate the motifs of his Hawaiian ancestors. He works in wood and stone with tools that he fashions himself. His driving force is cultural awareness and through his art he tells of the old ways. He lives simply with his wife and three daughters near an old fishpond on eastern Molokai. His work is known for its simplicity and is available at art shows periodically held throughout the islands.

Hawaiian Maiden *by John Costello*

Al Furtado is a freelance artist working in Honolulu. He specializes in capturing the movement of Hawaiian dance. His depictions are often larger than life with a strong sense of vitality and motion.

Daniel Wang was born in Shanghai where he learned the art of Chinese watercolors. Although born deaf and mute, he speaks loudly, clearly and beautifully through his art. Daniel has a special technique in which the palm of his hand becomes his artistic tool. He feels that he can transmit intense inner emotions directly from his body to the canvas.

The following is a potpourri of distinguished artists displayed at various galleries around the islands. Any work bearing their name is authentic island art considered to be superior by fellow artists. William Waterfall, photographer (see p.260); Satoru Abe, sculptor; Ruthadell Anderson, weaver; Betty Tseng Yu-ho Ecke, *dsui* painter; Claude Horan, sculptor, ceramics; Erica Karawina, stained glass; Ron Kowalke, painter; Ben Norris, painter; Louis Pohl, printmaker; Mamoru Sato, sculptor; Tadashi Sato, painter;

Reuben Tam, painter; Jean Williams, weaver; John Wisnosky, painter; John Young, painter.

ART TO BUY

Wild Hawaiian shirts or bright muumuus, especially when worn on the Mainland, have the magical effect of making wearers "feel" like they're in Hawaii, while at the same time eliciting spontaneous smiles from passer-by. Maybe it's the colors, or perhaps it's just the "vibe" that signifies "party time" or "hang loose," but nothing says Hawaii like alohawear does. There are more than a dozen fabric houses in Hawaii turning out distinctive patterns, and many dozens of factories creating their own personalized designs. Oftentimes these factories have attached retail outlets, but in any case you can find hundreds of shops selling alohawear. Aloha shirts were the brilliant idea of a Chinese merchant in Honolulu, who used to hand-tailor them and sell them to the tourists who arrived by ship in the glory days before WW II. They were an instant success. Muumuus or "Mother Hubbards" were the idea of missionaries, who were appalled by Hawaiian women running about *au naturelle* and insisted on covering their new Christian converts from head to foot. Now the roles are reversed, and it's Mainlanders who come to Hawaii and immediately strip down to as little clothing as possible.

Alohawear
At one time exclusively made of cotton, or from manmade yet naturally based rayon, these materials were and still are the best for any tropical clothing. Beware, however: polyester has slowly crept into the market! No material could possibly be worse than polyester for the island climate, so when buying your alohawear make sure to check the label for material content. Muumuus now come in various styles and can be worn for the entire spectrum of social occasions in Hawaii. Aloha shirts are still basically cut the same as always, but the patterns have undergone changes, and apart from the original flowers and ferns, modern shirts might depict an island scene giving the impression of a silkscreen painting. A basic good-quality muumuu or aloha shirt starts at about $25 and is guaranteed to be worth its price in good times

and happy smiles. The connoisseur might want to purchase *The Hawaiian Shirt, Its Art and History,* by R. Thomas Steele. It's illustrated with more than 150 shirts that are now considered works of art by collectors the world over.

Scrimshaw

This art of etching and carving on bone and ivory has become an island tradition handed down from the times of the old whaling ships. Although scrimshaw can be found throughout Hawaii, the center remains in the old whaling capital of Lahaina. Here along Front Street are numerous shops specializing in scrimshaw. Today, pieces are carved on fossilized walrus ivory that is gathered by Eskimos and shipped to Hawaii. It comes in a variety of shades from pure white to mocha, depending upon the mineral content of the earth in which it was buried. Elephant ivory or whalebone is no longer used because of ecological considerations, but there is a "gray market" in Pacific walrus tusks. Eskimos can legally hunt the walrus. They then make a few minimal scratches on the tusks which technically qualifies them to be "Native American art," and free of most governmental restrictions. The tusks are then sent to Hawaii as art objects, but the superficial scratches are immediately removed and the ivory is reworked by artisans. Scrimshaw is

made into everything from belt buckles to delicate earrings and even into coffee-table centerpieces. The prices can go from a few dollars up into the thousands.

Woodcarvings

One Hawaiian art that has not died out is woodcarving. This art was extremely well developed among the old Hawaiians and they almost exclusively used koa because of its density, strength, and natural luster. It was turned into canoes, woodware, and furniture for the *ali'i.* Koa is becoming increasingly scarce, but many items are still available, though costly. Milo and monkeypod are also excellent woods for carving and have largely replaced koa. You can buy tikis, bowls, and furniture at numerous shops. Countless inexpensive carved items are sold at variety stores, such as little hula girls or salad servers, but most of these are imported from Asia or the Philippines and can be bought at any variety store.

Weaving

The minute you arrive in Hawaii you should shell out $2 for a woven beach mat. This is a necessity, not a frivolous purchase, but it definitely won't have been made in Hawaii. What is made in Hawaii is *lau hala.* This is traditional Hawaiian weaving from the leaves *(lau)* of the pandanus *(hala)* tree. These leaves vary greatly in length, with the largest over six feet, and they have a thorny spine that must be removed before they can be worked. The color ranges from light tan to dark brown. The leaves are cut into strips from one-eighth to one inch wide and are then employed in weaving. Any variety of items can be made or at least covered in *lau hala.* It makes great purses, mats, baskets, and table mats.

Woven into a hat, it's absolutely superb but should not be confused with a palm-frond hat. A *lau hala* hat is amazingly supple and even when squashed will pop back into shape. A good one is expensive ($25) and with proper care will last for years. All *lau hala* should be given a light application of mineral oil on a monthly basis, especially if it's exposed to the sun. For flat items, iron over a damp cloth and keep purses and baskets stuffed with paper when not in use. Palm fronds also are widely used in weaving. They, too, are a great natural raw material, but not as good as *lau hala.* Almost any item such as a beach bag

ART INFORMATION

Organization	Address and Telephone	Remarks
Arts Council of Hawaii	Box 50225 Honolulu, HI 96850 tel. 524-7120	A citizens' advocacy group for the arts providing technical assistance and information. Publishes the *Cultural Climate* newsletter covering the arts of Hawaii. Includes a calendar of events, feature articles, and editorials. Membership fee, $15, includes newsletter; nonmembers, $.50 per issue.
Bishop Museum	1355 Kalihi St. Box 19000-A Honolulu, HI 96819 tel. 847-3511	World's best museum covering Polynesia and Hawaii; exhibits, galleries, archives, demonstrations of Hawaiian crafts, and a planetarium. On premises, Shop Pacifica has books and publications on Hawaiian art and culture. Shouldn't be missed. See p. 234.
Contemporary Museum of Art	2411 Makiki Heights Rd. tel. 526-1322	Focuses on exhibitions rather than collections, although works by David Hockney are on permanent display. Changing exhibits reflect different themes in contemporary art. Under the direction of Fritz Frauchinger. Open Monday through Saturday, 10 a.m.-4 p.m., noon-4 p.m. Sunday, closed Tuesday, admission $3.
East-West Center Learning Institute	Burns Hall 4076 1777 East-West Rd. Honolulu, HI 96848 tel. 948-8006	At U of H campus. Dedicated to the sharing, exhibiting, and appreciation of arts, culture, and crafts from throughout Asia and the Western world. Their free bi-monthly Centerviews includes an event calendar and tropical editorials on the Pacific. See p. 234.
East West Journal	1633 Kapiolani Blvd. Honolulu, HI 96814	Yearly guide to exhibition galleries featuring the work of locally renowned artists.
Hawaii Craftsmen	Box 22145 Honolulu, HI tel. 523-1974	Increases awareness of Hawaiian crafts through programs, exhibitions, workshops, lectures, and demonstrations.
Honolulu Academy of Arts	900 S. Beretania St. Honolulu, HI 96814 tel. 538-3693	Collects, preserves, and exhibits artworks. Offers public art education programs related to their collections, plus tours, classes, lectures, films, and a variety of publications. See p. 237.

Honolulu Symphony Society	1000 Bishop St. Honolulu, HI 96813 tel. 537-6171	Provides professional-level music, primarily symphonies and concerts.
Pacific Handcrafters Guild	Box 15491 Honolulu, HI 96818 tel. 923-5726	Focuses on developing and preserving handicrafts in Hawaii and the Pacific. Sponsors four major craft fairs annualy.
Polynesian Music & Dance Assoc.	93 Lowcrest Blvd. Scarborough, Ontario, Canada MIT IK7 tel. (416) 492-4222	Promotes interest and participation in Polynesian dance and culture. Offers group tours, music and dance lessons, quarterly newsletter.
State Foundation on Culture and the Arts	335 Merchant Street Room 202 Honolulu, HI 96813 tel. 548-4145	Preserves Hawaii's cultural and artistic heritage. Publishes *Hawaii Cultural Resource Directory,* listing art organizations, galleries, councils, co-ops, and guilds. Very complete.
University of Hawaii at Manoa Art Gallery	2535 The Mall Honolulu, HI 96822 tel. 948-6888	Showcase for contemporary artwork. Theme changes periodically. See p. 233.

woven from palm makes a good authentic yet inexpensive gift or souvenir, and are available in countless shops.

Gift Items

Jewelry is always an appreciated gift, especially if it's distinctive, and Hawaii has some of the most original. The sea provides the basic raw materials of pink, gold, and black coral, and it's so beautiful that it holds the same fascination as gemstones. Harvesting the coral is very dangerous work. The Lahaina beds off Maui have one of the best black coral lodes in the islands, but unlike reef coral these trees grow at depths bordering the outer limits of a scuba diver's capabilities. Only the best can dive 180 feet after the black coral, and about one diver per year dies in pursuit of it. Conservationists have placed great pressure on the harvesters of these deep corals and the state of Hawaii has placed strict limits and guidelines on the firms and divers involved.

Pink coral has long been treasured by man. The Greeks considered it a talisman for good health, and there's even evidence that it has been coveted since the Stone Age. Coral jewelry is on sale at many shops throughout Hawaii and the value comes from the color of the coral and the workmanship.

Puka (shells with little naturally occurring holes) and *opihi* shells are also made into jewelry. Many times these items are very inexpensive, yet they are authentic and great purchases for the price. Hanging macramé planters festooned with seashells are usually quite affordable and sold at roadside stands along with shells.

Hawaii produces some unique food items that are appreciated by most people. Various-sized jars of macadamia nuts and butters are great gifts, as are tins of rich, gourmet-quality Kona coffee, the only coffee produced in the U.S. Guava, pineapple, passion fruit, and mango are often gift-boxed into assortments of jams, jellies, and spicy chutneys. And for that special person in your life, you can bring home island fragrances in bottles of perfumes and colognes in the exotic odors of gardenia, plumeria, and even ginger. All of the above items are reasonably priced, lightweight, and easy to carry.

*leis for sale, Honolulu
c. 1920*
HAWAII STATE ARCHIVES

LANGUAGE OF THE LEI

The goddess Hiiaka is Pele's youngest sister, and although many gods were depicted wearing flower garlands, the lei is most associated with her. Perhaps it was because Hiiaka was the goddess of mercy and protection, qualities which the lei seemed to symbolize. Hiiaka traveled throughout the islands destroying evil spirits wherever she found them. In the traditional translation of "The Song of the Islands" by Rev. Samuel Kapu, the last verses read, "We all call to you, answer us O Hiiaka, the woman who travels the seas. This is the conclusion of our song, O wreaths of Hawaii, respond to our call." A special day, May 1, is Lei Day in Hawaii. It started in 1928 as a project of Don Blanding, an island poet.

Hardly a more beautiful tradition exists anywhere in the world than placing a flower garland around the neck of someone special. The traditional time to give a lei is when someone is arriving or departing the islands, so every airport has lei sellers, mostly older women who have a little booth at the entrance to the airport. But leis are worn on every occasion, from marriages to funerals, and are as apt to appear around the lovely neck of a hula dancer as a floral hat band on the grizzled head of an old *paniolo,* or even draped around his horse's neck. In old Hawaii leis were given to the local *ali'i* as a sign of affection. When two warring chiefs sat together and

wove a lei, it meant the end of hostilities and symbolized the circle of peace.

Lei Making

Any flower or blossom can be strung into a lei, but the most common are carnations or the lovely smelling plumeria. Leis, like babies, are all beautiful, but special ones are highly prized by those who know what to look for. Of the different stringing styles, the most common is *kui*—stringing the flower through the middle or side. Most "airport-quality" leis are of this type. The *humuhumu* style, reserved for making flat leis, is made by sewing flowers and ferns to a *ti,* banana, or sometimes to a *hala* leaf. A *humuhumu lei* makes an excellent hatband. The *wili* is the winding together of greenery, ferns, and flowers into short bouquet-type lengths. The most traditional form is *hili,* which requires no stringing at all but involves braiding fragrant ferns and leaves such as *maile.* If flowers are interwoven, the *hili* becomes the *haku* style, the most difficult and most beautiful type of lei.

The Lei Of The Land

Every major island is symbolized by its own lei made from a distinctive flower, shell, or fern. Each island has its own official color as well, though it doesn't necessarily correspond to the color of the island's lei. The island of Hawaii's lei is made from the red (or rare creamy white or orange) *lehua* blossom. The *lehua* tree grows from sea level to 9,000 feet and produces an abundance of tufted flowers. The official color of Hawaii Island, like the lava from its active volcanoes, is red.

Kauai, oldest of the main islands, is represented by the *mokihina* lei and the regal color purple. The *mokihina* tree produces a small cube-like fruit that smells like anise. Green when strung into Kauai's lei, they then turn a dark brown and keep their scent for months.

Maui is the pink island; its lei is the corresponding small pink rose called the *lokelani*. Not native but imported, in recent years they've fallen prey to a rose beetle. When they're scarce, a substitute *roselani* is used for Maui's lei.

Molokai is the silvery green island, and its lei is fashioned from the green leaves and small white flowers of the *kukui* tree. After it's shaped and polished, the *kukui* makes some of the most permanent and beautiful *leis* for sale in Hawaii. *Kukui* nut *leis* are quite common and make excellent gifts. Although not the official lei of any island, they could easily be the official lei representing all the islands.

Lanai has one of the most traditional forms of *leis* in Hawaii. Both its color and its lei are represented by the orange *kaunaoa*. This plant commonly grows along the beach and roadside and its orange, leafless stems are twisted into strands to form a lei. Oahu, the color of the sun, is garlanded by the yellow *ilima*. This flower is reminiscent of the *o'o* bird whose yellow feathers made the finest capes in Hawaii. The *ilima* often bears double yellow flowers and will infrequently produce a light red flower too rare to be used in leis.

Kahoolawe, the sacred island now used as a naval target range is given the color gray (hopefully not as in "battleship") and is represented by the silvery leaves and small white sweet-scented flowers of the *hinahina*. This heliotrope grows on sandy beaches just above the high-water mark, and is a very common plant throughout the Pacific.

Niihau, the Forbidden Island, is home to some of the last remaining pure-blooded Hawaiians, and takes the color white. The island's lei is the rare *pupu* shell. This shell is white, less than one-half inch long, and sometimes has brown spots. The shell was the home of a mollusk that died on the offshore reef. These *pupu* leis, considerd fine jewelry, fetch a handsome price. Very cheap facsimiles of *pikake*-shell leis are sold everywhere, and most have been imported from the Cook and Society Islands of the South Pacific.

The last island is the semi-submerged volcano of Molokini, just off Maui's south shore. Molokini is represented by the very traditional lei made from *limu kala,* a brown coarse seaweed with feathery spiny leaves that makes a boa-type lei.

Besides these island leis two others must be mentioned. A lei made from *maile* is perhaps the most traditional of all. *Maile* is an ordinary green

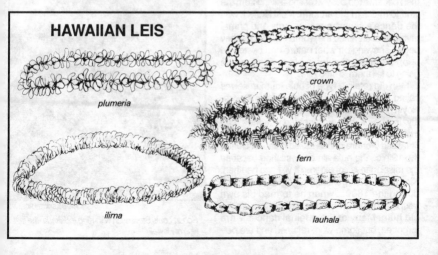

HAWAIIAN LEIS

plumeria

crown

ilima

fern

lauhala

leafy vine. Its stiff bone-like inner stem is removed, leaving the leaves and pliable bark intact, which are then twisted into a lei. They might be ordinary to look at, but they have a delicious smell that is Hawaii. *Maile* is often used in conjunction with flowers to make top-notch leis. Lauae is a common fern with large coarse shiny leaves. It is used to fluff out many leis and when the leaves are bruised they have a mild scent of *maile*. Leis have two qualities that are unsurpassed: they feel just as good to give as they do to receive.

HULA

The hula was and is more than an ethnic dance; it is the soul of Hawaii expressed in motion. It began as a form of worship during religious ceremonies and was only danced by highly trained men. It gradually evolved into a form of entertainment, but in no regard was it sexual. The hula was the opera, theater, and lecture hall of the islands all rolled into one. It was history portrayed in the performing arts. In the beginning an androgynous deity named Laka descended to Earth and taught men how to dance the hula. In time the male aspect of Laka departed for the heavens, but the female aspect remained. The female Laka set up her own special hula *heiau* at Haena Point on the Na Pali coast of Kauai, where it still exists. As time went on women were allowed to learn the hula. Scholars surmise that men became too busy wresting a living from the land to maintain the art form. Most likely, it was the dance's swaying movements and primal rhythm that attracted the women. And once they began showing off what nature had bestowed upon them, what chief in his right mind was going to tell them to stop?!

Men did retain a type of hula for themselves called *lua*. This was a form of martial art employed in hand-to-hand combat. It included paralyzing holds, bone-crunching punches, and thrusting with spears and clubs. It evolved into a ritualized warfare dance called hula *kui*. During the 19th c., the hula almost vanished because the missionaries considered it vile and heathen. King Kalakaua is generally regarded as saving it during the 1800s, when he formed his own troupe and encouraged the dancers to learn the old hula. Many of the original dances were forgotten, but some were retained and are per-

formed to this day. Although professional dancers were highly trained, everyone took part in the hula. *Ali'i*, commoners, young, and old all danced. The early drawings of ships' artists like Arago, Choris, and Webber all recorded hula scenes. Old folks even did it sitting down if their legs were too weak to perform the necessary gyrations.

Hula Training

Only the most beautiful, graceful, and elegant girls were chosen to enter the hula *halau* (school). At one time, the *halau* was a temple in its own right and the girls who entered at the age of four or five would emerge as accomplished dancers in their early teens to begin a lifelong career of the highest honor. In the *halau*, the *haumana* (pupils) were under the strict and total guidance of the *kumu* (teacher) and many *kapu* were placed upon them. The hula was a subordination of gross strength into a sublime coupling of grace and elegance. Once a woman became a proficient and accomplished dancer, her hula showed a personal, semi-spontaneous interpretation based upon past experiences. Today, hula *halau* are active on every island, teaching hula, and keeping the old ways and culture alive. Performers still spend years perfecting their techniques. They show off their accomplishments during the fierce competition of the

HAWAII STATE ARCHIVES

Robert Louis Stevenson with King Kalakaua, the last king of Hawaii

Merrie Monarch Festival in Hilo every April. The winning *halau* is praised and recognized throughout the islands.

The Special World Of Hula

Hawaiian hula was never performed in grass skirts; tapa or *ti*-leaf skirts were worn. Grass skirts came to Hawaii from the Gilbert Islands, and if you see grass and cellophane skirts in a "hula revue," it's not traditional. Almost every major resort offering entertainment or a luau also offers a "hula review." Most times, young island beauties accompanied by local musicians put on a floor show for the tourists. It'll be fun, but it won't be traditional. A hula dancer has to learn how to control every part of her/his body including the facial expressions, which help to set the mood. The correct chanting of the *mele* is an integral part of the performance. These story chants, combined with accompanying musical instruments, make the hula very much like opera, especially similar in the way the tale unfolds. The hands are extremely important and provide instant background scenery. For example, if the hands are thrust outward in an aggressive manner, this can mean a battle; if they sway gently overhead, they refer to the gods or to creation; they can easily become rain, clouds, the sun, sea, or moon. Watch the hands to get the gist of the story, though in the words of one wiseguy, "You watch the parts you like, and I'll watch the parts I like!" Swaying hips, depending upon their motion, can be a long walk, a canoe ride, or sexual intercourse. The foot motion can portray a battle, a walk, or any kind of conveyance. The overall effect is multi-directional synchronized movement.

Hula Music

Accompaniment is provided by chants called *mele* or *oli* and by a wide variety of basic instruments. The *ipu* is a primary hula instrument made of two gourds fastened together. It's thumped on a mat and slapped with the hand. In the background is the steady rhythm of the *pahu*, a large bass drum made from a hollowed coconut or breadfruit tree log, and covered with a sharkskin membrane. Hawaii's largest drum, it was sometimes placed on a pedestal and used in ceremonies at the *heiau*. The *uli uli* is a gourd or coconut filled with shells or pebbles and used like *mariachis,* while *ili ili* are merely stones

clicked together like castanets. The *punui* is a small drum made from a half coconut shell and beaten in counterpoint to the *ipu*. Oftentimes it was played by the hula dancer, who had it fastened to her body as a knee drum. The *puili* is a length of bamboo split at one end to look like a whisk, and struck against the body to make a rattling noise, while the *kaekaekee* and *kalau* are bamboo cut to various lengths and struck to make a rudimentary xylophonic sound. Two unique instruments are the *kupee niho ilio,* a dog's tooth rattle worn as an ankle bracelet by men only, now replaced by sea shells, and an *ohe hano ihu,* a nose flute of bamboo that was played in accompaniment while the person chanted. Not all of these instrument are actually necessary to perform a hula. All that's really needed is a dancer and a chant.

THAT GOOD OLD ISLAND MUSIC

The missionaries usually take a beating when it's recounted how much Hawaiian culture they destroyed while civilizing the natives. However, they seemed to have done one thing right. They taught the Hawaiians the diatonic scale and immediately opened a door filled with latent and superbly harmonious talent. Before the missionaries, the Hawaiians knew little about melody. Though sonorous, their *mele* were repetitive chants where the emphasis was placed on historical accuracy and not on "making music." The Hawaiians, in short, didn't *sing*. But within a few years of the missionaries' arrival, they were belting out good old Christian hymns and one of their favorite pastimes became group and individual singing.

Early in the 1800s, Spanish *vaqueros* from California were imported to teach the Hawaiians how to be cowboys. With them came guitars and moody ballads. The Hawaiian *paniolo* (cowboys) quickly learned both how to punch cows and to croon away the long lonely nights on the range. Immigrants that came along a little later in the 19th century, especially from Portugal, helped create a Hawaiian-style music. Their biggest influence was a small four-stringed instrument called a *braga* or *cavaquinho*. One owned by Augusto Dias was the prototype of a homegrown Hawaiian instrument that became known as the ukulele. "Jumping flea," the translation of ukulele, is an appropriate name devised by the Hawaiians when they saw how nimble the fingers were as they "jumped" over the strings.

The Merry Monarch, King Kalakaua, and Queen Liliuokalani were both patrons of the arts who furthered the Hawaiian musical identity at the turn of the century. Kalakaua revived the hula and was also a gifted lyricist and balladeer. He wrote the words to "Hawaii Pono," which became the national anthem of Hawaii and later the state anthem. Liliuokalani wrote the hauntingly beautiful "Aloha Oe," which is often pointed to as the "spirit of Hawaii" in music. Detractors say that its melody is extremely close to the old Christian hymn, "Rock Beside the Sea," but the lyrics are so beautiful and perfectly fitted that this doesn't matter.

Just prior to Kalakaua's reign a Prussian bandmaster, Capt. Henri Berger, was invited to head the fledgling Royal Hawaiian Band, which he turned into very respectable orchestra lauded by many visitors to the islands. Berger was openminded and learned to love Hawaiian music. He collaborated with Kalakaua and other island musicians to incorporate their music into a Western format. He headed the band for 43 years until 1915, and was instrumental in making music a serious pursuit of talented Hawaiians.

Popular Hawaiian Music

Hawaiian music has a unique twang, a special feeling that says the same thing to everyone that hears it: "Relax, sit back in the moonlight, watch the swaying palms as the surf sings a lullaby." This special sound is epitomized by the bouncy ukulele, the falsetto voice of Hawaiian crooners, and by the smooth ring of the "steel" or "Hawaiian" guitar. The steel guitar is a variation that was originated by Joseph Kekuku in the 1890s. Stories abound of how Joseph Kekuku devised this instrument; the most popular versions say that Joe dropped his comb or pocket knife on his guitar strings and liked what he heard. Driven by the faint rhythm of an inner sound, he went to the machine shop at the Kamehameha School and turned out a steel bar for sliding over the strings. To complete the sound he changed the cat-gut strings to steel and raised them so they wouldn't hit the frets. Voilà!—Hawaiian music as the world knows it today.

The first melodious strains of **slack-key guitar** can be traced back to the time of Kamehameha III, when Spanish cowboys (the forerunners of Hawaiian *paniolo*) from California were brought to the kingdom to run the wild cattle that had grown steadily in numbers ever since killing them was made *kapu* by Kamehameha I. The white man's gift had become a menace, growing in numbers to the point where they were even attacking grass houses for fodder. The Spanish cowboys roped, branded, and corralled them, and living up to the cowboy image, would pass lonesome nights on the range singing and playing their guitars. The Hawaiians who made excellent cowboys, and their ears, recently tuned by the missionaries, picked up the melodies accompanied by the strange new instrument, and quickly *Hawaiianized* them. The Spanish had their way of tuning the guitar, and played difficult and aggressive music that did not sit well with Hawaiians, who were much more gentle and casual in their manners.

Hawaiians soon became adept at making their own music. At first, one person played the melody, but it lacked fullness. There was no body to the sound. So, as one *paniolo* fooled with the melody, another soon learned to play bass, which added depth. But, a player was often alone, and by experimenting learned that he could get the right hand going with the melody, and at the same time could play the bass note with the thumb to improve the sound. Singers also learned that they could "open tune" the guitar to match their rich voices.

Due to *kahunamism,* Hawaiians believed that knowledge was sacred, and what is sacred should be treated with utmost respect, which meant keeping it secret, except from sincere apprentices. Guitar playing became a personal artform, whose secrets were closely guarded, and handed down only to family members, and only to those who showed ability and determination. When old-time slack-key guitar players were done strumming, they loosened all the strings so that no one could figure out how they had it tuned. If they were playing, and some folks came by that were interested and weren't part of the family, the Hawaiians stopped what they were doing, put the guitar down, and put their foot on it across the strings to wait for the person to go away. As time went on, more and more

Hawaiians began to play slack key, and a common repertoire emerged.

An accomplished musician could easily figure out the simple songs, once they had figured out how the family had tuned the guitar. One of the most popular tunings was the "open G." Old Hawaiian folks called it the "taro patch tune." Different songs came out, and if you were in their family and were interested in the guitar, they took the time to sit down and teach you. The way they taught was straightforward, and a test of your sincerity at the same time. The old master would start to play. They just wanted you to listen, get a feel for the music, not any more than that. You brought your guitar and *listened*. When you felt it, you played it, and the knowledge was transferred. Today, only a handful of slack-key guitar players know how to play the classic tunes classically. The best-known and perhaps greatest slack-key player was Gabby Pahinui, with The Sons of Hawaii. He passed away recently, but left many recordings behind. A slack-key master still singing and playing is Raymond Kane. Raymond now teaches a handful of students his wonderful and haunting music. Not one of his students are from his own family, and most are *haole* musicians trying to preserve the classical method of playing.

Hawaiian music received its biggest boost from a remarkable radio program known as "Hawaii Calls." This program sent out its music from the Banyan Court of the Moana Hotel from 1935 until 1975. At its peak in the mid-1950s, it was syndicated on over 700 radio stations throughout the world. Ironically, Japanese pilots heading for Pearl Harbor tuned in island music as a signal beam. Some internationally famous classic tunes came out of the '40s and '50s. Jack Pitman composed "Beyond the Reef" in 1948; over 300 artists have recorded it and it has sold well over 12 million records. Other million-sellers include: "Sweet Leilani," "Lovely Hula Hands," "The Crosseyed Mayor of Kaunakakai," "The Hawaiian Wedding Song."

By the 1960s, Hawaiian music began to die. It was just too corny for those turbulent years. Hawaiian music was too light, belonging to the older generation and the good times that followed WW II. One man was instrumental in keeping Hawaiian music alive during this period. Don Ho, with his Tiny Bubbles, became the token Hawaiian musician of the '60s and early '70s. He's persevered long enough to become a legend in his own time, and his Polynesian Extravaganza still packs them in six nights a week in Honolulu. Al Harrington, "The South Pacific Man," has another Honolulu "big revue" that draws large crowds. Of this type of entertainment, perhaps the most Hawaiian is Danny Kaleikini who entertains his audience with dances, Hawaiian anecdotes, and tunes on the traditional Hawaiian nose flute.

The Beat Goes On

Beginning in the mid-'70s, islanders began to assert their cultural identity. One of the unifying factors was the coming of age of "Hawaiian" music. It graduated from the "little grass shack" novelty tune and began to include sophisticated jazz, rock, and contemporary rhythms. Accomplished musicians whose roots were in traditional island music began to highlight their tunes with this distinctive sound. The best embellish their arrangements with ukuleles, steel guitars, and traditional percussion and melodic instruments. Some excellent modern recording artists have become island institutions. The local people say that you know if the Hawaiian harmonies are good if they give you "chicken skin."

Each year special music awards, Na Hoku Hanohano, or *Hoku* for short, are given to distinguished island musicians. The following are recent *Hoku* winners considered by their contemporaries to be among the best in Hawaii. If they're playing while you're there, don't miss them. They include: **Brothers Cazimero**, whose "Island in Your Eyes," won Best Contemporary Hawaiian Album. The Brothers are blessed with beautiful harmonic voices, but they are becoming increasingly commercial. **Krush**, whose "More and More," won the *Hoku* for *Best Contemporary Album*; **The Peter Moon Band**, contemporary but 100 percent quality with a strong traditional sound. **Karen Keawehawai'i**, whose "With Love, Karen" won the *Hoku* for Best Female Vocalist, has a sparkling voice and can be very funny when the mood strikes her. **Henry Kapono**, formerly of Cecelio and Kapono, keeps a low profile, but is an incredible performer and excellent songwriter. His shows are non-commercial and very special. **Cecilio** is now teamed up with **Maggie Herron,** who are

RADIO STATIONS

Station	Dial Number	Remarks
OAHU		
KCCN	AM 1420	Hawaiian music 24 hours. Indiscriminate selections will either delight or exasperate.
KDEO	AM 940	Country
KDUK	AM 980	Rock. Surfline report at tel. 538-7131
MAUI		
KHEI	AM 1100	Rock
KUIB	FM 94	Rock
KAIM	AM 870, FM 95.5	
KAOI	FM 95	Stereo
HAWAII		
KBIG	FM 98	Excellent stations, sound like FM with very few commercials
KHLO	AM 850	
KIPA	AM 620	
KKON	AM 790	Contemporary
KPUA	AM 970	Contemporary
KOAST	FM 92.1	Contemporary
KAUAI		
KIPO	AM 93.5, FM 93.5	Contemporary
KAUI	AM 720	Contemporary

hot together and have a strong following in Honolulu. **The Makaha Sons of Niihau** captured the *Hoku* for Best Traditional Hawaiian Album, and Best Group. Their sound, led by Israel Kamakawiwoole, is the best. They shouldn't be missed. **The Beamer Brothers** are excellent performances, and can be seen at various nightspots.

Some top-notch newcomers that are gaining popularity are: Ledward Kaapana; Mango; Oliver Kelly; Ka'eo; Na Leo Pilimehana, whose "Local Boys" recently won a *Hoku* for Best Single; Freitas Brothers; Brickwood Galuteria, who won a double *Hoku* for Best Male Vocalist and Most Promising Artist; and Third Road Delite.

Classical And Chamber Music
A wide assortment of classical and chamber music is offered in Hawaii. The following organizations sponsor concerts throughout the year: Chamber Music Hawaii, 905 Spencer St., No. 404, Honolulu, HI 96822 (tel. 531-6617); Classical Guitar Society of Hawaii, 1229 D. Waimanu, Honolulu, HI 96814 (tel. 537-6451); The Ensemble Players Guild, Box 50225, Honolulu, HI 96850 (tel. 735-1173); Hawaii Concert Society, Box 663, Hilo, HI 96721 (tel. 935-5831); Honolulu Symphony Society, 1000 Bishop St., Suite 901, Honolulu, HI 96813 (tel. 537-6171); Kauai Concert Assoc., 5867 Haaheo Pl., Kapaa, HI 96746 (tel. 822-7593); Maui Philharmonic Society, 2274 S. Kihei Rd., Kihei, HI 96753 (tel. 879-2962).

FESTIVALS, HOLIDAYS, AND EVENTS

In addition to all the American national holidays, Hawaii celebrates its own festivals, pageants, ethnic fairs, and a multitude of specialized exhibits. They occur throughout the year, some particular to only one island or locality, while others such as Aloha Week and Lei Day are celebrated on all the islands. Some of the smaller local happenings are semi-spontaneous, so there's no *exact* date when they're held. These are some of the most rewarding, because they provide the best times to have fun with the local people. At festival time, everyone is welcome. Check local newspapers and the free island magazines for exact dates of some events.

JANUARY

Early January
Start the New Year off right by climbing to the top of Koko Crater on Oahu for the *Hauoli Makahiki Hou,* a great way to focus on the horizons of the coming year and a great hangover remedy. Check with HVB for details. Or, continue the party with the **Sunshine Music Festival** rock concert at Diamond Head Crater.

Thump in the New Year with a traditional Japanese **Mochi Pounding Festival** at Volcano Art Center, Volcanoes National Park, Hawaii.

Sporting Events
January's first Saturday brings the **Hula Bowl Game** to Aloha Stadium, Honolulu. This annual game is a college all-star football classic. Aloha Stadium, tel. 488-7731 for details.

The **Molokai Challenge,** a new biathlon is held along Molokai's amazing North Coast. Watch a three mile run and a kayak race against time and the power of the sea.

The **Kauai Loves You Triathlon** is at lovely Hanalei Bay, Kauai. Amateurs and professionals are welcome. Covered by CBS, it can occur in December.

The athletes gear up with the Big Island **Triathlon Invitational** held in late December or early January. This is a three day event that ranges all over the island and includes an overnight stay at Volcanoes National Park.

The Volcano Wilderness Marathon and Rim Runs, where the truly energetic run 26 miles through the desolate Kau desert and 10 miles around the Caldera Crater Rim. Over 1,000 runners participate

The grueling **Maui Triathlon,** Kaanapali, Maui, is a very competitive sporting event with world-class athletes running for top prizes.

NFL Pro Bowl at Aloha Stadium, Honolulu is the annual all-star football game offering the best from both conferences. Aloha Stadium, tel. 488-7731 for details.

Late January

Robert Burns Night at the Ilikai Hotel, Honolulu is when local and visiting Scots from Canada and the Mainland celebrate the birthday of Scotland's poet Robert Burns.

The **Cherry Blossom Festival** in Honolulu can begin in late January and last through March. The fun includes a Japanese cultural and trade show, tea ceremony, flower arranging, queen pageant, and coronation ball. Check newspapers and free tourist magazines for dates and times of various Japanese cultural events.

The **Narcissus Festival** in Honolulu's Chinatown starts with the parade and festivities of Chinese New Year which can be anytime from mid-January to early February. The city sparkles with lion dances in the street, fireworks, a beauty pageant, and a coronation ball.

FEBRUARY

Early February

The **Punahou School Carnival,** in Honolulu, with its arts, crafts, and a huge rummage sale, is held at one of Hawaii's oldest and most prestigious high schools. Great ethnic foods and you'd be surprised at what Hawaii's oldest and most established families donate to the rummage sale.

The **Hawaiian Open International Golf Tournament** tees off in Honolulu at the exclusive Waialae Country Club. $500,000 prize money lures the best PGA golfers to this tournament which is beginning its second decade.

February offers everything from the links to skiing at the **Mauna Kea Ski Meet** atop the Big Island's 13,000-foot volcano—weather and snow conditions dictate the exact time, which can vary from early January to March. Skiers from around the world compete in cup skiing, and cross country.

Mid To Late February

The **Carole Kai Bed Race** is a fund-raising race of crazies, pushing decorated beds down Front Street in Lahaina, Maui, and at the Kukui Grove

Center in Lihue, Kauai. It's held in Honolulu in early March.

The **Haleiwa Sea Spree** on Oahu's North Shore is a four day action- packed event with surfing championships, outrigger canoe races, and ancient Hawaiian sports. An around-the-island bicycle race tops it off.

Enjoy the authentic Western flavor of the **Great Waikoloa Horse Races and Rodeo** at Waikoloa Stables, Waikoloa, Hawaii. Major rodeo events draw skilled **paniolo** from around the islands.

The **Annual Keauhou-Kona Triathlon** at Keauhou Bay, Big Island, equals half the Ironman requirements. Open to athletes unable to enter Ironman, and to anyone in good health, it allows relay team racing for the grueling events.

The **Captain Cook Festival** is held at Waimea, Kauai, the spot where this intrepid Pacific explorer first made contact. Food, entertainment, and a partial marathon add to the fun.

Buffalo's Annual Big Board Surfing Classic at Makaha Beach, Oahu, features the best of the classic board riders along with an authentic cultural event complete with entertainment, crafts, and food. The two day competitions are held the last weekend in February and again on the first weekend in March.

MARCH

Early March brings the **Annual Maui Marathon** along island roads from Wailuku to Lahaina, Maui. For information contact the Valley Isle Road Runners at tel. 242-6042.

The **Kukini Run** follows an ancient trail through Kahakuloa Valley on Maui's northwest coast.

The **Carole Kai Bed Race** heads down Kalakaua Avenue in Waikiki. A free concert is given at the Waikiki Shell the night before. Appearances by Hawaii's name entertainers are part of this fun-filled charity fund-raiser.

Mid March rumbles in with the **Kona Stampede** at Honaunau Arena, Honaunau, Kona, Hawaii. *Paniolo* provide plenty of action during the full range of rodeo events. For information call 885-7628.

The more *genteel* **Polo Season** starts in March and lasts until September. International teams come to Dillingham Field, Mokuleia, Oahu, for the competition.

Bagpipes herald late March at the **Hawaiian Highland Gathering,** Richardson's Field, Pearl Harbor, Oahu. Clans gather for Scottish games, competitions, ethnic foods, highland dancing, and pipe bands. Enjoy Scotsmen in kilts and leis too.

Music And Dance
The **Hawaiian Song Festival and Song Composing Contest** at Kapiolani Park Bandstand in Waikiki determines the year's best Hawaiian song and attracts top-name entertainers.

Honolulu's **Emerald Ball** is an elegant affair sponsored by the Society of the Friendly Sons of St. Patrick and features dinner and dancing to a big-name band. At this time the St. Patrick's Day Parade winds along Kalakaua Ave., in Waikiki.

Competition among secondary grade students of Hawaiian ancestry marks the **Kamehameha School Annual Song Contest** held at the Blaisdell Center Arena, Honolulu. For information call Kamehameha Schools at tel. 842-8211.

March For Women
Mid-month features feminine beauty, grace, and athletic ability at the **Miss Maui Pageant** at Baldwin High School, Wailuku, Maui; **Miss Kauai Pageant** at the Kauai War Memorial Convention Hall, Lihue; the **Miss Aloha Hawaii Pageant** at Hilo Civic Auditorium, Hilo, Hawaii.

The prestigious **LPGA Women's Kemper Open** chooses one of the islands' best golf courses for this annual event that features the Helene Curtis Pro-Am, and draws the world's best women golfers.

March For The Prince
The end of March is dedicated to Prince Kuhio, a member of the royal family and Hawaii's first delegate to the U.S. Congress. **Prince Kuhio Day** is a state holiday honoring Hawaii's Prince Kuhio held on March 26, his birthday. Celebrations are held at the Prince Kuhio Federal Building, Oahu. Call 546-7573 for details.

The **Prince Kuhio Festival** at Lihue, Kauai, features festivities from the era of Prince Kuhio along with canoe races and a royal ball.

The **Prince Kuhio Rodeo** is held at Po'oku Stables, in Princeville, Kauai. Call 826-6777 for details.

APRIL

Easter Sunday's **Sunrise Service** at the National Memorial Cemetery of The Pacific, Punchbowl Crater, Honolulu, is a moving ceremony that shouldn't be missed if you're in the islands at that time.

The **Annual Hawaiian Festival of Music** at Waikiki Shell, Honolulu, is a grand and lively music competition of groups made from all over the islands and the mainland. This music-lovers' smorgasbord offers everything from symphony, to swing and all beats in between. Call 637-6566 for information.

Wesak or Buddha Day is on the closest Sunday to April 8, and celebrates the birthday of Gautama Buddha. Ornate offerings of tropical flowers are placed at temple altars throughout Hawaii. Enjoy the sunrise ceremonies at Kapiolani Park, Honolulu, with Japanese in their best kimonos along with flower festivals, pageants, and dance programs in many island temples.

Mid To Late April
The **Aloha Basketball Classic** at the Blaisdell Center Arena, Honolulu, brings top college seniors who are invited to Hawaii to participate in charity games made up of four teams. Blaisdell Center, tel. 527-5400.

The **Paniolo Ski Meet** is exciting skiing atop the Big Island's Mauna Kea, conditions permitting.

The **Merrie Monarch Festival** in Hilo sways with the best hula dancers that the islands' hula *halau* have to offer. Gentle but stiff competition features both ancient and modern dances. The festival runs for a week on a variable schedule from year to year. It's immensely popular with islanders, and hotels, cars, and flights are booked solid. Call 935-9168 for information.

The **Kona Sports Festival** Kailua-Kona, Hawaii, is a solid week of sports entertainment and frivolity held toward the end of the month.

MAY

Early May

May 1 is May Day to the communist world, but in Hawaii red is only one of the colors when everyone dons a lei for **Lei Day.** Festivities abound throughout Hawaii, but there are special "goings on" at Kapiolani Park, Waikiki.

The **Captain Cook Festival** at Kailua-Kona offers Hawaiian games, music, and fishing.

Costumed pageants, canoe races, and a beard-judging contest commemorate times past at the **Lahaina Whaling Spree,** Lahaina, Maui.

The **Pacific Handcrafters Guild Fair** at Ala Moana Park, Honolulu, is a perfect opportunity to see the "state of the arts" in Hawaii when the islands' best artists gather in one spot to sell their creations.

Look skyward on May 5, **Japanese Boys' Day,** and you'll see paper carp *(koi)* flying from rooftops. Carp symbolize the manly virtues of strength and courage. The number of *koi* kites correspond to the number of sons in the family with the largest on top for the eldest, and then down the line.

Mid To Late May

Armed Forces Week brings military open houses, concerts, and displays in and around the islands. Hawaii is the most militarized state in the Union and this fact becomes obvious. Call Military Relations, tel. 438-9761 for details.

Filipino Fiesta is a month-long celebration of the islands' Filipino population. Food, various festivities, and a beauty contest are part of the fiesta.

Costumed riders from the annals of Hawaiian history ride again at **Hawaii on Horseback.** Horsemanship and a western flair mark these days held in and around Waimea, and the Parker Ranch on the Big Island.

Annual Western Week at Honokaa on the Big Island is a fun-filled week with a Western theme. It includes a cookout, parade, rodeo, and dance.

Memorial Day in Hawaii is special with military services held at Honolulu's, National Memorial Cemetery of the Pacific on the last Monday in May. Call 546-3190 for details.

Agricultural exhibts, down-home cooking, entertainment, and fresh produce are presented for four weekends starting in late May at the **50th State Fair,** at Aloha Stadium, Honolulu, tel. 536-5492.

JUNE

Early June

The **Kauai County Fair** at the Kauai War Memorial Convention Hall, Lihue, is a typical county fair offering the best in agriculture that the island has to offer.

Hawaii's best artists and craftsmen come to the **Mission Houses Museum Fancy Fair** in Houolulu. Browse while enjoying homemade food and entertainment. Call 531-0481 for details.

King Kamehameha Day

June 11 is a state holiday honoring Kamehameha the Great with festivities on all islands. Check local papers for times and particulars. The following are the main events: Oahu holds a lei-draping ceremony at King Kamehameha statue at the Civic Center in downtown Honolulu, along with parades complete with floats and pageantry featuring a *ho'olaule'a* (street party) in Waikiki; Kailua-Kona on the Big Island is hospitablè with a *ho'olaule'a,* parades, art demonstrations, entertainment, and contests; on Kauai enjoy parades, *ho'olaule'a,* arts, and crafts centered around the Kauai County Building; Maui's Lahaina and Kahului are decked out for parades, and pageants. Also, the Kamehameha Day Invitational Archery Tournament is held at the Kahului Armory and Valley Isle Archers Field Range.

The **Kamehameha Ski Meet** is in early June when bikini-clad contestants add a little extra spice on those bouncy moguls.

Mid To Late June

The Brigham Young University at Laie, Oahu, swings with the **Annual King Kamehameha Traditional Hula And Chant Competition.**

The **Annual Upcountry Fun Fair** at the Eddie Tam Center, Makawao, Maui, is an old-fashioned farm fair right in the heart of Maui's *paniolo* country. Crafts, food, and competitions are part of the fair.

The **Annual Hawaiian Festival Of Music** at the Waikiki Shell, Honolulu, is a repeat of the April festivities, but no less of a music lover's delight as local and Mainland bands compete in mediums from symphony to swing.

Hilo, Hawaii flashes its brilliant colors with the **Annual Hilo Orchid Society Show** at the Hilo Civic Auditorium, and the **Annual Big Island Bonsai Show,** Wailoa Center, Hilo (both sometimes scheduled for early July).

Dancing is part of the **Annual Japan Festival** in Honolulu at Kapiolani Park and the Blaisdell Center. Also, *Bon Odori,* the Japanese festival of departed souls, featuring dances and candle-lighting ceremonies are held at numerous Buddhist temples throughout the islands. A special *bon odori* festival is offered at Haleiwa Jodo Mission, Haleiwa, Oahu. These festivities change yearly and can be held anytime from late June to early August.

JULY

The week of the **Fourth of July** offers the all-American sport of rodeo along with parades on every island. Don't miss the following if possible. **July 4 Parker Ranch Rodeo And Horseraces,** Paniolo Park, Waimea, Hawaii. The epitome of rodeo by Hawaii's top cowboys, the setting is the Parker Ranch, the largest privately owned ranch in all of America, including Texas, *pardner!* Call 885-7655.

The **Annual Naalehu Rodeo,** Naalehu, Hawaii, offers rodeo events, motorcycle and dune buggy races, **luau,** food booths and Hawaiian entertainment.

Makawao Statewide Rodeo at the Oskie Rice Arena, Makawao, Maui, is an old-time up-country rodeo that can't be beat for fun and entertainment anywhere in the country. Call 572-8102.

The **Hawaiian Islands Tall Ships Parade** floats off Oahu on the 4th of July. Tall-masted ships from throughout the islands parade from Koko Head to Sand Island and back to Diamond Head. A rare treat and taste of days gone by.

July Sports
Sporting events throughout July feature races and competitions both on land and in the sea. The **Big Island Marathon** in Hilo is a full and half marathon starting and ending at the Hilo Hawaiian Hotel.

The **Tin Man Triathlon,** Honolulu, gathers over 1,000 triathletes to swim 800 meters, bike 25 miles and finish with a 10,000-meter (6.2

miles) run around Diamond Head and back to Kapiolani Park in Waikiki. Call 533-4262.

Run To The Sun from Kahului, Maui, is a grueling $37\frac{1}{2}$-mile ultra-marathon from sea level to Maui's 10,000-foot Haleakala. Held in June or August. Call 242-6042.

The **Annual Pan Am Windsurfing Pacific Cup** is held at various beaches around Oahu, determined by wind conditions.

Boats from ports around the world sail to Oahu for the **Pan Am Clipper Cup Series.** They navigate a series of triangles off Waikiki, along with one nonstop race from Ala Wai Harbor to Molokai, and an around-the-state nonstop race.

The **Trans Pacific Race** from Los Angeles to Honolulu sails during odd-numbered years. Yachties arrive throughout the month and converge on Ala Wai Yacht basin where "party" is the password. They head off for Hanalei Bay, Kauai, to begin the year's yachting season.

Four-man teams of one pro and three amateurs compete in the 54-hole **Mauana Kea Beach Hotel's Annual Pro-Am Golf Tournament** held at the hotel links along the Big Island's Kohala Coast.

Mid To Late July
The **International Festival Of The Pacific** in mid-July features a "Pageant of Nations" in Hilo. Folk dances, complete with authentic costumes from throughout Asia and the Pacific, add a rare excitement to the festivities. Contact the Japanese Chamber of Commerce, tel. 961-6123, for details.

The **Prince Lot Hula Festival** in Honolulu is a great chance for visitors to see "authentic" hula from some of the finest hula halau in the islands. Held at Moanalua Gardens, tel. 839-5334.

Hundreds of ukulele players from throughout the islands come to the Kapiolani Park Bandstand, Waikiki for, the **Annual Ukulele Festival.**

Take the opportunity to see the "state of the arts" all in one locality. Browse, buy, and eat ethnic foods at various stalls of the **Pacific Handcrafters Fair** at Thomas Square, Honolulu.

The beauty and grace of one of Hawaii's ethnic groups is apparent at the **Miss Hawaii Filipina Pageant,** Naniloa Hotel, Hilo.

The **Annual Honomu Village Fair,** Honomu, Hawaii, starts with a 46-mile Volcano to Honomu team relay race followed by mountainball, and volleyball. There's plenty of local foods, and arts and crafts.

AUGUST

Early August
Honolulu Zoo Day in Waikiki is a day of family fun where "kids" of all ages get an up-close look at the animals, along with a full day of entertainment.

The **Annual Hanalei Stampede** is held at the Po'oku Stables, Princeville, Kauai.

Recent hula graduates from Honolulu's Summer Fun classes perform at the **Hula Festival,** Kapiolani Park, Waikiki. Dancers of all ages, shapes, and sizes perform some amazing bodily gyrations.

Chamber music by nationally acclaimed artists fills the Kapalua Bay Hotel on Maui for the **Kapalua Music Festival,** one of Hawaii's few formal occasions.

The first August weekend is **Establishment Day** with traditional hula and lei workshops presented at the Big Island's Puukohala Heiaua where traditional artifacts are also on display.

Mid-August
The **Kona Hawaiian Billfish Tournament** in the waters off Kona, Hawaii brings American teams seeking entry to the **Annual Hawaiian International Billfish Tournament,** held about one week later. Contact Peter Fithian, tel. 922-9708.

Hula, artifacts, workshops in lei-making, Hawaiian language, and other ancient skills are the focus of **Establishment Day** at Puukohala Heiau on the Big Island. The day is extremely educational and packed with family fun. Puukohala Heiau, tel. 882-7218.

The macadamia nut harvest is celebrated with sporting events, horse racing and a "Harvest Ball" at the **Macadamia Nut Harvest festival,** Honokaa, Hawaii. Call 755-7792.

August 17 is **Admissions Day,** a state holiday recognizing the day that Hawaii became a state.

Late August
The **Hawaiian Open State Tennis Championships** are held at various courts around Honolulu and offer substantial prizes.

At the **Kauai County Fair** gardeners, stockmen, and craftspeople of the "Garden Island" display their wares at the War Memorial Center in Lihue. There is pageantry, great local foods, and terrific bargains to be had.

Terminally cute children from ages five to 12 dance for the **Queen Liliuokalani Keiki Hula Competition** at the Kamehameha Schools, Honolulu.

SEPTEMBER

In early September don't miss the **Parker Ranch Round-Up Rodeo,** Paniolo Park, Waimea, Hawaii, or the **Maui County Rodeo,** Makawao, Maui. Call Brenden Balthazar, tel. 572-8102 for details.

Athletes compete in the **Waikiki Rough Water Swim,** a two mile open ocean swim from Sans Souci Beach to Duke Kahanamoku Beach. Open to all ages and ability levels. Also, the **Garden Island Marathon And Half Marathon** starts at the Sheraton Hotel, Kapaa, Kauai.

Mid-September
The **Annual Seiko Super Tennis Tournament** at Wailea, Maui, is a championship tennis competition with leading professional team players.

The **Million Dollar Golden Marlin Fishing Tournament** catches plenty of fishermen at Kailua-Kona, Hawaii.

The **Hawaii County Fair** at Hilo, Hawaii, is an old-time fair held on the grounds of Hilo Civic Auditorium.

Aloha Week
Late September brings festivities on all of the islands, as everyone celebrates Hawaii's own "intangible quality," aloha. There are parades, luaus, historical pageants, balls, and various entertainment. The spirit of aloha is infectious and all are welcomed to join in. Check local papers and tourist literature for happenings near you.

The **Molokai To Oahu Canoe Race** for women (men in October) takes off at the end of September in Hawaiian-style canoes from a remote beach on Kauai to Fort DeRussy in Honolulu. In crossing, the teams must navigate the always-rough Kaiwi Channel.

OCTOBER

Early October
A fall show of the best works of guild members perfect for early-bird Christmas shopping is featured at the **Pacific Handcrafters Guild,** Ala Moana Center Gallery, Honolulu.

The **Maui County Fair** at the fairgrounds in Kahului is the oldest in Hawaii! Call 877-3432.

The **Makahiki Festival** at Waimea Falls Park, an 800-acre tropical preserve on Oahu, features Hawaiian games, crafts, and dances reminiscent of the great *makahiki* celebrations of ancient Hawaii.

The **Molokai To Oahu Canoe Race** for men (women in Sept.) navigates Hawaiian-style canoes across the rough Kaiwi Channel from a remote beach on Molokai to Fort DeRussy, Honolulu.

Oktoberfest. Where else would you expect to find German *oompah* bands, succulent *weiner-schnitzel und bier* than in Honolulu? At the Budweiser Warehouse, 99-877 Iwaena St., Halawa Park, from noon until 10 p.m.

Mid To Late October
Watch the boys from throughout Oceania smash, clash, and collide in the rough-and-tumble **Pan Am International Rugby Club Tournament** held at Queen Kapiolani Park, Honolulu, during odd-numbered years.

The **Annual Orchid Plant And Flower Show** displays Hawaii's copious and glorious flowers at the Blaisdell Center Exhibition Hall, Honolulu, tel. 527-5400.

The later part of the month is a superb time to visit the world's best museum of Polynesian and Hawaiian culture during the **Bishop Museum Festival.** Arts, crafts, plants, and tours of the museum and planetarium provide a full day of fun and entertainment for the family. Bishop Museum, Honolulu, tel. 847-3511.

When they really "wanna have fun" super-athletes come to the **Ironman World Triathlon Championship** at Kailua-Kona, Hawaii. A 2.4-mile open-ocean swim, followed by a 112-mile bike ride and topped off with a full marathon is their idea of a good day. Ironman Office, tel. 528-2050.

The **Kapalua International Championship Of Golf,** at Kapalua, Maui, is one of the best pro tournaments, drawing the world's best golfers

for one of the world's largest purses. Runs to early November. Kapalua International, tel. 669-4844.

NOVEMBER

Early November
Taste the best and only coffee commercially grown in the U.S. at the **Annual Kona Coffee Festival,** Kailua-Kona, Hawaii. Parades, arts and crafts, ethnic food and entertainment are part of the festivities.

Na Mele O'Maui Festival, Kaanapali and Lahaina, Maui, is a time when old Hawaii comes alive through art, dances, and music.

At the **Ho'olaulea in Waianae,** Wainae, Oahu, the military lets down its hair and puts on a display accompanied by top entertainers, food and music in this very ethnic area. All-day event. Army Community Relations, tel. 438-9761.

Mid-November
Here's your chance to see polo at the **Michelob Polo Cup And Bar-B-Que,** Olinda Polo Field, Makawao, Maui. Call 877-5541.

The **Annual King Kalakaua Keiki Hula Festival** is for children from around the state who come to Kailua-Kona, Hawaii to perform their hula. Plenty of fun, but the competition is serious.

November 11, **Veterans Day,** is a National holiday celebrated by a large parade from Fort DeRussy to Queen Kapiolani Park, Waikiki (all islands have a parade). For information, American Legion, tel. 949-1140.

Christmas In November
Hui Noeau Christmas Craft Fair is an annual event offering gifts, decorations, and food for those hungry shoppers. Held at Kaluanui Museum, Makawao, Maui. Call 979-2873

Christmas In The Country atop Hawaii's volcano is a delight where merrymakers frolic in the crisp air around a blazing fire, drinking hot toddys. Also, plenty of arts and crafts, food, and Santa for the *keikis.* Volcano Art Center, Hawaii Volcanoes National Park, Hawaii, 976-7676.

The **YWCA Festival Of Trees** presents Christmas crafts, ornaments, and decorated trees on display and for sale at the YMCA, Hilo, Hawaii, tel. 935-7141.

Quality items are offered by Hawaii's top craftsmen in an open air bazaar at the **Annual**

Christmas Fair of the Mission Houses Museum, Honolulu. Call 531-0481.

Late November
The best surfers in the world come to the best surfing beaches on Oahu for the **Hawaiian Pro-Surfing Championships.** Wave action determines sites except for the **Men's Masters** which is always held at Banzai Pipeline, North Shore, Oahu. Big money and national TV coverage bring out the best in everyone. Call 926-0611.

The Honolulu Academy of Art, Honolulu, tel. 538-3693, showcases some of Hawaii's finest contemporary artists at its **Artists Of Hawaii Annual Exhibition.**

DECEMBER

Early December
The **Kauai Junior Miss Presentation,** Kauai War Memorial Convention Hall, Lihue, is where young hopefuls get their first taste of the "big time."

The **Hawaii International Film Festival** at the East West Center, Honolulu, screens some of the best art films from the "East," "West," and Oceania. Call 944-7203 for details.

Christmas Celebrations
Christmas Fantasyland Of Trees at Honokaa, Hawaii, is an early showing of gaily decorated trees. The right Christmas spirit auctions them off for charity. Call 775-0345.

The **Festival Of Trees** is when the business community pitches in and offers gaily decorated trees with the proceeds to charity. It's held at the Coco Palms Hotel Queen's Audience Hall, Lihue, Kauai.

The **Kauai Museum Holiday Festival** is an annual Christmas event known for attracting the island's best in hand-crafted items and home-baked goodies. At the Kauai Museum, Lihue, Kauai, tel. 245-6931.

The **Kamehameha Schools Christmas Concert** is open to everyone and lifts the Christmas spirit at the Blaisdell Center Concert Hall, Honolulu, tel. 842-8211.

The open-air **Pacific Handcrafders Guild Christmas Fair,** Thomas Square, Honolulu presents the best by the best, just in time for Christmas. Pacific Handcrafters, tel. 923-5726.

Mid To Late December
The **Annual Honolulu Marathon** is an "institution" in marathon races, attracting the best runners from around the world. TV coverage. For information, call 723-7200.

The people of Hilo celebrate a New England Christmas in memory of the missionaries with **A Christmas Tradition.** Held at the Lyman House Memorial Museum, Hilo, tel. 935-5021.

A Christmas Tradition features the distinctive touches of a New England-style Christmas at the Lyman House Memorial Museum, Hilo, tel. 935-5021.

Bodhi Day is ushered in with ceremonies at Buddhist temples to commemorate Buddha's day of enlightenment. All islands.

The **Christmas Concert** by the Kauai High School Band and Chorus performs a medly of classic, contemporary and Hawaiian Christmas carols and tunes. At the Kauai War Memorial Convention Hall, Lihue, tel. 245-6422.

On **New Years Eve** hold on to your hat, because they do it up big in Hawaii. Merriment and alcohol flow all over the islands. Firecrackers are illegal, but they go off everywhere. Beware of hangovers and "amateur" drunken drivers.

December Sports
At the **Mauna Kea Beach Hotel's Annual Invitational Golf Tournament** men and women play at this fabulous golf course on the Kohala Coast, Hawaii, tel. 882-7222.

The **Kapalua-Betsey Nagelson Tennis Invitational** is a select field of women pros and amateurs. At Kapalua, Maui, Tennis Garden, tel. 669-5677.

The **Annual Rainbow Classic** is an invitational tournament of collegiate basketball teams. Blaisdell Center Arena, Honolulu, tel. 948-7523.

The **Aloha Bowl Game** is collegiate football with top teams from the Mainland coming to Aloha Stadium, Honolulu, tel. 488-7731.

PERFORMING ARTS EVENTS

The following offer top-notch performances at various times throughout the year: **Honolulu Symphony,** tel. 537-6191; **Hawaii Opera Theatre,** tel. 521-6537; **Honolulu Community Theatre,** tel. 734-0274; **Hawaii Performing Arts Company Theatre,** tel. 988-6131.

GETTING THERE

With the number of visitors each year approaching six million, and double that number of travelers just passing through, Hawaii is one of the easiest places in the world to get to . . . by plane. About 10 large U.S. airlines (and other small ones) fly to and from the islands; about the same number of foreign carriers, mostly from Asia and Oceania, touch down on a daily basis. In 1978 airlines were "deregulated." In 1984, the reign of the Civil Aeronautics Board (CAB), which controlled exactly which airlines flew where and how much they could charge, ended. Routes, prices, and schedules were thrown open to free competition. Airlines that had previously monopolized preferred destinations found competitors prying loose their strangleholds. Thus, Hawaii is now one of the most hotly contested air markets in the world. The competition between carriers is fierce, and this makes for "sweet deals" and a wide choice of fares for the money-wise traveler. It also makes for pricing chaos. It's impossible to give airline prices that will hold true for more than a month, if that long. But it's comforting to know that flights to Hawaii are cheaper today than they have been in years, and mile for mile are one of the best travel bargains in the industry. What's really important is to be familiar with the alternatives at your disposal, so you can make an informed travel selection. Now more than ever you should work with a sharp travel agent who's on your side.

Brief Airline History

On May 20-21, 1927, the people of the world were mesmerized by the heroic act of Charles Lindbergh, The Lone Eagle, as he safely piloted his sturdy craft, *The Sprit of St. Louis,* across the Atlantic. With the Atlantic barrier broken, it took only four days for Jim Dole, of pineapple fame, to announce an air race from the West Coast to Hawaii. He offered the same first prize of $25,000 that Lindbergh had claimed, and to sweeten the pot he offered $10,500 for second place. The **Dole Air Derby** applied only to civilian flights, though the military was already at work attempting the Pacific crossing.

In August 1925, a Navy flying boat took off from near San Francisco, piloted by Commander John Rodgers. The seaplane flew without difficulty across the wide Pacific's expanse, but ran out of gas just north of the Hawaiian Islands and had to put down in a stormy sea. Communication devices went dead and the mission was given up as lost. Heroically, Rodgers and his crew made crude sails from the wing's fabric and sailed the plane to within 12 miles of Kauai, where they were spotted by an incredulous submarine crew. On June 28, 1927, Army Lieutenants Maitland and Hegenberger successfully flew a Fokker trimotor land plane, *The Bird of Paradise,* from Oakland to Oahu in just under 26 hours.

On July 14, 1927, independent of the air derby, two indomitable pilots, Smith and Bronte, flew their *City of Oakland* from its namesake to a forced landing on the shoreline of Molokai. On August 16, 1927, eight planes lined up in Oakland to start the derby. The first to take off was the *Woolaroc,* piloted by Art Goebel and Bill Davis. It went on to win the race and claim the prize in just over 26 hours. Second place went to the appropriately named *Aloha,* crewed by Martin Jensen and Paul Schluter, coming in two hours behind the *Woolaroc.* Unfortunately, two planes were lost in the crossing and two more in the rescue attempt, which accounted for 12 dead. However, the race proved that flying to Hawaii was indeed feasible.

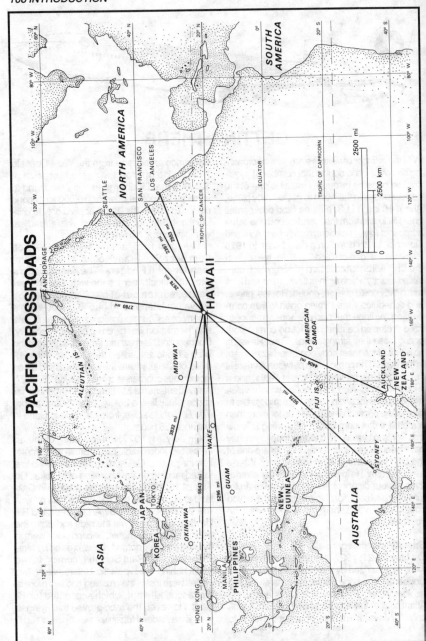

PACIFIC CROSSROADS

WINGS TO HAWAII

There are two categories of airlines that you can take to Hawaii: **domestic,** meaning American-owned, and **foreign**-owned. An American law, penned at the turn of the century to protect American shipping, says "only" an American carrier can transport you to and from two American cities. In the airline industry, this law is still very much in effect. It means, for example, that if you want a roundtrip San Francisco/Honolulu, you *must* fly on a domestic carrier, such as United or Pan Am. If, however, you are flying San Francisco to Tokyo, you are at liberty to fly a "foreign" airline such as Japan Air Lines, and you may even have a stopover in Hawaii, but you must continue on to Tokyo or some other foreign city and can not fly JAL back to San Francisco. Canadians have no problem flying Canadian Pacific roundtrip from Toronto to Honolulu because this route does not connect two American cities, and so it is with all foreign travel to and from Hawaii. Travel agents all know this, but if you're planning your own trip be aware of this fact and know that if you're flying roundtrip it must be on a domestic carrier.

Kinds Of Flights

The three kinds of flights are the "milk run," direct, and nonstop. Milk runs are the least convenient. On these, you board a carrier, say in your home town, fly it to a gateway city, change planes and carriers, fly on to the West Coast, change again, and then fly to Hawaii. They're a hassle—your bags have a much better chance of getting lost, you waste time in airports, and to top it off, they're not any cheaper. Avoid them if you can.

On direct flights you fly from point A to point B without changing planes; it doesn't mean that you don't land in between. Direct flights do land usually once to board and deplane passengers, but you sit cozily on the plane along with your luggage and off you go again. Nonstop is just that, but can cost a bit more. You board and when the doors open again you're in Hawaii. All nonstop flights from the West Coast gateway cities are "God willing," because there is only the Pacific in between!

Travel Agents

At one time people went to a travel agent the same way they went to a barber or beautician . . . loyally sticking with one. Most agents are reputable professionals who know what they're doing. They should be members of the American Society of Travel Agents (ASTA) and licensed by the Air Traffic Conference (ATC). Most have the inside track on the best deals, and they'll save you countless hours calling 800 numbers and listening to elevator music while on hold. Unless you require them to make very special arrangements, their services are free—the airlines and hotels that they book you into pay their commission.

If you've done business with a travel agent in the past, and were satisfied with his services and prices, by all means stick with him. If no such positive rapport exists, then shop around. Ask friends or relatives for recommendations; if you can't get any endorsements go to the Yellow Pages. Call two or three travel agents to compare prices. Make sure to give them all equal information and be as precise as possible. Tell them where and when you want to go, how long you want to stay, class you want to travel, and any special requirements. Write down their information. It's amazing how confusing travel plans can be when you have to keep track of flight numbers, times, prices, and all the preparation info. When you compare, don't look only for the cheapest price. Check for convenience in flights, amenities of hotels, and any other fringe benefits that might be included. Then make your choice of agent, and if he's willing to give you individualized service, stick with him from this point on.

Agents become accustomed to offering the same deals to many clients because they're familiar with making the arrangements and they worked well in the past. Sometimes these are indeed the best, but if they don't suit you, don't be railroaded into accepting them. Any good agent will work with you. After all, it's your trip and your money.

Package Tours

As an independent traveler, practical package deals that include flight, car, and lodging only are OK. Agents put these together all the time and they just might be the best, but if they don't suit you make arrangements separately. A package tour is totally different. On these you get your hand held by an escort, eat where they want you to eat, go where they want you to go, and watch Hawaii slide by past the window of your bus. For some people, especially older folks or groups, this might be the way, but everyone else should avoid them. You'll see Hawaii best on your own, and if you want a tour you can arrange one there, often cheaper. Once arrangements have been made with your travel agent, make sure to take all receipts and letters of confirmation (hotel, car) with you to Hawaii. They probably won't be needed, but if they are nothing will work better in getting results.

Fares

There are many categories of airline fares, but only three generally apply to the average traveler: 1st class, coach, and excursion (APEX). Traveling **1st class** seats you in the front of the plane, gives you free drinks and movie headsets, a wider choice of meals, more leg room, and access to VIP lounges if they exist. There are no restrictions, payment penalties on advance booking, minimum stays, or rebooking return flights.

Coach, the way that most people fly, is totally adequate. You sit in the plane's main compartment behind 1st class. Your seats are comfortable, but you don't have as much leg room or such a wide choice of meals. Movie headsets and drinks cost you a few dollars, but that's about it. **Coach** offers many of the same benefits as 1st class and costs about 30 % less. You can buy tickets up to takeoff; you have no restrictions on minimum or maximum stays; you receive liberal stopover privileges, and you can cash in your return ticket or change your return date with no penalties.

Excursion or **advance payment excursion (APEX)** fares are the cheapest. You are accommodated on the plane exactly the same as if you were flying coach. There are, however, some restrictions. You must book and pay for your ticket in advance (seven to 14 days). At the same time, you must book your return flight, and under most circumstances can't change either without paying a penalty. Also, your stopovers are severely limited and you will have a minimum/maximum stay

period. Only a limited number of seats on any one plane are set aside for APEX fares, so book as early as you can. Also, if you must change travel plans, you can go to the airport and get on as a standby passenger using a discounted ticket even if the airline doesn't have an official standby policy. There's always the risk that you won't get on but you do have a chance, as well as priority, over an actual standby customer.

Standby is exactly what its name implies: you go to the airport and wait around to see if any flights going to Hawaii have an empty seat. You can save some money, but cannot have a firm itinerary or limited time. Since Hawaii is such a popular destination standbys can wait days before catching a plane. A company called **Stand Bys Ltd.** offers an up-to-the-minute newsletter and an 800 number which gives you information on charter flights that haven't sold out. The service costs $45 per year, but you can save from 15-60 % on most tickets. Write Stand Bys Ltd., 26711 Northwestern Hwy., Southfield, MI 48034 tel. (313) 352-4876.

Active and retired **military personnel** and their dependents are offered special fares on airlines and in military hostels. An excellent resource book listing all of these special fares and more is *Space-A*, ($11.75 for book and first-class postage) available from Military Travel News, P.O. Box 9, Oakton, VA 22124. Plenty of money-saving tips.

Charters

Charter flights were at one time only for groups or organizations that had memberships in travel clubs. Now they're open to the general public. A charter flight is an entire plane or a "block" of seats purchased at a quantity discount by a charter company and then sold to customers. Because they are bought at wholesale prices, charter fares can be the cheapest available. As in package deals, only take a charter flight if it is a "fly only," or perhaps includes a car. You don't need one that includes a guide and a bus. Most importantly, make sure that the charter company is reputable. They should belong to the same organizations (ASTA and ATC) as most travel agents. If not, check into them at the local chamber of commerce.

More restrictions apply to charters than any others. You must pay in advance. If you cancel after a designated time, you can be penalized severely or lose your money entirely. You can not change departure or return dates and times. However, up to 10 days before departure the charter company is legally able to cancel, raise the price by 10 %, or change time and dates. They must return your money if cancellation occurs, or if changed arrangements are unacceptable to you. Mostly they are on the up and up and flights go smoothly, but there are horror stories. Be careful. Be wise. Investigate!

Tips

Flights from the West Coast take about five hours; you gain two hours over Pacific Standard time when you land in Hawaii. From the East Coast it takes about 11 hours and you gain five hours over Eastern Standard Time. Try to fly Monday through Thursday, when flights are cheaper and easier to book. Pay for your ticket as soon as your plans are firm. If prices go up there is no charge added, but merely booking doesn't guarantee the lowest price. Make sure that airlines, hotels, and car agencies get your phone number too, not only your travel agent's, in case any problems with availability arise (travel agents are often closed on weekends). It's not necessary, but it's a good idea to call and reconfirm flights 24-72 hours in advance.

First-row (bulkhead) seats are good for people who need more leg room, but bad for watching the movie. Airlines will give you special meals (vegetarian, kosher, low cal, low salt) often at no extra charge, but you must notify them in advance. If you're "bumped" from an overbooked flight, you're entitled to a comparable flight to your destination within one hour. If more than an hour elapses, you get denied-boarding compensation which goes up proportionately with the amount of time you're held up. Sometimes this is cash or a voucher for another flight to be used in the future. You don't have to accept what the airlines offer on the spot, if you feel they aren't being fair.

Traveling With Children

Fares for children 2-12 are 50 % of the adult fare; children under two not occupying a seat travel free. If you're traveling with an infant or active toddler, book your flight well in advance and request the bulkhead seat or first row in any sec-

tion and a bassinet if available. Many carriers have fold-down cribs with restraints for baby's safety and comfort. Toddlers appreciate the extra space provided by the front-row seats. Be sure to reconfirm and arrive early to assure getting this special seating. On long flights you'll be glad that you took these extra pains.

Although most airlines have coloring books, puppets, etc., to keep your child busy, it's always a good idea to bring your own. These can make the difference between a pleasant flight and a harried ordeal. Also, remember to bring baby bottles, formula, diapers, and other necessities as many airlines may not be equipped with exactly what you need. Make all inquiries ahead of time so you're not caught unprepared.

Baggage

You are allowed two free pieces of luggage and a carry-on bag. The two main pieces can weigh up to 70 pounds each with an extra charge levied for extra weight. The largest can have an overall added dimension (height plus width plus length) of 62 inches and the second can be up to 55 inches. Your carry-on must fit under your seat or in the overhead storage compartment. Purses and camera bags are not counted as carry-ons and may be taken aboard. Surfboards and bicycles are about $15 extra. Although they make great mementos, remove all previous baggage tags from your luggage; they can confuse handlers. Attach a sturdy holder with your name and address on the handle, or use a stick-on label on the bag itself. Put your name and address inside the bag, and the address where you'll be staying in Hawaii if possible. Carry your cosmetics, identification, money, prescriptions, tickets, reservations, change of underwear, camera equipment, and perhaps a change of shirt or blouse in your carry-on.

Visas

Entering Hawaii is like entering anywhere else in the U.S. Foreign nationals must have a current passport and proper visa. An ongoing or return air ticket as well as sufficient funds for the proposed stay in Hawaii are also requirements of foreign nationals by U.S. Immigration. Canadians do not need a visa or passport, but must have proper identification such as passport, driver's license, or birth certificate.

When To Go

The prime tourist season starts two weeks before Christmas and lasts until Easter. It picks up again with summer vacation in early June and ends once more in late August. If possible avoid these times of year. Everything is usually booked solid and prices are inflated. Hotel, airline, and car reservations, which are a must, are often hard to coordinate. You can save between 10 and 50% and a lot of hassling if you go in the artificially created **off season,** from September to early December, and mid-April (after Easter) till early June. You'll not only find the prices better, but the beaches, hikes, campgrounds, and even restaurants will be less crowded. The people will be happier to see you too.

DOMESTIC CARRIERS

The following are the major domestic carriers to and from Hawaii. The planes used are primarily DC-10s and 747s, with a smaller 727 flown now and again. A list of the "gateway cities" from which they fly direct and nonstop flights is given, but "connecting cities" are not. All flights, by all carriers, land at Honolulu International Airport except for limited direct flights to Maui and Hawaii. Only the established companies are listed. Entrepreneurial small airlines such as the now-defunct Hawaii Express pop up now and again and specialize in dirt-cheap fares. There is a hectic frenzy to buy their tickets and business is great for a while, but then the established companies lower their fares and the gamblers fold.

Hawaiian Air

One of Hawaii's own domestic airline has entered the Mainland market. They operate a daily flight from Los Angeles and San Francisco to Honolulu, with periodic flights from Anchorage, Las Vegas, Portland, and Seattle. The "common fare" ticket price includes an ongoing flight to any of the Neighbor Islands, and if leaving from Hawaii, a free flight from a Neighbor Island to the link-up in Honolulu. Hawaiian Air's trans-Pacific schedule features flights between Honolulu and points in the South Pacific nearly every day: flights depart for Pago Pago, American Samoa, half continuing on to Apia, Western Samoa, the rest to Tonga, with additional flights to New Zealand, Guam, Tahiti, and Rarotonga. Hawaiian Air offers special discount deals with Dollar rental cars and select major island hotels. Contact Hawaiian Air at (800) 367-5320.

United Airlines

Since their first island flight in 1947, United has become top dog in flights to Hawaii. Their Mainland routes connect over 100 cities to Honolulu. The main gateways are direct flights from San Francisco, Los Angeles, San Diego, Seattle, Portland, Chicago, New York, Denver, and Toronto. They also offer direct flights to Maui from San Francisco, Los Angeles, and Chicago, and from Los Angeles to the Big Island. United offers a number of packages, including flight and hotel on Oahu, and flight, hotel, and car on the neighboring islands. They interline with Aloha Airlines and deal with Hertz rental cars. They're the "big guys" and they intend to stay that way—their packages are hard to beat. Call (800) 241-6522.

American Airlines

Offers direct flights to Honolulu from Los Angeles, San Francisco, Dallas, and Chicago. They also fly from Los Angeles and San Francisco to Maui, with a connection in Honolulu. Call (800) 433-7300.

Continental

Flights from all Mainland cities to Honolulu go via Los Angeles and San Francisco. Also available are direct flights from Australia and New Zealand to Honolulu. Call (800) 525-0280 or (800) 231-0856 for international information.

Northwest Orient

Northwest flies from Los Angeles, San Francisco, and Portland via Seattle. There are onward flights to Tokyo, Osaka, Okinawa, Manila, Hong Kong, Taipei, and Seoul. Call (800) 225-2525.

Delta Airlines

In 1985, Delta entered the Hawaiian market; when it bought out Western Airlines its share became even bigger. They have nonstop flights to Honolulu from Dallas/Ft. Worth, Los Angeles, San Francisco, and San Diego, and now flights to Kahului, Maui, via Los Angeles or Honolulu. Call (800) 221-1212.

The Honolulu Advertiser EXTRA

Hawaii's Territorial Newspaper

HTH. YEAR, NO. 17.124—14 PAGES   HONOLULU, TERRITORY OF HAWAII, U.S.A., WEDNESDAY MORNING, APRIL 17, 1935.   PRICE FIVE CENTS

CLIPPER LANDS AT 8:00

Thousands See Flight's Start At Golden Gate

Heavily - Laden Ship In Graceful Takeoff from Bay Waters; Routine Job to Crew

Reaches Honolulu At 7:04; Cruises Over Island Until Crowds Arrive At Air Base

Giant Plane Sets New Record for Westbound Hop; Could Easily Have Made Better Time But Delayed Landing for Spectators

An Early Morning Caller

Advertiser Signs Wood | Here's Log Of Clipper Since Hop From Coast | Receptions Ready Today

Pan American Airlines, now out of business in the Pacific, opened Hawaii to mass air travel with this historic flight on Wednesday, April 17, 1935. The flight from Alameda Airport to Pearl Harbor took 19 hours and 48 minutes.

Pan Am

Pan Am's flights to Honolulu from New York, Miami, San Francisco, San Diego, and other Mainland cities all go through Los Angeles. Onward flights go to major Asian cities. Call (800) 843-8687.

America West

America West started as a regional carrier in Arizona making milk runs between Phoenix and Los Angeles. In November 1989, it entered the Hawaii market. Fares are comparable to the larger airlines and will allow Midwesterners to fly to either Phoenix or Las Vegas, and then straight on to Honolulu from there. They're flying brand-new 747s, and as an employee-owned airline have made an excellent reputation for service, friendliness, and on-time scheduling. For information call (800) 247-5692.

FOREIGN CARRIERS

The following carriers operate throughout Oceania but have no U.S. flying rights. This means that in order to vacation in Hawaii using one of these carriers, your flight must originate or terminate in a foreign city. You can have a stopover in Honolulu with a connecting flight to a Neighbor Island. For example, if you've purchased a flight on Japan Air Lines from San Francisco to Tokyo, you can stop in Hawaii, but you then must carry on to Tokyo. Failure to do so will result in a stiff fine, and the balance of your ticket will not be refunded.

Canadian Airlines International

Nonstop flights from Canada to Honolulu originate in Vancouver, Toronto, and Calgary; nonstop Pacific flights go to Fiji, Auckland, and Sydney, with connecting flights to other Pacific cities. Call (800) 426-7007.

Air New Zealand

Flights link New Zealand, Australia, and Fiji with Los Angeles via Honolulu. Also offered is a remarkable APEX fare from Los Angeles to New Zealand, with stops in Honolulu and Fiji, and a Super Pass fare that lets you stop in eight cities between Los Angeles and Australia. Occasionally, other special fares are offered. Call (800) 262-1234 for current information.

Japan Air Lines

The Japanese are the second largest group, next to Americans, to visit Hawaii. JAL flights to Honolulu originate in Tokyo, Nagoya, and Osaka. There are no JAL flights between the Mainland and Hawaii. Call (800) 525-3663.

All Nippon Airways

Flights from Tokyo via Honolulu and Los Angeles to San Francisco. Occasional charter flights are offered from Tokyo to Honolulu. Call (800) 235-9262 for current information.

Philippine Airlines

Flights to and from Los Angeles and San Francisco to Manila via Honolulu. Connections in Manila to most Asian cities. Call (800) 435-9725.

American Hawaiian Cruises' SS Independence

Qantas
Daily flights from San Francisco and Los Angeles to Sydney via Honolulu. Stopovers are possible in Fiji and Tahiti. Call (800) 622-0850.

China Airlines
They maintain routes from Los Angeles to Taipei with stopovers in Honolulu and Tokyo possible, but they are not available year-round. Connections from Taipei to most Asian capitals. Call (808) 652-1428.

Korean Air
Some of the least expensive flights to Asia. Flights leave only from Los Angeles, stopping in Honolulu, with either a direct flight to Seoul or a stopover in Tokyo. Connections to many Asian cities. Call (800) 421-8200.

Singapore Airlines
Flights to and from San Francisco and Los Angeles to Singapore via Honolulu and either Hong Kong or Taipei. Free stopovers for seven-day advance-purchase tickets. Call (800) 742-3333.

Air Tungaru
Limited flights from Kiribati to Honolulu via Christmas Island and Tarawa. In Hawaii, call 735-3994.

Air Nauru
The South Pacific's richest island offers flights throughout Polynesia, including most major Hawaiian islands, with connections to Japan, Taipei, Hong Kong, Manila, Singapore, and Australia. In Hawaii, call 531-9766.

TRAVEL BY SHIP

At one time Hawaiians lined the pier in Honolulu waiting to greet the cruise ships bringing visitors. It was the only way to get to Hawaii, but those days are long gone. Now only one American company and a few foreign lines make the crossing.

American Hawaii Cruises
This American cruise ship company operates two 800-passenger ships, the SS *Independence,* and the SS *Constitution.* Primarily, these ships offer similar seven-day itineraries that circumnavigate and call at the four main islands. Their price ranges from an inside "thrifty cabin" at $1095 to a luxury suite for $3695. Children under 16 are often given special rates, and cruise free from June to September when they share a cabin with their parents. You come aboard in Honolulu after arriving by plane arranged by American Hawaii Cruises. Each ship is a luxury seagoing hotel and gourmet restaurant; swimming pools, driving ranges, tennis courts, health clubs, movies, and nightclubs are all part of the amenities. For details contact: American Hawaii Cruises, 550 Kearny St., San Francisco, CA 94108, tel. (800) 227-3666, from Canada call collect (415) 392-9400.

Alternatives
Other companies offering varied cruises are **P&O Lines**, which operates the *Sea Princess* through the South Pacific, making port at Honolulu on its way from the West Coast once a year.

Royal Cruise Line out of Los Angeles, or Auckland alternatively, sails the *Royal Odyssey*, which docks in Honolulu on its South Pacific and Orient cruise, and charges from $2200 to $4000

The **Nauru Pacific Line** offers freighter/passenger service from San Francisco to Micronesia via Honolulu, six-week intervals year-round.

The **Holland America Line** sails the *Rotterdam* on its 108-day Grand Circle cruise, departing Fort Lauderdale, passing around South America and calling at Honolulu as it heads for Asia. Prices are from $20,000 to $70,000. call (800) 426-0327.

Society Expeditions offers a 42-day cruise throughout the South Pacific departing from Honolulu. Fares are from $3000 to $9000. call (800) 426-7794.

Information
Most travel agents can provide information on the above cruise lines. If you're really interested in traveling by ship contact: **Freighter Travel Club of America**, Box 12693, Salem, Oregon U.S.A.; or **Ford's Freighter Travel Guide**, Box 505, 22151 Clarendon St., Woodland Hills, CA U.S.A.

TOUR COMPANIES

Many tour companies offer packages to Hawaii in large city newspapers every week. They advertise very reasonable airfares, car rentals, and accommodations. Without trying, you can get roundtrip airfare from the West Coast and a week in Hawaii for $400 using one of these companies. The following companies offer great deals and have excellent reputations. This list is by no means exhaustive.

Council Travel Services
These full-service budget-travel specialists are a subsidiary of the nonprofit Council on International Educational Exchange, and the official U.S. representative to the International Student

Travel Conference. They'll custom-design trips and programs for everyone from senior citizens to college students. Bona fide students have extra advantages, however, including the availability of the International Student Identification Card (CISC), which often gets you discount fares and entrance fees. Groups and business travelers are also welcome. However, they deal with Hawaii mainly as a stopover en route to Asia. For full information, write to the main offices at Council Travel Services, 919 Irving St., #102, San Francisco, CA 94122, tel. (415) 566-6222. Other offices are in Austin, Berkeley, Boston, Long Beach, Los Angeles, Miami, New York, Portland, San Diego, and Seattle.

Student Travel Network
You don't have to be a student to avail yourself of their services. Their main office is at 2500 Wilshire Blvd., #920, Los Angeles, CA 90057, tel. (213) 380-2184. In Honolulu they're at 1831 S. King St., Honolulu, HI 96826, tel. 942-7755. STN also maintains offices in San Diego, San Francisco, and Northridge, California, Toronto, and Vancouver, as well as throughout Australia and Europe.

Nature Expeditions International
These quality tours have nature as the theme. Trips are 15-day, four-island natural history expeditions, with an emphasis on plants, birds, and geology. Their guides are experts in their fields and give personable and attentive service. Operations are temporarily suspended, but plans are to revive these trips in 1990. Contact Nature Expeditions International at 474 Willamette, Box 11496, Eugene, OR 97440, , tel. (503) 484-6529 for current status.

SunTrips
This California-based tour and charter company sells vacations all over the world. They're primarily a wholesale company, but will work with the general public. SunTrips often works with American Trans-Air, tel. (800) 225-9920, when flying to Hawaii. American Trans-Air answers their phones Monday through Friday during normal business hours only. When you receive your SunTrip tickets, you are given discount vouchers for places to stay that are convenient to the air-

port of departure. Many of these hotels have complimentary airport pickup service, and will allow you to park your car, free of charge, for up to 14 days, which saves a considerable amount on airport parking fees. SunTrips does not offer assigned seating until you get to the airport. They recommend that you get there two hours in advance, and they ain't kidding! This is the price you pay for getting such inexpensive air travel. SunTrips has a deal with Tropical Car Rental, which is an excellent Hawaii based company. Remember that everyone on your incoming flight is offered the same deal, and all make a beeline for the Tropical shuttle van after landing and securing their baggage. If you have a traveling companion, work together to beat the rush by heading directly for the van as soon as you arrive, leaving your companion to fetch the baggage. Pick your car up, and then return for your partner and the bags. Even if you're alone and you're snappy enough, you could get over to the car rental center, and return for your bags without having them sit very long on the carousel. Contact SunTrips, 100 Park Center, Box 18505, San Jose, CA 95158, tel. (800) 662-9292, 941-2697 in Honolulu.

Pacific Outdoor Adventures

This truly remarkable tour company operated by John Grey and Bob Wilson offers the best in nature tours. The emphasis is on the outdoors with hiking, camping, and kayaking central. These professional guides go out of their way to make your trip totally enjoyable and safe. Their specially designed kayaks are seaworthy in all conditions and for all ability levels. They focus on giving you a fun-filled "edutainment" adventure, where you can immerse yourself in the local culture, geography, and natural wonder of the areas visited. Although based in Hawaii with a full schedule of trips to the outer islands, Pacific Outdoor Adventures heads for fantastic and little-visited destinations throughout the Pacific. Prices are absolutely unbeatable for the experience offered and arrangements for packages can be made that include everthing from airfare to accommodations and gourmet meals. For a full list of itineraries contact Pacific Outdoor Adventures at P.O. Box 61609, Honolulu, HI 96839, tel. (808) 988-3913, toll-free (800) 52-KAYAK. If an unforgettable outdoor adventure is your goal, you can't go wrong!

Ocean Voyages

A unique company offering seven- and 10-day itineraries aboard a variety of yachts in the Hawaiian Islands. The yachts, equipped to carry from two to 10 passengers, ensure individualized sail training. The vessels sail throughout the islands exploring hidden bays and coves, and berth at different ports as they go. This opportunity is for anyone who wishes to see the islands in a timeless fashion, thrilling to sights experienced by the first Polynesian settlers and Western explorers. For rates and information contact Ocean Voyages, 1709 Bridgeway, Sausalito CA. 94965, tel. (415)-332-4681.

Island Holiday Tours

An established Hawaii-based company that offers flights with American and United, and rental cars through Budget. Arrangements can also be made for tours, luaus, helicopter rides, etc., on all islands. Contact Island Holiday Tours, 2255 Kuhio Ave., Honolulu, HI 96815, tel. (800) 448-6877.

Pleasant Hawaiian Holidays

A California-based company specializing in Hawaii. Arrangements are made for flights, accommodations, and transportation only. At 2404 Townsgate Rd., West Lake Village, CA 91361, tel. (800) 242-9244.

Unique Outdoor Tours/Experiences

Sierra Club Trips take nature lovers to Hawaii who are interested in an outdoor experience. Various trips include hikes over Maui's Haleakala, a kayak trip along the Na Pali coast of Kauai, or a family camping spree in Kauai's Kokee region. All trips are led by experienced guides and are open to Sierra Club members only ($33 per year to join). For information contact the Sierra Club Outing Dept., 730 Polk St., San Francisco, CA 94109, tel. (415) 776-2211.

Earthwatch allows you to become part of an expeditional team dedicated to conservation and the study of the natural environment. An expedition might be the study of dolphins in Kewalo Basin Marine Mammal Laboratory, or observing the ubiquitous mongoose from an observation hut high atop Mauna Kea. Basically, you are an assistant field researcher and your lodgings can be a dorm room at the University of Hawaii, and your meals can come from a remote camp kitchen. Fees vary and are tax deductible. If you are interested in this learning experience, con-

tact Earthwatch, 680 Mt. Auburn St., Box 403-P, Watertown, MA 02272, tel. (617) 926-8200.

DIRECTORY OF HAWAII'S BIKE STORES

OAHU

B & L Bicycle Repair Shop
Mililani Shopping Mall
95-390 Kuahelani
Mililani, HI 96789
625-2222

The Bike Shop
1149 S. King, Hon., HI 96814
531-7071
Kuapa Kai Cntr.,
Hon., HI 96825; 396-6342
98-019 Kam Hwy.,
Aiea, HI 96701; 487-3615

The Bike Way
655 Kapiolani,
Hon., HI 96813
(Next to Columbia Inn)
538-7433

Bikefactory Sportshop
724 Keeaumoku,
Hon., HI 96814; 946-8927

Eki Cyclery
Ala Moana Center
1450 Ala Moana,
Hon., HI 96814; 946-5444
1603 Dillingham,
Hon., HI 96817; 847-2005

Hawaiian Island Creations
Ala Moana Center
1450 Ala Moana,
Hon., HI 96814; 941-4491
Pearlridge Center
Aiea, HI 96701; 488-6700
354 Hahani,
Kailua, HI 96734; 262-7277

Island Triathlon & Bike
569 Kapahulu,
Hon., HI 96815; 732-7227
3312 Campbell,
Hon., HI 96815; 734-8398

McCully Bicycle & Sporting Goods
2124 S. King, Hon. HI 96826
(Next to Pay'n Save)
955-6329

University Cyclery
1728 Kapiolani,
Hon., HI 96814
(mauka corner of Atkinson & Kapiolani) 944-9884

Wahiawa Bicycle Shop
823 Olive,
Wahiawa, HI 96786
(At the top of Olive Ave.)
622-5120

Waipahu Bicycle & Sporting Goods
94-320 Waipahu Depot,
Waipahu, HI 96797
(Across from Arakawa's)
671-4091

MAUI
The Island Biker
Kahului Shopping Center,
Kahului, HI 96793; 877-7744

The Cycle & Sport Shop
111 Hana Hwy., Kahului, HI 96793; 877-5848
West Maui Center, Lahaina, HI 96791; 661-4191

HAWAII
B & L Marine, Bike & Sports
74-5504A Kaiwi,
Kailua, HI 96740
329-3309

Bicycle Warehouse
74-5539 Kaiwi,
Kailua, HI 96740
329-9424

The Bike Shop
258 Kam Ave.,
Hilo, HI 96720; 935-7588

Competitive Edge Triathlon Center
75-5744 Alii Dr.,
Kailua, HI 96740; 329-8141

Dave's Triathlon Shop
74-5588 Pawai,
Kailua, HI 96740; 329-4522

Mid Pacific Wheels
2200 Konoelehua Ave.,
Kawailani, HI 96720
959-7606

KAUAI
Bicycle John
4028-B Rice St.,
Lihue, HI 96766; 245-7579

Bicycles Kauai Inc.
1379 Kuhio Hwy.,
Kapaa, HI 96746; 822-3315

Kauai Sports
Kukui Grove
Shopping Center
3-2600 Kaumualii Hwy.,
Suite #3013,
Lihue, HI 96766; 245-8052

The Central Bike Shop
2-2488 Kaumualii Hwy,,
Kalaheo, HI 96741
332-9122

> * N.B. The above are full service bike stores. For rentals and tours see bicycles in the individual island chapters.

Bicycle Tours

For those interested in peddling around the Hawaiian Islands contact one of the following for their specialized bike trips. **Island Bicycle Adventures,** 569 Kapahulu Ave., Honolulu, HI 96815, tel. 734-0700, or (800) 233-2226. The owners and tour leaders are intimately familiar with bicycle touring on all islands, and are members of the Hawaii Bicycling league. They offer tours to Maui, the Big Island, and Kauai; **Backroads Bicycle Touring,** Box 1626, San Leandro, CA 94577, tel. 415-895-1738 are also experts in the field of bike touring, but at this time only tours the Big Island are offered.

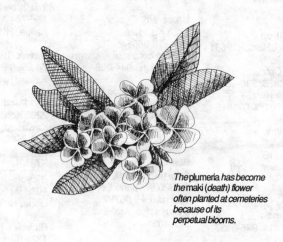

The plumeria *has become the* maki (death) *flower often planted at cemeteries because of its perpetual blooms.*

GETTING AROUND

Inter-island air travel is highly developed, economical, and ridiculously convenient. You can go almost anywhere at anytime on everything from wide-bodied jets to single-engine air taxis. But ironically, in an island community complete with its sea history, modern shipping, and port towns, you cannot go between islands on regularly scheduled ships, boats, or floating conveyances of any nature. You can charter a pleasure boat for a tremendous fee, or maybe bum a ride between the Neighbor Islands on a passing yacht, but nothing is available on a regular schedule. A hovercraft that once serviced the islands is now defunct. Periodically, there is a cry to reinstate some sort of coastal and inter-island boat or ferry service. Some say that visitors and islanders alike would enjoy the experience and be able to travel more economically. Others argue the Hawaiian waters are as dangerous and unpredictable as ever, and no evidence of need or enough passengers exists. A few skippers run pleasure craft between Maui-Molokai-Lanai and are willing to take on passengers, but this is a hit-and-miss situation based on space. These special situations are discussed under "By Boat" p. 126, and in the appropriate travel chapters under "Getting Around.".

By Air

Hawaiians take flying for granted, using planes the way most people use buses. A shopping excursion to Honolulu from a Neighbor Island is commonplace, as is a trip from the city for a picnic at a quiet beach. The longest flight, just over an hour, is from Kauai to Hawaii, including a stopover at one of the islands in between. The moody sea can be uncooperative , but the skies above Hawaii are generally clear and perfect for flying. Their infrequent gloomier moments can delay flights, but the major airlines of Hawaii have a perfect safety record ever since Hawaiian Air's maiden flight in 1929. The fares are competitive, schedules convenient, and the service friendly.

Brief History

Little more than a motorized kite, the *Hawaiian Skylark* was the first plane ever to fly in Hawaii. On New Year's Day, 1911, it circled a Honolulu polo field, where 3,000 spectators, including Queen Liliuokalani, witnessed history. Hawaiians have been soaring above their lovely islands ever since. The first paying customer, Mrs. Newmann, took off on a $15 joy ride in 1913 with a Chinese aviator named Tom Gunn. In February 1920, Charles Fern piloted the first inter-island customer roundtrip from Honolulu to Maui for $150. He worked for Charles Stoffer, who started the first commercial airline the year before with one Curtiss biplane, affectionately known as "Charlie's Crate." For about 10 years sporadic attempts at inter-island service amounted to little more than extended joy rides to deliver the day's newspaper from Honolulu. The James Dole Air Race in 1927 proved that transpacific flight was possible (see pg. 107), but inter-island passenger service didn't really begin until Stanley C. Kennedy, a WW I flier and heir to Inter-Island Steam Navigation Co., began Inter-Island Airways in January 1929. For a dozen years he ran Sikorsky Amphibians, considered the epitome of safety. By 1941 he had converted to the venerable workhorse, the DC-3, and changed the company name to **Hawaiian Air**.

By 1948, Hawaiian Air was unopposed in the inter-island travel market, because regularly scheduled boats had already become obsolete. However, in 1946 a fledgling airline named Trans-Pacific opened for business. A nonscheduled airline with only one war surplus DC-3, they carried a hunting party of businessmen to Molokai on their maiden flight. By June 1952, they were a regularly scheduled airline in stiff competition with Hawaiian Air and had changed their name to **Aloha Airlines**. Both airlines had their financial glory days and woes over the next decade; by the end of the '60s both were flying inter-island jets.

A healthy crop of small unscheduled airlines known as "air taxis" always darted about the wings of the large airlines, flying to minor airfields and performing flying services that were uneconomical for the bigger airlines. Most of these tiny, often one-plane air taxis were swatted from the air like gnats whenever the economy went sour or tourism went sluggish. They had names like Peacock and Rainbow, and after a brief flash of wings, they were gone.

INTER-ISLAND CARRIERS

The only effective way for most visitors to travel between the Hawaiian islands is by air (also see "Inter Island Ferry," p. 126). Luckily, Hawaii has excellent air transportation that boasts one of the industry's safest flight records.

Hawaiian Air, tel. (800) 882-8811 statewide, (800) 367-5320 on the Mainland, is not only the oldest airlines on Hawaii, it is also the biggest. It flies more aircraft, to more airports, more times per day than any other airline in Hawaii. It services all islands, including Molokai and Lanai. Hawaiian Air boasts a top-notch fleet of DC-9 jets for its longer flights, and modern Dash-7, turbo-props (50 passenger) for its shorter runs. From Honolulu to Kauai, 26 nonstop flights go from 5:40 a.m. to 8 p.m.; to Maui flights begin at 5:40 a.m. with one every 20 minutes or so until 8:05 p.m., also regularly scheduled flights to Kapalua, West Maui Airport; to Hilo flights every 40 minutes from 5:50 a.m. to 6:55 p.m. and to Kona from 5:55 a.m. to 6:45 p.m. Also, daily flights to Lanai and Molokai.

Aloha Airlines, tel. (800) 367-5250, or (800) 352-3503 statewide, connects Oahu to Kauai, Maui, and both Kona and Hilo on Hawaii. Aloha's routes aboard its all-jet fleet of Boeing 737s go to all four major islands but not to Lanai and Molokai. Flights include: to Kauai from Honolulu, 22 nonstop flights from 5:40 a.m. until 6:10 p.m.; to Maui, about 30 flights daily, with one departing every 20 minutes or so from 5:40 a.m. to 8:15 p.m.; to Kona, about 20 flights daily from 5:40 a.m. to 7 p.m.; and to Hilo, 12 flights from 5:50 a.m. to 7 p.m.

Practical Information, Fares And Tips

On Oahu, the inter-island carriers are located at the newly remodeled inter-island Terminal at Honolulu International Airport. It's to the right or *ewa* of the main terminal as you face it. The baggage allowance is two "normal-sized" pieces of luggage. Golf bags count as one piece. Over-

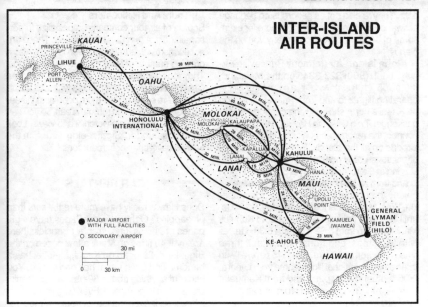

sized and extra bags or boxes are charged $5-10 more. Bicycles and surfboards cost $10-25 and can't be substituted as luggage. Although 60 minutes is recommended, if you check in under 30 minutes prior to flight time you can lose your seat.

The airlines have competitive prices with inter-island flights at about $55 O/W. You can also save money (about $15) if you **take the first or last daily scheduled flight.** This offer usually applies only to flights to and from Honolulu, but check as policy often changes. Another alternative is to **purchase a booklet of six flight vouchers.** You save about $7 per ticket, and they are transferable. Just book a flight as normal and present the filled-in voucher to board the plane. Perfect for families or groups of friends, they can be purchased at any ticket office or at Honolulu International. The inter-island airlines offer **joint fare:** if you book a roundtrip ticket with a specific major Mainland airlines, the Hawaiian inter-island airlines give you a fare reduction (not applicable to charter flights, or stopover flights on non-American carriers). Check with your travel agent to see which airlines are currently offering joint fares.

COMMUTER AIRLINES

Hawaii has a good but dwindling selection of "commuter airlines" offering regularly scheduled flights, air tours, and special flights to small airports that the big carriers don't service. They're so handy and personalized that they might be considered "air taxis." All use smaller aircraft that seat about 12 people, and fly low enough so that their normal inter-island flights are like an air tour. Stories abound of passengers being invited to ride copilot, or of a pilot going out of his way to show off a glimmering coastline or a beautiful waterfall. Many times you get the sense that it's "your" flight and that the airline is doing everything possible to make it memorable.

Fares, Schedules, And Tips

The following is offered merely as general advice to help you make a choice. Specific schedules are listed in the "Getting There" sections of the travel chapters. The commuter airlines are limited in plane size and routes serviced. Among themselves, prices are very competitive, but, except on their specialty runs, they tend to be more expensive than the three major inter-island carriers. They're also not as generous on baggage allowance, and you'll be charged more for extra, some of which may not accompany you on the plane.

Aloha Island Air (formerly Princeville Airways), tel. (800) 323-3345 on the Mainland, (800) 255-7198 statewide, is a commuter airline operating flights to and from Princeville Airport on Kauai's north shore. Flying comfortable 18-passenger Twin Otter De Havilland aircraft, they connect the resort community of Princeville with airports on all the islands. Part of their schedule offers seven daily nonstop flights from Honolulu starting at 6 a.m. and ending at 5:15 p.m. Flights to and from all Neighbor Island airports leave regularly throughout the day. Flights from Kapalua, West Maui, come four times a day, 9:10 a.m. until 3:35 p.m., all with one stop; from Kahului, Maui, they run from 8:35 a.m. until 3:30 p.m., all with two stops; and from Hana, Maui, three times daily from 8:10 a.m. until 2:45 p.m., all with three stops. Additional flights come from Lanai at 9:05 a.m. and 4:10 p.m., and from Kamuela, Hawaii, at 7:30 a.m. and 1:40 p.m., all going through Honolulu.

Reeves Air, tel. Oahu 833-9555, Maui 871-4624, has regularly scheduled flights between Honolulu, Maui, and Molokai on a daily basis as well as charter service to get you there when you want to go. Their prices are higher, but it's like hiring your own private air taxi.

Big Island Air, tel.329-4868, or (800) 367-8047, ext. 207, operates out of Kailua-Kona and has a regularly scheduled flight between Kona and Hilo on the Big Island only. The R/T flight leaves and returns daily between 11 a.m. and 12 noon. Check for specifics. Big Island Air also features jet charter service, and flight/see tours around the Big Island.

Practical Information

On Oahu, commuter airlines are located at the small, open-air "Commuter Terminal," at Honolulu International, left of the main terminal as you face it. Commuter airlines allow two normal-sized bags, but they are concerned with weight—up to 44 pounds no problem; between 44 and 80 pounds, free, but on a space-available basis; over 80, space-available but you pay extra; some airlines vary. Check-in is 30 minutes prior to departure; if you're not there at least 10 minutes before take-off, your seat can be sold.

Air Tours And Helicopters

Scores of air-tour companies specialize in personalized flights around the islands. These are not economical as travel between islands. Also a growing number of helicopters fly in the islands. They too offer air tours and adventures: Waimea Canyon, Haleakala, and Kilauea when it's spouting lava are some of their more popular sightseeing tours. Many land in remote areas, so you can enjoy your own private waterfall and views. Look for listings under "Sightseeing Tours" in the various travel chapter Introductions.

CAR RENTALS

Does Hawaii really have more rental cars than pineapples? Oahu's Yellow Pages have eight pages of listings for car rental agencies; there are over 40 firms on Maui, a few dozen on the Big Island, 20 or so on Kauai, Molokai has a handful, and even Lanai has one or two. You can rent anything from a 60-passenger Scenic-cruiser, to a 60cc moped. Even so, if you visit the islands during a peak tourist frenzy without reserving your wheels in advance, you'll be marooned at the airport.

There's a tremendous field of cars and agencies from which to choose and they're cheaper than anywhere else in America. Special deals come and go like tropical rain showers; swashbuckling price slashings and come-ons are all over the rental car market. A little knowledge combined with some shrewd shopping around can save you a bundle. And renting a car is the best way to see the islands if you're going to be there for a limited time. Outside of Oahu, it

simply isn't worth hassling with the poor public transportation system, or relying on your thumb.

Car Rental Categories

When you arrive at any of Hawaii's airports, you'll walk the gauntlet of car rental booths and courtesy phones shoulder to shoulder along the main hallways. Of the three categories of car rental agencies in Hawaii, each has its own advantage. The first category is the big international firms like National, Hertz, Avis, and Budget. These big guys are familiar, easy to work with, sometimes offer special fly/drive deals with airlines, and live up to their promises. If you want your rental experience to be hassle-free, they're the ones. Also, don't be prejudiced against them just because they're so well known; sometimes they offer the best deal.

Hawaii has spawned a good crop of statewide car rental agencies such as Tropical, Robert's, and Holiday Hawaii. These companies and their cars are also reliable, easy to book through a travel agent, and give good service. Their bargain prices and special deals make it worthwhile to price them. The third category is the local entrepreneurial rental agencies. Their deals and cars can range, like rummage-sale treasures, from great finds to pure junk. Some, like Hawaii Rent a Car, El Cheapo, and Molokai U Drive, are reliable and good. These companies have the advantage of being able to cut deals on the spot. If nothing is moving from their lot on the day you arrive, you might get a real bargain. Unfortunately, mixed in this category is a hodgepodge of the fly-by-nights. Some of these are small, but adequate, while others are a rip-off. Their cars are bad, their service is worse, and they have more hidden costs than a Monopoly board.

Requirements

A variety of requirements are imposed on the renter by car agencies, but the most important clauses are common. Some of the worst practices being challenged are: no rentals to people under 25 and over 70, and no rentals to military personnel or Hawaiian residents! Before renting, check that you fulfill the requirements. Generally, you must be 21, although some agencies rent to 18-year-olds, while others still require you to be 25. You must possess a valid driver's license, with licenses from most countries accepted, but to be safe if you are not American, get an International Driver's License. You should have a major credit card in your name. This is the easiest way, though some companies take a deposit, but it will be very stiff. It could easily be $50 per day on top of your rental fees and sometimes much more, and a credit check on the spot, complete with phone calls to your employer and bank, may be required. If you damage the car, charges will be deducted from your deposit, and the car company itself determines the extent of the damages. Some companies *will not* rent you a car without a major credit card in your name, no matter how much of a deposit you are willing to leave.

When To Rent

On this one, you'll have to make up your own mind, because it's a "bet" that you can either win or lose big. But it's always good to know the odds before you plop down your money. You can reserve your car in advance when you book your air ticket, or play the field when you get there. If you book in advance, you'll obviously have a car waiting for you, but the deal that you made is the deal that you'll get—it may or may not be the best around. On the other hand, if you wait you can oftentimes take advantage of excellent on-the-spot deals. Obviously, however, you're betting that cars are available. You might be totally disappointed, and not be able to rent a car at all, or you might make a honey of a deal.

If you're arriving during the peak seasons of Christmas, Easter, and late summer vacation, *absolutely book your car in advance.* They are all accounted for during this period, and even if you can find a junker from a fly-by-night, they'll price-gouge you mercilessly. If you're going off-peak, you stand a good chance of getting the car you want, at the price you want. It's generally best to book ahead, but the majority of car companies have free 800 numbers (listed below). At least call them for an opinion of your chances of getting a car when you intend to arrive.

Rates

If you pick up a car rental brochure at a travel agent, notice that the price for Hawaii rentals are about the lowest in the U.S. The two rate options for renting are **mileage,** or **flat rate.** A third type, mileage/minimum, is generally a bad idea unless you plan to do some heavy-duty driving. Mileage rate costs less per day, but you are charged for every mile driven. Mileage rates are best if you drive less than 30 miles per day—but even on an island that isn't much! The flat rate is best with a fixed daily rate and unlimited mileage. With either rate, you buy the gas; don't buy the cheapest because the poor performance from low octane eats up your savings.

Discounts of about 10-15% for weekend, weekly, and monthly rates are available. It's sometimes cheaper to rent a car for the week even if you're only going to use it for five days. Both weekly and monthly rates can be split between neighboring islands, but this will only apply if the firm has inter-island offices, and this usually eliminates the small local guys. Extra costs are assessed if you drop off the car at a different spot from where you rented it; a common one is a Hilo pick-up and a Kona drop-off on the Big Island. Don't be surprised if some car companies want an extra fee if you drop your Waikiki rental at the Honolulu Airport, even if they have a facility there.

Warning: If you keep your car beyond your contract, you'll be charged the highest daily rate unless you notify the rental agency beforehand. Don't keep your car longer than the contract without notifying the company. They are *quick* to send out their repossession specialists. You might find your car gone, a warrant for your arrest, and an extra charge. A simple courtesy call notifying them of your intentions saves a lot of headaches and hassle.

What Wheels To Rent

The super-cheap rates on the eye-catcher brochures refer to subcompact standard shifts. The price goes up with the size of the car and with an automatic transmission. Like options on a new car, the more luxury, the more you pay. If you can drive a standard shift, get one! They're cheaper to rent and operate. Because many Hawaiian roads are twisty affairs, you'll appreciate the down-shifting ability and extra control of a standard shift. AM/FM radios are good to have for entertainment, and for getting weather and surf conditions. If you have the choice take a car with cloth seats instead of sticky vinyl.

The average price of a subcompact, standard shift, without air conditioning is $25 per day with a weekly rate of $90 (add about $8 per day—$50 per week—for an automatic) but rates vary widely. Luxury cars are about $10 a day more

with a comparable weekly rate. Most of the car companies, local and national, offer special rates and deals. If you fly Hawaiian Air on their Mainland or inter-island service, you can get a car with Tropical or Holiday for less than $15 per day. Budget sometimes runs fly/drive specials with United and Western, and Hertz has a truly "Affordable Hawaii" package that gives you an excellent weekly rate if you meet the pre-requirements. These deals fluctuate too rapidly to give any hard and fast information except that they are common, so make sure to inquire. Also, peak periods have "black outs" where normal good deals no longer apply.

Insurance

Before signing your car rental agreement, you'll be offered "insurance," for around $8 per day. Since insurance is already built into the contract (don't expect the rental agency to point this out), what you're really buying is a waiver on the deductible ($500-$1000), in case you crack up the car. If you have insurance at home, you will almost always have coverage on a rental car, including your normal deductible, but not all policies are the same, so check with your agent. Also, if you haven't bought their waiver, and you have a mishap, the rental agencies will put a claim against your major credit card on the spot for the amount of deductible, even if you can prove that your insurance will cover. They'll tell you to collect from your insurance because they don't want to be left holding the bag on an across-the-waters claim. If you have a good policy with a small deductible, it's hardly worth paying the extra money even if you do have a claim against you; you'll eventually recover it, but if your own policy is inadequate, buy the insurance. Also, most major credit cards offer complimentary car rental insurance as a repayment for using their cards to rent the car. Simply call the toll-free number of your credit card company to see if this service is included.

Driving Tips

Protect your children as you would at home with car seats. Their rental prices vary considerably: Alamo offers them free of charge; National charges $3 per day; Hertz needs 48 hours' notice; Dollar gives them free but they're not always available at all locations; and almost all the agencies can make arrangements if you give them enough notice. Check before you go and if all else fails, bring one from home.

There are few differences between driving in Hawaii and on the Mainland. Just remember that many people on the roads are tourists and can be confused about where they're going. Since many drivers are from somewhere else, there's hardly a "regular style" of driving in the islands. A farmer from Iowa accustomed to poking along on back roads can be sandwiched between a frenetic New Yorker who's trying to drive over his roof and a super-polite but horribly confused Japanese tourist who normally drives on the left.

In Hawaii, drivers don't honk their horns except to say hello, or in an emergency. It's considered rude, and honking to hurry someone might earn you a knuckle sandwich. Hawaiian drivers reflect the climate: they're relaxed and polite. Oftentimes, they'll brake to let you turn left when they're coming at you. They may assume you'll do the same, so be ready, after a perfunctory turn signal, for a driver to turn across your lane. The more rural the area, the more apt this is to happen.

It may seem like common sense, but remember to slow down when you enter the little towns strung along the circle-island routes. You have the tendency to bomb along on the highway and flash through these towns, missing some of the islands' best scenery. Also, rural children expect *you* to be watchful, and will assume that you are going to stop for them when they dart out into the crosswalks.

The **H-1 and H-2 freeways** throw many Mainlanders a Polynesian "screw ball." Accustomed to driving on super highways, Mainlanders assume that these are the same. They're not. Oahu's super highways are much more twisted, turned, and convoluted than most Mainland counterparts. Subliminally they look like a normal freeway, except that they've been tied into a Hawaiian knot. There are split-offs, crossroads, and exits in the middle of the exits. Stay alert and don't be lulled into familiar complacency.

B-Y-O Car

Unless you'll be in Hawaii for a bare minimum of six months, and spending all your time on one island, don't even think about bringing your own car. It's an expensive proposition, and takes time

and plenty of arrangements. From California, it costs at least $600 to Honolulu, with an additional $100 to any other island. It would be better to buy and sell a car there, or lease for an extended period to save on rental costs. If you want to bring your own car write for information to: Director of Finance, Division of Licenses, 1455 S. Beretania St., Honolulu, HI 96814.

Four-wheel-drives, 4WDs

For normal touring, it is totally unnecessary to rent 4WDs in Hawaii except on Lanai, where they're a must, or if you really want to get off the beaten track. They are expensive ($65 per day), uneconomical, and you simply don't need them. However, if you want one, most car rental agencies have them. Because their numbers are limited, reservations are absolutely necessary.

AGENCY INFORMATION

The following is a partial list of the car rental agencies operating in Hawaii. The phone numbers given are toll-free 800 numbers when available, or the head-office numbers when not. Remember that 800 numbers sometimes vary according to your area code, so if you can't make connection please call your 800 operator (1-800-555-1212). Local addresses and phone numbers, by island, are listed in the "Getting Around" sections of the travel chapters, as are small local car rental agencies and specialty transport such as bicycles and mopeds.

Car Pickup

The vast majority of agencies listed have booths at all of the airport terminal buildings throughout Hawaii. If they don't, they have clearly marked courtesy phones in the lobbies. Just pick it up and they'll give directions on where to wait, and then come to fetch you with their shuttle.

NATIONAL AND INTERNATIONAL AGENCIES

The following rent vehicles on all islands except Molokai and Lanai. (Avis rents cars on Molokai).

National Car Rental, tel. (800) 227-7368; Alaska and Hawaii, tel. (800) 328-6321. Features GM cars, others available. Drive/stay packages with Hawaiian Pacific Resorts. Equal rates throughout islands. Minimum age 21, will rent without credit card.

Hertz, tel. (800) 654-3131. Fly/drive special with United. Also, "Affordable Hawaii," a special that really lives up to its name. Minimum age 18, but must have credit card in your own name or special Hertz voucher.

Avis, tel. (800) 331-1212; Alaska and Hawaii, tel. (800) 645-6393. Fly/drive packages with American and United. Minimum age 18, but must have major credit card.

Budget (Sears), tel. (800) 527-0700. Drive-/stay packages with various resorts and tour companies. Fly/drive packages with United and Western. Free coupon books. Minimum age 21.

Dollar, tel. (800) 421-6868, also Alaska and Hawaii. Minimum age 21 with major credit card, but manager may make special arrangement on the spot.

Thrifty, tel. (800) 331-4200; Alaska and Hawaii, tel. (800) 331- 9191. No rentals on the Big Island. Fly/drive packages with Continental and Northwest.

American International, tel. (800) 527-0202; Alaska and Hawaii, tel. (800) 527-0160.

Gray Line, tel. (800) 367-5360.

STATEWIDE AGENCIES

The following are statewide car rental agencies with excellent reputations, offering rentals on all major islands. (Molokai and Lanai, only when listed.)

A Hawaii-based company with an excellent reputation is **Tropical Rent a Car,** tel. 836-1176, Waikiki tel. 949-2002, (800) 367-5140 nationwide, (800) 352-3923 from Neighbor Islands. Being based in Hawaii, they can take care of any problem on the spot without hassle. Tropical's personnel go out of their way to make your rental go smoothly by adding that "aloha touch." Prices are very competitive, and they can put you into anything from an economy car with no a/c to a convertible, Cadillac, or European sports car.

Holiday, tel. (800) 367-2631; Oahu, 836-1974. Fly/drive special with Hawaiian Air. The same founder as Tropical, offering personalized island service and a VIP lounge.

Roberts, All islands, tel. 947-3939. Well-established island company who will rent to 18-year-olds, with conditions.

Molokai Island U Drive, Molokai only, tel. 567-6156. Good local company.

Oshiro Service U Drive, Lanai only, tel. 565-6952. Jeeps, cars, advice on road conditions. Excellent and friendly advice from the owner, Glenn Oshiro.

Lanai City Service, Lanai only, tel. 565-6780. A subsidiary of Trilogy Expeditions. Rents Toyotas, Jeeps, pickups, and vans.

BY BOAT

Inter-island Ferry

From time to time ferry companies have operated in Hawaii, but very stiff competition generated by the airline industry and the notoriously rough waters of the Hawaiian channels have combined to scuttle their opportunity for success. A new company has opened, making daily runs between, Molokai (Kaunakakai), and Maui (Lahaina) aboard their 118-foot vessel *The Maui Princess*. The boat, a converted oil-platform-personnel carrier from Louisiana, has been re-outfitted for Hawaii and includes a sun deck and hydraulic stabilizers which take some of the roll out of the rocky crossing. In effect, it's still a work boat, carrying workers from Molokai to Lahaina, along with some light cargo. As beautiful as the Hawaiian Islands are from the air, this is a wonderful opportunity to have an experience from sea level. The cabin is comfortably air-conditioned, and the crew, all local people, play guitar, ukulele, and sing old island tunes, helping to raise everyone's spirits. The majority of the people riding the shuttle are islanders, so if you're looking for a colorful and cultural experience, this is one of the best opportunities. The snack bar serves burgers and sandwiches for under $2, while beer is only $1.50 and the very stiff mixed drinks are around $2.

In Lahaina you are met about 300 yards offshore by the *Lin Wa,* a sister ship usually used as a local tourist cruiser. Since Lahaina Harbor is so small, the *Maui Princess* cannot enter. Passengers and luggage are offloaded *at sea* as the crews perform some amazing feats of balance, handling all manner of cargo between the pitching, yawing boats. Upon arrival in Lahaina, prearrange a pickup by the car companies (most have offices in nearby Kaanapali) or you'll be stranded. The *Maui Princess* is often late and the car companies close by 6:30 p.m., another

MAUI PRINCESS
SAILING SCHEDULE

For information and reservations:
on Molokai call 553-5736
on Maui call 661-5857
Mainland toll-free (800) 533-5800

Depart:	Kaunakakai, Molokai	5:45 a.m.
Arrive:	Lahaina, Maui slip 3	7:15 a.m.
Depart:	Lahaina, Maui slip 3	7:30 a.m.
Arrive:	Kaunakakai, Molokai	8:45 a.m.
Depart:	Kaunakakai, Molokai	3:45 p.m.
Arrive:	Lahaina, Maui slip 3	4:45 p.m.
Depart:	Lahaina, Maui slip 3	5:00 p.m.
Arrive:	Kaunakakai, Molokai	6:45 p.m.

logistical problem. The trip is tough, but adds a realness of arriving on an island that you don't get from a plane. Fares are $42 RT, children half price. Bicyclists will be especially happy, because there is no extra fee charged to transport your wheels. For information and reservations call (800) 833-5800, on Molokai 553-5736, on Maui 661-8397.

PUBLIC TRANSPORTATION

There is very limited public transportation in Hawaii except for the exemplary **TheBus** on Oahu. TheBus (tel. 531-1611) can take you just about anywhere that you want to go on Oahu for only $.60. Carrying over 200,000 passengers per day, it's a model of what a bus system should be. The **Hele On Bus Company** (tel. 935-8241 or 961-8343) is a woefully slow bus system that tries to service the Big Island. It's cheap and OK for short hops, but too infrequent and slow for long distances. Travelers say that they consistently make better time hitchhiking between Hilo and Kona than waiting for Hele On to waddle by. The **Blue Shoreline Bus** (tel. 661-3927) is like a convenience shuttle that services the tourist-oriented southwest coast of Maui between Napili and Lahaina. It does the job for its limited area. Another on Maui, the **Grayline** (tel. 877-5507), runs between Kahalui, Kihei, and Lahaina. It's expensive and its service is mostly

limited to peak daytime hours. On Kauai, all that is available is **Aloha Jitney** (tel. 822-9532) and it runs from Nawiliwili Bay, just south of Lihue, for eight miles to the Coconut Plantation Shopping Center in Waipouli near Kapaa. It runs only from 9:30 a.m. to 4:30 p.m. and is really a service for shoppers. Molokai and Lanai have no public transportation, but as on all the islands, taxis are available. There are novelty pedicabs in Waikiki, many hotel shuttles to and from airports, and convenience buses from some major resorts to nearby beaches and shopping centers, but that's about all the "public transportation" in Hawaii.

Ongoing Public Transportation
For those continuing on to the Mainland and wishing to procure a **Greyhound** "Ameripass" (sorry, not valid in Hawaii), this can be done in Hawaii. Write or visit Greyhound International, 550 Paiea St., Suite 104, Honolulu, HI 96819, tel. 893-1909. Send a $75 money order with the name of the person using the pass (for up-to-the-minute prices call any Greyhound terminal) for seven days unlimited travel in the U.S. For $12 per day more, you get an extension if the pass is renewed before the initial seven-day period runs out.

HITCHHIKING

Hitchhiking varies from island to island, both in legality and method of "thumbing a ride." On Oahu, hitchhiking is legal, and you use the tried-and-true style of facing traffic and waving your thumb. But you can only hitchhike from bus stops! Not many people hitchhike and the pickings are reasonably easy, but TheBus is only $.60 for anywhere you want to go and the paltry sum that you save in money is lost in "seeing time." It's semi-legal (the police don't bother you) to hitch on Kauai and Hawaii. Remember that Hawaii is indeed a "big" island; be prepared to take some time getting from one end to the other. Though on Lanai and Molokai hitching is illegal, hardly any policemen are to be seen. If they stop, it will probably be just to warn you, but note that the traffic is light on both islands. On Maui, thumbing a ride is illegal and the police will hassle you. You must learn a new and obviously transparent charade to hitch successfully. Basically: thumb at your side, stand by the road, face traffic, and smile. Everyone knows you're hitching, but that's the game.

You will get a ride eventually, but in comparison to the amount of traffic going by it isn't easy. Two things against you: many of the people are tourists and don't want to bother with hitchhikers, and many locals don't want to bother with non-local hitchhikers. When you do get a ride, most of the time it will be from a *haole* who is either a tourist on his own or a recent island resident. If you are just hitchhiking along a well-known beach area, perhaps in your bathing suit and obviously not going far, you can get a ride more easily. Women should exercise caution, like everywhere else in the U.S., and avoid hitchhiking alone.

Ti *plants are always found around* heiau, *where their leaves are still used to wrap stones as simple offerings to the gods.*

WHAT TO TAKE

It's a snap to pack for a visit to Hawaii. Everything is on your side. The weather is moderate and uniform on the whole, and the style of dress is delightfully casual. The rule of thumb is to pack lightly: few items, and light clothing both in color and weight. What you need depends largely on your itinerary and desires. Are you drawn to the nightlife, the outdoors, or both? If you forget something at home, it won't be a disaster. You can buy everything you need in Hawaii. As a matter of fact, Hawaiian clothing, such as muumuus and aloha shirts, are some of the best purchases you can make, both in comfort and style. It's quite feasible to bring only one or two changes of clothing with the express purpose of outfitting yourself while there. Prices on bathing suits, bikinis, and summer wear are quite reasonable.

A Matter Of Taste

A grand conspiracy in Hawaii adhered to by tourist, traveler, and resident is to "hang loose" and dress casual. Very rare occasions in Hawaii such as a symphony or a grand ball call for formal dress. Men don't need a suit and tie, and women don't need evening wear. Even the hoity-toity hotels and restaurants don't require them, so go with the flow and dress easy. Nowhere else do a dress shirt and slacks and a simple little dress go so far. During the day around the beach, you won't need more than a bathing suit. You might want a top to put on if you slip into a restaurant for lunch, but that's about it. For getting around during the day or evening, shorts are fine; for going out to dinner a pair of slacks or casual dress will do it.

Alohawear

Best of all, alohawear is all you need for virtually every occasion and for comfort. The classic muumuu is large and billowy so the cloth doesn't press against the skin, and aloha shirts are made to be worn out of the pants. The best of both are made of cool cotton. Not all muumuus are of the "tent persuasion." Some are very fashionable and form-fitted with peek-a-boo slits up the side, down the front, or around the back. *Holomuu* are fitted at the waist with a flowing skirt to the ankles. They're elegant and perfect for "stepping out." You'll notice many island women prefer *holomuu*. The colors are more subdued than those of tourists, and the bodice is fringed with lace. Oftentimes island women wear a flower hatband to set off their ensemble. If the occasion calls for it, men will formalize their outfit by tucking their aloha shirt into their pants. This also means that instead of wearing sandals they'll probably wear shoes. Women in muumuus and men in aloha shirts can go everywhere and do everything in Hawaii in perfect taste.

Basic Necessities

As previously mentioned, you really have to consider only two modes of dressing in Hawaii: beachwear and casual clothing. The following is designed for the mid-range traveler carrying one suitcase or a backpack. Remember there are laundromats and you'll be spending a considerable amount of time in your bathing suit. Consider the following: one or two pairs of light cotton slacks for going out and about, and one pair of jeans for trekking, or better yet, corduroys which can serve both purposes; two to three casual sundresses—muumuus are great; three or four pairs of shorts for beachwear and for sightseeing; four to five short-sleeved shirts or blouses and one long-sleeved; three to four colored and printed T-shirts; a beach cover-up, short terry-cloth-type is best; a brimmed hat for rain and sun—the crushable floppy type is great for purse or daypack; two to three pairs of socks are sufficient, nylons you won't need; two bathing suits, nylon ones dry quickest; plastic bags to hold wet bathing suits and laundry; five to six pairs of underwear; towels (optional, because hotels provide them, even for the beach); a first-aid kit (see below), pocket size is sufficient; suntan lotion; insect repellent; a daypack or large beach purse; and don't forget your windbreaker, perhaps a shawl for the evening, and a universal jogging suit.

In The Cold And Rain

Two occasions for dressing warm are visiting the top of mountains and going on boat rides where wind and ocean sprays are a factor. You can conquer both with a jogging suit (sweat suit) and a featherweight, water-resistant windbreaker. Haleakala on Maui, or Mauna Kea and Mauna Loa on the Big Island, can be downright chilly. If you're going to camp or trek, you should add another layer, the best being a woolen sweater. Wool is the only fiber that retains most of its warmth-giving properties even if it gets wet. If your hands get cold, put a pair of socks over them. Tropical rain showers can happen at any time, so you might consider a fold-up umbrella.

Shoes

Dressing your feet is hardly a problem. You'll most often wear *zoris* (rubber thongs) for going to and from the beach, leather sandals for strolling and dining, and jogging shoes for trekking and sightseeing. A few discos require leather shoes, but it's hardly worth bringing them just for that. If you plan on heavy-duty trekking, you'll definitely want your hiking boots. Lava, especially *a'a,* is murderous on shoes. Most backcountry trails are rugged and muddy, and you'll need those good old lug soles for traction. If you plan moderate hikes, you might want to bring rubberized ankle supports to complement your jogging shoes. Most drugstores sell them, and the best are a rubberized sock with toe and heel cut out.

Specialty Items

Following is a list of specialty items. They're not necessities but most definitely come in handy. A pair of binoculars really enhances sightseeing—great for watching birds, sweeping panoramas, and almost a necessity if you're going whale-watching. A folding Teflon-bottomed travel iron makes up for cotton's one major shortcoming—wrinkles—and you can't always count on hotels having irons. Nylon twine and miniature clothespins are used for drying garments, especially bathing suits. Commercial and hotel laundromats abound, but you can get by with hand washing a few items in the sink. A transistor radio/tape recorder provides news, weather, entertainment, and can be used to record impressions, island music, and a running commentary for your slide show. Hair dryer: although the wind can be relied on to dry, it leaves a bit to be desired in the styling department. An inflatable raft for riding waves, along with flippers, mask, and snorkel, can easily be bought in Hawaii, but don't really weigh that much or take up much space in your luggage. If you'll be camping or boating with only sea water available, take along

Sea Saver Soap. This soap will lather in salt water, and rinse away taking the sticky residue with it.

For The Camper

If you don't want to take it with you, all necessary camping gear can be purchased or rented while in Hawaii. Besides the above, you should consider taking the following: framed backpack or the convertible packs that turn into suitcases; daypack; matches in a waterproof container; all-purpose knife; mess kit; eating utensils; flashlight (remove batteries); candle; nylon cord; and sewing kit (dental floss works as thread). Take a first-aid kit containing Band-Aids, all-purpose an-

tiseptic cream, alcohol swabs, tourniquet string, cotton balls, elastic bandage, razor blade, telfa pads, and a small mirror to view private nooks and crannies. A light sleeping bag is good, although your fleecy jogging suit with a ground pad and covering of a light blanket or even your rain poncho are sufficient. Definitely bring a down sleeping bag for Haleakala or mountainous areas, and in a film container pack a few nails, safety pins, fishhooks, line, and bendable wire. Nothing else does what these do and they're all handy for a million and one uses. See "Camping And Hiking" pg. 158 for more information on what to bring.

ohia lehua

HEALTH AND WELL-BEING

In a recent survey published by *Science Digest,* Hawaii was cited as the healthiest state in the Union in which to live. Indeed, Hawaiian citizens live longer than anywhere else in America: men to 74 years and women to 78. Lifestyle, heredity, and diet help, but more importantly, Hawaii is an oasis in the middle of the ocean, and germs just have a tougher time getting there. There are no cases of malaria, cholera, or yellow fever. Because of a strict quarantine law, rabies is also nonexistent. On the other hand, tooth decay, perhaps because of a wide use of sugar and enzymes present in certain tropical fruits, is 30% above the national average. With the perfect weather, a multitude of outdoor activities, soothing negative ionization from the sea, and a generally relaxed and carefree lifestyle, everyone feels better there. Hawaii is just what the doctor ordered: a beautiful natural health spa with the best air quality in the country.

Pollution In Paradise

Calling Hawaii the healthiest state in America doesn't mean that it has totally escaped pollution. It is the only state, however, where the natural beauty is protected by state law, with a statewide zoning and a general development plan.

For example, the absence of billboard advertising is due to the pioneering work of a women's club, "The Outdoor Circle," which was responsible for an anti-billboard law passed in 1927. It's strictly enforced, but unfortunately high-rise and ill-advised development have obscured some of the lovely views that these far-sighted women were trying to preserve. Numerous environmental controversies, including nuclear proliferation, and the ill effects of rampant development, rage on the islands.

The most obvious infringements occur on Oahu, with 80% of the islands' population, which places the greatest stress on the environment. An EPA study found that almost 20% of Oahu's wells have unacceptably high concentrations of DBCP and TCP. Because of Hawaii's unique water lenses (fresh water trapped by layers of lava), this fact is particularly onerous. The "Great Oahu Milk Crisis" of 1982 saw dairies shut down when their milk was found to have abnormally high concentrations of heptachlo, a chemical used in the pineapple industry. When tops of pineapple plants were sold as fodder, the milk became tainted.

Widespread concern exists over a 1,500-unit development on the Waianae coast known as

West Beach. Environmentalists say that it will not only put a major strain on diminishing water resources, but impinge on one of the last fruitful fishing areas near long-established homes of native Hawaiians. A new freeway known as H-3 will cut across an ecologically sensitive mountain range, and an alternative biomass energy plant is denuding the islands of its remaining indigenous *ohia* trees. And just to be pesky, the Mediterranean fruit fly made its appearance and Malathion had to be sprayed. Compared to many states, these conditions are small potatoes, but it lucidly points out the holistic global concept that no place on Earth is immune from the ravages of pollution.

Handling The Sun

A burning issue with most visitors to Hawaii is the sun. Don't become a victim of your own exuberance. People can't wait to strip down and lie on the sand like a beached whale, but the tropical sun will burn you to a cinder if you're not cautious. The burning rays come through easier in Hawaii because of the sun's angle, and you don't feel them as much because there's always a cool breeze. The worst part of the day is from 11 a.m. until 3 p.m. You'll just have to force yourself to go slowly. Don't worry; you'll be able to flaunt your best souvenir, your golden Hawaiian tan, to your green-with-envy friends when you get home. It's better than showing them a boiled lobster body with peeling skin! If your skin is snowflake white, 15 minutes per side on the first day is plenty. Increase by 15-minute intervals every day, which will allow you a full hour per side by the fourth day. Have faith; this is enough to give you a deep golden uniform tan.

Haole Rot

A peculiar condition caused by the sun is referred to locally as *haole* rot. It's called this because it supposedly affects only white people, but you'll notice some dark-skinned people with the same condition. Basically, the skin becomes mottled with white spots that refuse to tan. You get a blotchy effect, mostly on the shoulders and back. Dermatologists have a fancy name for it, and they'll give you a fancy prescription with a not-so-fancy price tag to cure it. It's common knowledge throughout the islands that Selsun Blue Shampoo has some ingredient that stops the mottling effect. Just wash your hair with it and

then make sure to rub the lather over the affected areas, and it should clear up.

Cockroaches And Bugs

Everyone, in varying degrees, has an aversion to vermin and creepy crawlers. Hawaii isn't infested with a wide variety, but it does have its share. Mosquitoes were unknown in the islands until their larvae stowed away in the water barrels of the *Wellington* in 1826 and were introduced at Lahaina. They bred in the tropical climate and rapidly spread to all the islands. They are a particular nuisance in the rainforests. Bring a natural repellent like citronella oil, available in most health stores on the islands, or a commercial product available in all groceries or drug stores. Campers will be happy to have mosquito coils to burn at night as well.

Cockroaches are very democratic insects. They hassle all strata of society equally. They breed well in Hawaii and most hotels are at war with them, trying desperately to keep them from being spotted by guests. One comforting thought is that in Hawaii they aren't a sign of filth or dirty housekeeping. They love the climate like everyone else, and it's a real problem keeping them under control. Many hotels post a little card in each room instructing you to call the desk if you spot a roach; they'll be happy to charge up to your room and annihilate it. Of a number of different roaches in Hawaii, the ones that give most people the jitters are big bombers over two two inches long. Roaches are after food crumbs and the like, and very infrequently bother with a human. Be aware of this if you rent a room with a kitchenette or condo. If you are in a modest hotel and see a roach, it might make you feel better to know that the millionaire in the $600-a-night suite probably has them too. Bring your own spray if you wish, call the desk if you see them, or just let them be.

Poisonous Plants

A number of plants in Hawaii, mostly imported, contain toxins. In almost every case you have to eat a quantity of them before they'll do you any real harm. The following is a partial list of the most common plants that you'll encounter and the parts to avoid: poinsettia, leaves, stems and sap; oleander, all parts; azalea, all parts; crown flower, juice; lantana, berries; castor bean, all parts; bird of paradise, seeds; coral plant, seeds.

HAWAII STATE ARCHIVES

by ship's artist Francis Olmsted, c. 1840

WATER SAFETY

Hawaii has one very sad claim to fame: more people drown here than anywhere else in the world. Moreover, there are dozens of yearly victims of broken necks, backs, and scuba and snorkeling accidents. These statements shouldn't keep you out of the sea, because it is indeed beautiful, benevolent in most cases, and a main reason to go to Hawaii. But if you're foolish, *moana* will bounce you like a basketball and suck you away for good. The best remedy is to avoid situations you can't handle. Don't let anyone dare you into a situation that makes you uncomfortable. "Macho men" who know nothing about the power of the sea will be tumbled into a Cabbage Patch doll in short order. Ask lifeguards or beach attendants about conditions, and follow their advice. If local people refuse to go in, there's a good reason. Even experts get in trouble in Hawaiian waters. Some beaches, such as Waikiki, are as gentle as a lamb and you would have to tie an anchor around your neck to drown there. Others, especially on the north coasts during the winter months, are frothing giants.

While beachcombing, or especially when walking out on rocks, never turn your back to the sea. Be aware of undertows (the waves drawing back into the sea). They can knock you off your feet. Before entering the water, study it for rocks, breakers, reefs, and riptides. Riptides are powerful currents, like rivers in the sea, that can drag you out. Mostly they peter out not too far from shore, and you can often see their choppy waters on the surface. If caught in a "rip," don't fight to swim directly against it; you'll lose and only exhaust yourself. Swim diagonally across it, while going along with it, and try to stay parallel to the shore. Don't waste all your lung power yelling, and rest by floating.

When bodysurfing, never ride straight in; come to shore at a 45-degree angle. Remember, waves come in sets. Little ones can be followed by giants, so watch the action awhile instead of plunging right in. Standard procedure is to duck under a breaking wave. You can even survive thunderous oceans using this technique. Don't try to swim through a heavy froth and never turn your back and let it smash you. Don't swim alone if possible, and obey all warning signs. Hawaiians want to entertain you and don't put up signs just to waste money. The last rule is, "If in doubt, stay out."

Yikes!

Sharks live in all the oceans of the world. Most mind their own business and stay away from shore. Hawaiian sharks are well fed—on fish—and don't usually bother with unsavory humans. If you encounter a shark, don't panic! Never thrash around because this will trigger their attack instinct. If they come close, scream loudly.

Portuguese men-o-war put out long floating tentacles that sting if they touch you. Don't wash it off with fresh water; this will only aggravate it. Hot salt water will take away the sting, as will alcohol, the drinking or rubbing kind, aftershave, and meat tenderizer (MSG), which can be found in any supermarket or Chinese restaurant. Coral can give you a nasty cut, and it's known for causing infections because it's a living organism. Wash it immediately and apply an antiseptic. Keep it clean and covered, and watch for infection.

Poisonous sea urchins, such as the lacquer-black *wana,* can be beautiful creatures. They are found in shallow tide pools and can only hurt you if you step on them. Their spines will break off, enter your foot and burn like blazes. There are cures. Vinegar and wine poured on the wound will stop the burning. If not available, the Hawaiian method is urine. It might be ignominious to have someone pee on your foot, but it'll put the fire out. The spines will disintegrate in a few days, and there are generally no long-term effects.

Hawaiian reefs also have their share of moray eels. These creatures are ferocious in appearance, but will never initiate an attack. You'll have to poke around in their holes while snorkeling or scuba diving to get them to attack. Sometimes this is inadvertent on the diver's part, so be careful where you stick your hand while underwater.

HAWAIIAN FOLK MEDICINE AND CURES

Hawaiian folk medicine is well developed, and its cures for common ailments have been used effectively for centuries. *Kahuna* were highly regarded for their medicinal skills, and native Hawaiians were by far some of the healthiest people in the world until the coming of the Europeans. Many folk remedies and cures are used to this day and, what's more, they still work! Some of the most common plants and fruits you encounter provide some of the best remedies. When roots, seeds, or special exotic plants are used, the preparation of the medicine is as painstaking as in a modern pharmacy. These prescriptions are exact and take an expert to prepare. They should never be prepared or administered by an amateur.

Lomi Lomi

This traditional Hawaiian massage is of exceptional therapeutic value. It has been practiced since very early times, and is especially useful in cases of fatigue, general body aches, preventive medicine, and sports injuries. When Otto von Kotzebue arrived in 1824, he noted, ". . . Queen Nomahana, after feasting heartily, turned on her back, whereupon a tall fellow sprang upon her body and kneaded it unmercifully with his knees and fists as if it had been the dough of bread. Digestion was so assisted that the queen resumed her feasting." *Lomi lomi* practitioners must be accredited by the state. One of the best is Auntie Margaret Machado, Box 221, Captain Cook, HI 96704, tel. 328-2472. Auntie Margaret exemplifies the best in the tradition of Hawaiian healers. She teaches classes in Hawaiian *lomi lomi* and the use of traditional herbs and cures. She and her husband Daniel *are* aloha.

Common Curative Plants

Arrowroot, for diarrhea, is a powerful narcotic used in rituals and medicines. The pepper plant *(Piper methisticum)* is chewed and the juice is spat into a container for fermenting. Used as a medicine in urinary tract infections, rheumatism, and asthma, it also induces sleep and cures headaches. A poultice for wounds is made from the skins of ripe bananas. Peelings have a powerful antibiotic quality and contain vitamins A, B, and C, phosphorous, calcium, and iron. The nectar from the plant was fed to babies as a vitamin juice. Breadfruit sap is used for healing cuts and as a moisturizing lotion. Coconut is used to make moisturizing oil, and the juice was chewed, spat into the hand and used as a shampoo. Guava is a source of vitamins A, B, and C. Hibiscus has been used as a laxative. *Kukui* nut oil is a gargle for sore throats, a laxative, and the flowers are used to cure diarrhea. *Noni* reduces tumors, diabetes, high blood pressure, and the juice is good for diarrhea. Sugar cane sweetens many con-

This "denizen of the deep" is much more afraid of you than you are of him.
Howard Lindeman

KUKUI (CANDLENUT)

Reaching heights of 80 feet, the kukui *(candlenut) was a veritable department store to the Hawaiians, who made use of almost every part of this utilitarian giant. Used as a cure-all, its nuts, bark, or flowers were ground into potions and salves and taken as a general tonic, applied to ulcers and cuts as an effective antibiotic, or administered internally as a cure for constipation or asthma attacks. The bark was mixed with water and the resulting juice was used as a dye in tattooing, tapa cloth making, canoe painting, and as a preservative for fishnets. The oily nuts were burned as a light source in stone holders, and ground and eaten as a condiment called* inamona. *Polished nuts took on a beautiful sheen and were strung as leis. Lastly, the wood itself was hollowed into canoes and used as fishnet floats.*

coctions, and the juice of toasted cane was a tonic for sick babies. Sweet potato is used as a tonic during pregnancy, and juiced as a gargle for phlegm. Tamarind is a natural laxative and contains the most acid and sugar of any fruit on Earth. Taro has been used for lung infections, thrush, and as suppositories. Yams are good for coughs, vomiting, constipation, and appendicitis.

Commonly Treated Ailments

For arthritis make a poultice of *koali* and Hawaiian salt; cover the area and keep warm. A bad-breath gargle is made from the *hapu'u* fern. The latex from inside the leaves of *aloe* is great for soothing burns and sunburn, as well as for innumerable skin problems. If you get chapped lips or windburned skin use oil from the *hinu honu*. A headache is lessened with *awa* or *ape*. Calm nervousness with *awa* and *lomi lomi*, Hawaiian-style massage. To get rid of a raspy sore throat chew the bark of the root of the *uhaloa*. A toothache is eased by the sticky narcotic juice from the *pua kala* seed, a prickly poppy.

MEDICAL AND EMERGENCY SERVICES

Emergency: Dial 911

The following are hospitals providing emergency-room, long-term, and acute care. **Oahu:** Kaiser Foundation Hospital, 1697 Ala Moana Blvd., Honolulu, tel. 949-5811. They have an emergency room and are closest to Waikiki. They demand payment before treatment; Queen's Medical Center, 1301 Punchbowl, Honolulu, tel. 538-9011; St. Francis Hospital, 2230 Liliha, Honolulu, tel. 547-6551. **Maui:** Kula Hospital, 204 Kula Hwy., tel. 878-1221; Maui Memorial, Kaahumanu Ave., Wailuku, tel. 244-9056. **Molokai:** Molokai General, Kaunakakai, tel. 553-5331. **Lanai:** Lanai Community Hospital, Lanai City, tel. 565-6411. **Hawaii:** Hilo Hospital, 1190 Waianuenue Ave., Hilo, tel. 961-4211; Kona Hospital, Kailua-Kona, tel. 322-9311. **Kauai:** Wilcox Memorial Hospital, 3420 Kuhio Hwy., Lihue, tel. 245-1100.

ALTERNATIVE MEDICINE

Most ethnic groups that migrated to Hawaii brought their own cures along. The Chinese and Japanese are especially known for their unique and effective medicines, such as herbal medicine, acupuncture and *shiatsu*. Hawaii also has a huge selection of chiropractors and its own form of massage called *lomi lomi*. The Yellow Pages on all islands list holistic practitioners, herbalists, and naturopaths.

Acupuncture

This time-honored Chinese therapy is available throughout the islands. On Oahu contact the Hawaiian Association of Certified Acupuncturists, Box 11202, Honolulu 96828, tel. 941-7771 for referrals to state-licensed acupuncturists throughout the islands.

Massage

All types of massage are available throughout the islands. If you look in the Yellow Pages, you'll find everything from *shiatsu* and *lomi lomi* to "escort services" that masquerade their real profession as massage (for these, see p. 139-40). It's easy to tell the ads of legitimate massage practitioners offering therapeutic holistic massage. Check listings under "holistic practitioners" as well as "massage."

HELP FOR THE DISABLED

A handicapped or physically disabled person can have a wonderful time in Hawaii; all that's needed is a little pre-planning. The following is general advice that should help with your planning.

Commission On The Handicapped

This commission was designed with the express purpose of aiding handicapped people. They are a source of invaluable information and distribute self-help booklets free of charge. Any handicapped person heading to Hawaii should write first or visit their offices on arrival. For a *Handicapped Travelers Guide* to each of the four islands, write or visit the head office at: Commission on the Handicapped, Old Federal Bldg., 335 Merchant St., no. 215, Honolulu, HI 96813, tel. 548-7606; on Maui, 54 High St., Wailuku, Maui, HI 96793, tel. 244-4441; on Kauai, Box 671, Lihue, Kauai 96766, tel. 245-4308; on Hawaii, Box 1641, Hilo, HI 96820, tel. 935-7257.

General Information

The key for a smooth trip is to make as many arrangements ahead of time as possible. Here are some tips concerning transportation and accommodations. Tell the companies concerned of the nature of your handicap in advance so that they can make arrangements to accommodate you. Bring your medical records and notify medical establishments of your arrival if you'll be needing their services. Travel with a friend or make arrangements for an aide on arrival (see below). Bring your own wheelchair if possible and let airlines know if it is battery-powered; boarding inter-island carriers requires steps. No problem. They'll board you early on special lifts, but they must know that you're coming. Many hotels and restaurants accommodate disabled persons, but always call ahead just to make sure.

Oahu Services

At Honolulu International, parking spaces are on the fourth floor of the parking garage near the elevator closest to the inter-island terminal. The **Wiki Wiki Bus** to town has steps. **Medical Services,** 24-hours, Honolulu County Medical Society, tel. 536-6988; airport medical services at tel. 836-3341; visitor information at tel. 836-6417. For getting around, the City of Honolulu has a free curb-to-curb service for disabled persons, called **Handi-Van.** You must make arrangements for a pass 24 hours in advance. For a free handicapped bus pass for disabled but ambulatory people, write, Handi-Van Pass, or Handicapped Bus Pass, 650 S. King St., Honolulu 96813, tel. 524-4626. A private special taxi company is **Handi-Cabs of the Pacific** in Honolulu at tel. 524-3866. **Avis** will rent cars with hand controls, tel. 836-5511. **Grant Wheelchair and Repair of Honolulu,** tel. 533-2794, will do just that and outfit cars with hand controls. For **medical equipment** the following Honolulu establishments rent all kinds of apparatus: **AAA Medical,** tel. 538-7021; **Abbey Rents,** tel. 537-2922; **Medical Supplies,** tel. 845-9522; **Honolulu Orthopedic,** tel. 536-6661. For **medical support and help** the following provide nurses, companions, and health aides—all require advance notice. **Hawaii Center for Independent Living,** tel. 537-1941; **Travel-Well International,** tel. 689-5420; **Voluntary Action Center,** tel. 536-7234.

Maui Services

On arrival at Kahului Airport, parking spaces are directly in front of the main terminal. The restaurant there has steps, so food will be brought to you in the cocktail lounge. No special emergency medical services, but visitor information is at tel. 877-6431. There is no centralized medical service, but **Maui Memorial Hospital** in Wailuku will refer, tel. 244- 9056. Getting around can be tough because there is no public transportaion on Maui, and no tours or companies to accommodate non-ambulatory handicapped persons. However, both Hertz and Avis rent cars with hand controls. Health care is provided by **Maui Center for Independent Living,** tel. 242-4966.

Medical equipment is available at Crafts Drugs, tel. 877-0111; Hawaiian Rentals, tel. 877-7684; and Maui Rents, tel. 877-5827. Special recreation activities referrals are made by Easter Seal Society, tel. 242-9323, or by the **Commission on Handicapped,** tel. 244-4441.

Kauai Services

At Lihue Airport, parking is available in an adjacent lot and across the street in the metered area. **Emergency services,** tel. 245-3773; visitor info, tel. 245-8183. For medical services, **Kauai Medical Group** at Wilcox Hospital will refer, tel. 245-1500. To get around, arrangements can be made if the following are contacted well in advance: **Office of Elderly Affairs,** tel.245-7230; **Akita Enterprises,** tel. 245-5344. **Avis** will install hand controls on cars, but they need a month's notice. **Holiday** will do the same, tel. 245-6944. There are very few cut curbs on Kauai and none in Lihue. Special **parking permits** (legal anywhere, anytime) are available from the police station in Lihue. **Medical equipment** rentals are available from: **American Cancer Society,** tel. 245-2942; **Pay'n Save,** tel. 245-6776; **Easter Seals,** tel. 245-6983. For medical support and help contact **Kauai Center for Independent Living,** tel. 245-4034.

Hawaii Services

At Hilo Airport there are no facilities for deplaning non-ambulatory people from propeller planes, only jets and on the jetways. Inter-island flights should be arranged only on jets. Ramps and a special elevator provide access in the bi-level terminal. Parking is convenient in designated areas. At Kona boarding and deplaning is possible for the handicapped. Ramps make the terminal accessible. To get around, Handi-Vans are available in Hilo, tel. 961-6722. **Kamealoha Unlimited** has specially equipped vans, tel. 966-7244. **Parking permits** are available from Dept. of Finance, tel. 961-8231. Medical help, nurses, and companions are arranged through **Big Island Center for Independent Living,** tel. 935-3777. Doctors are referred by **Hilo Hospital,** tel. 961-4211, and **Kona Hospital,** tel. 322-9311. **Medical equipment** is available from **Kamealoha Unlimited,** tel. 966-7244; **Medi-Home,** tel. 969-1123; **Pacific Rentall,** tel. 935-2974.

THE HEAVY STUFF

Though the small towns and villages are as safe as you can find anywhere in America, Hawaii isn't all good clean fun. Wherever there's a constant tourist flow, a huge military presence, and high cost of living, there will be those people that mama warned you about. Most of the heavy night action occurs in Waikiki around Kuhio and Kalakaua avenues, and on Chinatown's Hotel Street (see p. 139). Something about the *vibe* exudes sexuality. The land is raw and wild, and the settings are intoxicating. All those glistening bodies under the tropical sun and the carefree lifestyle are super-conducive to you know what! Hawaii has long been known as a great place for boy meets girl, or whatever, but there is also "play for pay" if you want it.

Hawaii's sugar and pineapple industries started to flag in the last decade and people had to do something to make ends meet. More than a few began to grow *pakalolo* (marijuana), now counted as one of the biggest cash crops in Hawaii. The *pakalolo* (literally "crazy smoke") is said to be first-rate, and will knock your purple socks off. Theft and minor assaults can be a problem, but they're usually not violent or vicious as in some Mainland cities. Mostly, it's locals with a chip on their shoulder and little prospects who will ransack your car or make off with your camera. A big Hawaiian or local guy will be obliged to flatten your nose if you look for trouble, but mostly it will be sneak thieves out for a fast buck.

You can go two ways on the "sleaze" scene in Hawaii: ignore it and remain aloof and never see any; or, look for and find it with no trouble. The following is neither a condemnation nor an endorsement of how you should act and what you should do. It's merely the facts and the choice is up to you.

Prostitution—The Way It Was

Ever since the first ship arrived in 1778, Hawaii has known prostitution. At that time, a sailor paid for a woman for the night with one iron nail. Funny, today they'll take a plastic card. Prostitution, rampant until the missionaries arrived in 1819, was indeed a major cause of the tragic population decline of the Hawaiian race. The tradition carried on into this century. Iwilei was a notorious red-light district in Honolulu at the turn of the century. The authorities, many of whom were clientele, not only turned a blind eye to this scene, but semi-legalized it. A policeman was stationed inside the "stockade" and police rules were listed on the five entrances. The women were required to have a weekly VD checkup from the Board of Health, and without a current disease-free certificate they couldn't work. Iwilei was even considered by some to be an attraction: when Somerset Maugham passed through the islands in 1916 on his way to Russia as a spy for England, he was taken here as if on a sightseeing tour. The long-established military presence in Hawaii has also helped to keep prostitution a flourishing business. During WW II, troops were entertained by streetwalkers, houses of prostitution, and at dance halls. The consensus of the military commanders is that prostitution is a necessary evil, needed to keep up the morale of the troops.

The Scene Today

The two areas notorious for prostitution today are Kuhio and Kalakaua avenues in Waikiki, which are geared toward the tourist, and Hotel Street in downtown Honolulu, for servicemen and a much rougher trade. All sorts of women solicit on Kuhio and Kalakaua avenues—whites, blacks, and Asians—but the majority are young white women from the Mainland. They cruise along in the old-fashioned style, meeting your eyes and giving you the nod. As long as they keep walking the police won't roust them. They talk business on the street, and then take their john to a nearby backstreet hotel, where he'll be required to pay for the room. Prices vary with the services sought. Rock bottom is $75 for a 15-minute "slam bam." The room might cost another $15.

The prostitutes on Waikiki number about 300, and are very easy to find, mostly hanging out across the street from the police station on Kalakaua. Oh! Those brazen hussies! Or, in front of the Hyatt, as if standing in front of a classy hotel will make them a class act. There was a great influx when Los Angeles cracked down for the 1984 Olympics, and Honolulu inherited many of her displaced streetwalkers. Most hookers prefer Japanese clientele, followed by the general tourist, and lastly, the always broke serviceman. In the terse words of one streetwalker queried about the preference for Japanese, she said, "They're small, clean, fast, and they pay a lot."

Sounds like a streetwalker's dream! If anyone in Waikiki can speak Japanese, a hooker can.

Most are not "equal opportunity employees." Western guys, whether white or black, don't stand much of a chance. They are after the Japanese in a sort of crazy payback. The Japanese fish American waters, and the "pros" of Waikiki hook big Japanese fish. A Honolulu policemen on his Kuhio Avenue beat said, "I can't do anything if they keep walking. It's a free country. Besides, I'm not here to teach anyone morals . . . .Last week a john "fell" out of an eight-story window and a prostitute was found with her throat slit . . . .I'm just on the front lines fighting herpes and AIDS. Just fighting herpes and AIDS, man." The average guy won't have any hassles with a Waikiki prostitute. Mostly it's a straightforward business transaction, but unlike the days of Iwilei there is absolutely no official control or testing for VD.

Chinatown's Hotel Street (see p. 261) is as rough as guts. The girls are shabby, the bars and strip joints are shabbier, and the vibe is heavy. Prices are cheaper, but if you visit a Hotel Street hooker, you'd be well advised to wear a condom and a scuba diving wet suit for protection. Women can find male prostitutes on most of the beaches of Honolulu and Waikiki. Mostly these transactions take place during the day. Although many men make a legitimate living as "beach boys" instructing in surfing and the like, many are really prostitutes. It's always up to the woman to decide how far her "lessons" proceed.

Massage Parlors, Etcetera

Besides streetwalkers, Honolulu and some of the Neighbor Islands have their share of massage parlors, escort services, and exotic dance joints. Most are in Honolulu, and some will even fly their practitioners to the Neighbor Islands if necessary. For massage parlors and "escort services" you can let your fingers do the walking—through 14 pages in the Honolulu Yellow Pages alone. Oddly enough, the "massage" listing is preceded by one for "marketing" and followed by one for "meat." Many legitimate massage practitioners in Hawaii can offer the best therapeutic massages in a variety of disciplines, including shiatsu, lomi lomi, and Swedish. Unfortunately, they share the same listings with the other kind of massage parlors. If the Yellow Pages listing reads something like "Fifi's Playthings—We'll rub it day or night, wherever it is," this should tip you off. Usually they offer escort services too, for both men and women. The initial cost is about $50 to have an "escort" come to your hotel. Once there, this young man or woman will negotiate his or her own deal for services (about $75). This protects the escort service business, because if you happen to be an undercover vice officer, the "escort" takes the rap and not the business, since of course they had no idea of what was really going on.

Honolulu also has a number of exotic dance clubs, many along Kapiolani Boulevard. Basically, they're strip joints with an extra twist. The dancers themselves are very attractive white women who have been brought over from the Mainland. They can easily make $100 per night dancing, and the majority are not prostitutes, although money, if it's enough, always talks. Their act lasts for three songs, and gets raunchier as it goes. They start off like the girl next door in a prom dress, and wind up writhing naked on the floor, gyrating to some imaginary phallic stimulus. If you invite a dancer to have a drink, it'll cost you $10, but it will be a real drink. This gets you nothing but conversation. The patron's drinks aren't as inflated as the scene would suggest, and some think it a bargain for the price of one drink to have a naked woman bumping and grinding just five feet away. Working the sexually agitated male crowd are women who can best be described as "lap sitters." They're almost always older Korean women who've been through the mill. They'll charge you $5 for a fake drink called *niko hana* (nothing), and then try to entice you over to a dark corner table, where they'll chisel $20 more, for all you can manage, or are brave enough to do, in a dark corner of a night club. Their chief allies are dim lights and booze. See p. 255.

ILLEGAL DRUGS

The use and availability of illegal, controlled, and recreational drugs are about the same in Hawaii as throughout the rest of America. Cocaine constitutes the fastest-growing recreational drug, and it's available on the streets of the main cities, especially Honolulu. Although most dealers are small-time, the drug is brought in by organized crime. The underworld here is mostly populated by men of Asian descent, and the Japanese

yakuza is said recently to be displaying a heightened involvement in Hawaiian organized crime. Cocaine trafficking fans out from Honolulu.

A new drug menace hitting the Honolulu streets is known as "ice." Ice is smokable methamphetamine that will wire a user for up to 24 hours. The high lasts longer, and is cheaper than cocaine or its derivative, "crack". Users become quickly dependent, despondent, and violent because ice robs them of their sleep, along with their dignity. Its use is particularly prevalent among late-night workers. Many of the violent deaths in Honolulu have been linked to the growing use of ice.

However, the main drug available and commonly used in Hawaii is marijuana, which is locally called *pakalolo*. There are also three varieties of psychoactive mushrooms that contain the hallucinogen psilocybin. They grow wild, but are considered illegal controlled substances.

Pakalolo Growing
About 20 years ago, mostly *haole* hippies from the Mainland began growing pot in the more remote sections of the islands, such as Puna on Hawaii and around Hana on Maui. They discovered what legitimate planters had known for 200 years: plant a broomstick in Hawaii, treat it right, and it'll grow. *Pakalolo*, after all, is only a weed, and it grows in Hawaii like wildfire. The lo-

cals quickly got into the act when they realized that they, too, could grow a "money tree." As a matter of fact, they began resenting the *haole* usurpers, and a quiet and sometimes dangerous feud has been going on ever since. Much is made of the viciousness of the backcountry "growers" of Hawaii. There are tales of booby traps and armed patrols guarding their plants in the hills, but mostly it's a cat and mouse game between the authorities and the growers. If you, as a tourist, are tramping about in the forest and happen upon someone's "patch," don't touch anything. Just back off and you'll be OK. Pot has the largest monetary turnover of any crop in the islands, and as such, is now considered a major source of agricultural revenue. There are all kinds of local names and varieties of pot in Hawaii, the most potent being "Kona Gold," "Puna Butter," and "Maui Wowie," though, these names are all becoming passé. You can ask a likely person for pot, but mostly dealers will approach you. Their normal technique is to stroll by, and in a barely audible whisper say, "Buds?"

Hawaiian *pakalolo* is sold slightly differently than on the Mainland. The dealers package it in heat-sealed "Seal-a-Meal" plastic bags. The glory days are over, and many deals, especially on the streets of Honolulu, are rip-offs.

THEFT AND HASSLES

From the minute you sit behind the wheel of your rental car, you'll be warned about not leaving valuables unattended and locking your car up tighter than a drum. Signs warning about theft at most major tourist attractions help to fuel your paranoia. Many hotel rooms offer coin-operated safes, so you can lock your valuables away and be able to relax while getting sunburned. Stories abound about purse snatchings and surly locals who are just itching to give you a hard time. Well, they're all true to a degree, but Hawaii's reputation is much worse than the reality. In Hawaii you'll have to observe two golden laws: if you look for trouble, you'll find it; and, a fool and his camera are soon parted.

Crime In Hawaii

The FBI recently compiled some amazing statistics. They compared the crime rates of 10 American cities including Honolulu, Atlanta, Dallas, New Orleans, Miami, Phoenix, and Los Ange-

WARNING
DO NOT LEAVE
PURSE, WALLET OR
CAMERA IN LOCKED
OR UNLOCKED CARS

les. According to the number of murders, robberies, assaults, and burglaries per 100,000 residents, in every comparison, Honolulu had the lowest rates by far. The islands of Maui, Kauai, and Hawaii display similar statistics showing crime rates lower than most U.S. areas of comparable size and population. Simply stated, Hawaii is safer than most places in America, but it isn't crime free. Population-wise, Chinese and Japanese have the lowest rate of felons; whites and Filipinos have criminals equal to their percentage of population; Hawaiians and part Hawaiians generate twice as many criminals as their population percentage, and Samoans contribute 6% of the islands' felons while making up only 1% of the population.

Theft

The majority of theft in Hawaii is of the "sneak thief" variety. If you leave your hotel door unlocked, a camera sitting on the seat of your rental car, or valuables on your beach towel, you'll be inviting a very obliging thief to pad away with your stuff. You'll have to learn to take precautions, but they won't have to be anything like those employed in rougher traveling areas like South America or Southeast Asia, just normal American precautions.

If you must walk alone at night, stay on the main streets in well-lit areas. Always lock your hotel door and windows and place all valuable jewelry in the hotel safe. When you leave your hotel for the beach, there is absolutely no reason to carry all your traveler's checks, credit cards, or a big wad of money. Just take what you'll need for drinks and lunch. If you're uptight about leaving any money in your beach bag, just stick it in your bathing suit or bikini. American money is just as negotiable if it is damp. Don't leave your camera or portable stereo on the beach unattended. Ask a person nearby to watch them for you while you go for a dip. Most people won't mind at all, and you can repay the favor.

While sightseeing in your shiny new rental car, which immediately brands you as a tourist, again, don't take more than what you'll need for the day. Many people lock valuables away in the trunk, but remember most good car thieves can jimmy it as quickly as you can open it with your key. If you must, for some reason, leave your camera or valuables in your car, lock them in the trunk or consider putting them under the hood. Thieves usually don't look there and on most modern cars, you can only pop the hood with a lever on the inside of the car. It's not fail-safe, but it's worth a try.

Campers face special problems because their entire scene is open to thievery. Most campgrounds don't have any real security, but who, after all, wants to fence an old tent or a used sleeping bag? Many tents have zippers that can be secured with a small padlock. If you want to go trekking and are afraid to leave your gear in the campgrounds, take a large green garbage bag with you. Transport your gear down the trail and then walk off through some thick brush. Put your gear in the garbage bag and bury it under leaves and other light camouflage. That's about as safe as you can be. You can also use a variation on this technique instead of leaving your valuables in your rental car.

Hassles

Another self-perpetuating myth about Hawaii is that "the natives are restless." An undeniable animosity exists between locals, especially those with some Hawaiian blood, and *haole*. Fortunately, this prejudice is directed mostly at the "group" and not at the "individual." The locals are resentful against those *haole* who came, took their land and relegated them to second-class citizenship. They realize that this is not the aver-

age tourist and they can tell what you are at a glance. Tourists usually are treated with understanding and are given a type of immunity. Besides, Hawaiians are still among the most friendly, giving, and understanding people on earth.

Haoles who live in Hawaii might tell you stories of their children having trouble at school. They could even mention an unhappy situation at some schools called "beat-up-a-*haole*" day, and you might hear that if you're a *haole* it's not a matter of if you'll be beaten up, but when. Truthfully, most of this depends upon your attitude and your sensitivity. The locals feel infringed upon, so don't fuel these feelings. If you're at a beach park and there is a group of local people in one area, don't crowd them. If you go into a local bar and you're the only one of your ethnic group in sight, you shouldn't have to be told to leave. Much of the hassle involves drinking. Booze brings out the worst prejudice on all sides. If you're invited to a beach party, and the local guys start getting drunk, make this your exit call. Don't wait until it's too late.

Most trouble seems to be directed toward white men. White women are mostly immune from being beaten up, but they have to beware of the violence of sexual abuse and rape. Although plenty of local women marry white men, it's not a good idea to try to pick up a local girl. If you're known in the area and have been properly introduced, that's another story. Also, girls out for the night in bars or discos can be approached if they're not in the company of local guys. If you are with your bikini-clad girlfriend, and a bunch of local guys are, say, drinking beer at a beach park, don't go over and try to be friendly and ask, "What's up?" You (and especially your girlfriend) might not want to know the answer to this question. Maintain your own dignity and self-respect by treating others with dignity and respect. Most times you'll reap what you sow.

"Some were rapacious exploiters, seeking to deceive, loot and leave. Hawaii has known them by the thousands through the years."

—Edward Joesting

BY ALPHONSE PELLION, c. 1819, HAWAII STATE ARCHIVES

ACCOMMODATIONS

Hawaii's accommodations won't disappoint anyone. An exceptionally wide range of places to stay varies both in style and in price range. You can camp on totally secluded beaches three days down a hiking trail, have a dream vacation at some of the undisputed top resorts in the world, or get a package deal including a week's lodging in one of many island hotels for less than you would spend at home. If you want to experience the islands as if you lived there, bed and breakfasts are becoming popular and easy to arrange. Condominiums are plentiful and great for extended stays for families who can set up home away from home, or even for a group of friends who want to save money by sharing costs. There are a smattering of youth hostels and YM/WCAs, home exchanges, and if you're a student, maybe a summer session at the University of Hawaii to mix education and fun.

Hawaii makes the greater part of its living from visitors, and all concerned desire to keep Hawaiian standards up and vacationers coming back. This means that accommodations in Hawaii are operated by professionals who know the business of pleasing people, which adds up to benefits for you. Rooms in even the more moderate hotels are clean; the standard of services range from adequate to luxurious pampering. With the few tips and advice given below, you should be able to find a place to stay that will match your taste with your pocketbook. For specifics, please refer to "Accommodations" in each of the travel chapters.

HOTELS

Even with the wide variety of other accommodations available, most vistors, at least first-timers, tend to stay in hotels. At one time, hotels were the only places to stay, and characters like Mark Twain were berthed at Kilauea's rude Volcano House, while millionaires and nobility sailed for Waikiki where they stayed in luxury at the Moana

Hotel or Royal Hawaiian, which both still stand as vintage reminders of days past. Maui's Pioneer Inn dates from the turn of the century, and if you were Hawaii-bound, these and a handful that haven't survived, were about all that was offered. Today, there are 60,000 hotel rooms statewide, and every year more hotels are built and older ones renovated. They come in all shapes and sizes, from 10-room family-run affairs to high-rise giants. A trend turned some into condominiums, while the Neighbor Islands have learned an aesthetic lesson from Waikiki and build low-rise resorts that don't obstruct the view and blend more readily with the surroundings. Whatever accommodation you want, you'll find it in Hawaii.

Types Of Hotel Rooms

Most readily available and least expensive is a bedroom with bath, the latter sometimes being shared in the more inexpensive hotels. Some hotels also offer a studio, a large sitting room that converts to a bedroom; suites, a bedroom with sitting room; and apartments that have a full kitchen plus at least one bedroom. Kitchenettes are often available, and contain a refrigerator, sink, and stove usually in a small corner nook, or fitted together as one space-saving unit. Kitchenettes cost a bit more, but save a bundle by allowing you to prepare some of your own meals. To get that vacation feeling while keeping costs down, eat breakfast in, pack a lunch for the day, and go out to dinner. If you rent a kitchenette, make sure all the appliances work as soon as you arrive. If they don't, notify the front desk immediately, and if the hotel will not rectify the situation ask to be moved or for a reduced rate. Hawaii has cockroaches (see p. 133), so put all food away.

Hotel Rates: Add Nine Percent Room Tax

Every year Hawaiian hotels welcome in the New Year by hiking their rates by about 10%. A room that was $30 this year will be $33 next year, and so on. Hawaii, because of its gigantic tourist flow and tough competition, offers hotel rooms at universally lower rates than most developed resort areas around the world. Package deals, especially to Waikiki, almost throw in a week's lodging for the price of an air ticket. The basic **daily rate** is geared toward double occupancy; singles are hit in the pocketbook. Single rates are cheaper than doubles, but never as low as half the double rate; the most you get off is 40%. **Weekly and monthly** rates will save you approximately 10% off the daily rate. Make sure to ask because this information won't be volunteered. Many hotels will charge for a double and then add an additional charge ($3 to $25) for extra persons. Some hotels, not always the budget ones, let you cram in as many as can sleep on the floor with no additional charge, so again, ask. Others have a policy of **minimum stay,** usually three days, but their rates can be cheaper.

Hawaii's **peak season** runs from just before Christmas until after Easter, and then again in early summer. Rooms are at a premium, and peak-season rates are an extra 10% above the normal daily rate. Oftentimes they'll also suspend weekly and monthly rates during peak season. The **off-peak** season is in late summer and fall, when rooms are easy to come by and most hotels offer off-peak rates. Here, subtract about 10% from the normal rate.

In Hawaiian hotels you always pay more for a good view. Terms vary slightly, but usually "ocean front" means your room faces the ocean and mostly your view is unimpeded. "Ocean view" is slightly more vague. It could be a decent view, or it could require standing on the dresser and craning your neck to catch a tiny slice of the sea sandwiched between two skyscrapers. Rooms are also designated and priced upward as **standard, superior, and deluxe.** As you go up, this could mean larger rooms with more amenities or can merely signify a better view.

Plenty of hotels offer the **family plan,** which allows children under a certain age to stay in their parents' room free, if they use the existing bedding. If another bed or crib is required, there is an additional charge. Only a limited number of hotels offer the **American plan,** where breakfast and dinner is included with the night's lodging. In many hotels, you get a refrigerator and a heating unit to make coffee and tea provided free.

Paying, Deposits, And Reservations

The vast majority of Hawaiian hotels accept foreign and domestic traveler's checks, personal checks preapproved by the management, foreign cash, and most major credit cards. Reservations are always the best policy, and they're easily made through travel agents or directly by contacting the hotel. In all cases, bring documentation of your confirmed reservations with you in case of a mix-up.

Deposits are not always required to make reservations, but they do secure them. Some hotels require the first night's payment in advance. Reservations without a deposit can be legally released if the room is not claimed by 6 p.m. Remember too, that letters "requesting reservations" are not the same as "confirmed reservations." In letters, include your dates of stay, type of room you want, and price. Once the hotel answers your letter, "confirm" your reservations with a phone call or follow-up letter and make sure that the hotel sends you a copy of the confirmation. All hotels and resorts have **cancellation requirements** for refunding deposits. The time limit on these can be as little as 24 hours before arrival, to a full 30 days. Some hotels require full **advance payment** for your length of stay, especially during peak season or during times of crowded special events such as the Merrie Monarch Festival in Hilo. Be aware of the time required for a cancellation notice *before* making your reservation deposit, especially when dealing with advance payment. If you have confirmed reservations, especially with a deposit, and there is no room for you, or one that doesn't meet prearranged requirements, you should be given the option of accepting alternate accommodations. You are owed the difference in room rates if there is any. If there is no room whatsoever, the hotel is required to find you one at another comparable hotel and refund your deposit in full.

Amenities

All hotels have some of them, and some hotels have all of them. Air conditioning is available in most, but under normal circumstances you won't need it. Balmy tradewinds flow through louvered windows and doors in many hotels. Casablanca room fans are better. TVs are often included in the rate, but not always. In-room phones are provided, but a service charge is usually tacked on, even for local calls. Swimming pools are very common, even though the hotel may sit right on the beach. There is always a restaurant of some sort, a coffee shop or two, a bar, cocktail lounge, and sometimes a sundries shop. Some hotels also offer tennis courts or golf courses either as part of the premises or affiliated with the hotel; usually an "activities desk"

can book you into a variety of daily outings. Plenty of hotels offer laundromats on the premises, and hotel towels can be used at the beach. Bellhops get about $1 per bag, and maid service is free, though maids are customarily tipped $1-2 per day and a bit more if kitchenettes are involved. Parking is free. Hotels can often arrange special services like babysitters, all kinds of lessons, and often special entertainment activities. A few even have bicycles and some snorkeling equipment to lend. They'll receive and send mail for you, cash your traveler's checks, and take messages.

CONDOMINIUMS

Hawaii was one of the first states struck by the condominium phenomenon; it began in the 1950s and has increased ever since. Now condos are almost as common as hotels, and renting one is just about as easy. Condos, unlike hotel rooms, are privately owned apartments which are normally part of a complex or highrise. The condo is usually an absentee owner's second or vacation home. An on-premises condo manager rents the vacant apartments, and is responsible for maintenance and security.

Things To Know

Staying in a condo has advantages and disadvantages from staying in a hotel. The method of paying for and reserving a condo is just about the same as for a hotel. However, requirements for deposits, final payments, and cancellation charges are much stiffer than in hotels. Make absolutely sure you fully understand all of these requirements when you make your reservations. The main qualitative difference between a condo and a hotel is in amenities. At a condo, you're more on your own. You're temporarily renting an apartment, so there won't be any bellhops, rarely a bar, restaurant, or lounge on the premises, though many times you'll find a sundries store. The main lobby, instead of having that grand entrance feel of many hotels, is more like an apartment house entrance, although there might be a front desk. Condos can be efficiencies (one big room), but mostly they are one- or multiple-bedroom affairs with a complete kitchen. Reasonable housekeeping items should be provided: linens, all furniture, and a fully equipped kitchen. Most have TVs and phones, but remember that the furnishings provided are all up to the owner. You can find brand-new furnishings that are top of the line, right down to "garage sale" bargains. Inquire about the furnishings when you make your reservations. Maid service might be included on a limited basis (for example once weekly), or you might have to pay for it if you require a maid.

Condos usually require a minimum stay, although some will rent on a daily basis, like hotels. Minimum stays when applicable are often three days, but seven is also commonplace, and during peak season, two weeks isn't unheard of. Swimming pools are common, and depending on the "theme" of the condo, you can find saunas, weight rooms, jacuzzis, and tennis courts. Rates are about 10-15% higher than comparable hotels, with hardly any difference between doubles and singles. A nominal extra is charged for more than two people, and condos can normally accommodate four to six guests. You can find clean, decent condos for as little as $200 per week, all the way up to exclusive apartments for well over $1,000 per week. Their real advantage is for families, friends who want to share, and especially long-term stays where you will always get a special rate. The kitchen facilities save a great deal on dining costs, and it's common to find units with their own mini-washers and dryers. Parking space is ample for guests, and like hotels, plenty of stay/drive deals are offered.

Hotel/Condominium Information

The best source of hotel/condo information is the **Hawaii Visitors Bureau**. While planning your trip, either visit one nearby or write to them in Hawaii. (Addresses are given in the "Hawaii Visitors Bureau" section.) Request a copy of their free and current *Member Accommodation Guide.* This handy booklet lists all the hotel/condo members of the HVB. Listings include the addresses, phone numbers, facilities, rates, and general tips. Understand that these are not all of the hotels/condos in Hawaii, just those that are members of the HVB.

BED AND BREAKFAST

Bed and Breakfasts are hardly a new idea. The Bible talks of the hospitable hosts who opened the gates of their homes and invited the wayfarer in to spend the night. Bed and Breakfasts (B&Bs) have a long tradition in Europe, and were commonplace in Revolutionary America. Now, lodging in a private home is becoming increasingly fashionable throughout America, and Hawaii is no exception. Not only can you *visit* Hawaii, you can *live* there for a time with a host family and share an intimate experience of daily life.

Points To Consider

The beauty of B&Bs is that every one is privately owned, and therefore uniquely different from any other. The range of B&Bs is as wide as the living standards in America. You'll find everything from semi-mansions in the most fashionable residential areas to little grass shacks offered by a down-home fisherman and his family. This means that it's particularly important for you to choose a host family with whom your lifestyle is compatible. Unlike a hotel or a condo, you'll be living *with* a host and most likely his or her family, although your room will be private, with private baths and separate entranceways being quite common. You don't just "check in" to a bed and breakfast. In Hawaii you go through agencies (listed below) which match host and guest. Write to them and they'll send you a booklet with a complete description of the bed and breakfast, its general location, the fees charged, and a good idea of the lifestyle of your host family. With the reservations application they'll include a questionnaire that will basically determine your profile: are you single? children? smoker? etc., as well as arrival and departure dates and all pertinent particulars. Since B&Bs are run by individual families, the times that they will accept guests can vary according to what's happening in their lives. This makes it imperative to write well in advance: three months is good; earlier (six months) is too long and too many things can change. Four weeks is about the minimum time required to make all necessary arrangements. Expect a minimum stay (three days is common) and a maximum stay. Bed and breakfasts are not "long-term" housing, although it's hoped that guest and host will develop a friendship and future stays can be as long as both desire.

Rates And Particulars

The B&B you choose can have all of the modern amenities including kitchen facilities, laundry gorgeous views, TV, and everything else necessary for a comfortable stay thrown in for one price, or it can be a trekker's cabin at the foot of Haleakala with little more than a cot, cookstove, and roof over your head. Generally, you can expect to spend $30-$65 per day, with weekly and monthly discounts. Local phone calls are free. Special rates combine various car rentals, flights, and sightseeing tours. Most agencies require a deposit to make reservations, with a nonrefundable cancellation fee because of the work involved. You do, however, get your deposit back, if you notify of cancellation before deadline. Get particulars straight, so that you don't lose money in case of a change of plans.

B&B Agencies

One of the most experienced agencies, **Bed And Breakfast Honolulu Statewide**, at 3242 Kaohinanai Dr., Honolulu, HI 96817, tel. 595-7533, or (800) 288-4666, owned and operated by Marylee and Gene Bridges, began in 1982. Since then, they've become masters at finding visitors the perfect accommodation to match their desires, needs, and pocketbook. Their repertoire of guest homes offers more than 400 rooms, with half on Oahu, and the other half scattered around the state. Accommodations from Marylee and Gene are more personally tailored than a hotel room. When you phone, they'll match your needs to their computerized in-house guidelines. B&B Honolulu Statewide also features bargain package deals for inter-island fly/car rentals. If you have special needs and are coming during peak season, reserve up to four months in advance; normal bookings are perfect with two-month's lead time. But don't count them out if you just show up at the airport. Rooms can't be guaranteed, but they'll do their best to find you a place to stay.

Another top-notch B&B agency is **Bed and Breakfast Hawaii**, operated by Evelyn Warner and Al Davis. They've been running this service since 1978, and their reputation is excellent. B&B Hawaii has a membership fee of $10 yearly. For this they mail you their "Directory of Homes," a periodic "hot sheet" of new listings, and all pertinent guest applications; add $1 handling. Write Bed and Breakfast Hawaii, Box 449, Kapaa, HI 96746. For phone info and reservations call (808) 822-7771.

Bed and Breakfast Maui Style is the oldest B&B agency operating on Maui. The friendly host, Jeanne Rominger, can arrange a stay on Maui as well as on any of the other islands, including Molokai. Accommodations range from a room in a private home to one-bedroom apartments. Write Bed and Breakfast Maui Style, P.O. Box 886, Kihei, HI 96753, tel. 879-7865.

Other well-known agencies are: **Go Native Hawaii,** who will send you a directory and all needed information by writing to 65 Halualani Pl., P.O. Box 11418, Hilo, HI 96721, tel. 935-4178. **Pacific Hawaii Bed And Breakfast** at 970 N. Kalaheo, Suite A218, Kailua 96734, tel. 262-6026 or (800) 999-6026, lists homes throughout the state, but especially around Kailua/Kaneohe on Oahu's upscale windward coast. Four specializing in beachfront villas, luxury condominiums, and exclusive estates are **Villas of Hawaii,** 4218 Waialae Ave., Suite 203, Honolulu 96816, tel. 735-9000; **All Islands B&B,** at 823 Kainui, Kailua HI 96734, tel. 263-2342, or (800) 542-0344, owned and operated by Ann Carlin and Peggy Frazier, is the newest and most energetic agency, with over 300 host homes, and lots of personalized attention; **Premier Connections of Hawaii,** at 1993 S. Kihei Rd, Suite 209, Kihei, Maui, HI 96753; and **Vacation Locations Hawaii,** P.O. Box 1689, Kihei, HI 96753, tel. 874-0077. Information on B&Bs can also be obtained from the **American Board of Bed and Breakfast Assn.,** Box 23294, Washington, D.C. 20026.

SPECIAL ACCOMMODATIONS

YM/WCAs are quite limited in Hawaii. They vary as far as private room and bath are concerned, so each should be contacted individually. Prices vary too, but expect to pay $15 single. Men or women are accepted at respective Ys unless otherwise stated. Oahu has 5 Ys, and Maui and Kauai each have one. You can get information by writing **YMCA Central Branch,** 401 Atkinson Dr., Honolulu 96814, tel. 941-3344; Maui YMCA, J. Walter Cameron Center, 95 Mahalani St., Wailuku, HI 96793, tel. 244-3153; YMCA of Kauai, Box 1786, Lihue, HI 96766. Call 742-1182 or 742-1200. Refer to "Accommodations" in the travel chapters for particulars on the Ys.

There is only one official **American YH** in Hawaii, located in Honolulu and always busy. Other unaffiliated YHs exist in Waikiki as well. You can make reservations (see "Accommodations" in

Honolulu and Waikiki for addresses). **Elderhostel,** 100 Boyston St., Suite 200, Boston MA 02116, offers non-credit courses at Hawaii Loa College, Oahu. The **University of Hawaii** has two six-week summer sessions beginning late May and and again in early July offering along with the course work reasonable rates in residence halls (mandatory meals) and in apartments on campus. For complete information see "Honolulu, Accommodations."

Home Exchanges

One other method of staying in Hawaii, open to homeowners, is to offer the use of their home for a home in Hawaii. This is done by listing your home with an agency that facilitates the exchange and publishes a descriptive directory. To list your home and to find out what is available, write: Vacation Exchange Club, 12006 111 Ave., Youngtown, AZ 85363; or, Interservice Home Exchange, Box 87, Glen Echo, MD 20812.

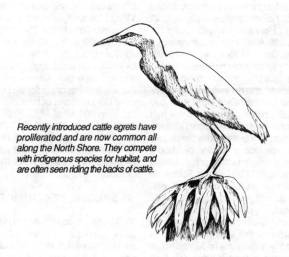

Recently introduced cattle egrets have proliferated and are now common all along the North Shore. They compete with indigenous species for habitat, and are often seen riding the backs of cattle.

FOOD AND DRINK

Hawaii is a gastronome's Shangri-La, a sumptuous smorgasbord in every sense of the word. The melting pot of ethnic groups that have come to Hawaii in the last 200 years have brought their own special enthusiasm and culture, and lucky for all, they didn't forget their cook pots, hearty appetites, and exotic taste buds. The Polynesians who first arrived found a fertile but barren land. Immediately they set about growing their taro, coconuts, and bananas, and raising chickens, pigs, fish, and even dogs, though these were reserved for the nobility. The harvests were bountiful and the islanders thanked the gods with the traditional feast called the luau. The underground oven, the *imu,* baked most of the dishes, and participants were encouraged to feast while relaxing on straw mats and enjoying the hula and various entertainments. The luau is as popular as ever, a treat that's guaranteed to delight anyone with a sense of eating adventure.

The missionaries and sailors came next and their ships' holds carried barrels of ingredients for the puddings, pies, dumplings, gravies, and roasts—the sustaining "American foods" of New England farms. The mid-1800s saw the arrival of boatloads of Chinese and Japanese peasants, who wasted no time making rice instead of bread the staple of the islands. The Chinese added their exotic spices, creating complex Sichuan dishes, as well as workingmen's basics like suey. The Japanese introduced sashimi, boxed lunches, delicate tempura, and rich, filling noodle soups. The Portuguese brought their luscious Mediterranean dishes with tomatoes and peppers surrounding plump spicy sausages, nutritious bean soups, and mouth-watering sweet treats like *malasadas* and *pao dolce* (sweet bread). Koreans carried crocks of zesty *kimchi,* and quickly fired up barbecue pits for *pulgogi,* a traditional marinated beef cooked over an open fire. Filipinos served up their mouthwatering *adobo* stews of fish, meat or chicken in a rich sauce of vinegar and garlic.

Recently, Thai and Vietnamese restaurants have been offering their irresistible dishes side by side with fiery burritos from Mexico and elegant marsala cream sauces from France. The ocean breezes of Hawaii not only cool the skin,

*Hawaiian family eating
poi, by A. Plum, c. 1846*
HAWAII STATE ARCHIVES

but on them waft some of the most delectable aromas on Earth, to make the tastebuds thrill and the spirit soar.

Special Note

Nothing is sweeter to the appetite than reclining on a beach and deciding just what dish will make your taste buds laugh that night. Kick back, close your eyes, and let the smells and tastes of past meals drift into your consciousness. The following should help you decide just exactly what it is that you're in the mood for and give you an idea of the dishes available in Hawaii, and their ingredients. Particular restaurants, eateries, stores, and shops will be covered in the travel chapters under "Food," and "Shopping."

HAWAIIAN FOODS

Hawaiian foods, oldest of all island dishes, are wholesome, well prepared, and delicious. All you have to do on arrival is notice the size of some of the local boys (and women) to know immediately that food to them is indeed a happy and serious business. An oft-heard island joke is that "local men don't eat until they're full; they eat until they're tired." Many Hawaiian dishes have become standard fare at a variety of restaurants, eaten one time or another by anyone who spends time in the islands. Hawaiian food in general is called *kaukau,* cooked food is *kapahaki,* and something broiled is called *kaola.* All of

these prefixes on a menu will let you know that Hawaiian food is served. Usually inexpensive, it'll definitely fill you and keep you going.

Traditional Favorites

In old Hawaii, although the sea meant life, many more people were farmers than fishermen. They cultivated neat garden plots of taro, sugar cane, breadfruit, and various sweet potatoes *(uala).* They husbanded pigs and barkless dogs *(ilio),* and prized *moa* (chicken) for their feathers and meat, but found eating the eggs repulsive. Their only farming implement was the *o'o,* a sharpened hardwood digging stick. The Hawaiians were the best farmers of Polynesia, and the first thing they planted was taro, a tuberous root that was created by the gods at the same time as man. This main staple of the old Hawaiians was pounded into poi, a glutinous purple paste. It comes in liquid consistencies referred to as "one-, two-, or three-finger poi." The fewer fingers you need to eat it, the thicker it is. Poi is one of the most nutritious carbohydrates known, but people unaccustomed to it find it bland and tasteless, although some of the best, fermented for a day or so, has an acidy bite. Poi is made to be eaten *with* something, but locals who love it pop it in their mouths and smack their lips. However, those unaccustomed to it will suffer constipation if they eat too much.

A favorite popular dessert is *haupia,* a custard made from coconut. *Limu* is a generic term for edible seaweed, which many people still gather from the shoreline and eat as a salad, or mix with ground *kukui* nuts and salt as a relish. A favorite Hawaiian snack is *opihi,* small shellfish (limpets) that cling to rocks. People gather them, always leaving some for the future. Cut from the shell and eaten raw by all peoples of Hawaii, as a testament to their popularity they sell for $150 per gallon in Honolulu. A general term that has come to mean hors d'oeuvres in Hawaii is *pu pu.* Originally the name of a small shellfish, now everyone uses it for any "munchy" that's considered a finger food. A traditional liquor made from *ti* root is *okolehao.* It literally means "iron bottom," reminiscent of the iron blubber pots in which it was fermented.

Luaus

Thick cookbooks are filled with common Hawaiian dishes, but you can get a good sampling at a well-done luau. The central feature is the *imu,* an underground oven. Basically, a shallow hole is dug and lined with stones upon which a roaring fire is kindled. Once the fire dies down and the stones are super-heated, the ashes are swept away and the *imu* is ready for cooking. At one time only men could cook in this fashion; it was *kapu* for women. These restrictions have long been lifted, but men still seem to do most of the pit cooking, while women primarily serve. The main dish at a luau is *kalua* pork. *Kalua* refers to any dish baked underground. A whole pig *(pua'a)* is wrapped in *ti* and banana leaves and placed in the hot center. Its stomach cavity is filled with more hot stones; surrounding the pig are little bundles of food wrapped in *ti* leaves. These savory bundles, *lau lau,* contain the side dishes: fish, chicken, poi, sweet potatoes, breadfruit, and even bananas. The entire contents are then covered with multiple layers of banana, *ti,* or sometimes ginger leaves and a final coating of earth. A long tube of bamboo may stick from the *imu* so that water (for steam) can be added. In about four hours the coverings are removed and the luau begins. You are encouraged to recline on *lau hala* mats placed around the central dining area, although tables and chairs are provided. There are forks and plates also, but traditionally it is proper to use your fingers and a sturdy banana leaf as a plate. Professional luau hosts pride themselves on their methods of cooking and their food, and for a fixed price you can gorge yourself like an ancient

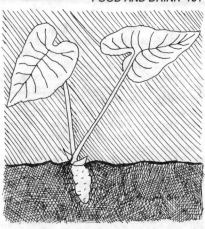

taro

ali'i. All luaus supply entertainment, and exotic drinks flow like the tides. Your biggest problem after one of these extravaganzas will be having the strength to rise up off your *lau hala* mat.

INTERNATIONAL DISHES

Chinese and Japanese cuisines have a strong influence on island cooking, and their well-known spices and ingredients are creatively used in many recipes. Other cuisines, such as Filipino, Korean, and Portuguese, are not as well known, but are now becoming standard island fare.

Chinese

Tens of thousands of fortune cookies yield their little springs of wisdom every day to hungry diners throughout Hawaii. The Chinese, who came to Hawaii as plantation workers, soon discovered a brighter economic future by striking out on their own. Almost from the beginning, these immigrants opened restaurants. The tradition is still strong, and if the smallest town in Hawaii has a restaurant at all, it's probably Chinese. These restaurants are some of the least expensive, especially at lunchtime when prices are lower. In them, you'll find the familiar chop sueys, chow meins, Peking duck, and fried rice. Takeout is common and makes a good, inexpensive picnic lunch.

Japanese

For the uninitiated, Japanese food is simple, aesthetically pleasing, and delicious. Sushi bars are plentiful, especially in Honolulu, using the freshest fish from local waters. Some common dishes include: teriyaki chicken, fish, or steak, which is grilled in a marinated *shoyu* (soy) sauce base; tempura, mouth-sized bites of fish and vegetables dipped in a flour and egg batter and deep fried; sukiyaki, vegetables, meat, mushrooms, tofu, and vermicelli which are brought to your table where you cook them in a prepared stock kept boiling with a little burner. You then dip the morsels into a mixture of egg and *shoyu; shabu shabu,* similar to sukiyaki without noodles and the emphasis on beef; *don buri,* ("various ingredients on rice in a bowl"), such as *ten don buri,* battered shrimp on rice; and various dishes of tofu, and *miso* soup, which provide some of the highest sources of non-meat protein. Japanese restaurants span the entire economic range, from some of the most elegant and expensive to hole-in-the-wall eateries where the surroundings are basic, but where the food is fit for a *samurai.* Above all, cleanliness is guaranteed.

Filipino

Most people have never sampled Filipino food. This cuisine is spicy with plenty of exotic sauces. The following are a sampling found in most Filipino restaurants: *singang,* sour soup made from fish, shrimp, or vegetables, that has an acidy base from fruits like tamarind; *adobo,* a generic term for anything (chicken and pork are standards) stewed in vinegar and garlic; *lumpia,* a Filipino spring roll; *pancit,* many variations of noodles made into ravioli-like bundles stuffed with pork or other meats; *lechon,* a whole suckling pig stuffed and roasted; *siopao,* a steam-heated dough ball filled with chicken or other tasty ingredients; and *halo halo,* a confection of shaved ice smothered in preserved fruits and canned milk.

Korean

Those who have never dined on Korean dishes are in for a sumptuous treat: *kalbitang,* a beef rib soup in a thin but tasty broth; *pulgogi,* marinated beef and vegetables grilled over an open flame; *pulkalbi,* beef ribs grilled over an open flame; *pibimbap,* a large bowl of rice smothered with beef, chicken, and vegetables that you mix together before eating; *kimchi,* fermented cabbage and hot spices made into a zesty "slaw"; *kimchi chigyae,* stew of *kimchi,* pork vegetables, and spices in a thick soup base.

TROPICAL FRUITS AND VEGETABLES

Some of the most memorable taste treats from the islands require no cooking at all: the luscious tropical and exotic fruits and vegetables sold in markets and roadside stands or found just hanging on trees, waiting to be picked. Make sure to experience as many as possible. The general rule in Hawaii is that you are allowed to pick fruit on public lands, but it should be limited to personal consumption. The following is a sampling of some of Hawaii's best produce.

Bananas

No tropical island is complete without them. There are over 70 species in Hawaii, with hundreds of variations. Some are for peeling and eating while others are cooked. A "hand" of bananas is great for munching, backpacking, or just picnicking. Available everywhere—and cheap.

Avocados

Brought from South America, avocados were originally cultivated by the Aztecs. They have a buttery consistency and a nutty flavor. Hundreds of varieties in all shapes and colors are available fresh year-round. They have the highest fat content of any fruit next to the olive.

Coconuts

What tropical paradise would be complete without coconuts? Indeed, these were some of the first plants brought by the Polynesians. When children were born, coconut trees were planted for them so they'd have fruit throughout their lifetime. Truly tropical fruits, they know no season. Drinking nuts are large and green, and when shaken you can hear the milk inside. You get about a quart of fluid from each. It takes skill to open one, but a machete can handle anything. Cut the stem end flat so that it will stand, then bore a hole into the pointed end and put in a straw or hollow bamboo. Coconut water is slightly acidic and helps to balance alkaline foods. Spoon meat is a custard-like gel on the inside of drinking nuts. Sprouted coconut meat is also an excellent food. Split open a sprouted nut, and inside is the yellow fruit, like a moist sponge cake. "Millionaire's salad" is made from the heart of a coconut palm. At one time an entire tree was cut down to get to the heart, which is just inside the trunk below the fronds and is like an artichoke heart except that it's about the size of a watermelon. In a downed tree, the heart stays good for about two weeks.

Breadfruit
This island staple provides a great deal of carbohydrates, but many people find the baked, boiled, or fried fruit bland. It grows all over the islands and is really thousands of little fruits growing together to form a ball.

Mangos
These are some of the most delicious fruits known to humans. They grow wild all over the islands; the ones on the leeward sides of the islands ripen from April to June, while the ones on the windward sides can last until October. They're found in the wild on trees up to 60 feet tall, and the problem is to stop eating them once you start!

Papaya
This truly tropical fruit has no real season but is mostly available in the summer. They grow on branchless trees and are ready to pick as soon as any yellow appears. Of the many varieties, the "solo papaya," meant to be eaten by one person, is the best. Split them in half, scrape out the seeds and have at them with a spoon.

solo papaya

breadfruit

Passionfruit
Known by their island name of *lilikoi,* they make excellent juice and pies. They're a small yellow fruit (similar to lemons but smooth-skinned) mostly available in summer and fall, and many wild ones grow on vines, waiting to be picked. Slice off the stem end, scoop the seedy pulp out with your tongue, and you'll know why they're called "passionfruit."

Guava
These small round yellow fruits are abundant in the wild where they are ripe from early summer to late fall. Considered a pest—so pick all you want. A good source of vitamin C, they're great for juice, jellies, and desserts.

Macadamia Nuts
The king of nuts was brought from Australia in 1892. Now it's the state's fourth largest agricultural product. Available roasted, candied, or buttered.

Litchi
Called nuts but really a small fruit with a thin red shell. They have a sweet and juicy white flesh when fresh, and appear like nuts when dried.

Fruit Potpourri
Beside the above, you'll find pineapple, oranges, limes, kumquats, thimbleberries, and blackberries, as well as carambolas, wild cherry tomatoes, and tamarinds.

FISH AND SEAFOOD

Anyone who loves fresh fish and seafood has come to the right place. Island restaurants specialize in seafood, and it's available everywhere.

HAWAIIAN GAME FISH

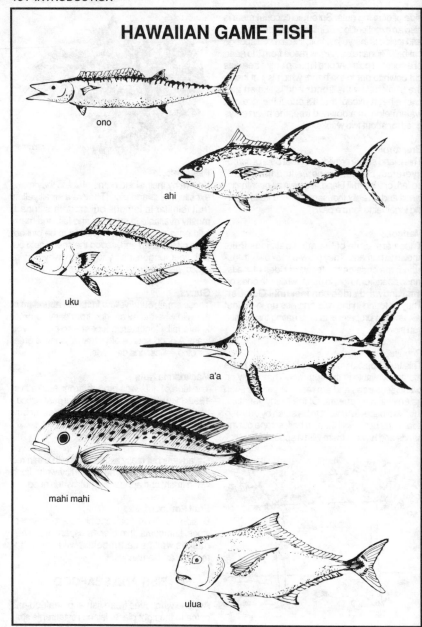

ono

ahi

uku

a'a

mahi mahi

ulua

Pound for pound, seafood is one of the best dining bargains in Hawaii. You'll find it served in every kind of restaurant, and often the fresh catch of the day is proudly displayed on ice in a glass case. The following is a sampling of the best.

Mahi Mahi

This excellent eating fish is one of the most common and least expensive in Hawaii. It's referred to as a "dolphin," but is definitely a fish and not a mammal at all. *Mahi mahi* can weigh 10-65 pounds; the flesh is light and moist, and the fish is broadest at the head. When caught it's a dark olive color, but after a while the skin turns iridescent—blue, green, and yellow. Can be served as a main course, or as a patty in a fish sandwich.

A'u

This true island delicacy is a broadbill swordfish or marlin. It's expensive even in Hawaii because the damn thing's so hard to catch. The meat is moist and white and truly superb. If it's offered on the menu, order it. It'll cost a bit more, but you won't be disappointed.

Ono

Ono means "delicious" in Hawaiian so that should tip you off to the taste of this "wahoo," or king mackerel. *Ono* is regarded as one of the finest eating fishes in the ocean, and its white flaky meat lives up to its name.

Manini

These five-inch fish are some of the most abundant in Hawaii and live in about 10 feet of water. They school and won't bite a hook but are easily taken with spear or net. Not often on a menu, but they're favorites with local people who know best.

Ulua

This member of the jack crevalle family ranges between 15 and 100 pounds. Its flesh is white and has a steak-like texture. Delicious and often found on the menu.

Fish Potpourri

Uku is a gray snapper that's a favorite with local people. The meat is light and firm and grills well. *Ahi,* a yellowfin tuna with a distinctive pinkish meat is a great favorite cooked, or uncooked in sushi bars. *Moi:* is the Hawaiian word for "king." This fish has large eyes and a shark-like head. Considered one of the finest eating fishes in Hawaii, it's best during the autumn months.

Some other island seafood found on the menu include *limu,* edible seaweed; *opihi,* small shellfish (limpets) that clings to rocks and is considered one of the best island delicacies, eaten raw; *aloalo,* like tiny lobsters; crawfish, plentiful in taro fields and irrigation ditches; *ahipalaka,* albacore tuna; various octopuses (squid or calamari); and sharks of various types.

MUNCHIES AND ISLAND TREATS

Certain "finger foods," fast foods, and island treats are unique to Hawaii. Some are a meal in themselves, but others are just snacks. Here are some of the best and most popular.

Pu Pu

Pronounced as in "Winnie the Pooh Pooh," these are little finger foods and hors d'oeuvers. They're everything from crackers to cracked crab. Often, they're free at lounges and bars and can even include chicken drumettes, fish kabobs, and tempura. A good display, and you can have a free meal.

Crackseed

A sweet of Chinese origin, those are preserved and seasoned fruits and seeds. Some favorites include coconut, watermelon, pumpkin seeds, mango, and papaya. They take some getting used to, but make great trail snacks. Available in all island markets. Also look for dried fish (cuttlefish) on racks, usually near the crackseed. These are nutritious and delicious and make a great snack.

Shave Ice

This real island institution makes the mainland "snow cone" melt into insignificance. Special machines literally "shave ice" to a fluffy consistency. It's mounded into a paper cone and you choose from dozens of exotic island syrups that are generously poured over it. You're given a straw and a spoon, and just slurp away.

Malasadas And Pao Dolce

Two sweets from the Portuguese. *Malasadas* are holeless doughnuts and *pao dolce* is sweet bread. They're sold in island bakeries and they're great for breakfast or just as a treat.

Lomi Lomi Salmon

This is a salad of salmon, tomatoes, and onions with garnish and seasonings. Often accompanies "plate lunches" and featured at buffets and luau.

MONEY-SAVERS

Only one thing is better than a great meal: a great meal at a reasonable price. The following are island institutions and favorites that will help you to eat well and keep prices down.

Kaukau Wagons

These are lunch wagons, but instead of being slick stainless steel jobs, most are old delivery trucks converted into portable kitchens. Some say they're a remnant of WW II, when workers had to be fed on the job; others say the meals they serve took their inspiration from the Japanese *bento,* a boxed lunch. You'll see them parked along beaches, in city parking lots, or on busy streets. Usually a line of local people will be placing their orders, especially at lunchtime, a tip-off that they serve a delicious, nutritious island dish for a reasonable price. They might have a few tables, but basically they serve "food to go." Most of their filling meals are about $3.50, and they specialize in the "plate lunch."

Plate Lunch

This is one of the best island standards. These lunches give you a sampling of authentic island food and can include "teri" chicken, *mahi mahi, lau lau,* and *lomi* salmon among others. They're on paper or styrofoam plates, are packed to go, and usually cost less than $3.50. Standard with a plate lunch is "two scoop rice," a generous dollop of macaroni salad or some other salad. A full meal, they're great for keeping down food prices and for making an instant picnic. Available everywhere from kaukau wagons to restaurants.

Saimin

Special "saimin shops," as well as restaurants, serve this hearty Japanese-inspired noodle soup on their menu. *Saimin* is a word unique to Hawaii. In Japan, these soups would either be called *ramin* or *soba,* and it's as if the two were combined to *saimin.* These are large bowls of noodle soup, a light broth with meat, chicken, or fish with vegetables stirred in. They cost only a few dollars and are big enough for an evening meal. The best place to eat saimin is in a little local hole-in-the-wall shop, run by a family.

Luaus And Buffets

As previously mentioned, the luau is an island institution. For a fixed price of about $30, you get to gorge yourself on a tremendous variety of island foods. On your luau day, skip breakfast and lunch and do belly stretching exercises! Buffets are also quite common in Hawaii, and like luaus they're "all you can eat" affairs. Offered at a variety of restaurants and hotels, they usually cost $8 and up. The food, however, ranges from quite good to only passable. At lunchtime, they're even cheaper, and they're always advertised in the free tourist literature, which often includes a discount coupon.

Tips

Even some of the island's best restaurants in the fanciest hotels offer "early-bird specials"—the regular-menu dinners offered to diners who come in before the usual dinner hour, which is approximately 6 p.m. You pay as little as half the normal price, and can dine in luxury on some of the best foods. Often advertised in the "free" tourist books, coupons for reduced meals might also be included: two for one, or limited dinners at a much lower price. Just clip them out. Hawaii has the full contingency of American fast-food chains including Jack in the Box, McDonalds, Shakey's Pizza, Kentucky Fried Chicken, and all the rest.

EXOTIC ISLAND DRINKS

To complement the fine dining in the islands, the bartenders have been busy creating their own tasty concoctions. The full range of beers, wines, and standard drinks is served in Hawaii, but for a real treat you should try some mixed drinks inspired by the islands. Kona coffee is the only coffee grown commercially in America. It comes from the Kona District of the Big Island and it is a rich, aromatic, and truly fine coffee. If it's offered on the menu, have a cup.

Drinking Laws

There are no "state" liquor stores; all kinds of spirits, wines, and beers are available in markets and shops, generally open during normal business hours, seven days a week. The drinking age is 18, and no towns are "dry." Legal hours for serving drinks depend on the type of establishment. Hours generally are: hotels, 6 a.m. to 4 a.m.; discos, and nightclubs where there is dancing, 10 a.m. to 4 a.m.; bars and lounges where there is no dancing, 6 a.m. to 2 a.m. Most restaurants serve alcohol, and in many that don't, you can bring your own.

Beer

A locally brewed beer is Primo. At one time brewed only in Hawaii, it's also made on the Mainland now. It's a serviceable American brew in the German style, but it lacks that full, hearty flavor of the European beers. Maui Lager, a new beer being brewed on Maui, is a different story.

It's a rich German-style beer made by brothers Klaus and Aloysius Klink. Maui Lager is made in Wailuku, at the Pacific Brewing Co., where tours can be arranged.

Exotic Drinks

To make your experience complete, you must order one of these colorful island drinks. Most look very innocent because they come in pineapples, coconut shells, or tall frosted glasses. They're often garnished with little umbrellas or sparklers, and most have enough fruit in them to give you your vitamins for the day. Rum is used as the basis of many of them. It's been an island favorite since it was introduced by the whalers of last century. Here are some of the most famous: mai tai, a mixture of light and dark rum, orange curaçao, orange and almond flavoring and lemon juice; chi chi, a simple concoction of vodka, pineapple juice and coconut syrup, real sleeper because it tastes like a milkshake; blue Hawaii, vodka and blue curacao; planter's punch, light rum, grenadine, bitters, and lemon juice, a great thirst quencher; singapore sling, a sparkling mixture of gin, cherry brandy, and lemon juice.

The coconut was very important to the Hawaiians and every part was utilized. A tree was planted when a child was born as a prayer for a good food supply throughout life. The trunks were used for building homes and heiau and carved into drums to accompany hula. The husks became bowls, utensils, and even jewelry. 'Aha, sennit rope braided from the husk fiber, was renowned as the most saltwater-resistant natural rope ever made.

CAMPING AND HIKING

A major aspect of the "Hawaii experience" is found in the simple beauty of nature and the outdoors. Visitors come to Hawaii to luxuriate at resorts and dine in fine restaurants, but everyone heads for the sand and surf, and most are captivated by the lush mountainous interior. What better way to savor this natural beauty than by hiking slowly through it or pitching a tent in the middle of it? Hawaii offers a full range of hiking and camping, and what's more, most of it is easily accessible and free. Camping facilities are located near many choice beaches and amid the most scenic areas in the islands. They range in amenities from full housekeeping cabins to primitive "hike-in" sites. Some restrictions to hiking apply because much of the land is privately owned, so you may require advance permission. But plenty of public access trails along the coast and deep into the interior would fill the itineraries of even the most intrepid trekkers. If you enjoy the great outdoors on the Mainland, you'll be thrilled by these "mini-continents," where in one day you can go from the frosty summits of alpine wonderlands down into baking cactus-covered deserts and emerge through jungle foliage onto a sun-soaked sub-tropical shore.

Note
Descriptions of individual state, county, and national parks, along with directions on how to get there, are given under "Camping And Hiking" in the respective travel chapters.

NATIONAL PARKS

Hawaii's two national parks sit atop volcanoes: **Haleakela National Park** on Maui, and **Hawaii Volcanoes National Park** centered around Kilauea Crater on the Big Island. Camping is free at both, and permits are not required except for cabins and campgrounds inside of Haleakala crater. Get free information by writing to the individual park headquarters listed below, or from **National Park Service,** 300 Ala Moana Blvd., Honolulu, HI 96850, tel. 546-7584.

Hawaii Volcanoes National Park
You won't need a permit to camp at the three overnight facilities at this amazing national park that spans one of the most active volcanoes in the world, but maybe an offering to Madame Pele would be a good idea. Registration at Park HQ is required if you intend to go trekking into the backcountry where you will need a wilderness

permit. There are three campgrounds in the park that you can drive to; though they operate on a first-come first-served basis, they're hardly ever filled. All have water, firepits, shelters, tables, and a seven-day limit, but no one counts too closely. Information, including pamphlets, brochures, and maps, is available on request from: **Park Headquarters,** Hawaii Volcanoes National Park, Hawaii, HI 96718, tel. 967-7311.

Haleakala National Park

Camping is free at Haleakala National Park on Maui. Permits are not needed to camp at Hosmer Grove, just a short drive from Park HQ, or at Oheo Stream Campground (formerly Seven Sacred Pools) near Kipahulu, along the coastal road 10 miles south of Hana. Camping is on a first-come, first-served basis, and there's an official three-day stay limit, but it's a loose count, especially at Oheo which is almost always empty. The case is much different at the campsites located inside Haleakala crater proper. On the floor of the crater are two primitive tenting campsites for which you'll need a wilderness permit. Because of ecological considerations, only 25 campers per night can stay at each site, and a three-night, four-day maximum stay is strictly enforced, with tenting allowed at any one site for only two nights. However, because of the strenuous hike involved, campsites are open most of the time. You must be totally self-sufficient and equipped for cold weather to be comfortable. Also, Paliku, Holua, and another site at Kapalaoa on the south rim offer fully self-contained cabins. To have a chance at getting a cabin you must make reservations, so write well in advance for complete information to: **Haleakala National Park,** Box 537, Makawao, HI 96768, tel. 572-9306.

STATE PARKS

Hawaii's 67 state parks are managed by the Dept. of Land and Natural Resources, through their Division of State Parks with branch offices on each island. These facilities include everything from historical sites like Iolani Palace in downtown Honolulu to wildland parks accessible only by trail. Some are only for looking at, some are restricted to day use, and at 16 or so

(which change periodically without notice) there is overnight camping. At seven of these 16 state parks, there are either A-frames, self-contained cabins, or group accommodations available on a fee basis with reservations necessary. At the others, camping is free, but permits are required. RVs are technically not allowed.

Permits And Rules

Camping permits, available free, are good for a maximum stay of five nights at any one park. A permit to the same person for the same park is again available only after 30 days have elapsed. Campgrounds are open every day on the Neighbor Islands, but closed Wednesday and Thursday on Oahu. Arrive after 2 p.m. and check out by 11 a.m., except again on Oahu where Wednesday check out is 8 a.m. You must be 18 for park permits, and anyone under that age must be accompanied by an adult. Alcoholic beverages are prohibited, along with nude sunbathing and swimming. Plants and wildlife are protected, but reasonable amounts of fruits and seeds may be gathered for personal consumption. Fires are allowed on cookstoves or in designated pits only. Dogs and other pets must be under control at all times and are not permitted to run around unleashed. Hunting and freshwater fishing are allowed in season with a license, and ocean fishing is permitted except where prohibited by posting. Permits are required for certain trails, pavilions, and remote camps, so check.

Cabins And Shelters

Housekeeping cabins, A-frames, and group lodges are available at seven state parks throughout the state (see "Camping And Hiking" travel chapters for charts). As with camping, permits are required with the same five-day maximum stay limitations. Reservations are necessary because of popularity, and a 50% deposit at time of confirmation is required. There is a three-day cancellation requirement for refunds, with payment made in cash, money order, certified check, or personal check only if the latter is received 30 days before arrival so that cashing procedures are possible. The balance is due on arrival; check in is 2 p.m., check out 11 a.m. Rates for A-frames, a single room with bunks and a picnic table, is a flat $7 per night, with a four-person maximum. Centrally located is a pavilion with a stove, refrigerator, restroom, and cold showers. Cabins are on a sliding scale of $10 for the 1st person, down to $5 for the six person maximum. These are completely furnished down to the utensils, with heaters for cold weather and private baths. Group accommodations (holding 32 to 64 people) are on an inexpensive, but slightly convoluted per-person, per-night basis: the maximum is $8 for the first person, first night, down to $1 for the 64th person after two nights. They're broken up into eight-person units which can be rented as such. Each has its own toilet and shower facilities but cooking is in a central mess hall.

State Park Permit-issuing Offices
Permits can be reserved two months in advance by writing a letter including your name, address, phone number, number in your party, type of permit requested, and duration of stay. They can be picked up on arrival with proof of identification. Office hours are 8 a.m. to 4:15 p.m., Monday through Friday. Usually, camping permits are no problem (Oahu excepted, see "Camping And Hiking," Oahu chapter) to secure on the day you arrive, but reserving ensures you a space and alleviates anxiety. The permits are available from the following offices: **Oahu,** Division of State Parks, 1151 Punchbowl St., Honolulu 96813, tel. 548-7455; **Hawaii,** Div. of State Parks, 75 Aupuni St., Hilo 96720, tel. 961-7200; **Maui and Molokai,** Div. of State Parks, 54 High St., Wailuku, 96793, tel. 244- 4354; **Kauai,** Div. of State Parks, State Bldg., 3060 Eiwa and Hardy Sts., Box 1671, Lihue, 96766, tel. 245-4444. For lodging at **Kokee State Park,** Kauai, write Kokee Lodge, Box 819, Waimea, HI 96796, tel. 335-6061.

COUNTY PARKS

The state of Hawaii is broken up into counties, and the counties control their own parks. Over 100 of these are scattered primarily along the coastlines, and are generally referred to as **beach parks.** Most are for day use only, where visitors fish, swim, snorkel, surf, picnic, and sunbathe, but over 36 beach parks have overnight camping. The rules governing their use vary slightly from county to county, but most have

about the same requirements as state parks. The main difference is that, along with a use permit, most county parks charge a fee for overnight use. Again, the differences between individual parks are too numerous to mention, but the majority have a central pavilion for cooking, restrooms, and cold-water showers (solar heated at a few), sometimes individual fire pits, picnic tables, and electricity (usually only at the central pavilion). RVs are allowed to park in appropriate spaces.

Fees And Permits
The fees are quite reasonable at $1-2 per night, per person, children about $.50 each. One safety point to consider is that beach parks are open to the general public and most are used with regularity. Quite a few people pass through, and your chances of encountering a hassle or rip-off are slightly higher (see p. 142 for safety tips). To get a permit and pay your fees for use of a county park, either write in advance, or visit one of the following issuing offices. Most will accept reservations months in advance, with offices generally open during normal working hours. For county parks write or visit the Dept. of Parks and Recreation, County Parks: **Oahu,** 650 S. King St., Honolulu, HI 96813, tel. 523-4525; **Maui,** War Memorial Gym, Wailuku HI 96793, tel. 244-5514; **Hawaii,** 25 Aupuni St., Hilo HI 96720, tel. 961-8311; **Kauai,** 4191 Hardy St., Lihue HI 96766, tel. 245-4982, or during off hours at Lihue Police Station, 3060 Umi St., Lihue 96766, tel. 245-6721; **Molokai,** County Bldg., Kaunakakai HI 96748, tel. 553-5141.

EQUIPMENT, INFORMATION, AND SAFETY

Equipment
Like everything else you take to Hawaii, your camping and hiking equipment should be lightweight and durable. Camping equipment size and weight should not cause a problem with baggage requirements on airlines: if it does, it's a tip-off that you're hauling too much. One odd luggage consideration you might make is to bring along a small **styrofoam cooler** packed with equipment. Exchange these for food items when you get to Hawaii; if you intend to car camp successfully and keep food prices down, you'll

definitely need a cooler. You can also buy one on arrival for only a few dollars. You'll need a lightweight **tent**, preferably with a rainfly, and a sewn-in floor. This will save you from getting wet and miserable, and will keep out mosquitoes, cockroaches, ants, and the few stinging insects on Maui. In Haleakala Crater, where you can expect cold and wind, a tent is a must; in fact you won't be allowed to camp without one.

Sleeping bags are a good idea, although you can get along at sea level with only a blanket. Down-filled bags are necessary for Haleakala, Mauna Kea, Mauna Loa, or any high altitude-camping—you'll freeze without one. **Camp stoves** are needed because there's very little wood in some volcanic areas, it's often wet in the deep forest, and open fires are often prohibited. If you'll be car camping, take along a multi-burner stove, and for trekking, a backpacker's stove will be necessary. The grills found only at some campgrounds are popular with many families that go often to the beach parks for an open-air dinner. You can buy a very inexpensive charcoal grill at many variety stores throughout Hawaii. It's a great idea to take along a **lantern**. This will give added safety for car campers. Definitely take a **flashlight**, replacement batteries, and a few small **candles**. A complete **first-aid kit** can be the difference between life and death, and is worth the extra bulk. Hikers, especially those leaving the coastal areas, should take **rain gear**, a plastic ground cloth, utility knife, compass, safety whistle, mess kit, water purification tablets, canteen, nylon twine, and waterproof matches. You can find plenty of stores that sell, and a few stores that rent, camping equipment; see the Yellow Pages under "Camping Equipment," and "Shopping" in the travel chapters.

Safety

There are two things in Hawaii that you must keep your eye on to remain safe: humans and nature. The general rule is, the farther you get away from towns, the safer you'll be from human-induced hassles. If possible, don't hike or camp alone, especially if you're a woman. Don't leave your valuables in your tent, and always carry your money, papers, and camera with you. (See "Theft"). Don't tempt the locals by being overly friendly or unfriendly, and make yourself scarce if they're drinking. While hiking, remember that many trails are well maintained,

but trailhead markers are often missing. The trails themselves can be muddy, which can make them treacherously slippery and oftentimes knee-deep. Always bring food because you cannot, in most cases, forage from the land. Water in most streams is biologically polluted and will give you bad stomach problems if you drink it without purifying it first, either through boiling or with tablets. For your part, please don't use the streams as a toilet.

Precautions

Always tell a ranger or official of your hiking intentions. Supply an itinerary and your expected route, then stick to it. Twilight is short in the islands, and night sets in rapidly. In June sunrise and sunset are around 6 a.m. and 7 p.m., in December these occur at 7 a.m. and 6 p.m. If you become lost at night, stay put, light a fire if possible, and stay as dry as you can. Hawaii is made of volcanic rock which is brittle and crumbly. Never attempt to climb steep *pali* (cliffs). Every year people are stranded and fatalities have occurred on the *pali*. If lost, walk on ridges and avoid the gulches which have more obstacles and make it harder for rescuers to spot you. Be careful of elevation sickness, especially on Haleakala, Mauna Loa, and Mauna Kea. The best cure is to head down as soon as possible.

Heat can cause you to lose water and salt. If you become woozy or weak, rest, take salt, and drink water as you need it. Remember, it takes much more water to restore a dehydrated person than to keep hydrated; take small frequent sips. Be mindful of flash floods. Small creeks can turn into raging torrents with upland rains. Never camp in a dry creek bed. Fog is only encountered at the 1,500- to 5,000-foot level, but be careful of disorientation. Generally, stay within your limits, be careful, and enjoy yourself.

Guidebooks

For a well-written and detailed hiking guide complete with maps, check out the *Hiking Hawaii Series* (a book for each island, plus a general book for all the islands) by Robert Smith, published by Wilderness Press, 2440 Bancroft Way, Berkeley, CA 94704. Another book by the same company is *Hawaiian Camping* by Shirley Rizzuto. Geared toward family camping, it's adequate for basic information and listing necessary addresses, but at times it's limited in scope.

Helpful Departments And Organizations

The following will be helpful in providing trail maps, accessibility information, hunting and fishing regulations, and general forest rules. The **Dept. of Land and Natural Resources,** Division of Forestry and Wildlife, 1151 Punchbowl, St., Honolulu, 96813, tel. 548-2861. Their "Recreation Map" (for each island) is excellent and free. The following organizations can provide general information on wildlife, conservation, and organized hiking trips: **Hawaiian Trail and Mountain Club,** Box 2238, Honolulu, 96804. The Trail and Mountain Club meets behind Iolani Palace on Saturdays at 10 a.m., and on Sundays at 8 a.m. Their hikes are announced in the *Honolulu Star Bulletin* in the "Pulse of Paradise" column; **Hawaiian Audubon Society,** Box 22832, Honolulu 96822; **Sierra Club,** 1100 Alakea St., Honolulu, 96813, tel. 538-6616. Also see p. 115-118.

Topographical And Nautical Charts

For in-depth topographical maps, write **U.S. Geological Survey,** Federal Center, Denver, CO 80225. In Hawaii, a wide range of topographical maps can be purchased at **Trans-Pacific Instrument Co.,** 1406 Colburn St., Honolulu, HI 96817, tel. 841-7538. For nautical charts, write **National Ocean Survey,** Riverdale, MD 20240.

map of the "Sandwich Isles" by Capt. Jean La Percuse, c. 1786

SPORTS AND RECREATION

Hawaii is a playground for young and old with sports, games, and activities galore. Everyone can find something they enjoy, and most activities are free, relatively cheap, or once-in-a-lifetime thrills that are worth the money. The sea is the ideal playground. You can swim, snorkel, scuba, surf, fish, sail, canoe, kayak, sailboard, bodysurf, parasail, cruise, or merely stroll along the shore picking shells or exploring tidepools. Every island offers tennis and golf, along with plenty of horseback riding, hiking, hunting, and freshwater fishing. Spectator sports like baseball, basketball, polo, and especially football are popular, and the Kona Coast of the Big Island is a mecca for world-class triathletes. Whatever your desire or physical abilities may be, there'll be some activity that strikes your fancy in Hawaii.

One of the best tonics for relaxation is to play hard at something you thoroughly enjoy, so you're deliciously tired and fulfilled at day's end. For you this might be hooking onto an 800-pound marlin that'll test you to the limit, or perhaps just giving yourself to the sea and floating on gentle waves. Hawaii is guaranteed to thrill the young, invigorate the once young, put a twinkle in your eye, and a bounce in your step.

Note: The following sports and activities breakdowns are designed to give you an idea of what's available. They'll all be covered in depth in the travel chapters under "Sports." There you'll also find specific entries for localized sports like horseback riding, jet-skiing, water-skiing, snow skiing, parasailing, kayaking, and much more. Whatever else you may do in Hawaii, you owe it to yourself to do one thing: enjoy it!

SCUBA AND SNORKELING

If you think that Hawaii is beautiful above the sea, wait until you explore below. The warm tropical waters and coral growth make it a fascinating haven for reef fish and aquatic plantlife. Snorkel and dive sites, varying in difficulty and challenge, are accessible from all islands. Sites can be totally hospitable where families, snorkeling for the first time, can have an exciting but safe frolic, or accessible only to the experienced diver. Every island has dive shops from which you can rent or buy all equipment, and where dive boats and instruction on all levels can be arranged. You'll soon discover that Hawaiian waters are remarkably clear with excellent visibility.

REEF FISH

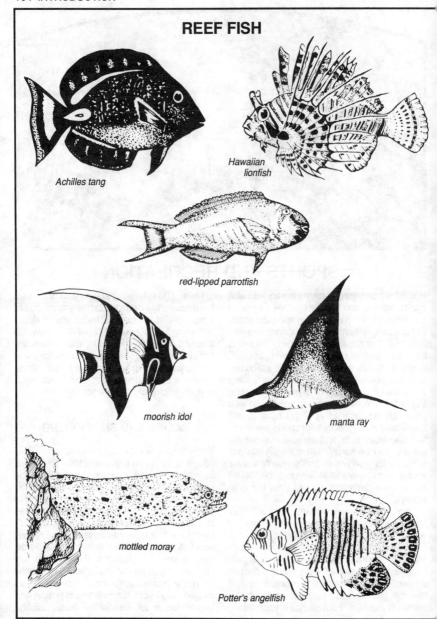

Achilles tang

Hawaiian lionfish

red-lipped parrotfish

moorish idol

manta ray

mottled moray

Potter's angelfish

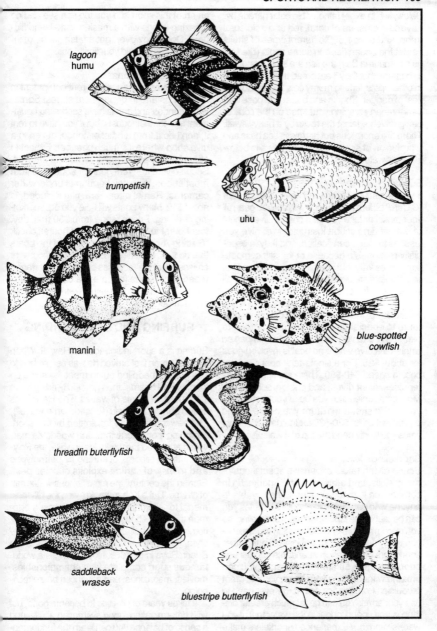

lagoon
humu

trumpetfish

uhu

manini

blue-spotted
cowfish

threadfin buterflyfish

saddleback
wrasse

bluestripe butterflyfish

Below, fish in every fathomable color parade by. Lavender clusters of coral, red and gold coral trees, and over 1,500 different types of shells carpet the ocean floor. In some spots (like Oahu's Hanauma Bay) the fish are so accustomed to humans that they'll eat bread from your hand. In other spots, lurking moray eels add the special zest of danger. Sharks and barracuda pose less danger than scraping your knee on the coral or being driven against the rocks by a heavy swell. There are enormous but harmless sea bass and a profusion of sea turtles. All this awaits below Hawaii's waters.

Scuba

If you're a scuba diver you'll have to show your "C Card" before local shops will rent you gear, fill your tanks, or take you on a charter dive. Plenty of outstanding scuba instructors will give you lessons towards certification, and they're especially reasonable because of the stiff competition. Prices vary, but you can take a four- to five-day semiprivate certification course including all equipment for about $175. Divers unaccustomed to Hawaiian waters should not dive alone regardless of their experience. Most opt for dive tours to special dive grounds guaranteed to please. These vary also, but an *accompanied* single-tank dive where no boat is involved goes for about $25. For a single-tank boat dive, expect to spend $40-$50. There are special charter dives, night dives, and photography dives. Most companies pick you up at your hotel, take you to the site, and return you home. Basic equipment costs $20-$30 for the day, and most times you'll only need the top of a wetsuit.

Snorkeling

Scuba diving takes expensive special equipment, skills, and athletic ability. Snorkeling in comparison is much simpler and enjoyable to anyone who can swim. In about 15 minutes you can be taught the fundamentals of snorkeling, so you're comfortable and confident in the water—you really don't need formal instructions. Other snorkelers or dive shop attendants can tell you enough to get you started. Because you can breathe without lifting your head, you get great propulsion from the fins and hardly ever need to use your arms. You can go for much greater distances and spend longer in the water than if you were swimming. Experienced snorkelers make

an art of this sport and you too can see and do amazing things with a mask, snorkel, and flippers. Don't, however, get a false sense of invincibility and exceed your limitations.

Gear And Excursions

Those interested can buy or rent equipment in dive shops and in department stores. Sometimes condos and hotels have snorkeling equipment free for their guests, but if you have to rent it, don't do it from a hotel or condo, but go to a dive shop where it's much cheaper. Expect to spend $7 a day for mask, fins, and snorkel. Scuba divers can rent gear for about $30 from most shops. A special option is underwater cameras. Rental of camera, film included, is about $10. Many boats will take you out snorkeling or diving. Prices range from $30 (half day, four hours) to $60 (full day, eight hours); check "Getting Around/Tours" for many of the boats that do it all, from deep-sea fishing to moonlight cruises. All of the "activities centers" can arrange these excursions for no extra charge; check "Getting Around/Sightseeing Tours" for names and numbers.

SURFING AND SAILBOARDING

Surfing is a sport indigenous to Hawaii. When the white man first arrived he was astonished to see natives paddling out to meet the ships on long carved boards, then gracefully riding them into shore on crests of waves. The Hawaiians called surfing *he'enalu* (to "slide on a wave"). The newcomers were fascinated by this sport, recording it on engravings and woodcuts marvelled at around the world. Meanwhile, the Polynesians left records of surfing as petroglyphs and in *mele* of surfing exploits of times past. Early in the century, the most famous waterman of all time, Duke Kahanamoku, won the Olympic medal for swimming. He then became a one-man traveling show, introducing surfing to California and Australia. Surfing later became a lifestyle, spread far and wide by the songs of the Beach Boys in the '60s. Now surfing is a world-famous sport complete with championships, movies, magazines, and advanced board technology.

It takes years of practice to become good, but with determination, good swimming ability, and a sense of balance you can learn the fundamen-

HAWAIIAN SHELLS

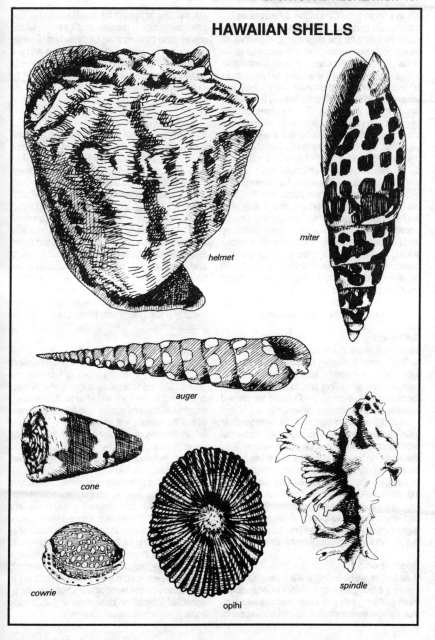

helmet

miter

auger

cone

opihi

cowrie

spindle

tals in a short time. One of the safest places offering ideal conditions to learn is Waikiki. The sea is just right for the beginner, and legions of beach boys offer lessons. At surf shops on all islands you can rent a board for very reasonable prices. The boards of the ancient *ali'i* were up to 20 feet long and weighed over 150 pounds, but today's board is made from ultralight foam plastic covered in fiberglass. They're about six feet long and weigh 12 pounds or so. Innovations occur every day in surfing, but one is the changeable "skeg" or rudder allowing you to surf in variable conditions. The sport of surfing is still male-dominated, but women champions have been around for years. The most famous surfing beach in the world is Sunset Beach and the Banzai Pipeline on North Shore Oahu. Every year the nationally televised Pro-Tour Surfing Championship is held there, usually in late November and December. It's only a matter of time before surfing becomes an Olympic sport. One of the most brilliant books ever written on surfing is *Surfing, The Ultimate Pleasure,* by Leonard Lueras and designed by Fred Bechlen. Published by Workman Publishing of New York, a copy can be found at almost every surf shop.

Sailboarding

Many people call this relatively new sport "windsurfing," which is actually the name of one of the most famous manufacturers of sailboards. A combination of surfing and sailing, the equipment is a rather large and stable surfboard mounted with a highly maneuverable sail. If it sounds difficult, most people find it slightly easier than surfing because you're mobilized by the wind and not at the mercy of the waves. You don't have to "read" the waves as well as a surfer, and like riding a bicycle, as long as you keep moving, you can hold your balance. Unlike surfing, which tends to be male-dominated, women, too, are excellent at sailboarding. Sailboards and lessons are available on all islands. They're slightly more expensive then surfboards to rent, but you should be in business for about $30.

Boogie Boards

If surfing or sailboarding are a bit too much for you, try a boogie board—foam boards about three feet long that you lie on from the waist up. You can get tremendous rides on boogie boards with the help of flippers for maneuverability. You can learn to ride in minutes and it's much faster, easier, and thrilling than bodysurfing. Boogie boards are for sale all over the islands and are relatively cheap. You can rent one from a dive or surf shop for a couple bucks, or buy your own for $10-15.

GONE FISHING

Hawaii has some of the most exciting and productive "blue waters" in all the world. You'll find a statewide "sport fishing fleet" made up of skippers and crews who are experienced professional anglers. You can also fish from jetties, piers, rocks, and from shore. If rod and reel don't strike your fancy, try the old-fashioned "throw net," or take along a spear when you go snorkeling or scuba diving. There's nighttime torch fishing that requires special skills and equipment, and freshwater fishing in public areas. Streams and irrigation ditches yield introduced trout, bass, and catfish. While you're at it, you might want to try crabbing for Kona and Samoan crabs, or working low-tide areas after sundown hunting squid (really octopus), a tantalizing island delicacy.

Deep-sea Fishing

Most game fishing boats work the blue waters on the calmer leeward sides of the islands. Some skippers, carrrying anglers who are accustomed to the sea, will also work the much rougher windward coasts and island channels where the fish bite just as well. Trolling is the preferred method of deep-sea fishing; this is done usually in waters of between 1,000-2,000 fathoms (a fathom is six feet). The skipper will either "area fish," which means running in a criss-crossing pattern over a known productive area, or "ledge fish," which involves trolling over submerged ledges where the gamefish are known to feed. The most advanced marine technology, available on many boats, sends sonar bleeps searching for fish. On deck, the crew and anglers scan the horizon in the age-old Hawaiian tradition—searching for seabirds clustered in an area, feeding on the very baitfish pursued to the surface by the huge and aggressive gamefish. "Still fishing," or "bottom fishing" with hand lines, yields some tremendous fish.

The Game Fish

The most thrilling gamefish in Hawaiian waters is marlin, generically known as "billfish" or *a'u* to the locals. The king of them is the blue marlin, with record catches well over 1,000 pounds. There are also striped marlin and sailfish, which often go over 200 pounds. The best times for marlin are during spring, summer, and fall. The fishing tapers off in January and picks up again by late February. "Blues" can be caught year-round, but, oddly enough, when they stop biting it seems as though the striped marlin pick up. Second to the marlin are tuna. *Ahi* (yellowfin tuna) are caught in Hawaiian waters of depths of 100-1,000 fathoms. They can weigh 300 pounds, but between 25 and 100 pounds is common. There's also *aku* (skipjack tuna) and the delicious *ono,* which average between 20 and 40 pounds.

Mahi mahi is another strong, fighting, deepwater gamefish abundant in Hawaii. These delicious fish can weigh up to 70 pounds. Shore fishing and baitcasting yield *papio,* a jack tuna. *Akule,* a scad, (locally called *halalu,)* is a smallish schooling fish that comes close to shore and is great to catch on light tackle. *Ulua* are shore fish and can be found in tidepools. They're excellent eating, average two to three pounds, and are taken at night or with spears. *O'io* are bonefish that come close to shore to spawn. They're caught baitcasting and bottom fishing with cut bait. They're bony, but they're a favorite for fish cakes and *poki.* *Awa* is a schooling fish that loves brackish water. It can get up to three feet long, and is a good fighter. A favorite for "throw netters," it's even raised commercially in fish ponds. Besides these there are plenty of goatfish, mullet, mackerel, snapper, various sharks, and even salmon.

Note: For Hawaiian Game Fish Chart, see p. 154.

"Blue Water" Areas

One of the most famous fishing spots in Hawaii is the **Penguin Banks** off the west coast of Molokai and the south coast of Oahu. "Chicken Farm" at the southern tip of the Penguin Banks are great trolling waters for marlin and *mahi.* The calm waters off the Waianae Coast of Oahu yield marlin and *ahi.* The Kona Coast of Hawaii with its crystal waters is the most famous marlin grounds in Hawaii. Every year the **Hawaiian International Billfish Tournament** draws anglers from around the world to Kona. The marlin are in 1,000 fathoms of water, but close in on the Kona Coast you can hook *ono* and handline for *onaga* and *kahala.* Maui fishermen usually head for the waters formed by the triangle of Maui, Lanai, and Kahoolawe where they troll for marlin, *mahi,* and *ono,* or bottom-fish for snapper. The waters around Kahoolawe are also good. Kauai has excellent fishing waters year-round, with *ono, ahi,* and marlin along the ledges. Large schools of *ahi* come to Kauai in the spring, and the fishing is fabulous with 200-pounders being known.

Charter Boats

The charter boats of Hawaii come in all shapes and sizes, but they are all manned by professional, competent crews and captains intimately knowledgeable of Hawaiian waters. Prices vary but expect to spend $80-$100 on a "share basis." The average number of fishermen per boat is six, and most boats rent all day for $600. You can also arrange half days, and bigger boats with more anglers cost as little as $35 per person. All tackle from 30 to 130 pounds is carried on the boats and is part of the service. Oftentimes soft drinks are supplied, but usually you carry your own lunch. It is customary for the crew to be given any fish that are caught, but naturally this doesn't apply to trophy fish; the crew is also glad to cut off some steaks and fillets for your personal use. Honolulu's Kewalo Basin, only a few minutes from Waikiki, has the largest fleet of charter boats. Pokai Bay also has a fleet and many charter boats sail out of Kaneohe Bay. On the Big Island, Kailua-Kona has the largest concentration of charter boats, with some boats out of Kawaihae. Maui boats come out of Lahaina or Maalaea Bay. Molokai has a small fleet berthed in Kaunakakai Harbor, and on Kauai most boats sail out of Nawiliwili Bay.

Freshwater Fishing

Due to Hawaii's unique geology, only a handful of natural lakes and rivers are good for fishing. The state maintains five "Public Fishing Areas" spread over Kauai, Oahu, and Hawaii (none on Maui, Lanai, or Molokai). Public fishing areas include: on Oahu, **Wahiawa Public Area,** a 300-acre irrigation reservoir primarily for sugar cane located near Wahiawa in central Oahu, and **Nuuanu Resevoir No. 4,** located in the Koolau

FRESHWATER FISH

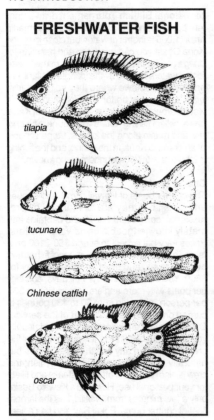

tilapia

tucunare

Chinese catfish

oscar

tucunare is a tough, fighting, good-tasting gamefish introduced from South America, similar to the oscar, from the same region. Both have been compared to bass, but are of a different family. *Tilapia* are from Africa and have become common in Hawaii's irrigation ditches. They're "mouth breeders" and the young will take refuge in their parents' protective jaws even a few weeks after hatching. Snakehead are eel-like fish that inhabit the reservoirs and are great fighters. Channel catfish can grow to over 20 pounds and bite best after sundown. There's also carp, and with their broad tail and tremendous strength, they're the poor man's gamefish. All of these species are best caught with light spinning tackle, or with a bamboo pole and a trusty old worm.

Fishing licenses are good from July 1 to June 30. Licenses cost: $7.50 for non-residents, $3.50 for tourists good for 30 days, $3.75 for residents and military personnel, $1.50 for children between nine and 15 years old, and free to senior citizens. Licenses are obtained from Division of Conservation and Resources Enforcement (Oahu, tel. 548-8766) or from most sporting goods stores. For free booklets and information write, Division of Aquatic Resources, 1151 Punchbowl St., Honolulu, HI 96813. All game fish may be taken year-round, except trout. Trout, only on Kauai, may be taken for 16 days commencing on the first Saturday of August. Thereafter, for the remainder of August and September, trout can be taken only on Sat., Sun., and state holidays.

Mountains above Honolulu; on Kauai, **Kokee Public Fishing Area,** located north of Kekaha, offers 13 miles of stream, two miles of irrigation ditches, and a 15-acre reservoir offering only rainbow trout; on Hawaii, **Waiakea Public Area** is a 26-acre pond within the city of Hilo, and **Kohala Reservoir** is on the north coast.

Freshwater Fish And Rules

Hawaii has only one native freshwater gamefish, the *o'opu.* This gobie is an oddball with fused ventral fins. They grow to be 12 inches and are found on all islands, especially Kauai. Introduced species include largemouth and smallmouth bass, bluegills, catfish, *tucunare,* oscar, carp, and *tilapia.* The only trout to survive is the rainbow, found only in the streams of Kauai. The

HUNTING

Most people don't think of Hawaii as a place to hunt, but actually it's quite good. Seven species of introduced game animals are regularly hunted, and 16 species of game birds. Not all species of game animals are open on all islands, but every island offers hunting. Please refer to "Sports" in the travel chapters for full details on hunting on particular islands.

General Hunting Rules

Hunting licences are mandatory to hunt on public, private, or military land anywhere in Hawaii. They're good for one year beginning July 1. They cost $7.50 residents, $15 non-residents, senior citizens free. Licenses are available from

feral pig

the various offices of The Division of Forestry and Wildlife (see below) and from sporting goods stores. This government organization also sets and enforces the rules, so contact them with any questions. Generally hunting hours are from a half-hour before sunrise to a half-hour after sunset. At times, there are "checking stations," where the hunter must check in before and after hunting.

Rifles must have greater than a 1,200-foot-pound muzzle velocity. Shotguns larger than .20 gauge are allowed, and muzzleloaders must have a .45 caliber bore or larger. Bows must have a minimum draw of 45 pounds for straight bows and 30 pounds for compounds. Arrows must be broadheads. Dogs are permitted only with some birds and game, and smaller caliber rifles and shotguns are permitted with their use, along with spears and knives. Hunters must wear orange safety cloth on front and back no smaller than a 12-inch square. Certain big game species are hunted only by lottery selection; contact the Division of Forestry and Wildlife two months in advance. Guide service is not mandatory, but is advised if you're unfamiliar with hunting in Hawaii. You can hunt on private land only with permission, and you must possess a valid hunting license. Guns and ammunition brought into Hawaii must be registered with the chief of police of the corresponding county within 48 hours of arrival.

Information

Hunting rules and regulations are always subject to change. Also, environmental considerations often change bag limits and seasons. Make sure to check with the Division of Forestry and Wildlife for the most current information. Request "Rules Regulating Game Bird Hunting, Field Trials and

Commercial Shooting Preserves," "Rules Regulating Game Mammal Hunting," and "Hunting in Hawaii." Direct inquiries to: Dept. of Land and Natural Resources, Division of Forestry and Wildlife Office, 1151 Punchbowl St., Honolulu 96813, tel. 548-2861; on Maui, 54 S. High St., P.O. Box 1015, Wailuku, 96793, tel. 244-4352; on Hawaii, Box 4849, Hilo 96720, tel. 961-7221; on Lanai, 338 8th St., Lanai City 96763, tel. 565-6688; on Kauai, 3060 Eiwa St., Box 1671, Lihue 96766, tel. 245-4444; on Molokai, Puu Kapeelua Ave., Hoolehua 96729, tel. 553-5415.

Game Animals

All game animals have been introduced to Hawaii. Some are adapting admirably and becoming well entrenched, while the existence of others is still precarious. **Axis deer** originated in India and were brought to Lanai and Molokai, where they're doing well. The small herd on Maui is holding its own. Their unique flavor makes them one of the best wild meats, and they're hunted on Molokai and Lanai in March and April, by public lottery. **Feral pigs** are escaped domestic pigs that have gone wild and are found on all islands except Lanai. The stock is a mixture of original Polynesian pigs and all that came later. Hunted with dogs and usually killed with a spear or long knife, pig hunting is not recommended for the timid or tenderhearted. These beasts' four-inch tusks and fighting spirit make them tough and dangerous. **Feral goats** come in a variety of colors. Found on all islands except Lanai, they have been known to cause erosion and are considered a pest in some areas, especially on Haleakala. Openly hunted on all islands, their meat when done properly is

Gambel's quail

Feral goats have over-populated and become pests. They roam from coast to mountaintop depleting vegetation and causing considerable erosion.

considered delicious. **Black-tailed deer** come from the Rocky Mountains. Forty were released on Kauai in 1961; the herd is now stabalized at around 400 and they're hunted in October by public lottery. **Mouflon sheep** are native to Corsica and Sardinia. They do well on Lanai and on the windswept slopes of Mauna Loa and Mauna Kea where they're hunted at various times by public lottery. **Feral sheep** haunt the slopes of Mauna Kea and Mauna Loa from 7,000 to 12,000 feet. They travel in flocks and destroy vegetation. It takes determination and a good set of lungs to bag one, especially with a bow and arrow. **Pronghorn antelope** on Lanai, **feral cattle** on the Big Island, and **rock wallabies** from Australia, who now make their home on Oahu, are not hunted.

Game Birds

A number of game birds are found on most of the islands. Bag limits and hunting seasons vary, so check with the Division of Forestry and Wildlife for details. **Ring-necked pheasants** are one of the best game birds found on all the islands. The **kalij pheasant** from Nepal is found only on the Big Island, where the **green pheasant** is also prevalent with some found on Oahu and Maui. **Francolins,** gray and black, from India and the Sudan, are similar to partridges. They are hunted with dogs on all islands and are great roasted. There are also **chukar** from Tibet, found on the slopes of all islands; a number of **quail**, including the **Japanese and California** varieties; **doves;** and the **wild Rio Grande turkey** which is found on all islands except Kauai

and Oahu (although a few of the "featherless variety" have been known to walk the streets of Waikiki).

GOLF AND TENNIS

People addicted to chasing that little white ball around the links are going to be delighted with Hawaii. You can golf every day of the year on over 60 golf courses scattered around the state. Many are open to the public, and are built along some of the most spectacular scenery in the world where the pounding surf, or flower-dappled mountains form the backdrop. Many courses have pros and pro shops, and a profusion of hotels offer "golfing specials." You'll find everything from Lanai's nine-hole Cavendish Golf Course, where you put your money in an envelope on the honor system, to the Mauana Kea Beach Golf Club, one of the most exclusive and exciting golf courses in the world. Master builders such as Robert Trent Jones have laid out links in the islands where major tournaments, such as the Kemper Open, are yearly events. Fees range from as little as $5.50 for some little nine-holers up to $75 and more at the more exclusive resorts.

Tennis courts are found on every island of Hawaii and enjoyed by locals and visitors on a year-round basis. County courts are open to the public, as are some hotel and private courts where fees range from complimentary to about $6 for non-hotel guests. Most courts are of laykold or plexipave asphalt. Many of the hotel, and some public, courts are lighted.

Note: Golf and tennis charts and listings appear under "Sports" in the travel chapters.

gray francolin

FACTS, FIGURES, AND PRACTICALITIES

This entire chapter is dedicated to the practical side of travel, the "nuts and bolts" you'll need to know to make your stay in Hawaii easier, more efficient, and more convenient. In it you'll find the names, addresses, and phone numbers of useful and helpful organizations and offices. Information, such as business hours, currency, and emergency phone numbers are listed, as well as a smattering of little-known facts and tidbits related to Hawaii. This information should help you get what you want, or at least point you in the right direction so you can get started. Good luck!

HAWAII VISITORS BUREAU

In 1903 the Hawaiian Promotion Committee thought tourism could be the economic wave of the future. They began the Hawaii Tourist Bureau, which became the **Hawaii Visitors Bureau.** The **HVB** is now a top-notch organization providing help and information to all of Hawaii's visitors. Anyone contemplating a trip to Hawaii should visit or write the HVB and inquire about any specific information they may require. Their advice and excellent brochures on virtually every facet of living, visiting, or simply enjoying Hawaii are free. The material offered is too voluminous to list, but for basics, request individual island brochures (including maps), and ask for their copies of "Member Accommodation Guide," and "Member Restaurant Guide." Allow two-three weeks for requests to be answered.

HAWAII VISITORS BUREAU OFFICES

Hawaii
The main HVB administration office is at Waikiki Business Plaza, 2270 Kalakaua Ave., Suite 801, Honolulu, HI 96815, tel. 923-1811. On Maui, 380 Dairy Rd., Kahului, HI 96732, tel. 244-9141. On Kauai, 3016 Umi St., Lihue HI 96799, tel. 871-8691. Hawaii has two branches: Hilo Plaza, 180 Kinoole St., Suite 104, Hilo HI 96720, tel. 961-5797, and 75-5719 W. Alii Dr., Kailua-Kona, HI 96740, tel. 329-7787.

North America
At 441 Lexington Ave., Room 1407, New York, N.Y. 10017, tel. (212) 986-9203; 1511 K St. N.W., Suite 415, Washington, D.C. 20005, tel. (202) 393-6752; 180 N. Michigan Ave. Suite 1031, Chicago, IL 60601, tel. (312) 236-0632; Central Plaza, 3440 Wilshire Blvd. Room 502, Los Angeles, CA 90010, tel. (213) 385-5301; Suite 450, 50 California St., San Francisco, CA 94111, tel. (415) 392-8173.

Canada
At 4915 Cedar Crescent, Delta, B.C., Canada V4M 1J9, tel. (604) 943-8555.

United Kingdom
c/o First Public Relations Ltd., 16 Bedford Sq., London WC 1B 3JH, England.

The "HVB Warrior" is posted alongside the roadway, marking sites of cultural and historical importance.

Australia
c/o Walshes World, 92 Pitt St., Sydney, N.S.W. 2000.

Asian Offices
Japan, 129 Kokusai Bldg., 4-1 Marunouchi 3-chome, Chiyoda-ku, Tokyo 100; **Indonesia,** c/o Pacific Leisure, Jalan Prapatan 32, Jakarta; **Hong Kong,** c/o Pacific Leisure, Suite 904, Tung Ming Bldg., 40 Des Voeux Rd., Central Hong Kong; **Philippines,** c/o Philippine Leisure Inc., Interbank Bldg., 111 Paseo de Roxas, Makati, Metro Manila; **Korea,** c/o Bando Air, Room 1510, Ankuk Insurance Bldg., 87, 1-ka, Eulchi-ro, Chung Ku, Seoul 100; **Singapore,** c/o Pacific Leisure, #03-01 UOL Bldg., 96 Somerset Rd., Sïngapore 0923; **Thailand,** c/o Pacific Leisure, 542/1 Ploenchit Rd., Bangkok; other offices are found through Pacific Leisure in **Kuala Lumpur, Penang,** and **Taipei.**

FOREIGN CONSULATES

All of the foreign consulates and diplomatic offices are located in Honolulu. Most major European, Asian, and Oceanic nations, along with many South American countries, have delegates in Honolulu. They are all listed under "Consulates" in the Oahu Yellow Pages. The following are only some of the phone numbers for foreign consulates in Hawaii.

Australia, tel. 524-5050; Japan, 536-2226; Nauru, 523-7821; Micronesia, 836-4775; France, 923-2666; Germany, 847-4411; India, 947-2618; Indonesia, 524-4300; Korea, 595-6109; New Zealand, 922-3853; Philippines, 595-6316; Thailand, 524-3888; W. Samoa, 734-3233.

TELEPHONES

Area Code: 808
The telephone system on all the main islands is modern and comparable to any systems on the Mainland. You can "direct dial" from Hawaii to the Mainland and 70 foreign countries. Undersea cables and satellite communications ensure top-quality phone service. Public telephones are found at hotels, street booths, restaurants, most public buildings, and at some beach parks. It is common to have a phone in most hotel rooms and condominiums, though a service charge is usually collected, even on local calls. The **area code** for all islands is **808.**

Rates
Like everywhere else in the U.S. it's cheaper to make long-distance calls on weekdays in the evenings. Rates go down at 5 p.m. and again at 11 p.m. until 8 a.m. the next morning. From Fri. at 5 p.m. until Mon. morning at 8 a.m., rates are also cheapest. Local calls from public telephones (anywhere on the same island is a local call) cost 20 cents. Calling between islands is a toll call, and the price depends on when and from where you call and for how long you speak. Emergency calls are always free. For directory assistance: local, 1-411; inter-island, 1-555-1212; Mainland, 1-area code-555-1212; toll free, 1-800-555-1212.

Helpful Numbers
POLICE——FIRE——AMBULANCE: On Oahu, Maui, and Kauai dial 911 from any phone. Lanai, police 565-6525, fire 565-6766, ambulance, 565-6411; Molokai, police, 553-5355, fire 553-5401, ambulance 553-5911; Hawaii, police (Hilo) 935-3311, fire 961-6022, ambulance 961-6022; all no charge.

Coast Guard Rescue: Oahu, 536-4336; Maui, 244-5256; Kauai, 245- 4521; Hawaii, 935-6370.

Civil defense: In case of natural disaster such as hurricanes or tsunamis call Oahu 523-

4121; Maui, 244-7721; Kauai, 245-4001; Hawaii, 935-0031.

Crisis and self-help centers: Oahu, 521-4555; Maui, 244-7407; Kauai, 245-7838; Hawaii, 329-9111.

Consumer protection: If you encounter problems finding accommodations, bad service, or downright rip-offs try the following, all on Oahu: Chamber of Commerce, 531-411; Hawaii Hotel Association, 923-0407; Office of Consumer Protection, 548-2540.

OTHER PRACTICALITIES

Time Zones
There is no "daylight saving time" observed in Hawaii. When daylight saving time is not in effect on the Mainland, Hawaii is two hours behind the West Coast, four hours behind the Midwest, and five hours behind the East Coast. Hawaii, being just east of the International Date Line, is almost a full day behind most Asian and Oceanic cities. Hours behind these countries and cities are: Japan, 19 hours; Singapore, 18 hours; Sydney, 20 hours; New Zealand, 22 hours; Fiji, 22 hours.

Electricity
The same electrical current applies in Hawaii as on the U.S. Mainland and is uniform throughout the islands. The system functions on 110 volts, 60 cycles of alternating current (AC). Appliances from Japan will work, but there is some danger of burn out, while those requiring the normal European current of 220 will not work.

MONEY AND FINANCES

Currency
U.S. currency is among the drabbest in the world. It's all the same size and color; those unfamiliar with it should spend some time getting acquainted so that they don't make costly mistakes. U.S. coinage in use is: $.01, $.05, $.10, $.25, $.50, and $1 (uncommon); paper currency is $1, $2, (uncommon), $5, $10, $20, $50, $100. Bills larger than $100 are not in common usage.

Banks
Full-service banks tend to open slightly earlier than Mainland banks, at 8:30 a.m. Mon. through Friday. Closing is at 3 p.m., except for late hours on Fri. when most banks remain open until 6 p.m. Of most value to travelers, banks sell and cash traveler's checks, give cash advances on credit cards, and exchange and sell foreign currency.

Traveler's Checks
TCs are accepted throughout Hawaii at hotels, restaurants, car rental agencies, and in most stores and shops. However, to be readily acceptable they should be in American currency. Some larger hotels that often deal with Japanese and Canadians will accept their currency. Banks accept foreign currency TCs, but it'll mean an extra trip and inconvenience. It's best to get most of your TCs in $20 denominations; anything smaller will mean too many, and anything larger can be hard to cash in smaller shops and boutiques. The most readily acceptable TCs in Hawaii (phone numbers—call collect if not an 800—for lost or stolen checks) include: American Express, 800-221-4950; MasterCard, (212) 974-5696; Visa, (800) 227-6830; Thomas Cook, (808) 523-0722; Citicorp, (516) 352-6000; and Bank of America, (800) 227-3460.

Credit Cards
More and more business is transacted in Hawaii using credit cards. Almost every form of accommodation, shop, restaurant, and amusement accepts them. For renting a car they're almost a must. With "credit card insurance" readily available, they're as safe as TCs and sometimes even more convenient. Write down the numbers of your cards in case they're stolen. Don't rely on them completely because there are some establishments that won't accept them, or perhaps won't accept the kind that you carry. The most readily accepted credit cards are MasterCard and Visa, followed by American Express, Diners Club, and Carte Blanche. Most banks will give you cash advances on your credit cards for a fee.

POST OFFICES

Post offices are located in all major towns and cities. Most larger hotels also offer limited postal services. Normal business hours are 8 or 8:30 a.m. until 4:30 or 5 p.m., Mon. through Fri., Sat. from 8 a.m. until noon.

MEASUREMENTS

Distance, weights, and measures

Hawaii like all of the U.S., employs the "English method" of measuring weights and distances. Basically, dry weights are in ounces and pounds; liquid measures are in ounces, quarts and gallons; and distances are measured in inches, feet, yards and miles. The metric system, based on units of 10, is known but is not in general use. The following conversion charts should be helpful.

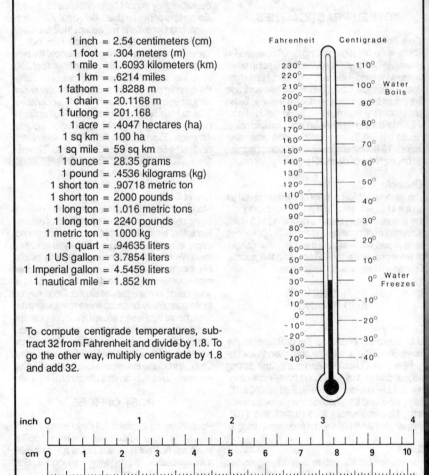

1 inch = 2.54 centimeters (cm)
1 foot = .304 meters (m)
1 mile = 1.6093 kilometers (km)
1 km = .6214 miles
1 fathom = 1.8288 m
1 chain = 20.1168 m
1 furlong = 201.168 m
1 acre = .4047 hectares (ha)
1 sq km = 100 ha
1 sq mile = 59 sq km
1 ounce = 28.35 grams
1 pound = .4536 kilograms (kg)
1 short ton = .90718 metric ton
1 short ton = 2000 pounds
1 long ton = 1.016 metric tons
1 long ton = 2240 pounds
1 metric ton = 1000 kg
1 quart = .94635 liters
1 US gallon = 3.7854 liters
1 Imperial gallon = 4.5459 liters
1 nautical mile = 1.852 km

To compute centigrade temperatures, subtract 32 from Fahrenheit and divide by 1.8. To go the other way, multiply centigrade by 1.8 and add 32.

Receiving Mail

The simplest way to receive mail is to have it sent to your lodgings if you're there long enough to receive it. Have it addresssed to you in care of your hotel or condo; include the room number if you know it. It'll be in your box at the front desk. If you plan frequent moves, or a multiple-island itinerary with short stays on each island, have mail sent "General Delivery" to a post office in a town you plan to visit. The P.O. will hold your mail in "general delivery" for 30 days. It takes about five days for a first-class letter to arrive in Hawaii from the Mainland. It's a good idea to notify the postmaster of the P.O. where you will be receiving mail when you expect to be there to pick it up. The third method is to have mail sent to you c/o American Express, 2222 Kalakaua Ave., Honolulu, HI 96815 (Hyatt Regency, Waikiki). This service is free for American Express card holders (sometimes they charge a small fee for others). They also forward mail for a $3 fee. You must visit Honolulu to pick up your mail, or phone them and send money to have it forwarded. Most people find this too awkward.

Zip Codes And Main Post Offices

The first three zip code digits, 967, are the same for all of Hawaii (except Honolulu is 968). The last two digits designate the particular post office. The following are the zip codes for the main P.Os. in Hawaii: Oahu, Honolulu (downtown, 3600 Aolele St.) 96820, Waikiki 96815; Kauai, Lihue 96766; Maui, Lahaina 96761, Kihei, 96753, Kahului, 96732; Molokai, Kaunakakai, 96748; Lanai, 96763; Hawaii, Hilo 96720, Kailua 96740.

NEWSPAPERS

Hawaii's two main English-language dailies are *The Honolulu Star Bulletin,* and *The Honolulu Advertiser.* The *Bulletin* has a circulation of just over 100,000, while the *Advertiser* is just under that figure. The Japanese-English *Hawaii Hochi* has a circulation of 10,000, and the Chinese *United Chinese Press* sells 1,000 per day. All are published on Oahu and available on other islands.

Weeklies And Magazines

There's a stampede of weeklies in Hawaii; all major islands have at least one and Oahu has at least six. On Kauai look for the *Kauai Times* and the slightly smaller *Garden Island.* The *Maui News,* published in Wailuku, reaches about 16,000 on Maui. The Big Island offers the *Hawaii Tribune Herald* out of Hilo with a circulation of 20,000, and *West Hawaii Today,* published in Kailua, reaches 6,000. All of these papers are great to see "what's happening" and to clip out money-saving coupons for restaurants, rentals, and amusements. A few military newspapers are printed on Oahu, along with the *Hawaii Times,* a Japanese-English paper reaching about 10,000 readers.

Over 20 magazines are published in Hawaii, but the ones with the most general interest are *Honolulu, Hawaii Business,* and *Waikiki Beach Press* (free).

Tourist Publications And Free Literature

On every island, at airports, hotel lobbies, shopping malls, and along the main streets are racks filled with free magazines, pamphlets, and brochures. Sometimes the sheer volume is overwhelming, but most have up-to-the-minute information on "what's happening," and many money-saving coupons. They're also loaded with maps and directions to points of interest. The best, published in a convenient narrow format, are *This Week ... Oahu, Maui, Kauai, Big Island,* published weekly. *Spotlight,* published weekly for the main islands is also good, offering information with a strong emphasis on sightseeing. *Guide to ...* all major islands is in normal magazine format, with good maps. There are also regional magazines such as *Maui Gold* and Harry Lyon's *Kona Coast* that are well worth checking out.

TIDBITS: OFFICIAL AND UNOFFICIAL

Official Hawaii

The state flower is the hibiscus. Over 5,000 species grow in Hawaii. It's tree is the *kukui.* This candlenut was one of the most useful trees of old Hawaii, providing food, medicine, and light. The bird is the *nene,* a modified goose that came to Hawaii eons ago and adapted to the rugged terrain, becoming a permanent resident and losing its instinct for migration. The humpback whale that visits Hawaii every year was made the official mammal in 1979. The nickname is "The Alo-

LARGEST CITIES/TOWNS

Island	Town/City	Pop.
Oahu	Aiea	33,000
	Honolulu	400,000
	Kailua	36,000
	Kaneohe	30,000
	Pearl City	43,000
	Wahiawa	17,000
	Waipahu	30,000
Maui	Kahului	13,000
	Kihei	5,700
	Lahaina	7,300
	Wailuku	10,300
Hawaii	Captain Cook	2,100
	Hilo	35,300
	Kailua-Kona	4,900
Kauai	Hanamalu	3,300
	Kapaa	4,500
	Kekaha	3,300
	Lihue	4,100
Molokai	Kaunakakai	2,300
Lanai	Lanai City	2,100
Nihau		250

ha State." The motto, *Ua mau ke ea o ka aina i ka pono* ("The life of the land is perpetuated in righteousness"), came from King Kamehameha III, when in 1843 Hawaii was restored to sovereignty after briefly being seized by the British. The anthem, "Hawaii Pono," was written by the "Merry Monarch," King Kalakaua, and put to music by the royal bandmaster, Henri Berger, in 1876. "Hawaii Pono" at one time was the anthem of the Kingdom of Hawaii and later the Territory before becoming the official state anthem.

Little-known Facts

The Hawaiian Islands, from Kure Atoll in the north to The Big Island in the south, stretch 1,600 miles. South Point *(Ka Lae)* on the Big Island is the southernmost point of the U.S. The islands are 25 million years old and are entirely made from volcanic activity. There's about as much land mass as New Jersey. Haleakala on Maui is the world's largest inactive volcano, while Hawaii's Mauna Loa is the world's largest active volcano, and Kilauea is *the* most active volcano in the world. Kauai's Mount Waialeale is the wettest spot on Earth, receiving over 600 inches of rain per year. Honolulu's Iolani Palace is the only "Royal Palace" in the U.S. Hawaii had the first company (C. Brewer), American school (Lahainaluna), newspaper *(Sandwich Island Gazette)*, bank (First Hawaiian) and church (Pukoo, Molokai) west of the Rocky Mountains.

Tidbits

American Captains Shaler and Cleveland brought the first horses aboard the *Lydia Byrd*, and introduced them at Lahaina in 1803. Two were given to Kamehameha the Great, who was not impressed. Tatooing was common in old Hawaii; many people had the date of the death of a loved one tatooed on their body, and gouged their eyes and knocked out their own teeth as a sign of mourning. The greatest insult was to inlay a spittoon with the teeth of a defeated enemy. The name of the channel between Maui and Kahoolawe, *Kealaikahiki,* means "the way to Tahiti." Voyagers got their bearings here for the long voyage south. "It will happen when Boki comes back" means something is impossible. Boki was a chief who sailed away in 1829 looking for sandalwood. He never returned. Only 20 of the 500 who sailed with him made it back to Hawaii.

OAHU

"... but a diversion, the most common is upon the water . . .
the men lay themselves flat upon an oval piece of plank . . .
they wait the time for the greatest swell that sets on shore,
and altogether push forward with their arms to keep on its
top, it sends them in with a most astonishing velocity. . .

—James King, c. 1779

INTRODUCTION

It is the destiny of certain places on Earth to be imbued with an inexplicable magnetism, a power that draws people whose visions and desires combine at just the right moment to create a dynamism so strong that it becomes history. The result for these "certain places" is greatness . . . and Oahu is one of these.

It is difficult to separate Oahu from its vibrant metropolis, Honolulu, whose massive political, economic, and social muscle dominates the entire state, let alone its home island. But to look at Honolulu *as* Oahu is to look only upon the face of a great sculpture, ignoring the beauty and subtleness of the whole. Just the words "Honolulu, Waikiki, Pearl Harbor" conjure up visions common to people the world over. Immediately imaginations flush with palm trees swaying, a healthy tan, bombs dropping with infamy, and a golden moon rising romantically over coiled lovers on a white-sand beach.

Oahu is called the "Gathering Place," and to itself it has indeed gathered the noble memories of old Hawaii, the vibrancy of a bright-eyed fledgling state, and the brawny power so necessary for its future. On this amazing piece of land adrift in the great ocean, 800,000 people live; five times that number visit yearly, and as time passes Oahu remains strong as one of those "certain places."

OVERVIEW

Oahu is partly a tropical garden bathed by soft showers and sunshine, and swaying with a gentle but firm rhythm. You can experience this feeling all over the island, even in pockets of downtown Honolulu and Waikiki. However, its other side is brash—dominated by the confidence of a major American city perched upon the Pacific Basin whose music is a pounding staccato jackhammer, droning bulldozer, and mechanical screech of the ever-building crane. The vast majority of first-time and return visitors land at Honolulu International and spend at least a few days on Oahu, usually in Waikiki.

People are amazed at the diversity of experiences the island has to offer. Besides the obvious (and endless) beach activities, there are museums, botanical gardens, a fantastic zoo

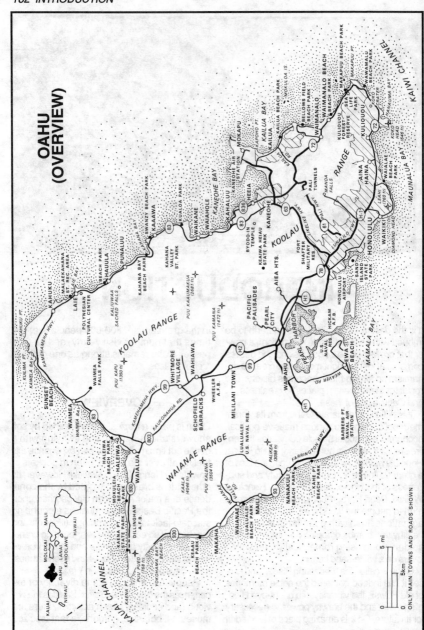

OAHU
(OVERVIEW)

ONLY MAIN TOWNS AND ROADS SHOWN

Waikiki

and aquarium, nightclubs, extravagant shows, free entertainment, cultural classes, theaters, sporting events, a major university, historical sights galore, an exotic cosmopolitan atmosphere, backcountry trekking, and an abundance of camping—all easily accessible via terrific public transportation. Finally, to sweeten the pot, Oahu can easily be the least expensive of the Hawaiian islands to visit.

Waikiki

Loosely, this world-famous beach is a hunk of land bordered by the **Ala Wai Canal** and running eastward to **Diamond Head.** Early last century these two golden miles were little more than a string of dirty beaches backed by a mosquito-infested swamp. Until 1901, when the Moana Hotel was built, only Hawaii's few remaining *ali'i* and a handful of wealthy *kamaaina* families had homes here. Now, over 125 hotels and condos provide more than 35,000 rooms, and if you placed a $20 bill on the ground, it would barely cover the land that it could buy!

This hyperactive area will delight and disgust you, excite and overwhelm you, but never bore you. Waikiki gives you the feeling that you've arrived *someplace*. Besides lolling on the beach and walking the gauntlet of restaurants, hotels, malls, and street merchants, you can visit the **Waikiki Aquarium** or **Honolulu Zoo.** Ever-present Diamond Head, that monolith of frozen lava so symbolic of Hawaii, is a few minutes' drive and a leisurely stroll to its summit. Head eastward around the bulge passing exclusive residential areas and you quickly find a string of secluded beaches. Around this tip you pass **Koko Head Crater,** a trekker's haven, **Hanauma Bay,** an underwater conservation park renowned for

magnificent family-class snorkeling, **Sea Life Park,** an extravaganza of the deep, and the sleepy village of **Waimanalo Beach.** Nearby at **Bellow's Beach** is camping, where it's hard to believe the city is just 12 miles back.

Downtown Honolulu

Head for downtown and give yourself a full day to catch all the sights. It's as if a huge grappling hook, attached to the heart of a Mainland city, hauled it down to the sea. But don't get the idea that it's not unique, because it is! You'll find a delightful mixture of quaintly historic and future-shock new, exotic, and ordinary. Town center is **Iolani Palace,** the only royal palace in America, heralded by the gilded statue of Kamehameha I. In an easy walking radius is the **State Capitol** and attendant government buildings. Chrome and glass skyscrapers holding the offices of Hawaii's economically mighty shade small stone and wooden structures from last century: **Mission Houses Museum, Kawaiiahao Church,** and **St. Andrew's Cathedral.**

Down at the harbor **Aloha Tower** greets the few passenger ships that still make port; nearby is the floating museum ship, *Falls of Clyde,* a nostalgic reminder of simpler times. Hotel Street takes you to old but not always venerable **Chinatown,** filled with alleyways housing tiny temples, herbalists, aromatic markets, inexpensive eateries, rough nightspots, dives, and the strong, distinctive flavor of transplanted Asia.

If the hustle and bustle gets to be too much, head for **Foster Botanical Gardens.** Or hop a special London bus for the serenity of the **Bishop Museum and Planetarium,** undoubtedly *the best* Polynesian cultural and anthropological museum in the world.

Pearl Harbor

Hawaii's only interstate, H-1, runs west of city center to Pearl Harbor. You can't help noticing the huge military presence throughout the area, and it becomes clear why Hawaii is considered the most militarized state in the Union. The attraction here, which shouldn't be missed, is the **USS *Arizona* Memorial.** The museum, visitors center, and tours, operated jointly by the U.S. Navy and the National Park Service, are both excellent and free.

Heading For The Hills

Behind the city looms the **Koolau Range.** As you head for these beckoning hills, you can side-trip over to the **University of Hawaii,** with its attendant **East West Center,** while passing through Manoa Valley, epitome of the "good life" in Hawaii. Route 61 takes you up and over Nuuanu Pali to Oahu's windward side. En route you'll pass **Punchbowl,** an old crater holding some of the dead from WW II and the Korean and Vietnam wars in the **National Cemetery of the Pacific.**

As you climb, the road passes the **Royal Mausoleum,** final resting place for some of Hawaii's last kings, queens, and nobility. Then comes **Queen Emma's Summer Palace,** a Victorian home of gentility and lace. Next is **Nuuanu Pali,** where Kamehameha drove 16,000 Oahu warriors over the cliff, sealing his dominance of the island kingdom with their blood. The view is hauntingly beautiful as the mountains drop suddenly to the coast of windward Oahu.

Windward Oahu

On the windward side, **Kailua** and **Kaneohe** have become suburban bedroom communities for Honolulu; this entire coast has few tourist accommodations, so it remains relatively uncrowded. The beaches are excellent, with beach parks and camping spots one after another, and the winds make this side off the island perfect for sailboarding. North of Kaneohe is **Valley of the Temples,** where a Christian cross sits high on a hill, and Buddha rests calmly in **Byodo-In Temple.**

Just up Rt. 83, the coastal highway, comes **Waiahole,** Oahu's outback, where tiny farms and taro patches dot the valleys, and local folks move with the slow beat of bygone days. A quick succession of beaches follow, many rarely visited by more than a passing fisherman. **Punaluu** town follows, offering some of the only accommodations along this coast, and a lovely walk to **Kaliuwaa,** the Sacred Falls. In **Laie** is the **Polynesian Cultural Center,** operated by the Mormon Church. **Brigham Young University** is here too, along with a solid Mormon temple that's open to visitors.

Northern Tip

North Shore is famous for magnificent surf. From **Sunset Beach** to **Haleiwa,** world-class surfers come to be challenged by the liquid thunder of the **Banzai Pipeline** and **Waimea Bay.** Art shops, boutiques, tiny restaurants, and secluded hideaways line these sun-drenched miles. At the far western end is **Dillingham Airfield** where you can take a glider or air tour of the island. The road ends with a very rugged jeep trail leading to **Kaena Point,** renowned for the most monstrous surf on the North Shore.

Northwest

The northwestern end of the island is the **Waianae Coast.** The towns of **Maili, Waianae,** and **Makaha** are considered the last domain of the locals of Oahu. This coastal area has escaped development so far, and it's one of the few places on the island where ordinary people can afford to live near the beach. Sometimes an attitude of resentment spills over against tourists; mostly though, lovely people with good hearts live here who will treat you as nicely as you're willing to treat them.

World-class surfing beaches along this coast are preferred by many of the best-known surfers from Hawaii. Many work as lifeguards in the beach parks, and they all congregate for the annual surfing championships held in Makaha. Here is a perfect chance to mingle with the people and soak up some of the last real aloha left on Oahu.

THE LAND

When Papa, the Hawaiian earth mother, returned from vacationing in Tahiti, she was less than pleased. She had learned through a gossiping messenger that her husband, Wakea, had been playing around. Besides simple philandering, he'd been foolish enough to impregnate Hina, a lovely young goddess who bore him island children. Papa, scorned and furious, showed Wakea that two could play the same game by taking a handsome young lover, Lua. Their brief interlude yielded the man-child Oahu, sixth of the great island children. Geologically, Oahu is the second oldest main island after Kauai. It emerged from beneath the waves as hissing lava a few million years after Kauai, and cooled a little quicker than Papa's temper to form Hawaii's third largest island.

LAND FACTS

Oahu has a total land area of 608 square miles, and measured from its farthest points is 44 miles long by 30 miles wide. The 112-mile coastline holds the two largest harbors in the state, **Honolulu** and **Pearl**. The **Koolau Mountains** run north-south for almost the entire length of the island, dramatically creating windward and leeward Oahu. The **Koolau Range** is smaller, confined to the northwestern section of the island. It too runs north-south, dividing the **Waianae Coast** from the massive **Leilehua Plateau** of the interior. **Mount Ka'ala**, at 4,020 feet in the northern portion of the Koolaus, is Oahu's highest peak. The huge Leilehua Plateau is still covered in pineapple and sugar cane, and lies between the two mountain ranges; it runs all the way from Waialua on the north shore to Ewa, just west of Pearl Harbor. At its widest point, around Schofield Barracks, it's more than six miles across.

Oahu's most impressive natural features were formed after the heavy volcanic activity ceased and erosion began to sculpt the island. The most obvious is the wall-like cliffs of the **Pali**—mountain heads eroded by winds from the east, valleys cut by streams from the west. Perfect examples of these eroded valleys are **Nuuanu** and **Kalihi**. Other impressive examples are **Diamond Head**, **Koko Head**, and **Punchbowl**, three "tuff-cone" volcanoes created after the heavy volcanic activity of early Oahu. A tuff cone is volcanic ash cemented together to form solid rock. Diamond Head is the most dramatic, formed after a minor eruption about 100,000 years ago and rising 760 feet from its base.

Oahu has the state's longest stream, **Kaukonahua**, which begins atop Puu Kaaumakua at 2,681 feet in the central Koolaus and runs westward for over 30 miles through the Leilehua Plateau. En route, it bypasses the **Wahiawa Reservoir** which, at 302 acres, forms the second largest body of fresh water in Hawaii. Nuuanu Pali Reservoir is another large body of water, and along with Wahiawa Reservoir provides excellent freshwater fishing spots (see p. 169), but there are no natural bodies of water on Oahu. Hikers should be aware of the uncountable streams and rivulets that can quickly turn from trickles to torrents, causing flash floods in valleys that were the height of hospitality only minutes before. Oahu's tallest waterfalls are 80-foot **Kaliuwaa** (Sacred Falls), just west of Punaluu, and **Waihee Falls**, in the famous Waimea Park on the North Shore, that has a sheer drop of over 40

AVERAGE MAXIMUM/MINIMUM TEMPERATURE AND RAINFALL

Town		Jan.	Mar.	May	June	Sept.	Nov.
Honolulu	High	80	82	84	85	82	81
	Low	60	62	68	70	71	68
	Rain	4	2	0	0	0	4
Kaneohe	High	80	80	80	82	82	80
	Low	67	62	68	70	70	68
	Rain	5	5	2	0	2	5
Waialua	High	79	79	81	82	82	80
	Low	60	60	61	63	62	61
	Rain	2	1	0	0	1	3

N.B. Rainfall in inches; temperature in Fahrenheit

feet. Oahu's main water concern is that usage is outstripping supply, and major municipal water shortages are expected by the year 2000 unless conservation measures and new technology are employed.

THE CLIMATE

Oahu, like all the Hawaiian islands, has equitable weather year-round with the average daily temperature about 80° F. The mountainous interior experiences about the same temperatures as the coastal areas because of the small difference in elevation. However, the **Pali** is known for strong, chilly winds that rise up the mountainside from the coast.

Precipitation is the biggest differentiating factor in the climate of Oahu. Generally, the entire leeward coast, from Makaha to Koko Head, is dry. Rain falls much more frequently and heavily in the Koolau Mountains and along the windward coast. Although rain can occur at any time of year, it is more plentiful in winter. Huge surf also pummels the North Shore during this period, closing off many beaches to the neophyte, but making them absolutely perfect for expert surfers. The maxim throughout the islands is "don't let rain spoil your day." If it's raining, simply move on to the next beach, or around to the other side of the island where it'll probably be dry. You can most often depend on the beaches of Waikiki and Waianae to be sunny and bright.

FAUNA

You would think that with Oahu's dense human population, little room would be left for animals. In fact, they are environmentally stressed, but they do survive. The interior mountain slopes are home to **wild pigs,** and a small population of **feral goats** survive in the Waianae Range. Migrating **whales** pass by, especially along the leeward coast where they can be observed from lookouts ranging from Waikiki to Koko Head. Half a dozen introduced game birds are found around the island, but Oahu's real animal wealth is its indigenous birdlife.

BIRDS

The shores around Oahu, including those off Koko Head and Sand Island, but especially on the tiny islets of Moku Manu and Manana on the windward side, are home to thriving colonies of marine birds. On these diminutive islands it's quite easy to spot a number of birds from the **tern** family including the white, gray, and sooty tern. All have distinctive screeching voices, and an approximate wingspan of 30 inches. Part of their problem is that they have little fear of humans. Along with the terns are **shearwaters.** These birds have a normal wingspan of about 36 inches and make a series of moans and wails, oftentimes while in flight. For some reason they're drawn to the bright lights of the city, where they fall prey to house cats and automobiles. Sometimes Moku Manu even attracts an enormous **Laysan albatross** with its seven-foot wingspan. **Tropic birds** with their lovely streamer-like tails are quite often seen along the windward coast.

To catch a glimpse of exotic birds on Oahu you don't have to head for the sea or the hills. The city streets and beach parks are constantly aflutter with wings. Black **myna birds** with their sassy yellow eyes are common mimics around town. **Sparrows,** introduced to Hawaii through Oahu in the 1870s, are everywhere, while *munia,* first introduced as cage birds from South East Asia, have escaped and are generally found anywhere around the island. Another escaped cage bird from Asia is the **bulbul,** a natural clown that perches on any likely city roost and draws attention to itself with loud calls and generally ridiculous behavior.

tropic bird

If you're lucky, you can also catch a glimpse of the *pueo* (Hawaiian Owl) in the mountainous areas of Waianae and the Koolaus. Also, along trails and deep in the forest from Tantalus to the Waianae Range you can sometimes see elusive native birds like the *elepaio, amakihi,* and the fiery red but very rare *i'iwi.*

Oahu also is home to a number of game birds mostly found in the dry upland forests. These include two varieties of **dove,** the **Japanese quail,** both the **green** and **ring-necked pheasant,** and **Erkel's francolin.** Hunting of these birds occurs year-round and information can be had by contacting the Oahu branch of the Division of Forestry and Wildlife.

NATIONAL WILDLIFE REFUGES

Two areas at opposite ends of the island have been set aside as national wildlife refuges (NWR): **James Campbell NWR,** above the town of Kahuku on the extreme northern tip; **Pearl Harbor NWR,** at the harbor entrance. Both were established in the mid '70s and are managed by the U.S. Fish and Wildlife Service. They serve mainly as wetland habitats for the endangered Hawaiian gallinule *(alae'ula),* stilt *(aeo),* and coot *(alae ke'oke'o).* Clinging to existence, these birds should have a future as long as their nesting grounds remain undisturbed.

These refuges also attract a wide variety of other birds, mostly introduced species such as **cattle egrets, herons,** a few species of **doves,** *munia, cardinals,* and the common **finch.**

Much of the area within the refuges are natural marshlands, but ponds, complete with water-regulating pumps and dikes, have been built. The general public is not admitted to these areas without permission from the refuge managers. For more information, and to arrange a visit, contact Refuge Manager, Hawaiian and Pacific Islands NWR, U.S. Fish and Wildlife Service, Federal Bldg., Room 5302, Box 50167, Honolulu, HI 96850.

Note: Oahu is like one huge tropical garden and has been planted with almost every type of flower, tree, fern, and fruit found in the islands. For a description of this flora please see the general introduction "Fauna and Flora."

GOVERNMENT

Oahu has been the center of government for about 150 years, since King Kamehameha III permanently established the royal court there in the 1840s. In 1873-74, King David Kalakaua built Iolani Palace as the central showpiece of the island kingdom. Liliuokalani, the last Hawaiian monarch, lived after her dethronement in the nearby residence, Washington Place. While Hawaii was a territory, and for a few years after it became a state, the palace was used as the capitol building, the governor residing in Washington Place. Modern Oahu, besides being the center of state government, governs itself as the **City and County of Honolulu.** The county not only covers the entire island of Oahu, but all the far-flung Northwest Islands, except for Midway, which is under federal jurisdiction.

State Representation

Oahu has four times as many people as the other islands combined. Nowhere is this more evident than in the representation of Oahu in the State House and Senate. Oahu claims 19 of the 25 state senators, and 39.7 of the 51 state representatives. (The 0.7 state representative covers the split district of the north Waianae area of Oahu, and the north shore of Kauai chips in with the remainder 0.3 of the representative). These lopsided figures make it obvious that Oahu has plenty of clout, especially Honolulu urban districts, which elect more than 50% of Oahu's representatives.

Frequent political battles ensue, since what's good for the city and county of Honolulu isn't always good for the rest of the state. More often than not, the political moguls of Oahu, backed by huge business interests, prevail. The Oahu state

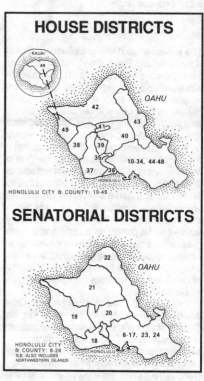

senators are overwhelmingly Democratic, except for three Republicans, all from the Honolulu urban districts. State representation is similar: only nine are Republicans, all from urban Honolulu or the suburban communities around Kailua.

ECONOMY

Economically, Oahu also dwarfs the rest of the islands combined. It generates income from government spending, tourism, and agriculture. A huge military presence, an international airport that receives the lion's share of visitors, and unbelievably, half of the state's best arable lands keep Oahu in the economic catbird seat. The famous Big Five Corporations all maintain their corporate offices in downtown Honolulu from which they oversee vast holdings throughout Hawaii and the Mainland. Located in about the same spots as when their founders helped to overthrow the monarchy, things are about the same as then, except that they're going strong, while the old royalty of Hawaii has vanished.

MILITARY AND GOVERNMENT SPENDING

Hawaii is the most militarized state in the Union, and Oahu is the most militarized island in the state. It all started in 1872, when General Schofield declared Pearl Harbor an essential base for maintaining military strength in the Pacific. Shortly after the turn of the century, Pearl was dredged by the Navy, the Army was firmly ensconced at Schofield Barracks, and Hawaii's military fate was sealed.

All four branches of the Armed Forces are represented on the island, and Camp H.M. Smith, overlooking Pearl Harbor, is HQ for CINCPAC, Commander in Chief, Pacific. CINCPAC oversees the largest strategic area in the world, ranging from both poles and from the west of South America across the entire Pacific to the Bay of Bengal. A full 25% of Oahu is owned or controlled by the military; the largest landholder is the Army, with over 100,000 acres. Much of this land, used for maneuvers, is off-limits to the public. Besides Pearl, so obviously dominated by battleship gray, the largest military lands are around Schofield Barracks, and the Kahuku-Kawailoa Training Area. About 62,000 military personnel, and at least that same number of their dependents, live on Oahu, which accounts for over 99% of the servicemen and women based in the state. Moreover, a corps of 20,000 civilians work directly for the armed services, with many more employed indirectly. Non-military government spending chips into the pot, and together the amount of money generated is astronomical.

TOURISM

The flow of visitors to Oahu has remained unabated ever since tourism outstripped sugar and pineapples in the early 1960s and became Hawaii's top money-maker. Of the nearly five million people that visit the state yearly, two-thirds stay on Oahu; almost all the rest, en route to the Neighbor Islands, at least pass through. Hotels directly employ over 15,000 workers, half the state's total, not including all the shop assistants, waiters and waitresses, taxi drivers, and everyone else needed to ensure a carefree vacation. Of Hawaii's 58,000 hotel rooms, Oahu claims 34,000. Tourism generates over $2 billion of yearly revenue, and this is only the amount that can be directly related to the hotel and restaurant trades. With the flow of visitors seemingly endless, Oahu has a bright economic future.

AGRICULTURE

You'd think that with all the people living on Oahu, coupled with the constant land development, there'd hardly be any room left for things to grow. But that's not the case. The land is productive, though definitely stressed. One startling example is in downtown Honolulu and Waikiki, where so many trees were removed to build parking lots that the asphalt becomes overheated from the lack of shade, allowing temperatures, once moderated by the trade winds, to rise demonstrably. Changing times and attitudes led to a "poi famine" that hit Oahu in 1967 because very few people were interested in the hard work of farming this staple. However, with half the state's best arable land, Oahu manages to produce a considerable amount of sugar cane, pineapple, and the many products of diversified agriculture.

Sugar lands account for 33,000 acres, most owned by the James Campbell Estate, located around Ewa, north and west of Pearl Harbor, with some acreage around Waimea and Waialua on the north shore. Pineapples cover 11,500

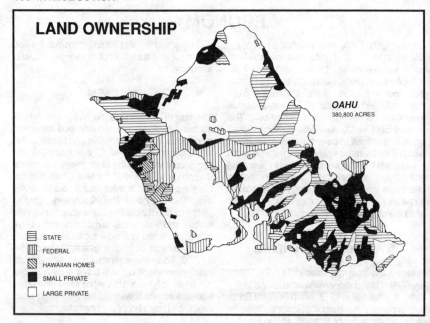

LAND OWNERSHIP

OAHU
380,800 ACRES

▤ STATE
▥ FEDERAL
▧ HAWAIIAN HOMES
■ SMALL PRIVATE
□ LARGE PRIVATE

acres, with the biggest holdings in the Leilehua Plateau belonging to Dole, a subsidiary of Castle and Cook. In the hills, entrepreneurs raise *paka-lolo,* which has become the state's most productive cash crop. Oahu is also a huge agricultural consumer, demanding more than four times as much vegetables, fruits, meats, and poultry to feed its citizens and visitors than the remainder of the state combined.

THE PEOPLE

For most visitors, regardless of where they've come from, Oahu (especially Honolulu) will be the first place they've ever encountered such an integrated multi-racial society. Various countries may be cosmopolitan, but nowhere will you meet so many individuals from such a diversity of ethnic groups, and mixes of these groups. You could be driven to your hotel by a Chinese-Portuguese cab driver, checked in by a Japanese-Hawaiian clerk, served lunch by a Korean waiter, serenaded by a Hawaiian-Italian-German musician, while an Irish-English-Filipino-French chambermaid tidies your room.

This racial symphony is evident throughout Hawaii, but it's more apparent on Oahu where the large population creates more opportunity for a racial hodgepodge. The warm feeling you get almost immediately upon arrival is that everyone belongs.

Population Figures

Oahu's 800,000 residents account for 80% of the state's population. All these people are on an island comprising only 10% of the state's land total, which adds up to nearly 1,600 people per square mile, eight times that of California. Sections of Waikiki can have a combined population of permanent residents and visitors as high as 90,000 per square mile, making cities like Tokyo, Hong Kong, and New York seem quite roomy by comparison. The good news is that Oahu *expects* all these people and knows how to accommodate them comfortably.

About 400,000 people live in greater Honolulu, generally considered the built-up area from Ewa to Koko Head. The next most populous urban centers after Honolulu are the Kailua-Kaneohe area with about 100,000 residents, fol-

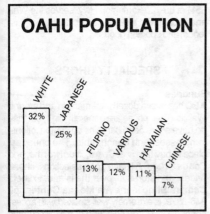

OAHU POPULATION

WHITE **32%**

JAPANESE **25%**

FILIPINO **13%**

VARIOUS **12%**

HAWAIIAN **11%**

CHINESE **7%**

lowed by Pearl City and Waipahu with a combined total of about 75,000 or so. With all of these people, and such a finite land resource, real estate on the island is sky high. A typical one-family home sells for $180,000, while a

condo averages about $110,000. And around plenty of prime real estate, these figures would barely cover the down payment!

So where is everybody? Of the major ethnic groups you'll find the Hawaiians clustered around Waianae and on the windward coast near Waiahole; the whites tend to be in Wahiawa, around Koko Head, in Waikiki, and in Kailua-Kaneohe; those of Japanese ancestry prefer the valleys heading toward the Pali, including Kalihi, Nuuanau, and Tantalus; Filipinos live just east of the airport, in downtown Honolulu, around Barbers Point, and in Wahiawa; and the Chinese are in Chinatown and around the Diamond Head area. Of the minor ethnic groups the highest concentration of blacks is in the Army towns around Schofield Barracks; Samoans live along with the Hawaiians in Waianae and the windward coastal towns, though the heaviest concentration is in downtown Honolulu not far from Aloha Tower; Koreans and Vietnamese are scattered here and there, but mostly in Honolulu.

SHOPPING

You can't come to Oahu and *not* shop. Even if the idea of it doesn't thrill you, the lure of almost endless shops offering every imaginable kind of merchandise will sooner or later tempt even the most "big-waste-of-time" mumbler through their doors. So why fight it? And if you're the other type, who feels as though a day without shopping is like being marooned on a deserted island, you can count on being rescued on Oahu, because everywhere on the horizon is "a sale, a sale!"

You can use "much much more" as either an aspersion or a tribute when describing Oahu, and nowhere does this qualifier fit better than when describing its shopping. Over a dozen major and minor shopping centers and malls are in Honolulu and Waikiki alone! Population centers around the island, including those in the interior, the South Shore, windward shore, and North Shore, all have shopping centers in varying degrees—at the very least, a parking lot rimmed with a half-dozen shops that can provide immediate necessities.

On the Neighbor Islands, a major shopping mall is usually found only in the island's main city, with mom 'n' pop stores and small super-

ettes taking up the slack. On Oahu, you've got these too, but you're never very far from some serious shopping centers. The tourist trade fosters the sale of art and artifacts, jewelry and fashions, and numerous boutiques selling these are strung around the island like a shell necklace. Food costs, in supermarkets, tend to be reasonable because Oahu is the main distribution center, and with all the competition, prices in general seem to be lower than on the other islands. If your trip to Hawaii includes a stop on Oahu, do most of your shopping here, because of the cut-rate prices and much greater availability of goods. When most Hawaiians go on a shopping spree, they head for Oahu.

The following listings are general; refer to "Shopping" in the travel sections for listings of specific shops, stores, and markets.

SHOPPING CENTERS

Honolulu Shopping Centers

Since it serves as the main terminal for TheBus, you could make a strong case that **Ala Moana Shopping Center** (see p. 255), under considerable renovation, is the heart of shopping on

Oahu. At one time billed as the largest shopping center in the country, today it settles for being the largest in the state, with its hundreds of stores covering 50 acres. It's on Ala Moana Blvd., just across from the Ala Moana Beach Park. **The Ward Warehouse** (see p.256) is just a few blocks west of the Ala Moana Center, at 1050 Ala Moana Boulevard. The **Ward Center** (see p. 257) on Ala Moana across from Ward Warehouse, is a relatively new shopping center that's gaining a reputation for some exclusive shops.

Waikiki Shopping

Shopping in Waikiki (see p. 294) is as easy as falling off a surfboard. In two or three blocks of Kuhio and Kalakaua avenues are no less than seven shopping centers. If that's not enough, there are hundreds of independent shops, plus plenty of street vendors. Main shopping centers include **Royal Hawaiian Shopping Center,** the **Waikiki Shopping Plaza,** and the **International Market Place,** an open-air shopping bazaar across from the Moana Hotel at 2330 Kalakaua Ave., open daily from 9 a.m. until the vendors get tired at night.

The **Hyatt Regency Shopping Center** is located on the first three floors of the Hyatt Regency Hotel, at 2424 Kalakaua Ave., tel. 922-5522. The **King's Village** is at 131 Kaiulani Ave., the **Waikiki Trade Center** is on the corner of Seaside and Kuhio avenues, and the **Rainbow Bazaar** is a unique mall located at the Hilton Hawaiian Hotel, at 2005 Kalia Road.

Around The Island

Heading east from Waikiki on Rt. 72, the first shopping stop is the **Niu Shopping Center** on your left, about four miles before Hanauma Bay. The **Times Supermarket** is known for good prices. Also on the left is the **Koko Marina Shopping Center** (see p. 312), just before Hanauma Bay, with a Liberty House, a few art galleries, and **Foodland Supermarket. Kailua** and **Kaneohe** bedroom communities also have their share of shopping malls. Numerous shops are found along the North Shore from Haleiwa to Waimea, including surf, art, boutiques, and plenty of fast food and restaurants. The **Pearlridge Center** (see p. 304) in Pearl City at the corner of the Kamehameha Highway and Waimano Home Road is a full shopping complex with over 90 stores. The **Waianae Mall** (see p.

351) at 86-120 Farrington Hwy. serves the Waianae coast with a supermarket, drug store, fast foods, and sporting goods.

SPECIALTY SHOPS

Sundries

ABC has over a dozen mini-marts in and around Waikiki. Their prices are generally high, but they do have some good bargains on suntan lotions, sunglasses, and beach mats. The cheapest place to buy **film** is at **Sears, Woolworths,** and **Longs Drugs.** All have good selections, cheap prices, and stores all over the island. **Francis Camera Shop** in the Ala Moana Center, tel. 946-2879, is extremely well stocked with accessories. For a large selection of military surplus and camping goods try the **Big 88** at 330 Sand Island Access Rd., tel. 845-1688.

If gadgetry fascinates you, head for **Shirokiya Department Store** at the Ala Moana and Pearlridge centers and in Waikiki. Besides everything else, they have a wonderful selection of all the jimjicks and doohickeys that Nippon has to offer. The atmosphere is somewhat like a trade fair.

Those who can't imagine a tour with anything on their feet but Birkenstock can have their tootsies accommodated, but they won't be entirely happy. If you get a sole blowout, **Birkenstock Footprints** at Ala Moana Center, tel. 531-6014, will re-sole them for $14, but they want a full week to do it. For one-day service, they'll refer you to a shoemaker, **Joe Pacific** at the Ala Moana Center, tel. 946-2998, but he wants a toe-twisting $25 for the service!

Bookstores

Oahu has plenty of excellent bookstores. In Honolulu, try the **Honolulu Book Shops** with three locations, one at the Ala Moana Center, tel. 941- 2274, one in downtown Honolulu at 1001 Bishop St., tel. 537-6224, and one at the Pearlridge Center, at tel. 487-1548. **Waldenbooks** is at the Pearlridge Center, tel. 488-9488, Kahala Mall, tel. 737-9550, and Waikiki Shopping Plaza, tel. 922-4154. For a fine selection of Hawaiiana try the **Bishop Museum and Planetarium Bookshop,** at the Bishop Museum, 1525 Bernice St., tel. 847-3511, and at the **Mission Houses Museum** in downtown Honolulu at 553 S. King St., tel. 531-0481.

carver at International Market Place, Waikiki

Three women, Rachel McMahan, Janice Beam, and Kathryn Decker, have shopped their fingers to the bone for you and have written a small but definitive book entitled *The Shopping Bag*. It lists and describes shops all over Oahu, from art supplies to toys and sporting goods.

Arts And Crafts

The following are a few of Oahu's many art shops and boutiques, just to get you started. An excellent place to find original arts and crafts at reasonable prices is along **The Fence** surrounding the Honolulu Zoo fronting Kapiolani Park. Island artists come here every weekend from 10 a.m. to 4 p.m. to display and sell their artwork. The **Honolulu Academy of Arts** at 900 S. Beretania, open Tues.-Sat. 10 a.m.-4:30 p.m., Sun. 1-5 p.m., is not only great to visit (free), but has a fine gift shop that specializes in Asian art.

The same high-quality and authentic handicrafts are available in both the **Hawaiian Mission Houses Museum** and **Bishop Museum** gift shops (see "Bookstores" above). For Oriental art try **Gallery Mikado** and **Garakuta-Do,** both in Waikiki's Eaton Square Complex. **Ka'ala Art,** tel. 637-7533, in Haleiwa (see p. 342) is a great one-stop shop for fine arts, pop art, and handicrafts, all by aspiring island artists. Also in Haleiwa, the **Fettig Art Gallery,** tel. 637-4933, is the oldest gallery on the North Shore, featuring works by Beverly Fettig and other island artists. The **Punaluu Gallery,** tel. 237-8325, is the oldest gallery on the windward coast. It's been there over 30 years and is now operated by candle maker extraordinaire Scott Bechtol.

Flea Markets And Swap Meets

These are the cheapest places to find treasures. Two operate successfully on Oahu and have a regular following. **Aloha Flea Market,** tel. 732-2437, is at Aloha Stadium every Wed., Sat., and Sun. from 7 a.m.-3 p.m. It's the biggest flea market on Oahu, selling everything from bric-a-brac to real heirlooms and treasures. **Kam Swap Meet,** tel. 488-5822, Kam Drive-In Theater, 98-850 Moanalua Rd., Pearl City, is open Wed., Thurs., Sat., and Sun. mornings. Regular stall holders to housewives cleaning out the garage offer great fun and bargains.

Food Shopping

Around the island plenty of mom 'n' pop grocery stores provide fertile ground for a cultural exchange, but they're expensive. Oahu's large supermarkets include **Times, Safeway, Foodland,** and **Star Markets.** Preference is highly individual, but Times has a good reputation for fresh vegetables and good prices. Japanese **Holiday Mart** has stores around the island. They've got some bargains in their general merchandise departments, but because they try to be everything, their food section suffers, especially the fruits and vegetables.

A **Floating Farmer's Market** appears at different times and places around Honolulu. For example, on Wednesday mornings from 9:45 to 10:45 a.m., it's across the street from the main library at 478 S. King St., in downtown Honolulu. The vendors are mostly Filipino, who drive up in small battered trucks and sell wonderful fresh vegetables from their home plots at very reasonable prices. Big shots who bring in fruits and vegies from California and the like have been trying to weed these little guys out. The Honolulu Dept. of Parks regulates the time and place for the market, and you can get more information at tel. 527-6060.

Chinatown offers the **People's Open Market** at the Cultural Plaza, located at the corner of Mauna Kea and Beretania streets. Besides produce, you'll find fresh fish, meats, and poultry; the **Oahu Fish Market** is in the heart of Chinatown along King Street. The shops are run-down but clean, and sell everything from octopus to kimchi.

Health Food Stores

Brown rice and tofu eaters can keep that special sparkle in their eyes with no problem on Oahu, where there are some excellent health food stores. Most have a snack bar where you can get a delicious and nutritious meal for bargain prices (see "Food" in the various travel sections.) **Down to Earth,** 2525 S. King St., tel. 947-7678, is an old standby where you can't go wrong; great stuff at great prices. **Kokua Co-op Natural Foods And Grocery Store,** at the corner of S. Beretania and Isenberg, tel. 941-1921 is open to the public Mon.-Sat. 9 a.m-8 p.m. and Sun. 10 a.m.-7 p.m. Full service store with organic and fresh produce, cheese, milk, juices, bulk foods, and breads. **Celestial Natural Foods,** at the Haleiwa Shopping Plaza on the North Shore, tel. 637-6729, is also top-notch. **Kailua Health Foods** at 124 Oneawa in Kailua, tel. 261-0353, is small but well stocked, especially with detoxification products. **Vim and Vigor** is a small chain of health food stores with locations around the island; the main one is at the Ala Moana Center, tel. 955-3600, and others at Pearlridge Center and the Kahala and Kamehameha centers.

GETTING THERE

The old adage of "all roads leading to Rome" applies almost perfectly to Oahu, though instead of being cobblestones, they're sea lanes and air routes. Except for a handful of passenger ships still docking at Honolulu Harbor, and some limited nonstop flights to Maui and the Big Island, all other passengers to and from Hawaii are routed through **Honolulu International Airport.** These flights include direct flights to the Neighbor Islands, which means stopping over at Honolulu International and continuing on the same plane, or more likely changing to an inter-island carrier whose fare is included in the original price of the flight. See "Getting There" in the General Introduction for more information.

HONOLULU INTERNATIONAL AIRPORT

The state's only international airport is one of the busiest in the entire country, with hundreds of flights to and from cities around the world arriving and departing daily. In a routine year, over 15 million passengers utilize this facility. The two terminals (directions given as you face the main entranceway) are: the main terminal, accommodating all international and Mainland flights, with a small wing at the far left end of the ground floor for a few commuter airlines; and the inter-island terminal in a separate building at the far right end of the main terminal.

The ground floor of the **main terminal** is mostly for arriving passengers, and contains the baggage claim area, lockers and long-term storage, car rental agencies, and international and domestic arrival doors which are separate. The second floor is for departing passengers, with most activity centered here, including ticket counters, shops, lounges, baggage handlers, and the entrance to most of the gates. From both levels you can board taxis and TheBus to downtown Honolulu and Waikiki.

International carriers usually park on the right side of the main terminal and use gates 26 through 31, while gates six through 31, on the left, are used by domestic carriers. The peak hours for the airport are 7-11 a.m. and 5-7 p.m.

The **inter-island terminal** services flights aboard Hawaiian, and Aloha Airlines to and from Honolulu. It has its own snack bars, car rental booths, transportation to and from the city, lounges, information windows, and restrooms. It is only a leisurely five minutes stroll between the two terminals, which is fine if you don't have much baggage; if you do, there are plenty of shuttles every few minutes. If you are at the small commuter airlines terminal at the opposite end of the complex, shuttles ($.50) come regularly, but if you need one in a hurry just ask someone at the ticket booths there to summon one for you.

Services, Information, Tips

The main **information booth** is located on the second level just near the central escalators. Besides general information, they have good maps of the airport, Oahu, Honolulu, and Waikiki. The inquiry booths lined up along the ground level and at the inter-island terminal are also friendly and helpful, but not always stocked with as many maps as the main information booth.

The **lost and found** is located on the ground level of the main terminal, and at the inter-island terminal. The **post office** is across the street from the main entranceway toward the inter-island terminal.

Lockers are located on both levels of the main terminal and at the inter-island terminal, with a **baggage storage room** only on the ground floor of the main terminal. Locker rental is $1 for a 24-hour period, with a refundable $5 key deposit. You can rent lockers for a month or longer, but you must prepay and leave a deposit. The baggage storage accepts no personal checks, no prepayments, and no pets or perishables. You *must* have your claim ticket to retrieve your belongings. The service is well run, efficient, and unfriendly.

Money can be a hassle at the airport, especially getting change, which is a downright rip-off, and very bad public relations for visitors. Unfortunately, no one will give you change, putting you at the mercy of $1 bill-change machines located throughout the airport. These machines happily dispense $.85 for every $1 you put in, so if you want to make a phone call, or the like, you're out of luck. The snack bars will only change money for you with a purchase. For a state that prides itself on the aloha spirit and depends on good relations with its visitors, this is a ridiculously poor way of greeting people, or giving them a last impression before they return home. The **foreign currency exchange** is on the second floor of the main terminal along the concourse behind the United ticket window. Here, and at a few smaller exchanges on the ground floor, the charge is one percent per transaction on foreign currency, and the same on traveler's checks no matter where they're from, with a minimum charge of $1.50.

To refresh and relax, you might visit the **Shower Tree**, on the second floor behind the United counter, next to the hairdresser. You can have a shower for $7.50, which includes soap,

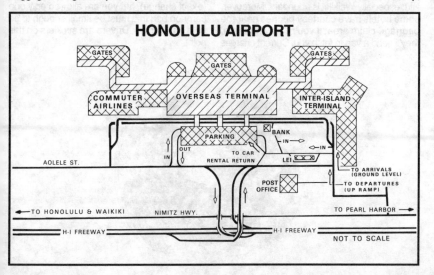

towel, shampoo, deodorant, and hair dryers; an eight-hour sleep in a private little room and a shower for $18.72; or a rest at $3 per hour. If this seems a bit pricy, just use the public bathrooms for a quick wash, then choose any one of three small gardens near the central concourse to take a little nap. If you're there just for a short snooze, airport security won't bother you.

Airport Transportation

Car rental agencies are lined up at booths on the ground floor of both terminals. Many courtesy phones for car rental agencies not at the airport are located in and around the baggage claim area; call for free vans to pick you up and take you to their nearby facility. This procedure even saves the hassle of maneuvering through heavy airport traffic—you usually wait at the island in the middle of the road just outside the baggage claim area. Make sure to specify the number of the area where you'll wait.

If you're driving to the airport to pick up or drop off someone, you should know about **parking.** If you want to park on the second level of the parking garage for departures, you must either take the elevator up to the fourth floor, or down to ground level, and from there cross the pedestrian bridge. There's no way to get across on levels two and three.

Public transportation to downtown Honolulu, especially Waikiki, is abundant. Moreover, some hotels have courtesy phones near the baggage claim area; if you're staying there, they'll send a van to fetch you. Current charges for taxis, vans, TheBus, and limos are posted just outside the baggage claim area, so you won't have to worry about being overcharged. **Taxis** to Waikiki cost about $15, not counting bags. **Grayline** runs a small bus or van to Waikiki for about $5 with no baggage charge. Also, a number of vans and motorcoaches leave from the central island in the roadway just outside the baggage claim. They charge $5, but a wait of up to 45 minutes for one is not out of the ordinary. Moreover, they drop passengers at hotels all over Waikiki, so if you're not one of the first stops by chance, it could be an hour or so after reaching Waikiki before you're finally deposited at your hotel.

Terminal Transportation, tel. 926-4747, offers hotel pick-up and a ride to the airport, including two standard pieces of luggage, for $5 adult, $2 child. **Em's Airport Shuttle,** tel. 545-1266, offers similar service from Waikiki every half-hour from 6 a.m. to 10 p.m. Or call **Airport Transportation,** tel. 261-7880 or 923-5700, adults $5, children 5-11 $2. They'll pick you up at a Waikiki hotel and bring you to the airport or vice versa.

You can take **TheBus** (# eight and # 20) to Waikiki via the Ala Moana Terminal, from which you can get buses all over the island. If you're heading north pick up bus numbers 20, 51, or 52 just outside the airport. TheBus only costs $.60 (exact change), but you are allowed only one carry-on bag that must be small enough to be held on your lap. Drivers are sticklers on this point.

GETTING AROUND

Touring Oahu is especially easy, since almost every normal (and not so normal) mode of conveyance is readily available. You can rent anything from a moped to a pedicab, and the competition is very stiff, which helps keep prices down. A few differences separate Oahu from the other islands. To begin with Oahu has a model public transportation system called TheBus— not only efficient, but very inexpensive. Also, Oahu is the only island that has a true expressway system, though along with it comes rush hour and traffic jams. A large part of Oahu's business is processing people, even if it's only to send them on to another island! The agencies operating these businesses on the island are masters at moving people down the road. With the huge volume of tourists that visit every year, it's amazing how smoothly it works. The following is a cross section of what's available and should help you to decide how you want to get around. Have fun! Also see p. 266 for more information about getting around in Waikiki.

CAR RENTALS

Every reputable national-, state-, and islandwide car rental agency is here, along with some car rental hucksters that'll hook you and land you like a *mahi mahi* if you're not careful. Most of the latter are located along the main tourist drags of Waikiki. The rule of thumb is, if their deal sounds too good to be true, it is. The competition is so fierce between the reputable agencies, however, that their deals are equally as good. Always check with your travel agency for big savings in fly/drive or stay/drive packages. Make sure your car comes with a flat daily rate and unlimited mileage. One of the hooks to lure you into renting a "bargain" car is to whack you with a mileage charge. Extra benefits from many firms include a free *Drive Guide* that has good maps and lists the island's main attractions; oftentimes you receive a booklet of coupons that entitle you to free or reduced prices on services, admissions, dining, and entertainment. Eight full pages of car rental agencies grace the Honolulu Yellow Pages, from firms that rent Mercedes convertibles down to low-budget operations with a few dented and dated Datsuns. Don't get the impression that the backyard firms are all rip-

offs. You can get some great deals, but you have to choose wisely and be willing to settle for a less than prestigious car.

Reserving a car on Oahu is doubly important because of the huge turnover that can occur at any time. Be aware of **drop-off charges;** for example, if you rent in Waikiki and leave the car at the airport, you'll be charged. It's convenient to rent a car at the airport. But it's also convenient to take an inexpensive shuttle to and from Waikiki, (see below) and rent there. Many of the firms have offices in Waikiki, and you can even rent a car from your hotel desk and have it delivered to you. This saves the obvious hassle of dealing with traffic and unfamiliar roads during arrival and departure, and avoids drop-off fees, but you don't always get the cheapest rates.

Agencies

A Hawaii-based company with an excellent reputation is **Tropical,** tel. 836-1176, in Waikiki tel. 949-2002, or (800) 367-5140 nationwide, (800) 352-3923 from the Neighbor Islands. Being based in Hawaii, they can take care of any problem on the spot without hassle. Tropical's personnel go out of their way to make your rental go smoothly by adding that "aloha touch." Prices are very competitive, and they can put you into anything from an economy car with no a/c, to a convertible, Cadillac, or European sports car.

National is one of the best with an airport location at 2965 N. Nimitz Hwy., tel. 836-2655, in Waikiki at 2160 Kalakaua Ave., tel. 922-6461, or toll-free at (800) 227-7368. Contact **Avis,** at the airport, tel. 836-5531, in Waikiki at tel. 836-5543, or (800) 331-1212; **Hertz,** has 11 locations around the island, including the airport at tel. 836-2511, or toll-free at (800) 654-8200. **Budget,** located at the airport, tel. 836-1700, with locations in Waikiki, or call central reservations at tel. 922-3600, or toll-free at (800) 527-0700.

Smaller but equally good firms include: **Sears,** accepting Sears credit cards, central reservations tel. 922-3805; **Thrifty,** airport tel. 836-2388, Waikiki tel. 923-7383, toll-free (800) 367-22-77; **Aloha Funway Rentals,** airport tel. 834-1016, Waikiki tel. 942-9696; **Holiday,** airport tel. 836-1974, Waikiki tel. 926-2752.

Cheaper firms offer bargain rates and older cars. Many of these rent without a major credit card, but require a stiff deposit. Sometimes they even rent to those under 21, but you'll have to show reservations at a major hotel. Some where you usually make out all right are: **Mal-Mat,** at 1111 Kapiolani Blvd., tel. 533-3986; **Alpert's Used Car Rentals,** tel. 955-4370; **Hawaii Discount,** tel. 536-1861; **AAA Rents,** 524- 8060.

If you're after a luxury car or a convertible try: **Convertibles Honolulu,** tel. 595-6170; and **Convertible Rentals,** featuring Mustangs, tel. 923-4131.

Four-wheel Drives And Mopeds

If you're into 4WDs try: **Odyssey Rentals,** tel. 947-8036; **United Car Rental,** tel. 922-4605; or **Aloha Funway Rentals,** tel. 834-1016.

Motorcycles and mopeds are available from: **Aloha Funway Rentals,** tel. 942-9696; **Continental Rent a Bike,** 923-7533; **Sunshine Moped Rentals,** tel. 923-6083; and **Odyssey Rentals,** tel. 947-8036.

OTHER ALTERNATIVES

Bicycles

Peddling around Oahu can be both fascinating and frustrating. The roads are well paved, but the shoulders are often torn up. Traffic in and around Honolulu is horrifying, and the only way to avoid it is by leaving very early in the morning. TheBus has no facilities for transporting your bike out of town, so an early departure is your only alternative. Once you leave the city, traffic, especially on the secondary interior roads, isn't too bad. Unfortunately, all of the coastal roads are heavily trafficked. You're better off renting a **cruiser** or **mountain bike,** which allow for the sometimes poor road conditions and open up the possibilities of off-road biking. But even experienced mountain bikers should be careful on Oahu trails, which are often extremely muddy and rutted. Pedaling around Waikiki, although congested, is usually safe, and a fun way of seeing the sights. Always lock your bike, and take your bike bag.

For info on biking on Oahu, contact **Hawaii Bicycling League,** Box 4403, Honolulu, HI 96813. This nonprofit corporation sponsors rides all over Oahu almost every weekend. Nonmembers are always welcome. The rides are multiple-level ability and are listed in the Hawaii Bicycling League's monthly newsletter, *Spoke-n-Words.* If you're into cycling and want a unique look at Oahu, don't miss these rides. See "Sightseeing Tours—Bicycling" for more info.

For bicycle rentals try: good old **Aloha Funway Rentals, tel. 942- 9696; The Bike Way,** at 655 Kapiolani Blvd., tel. 538-7433. For sales and repairs try: **The Bike Shop,** featuring Fuji, Mongoose, and Schwinn, at 1149 S. King St., tel. 531-7071; **McCully Bicycle,** featuring Specialized, Miyata, and Takara, at 1018 McCully St., tel. 955- 6329; and **The Bike Way,** featuring Bianchi and Univega, at 655 Kapiolani, tel. 538-7433.

TheBus

If Dorothy and her mates had TheBus to get them down the Yellow Brick Road, she might have chosen to stay in Oz and forget about Kansas. TheBus, TheBus, ThewonderfulBus is the always-coming, slow-moving, go-everywhere friend of the budget traveler. Operated by Mass Transit Lines (MTL) Inc., it could serve as a model of efficiency and economy in any city of the world. What makes it more amazing is that it all came together by chance, beginning as an emergency service in 1971. These brown, yellow, and orange coaches go up and down both the windward and leeward coasts and through the interior, while passing through all of the major and most of the minor towns in between, and most often stopping near the best sights.

The **direction** in which TheBus travels is posted after the number and the name of the town. They are designated as EB (eastbound toward Diamond Head) and WB (westbound towards the airport). The **fare** is only \$.60, paid in exact change upon entering. Even putting a \$1 bill into the box and not expecting change is unacceptable. Students under age 19 and over six are charged \$.25, while kids under five who can sit on their parent's lap aren't charged at all. Adult **monthly bus passes,** good at any time and on all routes, are \$15, students \$7.50, and senior citizens over age 65 are free. But they (seniors) must furnish proof of age. Passes are available at Foodland and Emjay stores, Pioneer Federal Banks, 7-11 convenience stores, all city halls, University of Hawaii (adult passes only), and at the MTL Bus Pass office at 725 Kapiolani Boulevard, tel: 531-1611 scheduling, or 524-4626 bus pass.

Transfers are free and are issued upon request when entering TheBus, but you can only use them for ongoing travel in the same direction, and on a different line (numbered bus). They are also timed and dated. For example, you can take #8 from Waikiki to the Ala Maona Terminal, get off and do some fast shopping, then use your transfer on #20 to continue on to Pearl Harbor.

Circling the island is a terrific way to see the sights and meet people all along the way. The circle route takes about four hours if you stay on, but you can use the transfer system to give yourself a reasonable tour of particular sights that strike your fancy. The **circle-island** bus is #52, but remember that there are two #52, going in different directions. The buses are labeled: **#52 Wahiawa Kaneohe,** going inland to Wahiawa, north to Haleiwa, along the north shore, down the windward coast to Kaneohe and back over the Pali to Honolulu; **#52 Kaneohe Wahiawa,** follows the same route but in the opposite direction. If you'll be taking this bus to Pearl Harbor, be absolutely sure to take #52 Wahiawa Kaneohe, because if you took the other, you'd have to circle the entire island before arriving at Pearl!

Get full information on TheBus by visiting the information booth at the Ala Moana Terminal where you can pick up fliers and maps. An excellent, inexpensive little guide is *Hawaii Bus and Travel Guide* by Milly Singletary, available in most bookstores. The following are some popular destinations and their bus numbers, all originating from the Ala Moana Terminal: **Airport,** #8 Airport, #20; *Arizona Memorial,* **Pearl Harbor,** numbers 20, 50, 51, 52 Wahiawa, (not #52 Kaneohe); **Bishop Museum,** #2 School; **Chinatown,** numbers 1, 2, 3, 4, 6, 8, 9, 11, 12, 50, 52 Wahiawa; **Fisherman's Wharf,** numbers 8 Airport, 20, 52 Kaneohe; Hanauma Bay, numbers 1, 57, beach bus weekends; **Honolulu (downtown),** numbers 1, 2, 3, 4, 9, 11, 12; **Pali Lookout,** not serviced; **Polynesian Culture Center,** both #52s, then a shuttle; **Queen Emma Palace,** #4; **Sea Life Park,** #57; **Waikiki Beach,** numbers 2, 4, 8, 14, 20.

A special "beach bus," an old battered green clunker, operates from June through August and runs from Waikiki to Waimanalo Beach, stopping at Hanauma Bay and Sandy Beach. It has racks for surfboards and leaves every hour (11

a.m. to 4 p.m.) from the corner of Monsarrat and Kalakaua avenues.

Taxis
The law says that taxis are not allowed to cruise around looking for fares, so you can't hail them. But they do and you can, and most policemen have more important things to do than monitor cabs. Best is to summon one from your hotel or a restaurant. All are radio-dispatched, and they're usually there in a flash. The fares, posted on the taxi doors, are set by law and are fair, but still expensive for the budget traveler. The rates do change, but expect about $1.50 for the flag fall, and then $.25 for each additional one-sixth mile. The airport to Waikiki is about $15. You pay extra for bags.

Of the many taxi companies, some with good reputations are: **SIDA,** a cooperative of owner-drivers, at tel. 836-0011; **Aloha State Taxi,** tel. 847-3566; **Charley's,** tel. 955-2211; **Discount Taxi,** tel. 841-0333. If you need some special attention like a Rolls-Royce limo, try: **Silver Cloud Limousines,** tel. 941-2901; for the handicapped and people in wheelchairs, **Handicabs,** tel. 524-3866. For **Pedicabs,** see p. 266.

Hitchhiking
On Oahu, hitchhiking is legal, and you use the tried-and-true style of facing traffic and waving your thumb. But you can only hitchhike from bus stops! Not many people hitchhike and the pickings are reasonably easy, but TheBus is only $.60 for anywhere you want to go and the paltry sum that you save in money is lost in "seeing time."

SIGHTSEEING TOURS

Guided land tours are much more of a luxury than a necessity on Oahu. Because of the excellent bus system and relatively cheap rental cars, you spend a lot of money for a narration and to be spared the hassle of driving. If you've come in a group and don't intend on renting a car, they also may be worth it. Sea cruises and air tours are equally luxurious, but provide glimpses of this beautiful island you'd normally miss. The following partial list of tour companies should get you started.

Note: For all activities including snorkeling, scuba, all water sports, horseback riding, parasailing, golf, tennis, etc., please refer to "Sports And Recreation."

Land Tours

If you're going to take a land tour, you must have the right attitude, or it'll be a disaster. Your tour leader, usually driving the van or bus, is part instructor, comedian, and cheerleader. There's enough "corn" in his jokes to impress an Iowa hog. On the tour, you're expected to become part of one big happy family, and most importantly, to be a good sport. Most guides are quite knowledgeable about Oahu and its history, and they honestly try to do a good job. But they've done it a million times before, and their performance can be as stale as week-old bread. The larger the tour vehicle and the shorter the miles covered, the worse it is likely to be.

If you still want a tour, take a full-day jaunt in a small van: you get to know the other people and the guide, who'll tend to give you a more in-depth presentation. Tips are cheerfully accepted. Also, be aware that some tours get kickbacks from stores and restaurants they take you to, where you don't always get the best bargains. Most companies offer free hotel pick-up and delivery. Lunch or dinner is not included unless specified, but if the tour includes a major tourist spot like Waimea Falls Park or the Polynesian Cultural Center, admission is usually included.

About eight different tours offered by most companies are variations on the same theme; since the prices are regulated, the cost is fairly uniform. The more popular are the **circle-island tour,** including stops at Diamond Head, Hanauma Bay, the windward and north shores, Waimea Falls, and perhaps the Mormon Temple and Dole Pineapple Plantation, for about $40, and half for children. A **night tour** to the Polynesian Cultural Center, including admission and dinner show, costs $50. **Picnic tours,** and tours to **Byodo-In Temple,** go for around $35. Tours to **Punchbowl** and the *Arizona* **Memorial** are around $20. A small tour worth considering is the **snorkel and swim** at Hanauma Bay, including transport to this underwater park, about four hours exploring, and your snorkel gear, for under $15.

Some reputable companies include: **Akamai Tours,** tel. 922-6485; **Polynesian Adventure Tours,** tel. 922-0888; **Robert's Hawaii Tours,**

tel. 947-3939, and **Gray Line Hawaii Ltd.,** tel. 922-5094 (large coaches accommodating 30 or more as well as smaller vans); **Transhawaiian Tours,** tel. 735-6467; **Charley's Tours,** tel. 955-3381; **E Noa Tours,** 941-6608; and **Four Wheel Drive Tours,** tel. 623-7021 (touring the rough road to Kaena Point).

The following are special tours that you should seriously consider. The **Walking Tour of Chinatown,** tel. 533-3181, by the Chinese Chamber of Commerce, leaves every Tues. at 9:30 a.m. from in front of their offices at 42 N. King Street. You get a narrated three-hour tour of Chinatown for about $3, and an optional Chinese lunch for around $4. **Walking Tour of Honolulu, the 1800s,** tel. 531-0481, is a two-hour tour led by a very knowledgeable volunteer from the Mission Houses Museum, who is probably a member of the Cousin's Society and a descendant of one of the original Congregationalist missionaries to Hawaii. You're led on a wonderfully anecdoted walk through the historical buildings of central Honolulu for only $4 for the tour alone, and $7 if you combine it with a museum tour, every Wed. and Fri. at 9:30 a.m., beginning from TheBus stop in front of the Capitol.

Ka'ao o Honolulu (stories of Honolulu) is an interpretive walking tour of the city's past. Run by Kapiolani Community College, Office of Community Services, adults $5, children 5-6 $2, students and seniors $4, tel. 739-9211. The tours are thematic and change regularly, but expect topics like "The Revolution of 1893," "The lighter side of old Honolulu," and the very popular "Ghosts of Honolulu." Master storyteller Glen Grant hosts many of the tours. Reserve!

Oahu By Bicycle

Free rides and tips for cycling are offered by the **Hawaiian Bicycling League** (see p. 198). Also, **Island Bicycle Adventures,** 569 Kapahulu Ave., Honolulu, HI 96815, tel. 732-7227, offers guided rides on Oahu, Maui, and the Big Island. These tours are led by Ken Reilly, Roberta Baker, and Frank and Laura Smith, all effective cycling instructors. They run three extensive tours: Maui Magic, five days touring Maui, $495; Hawaii Highlights, 10 days on the Big Island, $795; Oahu Explorer, a two-day leisurely circuit, $159. Good quality KHS 12-speeds are provided at an additional $10 per person per day.

Helmets, insurance, and all accommodations and meals are included in the price. Write for full details to the above address.

Oahu By Air

When you soar above Oahu, you realize just how beautiful this island actually is, and considering that the better part of a million people live in this relatively small space, it's amazing just how much undeveloped land still exists in the interior and even along the coast. The following are some air tours worth considering. Remember that small, one- or two-plane operations come and go as quickly as cloudbursts. They're all licensed and regulated for safety, but if business is bad, the propellers stop spinning.

Novel air tours are offered from Dillingham Airfield, up on the northwest section of Oahu, a few miles down the Farrington Hwy. from Waialua. Up here you can soar silently above the coast with **Glider Rides**, tel. 677-3404, an outfit offering one- or two-passenger, piloted rides infinitely more exciting than the company's name. A plane tows you aloft and you circle in a five-mile radius with a view that can encompass 80 miles on a clear day. The rides are available daily, first-come, first-served, from 10 a.m. to 5 p.m. Cost is around $40 single, $60 double, and flights, depending upon air currents, last about 20 minutes (see p. 336).

Surf Air Tours, tel. 637-7003, offers plane rides along the North Shore for a reasonable $49 per person that last a half-hour, while a one-hour circle-island tour costs $79. The aircraft are very dependable Cessna 172s or 206s, and the pilots narrate while positioning the plane so that you can take some good photos. The operation is professional but low-key, like taking a spin with a guy in his private plane.

Islands in the Sky is a one-day flying extravaganza that covers all the main islands except the Big Island, offered by the most reputable island-based airline, **Hawaiian Air**, tel. 537-5100. For about $200 they fly you to the seven islands, and include a breakfast, lunch, and ground excursion to Hana on Maui and the Fern Grotto on Kauai. It's a long full day, and one to remember.

Panorama Air Tours, tel. 836-2122 or (800) 367-2671, have tailor-made tours of Oahu and an all-encompassing "flightsee Hawaii tour" similar to Hawaiian Air's for about the same price.

They fly smaller two-engined aircraft, and include the Big Island, Maui, and Kauai with a ground stop on each.

Helicopter companies rev up their choppers to flightsee you around the island, starting at $50 for a short trip over Waikiki. Prices rise from there as you head for the North Shore. Chopper companies include: **Hawaii Pacific Helicopters**, tel. 836-1561; **Kenai Air Hawaii**, one of the oldest and most reputable companies in the islands, tel. 836-2071; and **Royal Helicopters**, tel. 941-4683.

Sails And Dinner Cruises

If you're taking a tour at all, your best bet is a sail or dinner cruise. They're touristy, but a lot of fun, and actually good value. Many times money-saving coupons for them are found in the free tourist magazines, and plenty of street buskers in Waikiki give special deals. The latter are mostly on the up and up, but make sure that you know exactly what you're getting. Most of these cruises depart from the Kewalo Basin Marina, near Fisherman's Wharf, at 5:30 p.m. and cruise Waikiki toward Diamond Head before returning about two hours later. On board are a buffet, open bar, live entertainment, and dancing. Costs vary but expect to spend about $40-50 per person. For cruises to Pearl Harbor and the *Arizona* Memorial see p. 301, and for snorkeling and fishing charters, p. 213 and 217.

Some of the better dinner sails and cruises follow. **Jada Yacht Charters**, tel. 955-0722, sail sister ships *Jada I* and *Jada II*, usually in tandem. Double-masted and with classic lines, they are the sharpest boats off Waikiki. Jada Charters takes you on a real sail, not a booze cruise where you stuff yourself on fried-to-death teriyaki chicken. They disembark from Ke'ehi Harbor, and will send a van to shuttle you from Waikiki. **Royal Hawaiian Holidays,** is a tour-booking company that can get you on a variety of cruises from a lunch to dinner sail. Prices are as low as $28, tel. 926-0623. The *Manu Kai* of the Hyatt Regency, tel. 922-9292, ext. 75145, takes hotel guests and the general public for a snorkel, sail, or cocktail cruise aboard this lovely 35-footer. **Aikane Catamarans**, tel. 522-1533, is an established company with a number of boats sporting a thatched roof and Polynesian revue. **Windjammer Cruises**, tel. 521-0036, sails a three-deck, 285-foot, four-masted fake sailing ship called the *Rella Mae* from Kewalo Basin. It looks good, but the sails are only for show. If you're sitting on Waikiki Beach and you see a rainbow-colored sail, it belongs to **Rainbow Cruises,** tel. 955- 3348. **Paradise Cruise,** tel. 536-3641, sails the *Pearl Kai* from Kewalo Basin on an evening sunset cruise. **Royal Hawaiian Cruises,** tel. 672-4141, boasts one of the least expensive cruises at $26, which includes a dinner, full bar, Polynesian revue, and dancing.

For something different try the **No Booze Cruise,** tel. 944-8033, sailing from Hula Kai Pier #11 aboard the *Adventure V* at 5:15 p.m. on Friday evening, and offers worship on the water on Sundays at 7:40 a.m. Live Christian music, soft drinks, and popcorn. Small fee on Friday and donation on Sunday. The **International Society for Krishna Consciousness** offers free rides on its *Jaludata,* along with free love feasts on Sunday at 4:30 p.m. For information, *Hare Krishna, Hare Rama,* call 595-3947. The *Ani Ani* belongs to **Glass Bottom Boats Hawaii,** tel. 537-1958, doing one-hour cruises along Waikiki; three cruises in the morning and three in the afternoon run on the hour, beginning at 9:30 a.m. and 1:30 p.m. The cost is under $10.

If you think that Oahu is beautiful topside, just wait until you see it below the waves. **Atlantis Submarines,** tel. 522-1710, cost about $50, departs from the Hilton Hawaiian Village where you board the Hilton Rainbow Catamaran that ferries you to the waiting sub. Once aboard, you're given a few instructions and then it's "run silent,

dinner sail, Waikiki

run deep, run excited." The sub is surprisingly comfortable. Seats are arranged so that everyone gets a prime view through the large windows, and the air is amazingly fresh. A thrill of a lifetime.

ACCOMMODATIONS

The innkeepers of Oahu would be personally embarrassed if you couldn't find adequate lodging on their island. So long as Oahu has to suffer the "slings and arrows" of development gone wild, at least you can find all kinds, qualities, and prices of places in which to spend your vacation. Of the nearly 60,000 rooms available in Hawaii, 35,000 are on Oahu, 30,000 of them in Waikiki alone! Some accommodations are living landmarks, historical mementos of the days when only millionaires came by ship to Oahu, dallying as if it were their own private hideaway. When the jumbo jets began arriving in the early '60s, Oahu, especially Waikiki, began to build frantically. The result was hotel skyscrapers that grew

faster than bamboo in a rainforest. These monoliths, which offered the "average family" a place to stay, marked a tremendous change in the social status of visitors to Oahu. The runaway building continued unabated for two decades, until the city politicians, supported by the hotel keepers themselves, cried "Enough!" and the activity finally slowed down.

Now a great deal of money is put into refurbishing and remodeling what's already built. Visitors can find breathtakingly beautiful hotels that are the best in the land, next door to more humble inns that can satisfy most anyone's taste and pocketbook. On Oahu, you may not get your own private beach with swaying palms and hula girls, but it's easy and affordable to visit one of the world's most exotic and premier vacation resorts. The following is merely an overview of the accommodations available on Oahu. For details and listings of specific accommodations, refer to the "Accommodations" section in the travel chapters.

What, Where, And How Much

At almost anytime of year, bargains, plenty of them, include **fly/drive/stay deals,** or any combination thereof, designed to attract visitors while keeping the prices down. You don't even have to look hard to find roundtrip airfare, room, and rental car for a week from the West Coast, all for around $500 based on double occupancy. Oahu's rooms are found in all sorts of hotels, condos, and private homes. Some venerable old inns along **Waikiki Beach** were the jewels of the city when only a few palms obscured the views of Diamond Head. However, most of Waikiki's hotels now are relatively new high-rises. In Waikiki's **Five-star** hotels, prices for deluxe accommodations with all the trimmings run about $150-200 per night.

But a huge inventory of rooms go for half that amount and less. If you don't mind being one block from the beach, you can easily find nice hotels for $30-40. You can even find these prices in hotels on the beach, though most tend to be a bit older and heavily booked by tour agencies. You, too, can get a room in these, but expect the staffs to be only perfunctorily friendly, and the hotels to be a bit worn around the edges. Waikiki's side streets also hold many apartment-hotels that are, in effect, condos. In these you get the benefit of a full kitchen for under $50. Stays of a week or more bring further discounts.

Central Honolulu has few acceptable places to stay except for some no-frills hotels in and around Chinatown. Bad sections of Hotel Street have dives frequented by winos and prostitutes, not worth the hassle for the few dollars saved. Some upscale hotels around Ala Moana put you near the beach, but away from the heavy activity of Waikiki. For those passing through, a few **overnight-style** hotels are near the airport.

The remainder of the island, outside Waikiki, was mostly ignored as far as resort development was concerned. In the interior towns, and along the south and most of the windward coasts, you'll be hard pressed to find a room because there simply aren't any. Even today, only a handful of hotels are found on the leeward coast, mostly around **Makaha.** The area has experienced some recent development with a few condos and some full resorts going up, but it remains mostly undeveloped. **Windward Oahu** does have established resorts, especially at Turtle Bay, Laie, and Punaluu, but most of the lodging there is in rentable beach houses and tiny, basic inns.

To round things off, there is a network of **bed and breakfast** homes (see p. 147), YM/WCAs, youth hostels, elderhostels, and summer sessions complete with room and board at the University of Hawaii (see "Honolulu Accommodations" for details). Oahu also offers plenty of spots to pitch a tent at both state and county campgrounds.

CAMPING AND HIKING

CAMPING

Few people equate visiting Oahu with camping. The two seem mutually exclusive, especially when you focus on the mystique of Waikiki, and the dominance of a major city like Honolulu. But between state, county, and private campgrounds, and even a military reserve or two, you have about 20 spots to choose from all over the island. Camping on Oahu, however, is a little different from camping on the Neighbor Islands, which are simply more amenable to camping. In an island state, they're considered "the woods, the sticks, the backcountry," and camping seems more acceptable there.

Although its totally legal to camp, and done by both visitors and residents, Oahu's camping problems are widely divergent, with social and financial implications. When the politically powerful tourist industry thinks of visitors, it imagines people sitting by a hotel pool, drinking mai tais, and dutifully spending money! Campers just won't cooperate in parting with their quota of dollars, so there's not much impetus to cater to their wants and needs. Moreover, Honolulu is an international city that attracts both the best and worst kinds of people. The tourist industry, supported by the civil authorities, has a mortal dread that low-lifers, loafers, and bums will ensconce themselves on Oahu's beaches. This would be disastrous for Oahu's image! Mainland cities, not so dependent upon tourism, can obviously be more tolerant of their citizens who have fallen through the social net. So in Oahu they keep a close eye on the campgrounds, enforcing the rules, controlling the situation. The campgrounds are patrolled, adding a measure of strictness along with a measure of security. Even decent people can't bend the rules and slide by a little, where they normally might on the Neighbor Islands.

An odd inherent social situation adds to the problem. Not too long ago, the local people either lived on the beach or used them extensively, oftentimes for their livelihood. Many, especially fishermen and their families, would set up semipermanent camps for a good part of the year. You can see the remnants of this practice at some of the more remote and ethnically claimed campgrounds. As Oahu, much more than the Neighbor Islands, felt the pressures of growing tourism, beachfront property became astronomically expensive. Local people had to relinquish what they thought of as *their* beaches. The state and county, in an effort to keep some beaches public and therefore undeveloped, created **beach parks**. This ensured that all could use the beaches forever, but it also meant that their access would be governed and regulated.

Local people, just like visitors, must follow the rules and apply for camping permits limited by the number of days that you can spend in any one spot. Out went the semipermanent camp and with it, for the local people, the idea of *our* beach. Now, you have the same rights to camp in a spot that may have been used, or even owned, in past generations, by the family of dark-skinned people next to you. They feel dispossessed, infringed upon, and bitter. And you, especially if you have white skin, can be the focus of this bitterness. This situation, although psychologically understandable, can be a monumental drag. Of course, not all island people have this attitude, and chances are very good that nothing negative will happen. But you must be aware of underlying motivations, so that you can read the vibes of the people around your camp spot.

If all of these "problems" haven't made you want to pull up your tent stakes and head into a more congenial sunset, you can have a great and inexpensive time camping on Oahu. All of this is just the social climate that you *may* have to face, but most likely, nothing unpleasant will happen, and you'll come home tanned, relaxed, and singing the praises of the great outdoors on Hawaii's capital island.

State Parks

Oahu boasts 23 state parks and recreation areas. The majority offer a beach for day use, walks, picnicking, toilets, showers, and pavilions. A few of these, including some very important *heiau,* along with **Washington Place,** the state capitol, **Iolani Palace, the Royal Mausolem,** and **Diamond Head** are designated as state monuments. Three state parks offer tent camping: **Sand Island State Park,** just a few

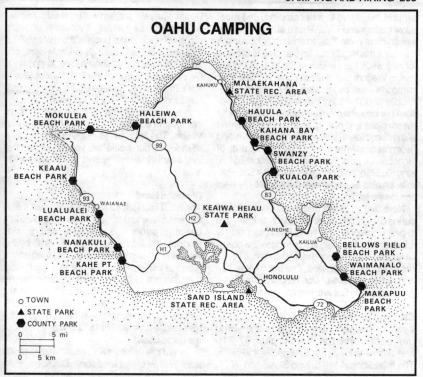

OAHU CAMPING

KAHUKU

MALAEKAHANA
STATE REC. AREA

MOKULEIA
BEACH PARK

HALEIWA
BEACH PARK

HAUULA
BEACH PARK

KAHANA BAY
BEACH PARK

99

SWANZY
BEACH PARK

KEAAU
BEACH PARK

KUALOA PARK

93

WAIANAE

KEAIWA HEIAU
STATE PARK

83

LUALUALEI
BEACH PARK

H2

KANEOHE

KAILUA

NANAKULI
BEACH PARK

H1

BELLOWS FIELD
BEACH PARK

KAHE PT.
BEACH PARK

WAIMANALO
BEACH PARK

HONOLULU

MAKAPUU
BEACH
PARK

SAND ISLAND
STATE REC. AREA

72

o TOWN
▲ STATE PARK
⬡ COUNTY PARK

0   5 mi

0   5 km

minutes from downtown Honolulu; **Keaiwa State Park,** in the interior on the heights above Aiea; and **Malaekahana State Park,** a mile north of Laie on the windward coast.

Oahu state parks close their gates and parking lots at night. Those *not* offering camping are open from 7 a.m. to 8 p.m., from May 1 to September 30, closing during the remainder of the year at 6:30 p.m. To camp at the three designated parks, you must acquire a permit (free) from the Dept. of Forestry, Division of State Parks, 1151 Punchbowl St., Honolulu 96813, tel. 548-7455. Office hours are 8 a.m. to 4:15 p.m. Oahu campsite permit reservations can be made no earlier than the fifth Wednesday before the first day of camping, but *must* be made at least one week in advance by writing a letter including your name, address, phone number, number of persons in your party, type of permit requested, and duration of your stay. The per-

mits can be picked up on arrival with proof of identification.

On Oahu campsites are at a premium and people line up at 8 a.m. on the first-floor breezeway on the Beretania Street side of the issuing office, just outside the double glass doors, where you are given a number on a first-come first-served basis. After this, go to the third floor where the office is located. **Note!** Camping is allowed *only* from 8 a.m. Friday to 8 a.m. Wednesday with the campgrounds shut down the other two days supposedly for regrowth. Camping is allowed for only five consecutive days in any one month, and don't forget a parking permit for your vehicle, which must remain within the locked park gates at night. *Alooohaaa!*

County Parks
The city and county of Honolulu has opened 13 (changes periodically) of its 65 beach parks

around the island to tent camping, and most allow trailers and RVs. These are the parks at which you're more likely to encounter hassles. A free permit is required, and camping is allowed for one week from Friday at 8 a.m. until the following Wednesday at 8 a.m., at which time your campsite must be vacated (no camping Wednesday and Thursday evenings). These campsites are also at a premium, but you can write for reservations and pick up your permits on arrival with proper identification. For information and reservations write or visit City and County of Honolulu, Dept. of Parks and Recreation, 650 S. King St., Honolulu, HI 96813, tel. 523-4525. Permits are also available from the satellite city halls around the island.

Note that all of the beach parks are closed during designated months (they differ from park to park) throughout the year. This is supposedly for cleaning, but really it's to reduce the possibility of squatters moving in. Make sure, if you're reserving far in advance, that the park will be open when you arrive! Don't count on the Parks and Recreation Department informing you!

Camping Gear And Rentals
If you've come without camping gear and wish to purchase some try: **War Surplus,** 97-719 Kamehameha Hwy., Pearl Ridge, tel. 456-5075; **The Bike Shop,** 1149 S. King St., tel. 531-7071. For rentals try **Omar the Tentman,** 1336 Dillingham Blvd., tel. 841-1057.

HIKING

The best way to leave the crowds of tourists behind and become intimate with the beauty of Oahu is to hike it. Although the Neighbor Islands receive fewer visitors, a higher percentage of people hike them than Oahu. Don't get the impression that you'll have the island to yourself, but you will be amazed at how open and lovely this crowded island can be. Some cultural and social hikes can be taken without leaving the city, like a stroll through Waikiki, or historical walking tours of downtown Honolulu and Chinatown. But others—some mere jaunts, others quite strenuous—are well worth the time and effort.

Remember that much of Oahu is privately owned, and you must have permission to cross this land or you may be open to prosecution.

Usually private property is marked by signs. Another source that might stomp your hiking plans with their jungle boots is the military. A full 25 percent of Oahu belongs to Uncle Sam, and he isn't always thrilled when you decide to play in his backyard. Some of the finest walks (like to the summit of Mt. Kaala) require crossing military lands, much of which has been altered by very unfriendly looking installations. Always check and obey any posted signs to avert trouble. The following listings are by no means all-inclusive, but should help you to choose a trail that seems interesting and within your ability level.

Diamond Head
The most recognized symbol of Hawaii, this is the first place you should head for a strikingly beautiful panorama of Waikiki and greater Honolulu. Called Leahi, ("Casting Point") by the Hawaiians, it was named Diamond Head after a group of wild-eyed English sailors espied what they thought to be diamonds glistening in the rocks. Hawaii had fulfilled so many other dreams, why not a mountain of diamonds?! Unfortunately, the glimmer was caused by worthless calcite crystals. No fortune was made, but the name stuck.

To get there, follow Kalakaua Avenue south from Waikiki until it leads onto Diamond Head Road, where a sign immediately points you to Diamond Head Crater. Pass through a tunnel and into the heavily militarized section in the center of the crater; the trail starts here. Although the hike is moderate, you should bring along water, flashlight (a must), and binoculars if you have them. Run by the Division of State Parks, the park is open daily from 6 a.m. to 6 p.m. A sign at the beginning describes the rigors you'll encounter, and informs that the trail is seven-tenths of a mile long and was built to the 760-foot summit of Leahi Point in 1908 to serve as a U.S. Coast Artillery Observation Station. It was heavily fortified during WW II, and part of the fun is exploring the old gun emplacements and tunnels built to link and service them.

Though only 10 minutes from Waikiki, wildflowers and chirping birds create a peaceful setting. When you come to a series of cement and stone steps, walk to a flat area to the left to find an old winch that hauled the heavy building materials to the top. Here's a wide panorama of the sea, and Koko Head, and notice too that atop every little hillock is an old gun emplacement. Next comes a short but dark (flashlight!) tunnel and immediately a series of 99 steps. You can avoid the steps by taking the trail to the left, but the footing is slippery and there are no guard rails. Following the steps is a spiral staircase that leads down into a large gun emplacement, through which you walk and come to another tunnel. If you haven't brought a flashlight, give your eyes a few minutes to adjust; there's enough light to make it. Once on top, another stairway and ladder take you to the very summit.

Judd Trail

This is an excellent trail to take to experience Oahu's "jungle" while visiting the historic and picturesque **Nuuanu Pali.** From Honolulu take H-1 and turn onto Route 61, the Pali Highway. Turn right onto the Old Pali Highway, then right again onto Nuuanu Pali Drive. Follow it for just under a mile to Reservoir # 2 spillway. The trail begins on the ocean side of the spillway and leads through fragrant eucalyptus and a dense stand of picture-perfect Norfolk pines. It continues through the forest reserve and makes a loop back to the starting point. En route you pass **Jackass Ginger Pool.** In the immediate area are "mud slides," where you can take a ride on a makeshift toboggan of *pili* grass, *ti* leaves, or a piece of plastic, if you've brought one. This activity is rough on your clothes, and even rougher on your body. The wet conditions after a rain are perfect for sliding. Afterward, a dip in Jackass Pool cleans the mud and refreshes at the same time. Continue down the trail to observe wild ginger, guava, and *kukui,* but don't take any confusing side trails. If you get lost head back to the stream and follow it until it intersects the main trail.

Tantalus And Makiki Valley Trails

Great sightseeing and hiking can be combined when you climb the road atop Tantalus. A range of trails in this area offer magnificent views. A few roads lead up Tantalus, but a good one heads past Punchbowl along Puowaina Drive; just keep going until it turns into Tantalus Drive. The road switchbacks past some incredible homes and views until it reaches the 2,013-foot summit, where it changes its name to Round Top Drive, then heads down the other side.

The best place to start is at the top of Tantalus at the **Manoa Cliff Trailhead,** where a number of intersecting trails give you a selection of adventures. Once on Round Top Drive, pass a brick wall with the name Kalaiopua Road imbedded in the stonework, and continue until you pass Forest Ridge Way, right after which is a large turnout on both sides of the road near telephone pole # 56. To the right is the beginning of half-mile-long **Moleka Trail,** which offers some excellent views and an opportunity to experience the trails in this area without an all-day commitment. The trails are excellently maintained, often by the local Sierra Club. Your greatest hazard here is mud, but in a moment you're in a graceful stand of bamboo, and in 10 minutes the foliage parts onto a lovely panorama of Makiki Valley with Honolulu in the background. These views are captivating, but remember to have "small eyes"—check out the varied colored mosses and fungi, and don't forget the flowers and fruit growing around you.

A branch trail to the left leads to Round Top Drive, and if you continue the trail splits into three: to the right is the **Makiki Valley Trail** that cuts across the valley starting at a Boy Scout camp on Round Top Drive and ending atop Tantalus; **Ualakaa Trail** branches left and goes for another half mile, connecting the Makiki Valley Trail with Puu Ualakaa State Park; straight ahead is the **Makiki Branch A Trail,** which descends for one-half mile, ending at the Division of Forestry Baseyard at the bottom of the valley.

On the mountainside of the Manoa Cliffs Trailhead is the **Connector Trail.** This pragmatic-sounding trail does indeed connect the lower trails with **Manoa Cliffs Trail,** skirting around the backside of Tantalus and intersecting the **Puu Ohia Trail,** which leads to the highest point on Tantalus and the expected magnificent view.

Maunawili Falls Trail

Maunawili Falls is on the other side of Nuuanu Pali, near Maunawili Town. This trail offers adventure into Oahu's jungle, with a rewarding pool and falls at the end. At the third red light as you head down the windward side of the Pali Highway, make a right onto Auloa Road. In a few hundred yards, take the left fork onto Maunawili Road and follow it toward the mountains through a residential area. Turn right onto Aloha Oe

Drive, follow it to the end, and make a right on Maleko Road. Take this to the end of the cul-de-sac. To the right is a wooden fence and walkway. A sign says "Private," so don't tresspass; instead go under the fence and start up what looks like a jeep trail but soon becomes a walking path. In 400 yards, at three telephone poles, the trail splits into three branches. Go straight ahead downhill until you intersect a trail that leads right along the creek. This trail is very muddy, but worth it. Follow it for about 15 minutes until you come to Maunawili Falls—deep enough to dive in. You can also see an upper falls. Above them is an open field perfect for an overnight camp. To the left a path leads past a small banana plantation, along an irrigation ditch cut into the mountainside, paralleled by a wooden walkway. Very few people venture into this safe but fascinating area.

Hauula Loop Trails
Built by the Workers Civilian Conservation Corp (WCCC) during the Depression, these manicured trails run up and down two ridges, and deep into an interior valley, gaining and loosing height as they switchback through the extraordinary jungle canopy. The **Gulch and Papali trails**, branches of the Hauula Loop Trail, start from the same place. The Hauula Trail is wide with good footing. There are a few stream crossings, but it's not muddy even after a heavy rain, which can shut down the Sacred Falls Trail just a few miles north. The hard-packed trail, covered in a soft carpet of ironwood needles, offers magnificent coastal views once you reach the heights, or you can look inland into verdant gulches and gulleys (valleys).

You'll be passing through miniature ecosystems very reminiscent of the fern forests on the Big Island, but on a much smaller scale. The area flora is made up of ironwoods, passion fruit, thimbleberries, *ohia,* wild orchids, and fiddlehead ferns. To get there, head for Hauula on coastal Route 83 (Kam Hwy.) and just past the 7-11 Store, between mile markers 21- 22, look inland for Hauula Homestead Road. Take it for a minute until you see the well-marked sign leading to the trails.

Sacred Falls
On coastal Route 83, between Hauula and Punaluu (mile markers 22-23), an HVB Warrior points you to Sacred Falls. Note that you *cannot* drive to the falls. An old commercial venture put out this misinformation, which persists to this day. The walk is a hardy stroll, so you'll need jogging shoes, not thongs. The area becomes a narrow canyon, and the sun sets early; don't start out past 3 p.m., especially if you want a dip in the stream. The trail was roughed up by Hurricane Ewa, and a sign along it says "Danger. Do not go past this point." Ignore it! The walking is a little more difficult but safe.

The area's Hawaiian name was Kaliuwaa ("Canoe Leak") and although the original name isn't as romantic as the anglicized version, the entire area was indeed considered sacred. En route, you pass into a very narrow valley where the gods might show disfavor by dropping rocks onto your head. Notice many stones wrapped with a *ti* leaf. This is an appeasement to the gods, so they're not tempted to brain you. Go ahead, wrap a rock; no one will see you! You hear the falls dropping to the valley floor. Above you the walls are 1,600 feet high, but the falls drop only 90 feet or so. The pool below is ample for a swim, but the water is chilly and often murky. A number of beautiful picnic spots are on the large flat rocks.

North Oahu Treks
Some of the hiking in and around northwest Oahu is quite difficult. However, you should take a hike out to **Kaena Point.** You have two choices: you can park your car at the end of the road past Dillingham Airfield on the north coast and hike in or you can park your car at the end of the road past Makua on the Waianae Coast and hike in. Both are about the same distance, and both are hardy but not difficult. The attraction of Kaena Point is huge surf, sometimes 30 feet high. The trail is only two miles, from each end, and few people come here except some local fishermen.

Peacock Flat is a good family-style trail that offers primitive camping. Follow Route 93 toward Dillingham Airfield and just before getting there turn left onto a dirt road leading toward the Kawaihapi Reservoir. If you want to camp, you need permits from the Division of Forestry and a waiver from the Mokuleia Ranch, tel. 637-4241, which you can get at their office, located at the end of a dirt road just before the one leading to Kawaihapi Reservoir. They also provide instructions and a key to get through two locked gates before reaching the trailhead, if you decide to go in from that end. Heading through the Mokuleia Forest Reserve, you can camp anywhere along the trail, or at an established but primitive campground at Peacock Flat. This area is heavily used by hunters, mostly after wild pig.

Dupont Trail takes you to the summit of Mt. Kaala, the highest point and by far the most difficult hike on the island. The last mile is downright dangerous, and has you hanging on cliff edges, with the bottom 2,000 feet below! This is not for the average hiker. Follow Route 930 to Waialua, make a left at Waialua High School onto a cane road, and follow it to the second gate, about 1.5 miles. Park there. You need a hiking permit from the Division of Forestry and a waiver from the Waialua Sugar Company, tel. 637-3521. Atop Kaala, although the views are magnificent, you'll also find a mushroom field of FAA satellite stations.

Hiking Groups And Information

The following organizations can provide information on wildlife, conservation, and organized hiking trips. **Hawaiian Trail and Mountain Club,** Box 2238, Honolulu 96804, meets behind Iolani Palace on Saturdays at 10 a.m., and Sundays at 8 a.m. Their hikes are announced in the *Honolulu Star Bulletin's* "Pulse of Paradise" column. **Hawaii Audubon Society** can be reached at Box 22832, Honolulu 96822. **Sierra Club,** 1212 University Ave., Honolulu 96826, tel. 946-8494, can provide you with a packet describing Hawaii's trails, charted by island, along with their physical characteristics and information on obtaining maps and permits. The packet costs $3, postage paid. Write the Division of Forestry, 1151 Punchbowl St., Room 325, Honolulu, HI 96813, tel. 548-2861, and ask for a copy of their *Island of Oahu Recreation Map*. It gives good information on hiking, camping, and hunting plus a description of most trails.

SPORTS

If it can be ridden, sailed, glided, flown, bounced, smashed with a racquet, struck with a club, bat, or foot, or hooked with the right bait, you'll find it on Oahu. And lots of it! The pursuit of fun is serious business here, and you can find anything, sportswise, that you ever dreamed of doing. The island offers tennis and golf, along with plenty of horseback riding, hiking, hunting, and freshwater fishing. Spectator sports like baseball, basketball, polo, and especially football are popular. Whatever your desire or physical abilities may be, there'll be some activity that strikes your fancy.

LAND SPORTS

Golf

With 24 private, public, and military golf courses scattered around such a relatively small island, it's a wonder that it doesn't rain golf balls. At present 15 links are open to the public, ranging from modest nine-holers to world-class courses whose tournaments attract the biggest names in golf today. Prices range from a token $2 up to $40 or more. Legendary courses like the superexclusive **Waialae Country Club** charge upwards of $20,000 membership fees, and have a reputation for such magnificently smooth greens that some of the snobbier members would rather stroke them than the mink upholstery in their Rolls-Royces. An added attraction of playing Oahu's courses is that you get to walk around on some of the most spectacular and manicured pieces of real estate on the island. Some afford sweeping views of the coast like the **Hawaii Kai Championship Course,** while others like the **Pali Golf Course** have a lovely mountain backdrop, or, like Waikiki's **Ala Wai Golf Course,** are set virtually in the center of all the downtown action.

The **Hawaiian Open Invitational Golf Tournament** held in late January or February at the Waialale Country Club brings the world's best golfers. Prize money is close to $1 million, and all three major TV networks cover the event. This is usually the only opportunity the average person gets to set foot on this course.

Military personnel, or those with military privileges, are welcome to golf at a number of courses operated by all four branches of the service. Calling the respective bases provides all necessary information.

Those who can't find their way to the links on their own might enjoy the services of **Alii Golf,** tel. 735-0060, or **Kato's Golf Tours,** tel. 947-

GOLF COURSES OF OAHU

COURSE	PAR	YARDS	FEES	CART
Ala Wai Golf Course 404 Kapahulu Ave. HI 96851 tel. 296-4653	70	6065	$8	$5.50
Bay View Golf Center 45-285 Kaneohe Bay Dr. Kaneohe, HI 96744 tel. 247-0451	54	2231	$5	$1
Hawaii Country Club Kunia Rd. Kunia, HI 96759 tel. 621-5654	71	5664	$17	Incl.
Hawaii Kai Championship Golf Course 8902 Kalanianaole Hwy. Honolulu, HI 96825 tel. 395-2358	72	6350	$40	Incl.
Hawaii Kai Executive Golf Course 8902 Kalanianaole Hwy. Honolulu, HI 96825 tel. 395-2358	55	2433	$9	$6
Honolulu Country Club 1690 Ala Puunalu St. Honolulu, HI 96818 tel. 833-4541	73	6808	$35	Incl.
Kahuku Golf Course *x* P.O. Box 143, Kahuku, HI 96731 tel. 293-5842	35	2699	$2	
Makaha Valley Country Club 84-627 Makaha Valley Rd. Waianae, HI 96792 tel. 695-7111	71	6369	$30	Incl.
Mid Pacific Country Club 266 Kaelepulu Dr. Kailua, HI 96734 tel. 261-9765	72	6812	$100	$20
Mililani Golf Club 95-176 Kualelani Ave. Mililani, HI 96789 tel. 623-2222	72	6815	$45	Incl.
Moanalua Golf Club * 1250 Ala Aolani St. Honolulu HI 96819 tel. 839-2411	36	2972	$12.50	$9
Oahu Country Club 150 Country Club Rd. Honolulu, HI 96817 tel. 595-3256	71	6000	$50	Incl.
Olomana Golf Links 41-1801 Kalanianaole Hwy. Waimanalo, HI 96795 tel. 259-7926	72	6081	$23.50	$10

GOLF COURSES OF OAHU (cont.)

COURSE	PAR	YARDS	FEES	CART
Pali Golf Course 45-050 Kamehameha Hwy. Kaneohe, HI 96744 tel. 261-9784	72	6493	$8	$5.50
Pearl Country Club 98-535 Kanonohi St. Aiea, HI 96701 tel. 487-3802	71	6924	$28	Incl.
Sheraton Makaha Resort and Country Club P.O. Box 896 Makaha Valley Rd. Waianae, HI 96792 tel. 695-9544	72	7091	$85	Incl.
Ted Makalena Golf Course 93059 Waipio Point Access Rd., Waipahu HI 96796 tel. 296-7888	71	5976	$8	$11
Turtle Bay Hilton and Country Club P.O. Box 187, Kahuku, HI 96731 tel. 293-8811	72	7036	$65	$9.50
Waialae Country Club x• 4997 Kahala Ave. Honolulu, HI 96816 tel. 734-2151	72	6529	$30	$8

N.B. *= 9-hole course   x=no club rentals   •=guests only

3010; both take you to a number of island courses and provide carts, greens fees, clubs, shoes, and roundtrip transportation as part of their services. For the rest, the following chart should help you tee off.

Tennis

Grease up the old elbow because Oahu boosts over 168 county-maintained tennis courts. Get a complete list of them by writing a letter of inquiry and enclosing a SASE to the Dept. of Parks and Recreation, Tennis Division, 3908 Paki Ave., Honolulu, HI 96815, tel. 923-7927. Also, plenty of hotel and private courts are open to the public or a fee, though a few hotels limit play to guests only. The chart on page 212 is a partial listing of what's available.

Horseback Riding

A different and delightful way to see Oahu is from the back of a horse. A few outfits operating

trail rides on different parts of the island include: **Gunstock's Ranch,** tel. 488-1593, offering rides over the ranch grounds on the North Shore; **Kualoa Ranch,** tel. 531-8531, by reservation only, on north windward Oahu; **Turtle Bay Hilton,** tel. 293-8693, on the North Shore, non-guests welcome; **Koko Crater Stables,** tel. 395-2682, with rides into Koko Head crater.

Spectator Sports

Oahu is home to a number of major sporting events throughout the year. Many are "invitationals" that bring the cream of the crop from both collegiate and professional levels. Here are the major sports happenings on the island.

Football is big in Hawaii. The University of Hawaii's Rainbows play during the normal collegiate season at Aloha Stadium near Pearl Harbor. In early January, the **Hula Bowl** brings together two all-star teams from the nation's collegiate ranks. You can hear the pads crack in

TENNIS COURTS OF OAHU

COUNTY COURTS

Under the jurisdiction of the Department of Parks and Recreation, 3908 Paki Avenue, Honolulu, HI 96815. Telephone 923-7927. Courts listed are in Waikiki and main towns only. There are approximately 30 additional courts around the island.

Location	Name of Court	No. of Courts	Lighted
Aiea	Aiea Recreation Center	2	Yes
Ewa	Ewa Beach Community Park	4	Yes
Kahala	Kahala Recreation Center	2	No
Kailua	Kailua Recreation Center	8	Yes
Kaimuki	Kaimuki Recreation Center	2	Yes
Kalakaua	Kalakaua Recreation Center	4	Yes
Kaneohe	Kaneohe District Park	6	No
Keehi	Keehi Lagoon courts	12	No
Koko Head	Koko Head District Park	6	Yes
Maunawili	Maunawili Park	2	Yes
Pearl City	Pearl City Recreation Center	2	Yes
Sunset Beach	Sunset Beach Neighborhood Park	2	Yes
Wahiawa	Wahiawa Recreation Center	4	Yes
Waialua	Waialua Recreation Center	4	Yes
Waianae	Waianae District Park	8	Yes
Waikiki	Ala Moana Park	10	Yes
Waikiki	Diamond Head Tennis Center	7	No
Waikiki	Kapiolani Tennis Courts	4	Yes
Waimanalo	Waimanalo District Park	4	No
Waipahu	Waipahu Recreation Center	4	Yes

HOTEL AND PRIVATE COURTS THAT ARE OPEN TO THE PUBLIC

Location	Name of Court	No. of Courts	Lighted
Honolulu	Hawaiian Regent Hotel (fee)	1	No
Honolulu	Ilikai Hotel, The Westin (fee)	7	Yes
Honolulu	King Street courts (fee)	4	Yes
Honolulu	Waikiki Malia Hotel (fee for non-guests)	1	No
Kailua	Windward Tennis Club (fee)	5	Yes
Waianae	Makaha Resort (fee)	4	Yes

February, when the NFL sends its best players to the **Pro Bowl.**

Basketball is also big on Oahu. The University of Hawaii's Rainbow Warriors play at the **Neal S. Blaisdell Center** in Honolulu at 777 Ward Street. Mid-April sees some of the nation's best collegiate hoopballers make up four teams to compete in the **Aloha Basketball Classic.**

You can watch the Islanders of the Pacific Coast League play **baseball** during the regular season at Aloha Stadium. Baseball goes back well over 100 years in Hawaii, and the Islanders receive extraordinary fan support.

Water sport festivals include surfing events, usually from November through February. The best-known are: the **Hawaiian Pro Surfing Championships;** the *Duke Kahanamoku Classic; Buffalo's Big Board Classic;* and the **Haleiwa Sea Spree,** featuring many ancient Hawaiian sports. You can watch some of the Pacific's most magnificent yachts sail into the **Ala Wai Yacht Basin** in mid-July, completing their run from Los Angeles in the annual **Trans Pacific Yacht Race.**

Hunting

Who would think that you could find any **wild game** on Oahu, not counting the two-legged variety. Mostly in the island's tough interior mountains are feral pigs and goats, two species of pheasants and doves, Erkel's francolin, and Japanese quail. You can hunt in 14 different areas with anything from spears to high-powered rifles. At this time no guide services are available on the island. See p. 170 for information on licences and regulations, or write Division of Forestry and Wildlife, 1151 Punchbowl St., Honolulu, HI 96813, tel. 548-2861.

WATER SPORTS

Snorkeling And Scuba

Oahu has particularly generous underwater vistas open to anyone donning a mask and fins. Snorkel and dive sites, varying in difficulty and challenge, are accessible from anywhere on the island. Sites can be totally hospitable, where families, and first-time snorkelers can have an exciting but safe frolic, or accessible only to the experienced diver. All over the island are dive shops from which you can rent or buy equipment, and where dive boats and instruction on all levels can be arranged. Particular spots are listed under "Beaches And Parks" in the travel sections, but some well-known favorites are Hanauma Bay, Black Point off Diamond Head, the waters around Rabbit Island, Sharks Cove on the North Shore, Wanalua Bay between Koko and Diamond Heads (good for green sea turtles), Magic Island near Ala Moana Beach Park, and some sunken ships and planes just off the Waianae coast.

If you're a scuba diver you'll have to show your C Card before local shops will rent you gear, fill your tanks, or take you on a charter dive. Plenty of outstanding scuba instructors will give you lessons towards certification, and they're especially reasonable because of the stiff competition. Prices vary, but you can take a three- to five-day semiprivate certification course including all equipment for about $275 (instruction book, dive tables, logbook extra charge). Divers unaccustomed to Hawaiian waters should not dive alone regardless of their experience. Most opt for dive tours to special dive grounds guaranteed to please. These vary also, but an *accompanied* single-tank dive where no boat is involved goes for about $65. For a single-tank boat dive, expect to spend $75. There are special charter dives, night dives, and photography dives. Most companies pick you up at your hotel, take you to the site, and return you home. Basic equipment costs $20-$30 for the day, and most times you'll only need the top of a wetsuit.

The following full-service dive shops charge around $65 for an introductory dive, $75 for a one-tank boat dive, and around $275 for a three-to-five-day certification course. Dive shops with a good reputation include: **Waikiki Diving,** at 1734 Kalakaua and at 420 Nahua, tel. 922-7188, which offers PADI certification. No snorkeling tours, but you can rent snorkeling equipment at $6 for 24 hours. Certification courses cost $300, open-water dives for beginners from shore are $50 one dive, $75 two dives. Try also **Steve's Diving Adventures,** 1860 Ala Moana Blvd., tel. 947-8900; **South Sea Aquatics,** 1050 Ala Moana Blvd; tel. 538-3854; **Hawaiian Divers,** 2344 Kam Hwy., tel. 845-6644; and **American Dive Oahu,** 3648 Waialae Ave., tel. 732-2877 for a full-service dive shop offering certification, shore and boat dives, and snorkeling adventures.

Surf and Sea, tel. 637-9887, is a complete dive shop on the North Shore in Haleiwa. **Aaron's Dive Shop,** at 602 Kailua Rd., Kailua, tel. 261-1211, open Mon.-Fri 8-8, Sat. till 6, Sun. till 5, is a full-service dive shop. Snorkel outfits run $7 for 24 hours. They have a four-day PADI certification course for $300. An introductory dive on a boat costs about $75, off the beach is $75 but you get two dives. **Leeward Dive Center,** 87-066 Farrington Hwy., Maili, tel. 696-3414, or (800) 255-1574, offers PADI and NAUI courses for $300. Introductory dives are $65, boat dives $65 for two tanks, $70 for night dives. **Aloha Dive Shop,** at Koko Marina (en route to Haunama Bay), tel. 395-5922, does it all, from snorkeling to boat dives. Excellent rates.

Snorkel Rental Equipment And Tours

Those interested can buy or rent equipment in dive shops and in department stores. Sometimes condos and hotels have snorkeling equipment free for their guests, but if you have to rent it, don't do it from a hotel or condo but go to a dive shop, where it's much cheaper (see above). Expect to spend $5-$8 a day for mask, fins, and snorkel. Many boats will take you out snorkeling or diving. Prices range from $40 (half day, four hours) to $70 (full day, eight hours), check "Getting Around—Sightseeing Tours," for many of the boats that do it all, from deep-sea fishing to moonlight cruises. A hotel's "activities center" can arrange these excursions for no extra charge. The following are outfits where you can rent equipment and/or take excursions (also see "Snorkel and Scuba" above). Do yourself a favor and wash all the sand off rented equipment. Most shops irritatingly penalize you $1 if you don't. All want a deposit, usually $30, that they put on a credit card slip and tear up when you return. Underwater camera rentals are now normally available at most shops, and go for around $10-$12 including film (24 shots), but not developing. Happy diving!

Hanauma Bay is a wonderful place to begin snorkeling, but it's very crowded. A number of outfits sponsor snorkel excursions to this underwater park. This is one of those times where you might consider going with a tour, and not on your own—it's cheap, and you don't have to worry about parking. A tour shouldn't cost any more than $15, and sometimes as little as $12 for a half day, including hotel pick-up and return, all snorkeling equipment, a beach mat, fish food, corrective lenses, vests, sometimes a complimentary soft drink, and free use of an underwater camera. Naturally, you're stuffed on a bus, and a normal tour lasts about three hours. If you go early in the morning, usually around 7 a.m., the bay will be much less crowded, and you can even save a few more dollars. The free tourist literature often has coupons that reduce these prices further! Hanauma Bay snorkeling tour operators include: **Pacific Interlude,** tel. 848-0949; **Hawaii Snorkeling,** tel. 944-2846; **Budget Snorkel,** tel. 947-2447; **Seashore Snorkeling,** tel. 395-8947; **Tommy's Tours,** tel. 944-8828; **Paradise Snorkeling Adventures,** tel. 923-7766.

Snuba Tours Of Oahu

No that's not a typo. **Snuba,** at 2233 Kalakaua Ave., B205A, Suite 1271, Honolulu, HI 96815, tel. 922-7762, offers a hybrid sport that is half snorkeling and half scuba diving. You have a regulator, a weight belt, mask, and flippers, and you're tethered to scuba tanks that float 20 feet above you on a sea-sled. The unofficial motto of Snuba is "secure but free." The idea is that many people become anxious diving under the waves encumbered by tanks and all the scuba apparatus. Snuba frees you. You would think that being tethered to the sled would slow you down, but actually you're sleeker and can make better time than a normal scuba diver. The sled is made from industrial-strength polyethylene and is $2\frac{1}{2}$ feet wide by $7\frac{1}{2}$ feet long, and consists of a view window and a belly in the sled for location of the scuba tank. If you get tired, just surface and use it as a raft. Snuba was invented by Mike Stafford of Placerville, California, as an aid to disabled people who wished to scuba. He got the idea from modern gold miners in the Mother Lode area who set a scuba tank on the side of the riverbank and run an air line down to the water to look for gold nuggets wedged under boulders. The first raft came off the assembly line in 1988.

Mick Riegel, the owner and operator of Snuba of Oahu, is one of the first to open a commercial venture in this newest of underwater sports. Mick conducts two morning tours, and one afternoon tour daily. From Monday through Friday, the dive spot of choice is at Hanauma Bay, but on weekends and holidays no commercial activity is allowed at the bay, so on those days, the morning surf report dictates the dive spot. Snuba will send its van to fetch you, and will return you to your hotel after the dive. The morning tour at $49.95 is designed for the beginner, and lasts 30 minutes underwater. You are given instruction, and two people are assigned as "buddies" on one sled. You get your first taste of the underwater experience within the reef. The afternoon dive costs $59.95, lasts one hour underwater, and you're allowed to go beyond the reef. On weekends and holidays tours include a picnic on the beach and cost $5 more.

Surfing
A local Waikiki beachboy by the name of Duke Kahanamoku won a treasure box full of gold medals for swimming at the Olympic games of 1912, and thereafter became a celebrity who toured the Mainland and introduced surfing to the modern world. Duke is the father of modern surfing, and Waikiki is its birthplace. All the Hawaiian Islands have incredibly good surfing conditions, but Oahu is best. Conditions here are perfect for rank beginners up to the best in the world. Waikiki's surf is predictable, and just right to start on, while the **Banzai Pipeline** and **Waimea Bay** on the north shore have some of the most formidable surfing conditions on Earth. **Makaha Beach** in Waianae is perhaps the best all-around surfing beach, frequented by living legends in this most graceful sport. If there is such a thing as "the perfect wave," Oahu's waters are a good place to look for it.

Summertime brings rather flat action all around the island, but the winter months are a totally different story, with monster waves on the North Shore, and heavy surf, at times even in the relative calm of Waikiki. *Never* surf without asking about local conditions, and remember that "a fool and his surfboard, and maybe his life, are soon parted." See Festivals And Events for local and international surfing competitions on Oahu.

Lessons? A number of enterprises in Waikiki offer beach services. Often these concessions are affiliated with hotels, and almost all hotel activities desks can arrange surfing lessons for you. An instructor and board go for about $15 per hour. A board alone is half the price, but as in skiing, a few good lessons to start you off are well worth the time and money. Some reputable **surfing lessons** along Waikiki are provided by: Outrigger Hotel, 2335 Kalakaua Ave. tel. 923-

0711; Hilton Hawaiian Village, 2005 Kalia Rd., tel. 949-4321; Halekulani Hotel, 2199 Kalia Rd., tel. 923- 2311; Big Al Surfing School, 2210 Kalia Rd., tel. 923-4375. Also check near the huge rack of surfboards along Kalakaua Ave., just near Kuhio Beach at the Waikiki Beach Center, where you'll find a number of beachboy enterprises at competitive rates. Fort DeRussy Beach Services, tel. 941-7004, is another good one, and in Haleiwa on the North Shore, try Surf and Sea, tel. 637-9887.

Sailboarding Lessons And Rentals
The fastest growing water sport, both in Hawaii and around the world, is **sailboarding.** Kailua Bay has perfect conditions for this sport, and you can go there any day to see sailboarders skimming the waves with their multihued sails displayed like proud peacocks (see p. 316.) Daily, a flotilla of sailboarders glide over its smooth waters, propelled by the always blowing breezes. Along the shore and in town a number of enterprises build, rent, and sell sailboards. There is also sailboarding along the North Shore (see p.344 for rentals there). Commercial ventures are allowed to operate along Kailua Beach only on weekdays and weekend mornings, but weekend afternoons and holidays are *kapu!* Here are some of the best.

Aloha Windsurfing, tel. 926-1185, sets up along the beach. Group lessons and board rentals are $35 for three hours, or $47 for five hours. Transportation from Waikiki, including all-day rental is $57, or $47 for rental only. They also rent kayaks at $10/first hour and $5 for each additional hour.

The **Froome Boating Company,** tel. 261-2961, at 789 Kailua Rd., on the corner of Kailua Road and the Pali Highway just as you're entering town, rents sailboards. They'll put it on the roof of your car with a rack provided. It's $29 for four hours, $35 for the day, $40 for 24 hours, full week $130. They also rent kayaks and wave skis, half day $25, full day $30, 24 hours $35. Hobies rent from $60 half day to $350 for the week for a 14- footer, a 16-footer is $80 half day, $400 week. Hobie Cat lessons available.

Kailua Sailboard Company, 130 Kailua Rd., tel. 262-2555, open 8:30 a.m.-5 p.m. daily, is a full-service sailboard store. Rentals are $27 per day (24 hours), half day $20, longer terms available. Beginning group lessons are $35 for a

Kailua Beach, the sailboarding capital of Oahu

three-hour session. During the week they have equipment right at the beach so you don't have to have a car to transport it. Weekends they provide a push cart, or a roof rack at no additional charge. They also have boogie boards for $7.50/day, wave skis $15/day, and two-person kayaks at $35.

Naish Hawaii, 160 Kailua Rd. (just off the beach), tel. 261-6067, and 155 A Hamakua Dr., tel. 262-6068, open 9-5 daily, are very famous makers of custom boards, production boards, sails, hardware, accessories, and repairs. At the beach store they also have T-shirts, bathing suits, beach accessories, hats, and slippers. The other location is the showroom. Naish is the largest and oldest sailboarding company in Hawaii. One of the major priorities of the Kailua Road store, known as the Naish Windsurfing School, is giving lessons. Early-bird specials from 8:30-10 a.m. are one person $25, two people $39; basic lessons for one person throughout the day is $35 for four hours including equipment. They also have a "kids' clinic" weekdays from 4-6 p.m. Naish has an excellent reputation as the biggest and the best.

Thrill Craft, Jet Skis, Parasailing, Etc.

Those into **jet-skiing** might try **Offshore Sports Hawaii,** tel. 395-3434, at the Koko Marina Shopping Center, near Hanauma Bay. Upstairs on the water side of the Koko Marina is **American Sports Ltd.,** tel. 395-5319, which offers jet skiing, snorkeling, and can book you into parasailing and scuba diving as well. Their special deal is jet-skiing, plus snorkeling, plus lunch (French fries or a Japanese *bento* if you prefer) for $49. **Waikiki Beach Services,** tel. 924-4941, rents jet skis along Waikiki. Their rates are $40 for one hour, or $60 for two people on one ski for one hour. If you like water-skiing, **Suyderhoud's Water Ski Center,** tel. 395-3777, also at the Koko Marina Shopping center, can provide all your equipment, rentals, and lessons. Also see "Sailboarding Lessons And Rentals" above, since many of those companies also rent other water equipment.

For a once-in-a-lifetime treat try **Aloha Parasail,** tel. 521-2446. Strapped into a harness complete with life jacket, you're towed aloft to glide effortlessly over the water. Aloha Parasail has free hotel pick-up. **Skyrider,** tel. 924-4941 straps you into a specially equipped chair big enough for two, with two-way radio and you-control-the-height mechanism.

For those with a very adventurous spirit and a lot of guts, **Tradewinds Hang Gliding,** tel. 396-8557, provides quality instruction in the guaranteed thrill of hang gliding. Beginning lessons on easy slopes $40, advanced with instructor $75. Happy landings!

Go Bananas Hawaii, 740 Kapahulu, tel. 737-9514, open 9-6 daily, is into kayaks, wave skis and water toys. They run day tours and overnight tours, but don't like to rent to beginners. But you can go for a guided day tour with at least three people at $30 per head. The store also sells aqua socks for walking on the reef, books, soaps, sunglasses, and T-shirts. Also see **Pacific Outdoor Adventures** p. 116, and "Sailboarding Lessons and Rentals p. 215 for more companies renting kayaks, Hobie Cats, and a variety of marine equipment.

Boogie Boards

Boogie boards are for sale all over the island and are relatively cheap. You can rent one from a dive or surf shop for a couple bucks, or buy your own for $35-70. The most highly acclaimed boogie-boarding beach on Oahu is Sandy Beach. It also has the dubious distinction of being the most dangerous beach in Hawaii, with more drownings, broken backs, and broken necks than anywhere in the state. Waikiki is tame and excellent for boogie boarding, while Waimanalo Beach (p. 311) is more for the intermediate boarder.

Water Sports Rental Gear

Sea Wind and Surf Shop in the 400 block of Royal Hawaiian Avenue rents surfboards, boogie boards, and snorkel sets from 8 a.m.-10 p.m. A surfboard is $8 for the day, boogie boards $6, snorkel set $5. They're a full-service shop where you can buy clothing as well. **Titou Rental Shop,** tel. 923-3627, in the Outrigger East Hotel along Kuhio Avenue, is open 8 a.m.-5 p.m. daily. They rent snorkel gear, boogie boards (cheapest is $7.50) for 24 hours, and surfboards. Surfboards are $15 a day. A snorkel package is $5.50 for 24 hours, $11 for three days. They don't give surf lessons, but can arrange them. Also see "Scuba And Snorkeling," and "Sailboarding" for more information.

FISHING

Deep-sea Fishing

Oahu's offshore waters are alive with game fish. Among these underwater fighters are marlin, *ahi, ono, mahi mahi,* and an occasional deepwater snapper. The deep-sea boats generally troll the Penguin Banks of the island and along the generally calm waters of the Waianae Coast, from Barber's Point to Kaena Point. Rates depend on the size of the boat, but an average 6-passenger boat on a private basis costs about $600. Most anglers opt to share the boat and split costs with others in the party. Expect to spend about $100 for a full day (7 a.m. to 4 p.m.) and $80 for a half day. All bait and tackle are provided, but you must bring your own lunch.

The vast majority of Oahu's fleet moors in **Kewalo Basin,** in Honolulu Harbor along Ala Moana Boulevard next to Fishermen's Wharf. The boat harbor is a sight in itself, and if you're contemplating a fishing trip, it's best to head down there the day before and have a yarn with the captains and returning fishermen. This way you can get a feel for a charter that will suit you best.

Charter organizations include: **Island Charters,** tel. 536-1555; **Happy Time Charters,** tel. 329-9530; **Sport Fishing Hawaii,** tel. 536-6577, with the largest fleet of all. Many private boats operating out of Kewalo Basin include: *Tina Rei,* tel. 536-5018; *Alii Kai,* tel. 521-3969; *Kahuna Kai,* tel. 235-6236; *Fish Hawk,* tel. 531- 8338; *Pacific Blue,* tel. 487-8448; *Sea Verse,* tel. 521-8829.

A few boats operate out of **Pokai Bay,** in Waiane on the northern leeward coast. One of the best is the *Kamalii Kai Too,* operated by Capt. Jim Hilton, tel. 696-7264. A few boats are even berthed in Haleiwa on the North Shore. One with an excellent reputation is the *Haole Queen,* tel. 637-5189, skippered by Lester Walls. Another good boat is the *Stacy-K,* with Capt. Bill Mattox, tel. 637-7060.

Freshwater Fishing

The state maintains two public freshwater fishing areas on Oahu. The **Wahiawa Public Fishing Area** comprises 300 acres of fishable waters in and around the town of Wahiawa. It's basically an irrigation reservoir used to hold water for cane fields. Species regularly caught here are large and smallmouth bass, sunfish, channel catfish, *tucunare,* oscar, carp, snakehead, and Chinese catfish. The other area is the **Nuuanu Reservoir # 4,** a 25-acre restricted watershed above Honolulu in the Koolau Mountains. It's open for fishing only three times per year in May, August, and November. Fish caught here include tilapia and Chinese catfish.

Licenses are obtained from the Division of Conservation and Resources Enforcement (Oahu, tel. 548-8766) or from most sporting goods stores. For free booklets and information write Division of Aquatic Resources, 1151 Punchbowl St., Honolulu, HI 96813.

PRACTICAL INFORMATION

Emergency And Health

Police, fire, and ambulance can be summoned from anywhere on Oahu by calling **911.** Reach the **Coast Guard** for search and rescue at tel. 536-4336 and the **Life Guard Service** at tel. 922-3888.

Full-service hospitals include: **Queen's Hospital,** 1301 Punchbowl St., Honolulu, tel. 538-9011; **Kaiser Foundation,** 1697 Ala Moana Blvd., Honolulu, tel. 949-5811.

Medical services and clinics include: **Doctors Emergency and Medical Services,** 1860 Ala Moana Blvd., tel. 943-1111, for emergencies and "house calls" to your hotel, 24 hours a day; in Waikiki call 926- 4777, at Hyatt Regency Hotel, and the Reef Tower Hotel. Call 923-9966 for **Japanese speaking doctors. Medi-Mart,** Waikiki, Royal Hawaiian Shopping Center, Bldg. A, Room 401, tel. 922-2335, open 9 a.m. to 6 p.m.; **Waikiki Health Center,** 277 Ohua Ave., tel. 922-4787, for low-cost care including pregnancy and confidential VD testing, open 9 a.m-8 p.m. Mon.-Thurs., until 4:30 p.m. Fri., until 2 p.m. Saturday. For dental referral call **Dentist Information Bureau** at tel. 536-2135, 24-hour service. You can get a free **blood pressure** check at the fire station in Waikiki, corner of Paki and Kapahulu streets, daily 9 a.m.-5 p.m.

Pharmacies around the island include: **Outrigger Pharmacy,** in the Waikiki Outrigger Hotel, 2335 Kalakaua Ave., tel. 923-2529; **Kuhio Pharmacy,** at the corner of Kuhio and Nahua, tel. 923-4466, full-service; **Longs Drugs,** in Honolulu at the Ala Moana Shopping Center, tel. 941-4433, and at the Kaneohe Shopping Center, tel. 235-4511; **Pay 'n Save** at 86-120 Farrington Hwy., Waianae, tel. 696-6387.

For **alternative health care** try: **Acupuncture Clinic,** Waikiki Medical Bldg., 305 Royal Hawaiian Ave. Rm. 208, tel. 923-6939, open Mon.-Fri. 9 a.m.-4 p.m.; **Honolulu School of Massage,** 1750 Kalakaua Ave., tel. 942-8552, open 10 a.m.-6 p.m., with some later hours; and **Ed Hoopai,** an excellent masseur whose motto is "You're in good hands," tel. 926-9045, at 250 Lewers St., second floor of the Outrigger Village Hotel, the suite above the pool. He deals basically in headaches, neck and shoulders, and lower backs. Half-hour for neck and shoulder or back is $22, one hour for full body is $36. Open

Mon.-Sat. 9 a.m.-6 p.m. and by appointment. **Colon Therapy of Hawaii,** 122 Oneawa St. Kailua, tel. 261-4511, offers detoxification and massage administered by Alcyone.

Chiropractic care: Chiropractic Referral Service, 700 Bishop St., tel. 521-5784, offers free information and referral to qualified chiropractors. **Chiropractic Dial-a-Tape** has taped messages for what ails, tel. 737-1111; on the leeward side is **Dr. Tom Smith,** 1222 Oneawa St., Kailua, tel. 261-4511, limited hours.

Visitor Information

A complete listing of **Hawaii Visitors Bureau** offices appears on page 173. The main Oahu HVB office is at 2270 Kalakaua Ave., Honolulu, HI 96815, tel. 923-1811. They also operate a number of information kiosks at the airport. The **Japanese Chamber of Commerce** has special information on things Japanese, tel. 949-5531; the **Chinese Chamber of Commerce,** offers information and tours on Chinatown, tel. 533-3181. **State Foundation on Culture and Arts,** 335 Merchant St. Rm. 202, tel. 548-4657, dispenses information on what's happening culturally on Oahu. For general information, or if you have a hassle, try the **Office of Information and Complaints,** tel. 523-4385 or 523-4381.

Reading Material

Besides a number of special-interest Chinese, Japanese, Korean, Filipino, and military newspapers, two major dailies are published on Oahu. The *Honolulu Advertiser,* tel. 525-8000, is the morning paper, and the *Honolulu Star Bulletin,* tel. 525-8000, is the evening paper. They combine to make a Sunday paper. A money-saving paper is the *Pennysaver,* tel. 521-9886, featuring classified ads on just about anything. Call for distribution points.

Don't miss out on the **free tourist literature** available at all major hotels, shopping malls, the airport, and stands along Waikiki's streets. They all contain up-to-the-minute information on what's happening, and a treasure-trove of free or reduced-price coupons for various attractions and services. Always featured are events, shopping tips, dining and entertainment, and sightseeing. The main ones are: *This Week Oahu,* the best and most complete; *On the Go, Hawaii,* general information about the island attractions; *Waikiki, On the Go,* focusing mostly on Waikiki; *Spotlight Hawaii,* with good sections on dining and sightseeing. Two free tabloids, *Waikiki Beach Press* and *Island News,* offer entertainment calendars and feature stories of general interest to visitors. *Oahu Drive Guide,* handed out by all the major car rental agencies, has some excellent tips and orientation maps. Especially useful to get you started from the airport.

For **bookstores,** see page 192.

Post Offices And Libraries

Many small post offices are found in various towns around the island. The main post office in downtown Honolulu is at 3600 Aolele St., tel. 422-0770; in Waikiki at 330 Saratoga Rd., tel. 941-1062; in Kailua at 335 Hahani, tel. 262-7205; in Waianae at 86-015 Farrington Hwy., tel. 696-4032; in Haleiwa at 66-437 Kam Hwy., tel. 637-5755; in Wahiawa at 115 Lehua, tel. 621-8496.

Oahu's libraries include: Hawaii State Library, in Honolulu at 478 S. King St., tel. 548-4775; Kailua Library, 239 Kuulei Rd., tel. 261-4611; Library for the Blind and Physically Handicapped, 402 Kapahulu Ave., tel. 732-7767; Waikiki branch library next door, at 400 Kapahulu, tel. 732-2777.

Weather And Surf Conditions

For a weather report call 836-0234; for surfing conditions, call 836-1952; for Hawaiian waters report, tel. 836-3921.

Helpful Numbers

Arizona Memorial, tel. 922-1626; **Babysitting services,** tel. 923-8337, in Waikiki at 922-5575; **Bishop Museum,** tel. 922-1626; **Council of Churches,** tel. 521-2666; **Dept. of Agriculture,** plants, produce, regulations, etc., tel. 836-1415; **directory assistance,** tel. 1-411; **Honolulu Harbor,** daily ship arrival recording, tel. 537-9260; **Honolulu International Airport,** tel. 836-1411/6431; **Time,** tel. 983-3211; **Whale Watch,** tel. 922-1626.

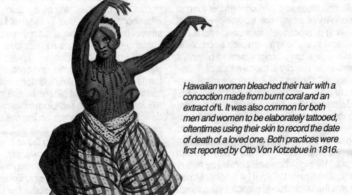

Hawaiian women bleached their hair with a concoction made from burnt coral and an extract of ti. It was also common for both men and women to be elaborately tattooed, oftentimes using their skin to record the date of death of a loved one. Both practices were first reported by Otto Von Kotzebue in 1816.

HONOLULU

Honolulu is *the* most exotic city in America. It's not any one attribute that makes this so, it's a combination of things. Honolulu's like an ancient Hawaiian goddess who can change her form at will. At one moment you see a black-eyed beauty, swaying provocatively to a deep and basic rhythm, and in the next a high-tech scion of the computer age sitting straight-backed behind a polished desk. The city is the terminus of "manifest destiny," the end of America's relentless westward drive, until no more horizons were left. Other Mainland cities are undoubtedly more historic, cultural, and perhaps, to some, more beautiful than Honolulu, but none come close to having all of these features in the same overwhelming combination. The city's face, though blemished by high-rises and pocked by heavy industry, is eternally lovely. The Koolau Mountains form the background tapestry from which the city emerges, the surf gently foams along Waikiki, the sun hisses fire-red as it drops into the sea; and Diamond Head beckons with a promise of tropical romance.

In the center of the city, skyscrapers rise as silent, unshakable witnesses to Honolulu's economic strength. In glass and steel offices, businessmen wearing conservative three-piece uniforms are clones of any found on Wall Street. Below, a fantasia of people live and work. In nooks and crannies are an amazing array of arts, shops, and cuisines. In a flash of festival the streets become China, Japan, Portugal, New England, old Hawaii, or the Philippines.

New England churches, royal palaces, bandstands, tall-masted ships, and coronation platforms illustrate Honolulu's history. And what a history! You can visit places where in a mere twinkle of time past, red-plumed warriors were driven to their death over an impossibly steep *pali,* where the skies were alive with screaming Zeros strafing and bombing the only American city threatened by a foreign power since the War of 1812. In hallowed grounds throughout the city lie the bodies of fallen warriors. Some are entombed in a mangled steel sepulcher below the waves, others from three wars rest in a natural bowl of bereavement and silence. And a nearby royal mausoleum holds the remains of those who were "old Hawaii."

Honolulu is the pumping heart of Hawaii. The state government and university are here. So are botanical parks, a fine aquarium and zoo, a floating maritime museum, and the world's fore-most museum on Polynesia. Art flourishes like flowers, as do professional and amateur entertainment, extravaganzas, and local and world-class sporting events. But the city isn't all good clean fun. The seedier side includes "girlie" shows, raucous GI bars, street drugs, and street people. But somehow this blending and collision of East and West, this hodgepodge of emotionally charged history, this American city superimposed on a unique Pacific setting works well as Honolulu, the "Sheltered Harbor" of man and his dreams.

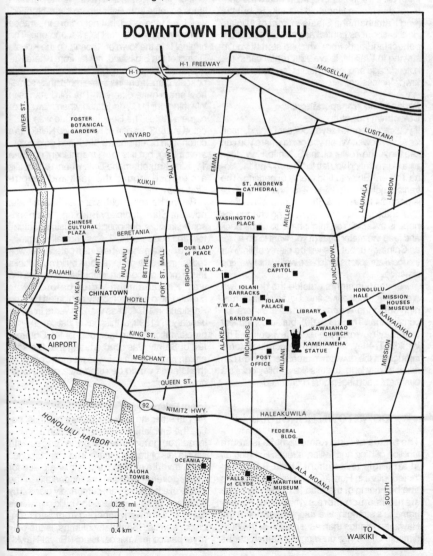

DOWNTOWN HONOLULU

SIGHTS

The best way to see Honolulu is to start from the middle and fan out on foot for the inner city. You can *do* downtown in one day, but the sights of greater Honolulu require a few days to see them all. It's a matter of opinion where the center of downtown Honolulu actually is, but the King Kamehameha Statue in front of Aliiolani Hale is about as central as you can get, and a perfect landmark from which to start. If you're staying in Waikiki, leave your rental car in the hotel garage and take TheBus (no. 2) for downtown sightseeing.

Parking And Transportation, Downtown Honolulu

If you can't bear to leave your car behind, head for Aloha Tower. When you get to where you can see the Aloha Tower off the S. Nimitz Hwy., look for a sign pointing you left to "Piers 4 And 11, Aloha Tower." Enter to find plenty of parking. The traffic is not as congested here, and the large lot is open 24 hours, at $.50 per hour, with a four-hour maximum on the meter. Bring change, as none is avilable. You might have to come back and feed the meter again if you want to go as far as Chinatown, but this will be plenty of time for the local attractions which are well within walking distance.

For various sights outside the downtown area, your rental car is fine. Some shuttles running out to the *Arizona* Memorial are more expensive than TheBus ($.60), but so convenient that they're worth the extra few coins. The **Waikiki Trolley,** tel. 526-0112, conducts tours throughout the downtown area. For $7, you can ride it all day long. It looks like a trolley but it's a bus that's been ingeniously converted.

DOWNTOWN HONOLULU

The **Statue of King Kamehameha** is at the junction of King and Mililani streets. Running off at an angle is **Merchant Street,** the oldest thoroughfare in Honolulu, and you might say its "the beginning of the road to modernity." The statue is much more symbolic of Kamehameha's strength as a ruler and unifier of the Hawaiian Islands than as a replica of the man himself. Of the few drawings of Kamehameha

that have been preserved, none is necessarily a good likeness. Kamehameha was a magnificent leader and statesman, but by all accounts not very good-looking. This statue is one of three. The original, lost at sea near the Falkland Islands en route from Paris where it was bronzed, was later recovered, but not before insurance money was used to cast this second one. The original is in the town of Kapaau, in the Kohala District of the Big Island, not far from where Kamehameha was born, but although they supposedly came from the same mold, they somehow seem quite different. The third stands in Washington, D.C., dedicated when Hawaii became a state. The Honolulu statue was dedicated in 1883, as part of King David Kalakaua's coronation ceremony. Its black and gold colors are striking, but it is most magnificent on June 11, King Kamehameha Day, when 18-foot leis are draped around the neck and the outstretched arms.

Behind Kamehameha stands **Aliiolani Hale,** now the State Judiciary Building. This handsome structure, designed by an Australian architect and begun in 1872, was originally commissioned by Kamehameha V as a palace, but was redesigned as a general court building. It looks much more grand than Iolani Palace across the way. Kamehameha V died before it was finished, and it was officially dedicated by King Kalakaua in 1874. Less than 20 years later, on January 17, 1893, at this "hall of justice," the first proclamation by the Members of the Committee of Safety was read, stating that the sovereign nation of Hawaii was no more, and that the islands would be ruled by a provisional government.

Iolani Palace

As you enter the park-like palace grounds, notice the Emblem of Hawaii in the center of the large iron gates. They're often draped with simple leis of fragrant *maile.* The quiet grounds are a favorite strolling and relaxing place for many government workers, especially in the shade of a huge banyan, purportedly planted by Kalakaua's wife, Kapiolani. The building, with its glass and ironwork imported from San Francisco, and its Corinthian columns, is the only royal palace in America. Iolani ("Royal Hawk")

Iolani Palace, the only royal residence in America

Palace, begun in 1879 under orders of King Kalakaua, was completed in December 1882 at a cost of $350,000. It was the first electrified building in Honolulu, and had a direct phone line to the Royal Boat House.

Non-Hawaiian island residents of the day thought it a frivolous waste of money, but here poignant scenes and profound changes rocked the Hawaiian islands. After nine years as king, Kalakaua built a **Coronation Stand** that temporarily sat in front of the palace, (now off to the left). In a belated ceremony, Kalakaua raised a crown to his head and placed one on his queen, Kapiolani. During the ceremony, 8,000 Hawaiians cheered, while Honolulu's foreign, tax-paying businessmen boycotted. On August 12, 1898, after only two Hawaiian monarchs, Kalakaua and Liliuokalani (his sister), had resided in the palace, the American flag was raised up the flagpole following a successful coup that marked Hawaii's official recognition by the U.S. as a territory. During this ceremony, royal Hawaiian subjects wept bitter tears, while the businessmen of Honolulu cheered wildly.

Kalakaua, later in his rule, was forced to sign a new constitution that greatly reduced his own power to little more than figurehead status. He traveled to San Francisco in 1891, where he died. His body was returned to Honolulu and lay in state in the palace. His sister, Liliuokalani, succeeded him; she attempted to change this constitution and gain the old power of Hawaii's sovereigns, but the businessmen revolted and the monarchy fell. Iolani Palace then became the main executive building for the provisional government, with the House of Representatives meeting in the throne room and the Senate in

the dining room. It served in this capacity until 1968.

Iolani Palace is open to one-hour **guided tours only,** Wed. to Sat. 9 a.m.- 2:15 p.m.; $4 adults, $1 children, with no children under five admitted. They're popular so make reservations at least a day in advance. Tickets are sold at a window at the Barracks, open Tues. to Sat. 8:30 a.m.- 2:15 p.m. The Palace shop is open 8:30 a.m.-3:30 p.m. Tues.-Saturday. For information and reservations call 522-0832.

Palace Grounds

Kalakaua, known as the "Merry Monarch," was credited with saving the hula. He also hired Henri Burger, first Royal Hawaiian Bandmaster, and together they wrote "Hawaii Pono," the state anthem. Many concerts were given from the Coronation Stand, which became known as the **Royal Bandstand.** Behind it is **Iolani Barracks** (Hale Koa), built in 1870 to house the Royal Household Guards. When the monarchy of Hawaii fell to provisional government forces in 1893, only *one* of these soldiers was wounded in a pathetic show of strength. The Barracks were moved to the present site from nearby land on which the State Capitol was erected.

To the right behind the palace are the **State Archives.** This modern building, dating from 1953, holds records, documents, and vintage photos. A treasure trove to scholars and those tracing their genealogy, it is worth a visit by the general public to view the old photos on display. Free, open Mon. to Fri. 7:45 a.m.- 4:30 p.m. Next door is the **Hawaii State Library,** housing the main branch of this statewide system. As in all Hawaii state libraries, you are entitled to a card on your first visit, and are then eligible to take out books. The central courtyard is a favorite lunch spot for many of the government workers. Some of the original money to build the library was put up by Andrew Carnegie. For information call 548-4775.

Government Buildings

Liliuokalani was deposed and placed under house arrest in the Palace for nine months. Later, after much intrigue that included a visit to Washington, D.C., to plead her case and an aborted counter-revolution, she sadly accepted her fate and moved to nearby **Washington Place.** This solid-looking structure fronts Beretania Street and was originally the home of sea captain John Dominis. It was inherited by his son John Owen Dominis, who married a lovely young Hawaiian aristocrat, Lydia Kapaakea, who became Queen Liliuokalani. She lived in her husband's home, proud but powerless, until her death in 1917. Washington Place is now the official residence of the governor of Hawaii.

To the left of Washington Place is **St. Andrew's Cathedral.** Built in 1867 as an Anglican church, many of its stones and ornaments were shipped from England; Hawaii's monarchs worshipped here, and the church is still very much in use. To the right is the **War Memorial.** Erected in 1974, it replaced an older memorial to the people who perished in WW II. A courtyard and benches are provided for quiet meditation.

Directly in front is the magnificent **Hawaii State Capitol,** built in 1969 for $25 million. The building itself is a metaphor for Hawaii: the pillars surrounding it are palms, the reflecting pool is the sea, and the cone-shaped rooms of the Legislature represent the volcanos of Hawaii. It's lined with rich *koa* wood from the Big Island, and is further graced with woven hangings and murals, with two gigantic, four-ton replicas of the State Seal hanging at both entrances. The inner courtyard has a 600,000-tile mosaic, "Aquarius," rendered by island artist Tadashi Sato, and on one side is a poignant sculpture of **Father Damien of the Lepers.** The state Legislature is in session January to March, and opens with dancing, music, and festivities at 10 a.m. on the third Wednesday in January, public invited. Peek inside, then take the elevator to the fifth floor for outstanding views of the city.

MISSION HOUSES MUSEUM

This living museum, on King Street across from Kawaiahao Church (oldest in Honolulu), is a complex including two main houses, a printing house annex, a library and a fine, inexpensive gift shop. It's operated by the **Hawaiian Mission Children's Society** (or Cousins' Society), whose members serve as guides and hosts. Many are direct descendants, or spouses of descendants, of the Congregationalist missionaries who built these structures. Tours are con-

MISSION HOUSES MUSEUM

left to right: Frame House, Printing House, Chamberlain House

ducted Tues.-Sat. 9 a.m.- 4 p.m., Sun. 12-4 p.m., closed Mondays. Guided tours of the Frame House 9:30 a.m.- 3:00 p.m.; $3.50 admission, tel. 531-0481. The museum hosts Hawaii's only **living history program.** Volunteers, all adept at acting, dress up in fashions of the period, and assume the roles of missionaries in 1830 Honolulu. Feel free to interact and ask questions, but remember that they stay in character, so the answers may surprise you. Saturdays only from 10 a.m.-3 p.m., admission for adults $3.50.

Construction

If you think that pre-cut modular housing is a new concept, think again. The first structure that you enter is the **Frame House,** the oldest wooden structure in Hawaii. Precut in Boston, it came along with the first missionary packet in 1819. Since the interior frame was left behind and didn't arrive until Christmas Day, 1820, the missionary families lived in thatched huts until it was erected. Finally the Chamberlain family occupied it in 1821. Many missionary families used it over the years, with as many as four households occupying this small structure at the same time. This is where the Christianizing of Hawaii truly began.

The missionaries, being New Englanders, first dug a cellar. The Hawaiians were very suspicious of the strange hole, convinced that the missionaries planned to store guns and arms in this "fort." Though assured to the contrary, King Liholiho, anxious to save face and prove his omnipotence, had a cellar dug near his home twice as deep and large. This satisfied everyone.

Notice the different styles, sizes, and colors of bricks used in the structures. Most of the ships of the day carried bricks as ballast. After unloading cargo, the captains either donated or sold the bricks to the missionaries, who incorporated them into the structures. A common local material was coral stone: pulverized coral was burned with lime to make a rudimentary cement, which was then used to bind cut-coral blocks. The pit that was used for this purpose is still discernible on the grounds.

Kitchen

The natives were intrigued with the missionaries, whom they called "long necks" because of their high collars. The missionaries, on the other hand, were a little more wary of their "charges." The low fence around the complex was symbolic as well as utilitarian. The missionaries were obsessed with keeping their children away from Hawaiian children, who at first ran around naked and played many games with overt sexual overtones. Almost every evening a small cadre of Hawaiians would assemble to peer into the kitchen to watch the women cook, which they found exceedingly strange because their *kapu* said that *men* did the cooking. In the kitchen, actually an attached cook house, the woodburning stove kept breaking down. More often than not, the women used the fireplace with its built-in oven. About once a week, they fired up the oven to make traditional New England staples like bread, pies, cakes, and puddings. The missionaries were dependent on the Hawaiians to bring them fresh water. Notice a large porous stone through which they would filter the water to remove dirt, mud, and sometimes brackishness.

The Hawaiians were even more amazed when the entire family sat down to dinner, a tremendous deviation from their beliefs that separated men and women when eating. When the missionaries assembled to dine or meet at the "long table," the Hawaiians silently stood at the open door to watch the evening soap opera. The unnerved missionaries eventually closed the door and cut two windows into the wall, which they could leave opened but draped. The long table took on further significance. The one you see is a replica. When different missionaries left the islands, they, like people today, wanted a souvenir. For some odd reason, they elected to saw a bit off the long table. As years went by, the table got shorter and shorter until it was useless.

Residents

The house was actually a duplex. Although many families lived in it, two of the best known were the Binghams and the Judds. Much of the furniture here was theirs. Judd, a member of the third missionary company, assumed the duties of physician to all the missionaries and islanders. He often prescribed alcohol of different sorts to the missionary families for a wide variety of ailments; many records remain of these prescriptions, but not one record of complaints from his patients. The Binghams and Judds got along very well, and entertained each other and visitors, most often in the Judds' parlor because they were a little better off. The women would often congregate here to do their sewing, which was in great demand, especially by members of the royal household. Until the missionary women taught island girls to sew, providing clothing for Hawaii's royalty was a tiresome and time-consuming obligation.

The missionaries were self-sufficient, and had the unbounded energy of youth, as the average age was only 25. The husbands often built furniture for their families. Reverand Bingham, a good craftsman, was pressed by Queen Kaahumanu to build her a rocking chair after she became enamored of one made for Mrs. Bingham. The queen weighed almost 400 pounds, so building her a suitable chair was no slim feat! Still, the queen could only use it in her later years when she'd lost a considerable amount of weight. After she died, the Bingham's asked for it to be returned, and it sits in their section of the house. Compare Bingham's chair to another in the Judds' bedroom, jury-rigged by a young missionary husband from a captain's chair. An understatement, found later in his diary, confirmed that he was not a carpenter.

When you enter the Judds' bedroom, note how small it is, and consider that two adults and five children slept here. As soon as the children were old enough, they were sent back to the Mainland for schooling, no doubt to relieve some of the congestion. Also notice that the windows were fixed, in the New England style, and imagine how close it must have been in these rooms. The Binghams' bedroom is also small, and not as well furnished. Bingham's shaving kit remains, and is inscribed with "The Sandwich Isles." In the bedroom of Mary Ward, a missionary woman who never married, notice that the roof was raised to accommodate her canopy bed.

Another famous family that lived in the complex were the Cookes. When the missionary board withdrew its support, the Cookes petitioned them to buy the duplex, which was granted. Shortly thereafter, Mr. Cooke, who had been a teacher, formed a partnership with one Mr. Castle, and from that time forward became Castle and Cooke, one of Hawaii's oldest and most powerful corporations. The largest building in the compound is **The Chamberlain House.** This barn-like structure was completed in 1831, and used as a warehouse and living quarters for Levi Chamberlain's family. Goods were stored in most of the structure, while the family occupied three modest rooms.

Printing House

The missionaries decided almost immediately that the best way to convert the natives was to speak to them in their own language, and to create a written Hawaiian language which they would teach in school. To this end, they created the **Hawaiian alphabet,** consisting of 12 letters, including the five vowels and seven consonants. In addition, to disseminate the doctrines of Christianity, they needed books, and therefore a printing press. On the grounds still stands the Printing House, built in 1841 but first used as annex bedrooms by the Hall family. The original printing house, built in 1823, no longer exists. In the Printing House is a replica of the Ramage press brought from New England, first operated by Elisha Loomis. He returned to the Mainland when he was 28, and soon died of TB, but not before he had earned the distinction of being the first printer west of the Rockies. Here were printed biblical tracts, text books, or anything that the king or passing captains were willing to pay to have printed. Although it took eight hours of hard work to set up one page to be printed, it is estimated that in the 20 years the press operated under the missionaries, over seven million pages were produced.

Gift Shop

While on the grounds make sure to visit the bookstore and gift shop. It's small, but has an excellent collection of Hawaiiana, and some very inexpensive but quality items, such as tapa bookmarks for only $.25, and an outstanding collection of Niihau shellwork, considered the finest in Hawaii. The shelves hold tasteful items like woodcarvings, bread boards, hats, weavings, chimes, flags of old Hawaii, and stuffed pillows with classic Hawaiian quilt motifs. Also a good collection of Hawaiian dolls, for kids and adults. Between the bookstore and the research library are restrooms. Also, consider a **Walking Tour of Honolulu,** offered by the museum, that guides you through downtown Honolulu for two hours, hitting all the historic sights with an extremely knowledgeable narration by one of the museum's guides (see p. 200). For further information write Hawaiian Mission Children's Society, 553 S. King St., Honolulu, HI 96813, tel. 531-0481.

KAWAIAHAO CHURCH

This church, so instrumental in Hawaii's history, is the most enduring symbol of the original missionary work in the islands. A sign welcomes you and bids the blessing, "Grace and peace to you from God our Father." The church was constructed from 1836 until 1842 according to plans drawn up by Hiram Bingham, its minister. Before this, at least four grass shacks of increasing size stood here. One was destroyed by a sailor who was reprimanded by Rev. Bingham for attending services while drunk; the old sea dog returned the next day and burned the church to the ground. Kawaiahao ("Water of Hao") Church is constructed from over 14,000 coral blocks quarried from offshore reefs. In 1843, following Restoration Day, when the British returned the Hawaiian Islands to sovereignty after a brief period of imperialism by a renegade captain, King Kamehameha III here uttered the profound words in a thanksgiving ceremony that were destined to become Hawaii's motto, *"Ua mau ke ea o ka aina i ka pono,"* "The life of the land is preserved in righteousness."

Other noteworthy ceremonies held at the church were the marriage of King Liholiho and his wife Queen Emma, who bore the last child born to a Hawaiian monarch. Unfortunately, little Prince Albert died at the age of four. On June 19, 1856, Lunalilo, the first king elected to the throne, took his oath of office in the church. A bachelor who died childless, he always felt scorned by living members of the Kamehameha clan, and refusing to be buried with them at the Royal Mausoleum in Nuuanu Valley, he is buried in a tomb in the church's cemetery. Buried along with him is his father Charles Kanaina, and nearby lies the grave of his mother Miriam Kekauluohi. In the graveyard lies Henri Burger, and many members of the Parker, Green, Brown, and Cooke families, early missionaries to the islands. Liliuokalani's body lay in state in the church before it was taken to the Royal Mausoleum. A jubilation service was held in the church when Hawaii became a state in 1959. Kawaiahao holds beautiful Christmas services with a strong Polynesian and Hawaiian flavor. Hidden away in a corner of the grounds is an unobtrusive adobe building, remains of a schoolhouse built in 1835 to educate Hawaiian children.

HAWAII MARITIME CENTER

The development of this center is a wonderful concept whose time has finally come. It's amazing that a state and former nation, whose discovery and very birth are so intimately tied to the exploration, navigation, and exploitation of the sea, has never had a center dedicated exclusively to these profoundly important aspects of its heritage. Now the Hawaii Maritime Center, at Pier 7, Honolulu Harbor, Honolulu, HI 96813, tel. 523-6151, is exactly that . . . and it needs your support as a visitor. The Center, along with its museum in the **Kalakaua Boathouse**, now consists of three attractions: Aloha Tower, the beacon of hospitality welcoming people to Hawaii for six decades; the classic, and last remaining, fully rigged, four-masted *Falls of Clyde* floating museum; and the reproduction of a Hawaiian sailing canoe, *The Hokule'a,* that recently sailed back in time using ancient navigational methods to retrace the steps of Hawaii's Polynesian explorers. Take bus #8 or 20 from Waikiki and you're deposited just in front. Admission $6, all attractions. Open 9 a.m.-5p.m. every day.

The Kalakaua Boathouse

The main building of the center is the two-storied Kalakaua Boathouse. Behind is Coasters, an American standard restaurant (see p. 248), and an area called Kalakaua Park, a garden and observation area perfect for lunch. Eighty-one steps lead to the "crow's nest," and "widow's walk," with great views of the harbor and city.

Upon entering you find a glass case filled with trophies and memorabilia from the days of King Kalakaua. His words have a sadly prophetic ring. "Remember who you are. Be gracious, but never forget from whence you came for this is where your heart is. This is the cradle of your life." Notice the phones installed throughout the capital in 1887, a few years before California had electricity. Kalakaua had previously installed telephones between his boathouse and the palace in 1878, just two years after Bell's invention. The bottom floor of the center recalls ancient fishing methods, and the traditional division of land and sea resources among the people.

King David Kalakaua

Another fascinating display traces the development of surfing through the ages, from original boards, more like seagoing canoes, at 18 feet long, until the modern debut of the fiberglass board. Spot a vintage album of *Surfin Safari* by The Beach Boys. Here, too, is a land surfing sled used for games during the Makahiki Festival. It measures six inches wide and 10-14 feet long. Trails to accommodate it were up to a mile long. Built on steep hills, they were paved in stone, layered with earth and topped with slippery grass. Once launched there was no stopping until the bottom. Yippee!

One corner of the museum is dedicated to tattooing, Polynesian and Western. It shows traditional tattoos worn by both men and women, and then how Western style became more popular, as Hawaii was a main berth for sailors, who sported these living souvenirs from around the world. **Mail buoys** sounds uninteresting, but these tidbits of old Hawaiiana, still alive today, are fascinating. Fashioned from gaily painted metal cans, passing ships, mainly from Peru and Equador, still radio Honolulu Harbor that they

are dropping one. Someone, anyone who heard the message, would fetch them. Inside are little gifts for the finder, who takes the enclosed mail and sends it on its way.

The second floor is dedicated to the discovery of Hawaii, both by the Polynesians and Westerners. Through ledgers, histories, and artifacts, it traces original discovery, Western discovery, the death of Capt. Cooke, and the roll of the sea otter pelt which brought the first whalers and traders after sandalwood. The whaling section is dripping with blood and human drama. Look at the old harpoons and vintage film footage. Yes, film footage, and photos. A remarkable display is of schrimshaw from the whaling days. Sailors would be at sea for five to seven years, and would have untold hours to create beauty in what were dismal conditions. Suspended from the ceiling are replicas of double-hulled sailing canoes. One corner is a replica of H. Hatfield and Co., a whaling supply store of the era. The rear of the second floor shows steam ships that cruised between Hawaii, Japan, and the East coast, a nature exhibit of weather, marinelife, and volcanos, and an auditorium with a video on the climatic conditions in Hawaii.

Aloha Tower

When this endearing and enduring tourist cliché was built in 1926 for $160,000, the 184-foot, 10-story tower was the tallest structure on Oahu. As such, this landmark, with clocks embedded in all four walls, and emblazoned with the greeting and departing word, Aloha, became the symbol of Hawaii. Before the days of air transport, ocean liners would pull up to the pier to disembark passengers at the foot of the tower, and on these "Steamer Days," festive well-wishers from throughout the city would gather to greet and lei the arriving passengers. The Royal Hawaiian Band would even turn out to welcome the guests ashore.

When you take the escalator up from the parking area, notice the huge U.S. Customs rooms that at one time processed droves of passengers. Today, the crowds are gone and the tower is quiet. Only a few harbormasters on the top floor oversee the comings and goings of cargo ships. When you enter the tower a sign claims that you can only get to the observation area on the top floor by elevator. You can walk up to the ninth floor if you want, but to get to the

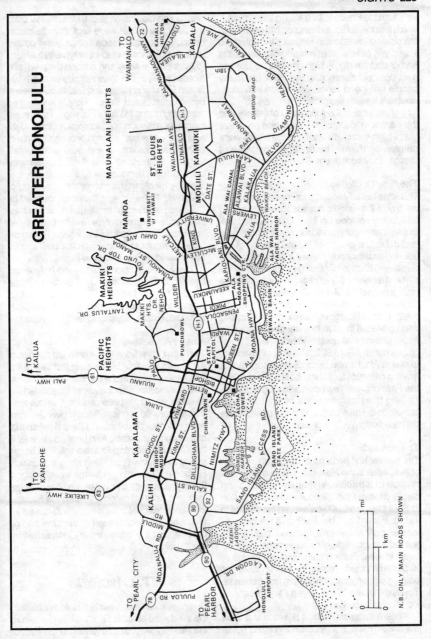

GREATER HONOLULU

N.B. ONLY MAIN ROADS SHOWN

very top does necessitate taking the elevator, which has the dubious distinction of being one of the slowest elevators in Hawaii. Once atop the tower, you get the most remarkable view of the harbor and the city. A high-rise planned for just next door will surely ruin the view, but many people with good sense, and luckily with some clout, are fighting this project. A remarkable feature of the vista is the reflections of the city and the harbor in many of the steel and reflective glass high-rises. It's as if a huge mural were painted on them. The tower is open free of charge, daily from 8 a.m.-9 p.m.

The Falls Of Clyde

This is the last fully rigged, four-masted ship afloat on any of the world's oceans. She was saved from being scrapped in 1963 by a Seattle bank that was attempting to recoup some money on a bad debt. The people of Hawaii learned of her fate and spontaneously raised money to have the ship towed back to Honolulu Harbor. The *Falls of Clyde* was always a worker, never a pleasure craft. It served the Matson Steamship Company as a cargo and passenger liner from 1898 until 1920. Built in Glasgow, Scotland, in 1878, she was converted in 1906 to a sail-driven tanker; a motor aboard was used mainly to move the rigging around. After 1920, she was dismantled, towed to Alaska and became little more than a floating oil depot for fishing boats. Since 1968, the *Falls of Clyde* has been a floating museum, sailing the imaginations of children and grownups to times past, and in this capacity has perhaps performed her greatest duty.

The *Hokule'a*

The newest and perhaps most dynamic feature of the Center is the *Hokule'a*. This authentic recreation of a traditional double-hulled sailing canoe captured the attention of the world when in 1976 it made a 6,000-mile round trip voyage to Tahiti. Piloted by Mau Piailug, a Caroline Islander, only ancient navigational techniques guided it successfully on its voyage. This attempt to relive these ancient voyages as closely as possible included eating traditional provisions only—poi, coconuts, dried fish, and bananas. Toward the end of the voyage some canned food had to be broken out!

Modern materials such as plywood and fiberglass were used, but by consulting many petro-glyphs and old drawings of these original craft, the design and lines were kept as authentic as possible. The sails, made from a heavy cotton, were the distinctive crab-claw type. In trial runs to work out the kinks and choose the crew, she almost sank in the treacherous channel between Oahu and Kauai and had to be towed in by the Coast Guard. But the *Hokule'a* performed admirably during the actual voyage. The experiment was a resounding technical success, but it was marred by bad feelings between members of the crew who argued and drew racial boundary lines. Both Hawaiian and white crew members found it impossible to work as a team, thereby mocking the canoe's name, "Star of Gladness." The tension was compounded by the close quarters of more than a dozen men living on an open deck only nine feet wide by 40 feet long. The remarkable navigator Piailug refused to return to Hawaii with the craft and instead sailed back to his native island.

The *Hokule'a,* sponsored by the Polynesian Sailing Society, will make Pier seven its home berth when not at sea. This double-hulled canoe, a replica of the ones that Captain Cook found so remarkable, should fascinate you too.

Nearby Attractions

Two other attractions in the area are not part of the Hawaii Maritime Museum: in fact they're the antithesis of what this fine museum stands for. One is a monstrosity of a dinner boat called the *Relame,* an old flat-bottomed ferry, whose four-masts were added for effect. If ever the sails were unfurled, it'd roll around like a drunken tub-of-lard on roller skates. Also berthed close by is the *Oceania* **Floating Restaurant.** This barge, towed all the way from Hong Kong to Honolulu Harbor in 1972, is billed as the world's largest floating restaurant. It would best be described as "modern Oriental rococo." Unlike the *Relame,* the structure is just bizarre enough to make it interesting. Businesses seem to come and go here, and at the moment the *Oceania* has an empty hold.

PALI HIGHWAY

Cutting across Oahu from Honolulu to Kailua on the windward coast is Rt. 61, better known as the Pali Highway. Before getting to the famous

Nuuanu Pali Lookout at the very crest of the Koolau Mountains, you can spend a full and enjoyable day sightseeing. Stop en route at Punchbowl's National Memorial Cemetery, followed by an optional side trip to the summit of Tantalus for a breathtaking view of the city (see p. 207). You can also visit the **Royal Mausoleum** in the vicinity. Take the H-1 Freeway to Vineyard Boulevard (exit 22), cross the Pali Hwy. to Nuunau Avenue and follow it to the mausoleum. If you continue up Nuuanu Avenue, it intersects the Pali Hwy. in a minute or two, but you'll have passed the Punchbowl turnoff. This small chapel, built in 1865 by Kamehameha IV, holds the bodies of most of the royal family who died after 1825. Their bodies were originally interred elsewhere but were later moved here. The mausoleum at one time held 18 royal bodies, but became overcrowded, so they were moved again to little crypts scattered around the grounds. Few tourists visit this serene place open weekdays from 8 a.m- 4 p.m., tel. 536-7602.

About two miles past the Punchbowl turnoff, heading up the Pali Hwy. (exit 21-B off H-1), an HVB Warrior points you to the **Walker Home** across from Nuuanu Congregational Church. It's famous for its gardens, and at one time visitors were welcome to come and tour them for a fee. It's hard to tell if this is still happening. The gates are open and no signs tell you to keep out, but an unsmiling housekeeper backed by a steely-eyed German shepherd make you want to wave from your car and keep rolling. Next comes Queen Emma's Summer Palace (see following) and the Daijingu Temple, a Baptist college, and a Catholic church. It seems as though these sects were vying to get farther up the hill to be just a little closer to heaven.

A sign, past Queen Emma's Palace, points you off to **Nuuanu Pali Drive.** Take it! This few-minutes' jog off the Pali Hwy. (which it rejoins) takes you through some wonderful scenery. Make sure to bear right as soon as you pull off and not up the Old Pali Hwy., which has no outlet. Immediately the road is canopied with trees, and in less than half a mile there's a bubbling little waterfall and a pool. The homes in here are grand, and the entire area gives a park-like effect. One of the nicest little roads that you can take while looking around, this side trip wastes no time at all.

Queen Emma's Summer Palace

This summer home is more the simple hideaway of a well-to-do family than a grand palace. The 3,000-square-foot interior has only two bedrooms and no facilities for guests. The first person to put a house on the property was John George Lewis. He purchased the land for $800 from a previous owner by the name of Henry Pierce, and then resold it to John Young II. The exterior has a strong New England flavor, and indeed the house was prefabricated in Boston. The simple square home, surrounded by a *lanai,* was built from 1843 to 1847, by John Young II, Queen Emma's uncle. When he died, she inherited the property, and spent many relaxing days here, away from the heat of Honolulu, with her husband King Kamehameha IV. Emma used the home little after 1872, and following her death in 1885 it fell into disrepair.

Rescued from demolition by the Daughters of Hawaii in 1913, it was refurbished and has operated as a museum since 1915. The Palace, at 2913 Pali Hwy., tel. 595-3167, is open daily 9 a.m.- 4 p.m., admission $4, children under 12 $.50. Although it's just off the Pali Highway, the one and only sign comes up quickly, and many visitors pass it by. If you pass the entranceway to the Oahu Country Club just across the road, you've gone too far.

As you enter, notice the tall *kahili,* symbols of noble rank in the entranceway, along with *lau hala* mats on the floor, which at one time were an unsurpassed speciality of Hawaii. Today they must be imported from Fiji or Samoa. The walls are hung with paintings of many of Hawaii's kings and queens, and in every room are distinctive Hawaiian artifacts, such as magnificent feather capes, fans, and tapa hangings.

The furnishings have a very strong British influence. The Hawaiian nobility of the time were enamored with the British. King Kamehameha IV traveled to England when he was 15 years old; he met Queen Victoria, and the two became good friends. Emma and Kamehameha IV had the last child born to a Hawaiian king and queen on May 20, 1858. Named Prince Albert after Queen Victoria's consort, he was much loved, but died when he was only four years old on August 27, 1862. His father followed him to the grave in little more than a year. The king's brother, Lot Kamehameha, a bachelor, took the throne, but died very shortly thereafter, marking the end of the Kamehameha line; after that, Hawaii elected her kings. Prince Albert's canoe-shaped cradle is here, made in Germany by Wilhelm Fisher from four different kinds of Hawaiian wood. His tiny shirts, pants, and boots are still laid out, and there's a lock of his hair, and one from Queen Emma. In every room there is royal memorabilia. The royal bedroom displays a queen-sized bed covered with an exquisite pink and purple tapa bedspread. There's vintage Victorian furniture, and even a piano built in London by Collard and Collard. A royal cabinet made in Berlin holds porcelains, plates, and cups. After Queen Emma died, it stood in Charles R. Bishop's drawing room, and was later returned. The grounds are beautifully manicured, and the house is surrounded by shrubbery and trees, many of which date from when the royal couple lived here. Restrooms are around back.

Walk around back past the basketball court and keep to the right. Soon you'll see a modest little white building. Look for a rather thick and distinctive rope hanging across the entranceway. This is the Shinto temple **Dai Jingu**. It's not nearly as spectacular as the giant trees in this area, but it is authentic and worth a quick look.

The Daughters of Hawaii have added a gift shop around back, which is open the same hours as the Palace. It's small but packed with excellent items like greeting cards, leis, travel guidebooks, beverage trays (reproductions of the early Matson Line menus), little Hawaiian quilt pillows, needlepoint, wraparounds from Tahiti, T-shirts with Queen Emma's Summer Palace logo, and Niihau shellwork, the finest in Hawaii.

Nuuanu Pali Lookout

This is one of those extra-benefit places where you get a magnificent view without any effort at all. Merely drive up the Pali Hwy. to the well-marked turnout and park. Rip-offs happen, so take all valuables. Before you, if the weather is accommodating, an unimpeded view of windward Oahu lies at your feet. Nuuanu Pali ("Cool Heights") lives up to its name; the winds here are chilly, extremely strong, and funnel right through the lookout. You definitely need a jacket or windbreaker. On a particularly windy day just after a good rainfall, various waterfalls tumbling off the *pali* will actually be blown uphill! A number of

roads, punched over and through the *pali* over the years, are engineering marvels. The famous "carriage road" built in 1898 by John Wilson, a Honolulu boy, for only $37,500, using 200 laborers and plenty of dynamite, was truly amazing. Droves of people come here, many in huge buses, and they all go to the railing to have a peek. Even so, by walking down the old road built in 1932 that goes off to the right, you actually get private and better views. You'll find the tallest point in the area, a huge needle-like rock. The wind is quieter here.

Nuuanu Pali figures prominently in Hawaii's legend history. It's said, not without academic skepticism, that Kamehameha the Great pursued the last remaining defenders of Oahu to these cliffs in one of the final battles fought to consolidate his power over all of the islands in 1795. If you use your imagination, you can easily feel the utter despair and courage of these vanquished warriors as they were driven ever closer to the edge. Mercy was not shown nor expected. Some jumped to their deaths rather than surrender, while others fought until they were pushed over. The estimated number of casualties varies considerably, from a few hundred to a few thousand, while some believe that the battle never happened at all. Compounding the controversy are stories of the warriors' families, who searched the cliffs below for years, and supposedly found bones of their kinsmen, that they buried. The Pali Lookout is romantic at night, with the lights of Kailua and Kaneohe in the distance, but the best nighttime view is from Tantalus Drive, where all of Honolulu lies at your feet.

PUNCHBOWL, NATIONAL CEMETERY OF THE PACIFIC

One sure sign that you have entered a place of honor is the hushed and quiet nature that everyone adopts without having to be told. That's the way it is the moment that you enter this shrine. The Hawaiian name, Puowaina ("Hill of Sacrifice"), couldn't have been more prophetic. Punchbowl is the almost perfectly round crater of an extinct volcano that holds the bodies of nearly 25,000 men and women who fell fighting for the United States, from the Spanish-American War to Vietnam. At one time, Punchbowl was a bastion of heavy cannon and artillery trained on Honolulu Harbor to defend it from hostile naval forces. In 1943 Hawaii bequeathed it to the federal government as a memorial; it was dedicated in 1949, when the remains of an unknown serviceman killed during the attack on Pearl Harbor were the first interred.

As you enter the main gate, a flagpole with the Stars and Stripes unfurled is framed in the center of a long sweeping lawn. A roadway lined with monkeypods adds three-dimensional depth to the impressionistic scene, as it leads to the steps of a marble, altar-like monument in the distance. The eye has a continuous sweep of the field, as there are no elevated tombstones, just simple marble slabs lying flat on the ground. The field is dotted with trees, including eight banyans, a special tree and symbolic number for the many Buddhists buried here. Brightening the scene are plumeria and rainbow shower trees, often planted in Hawaiian graveyards because they produce flowers year-round as perennial offerings from the living to the dead when they can't personally attend the grave. All are equal here; the famous like Ernie Pyle, the stalwart who earned the Congressional Medal of Honor, and the unknown who died alone and unheralded on muddy battlefields in Godforsaken jungles. To the right, just after you enter is the office, open Mon. to Fri. 9 a.m.- 5 p.m. with brochures, and restrooms. Tour buses, taxis, and limousines are lined up here. Don't leave valuables in your car.

The Monument

Like a pilgrim, you climb the steps to the monument, where on both sides marble slabs seem to whisper the names of the 20,000-plus servicemen, all MIAs whose bodies were never found but whose spirits are honored here. The first slabs on the right are for the victims of Vietnam, on the left are those from WW II, and you can see that time is already weathering the marble. They lie together, as they fought and died . . . men, boys, lieutenants, captains, private soldiers, infantrymen, sailors . . . from everywhere in America. "In proud memory . . . this memorial has been erected by the United States of America."

At the monument itself, built in 1966, is a chapel and in the middle is a statue of a woman, a woman of peace, a heroic woman of liberty. Around her on the walls are etched maps and battles of the Pacific War whose names still

evoke passion: Pearl Harbor, Wake, Coral Sea, Midway, Iwo Jima, the Gilbert Islands, Okinawa. Many of the visitors are Japanese. Many of Hawaii's war dead are also Japanese. Four decades ago we battled each other with hatred and malice. Today, on bright afternoons we come together with saddened hearts to pay reverence to the dead.

To get to Punchbowl take the H-1 Freeway to Rt. 61, the Pali Highway, and exit at 21-B. Immediately get to the right, where a sign points you to Punchbowl. You'll make some fancy zigzags through a residential area, but it's well marked and you'll come to Puowaina Street, which leads you to the main gate. Make sure to notice landmarks going in, because as odd as it sounds, no signs lead you back out and it's easy to get lost.

UNIVERSITY OF HAWAII

You don't have to be a student to head for the University of Hawaii, Manoa Campus. For one, it houses the **East-West Center,** where nations from Asia and the Pacific present fascinating displays of their homelands. Also, Manoa Valley itself is one of the loveliest residential areas on Oahu. To get to the main campus follow the H-1 Freeway to exit 24B (University Avenue). Don't make the mistake of exiting at the University's Makai Campus. Follow University Avenue to the second red light, Dole Avenue, and make a right onto campus. Stop immediately at one of the parking lots and get a parking map! Parking restrictions are strictly enforced, and this map not only helps to get you around, but saves you from fines or having your car towed away. Parking is $.50 an hour, even for visitors, so think about taking TheBus, which services this area quite well.

Student Center

Make this your first stop. As you mount the steps, notice the idealized mural of old Hawaii: smiling faces of contented natives all doing interesting things. Inside is the **Information Center,** which dispenses info. not only about the campus, but also what's happening socially and culturally around town. They even have lists of cheap restaurants, discos, and student hangouts. Next door are typewriters available to nonstudents at $2 per day. The food in the cafeteria is institutional but cheap, and has a Hawaiian twist. The best place to eat is at the **Manoa Gardens** in the Hemingway Center where you can get a tasty stir-fry or good vegetarian dish for $3.50 and up.

The **University Bookstore** is excellent, open Mon. to Fri. 8:15 a.m.- 4:15 p.m., Sat. 8:15-11:45 a.m. The bookstore is worth coming to for its excellent range of specialty items like language tapes and its extensive assortment of travel guidebooks. The **University Art Gallery** is on the third floor, and is worth a look. Free! The exhibits change regularly. Next to the gallery is a lounge filled with overstuffed chairs and big pillows, where you can kick back and even take a quick snooze. This is not a very social campus. By 4:30 or 5 p.m. the place is shut up and no one is around. Don't expect students gathered in a common reading room, or the activity of social and cultural events. When school lets out at the end of the day, people simply go home.

East-West Center
Follow Dole Avenue to East-West Road and make a left. Free tours, Mon. to Fri. at 1:30 p.m., originate from Bachman Hall at the corner of University and Dole avenues. For more info contact the East-West Center, 1777 East-West Rd., Honolulu, HI 96848, tel. 944-7111. The Center's 21 acres were dedicated in 1960 by the U.S. Congress to promote better relations between the countries of Asia and the Pacific with the U.S. Many nations, as well as private companies and individuals, fund this institution of cooperative study and research. John Burn's Hall's main lobby dispenses information on what's happening, along with self-guiding maps. Thomas Jefferson Hall, fronted by Chinese lions, has a serene and relaxing Japanese garden behind, complete with a little rivulet and a teahouse named Jakuan, "Cottage of Tranquility." The murals inside are excellent, and it also contains a large reading room with relaxing couches.

The impressive Thai Pavilion was a gift from the king of Thailand, where it was built and sent to Hawaii to be reconstructed. This 23-ton, solid teak *sala* is a common sight in Thailand. The Center for Korean Studies is also outstanding. A joint venture of Korean and Hawaiian architects, its inspiration was taken from the classic lines of Kyongbok Palace in Seoul. Most of the buildings are adorned with fine artworks: tapa hangings, murals, calligraphy, paintings, and

sculpture. The entire center is tranquil, and along with the John F. Kennedy Theater of Performing Arts just across the road, is indeed fulfilling its dedication as a place of sharing and learning, culture and art.

BISHOP MUSEUM (STATE MUSEUM OF NATURAL AND CULTURAL HISTORY)

This group of stalwart stone buildings holds the greatest collection of historical relics and scholarly works on Hawaii and the Pacific in the world. Referring to itself as a "museum to instruct and delight," in one afternoon walking through its halls you can educate yourself about Hawaii's history and people and enrich your trip to the islands tenfold.

Officially named Bernice Pauahi Bishop Museum, its founding was directly connected to the last three royal women of the Kamehameha Dynasty. Princess Bernice married Charles Reed Bishop, a New Englander who became a citizen of the then-independent monarchy in the 1840s. The princess was a wealthy woman in her own right, with lands and an extensive collection of "things Hawaiian." Her cousin, Princess Ruta Keelikolani, died in 1883, and bequeathed Princess Bernice all of her lands and Hawaiian artifacts. Together, this meant that Princess Bernice owned about 12% of all Hawaii! Princess Bernice died less than two years later, and left all of her land holdings to the **Bernice Pauahi Bishop Estate,** which founded and supported the Kamehameha School, dedicated to the education of Hawaiian children. (Though this organization is often confused with the Bishop Museum, they are totally separate. The school shared the same grounds with the museum, but none of the funds from this organization were, or are, used for the museum.) Bernice left her personal property, with all of its priceless Hawaiian artifacts, to her husband Charles. Then, when Queen Emma, her other cousin, died the following year, she too desired Charles Bishop to combine her Hawaiian artifacts with the already formidable collection and establish a Hawaiian museum.

True to the wishes of these women, he began construction of the museum's main building on December 18, 1889, and within a few years the museum was opened. In 1894, after 50 years in

Hawaii, Bishop moved to San Francisco where he died in 1915. He is still regarded as one of Hawaii's most generous philanthropists. In 1961, a science wing and planetarium were added, and two dormitory buildings are still used from when the Kamehameha School for Boys occupied the same site.

Getting There
To get there, take exit 20A off the H-1 Freeway, which puts you on Rt. 63, the Likelike Highway. Immediately get into the far right lane. In only a few hundred yards, turn onto Bernice Street where you'll find the entrance. Or, exit H-1 onto Hofftailing Street, Rt. 61, exit 20B. Keep your eyes peeled for a clearly marked but small sign directing you to the museum. TheBus #2 (School-Middle Street) runs from Waikiki to Kapalama Street, from which you walk two blocks.

Admission And Information
The museum is located at 1525 Bernice St., Honolulu, HI 96817, tel. 847- 3511, and is open seven days per week from 9 a.m.- 5 p.m. The official entrance has been changed. It's now at the new building just near the planetarium, not at the old lava stone building. Admission is $5.95 adults, six and younger free, but some exhibits and the planetarium are closed to children under six. It's sometimes best to visit on weekends because many weekdays bring teachers and young students who have more enthusiasm for running around than checking out the exhibits. Food, beverages, smoking, and flash photography are all strictly prohibited in the museum. The natural light in the museum is dim, so if you're into photography you'll need super-fast film (400 ASA performs only marginally). Before leaving the grounds make sure to visit **Atherton Halau,** where a hula is performed Mon.-Sat. at 10:15 a.m. and 2 p.m. Throughout the week, the hall offers demonstrations in various Hawaiian crafts like lei-making, featherwork, and quilting. The **planetarium** opens up its skies daily at 11 a.m. and 2 p.m.

There are special nighttime shows and family discount days offered, call 847-3511 for details. The snack shop has reasonable prices, and **Shop Pacifica,** the museum bookstore and boutique, has a fine selection of materials on Hawaii and the Pacific, and some authentic and inexpensive souvenirs. The **museum cafe** has

HAWAII STATE ARCHIVES

Princess Bernice

a limited menu with dishes like Hawaiian fruit salad $3.50, hamburger $2.85, teriyaki burger $2.65, and snacks like chili dogs, muffins, chips, and drinks.

Exhibits
It's easy to become overwhelmed at the museum, so just take it slowly. The number of exhibits is staggering: over 100,000 artifacts, almost 20 million (!) specimens of insects, shells, fish, birds, and mammals, plus an extensive research library, photograph collection, and fine series of maps. The main gallery is highlighted by the rich tones of *koa,* the showpiece being a magnificent staircase. Get a map at the front desk that lists all of the halls, along with a description of what theme is found in each, and a suggested route to follow. The following are just a potpourri of the highlights that you'll discover.

To the right of the main entranceway is a fascinating exhibit of the old Hawaiian gods. Most are just called "wooden image" and date from the early 19th century. Among them are: Kamehameha's war-god, *Ku;* the tallest Hawaiian sculpture ever found, from Kauai; and an image of a god from a temple of human sacrifice; and lesser gods, personal *aumakua* that controlled the lives of Hawaiians from birth until death. You wouldn't want to meet any of them in a dark alley! Outside, in what's called the **Hawaiian Courtyard,** are implements used by the Hawaiians in everyday life, as well as a collection of plants that have all been identified. The first floor of the main hall is perhaps the most interesting because it deals with old Hawaii. Here are magnificent examples of *kahili,* feathered capes, plumed helmets . . . all the insignia and regalia of the *ali'i.* A commoner sits in a grass shack, a replica of what Capt. Cook might have seen.

Don't look up! Over your head is a 55-foot sperm whale hanging from the ceiling. It weighed over 44,000 pounds alive. You'll learn about the ukelele, and how vaudevillians spread its music around the world. Hula- skirted damsels from the 1870s peer provocatively from old photos, barebreasted and with plenty of "cheesecake." Tourists bought these photos even then, although the grass skirts they're wearing were never a part of old Hawaii, but were brought by Gilbert Islanders. See authentic hula instruments like a "lover's whistle," a flute played through the nose, and a musical bow, the only stringed pre-European Hawaiian instrument.

Don't miss the *koa* wood collection. This accomplished artform produced medicine bowls, handsome calabashes, some simple home bowls, and others reputed to be the earthly home of the wind goddess, and had to be refitted for display in Christianized Iolani Palace. A model *heiau* tells of the old religion, and the many strange *kapu* that governed every aspect of life. Clubs used to bash in the brains of *kapu*-breakers are next to benevolent little stone gods, the size and shape of footballs, that protected humble fishermen from the sea. As you ascend to the upper floors, time becomes increasingly closer to the present. The missionaries, whalers, merchants, laborers, and Westernized monarchs have arrived. Yankee whalers from New Bedford, New London, Nantucket, and Sag Harbor appear determined and grim-faced as they scour the seas, harpoons at the ready. Great blubber pots, harpoons, and figureheads are preserved from this perilous and unglamorous life. Bibles, thrones, the regalia of power and of the new god are all here.

MUSEUMS, GALLERIES, GARDENS, AND TOURS

Military Museums

The museum at **Battery Randolph,** with the hulks of tanks standing guard, is one long cor-

ridor where you feel the strength of the superthick reinforced walls of this once-active gun emplacement. Located at Fort DeRussy, on the corner of Kalia and Saratoga roads, free guided tours are available, open Tues.-Sun., 10 a.m.-4:30 p.m., tel. 543-2687. U.S. Battery Randolph once housed two 14-inch coast artillary rifles meant to defend Honolulu and Pearl harbors. The architecture is typical of the Taft Period forts constructed between 1907 and 1920. The battery is listed in the National Register of Historic Places. Upon entering is a shop dedicated to *things military,* flying jackets to wall posters. Walk the halls to learn the military history of Hawaii traced as far back as Kamehameha I. Here are rifles, swords, and vintage photos of Camp McKinley, a turn-of-the-century military station in the shadow of Diamond Head.

A side room holds models of artillary used to defend Waikiki from times when Battery Randolph was an active installation. One room shows how the guns worked in a method called "disappearing guns." The gun would raise up and fire and then disappear. The recoil of the gun would lock it back in position, and after it was reloaded a 50-ton counterweight would pop it up ready to fire. The explosive sound would rattle the entire neighborhood so they were seldom test-fired.

Exhibits show the fledgling days of Army aviation in Hawaii when on July 13, 1913, 14 officers began a military flying school. There are beautiful models of military equipment, especially one of an old truck unit. Then comes the ominous exhibit of "Rising Japan" with its headlong thrust into WW II. Hawaii, grossly overconfident, felt immune to attack because of the strong military presence. Photos from the '30s and '40s depict the carefree lifestyle of visiting celebrities like Babe Ruth and Shirley Temple, which ended abruptly on Dec. 7, 1941, in the wreckage of Pearl Harbor.

An entire room is dedicated to the Pearl Harbor attack and is filled with models of Japanese planes, aircraft carriers, and real helmets and goggles worn by the Zero pilots. Most interesting are the slice-of-life photos of Hawaii mobilized for war: defense workers, both men and women, sailors, soldiers, entertainers, street scenes. Pamphlets from the time read, "Know Your Enemies," and there's a macabre photo of people gathered at a stadium to see the demonstration of the devasting effect of flame throwers that would be employed upon the Japanese enemy. Bob Hope is here entertaining the troops, while a 442nd Regimental Battle Flag bears testament to the most decorated unit in American history, comprised mostly of *nissei* Japanese from Hawaii. Then come photos and exhibits from the soulwrenching conflicts in Korea and Vietnam. Finally a room, like a whispering tomb, tells of the heroics of Hawaiian soldiers who have been awarded the Congressional Medal of Honor, almost all posthumously.

Make sure to go outside to the upper level exhibit where you'll see one of the old guns still pointing out to sea, which seems incongruous with sunbathers just below on the quiet and excellent stretch of beach. On the upper deck are depth charges, torpedoes, and shells, along with a multimedia slide show. Your eyes will take a few minutes to refocus to the glorious sunshine of Waikiki after the cold gloom of the bunker. Perhaps our hearts and souls could refocus as well.

Honolulu Academy Of Arts

This museum has a brilliant collection of classic and modern art, strongly emphasizing Asian artwork. James Michener's outstanding collection of Japanese *ukiyoe* is here. The story goes that an unfriendly New York cop hassled him on his way to donate it to a N.Y.C. museum, while a Honolulu officer was the epitome of aloha when Michener was passing through, so he decided that his collection should reside here. This collection is currently displayed about six months per year, but a decision has been made to display it year-round. Magnificent Korean ceramics, Chinese furniture, Japanese prints, along with Western masterworks from the Greeks to Picasso, make the Academy one of the most rounded art museums in America. Some collections are permanent while others change, so the museum remains dynamic no matter how many times you visit.

Enjoy the magnificent building and grounds as well as the glorious artwork. It's a perfect building designed by architect Bertrum Goodhugh and benefactor Mrs. Charles Montague expressly as a museum. The design is a combination of East and West with a Hawaiian roof, and thick white stucco walls reminiscent of the American Southwest. Enter through the foyer

and pass to the courtyard that gets you away from the hustle and bustle of downtown. It's great for a little respite from noise. Pass through double French doors to the thick white-walled galleries that create a perfect atmosphere for displaying fine works of art. Discover delights like Paul Gauguin's *Two Nudes on a Tahitian Beach,* Whistler's *Arrangement in Black No. 5,* and John Singer Sargent's *Portrait of Mrs. Thomas Lincoln Hansen Jr.* An entire wing is dedicated to religious art, while another holds furniture from medieval Europe. The courtyards are resplendent with statuary from the 6th Century A.D. and a standing figure from Egypt, circa 2500 B.C. The Hawaiian climate is perfect for preserving artworks.

Stop at the **Academy Shop,** specializing in art books, museum repros, Hawaii out-of-prints, jewelry, notebooks, and post cards, open 1-4 Tues.-Sat. and 1-5 Sunday. The Garden Cafe, open 11:30 a.m.-1 p.m. Tues.-Fri., Thursday supper at 6:30 p.m., is in a garden under a canopy. They have a light but terrific menu, and besides, a trip to the Academy demands a luncheon in the cafe. For menu and details see p. 250.

Museum hours are Tues.-Sat. 10 a.m.- 4:30 p.m., Sun. 1-5 p.m., closed Monday. Free, donations only. Guided tours are conducted at 11 a.m. Tues., Wed., Fri., Sat., and at 1 p.m. on Thurs. and Sunday. The Academy of Arts is at 900 S. Beretania St. (TheBus #2), opposite Thomas Square, tel. 538-1006.

The Contemporary Museum

Under the direction of Fritz Frauchinger, at 2411 Mikiki Heights Rd., tel. 526-1322, the museum welcomes you with two copper-green gates that are sculptures themselves. This open and elegant structure, the former Spalding House, has yielded six galleries, a shop, and an excellent gourmet restaurant (see p. 250). Acquired through the generosity of the Honolulu Advertiser's stockholders, it was donated to the museum as a permanent home in 1988. Surrounding it are three magnificent acres sculpted into Oriental gardens perfect for strolling and gazing at the sprawl of Honolulu far below. The focus is on exhibitions, not collections, although works by David Hockney are on permanent display. Always-changing exhibits reflect different themes in contemporary art. Open Mon.-Sat. 10

a.m.- 4 p.m., Sun. noon-4 p.m., closed Tues., admission $3.

Tennent Art Foundation
At 201-203 Prospect St., on the *ewa* slope of Punchbowl, the foundation is open Tues.-Sat. 10 a.m.- noon, and Sun. 2-4 p.m., tel. 531-1987. It's free. There is a library and the walls hold the paintings of Madge Tennent, one of Hawaii's foremost artists, as well as many other contemporary works. It's beautiful and quiet and worth a visit.

Foster Botanical Gardens
Fifteen acres of exotic trees, many of which have been growing in this manicured garden for over 100 years, at one time this was the private estate of Dr. Hillebrand, physician to the royal court, who brought many of the seedlings from Asia. Two dozen of these trees enjoy lifetime protection by the state. At 180 N. Vineyard St., tel. 531-1939, open daily 9 a.m.- 4 p.m., it's free with self-guiding brochures. Guided tours Mon., Tues., and Wed. at 1:30 p.m.; many nature hikes on Oahu and the Neighbor Islands are sponsored by the gardens.

Manoa Road
Leading past the University of Hawaii into Manoa Valley, is a lovely residential area. En route you pass **Punahou School,** one of the oldest and most prestigious high schools in Hawaii. Built in 1841 from lava rock, children of the missionary families of wealthy San Franciscans attended, getting the best possible education west of the Rockies. Manoa Road turns into Oahu Avenue. **Waioli Tea Room,** 3016 Oahu Ave., owned and operated by the Salvation Army, is a small park; their snack bar features fresh- baked pastries and serves lunch daily from 11 a.m.- 2 p.m. Also featured here is the **Little Grass Shack** transported from Waikiki that Robert Louis Stevenson supposedly lived in. Visit the chapel with its distinctive stained-glass windows. Waioli Tea Room is open daily, except Monday, from 8 a.m.- 3:30 p.m., luncheon served from 11 a.m.- 2 p.m. For reservations call 988-2131.

The Dole Cannery Square
Look for the giant pineapple rising 200 feet into the air. A landmark of Honolulu, it was built in Chicago and erected here in 1928. It is still used as a reservoir and holds 100,000 gallons of water that's piped throughout the Dole Cannery, whose outer buildings were transformed in 1988 to a mini-mall which complements the ongoing Dole Cannery Tour. Located at 650 Iwilei Rd., tel. 548-4837, 45-minute tours are conducted daily from 9 a.m.- 5 p.m., with the last departing at 3 p.m. Admission is $5; children under 12 are free. Free parking is provided if you take your car, but ride the **Pineapple Transit,** tel. 523-DOLE, a van that runs from 8:30 a.m.- 3:30 p.m., picking up at many Waikiki hotels, $.50 one way. Upon entering the atrium area, look high on the walls to see reproductions of Dole Pineapple can labels. They're pop art, and convey a feeling of simpler times past. Here also is the **Food Court** providing snacks, salads, sandwiches, and soups for a quick lunch.

The tour itself begins with a stereophonic slide show that instructs on the development of pineapple in Hawaii. Plenty of memorabilia and vintage photos help create a sense of the past. You're then conducted right into the factory where workers are busy packing the fruit, and where you learn the process of how it makes it to the kitchen table. Observe the newest generation of the marvelous Ginaca machine, first built in 1913 by Henry Ginaca, a draftsman hired by James Dole to modernize the industry. This whirring wonder can peel, core, cut, slice, and dice 100 fruits per minute. Within 20 minutes of reaching the machine, the canned fruit's ready for the grocer's shelf. After the tour, you're taken to a tasting room where you're offered complimentary . . . guess what?

On the second floor you'll find a cluster of shops laid out as traditional storefronts and featuring items made in Hawaii. Stop at the **Dole Logo Shop** for a T-shirt with a replica of a vintage pineapple can label, along with hats, gift items, and glassware all bearing the Dole logo. The **Island Moo Moo Works,** popular with local people, has racks of affordable muumuus and alohawear. The **Jungle Jerky Shop** has jerky of all sorts and sells stuffed animals, all life-sized, as well as cotton cloth flowers. New shops like **Mamo Howell** and **Island Princess** will add elegance with their fashions, or you can take care of your sweet tooth at **Sharyn's Hawaiian Island Cookies.** One of the nicest shops is the **Village Beach Shop.** They're a complete resort-wear store with plenty of muumuus, sandals, and even boogie boards to choose from. They have a fine selection of T-shirts with gold designs by Ericka Paeis, a very creative and distinctive designer in the crowded field of Hawaiian T-shirts.

Paradise Park

These 13 acres of lush tropical plants explode in the 160 inches of annual rainfall that cascades into this farthest section of Manoa Valley. Magnificent blooms compete with the wild plumage of 50 species of exotic birds. You first walk into a giant bird cage laced with paths. The birds perform circus acts at scheduled intervals; some could easily win a spot with Barnum and Bailey for their tricks. This is purely make-believe Hawaii, good for a few hours of family fun. The Chuck Machado Luau is held here on Sunday evenings, and Henri Hawaii's Restaurant, on the premises, has good food at not too inflated prices at 3737 Manoa Rd., tel. 988-6686. Admission is $7.95 adults, $5.95 children, open daily 9:30 a.m.- 5:30 p.m., allow two to three hours to see the entire park. Drive or take TheBus, no. 8-Paradise Park, from Ala Moana Center. Also, a special tour bus from Waikiki is available.

Moanalua Gardens

Those private gardens of the Damon Estate, at 1352 Pineapple Pl., tel. 839-5334, were given to the original owner by Princess Bernice Bishop in 1884. Just off the Moanalua Freeway, and open to the public, these gardens are not heavily touristed, a welcome respite from the hustle and bustle of the city. Some magnificent old trees include a Buddha tree from Ceylon, and a monkeypod called "the most beautifully shaped tree" in the world by *Ripley's Believe It or Not*. The Moanalua Foundation also sponsors walks deep into Moanalua Valley for viewing the foliage of "natural Hawaii." The free guided walks begin at 9 a.m. usually on weekends; make arrangements by calling 839-5334.

HONOLULU BEACHES AND PARKS

The beaches and parks listed here are found in and around Honolulu's city limits. World-famous Waikiki has its own entire section (see p. 270). The good thing about having Waikiki so close is that it lures most bathers away from other city beaches, which makes them less congested. The following list contains most of Honolulu's beaches, ending at Fort DeRussy Beach Park, just a few hundred yards from where the string of Waikiki's beaches begin. Also see Aiea, p. 303

Sand Island State Recreation Area

As you enter this 140-acre park by way of the Sand Island Access Road, clearly marked off the Nimitz Highway, you pass through some ugly real estate—scrapyards, petrochemical tanks, and other such beauties. Don't get discouraged, keep going! Once you cross the metal bridge, a favorite fishing spot for local people, and then pass the entrance to the U.S. Coast Guard base, you enter the actual park, 14 acres landscaped with picnic and playground facilities. Follow the road into the park; pass two observation towers that have been built in the middle of a grassy field from where you get an impressive view of Honolulu, with Diamond Head making a remarkable counterpoint. The park is excellently maintained, with pavilions, coldwater showers, walkways, and restrooms. For day use only, the park closes at 6:30 p.m. The camping area is usually empty (state permit required, see pp. 159 and 205). The sites are out in the open, but a few trees provide some shade.

Unfortunately, you're under one of the main glide-paths for Honolulu International Airport. Many local people come to fish, and the surfing is good, but the beaches for snorkeling and swimming are fair at best. Some of the beach area is horrible, piled with broken stone, rubble, and pieces of coral. However, if you follow the road past the tower and park in the next lot, turn right and follow the shore up to a sandy beach. The currents and wave action aren't dangerous, but remember that this part of the harbor receives more than its share of pollutants. For delicious and inexpensive plate lunches, make sure to stop at Penny's just next door to Dirty Dan's Topless Go-Go Bar on your way down the access road (see p. 249 and p. 255).

La Mariana Yacht Sailing Club

This small marina at 50 Sand Island Access Road is a love song in the middle of an industrialized area. The marina is Annette La Mariana Nahinua's labor of love that has remained true since 1955. You can read her fantastic story on the menu of the marina's **Hideaway Restaurant** (p. 250), which is the only real restaurant on Sand Island. In 1955 this area was forgotten, forsaken, and unkempt. Ms. Nahinua, against the forces of nature, and the even more unpredictable and devastating forces of bureaucracy, took this land and turned it into a yacht harbor. The main tools were indefatigable determination, God listening to her prayers, and a shovel and rake. It's one of the last enclaves of old Hawaii, a place to come for dinner, a drink, or just to look at the boats. The nighttime bartender, Mr. Lee, is friendly but stoic after decades of seeing and hearing it all. Annette, the founder, is now a little gray-haired woman, a motherly type in Birkenstocks, who lives right here above the Hideaway. In the daytime she wanders around spreading her magic while talking to old salts or new arrivals.

The marina is adjacent to an open waterway, which means that you don't have to pay for anchorage. It comes under the old "rights of sailors" to find a free port in which to berth. This unique setup has created an atmosphere in which a subculture of people have built subsistence shacks on the little islands that dot the bay. Some also live on old scows, shipshape yachts, or on very imaginative homemade crafts, afloat and semi-afloat on this tranquil bay. Many are disillusioned and disenfranchised Vietnam vets who have become misanthropes. You'll see the Stars and Stripes flying from their island hooches. Others are yachties who disdain being landlubbers, while others are poor souls who have fallen through the social net. La Mariana is a unique statement of personal freedom in a city where unique statements are generally not tolerated.

Kakaako (Point Panic) Beach Park

This small facility was carved out of a piece of land donated by the University of Hawaii's Biomedical Research Center. Next to Kewalo Basin Harbor, follow Ahuii Street, off Ala Moana Boulevard. You'll come to some landscaped grounds with a cold-water shower and a path leading to the bathing area. Kewalo Basin, developed in the '20s to hold Honolulu's tuna fleet, is home to many charter boats. If you're lucky, you may even spot a manta ray which are known to frequent these waters. This area is poor for swimming, known for sharks, but great

for bodysurfing. Unfortunately, novices will quickly find out why it's called Point Panic. A long seawall with a sharp dropoff runs the entire length of the area. The wave action is perfect for riding, but all wash against the wall. Beginners stay out! The best reason to come here is for the magnificent and unobstructed view of the Waikiki skyline and Diamond Head.

Ala Moana Park

Ala Moana ("Path to the Sea") Beach Park is by far Honolulu's best. Most visitors congregate just around the bend at Waikiki, but residents head for Ala Moana, the place to soak up the local color. During the week, this beautifully curving white-sand beach has plenty of elbow room. Weekends bring families that come for every water sport Oahu offers. The swimming is great, with manageable wave action, plenty of lifeguards, and even good snorkeling along the reef. Board riders have their favorite spots, and bodysurfing is excellent. The huge area has a number of restrooms, food concessions, tennis courts, softball fields, a bowling green, and parking for 500 cars. Many Oahu outrigger canoe clubs practice in this area, especially in the evening; it's great to come and watch them glide along. A huge banyan grove provides shade and strolling if you don't fancy the beach, or you can bring a kite to play aloft with the trade winds. Ala Moana Park stretches along Ala Moana Avenue, between the Ala Wai and Kewalo Basin boat harbors. It's across from the Ala Moana Shopping Center, so you can rush right over if your credit cards start melting from the sun.

Aina Moana ("Land from the Sea") **Recreation Area** used to be called Magic Island because it was reclaimed land. It is actually the point of land stretching out from the eastern edge of Ala Moana, and although it has a different name, appears to be part of Ala Moana. All the beach activities are great here, too.

Kahanamoku Beach

The stretch of sand in front of the Hilton Hawaiian Village is named after Hawaii's most famous waterman, Duke Kahanamoku. The manmade beach and lagoon were completed in 1956. A system of pumps pushes water into the lagoon to keep it fresh. The swimming is great, and plenty of concessions offer surfboards, beach equipment, and catamaran cruises.

Fort DeRussy Beach

This is the last beach before reaching the Waikiki beaches proper. You pass through rights-of-way of the Fort DeRussy military area where you'll find restrooms, picnic facilities, volleyball courts, and food and beverage concessions. Lifeguard service is provided by military personnel—no duty is too rough for our fighting men and women! A controversy has raged for years between the military and developers who covet this valuable piece of land. The government has owned it since the turn of the century, and has developed what once was wasteland into the last stretch of noncement, non- high rise piece of real estate left along Waikiki. Since the public has access to the beach, and since Congress voted a few years back that the lands can not be sold, it'll remain under the jurisdiction of the military. **Battery Randolph,** on the military grounds, is open to the public as a military museum.

ACCOMMODATIONS

The vast majority of Oahu's hotels are strung along the boulevards of Waikiki. Most are neatly clustered, bounded by the Ala Wai Canal, and run eastward to Diamond Head. These hotels will be discussed in the Waikiki section. The remainder of greater Honolulu has few hotels, but what do exist are some of Oahu's cheapest. Most are clean, no-frills establishments, with a few others at the airport, or just off the beaten track.

Oahu's YM/WCAs And YH

Oahu has a number of YM/WCAs from which to choose, and the only official youth hostel in the state. They vary as far as private room and bath are concerned, facilities offered, and prices. Expect to pay about $30 s with a shared bath, and about $32.50 d with a private bath.

The **YMCA Central Branch** (men only) at 401 Atkinson Dr., Honolulu 96814, tel 941-3344, is the most centrally located and closest to Waikiki. You can call ahead, but there are no reservations, no curfew, and no visitors after 10 p.m.; it has an outside pool, singles, doubles, and private baths. This Y is located just across from the eastern end of Ala Moana Park, only a 10-minute walk to Waikiki.

YMCA Nuuanu (men only), 1441 Pali Hwy., Honolulu 96813, tel. 536- 3556, just near the intersection of S. Vineyard Blvd., is a few minutes' walk from downtown Honolulu. You'll find a modern, sterile facility with a pool, shared and single rooms, and private or communal showers; reservations accepted.

Armed Services YMCA, open to military personnel and civilian, both men and women, at 250 S. Hotel St., Honolulu, tel. 524-5600. No reservations, but a pool, single and double rooms, plenty of sporting facilities, and child care!

YMCA Atherton Branch, 1810 University Ave., Honolulu, tel. 946-0253. Near the University of Hawaii, men and women students are given preferential treatment. Dormitory style, no recreational facilities. Cheapest in town, but there's a three-night minimum, and a one-time membership fee.

YWCA Fernhurst, 1566 Wilder Ave., Honolulu 96822, tel. 941-2231, just off Manoa Rd., across from the historical Punahou School. Singles and doubles with shared bath, women only. Weekly rates. Breakfast and dinner included (except Sunday) for low price. Doors closed at 11 p.m., but the night guard will admit later. Limited reservations depending on availability with deposit. Women can stay for up to one year, and many women from around the world add an international flavor.

The only official American Youth Hostel in Hawaii (more listed under Waikiki) is the **Honolulu International Youth Hostel,** 2323 A Seaview Ave., Honolulu, HI 96822, tel. 946-0591, located near the University of Hawaii. This YH is always busy, but will take reservations. AYH members with identity cards are given priority, but nonmembers are accepted on a space-available day-by-day basis. For information and reservations write to the manager, and include SASE and a night's lodging deposit. For information and membership cards write American Youth Hostels, 1332 I St., N.W., Suite 895, Washington D.C. 20005.

Elderhostel, 100 Bolyston St., Suite 200, Boston, MA 02116, offers noncredit courses at

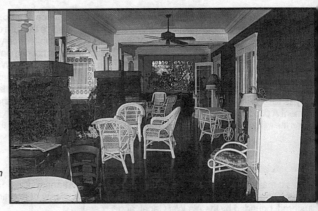

Manoa Valley Inn

Hawaii Loa College, Oahu. For people 60 years and older. Fees begin at $175 and include course, room, and board.

University Of Hawaii

Two six-week summer sessions beginning late May and in early July are offered to bona fide students of accredited universities at the University of Hawaii at Manoa, Oahu. Reasonable rates in residence halls (mandatory meals) and in apartments on campus; special courses with emphasis on Polynesian and Asian culture and languages, including China and Japan. Unbeatably priced tours and outings to points throughout the islands for students and the general public at the Summer Session Activities Office. For information, catalog, and enrollment, write Summer Session Office, University of Hawaii, 2500 Dole St., Krauss Hall 101, Honolulu, HI 96822, tel. 944-1014 or 949-0771.

Moderate/Expensive Hotels

The **Kobayashi Hotel** at 250 N. Beretania St., Honolulu, HI 96817, tel. 536-2377, is in Chinatown, and an old standby as an inexpensive but clean hotel. It's away from all the Waikiki action, and the spartan, linoleumed rooms rent for under $37. Plenty of travelers pass through here, and the hotel's restaurant serves authentic Japanese food at moderate prices.

The **Nakamura Hotel** is a little bit more *uptown* both price- and location-wise. It's at 1140 S. King St., Honolulu, HI 96814, tel. 537-1951. The rooms are well appointed, carpeted, and have large bathrooms. Some a/c rooms face

busy King Street; the *mauka* side rooms are quieter, with plenty of breezes to keep you cool. Often you can find a room at this meticulously clean hotel when others are booked out, only because it's out of the mainstream.

The **Pagoda Hotel,** 1525 Rycroft St., Honolulu, HI 96814, tel. (800) 367-6060, on Oahu 941-6611, behind Ala Moana Park between Kapiolani Blvd. and S. King Street. Because this hotel is away from the "action," you get very good value for your money. Rooms with kitchenettes start at about $55, with two-bedroom suites at around $90. All rooms have TV, a/c parking, swimming pool, and the well-known Pagoda Restaurant.

Another in the same category is the **Hawaii Dynasty Hotel,** at 1830 Ala Moana Blvd., tel 955-1111. Rooms here are clean, decent, away from the action, and reasonably priced.

The **Ala Moana Americana,** 410 Atkinson Dr., Honolulu, HI 96814, tel. (800) 228-3278, or Oahu 955-4811, is another hotel where you're just off the Waikiki strip. It's located just behind Ala Moana Park between Ala Moana and Kapiolani boulevards, with a walking ramp connecting it directly with the Ala Moana Shopping Center. Rooms start at $90 and go up to around $250 for a two-bedroom suite (six people). There's a/c, TV, swimming pools, an all-night coffee shop, and the Summit Supper Club on the top of this 36-story hotel.

Manoa Valley Inn

The Manoa Valley Inn, at 2001 Vancouver Dr Honolulu, HI 96822, tel. 947-6019, (800) 634

\$115 is a magnificent opportunity to lodge in turn-of-the-century elegance. Formerly the John Guild Inn, this bed and breakfast was completely restored in 1982 and is listed on the National Register of Historic Places. Innkeeper Marianne Schultz offers a double bed with a shared bath, including continental breakfast, at a very reasonable \$80, or a private suite for \$145. You walk through French doors backed by lace curtains, and the magic begins. Overhead is a small tear-drop chandelier, and on the floor a Persian carpet. A solid Edwardian cloak rack stands like a silent and reliable footman ready to receive your muddy riding boots. The mood of the period is sustained by the wallpaper throughout, variations on a theme, floral, pastoral, turn-of-the-century, in pinks, tans, lavenders, and grays.

After registering in the main foyer, turn right into what was the dining room. Here is a hand-crafted pool table with a thick slate bottom that plays very well. To the right is a sturdy sideboard that holds the exemplary continental breakfasts that are prepared in the kitchen just behind. In the morning, the aroma of fresh-brewed coffee wafts up the stairs. You can enjoy Kona, Colombian blend, and macadamia nut coffee, or choose from a selection of herbal teas, or hot chocolate. The morning selections are bran muffins, croissants, little sticky buns, fresh fruit of the season, and hand-squeezed juices. The daily and Sunday newspapers lie around. Pick one and sink into the billowy cushions of a wicker chair on the lava-rock-colonnaded back porch. Still purring is an old fridge from the '30s that's stocked with mineral waters and sodas. Both inside and out, you'll find coffee tables surrounded by overstuffed chairs, and nearby decanters of port and sherry and dishes filled with chocolates. Every evening, wine and gourmet cheese, along with crackers and fresh fruits, are presented. All complimentary to guests.

The original structure was a very modest, two-story, box-like home. It was situated on seven acres, but the demand for land by growing Honolulu has whittled it down to the present half acre, or so. The grounds are well kept, but small, so don't expect sweeping grand lawns. The original owner was Milton Moore, an Iowa lumberman. He sold it to John Guild in 1919, a secretary to Alexander and Baldwin, who basically created the structure that you see today. The home went through several owners and even did a stint as a fraternity house. It ended up as low-priced apartment units until it was rescued and refurbished by Rick Ralston, the owner of Crazy Shirts, one of Hawaii's successful self-made men, and a patron of arts and antiques. He outfitted the house from his warehouse of antiques with furnishings not original to the house, but true to the period. The original structure was built in 1915. In 1919 the third floor was added, along with the back porch.

Inside, standing lamps wear shades, like the fringed miniskirts of roaring '20s flappers. A dignified but daffy grandfather clock, always confused about the exact time, chimes whenever it's in the mood. Everywhere, on marble-topped credenzas or sideboards, are silver teapots, *objects de'art,* and porcelain statuary. The main common room is dominated by a burly fireplace. On the mantel are bronze statues, and above hangs a painting depicting leisure activities of the gentry of the turn of the century. Notice the glass cabinets filled with a collection of vintage hula dolls, and lovely pieces like tables with wooden inlays. Here and there, arranged for when conversation was the evening's entertainment, are couches and carved Queen Anne chairs. Lamps diffuse light through stained-glass shades. An old piano with sheet music of songs made famous by Judy Garland, Bing Crosby, and Rosemary Cluny waits to be tinkled. The sun parlor is beveled glass, lace curtains, ferns and exotic plants on pedestals. A nickleodeon is always ready to belt out a tune for a coin. A partner's desk, designed for two people to sit and face each other (19th-century embezzlement insurance?) is there for writing cards and letters. In the corner is a TV with cable and a VCR.

Climb the wide wooden staircase. Upstairs, each room has a slightly different theme. There's the John Guild Suite, the only suite in the house with a sitting room. Inside recline on a velvet couch while perusing old books on Hawaiian commerce, or even flipping through the 1940 phone book. The sitting room has a pigeon hole secretary, and a big carved mirror. The color scheme of drapes and wallpaper is shades of rose and pink. In the bedroom is a king-sized bed with a carved headboard, matching side tables, and two stained-glass lamps. Enter the bathroom to find a separate bathtub and shower, and everything in marble. This is a *real* bathtub, designed for you to immerse yourself in a full reclining position.

Another common area on the second floor is more private than in the main living room. It was at one time an open-air room that was enclosed in 1919, and a bay window installed. At Christmas it's resplendent with a table-top tree and lined with poinsettias. The third floor has rooms with a shared bathroom. Furniture in each room is different. The W.F. Dillingham Room has two large poster beds and substantial mahogany furniture; in another, the J.D. Dole Room, a

white wrought-iron bed, pink doilies, and pictures of children walking along with their dogs make it more feminine. A cottage with a white on white theme offers seclusion and privacy away from the main house. Unfortunately, the bed covered by an elegant lace bedspread is a bit short, and it is not recommended for people over six feet tall.

The rooms are air conditioned in the same way as the day they were built, beautiful breezes through open windows. That's what Manoa Valley is known for.

the hibiscus, Hawaii's state flower

FOOD

The restaurants mentioned below are outside of the Waikiki area, although many are close, even within walking distance. Others are located near Ala Moana, Chinatown (see p. 261 for restaurants), downtown, and the less touristed areas of greater Honolulu. Some are first-class restaurants, others, among the best, are just roadside stands where you can get a satisfying plate lunch. The restaurants are listed according to price range and location, with differing cuisines mixed in each range. Besides the sun and surf, it's the amazing array of food found on Oahu that makes it extraordinary.

SHOPPING CENTER DINING

Ala Moana Shopping Center
The following are all located at the Ala Moana Shopping Center (see p. 255), which has recently undergone a full face lift. Most are located in the **Makai Food Court,** a huge central area where you can inexpensively dine on dishes from San Francisco to Tokyo. Counter-style restaurants serve island favorites, reflecting the multi-ethnic culinary traditions from around the Pacific. You take your dish to a nearby communal dining area, which is great for people-watching. The **China House** is open daily for lunch and dinner, tel. 949-6622. This enormous dining hall offers the usual selection of Chinese dishes, but is famous for its dim sum (served 11 a.m. to 2 p.m.); you pick and choose bite-sized morsels from carts.

La Cocina, open daily for lunch and dinner, tel. 949-9233, serves Mexican food for under $5 with complimentary chips and salsa. Dining facilities and takeout service. Less spicy offerings to suit American tastes.

Michel's Baguette, first floor ocean side. Open weekdays from 7 a.m.-9 p.m., Sat. till 5:30 p.m., Sun. 8 a.m.-5 p.m., tel. 946-6888. They specialize in French bread, pastries, and croissants baked on the premises. A good selection of tasty soups, salads, and sandwiches, it.s a change from the ordinary burger.

Patti's Chinese Kitchen, first floor facing the sea, tel. 946- 5002, has all the ambience you'd expect from a cafeteria-style Chinese fast-food joint, plus lines about a block long. But don't let either discourage you. The lines move incredibly quickly, and you won't get gourmet food, but it's tasty, plentiful, and cheap. The "Princess-Queen Special" is steamed rice, fried rice or noodles, a chow mein plus two entrees like sweet and sour pork, or a chicken dish—for around $3. The Queen is the same, but add an entree—under $4. You can even have four entrees which fills two large paper plates. The princesses who eat this much food aren't tiny-waisted damsels waiting for a rescuing prince—they can flatten anyone who hassles them on their own.

The Ward Warehouse
This shopping center (see p. 256) has a range of restaurants, from practical to semi-chic, all reasonably priced. **Beni Kai** is a Japanese restaurant that's beautifully appointed with a rock garden at the entranceway that continues to the inside. It's bright and airy, neo-Japanese traditional. Prices are reasonable with set menu dishes like *unagi kabayaki* for $12.95, or miso-fried fish at $9.25. They have a wide selection of *don buri, yakitori,* and tempura for around $6. Open Mon.-Sat. 11 a.m.-2 p.m. for lunch, and for dinner from 5 p.m.

Nearby is the opposite side of the coin. A small lunch stand sells saimin and *yakitori* for under $4. Mostly you stand and eat, but there are a few tables in the common mall area. Also, for fast foods you'll find **Cookie Kitchen** and **Dave's Ice Cream,** supposedly the favorite of local people who compare it with the much-touted Lappert's. It's locally made and supposedly the best. In the mall you'll find **Harpo's,** your basic pizza parlor, and **The Old Spaghetti Factory,** serving a wide variety of pasta not quite like Mama makes, but passable, and at a reasonable price.

For those into health foods try **Aloha Health Food,** primarily a vitamin and mineral store, but they do have some prepared food and drinks in a cooler. Right across is **Coffee Works,** specializing in gourmet coffee and tea. They have a bakery and sandwiches for under $5, croissants $1.50. So take your vitamins on one side and get jazzed on the other. The **Farmer's Market** is not in the Ward Warehouse, but just across the street, at 1020 Auahi, where you can pick up fresh produce and flowers.

Orson's Restaurant is a seafood house on the second floor. It's actually quite elegant considering the location, with a prize-winning sunset view of the small boat harbor at Kewalo Basin across the way. The inside, too, is richly appointed in woods and glass. Prices are $12-15 for the fresh catch of the day complimented by an extensive wine list.

The **Chowder House** on the ground floor has fresh-grilled *ahi* for $8.25, snow crab salad $5.95, Manhattan clam chowder $2.25, clams and oysters on the half shell $6, bay shrimp cocktail $2.95, deep-fried shrimp $5.85, and daily specials from $5-8.

The Ward Center

This upscale shopping center is directly across the street from Ala Moana Park, and next door to the Ward Warehouse. The following are some of its restaurants and eateries, where you can enjoy not only class, but quality as well.

R. Fields Wine Co. is not really a restaurant, but a purveyor of exquisite food, fine wines, crackers, cookies, cheeses, imported pastas, and caviar. Most of the wines are top shelf from California like King Cellars, Dominus, Opus I, Sutter Home (a fluke, left over from their catering business), and Robert Mondavi, with a nice vertical of their reserve wines going back to 1968. Also older French wines, as well as German wines.

Chocoholics would rather visit the **Honolulu Chocolate Company** than go to heaven. Mousse truffles, Grand Marnier truffles, chocolate eggs with pistachio or English walnut will all send you into eye-rolling rapture. If you enter, forget any resolve about watching your weight. You're a goner!

For a quick lunch try **Mocha Java** or **Crepe Fever.** Both are yuppie, upscale, counter-service-type places with a few tables. Both have a selection of sandwiches with an emphasis on vegetarian. Crepe Fever has stuffed whole croissants, and grain sandwiches. If you want a designer lunch, that's the place to go. For a double-fisted American sandwich with all the trimmings try **Big Ed's,** a deli serving no-nonsense corned beef $5.35, ham $4.50, tuna salad $4.25, or polish sausage. Takeout as well as sit down, actually a good seating area away from the bustle at the south end of the shopping center.

Al Fresco's on the corner in the Ward Center is an upscale semi-deli and restaurant whose tables spill out into a little courtyard. Stay simple with a small pizza at $8.95, a Caesar's salad for $6.95, or move onto smoked chicken with mustard herb butter pasta for $13.95, pesto with smoked salmon $13.95, boneless chicken breast $14.95. Specials every day like grilled eggplant for $8.95 up to blackened *onaga* $19.95. This Mediterranean-style cafe is gourmet; while perhaps not designed for an elegant evening, it will give you fine dining at reasonable prices for what you're getting.

The premier, or at least best-known, restaurant in the complex is **Keo's Thai Restaurant,** known for its mouthwatering Thai dishes and for its beautiful decor. The menu is extensive with plenty of dishes for non-meateaters. Prices range but can be quite reasonable for Thai noodles, chicken, shrimp, or vegetarian $6.95-8.95, house salad $4.95, green papaya salad $4.95, spring rolls (four) $4.95, and tofu, shrimp or chicken satay for under $9. Try the delicious soups like spicy lemon grass or Thai ginger for $3.75 per serving. Entrées like the Evil Jungle Prince has quite a spicy reputation, or tame down with Asian watercress stir-fried with garlic yellow bean sauce, and beef, shrimp, or vegies from $6.95-8.95. Keo's has another location and operates the Mekong I & II, simpler and less expensive restaurants. Keo's is known for its beautiful flower displays of torch ginger, orchids or plumeria on every table, and you may eat inside or outside.

The **Yum Yum Tree** is an affordable American standard restaurant that features pies and cakes from its bakery, along with homestyle fresh pasta. They have an extensive dining area, quite cheerful with dark wood floors, ferns, hanging greenery, and an open-beam ceiling. Breakfast is 7 a.m.-12 p.m., lunch 11 a.m.-5 p.m., dinner 5 p.m. to midnight, cocktails 7 a.m.-closing. Adjacent is **Compadres Mexican Restaurant,** tel. 523-1307, with the standards of burritos, tostadas, enchiladas, and tacos at reasonable prices. This small chain with restaurants in California and Australia, also serves fresh fish *éla Mexicana*, and has one of the largest selections of tequilla in the Pacific.

Don't let the name **Andrew's Restaurant,** tel. 523-8677, fool you. It's actually an excellent Italian and European restaurant on the second floor that makes its own pasta. Starters include *calamari fritto* $6.25, wilted spinach salad $3.50, and minestrone $3, entrees are canneloni $13.95, frogs legs $16.75, a variety of veal dishes for under $20, and complete dinners with all the trimmings for $17-25.

Upstairs too is **Monterey Bay Canners Seafood Restaurant,** which features all-you-can eat salad, soup, and hot potato bar for $5.95 from 11 a.m.-3 p.m. They have the cheapest prices in the shopping center. Specials are sautéed tiger prawns, an *ono* sandwich and chowder, Cajun combo, and lobster with black bean sauce, all under $8. From the broiler try Alaskan halibut $13.95, New York steak and scampi $19.95, traditional favorites like teriyaki chicken breast $10.95, and some pastas. Then they have what they call the Fisherman's Choice luncheon entrees like *ono,* halibut, teri chicken, and catfish for $7.95. Entertainment nightly provided by "Carlos." Not bad at all for a small California chain with other locations at the Outrigger in Waikiki and at Pearlridge Shopping Center.

Restaurant Row

This new-age complex at 500 Ala Moana (across from the Federal Building) points the way to "people-friendly" development in Honolulu's future. It houses shops and businesses, but mostly restaurants, all grouped together around a central courtyard and strolling area. Some restaurants are elegant and excellent, while others are passable and plain. But they are all in a congenial setting, and you can pick your palate and style preference as easily as you'd pick offerings at a buffet. Start at the central fountain area with its multicolored modernistic Lego-inspired tower. Every Saturday at 8 p.m. jazz is offered here overlooking the waterfront.

The **Sunset Grill,** tel. 521-4409, is on the corner. With wraparound windows, a long and open bar, and comfortable maple chairs, it lives up to its name. This is the place to come for a quiet evening drink in the downtown area. The food is prepared in full view on a *kiawe*-fired grill, wood-roasting oven, and Italian rotisserie. Choices include a variety of pasta, gourmet salads, calamari, fresh fish, oysters, chicken, veal, and lamb. Lunch is a wide variety of plump juicy sandwiches of turkey, sausage, beef, fish, or chicken. The chefs at the Sunset aren't afraid to blend East with West using basil, vinaigrette, Gorgonzola, salsa, black bean sauce, strawberries, curry, oyster sauce, hollandaise, and tangy peppers in a wide variety of creations. Open

daily from 11 a.m., weekends from 9 a.m., with a late-night menu on weekends.

The Rose City Diner will take you to a more innocent America when bobby-soxers sat on the hoods of their boyfriends' Chevys and listened to Buddy Holly on the AM radio. Fabian, Dion, Annette, or Ricky would feel right at home ordering burgers and BLT's from this classic menu, except that they would be better than ever. The roller-skating waitresses wear pink uniforms with white aprons and jaunty hats. The booths, like a cool Elvis outfit, are pink and black. The walls are covered with pictures of five decades of actors and musicians: Satchmo, Jimmy Stewart, Ronald Reagan, Bogart, Elvis, Marlon, Sophia, Rock, Marilyn, Jane, Hitchcock, Lucy, Dezi, Fred, and Ethel—they're all here. Booths have table-top jukeboxes. Try a slider burger with grilled onions, miniburgers served in a basket on French fries, bird on a bun (teriyaki chicken with swiss cheese and Thousand Island dressing), a chili sundae (chili, sour cream, onions, and cherry tomato on top), and wash it down with root beer floats, cherry cokes, and frothy malts. Open for breakfast, lunch, and dinner, 24 hours.

One of the simple restaurants is **Marie Callender's,** featuring heartland American pot pies, burgers, pasta, salads, and breakfast specials. The strawberry pie is delicious. Fast-food pawns will be happy to hear that **Burger King** is here too. **R. Fields Wine Co.,** for a do-it-yourself meal, is here with its gourmet wines, crackers, cheeses, escargot, caviar, and paté. **Cheers** is a small bar open 11 a.m.-2 a.m. Stuck in the corner, it tries to live up to its TV namesake by welcoming the local execs and secretaries in for an after-work drink and chat. It's comfortable, friendly, sports-oriented, and smoky.

In the middle of the complex is **The Row,** an outdoors bar with finger food. The **Honolulu Chocolate Co.** is next. Like a smug little devil, it tempts with chocolate truffles, mocha clusters, and fancy nut rolls. So sin! You're on vacation. The **Paradise Bakery Cafe** is a simple counter restaurant with pies, coffee, and donuts.

Trattoria Manzo, tel. 522-1711, owned by Tony Manzo, offers very special Italian dishes from the Abruzzi, a coastal and mountainous region along the Adriatic known for its hearty cooking. Choose an antipasto from Italian cold cuts to clams in red wine sauce for $7 and under. Assorted soups and salads range from $3 to $6 for *insalata calamari.* Select your favorite pasta, and then cover it with one of 20 delectable sauces, all under $10. Chicken, veal, and steak are grilled, simmered in wine sauce, or made into parmigiana, or choose a traditional lasagna, *gnocchi,* or a good old pizza. The interior is sharp with neon strips, and black marble tables and chairs.

The Black Orchid, tel. 521-3111, is the loveliest flower in the "Row." It's an art deco neospeakeasy arranged perfectly for intimate romance or friendly socializing by interior decorator Meriam Braselle. Waiters are in tuxes, and all the ladies having dinner are offered a rose. Billie Holiday would look sleek in a sequined dress at the black marble bar. Bogie and his mobsters might survey the scene from one of the raised upholstered booths, while Fred Astaire glides past reflecting glasswork to a table for two in the corner. The walls, covered in murals by Tamara, suggest this classic nightclubbing era. The restaurant is open for lunch and dinner daily, and is extremely popular. Dinner reservations, especially on weekends, are a must. During the evening, both men and women would feel most comfortable in their sharpest evening wear. Jackets are suggested, but collared shirts and dressy slacks will do.

San Francisco-trained chef Nick Sayada makes a cioppino as delicious as the best found on Fishermen's Wharf. Tom Selleck, one of the owners, loves the black and blue *ahi sashimi,* crisped in fiery Cajun spices. Starters include oyster, clam, and mussel bisque, or warm red cabbage salad with goat cheese. Entrees are rack of lamb in wine sauce, grilled swordfish, veal piccatta, fresh pasta, lobster and more lobster live from Maine, in cream, black bean sauce, or in fettuccini. Molokai sends venison, while the best island beef, fish, and poultry are grilled, sautéed, roasted, and baked in heady sauces and spices. An extensive wine list will add the right smoothness and zest to the gourmet meal. Desserts are handmade ice cream, exquisite flaky pastries, and pies like banana made with vanilla mousse.

The lunch and dinner menu change weekly, the lounge menu is available until 3 a.m., and the morning catch decides the fresh fish of the day. There is daily entertainment in the lounge, with dancing to live music until 4 a.m. Vocalist Azure McCall brightens the evening with a fine selection of jazz, and swing numbers, while the contemporary sounds of Norm Compton with Armed and Dangerous keeps you dancing all night. If you are looking for *the* special setting for a night out, pick The Black Orchid.

INEXPENSIVE DINING AROUND TOWN

The following restaurants are located in and around the greater Honolulu area.

The **University of Hawaii,** Manoa Campus, hosts a number of restaurants, ranging from an inexpensive cafeteria to international cuisine at the East-West Center. Inexpensive to moderate restaurants include: **Manoa Gardens,** salad and snacks; **Campus Center Dining Room,** for full meals; and the **International Garden,** at Jefferson Hall in the East-West Center. For a great little lunch in a quiet setting in this area see the Waioli Tea Room page 238.

At the Hawaii Maritime Museum (see p. 227) you'll find **Coasters Restaurant** tucked away in the rear overlooking Honolulu Harbor. American standards with a full complement from the sandwich board. Not great food, but a great setting and away from the bustle of Honolulu. More interesting and definitely more local is **Pier Eight Restaurant** sandwiched under the huge elevated pier area just nearby the Maritime Center. Basic Chinese fast food to go, open daily 10 a.m.-5 p.m.

King's Bakery and Coffee Shop is a favorite of local people, at 1936 S. King St. and Pumehana, tel. 941-5211 (one of three locations). They're open 24 hours, and get very busy around 6 p.m. when they allow only groups of two or more to sit in the few booths; the rest eat at the counter. The menu is American/Hawaiian/Oriental. Full meals are around $5. Not great, but good and wholesome. The bakery has seven-grain bread, whole wheat, but mostly white fluffy stuff with tons of powdered sugar. However, they do offer "tofuti," a soft ice creamlike dessert made from healthful tofu. Their other locations are at the Kaimuki Shopping Center and Eaton Square. Across the street from King's Bakery are two inexpensive eateries, **McCully Chop Suey,** and **Yoshi's Sushi Yakiniku Restaurant.**

Down to Earth Natural Foods, open Mon. to Sat. 10 a.m.-8:30 p.m., Sun. 10 a.m.-6 p.m., at 2525 S. King St., tel. 947-7678, is a kind of "museum of health food stores" serving filling, nutritious health food dishes for very reasonable prices. Sandwiches, like a whopping avocado, tofu, and cheese, are under $5. Daily full-meal specials, like vegie stroganoff, eggplant parmigiana, and lasagna are around $4, including salad. There are plenty of items on the menu that will fill you up for under $3. Healthwise, you can't go wrong! Just up the street at 2471 S. King, across from the Star Garden Market, is the tiny **Saimin Bowl Restaurant.** Their name says it all, and you can have a huge steaming bowl of soup for a few dollars.

Kokua Co-op Natural Foods And Grocery Store, at the corner of S. Beretania and Isenberg, tel. 941-1921, is open to the public Mon.-Sat. 9 a.m-8 p.m., Sun. 10 a.m.-7 p.m. A full-service store with organic and fresh produce, cheese, milk, juices, bulk foods, and breads.

Sekiya's Restaurant and Deli at 2746 Kaimuki Ave., tel. 732-1656, looks like a set from a 1940s tough-guy movie. The food is well prepared and the strictly local clientele will be amazed that you even know about the place.

Hale Vietnam, 1140 12th Ave. in Kaimuki, tel. 735-7581, is building an excellent reputation for authentic and savory dishes, at very moderate prices. It gets the highest praise from local people who choose it again and again for an inexpensive evening of delicious dining.

For a quick *bento* or sushi to go, try **Matsuri Sushi,** tel. 949-1111, at the corner of Kapiolani Blvd. and McCully. This quick stop is perfect to pick up lunch on your way out of the Waikiki area.

Suehiro's at 1824 S. King, open daily for lunch and dinner, with takeout service, tel. 949-4584, gets the nod from local Japanese people. The menu here is authentic, the decor strictly Americana, and the food well prepared and moderately priced.

People's Cafe, 1300 Pali Hwy., is open Mon. to Sat. 10 a.m.-7:30 p.m., tel. 536-5789. Two going on three generations of the same Japanese family have been serving the full range of excellent and inexpensive Hawaiian food at this down-home restaurant. It's not fancy, but the food is good, and the surroundings clean.

Coco's Coffee House at the corner of Kalakaua and Kapiolani is an American standard that's open all night. It's like a million others in the U.S. where you can order a hot roast beef sandwich for a few bucks, or just sip a coffee into the wee hours, staying out of the weather.

Another of the same is the **Hungry Lion,** tel. 536-0148, at 1613 Nuuanu Avenue Open 24 hours, it serves everything from Oriental food to steaks. Many local people come here after a night out. Nothing special, but decent wholesome food on formica tables.

M's Coffee Tavern is a favorite with downtown office workers for great lunches, excellent coffee, and cocktails, at 124 Queen St., tel. 531-5739.

Walli Wok, tel. 943-1WOK, is a Chinese Restaurant that delivers, but you must spend a minimum of $8. They'll come to anywhere in the downtown and Waikiki area, and are perfect for condo dinners, or late-night snacks. The food is passable, and the servings ample.

Two inexpensive yet authentic restaurants next door to each other at 1679 Kapiolani Blvd., are the **Kintoki Japanese Restaurant,** tel. 949-8835, and the **Sukyung Korean Restaurant.** This semi-seedy area has plenty of "girlie bars," but the food is good and authentic, with most items priced below $5.

Penny's Plate Lunches, on the Sand Island Access Rd. next to Dirty Dan's Topless Go-Go Joint, is one of the least expensive and most authentic Hawaiian plate-lunch stands you can find. The most expensive lunch is *(lau lau),* pork and butterfish wrapped in a *ti* leaf, at around $3.50. You can also try baseball-sized *manapua* for around $.60. Penny's is out of the way, but definitely worth a stop.

You can't get much cheaper than free, and that's what the **International Society for Krishna Consciousness** offers every Sunday at 5:30 p.m. for its vegetarian smorgasbord. Their two-acre compound is just off the Pali Hwy. at 51 Coelho Way, tel. 595-4913. Of course there're a few chants for dessert. *Hare Krishna!*

Downtown Honolulu

In central Honolulu, mostly along Bishop Street's financial district, you'll find excellent and inexpensive restaurants that cater to the district's lunch crowd. (For restaurants in Chinatown, see p. 261.) One of the best is the **Croissanterie**, tel. 533-3443, at 222 Merchant St., open Mon.-Fri. 6 a.m.-9 p.m., Sat. to 4 p.m., closed Sunday. They serve up gourmet coffee and baskets of croissants stuffed with everything from tuna to strawberries and cream. There're salads, soups, Japanese food, and a pasta table with lasagna and linguini with salad and garlic bread for under $5. The vintage building, which recently housed a bookstore, has brick walls, hardwood floors, and straight-backed cane chairs, all part of the decor in this sidewalk-style European cafe.

Another good place is **Al's Cafe** in the 1100 block of Bishop, open Mon.-Fri. 6 a.m.-4 p.m., Sat. 7 a.m.-1 p.m. Daily lunch specials like tuna or ham and cheese sandwiches and a medium soft drink or coffee for $3. Fast food in the area is **Jack in the Box, Taco Bell,** and **Pizza Hut** across the street from Woolworth's on Hotel Street. Heading down Hotel toward Chinatown you'll pass **Kathy's Kitchen,** at Bethel and Pauahi, where for around $4 you can get a plate lunch.

Art And The Sandwich
In Honolulu there are a few opportunities to feed your mind and soul along with satiating your appetite.

The **Garden Cafe,** tel. 531-8865, at the Honolulu Academy of Arts, 900 S. Beretania, is a classy place for lunch. Open 11:30 a.m.-1 p.m. Tues. to Fri., Thurs. supper at 6:30 p.m., it's set up in a garden of this excellent museum under a canopy. The cafe serves *different* soups like ice pumpkin soup with parsley, salads such as crunchy pea or orange, and sandwiches of ham with pepper jelly. Desserts run $1.50 with full luncheon at $6.50. The food is delicious, but be aware that the portions are not for the hungry, being designed primarily for patrons of the arts who seem to be wealthy matrons from the fashionable sections of Honolulu who are all watching their waistlines.

Don't let the Porsches, Mercedeses, and BMWs parked vanity plate to vanity plate in the parking lot discourage you from enjoying the **Contemporary Cafe,** tel. 523-3362, at the Contemporary Art Museum, 2411 Makiki Heights Drive. The small but superb menu is as inspired as the art in the museum, and the prices are astonishingly inexpensive. Dine inside or out, or perch on the porch. Appetizers are paté, mussels, escargot, or smoked salmon for under $4. Soups and salads are wilted spinach, chilled chicken breast, Greek salad, and shrimp Louie for $4-6. Sandwiches are a fine selection including smoked breast of turkey, or *ahi* Caesar for

under $5. Desserts run from cheesecake to pecan pie, and beverages include homemade lemonade, and cappuccino. For a wonderful cultural outing combined with a memorable lunch, come to the Contemporary Cafe. It's just so . . . contemporary!

Fast Foods And Treats
Fast-food fanciers and fanatics have nothing to fear on Oahu. There're enough quick eateries to feed an army, mainly because there is an Army, plus a Navy and Marine Corps of young men and women on the island, not to mention the army of tourists. If you're after pizza, burgers, shakes, and fries, choose from 36 **McDonald's,** 13 or so **Jacks-in-the-Box,** 24 **Pizza Huts,** 10 or so **Zippy's,** six **Wendy's,** a few **Farrell's** and good old **Dairy Queens.**

For **shave ice** try the **Waiola Store** on the corner of Paani and Waiola. You can get it in Waikiki, but for the real stuff in its syrupy glory come here. Open Mon.-Sat. 7 a.m.-9 p.m., Sun. 8 a.m.-7:30 p.m. If you go to the Willows just around the corner (see p. 251) this is a great place to come for an authentic island treat.

MODERATE
DINING AROUND TOWN

The following listings are for restaurants where two can dine for around $30. This does not include drinks.

Castagnola's Restaurant, tel. 988-2969, in the Manoa Marketplace, is quickly gaining a reputation as an authentic Italian restaurant offering dishes at a reasonable price. Away from the action, they're quiet and cozy. The decor is peasantish, with Chianti bottles, ropes of garlic, and checkered tablecloths. Two could dine on antipasti, soup, pasta, and a glass of wine for $25.

The Hideaway Restaurant at La Mariana Yacht Sailing Club, 50 Sand Island Access Rd. (see p. 239) is the only real restaurant on Sand Island. Henry, for many years a ship's cook, can cook everything well—maybe not great, but well. If a Chinese person came here and wanted chop suey Henry could do it. If a guy wanted steak and potatoes, you got it! Pasta? Here it is! The Hideaway is an out-of-the-way place, local, and real Hawaiiana. This is where all the yachties come. They serve appetizers, even escargot for $6.75, chicken wings $5.25, sautéed mushroom buttons $5.25. From the broiler, rib-eye steak is $11.50. The most expensive is an eight-ounce filet mignon $14.95. From the sea, deep-fried scallops $10.50, shrimp scampi served over linguini $10.95, ahi fresh fillet or steak cut for $10.95. That's the cheapest fresh *ahi* around.

Henry is also known for his onion rings. They're not on the menu, you have to know about them. Now you know. The Sunday brunch is excellent, but basic—eggs, potatoes, a slab of ham, rice, and toast for $3.50. Hard to beat. Inside hang Japanese glass floats that at night are diffused with different colors, providing mood lighting for the cozy black booths and wooden tables with high-backed wicker chairs.

Shiruhachi at 1901 Kapiolani Blvd., tel. 947-4680, is a completely authentic Japanese sushi bar operated by Hiroshi Suzuki. As a matter of fact, until recently 90 percent of the clientele were Japanese, either visiting businessmen or locals in the know, and the menu was only in Japanese. However, everyone is more than welcome. With a beer, you get free *otsumami* (nibbles) with a wide selection of sushi and other finger foods like *yakitori* at about $2 for two skewers. A separate section of the restaurant turns into a cocktail lounge, somewhat like an *akachochin,* a neighborhood Japanese bar where people go to relax. There's taped music and a dance floor. If you're into authentic Japanese, this is a great one.

Auntie Pasto's at 1099 S. Beretania and the corner of Pensacola, tel. 523-8855, is open daily for lunch, dinner, and late nights. The vibe is upbeat pizza parlor, where you can even bring your own wine. Most of the Italian menu is around $6; the specialty is a fish stew loaded with morsels for about $12. Their large salad with garlic bread is cheap, and enough for two. No reservations necessary, quiet, comfortable.

Willows is at 901 Hausten, just behind Kapiolani Blvd. on the north side of the Ala Wai Canal, tel. 946-4808. Like a tiny tropical oasis surrounded by the cement of the city, there's a willow-shaped pool bubbling with uncountable carp. Once inside, the garden opens up, and there are even strolling musicians singing Hawaiian standards. Local people love it, a definite tip-off. The food is Hawaiian/Oriental/American. And the dessert pies are great! It's best known for its Sunday brunch from 10 a.m.-1 p.m., when the huge restaurant is filled with local families. The few minutes' drive from Waikiki keeps most tourists away.

For lunch start with Johnny B's Mushrooms (fresh whole mushrooms seasoned with a special butter) for $4, teriyaki meat sticks $5, or Puna's Favorite Salad of the Sea (whole gulf shrimp, crab meat, gently poached scallops nestled in a bed of lettuce topped with a fruit garnish) for $11.50. Enter along a covered walkway. The decor is upgraded South Seas with natural wood beams. Basically you're dining outside. The tables are set with pink tablecloths, and the chairs are bent bamboo with red fluffy pillows, with many under gay umbrellas. The grounds are an integral part of the decor. All around are exotic plants, some hanging. In the main dining room the ceiling is solid wood, open-beamed with a skylight and ceiling fans. The post and beams are gnarled twisted logs with their natural bark intact. One wall is solid lava, and the effect is very pleasing. This open, breezy, restaurant is basic Hawaiian, at a good price.

TGI Fridays is a raucous singles' bar known for some delectable morsels such as stuffed potatoes, quiches, and the like. It's across the street from the Blaisdel Center at 950 Ward Ave., open daily 11 a.m.-1 a.m., tel. 523-5841. Plenty of swingers and college students keep the joint jumpin'.

Wo Fat's at 115 N. Hotel St., tel. 533-6393, has had a little experience satisfying customers—the oldest eatery in Chinatown, it's been at the same location for over 80 years, and open for business for 100! Besides serving delicious food from a menu with hundreds of Cantonese dishes, the building itself is monumentally ornate. You're entertained just checking out the decor of lanterns, dragons, gilt work, and screens. Most dishes are reasonably priced and start at around $5. This restaurant is highly respected by the people of Chinatown, and is part of the Chinatown Tour offered by the Chamber of Commerce. (See p. 260.)

EXPENSIVE DINING AROUND TOWN

Sometimes only the best will do, and Honolulu can match any city for its fine restaurants. More fine dining is found in Waikiki, see p. 280.

Won Kee Seafood Restaurant, 100 N. Beretania, is a splurge joint where you get delicious seafood. Free parking on Mauna Kea Street. This is the place for Honolulu's in-the-know crowd. Tasteful and elegant surroundings.

Fishermen's Wharf Restaurant, Ala Moana Blvd. at Kewalo Basin, tel. 538-3808, serves lunch and dinner, reservations necessary. Tough parking, but free with validation in local lots. The restaurant has two sections: upstairs is the **Captain's Bridge** and downstairs is the **Seafood Grotto.** The greatest thing about this restaurant is its location, right on Fishermen's Wharf with plenty of bobbing boats at anchor and local color just outside the windows. The waitresses wear cutesie-pie sailor suits, the waiters striped jerseys. The service is adequate but not special, mostly due to the number of people served—always packed! For a renowned fish restaurant too many offerings are plain old deep-fried. For example, the shrimp stuffed with cheese and crab meat is merely breaded and popped in the fryer. Good, but not special. The cheapest item on the menu is spaghetti, not linguini, with canned clam sauce. Two can dine for around $30, to say you've been there, but you'll hardly hurry back.

The **Chart House** at 1765 Ala Moana Blvd. near Ala Wai Yacht Harbor, is open daily 4 p.m. (Sun. 5 p.m.) till 2 a.m., tel. 941-6660. They offer a happy hour until 7 p.m., *pu pus* until midnight, and nightly entertainment. Shellfish specialities start at $15, with chicken and beef dishes a few dollars cheaper.

India House, 2632 S. King St., is open daily for lunch and dinner, tel. 955-7552. Extraordinary Indian dishes prepared by chef Ram Arora. A wide selection of curries, vegetarian dishes, special *naan* bread, kabobs, and fish *tikka.* Specialty desserts of homemade ice cream and toppings.

Windows of Hawaii sits atop the Ala Moana Bldg. at 1441 Kapiolana Blvd., serving American and continental. Great views from this revolving restaurant. Lunch (sandwiches) for under $8, and complete dinners from $15. Extremely popular for sunset. Reservations, tel. 941-9138. Champagne brunch Sat. and Sun. 10 a.m.-2 p.m

Keo's Thai Restaurant, 625 Kapahulu, open nightly from 5:30-11:00 p.m., tel. 737-8240, has become an institution. It serves great Thai food at expensive prices. They pride themselves on the freshest ingredients, spices tuned up or down to suit the customer, and Keo's recipes taught to each chef personally. There's always a line, with a few benches in the parking lot for waiting customers, but no reservations are taken. The 8-page menu offers most of Thailand's delectables, and vegetarians are also catered to. You can save money and still have the same quality food at **Mekong II,** 1726 S. King, lunch and dinner, tel. 941-6184. Owned by Keo's, it's not as fancy.

Nuuanu Onsen, 87 Laimi Rd., (right off the Pali Hwy., just before Queen Emma's Summer Palace), tel. 538-9184, is one of Honolulu's best-kept secrets. This authentic Japanese teahouse serves a gourmet fixed menu. You leave your cares along with your shoes at the entrance, and are escorted by a kimono-clad waitress to your lacquered table, where you sit on *tatami* mats and enjoy the serenity of the garden framed by the shoji screens. The hostess plays geisha-like teahouse games if you like. Here, you enjoy the experience as much as the meal.

LUAUS

To have fun at a luau you have to get into the swing of things. Basically a huge banquet, you eat and drink until you're contentedly uncomfortable, somewhat like Thanksgiving on the beach. Entertainment is provided by local performers in what is invariably called a "Polynesian Revue." This includes the tourist's hula, the fast version with swaying hips and dramatic lighting, a few wandering troubadors singing Hawaiian standards, and someone swinging swords or flaming torches. All the Hawaiian standards like poi, *haupia, lomi* salmon, *laulau,* and *kalua* pig are usually served. If these don't suit your appetite, various Oriental dishes, plus chicken, fish, and roast beef do. If you leave a luau hungry, it's your own fault!

Luaus range in price from $40-50 per person. The price oftentimes includes admission to the theme parks at which many are now presented. The least expensive, most authentic, and best luaus are often put on by local churches or community groups. They are not held on a regular basis, so make sure to peruse the free tourist literature where they advertise. The following luaus are institutions and have been operating for years. If you ask a local person "Which is the best?" you won't get two to agree. It's literally a matter of taste.

The **Royal Hawaiian Luau** on the Ocean Lawn of the Royal Hawaiian Hotel, every Mon. from 6-9 p.m. tel. 923-7311, *is* the classic Hawaiian feast complete with authentic foods, entertainment, and richly spiced with aloha. Authenticity is added by lawn seating on traditional *lau hala* mats (table seating too) while the sun sets on Waikiki Beach and the stars dance over Diamond Head. Entertainment is an hour-long Polynesian extravaganza featuring Tahitian and traditional hula, a Samoan fire dance, bold rhythmic drumming, and singing by Sam Bernard. The buffet is a lavish feast of *kalua* pig, salmon, *mahi mahi,* steak, and sides of poi, *haupia,* and a sinful but scrumptious table of desserts like coconut cake, *lilikoi* chiffon pie, banana bread, and guava chiffon pie. You are presented with a fresh flower lei and welcomed at the open bar for mai tais and other tropical drinks. $49.50 adults, $39.50 children under 12.

Chuck Machado's is every Tues., Fri., and Sun. at 7 p.m., tel. 836-0249, at the Waikiki Outrigger Hotel. It's a great show that you can enjoy just by strolling on the nearby beach. **Paradise Park Luau,** Mon., Wed., and Thurs., a full day beginning at 2 p.m. with free transportation and admission to the park, tel. 944-8833.

Germaine's Luau, often claimed by local people to be *the best,* is held at Ewa Beach, tel. 946-3111. **Paradise Cove Luau** boasts a private beach with a shuttle bus departing Waikiki at 4 p.m. and returning by 10 p.m., tel. 945-3571. The **Great Hawaiian Luau** is held at Makapuu Point, tel. 926-8843.

ENTERTAINMENT

Dancing, Disco, And Lounge Acts

Anna Bannana's, at 2440 S. Beretania, tel. 946-5190, is the "top banana" for letting your hair down and boogieing the night away. It's out by the university just across from Star Market. This dance joint has a laidback atmosphere, reasonable beer prices, a $3 cover which goes to the band, no dress code, and a friendly crowd. Dancing is upstairs, light dining downstairs, and a backyard to cool off between sets. Great place, great fun!

The **Club Jubilee,** at 1007 Dillingham Blvd., tel. 845-1568 sways with Hawaiian music every night but Monday. Listen to hula tunes on traditional and quickly fading slack key guitar. People from the audience, when moved by the music, will take to the dance floor or the stage for an impromptu performance. What they lack in polish they make up for in sincerity. Everybody's welcome. Beer around $2.50, with plenty of *pu pus,* like watercress with mayonnaise and soy sauce, along with regular island munchies.

University of Hawaii students trumpet the mating call at **Moose McGillycuddy's,** at 1035 University Ave., tel. 944-5525, especially every Thursday, which is Ladies Night. Standard but good food priced for the student pocketbook, and plenty of dancing.

The **Black Orchid,** at Restaurant Row, the hottest new nightclub/ restaurant in Honolulu (see p. 248), has live music nightly, fantastic food, and a classic "neo-Bogart" atmosphere.

Studebaker's at Restaurant Row (see p. 247) is a neon-lit, chrome deco bar with two red Studebakers in the window. Daytime it's a restaurant, but in the evening it's a disco and bar. From 4-7 p.m. enjoy the best deal with a one-drink minimum, and $1.50 buffet which can easily be a light dinner. The bartenders and cocktail waitresses climb on stage every hour and jitterbug for the audience demonstrating classic "American Bandstand" routines and steps. One wall of glass bricks diffuses the light, and from the outside makes all the dancers look as if they're in a fishbowl. *Uptown* dress code, male and female peacocks welcome. No one under 23 admitted.

Rumors, in the Ala Moana American Hotel, 410 Atkinson St., tel. 955-4811, is an established disco that cranks up around 9 p.m. and features the newest in dance and rock videos. Also, the restaurant atop the building, Windows of Hawaii, supplements your dinner with an evening lounge act.

Tony Roma's, 98-150 Kaonohi St. in the Westridge Mall, Aiea Town, tel. 487-9911, offers a lounge act Sun. to Fri., and daily happy hour from 4:30-8:30 p.m. and a special *pu pu* menu.

TGI Fridays, 950 Ward Ave., tel. 523-5841, is a lively night spot. Good food, large portions, reasonable prices, and music. **Pecos River Cafe,** at 99-016 Kamehameha Hwy., tel. 487-7980, has country music featuring Nick Masters and the Mustangs.

Freebies

At **Centerstage,** Ala Moana Center, various shows are presented—mostly music (rock, gospel, jazz, Hawaiian) and hula. Performances usually start at noon. The **Young People's Hula Show,** every Sun. at 9:30 a.m., is fast becoming an institution. Here, hula is being kept alive, with many first-time performers interpreting the ancient movements that they study in their *halau.*

The **Royal Hawaiian Band,** founded over 100 years ago, performs Fri. at noon on the Iolani Palace Bandstand.

Hilo Hattie, 700 Nimitz Highway, the largest manufacturer of alohawear in the state, conducts free tours of the factory complete with hotel pick-up. Up to 80,000 garments are on display in the showroom. It's hard to resist spending: prices and craftsmanship are good, and designs are the most contemporary. Open daily 8:30 a.m.-5 p.m., tel. 537-2926.

The giant pineapple watertower off Iwilei Road guides you to the **Dole Pineapple Factory,** which has been completely refurbished into a mini-mall with distinctive Hawaiian shops and a cafeteria. Here, millions of Hawaii's fruit are sliced, juiced, and canned for shipment around the world. Free samples are available. Least activity is during the winter months, but something fascinating is always going on. In the summertime, at the height of the harvest, this factory can process over three million cans of fruit per day! No reservations needed for small groups. Contact the Dole Company at 650 Iwilei Rd., tel. 536-3411, open 9 a.m. to 3 p.m., small admission.

Girlie Bars And Strip Joints

You'll have no excuse if your maiden Aunt Matilda or local chapter of Friendly Feminists ever catches you going into one of these joints, sonny boy! There's not even a hint of a redeeming social value here, and the only reason they're listed is to let you know where *not to go* if you're offended by raunchy sex shows. Many of these "lounges," as they're called, are strung along the 1600 and 1700 blocks of Kapiolani Blvd., and in the little alleys running off it. Mostly, tough-looking Oriental men own or operate them, and they open and shut quicker than a streetwalker's heart. Inside are two types of women: the dancers and the "lap sitters," and there's definitely a pecking order in these henhouses. (For a full description, see p. 140.) Most patrons are local men or GI types, with only a smattering of tourists. Personal safety is usually not a problem, but a fool and his money are soon parted in these bars.

Here are some *without* the bad reputations that frequently go along with this type of clip joint. **Misty II Lounge,** operated by a Vietnamese guy named Dean, has been there five years, an eternity in this business; Dean immediately fires any girl with bad vibes. This club is at 1661 Kapiolani Blvd., tel. 944-1745. Just behind it in the little alleyway are the **Orchid, Musume,** and **Winners Club**—all about the same. Two clubs considered to be good ones by their patrons are **Butterfly Lounge,** 903 Keamoku, tel. 947-3012, and the **Stop Lite Lounge,** at 1718 Kapiolani, tel. 941-5838.

Chinatown's **Hotel Street** has hookers, both male and female, walking the heels off their shoes. They cruise during the day, but the area really comes alive at night. Mostly, these people are down-and-outers who can't make it against the stiff competition along the main areas of Waikiki. The clientele is usually servicemen and hardcore locals. A few clubs in this area offer strippers. Always be prepared for fights and bad vibes in any of these joints. A few that tourists have entered and survived include the **Zig Zag, My Way,** and **Hubba Hubba Lounge** (see p.261)

Dirty Dan's, 205 Sand Island Access Rd., tel. 841-9063, is an old-fashioned topless go-go bar, the same as the famous one in San Diego. It's frequented mostly by GIs and can get pretty rowdy, especially late on weekends. The place is clean and prides itself on giving you a fair shake. It's not at all like the grab joints listed above. The women here are young and beautiful and *not* allowed to fraternize with the clientele. You can look, but you *cannot* touch. This helps to keep away the sleaze element. Draft and bottled beer are reasonably priced.

SHOPPING

If you don't watch the time, you'll spend half your vacation moving from one fascinating store to the next. Luckily, in greater Honolulu the majority of shopping is clustered in malls, with specialty shops scattered around the city, especially in the nooks and crannies of Chinatown (see p. 260). For a general overview of what the island has for sale, along with listings for bookstores, flea markets, sundries, and art shops, see p. 193. For food shopping see p. 193.

Ala Moana Shopping Center

This is the largest shopping center in the state, and if you want to get all of your souvenir hunting and special shopping done in one shot, this is the place. It's on Ala Moana Blvd., just across from the Ala Moana Beach Park, open weekdays from 9:30 a.m.-9 p.m., Sat. 9:30 a.m.-5:30 p.m., Sun. 10 a.m.-5 p.m., tel. 946-2811. Recently, the Ala Moana Shopping Center has taken off its comfortable Hawaiian shirt and shorts and donned designer fashions by Christian Dior and Charles Jordan. Local people are irritated, and they have a point, to a point. The Center has plenty of down-home shopping left, but it now caters as much to the "pent house" as it does to the "one room efficiency." It used to be where the people shopped, but now portions are being aimed at the affluent tourist, especially the affluent Japanese tourists who flaunt designer labels like politicians flaunt pretty secretaries. If anything, the shopping has gotten better, but you'll have to look around a bit more for bargains.

Plenty of competition keep prices down, with more than enough of an array to suit any taste and budget. About 100 stores include all of Hawaii's major department stores like **Sears, Penny's,** and **Liberty House.** Utilitarian shops like shoe makers, eateries, banks, and boutiques feature everything from flowers to swim fins. It's also a great place to see a cross section of Hawaiian society. Another pleasantry is a free hula show every Sunday at 9:30 a.m. on the **Centerstage** (see p. 254). The **Hawaii Visitors Bureau** maintains an information kiosk just near Centerstage. The following is a mere sampling of what you'll find.

The restaurants in the **Makai Food Court** are exceptional, if not for taste, at least for price, and an unbelievable variety of cuisine. In a huge open area you'll find dishes from Bangkok to Acapulco, from Tokyo to San Francisco. Most of these restaurants are counters for ordering, with tables in a common dining area. Great for people-watching, too!

A good one-stop store with plenty of souvenir-quality items at affordable prices is good old **Woolworth's.** They have all of the same sundries as Mainland stores, but plenty of Hawaiian and Oriental baubles fill the shelves, too. The film prices are some of the best.

House of Music sells records and tapes. This is a good store to shop for those island sounds that'll immediately conjure up images of Hawaii whenever they're played. Ground floor, tel. 949-1051.

The Honolulu Book Shop, tel. 941-2274, has the largest selection of books in the state, especially their Hawaiiana section. Books make inexpensive, easy-to-transport, and long-lasting mementos of your trip to Hawaii. Ground level near Centerstage.

Francis Camera Shop, tel. 946-2879, is a well-stocked camera store with a fine selection of merchandise sure to please the most avid camera buff. If you need something out of the ordinary for your camera bag, this is a good place to come. The staff is friendly and will spend time giving you advice. However, the best place to buy film is at **Sears** (no credit cards). **Woolworth's** and **Long's Drugs** also have good prices, but for cheap and fast developing try **Fromex Photo,** tel. 955-4797, street level, ocean side.

The Crackseed Center, tel. 949-7200, offers the best array of crackseed (spiced nuts, seeds, and fruits) that have been treats for island children for years. There're also dried and spiced scallops at $68 per pound and cuttlefish at $2.50 per pound—such a deal! Prices are inflated

here, but their selection can't be beat, and you can educate yourself about these same products in smaller stores around the island. Crackseed is not to everyone's liking, but it does make a unique souvenir. Spirolina hunters can get their organic fix at **Vim and Vigor** featuring vitamins, supplements, and minerals.

Shirokaya is a Japanese-owned department store between Penney's and Liberty House on the mountain side of the complex. They have a fascinating assortment of gadgetry, knick-knacks, handy items, and nifty stuff that Nippon is so famous for. It's fun just to look around, and the prices are reasonable. Japanese products are also available at **Iida's,** a local store dating back to the turn of the century, featuring garden ornaments and flower-arrangement sets, tel. 946-0888.

Specialty shops in the Center include: **The Ritz Department Store** with high fashions for men and women; **Hawaiian Island Creations, Products of Hawaii,** and **Irene's,** all selling a wide assortment of island-made goods and souvenirs, from cheap to exquisite; **India Imports,** many unique items from the subcontinent, and eelskin products; **Tahiti Imports** with bikinis, muumuus, and a wide selection of handicrafts from throughout Polynesia; **Jeans Warehouse** for you aloha buckaroos; and **San Francisco Rag Co.** for nice rags sewn together well. For food see p. 245.

The Ward Warehouse

Located just a few blocks west of Ala Moana Center, at 1050 Ala Moana Blvd., open weekdays 10 a.m.-9 p.m., Sat. 10 a.m.-5 p.m., Sun. 11 a.m.-4 p.m., tel. 531-6411. This modern two-story complex lives up to its name as a warehouse, with a motif from bygone days when stout wooden beams were used instead of steel. The wide array of shops here includes an array of inexpensive restaurants (see p. 245), but the emphasis is on arts and crafts, with no less than 10 shops specializing in this field.

Greenhouse Magic is dazzling in silk flowers and plants. **Imports International** has nifty items from around the world—clothing, rugs, knickknacks, wicker baskets, tasteful postcards, jewelry, clothing for women, and shirts for men. Also hand-painted ducks, frogs, and parrots are everything from ties to center pieces. Next door is **Future Heirlooms Collectibles** with pottery, baskets, and ceramics from Asia. Wonderful but expensive ethnic clothing comes from Thailand, Indonesia, and Malaysia. Gaily decorated they come as vests, pants, coats, and jackets, all 100% cotton.

The Art Board is excellent for poster art, with racks of limited editions from which to choose. Postcards by some of the islands' best artists and a good crystal collection keep the vibes positive in this small but jam-packed shop. **Ono Gallery** sparkles with jewelry, hanging stained glass, wooden boats, candles, bronzes, and sculpture. Give the tots their first lesson in impulse buying at **Hello Kitty's,** a toy store, or at **Kris Kringle's Den.** Show them how a pro does it at **B.B. Sports, Blue Ginger, Imports Intl., In The Sun,** or **Royal Alima.**

Kids of all ages will love **Neon Leon,** where you can buy masks, flying bats, puppets, a lot of neon, fake buns, and a pineapple head if you've left yours at home. **Books, Comics, And Games** for serious funmakers is on the second floor, while **Waldenbooks** has a tremendous selection of printed material on the first. Repent past gluttonies at **Aloha Health Food,** primarily a vitamin and mineral store. Or dress your feet at **Thongs and Things** with everything in thongs from spiked golfing thongs to Teva sandals, the best all-around footwear for the island. Upstairs is **Birkenstock Footprints,** with their wonderfully comfortable ugly-ducklings.

Perhaps the premier shop in the Warehouse is the **Artists Guild,** with very fine art by local artists. Most work has either a Hawaiian theme or utilizes island materials. Woodworkers, like Allen Wilkenson, fashion beautiful koa rocking chairs for $1900 or a table from koa, maple, and rosewood for $6800. Less expensive but terrific pieces are handwoven women's blouses by Gwendolyn for about $60 each. Shelves of pottery start from $20, with natural woven baskets from $50. Lynn Walton has been showing her work here for about 10 years. She does acrylic paintings similar to Pegge Hopper's, though she's been painting longer. A slight controversy as to who got it from whom doesn't detract from the beauty of this work. Leighton Lam, a resin artist who makes everything from jewelry to fine arts is well represented. Lucille Cooper works in raku and goes beyond pottery to sculpture. Rick Mills, a professor at the University of Hawaii, shows his glasswork here. Browse, buy, or pick up a memento like hand mirrors, boxes, combs, and earrings for under $15.

Ward Center

Across the street from the Ward Warehouse, this relatively new shopping center is gaining a reputation for some exclusive shops. Open weekdays 10 a.m.-9 p.m., Sat. 10 a.m.-5 p.m., Sun. 11 a.m.-4 p.m., tel. 531-6411. The Ward Center is appointed in light wood, and accentuated by brick floors that give the feeling of an intimate inside mall, although much is outside. For the excellent restaurants here see page 246.

R. Fields showcases fine wines and exquisite foods, crackers, cookies, cheeses, imported pastas, and caviar. **Images International Of Hawaii** is an exclusive art shop where you'd like to become a patron of the arts. They feature Tatsuo Ito, a master of *rimpa,* characterized by the use of 24-karat gold on fans forming a three-piece panel three by six feet. Scenes are traditional Japanese motifs of *sakura,* wisteria, cranes, chrysanthemums, and waves. Contrast this with a remarkable Lucite sculpture by Frederik Hart called *Contemplation.* Another gallery is at the Hyatt Regency in the lobby area, where they feature the work of Hisashi Otsuka.

Ladies will find exclusive fashions at **Pappagallo, Imago,** and **Susan Marie of Honolulu.** Men can outfit themselves in the most stylish fashions at **Ross Sutherland.** Promenade in style with a lid from **The Honolulu Hat Co.,** accented by a diamond stickpin from the **Imperial Collection.**

The Colonnade is a cluster of shops inside the Ward Center. It includes **Regency Shoes, Lady Judith,** and **Art A La Carte.** Just down the way is **Willowdale Galleries,** twinkling with elegant antiques. It's like looking into a giant china closet full of the best place settings and crystal. Stuck back in a remote corner, where mystics feel more at home, is **Sedona,** a metaphysical new-age store. They have oils, crystals, agates, books, and consciousness-lifting tapes. Recharge your spiritual batteries with psychic readings by Pamela Higa, who gives "self empowerment sessions and intuitive services," tel. 262-9674.

Downtown Shopping

If you're touring the historical sights of downtown Honolulu, take a short stroll over to the corner of

Bishop and King streets, as good a place as any to call the center of the financial district. The names atop the buildings, both vintage and new, trace "big business" in Hawaii. There's good food to be enjoyed in the restaurants in this area (see p. 249) along with some shops stuck away in the corners of the big buildings. For Chinatown shopping see p. 260. Also, an enjoyable time can be had at the **Dole Cannery Square,** with shopping in its new mini-mall, see page 238. **Long's Drugs,** tel. 534-4551, is at 1088 Bishop, and almost next door is **Woolworth's,** tel. 524-8980, for any sundries and necessities.

The full-service **Honolulu Bookshop** is on the corner of Bishop and Hotel, tel. 534-6224. The selections are excellent. **Nautilus Of The Pacific** is at 1141 Bishop, specializing in estate jewelry and Hawaiian heirlooms, with plenty of sculptures and ceramics from Japan and China. **Hawaiian Islands Stamp and Coin,** tel. 531-6251, at 1111 Bishop St., street level in the International Savings Building, displays rare coins, stamps, and paper money of the U.S., Hawaii, and worldwide. **Discount Store,** at 65 S. Hotel St., sells TVs, VCRs, radios, and electronic gear. **Amar's Sporting Goods,** tel. 536-0404, at the corner of Bethel and Pauahi, is one of the bigger sporting goods stores on Oahu.

Bargains And Discounts

For discounts and bargains, try the following: **Crazy Shirts Factory Outlet,** at 99-969 Iwaena St., Aiea, tel. 487-9919, or 470 N. Nimitz Hwy., Honolulu, tel. 521-0855, seconds and discontinued styles, with a minimum savings of 50 percent. **Swimsuit Warehouse,** 870 Kapahulu Ave., Honolulu, tel. 735-0040, has women's swimsuits under $20, plus shorts and tops. **The** **Muumuu Factory,** 1526 Makaloa St., offers great sales—get there early and bring your helmet and shoulder pads to fight off the crowds. The **Hawaii Fashion Facotry** at 1031 Auahi St., 2nd floor, is just between the Ward Center and the Ward Warehouse. Fashions at factory prices with the public welcome to visit the showrooms. **Goodwill Thrift Shop,** at 83 N. King, tel. 521-3105, displays the same bargains as on the Mainland, but with a wide assortment of alohawear. **Nearly New Thrift Shop,** 1144 Koko Head Ave., tel. 732-3272, has consignment sales of quality merchandise. **Symphony Thrift Shop,** 1923 Pensacola, tel. 524- 7157, is a consignment shop for used clothing in excellent condition, and usually name brands. **The Discount Store,** 188 S. Hotel St., tel 537- 4469, boasts excellent prices on tape recorders, tapes, batteries, and electrical equipment. For **flea markets,** see page 193.

Miscellaneous

Everyone, sooner or later, needs a good hardware store. You can't beat the selection at **Kilgo's,** 180 Sand Island Rd., tel. 845-3266. They have it all.

For camera and photo supplies **Central Camera** is a fine store in the downtown area where the salespeople are very helpful. Across from Hawaiian Telephone at 1164 Bishop St., tel. 536-6692. Open 8:30 a.m.-4 p.m. Mon.-Fri. and 8:30-11 a.m. Saturday. (Also see Ala Moana Shopping Center, p. 255). For **sporting goods,** try: **Big 88,** 330 Sand Island Rd., tel. 845-1688, many military items; **Amar Sporting Goods,** 1139 Bethel St., tel. 536-0404, sporting goods, sportswear, and a full range of accessories and equipment.

parrot fish

CHINATOWN

Chinatown has seen ups and downs in the last 130 years, ever since Chinese laborers were lured from Kwangtung Province to work as contract laborers on the pineapple and sugar plantations. They didn't need a fortune cookie to tell them that there was no future in plantation work, so within a decade of their arrival they had established themselves as merchants, mostly in small retail businesses and restaurants. Chinatown is roughly a triangle of downtown Honolulu bordered by Nuuanu Street on the east, N. Beretania Street on the north, and S. King Street forming the hypotenuse. Twice this area has been flattened by fire, once in 1886 and again in 1900. The 1900 fire was deliberately set to burn out rats that had brought bubonic plague to the city. The fire got out of control and burned down virtually the whole district. Some contended that the fire was allowed to engulf the district in order to decimate the growing economic strength of the Chinese. Chinatown reached its heyday in the 1930s when it thrived with tourists coming and going from the main port at the foot of Nuuanu Street.

Today, Chinatown is a mixed bag of upbeat modernization and run-down, sleazy storefronts. Although still strongly Chinese, there are Japanese, Laotians, Vietnamese, and even an Irish pub, O'Toole's, on Nuuanu Avenue. This is

Asia come to life: meat markets with hanging ducks, and Chinese, Korean, Japanese, and Vietnamese food with their strange aromatic spices all in a few blocks. The entire district takes only 10 minutes to walk, and is a world apart from tourist Oahu. Crates, live chickens, incredible shops, down-and-outers, tattoo parlors, and temples are found in this quarter. When Hotel Street meets River Street, with the harbor in the background, it all abruptly ends. This is a different Honolulu, a Pacific port, crusty and exciting.

Around Chinatown

Look for the pagoda roof of **Wo Fat's** on the corner of Hotel and Maunakea streets. This is the oldest chop suey house in Honolulu, started in 1886 by Mr. Wo Fat, a baker. It's a good landmark for starting your tour. If you want to clear your head from the hustle and bustle visit the **Kuan Yin Temple,** where Buddha is always praised with some sweet-smelling incense. For peace and quiet, or to check out some old-timers playing checkers or dominoes, cross the river and enter **Aala Triangle Park.** Treat yourself by walking a few minutes to **Foster Botanical Park** at 180 N. Vineyard for a glimpse of rare and exotic flora from around the world. See page 238. While walking River Street, bordering Nuuanu

Stream, behind the Cultural Plaza, notice what most people think is a temple, but is really **Izumo Taisha Jinja,** a Japanese Shinto shrine. All the accoutrements of a shrine are here—roof, bell, prayer box. This one houses a male deity. You can tell by the cross on the top. There's a ferrous concrete example of a *torii* gate. **Lum Sai Ho Tong** across the street from the Shinto shrine is a basic Chinese Buddhist temple, very small. Below it is Edwin's Upholstery Shop, part of the temple.

You can easily do Chinatown on your own, but for a different slant and some extremely knowledgeable guides try the **Chinese Chamber of Commerce Tour,** tel. 533-3181, that's been operating as a community service for almost 30 years. They'll guide you around Chinatown for only $4, with an optional $5 lunch at Wo Fat's. Or try the **Hawaiian Heritage Center Tour** from 1026 Nuuanu Ave., tel. 521-2749, every Mon., Wed., and Fri. at 9:30 a.m., for $4, and a lunch at Wo Fat's for $5. An excellent source of general information is the **Hawaii Chinese History Center,** 111 N. King St., Honolulu, HI 96817.

Shopping

For shopping head to the **Cultural Plaza,** on the corner of Mauna Kea and Beretania streets, but note that it has been struggling lately and shops come and go with regularity. It's more fun to look at than to shop. You'll find **Vin Ching Jade Center,** and **Dragongate Bookstore. Excellent Jewelry Factory,** and **Peninsula Jewelry.** The Cultural Plaza **Moongate Stage** is the center piece. Here they perform Chinese dance and plays, and herald in the Chinese New Year. If there is a presentation (free), attend.

Nearby you'll find the **People's Open Market,** a co-operative of open-air stalls selling just about everything that Chinatown has to offer at competitive prices. Follow your nose to the pungent odors of fresh fish at **Oahu's Fish Market** on King Street, where ocean delectables can be had for reasonable prices.

Pauahi Nuuanu Gallery, open weekdays 10:30-4, Sat. 9-1, at the corner of Pauahi and Nuuanu streets, is owned and operated by Lorna Dunn. It's small, but so are diamonds, and inside it's loaded with Hawaiian arts and crafts. The most impressive are the wooden bowls—light as a feather and thin as glass, made by Mi-

chael Ilipuakea Dunn, Lorna's son. Besides bowls there are little wooden jewelry boxes by Michael. Mythical carvings by Richard Morgan Howell depict Hawaiian legends in wood and stone. Bruce Clark and Rick Mills, an instructor at the University of Hawaii, are glasswork artists. The painters represented are Laka Morton, a Kauai artist, Jianjie Jie, and Douglas Tolantino, a Filipino-Hawaiian, with heavy oils by Ellen Joseph Gilmore. Expensive prices, but quality work.

Waterfall Galleries, owned by award-winning photographer William Waterfall, are at 1160A Nuuanu St., tel. 521-6863. William runs the gallery, takes the photos, and collects the artwork that's here. The photography is all original. Plenty of the artwork comes from Asia, especially Balinese carvings, and celadon pottery from Thailand which is done in woodburning kilns, and signed by the potter. William, while doing travel assignments, buys the artworks and schleps them back. His gallery is full of sculptures, bas-reliefs, and masks from previous trips. So you don't know what you'll get when you come in here, but you can count on it being tasteful and original.

Pegge Hopper Gallery is next door to Waterfall Galleries. Ms. Hopper is one of the three most famous working artists in all of Hawaii. Her original works grace the walls of the most elegant hotels and homes in the islands. If you would like to purchase one of her bold and amazing serigraphs, this shop has the best and widest selection.

Cindy's Flower Shop is just next to Wo Fat's, and they have fresh leis at cheap prices. Located right where S. Beretania turns into N. Beretania, at Smith street across from the Honolulu Towers, are a garland of flower shops like Lita's Leis and Maunakea Leis, famous for good products and prices. At River and S. Beretania is an open **people's market** every Monday from 10 a.m.-11:15 a.m., selling fresh produce from local gardens.

The **Wingon Co.** at 131 Hotel has porcelain ware, but the feature is the big crocks of crack seed. If you want it the way it *was* made, this is it.

Yuan Chai Tong Ltd. Oriental Herbs and **Dr. W.S. Lam** licensed acupuncturist occupy a storefront on the corner of River and N. King. Nearby on Maunakea is **Fook Sau Tong's,** another Chinese herb specialist. Look in the window to see coiled snake skin, a few dried-out snakes, some flat-looking lizards, and who-knows-what. They'd better be good for you. If you need a bounce put back in your step, maybe some tonics that resemble road tar and a few needles in the ear are just what the doctor will order.

Down Smith Street is **Kam Mau Co.,** whose shelves are stacked with every conceivable (and inconceivable) Oriental food. This is a great place to sample authentic crack seed. If your tummy revolts or if you need a quick tonic head next door to **Lai An Tong's** herb shop where some mashed antelope antler or powdered monkey brain will set you straight again.

On the corner of Maunakea and Hotel you'll find **New World Fashions,** men and women's wear—quality, value, and low prices.

Chinatown Nights
Chinatown is relatively safe, especially during the daytime, but at night, particularly along infamous Hotel Street, you have to be careful. When the sun sinks, the neon lights, and the area fires up. Transvestites and hookers slide down the street, shaking their wares and letting you know that they're open for business. Purchasing might leave you with a few souvenirs that you'd never care to *share* with the folks back home.

Not many tourists come this way. But walking down Hotel street is really an adventure in and of itself. If you stay on the main drag, right down the middle, you'll be OK. There are a lot of nondescript places like **China Bar,** that open to the street like a wound oozing the odor of stale beer and urine. At Hotel and Nuuanu you find the Honolulu Police Department downtown substation. And then the smut begins. It seems as though you get the cops and the smut at the same places.

The **Hubba Hubba Club,** with its live nude shows, no cover, and not-too-inflated drinks is the best of Hotel Street. This is not a place for candy asses, wimps, or missionaries. Simply put, there are naked women in here doing exotic and bizarre acts. The Hubba Hubba is basically a clip joint on the up and up. Inside are flashing lights, a runway, and $3 beers, with only mild pressure as you sit and watch the act. If you invite one of the dancers to sit with you it's $10. The women, for what they get paid (not much),

really put a lot into it. They all have costumes and acts and basically they do four songs. They start off in everything from space-age erotica to old-fashioned white gowns and then off they go. Most wear garter belts for tips and perform their act within breathing distance.

As you walk down Hotel Street toward the river it gets sleazier. Next comes the **Zig Zag Club,** which is basically a gin joint. Interspersed is an assortment of peep shows, followed by the **Swing Club,** with disco dancing from 10:30 a.m.-2:30 a.m., and then **Two Jacks Bar** (bar and cabaret). **Elsie's Bar,** at 145 N. Hotel St., open 6 a.m.-2 a.m., looks meaner than a tattooed snake, but it's a safe place. So if you want to have a night of fun and relaxation come in here. They offer Hawaiian music by the Puamana Serenaders along with fairly decent Hawaiian food. A few doors down are steps leading upstairs to the **Original Bath Palace.** The *original* place where drunken fools were taken to the cleaners.

Food
You can eat delicious ethnic food throughout Chinatown. If not Honolulu's best, the entire district, food-wise, is definitely Honolulu's cheapest. On almost every corner you've got places like **Mini Garden Noodle and Rice Shop** and **Cafe Paradise** for breakfast, lunch, and dinner. They're basic and cheap eateries whose ambiance is a variation of formica topped-tables and linoleum floors. In almost all, the food is authentic, with most featuring Oriental foods. You can easily get meals here for $3 to $5. Some eateries appear greasier than the Alaska Pipeline, so you'll have to vibe them out. The local people eat in them regularly, and most are clean enough. An example is **Neon's Filipino Restaurant** on S. Hotel near the Hubba Hubba Club. The sign says "Come in and have a halo halo, consists of many delicious fruits and flavor of canned juices. And by the way order a piece of custard." They serve Filipino dishes like *mongo ampalaya,* shrimp *pinakabet,* and *pancit* Canton for around $5.

Right at the corner of N. Hotel and Maunakea, you'll see **Wo Fat's Chinese Chop Suey,** tel. 533-6393, the oldest chop suey house in Hawaii, where you're guaranteed an authentic meal at reasonable prices. A visit to Chinatown is incomplete without lunch at Wo Fat's, or at least a tour of this extremely ornate restaurant. The three floors are covered with paintings of dragons, birds, flowers and a variety of land and seascapes. Murals, carvings, and hanging lanterns create the mood of "rococo Chinese." The menu is like a small phone book with literally hundreds of choices of fish, fowl, beef, and vegetarian dishes. It's hard to spend more than $10 per person, with many dishes considerably less.

Doong Kong Lau offers hakka cuisine and sizzlers. It's on the river side of the Cultural Plaza, open Mon. 9 a.m.-9:30 p.m., Tues.-Sun. 8 a.m.-9:30 p.m., tel. 531-8833. Inside it's utilitarian with leatherette seats and formica tables. You come here for the food. Savories include stir-fried squid with broccoli for $5.95, stir-fried scallops with garlic sauce for $7.95, stir-fried oysters with black beans for $6.95, sizzle plates like seafood combo at $7.95, shark fin with shredded chicken $16.50. The menu reads, "The chief recommends deep fried shrimp with toast." Who's to argue with the chief! **Won Kee Seafood Restaurant** is another restaurant in the Cultural Plaza. Locals swear by it, especially the lunch specials for $4.95.

The **Royal Kitchen**, tel. 524-4461, in the Cultural Plaza, is very popular with local families and business people. They're especially known for their takeout baked *manapua,* soft dough with pork and spices, and for their Chinese sausage, *lupcheung.* Open very early in the morning.

And stuck right in the center of Asia, what else would you expect to find but **Eleno's Mexican Restaurant.** Basic Mexican food like tacos, tostadas, enchiladas, and refills of chips and salsa, all around $5.

Pho May Vietnamese Restaurant at 1029 Maunakea St., tel. 533-3522, open daily 9-9, is a family-operated restaurant, and it is excellent. There is no ambiance, but the food more than

makes up for it. Nothing is over $5. Specialties include Vietnamese soups of steak, well-done brisket and flank, tendon and tripe for $3.95, French bread and beef juicy cube for $3.95, and hot-and-sour soup for two bucks. With the soup they give you a stalk of fresh basil that you break up yourself, a spice that resembles cilantro, and sprouts that you add to the soup. Try shrimp and pork salad $4, or crabmeat fried wonton for $4, and chicken curry $4. Try the curry chicken—terrific. For well under $10 you'll waddle away totally satiated.

There's a really decent-looking Vietnamese restaurant called **Sau Duong** at 58 N. Hotel, tel. 538-7658. Home-cooked dishes like sour soup with fish $8, lemon grass-spiced pork chop $5.50. House specialties like fine sliced papaya salad with shrimp and pork $3.75. Open for breakfast, lunch, and dinner.

To Chau Vietnamese Restaurant, at 1007 River, tel. 533-4549, and **Ha Bien** next door to "Tattoo Parlor" serve basic Vietnamese fare for under $5 for most dishes. They're around the corner from the action of Hotel Street, and are family-oriented. Ha Bien is open strange hours, Mon. 8 a.m.-4 p.m., open the remainder of the week until 6 p.m.

Another Vietnamese restaurant is **My Canh**, tel. 599-1866, at 164 N. King St., open Mon.-Sat. 9-5, Sun. 9-3. Their menu reads "you can select one specialty of the heart warming combination of the followings: rare steak well cooked, brisket and tendon, regular is $3.75, special is $4. BBQ meat spring for roll rice vermicelli $4.25."

One place that you shouldn't miss is **Shung Chong Yuein,** a Chinese cake shop at 1027 Maunakea. Look in to see yellow sugar cakes, black sugar cakes, shredded coconut with eggs, salted mincemeat, Chinese ham with egg, lotus seeds, and steamed buns.

"It is the meeting place of East and West. The very new rubs shoulders with the immeasurably old. And if you have not found the romance you expected you have come upon something singularly intriguing."

—W. Somerset Maugham

WAIKIKI

Waikiki ("Spouting Water") is like a fresh young starlet from the sticks who went to Hollywood to make it big, and did, though maybe too fast for her own good. Everyone always knew that she had a double-dip of talent and heart, but the fastlane has its heartaches, and she's been banged around a little by life. Even though her figure's fuller, her makeup's a little askew, and her high heels are worn down, she has plenty of chutzpah left, and when the curtain parts and the lights come up, she'll play her heart out for her audience.

Waikiki is a classic study of contradictions. Above all, it is a result of basic American entrepreneurism taken to the nth degree. Along the main strip, high-powered businessmen cut multimillion-dollar deals, but on the sidewalks it's a carnival midway with hucksters, handbillers, and street people selling everything decent and indecent under the tropical sun. To get a true feeling for Waikiki, you must put this amazing strip of land into perspective. The area covers only seven-tenths of a square mile, which at a good pace, you can walk in 15 minutes. On any given day, about 110,000 people crowd its beaches and boulevards, making it one of the most densely populated areas on Earth. Sixty thousand of these people are tourists; 30,000 are workers who commute from various towns of Oahu and cater to the tourists, and the remaining 20,000 actually call Waikiki home. The turnover is about 80,000 new tourists per week, and the pace never slackens. To the head shakers, these facts condemn Waikiki as a mega-growth area gone wild. To others, these same figures make Waikiki an energized, fun-filled place to be, where "if you don't have a good time, it's your own fault."

For the naive or the out-of-touch looking for "grass-shack paradise," the closest they'll come to it in Waikiki is painted on a souvenir ashtray. Those drawn to a smorgasbord of activities, who are adept at choosing the best and ignoring the rest, can't go wrong! People and the action are as constant in Waikiki as the ever-rolling surf.

History

The written record of this swampy area began in the late 1790s. The white man, along with his historians, cartographers, artists, and gunpowder, were already an undeniable presence in the islands. Kalanikupule, ranking chief of

Oahu, hijacked the *Jackall,* a small ship commanded by Capt. Brown, with which he intended to spearhead an attack against Kamehameha I. The chief held the *Jackall* for a while, but the sailors regained control just off Diamond Head and sent the Hawaiians swimming for land. The ship then hastened to Kamehameha to report the treachery, and returned with his armada of double-hulled canoes, which beached along Waikiki. The great king then defeated Kalanikupule at the famous battle of Nuuanu Pali, and secured control of the island. Thereafter Waikiki, pinpointed by Diamond Head, became a well-known landmark.

Waikiki's interior was low-lying swampland, long known to be good for fishponds, taro, rice, and bananas, but hardly for living. The beach, however, was always blessed with sunshine and perfect waves, especially for surfing, a sport heartily loved by the Hawaiians. The royalty of Hawaii, following Kamehameha, made Honolulu their capital, and kept beach houses at Waikiki. They invited many visiting luminaries to visit them at their private beach. All were impressed. In the 1880s, King Kalakaua was famous for his beach house hospitality. One of his favorite guests was Robert Louis Stevenson, who spent many months here writing one of his novels. By the turn of the 20th century Waikiki had become a highly exclusive vacation spot.

In 1901 the Moana Hotel was built, but immediately a protest was heard because it interfered with the view of Diamond Head. In 1906, Lucius Pinkham, then director of Hawaii's Board of Health, called the mosquito-infested area "dangerous and unsanitary," and proposed to drain the swamp with a canal so that "the whole place can be transformed into a place of unique beauty." By the early 1920s, the Ala Wai Canal was built, its dredgings used to reclaim land, and Waikiki was demarcated. By the end of the 1920s, the Royal Hawaiian Hotel, built on the site previously occupied by the royal beach house, was receiving very wealthy guests who arrived by ocean liner, loaded down with steamer trunks. They ensconced themselves at Waikiki, often staying for the duration of the season.

For about 40 years, Waikiki remained the enchanted domain of Hollywood stars, dignitaries, and millionaires. But for the brief and extraordinary days of WW II, which saw Waikiki barricaded and barb-wired, GIs—regular guys from the Mainland—were given a taste of this "reserved paradise" while on R&R. They brought home tantalizing tales of wonderful Waikiki, whetting the appetite of middle America.

Beginning just before statehood and continuing through the '60s to the mid-'70s, hotels and condos popped up like fertilized weeds, and tourism exploded with the advent of the jumbo jet. Discounted package tours began to haul in droves of economy-class tourists. Businesses catering to the tastes of penny-pinchers and first-timers elbowed their way into every nook and cranny. For the first time Waikiki began to be described as tacky and vulgar. For the old-timers, Waikiki was in decline. The upscale and repeat visitors started to snub Waikiki, heading for hidden resorts on the Neighbor Islands. But Waikiki had spirit and soul, and never gave in. In the last few years, its declining hotels started a campaign to regain their illustrious images. Millions upon millions of dollars have poured into renovations and remodelings. Luxury hotels renting exclusive and expensive rooms have reappeared, and are doing a booming business.

Waikiki Today

The Neighbor Islands are pulling more and more tourists away, and depending on point of view, this is either boon or bust for Waikiki. Direct flights to Maui and the Big Island allow more tourists than ever to bypass Oahu but still a whopping 80 percent of the people visiting the islands spend at least one night in a Waikiki hotel, which offer the lowest room rates in Hawaii. The sublime and the gaudy are neighbors in Waikiki. Exclusive shops are often flanked by buskers selling plastic hula dolls. Burgers and beer mingle their pedestrian odors with those of Parisian cuisine. Though Waikiki in many ways is unique, it can also come off as "Anytown, U.S.A." But most importantly it somehow works, and works well. You may not find "paradise" on Waikiki's streets, but you will find a willing "dancing partner," and if you pay the fiddler, she'll keep the beat.

Non-Americans, especially Japanese, still flock for dream vacations, mostly staying at Waikiki hotels, 25 percent of which are owned by Japanese firms. Mainlanders and locals alike are disgruntled when they see the extent to which Waikiki has become a Japanese town. It's one of the only cities in America where you can have trouble ordering a meal or making a purchase if you don't speak Japanese! The visiting Japanese have been soundly warned by the tour operators before they arrive to never talk to strangers, especially someone on the street. Unfortunately for them, this means a vacation in which they never really leave Japan. They're herded into Japanese-owned shops and restaurants where prices are grossly inflated, and from which the tour operators get kickbacks. Local shopkeepers, not on the list, are aggravated. They say that the once-timid Japanese visitor will now show irritation if the shopkeeper doesn't speak Japanese, and will indignantly head for the door if there is no one provided to deal with them in their native tongue. Also, these visitors have been taught to bargain with American shopkeepers, who they are told inflate prices. This makes for some rugged interaction when the price is already fair, but the Japanese visitor won't believe it. Although a survey was done that says the Japanese tourist spends an average of $200/day, as opposed to a Mainlander who spends $100/day, the Japanese really don't spread their money around as much as you would think. The money spent in Japanese shops primarily goes back to Japan. It's an incestuous system that operates in Waikiki.

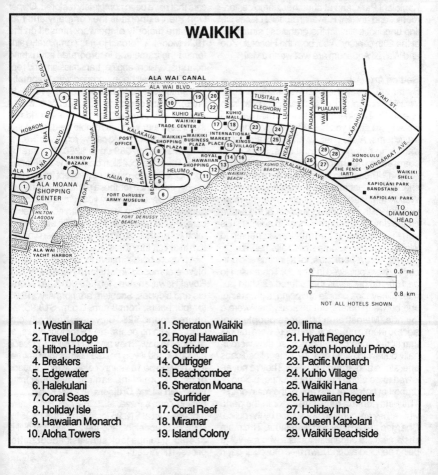

WAIKIKI

NOT ALL HOTELS SHOWN

1. Westin Ilikai
2. Travel Lodge
3. Hilton Hawaiian
4. Breakers
5. Edgewater
6. Halekulani
7. Coral Seas
8. Holiday Isle
9. Hawaiian Monarch
10. Aloha Towers
11. Sheraton Waikiki
12. Royal Hawaiian
13. Surfrider
14. Outrigger
15. Beachcomber
16. Sheraton Moana Surfrider
17. Coral Reef
18. Miramar
19. Island Colony
20. Ilima
21. Hyatt Regency
22. Aston Honolulu Prince
23. Pacific Monarch
24. Kuhio Village
25. Waikiki Hana
26. Hawaiian Regent
27. Holiday Inn
28. Queen Kapiolani
29. Waikiki Beachside

SIGHTS

To see Waikiki's attractions, you have to do little more than perch on a bench or loll on a beach towel. Its boulevards and beaches are world-class for people-watching. Some of its strollers and sunbathers are *visions,* while others are real *sights.* And if you keep your ears open, it's not hard to hear every American accent and a dozen foreign languages. Some actual sights are intermingled with the hotels, boutiques, bars, and restaurants. Sometimes, too, these very buildings *are* the sights. Unbelievably, you can even find plenty of quiet spots—in the gardens of Kapiolani Park, and at churches, temples, tea-rooms, and ancient Hawaiian special places sitting unnoticed amidst the grandiose structures of the 20th century. Also, both the Honolulu Zoo and Waikiki Aquarium are well worth a visit.

Getting Around

By far and away the best way to get around Waikiki is on foot. For one, it's easily walked from one end to the other in less than 20 minutes, and walking will save you hassling with parking and traffic jams. Also, TheBus and taxis are abundant, and along with rental cars, have been covered in the Introduction under "Getting Around." Those who have opted for a rental car should note that many of the agencies operate Waikiki terminals, which for some can be more convenient than dropping your car at the airport on the day of departure. Check to see if it suits you. The following information is specific to Waikiki, and offers some limited alternatives.

In mid-1987, **pedicabs,** for all intents and purposes, were outlawed in Waikiki. There used to be 150-160 pedicabs that offered as short taxi rides. They took people shopping, sightseeing, and between hotels, but basically they were a joy ride. Mainstream business people considered them a nuisance, and there were rumors that some drivers dealt drugs, so they were finally outlawed. Now only 10-12 legal pedicabs operate in and around Waikiki. They're not allowed to go along Kalakaua Avenue, pickup or dropoff at hotels, or use any of the main drags. They stay on the back streets or in the park, where they are constantly watched by the police. Charges are a hefty $3 per minute. The main customers are Japanese tourists who marvel at being peddled around town by a muscular *gaijin*

in a rickshaw-type conveyance never seen in their own homeland any longer.

The **Waikiki Trolley,** tel. 526-0112, offers tours that'll take you throughout Waikiki and downtown Honolulu. A day pass costs $7, and you can get on and off as much as you like. The trolley is really an open-air bus, but it's well done and plenty of fun.

The most distinctive and fun-filled cars on Oahu are the hotrods available from **Cruisin' Classics,** 2139 Kuhio Ave., tel. 923-6446. They have a fleet of American and European classic cars that have been completely restored. Owner Don Pierce operates the company and has done the majority of the work himself on the 1928 Model-A Fords. He has completely reinforced the frame and incorporated a Mustang front suspension, engine, transmission, and rear end. They've all been updated with automatic transmissions, and power steering (easy to drive). All are equipped with AM/FM cassette players and *oouugah* horns. Pick a roadster that'll seat four with the rumble seat, or a four-door convertible touring car, which seats five.

Prices start at $89 up to $250 for a stretch limo. They offer collision damage waiver for an additional $14.95, or you can accept full responsibility. Insurance for these particular cars is not automatically covered by your credit card company which is often the case with normal rental cars. If your hotel is in the Waikiki area they'll fetch you in their stretch limo, and when you return their car, they'll take you back to your hotel.

A reasonable alternative for Waikiki is to rent a bicycle or moped. **Interisland Rentals,** at 535 Royal Hawaiian Ave., tel. 946-0013 has scooters and bicycles. Scooters are normally $12.95 for four hours, from 8 a.m.-6 p.m. $18.95, 24 hours around $25. Bicycles, basically city cruisers with no gears, are $9 for four hours, or $12 for the day. They also have cars and jeeps available, and if you need a helmet they're free. You have to be 18 years or older to rent mopeds or cars. More of the same is available from **Hawaiian Island Cruisers,** at 2139 Kuhio Ave., behind Zorro's Pizza, tel. 926-8725. Brand-new mopeds start at $13.95 for four hours, $15.95 for six, $19.95 for eight, and the 24-hour special is $24.95. If things look slow ask about better prices. They'll deal!

Waikiki does an excellent job of conveying traffic, both auto and pedestrian, along Kalakaua Avenue, the main drag fronting Waikiki. They've installed, very clear, yet unattractive, combinations of stoplights and street names. These are metal L-shaped beams, painted a dull brown, that straddle the roadways clearly pinpointing your location. Unfortunately, they match the area about as well as work boots match a hula dancer. To give the feeling of an outdoor strolling mall, sidewalks along Kalakaua have been widened and surfaced with red brick.

The **Kapiolani Park Kiosk** is on the corner of Kapahulu and Kalakaua avenues. The kiosk uses vintage photos to give a concise history of Kapiolani Park. An overview map shows all the features of the park. Information is available here concerning events at the Aquarium, Zoo, Waikiki Shell, the Kodak Hula Show, the Art Mart (a collection of island artists selling their creations along the Zoo Fence, (see p. 294), and the Kapiolani Bandstand, where you're treated to free concerts by top-name bands and orchestras (see p. 293).

DIAMOND HEAD

If you're not sandwiched in a manmade canyon of skyscrapers, you can look eastward from anywhere in Waikiki and see Diamond Head. Diamond Head *says* Waikiki. Western sailors have used it as a landmark since the earliest days of contact, and the Hawaiians undoubtedly before that. Ships' artists etched and sketched its motif long before the names of the new-found lands of Hawaii, Waikiki, and Oahu were standardized, and appeared on charts as *Owyhee, Whytete,* and *Woohoo.* The Hawaiian name was Leahi ("Brow of the Ahi"); legend says it was named by Hi'iaka, Madame Pele's younger sister, because she saw a resemblance in its silhouette to this yellowfin tuna. The name "Diamond Head" comes from a band of sailors who found calcite crystals on its slopes and thought they'd discovered diamonds. Kamehameha I immediately made the mountain *kapu* until his adviser John Young informed him that what the seamen had found, later known as "Pele's tears," were worthless except as souvenirs. Diamond Head was considered a power spot by the Hawaiians. Previously, Kamehameha had worshipped at a *heiau* located on the western

slopes, offering human sacrifice to his blood-thirsty war-god, Ku.

Geologically, the 760-foot monolith is about 350,000 years old, formed in one enormous explosion when sea water came into contact with lava bubbling out of a fissure. No new volcanic activity has been suspected in the last 200,000 years. The huge rock is now Hawaii's state monument and a national natural landmark. Its crater serves as a Hawaii National Guard depot; various hiking trails to the summit bypass installations left over from WW II (see p. 206). Getting there takes only 15 minutes from Waikiki, either by TheBus no. 57 or by car along Diamond Head Road. The southeast *(makai)* face has some of the most exclusive and expensive real estate in the islands. The Kahala Hilton Hotel here is regarded by many to be one of the premier hotels in the world, and nearby is the super-snobbish Waialae Country Club. Many private estates—homes of multimillionaires, Hollywood stars, and high-powered multinational executives—cling to the cliffside, fronting ribbons of beach open to the public by narrow rights-of-way that oftentimes are hemmed in by the walls of the estates.

KAPIOLANI PARK

In the shadow of Diamond Head is Kapiolani Park, a quiet 140-acre oasis of greenery, just a coconut's roll away from the gray cement and flashing lights of Waikiki. It has proved to be one of the best gifts ever received by the people of Honolulu, ever since King Kalakaua donated this section of crown lands to them in 1877, requesting it be named after his wife, Queen Kapiolani. In times past it was the sight of horse and car races, polo matches, and Hawaii's unique *pa'u* riders, fashionable ladies in long flowing skirts riding horses decked out with lei. The park was even the sight of Camp McKinley, the U.S. Army HQ in the islands from 1898 to 1907.

It remains a wonderful place for people to relax and exercise away from the hustle of Waikiki. The park is a mecca for jogging and aerobics, with many groups and classes meeting here throughout the day. It also serves as the starting point for the yearly **Honolulu Marathon,** one of the most prestigious races in the world. The beach part of the park, called Sans Souci, is very popular with local people and those wishing to escape the crowds, just a few beach blanket-lengths away (see p. 271).

Its **Waikiki Shell,** an open-air amphitheater, hosts many visiting musical groups, especially during Aloha Week. The Honolulu Symphony is a regular here, providing free concerts especially on summer evenings. Nearby, the **Kapiolani Bandstand** hosts the Royal Hawaiian Band on Sunday afternoons. Also, under the shade of the trees toward Waikiki Beach, plenty of street entertainers, including clowns, acrobats, and jugglers, congregate daily to work out their routines to the beat of conga drums and other improvised music supplied by wandering musicians. Families and large groups come here to picnic, barbecue, and play softball. The park grounds are also home to the free **Kodak Hula Show** (see p. 293), Elks Club, prestigious Outrigger Canoe Club founded at the turn of the century, Waikiki Aquarium, and 45-acre Honolulu Zoo.

Just in front of the zoo, by the big banyan, are hundreds and hundreds of pigeons, the "white phantoms of Waikiki." In the morning they are especially beautiful darting through the sunshine like white spirits. Go to the Stop N Go or the ABC Store at the corner of Kapahulu and Kapiolani and buy birdseed. Take a few handfuls and stand among the pigeons. They will perch on your arms, shoulders, and head and peck away. If you're not wearing toed shoes be advised that if you drop seed between your toes, you'll get an instant and free pedicure by the hungry birds. This is great fun and free!

WAIKIKI AQUARIUM

The first Waikiki Aquarium was built in 1904, its entranceway framed by a *torii* gate. Today's aquarium was built and stocked in 1954, and a plan is now underway to rebuild and refurbish it with a new entranceway, "touch tanks," and an opening directly to the sea. The aquarium, located at 2777 Kalakaua Ave. (TheBus #2), tel. 923-9741, is open daily 9 a.m.-5 p.m., $2.50 donation for adults, children under 16 and seniors free. A self-guiding book describing the marinelife is available for $5, and an audio tour ("magic wand" device) in English and Japanese is $.50.

Although over 300 species of Hawaiian and South Pacific fish, flora, and mammals live in its sparkling waters, the aquarium is much more

than just a big fishtank. The floor plan contains four galleries of differing themes, and a seal tank. The **South Seas Marine Life** exhibit shows fish found in waters from Polynesia to Australia. The tanks hold sharks, turtles, eels, rays, clams, a seahorse, and colorful coral displays. Another exhibit, **Micronesia Reef Builders,** is perhaps the most amazing of all. It contains live coral that seem more like extraterrestrial flowers than specimens from our own seas. Some are long strands of spaghetti with bulbous ends like lima beans, others are mutated roses, or tortured camellias, all moving, floating, and waving their iridescent purples, golds, and greens in a watery bouquet.

When you hear a coach's whistle blow, the seals are about to perform their antics. Watch these natural hams from the side of their newly renovated tank. These Hawaiian monk seals are one of only two species of tropical seals on Earth. Endangered, there are only about 1,500 individuals still surviving. The performances are more of a detailed description of the seals and their dwindling environment. This is a very special opportunity, and extremely worthwhile. (See pp. 13 and 354).

The aquarium contains a bookshop with a tremendous assortment of titles on fish, birds, reptiles, amphibians, and the flora of Hawaii. Restrooms are behind the bookshop area as you face the main gate. The University of Hawaii offers seminars and field trips through the aquarium, everything from guided reef walks to minicourses in marine biology. Information is available at the aquarium.

Just near the aquarium is the **Waikiki Natatorium,** a saltwater swimming pool built in 1927 as a WW I memorial, allowed to decay over the years until it was closed in 1980. Plans constantly afoot in the House of Representatives call for a restoration.

HONOLULU ZOO

The trumpeting of elephants and chatter of monkeys emanates from the jungle across the street at the Honolulu Zoo, 151 Kapahulu Ave., tel. 923-7723, open daily 8:30 a.m.-4:30 p.m., with special shows in summer at 6 p.m., admission $3, yearly pass $5. As you walk along or ride the tram, you find the expected animals from around the world: monkeys, giraffes, lions, big cats, a hippo, even a grizzly bear. The Honolulu Zoo has the *only* reptiles in Hawaii—three snakes in the Reptile House. Many islanders love this exhibit, because snakes in Hawaii are so exotic! But the zoo is much more than just a collection of animals. It is an up-close escapade through the jungle of Hawaii, with plants, trees, flowers, and vines all named and described. Moreover, the zoo houses Hawaii's indigenous birdlife, which is fast disappearing from the wild: Hawaiian gallinules, coots, hawks, owls, and the *nene,* the state bird, which is doing well in captivity, with breeding pairs being sent to other zoos around the world. The zoo is also famous for its Manchurian cranes, extremely rare birds from Japan, and for successfully mating the Galapagos turtle. A **petting zoo** of barnyard animals is great for kids. A concession stand serves typical junk food and soft drinks.

FREE SIGHTS AND CURIOSITIES

On the beach near the Surfrider Hotel are the *kahuna* stones, a lasting remnant of old Hawaii. The Hawaiians believed these stones were imbued with mana by four priests from Tahiti: Kinohi, Kahaloa, Kapuni, and Kapaemahu. They came to visit this Polynesian outpost in ancient times and left these for the people, who have held them in reverence ever since.

The **Urusenke Teahouse** is an authentic teahouse donated to Hawaii by the Urusenke Foundation of Kyoto. It is located at 245 Saratoga Rd, which lies along the Waikiki side of Fort DeRussy. Every Wed. and Fri. from 10 a.m.-12 p.m., teamaster Yoshibuma Ogawa performs the ancient and aesthetic art of *chanoyu* (tea ceremony). The public is invited (free) to partake of the frothy *matcha,* a grass-green tea made from the delicate tips of 400-year-old bushes. To find delight and sanctuary in this centuries-old ritual among the clatter and noise of Waikiki offers a tiny glimpse into the often puzzling duality of the Japanese soul.

As you walk along Kalakaua Avenue, directly across from Waikiki Beach proper is **St. Augustine Catholic Church.** This modernistic building squashed between high-rises is worth a quick look. The interior, serene with the diffused light of stained glass, looks like a series of A-frames.

Believe it or not, you should pass through the McDonald's at the Royal Hawaiian Shopping Center to see a permanent collection of Hawaiian art on display. Among the exhibits are carvings, paintings, macramé, and featherwork. Many of the works are by Rocky Kaiouliokahihikoloehu Jensen, a famous island artist.

If you are fascinated by the military and its history, visit **Battery Randolph** at Fort DeRussy, at the corner of Kalia and Saratoga roads. Plenty of displays and historical artifacts, free guided tour, open Tues.-Sun., 10 a.m.-4:30 p.m., tel. 543-2687. See also page 236.

Even if you're not a guest at the following hotels, you should at least drop by their lobbies for a quick look. Dramatically different, they serve almost as a visual record of Waikiki's changing history. The **Moana Hotel,** the oldest, dating from 1901, is a permanent reminder of simpler times when its illustrious clientele would dance the night away at an open-aired nightclub suspended over the sea. The Moana houses the Banyan Court Room, named after the enormous banyan tree just outside. From here, "Hawaii Calls" beamed Hawaiian music to the Mainland by shortwave for 40 years beginning in 1935. In its heyday, the show was carried by over 700 stations. The hotel's architecture is a classic example of the now quaint "colonial style."

Across the street are the giant, modernistic, twin towers of the **Hyatt Regency.** The lobby, like most Hyatts, is wonderful, with a huge waterfall and a jungle of plants, all stepped down the series of floors, making an effect like the "Hanging Gardens of Babylon." The **Pacific Beach Hotel,** at 2490 Kalakaua Ave., is a first-rate hotel and a great place to stay in its own right. But if you don't, definitely visit the lobby where the Oceanarium Restaurant has three full floors dedicated to an immense aquarium holding 280,000 gallons of sea water. The old mafia dons used to send their rivals to "sleep with the fishes"—here, you have an opportunity to dine with the fishes. Usually you go snorkeling to watch the fish eat, but in this particular instance the fish watch you eat.

The **Royal Hawaiian Hotel,** built in 1927 on the site of the old royal beach house, once had fresh pineapple juice running in its fountains. Now surrounded by towering hotels, it's like a guppy in a sea of whales. However, it does stand

Waikiki

out with its Spanish-Moorish style, painted in distinctive pink. In the old days, only celebrities and luminaries came to stay—who else could afford $3 per day? Although it's younger than the Moana, many consider it the grande dame of Hawaiian hotels. The entranceway is elegantly old-fashioned, with rounded archways, overstuffed couches, and lowboys. You pass through the lobby on a shocking cerise and green rug. All the rooms are appointed in this trademark pink, with matching towels, sheets, and pillowcases. When you visit the Royal Hawaiian, the most elegant lobby is not where you check in. Rather, turn right from there and follow the long hallway toward the sea. This becomes an open breezeway, with arches and columns in grand style. You'll come to a small circular area in the hotel. Here is the heart, with Diamond Head framed in the distance.

WAIKIKI BEACHES AND PARKS

In the six miles of shoreline from Gray's Beach fronting the Halekulani Hotel in central Waikiki to Wailupe Beach Park in Maunalua Bay just east of the Kahala Hilton are at least 17 choice spots for enjoying surf activities. Most of the central Waikiki beaches are so close to each other that you can hardly tell where one ends and another begins. All of these are generally gentle, but as you head east the beaches get farther apart and have their own personalities. Sometimes they're

rough customers. As always, never take *moana* for granted, especially during periods of high surf. To get information on beaches and their conditions, call Honolulu Water Safety, tel. 922-3888; handicapped people can get information on specialized beach facilities and parks by calling 523-4182. Now that you've finally arrived at a Waikiki beach, the one thing left to do is kick back and R-E-L-A-X.

Waikiki Beach stretches for two miles, broken into separate areas. A multitude of concession stands offer everything from shave ice to canoe rides. It's not news that this beach is crowded. Sometimes when looking at the rows of glistening bodies, it appears that if one person wants to tan his other side, everybody else has to roll over with him. Anyone looking for seclusion here is just being silly. Take heart—a big part of the fun is the other people.

Umbrella stands set up along Waikiki Beach fronting Kalakaua rent boogie boards, surfboards, paddle boats, and snorkel gear. They're convenient, but their prices are much more ($5 for two hours) than many shops offering the same equipment (see p. 213-214). The guys by the big banyan tree are slightly cheaper than those set up by the breakwater just before Kapiolani Park. However, all offer decent prices for surfing lessons ($15 per hour including board and lesson, standing guaranteed), and a $5 ride on an outrigger canoe which gets you three waves and about 20 minutes of fun. Bargaining is acceptable.

Gray's Beach

This westernmost section's name comes from Gray's-By-The-Sea, a small inn once located here. The narrow white-sand beach lies in front of the Halekulani Hotel that replaced it. Take Lewers Street off Kalakaua Avenue and park along Kalia Road; a right-of-way is between the Reef and Halekulani hotels. The sea is generally mild here and the swimming is always good, with shallow waters and a sandy bottom. Offshore is a good break called **No. 3's,** a favorite with surfers.

Next door is **Royal-Moana Beach,** lying between Waikiki's oldest manmade landmarks, the Moana and Royal Hawaiian hotels. Access is unlimited off Kalakaua Avenue. The inshore waters here are gentle and the bottom is sandy and generally free from coral. Offshore are three popular surfing areas, **Popular's, Queen's,** and **Canoes.** Many novices have learned to surf here because of the predictability of the waves, but with so many rookies in the water, and beach activities going on all around, you have to remain alert for runaway boards and speeding canoes.

Waikiki Beach Center
And Prince Kuhio Beach Center

When people say "Waikiki Beach," this is the section to which they're referring. Both beaches front Kalakaua Avenue, and a long sand retaining wall called **Slippery Wall** fronts both beaches, creating a semi-enclosed saltwater pool. Here, you'll find surfing, canoeing, snorkeling, and safe year-round swimming along the gently sloping, sandy-bottomed shoreline. There are comfort stations, concession stands, and lifeguards. Be careful of the rough coral bottom at the Diamond Head end of Kuhio Beach. Covered with a coating of oil-slick seaweed, Slippery Wall definitely lives up to its name. Though local youngsters play on the wall, the footing is poor and many knees have been scraped and heads cracked after spills from this ill-advised play. The surf on the seaward side of the wall churns up the bottom and creates deep holes that come up unexpectedly, along with an occasional rip current.

Kapiolani Beach Park

This is the only park along Waikiki with facilities for barbecueing and picnicking. Although it's only a short stroll down the beach from Waikiki, it gets much less use. This is where local families and those in the know come to get away from the crowds. In the park and along the beach are restrooms, volleyball courts, picnic tables, lifeguard towers, a bath house, and concession stand. Activities include surfing, fishing, snorkeling, and year-round safe swimming. Just be careful of the rocky bottom that pops up unexpectedly here and there. Kapiolani Park incorporates **Sans Souci Beach** at the eastern end. This beach, in front of the Colony Surf and Kamaina hotels, has unlimited access. Changing facilities are found at the deteriorating Honolulu Natatorium, a saltwater pool built in the '20s. Many families with small children come to Sans Souci because it is so gentle.

The **Natatorium** is in a sad state. Battles rage on whether it should be refurbished or torn down. Unless something has been done by the time you arrive, it's better to avoid its murky waters. Be careful of the rocky areas and dangerous dropoffs along the channel, especially in front of the Natatorium. **Kapiolani Park Center** is the beach closest to Waikiki. The swimming is good here, with the best part at the Waikiki end. The beach is at its widest, and the bottom is gently sloping sand. The area called **The Wall** has been designated as a special bodysurfing area. Supposedly, board riders are restricted from this area, but if the surf is good they're guaranteed to break the rules. Experts can handle it, but novices, especially with runaway boards, are a hazard.

Around Diamond Head

Kaluahole Beach is located at the Waikiki side of Diamond Head. The water conditions are safe all year-round, but the beach is small and lies along a seawall. Once a large beach, it was paved over for building purposes. It has one public right-of-way, poorly marked and sandwiched between private homes. It's almost at the end at 3837 Kalakaua Avenue. The surfing in this area is generally good, and the breaks are known as "Tongg's," named after a local family that lived along this shore.

Diamond Head Beach Park is an unlimited access area along Beach Road (marked). It covers almost two acres of undeveloped shoreline. Unfortunately, the beach is very narrow and surrounded by unfriendly rock and coral. The waters, however, are quite protected and generally safe, except in periods of high surf. This area is good for fishing and finding quiet moments.

Kuilei Cliffs Beach Park lies below Diamond Head Road, with access available from three lookout areas along the road. You must walk down the cliff trails to the beaches below. Here are plenty of secluded pockets of sand for sunbathing, but poor swimming. The surf is generally rough, and the area is always frequented by surfers. Offshore is hazardous with submerged rocks, but this makes it excellent for diving and snorkeling—for experts only! Currents can be fierce, and you can be dashed against the rocks. Whales can sometimes be spotted passing this point, and to add to the mystique, the area is considered a breeding ground for sharks. Most visitors just peer down at the surfers from Diamond Head Road, or choose a spot of beach for peace and quiet.

Farther east is **Kaalawai Beach.** The swimming is good here and generally safe because of a protecting reef. Many locals come to this area to fish, and it is good for bodysurfing and snorkeling. The waters outside the reef are excellent for surfing, and produce some of the biggest waves on this side of the island. Access is by public right-of-way, marked off Kulumanu Place, a small side road running off Kahala Avenue, or by walking along the shoreline from Kuilei Beach.

Kahala Beach, lying along Kahala Avenue, can be reached by a number of marked rights-of-way located between the high fences of estates in the area. The swimming is not particularly good, but there are plenty of pockets of sand and protected areas where you can swim and snorkel. Local people come to fish, and the surfing is good beyond the reef. The Kahala Hilton is located along this beach at the eastern end. The public can use "their" beach by walking from Kahala Beach. The swimming here is always safe and good because the hotel has dredged the area to make it deeper. Concession stands and lifeguards are provided by the hotel.

Wailupe Beach Park lies on the Waikiki side of Wailupe Peninsula in Maunalua Bay, and will be the last beach covered in this chapter. This beach park, clearly marked off the Kalaniana'ole Highway, provides restrooms and picnic facilities. The swimming is safe, but the bottom can have either oozy mud or sharp coral in spots. Be careful of the boat channel surrounding the area because the deep dropoff is very abrupt.

ACCOMMODATIONS

Waikiki is loaded with places to stay: 170 properties holding 34,000 rooms jammed into one square mile. And they come in all categories of hotels and condos, from deluxe to dingy. Your problem won't be finding a place to stay, but choosing from the enormous selection. During "peak season," (Christmas to Easter and again in summer) you'd better have reservations, or you could easily be left out in the *warm*. The good news is that, room for room, Waikiki is the cheapest place to stay in the state. Hotels along the beach tend to be slightly more expensive than their counterparts on a side street or back lane. The beachfront hotels have the surf at the doorstep, but those a block away have a little more peace and quiet. The following listings are not exhaustive. They couldn't be! Here is just the best from all categories which you can use as a barometer to measure what's available.

INEXPENSIVE

Youth Hostels

Waikiki's two youth hostels are within a five minute walk from each other. Both cater to international travelers who are doing it on an economy budget. Plenty of travelers, especially from Australia and New Zealand, use the hostels. Both are friendly, comparably priced, well maintained, and offer advice on inexpensive dining and activities in and around Waikiki. Jack, the manager of Hale Aloha, is particularly helpful.

Hale Aloha Youth Hostel is located in Waikiki at 2417 Prince Edward St., Honolulu, HI 96815, tel. 926-8313. Walk down Kalakaua until you see the Hyatt Regency. Two streets directly behind is Prince Edward. Directions are also available at the Airport Information Counter. A dorm room bunk is $12. Couples only can rent a studio for $25, which has to be reserved at least two weeks in advance with first night's deposit. No credit cards. The business office is open 8-10 a.m., and 5-9 p.m. The hostel closes at 11 p.m. and all must leave daily from 10 a.m.-5 p.m. Maximum three-day stay, especially during peak seasons, can sometimes be extended at the discretion of the house parent. Requests must be made before 7:30 p.m. the previous day. Baggage may be left for the day for $1. No key deposits will be returned for keys not returned by 10 a.m. Visitors are not allowed at any time. No alcohol or smoking. Chores are required. Lockers available.

International Club Hostel Waikiki at 2413 Kuhio Ave., tel. 924-2636, has kitchen and laundry facilities and relaxed island-style lounge. Prices: dorm-style (5 beds in each) $15 per night. Care deposit $10, returned to you when you give back the key. Double rooms, $20, no key deposit. They accept reservations. When the YHs are full try the **Waikiki Prince** just next door to Hale Aloha, at 2431 Prince Edward St., tel. 922-1544. Listed as a hostel, it is about the cheapest in Waikiki at about $25-35/night during low season.

Honolulu's YM/WCAs and official American Youth Hostel are near, but not technically in Waikiki. Find a complete list under "Honolulu—Accommodations," p. 241.

Waikiki Hana Hotel

This hotel at 2424 Koa Ave., Honolulu, HI 96815, tel. 926-8841, (800) 367-5004, sits just behind the massive Hyatt Regency on a quiet side street. The hotel has just 73 rooms, so you don't get lost in the shuffle, and the friendly staff go out of their way to make you feel welcome. The Waikiki Hana is surrounded by high-rise hotels, so there's no view, but the peace and quiet just one block from the heavy action more than makes up for it. Rooms start at a very reasonable $62, to $89 for a superior with kitchenette. All rooms have telephone, a/c, color TV, electronic safes, and are gaily appointed with bright bedspreads and drapes. The **Super Chef Restaurant,** on the ground floor of the hotel, is one of the best in Waikiki for atmosphere, food, and very reasonable prices (see p. 284). On-sight parking is another good feature in crowded Waikiki. For a quiet, decent, but basic hotel in the heart of Waikiki, the Waikiki Hana can't be beat!

Waikiki Beachside Apartment Hotel

This hotel, at 2556 Lemon Rd., Honolulu, HI 96815, tel. 923-9566, is owned and operated by Mr. and Mrs. Wong, who keep a close eye on who they admit as they run a very decent and clean hotel. They rent weekly and monthly, charging from $250 to $1000, off-season cheaper. Per diem rooms are sometimes available, but you have to speak to Mrs. Wong first. Furnished units have full kitchens and baths with twin beds and a convertible sofa. Up to three people no extra charge. Laundry facilities but no maid service. Reservations reluctantly accepted (they like to see you first). Parking extra.

Outrigger Coral Seas Hotel

The Outrigger Coral Seas, at 250 Lewers St., Honolulu, HI 96815, tel. 923- 3881, (800) 367-5170, is an old standby for budget travelers, designed that way by Mr. Pat Kelly, an octagenarian who lives down the street and wanted to provide a good cheap place for people to stay in Waikiki. This is the epitome of the economy tourist hotel and houses Perry's Smorgasbord. It's one of the Outrigger Hotels, and seems to get all the hand-me-downs from the others in the chain. There's a restaurant, cocktail lounge, TV, pool, and parking. Rates are an economical $45 s, $55 d, $15 extra person, and just a few dollars more for a kitchenette. Not to everyone's taste, but with plenty of action and the beach only a few steps away.

Edgewater Hotel

The Edgewater, at 2168 Kalia Rd., tel. 922-6424, is another budget standby in the palpitating heart of Waikiki. Rates begin at a reasonable $45 s, to $110 for a suite, $15 extra person. Facilities include swimming pool, good Italian restaurant, parking, TV, and maid service. Kitchenettes slightly extra.

Royal Grove Hotel

The Royal Grove, at 151 Uluniu Ave., tel. 923-7691, run by the Fong family, gives you a lot for your money. You can't miss its paint-sale pink exterior, but inside it's much more tasteful. The older and cheaper wing is about $35 per room, the newer upgraded wing with a/c is around $45.

Most are studios and one-bedroom apartments with full facilities. A tiny pool in the central courtyard offers some peace and quiet away from the street. The Royal Grove passes the basic tests of friendliness and cleanliness. It's used but not abused. During low season, Sept. 1-Dec. 15, they offer reduced weekly and monthly rates.

MODERATE

The **Queen Kapiolani Hotel,** 150 Kapahulu Ave., Honolulu, HI 96815, tel. (800) 367-5004, on Oahu tel. 922-1941. With its off-the-strip location and magnificent views of Diamond Head, this is perhaps the best, and definitely the quietest, hotel for the money in Waikiki. You're only seconds from the beach, and the hotel provides a spacious lobby, parking, restaurant, TV, a/c, shops, and a swimming pool. Rates begin at $72 standard, to $102 for a superior; a few rooms have kitchenettes. The main lobby is being rejuvenated with a $2 million face lift. The stately marble columns have been redone, new wallpaper has been applied, and the shopping area is being upgraded. The overall effect is an open and airy frame with the still life of Diamond Head in the background. Select rooms have been made first-class with new carpeting, draperies, furnishing, and amenities. Most will boast a spectacular view of Diamond Head. Excellent choice for the money, for reservations write directly or to Hawaiian Pacific Resorts, 1150 S. King St., Honolulu, HI 96814, tel. 531-5235. Also, featured in the Peacock Dining Room, is one of the best buffets in Waikiki, (see p. 284).

You can't beat the value at the **Pacific Monarch Hotel/Condo.** Directly behind the Hyatt Regency at 142 Uluniu Ave., Honolulu, HI 96815, tel. 923-9805, (800) 367-6046, it offers some great features for a moderately priced hotel. Fully furnished studios begin at $75, one-bedroom apartments from $110, all a/c, with on-site parking, standard rooms available, too. The rooms are bright and cheery with full bath, living/dining area, and cable TV. End units of each floor are larger, so request one for a large or shared party. The swimming pool, with a relaxing jacuzzi, perches high over Waikiki on the 34th floor of the hotel, offering one of the best city scapes in Honolulu. The lobby is sufficient but small. It's accented with a lava fountain and two giant brass doors. A security key allows guests through the main door to the elevators. Save money and have a great family experience by setting up temporary housekeeping at the Pacific Monarch.

You can capitalize on the off-beach location of The **Honolulu Prince,** at 415 Nahua St., Honolulu, Hi 96815, tel. 922-1616, (800) 922- 7866, where you'll find a hotel/condo offering remarkably good value for your money. One of the newest editions to Aston Resorts, the hotel/condo invites you into its fully furnished one- and two-bedroom suites. All offer a/c, color cable TV, fully equiped kitchens, and daily maid service. Prices begin at $74 for a standard room, $115 one bedroom, and $130 two bedroom, with substantial discounts during low season. The apartments are oversized with a huge sitting area that includes a sofa bed for extra guests. The Honolulu Prince is not fancy, but it is clean, decent, and family-oriented. A fine choice for a memorable vacation at affordable prices.

The **Breakers Hotel,** 250 Beach Walk, Honolulu, HI 96815, tel. 800-426-0494, on Oahu 923-3181, is a family-style hotel. Only minutes from the beach, somehow it keeps the hustle and bustle far away. Every room has a kitchenette and overlooks the shaded courtyard of coconut and banana trees. Facilities include a/c, TV, pool, and parking. Studios begin at $75, one bedroom at $110, all fully furnished.

The **Waikikian Hotel,** 1811 Ala Moana Blvd., Honolulu, HI 96815, tel. 949-5331, or (800) 367-5124, is at the north end of Waikiki near the Ala Moana Boat Harbor and is surrounded by ultramodern high rise hotels. This character laden hotel is only two stories, and is an enclave of peace amidst hustle and bustle. There is a feeling of days gone by as you move down the charming walkway through painstakingly cared for grounds. Ferns, palms, and flowers line the walk, and at night it is accentuated with lighted torches. If you know what to expect you'll be happy with this hotel. Don't expect luxury, but do expect a double dip of character. The grounds front the safe Hilton Hawaiian Village Lagoon with a short walk to the waves of Waikiki. Prices are reasonable at $69 with family suites for $135.

Outrigger Hotels have 20 locations in and around Waikiki offering thousands of rooms. Many of the hotels are on quiet side streets, others are on the main drags, while still more perch on Waikiki Beach. Although they're not luxurious, they do offer good accommodations and all have pools, restaurants, parking, a/c, TV, and parking. Rates vary slightly from hotel to hotel: some have kitchen facilities and cost $75 d to $300 for a suite, $10-15 extra person. For information call (800) 367-5170, in Canada (800) 826-6786, or write to central reservations, 2335 Kalakaua Ave., Honolulu, HI 96815.

Ilima Hotel, 445 Nohonai St., Honolulu, HI 96815, tel. (800) 421- 0767, on Oahu tel. 923-1877, fronts the Ala Wai Canal overlooking the Ala Wai Golf Course. This condo-style hotel is a few blocks from the beach—quiet atmosphere and budget rates. They have just completed a $1.5 million renovation, featuring waveless waterbeds in their deluxe suites. Studio units begin at a reasonable $45 s, $8 extra person, and one bedroom $75, two bedroom $85. All units have full kitchens, a/c, TV, along with a pool, parking, and maid service. Good value.

Miramar Hotel, 2345 Kuhio Ave., Honolulu, HI 96815, tel. (800) 367-2303, on Oahu tel. 922-2077, is in the heart of Waikiki. The hotel, refurbished and renamed in the last few years, offers generous-sized rooms, with lanai, pool, restaurant, a/c, TV, and parking. Rates range from $65 s to $75 d, $15 extra person.

Waikiki Shores Apartments, 2161 Kalia Rd., Honolulu, HI 96815, tel. 800-367-2353, on Oahu, tel. 926-4733, has studios, one-, and 2-bedroom apartments, minimum stay three nights. No children under 12, weekly maid service, parking. All units have full kitchens; studios $75, $130-260 for a two-bedroom.

Holiday Inn Waikiki Beach, 2570 Kalakaua Ave., Honolulu, HI 96815, tel. (800) 465-4329, on Oahu tel. 922-2511. No surprises at a good old Holiday Inn offering a/c, TV, pool, parking, restaurants, and maid service. Standard rooms begin at around $95, $120 for deluxe, and $1000 for the penthouse. Extra person $15. The Holiday Inn is at a good location just near Kapiolani Park and away from the heavy bustle.

A reasonably priced accommodation is the **Coconut Plaza Hotel** at 450 Lewers St., tel. 923-8828, (800) 882-9696. Rates are about $100 for a double during peak season. Off-season is cheaper, with a special day rate of $50 for bona fide business travelers. A continental breakfast is free daily in the lobby, with a free mai tai party on Fridays. Fully a/c with a hotel pool.

The **Waikiki Joy** at 320 Lewers St., Honolulu, HI 96815, tel. 923- 2300 or (800) 367-8047, ext. 230, used to be an old funky hotel. A Japanese firm recently bought it and refurbished it into yuppie heaven. It has a new facade, and all rooms have been redone in shades of white on white. Amenities include pool, color TV, VCR, and some rooms with private jacuzzi. Rates are from $110 to $250.

DELUXE

Hilton Hawaiian Village

The Hilton, at 2005 Kalia Rd., Honolulu, HI 96815, tel. 949-4321 or (800) 445-8667, is at the far western end of Waikiki, just below Fort DeRussy. This is a glorious first-rate hotel, an oasis of tranquility as it sits in its own quiet corner of Waikiki. Enter along 200 yards of the private hotel driveway, passing the Village, a small mall with exclusive shopping and dining (see p. 289). Facing you are the Hilton's "towers," the Tapa, the Diamond Head, the Rainbow, and the prestigious Alii Tower. Rainbow Tower, so called because of the huge multistoried rainbow on the entire side of this building, is, according to the *Guinness Book of World Records,* the tallest ceramic-tile mosaic in the world. Rooms in all are deluxe with magnificent views. Amenities include color TV, a/c, self service bar, refrigerator, and safe.

The Alii Tower pampers you even more with a private pool with nightly gourmet *pu pu,* turn-down service, fresh flowers, fruit baskets, concierge service, fitness center, sauna, and bath accessories. Rates are from $140-235 throughout the Village, and from $225-335 in the Alii Tower.

The towers form a semicircle fronting the beach, not a private beach because none can be private, but about as private a public beach as you can get. Few come here unless they're staying at the Hilton. It's dotted with palms—tall royal palms for elegance, shorter palms for shade. The property has three pools. The main pool, surrounded by luxuriant tropical growth, is the largest in Waikiki. The lagoon area is the music of water in bubbling rivulets, tiny waterfalls, and reflecting pools. Torches of fire and

Moana Hotel

ginger, banana trees, palms, ferns, and rock gardens are the grounds. The Hilton is a complete destination resort where you can play, relax, shop, dine, dance, and retreat. It's a hotel that knows what it's about and has found its center.

The *action* of Waikiki is out there, of course, just down the driveway, but you don't feel it unless you want to. Relax and enjoy the sunset accompanied by music at anyone of 10 lounges like the **Shell Bar,** or in the main foyer where another small casual bar swings to the tunes of a piano stylist. Exotic and gourmet dining from throughout the Pacific rim is available at the Village's 10 restaurants, especially the hotel's signature **Bali By the Sea** and **Golden Dragon** restaurants (see p. 289). As you pull into the driveway there's a geodesic dome, like a giant stereo speaker, where **Don Ho and his Polynesian Extravaganza** perform nightly (see p. 292). The Hilton Hawaiian Village has everything to keep its temporary "villagers" contented and happy.

Hawaiian Regent Hotel
The Hawaiian Regent, at 2552 Kalakaua Ave., Honolulu, HI 96815, tel. 922- 6611, (800) 367-5370, has a long history of treating guests like royalty. The hotel now stands on what was the original site of Queen Liliuokalani's summer cottage. The Regent was the first major Hawaiian project of master designer Chris Hemmeter, famed for his magnificent Westin Kauai and

Hyatt Regency Waikaloa hotels. The grand tradition of the hotel is reflected in the open sweeping style that marks a Hemmeter project. After almost two decades, the Regent appears extremely modern becasue its design was so visionary when it was built.

With almost 1,400 units, the hotel ranks as the third largest hotel in Hawaii after the Hilton Hawaiian Village and the Sheraton Waikiki. Rates are from $110 for a standard room to $350 for a deluxe suite. Children are especially taken care of with the "Keiki K.A.I. Club," a summer program, and honeymooners can choose a junior suite with special amenities for a reduced price. All rooms are oversized and include cable TV, a/c, nightly turn down service, and in-room safes. You can step across the street to mingle with the fun-seekers on Waikiki Beach, or relax in one of the hotel's two pools. A championship Laykold tennis court is open from sunrise to sunset with lessons and rackets available.

The hotel offers a variety of exclusive shops in an off-lobby mall area like Shiokiya and Sandcastles for alohawear and evening wear. An onsite beauty shop and Japanese acupressure/massage service are there to revitalize you after a hard day of having fun in the sun. The Regent is renowned for its fine dining, entertainment, and late-night disco. The **Lobby Bar** is a perfect spot to perch while listening to relaxing Hawaiian music every evening. **The Cafe Regent,** an open-air restaurant just off the main lobby, is open for a breakfast, buffet, and lunch selections from 6 a.m.-2:30 p.m. The **Tiffany Restaurant,** dinner only, has casual dining in an elegant atmosphere of stained-glass ceiling and shuttered windows (see p. 284). The **Ocean Terrace,** designed for kicking back and watching life go by, is a poolside bar serving sandwiches and hamburgers at very good prices. The premier restaurant of the hotel, and one of Waikiki's consistent best, is the award-winning **The Secret,** Previously known as the Third Floor, (see p. 288) where you can not only dine in Polynesian splendor, but be treated to a magnificent selection of wines collected by Richard Dean, one of only two *sommeliers* in all of Hawaii.

Enjoy a daily international buffet, or spectacular Sunday brunch at **The Summery,** or a traditional Japanese meal at the **Regent Marushin.** You won't be told to hush while you dance or relax to the sounds of live music in **The Library.** And, if you have "dancing feet" head for **The Point After,** one of Waikiki's swingingest high-tech discos that will rock you until the wee hours. Women will enjoy showing the boys how to really hoop and holler as they review the "hunks" in Hawaii's own **All-Male Dance Review** at the Point After nightly Tues.-Saturday. If you're after peace and quiet head for the **Garden Courtyard,** a multipurpose area in the center of the hotel. Sit among flowers and full grown coconut and bamboo trees. Every Mon., Wed. and Fri. from 10 a.m.-12 p.m. learn lei making, the hula, or even Hawaiian checkers by *kapuna* who come just to share their aloha. The Hawaiian Regent is a first-class hotel that really knows how to make you feel like a visitng monarch. Rule with joy!

Sheraton Moana Surfrider Hotel

The Moana, at 2365 Kalakaua Ave., Honolulu, HI 96815, tel. (800) 325-3535, on Oahu tel. 922-3111, is the oldest and most venerable hotel in Waikiki (see p. 269). Now operated by Sheraton Hotels, it has just completed a $50 million upgrade, which has restored the class and beauty for which the Moana has long been famous. More than just recapturing turn-of-the century grandeur, the Moana has surpassed it by integrating all of the modern conveniences. The original Italian Renaissance style is the main architectural theme, but like a fine opera, it joins a variety of architectural themes that blend into a soul-satisfying finale. The restoration has con-

nected the three main buildings, the Moana, Ocean Lanai, and Surfrider, to form an elegant complex of luxury accommodations, gourmet dining, and distinctive shopping. The Moana, filled with memories of times past, is magical. It's as if you stood spellbound before the portrait of a beautiful princess long deceased, when suddenly her radiant look-alike granddaughter, dazzling in jewels and grace, walks into the room.

You arrive under the grand columns of a porte cochere where you are greeted by doormen in crisp white uniforms, and hostesses bearing leis and chilled pineapple juice. The lobby is a series of genteel parlor arrangements conducive to very civilized relaxation. Art, urns, chandeliers, sofas, koa tables, flowers, vases and pedestaled glass topped tables wait in attendance. A brass birdcage elevator takes you to the second floor where a room filled with 80 years of Moana memorabilia whispers names and dates of the Moana's grand past. After a fresh chilled glass of pineapple juice, you are escorted to check-in.

Upstairs, the rooms are simple elegance. Queen-size beds, overstuffed chairs and fat fluffy pillows and bedspreads extend their waiting arms. All rooms have a/c, a remote-control master keyboard for TV, lights, and music. But this is the Moana! Sachet-scented closets hold *yukata,* terry slippers, and satin hangers. Fresh coffee with percolator is provided, along with a self-serve mini-bar, and daily newspaper. Bathrooms are tile and marble appointed with huge towels and stocked with fine soaps, shampoos, creams, makeup mirrors, and a bathroom scale which you can hide under the bed.

Being the first hotel built in Waikiki, it sits right on the beach with one of the best views of Diamond Head along the strip. A swimming pool with sundeck is staffed with attentive personnel, and the activities center can book you on a host of activities including a classic outrigger canoe ride or a sunset sail on a catamaran. Three restaurants, a grand ballroom, snack bar, and two lounges take care of all your dining needs. Rooms in the Moana wing overlook Banyan Court, scene of a nightly entertainment such as a Polynesian Revue, or chamber music provided by a pianist or harpist. Open the windows, allowing the breezes to billow the lace curtains while the waves of Waikiki join with the music below in a heavenly serenade. Rooms are

$145-170 standard, $235-260 superior. A superb hotel offering old-fashioned service.

Royal Hawaiian Hotel

At 2255 Kalakaua Ave., Honolulu, HI 96815, tel. (800) 325-3535, on Oahu tel. 923-7311, the Royal Hawaiian is second oldest, and it too provides an ongoing experience in turn-of-the-century charm. A basic bedroom starts at around $195 s, with suites ranging from $300 to over $1600. The Moana and Royal Hawaiian are worth a visit even if you don't stay there. (See p. 269)

The Royal Hawaiian has just completed a $25 million restoration, which has recaptured the grand elegance of days past. Doors first opened in 1927, at a cost of $4 million, an unprecedented amount of money in those days for a hotel. The Depression brought a crushing reduction to Hawaiian tourism, bringing the yearly total down from a whopping 22,000 to under 10,000 (today more visitors arrive in one day) and the Royal became a financial loss. During WW II, with Waikiki barb-wired, the Royal was leased to the Navy as an r&r hotel for sailors from the Pacific Fleet. After the war, the hotel reverted to Matson Lines, the original owner, and reopned in 1947 after a $2 million renovation. Sheraton Hotels purchased the Royal in 1959, built the Royal Tower Wing in 1969, sold the hotel in 1975, but remained as operating managers.

Original doors were one solid and one louvered so you could catch the ocean breezes and still have privacy. Today, the hotel is fully air conditioned so the old doors have been removed and new solid rosewood doors carved in the Philippines have been added. Rooms might have four-poster beds, canopies, twins, or kings, depending upon your preference. All rooms have remote-control TV, refrigerators, electronic safes, and computer hookups on telephones for lap-top computers. Furniture is French provincial, with bathrooms fully tiled. Completely renovated rooms in the original section have kept the famous pink motif, but are slightly more pastel. They have a marble tile bathroom, a brass butler, louvered drawers, and a huge bed. The tall ceilings are even more elegant with molded plaster cornices. Guests are treated to banana bread on arrival, daily newspaper, and turn-down service with a complimentary late-night sweet treat. Preferential tee-off times at the Makaha Resort are also offered. Each floor of

Royal Hawaiian Hotel

the original Royal has a pool elevator, so guests in beachwear don't clash with the early evening black-tie set. A Hospitality Suite is provided for early morning check-ins, or late check-outs. It offers guests, at no extra charge, shower facilities, maid service six times during the day, coffee-making facilities, and a sitting and lounging area.

Some of the prestige suites are truly luxurious, costing just under $2000 per night. They feature huge balconies, with tiled floors, where a party of 25 could easily be entertained. The tastefully carpeted bedrooms boast a quilt-covered bed heaped with a half dozen pillows. The huge bathrooms overlook the beach and have a small built-in jacuzzi. In the massive Governor's Suite is a formal dining room, two huge bedrooms, two magnificent sitting areas, one a formal parlor, and the other an "informal" rec-room. The Royal Towers, an addition dating from 1969, are preferred by many guests because every room has an ocean view. From the balcony of most, you look down onto the swimming pool, the beach, palm trees, and Diamond Head in the distance.

If you stay at the Royal Hawaiian, you can dine and sign at the Moana, Surfrider, Sheraton Waikiki, or Princess Kaiulani, all operated by Sheraton Hotels. One of the best features of the Royal, open to guest and non-guest, is the remarkable luau every Monday night (see p. 253), and the extraordinary food and entertainment provided nightly by the Brothers Cazimero in the hotel's famous and elegant Monarch Dining Room (see p. 291).

Hyatt Regency

The Hyatt, at 2424 Kalakaua Ave., Honolulu, HI 96815, tel. (800) 228-9005, on Oahu tel. 922-9292, is magnificent. If the frenetic pace gets to be too much, just head for the peaceful lobby with pine trees and cascading waterfall. The hotel offers a/c, TV, lounges, shops, restaurants, swimming pool, and parking. Basic rooms start at around $130 d, $15 extra person, and go to $1,000 for a suite. An excellent choice for an expensive hotel.

LUXURY

Waikiki is home to two of the finest hotels in the world. The **Halekulani Hotel,** in mid-Waikiki at 2199 Kalia Rd., Honolulu, HI 96815, tel. (800) 367-2343, on Oahu tel. 923-2311, was an experiment in impeccable taste that paid off. A few years ago the hotel was built with the belief that Waikiki could still attract the luxury-class visitor. Since opening, the hotel, recognized as a member of the Leading Hotels of the World, has been constantly filled. It's a hotel that takes care of the smallest details like cloth hand towels, even in the lobby restrooms. When you arrive you are escorted to your room where you register. Soon, a bellman appears bearing a silver tray nestling a fine china plate on an embroidered linen cloth which holds an array of chocolates, compliments of the house. Each room, done in seven shades of white has three telephones, a bathroom as large as many hotel rooms, bath towels the size of parlor rugs, and a private lanai. Each night a little white box tied with silver string is placed on your pillow, and inside is a gift from the management. Prices begin at around $190 d, and go to around $325, suites $650, $35 extra person. If you want to splurge on one night of luxury, the Halekulani is unforgettable.

Long considered one of the finest hotels in the world is the **Kahala Hilton,** 5000 Kahala Ave., Honolulu, HI 96816, tel. (800) 367-2525, on Oahu tel. 734-2211. Technically not in Waikiki, but a few minutes' drive east. The hotel was built almost 30 years ago and is proud that most of its key workers have been there from the first days. A large number of guests return yearly, and have formed friendships with the staff. Located away from Waikiki and surrounded by the exclusive Waialae Country Club (not even hotel guests are welcome unless they are members), the hotel gives a true sense of peace and seclusion. It has an excellent formal restaurant, The Maile, a private beach, swimming pools, all water-sport gear available, a saltwater pond holding three porpoises, and a lovely breezy lobby. The rooms, large with sweeping ocean and mountain views, rent for $180-400 d, $495-1700 for a suite. The Kahala obviously isn't for everyone, but there's no doubt that you definitely get all that you pay for.

FOOD

The streets of Waikiki are an international potluck, with over a dozen cuisines spreading their tables. Because of the culinary competition, you can choose restaurants in the same way that you peruse a buffet table, for both quantity and quality. Within a few hundred yards are all-you-can-gorge buffets, luaus, dinner shows, fast foods, ice cream, and jacket-and-tie restaurants. The free tourist literature runs coupons, and placards advertise specials for breakfast, lunch, and dinner. Bars and lounges often give free *pu pus* and finger foods that can easily make a light supper. As with everything in Waikiki, its restaurants are a close-quartered combination of the best and the worst, but with only a little effort it's easy to find great food, great atmosphere, and mouthwatering satisfaction. For a list of luaus in greater Honolulu including Waikiki see p. 252.

Note: At many of the moderately priced restaurants listed below and at all of the expensive restaurants *reservations are highly recommended*. It's much easier to make a two-minute phone call than it is to have your evening spoiled, so please call ahead. Also, many of the restaurants along the congested Waikiki strip provide valet parking (usually at no charge), or will offer validated parking at a nearby lot. So check when you call to reserve. Attire at most Hawaiian restaurants is casual, but at the better restaurants it is dressy casual, which means close-toed shoes, trousers, and a collard shirt for men, and a simple but stylish dress for women. At some of the very best restaurants you won't feel out of place with a jacket, but ties are not usually worn.

INEXPENSIVE

Eggs And Things, tel. 949-0820, is a late-night institution open from 11 p.m.- 2 p.m. the following afternoon, at 1911 Kalakaua Ave. just where it meets McCully. A number of discos like The Wave and Pink Cadillac are just around the corner, so the clientele in the wee hours are partiers and revelers. The decor is wooden floors and formica tables, but the waitresses are top notch and friendly. The food is absolutely excellent and it's hard to spend over $6. Daily specials are offered from 1-2 a.m., while morning specials from 5-8 a.m. get you three pancakes and two fresh eggs cooked as you like for $1.99.

Waffles and pancakes are scrumptious with homemade fresh fruit or coconut syrup. Besides the eggs and omelettes the most popular item is fresh fish, which is usually caught by the owner himself, Mr. Jerry Fukunaga, who goes out almost every day on his own boat. It's prepared Cajun-style, or sauteed in garlic and butter, with two fresh eggs and a choice of pancakes, rice, or home-fried potatoes. Prices vary according to market price from $6.75 to $8. Casual attire acceptable, BYO booze OK.

Around the corner is **The Dynasty Restaurant,** tel. 947-3771, at 1830 Ala Moana Boulevard. They have a large and varied selection of Chinese food that is acceptable but not memorable. They are, however, open 24 hours, which is the main reason for going there.

Da Smokehouse, tel. 946-0233, 470 Ena Rd., open daily from 11:30 a.m. to midnight, is one of those places where the food is excellent, but you wouldn't want to eat there. Why? Because it is primarily a takeout restaurant with only a few booths stuck in the back where *da* smoke and *da* grease from *da* wood-fired smoker *is da* decor. Your choices are smoked beef, pork, chicken and ham all served picnic style with two choices of homemade potato salad, baked beans, rice, or cole slaw. Price ranges $3.50 to $10 for charbroiled smoked prime rib. The combo plate of all of the above that can easily feed four is only $15. No liquor so BYO. Free delivery makes Da Smokehouse a perfect alternative to inflated room service prices at surrounding hotels, or for a home-cooked dinner in your condo. You'll love it!

Country Life Restaurant, at 421 Nahua St., is a new, all-natural food restaurant operated by the Seventh-day Adventists. The cuisine is fresh, wholesome, and totally vegetarian, using no animal products whatsover. Meals are a set price of $3.99 to $4.49 per pound, so you can fill your plate with anything on the menu that seems appetizing. Entrees change daily and can be anything from lasagna to pecan loaf with cashew gravy. Desserts are delicious, sugarless, and wholesome including blackberry cobler, and an assortment of whole grains and fruits. The salad bar couldn't be fresher, and is even more delicious with an assortment of homemade spreads.

Ruffage Natural Foods, at 2442 Kuhio, tel. 922-2042, is one of a very few natural food restaurants in Waikiki. They serve non-fish sushi, a wide assortment of tofu sandwiches, natural salads, tofu burgers, and smoothies. Everything is less than $5. It's a small hole-in-the-wall type eatery that's easy to miss. A few tables outside under a portico is the ambiance.

Ezogiku is a chain of Japanese restaurants. Open til the wee hours, these no-atmosphere restaurants serve inexpensive hearty bowls of Sapporo *ramen* (renowned as the best), curry rice, and *gyoza.* They have multiple locations around Waikiki at 2083 Kuhio Ave., 2420 Koa Ave., 2546 Lemon Rd., and 2141 Kalakaua Avenue. Ezogiku is a no-frills kind of place. Small, smoky, counter seating, and totally authentic. They're so authentic that on their dishes they spell *ramen* as *larmen.* You not only eat inexpensively, but you get a very authentic example of what it's like to eat in Japan . . . cheaply. Eat heartily for around $6.

The Jolly Roger is an American standard restaurant with a Hawaiian flair. If you're after good old tuna salad sandwiches, hot roast beef, a tostada even, or just plain soup and salad, this would be your best bet in Waikiki. The Jolly Roger has two locations, at 2244 Kalakaua (always too crowded so the service suffers), and 150 Kaiulani, where it's slightly quieter. Actually the Kaiulani restaurant borders on tasteful with a dark green decor accented with bronze, pleasant booth seating, and a profusion of ferns and hanging plants. Both open from 6:30-1 a.m. Breakfasts are waffles, pancakes, omelettes, and meats, but try their *orange bread* as standard or French toast. Lunch specials are hamburger steak $4.95, with dinners well under $10. Happy hour from 6 a.m.-6 p.m. pours exotics for $1.75, draft beer $1.50, free *pu pus* from 4-6 p.m. Nightly entertainment in the bar section, especially The Blue Kangaroo at the Kalakaua Avenue Jolly Roger (see p. 290).

Man Lee's Chinese Restaurant, 124 Kapahulu, tel. 922-6005, is a basic Chinese restaurant that offers specials. Breakfast is a bargain with hotcakes, eggs, sausage, and coffee for around $2.99. The atmosphere is quiet since it's around the corner from most of the action. A belly-filler only.

Wong and Wong, at 1023 Maunakea, tel. 521-4492, is a simple and basic Chinese restaurant where you can have a good and filling meal at a reasonable price. Many people who live and work in and around Waikiki choose to go here for Chinese food.

Perry's Smorgy at 2380 Kuhio Ave., tel. 926-9872, and at the Coral Seas Hotel, 250 Lewers St., tel. 923-3881, is the epitome of the budget travelers' "line 'em up, fill' em up, and head 'em out" kind of restaurant. There is no question that you'll waddle away stuffed, but forget about any kind of memorable dining experience. When you arrive, don't be put off by the long lines. They move! First, you run a gauntlet of salads, breads, and potatoes, in the hopes that you'll fill your plate. Try to restrain yourself. Next comes the meat, fish, and chicken. The guys serving up the roast beef are masters of a whole lot of movement and very little action. The carving knife whips around in the air, but does very little damage to the joint of beef. A paper-thin slice is finally cut off and put on your plate with aplomb. The carver then looks at you as if you were Oliver Twist asking for more. Added pressure comes from the long line of tourists behind, who act as if they have just escaped from a Nazi labor camp. The breakfast buffet is actually very good with all the standard eggs, meats, juices, and rolls, and the food in general, considering the price, is more than acceptable.

Pizzeria Uno at 2256 Kuhio (and Seaside), tel. 926-0646, is part of a small chain that allows each of its locations to be individual, although the deep-dish "Chicago-style" pizza remains the same. Open daily 11 a.m.-midnight, live entertainment Wed.-Sat., express lunch Mon.-Fri. 11-3, with specials including soup or salad. Appetizers like pizza skins, potato-flavored pizza wedges with onions and zesty cheese for $4.75, and individual-size pizzas for $5.95 keep prices down. Large pizzas like "Spinoccoli" are different with spinach, fresh broccoli, a blend of cheeses, and a little garlic for $10.95. Also, burgers and sandwiches, with names like "The Big Frankie," no teenie weanie, mark Pizzeria Uno as a casual fun-filled restaurant. Happy hour, 11 a.m.-6 p.m. is a good value with draft beer at $.95, and all tropical drinks for $1.95. Breakfast is a "sunrise special," two golden-brown pancakes, two strips of bacon, and an egg for $1.99 from 6 a.m.-noon. Modern and upbeat with black and white decor, It's on the beaten track, but worth a stop.

The **Waikiki Seafood and Pasta Co.,** is at the Outrigger Surf Hotel, 2280 Kuhio Avenue. Dinners are good but not memorable, and range from inexpensive to reasonable. Fresh pasta starts from golden herb pasta for $5.95, pasta of the day $6.95. Other dishes are calamari marinara $9.95, veal piccata $12.95, calamari steak Italiana $10.95. Specials like vegie lasagna are $6.95 with the most expensive at $14 for veal parmigiana. Good value, and acceptable food. A change from deep-fried *mahi mahi*.

Peking Garden, 307 Royal Hawaiian Ave., tel. 922-3401, is a hole-in-the-wall eatery just behind the Waikiki Medical Center heading *mauka*. They serve Chinese-American food basically in the form of filling plate lunches for around $3.50. A good choice is the Peking fried chicken.

Shorebird Beach Broiler is on the beach behind the Reef Hotel at 2169 Kalia Rd., tel. 922-2887, giving this budget restaurant the best gourmet location in all of Waikiki. Here you'll find a limited but adequate menu of cook-your-own selections for under $12 (discount tickets save you more). Open breakfast, lunch and dinner from 5 p.m. Walk through the lobby to the beach for a remarkable sunset while dining. Included is a good fresh salad bar of vegetables and fruits. Beverages are included, but you pay extra for bread. Nightly there's disco dancing from 9 p.m.- 2 a.m. Good value and a pleasing setting.

Ferdinand's in the Coral Reef Hotel, 2299 Kuhio Ave., tel. 923- 5581, is a no-nonsense place running specials and discount tickets. Basically it's an American standard restaurant with a Hawaiian flavor. An attempt is made at entertainment, a Don Ho clone singing in the background. The food is decent but not memorable; with discounts two can eat for around $15. Besides inexpensive food, they have inexpensive drinks at happpy hour, beers $1 or $1.25. They also have free *pu pus* from 4-6 p.m. The breakfast special is a choice of two pancakes or toast and jelly and bacon or sausage, or an egg any style for $1.99.

The **Holiday Inn** at 2570 Kalakaua Ave., has very reasonable dining. Breakfast specials for $1.99 get pancakes, eggs, and bacon. Dinners are specials for $10 and under like roast beef at $8.95. Basic American food in the street-level dining room.

Hamburger Mary's at 2109 Kuhio, tel. 922-6722, has two claims to fame. It serves homestyle food at reasonable prices, and has long been famous as a gay and lesbian hangout. The decor, given the open structure of the building facing Kuhio, is actually quite nice. The front is a terrace with a brick floor, round tables, and wrought-iron chairs. The *inside* area has a little grass shack motif, with curios hanging from the ceiling—old glass bottles, chandeliers, a flying angel, even an old surfboard. The back room holds a pool table and a dance floor. Rock and roll is always happening. Breakfasts are served all day long. At lunch they feature salads such as a fresh garden salad for $5.25, or stuff your own (your choice of papaya, avocado, or tomato stuffed with chicken, tuna, cream cheese, or cheddar cheese) for $7.25. Big hearty Hamburger Mary sandwiches are the Mary burger $4.25, avocado burger $6.25, meatless sandwiches like avocado or cheddar cheese for under $6. Soups and sides are plentiful, but try a bowl of homemade beef chili for $3.50. A great people-watching spot with good food at moderate prices.

Waikiki Malia Hotel Restaurant, 2211 Kuhio Ave., tel. 923-7621. Open 24 hours, specials for around $7.95; crisp salad bar and a huge well-done baked potato with dinner. Beverages are not included, but it's a good value.

It's Greek To Me, at the Royal Hawaiian Shopping Center, 2201 Kalakaua Ave., tel. 922-2733 is a combination sandwich bar and restaurant serving traditional Greek food such as *falafel, moussaka,* and *souvlaki.* Fatso sandwiches are about $6.50, while the dinners are generally under $10. Also, pizza, steaks, and some Mediterranean dishes. This open sidewalk cafe is perfect for a casual meal right after the beach.

The Islander Coffee House on Lewers St., tel. 923-3233, in the Reef Towers Hotel, has inexpensive breakfasts of two pancakes, eggs, and bacon for $2.29. They also offer steak and eggs Benedict for $3.89, chef salad $5.65, hamburgers under $5, and specials every day for inexpensive prices. No dining experience whatsoever, but down-home prices in the heart of Waikiki.

The **Mongolian Barbecue** at the Kuhio Mall, 2301 Kuhio Ave., tel. 923-2445, open daily 11 a.m.-10 p.m., would make Genghis Khan smile. He could feed his army for peanuts. There is no decor, but this is a very good and inexpensive place to eat. For $12.95 you get the "Full Mongolian," for which you select your own fresh meats of beef, chicken, pork, and lamb, vegies, sauces, and spices from chilled serving trays. Then you watch them cook your order in the fire pit. Included is rice and a famous homemade sesame bun. If you can handle it, you can go back for a second round. Children under 12 get the same treatment for $7.95. If it sounds like too much try the "Quick Mongolian" for $5.95, which is the same but the items are selected for you by the servers, and no seconds. The "Mini-Mongolian" for $4.95 is your choice of beef, lamb, chicken, or pork with vegies, served with rice or homemade bun. Limited fish selections as well.

INEXPENSIVE: KAPAHULU AVENUE

Once Kapahulu Avenue crosses Ala Wai Boulevard, it passes excellent inexpensive to moderately priced restaurants, strung one after the other.

The first is **Rainbow Drive-In,** at the corner of Kanaaina Avenue. It's strictly local, with a kids' hangout feel, but the plate lunches are hearty and well done for under $4. Another of the same, **K C Drive-In** just up the road a few blocks at 1029 Kapahulu, specializes in waffle-dogs, shakes, and even has carhops. Both are excellent stops to pick up plate lunches on your way out of Waikiki heading for the H-1 Freeway.

The first sit-down restaurant on the strip is **Irifune** Japanese Restaurant, at 563 Kapahulu, tel. 737-1141, directly across from **Zippy's,** a fast-food joint. Irifune serves authentic, well-prepared Japanese standards in its small dining room. Most meals begin at $6, with a nightly special for around $8. You're also given a card that is punched every time you eat there; after 20 meals, you get one free.

The next is **Ono Hawaiian Foods,** an institution in down-home Hawaiian cooking. This is the kind of place that a taxi driver sends you to when you ask for the real thing. It's clean, basic, with the decor being photos of local performers hung on the wall. If you want to try *lomi* salmon, poi, or *kalua* pig, this is *da kine place, brah!* Prices are

cheap. Open Mon.-Sat. 10:30 a.m.-7:30 p.m., 726 Kapahulu, tel. 737- 2275. And, if you have a sweet tooth just up the road is **Leonard's Bakery** that specializes in *malasadas* and *pao dolce.*

The **Rama Thai Restaurant** is on the corner of Kapahulu and Winam streets, across from New World Chinese Restaurant. Open daily for lunch, and dinner from 5:30-10 p.m., tel. 735-2789. The interior is *uptown* with some track lighting and linen tablecloths, but the prices and food are still *down-home Bangkok.* Wonderful choice is satay beef appetizer for $6.95, chicken and ginger soup in coconut milk spicy broth $6.95, and red Thai curried beef, chicken, or scallops for $6.95. Almost half of the menu is vegetarian. All items are 'a la carte, so it's not that cheap; a complete meal costs around $15. The fish-ball soup is out of this world, with plenty for two. The tofu in coconut milk is also a great choice.

To round out the multicultural cuisines of Kapahulu Avenue, try **Plaza Manila,** at 750 Palani Ave. and Kapahulu. Open daily except Mon., from 11 a.m.-10 p.m., tel. 734-0400. Traditional Filipino dishes with many American and Hawaiian standards.

Fast Foods And Snacks

There are enough formica-tabled, orange-colored, golden-arched, belly-up-to-the-window places selling perfected, injected, and inspected ground cow, chicken, and fish to feed an army . . . and a navy, and marine corps too. Those needing a pre-fab meal can choose from the royal **Burger King,** and **Dairy Queen, Jack-in-his-Box, Ronnie McDonald, Pizza Hut-2-3-4, Wendy's,** and dippy **Zippy's Drive-In.** Addicts find your own pushers!

Farrels Restaurant at the International Market Place and the Royal Hawaiian Center serves ice cream and a good selection of sandwiches and soups for decent prices. Along Kalakaua Avenue are **Baskin Robbins,** and **Haagen Daz.** For cheap Italian try the **Noodle Shop** in the Waikiki Sand Villa Hotel, tel. 922-4744.

Minute Chef, across from the Sheraton Moana Surfrider Hotel, on Kalakaua Ave., has hamburgers for $.99 cents, cheese burgers $1.19, sandwiches $2.50, and roast beef for about $3.99. A change of pace from the sty-rofoam box-type fast foods. Not bad, for cheap fast food.

Zorro's, with eight or so locations in and around Honolulu (two on Kuhio Ave. in Waikiki), tel. 926-5555, is your basic pizza parlor that in-cludes a limited menu of pasta, sandwiches, and salad. The standard 16-inch pizza ranges from $10.99 to $19.89 depending upon toppings. Pastas are all under $6, and sandwiches under $5. Open from 10 a.m.-4 a.m. with free delivery.

The Patisserie at 2330 Kuhio (about three more scattered around town), tel. 922-9752, offer fresh French pastries, coffee, and sand-wiches. They're not bad for this neck of the woods. Fairly decent food at acceptable prices. Good for early mornings if you want just a light breakfast.

Fatty's Chinese Fast Food, 2345 Kuhio, tel. 922-9600, is very inexpensive. For about $3.50 you get a giant plate of Chinese fast food. A belly filler only, but not bad.

MODERATE

Peacock Dining Room, at the Queen Kapiolani Hotel, 150 Kapahulu, tel. 922-1941, open 5:30-9 p.m., offers one of the most outstanding buffets in Waikiki for both price and quality. Different nights feature different cuisines. All are special but the Japanese buffet on Wednesday and Thursday and the seafood buffet on Friday are extraordinary. All range from $12.95 to $15.95. The room itself is very tasteful with white table-cloths and full service. Every time you return to the buffet just leave your empty plate and it will be taken away for you. Help yourself from an amazing array of entrees that are expertly pre-pared. The salad bar is extremely varied, and the desserts will make you wish that you saved room. This is an excellent value.

Tiffany's Steakhouse at the Hawaiian Re-gent, 2552 Kalakaua, tel. 922-6611, dinner from 6-9:30 p.m., is a casual restaurant featuring thick juicy steaks, a varied and ample salad bar, and a good selection of fresh fish and seafood selec-tions. Evenings are magical because of a stained-glass ceiling illuminated with backlight-ing. The furnishings are European contempor-ary that counter-point louvered windows all around. Tables are set with pink tablecloths and

heavy crystal ware while subdued lighting and ceiling fans add comfort and romance to your meal. The menu begins with escargot $6.95, soups and chowder under $4, and a seafood bar for $6.95. The house specialties are generous portions of prime rib $19.95, filet mignon $21, short rib $18.50, tempura $18.50, and seafood Newburg $17.95. The a la carte salad bar is $7.95. Tiffany's is that special blend of elegant and casual where you can dine in style and still be presented with a moderate check.

The **Super Chef Restaurant,** tel. 926-7199, at the Waikiki Hana Hotel 2424 Koa Ave., is a sleeper. It is definitely one of *the* best mod-erately/inexpensively priced restaurants in Wai-kiki where you can get an *almost* gourmet meal for a terrific price. Being in a small hotel on a side street keeps the crowds away, so the quality of the food and service never suffers. The restau-rant decor is not spectacular, but it is classy with small linen-covered tables and drum-seat chairs in a open and cheery room. The staff is very friendly, and the chefs prepare each meal in-dividually behind a tile counter. Breakfast is from 6:30-10:30 a.m. when they feature buttermilk pancakes, bacon and ham, or Portuguese sau-sage, with a large juice for just $2.25, or choose a *wiki wiki* breakfast of pastry, juice, and Kona coffee for only $1.75. No lunch menu and dinner is from 5-10 p.m. One special is a complete din-ner of steak with two lobster tails for only $11.95, or rack of lamb for $8.95. What's the catch? The portions are moderate but definitely not minis-cule, and on top of it the cooking is just a half step below excellent. Definitely worth a try.

Carlos Castaneda wouldn't even notice as he walked past two psychedelic green cactuses into **Pepper's,** at 150 Kaiulani Ave., tel. 926-4374 open daily for lunch from 11:30 a.m.-4 p.m., dinner from 4 p.m.-1:30 a.m.! The interior is Yuppie-Mex with a wraparound rectangular bar with a fat wooden rail, and low ceilings done in a Mexican-style stucco. The specialties of the house are prepared in a smoke-fired oven for that hearty outdoor flavor in the heart of "Rancho Waikiki." Light meals are chicken taco salad for $4.50, the Pepper club $4.94, and tuna melts $4.95, with a good selection of salads. But you can get these anywhere so go "south of the border" for burrito madness for $7.50, a com-plete flautas dinner for $7.95, or selections from the mesquite grill like marinated chicken breast

$10.95, baby-back ribs (full slab) for $14.95. You can also pick Mexican favorites like tacos, enchiladas, and fajitas, all served with rice, beans, and Mexican salad. Nothing on the Mexican side is more than $10.95, with most around $7. Interface your face with good food at a decent price at Pepper's, *hombre*.

Eating at **Caffe Guccinni** is like following a Venetian gondolier to his favorite restaurant. It's not fancy but the food is good and plentiful, and the pasta is made fresh daily. The staff is usually a cook and a waiter who seats you at one of a half dozen tables that are mostly outdoors. At 2139 Kuhio Ave., tel. 922-5287, daily from 3-11p.m., they're easy to miss because they're stuck back off the street, which means a nice and quiet area. Prices are garlic bread $2, Caesar's salad $5.50, or house specialties (with soup or salad), like eggplant parmigiana $8.50, pasta contesto $8.50, spaghetti and meatballs $9.50, and manicotti $9.75. The cappuccino and espresso are freshly brewed and extraordinarily good. For dessert have *cannoli*, a flaky pastry stuffed with ricotta and smothered with slivers of almond and chocolate—excellent.

Hernando's Hideaway, at 2139 Kuhio, tel. 922-7758, open daily 11 a.m.-10 p.m., sits well off the street and is a very casual Mexican restaurant where the emphasis is on plenty of good food and having a good time. Tables are mostly outside under an awning and covered with butcher-block paper so you can crayon your heart away and get rid of your anxieties by scribbling all over the table. Every day is a special drink day, and there is live entertainment on Wednesday and Sunday. Happy hour brings $2 margaritas. Throughout the week there're bikini contests, and ladies' night on Wednesdays. All this activity attracts a younger crowd of both resort workers and vacationers. The menu is average Mexican dishes from nachos to tostadas. You can eat until you're as stuffed as a burrito for under $8. Olé!

The **New Orleans Bistro**, at 2139 Kuhio, tel. 926-4444, open from 11 a.m.-midnight, along with its zesty Cajun and creole dining, offers jazz nightly. The chef, from New Orleans, has put together a small but superb sampler menu of the finest in Cajun cooking. The prices are a touch expensive, but if you're bored with the average offerings of mahi mahi and teri chicken, you'll be glad that you found the Bistro. They've done the

most with this limited location. The tables, covered in pink tablecloths, are arranged so that there is an intimate and romantic feeling, and somehow the hustle and bustle of Kuhio has been minimized. Appetizers begin at $4.95 and sharpen your palate with deep-fried calamari, or oysters Bienville, and Gulf Coast oysters baked on the half shell topped with New Orleans classic cream sauce and laced with shrimp for $10.95. Salads are basically $5 and include beefsteak tomato (Maui Feast) and house salad of hearts of palms $4.95. Entrees are mesquite-grilled lemon herb chicken $12.95, Louisiana fresh fried catfish $14.95, blackened fish du jour (seasonal price), or smoked Kalua shrimp and angel hair pasta $15.95. If reptiles and amphibians pique your fancy there're frog legs and alligator tenderloins barbecued, blackened, or deep-fried with cocktail sauce, served with Cajun rice and vegies for $19.95. A good choice for a *different* dining experience.

Bobby McGee's Conglomeration, at the Colony East Hotel, 2885 Kalakaua, tel. 922-1282, open Mon.-Thurs. 5:30-10 p.m., Fri., Sat., and Sun. 5-11 p.m. This is a riproaring fun-filled place for the entire family. One of those rare combinations that caters to all ages and all pocketbooks, and foodwise it won't let you down. The waiters and waitresses are all in costume, so you might be served your meal by Batman or Annie Oakley. The interior has numerous rooms, so you can sit close to the disco dance floor in case you have the overwhelming urge to twist off a few calories, or you can sit in a quiet room well away from the music. Create your own combos by mixing and matching selections like fried clam strips, top sirloin, deviled crab, island chicken. Pick any two for $14.95, any three for $16.95, each additional $3.95. Also traditional dishes are top sirloin for $13.75, *mahi mahi* macadamia for $8.95, or lasagna for $8.25. Children's menu for under $5. Plus an assortment of sandwiches for $5. All entrees come with the salad bar which is set up in an old bathtub. If you can't make up your mind where to dine, Bobby McGee's is a sure bet.

The Blue Water Cafe, 2350 Kuhio Ave., tel. 926-2191, open from 7 a.m.-10 p.m., dancing from 10 p.m.-4 a.m., is basic and cozy with heavy oak tables, brass rails, and wooden arm chairs. With a name like Blue Water you'd think they were big on fish, but they're the home of the "one pound Porter house steak" for only $9.95. They also serve Maine lobster with garlic and butter pasta for $19.95, and the chef's specials like strips of tenderloin sauteed with mushrooms and onions $10.95 and Pacific red snapper $10.95. Happy hour is 11-7 and 9-midnight, $1.50 for standards in the lounge only. The large-screen TV used nightly in the disco shows Hawaiian activities during the day and evening. So while you're chomping your steak you can be learning about Hawaii too!

Pieces of Eight in the Coral Seas Hotel, tel. 923-6646, is open daily 5-11 p.m., happy hour is 4-6 p.m., piano bar nightly. This steak and seafood house has managed to create a comfortable and relaxed atmosphere where they serve up excellent steaks and very good fish dishes at a moderate price. The decor is dark wood and burnished brass in a romantically lit main room. A piano stylist tinkles in the background. It's the perfect combination of restaurant that will match itself to your mood. Come for that special night out or just a casual evening meal. "Early birders" from 5-6:30 p.m. can peck selections like garlic chicken or fish n' chips with salad bar for $5.95. Entrees are 10-ounce top sirloin $11.95, ground beef sirloin $8.50, filet mignon $15.95, mahi mahi amandine for $10.95. All dinners include choice of potato, rice, or bread and salad bar at $2.50 extra. A great choice for good food and a pleasant setting at affordable prices.

The House of Hong, 260 Lewers St., tel. 923-0202, is open daily 11 a.m.-10:30 p.m., Sun. from 4 p.m., piano bar nightly except Sunday. Not bad for a standard, no surprises Chinese restaurant. The decor borders on tasteful with some tables outfitted in starchy white tablecloths accented by inlaid murals and painted ceilings of China scenes. The Cantonese lunch special is weekdays from 11 a.m.-3 p.m. for $4.95, and early-bird specials from 4-6 p.m. offer dishes like egg flower soup, chicken chow mein, sweet and sour pork, crispy wonton, fried rice, fortune cookie, and Chinese tea for $9.95. Not great, but no complaints except for a *sometimes* pushy doorman who tries to hustle you inside.

The **Oceanarium** at the Pacific Beach Hotel, 2490 Kalakaua Ave., tel. 922-1233, offers a sundown special from 5-6:30 p.m. for $10-12 including *mahi mahi,* teri steaks and chicken, chicken fetuccini, and barbecued ribs. They even have a seafood sampler for $12.95. Full breakfast and lunch menus. For lunch, try the tropical fruit plate $7.50 or an entree like Cajun five-spice chicken for $7.50. Dinner appetizers like Cajun calamari begin at $4.25, New York peppercorn steak for $19.95, or special combos like Hawaiian lobster for $21.95. Also fresh island catches at market prices. The Ocenarium is done in elegant muted colors as if you were under water. See p. 269 for a description of the massive 280,000-gallon aquarium that is the decor.

Trattoria, in the Edgewater Hotel, 2168 Kalia Rd., tel. 923-8415, serves savory dishes from Northern Italy. Particularly good are the veal plates with an appropriate bottle of Italian wine.

Benihana of Tokyo at the Hilton Rainbow Bazaar, 2005 Kalia Rd., tel. 955-5955, is a medium-priced Japanese restaurant for those who are jittery about the food and prices. Meals are designed to fit *gaijin* taste, and cooks flash their knives and spatulas at your table—as much a floor show as a dining experience. Good, basic Japanese food, *teppan*-style.

Rascals on Kuhio, at the Kuhio Mall, 2301 Kuhio Ave., tel. 922-5566, is open for dinner only, and doubles as a nightclub with late-night suppers served until 3 a.m. and dancing until 4 a.m. Varied menu of seafood, featuring Cajun-style shrimp soup.

Popo's Margarita Cantina, International Market Place, tel. 923-8373, and **Compadres Mexican Bar and Grill,** Outrigger Prince Hotel, 2500 Kuhio Ave., tel. 924-4007, offer tacos, enchiladas, chips and salsa, done in a reasonably good Mexican style with good value on the combination plates.

Mandarin Palace, the Miramar Hotel, 2345 Kuhio Ave., tel. 926-1110, for lunch and dinner. Highly rated for its Oriental cuisine in a full-blown Chinese atmosphere.

Seafood Emporium, Royal Hawaiian Shopping Center, 2201 Kalakaua Ave., tel. 922-5477. Moderately priced for seafood, with one of the island's largest selections of domestic and imported fish. A good choice for a reasonable lunch or dinner.

The Great Wok of China, Royal Hawaiian Center, 2201 Kalakaua Ave., tel. 922-5373. Decent food, it's fun to eat here as chefs prepare food at your table in, you guessed it, woks. A good assortment of meat, seafood, and vegetable dishes, guaranteed not to be the steam-table variety.

Spat's, Hyatt Regency, 2424 Kalakaua, tel. 922-9292, is a fun restaurant doubling as a disco, featuring passable Italian cuisine, with decent veal dishes and pasta.

If local people want a buffet they head for **Kengos's Buffet,** 1529 Kapiolani Blvd, tel. 941-2241, which is a sure sign that you get value for your money. Friday evenings are extremely popular with a special seafood buffet for $14.95. If you're heading for Kengo's go at lunchtime because you get the exact same buffet for $7.50. Every day is slightly different, but you can count on a huge assortment of food that is sure to please.

EXPENSIVE

Sergio's, at the Ilima Hotel, 445 Nohonani, open daily for dinner only from 5:30-11:30 p.m., tel. 926-3388, is one of the finest restaurants over all, and *the* best Italian restaurant in Honolulu. The dishes are culinary masterpieces, painstakingly prepared using only the freshest ingredients that have been imported from around the world. Like the true works of art that they are, the dishes are elegantly presented by a professional and knowledgeable staff. The interior is romantic, subtle, and simple, with a combination of booths and tables. Sergio prepares foods from all regions of Italy, blending and matching hearty peasant soups, fresh salads, and antipasti garnished with aromatic cheeses and spicy prepared meats, pasta dishes, entrees, and desserts. The more than a dozen choices of pasta come with sauces of savory meat, or delicate vegetables, and seafood. Entrees are chicken, beef, and fresh fish that make your taste buds rise and shout "Bravo! Sergio! Bravo!"

If food was fine art, and the French definitely regard it as such, the dishes prepared at **Michel's** would deserve their rightful place at the Louvre. Located at the Colony Surf Hotel, 2895 Kalakaua Ave., tel. 923-6552, open daily from 7 a.m.-10 p.m. Michel's is literally on the beach, so your appetite is piqued not only by sumptuous morsels, but by magnificent views of the Waikiki skyline boldly facing the Pacific. The interior is "neo-French elegant," with the dining rooms appointed in soft pastels, velour chairs with armrests, white tablecloths, crystal chandeliers, heavy silver service, and tasteful paintings. The bar is serpentine and of polished koa. Michel's

Sunday brunch is legendary. Choose an entree and the remainder of the brunch comes with it. Suggestions are baked avocado with crab meat for $22, or renowned eggs Benedict for $17. You get a choice of broiled fresh grapefruit with sherry, sliced oranges and melon, fresh Hawaiian pineapple slices, Puna papaya with limes, along with a sparkling champagne cocktail, and baskets of banana or blueberry muffins and Kona coffee.

Daily breakfasts are a wild mushroom omelette for $8.50, or breakfast steak and eggs for $14.50, Belgian waffles $9.50, buttermilk pancakes $7.50. Lunch is appetizers like baked oysters Michel for $8, or Michel's Reuben sandwich for $9. Fruits of the sea are steamed king crab leg for $18, and from the grill come spring lamb chops $17. Dinner is *magnifique* with fresh Maine lobster on ice $25, delicate baby coho salmon garnished with shrimp served in its own sauce $30, or tournedos rossini, a center cut of tenderloin with goose liver and truffles. The dining experience at Michel's is completely satisfying with outstanding food and outstanding service, all in an outstanding setting.

One of the most laudable achievements in the restaurant business is to create an excellent reputation and then to keep it. **Nick's Fishmarket** at the Waikiki Gateway Hotel, 2070 Kalakaua, tel. 955-6333, open nightly for dinner from 6-11:30 p.m., has done just that . . . and keeps doing it. Many gourmets consider Nick's *the* best dining in Waikiki, and it's great fun to find out if they know what they're talking about. Owner Randy Schoch pays personal attention to every detail at Nick's, while executive chef Edward Fernandez creates the culinary magic. Tuxedoed waiters, knowledgeable about every dish and the extensive wine list, add a just-right touch of elegance. Start with fresh-baked clams casino $8.95, smoked salmon $9.50, or if you're in the mood how about beluga caviar for only $70. For soup order the Fish Market Chowder, or Chef Fernandez's famous chicken noodle soup. Salads are wonderful too with Nick's special salad, or Caesar salad prepared at your table for $7.50. Seafood and fish entrees are unbeatable. Choose from a wide assortment of island fish like *ono, ahi,* and *opakapaka* that are broiled, baked, seared, or served in a rich Amandine or dill sauce. Fresh Maine lobster, bouillabaisse of lobster, crab, and shrimp, or fresh catfish Cajun style will make you rejoice. Although Nick's is primarily fish, don't overlook the veal, steaks, and chicken with sides of pasta. An excellent choice is one of Nick's complete dinners featuring entree, soup or salad, vegetables, and hot drink for $26.95. Dancing and listening music is nightly with No Excuse from 9 p.m.-1:30 a.m. Tues.-Sat., while Leroy Kahuku plays island favorites on his mellow guitar on Sun. and Mondays. If you had only one evening in Waikiki and you wanted to make it memorable, you'd have a hard time doing better than Nick's Fishmarket.

The Secret, previously known as the Third Floor, is the signature restaurant at the Hawaiian Regent, 2552 Kalakaua, tel. 922-6611, open nightly from 6-9:30 p.m. As you enter, you pass an arrangement of cornucopia holding fresh fruits and fish, while others brim over with gourds, Indian corn, bread turtles and alligators. A wheel barrow is loaded with nuts. The decor in the main room is high-back, peacock, wicker chairs, where you're wrapped in the arms of bamboo in a booth-like atmosphere. The room is of open-beam construction overlooking Waikiki Beach. In the center is a *koi* pond with gas torches lit for that extra touch. Hanging from the ceiling are banners that give you the feeling of being at a medieval feast, Polynesian style. Strolling minstrels, The Anacan's, play a seemingly infinite melody of moody contemporary tunes, while a harpist gives an impression of heavenly strains on Monday evenings. Waiters are extremely professional, providing insightful tips to the menu that they have memorized. The Secret is renowned for its fine wines, with over 340 selections that are expertly managed by Richard Dean, one of only two master *sommeliers* in all of Hawaii. Within the restaurant is a wine room that can hold a private party of 12 that may choose from a special menu. As you peruse the menu you are presented with a plate of freshly baked Indian *naan* bread. Select the hors d'oeuvres bar, which has smoked salmon, caviar, and duck paté, enough for a meal for a reasonable $12. Specialties are a *Casserole des fruits de Mer* (lobster, scallops, shrimp, and *opacapaca* in fennel sauce) for $29.50, scampi provençal $31.25, rack of spring lamb $32, and medallions of venison for $29. The Secret has a long and well-deserved reputation as one of the finest eating establishments in Waikiki. A romantic dinner here will long be remembered.

Matteo's, in the Marine Surf Hotel, 364 Seaside, tel. 922-5551, open from 6 p.m.-2 a.m., is a wonderfully romantic Italian restaurant that sets the mood even outside by welcoming you with a red canopy and brass rail that leads to a carved door of koa and crystal. Inside is dark and stylish, with high-backed booths, white tablecloths, and marble-top tables. On each is a rose, Matteo's signature. Dinners begin with hot antipasti such as stuffed mushrooms à la Matteo $6.50, seafood combo $11.50, or cold antipasto for two for $10.95. Light fare of *ensalada e zuppa* (salad and soup) like special salad $5.75, heart of romaine lettuce $6.75, clam soup $9.50, matched with garlic bread $1.50 or pizza bread $2.50, makes an inexpensive but tasty meal. Entree suggestions are chicken *rollatini* $16.50, veal *rollatini* (rolled veal stuffed with bell peppers, mushrooms, onions, spinach, and mozarella) for $20.95, or *bragiola* (rolled beef with mozarella cheese, garlic, fresh basil, and baked with marinara sauce) for $15.95. Complete dinners come with Matteo's special salad, pasta, vegetables, and coffee or tea and include *mahi mahi* Veronica (sauteed fish in lemon sauce and seedless grapes) $22.95, or veal parmigiana $23.95. Pastas are very reasonable and dishes include *gnocchi* $12.95, manicotti a la Matteo's $10.95. An extensive wine list complements the food. If you are out for a special evening of fine dining and romance, Matteo's will set the mood, and the rest is up to you.

Colony Steak House, at the Hyatt Regency, 2424 Kalakaua, tel. 922-9292. As the name implies, they specialize in excellent cuts of steak that you personally choose, as well as fish and a truly superb salad bar. **Bagwell's,** also in the Hyatt Regency, tel. 922-9292, is a superb French restaurant with an imaginative menu and great wine list. The chef is Yves Menoret, formerly of Alexis in San Francisco. The prices are richer than French pastry.

Restaurant Suntory, Royal Hawaiian Shopping Center, tel. 922-5511, is a very handsome restaurant with different rooms specializing in particular styles like *shabu shabu, teppanyaki,* and sushi. The prices used to be worse, but they're still expensive. However, the food preparation and presentation are excellent, and the staff is very attentive.

Furusato Sushi, right next to the Hyatt Regency at 2424 Kalakaua Ave. tel. 922-4991, and

Furusato Tokyo Steak downstairs are both expensive but top-notch Japanese restaurants. The food and service are authentic, but they are geared toward the Japanese tourist who expects, and almost demands to pay high prices. In the steakhouse expect steak since very little else is on the menu. Upstairs is sushi. Free valet parking is great for this congested part of Waikiki.

The **Hilton Hawaiian Village** at 2005 Kalia Rd., is one of the finest destination resorts in Hawaii. Its two signature restaurants, both *Travel Holiday* award winners, complement the resort perfectly. **Bali By The Sea,** tel. 941-2254, open daily for dinner from 6-10 p.m., may sound like Indonesian cuisine, but it's more continental than anything else. The setting couldn't be more brilliant. Sit by the open windows so that the sea breezes fan you as you overlook the gorgeous Hilton beach with Diamond Head off to your left. The room is outfitted in a blue paisley carpet, high-backed, armrest-type chairs, white tablecloths, and classical place settings with silver service. Upon ordering, you are presented with a complimentary platter of hors d'oeuvres. Choose appetizers like gratin of oysters with Julienne of duck, or fettucini with wild mushrooms with prosciutto and sun-dried tomatoes. Soups are bisque of shrimp and lobster or a classic French onion. Entrees are a magnificent selection of fish from Hawaiian waters baked, sautéed, or broiled and then covered in a variety of sauces from fresh basil to mint and tomato vinaigrette. Meat entrees are breast of chicken and lobster, or medallions of venison simmered in pears, cranberry and *poivrade* sauce. The meal ends with a fine presentation of desserts, or a complimentary steaming chocolate Diamond Head. Bali by the Sea is a superb choice for an elegant evening of fine dining.

The **Golden Dragon,** tel. 946-5336, open nightly for dinner from 6- 10 p.m., would tempt any knight errant to drop his sword and to pick up chopsticks. This too is a fine restaurant where the walls are decorated with portraits of emperors, and the plates carry the Golden Dragon motif. The interior color scheme is a striking vermilion and black, with the chairs and tables shining with a lacquerware type of patina. The floor is dark koa. Outside, the terrace has pagoda-style canopies under which you may dine. Obviously the Golden Dragon isn't your average *chop suey* house, but the menu has all of the standard Chinese fare from lemon chicken to . . . well, chop suey, but it doesn't end there. The food is expertly prepared, and two fine choices are the exotic Imperial Beggar's Chicken (for two), which takes 24 hours' notice to prepare and Chef Dai's Selection (for two), which includes lobster in black bean sauce, shrimp, almond duck, beef in rice wine, duck fried rice, and a special dessert all for only $40. For a first-class restaurant with impeccable food and service, the prices at the Golden Dragon are very, very reasonable.

The **Surf Room,** is in the Royal Hawaiian Hotel, 2259 Kalakaua Ave., tel. 923-7311. The menu is solid but uninspired. However, the setting couldn't be lovelier, and the huge buffet is staggering.

Hy's Steak House, 2440 Kuhio Ave., tel. 922-5555, is one of those rare restaurants that is not only absolutely beautiful, but serves great food as well. Decorated like a Victorian sitting room, its menu offers things other than steaks and chops, but these are the specialties and worth the stiff-upper-lipped price.

ENTERTAINMENT

Waikiki swings, beats, bumps, grinds, sways, laughs, and gets down. If Waikiki has to bear being called a carnival town, it might as well strut its stuff. Dancing (disco and ballroom), happy hours, cocktail shows, cruises, lounge acts, Polynesian extravaganzas, and the street scene provide an endless choice of entertainment. Small-name Hawaiian trios, soloists, piano men, and sultry singers featured in innumerable bars and restaurants woo you in and keep you coming back. Big-name island entertainers and visiting international stars play the big rooms. Free entertainment includes hula shows, ukulele music, street musicians, jugglers, artists, and streetwalkers. For a good time, nowhere in Hawaii matches Waikiki. Also see page 254 for other listings in and around greater Honolulu.

Bars, Happy Hours, And Lounge Acts

Plaza Lounge, tel. 922-6885, in the Waikiki Shopping Plaza, presents Mel Cabang, a fat, bald, and funny-as-hell Filipino singer-comedian. He plays with the audience, like Don Rickles, but he's so *gestalt* that you can't believe it. His risqué repartee, fine guitar-playing, and surprisingly good voice don't quite seem to fit his face. Tuesday to Sat. from 9 p.m., no cover, $2 per drink.

Brother Noland is a local talent who appears around town, but most often performs at the lounge in the Waikiki Sheraton, tel. 922-4422. He's the cutting edge for ethnic Hawaiian groups playing hot reggae, originals, and plenty of Stevie Wonder, solo or with a group, and shouldn't be missed.

Steve and Theresa are excellent Hawaiian musicians. Their sound is a melodious mixture of traditional and contemporary. Accomplished musicians with beautiful voices, they often appear at La Mex in the Royal Hawaiian Shopping Center, tel. 923-2906.

In the Park Shore Hotel, 2586 Kalakaua Ave., The Bar is a quiet, relaxing place to have a drink. A talented pianist and organist, Andre Branch, plays nightly. Free.

The **Irish Rose Saloon** at 227 Lewers, presents live entertainment nightly with dancing till 4 a.m., and features sporting events on their big-screen TV. Happy hour is from 3-8 p.m. Right across the street from the Outrigger Coral Seas

Hotel, just at the entrance of the Al Herrington Show.

A great little homey bar called the **Brass Rail** serves up cold draft beer and deli sandwiches. They're into sports and especially Monday Night Football, which usually begins in Hawaii at 7:30 p.m. Located on the ground floor of the Outrigger Waikiki Hotel, at 2335 Kalakaua.

The **Rose and Crown Pub** in King's Village has a pianist playing sing-along favorites in what is a very close rendition of an English-style pub. They have daily specials, for example, on Saturday if you wear your Rose and Crown hat you have happy hour prices all night long. So drink hearty, and hold on to your hat! The crowd is a good mixture intent on swilling beer and partying. Noisy, raucous, and fun.

Key Largo is a *bar,* and bars are not so easy to find in Waikiki. Stuck away at 142 Uluniu St., it attracts a mostly local crowd, especially Wed.-Sat. when they feature live rock 'n' roll bands. Key Largo doesn't have the vibe of a rough joint, but it is the sort of place where a fool and his teeth can easily be parted.

Jolly Roger Restaurant at the 2244 Kalakaua and 150 Kaiulani (see p. 281) presents a changing mixture of live music nightly in their lounge open until 2 a.m. A good spot for listening to music and enjoying conversation around the bar.

The Grapevine, corner of Prince Edward and Uluniu streets, presents low-key live music. Artists change, but expect a guitarist playing soulful Hawaiian music.

In the International Market Place, the **Cock's Roost Steak House** offers free entertainment, with no minimum or cover. Nearby, the **Crow's Nest**, above the Jolly Roger Restaurant, at 2244 Kalakaua, features local and visiting entertainers. If Blue Kangaroo, a hilarious comedy act, is playing, don't miss them. The entertainers, Mike Drager and Jay Cook, have been singing and playing their guitars and various other stringed instruments together for over 25 years. They first played at the Crow's Nest in 1972, and in their own words "can't believe the sumbitch lasted this long." Their ribald songs are extremely egalitarian . . . they insult all races, creeds, and sexes equally. As the night gets later their humor gets raunchier. Be forewarned, and have a ball.

the distinctive wall
mural at The Wave

The Brothers Cazimero have an excellent and well-deserved reputation as one of Hawaii's finest duos, singing a lovely blend of Hawaiian and contemporary music. You can usually catch them at the Royal Hawaiian Hotel's Monarch Room. Dinner and cocktail shows are from 7 p.m. Tues.-Saturday. Alohawear is fine, tel. 923-7311.

Trappers in the Hyatt Regency is an intimate jazz nightclub, with overstuffed chairs and cozy booths; continuous jazz from 5:30 p.m.

Baron's Studio, Waikiki Plaza Hotel, tel. 946-0277, is home to jazz vocalist Azure McCall. Open nightly, quiet drinks, fine background tunes.

The **Polynesian Pub,** 2490 Kalakaua, tel. 923-3683, offers happy hour nightly and contemporary Hawaiian music. Right-priced drinks, no cover.

The **Garden Bar,** Hilton Hawaiian Village, tel. 949-4321, features John Norris and the New Orleans Jazz Band on Sun. from 2-6 p.m.

Discos, Dancing And Nightclubs

Ballroom dancers will enjoy **Tea Dancing at the Royal** in the Monarch Room of the Royal Hawaiian Hotel, featuring the 14-piece Del Courtney Orchestra, Mon. from 5:30-8:30 p.m. The **Maile Lounge** at the Kahala Hilton, tel. 734-2211, offers live music for ballroom dancing nightly.

Nick's Fishmarket at the Gateway Hotel, 2070 Kalakaua (see p. 287), swings with contemporary dance music until 1:30 a.m. A mixed crowd, but mostly a mature crowd who have stayed on to dance after a magnificent meal that Nick's is known for. Music is provided by No Excuse, headliners that make Nick's their home when not on tour.

The **Paradise Lounge** in the Rainbow Tower of the Hilton Hawaiian Village is a jazz nightclub, perfect for a night of relaxing entertainment. They have a pianist nightly and a polished wooden dance floor. Weekends brings a variety of jazz ensembles for your listening and dancing pleasure. Perfect for a romantic evening.

The Wave is a rock 'n' roll and new wave hotspot with live music nightly, 1877 Kalakaua Ave., tel. 941-0424. It has become an institution of late-night fun and dancing. The crowd is mixed, and you can either choose to dance, or perch upstairs in the balcony behind glass where you can check out the dancers below, or have a few drinks and some conversation. The Wave is a sure bet for a night of fun.

Pink Cadillac at 478 Ena is just around the corner from the Wave. Open till 2 a.m., its large dance floors rock with merrymakers ages 18 and up. It's a happening place for younger rockers. Alcohol is served, but if you are under 21 you'll be braceletted, which means you can't drink. The cover charge is $10 for ages 18-21, $5 over 21.

The following are disco nightclubs in and around Waikiki. Most have videos, a theme, a dress code of alohawear and shoes, no sandals, and start hopping around 9 p.m. with the energy cut off around 4 a.m.

The **Jazz Cellar,** 205 Lewers St., features mostly live rock and roll and some jazz. The place jumps till 4 a.m. and has plenty of special nights like Thirsty Tuesdays and Ladies' Night. Put on your dancin' shoes, casual attire, tel. 923-9952.

Lewers Street Annex at 270 Lewers is a basic disco dance spot featuring Top-40 tunes. The clientele is mostly young visitors and some local workers who stop in for a late-night drink. A special feature is their "12 o'clock high," basically happy hour prices from 12 noon-12 midnight. Standard drinks $1.50, domestic beers $1.50, margaritas and mai tais $1.50. Good for casual drinking, dancing, and meeting people.

The Infinity at the Sheraton Waikiki presents golden oldies and contemporary live music nightly from 8 p.m. Good dance floor.

The **Blue Water Cafe,** 2350 Kuhio Ave, once the home of live music, now has disco and videos. It's distinguished by it's copper and brass appointments, including full copper doors to the restrooms, pillars that are covered in copper and a ceiling that looks like closely fit barrel staves. Waitresses are particularly good-looking.

The **3-D Ballroom,** 2260 Kuhio, is a crummy little joint two floors up with super-loud music for teeny-boppers and punkers.

The Point After, 2552 Kalakaua Ave., tel. 922-6611. Fatso sofas in this football-theme nightspot. A local favorite with a dress code.

Spats in the Hyatt Regency, tel. 922-9292, is an Italian restaurant that turns into a disco around 9 p.m. The decor is 1920s art deco. Classy, well known, and swinging.

Red Lion Dance Palace, 240 Lewers St., tel. 922-1027, offers high-tech video and disco and a pool bar. Beachwear OK, from 2 p.m.-4 a.m.

Masquerade and **Phaze,** next door to each other at the corner of McCully and Kalakaua avenues, feature a heavy sound system and wild light shows. Cutting-edge videos, great dance floors, and wild tunes till 4 a.m.

Cilly's, 1909 Ala Wai Blvd., tel. 942-2942, **Annabelle's** at the Westin Ilikai, 1777 Ala Moana Blvd., tel. 949-3811, and **Steel Wings,** also at the Westin Ilikai, are well-known discos where you can't help having a good time. All have reputations as swinging nightspots.

Exotic live dancers, like exotic live plants, need a unique atmosphere in which to bloom. Both seem to crave light, one sunlight, the other a spotlight. Most of the flashy fleshy nightspots of Waikiki used to be a few blocks away along Kapiolani Blvd. (see p. 139) but they have been moving ever closer to the heart of Waikiki. Now they are strung along Kuhio Avenue, where they're easily recognizable by their garish neon lights which advertise their wares. The Kuhio Avenue exotic dance spots are supposedly a step up in class from their Kapiolani Boulevard counterparts, but when their dancers strip to the buff, the difference is hardly noticeable . . . or very noticeable, depending upon point of view. The names of the strip joints really don't matter, just look for the signs of "exotic dancers." Usually a $10 cover and $5 for a drink.

Dinner Shows
And Polynesian Extravaganzas

Free tickets to these extravaganzas are handed out by condo time-share outfits stationed in booths along the main drags. For attending their sales presentations, usually 90 minutes, you can get tickets to the Don Ho Show, among others—but they might be the toughest freebies you've ever earned. The presentation is a pressure cooker. The sales people are pros, who try every imaginable technique to get you to sign. If you're really interested in time-sharing, the deals aren't too bad, but if you're there only for the tickets, what a waste of time!

The **Don Ho Show** at the Hilton Hawaiian Village has been attracting huge crowds for years, leaving some thrilled, appalling others. There are some truly dazzling costumes and plenty of glitzy Hawaiian acts, complete with music and dance. Don Ho, a talented vocalist and veteran performer, is either totally relaxed in his role or dulled by its repetition. Some consider his sexual humor in bad taste, but it's no different from what you hear in most nightclubs. After all, the show isn't a prayer meeting. Don Ho plays with the audience, especially the older folks, making pointed jokes about Mainlanders. Of course everyone roars with laughter—blame it on the potent mai tais. There are two shows Sun.-Fri.: the dinner show from 6:30-8:30 p.m. for about $70 per couple, and the cocktail show from 8 p.m. about $35 per couple, includes one drink. For details and reservations, call 949-4321.

Al Harrington, billed as "The South Pacific Man," has also been attracting crowds for years at the Polynesian Palace in the Reef Towers

Hotel on Lewers St., tel. 923-9861. Another wonderfully costumed Polynesian extravaganza takes you on a musical tour through the South Pacific. Personable Harrington takes time to make everyone feel comfortable, and though he too has been doing the show for years, he manages to keep sparkle in his performance. Two dinner shows and two cocktail shows nightly except Saturdays. The buffet dinner is reputed to be exceptional. Prices are about $70 per couple for the dinner show, half that for the cocktail shows.

The Kahala Hilton, tel. 734-2211, presents **An Evening With Danny Kaleikini**. This extraordinary island entertainer has been captivating audiences here for almost 20 years. This show has class; it doesn't draw the large budget-oriented crowds. Two shows nightly except Sun., dinner show at 7 p.m., cocktail show at 9 p.m.

Tavana's Polynesian Spectacular in the Long House of the Hilton Hawaiian Village, tel. 923-0211, combines Polynesian music, song and dance, dramatic effects, and costumes. Two shows nightly: dinner seating at 5:30 and 8:30 p.m., cocktails at 6:30 and 9 p.m.

Dick Jensen, The Hula Hut, 286 Beachwalk, tel. 923-3838, is a dinner show with an all-you-can-eat buffet. Seating at 8 p.m., $30 per person, cocktail show 8:45 p.m., $18 per person, one cocktail included.

Free Entertainment

Check the newpapers and free tourist literature for times to the following events.

The **Royal Hawaiian Band** plays free concerts on Sunday afternoons at the bandstand in Kapiolani Park, oftentimes with singers and hula dancers. Also in the park, free concerts are periodically given by a variety of local and visiting musicians at the Waikiki Shell.

The **Kodak Hula Show** is free, though it's a hassle to get in. The show is held on Tues., Thurs., and Fri. at 10 a.m. in Kapiolani Park. Ex-tremely popular, people start lining up at 8 a.m.; be there by 9 if you want a seat. You sit on bleachers with 3,000 people, while Hawaiian *tutu* bedecked in muumuus, leis, and smiles play ukeleles and sing for the *ti*-leaf-skirted dancers. You can buy film and even rent a camera, as befits the show's sponsor, the Eastman Kodak Company—snap away with abandon. The performance dates back to 1937, and some of the original dancers, now in their 80s, still participate. At the finale, the dancers line up on stage with red-lettered placards that spells out H-A-W-A-I-I, so you can take your own photo of the most famous Hawaiian postcard. Then the audience is invited down for a free hula lesson. People that are too hip hate it, *kamaainas* shy away from it, but if you're a good sport, you'll walk away like everyone else with a big smile on your face.

A potpourri of contemporary entertainment is also found in Kapiolani Park on weekends. Just across from the zoo, musicians, jugglers, clowns, unicyclists, and acrobats put on a free, impromptu circus. Some of the best are B.J. Patches, Twinkles, and Jingles from a local troupe called Clown Alley.

The ukelele tree in front of the Reef Hotel, 2169 Kalia Rd., has heard the lovely melodies of Hawaii for 50 years. Every Sun. at 8 p.m. local musicians and sometimes well-known guests come to play and be heard.

The **Royal Hawaiian Shopping Center** provides free entertainment throughout the week: quilting, *lau hala* weaving, pineapple cutting, and free hula lessons every Friday at 10 a.m. with Aunti Maiki Aiu Lake.

Aunty Bella's Leis, 2200 Kalakaua Ave., gives free lei-making classes Mon., Wed., and Fri. at 10:30 a.m. The flowers are free and you keep the lei that you string.

At the Shore Bird Restaurant, 2160 Kalia, a **female bikini beauty** contest on Sun. at 4 p.m. You can win $400 for first prize, second prize $150, third $50. All finalists receive dinner for two at the Shore Bird Beach Broiler and much more.

SHOPPING

The biggest problem concerning shopping in Waikiki is to keep yourself from burning out over the endless array of shops and boutiques. Everywhere you look someone has something for sale, and with the preponderance of street stalls lining the boulevards, much of the merchandise comes out to greet you. The same rule applies to shopping as it does to everything in Waikiki—class next door to junk. Those traveling to the Neighbor Islands should seriously consider a shopping spree in Waikiki, which has the largest selection and most competitive prices in the islands. A great feature about shopping in Waikiki is that most shops are only a minute or two from the beach. This enables your sale-hound companion to hunt while you relax. There's no telling how much money your partner can save you! "Ingrate! This bathing suit could have cost $50, but I got it for $25. See, you saved $25 while you were lying here like a beached whale." Everyone concerned should easily be mollified. Charge!

The Fence

The best place to find an authentic island-made souvenir at a reasonable price is at **The Fence,** located along the fence of the Honolulu Zoo fronting Kapiolani Park. The new offical name is **Artists of Oahu/Sunday Exhibit.** Some of the island's best artists congregate here to display and sell their works on Wednesday and weekends from 10 a.m.-4 p.m. Individual artists are only allowed to display one day a week. The Fence was the good idea of Honolulu's current mayor, Frank Fasi, who decided that Oahu's rich resource of artists shouldn't go untapped. There are plenty of excellent artists whose works are sure to catch your fancy. Here are some of the best.

John Costello does colorful island-inspired paintings in pointillism, many of which have a fantastic, dreamlike quality. **Mary Ann Abel,** whose pen and inks of things Hawaiian, especially children's faces, are inspired. **Daniel Wang,** one of the few practicing deaf artists in the U.S., specializes in a remarkable palm painting technique done on rice paper with Chinese inks and watercolors. **Bob Reeves** works with island woods and specializes in koa frames.

Caridad Sumile does beautiful paintings and portraits in watercolors and acrylics.

Marge Claus has a colorful batik style. **Patrick Doell** has a very realistic, almost picture-postcard style. **Maggie Kobayashi** incorporates the female form with nautical suggestions and loves doing mermaids. **"June of Art," Hoegler-Reda** piles on layers of paint to achieve a three-dimensional quality. **Leonard Wood** loves animals and renders them in quiet pastels.

Cathy Thompson does dreamy, impressionistic lily ponds. **Joe Hunt** loves the "joy of life" and renders lively paintings of color and movement. **Edna Loo** does whimsical vignettes of children in Hawaiian settings. **Dianne Jeanine** paints soft flowing watercolors of flowers, sunsets, and seascapes. **Francine McGee** uses layers of glazing with modern transclucent colors to achieve Old Master-like seascapes. **Theresia Brinsen** is noted for the brilliance of the knife-technique in land- and seascapes. **Peggy Pai Laughlin** does batik and oil on silk and free-stitch embroidery.

Gifts And Souvenirs

If you would really like to return from the islands with a unique gift try **Hawaiian Pillows and Kits,** tel. 734-5032. The pillowcases are excellent renditions of the distinctive style of quilting developed in Hawaii after being introduced by the missionaries of last century. Rose Tam-Hoy, the owner, shows her handiwork at the Sheraton Moana's Banyan Courtyard on Fridays and at various other hotels throughout the week. Rose is a wealth of knowledge on Hawaiian quilting, and is happy to offer demonstrations and lessons.

Another islander demonstrating and selling Polynesian crafts is Faitu Powell of **Powell's Souvenirs,** tel. 926-6797. Faitu also sets up a small display at the Moana on Friday, and across the way at the Princess Kaiulani on Saturdays. She specializes in handmade hula skirts, leis, head bands, *haku,* and a variety of handicrafts. All of her souvenirs are authentic.

Fine Japanese art can be seen and purchased at two outstanding shops in Waikiki's Eaton Square, **Gallery Mikado** and **Gara Kuta-Do.**

John Costello, artist

ABC Stores scattered throughout Waikiki were founded by a local man, Sid Kosasa, who learned the retail business from his father. This "everything store" sells groceries, sundries, and souvenirs. Prices are good, especially on specials like lotions and beach mats. Very convenient.

You can purchase colorful, dramatic **Hawaiian calendars** drawn by Herb Kane, a well-known local artist, at all of the Burger King outlets. Fine mementos, they sell for under $3.

On Kalakaua between Kealohilani and Ohua streets above the ABC Store is **Lowest Factory Prices.** They've got very good prices on all-cotton shirts and muumuus, a rarity. Every price tag offers 10% off.

Those who just couldn't return home without a deep Hawaiian tan can be helped by visiting **Waikiki Aloe.** They specialize in skin-care products, lotions, and tanning supplies. In the Royal Hawaiian Shopping Center and the Kuhio Mall.

The **Waikiki Business Plaza,** 2270 Kalakaua Ave., houses a number of jewelry stores. In one stop you can get a pretty good idea of prices and availability. Look for jewelry boxes laden with jade, gold, turquoise, pearls, coral, *puka* shells, and eel, snake, and leather goods.

Military Shop of Hawaii has an entire wall dedicated to military patches, along with clothes, memorabilia, and collectibles. At 1921 Kalakaua Ave., tel. 942-3414.

Those with good taste but a limited budget should check out **Hawaiian Wear Unlimited,** liquidators of alohawear from most of Hawaii's big manufacturers. Located at the Royal Hawaiian Shopping Center, daily 9 a.m.-10 p.m. Also, **Robin Claire** "resale boutique" sells used designer clothing. At 1901 Kapiolani Plaza, tel. 941-8666.

Kite Fantasy, 2863 Kalakaua Ave., tel. 922-KITE, is sure to have an aerial toy to tickle your fancy. Kapiolani Park across the road is one of the best spots around to fly a kite, and they give free kite-flying lessons regardless of whether you purchase a kite or not; daily display at 11 a.m. and 2 p.m. Next door to the old Natatorium and the New Otani Hotel, you'll see multicolored kites floating in the breeze. Inside they have the "finest collection of kites, windsocks, and toys" in Hawaii. The phenomenal winds in Hawaii that generate good waves and good windsurfing conditions, also generate excellent kite-flying conditions. Hardly a day goes by that there isn't wind enough to get a kite up. And, because the winds are so gusty and changeable, it makes for some fantastic kite-flying acrobatics. Nearby in the park is what they call the Kite Tree, where kite flyers congregate in the evening. So if you're interested, go fly a kite!

Waikiki Fashion Center, 2310 Kuhio, next door to Zorro's, sells alohawear like plenty of other stores, but the prices are pretty good, and they even feature an ad for $5 off with a purchase of $20 or more.

For a full range of **photo supplies** at bargain prices try: **Woolworth's,** 2224 Kalakaua Ave.;

Fox Photo in the International Market Place and the Waikikian and Reef Towers hotels; and **Photo Stores** here and there along Kalakaua, Kuhio, Kalia, and Lewers streets. **Island Camera and Gift Shop,** on Kalakaua across from the Moana Hotel, is a small, but a full-service camera store. Handbillers often give money-saving coupons to a variety of photo stores.

Duty-free goods are always of interest to international visitors. You can find a duty-free store on Royal Hawaiian Ave., just behind Woolworth's. Also, if you want to see a swarm of Japanese jostling for position in a tiny little store trying to feed a buying frenzy, that's the spot.

Waikiki Shopping Centers
The largest credit card oasis is the **Royal Hawaiian Shopping Center.** This massive complex is three stories of nonstop shopping, running for three blocks in front of the Sheraton and Royal Hawaiian hotels. It's open daily 9 a.m.-10 p.m., til 9 p.m. on Sun., tel. 922-0588. This complex provides an excellent mixture of small intimate shops and larger department stores. There's a **post office** on the second-floor "B" building. The second and third floors of this shopping center are pretty quiet. It's off the street so not as many tourists find there way here. It's a good place to do some comparative browsing before making your purchases.

Where the Royal Hawaiian Shopping Plaza ends the **Waikiki Shopping Plaza** begins, but on the other side of the street. Here, you'll find multilevel shopping. The mall's centerpiece is a five-story waterfall, an impressive sculpture of water and plexiglass. Another feature of this mall is **Waikiki Calls,** a free hula show. The plaza is open daily 9 a.m.-11 p.m., tel. 923-1191.

The **International Market Place** is an open-air shopping bazaar that feels like Asia. Its natural canopy is a huge banyan, and the entire complex is across from the Moana Hotel at 2330 Kalakaua Ave., open daily from 9 a.m. until the vendors get tired at night, tel. 923-9871. Among some fine merchandise and a treasure or two is great junk! If you're after souvenirs like bamboo products, shellwork, hats, mats, lotions, alohawear, and carvings, you can't do better than the International Market Place. The worst thing is that everything starts to look the same, the

best is that the vendors will bargain. Make offers. If you successfully work your way through the gauntlet of shops without getting scalped, you may be able to find out what the future may bring by stopping at the Enchanted Tree. Here you can get psychic readings and healings. Mini readings $10, six-month reading $15, one-year reading $20, family reading $25, and life reading $35. Located under the big banyan.

Directly behind the marketplace is the **Kuhio Mall,** at 2301 Kuhio Avenue. Basically the same theme with open-air shops: gifts, fashions, food, and handmade artifacts. Enjoy the free Polynesian Show nightly at 7 and 8 p.m. This is a little older, funkier mall, one grade up from what you would find in the International Market Place and Duke's Alley. You'll find among others **S.K. Takahashi,** jewelry and gifts, and the **Waikiki Aloe Center** where you can watch their lab at work. If you wanted a low- key place to discover "treaure junk" this mall is good. It's even better than the Waikiki Marketplace because it's more low key. There aren't nearly as many people here and the salespeople are not as pushy.

Walk to the rear of the mall and go upstairs to what's called the **Craft Court.** You'll find crafts and plants made or grown in Hawaii sold by a small co-op of shops. Inside are *haku* lei (flat) that work as a hat band, a butterfly gallery, with specimens gathered from insect breeding farms, silk flower arrangements, and plants certified for export (blooming and nonblooming varieties of anthurium, ginger, plumeria, orchids), and flower bouquets. Judy Vess has a shop here selling hand-blown pyrex glass teardrops. Inside the tear-shaped glass is sterilized ocean water, sands from Hawaii, and five little sea shells from three different islands. Another shop sells a replica of a double-hulled canoe that looks very authentic, but is made from rolled newspaper. It's been laquered and shellacked, so it has a realistic brown patina to it, complete with the distinctive crab claw sail. Weaving and pottery selections are very reasonable. If you want something at Christmas time to remind you of Aloha Santa, they have Christmas wreaths made out of local forest products.

For those who can't stand to waste an opportunity to shop, they can do so while passing through **Duke's Alley,** a short cut between

Kuhio and Kalakaua avenues. Here you'll find a row of stalls selling basically the same merchandise as in the International Market Place.

The **Hyatt Regency Shopping Center,** also called the **Atrium Shops,** is located on the first three floors of the Hyatt Regency Hotel, 2424 Kalakaua Ave., tel. 922-5522, open daily 9 a.m.-11 p.m. The 70 or so shops here are mighty classy: if you're after exclusive fashions or a quality memento, this is the place. There's a continental-style sidewalk cafe, backed by a cascading indoor waterfall. Often free entertainment and fashion shows are put on by the various shops.

Smaller Malls

King's Village, at 131 Kaiulani Ave., just next to the Hyatt Regency, takes its theme from last century, where boardwalks pass 19th-century look-a-like shops, complete with a changing-of-the-guard ceremony nightly at 6:15 p.m. This attractive complex offers free entertainment, and attracts some of the best local street artists who usually set up their stands at night. The **Waikiki Trade Center** is on the corner of Seaside and Kuhio avenues with some of Waikiki's most elegant shops, featuring sophisticated fashions, exquisite artworks, and fine dining. The **Rainbow Bazaar** is a unique mall located at the Hilton Hawaiian Hotel, 2005 Kalia Road. Fun just to walk around, shops feature three main themes: Imperial Japan, Honk Kong Alley, and South Pacific Court.

The **Waikiki Bazaar** is on Kalakaua across from a brand-new building called A.N.A. Kalakaua Center, a multihued building in pastels. It's beautiful. Reminiscent of newer constructions seen in Japan. The Bazaar is bizarre. Upstairs, and in little booths are an orgy of porno shops. A person who couldn't read Japanese *katakana* wouldn't know that they said "porno." The Bazaar is there expressly for the use of Japanese tourists.

Street Artists And Vendors

You don't have to try to find something to buy in Waikiki—in fact, if you're not careful, the mer-

chandise will come after you! This takes place in the form of street vendors, who have been gaining a lot of attention lately. Some view them as a colorful addition to the beach scene, others as a nuisance. These carnival-type salespeople set up their mobile booths mainly along Kalakaua Avenue, with some on Kuhio Avenue and the side streets in between. In dealing with them you can have a positive experience if you remember two things: they have some pretty nifty junk, and you get what you pay for.

Also, street artists set up their palettes along busy thoroughfares, and especially at the entrances to small shopping malls. Most draw caricatures of patrons in a few minutes for a few dollars—fun souvenirs. An outstanding street artist is Mai Long, a Vietnamese man who sets up in King's Alley and does superb profiles or full face all in color for less than $10.

Right here under the Waikiki banyan is a gentleman named Coco who makes coconut-frond hats, basically a dying art. Just near the canoe rides, you'll see his hats and baskets. Depending on the hat, you can get one for $15 or so. The baskets, good for holding fruit, incidentals, or whatever, are a real souvenir of Hawaii. With Coco making them right before your very eyes, you can't get more authentic than that. Coco says you can still learn how to weave in the Hawaiian tradition. His dad, Uncle Harry Kuikai, weaves at the Royal Hawaiian Shopping Center every Tues. and Thurs. from 9:30- 11:30a.m. He'll teach you the basics of weaving and you can make your own souvenir (free). For longer-term tourists, there's an eight-week weaving class sponsored by the Kamehameha School. Just call the high school and inquire as to time and fees.

As you walk around Waikiki you'll see plenty of street-side booths offering unbelievable prices like "rent a car for $5, a jeep for $15, Pearl Harbor Cruise $5, Don Ho Show $20". Why so cheap? They're basically an advertising firm that signs you up to listen to a 90-minute spiel on a time-share condo. What happens during and after the 90-minute hard pitch is up to you, but you do get the payoff at the end.

CENTRAL OAHU

For most uninformed visitors, central Oahu is a colorful blur as they speed past in their rental cars en route to the North Shore. Slow down, there are things to see! For island residents, the suburban towns of Aiea, Pearl City, Mililani, and Wahiawa are home. Both routes heading north from Honolulu meet in **Wahiawa,** the island's most central town. The roads cross just near the entrance to **Schofield Barracks,** a warm-up target for Japanese Zeros as they flew on their devastating bombing run over Pearl Harbor.

Wahiawa was of extreme cultural and spiritual importance to the early Hawaiians. In town are **healing stones,** whose mystic vibrations were said to cure the maladies of sufferers. In a field not far from town are the *Kukaniloko,* the royal birthing stones, where the ruling *ali'i* labored to give birth to the future noblemen of the islands. While in town you can familiarize yourself with Oahu's flora by visiting the **Wahiawa Botanical Garden,** or take a quick look at a serene Japanese temple.

As you gain the heights of the **Leilehua Plateau,** sandwiched between the Waianae and Koolau ranges, a wide expanse of green is planted in cane and pineapple. Just like on supermarket shelves, Del Monte's **Pineapple Variety Garden** competes with Dole's **Pineapple Pavilion,** a minute up the road. As a traveler's way station, central Oahu blends services, amenities, and just enough historical sites to warrant stretching your legs, but not enough to bog you down for the day.

WAHIAWA AND VICINITY

Wahiawa is like a military jeep: basic, ugly, but indispensable. This is a soldiers' town, with servicemen from Schofield Barracks or nearby Wheeler AFB shuffling along the streets. Most are young, short-haired, short-tempered, and dressed in fatigues. Everywhere you look are cheap bars, burger joints, run-down discos perfumed with sweat and spilled beer, and used-furniture stores. Route 99 turns into Rt. 80 which goes through Wahiawa, crossing California Avenue, the main drag, then rejoining Rt. 99 near the Del Monte Pineapple Garden. Wahiawa has seemingly little to recommend it, and maybe because of its ugliness, when you do find beauty it shines even brighter.

SIGHTS

Wahiawa Botanical Gardens

In the midst of town is an oasis of beauty, 27 acres of developed woodlands featuring exotic trees, ferns, and flowers gathered from around the world. Located at 1396 California Ave., they're open daily except Christmas and New Year's, from 9 a.m.-4 p.m., admission free. The parking lot is marked by an HVB warrior; walk through the main entranceway and take a pamphlet from the box for a self-guiding tour. When it rains, the cement walkways are treacherously slippery, especially if you're wearing thongs. The nicer paths have been left natural, but they can be muddy. Inside the grounds are trees from the Philippines, Australia, Africa, and a magnificent multihued Mindanao gum from New Guinea. Your senses will be bombarded with fragrant camphor trees from China and Japan, and the rich aroma of cinnamon. Everywhere are natural bouquets of flowering trees, entangled by vines and highlighted by rich green ferns. Most specimens have been growing for a minimum of 40 years, so they're well established.

The Healing Stones

Belief in the healing powers of these stones has been attracting visitors since ancient times. When traveling down Ohai Street (Rt. 80) take a left on California Avenue, and follow it to Kaalalo Place. To glimpse the religion of Hawaii in microcosm, in a few blocks you pass the Riusenji Soto Buddhist Mission, followed by the healing stones, next door to Olive United Methodist Church. If you've never experienced a Buddhist temple, make sure to visit the grounds of **Riusenji Soto Mission.** Usually no one is around, and even if the front doors are locked you can peer in at an extremely ornate altar graced by Buddha, highlighted in black lacquer and gold. On the grounds look for a stone *jizo,* patron of travelers and children. In Japan he often wears a red woven hat and bib, but here he has on a straw hat and muumuu.

An HVB Warrior marks the stones, just past the Kaalala Elementary School, across the street from a beautiful eucalyptus grove. A humble cinder-block building built in 1947 houses the stones. When you swing open the iron gate it strikes a deep mournful note, as if it were an instrument designed to announce your presence

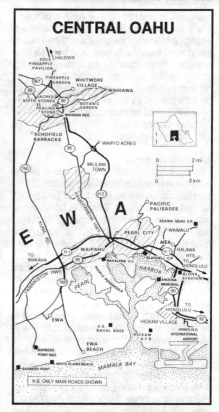

and departure. Inside the building, three stones sit atop rudimentary pedestals. Little scratches mark the stones, and an offertory box is filled with items like oranges, bread, a gin bottle, coins, and candy kisses. A few votive candles flicker before a statue of the Blessed Virgin.

Kukaniloko, The Birthing Stones

Follow Rt. 80 through town for about a mile. At the corner of Whitmore Avenue is a red light: right takes you to Whitmore Village and left puts you on a dirt track that leads to another eucalyptus grove marking the birthing stones. About 40 large boulders are in the middle of a field with a mountain backdrop. One stone looks like the next, but on closer inspection you see that each has a personality. The royal wives would come here, assisted by both men and women of the ruling *ali'i,* to give birth to their exalted offspring. The baby's umbilical cord, a sacred talisman, would be hidden in the cracks and crevices of the stones. Near the largest palm tree is a special stone that appears to be fluted all the way around, with a dip in the middle. It, along with other stones nearby, seem perfectly fitted to accept the torso of a woman in a reclining position. Notice that small fires have been lit in the hollows of these stones, and that they are discolored with soot and ashes.

Schofield Barracks

Stay on Rt. 99, skirt Wahiawa to the west, and go past the entrance to Schofield Barracks. Schofield Barracks dates from the turn of the century, named after Gen. John Schofield, an early proponent of the strategic importance of Pearl Harbor. A sign tells you that it is still the "Home of the Infantry, Tropic Lightning." If you enter here through the McComb Gate, you can visit the **Tropic Lightning Museum** with memorabilia going back to the War of 1812. There are planes from WW II, Chinese rifles from Korea, and deadly *pungi* traps from Vietnam.

The museum has lost many of its exhibits in recent years. They've been taken to the Army Museum in Waikiki. But the base is still interesting to visit and remains one of the prettiest military installations in the world. With permission, you can proceed to the Kolekole Pass, from where you get a sweeping view of inland and coastal Oahu. While heading north on 99 as you pass Schofield Barracks, notice a few run-down shops about 50 yards past the entrance. Stop here and look behind the shops at a wonderful still life created by the Wahiawa Reservoir (good fishing, see p. 185).

Pineapples

A few minutes past the entrance to Schofield Barracks, Rt. 803 bears left to Waialua, while Rt. 99 goes straight ahead and begins passing rows of pineapple. At the intersection of Rt. 80 the **Del Monte Variety Garden.** You're free to wander about and read the descriptions of the history of pineapple production in Hawaii, and of the genetic progress of the fruit made famous by the islands. This exhibit is much more educational and honest than the **Dole Pineapple Pavilion** just up the road, the one with all the tour buses lined up outside. You too can enter and pay $1.50 for a sad little paper plate half filled with pineapple chunks. Or how about $.60 for a glass of canned pineapple juice from a dispenser that you'd find in any fast-food store. Unless the pineapple harvest has been abundant, you can't even buy a fresh fruit, and when you can, they're no cheaper or fresher than those in any grocery store. The Dole Pineapple Pavilion is firmly entrenched along the tourist route, but as a positive public relations scheme it is a blunder!

PRACTICALITIES

Food And Shopping

Kemoo Farm at 1718 Wilikina Dr., tel. 621-8481, just past the entrance to Schofield Barracks, has been a *kamaaina* favorite since 1935. The restaurant has a soothing bucolic feeling, perched on the banks of manmade Wahiawa Reservoir. Servings are family style with homemade bread, fresh trout, and rich gravies dolloped over roast beef or duck. Sunday and Wednesday feature a brunch complete with island entertainment. Reservations are necessary for these days, and advisable for the remainder of the week. Dinner and drinks for two runs about $50.

Dot's Restaurant, off California Ave. at 130 Mango St., tel. 622-4115, is a homey restaurant specializing in American-Japanese food that gives a good square meal for your money. The interior is a mixture of Hawaiian/Oriental in dark brown tones. Lunch specials include butterfish, teriyaki chicken, pork, or beef plates all for around $4.50. Miso soup is $2, and simple Japanese dishes go for about $3.50. The most expensive item on the menu is steak and lobster for $15. Dot's is nothing to write home about, but you definitely won't go hungry.

If you're into fast foods, no problem. The streets are lined with **Jack in the Box,** elbowing **Ronald McDonald,** who's trying to outflash the old **Burger King.**

The streets of Wahiawa are lined with stores that cater to residents, not tourists. This means that the prices are right, and if you need supplies or necessities, this would be a good place to stock up. On the corner of California and Oahi streets is a **Coronet Store,** an old-fashioned five and dime, where you can buy anything from suntan lotion to a crock pot. The **Big Way Supermarket** is at the corner of California and Kilani avenues.

AIEA, PEARL CITY, AND VICINITY

The twin cities of Aiea and Pearl City, except for the USS Arizona Memorial and perhaps a football game at Aloha Stadium, have little to attract the average tourist. Mainly they are residential areas for greater Honolulu, and for the large numbers of military families throughout this area.

PEARL HARBOR: USS *ARIZONA* MEMORIAL

Even as you approach the pier from which you board a launch to take you to the USS *Arizona,* you know that you're at a shrine. Very few spots in America carry such undeniable emotion so easily passed from one generation to another: here, Valley Forge, Gettysburg, not many more. On that beautiful, cloudless morning of December 7, 1941, at one minute before 8 o'clock, the United States not only entered the war, but lost its innocence forevermore.

The first battle of WW II for the U.S. actually took place about 90 minutes before Pearl Harbor's bombing when the USS *Ward* sank an unidentified submarine sliding into Honolulu. In Pearl Harbor, dredged about 40 years earlier to allow superships to enter, the heavyweight champions of America's Pacific fleet were lined up flanking the near side of Ford's Island. The naive deployment of this "Battleship Row" prompted a Japanese admiral to remark that never, even in times of maximum world peace, could he dream that the military might of a nation would have its unprotected chin stuck so far out, just begging for a right cross to the jaw. When it came, it was a roundhouse right, whistling through the air, and what a doozy!

Well before the smoke could clear and the last explosion stopped rumbling through the mountains, 3,581 Americans were dead or wounded, six mighty ships had sunk into the ooze of Pearl, 12 others stumbled around battered and punch-drunk, and 347 warplanes were useless heaps of scrap. The Japanese fighters had hardly broken a sweat, and when their fleet, located 200 miles north of Oahu, steamed away, the "east wind" had indeed "rained." But it was only the first squall of the American hurricane that would follow.

Getting There

There are a few options on how to visit Pearl Harbor and the USS Arizona Memorial. If you're driving, the entrance is along Rt. 99, the Kamehameha Highway, about a mile south of Aloha Stadium; well-marked signs direct you to the parking area. If you're on H-1 west, take exit 15A, and follow the signs. You can also take TheBus, nos. 50, 51, and 52 from Ala Moana Center, or no. 20 Airport, from Waikiki, and be dropped off within a minute's walk of the entrance. Depending upon stops and traffic, this can take well over an hour. **Arizona Memorial Shuttle Bus,** a private operation from Waikiki, takes about 20 minutes and will pick you up at your hotel, tel. 926-4747, about $2.50 one way, reservations necessary. Returning, no reservations are necessary; just buy a ticket from Gloria, the lady selling them under the green umbrella in the parking lot.

The **Arizona Memorial Visitor Center** is a joint venture of the U.S. Park Service and the Navy, and is free! The Park Service runs the theater and museum, and the Navy operates the shuttle boats that take you out to the memorial shrine. The complex is open daily except Mondays from 8 a.m. to 3 p.m., when you can visit the museum and the theater, and take the shuttle boats out to the memorial. If the weather is stormy, or waves rough, they won't sail so call 422-0561 or 422-2771. As many as 3,000 people visit per day, and your best time to avoid delays is before 9:30 a.m. Also, a number of boats operate out of Kewalo Basin doing **Pearl Harbor Cruises.** Costing about $10 for an extensive tour of Pearl Harbor, they are not allowed to drop passengers off at the memorial itself.

Bookstore And Theater

As you enter, you're handed a numbered ticket. Until it's called, you can visit the bookstore/gift shop and museum. The bookstore specializes in volumes on WW II and Hawaiiana. The museum is primarily a pictorial history, with a strong emphasis on the involvement of Hawaii's Japanese citizens during the war. There are instructions of behavior to "all persons of Japanese ancestry," from when bigotry and fear prevailed early in the war, as well as documentation of the

Under attack: The Japanese attack on Pearl Harbor set off a chain of events which would make the U.S. the domineering power of the Pacific.
NATIONAL ARCHIVES

442nd Batallion, made up of Japanese soldiers, and their heroic exploits in Europe, especially their rescue of Texas's "lost batallion." Preserved newspapers of the day proclaim the "Day of Infamy" in bold headlines.

When your number is called you proceed to the comfortable theater where a 20-minute film includes actual footage of the attack. The film is historically factual, devoid of an overabundance of flag waving and mom's apple pie. After the film you board the launch: no bare feet, no bikinis or bathing suits, but shorts and shirts are fine. Twenty years ago visitors wore suits and dresses as if going to church!

The Memorial
The launch, a large vessel handled and piloted with professional deft usually by women Naval personnel, heads for the 184-foot-long alabaster memorial straddling the ship that still lies on the bottom. Some view the memorial as a tombstone; others see it as a symbolic ship, bent by struggle in the middle, but raised at the ends pointing to glory. The USS *Arizona* became the focus of the memorial because her casualties were so severe. When she exploded, the blast was so violent that it lifted entire ships moored nearby clear out of the water. Less than nine minutes later, with infernos raging and huge hunks of steel whizzing through the air, the *Arizona* was gone. Her crew went with her; nearly 1,100 men were sucked down to the bottom, and only 289 somehow managed to struggle to

the surface. To the left and right are a series of black and white moorings with the names of the ships tied to them on the day of the attack.

The deck of the memorial can hold about 200 people; a small museum holds the ship's bell, and a chapel-like area displays a marble tablet with the names of the dead. Into a hole in the center of the memorial, flowers and wreaths are dropped on special occasions. Part of the superstructure of the ship still rises above the waves, but it is slowly being corroded away by wind and sea water. The flag, waving overhead, is attached to a pole anchored to the deck of the sunken ship. Sometimes, on weekends, survivors from the attack are aboard to give firsthand descriptions of what happened that day. Many visitors are Japanese nationals, who often stop and offer their apologies to these Pearl Harbor survivors, distinguished by special military-style hats. The Navy ordered that any survivor wishing to be buried with his crew members had that right. In 1982 a diver took a stainless-steel container of the ashes of one of the survivors to be laid to rest with his buddies.

Nearby Attractions
The **USS *Bowfin*,** a WW II submarine moored within walking distance of the *Arizona* Memorial Center, has been turned into a self-guiding museum. It's open from 9:30 a.m.- 4:30 p.m., admission $3 adults, $1 children ages 6-12. In the little compound leading to the sub is a snack bar with some tables, a few artillery pieces, and a

torpedo or two. As you enter, you're handed a telephone-like receiver; a recorded transmitted message explains about different areas on the sub. The deck is made from teak wood, and the deck guns could go fore or aft depending on the skipper's preference. You'll also notice two anchors; one, under a fresh coat of paint was salvaged from the pink sub used in the film *Operation Petticoat.*

As you descend, you feel as if you are integrated with a machine, a part of its gears and workings. In these cramped quarters of brass and stainless steel lived 90 to 100 men, all volunteers. Fresh water was in short supply, and the only man allowed to shower was the cook. Officers were given a dipper of water to shave with, but all the other men grew beards. With absolutely no place to be alone, the men slept on tiny stacked shelves, and only the officers could control their light switches. The only man to have a miniscule private room was the captain.

Topside, twin 16-cylinder diesels created unbelievable noise and heat. A vent in the passageway to the engine room sucked air with such strength that if you passed under it, you'd be flattened to your knees. When the sub ran on batteries under water, the quiet became maddening. The main bunk room, not much bigger than an average bedroom, slept 36 men. Another 30 or so ran the ship, while another 30 lounged. There was no night and day, just shifts. Coffee was constantly available, as well as fresh fruit, and the best mess in all the services. Subs of the day had the best radar and electronics available. Aboard were 24 high-powered torpedoes, and ammo for the topside gun. Submariners, chosen for their intelligence and psychological ability to take it, knew that a hit from the enemy meant certain death. The USS *Bowfin* is fascinating and definitely worth a visit.

The Navy holds an **open house** on one of its ships berthed at Pearl Harbor on the first Saturday of each month. For information call 474-8139. You must enter through the main Nimitz Gate, and then follow the signs to the ship, which is usually at the Bravo or Mike piers. On your way to the docking area you stop at the Family Services area where you can pick up some snacks or ice cream at a Baskin-Robbins concession. The sailors conducting the tour are polite and knowledgeable, and the tour is free. Those never in the service can always spot the

officers—the guys with the white shoes. Take TheBus to the Nimitz Gate, or if you've visited the *Arizona* Memorial, a convenient shuttle connects for only $.50.

The **Pacific Submarine Museum** is also reached through the Nimitz Gate. It's free but you need a pass from the gate. It's open Wed.-Sun. 9:30 a.m.- 5 p.m., tel. 471-0632.

BEACHES AND SIGHTS

As you travel up Aiea Heights Road, an exit off H-1, you get a world-class view of Pearl Harbor below. It's not glorious because it is industrialized, but you do ride through suburban sprawl Hawaiian style until you come to the end of the road at **Keaiwa Heiau State Recreation Area.** In the cool heights above Aiea Town, these ancient grounds have a soothing effect the minute you enter. Overnight tent camping is allowed here, with exceptionally large sites (permit needed, see page 159); for the few other visitors, the gates open at 7 a.m. and close at 6:30 p.m. As you enter the well-maintained park (a caretaker lives on the premises), tall pines to the left give a feeling of alpine coolness. Below, Pearl Harbor lies open, like the shell of a great oyster.

Keaiwa Heiau was a healing temple, surrounded by gardens of medicinal herbs tended by Hawaii's excellent healers, the *kahuna lapaau.* From the gardens, roots, twigs, leaves, and barks were ground into potions and mixed liberally with prayers and love. These potions were amazingly successful in healing Hawaiians before the white man brought his diseases. Walking onto the stone floor of the *heiau,* it's somehow warmer and the winds seem quieter. Toward the center are numerous offerings, simple stones wrapped with a *ti* leaf. Some are old, while others are quite fresh. Follow the park road to the **Aiea Loop Trail,** which heads back 4½ miles roundtrip onto one of the ridges descending from the Koolaus. Pass through a forest of tall eucalyptus trees, viewing canyons to the left and right. Notice, too, the softness of the "spongy bark" trees growing where the path begins. Allow three hours for the loop.

Blaisdell Beach Park's waters, which can be considered part of Pearl Harbor, are too polluted for swimming. It's sad to think that at the turn of the century it was clear and clean enough to support oysters. Pearl Harbor took its name from

Waimomi, "Water of Pearls," which were indeed harvested from the oysters and a certain species of clam growing here. Today, sewage and uncountable oil spills have done their devastation. Recently, oysters from the Mainland's East Coast have been introduced, and are being harvested from the mud flats. Supposedly, they're fit to eat. Facilities include a pay phone, tables, and restrooms. Access is off Rt. 99 just past Aloha Stadium and before you enter Pearl City.

Keehi Lagoon Beach Park is also polluted, but some people do swim here. The park is at the northern tip of Keehi Lagoon, at 465 Lagoon Dr., just past the **Pacific War Memorial** on Rt. 92 (the Nimitz Highway). Here are restrooms, picnic facilities, and a pay phone. Local people use the area for pole fishing and crabbing.

PRACTICALITIES

Accommodations

Except for long-term, accommodations are virtually non-existent in this area. Luckily **bed and breakfast** homes provide some alternatives. One of the most interesting is the home of Corry and Helga Trummel, who reside in Pacific Palasades above Pearl City. What started out as a tract house has become a living museum. Helga has been collecting and inheriting art since she was a little girl in prewar Germany. Every nook and cranny has a curio from Europe, Asia, or Hawaii and Helga loves to share her artworks and the fascinating stories of her youth. The first floor is completely dedicated to the guests. There's a music room, a library with a fine collection of books on WW II and the western states, two bedrooms and a separate cottage in the back. Out here too is a small pool, dry sauna, and an observation platform high on the hill. Inside, as you mount the steps to the second floor your're greeted by a wooden statue of a woman with a bowl on her head, original oil paintings, and a grandfather clock, all from last century. Enter the breakfast nook and suddenly you're in a German hunting lodge. The green and white table and benches painted with flowers are over 100 years old. Gaze around to see a stuffed bear, antique sitar, a mountain goat, stag, stuffed ducks, a collection of beer steins, a white moose head, a pronghorn, and a

bar. All in what once was a tract house kitchen! The main house is furnished like a very rich German chocolate cake, maybe not to everyone's taste, but definitely filling. Make reservations by contacting Bed & Breakfast Hawaii (see p. 147 for a full listing).

The **Pepper Tree Apartment Hotel,** at 98-150 Lipoha Pl., Aiea, HI 96701, tel. 488-1993, offers furnished studios and apartments all with complete kitchens and baths, TV, and phones. A laundromat and swmming pool are also available. Many military personel use this facility as temporary housing.

Shopping, Dining, And Services

The main shopping center in Aiea is the **Pearl Ridge Shopping Center,** with hundreds of stores, restaurants, and speciality shops. Prices here are geared toward island residents, not tourists, so you have a good chance of coming away with a bargain.

Buzz's Steak House, 98-751 Kuahao Pl. (at the corner of Moanoloa and Kahumanu), tel. 487-6465, is futuristic, like something a kid would build with an erector set. It'd be perfect if it were down by the sea, where you could see something, but from where it's located you can peer at Pearl Harbor in the distance, or have a world-class view of the freeway. The steakhouse is owned and operated by an old island family whose business grew into a small chain of restaurants from their original location in Kailua. This is one of the remaining three. Buzz's is an institution where islanders go when they want a sure-fire good meal. There's a salad bar and you prepare your own charbroiled steaks and fish. The prices are reasonable.

The **Waimalu Shopping Plaza,** located along Kaahumanu St. between the Kamehameha Hwy. (Rt.99) and the H-1 Freeway, has a small cluster of shops and restaurants. There's a **Times Supermarket,** open 24 hours with its pharmacy and deli, and the **Good Health Store,** open 9 a.m.-7 p.m., Sat. 11 a.m.-6 p.m., selling food supplements and minerals. In the same complex is **Stuart Anderson's Cattle Co.,** tel. 487-0054, open daily for lunch and dinner, lounge until 2 a.m. weekends, serving huge steaks and all the trimmings. Here too is **Melnita's Kitchenette,** tel. 487-2467, with basic and inexpensive Filipino food. Melnita's features Pampango cuisine, open for lunch and dinner, takeout and catering.

Across the road is the **Elephant and Castle Restaurant,** at 98-1247 Kaahumanu, tel. 487-5591, open for breakfast, lunch and dinner. This restaurant has done an excellent job of creating an English-style pub atmosphere. The interior is cool and rich with red velvet, heavy chairs, tapestries, open beams, and a pool table and dart boards in the pub area. Nightly, it's one of the best places for a beer and a chat in the area. The food is good too. For example, try English fish and chips for $4.95, burger platter $5, hot sandwiches $5, soup and sandwich $4.75. Specials on weekends are English prime rib dinner, queen size $10.95, king $14.95, New York steak $14.95, seafood scampi $10.95. Enjoy merry old England, Hawaiian style.

The **Pearl City Tavern,** at 905 Kamehameha Hwy. (corner of Waimano Home Dr.) tel. 455-1045, is *the best* restaurant in the Pearl City/Aiea area. The cuisine is a combination of seafood, steaks, sushi, and mainstream Japanese. They're famous for their "monkey bar," which features rhesus monkeys behind the bar in a glass cage. After a couple of stiff belts some customers mistakenly think that they're looking into a mirror. There's a fish tank bubbling away and a separate tank for live Maine lobsters, a specialty of the house. Choose a table or romantic booth in the huge dining room appointed with Japanese scrolls, a huge lantern, and shoji screens. For lunch try escargot $5.50, seafood *pu pu* $2.15, chef salad $8, shrimp Louie $7.50, or a bowl of Boston clam chowder for only $1.50. Dinner is delicious with a choice of chicken Oriental salad $6, prime rib $15.75, filet of *mahi mahi* $15, or seafood Newburg $15.75. Or choose three different entrees for $25 from: soft shell crab, shrimp and scallops, king crab legs, and roast prime rib. Dinners include won ton soup or salad, potatoes, french bread and butter. Complete Japanese dinners are miso soup, and trimmings, rice and tea, and a choice of any three of the following entrees: broiled fish, sashimi, beef teriyaki, butterfish *misoyaki,* or chicken teriyaki at $17.25 per person. If you're in the Pearl Ridge/Aiea area and want a special night out, this is the place!

triton shell

SOUTHEAST OAHU
KOKO HEAD TO WAIMANALO

It's amazing how quickly you can leave the frenzy of Waikiki behind. Once you round the bend past Diamond Head and continue traveling east toward Koko Head, the pace slackens measurably... almost by the yard. A minute ago you were in traffic, now you're cruising. It's not that this area is undeveloped; other parts of the island are much more laid-back, but none so close to the action of the city. In the 12 miles you travel from Honolulu to Waimanalo, you pass the natural phenomenon of Koko Crater, a reliable blowhole, the most aquatically active underwater park in the islands, and a string of beaches, each with a different personality.

Man has made his presence felt, too. The area has some of the most exclusive homes on the island, as well as Hawaii Kai, a less exclusive project developed by the visionary businessman Henry Kaiser, who 20 years ago created this harbinger of things to come. There's Sea Life Park, offering a day's outing of fun for the family, plus shopping centers, the mostly Hawaiian town of Waimanalo, and Bellows Air Force Base, unused by the military and now one of the finest camping beaches on the island. Besides camping, few accommodations are found out here, and few restaurants. This lack of development preserves the area as scenic and recreational, prized attributes that should be taken advantage of before this sunny sandbox gets paved over.

SIGHTS, BEACHES, AND PARKS

The drive out this way accounts for half of the 360 degrees of what is called **The Circle Route.** Start by heading over the Pali Highway down to Kailua, hitting the sights on the way, or come this way first along Diamond Head Road to Rt. 72 as you make the loop back to the city. The only consideration is what part of the day you'd rather stop at the southeast beaches for a dip. For the most part, the beaches of this area *are* the sights, so both are combined in this one section. The road abounds with scenic points and overlooks. This is the part of Oahu that's absolutely beautiful in its undevelopment. It's hard to find a road on any of the Hawaiian islands that's going to be more scenic than this. At first the countryside is dry because this is the leeward side. But as you approach Waimanalo it gets much more tropical. The road is a serpentine ribbon with one coastal vista after another, a great choice for a joy ride just to soak in the sights. The following listings assume that you follow Rt. 72 from Waikiki to Waimanalo. For beaches between Waikiki and the following, please see p. 271.

Maunalua Bay

Maunalua ("Two Mountain") Bay is a four-mile stretch of sun and surf between Diamond Head and Koko Head, with a beach park about every half mile. The first is **Waialae Beach County Park** in Kahala. Go straight ahead on Kahala Avenue for one minute instead of going left on Rt. 72 to join H-1 on to Haunama Bay. This section is the Beverly Hills of Honolulu, as many celebrities like Tom Selleck and Carol Burnett have homes here. The least expensive home in this section would easily be pushing $1 million. Waialae is a popular windsurfing spot, crowded on weekends. It's a small beach park with basic amenities in a beautiful location where Makapuu Head wraps around and gives the impression that there are two islands off in the distance, but it's just the way Oahu bends at this point.

Next comes **Kawaikui Beach Park.** No lifeguard, but the conditions are safe year-round, and the bottom is shallow, muddy, and overgrown with seaweed. In times past, islanders came to the confluence of a nearby spring to harvest special *limu* that grow only where fresh water meets the ocean. You'll find unlimited access, parking stalls, picnic facilities, and restrooms. Few people use the park, and it's ideal for sunning, but for frolicking in the water, give it a miss.

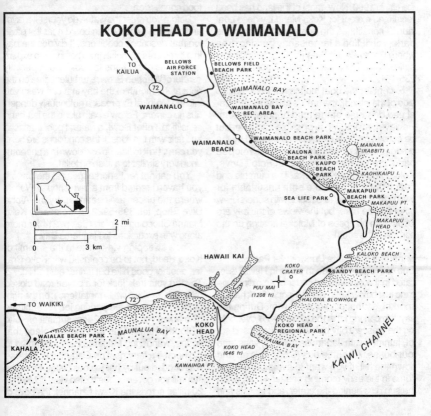

KOKO HEAD TO WAIMANALO

In quick succession come **Niu and Paiko beaches,** lying along residential areas. Although there is public access, few people take advantage of them because the swimming, with a coral and mud bottom, is less than ideal. Some residents have built a pier at Niu Beach past the mudflats, but it's restricted to their private use. Paiko Lagoon is a state bird sanctuary; binoculars will help with sightings of a variety of coastal birds.

The residential area in the hills behind **Maunalua Bay Beach Park** is Hawaii Kai, built by Henry Kaiser, the aluminum magnate. The controversial development was often denigrated as "suburban blight." Many felt it was the beginning of Oahu's ruination. The park fronts Kuapa Pond, at one time a huge fishpond, later dredged by Kaiser who used the dredged material to build the park which he donated to the city in 1960. Now, most of the land has been reclaimed except for Koko Marina, whose boat launch constitutes the primary attraction of the park. You'll find a large sandy parking area where **Paradise Jet Skis** (look for a tent) rents self-powered skis, pricey at $40 per hour, tel. 235-1612.

Except for the boat launch (only one on this side of the island), the area is of little recreational use because of the mud or coral bottom. However, swimming is possible and safe, but be careful of the sudden drops created by the dredged boat channels. Two undeveloped parks are located at the end of Poipu Drive, **Kokee and Koko Kai parks.** The currents and beach conditions make both unsuitable for swimming, but they're popular with surfers. Few others come here, but the views of the bay are lovely with glimpses of Molokai floating on the horizon to the south.

Hanauma Bay State Underwater Park

One of the premier beach parks in Hawaii is located in the sea-eroded crater of an extinct volcano just below Koko Head. People flock here to snorkel, scuba, picnic, and swim. During the day, the parking lot at the top of the hill overlooking the crescent bay below looks like a used car lot, jammed with Japanese imports, vans, and tour buses. A shuttle bus ($.50) runs up and down the hill. If you want to avoid the crowds come in the early morning or after 4 p.m. when the sun dips behind the crater, and tourists and buses leave on cue. There's still plenty of daylight, so plan your trip accordingly. The **Hanauama Express** is a red, white, and black bus that cruises Kuhio and Kalakaua avenues. It comes by about once every 15 minutes and stops at all the major hotels. For $1.50 they'll take you to Hanuama Bay so you can avoid the drive and the hassle with parking once at the bay.

The reef protects the bay and sends a maze of coral fingers right up to the shoreline. A large sandy break in the reef, **Keyhole,** is a choice spot for entering the water and for swimming. The entire bay is alive with tropical fish. Many have become so accustomed to snorkelers that they've lost their fear entirely, and willingly accept food from your fingers—some so rudely you had better be careful of getting your fingers nibbled. The county provides lifeguards, restrooms, showers, picnic facilities, pavilion, and food concession.

Before you enter the water, do yourself a favor and read the large bulletin board near the pavilion that describes conditions. It divides the bay into three areas ranging from beginner to expert, and warns of sections to avoid. Be especially careful of **Witches Brew,** a turbulent area on the right at the mouth of the bay that can wash you into the **Molokai Express,** a notoriously dangerous rip current. Follow a path along the left-hand seacliff to **Toilet Bowl,** a natural pool that rises and falls with the tides. If the conditions are right, you can sit in it to float up and down in a phenomenon very similar to a flushing toilet.

You cannot rent snorkel gear at the park. If you haven't rented from a dive shop in Waikiki where the prices are cheapest, try the Aloha Dive Shop, tel. 395-5922, in the nearby Koko Marina Shopping Center. (See p. 214 for more along with excursions to Hanuama Bay.)

For a sweeping view, hike to the summit of Koko Head, not to be confused with Koko Crater, another good hike but farther east on Rt. 72. To start your trek, look for a paved road closed off to vehicles by a white metal fence, on the right before the road to the parking lot. A 15-minute hike takes you to the 642-foot summit of Koko ("Blood") Head. This was the last place that young, wandering Madame Pele attempted to dig herself a fiery nest on Oahu; as usual, she was flooded out by her jealous sister. From the summit you get an unobstructed view of Molokai 20 miles across the Kaiwi Channel, the bowl of

Hanauma Bay at your feet, and a sweeping panorama of Diamond Head and the Koolau Mountains. Below are two small extinct craters, Nono'ula and Ihi'ihilauakea.

Koko Crater
Koko Crater's official name is Kohelepelepe ("Fringed Vagina"). Legend says that Pele's sister, Kapo, had a magical flying vagina that she could send anywhere. Kamapua'a, the pig-god, was intent on raping Pele, when Kapo came to her aid. She dispatched her vagina to entice Kamapua'a, and he followed it to Koko Head where it made the crater, and then flew away. Kamapua'a was unsuccessful when taking a flying leap at this elusive vagina.

You can either hike or drive to the crater. To begin the hike, look for the road to the "Hawaii Job Corp Training Center" just across from Hanauma Bay. Follow the road down past a rifle range and park at the job training building. Behind is an overgrown tramway track. The remaining ties provide a rough but adequate stairway to the top. At the 1,208-foot summit is an abandoned powerhouse and tramway station. The wood is rotted and the floors are weak! The crater itself lies 1,000 feet below. An easier but less exciting route is to follow Rt. 72 for two miles to Wawamalu Beach near the Hawaii Kai Golf Course, and then take a left on Kealahou Street. En route you pass **Koko Crater Stables,** tel. 395-2628, which offers guided trail rides into the crater. Park your car here, and nearby is a walking path that leads into the crater. On the floor of Koko Crater is a botanical garden that, due to the unique conditions, specializes in succulents.

Halona Cove
As you round a bend on Rt. 72 you come to the natural lookout of Halona Cove, which means "The Peering Place," an excellent vantage point from which to see whales in season. Just before Halona, a sign will point you to the **Honolulu Japanese Casting Club,** with a stone wall and a monument. The monument at one time was of O Jisan, the Japanese god of protection, destroyed by overzealous patriots during WW II. The current monument was erected after the war, and O Jisan was carved into it. Below is a secluded little beach that's perfect for sunbathing. The only way to it is to scramble down the

The lifeguards do a great job at Sandy Beach.

cliff. Swim only on calm days, or the wave action can pull you out to sea and then suck you into the chamber of the famous **Halona Blowhole** just around the bend. There's a turnout at the blowhole for parking. The blowhole is a lava tube at the perfect height for the waves to be driven into it. The water compresses, and the pressure sends a spume into the air. Be extremely cautious around the blowhole. Those unfortunate enough to fall in face almost certain death.

Sandy Beach Park
Sandy Beach is one of the best bodysurfing beaches on Oahu, and the most rugged of them all. More necks and backs are broken on this beach than on all the other Oahu beaches combined. But because of the east-breaking waves, and bottom, the swells are absolutely perfect for bodysurfing. The lifeguards use a flag system to inform you about conditions. The **red flag** means "stay out." When checking out Sandy Beach, don't be fooled by bodysurfers who make it appear easy. These are experts, intimately familiar with the area, and even they are injured at times. Local people refer to the beach as "Scene Beach" because this is where young people come to strut their stuff. This is where the boys are because this is where the girls are. There are restrooms, a large parking area, and two lifeguard towers. Rip-offs have happened,

so don't leave valuables in your car. *Kaukau* wagons park in the area selling a variety of refreshments.

As the road skirts the coastline, it passes a string of beaches which look inviting but are extremely dangerous because there is no protecting reef. The best known is **Wawamalu**, where people come to sunbathe only. Across the road is **Hawaii Kai Golf Course,** tel. 395-2356. You have a choice of two courses: the Championship, offering a full round of golf with beautiful views, challenging holes, and excellent greens; or the Executive, a shorter par-3 course for those with limited time. This is an excellent public course, but the greens fee is high.

Makapuu Beach Park

This beach park is below Makapuu ("Bulging Eye") Point, a projection of land marking Oahu's easternmost point, and a favorite launching pad for hang gliding. Makapuu is *the* most famous bodysurfing beach in the entire state, but it can be extremely rugged; more people are rescued here than at any other beach on Oahu (except Sandy Beach). In winter the conditions are hazardous, with much of the beach eroded away, leaving exposed rocks. With no interfering reef, the surf can reach 12 feet—perfect for bodysurfing, if you're an expert. Board riding is prohibited. In summer, the sandy beach reappears, and the wave action is much gentler, allowing recreational swimming. There are restrooms, lifeguard towers with a flag warning system, and picnic facilities.

Offshore is **Manana** ("Rabbit") **Island.** Curiously, it does resemble a rabbit, but it's so named because rabbits actually live on it. They were released there in the 1880s by a local rancher who wanted to raise them but who was aware that if they ever got loose on Oahu they could ruin much of the croplands. During the impotent counterrevolution of 1894, designed to reinstate the Hawaiian monarchy, Manana Island was a cache for arms and ammunition buried on its windward side. Nearby is tiny Kaohikaipu ("Turtle") Island that, along with Manana, is reserved as a seabird sanctuary.

Sea Life Park

This is a cluster of landlocked tanks holding an amazing display of marine animals that live freely in the ocean just a few hundred yards away. Offshore is Rabbit Island. Admission is $7.75, children ages 7-12 $5, "behind-the-scenes tour" $9, tel. 259-7933, open daily 9:30 a.m.-5 p.m., Fri. until 10 p.m. The best bus to take is #57 from Ala Moana Center, or #58, which comes straight up Kuhio Avenue. The park hosts a variety of shows by trained seals, whales, dolphins, and the Ocean Science Theater. The Hawaiian Reef Tank is a 300,000-gallon fish bowl where you can see the fish being hand fed; Whaler's Cove is where the park's whales perform acrobatics and other tricks.

Outside the entrance turnstile is a shopping complex, and The Galley Restaurant. Also, the **Pacific Whaling Museum** is here and free to the public. It houses one of the largest collections of whaling artifacts and memorabilia in the Pacific. The Whaler's Cove has a replica of a whaling ship called the *Essex Nantucket.* Sea lion food is available, and there's a public feeding daily at 11:30 a.m., 1:30 p.m. and 3:30 p.m., also 5 p.m. on Friday. Sea Life Park is a great learning experience for a family or anyone interested in sealife, especially if you're going to be into snorkeling or scuba.

Kaupo Beach Park

This is the first park that you come to along the southeast coast that is safe for swimming. It is between Sea Life Park and Waimanalo. The park is undeveloped and has no lifeguards, so you must exercise caution. The shore is lined with protective reef or rocks, and the swimming is best beyond the reef. Close to shore, the jutting rocks discourage most swimmers. Surfers frequent Kaupo, especially beginners, lured by the ideal yet gentle wave action.

Kaiona Beach Park

Just before you enter the ethnically Hawaiian town of Waimanalo, you pass **Kaiona Beach Park,** which you can spot because of the semipermanent tents pitched there. Local people are very fond of the area, and use it extensively. Look inland to view some remarkable cliffs and mountains that tumble to the sea. The area was at one time called Pahonu, "Turtle Fence," because a local chief who loved turtle meat erected a large enclosure in the sea into which any turtle that was caught by local fishermen had to be deposited. Parts of the pond fence can still be seen. Facilities include restrooms, showers, and a picnic area. Swimming is safe year-round, and tent and trailer camping are allowed with a county permit.

Waimanalo

This small rural town was at one time the center of a thriving sugar plantation owned by the *hapa* Hawaiian nobleman, John Cummins, who was responsible for introducing rabbits to Manana Island. It has fallen on hard times ever since the plantation closed in the late 1940s, and now produces much of Honolulu's bananas, papayas, and anthuriums from small plots and farms. The town sits in the center of Waimanalo Bay, which is the longest (3½ miles) stretch of sand beach on Oahu. To many people, especially those from Oahu, it is also the best. Few but adequate travelers' services are in town (see "Services" below).

The **Olomana Golf Course,** tel. 259-7926, is a 6,000-yard, relatively easy, par-71 course, inexpensive and close to town. You think you're in Waimanalo when you pass a 7-eleven Store and McDonald's in a built-up area, but that isn't it. You keep going about a mile or two and and then you'll come to the older section of town which is Waimanalo proper.

Waimanalo County Beach Park, as you enter town by the 7-11 and McDonald's, provides camping with a county permit. The beach is well protected and the swimming is safe year-round. Snorkeling is good, and there are picnic tables, restrooms, and recreational facilities including a ball park and basketball courts. This park is right in town, and not secluded from the road. Although the facilities are good, the setting could be better.

Just outside of town is **Waimanalo Bay State Recreation Area,** which remains largely undeveloped, and is much better situated. The access road is hard to spot, but just after McDonald's look for a tall wire fence with the poorly marked entrance in the center. It is good for picnicking and swimming, which can sometimes be rough. The area, surrounded by a dense ironwood grove, is called "Sherwood Forest," due to many rip-offs by thieves who fancy themselves as Robin Hood, plundering the rich and keeping the loot for themselves. Guess who the rich guys are? Fortunately, this problem of breaking into cars is diminishing, but take necessary precautions. This is the best beach on this section of the island.

Bellows Beach County Park, a one-time active Air Force base, is now one of Oahu's finest beach parks, and there's camping too! As you enter a sign warns that "This military installation is open to the public only on the following days: weekends—12 noon Friday to 6 a.m. Monday; federal and state holidays—6 a.m. to 6 a.m. the following day. Camping is authorized in this park by permit from the City and County of Honolulu, Parks and Recreation Board, only." They mean it! The water is safe for swimming year-round, but lifeguards are on duty only during the above-stated hours. Bodysurfing and board surfing are also excellent in the park, but snorkeling is mediocre. Surfboards are not allowed in the area between the two lifeguard towers. After entering the main gates, follow the road for about two miles to the beach area. You'll find picnic tables, restrooms, and cold-water showers. The combination of shade trees and adjacent beach make a perfect camping area. The park is marked by two freshwater streams, Waimanalo and Puha, at either end.

SERVICES

Except for the excellent camping, you're limited when it comes to accommodations in this area. **Hawaiian Family Inns,** a small cooperative of private homes in and around Hawaii Kai, provides European-style bed and breakfast. Each home differs slightly, but most have a private entrance, bath, yard and beach privileges, and some kitchen facilities. Daily rates are a reasonable $35, less during the off-season, with weekly and monthly discounts available. The three homes involved can be reached by calling 395-3710, 395-4130, or 395-8153.

The first place to pick up supplies as you head east on Rt. 72 is at the **Times Super Market** in the **Niu Valley Shopping Center,** located about halfway between Diamond Head and Koko Head. The store is open until 11 p.m., and they have some of the best food prices on the island. **Dave's Ice Cream** and a small restaurant, **The Swiss Inn,** are about all that's here.

Roy's Restaurant, 6600 Kalanianaole Hwy., tel. 396-7697, just before Hawaiikai Dr., features L.A. *nouveau cuisine.* The presentation is very Japanese, colorful, and pleasing to the eye. The crab cake, minced with celery and red bell pepper, flash-fried and served with a cream sauce, is out of this world. The lamb in a deep rich gravy is an excellent choice, or try the blackened *ahi* with a *wasabi* mustard sauce. Reasonably expensive.

Koko Marina Shopping Center

Located along the highway in Hawaii Kai, this center is the largest and easiest access shopping center that you'll find on the way to Hanauma Bay. For photo supplies and sundries, try Thrifty Drugs, Ben Franklin's, Clic Photo, and Surfside Camera. There are two banks, a **Waldenbooks** and a satellite city hall for camping permits (tel. 395-4481). **Foodland** provides most supplies for picnics and camping, and you can dine at Chuck's Steak House, McDonald's, Magoo's Pizza, Baskin-Robbins Ice Cream, Sizzler, Kentucky Fried Chicken, and Kozo Sushi. More expensive restaurants include **Stromboli Ristorante,** with fresh pasta, and **Pacific Broiler,** quite picturesque near the waterway, with salads for under $5, fresh fish dishes for $15, and pastas from $12-15.

The **Aloha Dive Shop** at the Koko Marina is a full-service dive shop. You can rent or buy snorkeling and scuba gear. So if you haven't picked up rentals from Waikiki and you're heading out to Hanauma Bay, come here. They have plenty of different dives. They start at $52 for beginners, certified divers for $62, and certification courses (three days) are $295, featuring all-boat diving at Manalua Bay and Koko Head and Diamond Head.

The Japanese own the Koko Marina Center. In the center are thrill ride (jet-skis, parasails, etc.) booking agencies that will take non-Japanese tourists, but are more for the Japanese tourists who come in here by the bus loads and immediately head out on one of these thrill rides. They've already booked in Japan, so it's all set up and off they go.

Upstairs on the water side of the Koko Marina is **American Sports Ltd.,** tel. 395-5319, that offer jet-skiing, snorkeling, and can book you into parasailing and scuba diving as well. Their special deal is jet-skiing, snorkeling, plus lunch for $49. Lunch is a sandwich and French fries, or for Japanese, *bento* if you prefer.

Waimanalo And Vicinity Practicalities

For a tasty and inexpensive lunch try any of a number of *kaukau* wagons around Sandy Beach. Get basics at **Mel's Market,** where you can pick up almost all camping supplies. Waimanalo town is growing up. As you enter you'll find a **7-11** and **McDonald's.** Keep going for a mile or so to find **Waimanalo Shopping Center** in the middle of town. Here are **Jack in the Box** and two gas stations. You can do all your business, pick up lunch and supplies, and head on down the road or go to the beach. In the shopping center is **visitor information, Woolworth's** and **Waimanalo Market.**

A good little restaurant here is **Waimanalo Cafe,** a down-home place with Naugahyde booths and formica tables selling American standard and Hawaiian foods. The Waimanalo Cafe features an assortment of plate lunches for $5. One of their best, if you're into meat, is an eight-ounce hamburger steak with fried onions, fries, and a salad for $4.95. So you can't beat the prices. The cafe actually has some atmosphere. Overhead are skylights and peculiar open beams painted green. While waiting for your meal walk up to the bar area. The back wall of the bar is loaded with unique bumper stickers. Have a read and a chuckle while your food is being prepared.

Pine Grove Village is an open-air bazaar where local people come to sell handmade products and produce. The majority of items are authentic and priced well below similar products found in Honolulu. Participants and times vary, but a group is usually selling daily until 6 p.m. Some excellent buys include local fruits and vegetables, leis, shellwork, hand-dipped candles, bikinis, jewelry, and leather goods. Price haggling is the norm; when the seller stops smiling, that's about the right price.

WINDWARD OAHU

Oahu's windward coast never has to turn a shoulder into a harsh and biting wind. The trades do blow, mightily at times, but always tropical warm, perfumed with flowers, balmy and bright. Honolulu is just 12 miles over the hump of the *pali,* but a world apart. When *kamaaina* families talk of going to "the cottage in the country," they're most likely referring to the windward coast. In the southern parts, the suburban towns of **Kailua** and **Kaneohe** are modern in every way, with the lion's share of the services on this side. Kailua has Oahu's best windsurfing beach and a nearby *heiau,* preserved and unvisited, while Kaneohe sits in a huge bay dotted with islands and reef. The coastal **Kamehameha Highway** (Rt. 83) turns inland to the base of the *pali,* passing the **Valley of the Temples,** resplendent with universal houses of worship. At **Kahaluu** starts a string of beaches running north, offering the full range of Oahu's coastal outdoor experience. You can meander side roads into the mountains near the Hawaiian villages of **Waiahole** and **Waiakane,** where the normal way of life is ramshackle cottages on small subsistence farms.

The coast bulges at **Ka a awa,** where the **Crouching Lion,** a natural stone formation,

seems ready to pounce on the ever-present tour buses that disturb its repose. Nearby is the **Plantation Spa,** an energized retreat where you can have your cosmic batteries recharged. **Punaluu** is famous for **Pat's,** the only resort in the immediate area, and for **Sacred Falls Park**, a short hike to a peak at Oahu's beautiful and natural heart (if it isn't muddy). Suddenly, you're in manicured **Laie** where Hawaii's Mormon community has built a university, a temple perfect in its symmetry, and the **Polynesian Cultural Center,** a sanitized replica of life in the South Seas, Disney style. The northern tip at Kahuku, site of one of Oahu's oldest sugar mills, is where the **North Shore** begins. Kahuku Point houses two refuges, one for wildlife, and the other for Oahu's only nudist camp, both protecting endangered species from mankind's prying eyes.

It makes little difference in which direction you travel the windward coast, but the following will be listed from south to north from Kailua to Kahuku. The slight advantage in traveling this direction is that your car is in the right-hand lane, which is better for coastal views. But, as odd as it may seem, this dynamic stretch totally changes its vistas depending upon the direction that you travel. You can come one way and then retrace your steps, easily convincing yourself that you've never seen it before. The road is clearly marked with mile markers. They decrease as you head north from Kaneohe on Rt. 83, the Kamehameha Highway. Also see "Camping and Hiking" (pp. 204-209) for trails in the area.

KAILUA AND VICINITY

The easiest way into Kailua ("Two Seas") is over the Koolaus on Rt. 61, the Pali Highway. As soon as you pass through a long tunnel just after Nuuanu Pali Lookout (see p. 232) and your eyes adjust to the shocking brilliance of sunshine, look to your right to see Mt. Olomana. Its 1,643- foot peak is believed to be the volcanic origin of Oahu, the first land to emerge from the seas. Below lies Kailua and the Kawainui Marsh, perhaps the oldest inhabited area on this side of the island. Kamehameha I, after conquering Oahu in 1795, gave all this land to his chiefs who had fought for him. The area became a favorite of the ruling *ali'i* until the fall of the monarchy at the turn of this century. The Kawainui Canal drains the marsh and runs through Kailua. A good vantage point from which to observe it is along Kalaheo Ave., the main road running along the coast in Kailua. Kailua has approximately 45,000 people, technically making it the state's largest windward city. It's developed with shopping centers, a hospital, and the *best* sailboarding beach in the state (see below). For a full description of sailboarding activities at Kailua Beach please refer to "Sports," p. 215. Four golf courses surround the town, and a satellite city hall dispenses camping permits.

SIGHTS

A good touring loop is to continue straight on Rt. 61 until it comes to the coast. Turn on Kalaheo Road, which takes you along the coast to Kailua Beach Park. In the waters offshore will be a spectacle of windsurfers, with their sails puffed out like the proud chests of multicolored birds. To the left of the beach is **Mokapu** ("Sacred Area") **Peninsula,** home of the Kaneohe Marine Corps Base. Notice that the rock that separates the peninsula creates a large natural archway navigable by sizable boats. Most of the little islands in the bay are bird sanctuaries. The farthest, **Moku Manu,** is home to terns and man-of-wars, birds famous for leading fishermen to schools of fish. Up on the coastal bluffs is a gray house with a flat roof, the residence of a local woman called the "Birdlady of Kailua." The woman has a reputation for taking care of any sick or injured birds that people bring to her. The entire home is carved from rock, including the chairs and table. Every once in a while tours are offered to the home for a few dollars. They're irregular, so check the local papers, and you may be lucky enough to be there at just the right time.

Aalapapa Drive gains the heights from the beach and takes you through an area of beautiful homes until you come to **Lanikai Beach.** At one time trees came down to the shoreline, but it has steadily eroded away. The Navy attempted to start a retaining reef by dumping bargeloads of white bath tile just offshore. Their efforts were not successful, but many homes in town now have sparkling new white-tiled bathrooms! As Aalapapa Drive loops back to town, it changes names to Mokulua; a pulloff here affords an expansive panorama of the bay below. By daytime it's enjoyable, but in the evening local kids come here to hang out and drink beer.

Ulupoa Heiau

This *heiau* was dedicated to the Ulu line of *ali'i,* who were responsible for setting up *heiau* dedicated to the sacred birth of chiefs. Oftentimes the umbilical cord was cut just as a drum was sounded, then the cord *(piko)* was placed in a shallow rock depression at a *heiau*. This temple was supposedly built by the legendary *menehune*. The stone craftsmanship is remarkable— measuring 140 feet wide and 30 feet high. Atop the temple is a pathway that you can follow. Notice small stones wrapped in *ti* leaves placed as offerings. To get there, as you approach Kailua on Rt. 61 look for a red light and a 7-eleven store. Turn left onto Uluoa Street, following it to Manu Aloha Street, where you turn right. Follow it to the end and park in the YMCA lot. A small lane leads from here to **Maunawili Falls** (see p. 207).

BEACHES

Along the shoreline of an exclusive residential area, just south of Kailua, sits **Lanikai Beach.**

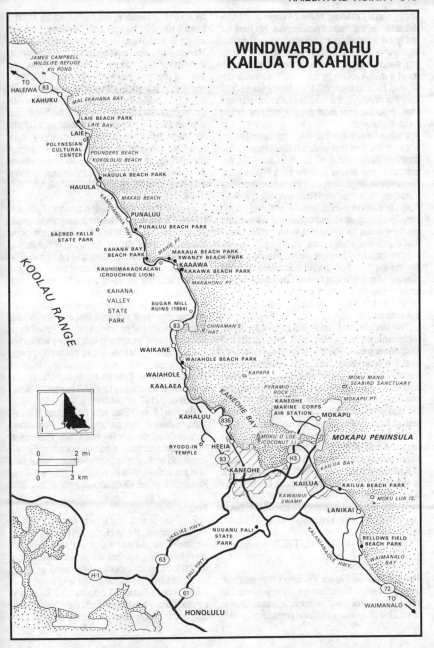

WINDWARD OAHU
KAILUA TO KAHUKU

JAMES CAMPBELL WILDLIFE REFUGE KII POND

TO HALEIWA

KAHUKU

MALEKAHANA BAY

LAIE BEACH PARK
LAIE BAY

LAIE

POLYNESIAN CULTURAL CENTER

POUNDERS BEACH
KOKOLOLIO BEACH

HAUULA BEACH PARK

HAUULA

KAMEHAMEHA HWY

MAKAO BEACH

PUNALUU

PUNALUU BEACH PARK

SACRED FALLS STATE PARK

MAHIE PT.

KAHANA BAY BEACH PARK

MAKAUA BEACH PARK
SWANZY BEACH PARK

KAUHIIMAKAOKALANI (CROUCHING LION)

KAAAWA

KAAAWA BEACH PARK

KAHANA VALLEY STATE PARK

MAKAHONU PT.

SUGAR MILL RUINS (1864)

KOOLAU RANGE

CHINAMAN'S HAT

WAIKANE

WAIAHOLE BEACH PARK

WAIAHOLE

KAPAPA I.

MOKU MANU SEABIRD SANCTUARY

KAALAEA

PYRAMID ROCK

KANEOHE MARINE CORPS AIR STATION

MOKAPU PT.

KAHALUU

KANEOHE BAY

MOKAPU

BYODO-IN TEMPLE

HEEIA

MOKU O LOE (COCONUT I.)

MOKAPU PENINSULA

KANEOHE

KAWAINUI SWAMP

KAILUA BAY

KAILUA

KAILUA BEACH PARK

MOKU LUA IS.

LANIKAI

LIKELIKE HWY

NUUANU PALI STATE PARK

KALANIANAOLE HWY

BELLOWS FIELD BEACH PARK

WAIMANALO BAY

PALI HWY

H-1

HONOLULU

TO WAIMANALO

0   2 mi
0   3 km

Three clearly marked rights-of-way run off Mokulua Drive, the main thoroughfare. No facilities but good snorkeling and swimming year-round, with generally mild surf and a long, gently sloping, sandy beach. The beach runs south for almost a mile, broken by a series of seawalls designed to hold back erosion. Many small craft use the sandy- bottomed shore to launch and land. Popular with local people, but not visited much by tourists.

Kailua Beach Park is the main beach in the area. In the last few years, it has become the sailboarding capital of Hawaii. Local people complain that at one time the beach was great for family outings, with safe conditions and fine facilities. Now the wind has attracted a daily flotilla of sailboarders, kayak racers, and jet-skiers. The congested and contested waters can be dangerous for the average swimmer. Many sailboarders are beginners, so if you're a swimmer, be careful of being run over. The conditions are similar to out-of-control skiers found on the slopes of many mountains. The sailboarding area is clearly marked with buoys, which recently were moved 100 yards northeast, making the area larger.

The park boasts a pavilion, picnic facilities, restrooms, showers, lifeguards, boat ramp, and food concession. The surf is gentle year-round, and the swimming safe. Children should be careful of the sudden dropoffs in the channels formed by the Kaelepulu Canal as it enters the sea in the middle of the beach park. Good surfing and diving are found around Popoi'a Island just offshore. Follow Rt. 61 through Kailua until it meets the coast, and then turn right on S. Kalaheo St. following it to the beach park. For sailboard rentals and instruction see p. 215.

Kalama Beach is reached by making a right onto N. Kalaheo. This beach has no facilities and is inferior to Kailua Beach Park, but the swimming is good, and sections of the beach have been made off-limits to any surf-riding vehicles.

PRACTICALITIES

Accommodations

The **Kailua Beachfront Vacation Homes** offer two completely furnished and ready-to-move-into rental homes with a minimum stay of five days. The one-bedroom home rents for $95-110 for up to four persons, the three-bedroom home from $190-220 for up to six persons. Located along S. Kalaheo, 10 properties from Kailua Beach Park. For peak seasons like Christmas and Easter reservations up to a year in advance are not unusual. Normally reserve three to six months in advance. Homes have telephones, color TVs, beach furniture, parking, maid service on request, and BBQs. The three-bedroom has a full kitchen with electric stove, a large refrigerator, dishwasher, washer and dryer, and all lanai furniture. The smaller house is complete except for dishwasher. For information and reservations write Kailua Beachfront Vacation Homes, 133 Kailuana Pl., Kailua, HI 96734, tel. 261-3484.

One of the finest guest homes in Kailua is **Sharon's Serenity.** This beautiful property sits on a quiet side street fronting the picturesque Kawainui Canal. Sharon goes out of her way to make you feel comfortable and welcome. The fridge is always filled with cold beer and soft drinks, and the coffee is always fresh-perked. Sharon also takes the time to sit with you, giving advice on where to dine, what to see, and a candid description of activities that are worthwhile. The meticulously clean, and beautifully appointed home features guest rooms with color TV, a spacious family room, swimming pool, lanai, and beautiful views of the *pali* and the bay. Sharon's Serenity is an excellent choice. To make reservations contact B&B Honolulu Statewide (see p. 147 for details.)

Pacific Hawaii Bed and Breakfast lists private homes in and around Kailua. Rates and homes differ dramatically, but all are guaranteed to be comfortable and accommodating. For information and location, write Pacific Hawaii Bed and Breakfast, 970 N. Kalaheo, Suite A-218, Kailua 96734, tel. (800) 999-6026 or 262-6026.

Food

For a quick snack at a juice bar try **Vim and Vigor,** a small island chain with a half dozen stores. This one's at the corner of Kailua Rd. and Hahani St., tel. 262-9911. Besides normal health food items, including Hain products, they serve sandwiches for under $3 and a variety of exotic smoothies for $1.50. Bread choices are whole grain, nine-grain, and pita. Open Mon.-Sat. 9 a.m.-5 p.m., Sun. 10 a.m.-4 p.m.

The **Kailua Shopping Center,** 540 Kailua Rd., has one of the very best restaurants in Kailua for value in the **Barbecue East,** tel. 262-8457, open Mon.-Sat. 11 a.m.-9 p.m., Sun. 1-9 p.m., last Sun. of the month 5-9 p.m. The prices are terrific, the service friendly, and the food is delicious in this formica and linoleum decor restaurant. It's really an international potpourri that Hawaii is famous for because with every plate you get Korean kimchi, Japanese miso soup, Hawaiian fish, American macaroni salad, and a bit of coleslaw. If that's not all the peoples of Hawaii accounted for, then what is? Specials include *ahi jun* or teriyaki, butterfish, or scallops *jun* for $6.95. The sashimi special is *ahi* sashimi with fried scallop, fried oysters, kalbi beef, barbecued chicken, and sides for $10.75. You can even have a sashimi mixed plate of barbecued chicken and beef, sashimi, and the works for only $7.45. Korean specials are *kalbi* beef, or *pulgogi,* or chicken *mando* and all the trimmings for $8.95. They also serve beer and wine. The best choice for the money in Kailua, but no decor whatsoever.

If you want to save even more, at the other end of the shopping plaza is **Okazu-ya,** just a takeout lunch window, Japanese and Korean style. In the same small complex is **Chef's Grill** Sandwich and Plate Lunch, and a **Baskin-Robbins** for your sweet tooth.

The 100 block of Hekili Street could be Kailua's version of Honolulu's Restaurant Row. Along this street is the **No Name Bar,** tel. 261-8725, just across from the bowling alley. The No Name Bar is for beer-drinking types who want a good meal as well. They have Sunday morning football at 7:30 a.m., and serious Monday night football at 6:30 p.m. Open Mon.-Fri. 3 p.m.-2 a.m., Sat. 11 a.m.-2 a.m., Sun. 3 p.m.-midnight, happy hour is 4-7 p.m., with live entertainment nightly. Choices include salads like cobb salad for $5.50, No-name salad of ham, turkey, Swiss, provolone, eggs, and cukes for $5.95. Mixed plates can be empañadas—fresh-baked pastry filled with chick peas, olives, Cheddar, and spicy Mexican sauce, $4.95, or sausage bread, $4.95 small, $6.50 large. Chili is $2.95., and sandwiches are under $5.

The **Princess Chop Suey** is your basic chop suey joint two doors down from the No Name. Open Mon.-Sat. 10:30 a.m.-9 p.m., Sun. 12-9

p.m., tel. 839-0575. With naugahyde booths and formica tables, everything is under $5.

Next door is **Sisco's Cantina,** tel. 262-7337, featuring complete Mexican cuisine, open 11 a.m.-10 p.m. Sun.-Thurs., 11 a.m.-11 p.m. Fri. and Saturday. Tostadas, tacos, burritos, enchiladas, and chiles rellenos are all under $8. More expensive dishes are shrimp Veracruz $12, fajitas $15.25, for two $18.95. All come with Mexican corn, sautéed Tex-Mex mushrooms and salad. Inside, the south-of-the-border atmosphere is created with hanging piñatas, stucco walls, and blue-tile tables. A minute down the street is **Detroit Italian Deli,** featuring subs and ice cream.

L'Auberge Swiss Restaurant at 117 Hekili St., tel. 262-4835, is *so* continental and one of the finest restaurants on the entire windward coast. Don't miss it. Owned and operated by the Baltzer family, the small dining room is known for crepes stuffed with delicious morsels like crab or mushrooms and garnished with a rich sauce. The fresh fish is excellent, and they sometimes serve Maui rabbit. Appetizers include homemade country paté $6, fresh oysters on the half shell, $7. Soup of the day is $2.50, and salads like hearts of Manoa vinaigrette is $3. The setting is not romantic, but they've done a great job creating a pleasant atmosphere with red and white checkered tablecloths.

Dinner is served Tues.-Sat. 6-10 p.m., Sun. 5:30-9:30, p.m.; for reservations call 263-4663 after 2 p.m. They have light Swiss dinners like bratwurst and *rosti* (pan fried veal-pork sausage with sauteed onions and potatoes) for $8.25, or veal and fresh mushrooms cooked in a cream sauce and served in a pastry shell with rice pilaf and fresh vegies for $8.50. Pasta prepared a different way each day varies in price. Swiss cheese fondue is $9.50, veal *scallopini marsala* is $15, and filet mignon Michelle is $16.50. Treat yourself to desserts like *meringue glace* ($2.75) or a chocolate snowball, a large scoop of ice cream dipped in chocolate and nuts and Kahlua-flavored caramel sauce ($3). Their special is Grandmother's Opfelchuechli, apple slices in liquor, fried in beer batter, dipped in cinnamon sugar, and served with vanilla cream sauce for $3.50. L'Auberge is simply fine dining at its best.

If you're interested in two distinctly different types of food you can try the **Sunshine Cafe,**

124 Oneawa St., tel. 261-0353, just across the street from **Taco Bell.** This former health food eatery is now a full-fledged luncheonette but still has a small selection of health food products. Open Tues.-Sat. 11 a.m.-8 p.m. At dinner they usually do several specials, which could be spinach lasagna, eggplant enchiladas, or spaghetti from $5.95- 6.95. Cindy, the owner, uses organic ingredients whenever available. Other selections are the King Neptune sandwich—tuna salad, tomato, sprouts ($3.75), smoked salmon ($4.95), garden burger (meatless burger patty made from grains, nuts, and cheeses compacted) for $3.75. Mexican twists like tasty tostadas are $4.50, and vegetarian chili is $1.75 up to $5.95 for an extra large; Pele's plate, chili served with brown rice, salad, and a whole wheat roll is $4.50. Cindy specializes in desserts, whipping up cobblers and deep-dish fruit pies sweetened with honey. A great lunch or light dinner for the health-conscious. Next door is **Ching Lee Chop Suey,** a downhome, inexpensive Chinese restaurant where you can have a complete meal for under $5.

Uluniu Street has inexpensive places to eat, one after the other. After making a left from Kuulei Road (Rt. 61) onto Oneawa, a main thoroughfare, turn right onto Uluniu just at the large Kailua Furniture. First is an authentic hole-in-the-wall Japanese restaurant, **Kailua Okazuya.** They specialize in *donburi,* a bowl of rice smothered with various savories. Try their *o yakodon buri,* chicken and egg with vegetables over rice for under $4. They serve plate lunches and a sushi special that can't be beat which includes fresh fish, shrimp, abalone, and octopus for only $5! Next door is **Insam Korean Restaurant,** with more of the same Korean style, and up the street is the **New Chinese Garden,** a basic Chinese restaurant with decent prices. None of these restaurants are remarkable, but will fill you up with good enough food for a very reasonable price.

The address of **Kolohe Restaurant** (Kolohe means "rascal"), at 415-F Uluniu St., open 11 a.m.-6:30 p.m. Mon.-Fri., tel. 261-3050, won't help you much in finding this authentic Hawaiian food restaurant. Instead look for the McDonald's off Kailua Rd., and walk behind across the municipal parking lot. Except for vintage photos of canoeists and old Hawaiiana on the walls, there is no decor, but that doesn't detract from the excellent and inexpensive cuisine. They offer a fixed menu of *kalua* pig, *pipikaula, lomi* salmon, and one-scoop rice for $4.75, along with a variety of mix-and-match combo plates for under $5. It doesn't sound very Hawaiian, but their chopped steak is absolutely delicious. Don't overlook strange-sounding items like fried aku or ahi bones, which are a local favorite. Kolohe Restaurant is the genuine article, and if you want real Hawaiian cuisine this is the best in Kailua.

You'll first notice **Someplace Else,** at the corner of Aulike and Kuule Rd., open 11 a.m.-2 a.m., food service till 10 p.m., no breakfast except Sun. brunch from 9 a.m., tel. 262-8833, because of the huge multicolored umbrellas in the outside patio area. This is Kailua's upscale yuppie restaurant. It's a jungle in there with hanging plants, ferns, and flowers in every nook and cranny. The works of a local artist, Jean Myoko Kuboto, who specializes in *gyotaku,* printmaking using a fish which is covered in ink and then stenciled onto paper, adorns the walls. Throughout the week specials are offered, with Tuesday being "*wahine* night" (girls' night), with $1 drinks, 5 p.m.-closing, and Wednesday is "over the hump night"—10 p.m.-midnight all drinks $1.75. Besides a full bar, there is an array of fruit smoothies for $1.75.

Lunch brings a broiled *ono* sandwich for $6.25, chicken almond salad ($5.25), or crab-stuffed tomato for $7.95. The extensive menu continues with omelettes, and appetizers like escargot ($5.95), stuffed mushrooms ($5.95), and clam chowder, French onion, gazpacho, and soup of the day for under $3. South-of-the-border selections are burritos, chimichangas and the like for around $7. The broiler fires up with top New York steak ($14.95), barbecued ribs ($11.95), and chicken marsala for under $10. If you are looking for a place to "do lunch," or an evening of civilized conversation, don't go anywhere until you've tried Someplace Else.

For Italian try **Florence's,** 20 Kainehe St., tel. 261-1987. Florence has cooked up a few pots of spaghetti over the past 30 years that have kept locals and tourist coming back for more. You receive a full dinner, including minestrone, salad, bread, beverage, a side of macaroni, and the entree of the day for $10. Not only inexpensive but *delicioso!* Open for lunch, too, with savory meatball sandwiches a great choice.

Buzz's Original Steakhouse, at 413 Kawailoa Rd., tel. 261-4661, is really *the* original steakhouse of this small island chain owned by the Schneider family. Buzz's is just across the road from Kailua Beach Park, situated along the canal. This restaurant is an institution with local families. It's the kind of place that "if you can't think of where to go, you head for Buzz's." The food is always good, if not extraordinary. They have top sirloin ($12.95), pork chops ($11.95), chicken teri ($10.75), fresh fish usually about $18, and *mahi mahi* ($11.95). Salad bar is included with all entrees, and separately for $6.95. Everything is charbroiled. A can't-go-wrong choice.

Saeng's Thai Cuisine, at 315 Hahani, tel. 263-9727, open Sat.-Sun. 5- 9:30 p.m., Mon.-Fri. 11 a.m.-2:30 p.m. and again from 5-9:30, offers spicy Thai food with an emphasis on vegetarian meals. Appetizers and starters are Thai crisp noodles ($4.25), sautéed shrimp ($7.95), salads like green papaya salad ($4.25), *yum koong* (shrimp salad) for $6.95, and chicken coconut soup ($5.95). Specialties include spicy stuffed calimari ($8.95), Thai red curry ($6.95), and à la carte beef, pork, and chicken dishes, all under $6. Vegetarians can pick from mixed vegies with yellow bean paste ($4.95), mixed vegies with oyster sauce ($4.95), or zucchini tofu ($4.95). Saeng Thai is a good change of pace at a decent price.

Orson's Bourbon House, along the main drag at five Hoolai St., tel. 262-2306, is just behind the Burger King on a little side street. This Cajun-style restaurant prepares blackened *ahi,* a medium-rare fish, (wonderful as appetizer, but can do as an entree for $7,) fried calamari ($5.95), and *mufaletas* (a sub sandwich New Orleans style). Special of the day could be fresh silver salmon sautéed for $12.50. The decor is fine dining with white starched tablecloths, and fresh flower bouquets, while the bar area is rich with koa wood trim. Nightly entertainment is provided by Joel Kerosaki from Mon.-Thurs., and Carol Atkinson from Fri.-Sun., who perform a mixture of Hawaiian, jazz, and contemporary tunes. A good selection for a quiet dinner.

Captain Bob's Picnic Sail, tel. 926-5077, tours Kaneohe Bay daily and features lunch and all you can drink on its three- to four-hour sail for

$35. You can work off lunch snorkeling or playing volleyball on the beach. The food is passable, but the setting offshore with the *pali* in the background is world class. Captain Bob also has a good reputation for community spirit, often taking local children's groups out on his boats. For most people desiring to see the waters along the windward coast while spending a pleasant afternoon, this is the best bet.

Shopping And Services

These two towns of Kailua and Kaneohe have the lion's share of shopping on the windward coast. You can pick up basics in the small towns as you head up the coast, but for any unique or hard-to-find items, Kailua/Kaneohe is your only bet. The area offers a few shopping centers. The **Windward Mall,** at 46-056 Kamehameha Hwy., Kaneohe, tel. 235-1143, open weekdays 9:30 a.m.-9 p.m., Sat. to 5:30 p.m., Sun. 10 a.m.-5 p.m., is the premier, full-service mall on the windward coast. Besides department stores like Liberty House and Sears, there are shops selling everything from shoes to health foods.

The **Kaneohe Bay Mall** across from the Windward Mall is a little more downhome, and features a Longs Drugs, especially good for photo supplies. The **Aikahi Park Shopping Center** along Kaneohe Bay Dr., at the corner of Mokapu Blvd., is a limited shopping center whose main shops are a Safeway and a Sizzler Restaurant. The **Kailua Shopping Center** at 540 Kailua Rd. also has limited shopping that includes a **Time's Supermarket,** open till 10 p.m., and a well-stocked **Honolulu Bookshop,** tel. 261-1996, open Mon.-Fri. 9:30-9, Sat. 9:30-5:30, Sun. till 5 p.m., for a full range of reading material. There's also a **Cornet Store** along Kailua Ave. for sundries, lotions, and notions, and a **Longs Drugs.**

Thursday mornings bring a **farmers' market** into town for only one hour from 8:50-9:50 a.m. Those in the know arrive early to get a number at their favorite stalls, which can sell out within minutes of opening. Great for fresh flowers and fruits.

You might pick up an heirloom at **Heritage Antiques,** daily 10-5:30, at the corner of Kailua Rd. and Amakua St., tel. 261-8700, which is overflowing with Oriental, Hawaiian, and Americana antiques. Here too are **jewelers,** H.W.

Roberts and J.K. Phillips, who specialize as gemologists as well.

You'll find just about anything at **Holiday Mart** on Hahani Road., or picnic supplies at the landmark **Kalapawai Store,** at the corner of Kailua and Kalaheo roads, which marks the best entrance to Kailua's sailboarding beaches.

Campers can reach the **satellite city hall** for information and permits by calling 261-8575. A

post office is at the corner of Kailua and Hahani, just across from the Hawaiian National Bank. Medical aid is available from **Castle Medical Center,** tel. 261-0841. A local **colonics therapist,** tel. 261-4511, is Alcyone at 122 Oneawa St., who specializes in detoxification programs and massage, and **Family And Urgent Medical Care** is at 660 Kailua Rd., tel. 263-4433.

KANEOHE AND VICINITY

The bedroom community of Kaneohe ("Kane's Bamboo") lies along Kaneohe Bay, protected by a huge barrier reef. Within the town is **Hoomaluhia Regional Park,** so large that guided hikes are offered on a daily basis. Offshore is Moku o' Loe, commonly called **Coconut Island.** It became famous as the opening shot in the TV show "Gilligan's Island," although the series itself was shot in California. In ancient times, it was kapu and during WW II served as an R&R camp for B-29 crews. Many of the crews felt the island had bad vibes, and reported having a streak of bad luck. In recent times, Frank Fasi, Honolulu's mayor, suggested that Hawaii's gate-crashing guests, Ferdinand and Imelda Marcos, should lease Coconut Island. It never happened.

SIGHTS

In the northern section of town is **He'eia Pier,** launching area for the *Coral Queen,* tel. 247-0375, a glass-bottomed boat that sails throughout the bay. It's a popular attraction, so make reservations. Fortunately, in recent years, the once crystal-clear bay, which was becoming murky with silt because of development, is clearing again due to conservation efforts.

A sandbar has been building in the center of Kaneohe Bay that has made a perfect anchorage for yachts and powerboats. These boat people drop anchor, jump off, and wade to the bar through waist-deep, clear waters. It has become an unofficial playground where you can fling a Frisbee, drink beer, fly a kite, or just float around. Part of the sandbar rises above the water and some BBQ chefs even bring their hibachis and have a bite to eat. Surrounding you is Kaneohe Bay with Chinaman's Hat floating off to your right, and a perfect view of the *pali*

straight ahead. The epitome of *la dolce vita,* Hawaiian style.

Senator Fong's Plantation, at 47-285 Pulama Rd., Kaneohe 96744 (near Kahaluu), tel. 239-6775, open daily 9 a.m.-4 p.m., for guided tram tours, adults $6.50, children $3, under five free. Hawaii's newest attraction is a labor of love created by Senator Hiram Fong, who served as the state senator from 1959 to 1976. Upon retirement he returned to his home, and ever since has been beautifying his gardens started over 35 years ago. The result is 725 acres of natural beauty.

For a fun-filled day on Kaneohe Bay, far from the crowds of Waikiki, try **North Bay Boat Club's** "A Day on the Bay," located on the grounds of Schrader's Windward Marine Resort, 47-039 Lihikai Dr., Kaneohe, tel. 239-5711, ext. 112. "Your day" includes hotel pick-up, BBQ lunch, open bar, sailboarding, kayaking, snorkeling, and sailing. Scuba introductory dives and jet-ski rides are also available at extra cost from **Wave Riders of Kaneohe,** tel. 239-5711, who offer a self-propelled tour around the bay on a jet-ski for $40 per hour, or $60 for two people for an hour.

All Hawaii Cruises, tel. 926-5077, features a snorkel/sail with Captain Bob, who has an excellent reputation with local people. Your adventure includes hotel pick-up, BBQ lunch, open bar, a four-hour sail, glass-bottom viewing, and reef walking. This is an excellent opportunity to view the awesome beauty of the windward coast.

BEACHES

Kaneohe Bay offers **Kaneohe Beach Park, He'eia State Park,** and **Laenani Beach Park,** all accessible off Rt. 836 as it heads northward

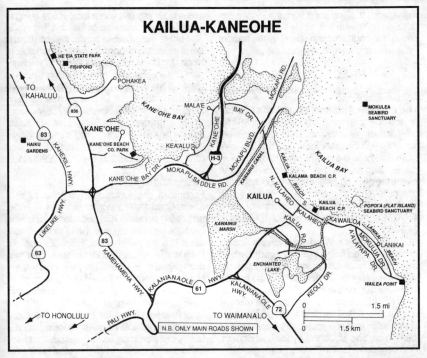

along the coast. All are better for the views of Kaneohe Bay than for beach activities. They have restrooms and a few picnic tables. The water is safe year-round, but it's murky and lined with mudflats and coral heads. The same conditions hold true for **Waiahole Beach Park** about four miles north, but this area is much less developed, quieter, and good for beachcombing.

He'eia State Park lies along Rt. 836 between Kaneohe and Kahaluu and is designated as an "interpretive park." It sits high on Kealohi Point overlooking He'eia Fishpond below. Kealohi translates as "The Shining," because it was a visible landmark to passing voyagers, but there is a much deeper interpretation. To the Hawaiians this area was a "jumping-off point into the spirit world." It was believed that the souls of the recently departed came to this point and leapt into eternity. The right side, He'eia-kei, was the side of light, while the left side, He'eia-uli, was the domain of darkness. The wise *kahuna* taught that you could actually see the face of God in the brilliant sun as it rises over the point.

On the grounds are a main hall, pavilion, restrooms, and various short walks around the entire area with magnificent views of Kaneohe Bay. The park contains numerous indigenous plants and mature trees, the perfect laboratory for the educational goals set by The Friends of He'eia State Park. As an interpretive park, programs are offered for the community and visitors alike. Bernadette Lono, the Director of Hawaiian Studies, gives personal tours of the area. Her family has been part of this *ahuapua* (ancient land division) for countless generations. Bernadette first acquaints you with the area by asking you to sit Hawaiian style on the grass. The earth or *aina* is fundamental to the Hawaiian belief system, and you should start connected to it. She goes on to explain the symbiotic relationship between inland farmers whose fields stretched to Eolaka, the top of *pali,* and the fishermen who plied the waters of Mokapu on the other side of the peninsula.

Below, He'eia Fishpond is now privately owned by a Mr. Brooks, who has taken over the management of the pond from the Bishop Estates on a 20-year lease. He will raise mullet *(ama),* the traditional fish raised by the ancient Hawaiians and *kapu* to all except the *ali'i.*

PRACTICALITIES

Accommodations

The **Bayview Apartment Hotel** has fully furnished one- and two-bedroom units at $64 for one bedroom, $82 for two. Three-day minimum stay, but you can stay for one or two if there's room. The hotel is a no-frills cinderblock building that is clean and friendly. There's parking, TV, swimming pool, no in-room phones, but an intercom calls you to the front desk. For reservations and information write Bayview Apartment Hotel, 44-707 Puamohala St., Kaneohe, HI 96744, tel. 247-3635.

The **Schrader's Windward Marine Resort** in Kaneohe has fully furnished apartments. It calls itself "a small rural resort," and although not far from city lights, it's definitely off the beaten track—literally on the edge of Kaneohe Bay, so close that it boasts fishing from the lanai of some apartments. Follow Rt. 836 from Kahaluu for a few minutes until you spot the Pineapple Hut (a tourist trap) and St. John's by the Sea Church. Turn here down Lihikai Drive to the resort.

There are 53 units here, but they differ greatly as they sprawl along the bay. The gray building, a housing project clone along the road front, is part of the place, and oddly enough are some of the most expensive units at $85-100 per night. All units have living rooms, color TV, phones, daily maid service, refrigerators and air-conditioning, but only 19 have stoves and these rent for $65-200 per night. The least expensive with a full kitchen is $65. The rooms are spotless but old. Because of the age of the building, it's as if you've gone back 30 years to old Hawaii. The resort houses a fair number of TLA people (Temporary Lodging for Military). This is the only place for them to stay on the island.

The best deal for the money is a one-bedroom away from the road and facing the bay. If you call

and specify any unit with a lanai you're going to get at least a partial view of the bay. The resort also offers motorboats, kayaks, sailboards, and small sailboats through its sister organization, North Bay Boat Club. Get a break at Wave Runners of Kaneohe (jet-skis) and Twilight Cruise, a narrated cruise of the bay every Tuesday evening on a pontoon boat. Discounts offered on long stays, in a package deal with Thrifty car rental.

For information write Schrader's Windward Marine Resort, 47-039 Lihikai Dr., Kaneohe, HI 96744, tel. (800) 367-8047, ext. 239, Canada (800) 423-8733, ext. 239, on Oahu 239-5711.

Dining And Nightlife

Fortunately, or unfortunately, Kaneohe is a bit of a wasteland as far as tourist services, nightlife, and eating out are concerned. Most people who live here head for the action in Honolulu. There are a few limited choices. Recently opened **Falia's** serves steak and lobster in their medium-priced dining room. They also offer vintage Hawaiian music with Blah Pahi Nui, who plays excellent slack-key guitar. **Fuji's Delicatessen,** at 45-270 Wm. Henry Rd., tel. 235-3690, is a local favorite known for its downhome Japanese, Korean, and Hawaiian cooking served family style on long communal tables. **Marie Callender's,** a national chain, has a restaurant at 46-056 Kamehameha Hwy., tel. 235-6655, and serves decent food in a pleasant atmosphere. They also feature Kaleo Okalani, three women with rich voices who harmonize beautifully.

If you're looking for a real cultural experience, head for **Bob's Saimin,** at 46-132-A Kahuhipa St., tel. 247-7878, especially late in the evening where you can get hearty bowls of soup and a selection of barbecued meats for inexpensive prices. The best deal in town is at **Kim Chee One,** at 46-010 Kamehameha Hwy., tel. 235-5560, which has a few sister restaurants scattered around Oahu. The setting is plain, but you'll have trouble finishing the excellent Korean mixed barbecue plate for $6.95, easily enough for two.

KAHEKILII HIGHWAY

Where Rt. 83 intersects the Likelike Highway on the southern outskirts of Kaneohe, it branches north and changes its name from the Kamehameha Highway to the Kahekilii Highway until it hits the coast at Kahaluu. This four-mile traverse passes two exceptionally beautiful valleys: Haiku Valley and the Valley of the Temples. Neither should be missed.

SIGHTS

Haiku ("Abrupt Break") **Gardens** is a lovely section of commercial area that includes a restaurant (see below) and some quiet condominiums. After you pass a community college, Haiku Road is past two red lights. Turn left here and proceed for about one-half mile until you see the entrance. The gardens date from the mid-1800s, when Hawaiian *ali'i* deeded 16 acres to an English engineer named Baskerville. He developed the area, creating a series of springfed lily ponds, a number of estate homes, and planting flowers, fruits, and ornamental trees. Later a restaurant was built, now owned by the Ing family, and the grounds became famous for their beauty, often used for outdoor weddings and special gatherings.

You're welcome to walk through the gardens. Proceed from the restaurant down a grassy area to a pond, where perhaps you'll attract an impromptu entourage of ducks, chickens, and guinea fowl that squawk along looking for handouts. Amidst the lush foliage is a grass shack used for weddings. A path leads around a larger pond whose benches and small pavilions are perfect for contemplation. The path leads under a huge banyan, while a nearby bamboo grove serenades with sonorous music if the wind is blowing.

Valley Of The Temples

The concept of this universal faith cemetery is as beautiful as the sculpted *pali* that serves as its backdrop. A rainy day makes it better. The *pali* explodes with rainbowed waterfalls, and the greens turn a richer emerald, sparkling with dewdrops. Don't miss the Valley of the Temples Memorial Park, 47-200 Kahekili Hwy., tel. 239-8811. Admission is $2 or *kamaaina* rates of $5 per carload, but you have to prove you're from

Hawaii. High on a hill sits a Christian chapel, an A-frame topped by a cross. The views can be lovely from up here, but unfortunately the large windows of the chapel perfectly frame some nondescript tract housing, and a Pay 'n' Save supermarket below. Great planning!

The crown jewel of the valley is **Byodo-In Temple** ("Temple of Equality"), a superbly appointed replica of the 900-year-old Byodo-In of Uji, Japan (depicted on the 10-yen coin). This temple dates from June 7, 1968, 100 years to the day when Japanese immigrants first arrived in Hawaii. It was erected through the combined efforts of an American engineering firm headed by Ronald Kawahara in accordance with a plan designed by Kiichi Sano, a famed Kyoto landscape artist. Remove your shoes before entering the temple. A three-ton brass bell, which you're invited to strike after making an offering, creates the right vibrations for meditation, and symbolically spreads the word of Amida Buddha.

The walls hold distinctive emblems of different Buddhist sects. Upstairs wings are roped off, with no entry permitted. Stand on the gravel path opposite the main temple. You'll see a grating with a circle cut in the middle. Stick your face in to see the perfectly framed contemplative visage of Buddha. Cross a half-moon bridge to the left of the temple and follow the path to a small gazebo. Here a rock, perfectly and artistically placed, separates a stream in two, sending the water to the left and right. The pagoda at the top of the path is called the Meditation House. Go to this superbly manicured area to get a sweeping view of the grounds. In front of the Meditation House is a curious tree; pick up one of the fallen leaves, and feel the natural velvet on the backside.

The grounds are alive with sparrows and peacocks, and from time to time you'll hear a curious-sounding "yip, yip, yip" and clapping hands. Follow it to discover Mr. Henry Oda, who will be surrounded by birds taking crumbs from his fingers, and a boiling cauldron of *koi* in the waters below with mouths agape demanding to be fed. He has taken over for the recently retired Mr. Hisayoshi Hirada, the original "Birdman of Byodo-In." Mr. Hirada translates his first name into "long live a good man," and he, well into his 80s, is living proof. Mr. Hirada began training the birds and carp of Byodo-In after his *first* retirement. He would come daily to feed the fish, clapping his hands while he did so. Soon the Pavlovian response took over. Simultaneously, a small and courageous bird, which Hirada-san calls Charlie, began taking crumbs from his fingers.

Mr. Oda does a great job of showing visitors around, but old-timers say that there is no one like Mr. Hirada, and if he happens to be there while you're visiting, you have been blessed by the great Buddha of Byodo-In. A small gift shop selling souvenirs, cards, and some refreshments is to the right of the temple. If you wish to photograph the complex, it's best to come before noon, when the sun is at your back as you frame the red and white temple against the deep green of the *pali*.

Kahaluu

This town is at the convergence of the Kahekilii Highway and the Kamehameha Highway (Rt. 83) heading north. Also, Rt. 836, an extension of the Kamehameha Highway, hugs the coastline heading down to Kailua-Kaneohe. It offers some of the most spectacular views of a decidedly spectacular coast, with very few tourists venturing down this side road. Kahaluu Town is a gas station and a little tourist trap selling junk just in case you didn't get enough in Waikiki. The Hygienic store sells liquor, groceries, soda, and ice, all you'll need for an afternoon lunch. The Waihee Stream, meandering from the *pali*, empties into the bay and deposits fresh water into the ancient **Kahaluu Fish Pond,** a picture-perfect tropical setting. So picture-perfect is the place that it has provided the background scenery to TV and Hollywood productions such as an episode from "Jake and the Fat Man," a setting for *Parent Trap II,* and the famous airport and village scene from *The Karate Kid.* All of the scenery has been torn down, but you can still overlook the fishpond by taking a short walk just behind the bank in town.

WAIAHOLE AND VICINITY

If you want to fall in love with rural, old-time Oahu, go to the northern reaches of Kaneohe Bay around Waihole and Waikane, a Hawaiian grass-roots area that has so far eluded development. Alongside the road are many more fruit stands than in other parts of Oahu. For a glimpse

of what's happening look for the Waiahole Elementary School, and turn left up Waiahole Valley Road. The road twists its way into the valley, becoming narrower until it turns into a dirt track. Left and right in homey, ramshackle houses lives downhome Hawaii, complete with taro patches in the backyards. Another road of the same type is about one-half mile up Rt. 83 just before you enter Waikane. If you're staying in Waikiki, compare this area with Kuhio Avenue only 45 minutes away!

Route 83 passes a string of beaches, most with camping. Offshore from Kualoa County Park is Mokoli'i ("Small Reptile") Island, commonly called **Chinaman's Hat** (between mile marker 30 and 31) due to its obvious resemblance to an Oriental chapeau. If the tides are right, you can walk out to it (sneakers advised because of the coral), where you and a few nesting birds have it to yourself. Kualoa Park has undergone extensive renovations. There is an expansive parking area, plenty of picnic tables, and a huge grassy area fronting the beach. The road passes through what was once sugar cane country. Most of the businesses failed last century, but you will see the ruins of the Judd Sugar Works a mile or so before reaching Ka'a'awa. The dilapidated mill stands although it was closed more than a century ago. Entering is not advised!

Kualoa County Regional Park

With the *pali* in the background, Chinaman's Hat Island offshore, and a glistening white strand shaded by swaying palms, Kualoa is one of the finest beach parks on windward Oahu. One of the most sacred areas on Oahu, the *ali'i* brought their children here to be reared and educated, and the area is designated in the National Register of Historic Places. It has a full range of facilities and services, including lifeguards, restrooms, and picnic tables. The park is open daily from 7 a.m.-7 p.m., with overnight camping allowed with a county permit (mandatory). The swimming is safe year-round along the shoreline dotted with pockets of sand and coral. The snorkeling and fishing are good, but the real treat is walking the 500 yards to Chinaman's Hat at low tide. You need appropriate footgear (old sneakers are fine) because of the sharp coral heads. The island is one of the few around offshore Oahu that is not an official bird sanctuary, although many shorebirds do use the island and should not be molested.

Because of its exposure to winds, Kualoa is sometimes chilly. Although the park is popular, it is not well marked. It lies along Rt. 83, and if you're heading north, look for a red sign to the Kualoa Ranch. Just past it is an HVB Warrior pointing to the park and Chinaman's Hat. Heading south the entrance is just past the HVB Warrior pointing to the Kualoa Sugar Mill ruins.

PRACTICALITIES

Food And Shopping

The **Haiku Gardens Restaurant,** true to its name, sits surrounded by a fragrant garden in a lovely, secluded valley (see p. 323). The restaurant is undergoing massive renovations and is supposed to open as a Chart House, a chain with an excellent reputation for good food at reasonable prices.

The **Hygienic Store** along Rt. 83 just past the Valley of Temples sells groceries and supplies. It's flanked by stalls selling fruits and shellwork at competitive prices.

Follow the Kahekilii Hwy. to Rt. 83 past Waiahole and Waikane, where you'll find some of the best roadside fruit stands on Oahu. One little stand just near the Waiahole Elementary School (mile marker 34.5) is manned on nonschool days by two young sisters, Zalia and Kahea. Their smiles alone are worth a stop. Just up Rt. 83 is another stand that features drinking coconuts. Do yourself a favor and have one. Sip the juice and when it's done, eat the custard-like contents. A real island treat, nutritious and delicious.

KA'A'AWA TOWN AND VICINITY

SIGHTS

When you first zip along the highway through town you get the impression that there isn't much, but there's more than you think. The town stretches back toward the *pali* for a couple of streets. On the ocean side is **Ka'a'awa Beach Park,** a primarily local hangout. Across the road is the post office, and the **Ka'a'awa Country Kitchen,** which serves breakfast and plate lunches, where you can easily eat for $5. They have a few tables, but the best bet is to get your plate lunch and take it across the street to the beach park. Next door is a **7-eleven** with gas and incidentals. Behind the post office is **Pyramid Rock,** obviously named because of its shape.

Oahu's *pali* is unsurpassed anywhere in the islands, and it's particularly beautiful here. Take a walk around. Stroll the dirt roads through the residential areas and keep your eyes peeled for a small white cross on the *pali* just near Pyramid Rock. It marks the spot where a serviceman was killed during the Pearl Harbor invasion. His spirit is still honored by the perpetually maintained bright white cross. While walking you'll be treated to Ka'a'awa's natural choir—wild roosters crowing any time they feel like it, and the din of cheeky parrots high in the trees. A pair of parrots escaped from a nearby home about 10 years ago, and their progeny are joyfully relishing life in the balmy tropics. If you'd like to mimic one of these fancy-free parrots see **The Plantation Spa** (p. 326) for a uniquely revitalizing experience in Ka'a'awa.

As you come around the bend of Mahie Point, staring down at you is a very popular stone formation, the **Crouching Lion.** Undoubtedly a tour bus or two will be sitting in the lot of the Crouching Lion Inn. As with all anatomical rock formations, it helps to have an imagination. Anyway, the inn is much more interesting than the lion. Built by George Larsen in 1928 from rough-hewn lumber from the Pacific Northwest, the huge stones were excavated from the site itself. The inn went public in 1951 and has been serving tourists ever since (for menu and prices see below).

Ka'a'awa And Kahana Bay Beaches

Three beach parks in as many miles lie between Ka'a'awa Point and Kahana Bay. The first heading north is **Ka'a'awa Beach Park,** a popular camping beach (county permits) with restrooms, lifeguards, and picnic facilities. An offshore reef running the entire length of the park makes swimming safe year-round. There's a dangerous rip at the south end of the park at the break in the reef.

Swanzy County Park, two minutes north, also has camping with a county permit. The sand and rubble beach lies below a long retaining wall, often underwater during high tide. The swimming is safe year-round, but is not favorable because of the poor quality of the beach. Swanzy is one of the best squidding and snorkeling beaches on the Windward coast. A break in the offshore reef creates a dangerous rip, and should be avoided.

Kahana Bay County Park is a full-service park with lifeguards, picnic facilities, restrooms, the area's only boat launch, and camping (county permit). Swimming is good year-round, although the waters can be cloudy at times, and a gentle shorebreak makes the area ideal for bodysurfing and beginner board riders. This entire beach area is traditionally excellent for *akule* fishing, with large schools visiting the offshore waters at certain times of year. It once supported a large Hawaiian fishing village; remnants of fishponds can still be seen. On the mountainside is **Kahana Valley State Park** amidst a mixture of ironwoods and coconut trees. Here are restrooms, fresh water, and picnic tables. Few visit here, and it's perfectly situated for a quiet picnic.

Huilua Fish Pond lies between Ka'a'awa and Punaluu, not far from the Paniola Cafe (about mile marker 25.8). Look to the mountainside for Trout Farm Road and immediately to your right, on the ocean side, is the fishpond. Spot a small bridge and a great launching area for a canoe, kayak, or flotation device. Once in, go left under the traffic bridge. Follow Kahana Stream as it gets narrower and narrower (but passable) as it heads inland. You can even use the overhanging ferns to pull yourself along. It's deep so be aware. If you go to the right, you'll reach the bay. It's fairly safe until you come to open ocean. The-Bus stop is directly across from the launching area so you can get off here, enjoy the sights, and then continue on.

PRACTICALITIES

The Plantation Spa

The Plantation Spa is essentially into three-part harmony . . . of body, mind, and spirit. By itself it can't make you sing, but it can provide the perfect space for you to re-attune to your own deep cosmic melody and, perhaps, with effort, to belt out a few glorious chords by the time you leave.

Plantation Spa

Set on seven lovely acres of what once was the summer estate of Mary King, heiress to Schilling Spices, it was originally created as a retreat, and it still is, but now even more so.

The spa began in 1987 when Bodile Anderson, the owner and operator, brought a long-held dream into reality. For years Bodile had led health seminars throughout Hawaii, taking her guests to various resorts. But something wasn't quite right. Bodile felt that she needed her own place, free from outside influences and interruptions because the tune she taught and the tune she sang was very subtle.

Mostly, Bodile shares her clean and sensible lifestyle with you, and claims that the way she lives is the way she was raised in her native Sweden. She's primarily self-taught, even taking excursions to visit Philippine faith healers, but she learned her basic techniques and philosophy from her friend Ebba Weararland, who, along with her husband Are, were pioneers in the self-health movement begun in Switzerland over 50 years ago.

Bodile is aided by a remarkably knowledgeable, skillful, and diverse staff who have come up with the perfect combination of pampering and working you into shape. In essence they are the *potters* and you are the willing clay. They will create a designer week of exercise (aerobics, hikes, swimming, and more), contemplation, meditation, relaxation, cultural pursuits, and right eating habits. From you they need a desire to show up and some enthusiasm.

The peaceful grounds, kept impeccably by Simaile and Taniella, two Tongan gentlemen, are an ally. You enter off the beach road passing through gates that open onto an expansive lawn that gives a buffer to the outside world. There's an outdoor weightroom, and to the rear of that some change rooms. Here too is a freeform swimming pool complete with jacuzzi to untie muscles, and the melody of a small waterfall to unjangle nerves. The grounds rise behind the main house to the second level, where there's a guesthouse with two separate rooms. If you follow still farther up the hill you come to what was the Orchidarium, which is now used for massage and herbal wraps, so that you emerge as fresh as a daisy.

Food, and its relationship to good health, is emphasized at the spa. The purification process begins with what you eat. If you choose, you can fast for anywhere from one to seven days, and you'll be monitored and counseled along the way. Many people have reported a great weight *loss* while experiencing an energy *gain* while on the spa's special fasting program. For others, meals are wholesome vegetarian, prepared with fresh and basic ingredients. All take a hand in preparing their specialties but the main cooks are Gini Maddocks and all-around hand Jeannine Lundgren, who will be your message therapist and fearless leader on morning beach walks.

Your week at the spa begins with reception and orientation at 4 p.m. on Sunday and ends the following Saturday at 10 a.m. The spa can pick you up at the airport, so don't rent a car. You won't be going anywhere else. All the rooms are the same price, $1250 for seven days, six nights, based on double occupancy, or $1550 for single occupancy. Prices include all meals, activities, facilities, and all normal programs. For reservations and information contact the Plantation Spa at 51-550 Kamehameha Hwy., Ka'a'awa, HI 96730, tel. 237-8685 or (800)422-0307.

The Crouching Lion Inn

There was a time when *everyone* passing through Ka'a'awa stopped at the Crouching Lion Inn. Now "everyone" has become "too many" ever since the tour buses started packing in here for lunch. The Inn, along Rt. 83 in Ka'a'awa, tel. 237-8511, is beautiful enough to stop at just to have a look, but if you wan't a reasonably quiet meal, avoid lunchtime and come in the evening. Dinners are pricey and include *mahi mahi* ($12), fisherman's catch ($20), rack of lamb ($19), or Hawaiian chopped steak ($12). If you're not hungry and just wish to enjoy the rustic inn, the cocktail lounge has lost its liquor license, but you can still order a coffee or soft drink.

PUNALUU AND HAUULA

PUNALUU

When islanders say Punaluu ("Coral Diving") they usually combine it into the phrase "Pat's at Punaluu" because of the famous resort that's been delighting local people and visitors for years (at mile marker 23.2). It's a favorite place to come for a drive in the "country." Punaluu is a long and narrow ribbon of land between the sea and the *pali*. Its built-up area is about a mile or so long, but only a hundred yards wide. It has gas, supplies, camping, and some of the cheapest accommodations anywhere on Oahu (see below). The **Punaluu Art Gallery**, operated by Scott Bechtol, famous candle artist, offers distinctive island art. On the northern outskirts of town, a sign points to **Sacred Falls,** an excellent hike, weather permitting (see p. 208).

A few hundred yards south of Pat's is **St. Joachim Church.** There's nothing outstanding about it, merely a one-room church meekly sitting on a plot of ground overlooking the sea. But it's real, homegrown, where the people of this district come to worship. Just look and you might understand the simple and basic lifestyle that still persists in this area.

The **Punaluu Art Gallery,** in Punaluu around mile marker 24, tel. 237-8325, open daily 10 a.m.-6 p.m., formerly owned by Dorothy Zoler, is the oldest art gallery on windward Oahu. The new owner, candle artist Scott Bechtol, remains dedicated to showcasing the works of an assortment of the finest artists that the North Shore has to offer. Scott is well known for his wonderful sculpted candles, all made from the finest beeswax. Some are lanterns shaped like a huge pita bread with the top third cut off. The remainder is sculpted with a scene that glows when the candle is lit. Others are huge tikis, dolphins, or flowers, all inspired by the islands. There's even a 10-foot whale! Some of the larger candles are $70, the man-size tiki is about $800, but smaller candles are only $5, and Scott's unique "crying tiki" sells for only $20. Scott creates all of this beautiful glowing art with just one precision carving tool . . . a Buck knife!

Other artists shown are Betty Jenks from Ka'a'awa, who does original miniature oils for $20, that are about the size of a compact mirror. Bill Cupit creates "bananascapes." Bill removes the outer bark from the banana tree, then he tears and cuts it to make a scene of boats or mountains. The result is a three-dimensional piece. Bill's wife is an artist who specializes in seascapes made with seaweed. Other beauty is added by Janet Holiday's silkscreen prints, Bruce Clark's woodcarvings, and Peter Hayward's oil paintings. The Punaluu Art Gallery is a jewel case of man-made beauty surrounded by natural beauty. They harmonize perfectly.

HAUULA

This speck of a town is just past Punaluu between mile markers 21 and 22. The old town center is two soda machines, two gas pumps, and two limited supply stores, Masa's and Ching Jong Leong's. Another store, Segarne's, sells cold beer and liquor. At the estuary of a stream is **Aukai Beach Park,** a flat little beach right in the middle of town. A **7-eleven** and a little church up on the hill with the *pali* as a backdrop add the seemingly mandatory finishing touches. Just near the bus stop on the south end, look for a local man who is usually there selling leis. The flowers and vines are fresh-picked from the immediate area, and the prices and authenticity are hard to beat.

Outdoor enthusiasts will love the little-used **Hauula Loop Trails.** These ridge trails head up the valleys gaining height along the way. They offer just about everything that you can expect for a Hawaiian trail, the mountains, the valleys, and vistas of the sea. Built by the CCC during the Depression, the trails are wide and the footing is great even in rainy periods which can shut down the nearby **Sacred Falls Trail.** (See p. 208 for a complete description). At the north end of town is the **Hauula Kai Center,** a small shopping center where you'll find the Lotus Inn Chop Suey, a Pay 'n' Save, Lindy's Food (a supermarket), the Bethlehem Baking Co., and a post office (See p. 330 for more details.)

BEACHES

Right along the highway is **Punaluu County Beach Park.** Punaluu provides shopping and the beach park has restrooms, cooking facilities, camping by permit (recently closed, so check), but no lifeguards. The swimming is safe year-round inside the protected reef. Local fishermen, usually older Filipino men who are surfcasting, use this area frequently. They're friendly and a great source of information for anyone trying to land a fish or two. They know the best baits and spots to dunk a line.

Hauula County Beach Park is an improved beach park with lifeguards, picnic facilities, restrooms, pavilion, volleyball court, and camping (permit). There's safe swimming year-round inside the coral reef, with good snorkeling, and surfing usually best in the winter months. Rip currents are present at both ends of the beach at breaks in the reef, and deep holes in a brackish pond are formed where Maakua Stream enters the sea. Across the road are the ruins of the historic **Lanakila Church** (1853), partially dismantled at the turn of the century to build a smaller church near Punaluu.

PRACTICALITIES

Accommodations
Two institutions at Punaluu are sure to please. Each is in a different economic and social category, but because they're off the beaten track, both offer great value. **Pat's at Punaluu** (mile marker 23.2) is more famous as a restaurant than as condominium apartments, but you'll be pleased with both. Daily rates are $54-62 cottage, $58-66 one bedroom, $102-120 three-bedroom, same rate up to four persons, extra person $10. At Pat's are a magnificent beach,

parking, TV, a fine restaurant, swimming pool, and weekly maid service. They offer a "room 'n' wheels" package, and discounts on long stays. Pat's is off the beaten track, so definitely call ahead to check room availability. Turning up and expecting a room is a foolish maneuver, and remember that this is a condo, not a hotel, so one-night stays are not the norm. Next to the restaurant is a small convenience store that may or may not look open. But inside (separate business) is a small desk, open 8:30 a.m.-1 p.m., where you register. Another rental office on the property is open until 9 p.m., but check-in after that costs extra since someone has to stay around to let you in. For information write Pat's at Punaluu Condo, 53-567 Kamehameha Hwy., Hauula, HI 96717, tel. 293-8111.

The **Countryside Cabins** are a wonderful, inexpensive, and definitely funky place to stay. They're owned and operated by a sparkling older woman, Margaret Naai. The entrance is hard to spot, but it's located *mauka* about halfway between Pat's of Punaluu and the Paniolo Cafe. Look for the small white sign that says "Cabins." You're greeted by a large black dog named Smokey. He's a big baby so don't worry. Margaret comes out with a rolled-up newspaper to fend Smokey off because he jumps on her: Smokey weighs 98 pounds, she only 96. Completely furnished studios are $25 daily, $175 weekly, $475 monthly. Unfurnished rooms are $20 nightly, $140 weekly, $300 monthly. Margaret will reserve a room for you if you send a $10 deposit. She's a peach, but she's getting on in years, so it would be best to send a SASE envelope with your deposit and not count on her to remember. For information and reservations, write Countryside Cabins, 53-224 Kamehameha Hwy., Hauula HI 96717, tel. 237-8169.

Food

An institution along the windward coast, **Pat's of Punaluu** has an extraordinary view of the coast. The interior is quite tasteful with open beams, ceiling fans, high-backed wicker chairs, and a long polished *koa* bar. The feeling is warm, peaceful, and very tropical. There's a little bandstand, some fish tanks, and a large lava rock wall that counterpoints the white stucco. Breakfast for $5 is huge, and a bargain. Lunch is a Pat's burger for $6.25, grilled teri chicken ($6.25), tropical fruit salad for $6.50 (also a lunch buffet

on weekdays). Dinner is quite gourmet with offerings of sashimi, escargot, or beer-battered *mahi mahi* for appetizers ($6-8). Soup, like seafood bisque, and a salad of fresh-tossed greens are around $4. Entrees include grilled choice New York steak ($16.95), grilled lamb ($12.75), fresh *opakapaka* ($17.95), and a complete chef dinner for $25, which changes regularly. Open for breakfast 8 a.m., lunch 11 a.m.-2 p.m., dinner from 5-9:30 p.m.

No trip to Pat's is complete without sampling the fresh tarts famous since 1945—your choice of banana, pineapple, or coconut ladled into an oven-fresh tart and mounded with whipped cream. Pat's is also famous for mai tais, made fresh ($5), and so laced with booze that if you intend on driving, only have one!

Pat's presents an authentic hula show Sat.-Sun. at 7 p.m. Contemporary dance music follows. Pat's, long renowned as a good old-fashioned Hawaiian-style restaurant, has been going through a transition in the last few years. Luckily, it is definitely back on the right track. The previous owners tried to make it a tourist trap complete with a mediocre cafeteria to cater to the tour-bus crowd. The new owners have reclaimed Pat's and saved it from a fate worse than deep-fried *mahi mahi*. They're restoring Pat's to its old island-style tradition, and doing an admirable job. Pat's is back, and is definitely worth a stop.

What tropical island would be complete without a cowboy cafe serving rattlesnake chili? The **Paniolo Cafe** along the highway in Punaluu (mile marker 23), tel. 237-8521, has a foot-stompin' dance floor with country music and just the right touch of cowboy class. A stuffed longhorn steer glares from one wall, a rattler, as thick as a wrestler's arm, from the other. You'll dine on barbecued beef, ribs, chicken, and an assortment of Mexican food all priced around $9.95. A whopping 12-ounce steak is $16, and the rattlesnake chili at $5 *is* authentic. Try their deep-fried bananas with wild honey for dessert. Or you could broil your own entrees like *mahi mahi,* a small steak, or teri chicken for under $10 including the salad bar.

The Paniolo is friendly and attracts a mixed crowd, along with a regular clientele of local people. No one is going to hassle you, but if you're looking for trouble you'll be served a good old knuckle sandwich, pardner! You can order 16-

ounce Mason jars of Miller Light or Bud for $2. Sashay to the tunes of the Bourbon Cowboys on Fri. and Sat. from 9-11:30 p.m. and again on Sunday afternoons. The Paniolo is a great bar, a commodity hard to find on Oahu, and the only one of its kind along the windward shore.

Shopping
The **Hauula Shopping Center** features **Pay 'n' Save** for everything from film to swim fins, and the **Village Food Mart** is open from 9-9 weekdays, 9-5 Sunday for all food needs. The **Hawaiian-Polynesian Cultural Supply**, tel. 293-1560, open 9:30 a.m.-5 p.m. weekdays, half day

Saturday, is a rare and unique hula supply store. They feature fine Polynesian crafts used in the hula like ip'u (gourd drums), hula skirts, headdresses, beads, and shell leis. There are other accoutrements and art items like koa bowls, carved turtles, and mother-of-pearl necklaces. All items are handmade in Tahiti, Samoa, Tonga, and Hawaii, basically from throughout Polynesia. T-shirts, sweatshirts, and suntan oil are also sold. All items offered are authentic, and the storekeepers are friendly and informative regarding the hula. A great store in which to browse and to pick up a unique and real souvenir.

LAIE TO KAHUKU

LAIE

The "Saints" came marching into Laie ("Leaf of the *le* Vine") and set about making a perfect Mormon village in paradise. What's more, they succeeded! The town itself is squeaky clean, with well-kept homes and manicured lawns that hint of suburban Midwest America. Dedicated to education, they built a branch of **Brigham Young University** (BYU) that attracts students from all over Polynesia, many of whom work in the nearby Polynesian Cultural Center. The students vow to live a clean life, free of drugs and alcohol, and not to grow beards. God doesn't like beards! In the foyer of the main entrance look for a huge mural depicting Laie's flag-raising ceremony in 1921, which symbolically established the colony. The road leading to and from the university campus is maze-like but easily negotiable.

The first view of the **Mormon Temple,** built in 1919, is very impressive. Square, with simple architectural lines, this house of worship sits pure white against the *pali,* and is further dramatized by a reflecting pool and fountains spewing fine mists. This tranquil, shrine-like church is open daily from 9 a.m.-9 p.m., when a slide show telling the history of the Laie colony is presented, along with a guided tour of the grounds. "Smoking is prohibited, and shirts (no halter tops) must be worn to enter." The temple attracts more visitors than any other Mormon site outside of the main temple in Salt Lake City.

Polynesian Cultural Center
The real showcase is the Polynesian Cultural Center. PCC, as it's called by islanders, began as an experiment in 1963. Smart businessmen said it would never thrive way out in Laie, and tourists didn't come to Hawaii for *culture* anyway. The PCC now rates as one of Oahu's top tourist attractions, luring about one million visitors annually. Miracles do happen! PCC is a non-profit organization, with proceeds going to the Laie BYU, and to maintaining the center itself.

Covering 42 acres, the primary attractions are seven model villages including examples from Hawaii, Samoa, the Marquesas, Fiji, New Zealand, Tonga, and Tahiti. Guides lead you through the villages either on a walking tour, or by canoe over artesian-fed waterways. A shuttle tram runs outside the center, and will take you on a guided tour to the BYU campus, the Temple, and a short tour of the community. The villages are primarily staffed with people from the representative island homelands. Remember that most are Mormons, whose dogma colors the attitudes and selected presentations of the staffers. Still, all are genuinely interested in dispensing cultural knowledge about their traditional island ways and beliefs, and almost all are characters who engage in lighthearted bantering with their willing audience. The undeniable family spirit and pride at PCC makes you feel welcome, while providing a clean and wholesome experience, with plenty of attention to detail.

The morning begins with the **Fiafia Festival,** a lei greeting that orients you to the Center. Next comes **Music Polynesia,** a historical evolution of island music presented by singers, musicians, and dancers. A brass band plays from 5:30 p.m., touring the different villages, and the **Pageant of Canoes** sails at 2 and 3 p.m. The largest extravaganza occurs during an evening dinner show called **This is Polynesia.** Beginning at 7:30 p.m., the center's amphitheater hosts about 3,000 spectators for this show of music, dance, and historical drama. The costumes and lighting are dramatic and inspired; it's hard to believe that the performers are not professionals. Soon to open is an *Imax,* a wraparound movie screen, that attempts to give you a real sense of what it's like to take a canoe around the shores of Fiji, or to tramp the mountains of New Zealand.

Food is available from a number of snack bars, or you can dine at the **Gateway,** which serves you a buffet dinner as part of a package including the Polynesian extravaganza. A luau and a Mission Buffet are offered now and again, usually at 5:30 p.m., so there's plenty of time to eat and then catch the show if you desire.

PCC is open daily except Sunday from 12:30 p.m. General admission to the center is $24.95 for adults, $9.95 children under 11, under five free. There are also a variety of other packages available including an all-day pass, with dinner buffet and evening show for around $50, children $40. For more information contact PCC at tel. 293-3333. TheBus # 52 leaves from Ala Moana to the center and takes about two hours. Most island hotels can arrange a package tour to PCC.

KAHUKU

This village, and it is a village, is where the *workers* of the North Shore live. Kahuku has little to recommend it, except that it is very real, and a lingering slice of what Hawaii was, not so long ago. Do yourself a favor and turn off the highway for a two-minute tour of the dirt roads lined by proudly maintained homes that somehow exude the feeling of Asia. Of course there is the Kahuku Superette for supplies, and **Huevos Restaurant,** open daily 7 a.m.-1 p.m., and again on Fri. and Sat. from 5:30-9 p.m., basic Mexican. Huevos is in a dilapidated old building in the center of town (follow signs) and is worth a visit just

Polynesian Cultural Center

to soak up the local scene. A little white *kaukau* wagon sits across the roadway from the school. They sell great food that they pick up in Chinatown everyday. They're here only during school hours, when you can pick up a tasty and inexpensive lunch.

Keep a sharp eye out for a truck and a sign featuring fresh shrimp for $5.95 just along the road. Follow it to **Ahi's Kahuku Restaurant,** operated by Roland Ahi and son, open daily 7 a.m.-9 p.m. The shrimp couldn't be fresher as it comes from Pacific Sea Farms, an aquaculture farm just a few minutes away. The longest that these plump babies have been out of the water is 48 hours, so you are definitely getting *the* best. In this no-frills but super-friendly restaurant, you can have your shrimp cooked to order as scampi, deep-fried, tempura, a cocktail, or sautéed. You get about five to seven shrimp, depending on the size. The shrimp is the *pièce de résistance,* but they have basic sandwiches like tuna and hamburger, both under $4, and entrees like spaghetti with meat sauce for $4.95, and steak and *mahi mahi* combo for $10.95. Complete meals come with a green salad, fresh vegetables, rice, and tea. They also serve beer and wine, and on Saturday nights feature a sing-along *kareoke,* where you can become an instant star.

On the north end of town is **The Mill Shopping Center,** which is really the town's old sugar mill that has been recycled. The interior is dominated by huge gears and machinery, power panels, and crushers that are the backdrop for a string of shops, a restaurant, and the Kahuku Theater. The 10-foot gears and conveyor belts have all been painted with bright colors and seem like a display of modern art pieces. Outside is a **Circle K** food store and gas station, **Lee's Gifts and Jewelry**, **Island Snow** for shave ice, **Tropical Memories Jeweler,** and a post office. Inside is the **Country Kitchen,** open 8 a.m. till 10 p.m. This restaurant has utilized the theme perfectly by situating a portion of its tables in an old caboose. They have a full range of sandwiches and burgers for under $5, and dinners like ham and broccoli supreme, $6.50. Country suppers are the likes of fried chicken, $9.45, roast turkey, $9.45, ribeye steak, $11.95, Mexican salad for $5.25, and grilled chicken breakfast salad for $5.75; special prices for seniors and children.

BEACHES

At the north end of Laie, you'll pass **TT Surf Shop,** about the only shop in this neck of the woods offering surfing equipment, boards, or boogie boards.

At the southern end of Laie is **Pounder's Beach,** so named by students of BYU because of the pounding surf. The park area is privately owned, open to the public, with few facilities (a few portable outhouses and picnic tables). This beach experiences heavy surf and dangerous conditions in the winter months, but its excellent shoreline break is perfect for bodysurfing. The remains of an old pier at which inter-island steamers once stopped is still in evidence.

Laie County Park is an unimproved beach park with no facilities, but a one-mile stretch of beach. The shoreline waters are safe for swimming inside the reef, but wintertime produces heavy and potentially dangerous surf. Good snorkeling, fishing, and throw-netting by local

fishermen; get there by following the stream from the bridge near the Laie Shopping Mall.

Kakela Beach is a privately owned facility where camping is allowed. Secure a reservation from Zion Securities, 55-510 Kamehameha Hwy., Laie, HI 96762, tel. 293-9201. Or check in with the caretaker if you arrive during daylight hours, when chances are good that you can find a spot without reservations. Camping is $5 per person per night. The area is improved with showers and picnic facilities. No BBQs but you can bring your own camp stove. This facility is private, under-used, and secure. Pitch your tent among the ironwoods overlooking the beach, which has good swimming and bodysurfing.

Malaekahana State Recreation Area

This is the premier camping beach along the north section of the windward coast. Separated from the highway by a large stand of shade trees, it offers showers, restrooms, picnic facilities, and camping (state permit). Offshore is Moku'auia, better known as **Goat Island.** You can reach this seabird sanctuary by wading across the reef during low tide. You'll find a beautiful crescent white-sand beach and absolute peace and quiet. The swimming inside the reef is good, and it's amazing how little used this area is for such a beautiful spot. Be aware that there are two entrances to the park. The north entrance, closest to Kahuku, puts you in the day-use area of the park, where there are restrooms and showers. Offshore, about 200-300 yards, is a small island. *You can not wade to this island. It is too far, and the currents are strong.* The entrance to the camping section is south a minute or two (around mile marker 17) and is marked by a steel gate painted brown and a sign welcoming you to Malaekahana State Recreation Area. You must be aware that the gates open at 7 a.m. and close at 6:45 p.m. Goat Island is only a stone's throw from shore. Reef walkers or tennis shoes are advised.

PRACTICALITIES

Accommodations

The **Laniloa Lodge Hotel** is just outside the Polynesian Culture Center, and has been recently given a face lift. Rooms are $60 s, $65 d, $70 for a triple, $75 for four, and $120-175 for a suite. They also offer $49 for a double room if you purchase two all-day tickets to the Polynesian Cultural Center. All rooms have a/c, TV, and there's parking, a pool, and a restaurant that closes early on Sundays, but McDonald's is next door. For information write Laniloa Lodge Hotel, 55-109 Laniloa St., Laie, HI 96762, tel. 293-9282 or (800) 526-4562.

Kekeala Hale is a condominium rental fronting Kekeala Beach, at 55-113 Kamehameha Hwy., Laie, HI, 96762 tel. 293-9700. They call themselves "private Polynesia at its best," and being as secluded as they are, they have a point. Cottages are over a thousand square feet with a full kitchen and bath, with one king and four twin beds in each unit. A tennis court on property is featured. Rates for cottages that sleep six to 12 (using foam pads) are $240 daily, $600 for a weekend, $1440 weekly. Rates for a cottage sleeping four to six is $120 daily, $720 weekly. All require a three-day minimum.

Lora Dunn's House is at 55-161 Kamehameha Hwy., Laie, HI 96762, tel. 293-1000 (between mile markers 19 and 20, ocean side). Lora admits people on a first-come first-served basis, but will happily take phone reservations for which she requires a deposit. Chances of turning up and finding a vacancy are poor, so at least call from the airport to check availability. A separate studio for two people is $175, while the downstairs self-contained unit of her home, which is larger and can accommodate four people, runs about $350 per week. Good value in a quiet, if not spectacular, setting.

Food

When you enter Laie you will be greeted by the Stars and Stripes flying over the entrance of the Polynesian Cultural Center. Next door is a whopper of a **McDonald's,** and in keeping with the spirit of Polynesian culture, looks like a Polynesian longhouse. Just next door is the **Laniloa Lodge,** whose restaurant features breakfast specials for under $4, and complete dinners with soup, salad, vegies, and Kona coffee for only $10.95. They're open every day from breakfast until 8 p.m., except Sunday when the restaurant closes at 2 p.m. The food is wholesome but ordinary at the Laniloa Lodge, tel. 293-5888.

A few minutes down the road, the **Haaula Shopping Center** provides a small variety of dining spots. At the **Lotus Inn Chop Suey,** tel. 293-5412, you'll get a tasty and filling meal daily from 10 a.m.-9 p.m. for under $6. A full menu of Cantonese-style food includes ginger chicken, shrimp, and beef. Happy hour runs from 3-7 p.m., when well drinks cost $1.25 and are accompanied by free *pu pu*. **Country Health Food,** specializing in sandwiches and smoothies, is open Mon.-Sat. 9 a.m.-7 p.m., tel 293-2153. They are almost as much of a restaurant as they are a health food store. Some tasty items are the garden salad $2.50, nachos for $3, and an assortment of freshly made sandwiches like the Tuna Terrific, $3.25, Avocado Supreme, $3.25, and Texas-style BBQ meat-free burger for $3.50. Energize with a full selection of herbal ice teas, fresh-squeezed orange juice or carrot juice. Smoothies are strawberry or coco-butternut shake, made with nonfat milk, cocoa protein, peanut butter, egg, and banana for $2.75. A great change of pace. The shopping center also features a **Domino's Pizza,** and the **Bethlehem Baking Company,** open daily 6:30 a.m.-6 p.m., with an assortment of yummies including sweet homemade breads of pineapple and coconut.

THE NORTH SHORE

This shallow bowl of coastline stretches from Kaena Point in the west to Turtle Bay in the east. **Mount Kaala,** verdant backdrop to the area, rises 4,020 feet from the Waianae Range, making it the highest peak on Oahu. The entire stretch is a day-tripper's paradise with plenty of sights to keep you entertained. But the North Shore is synonymous with one word: surfing. Thunderous winter waves, often measuring 25 feet (from the rear!), rumble along the North Shore's world-famous surfing beaches lined up one after the other—**Waimea Bay, Ehukai, Sunset, Banzai Pipeline.** They attract highly accomplished athletes who come to compete in prestigious international surfing competitions. In summertime *moana* loses her ferocity and lies down, becoming gentle and safe for anyone.

Haleiwa, at the junction of the Farrington Highway (Rt. 930) heading west along the coast and the Kamehameha Highway (Rt. 83) heading east, is fast becoming the central town along the North Shore. The main street is lined with restaurants, boutiques, art gallerys, small shopping malls, and sports equipment stores. **Waialua,** just west, is a "sugar town" with a few quiet condos for relaxation. Farther west is **Dillingham Airfield,** where you can arrange to fly above it all in a small plane or soar silently in a glider. The road ends for vehicles not far from here, and then your feet have to take you to Kaena Point, where *the* largest waves pound the coast. Heading east, you'll pass a famous *heiau* where human flesh mollified the gods. Then come the great surfing beaches and their incredible waves. Here and there are tidepools rich with discovery, a monument to a real local hero, and **Waimea Falls Park,** the premier tourist attraction of the North Shore.

BEACHES AND SIGHTS

The main attractions of the North Shore are its beaches. Interspersed among them are a few sights definitely worth your time and effort. The listings below run from west to east. The most-traveled route to the North Shore is from Honolulu along the H-2 freeway, and then directly to the coast along Rt. 99 or Rt. 803. At Weed Circle or Thompson Corner, where these routes reach the coast, turn left along the Farrington Highway following it to road's end just before Kaena Point, or right along the Kamehameha Highway (Rt. 83), which heads around the coast all the way to Kailua.

Be aware that *all* North Shore beaches experience very heavy surf conditions with dangerous currents from October through April. The waters, at this time of year, are not for the average swimmer. Please heed all warnings. In summertime, leap in!

ALONG THE FARRINGTON HIGHWAY

Waialua

The first town is Waialua ("Two Waters"). Take Waialua Beach Road just off the Weed Traffic Circle coming north on Rt. 99, or follow the signs off the Farrington Highway. At the turn of the century, Waialua, lying at the terminus of a sugar-train railway, was a fashionable beach community complete with hotels and vacation homes. Today, it's hardly ever visited, and it's not uncommon to see as many horses tied up along main street as it is to see parked cars in this real one-horse town. Sundays can also attract a rumble of bikers who kick up the dust on their two-wheeled steeds.

The sugar mill, an outrageously ugly mechanical monster, is still operating and is central to the town. Quiet Waialua, with its main street divided by trees running down the middle, *is* rural Oahu. There's a general store for supplies, post office, and snacks at the **Sugar Bar,** a restaurant in the old Bank of Hawaii building. If you're returning to Haleiwa take Haleiwa Road, a back way through residential areas. Look for Paalaa Road on the right and take it past a small Buddhist temple that holds an *o bon* festival honoring the dead, traditionally observed in July.

Mokuleia Beach Park And Dillingham Airfield

Mokuleia is the main public access park along the highway. It provides picnic facilities, restrooms, lifeguards, playground area, and camping (county permit). In summertime, swimming is possible along a few sandy stretches protected by a broken offshore reef. Mokuleia Army Beach, across from the airfield, is a wider strand of sand. It's very private, and the only noise interrupting your afternoon slumber might be planes taking off from the airfield. A minute farther toward Kaena is an unofficial area with a wide sand beach. During the week you can expect no more than half dozen people on this 300-yard beach. Remember that this is the North Shore

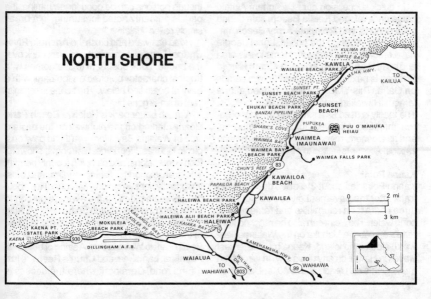

and the water can be treacherous. Careful! Five minutes past the airfield, the road ends. This is a good place to check out giant waves.

Across the road is **Dillingham Airfield,** small but modern, with restrooms near the hangars and a new parking area. A public phone is available in hangar G-1. Most days, especially weekends, a few local people sell refreshments from their cars or trucks. The main reason for stopping is to take a small plane or glider ride. **Glider Rides,** tel. 677-3404, take you on a 20- to 30-minute flight for $40 single, $60 double. The owner is Bill Star, who has been flying from here since 1970. They fly seven days a week starting at about 10 a.m. on a first-come, first-served basis. They suggest you bring a camera, and arrive before 5 p.m. to get the best winds. There's always a pilot with you to make sure that your glider ride is a *return* trip. Another glider operation is **Mile High Glider Rides.** They fly for 30 minutes, and they offer a sit-up-front-and-try-the-controls-type ride complete with acrobatics and instruction. They fly out of hangar No. 10, and charge about $80 per ride. **Surf Air Tours,** tel. 637-7003, flies Cessna 172s or 206s for a half-hour along the North Shore for $30 per person, or on a longer "circle-island tour" for $50 per person. It's worthwhile, but the glider ride is more exceptional.

In quick succession after Dillingham Airfield come undeveloped **Kealia Beach,** safe during calm periods, and **Mokuleia Army Beach,** improved and open to the public. Local people have erected semipermanent tents in this area and guard it as if it were their own. **Camp Harold Erdman** is next, one of the best-known camps on Oahu. This YMCA facility is named after a famous Hawaiian polo player killed in the '30s. The facility is used as a summer camp for children, throughout the year for special functions, and as a general retreat area by various organizations. Access is limited to official use.

Kaena Point

Kaena Point lies about 2½ miles down the dirt track after the pavement gives out. Count on three hours for a return hike and remember to bring water. The Point can also be reached from road's end above Mahuka on the Waianae (leeward) side of the island. Kaena has *the* largest waves in Hawaii on any given day. In wintertime these giants can reach above 40 feet, and their

power, even when viewed safely from the high ground, is truly amazing. Surfers have actually plotted ways of riding these waves, which include being dropped by helicopter with scuba tanks. Reportedly, one surfer named Ace Cool has already done it. For the rest of us mortals . . . "who wants to have that much fun anyway!" Kaena Point is the site of numerous *heiau.* Due to its exposed position, it, like similar sites around the islands, was a jumping-off point for the "souls of the dead." The spirits were believed to wander here after death, and once all worldly commitments were fulfilled, they made their "leap" from earth to heaven. Hopefully, the daredevil surfers will not revive this tradition!

HALEIWA AND VICINITY

Haleiwa ("Home of the Frigate Birds") has become the premier town of the region, mainly because it straddles the main road and has the majority of shopping, dining, and services along the North Shore. **Haleiwa Ali'i Beach Park** is on the western shores of Waialua Bay, which fronts the town. This beach park is improved with restrooms, lifeguard tower, and small boat launch. Lifeguards man the tower throughout the summer, on weekends in winter. The shoreline is rocks and coral with pockets of sand, and although portions can be good for swimming, the park is primarily noted for surfing, in a break simply called "Haleiwa."

Head eastward and cross the **Anahulu River Bridge.** Park for a moment and walk back over the bridge. Look upstream to see homes with tropical character perched on the bank with a bevy of boats tied below. The scene is reminiscent of times gone by.

A much better park is **Haleiwa Beach Park,** clearly marked off the highway on the eastern side of Waialua Bay. Here you'll find pavilions, picnic facilities, lifeguards, restrooms, showers, food concessions, and camping (county permit). The area is good for fishing, surfing, and most importantly, for swimming year-round! It's about the only safe place for the average person to swim along the entire North Shore during winter.

Kawailoa Beach is the general name given to the area stretching all the way from Haleiwa Beach Park to Waimea Bay. A string of beaches, **Papailoa, Laniakea,** and **Chun's Reef,** are just off the road. Cars park where the access is good. None of these beaches is suitable for the recreational swimmer. All are surfing beaches, with the most popular being Chun's Reef.

WAIMEA BAY AND VICINITY

The two-lane highway along the North Shore is pounded by traffic; be especially careful around Waimea Bay. The highway sweeps around till you see the steeple of **St. Peter and Paul Mission** with the bay below. The steeple is actually the remnants of an old rock-crushing plant on the site. **Waimea Bay Beach Park** has the largest rideable waves in the world. This is the heart of surfers' paradise. The park is improved with a lifeguard tower, restrooms, and a picnic area.

During a big winter swell, the bay is lined with spectators watching the surfers ride the monumental waves. In summertime, the bay is calm as a lake. People inexperienced with the sea should not even walk along the shorebreak in winter. Unexpected waves come up farther than expected, and a murderous rip lurks only a few feet from shore. The area is rife with tales of heroic rescue attempts, many ending in fatalities. A plaque commemorates Eddie Aikau, a local lifeguard credited with making thousands of rescues. In 1978, the *Hokulea,* the Polynesian Sailing Society's double-hulled canoe, capsized in rough seas about 20 miles offshore. Eddie was aboard, and launched his surfboard to swim for help. He never made it, but his selfless courage lives on.

Waimea Falls Park

Look for the well-marked entrance to Waimea Falls Park, mountainside from the bay. You can drive for quite a way into the lush valley before coming to the actual park entrance. As you enter, a local man sells Hawaiian coconut-frond hats. These are the authentic article, priced right at around $6. The park is primarily a botanical garden with a fascinating display of flowers and plants, all labeled for your edification. If you choose not to walk, open-air tour buses take you through the grounds narrating all the way. The highlight is professional diving from the 55-foot rock walls into the pool below Waimea Falls. This event, along with the ancient hula (excellent, and authentic), a display of Hawaiian games, and feeding of wildlife are scheduled

four times throughout the day, so whenever you arrive you'll have an opportunity to see them. Nature paths, great for carefree roaming, lead into the valley. Admission is $9.95 adults, $6 juniors, and $2 children, open daily 10 a.m.-5:30 p.m., tel. 638-8511. The **Proud Peacock** (see p. 341) serves dinner until 9 p.m. Monthly (check the free tourist literature), on the Friday night closest to the full moon, beginning at 8:30 p.m., the park offers a free guided moon-viewing tour.

Pupukea Beach Park

A perfect place to experience marinelife is the large tidepool next to Pupukea Beach Park, the first one north of Waimea Bay, across the street from the Shell gas station. A long retaining wall out to sea forms a large and protected pool at low tide. Wear footgear and check out the pools with a mask. Don't be surprised to find large sea bass. A sign warns against spearing fish, but the local people do it all the time. Be careful not to step on sea urchins, and stay away from the pool during rough winter swells, when it can be treacherous. The beach park has restrooms, picnic facilities, and fair swimming in sandy pockets between coral and rock, but only in summertime. County camping with a permit *was* allowed in this beach park, and may be available again.

The middle section of the park is called **Shark's Cove,** though no more sharks are here than anywhere else. The area is terrific for snorkeling and scuba in season. Look to the mountains to see **The Mansion** (see below), and next to it the white sculpture of the **World Unity Monument.** If you had to pick a spot from which to view the North Shore sunset, Pupukea Beach Park is hard to beat!

Further down the road, as you pass mile marker nine you can't help noticing a mammoth redwood log that has been carved into a giant statue representing an ancient Hawaiian. Peter Wolfe, the sculptor, has done a symbolic sculpture for every state in the union, this being his 50th. This statue is extremely controversial. Some feel that it looks much more like an American Indian than a Hawaiian, and that the log used should have been a native *koa* instead of an imported redwood from the Pacific Northwest. Others say that its *intention* was to honor the living and the ancient Hawaiians, and that is what's important. Just off to the left is a small shop selling plants, towels, and shellwork from the Philippines.

Puu O Mahuka Heiau

Do yourself a favor and drive up the mountain road leading to the *heiau* even if you don't want to visit it. The vast and sweeping views of the coast below are incredible. About one mile past Waimea Bay the highway passes a Foodland on the right. Turn here up Pupukea Road and follow the signs. Ignore the warning at the beginning of the access road; it's well maintained.

Puu O Mahuka Heiau is large, covering perhaps five acres. Designated as a state historical site, its floorplan is huge steps, with one area leading to another just below. The *heiau* was the site of human sacrifice. People still come to pray as is evidenced by many stones wrapped in *ti* leaves placed on small stone piles lying about the grounds. In the upper section is a raised mound surrounded by stone in what appears to be a central altar area. The *heiau* stonework shows a high degree of craftsmanship throughout, but especially in the pathways. The lower section of the *heiau* appears to be much older, and is not as well maintained.

Drive past the access road leading to the *heiau* and in a minute or so make a left onto Alapio Road. This takes you through an expensive residential area called **Sunset Hills** and past a home locally called **The Mansion**—look for the English-style boxwood hedge surrounding it. The home was purported to be Elvis Presley's island hideaway. Almost next door are the grounds of the **Nichiren Buddhist Temple,** resplendent with manicured lawns and gardens. This area is a tremendous vantage point from which to view Fourth of July fireworks that light up Waimea Bay far below.

THE GREAT SURFING BEACHES

Sunset Beach runs for two miles, the longest white-sand beach on Oahu. Winter surf erodes the beach, with coral and lava fingers exposed at the shoreline, but in summertime you can expect an uninterrupted beach usually 200-300 feet wide. The entire stretch is technically Sunset Beach, but each world-famous surfing spot warrants its own name though they're not clearly marked and are tough to find . . . exactly. Mainly, look for cars with surfboard racks parked along

the road. The beaches are not well maintained either. They're often trashed, and the restrooms, even at Waimea Bay, are atrocious. The reason is politics and money. Efforts all go into Waikiki, where the tourists are. Who cares about a bunch of crazy surfers on the North Shore? They're just a free curiosity for the tourists' enjoyment!

The **Banzai Pipeline** is probably the best-known surfing beach in the world. Its notoriety dates from *Surf Safari,* an early surfer film made in the 1950s, when it was dubbed "Banzai" by Bruce Brown, maker of the film. The famous tube-like effect of the breaking waves comes from a shallow reef just offshore which forces the waves to rise dramatically and quickly. This forces the crest forward to create "the Pipeline." A lifeguard tower near the south end of the beach is all that you'll find in the way of improve-

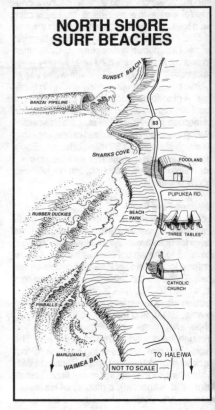

NORTH SHORE SURF BEACHES

SUNSET BEACH

BANZAI PIPELINE

83

SHARKS COVE

FOODLAND

PUPUKEA RD.

RUBBER DUCKIES

BEACH PARK

"THREE TABLES"

CATHOLIC CHURCH

PINBALLS

MARIJUANA'S

WAIMEA BAY

TO HALEIWA

NOT TO SCALE

nents. Parking is along the roadway. Look for Sunset Beach Elementary School on the left, and the Pipeline is across the road. You can park in the school's lot on nonschool days.

Ehukai Beach Park is the next area north. It has a lifeguard tower and restroom, and provides one of the best vantage points from which to watch the surfing action on the Pipeline and Pupukea, the area to the right.

Don't expect much when you come to **Sunset Beach Park** itself. Except for a lifeguard tower, there is nothing. This beach is the site of yearly international surfing competitions. Almost as famous as the surfing break is the **Sunset Rip,** a notorious current offshore that grabs people every year. Summertime is generally safe, but never take *moana* for granted.

PRACTICALITIES

ACCOMMODATIONS

Places to stay are quite limited along the North Shore. The best deals are renting beach homes or rooms directly from the owners, but this is a hit- and-miss proposition, with no agency handling the details. You have to check the local papers. The homes vary greatly in amenities. Some are palaces, others basic rooms or shacks, perfect for surfers or those who consider lodging as secondary. Check the bulletin boards outside the Surf and Sea Dive Shop in Haleiwa and Foodland supermarket.

Expensive

The **Turtle Bay Hilton** is a first-class resort on Turtle Bay, the northern extremity of the North Shore, Box 187, 57-091 Kamehameha Hwy., Kahuku, HI 96731, tel. 293-8811. Once a Hyatt hotel, it was built as a self-contained destination resort. It's surrounded by sea and surf on Kuilima Point, which offers protected swimming year-round. All are welcomed at the beach, so if you come for a day, park in the hotel parking lot and validate your ticket at one of the hotel restaurants to only pay $1 for parking. TheBus also stops at the hotel. The entrance to the hotel is grand, as it's lined with six-foot-high hibiscus and a formal lawn. The resort is complete with a golf course, tennis courts, pool, full water activities including sailboarding and scuba lessons, horseback riding, shopping, and the fanciest dining on the North Shore. Since the hotel is isolated, you should *always* call ahead to book any of these activities, even for guests staying at the hotel. There's very little shopping in this area, so if you're after film, or basic picnic supplies, stop at the hotel's mini mall. All rooms are ocean view, but not all are oceanfront. Oceanfront is slightly more expensive, but is worth the price especially

from January to April when humpback whales cavort in the waters off the point. Rooms are furnished with full baths, a mini fridge, dressing room, a large vanity, ample closets, a/c, and cable TV. Junior suites come complete with a library, large bathroom and changing room, two couches, a sitting area, queensized bed, and a large enclosed lanai. Rates based on double occupancy begin at $135 for a studio, extra person $15, $235 cottage, $300-950 for a suite. Room rates may seem high, but you actually get much more than what you would pay for a mainstream hotel of similar stature. The Hilton family plan allows children free when they stay in a room with their parents. See "Food" below for a full listing of the fine dining offered at the Turtle Bay Hilton.

The most important features of the **Mokuleia Beach Colony,** at 68-615 Farrington Hwy., Waialua, HI 96791, is what's missing . . . hustle, bustle, and noise. This secluded condo, backdropped by mountains, fronted by the sea, and nestled next to a stately white-fenced polo field, is the epitome of serenity whose colors are emerald green and sky blue, and whose music is the rolling surf. Each privately owned *hale* is split into two 700-square-foot open-floor-plan units that are fully furnished. All have a screened lanai which doubles as a day room, a living room area, modern kitchen, bedroom, and a full bath. Cooling is provided by ceiling fans and shuttered windows and screens that catch the balmy breezes. Tennis courts and a pool are part of the complex. Average prices range from $550- 600 weekly. Sundays usually bring sky divers and hang gliders who land in the polo field next door except during polo season, which brings a match every Sunday from March through August. The Colony has formed an association which handles rentals. To book a *hale* contact Bobbie Kane, c/o Kane International, 2828 Paa

St., Suite 2130, Honolulu, HI 96819, tel. 833-1600, fax (808) 834-0577.

Ke Iki Hale is a small condo complex operated by Alice Tracy, 59- 579 Ke Iki Rd., 96712, tel. 638-8229. Pass the Foodland Supermarket heading north, and look for a school sign. Turn left here to the beach to find the condo. The property has 200 feet of private beach with a sandy bottom that goes out about 300 feet (half that in winter). The condo is quiet with a home-away-from-home atmosphere. Rates are: one-bedroom beachfront, $125 per day, $700 per week, $2,400 per month; two-bedroom beachfront $125 per day, $775 per week, $2,500 per month. Units on the grounds with no beachfront are about 25% less.

Surfer Rentals

The North Shore of Oahu is long famous for its world-class surfing. The area attracts enthusiasts from around the world who are much more concerned with the daily surfing report than they are with deluxe accommodations. The Kamehameha Highway is dotted with surfer rentals from Haleiwa to Turtle Bay. Just outside their doors are the famous surfing breaks of Marijuana's, Rubber Duckies, and Pinballs, all famous and known to world-class surfers. Some of these accommodations are terrific, while others are barely livable. Here's a sample of what's offered.

The **Plantation Village** at 59754 Kamehameha Hwy., Haleiwa 96712, tel. 638-8663, lies across from Three Tables Beach by Shark's Cove, between mile markers six and seven. It's on TheBus line and only a five-minute walk from a Safeway store for supplies. The Plantation Village, once a real Filipino working village, has cottages by the sea, secure behind a locked gate, and furnished with cable, stereo, linens, dishes, washers and dryers, ice machines, and cleaning service. There is a full kitchen and even a cook whom you pay separately for preparing your meals if you wish. Many of the fruit trees on the grounds provide the guests with complimentary bananas, papayas, breadfruit, or whatever is happening. Prices are $15 for a shared room and bath with two or three others. Ask for Unit-2, which is the same price, but a tiny private room. The small (300 square foot) private cottages, once the homes of real plantation workers, sleep two and are $50 per night. A $100 per night deluxe cottage sleeps four, and you get a large front lanai, two couches, wicker furniture in a sitting room, cable TV, a/c, fan, full bath with vanity and kitchen fully furnished with microwave, stove, and fridge. The Plantation Village is geared to long stays and has a one-week minimum policy. They will come to the airport to pick you up for $25, which is great if you have a surfboard and gear. During surfing season the place is booked out. Reserve two months in advance; full deposit during high season (Dec.-Feb.), one half deposit other months. No refund policy in high season.

The Vacation Inn and Hostel, 59-788 Kam Hwy., Haleiwa, HI 96712, tel. 638-7838, specializes in budget accommodations for surfers, backpackers, and families. Owned and operated by the Foo Family, the main building in this small cluster of buildings is at mile marker six, the fourth driveway past the church tower coming from Waimea Bay. There are a number of facilities and room styles which could put you on the beach or mountainside, depending on availability and your preference. Basic rates are $12 for a bunk in the hostel-style rooms, which includes cooking and laundry facilities, and TV in the communal room. Each room has four bunks, microwaves, shower, and bath. The feeling is definitely not deluxe, but it is adequate. A complex on the beach offers a $65 room which sleeps four, has a complete kitchen, two double beds, a roll-out couch, ceiling fan, and a world-class view of the beach from your lanai. The back house, on the mountainside, is further away from traffic and is amongst the trees. It's on stilts, and has an open ceiling and rustic common area. Rates are $33 for the main rooms (two people), a private loft for $25 (it would be hot up there), or share a bunk for $12. The Vacation Inn has only one rule: use common sense, and clean up after yourself. They provide free boogie boards and snorkeling gear, and will rent you bikes and surfboards. Airport transportation is $5, $25 if it's a special trip. Everyone's friendly and laid-back. Book ahead. A good choice.

Between mile markers nine and 10 look for a small sign that says "Rooms". In this very basic accommodation you can rent for a night, a week, or a month ($400). There's no name, but call 638-8895 for info. Expect communal cooking facilities, shared bath, and no maid service. This is basically a crash pad for surfers and travelers

Not recommended for anyone interested in anything but basic and cheap.

FOOD

Inexpensive

McDonald's golden arches rise above Haleiwa as you enter town. Historic Haleiwa Theater was torn down so that the world could have another Egg McMuffin. Here too is a 7-11 convenience store. Almost next door is Pizza Hut. Besides pizza, their salad bar isn't bad.

Between the two, but a culinary world apart, Celestial Natural Foods, tel. 637-6729, open weekdays 9 a.m.-6:30 p.m., Sun. 10-6, sells natural and health foods, and vegetarian meals at the snack bar. Smoothies are $2.50; most sandwiches and a variety of salads are under $3.50.

Cafe Haleiwa, a hole-in-the-wall eatery on your left just as you enter town, serves one of the best breakfasts on Oahu. Their "dawn patrol" from 6-7 a.m. includes eggs and whole-wheat pancakes for $2.50. Specials of the house are whole-wheat banana pancakes, French toast, spinach and mushroom quiche, and steaming-hot Kona coffee. One of the partners, Jim Sears, is called "the wizard of eggs" and has built up a local following. The cafe attracts many surfers, so it's a great place to find out about conditions.

If you're tired or just need a pick-me-up head for the North Shore Marketplace (after McDonald's, mountainside) where you'll find the Coffee Gallery, open from 5:30 a.m.-9:30 p.m. They pour gourmet coffees and offer a selection of deli sandwiches and salads for under $5. The China Inn here serves a variety of inexpensive dishes like sweet and sour pork $3.50, sweet and sour fish $3.25, and hamburgers. Take it out to the shade of the lanai. A minute past is the Haleiwa Chinese Restaurant, tel. 637-3533, open daily 10 a.m.-9 p.m. The interior is basic but the food is very good. Their steamed sea bass and kung pao chicken are both excellent. A gigantic bowl of tofu soup is $4, while most main courses are under $6. One of the best inexpensive eateries on the North Shore.

You can tell by the tour buses parked outside that Matsumoto's is a very famous store on the North Shore. What are all those people after? Shave ice. This is one of the best places on Oahu to try this island treat. Not only do the tourists come here, but local families often take a "Sunday drive" just to get Matsumoto's shave ice. Try the Hawaiian Delight, a mound of ice smothered with banana, pineapple, and mango syrup.

The Country Drive-In is across from Haleiwa Shopping Center. They have plate lunches (20 varieties), smoothies, and country breakfasts like corned beef hash and fried eggs with breakfast meat for $2.25. Quick and good.

The tiny town of Waialua (see p. 335) is home to The Sugar Bar, located in the old Bank of Hawaii Building. They feature an international cuisine, hot dogs from America to bratwurst from Germany. Magnifique!

East from town across from Shark's Cove is the Shark's Shack, a usually open lunch wagon that'll fix you a sandwich or rent you snorkeling gear. Next door is Pupukaia Shave Ice for an island treat. Farther toward Sunset Beach (around mile marker nine) look for Diamico's Pizza, open for breakfast, lunch, and dinner, and the Sunset Beach store, home of Ted's Bakery.

Moderate/Expensive

Steamer's in the Haleiwa Shopping Plaza, tel. 637-5071, is a clean and modern restaurant serving seafood, beef, and chicken. There's plenty of brass, paneled walls, and low lighting. Lunches are especially good with a wide choice of omelettes from $5, including one made from crab, shrimp, and mushrooms; all come with blueberry or French muffins. Whet your appetite with sushi, steamed clams, or have full fish dinners starting at $10. Dining daily 11 a.m.-11 p.m., bar until 2 a.m.

Rosie's Cantina, also in the plaza, open Sun.-Thurs. 7 a.m.-10 p.m, Fri.-Sat. 7-11 p.m., prepares hearty Mexican dishes for a good price. The inside is "yuppie Mex" with brass rails, painted overhead steam pipes, and elevated booths. Expect to pay $4 for enchiladas and burritos, while meat dishes are $8-9. Order the enchilada stuffed with crab for $9; add a salad and two could easily make this a lunch. Pizza Bob's across the way has an excellent local reputation, and its little pub serves up delicious pizza, salad, lasagne, and sandwiches.

The Proud Peacock, Waimea Falls Park, tel. 638-8531, is open daily for lunch and dinner. It's fun to dine here even if you don't enter the park. From the dining room, you can look into some of the nicest gardens while feeding crumbs to the peacocks. The beautiful mahogany bar was made in Scotland almost 200 years ago. You can have a light soup and salad, but their seafood *pu pu* platter is hard to beat. Roast pork and roast beef are well-prepared favorites here. A Moonlight Buffet from 5-9 p.m. is served to adults for $9.95, children 12 and under $5.95, on two full-moon nights a month. Included are prime rib, chicken, *mahi mahi,* and Hawaiian-style pork. Guided tours begin at 8:30 p.m. sharp.

Jameson's By the Sea, 62-540 Kamehameha Hwy., tel. 637-4336, is open daily for lunch, dinner, and cocktails. It's at the north end of Haleiwa overlooking the sea. Its outdoor deck is perfect for a romantic sunset dinner while inside the romantic mood is continued with track lighting, shoji screens, cane chairs with stuffed pillows, candle with shades, and tables resplendent with fine linen. Appetizers include a salmon plate for $7.95, stuffed mushrooms with escargot $5.50, and fresh oysters $7.95. Chowder and salad are under $4. Try the Yokohama soup, and salad with any of the delicious homemade dressings. Desserts are glorious. Have the lemon macadamia chiffon pie for $3.50. Main dishes like mahi mahi, stuffed shrimp, shrimp curry with mango chutney, and sesame chicken range from $14 to $19. The fresh catch is priced daily. The bar is quiet at night and serves a variety of imported beers; try South Pacific, imported from New Guinea. The service is top-notch; the dining room closes at 10 p.m. and the bar an hour later. Reservations are highly recommended. Request a window seat for sunset.

The **Sea View Inn,** 66-011 Kamehameha Hwy., Haleiwa, tel. 637-4165, is a green cinderblock building on the left before you cross the Anahulu River bridge. It's hard to tell if they are open since they have been in a period of transition lately. The word is that the restaurant will become a Chart House, which is a chain known for good food at decent prices.

Classy Dining
If you're looking for gourmet dining in an incredibly beautiful setting head for the Turtle Bay Hilton. **The Cove Restaurant,** open 6-9:30 p.m. (reservations advised), is the signature restaurant at the resort and welcomes you for an evening of fine dining. Slowly stroll a wooden walkway leading past tiny waterfalls and a profusion of plants to the main room that overlooks the manicured grounds and pool. Start with onion soup with provolone $5.75, Tahitian crab soup $6, or a variety of fresh island salads for $6. Move on to filet mignon $21.50, veal chops $22, fresh tiger prawns and lobster $30, and a choice of fresh catch for $23. Enjoy dessert while peering through floor-to-ceiling windows that frame the living mosaic of Turtle Bay turned brilliant by a legendary North Shore sunset.

The **Seatide Room** is synonymous with Sunday brunch. It enjoys a wonderful reputation and if friends or family come visiting, islanders take them here to impress. Brunch is buffet style from 9 a.m.-2 p.m. and features mounds of fresh fruits and pastries, fresh-squeezed fruit juices, imported cheeses, eggs Florentine and Benedict, fresh fish, seafood, sashimi, shrimp, crab claws, and flowing champagne. Reservations not taken, $21 adults. Expect a wait, which goes easily as you enjoy the magnificent scenery.

The **Palm Terrace** is the most "ordinary" of the hotel's restaurants, but *good* ordinary. Open from 6:30 a.m.-11:00 p.m., it serves hearty American favorites from all 50 states. For example you can order a plate of potato *latka* combined with *lomi* salmon which would put a smile on the face of a Jewish *bubby* from the Bronx, and on the face of a Hawaiian *tutu* from Hilo. The views overlooking Turtle Bay combined with excellent value for the money makes the Palm Terrace the best *ordinary* restaurant on the North Shore.

The **Bay View Lounge** is a casual restaurant/nightclub offering a deli-luncheon buffet. It's open 11:30 a.m.-1 a.m. and serves complimentary *pu pu* around sunset, which is a perfect time to drop in. On weekends the Bay View Lounge is the hotspot disco, ID's required after 9 p.m. dress code is collared shirts and close-toed shoes.

SHOPPING AND SERVICES

As you enter Haleiwa from the west, you'll pass a **Shell** gas station, and **The North Shore Market Place,** with a full-service **post office.** Across the road is **Excell Wet Suits And Water Sports,** a full-service surf shop that rents snorkeling gear.

Ka'ala Art, open 9 a.m.-6 p.m. daily, tel. 637-7065, as you enter Haleiwa (across from Mc-

Donald's), is a perfect place to stop, with some of the best shopping on the North Shore. The brothers Costello, John and Kevin, who own and operate the shop, are knowledgeable, longtime residents of the North Shore who don't mind dispensing directions and information. The premiere items are John's original artwork, wonderful paintings that are impressionistic and magical, with many of these unique designs silk-screened onto 100% cotton T-shirts or made into inspiring posters. John has also turned his hand to carvings of dolphins and other Hawaiian themes. Also featured are fine carvings from Tonga, Tahiti, and Fiji that John has hand-selected on his travels. Small but wonderful items are tapa cloth made by a Tongan woman named Sella who lives nearby, batiks from Thailand, and jewelry made locally and from Asia. The Costello brothers travel to buy, and they have a keen eye for what's happening and distinctive. When you come in here you'll be in for a treat. It looks as if a rainbow has spilled in a corner of the shop where 100% cotton pareo ($12-35) from Hawaii, Tahiti, and Indonesia vibrate in living color. Their "art-clothing" includes a rack of bikinis, locally made in 100% cotton for $14-40, hats, tops for women, beach shoes, towels, slippers, and men's batik shirts for $34. Two of the best local artists displayed are Mango and Caridad Sumile. There's a fine postcard selection, candles, and a smidgen of touristy junk just to remind you that you're still on Oahu.

The **North Shore Marketplace,** along the Kam Highway between McDonald's and the Haleiwa Shopping Center, is a small complex with some interesting shops. **The Coffee Gallery,** selling gourmet coffees, is open daily from 5:30 a.m.-9:30 p.m. Next door the **Island Wear Factory Outlet** has inexpensive alohawear. The most interesting shop is **Jungle Gem's,** tel. 637-6609, open 9:30 a.m.-5 p.m., with a metaphysical assortment of crystals, crystal balls, African trading beads, gems, jewelry, and thunder eggs. The owners, Brent Landberg and Kimberely Moore, are knowledgeable gemologists and jewelers who do much of the fine work on display. Shop assistant Darja Cocca is a **licensed massage therapist,** tel. 638-5661, P.O. Box 1237 Haleiwa 96712, whose specialties are Swedish deep-tissue massage and acupressure, which she combines with live food

Ka'ala Art

cleanses and yoga therapy. Darja definitely has the "gift of touch," and she will *hand tailor* a program designed for you. Her prices are reasonable, and the experience is extra-ordinary.

Next door is another fine shop, **More Or Less Beach Wear,** tel. 638-6859, open 9 a.m.-6 p.m. daily, where they make custom bathing suits and sell hand-painted T-shirts by local artists. The owner and chief designer, Lucinda Vaughen, will take a personal hand in fitting and designing just the right suit for you. **Raging Isle Sports,** tel. 637-7707, 10 a.m.-6 p.m. daily, is primarily a surf shop and manufacturer of Barnfield's Raging Isle Boards, but they rent and sell bikes, and you can pick up items from a pair of shorts to a tennis racket. The bikes are an assortment of beach cruisers and mountain bikes that rent from $10-20 daily, and $55-115 weekly. They also service and repair bikes.

As you move down the Kamehameha Highway from west to east you'll pass in rapid succession the **Haleiwa Flower Shop** on the left selling lei and fresh-cut flowers. Next comes **Oo-**

genesis Boutique, with original fashions for women, and almost next door is **Haleiwa Acupuncture Clinic**, tel. 637-4449, with Richard Himmelmann, in cooperation with Healing Touching Massage by Brenda McKinnon, and chiropractic care by Dr. Edward Bowles, who will make house calls. Next to the clinic **Race Hawaii**, tel. 637-SURF, open 9 a.m.-6 p.m. daily, 8 a.m.-7 p.m. during top season, is a famous surfboard design shop owned by Scott Bucknall who has patented the x-fin scag design. They rent boards during the surf season and sell bathing suits, biking pants, and T-shirts bearing their logo. On the right is **A Guy Selling Shells**. He specializes in hanging baskets, made from bubble shells and cowrie. Prices range from $50 down to $5, with most coming from the Philippines.

Proceeding along you'll come to **Hawaii Surf And Sail**, open 8:30 a.m.-7:30 p.m., tel. 637-5373. They have surfboards (rental $10/day), sailboards, and accessories. The **Consignment Shop**, behind the Country Kitchen, sells well-chosen junk and previously owned ladies' apparel and accessories, artwork, clothing, and towels. Nearby look for a sign to **Fantasy Cycles**, open 10 a.m.-7 p.m., Sun 10 a.m.-3 p.m., owned by Bob Frattin. He rents bikes for $10 day or $45/week. Bob will start off entry-level riders with a map and riding pointers. Bob will also take riders on trail tours that includes lunch. Must be experienced, not for the beginner or couch potato. **Ila Ila Gallery** is across the street from the Protestant church, founded in 1892, and next door to Aoki's Shave Ice. This co-op shows the efforts of local artists who have been juried in order to place their artwork on consignment there. Featured are the fine candle sculptures of **Scott Bechtol** (see p. 327.

Past Matsumoto's Store look for the **Fetig Art Gallery**, tel. 637-4933. Most of the work is by Beverly Fetig, who has been painting the islands for a quarter century. For the last few years she's been painting European scenes, which occupy a room by themselves. The gallery is the oldest on the North Shore, and most of the artists are well known. Prices for original works start at $45 and go up to around $4000. Only a few prints, by well-known artists and numbered, start at around $175. Even if you can't afford paintings from the Fetig Gallery, it's a good place to see the state of the arts on the North Shore.

The **Haleiwa Shopping Center** provides all the necessities in one-stop shopping: boutiques, pharmacy, photo store, and general food and merchandise. It's in the center of Haleiwa, tel 622-5179. Some shops are: **Rix** with jewelry, women's fashions, and alohawear; **Flavormania**, a gourmet ice cream palace; **Et Cetera's**, a tiny but jam-packed souvenir store with woodcarvings, teas, alohawear, and shells; **Space And Lace** sells hats, slippers, shoes, towels and sunglasses; **Liquor Galley**, open daily 9 a.m.-midnight is a full-service liquor store; and **Haliewa Family Health Center**, a walk-in clinic tel. 524-2527, open 8 a.m.-5 p.m. daily, closed Sunday.

Wyland Gallery, across the street from the shopping plaza, is open daily 9 a.m.-6 p.m., tel 637-7498. Wyland is a famous environmental artist known for his huge whale and marinelife murals, in addition to watercolors and fine oil paintings. The gallery is large, spacious, and well lit. Everything has a Hawaiian or sea theme, and there's even a huge fish tank filled with tropical fish. Delight at the magnificent bronze sculptures by Dale Evers, depicting whales and manta rays in sublime frozen movement. There're modern sepiatone photos by Kim Taylor Reese, watercolors of Hawaiian maidens by Janet Stewart, lithographs by Roy Tabora of palms trees and cliffs with Michelangelo skies, bronze dolphins by Christopher Bell, wood sculptures by Kerry Sweet, Margaret Keene's lithographs of children with big eyes, and Sue Phillipson's oils of island flowers. You can walk away with a limited-edition lithograph by Wyland with original watercolor mark framed in *koa* for $940. If the original artwork is too expensive, there're posters, mini-prints, and postcards. Wyland's gold jewelry sculpture is beautiful, distinctive, and affordable.

For food and picnic supplies try the **Haleiwa IGA**, tel. 637-5004, or **Foodland**, along the highway past Waimea Bay, tel. 638-8081.

For a full range of surfing, snorkeling, and diving equipment try **Surf and Sea** near the Union 76 gas station in Haleiwa. They've got boogie boards, masks and fins, tanks, weights, surfboards, and sailboards. They can even arange flights from Dillingham Airfield.

For general North Shore **information** peruse the bulletin boards outside of Surf and Sea and the Foodland Supermarket.

THE LEEWARD COAST

The Waianae ("Mullet Waters") Coast, the leeward face of Oahu, is separated physically from the rest of the island by the Waianae Range. Spiritually, culturally, and economically, the separation is even more profound. This area is Oahu's last stand for ethnic Hawaiians, and for that phenomenal cultural blending of people called *locals*. The idea of "us against them" permeates the consciousness of the area. Guidebooks, government pamphlets, and word of mouth warn tourists against going to Waianae because "the natives are restless." If you follow this poor advice, you not only miss the last of undeveloped coastal Oahu, but the absolute pleasure of meeting people who will treat you with genuine aloha. Along the coast are magnificent beaches long known for their surf, new condos and developments nestled in secure valleys, prime golfing, and inland, roads that'll take you to the roof of Oahu. Waianae is the home of small farms, run-down shacks, and families that hold luau on festive occasions, where the food and entertainment are the real article. Anyone lucky enough to be invited into this quickly disappearing world will be blessed with one of the last remaining authentic cultural experiences in Hawaii.

The possibility of hassles shouldn't be minimized because they do happen, but every aggressor needs a victim. The biggest problem is thievery, of the sneak-thief variety. You're marked as a tourist because of your new rental car. If you leave valuables in it, or lying unattended on the beach, they have a good chance of disappearing. But who does silly things like this *anywhere* in the U.S.? You won't be accosted, or held up at gunpoint, but if you bother a bunch of local guys drinking beer, you're asking for trouble. Moreover, the toughness of Waianae is self- perpetuating, and frankly the locals *like* the hard reputation. A few years back a feature writer reported that when he visited Waianae some toughs threw rocks at him. No one had ever reported this before, but after a big stink was made about it, more and more people had rocks thrown at them when they visited here. In recent years *pakalolo* has had a tremendous effect on the area. Local guys began growing and smoking it. This brought some money back into the depressed region, and it changed the outlook of some of the residents. They felt a camaraderie with other counterculture people, many of whom happened to be *haoles*. They could relax and not feel so threatened with pursuing an often elusive materialistic path. Many became more content with their laid-back lifestyle, and genuinely less interested with the materialistic trip all the way around.

In truth, *we* shouldn't be warned about *them*, but vice versa. The people of Waianae are the ones being infringed upon, and it is they who, in the final analysis, will be hassled, ripped off, and ultimately dispossessed. Recent articles by Oahu's Development Conference strongly state that future development will center on the island's northwestern shore . . . the Waianae Coast! A few rocks are poor weapons against developmental progress, which is defined by the big boys with the big dreams and the big bucks to back them up.

BEACHES AND SIGHTS

The Waianae Coast is very accessible. One road takes you there. Simply follow the H-1 freeway from Honolulu until it joins the Farrington Hwy. (Rt. 93). It runs north, opening up the entire coast. A handful of side roads lead into the interior, and that's about it! A strange recommendation, but sensible on this heavily trafficked road, is to drive north to the end of the line and then stop at the scenic sights on your way back south. This puts you on the ocean side of the highway where you won't have to worry about cutting across two lines of traffic, which can be a steady stream making it tough to navigate. TheBus No. 51 runs the entire Waianae Coast, and stops at all of the following beaches.

Note: Many of the beach parks along this coast offer **camping,** but their status periodically changes to **no camping** without notice. Many of the other campers are local people in semipermanent structures; the reason that the status changes quickly is to prevent these people from squatting. Also, remember that this is the leeward coast, which gets plenty of sunshine. Many of the beach parks do not have shade trees, so be prepared. June is the prettiest month because all the flowers are in bloom, but it's one of the worst times for sunburn. The entire coast is great for snorkeling, with plenty of reef fish. However, keep your eyes on the swells, and always stay out during rough seas, when waves can batter you against the rocks. The parks listed below run from south to north.

HEADING NORTH

Barber's Point Beach Park

The first beach is Barbers Point Beach Park, at the end of Kalaeloa Boulevard. Turn down it where H-1 and the Farrington Hwy. join. The Point was named after Capt. Henry Barber, who was shipwrecked here in 1795. Few people, even island residents, visit this beach park. It's in an industrial area and the shoreline is rocky. One pocket of white-sand beach is open to the public, though it fronts a private residence. The swimming is safe only in summer, and you'll find picnic facilities, restrooms, and camping (county permit).

Kahe And Hawaiian Electric Beach Park

Kahe and Hawaiian Electric beach parks are just where the Farrington Hwy. curves north along the coast. They're the first two *real* Waianae beaches, and they're symbolic. You come around the bend to be treated to an absolutely pristine view of the coast with the rolling sea, white-sand beach, cove, and the most hideous power plant you've ever seen. Kahe Beach Park offers restrooms, pavilion, and picnic facilities. The beach is poor except for a section just east of the improved park. Swimming is dangerous except on calm summer days. The Hawaiian Electric Beach Park, across from the power plant, is known as "Tracks" to island surfers because of the railroad tracks that run along the shore here. Facilities include picnic tables, pavilion, restrooms, showers, and parking along the highway. The white-sand beach is wide, and the swimming generally safe. The mild waves are perfect for learning how to surf. If you keep your eyes trained out to sea, the area is beautiful. Don't look inland!

Nanakuli Beach Park

Nanakuli Beach Park is on the southern outskirts of Nanakuli ("Pretend To Be Deaf") Town, which is the first real town of the Waianae Coast. If you get to the red light you've gone a little too far. The beach park is community-oriented with recreational buildings, basketball courts, baseball dia-

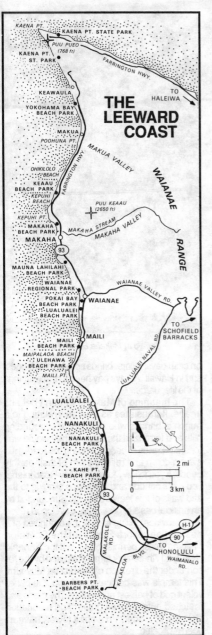

THE
LEEWARD
COAST

mond, and kiddies' play area. Camping has been permitted with a county permit. Lifeguards work on a daily basis, and the swimming is generally safe except during periods of high winter surf. The northern end of the beach, called Kalanianaole, is generally calmer than the southern end. They're divided by a housing project, but connected by a walkway. The southern section is fronted by a cliff with a small cove below. During periods of calm surf, the waters are crystal clear and perfect for snorkeling.

Ulehawa Beach Park

Ulehawa Beach Park, just north of Nanakuli, offers restrooms, picnic facilities, lifeguards, and sometimes camping. The best swimming is in a sandy pocket near the lifeguard tower. Surf conditions make for good bodysurfing. Most of the park, along a rocky cliff, is undeveloped. Here you'll find unlimited fishing spots. A shallow lagoon is generally safe for swimming year-round. As always, it's best to check with the local people on the beach.

Maili Beach Park

Maili Beach Park is at the southern end of Maili ("Many Small Stones") Town. It lies between two streams coming down from the mountains. Amenities include restrooms, picnic facilities, lifeguard tower, and camping . . . sometimes! The best swimming is in front of the lifeguard tower. The beach is broken into three parts by a housing development. In wintertime the beach disappears, but it returns wide and sandy for the summer. Most of the park is undeveloped. In town is a **7-eleven** and gas stations. As you drive through town notice a giant outcropping, Maili Point, which meets the sea like a giant fist. It has the same dominant presence as Diamond Head. When you go through town you'll see what's been happening around here since development has come to Waianae. Pull off at Maili Beach Park, and to your right are the modest homes of local people. Look up the coast to where the mountains come down to the sea. Out on that headland you can see a giant resort and on the bending backbone leading up to it modest homes of the local people. The beach is at least 300 yards long, and family-oriented. Plenty of coral pockets offer good snorkeling. Don't just jump in. Ask the locals or swing by the lifeguard tower to make sure that it's safe.

Lualualei Beach Park

Lualualei Beach Park has restrooms, camping sometimes, and picnic facilities. The entire park is largely undeveloped and lies along low cliffs and raised coral reef. Swimming is almost impossible. It's primarily good for fishing and lookng.

Pokai Beach Park

Pokai Beach Park is one of the nicest along the Waianae Coast, located just south of Waianae Town. It provides restrooms, camping sometimes, lifeguards, and boat ramp, which brings plenty of small craft into the area. Don't be surprised to see a replica of a double-hulled canoe often used for publicity purposes. It last appeared in a beer commercial. The park is clean, well maintained, reasonably secure, and family-oriented. There's surfing, snorkeling, and safe swimming year-round. If you're heading for one beach along Waianae, this is a top choice.

To get a look at a small working harbor or to hire a fishing boat, visit **Waianae Boat Harbor** as you head north from town. Huge installed stones form an impressive manmade harbor, with everything from luxury yachts to aluminum fishing boats. To head inland take **Waianae Valley Road.** You quickly gain the heights of the Waianae Range, and eventually come to a sentry box with a soldier inside. From here Kolekole Road is closed to the public, but if you stop and identify yourself, you'll be given permission to go to **Kolekole Pass.** The awesome view is well worth the trip.

Makaha Beach Park

Makaha Beach Park is famous for surfing, and as you approach, you can't help spotting a dominant headland called **Lahi Lahi,** which was a one-time island. Called "Black Rock" by the local fishermen, and used as a landmark, it still marks Makaha. Surfing competitions have been held here since the Makaha International Surfing Competition began in 1952. In recent years, a local lifeguard named Richard "Buffalo" Keaulana, known to all who've come here, has begun the Annual Buffalo Big Board Riding Championship. Paul Strauch Jr., inventor of the "hang five," comes to Makaha whenever he has a chance, along with Buffalo's sons and other pro surfers, many of whom live in the area. The swimming can be dangerous during high surf, but excellent

Buffalo at Makaha Beach Park

on calm days. Winter brings some of the biggest surf in Hawaii. Always pay heed to the warnings of the lifeguards.

The meaning of Makaha doesn't help its image. It translates as "Fierce," relating to a bunch of bandits who lived in the surrounding hills and terrorized the region. They would wait for small bands of people walking the road, then swoop down and relieve them of their earthly goods. If you follow Makaha Valley Road inland, you pass condos and high-rises clinging to the arid walls of this leeward valley. Surrounded by an artificial oasis of green, this developed resort area provides golfing and all the amenities of a destination resort. Stop in at the Sheraton Makaha to ask permission to visit the **Kaneaki Heiau,** a 17th-century temple restored by the resort under the direction of the Bishop Museum. This temple was dedicated to Lono, the benevolent god of harvest and fertility. The grass and thatched huts used as prayer and meditation chambers, along with a spirit tower, have all been replicated.

Once past Makaha, the road gets rugged, with plenty of private places to pull off. This crab claw of land, which ends at Kaena Point, forms a bay. The seascape demands attention but look into the interior. The mountains seem naturally terraced as they form dry, deep valleys. All are micro habitats, each different from the other. On top of one notice a gigantic golf ball, really a radar tracking station, that lets you know that you're coming to the end of the passable road.

Keaau Beach Park

Keaau Beach Park has restrooms, picnic facilities, and camping (county permit). The improved part of the park has a sandy beach, but mostly the park is fronted by coral and lava, and is frequented mostly by fishermen and campers. The unimproved section is not good for swimming, but it does attract a few surfers, and is good for snorkeling and scuba but only during calm periods. The improved section is a flat grassy area with picnic tables, shade trees, and pavilions.

Yokohama Bay

Yokohama Bay is the end of the line. The pavement ends here, and if you're headed for Kaena Point (see p. 336) you'll have to walk. Yokohama Bay is a long stretch of sandy beach that is mostly unimproved. A lava-rock bathhouse is on the right, just after the entrance. The area was named because of the multitude of Japanese fishermen who came to this lonely site to fish. It's still great for fishing! The swimming can be hazardous because of the strong wave action and rough bottom, but the snorkeling is superb. Mostly the area is used by surfers and local people, including youngsters who dive off the large lava rocks. This is inadvisable for people unfamiliar with the area. Yokohama is a great place to come if you're after a secluded beach. Weekdays, you'll have it to yourself, with a slightly greater number of people on the weekends. Definitely bring cold drinks, and remember that there are no shade trees, so a hat or beach umbrella is a necessity. Many camp here unofficially.

Notice a rugged beach area, marked by dumped household appliances, just south of Yokohama Bay. Notice broken-down vans and makeshift tents of ripped tarps put up by local people who have staked out this area and who live here semipermanently. If you're looking for trouble, you've found the right spot.

Kaneana Cave is a few minutes south on your left as you head back down the coast. You probably didn't notice it on your way north because of the peculiar land formation that conceals the mouth in that direction. Unfortunately, people have come here with spray cans and trashed the cave. If you can overlook that, it's a phenomenon—a big one. You can spot it by looking for three cement blocks, like road dividers, right in front of the entrance. It's at the foot of a 200-foot outcropping of stone. When you see local people defacing the natural beauty like this, it's hard to believe that the Hawaiians had such a spirit bond with the *aina*.

PRACTICALITIES

ACCOMMODATIONS

Except for camping, there are no inexpensive places to stay along the Waianae Coast. Some local people let rooms for a good rate, but there is no way to find this out in advance. Your best bet is to check out the **bulletin board** at the Food Giant Supermarket in Waianae. Accommodations range from moderate to expensive, with Makaha Valley being the most developed resort area of Oahu outside of Waikiki. Except for the Sheraton Makaha Resort, all are condos and require a minimum stay of seven days.

The **Maili Cove** rents one-bedroom apartments for $350-450 per week. They have a swimming pool, parking, and TV, along with a few hotel units. Located at 87-561 Farrington Hwy., Waianae, HI 96792, tel. 696-4447.

The **Makaha Beach Cabanas** are in Makaha along the beach just past the high school. All units have a lanai overlooking the water. They're not fancy but are spotlessly clean and serviceable. All units are fully furnished with complete kitchens; from $350 per week. Contact the Makaha Beach Cabanas, 84-965 Farrington Hwy., tel. 696-7227.

The **Makaha Shores** are privately owned units that overlook a beautiful white-sand beach and provide great viewing of the surfers challenging the waves below. All units are fully fur-

typical camping beach,
Leeward Coast

nished with weekly rates of $290 studio, $400 one-bedroom, and $500 two-bedroom. Contact the condo at 84-265 Farrington Hwy., Makaha 96792, tel. 696-7121.

The least expensive accommodations are at the **Makaha Surfside.** The beach is rocky near the condo, but it makes up for this with two pools and a sauna. All units are individually owned and fully furnished. Weekly rates begin at $290 studio to $400-475 for a one-bedroom. Daily rates range from $40 to $55. For information write Makaha Surfside, 85-175 Farrington Hwy., Makaha 96792, tel. 696-2105.

Makaha Valley Towers rise dramatically from Makaha Valley, but they don't fit in. They're either a testament to man's achievement or ignorance, depending on your point of view. In keeping with the idea of security, you drive up to a gate manned by two guards. You're stopped, asked your business, and sent unsmilingly on your way. The condo provides fully furnished units, a/c, TV, and pool. Weekly rates are $365 studio, $400-500 one-bedroom. If you're staying in this ill-fitting high-rise, at least try to get a top floor where you can take advantage of the remarkable view. For rates and information: Makaha Valley Towers, 84-740 Kili Dr., Makaha 96792, tel. 695-9055.

The **Sheraton Makaha Resort** is famous for its hideaway golf course, among the top five on Oahu. The 6,400-foot par-72 course is relatively flat and costs $15 guest, $40 non-guest, plus $10 for a mandatory cart. The Sheraton has done an exemplary job with the units, some of

the nicest on the island. This is a true destination resort with a complete list of activities including horseback riding, tennis, two swimming pools, and a full complement of hotel-sponsored beach and water activities (although the ocean is a few miles away). Rooms begin at $85 d to $250 for a suite. For information and reservations, write Sheraton Makaha Resort, Box 896, Waianae, HI 96792, tel. (800) 325-3535, on Oahu 695-9511.

FOOD

For anyone with an urge to eat a two-scoop plate lunch, no problem. Little drive-in lunch counters are found in almost every Waianae town. Each serves hearty island food such as teriyaki chicken, pork, or *mahi mahi* for under $5. A good one is the **Nanakuli Drive-In** in the middle of town. **Makaha Drive-In** is more of the same. Another popular spot is **Red Baron Pizza** in the Waianae Shopping Center, tel. 696-2396.

You also see plenty of fruit sellers parked along the road. Their produce couldn't be fresher, and stopping provides you not only with the perfect complement to a picnic lunch but with a good chance to meet some local people.

For your shopping and dining needs in Nanakuli, try the **Pacific Shopping Mall** where you'll find the **Nanakuli Chop Suey Restaurant,** open 10 a.m.-8:30 p.m., tel. 668-8006, serving standard Chinese fare at local down-home prices (chicken dishes under $5, beef or pork to $4.75.) Just behind McDonald's is the **Eden**

BBQ Lounge with sit-down and takeout Korean food at moderate prices, tel. 668-2722, open 10-9 daily. In town is **Big Daddy's Plate Lunch,** where you can dine on island standards with a mandatory two-scoop rice for around $5.

The **Waianae Mall** is a complete shopping facility. Don't worry about bringing supplies or food if you're on a day excursion. You'll find all that you need at the mall, which includes Cathay Deli, Red Baron Pizza, Subway Sandwiches, Woolworth's, Big-Way Supermarket, and Pay 'n' Save Drugs. Have no fear if you're addicted to fast foods. Some major franchises have decided that your trip to leeward Oahu wouldn't be complete without something processed in a styrofoam box. **Burger King** is in the mall, and in town **McDonald's** golden arches rise alongside the highway just across from **Taco Bell**. If you're looking for ethnic flavor try the **Bayside Drive In** for a plate lunch, or the local **Tamura Supermarket.** You'll spot a number of gas stations in the middle of town, along with a **Domino's Pizza, Circle K,** and a 7-11 convenience store.

Makaha has **Makaha Drive In,** a plate lunch stand, **Woolworth's,** and a shopping basket of neighborhood markets.

The **Fogcutter** is a semicasual place offering steaks and seafood, at 84-111 Orange St., Makaha, tel. 695-9404. Prices are reasonable and the food is good. To pinpoint the Fog Cutter, one of the only sit-down places to eat in Makaha, look for the Cornet Store on the right as you head north through town. The first right past it is Orange Street, where you're welcomed by two old smokestacks. The restaurant offers lunch, dinner, and cocktails. Prepared beef is priced at $1.45 per ounce (pick your own size), with chicken dishes at $10. The Captain's seafood mix (shrimp, *mahi,* scallops, and crab) is priced right at $12.25. All dinners include salad bar and

homemade clam chowder or Portuguese bean soup. Hours 11-2 lunch, 6-10 dinner. The bar is friendly with a nautical theme highlighted by captains' chairs, charts, a ship's compass, and sailing paraphernalia.

The **Rusty Harpoon** is between Waianae and Maili overlooking the sea. It probably serves the best food for the money along the coast. In keeping with the name the airy interior is rustically nautical, complete with hurricane lamps and of course a few harpoons. The menu is chicken, fish, and beef, but the best deals are the Hawaiian plates. Lunch prices are excellent at around $5, but expect double that for the dinner menu.

The **Sheraton Makaha** has a number of restaurants ranging from sandwich bars to elegant dining. The Kaala Room features an impressive menu of fresh fish, steaks, and continental cuisine. Get a table with a long sweeping view of the valley, wonderful at sunset. Daily for dinner, tel. 695-9511. The hotel's Pikakae Cafe serves breakfast, lunch, and dinner with an assortment of sandwiches and international dishes.

The **Food Giant** grocery store in Waianae has a good selection of Oriental and Hawaiian food. To know what's happening along the Waianae Coast check out the bulletin board in front. The **Waianae Hawaiian Cultural and Art Center** offers workshops in lei-making, *lau hala* weaving, hula, and the Hawaiian language. They welcome people either to observe or participate in their programs. For times and schedules contact the **State Foundation of Culture and Arts,** tel. 548-4145.

Pokai Pottery on Pokai St., Waianae, is owned and operated by Bunkie Eakutis. His studio is attached to his home where he makes ceramics sold around the island through the Artists' Guild.

THE NORTHWESTERN ISLANDS

Like tiny gems of a broken necklace, the Northwestern Hawaiian Islands spill across the vast Pacific. Popularly called the **Leewards,** most were discovered last century, oftentimes by hapless ships that ground to a sickening halt on their treacherous, half-submerged reefs. Their captains left their names: Lisianski, Kure, French Frigates, Hermes, and Pearl. Even today, craft equipped with the most modern navigational devices must be wary in these waters. They remain among the loneliest outposts on the face of the Earth.

OVERVIEW

Land And Climate

The Leewards are the oldest islands of the Hawaiian chain, believed to have emerged from the sea at least six million years ago; some experts say 25 million years! Slowly they floated northward past the suboceanic hotspot as the other islands were built. Measured from **Nihoa Island,** about 100 miles off the northern tip of Kauai, they stretch for just under 1,100 miles to **Kure Atoll,** last of the **Midway Islands.** There are 13 islets, shoals, and half-submerged reefs in the chain. Most have been eroded flat by the sea and wind, but a few tough volcanic cores endure. Together they make up a land mass of approximately 3,400 acres, the largest being the Midways at 1,280 acres, and the smallest the **Gardner Pinnacles** at just over 2½ acres. The climate is similar to that of the main islands with a slightly larger variance. Temperatures sometimes dip as low as 50° F and climb as high as 90° F.

Administration And History

Politically, the Leewards are administered by the city and county of Honolulu, except for the Midway Islands, which are under federal jurisdiction. None are permanently inhabited, except for some lonely military and wildlife field stations on

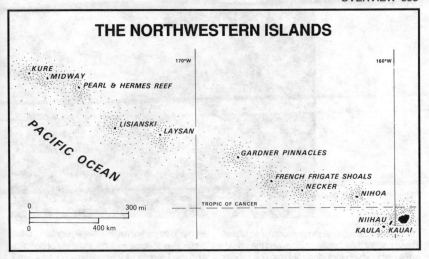

THE NORTHWESTERN ISLANDS

Midway, Kure, and the French Frigate Shoals. All are part of the **Hawaiian Islands National Wildlife Refuge,** established at the turn of the century by Theodore Roosevelt. In precontact times, some of the islands supported a Tahitian culture markedly different from the one that emerged on the main Hawaiian islands. Necker Island, for example, was the only island in the entire Hawaiian archipelago on which the inhabitants carved stone figures with a complete head and torso. On many of the others, remnants of *heiau* and agricultural terracing attribute to their colonization by pre-contact Hawaiians. Over the years, natives as well as Westerners have exploited the islands for feathers, fertilizer, seals, and fish.

The islands are closely monitored by the U.S. Fish and Wildlife Agency. Permission to land on them is granted only under special circumstances. Studies are underway to determine if the waters around the islands can support some commercial fishing, while leaving a plentiful supply of food for the unique wildlife of these lonely islands.

Wildlife
Millions of seabirds of various species have found permanent sanctuary on the Leewards, using them as giant floating nests and rookeries. Today the populations are stable and growing, but it hasn't always been so. On Laysan, at the

turn of the century, egg hunters came to gather uncountable albatross eggs, selling the albu-

unique figurine of Neckar Island

monk seal

men to companies making photographic paper. They brought their families along, and their children's pets, which included rabbits. The rabbits escaped and multiplied wildly. In no time they invaded the territories of the **Laysan honeycreeper, rail,** and **millerbird,** rendering them extinct. Laysan has recovered and is refuge to over six million birds, including the rare and indigenous **Laysan teal** and **finch.**

An amazing bird using the rookeries is the **frigate bird.** The male can blow up its chest in a mating ritual like a giant red heart-shaped balloon. Also known as **man-of-war birds,** they oftentimes pirate the catches of other birds, devour chicks, and even cannibalize their own offspring.

Some of the most prolific birds of the Leewards are terns, both the delicate all-white **fairy tern** and its darker relative the **sooty tern.** Other distinctive species include a variety of boobies, and the **Laysan albatross,** which has a wingspan of 10-12 feet, the world's largest.

Besides birds, the islands are home to the **Hawaiian monk seal,** one of only two species of indigenous Hawaiian mammals. These beautiful and sleek animals were hunted to near extinction for their skins. Man encroached on their territory more and more, but now they are protected as an endangered species. About 1,000 individuals still cling to existence on various islands.

The **green turtle** is another species that has found a haven here. They were hunted to near extinction for their meat and leather, and of the few colonies around the world, the largest in the U.S. is on the French Frigate Shoals.

MAUI

KAHOOLAWE, LANAI, AND MOLOKAI

"How shall we account for this nation spreading itself so far over this vast ocean? We find them from New Zealand to the south, to these islands to the north and from Easter Island to the Hebrides; . . . how much farther is not known . . ."

—Captain James Cook

INTRODUCTION

The Kumulipo, the ancient genealogical chant of the Hawaiians, sings of the demigod Maui, a half-human mythological sorcerer known and revered throughout Polynesia. Maui was a prankster on a grand scale who used guile and humor to create some of the most amazing feats of "derring-do" ever recorded. A Polynesian combination of Paul Bunyan and Hercules, Maui's adventures were known as "strifes." He served mankind by fishing up the islands of Hawaii from the ocean floor, securing fire from a tricky mud hen, lifting the sky so humans could walk upright, and slowing down the sun god by lasooing his genitals with a braided rope fashioned from his sister's pubic hair. Maui accomplished this last feat on the summit of the great mountain Haleakala ("House of the Sun"), thus securing more time in the day to fish and to dry tapa. Maui met his just but untimely end between the legs of the great goddess, Hina. This final prank, in which he attempted to crawl into the sleeping goddess' vagina, left his feet and legs dangling out, causing uproarious laughter among his comrades, a band of warrrior birds. The noise awakened Hina, who saw no humor in the situation. She unceremoniously squeezed Maui to death. The island of Maui is the only island in Hawaii and throughout Polynesia named after a god. With such a legacy the island couldn't help but become known as *Maui no ka oi,* (Maui is the best!)

OVERVIEW

In a land of superlatives, it's quite a claim to call your island *the* best, but Maui has a lot to back it up. Maui has more miles of swimmable beach than any of the other islands. Haleakala, the massive mountain that *is* East Maui, is the largest dormant volcano in the world. Its hardened lava that rises over 30,000 feet from the sea floor makes it one of the heaviest concentrated masses on the face of the earth. Legitimate claims are made that Maui grows the best onions and potatoes, but the boast of the best *pakololo* may only be a pipe dream, since all islands have great soil, weather, and many enterprising gardeners. Some even claim that Maui gets more sunshine than the other islands, but that's hard to prove.

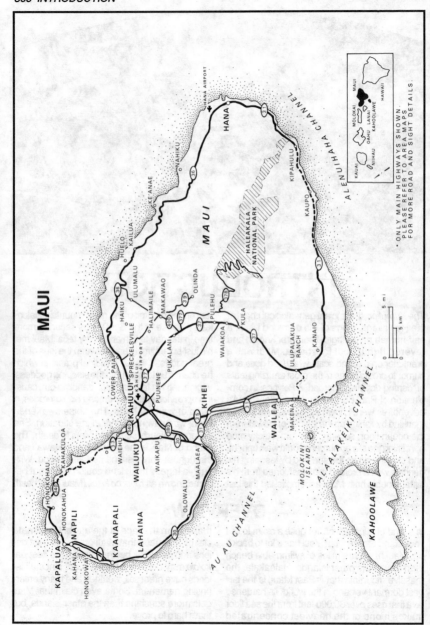

MAUI

ONLY MAIN HIGHWAYS SHOWN
PLEASE REFER TO AREA MAPS
FOR MORE ROAD AND SIGHT DETAILS.

KAUAI MAUI
MOLOKAI
OAHU LANAI
NIIHAU KAHOOLAWE HAWAII

5 mi

5 km

ALENUIHAHA CHANNEL

HANA AIRPORT
HANA
NAHIKU
KEANAE
KAILUA
HUELO
HAIKU
ULUMALU
OLINDA
MAKAWAO
HALIIMAILE
ULUPALAKUA RANCH
KANAIO
KAUPO
KIPAHULU
HALEAKALA NATIONAL PARK

MAUI

KULA
PULEHU
PUKALANI
WAIAKOA
KIHEI
MAKENA
WAILEA

KAHULUI
KAHULUI AIRPORT
SPRECKELSVILLE
LOWER PAIA
PUUNENE
WAILUKU
WAIKAPU
MAALAEA
WAIEHU
WAIHEE
KAHAKULOA
HONOKOHAU
HONOKAHUA
KAPALUA
NAPILI
KAHANA
HONOKOWAI
KAANAPALI
LAHAINA
OLOWALU

MOLOKINI ISLAND

ALALAKEIKI CHANNEL

AU AU CHANNEL

KAHOOLAWE

Maui's Body

If you look at the silhouette of Maui on a map, it looks like the head and torso of a man bent at the waist and contemplating the uninhabited island of Kahoolawe. The head is West Maui. The profile is that of a wizened old man whose wrinkled brow and cheeks are the **West Maui Mountains.** The highest peak here is **Puu Kukui,** 5,778 feet high and located just about where the ear would be. If you go to the top of the head, you'll be at Kapalua, a resort community recently carved from pineapple fields. Fleming Beach begins a string of beaches that continues down over the face, stopping at the neck, and picking up again on the chest, which is southeast Maui. Kaanapali is the forehead; this massive beach continues almost uninterrupted for four miles. In comparison, this area alone would take in all of Waikiki, from Diamond Head to Ala Moana. Sugar cane fields fringe the mountain side of the road, while condos are strung along the shore. The resorts here are cheek to jowl, but the best are tastefully done with views and access to the beach.

Lahaina would be located at the Hindu "third eye." This town is where it's "happening" on Maui, with concentrations of crafts, museums, historical sites, restaurants, and night spots. Lahaina has always been somewhat of a playground, used in times past by royal Hawaiian *ali'i* and then by Yankee whalers. The "good-times" mystique still lingers. At the tip of the nose is Olowalu, where a lunatic Yankee trader, Simon Metcalf, decided to slaughter hundreds of curious Hawaiians paddling toward his ship just to show them he was boss. From Olowalu you can see four islands: Molokai, Lanai, Kahoolawe, and a faint hint of Hawaii far to the south. The back of Maui's head is an adventurer's paradise, complete with a tourist-eliminating rugged road posted with overexaggerated Proceed No Farther signs. Back here are tremendous coastal views, bird sanctuaries, *heiau,* and Kahakuloa, a tiny fishing village reported to be a favorite stomping ground of great Maui himself.

The Isthmus

A low flat isthmus planted primarily in sugar cane is the neck that connects the head of West Maui to the torso of East Maui, which is Haleakela. The Adam's apple is the little port of Maalaea, which has a good assortment of pleasure and fishing boats, and provides an up-close look at a working port not nearly as frenetic as Lahaina. The nape of the neck is made up of the twin cities of Wailuku, the county seat, and Kahului, where visitors arrive at Maui's airport. These towns are where the "people" live. Some say the isthmus, dramatically separating east and west, is the reason Maui is called the "Valley Isle." Head into Iao Valley from Wailuku, where the West Maui Mountains have been worn into incredible peaked monolithic spires. This stunning valley played a key role in Kamehameha's unification of the Hawaiian Islands, and geologically seems to be a more fitting reason for Maui's nickname.

East Maui/Haleakala

Once you cross the isthmus you're on the immensity of Haleakela. This mountain is a true microcosm and makes up the entire bulging, muscled torso. Its geology encompasses alpine, desert, jungle, pastureland, and wasteland. The temperature, determined by altitude, ranges from subfreezing to subtropical. If you head east along the spine, you'll find world-class sailboarding beaches, artist villages, last-picture-show towns, and a few remaining family farms planted in taro. Route 36, the only coastal road, rocks and rolls you over its more than 600 documented curves, and shows you more waterfalls and pristine pools than you can count. After crossing more than 50 bridges, you come to Hana. Here, the "dream" Hawaii that people seek still lives. Farther along is Oheo Stream and its pools, erroneously known as "The Seven Sacred Pools." However, there is no mistaking the amazing energy vibrations in the area. Close by is where Charles Lindbergh is buried, and many celebrities have chosen the surrounding hillsides for their special retreats and hideaways.

On Haleakala's broad chest are macho cowboy towns complete with Wild West rodeos contrasting with the gentle but riotous colors of carnation and protea farms. Polipoli State Park is here, a thick forest canopy with more varieties of imported trees than anywhere in Oceania. A weird cosmic joke places Kihei just about where the armpit would be. Kihei is a mega-growth condo area ridiculed as an example of what developers shouldn't be allowed to do. Oddly enough, Wailea, just down the road, exemplifies a reasonable and aesthetic planned community and is highly touted as a "model" development

AVERAGE MAXIMUM/MINIMUM TEMPERATURE AND RAINFALL

Island	Town		Jan.	Mar.	May	June	Sept.	Nov.
Maui	Lahaina	high	80	81	82	83	84	82
		low	62	63	68	68	70	65
		rain	3	1	0	0	0	1
	Hana	high	79	79	80	80	81	80
		low	60	60	62	63	65	61
		rain	9	7	2	3	5	7
	Kahului	high	80	80	84	86	87	83
		low	64	64	67	69	70	68
		rain	4	3	1	0	0	2

area. Just at the belly button, close to the *kundalini,* is Makena, long renowned as Maui's "alternative beach." It's the island's last "free" beach with no restrictions, no park rangers, no amenities, and sometimes, no bathing suits.

Finally, when you pilgrimage to the summit of Haleakala, it'll be as if you've left the planet. It's another world: beautiful, mystical, raw, inspired, and freezing cold. When you're alone on the crater rim with the world below garlanded by the brilliance of sunrise or sunset, you'll know that you have come at last to great Maui's heart.

THE LAND

Maui is the second largest and youngest of the main Hawaiian Islands, next to Hawaii. It is made up of two volcanoes: the **West Maui Mountains** and **Haleakala.** The West Maui Mountains are geologically much older than Haleakala, but the two were joined by subsequent lava flows that formed a connecting low, flat isthmus. **Puu Kukui** at 5,778 feet is the tallest peak of the West Maui Mountains. It's the lord of a mountain domain whose old weathered face has been scarred by an inhospitable series of deep crags, valleys, and gorges. Haleakala, in comparison, is an adolescent with smooth, rounded features. This precocious kid looms 10,023 feet above sea level and is four times larger than West Maui. Its incredible mass, as it rises over 30,000 feet from the ocean floor, is one of the densest on Earth. Its gravitational pull is staggering and it was considered a primary

power spot in old Hawaii. The two parts of Maui combine to form 728.8 square miles of land with 120 linear miles of coastline. At its widest, Maui is 25 miles from north to south, and 40 miles east to west. The coastline has the largest number of swimmable beaches in Hawaii, and the interior is a miniature continent with almost every conceivable geological feature evident.

Climate
Maui has similar weather to the rest of the Hawaiian Islands, though some afficionados claim that it gets more sunshine than the rest. The weather on Maui depends more on where you are than on what season it is. The average yearly daytime temperature hovers around 80° F and is moderated by the tradewinds. Nights are just a few degrees cooler. Since Haleakala is a main feature on Maui, you should remember that altitude drastically affects the weather. Expect an average drop of three degrees for every 1,000 feet of elevation. The lowest temperature ever recorded in Hawaii was atop Haleakala in 1961 when the mercury dropped well below freezing to a low of 11%.

Precipitation
Rain on Maui is as much a factor as it is in all of Hawaii. On any day, somewhere on Maui it's raining, while other areas experience drought. A dramatic example of this phenomenon is to compare Lahaina with Mount Puu Kukui, both on West Maui and separated by only seven miles. Lahaina, which translates as "Merciless

Sun," is hot, arid, and gets 17 inches of rainfall annually, while Puu Kukui can receive close to 40 *feet* of rain! This rivals Mt. Waialeale on Kauai as the wettest spot on earth. The windward (wet) side of Maui, outlined by the Hana Road, is the perfect natural hothouse. Here, valleys sweetened with blossoms house idyllic waterfalls and pools that visitors treasure when they happen upon them. On the leeward (dry) side are Maui's best beaches: Kapalua, Kaanapali, Kihei, Wailea, and Makena. They all sit in Haleakala's "rain shadow." If it happens to be raining at one, just move a few miles down the road to the next. Anyway, the rains are mostly gentle and the brooding sky, especially at sundown, is even more spectacular than normal.

FLORA AND FAUNA

Maui's indigenous and endemic plants, trees, and flowers are both fascinating and beautiful. Unfortunately, they, like everything else that was native, are quickly disappearing. The majority of flora found interesting by visitors was either introduced by the original Polynesians or later by white settlers. Maui is blessed with state parks, gardens, undisturbed rainforests, private reserves, and commercial nurseries; combined they offer brilliant and dazzling colors to the landscape.

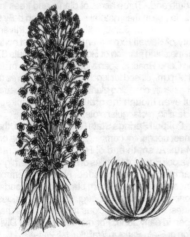

Silversword
Maui's official flower is a tiny pink rose called a *lokelani*. Its unofficial symbol, however, is the silversword. The Hawaiian name for silversword is *ahinahina* which translates as "gray gray," and the English name derives from a silverfish, whose color it's said to resemble. The silversword is from a remarkable plant family that claims 28 members, with five in the specific sil-

versword species. It's kin to the common sunflower, and botanists say the entire family evolved from a single ancestral species. The members of the silversword family can all hypothetically interbreed and produce remarkable hybrids. Some plants are shrubs, while others are climbing vines, and some even become trees. They grow anywhere from desert conditions to steamy jungles. On Maui, the silversword is only found on Haleakala, above the 6,000-foot level, and is especially prolific in the crater. Each plant lives from five to 20 years and ends its life by sprouting a gorgeous stalk of hundreds of purplish-red flowers. It then withers from a majestic six-foot plant to a flat gray skeleton. An endangered species, silverswords are totally protected. They protect themselves, too, from radiation and lack of moisture by growing fuzzy hairs all over their swordlike stalks. You can see them along the Haleakala Park Road at **Kalamaku Overlook,** or by hiking along **Silversword Loop** on the floor of the crater.

Protea
These exotic flowers are from Australia and South Africa. Because they come in almost limitless shapes, sizes, and colors, they captivate everyone who sees them. They are primitive, almost otherworldly in appearance, and they exude a life force more like an animal than a flower. The slopes of leeward Haleakala between 2,000 and 4,000 feet is heaven to protea—the growing conditions could not be more perfect. Here are found the hardiest, highest-quality protea in the world. The days are warm, the nights are cool and the well-drained volcanic soil has the exact combination of minerals that protea thrive on. Haleakala's crater even helps by creating a natural air flow which produces cloud cover, filters the sun, and protects the flowers. Protea make excellent gifts that can be shipped anywhere. As

fresh-cut flowers they are gorgeous, but they have the extra benefit of drying superbly. Just hang them in a dark, dry, well-ventilated area and they do the rest. You can see protea, along with other botanical specialties, at the following: **Kula Botanical Garden** (see below), **Upcountry Protea Farm** on Upper Kimo Drive one mile off Haleakala Hwy. (Route 377), **Hawaii Protea Co-op,** next to Kula Lodge on Crater Road, and **Protea Gardens of Maui,** on Hapapa Road off Route 377 not far from Kula Lodge.

Carnations

If protea aren't enough to dazzle you, how about fields of carnations? Most Mainlanders think of carnations stuck in a groom's lapel, or perhaps have seen a table dedicated to them in a hothouse, but fields full of carnations! The Kula area produces carnations that grow outside nonchalantly in rows, like cabbages. They fill the air with an unmistakable perfume, and they are without doubt a joy to behold. You can see family and commercial plots throughout the upper Kula area.

Prickly Pear Cactus

Interspersed in countless fields and pastures on the windward slope of Haleakala, adding that final nuance to cattle country, are clusters of prickly pear cactus. The Hawaiians call them *panini,* which translates as "very unfriendly," undoubtedly because of the sharp spines covering the flat thick leaves. These cactus are typical of those found in Mexico and the southwestern U.S. They were introduced to Hawaii before

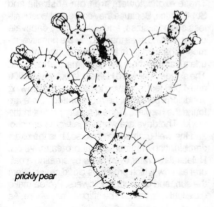

prickly pear

1810 and established themselves, coincidentally, in conjunction with the cattle being brought in at that time. It's assumed that Don Marin, a Spanish adviser to Kamehameha I, was responsible for bringing in the cactus. Perhaps the early *paniolo* felt lonely without them. The *panini* can grow to heights of 15 feet and are now considered a pest, but nonetheless look as if they belong. They develop small pear-shaped fruits which are quite delicious. Hikers who decide to pick them should be careful of small yellowish bristles that can burrow under the skin and become very irritating. The fruits turn into beautiful yellow and orange flowers.

Botanical Gardens, Parks, And State Forests

Those interested in the flora of Maui would find a visit to any of the following both educational and entertaining. In the Kula area visit: **Kula Botanical Gardens,** tel. 878-1715, clearly marked along Route 377 (Haleakala Hwy.) just a mile from where Route 377 joins Route 37 at the south end. Three acres of plants and trees include koa in their natural settings. Open daily 9 a.m. to 4 p.m., $2.50, self-guided tour. **University of Hawaii Expermental Station,** just north of the south junction of Route 377 and Route 37 on Copp Road, is open Mon. to Fri., 7:30 a.m. to 3:30 p.m., closed for lunch, free. Twenty acres of constantly changing plants that are quite beautiful even though the grounds are uninspired, scientific, rectangular plots.

Polipoli Springs State Recreation Area, the finest upcountry camping and trekking area on Maui. At south end of Route 377, turn onto Waipoli Road for 10 miles of bad road. Overnight camping is recommended. Native and introduced birds, magnificent stands of redwoods, conifers, ash, cypress, sugi, cedar and various pines. Known for delicious methley plums that ripen in early June. For more info contact Division of State Parks in Wailuku, tel. 244-4354.

Keanae Arboretum, about 15 miles west of Hana on the Hana Hwy. (Route 360), is always open, no fee. Native, introduced, and exotic plants, including Hawaiian food plants, are in a natural setting with walkways, identifying markers, tropical trees, and mosquitos. Educational, a must.

Helani Gardens, one mile west of Hana, open daily 10 a.m. to 3:30 p.m., adults $2. These 60 acres of flower beds and winding jeep trails are the lifetime project of Howard Cooper, lovingly tended, exotic jungle, terrific!

Maui Zoo and Botanical Garden, in Wailuku, is easily accessible. Get a basic introduction to flora at this tiny zoo, good for tots, and mildly interesting. In Central Maui try: **Kepaniwai Park,** on Route 32 leading to Iao Needle. This tropical setting displays formalized gardens from different nations. Open daily, no fee. Finally, for an extremely civilized treat, visit the formal gardens of the **Hyatt Regency Hotel** in Kaanapali, open to the public. The architecture and grounds are impeccable.

Maui's Endangered Birds

Maui suffers the same fate as the other islands. Its native birds are disappearing. Maui is the last home of the crested honeycreeper (akohe'kohe). It lives only on the windward slope of Haleakala from 4,500 to 6,500 feet. It once lived on Molokai, but no longer. It's rather a large bird, averaging over seven inches long, and predominantly black. Its throat and breast are tipped with gray feathers, while it's neck and underbelly are a bright orange. A distinctive fluff of feathers forms a crown. It primarily eats ohia flowers and it's believed that the crown feathers gather pollen and help to propagate the ohia. The parrotbill is another endangered bird found only on the slopes of Haleakala above 5,000 feet. It has an olive-green back and a yellow body. Its most distinctive feature is its parrot-like bill which it uses to crack branches and pry out larvae.

Two waterbirds found on Maui are the Hawaiian stilt (ae'o) and the Hawaiian coot (alae ke'-oke'o). The stilt is about 16 inches tall and lives on Maui at Kanaha and Kealia ponds. Primarily black with a white belly, its sticklike legs are pink. The adults will pretend to be hurt, putting on an excellent performance of the "broken wing" routine, in order to lure predators away from their nests. The Hawaiian coot is a web-footed water bird that resembles a duck. It's found on all the main islands but mostly on Maui and Kauai. Mostly a dull gray, it has a white bill and tail feathers. It builds a large floating nest and vigorously defends its young.

The dark-rumped petrel is slightly different than other primarily marine birds. This petrel is found around the Visitors Center at Haleakala Crater about one hour after dusk from May through October. The amakihi and the iiwi are endemic birds that aren't endangered at the moment. The amakihi is one of the most common native birds. It's a yellowish-green bird that frequents the high branches of ohia, koa, and sandalwood looking for insects, nectar, or fruit. It's less specialized than most other Hawaiian birds, the main reason for its continued existence. The iiwi is a bright red bird with a salmon-colored, hooked bill. It's found only on Maui, Hawaii, and Kauai in the forests above 2,000 feet. It, too, feeds on a variety of insects and flowers. The iiwi is known for its harsh voice that sounds like a squeaking hinge but is also capable of a melodious song.

Other indigenous birds found on Maui are the wedge-tailed sheerwater, white-tailed tropic bird, black noddy, American plover, and a large variety of escaped exotic birds.

Pueo

This Hawaiian owl is found on all of the main islands, but mostly on Maui, especially in Haleakala Crater. The pueo is one of the oldest examples of an aumakua (family-protecting spirit) in Hawaiian mythology. It was an especially benign and helpful guardian. Old Hawaiian stories abound in which a pueo came to the aid of warriors in distress, who would head for a tree in which a pueo had alighted. Once there, they were safe from their pursuers and were under the protection of "the wings of an owl." Many introduced barn owls in Hawaii are easily distinguished from a pueo by their distinctive heart-shaped faces. The pueo is about 15 inches tall with a mixture of brown and white feathers. The eyes are large, round, and yellow; the legs are heavily feathered, unlike a barn owl. Pueo chicks are a distinct yellow color.

Nene

The nene, or Hawaiian goose, is found only on the slopes of Mauna Loa and Mauna Kea on the Big Island, and in Haleakala Crater on Maui. It was extinct on Maui until a few birds were returned there in 1957. By the 1940s less than 50 birds were living in the wild; now approximately 125 birds are on Haleakala, and 500 on the Big Island. Although the birds can be raised successfully in captivity, their life in the wild is still in question. Some ornithologists even debate whether the nene ever lived on Maui. The nene is believed to be a descendent of the Canadian

The nene, *the state bird, lives only on Haleakala and on the slopes of Mauna Loa and Mauna Kea on the Big Island.*

goose, which it resembles. It's perfectly at home away from water, foraging and nesting on rugged and bleak lava flows. The *nene* is a perfect symbol for Hawaii: let it be and it will live!

THE HUMPBACKS OF MAUI

Humpbacks get their name from their style of exposing their dorsal fin when they dive, which gives them a humped appearance. About 7,000-8,000 humpback whales are alive today, down from an estimated 100,000 at the turn of the century. The remaining whales are divided into three separate global populations: North Atlantic, North Pacific, and South Pacific groups. About 500 North Pacific humpbacks migrate from coastal Alaska starting in November. They reach their peak in February, congregating mostly in the waters off Maui, with a smaller group heading for the waters off Kona on Hawaii. An adult humpback is 45 feet long and weighs in at a svelte 40 tons (80,000 pounds). They come to Hawaii mainly to give birth to a single 2,000-pound, relatively blubberless calf. They nurse their calf for about one year and become impregnated again the next. While in Hawaiian waters humpbacks generally don't eat. They wait until returning to Alaska where they gorge themselves on krill. It's estimated that they can live off their blubber without peril for six months. They have an enormous mouth stretching a third the length of their bodies which is filled with over 600 rows of baleen, a prickly, fingernail-like substance. Humpbacks have been known to blow air under water to create giant bubble-nets that help to corral krill. Then they rush in with mouth agape and dine on their catch.

Like all cetaceans they breathe consciously, not involuntarily like humans; like other baleen whales they feed in relatively shallow waters and therefore sound (dive) for periods lasting a maximum of about 15 minutes. In comparison, a sperm whale (toothed bottom-feeder) can stay down for over an hour. On the surface a humpback breathes about once every two minutes, and sometimes sleeps on the surface or just below it for two hours. A distinctive feature of the humpback is the 15-foot flipper which it can bend over its back. The flippers and tail flukes have white markings that always differ between individuals and are used to recognize the humpbacks from year to year. The humpback is the most "aquabatic" of all whales and it is a thrilling sight to see one of these playful giants leap from the water and create a monumental splash.

Humpback's Song
All whales are fascinating, but the humpbacks have a special ability to sing unlike any others. They create their melodies by grunting, shrieking, and moaning. No one knows exactly what the songs represent, but it's clear they're a definite form of communication. The singers appear to be "escort males" that tag along with, and seem to guard, a mother and her calf. The songs are exact renditions that last 20 minutes or more and are repeated over and over again for hours. Amazingly, all the whales know and sing the same song, and the song changes from year to year. The notes are so forceful that they can be heard above and below the water for miles. Some of the deep base notes will even carry underwater for 100 miles! Scientists devote careers to recording and listening to the humpbacks' songs. As yet they're unexplained, but anyone who hears their eerie tones knows that he is privy to a wonderful secret and that the songs are somehow a key to understanding the consciousness of the great humpback.

The Brig *Carthaginian*

Just to the right of the Loading Dock in Lahaina Harbor is a restored 19th-century square-masted ship, the *Carthaginian*. It's a floating museum dedicated to whales and whaling, featuring an excellent audio-visual display narrated by actor Richard Widmark. The *Carthaginian* ($2) is open daily 9:30 a.m. to 5 p.m., but to enjoy the entire display allow at least an hour. As you descend into the hold of the ship and bright sunlight fades to cool shadow, you become a visitor into a watery world of the humpback whale. The haunting, mysterious songs of the humpback provide the background music and set the mood. Sit on comfortable captains' chairs and watch the display. The excellent photos of whales are by Flip Nicklin, courtesy of the National Geographic Society. The *Carthaginian* is a project of the Lahaina Restoration Foundation, Box 338, Lahaina, HI 96761 tel. 661-3262. The foundation is a nonprofit organization dedicated to educational and historical restoration in Lahaina.

Whalewatching

If you're on Maui from late Nov. to early May, you have an excellent chance of spotting a humpback. You can often see a whale from a vantage point on land but this is nowhere near as thrilling as seeing them close-up from a boat. Either way, binoculars are a must. Telephoto and zoom lenses are also useful and you might even get a nifty photo in the bargain. But don't waste your film unless you have a fairly high-powered zoom: fixed-lens cameras give pictures with a lot of ocean and a tiny black speck. If you're lucky enough to see a whale breach (jump clear of the water), keep watching—they often repeat this a number of times. If a whale dives and lifts its fluke high in the air, expect it to be down for quite a while (15 minutes) and not come up in the same spot. Other times they'll dive shallowly, then bob up and down quite often. From shore you're likely to see whales anywhere along Maui's south coast. If you're staying at any of the hotels or condos along Kaanapali or Kihei and have an ocean view, you can spot them from your lanai or window. A good vantage spot is Papawai Point along Route 30 and up the road heading west just before the tunnel. Maalaea Bay is another favorite nursing ground for mothers and their calves;

you also get to see a small working harbor up close. An excellent viewpoint is Makena Beach on the spit of land separating Little and Big Beaches (local names). If you time your arrival near sunset, even if you don't see a whale, you'll have a mind-boggling light show. For general information see p. 16; for Maui whalewatching cruises see p. 382.

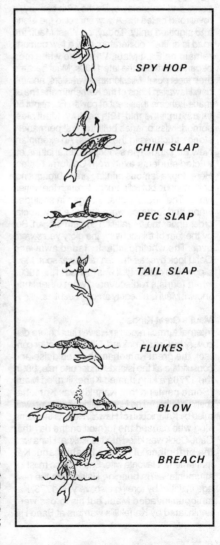

SPY HOP

CHIN SLAP

PEC SLAP

TAIL SLAP

FLUKES

BLOW

BREACH

HISTORY

The Kumulipo sings that Maui was the second island child of Wakea and Papa. Before the coming of the white man and his written record, it's clear that the island was a powerful kingdom. Wars raged throughout the land and kings ruled not only Maui, but the neighboring islands of Lanai and Kahoolawe. By the 16th century, a royal road called the Alaloa encircled the island and signified unity. Today, on West Maui, the road is entirely obliterated: only a few portions remain on East Maui. When the white men began to arrive in the late 1700s, Maui became their focal point. Missionaries, whalers, and the new Hawaiian kings of the Kamehameha line all made Lahaina their seat of power. For about 50 years, until the mid-19th century, Maui blossomed. Missionaries built the first permanent stone structures in the islands. An exemplary New England-style school at Lahianaluna attracted students even from California cities. Here, too, a famous printing press brought not only revenue but refinement, through the written word. The sugar industry began in secluded Hana and fortunes were made; a new social order under the "Plantation System" began. But by the turn of this century, the glory years were over. The whaling industry faded away and Oahu took over as the central power spot. Maui slipped into obscurity. It was revived in the 1960s when tourists rediscovered what others had known: Maui is a beauty among beauties.

Maui's Great Kings

Internal turmoil raged in Hawaii just before discovery by Capt. Cook in 1778. Shortly after contact, the great Kamehameha would rise and consolidate all the islands under one rule, but in the 1770s a king named Kahekili ruled Maui. (Some contend that Kahekili was Kamehameha's father!) The Hana district, however, was ruled by Kalaniopuu of Hawaii. He was the same king who caused the turmoil on the day that Capt. Cook was killed at Kealakekua. Hana was the birthplace of Queen Kaahumanu, Kamehameha's favorite wife. She was the most instrumental ali'i in bringing Hawaii into the new age initiated by foreign discovery. In 1776, Kalaniopuu invaded Maui, but his forces were annihilated by Kahekili's warriors at Sand Hill

near Wailuku, which means "Bloody Waters." On November 26, 1778 Capt. Cook spotted Maui, but bypassed it because he could find no suitable anchorage. It wasn't until May 28, 1786 that a French expedition led by Commander La Perouse came ashore near Lahaina after finding safe anchorage at what became known as La Perouse Bay. Maui soon became a regular port of call. In 1790 Kamehameha finally defeated Kahekili's forces at Iao Needle and brought Maui under his domain. The great warrior Kahekili was absent from the battle, where Kamehameha used a cannon from the Fair American, a small ship seized a few years before. Davis and Young, two marooned seamen, provided the technical advice for these horrible but effective new weapons.

Maui's Rise

The beginning of the 19th century brought amazing changes to Hawaii and many of these came through Maui—especially the port of Lahaina. In 1793, Capt. Vancouver visited Lahaina and confirmed La Perouse's report that it was a fine anchorage. In 1802 Kamehameha stopped with his enormous "Pelelu Fleet" of war canoes on his way to conquer Oahu. He lingered for over a year collecting taxes and building his "Brick Palace" at Lahaina. The bricks were poorly made, but this marked the first Western-style structure in the islands. He also built a fabulous straw house for his daughter Princess Nahienaena that was so well constructed it was later used as the residence of the U.S. Consul. In 1819 the first whaler, The Bellina, stopped at Lahaina and marked the ascendancy of Hawaii as the capital of the whaling industry that lasted until the majority of the whaling fleet was lost in the Arctic in 1871. During its heyday, over 500 ships visited Lahaina in one year. Also in 1819, the year of his death, Kamehameha built an observation tower in Lahaina so that he could watch for returning ships, many of which held his precious cargo. In that prophetic year the French reappeared, with a warship this time, and the drama began. The great Western powers of the period maneuvered to upstage each other in the quest for dominance of this Pacific jewel.

Na Pali Coast (Robert Nilsen)

1. Waipio Valley (J.D. Bisignani)   **2.** Hanakapiai Beach (Robert Nilsen)

1. lantana (J.D. Bisignani) **2.**plumeria (J.D. Bisignani) **3.** anthurium (J.D. Bisgnani)

1. Byodo-In (J.D. Bisignani)   **2.** Rural church (Bob Cowan)

1. waterfall at Hawaii Tropical Botanical Gardens (J.D. Bisignani)
2. Waimea Canyon (J.D. Bisignani) 3. Hanalei Valley (Robert Nilsen)

1. the Puna coast (J.D. Bisignani)   **2.** Hana Road waterfalls (J.D. Bisignani)
3. Road to MacKenzie Park (J. D. Bisignani)

The Missionaries

In 1823 the first Christian mission was built in Lahaina under the pastorage of Rev. Richards, and the great conversion of Hawaii began in earnest. In that year Queen Keopuolani, the first great convert to Christianity, died. She was buried in Lahaina not according to the ancient customs accorded to an *ali'i*, but as a reborn child of Christ. The Rev. Richards and Queen Kaahumanu worked together to produce Hawaii's first Civil Code based on the Ten Commandments. The whalers fought the interference of the missionaries to the point where attempts were made on Rev. Richards' life, including a naval bombardment of his home. Over the next decade, the missionaries, ever hard at work, became reconciled with the sailors, who donated funds to build a Seaman's Chapel. This house of worship was located just next to the Baldwin Home, an early permanent New England-style house which still stands on Front Street. The house originally belonged to the Spaulding family, but the Baldwins were such an influence that it was known by their name. Lahainaluna High School, situated in the cool of the mountains just north of Lahaina, became the paramount institution of secondary learning west of the Rocky Mountains. The newly wealthy of Hawaii and California sent their progeny here to be educated along with the nobility of the Kingdom of Hawaii.

Maui Fades

If the following 30 years of Maui's historical and sociological development were put on a graph, it would show a sharp rise followed by a crash. By mid-century, Maui boasted the *first* Constitution, Catholic Mass, Temperance Union, Royal Palace, and steamship service. A census was taken and a prison built to house reveling seamen. Kamehameha III moved the capital to Honolulu and the 1850s brought a smallpox epidemic, the destruction of Wainee Church by a "ghost wind," and the death of David Malo, a classic historian of pre-contact Hawaii. By the late 1860s, the whaling industry was dead, but sugar would rise to take its place. The first successful sugar plantation was started by George Wilfong in 1849 along the Hana coast, and the first great sugar mill was started by James Campbell in 1861. The 1870s saw the planting of Lahaina's famous Banyan Tree by Sheriff W.O. Smith, and the first telephone and telegraph cable linking Paia with Haiku.

The 20th Century

When the Pioneer Hotel was built in 1901, Lahaina was still important. Claus Spreckels, "King Sugar" himself, had large holdings on Maui and along with his own sugar town, Spreckelsville, built the Haiku Ditch in 1878. This 30-mile ditch brought 50 million gallons of water a day from Haiku to Puunene so that the "green gold" could flourish. This entrepreneur was able to buy the land for his sugar plantation cheaply. The highly superstitious Hawaiians of the time didn't value this particular plot of land, believing that the souls of those that had not made the leap to heaven were condemned to wander this wasteland. To them it was obviously cursed, supporting only grasses and scrub bushes, and they felt that they were getting the bargain, offloading it to this unsuspecting *haole*. Moreover, Spreckels was a gambler. In a series of late-night poker games with Kamehameha III he was able to win the water rights to a dozen or so streams in the area, thereby creating the possibility for his Haiku Ditch. Sugar and Maui became one.

Then, because of sugar, Lahaina lost its dominance and Paia became the town on Maui during the 1930s, where it housed plantation workers in camps according to nationality. Maui slid more and more into obscurity. A few luminaries brought some passing fame: Tandy MacKenzie, for example, born in Hana in 1892, was a gifted operatic star whose career lasted until 1954. In the 1960s, Maui, as well as all of Hawaii, became accesssible to the average tourist. It was previously discovered by men like Sam Pryor, retired vice-president of Pan Am who made his home in Hana and invited Charles Lindbergh to visit, then to live and finally die in this idyllic spot. In the mid-'60s, the Lahaina Restoration Foundation was begun. It dedicated itself to the preservation of Old Lahaina and other historical sites on the island. It now attempts to preserve the flavor of what once was while looking to future growth. Today, Maui is once again in ascendancy, the second most visited island in Hawaii after Oahu.

GOVERNMENT

The boundaries of Maui County are a bit oddball, but historically oddball. Maui County encompasses Maui Island, as well as Lanai, Molokai, and the uninhabited island of Kahoolawe. The apparent geographical oddity is an arc on East Maui, from Makawao past Hana and along the south coast almost to Kihei, which is a "shared" political area, aligned with the Kohala District of the Big Island since Polynesian times. These two districts were joined with each other, so it's just a traditional carryover. The real strangeness occurs in Maui's 5th Senatorial District and its counterpart, the 10th Representative District. These two political areas include West Maui and the islands of Lanai and Molokai. West Maui, with Kaanapali, Lahaina, and Kapalua, is one of the most developed and financially sound areas in all of Hawaii. It's a favorite area with tourists and is the darling of developers. On the other hand, Lanai has a tiny population that is totally dependent on a one-company "pineapple economy." Molokai has the largest per capita concentration of native Hawaiians, a "busted economy" with a tremendous share of its population on welfare, and a grass-roots movement determined to preserve the historical integrity of the island and the dignity of the people. You'd have to be a political magician to fairly represent all of the constituents in these widely differing districts.

Maui's Representatives: Hawaii's State Legislature is comprised of 76 members, with the House of Representatives having 51 elected seats, and the State Senate 25. Members serve two- and four-year terms respectively. All officials come from 76 separate electorates based on population. Maui is represented by three state senators, who've usually been Democrats, and five state representatives, who've been Democrats as well.

ECONOMY

Maui's economy is a mirror image of the state's economy: it's based on tourism, agriculture, and government expenditures. The primary growth is in **tourism.** Over 12,000 rooms are available on Maui in all categories, and they're filled 70% of the time. On average, Maui attracts close to a million tourists per year, and on any given day

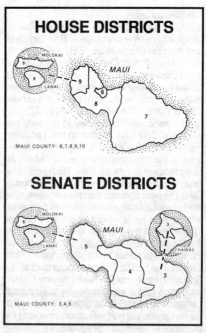

HOUSE DISTRICTS

MOLOKAI
9
LANAI
9
MAUI
9
6
8
7

MAUI COUNTY: 6,7,8,9,10

SENATE DISTRICTS

MOLOKAI
5
LANAI
5
MAUI
5
3
HAWAII
4
3

MAUI COUNTY: 3,4,5

there are about 15,000 visitors enjoying the island. The building trades are still booming, and though the majority of the rooms are in Kihei-Wailea, the Kaanapali area is catching up fast.

Agriculturally, Maui generates revenue through cattle, sugar, pineapples, *pakololo,* and flowers. **Cattle grazing** occurs on the western and southern slopes of Haleakala, where 20,000 acres are owned by the Ulupala Kua Ranch and over 32,000 acres by the Haleakala Ranch. The upper slopes of Haleakala around Kula are a gardener's dream. Delicious onions, potatoes, and all sorts of garden vegetables are grown but are secondary to large plots of gorgeous flowers, mainly carnations and the amazing protea.

Sugar, actually in the grass family, is still very important to Maui's economy, but without federal subsidies it wouldn't be a viable cash crop. The largest acreage is in the central isthmus area, which is virtually all owned by the Alexander and Baldwin Company. There are also large sugar tracts along Kaanapali and the west coast that are owned by Amfac and Maui Land and Pineapple. Those lodging in Kaanapali will

MAUI POPULATION

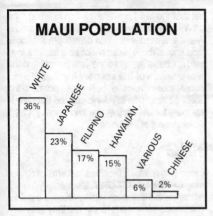

- WHITE 36%
- JAPANESE 23%
- FILIPINO 17%
- HAWAIIAN 15%
- VARIOUS 6%
- CHINESE 2%

become vividly aware of the sugar fields when they're burned off just prior to harvesting. Making these unsightly burnings even worse is the fact that the plastic pipe used in the drip irrigation of the fields is left in place. Not cost-efficient to recover, it is burned along with the cane, adding its noxious fumes to the air.

Pineapples grow in central East Maui between Paia and Makawao where Alexander and Baldwin own most of the land. Another area is the far west coast north of Napili where Maui Land and Pineapple controls most of the holdings. Renegade entrepreneurs grow patches of *pakalolo* wherever they can find a spot that has the right vibes and is away from the prying eyes of the authorities. Deep in the West Maui Mountains and along the Hana coast are favorite areas.

Government expenditures in Maui County are just over $40 million per year. A small military presence on Maui amounts to a tiny Army installation near Kahului; and the Navy owning the target island of Kahoolawe. With tourists finding Maui more and more desirable every year, and with agriculture firmly entrenched, Maui's economic future is bright.

Tourism-related Problems

Two prime examples of the best and the worst development can be found on Maui's south shore at Kihei and Wailea, less than five miles apart. In the late '60s Kihei experienced a de-

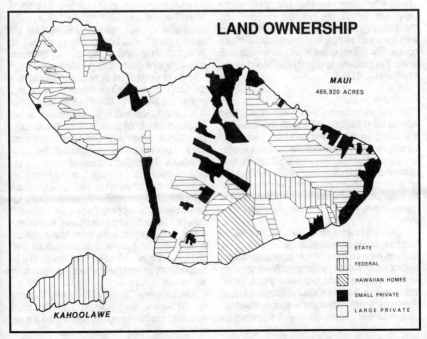

LAND OWNERSHIP

MAUI
465,920 ACRES

- STATE
- FEDERAL
- HAWAIIAN HOMES
- SMALL PRIVATE
- LARGE PRIVATE

KAHOOLAWE

velopment-inspired "feeding frenzy" that made the real sharks off its shore seem about as dangerous as Winnie the Pooh. Condos were slapped up as fast as cement can dry, their architecture reminiscent of a stack of shoeboxes. Coastline renowned for its beauty was overburdened, and the view was wiped out in the process. Anyone who had the bucks built, and now parts of Kihei look like a high-rise, low-income, federally funded housing project. You can

bet that those who made a killing building here don't live here. Conversely, just down the road is Wailea, a model of what development could (and should) be. The architecture is tasteful, lowrise, unobtrusive, and done with people and the preservation of the scenery in mind. It's obviously more exclusive, but access points to the beaches are open to everyone, and the view is still there for all to enjoy, pointing the way for the development of the future.

SHOPPING

In this chapter you'll find general information about shopping on Maui for general merchandise, books, arts, crafts, and specialty items. Specific shops are listed in the "Shopping" section of each travel chapter. Here, you should get an overview of what's available and where, with enough information to get your pockets twitching and your credit cards smoldering! Happy bargain hunting!

SHOPPING MALLS

Those who enjoy one-stop shopping will be happy with the choices in Maui's various malls. You'll find regularly known department stores as well as small shops featuring island-made goods. The following are Maui's main shopping malls. For food markets and health food stores see "Food And Drink."

Kahului/Wailuku

Along Kaahumanu Avenue, you'll find **Kaahumanu Mall,** tel. 877-3369, the largest on the island. Here's everything from **Sears** and **Liberty House** to **Sew Special,** a tiny store featuring island fabrics. The mall is full service with apparel stores, shoe stores, computer centers, art shops, music stores, and **Waldenbooks.** You can eat at numerous restaurants, buy ice cream cones, or enjoy a movie at **Holiday Cinema.**

Down the road is **Maui Mall,** tel. 877-5523, featuring photo centers, **Longs** for everything from aspirin to film, **Woolworth's, Waldenbooks,** tel. 877-0181, gourmet coffee and sandwiches, and sports and swimwear shops. Cross the street to the **Old Kahului Store,** a refurbished mini-mall with apparel shops, a restaurant, and surf shops. Sandwiched between

these two modern facilities is **Kahului Shopping Center,** tel. 877-5527. It's definitely "downhome" with old-timers sitting around outside. The shops here aren't fancy, but they are authentic and you can make some offbeat purchases by strolling through.

Lahaina And Vicinity

You can't beat Lahaina's Front Street for the most, best, worst, artistic, and tacky shopping on Maui. This is where the tourists are, so this is where the shops are . . . shoulder to shoulder. The list is endless, but you'll find art studios, kites, T-shirts galore, scrimshaw, jewelry, silks, boutiques, leathers, souvenir junk, eel skins, and even a permanent tattoo memory of Maui. No wimps allowed! Lahaina has the best special-interest shopping on Maui in various little shops strung out along Front Street (see "Shopping" in the Lahaina section). The following are the local malls: **The Wharf,** tel. 661-8748, on Front Street has a multitude of eating establishments, as well as stores and boutiques in its multilevel shopping facility. When you need a break, get a coffee and browse the fine selections at The Whaler's Book Shoppe—great selections and a topnotch snack bar. **Lahaina Market Place,** tel. 667-2636, tucked away on Front Street, features established shops along with open-air stalls. **Lahaina Square Shopping Center,** tel. 242-4400, between Route 30 and Front Street, has various shops, and is probably the most *local* of the Lahaina malls. The **505 Front Street Mall,** tel. 667-2514, is at the south end of Front Street, and offers distinctive and quiet shopping away from the frenetic activity.

The Lahaina Cannery Shopping Mall, tel. 661-5304, is a newly opened center on Lahaina's west end, featuring restaurants, boutiques, specialty shops, fast food, and plenty of bargains. It's the largest mall on West Maui and has some of the best shopping under one roof on the island.

Kaanapali

Whaler's Village, tel. 661-4567, is a Kaanapali mall which features a decent open-air, self-guided museum as you walk around its shops. There are various eateries, bottle shops, and a cinema. It's a great place to stroll, buy, and learn a few things about Maui's past. The **Sheraton** and **Marriott Hotel** both have shopping, but the best is at the **Hyatt Regency.** You'll need a suitcase stuffed with money to buy anything, but it's a blast just walking around the grounds and checking out the big-ticket items.

Kihei And Wailea

Azeka Place, tel. 879-4449, is just along Kihei Road. There's food shopping, a **Liberty House,** a dive shop, and an activities center. Strung along Kihei Road, one after another, are **Kukui Mall,** which opened in early 1989, **Rainbow Mall,** and next door the **Kamaole Shopping Center,** both with dining, unique boutiques, and food and liquor stores. **Wailea Shopping Village,** tel. 879-4474, has an assortment of both chic and affordable boutiques in this exclusive mall just near the **Intercontinental** and **Stouffer's resorts.**

Specialty Stores And Neat Things

Some truly nifty and distinctive stores are wedged in among Maui's run-of- the-mill shopping centers, but for real treasures you'll find the solitary little shop the best. Lahaina's Front Street has the greatest concentration of top-notch boutiques, but others are dottted here and there around the island. The following is only a sampling of the best; many more are listed in the individual chapters.

Tattered sails on a rotted mast, tattooed sea-dogs in wide-striped jerseys, grim-faced Yankee captains squinting at the horizon, exotic, probably extinct, birds on the wing, flowers and weather-bent trees, and the beautiful, simple faces of Polynesians staring out from ancient days are faithfully preserved at **Lahaina Print-sellers Ltd.** Here is one of the newest and most unusual purveyors of art on Maui. Their shops, like mini-museums, are hung with original engravings, drawings, maps, charts, and naturalist sketches ranging in age from 150 to 400 years. Each, marked with an authenticity label, can come from anywhere in the world, but the Hawaiiana collection is amazing in its depth. Many works feature a nautical theme, reminiscent of the daring explorers who opened the Pacific. The Lahaina Printsellers, whose shops are rather new, have been collecting for over 15 years and are the largest collectors of material relating to Capt. Cook in the entire Pacific Basin. Prices range from $25 for the smallest antique print up to $15,000 for a rare museum-quality work. The Lahaina Printsellers keep Maui's art alive by representing modern artists as well, like Richard Fields, whose works are destined to become classics. The production end of the Lahaina Printsellers is located at the historic Hale Aloha, an old-time meeting house, at 636 Luakini St., Lahaina, tel. 661-5120. Two shops are in malls, one at the Whaler's Village in Kaanapali, tel. 667-7617, and the other at the Wailea Shopping Village, tel. 879-1567. Perhaps the most interesting shop is at the historic Seamen's Hospital, tel. 667-7843, along Lahaina's Front Street. Here, some of the sailors who opened the Pacific, and whose exploits are commemorated on the walls, lay sick and dying, never to return home.

For a unique memento of Maui have your photo taken by Barrie Matthews or Dave Vanzo of **Birds Of Paradise,** tel. 874-0824. You'll become the human perch for their three feathered friends, two macaws and a sassy cockatoo. The birds are very tame, natural hams, and the only thing on Maui guaranteed to be more colorful than your Hawaiian shirt. For only $15, five shots, or $20 for 10 shots, they'll come to your hotel, condo, or meet you on the beach and the next day deliver the photos, which come with mounts to make personalized postcards.

Paia is quickly becoming the unofficial art center of Maui, along with being the windsurfing capital of Hawaii. Lahaina has slicker galleries, but you come much closer to the source in Paia. The **Maui Crafts Guild** is an exemplary crafts shop that displays the best in local island art. All artists must be selected by active members before their works can be displayed. All materials used must be natural, with an emphasis on those found only in Hawaii. Quickly comes **Paia Gallery,** hung with distinctive island works, and up the street is **Exotic Maui Woods** and the workshop of Eddie Flotte, a modern Maui master. A few miles past Paia you turn up an old road to the **Old Pauwela Cannery,** where artists like Piero Resta have honeycombed studios into this massive old building.

Upcountry's Makawao is a wonderful and crazy combination of old-time *paniolo,* matured hippies who now worry about drugs and their kids, and sushi-munching yuppies. This hodgepodge makes for a town with tack shops, hardware stores, exclusive boutiques, art shops, gourmet coffee shops, and non-dairy guaranteed-to-be-good-for-you ice cream stores. All are strung along two Dodge City-like streets.

Near Kahului visit the **Pink and Black Coral Factory.** Local craftsmen make distinctive coral jewelry from the amazing corals found under Maui's seas. Some divers lose their lives each year while harvesting these fantastic corals. **Maui Swap Meet** convenes at Maui County Fairgrounds, in Kahului off Puunene Avenue (Hwy. 35); open every Sat. 8 a.m to 1 p.m. Admission 50 cents. Great junk! Wailuku is Maui's attic turned out on the street. About five odd little shops on Market Street diplay every kind of knickknack, curio, art treasure, white elephant, grotesque and sublime piece of furniture, jewelry, stuffed toy, game, or oddity that ever floated, sailed, flew, or washed up on Maui's beaches.

MUSEUMS, GARDENS, ETC.

Alexander & Baldwin Sugar Museum, 3957 Hansen Rd., Lahaina, tel. 871- 8058.

Baldwin House, Front St., Lahaina. Open daily from 9:30 a.m. to 5 p.m., tel. 661-3262. Two-story home of medical missionary Dwight Baldwin.

Brig *Carthaginian* **Floating Museum,** Lahaina Harbor, Lahaina. Open daily 9 a.m. to 5 p.m. Replica of a 19th-century brig. Features whaling artifacts and exhibits on the humpback whale.

Hale Hoikeke Museum, 2375 A Main, Wailuku, tel. 244-3326. Hawaiian history museum. Art gallery featuring Kahoolawe artifacts and the renowned paintings of Edward Bailey.

Hale Pa'i Printshop Museum, P.O. Box 338, Lahaina, tel. 667-7040. Located on grounds of Lahainaluna school. Operational relics of original printing press. Original Lahainaluna press publications, exhibit of Lahainaluna school past and present.

Hana Cultural Center, Box 27, Hana, tel. 248-8070. Preserves and restores historical sites, artifacts, photos, documents, etc. Construction of museum facilities in Hana.

Kahanu Gardens, at Ulaina Road in Hana. This 20-acre garden, part of the National Tropical Botanical Garden, contains commercial and decorative varieties of tropical plants, as well as Piilanihale Heiau, one of the largest in all of Hawaii. Open Tues.-Sat. 10:00 a.m. to 2:00 p.m., admission $5.00

Helani Gardens, privately owned, a 70 acre drive-through garden on the western outskirts of Hana, well marked. Self guided tours. Open daily, 10 a.m. to 4 p.m.

Kula Botanical Gardens, Hwy. 377 to Upper Kula Road, tel. 878-1715. Open daily 9 a.m. to 4 p.m. Excellent arrangements of tropical plants and flowers. Upcountry Maui.

Lahaina Arts Society, P.O. Box 991, Lahaina, tel. 661-0111. To perpetuate and further Hawaiian culture, the arts, crafts. Two galleries, annual scholarship, and traveling exhibitions help maintain Lahaina district courthouse.

Lahaina Restoration Foundation, P.O. Box 991, Lahaina, HI 96761, tel. 661-3262. James C. Luckey, director. Open Mon. to Sat. 10 a.m. to 4 p.m. Organization dedicated to the preservation of historical Lahaina. Sponsors restorations, archaeological digs, and renovation of cultural and historical sites. Operates Baldwin Home, Brig *Carthaginian,* among others.

Maui Historical Society, P.O. Box 1018, Wailuku, tel. 244-3326. Open 25 hours per week. Same as or part of Hale Hoikeke Museum. Promotes interest in and knowledge of history of Hawaii and Maui County. Six free lectures per year.

Whaler's Village Museum, Whaler's Village Shopping Center, Kaanapali, tel. 667-9564. Whaling artifacts, 30-foot sperm whale skeleton set among gift shops. Self-guided learning experience while you shop.

ART INFORMATION

Arts Council of Hawaii, P.O. Box 50225, Honolulu, HI 96850, tel. 524-7120, Karl Ichida, Exec. Director. This is a citizens' advocacy group for the arts which provides technical assistance and information to individuals and groups. It publishes the *Cultural Climate*, a newsletter that covers what's happening in the arts of Hawaii. It includes a calendar of events, feature articles, and editorials. Anyone interested in Hawaiian arts can become a member of ACH for only $15, which entitles you to receive the "Cultural Climate." Nonmembers can pick it up for 50 cents an issue.

Pacific Handcrafters Guild, P.O. Box 15491, Honolulu, HI 96818, tel. 923-5726. The guild's focus is on developing and preserving handcrafts in Hawaii and the Pacific. They sponsor four major craft fairs, two guild-sponsored fairs, and two gallery shows annually.

State Foundation on Culture and the Arts, 335 Merchant St., Room 202, Honolulu, HI 96813, tel. 548-4145. Begun by the State Legislature in 1965, its goals are to preserve Hawaii's diverse cultural heritage, promote the arts and artists and to make cultural and artistic programs available to the people. Their budget includes the purchasing of artworks (one percent of the construction cost of any state buildings goes for art). Many of their purchases hang for a time in the governor's office. They publish the very complete "Hawaii Cultural Resource Directory," which lists most of the art organizations, galleries, councils, co-ops, and guilds throughout Hawaii.

GETTING THERE

Maui attracts over a million visitors per year. A limited number of direct flights from the Mainland are offered, but most airlines servicing Hawaii, both domestic and foreign, land at Honolulu International Airport and then offer connecting flights on inter-island carriers from there; in most cases they're part of the original ticket price with no extra charge. Different airlines have "interline" agreements with different Hawaiian carriers so check with your travel agent. All major and most smaller inter-island carriers service Maui from throughout Hawaii with over 100 flights per day in and out of Kahului Airport.

Maui's Airports
There are three commercial airports on Maui, but the vast majority of travelers will be concerned with **Kahului Airport,** which accommodates 95% of the flights in and out of Maui. Kahului Airport is only minutes from Kahului town, on the northcentral coast of Maui. A full-service facility with most amenities, it has car rental agencies, information booths, lockers, and limited public and private transportation. Major roads lead from Kahului Airport to all primary destinations on Maui.

Hawaiian Airlines opened **Kapulua-West Maui Airport** in early 1987. This brand-new facility is conveniently located between Kaanapali and the Kapalua resort areas, on the *mauka* side of the Honoapiilani Hwy. at Mahinahina, just a few minutes from the major Kaanapali Hotels. This is definitely the airport that

you want to use if you are staying anywhere on West Maui, if possible. Besides Hawaiian Air, which will operate 22 daily flights connecting West Maui with the rest of Hawaii, seven other commuter airlines have contracted to use the facility, but for now only Aloha Island Air and Panorama Air Tours have a booth. The facility opens West Maui to its first-ever service to all the Hawaiian Islands, the South Pacific, and the Mainland's West Coast. The brand-new facility is very user-friendly with a snack bar, sundries, and car rental agencies or courtesy phones for car rental pickup. A free trolley bus connects you with major Kaanapali hotels.

The third is **Hana Airport,** an isolated strip on the northeast coast just west of Hana with no amenities, facilities, or transportation. People flying into Hana Airport generally plan to vacation in Hana for an extended period and have made prior arrangements for being picked up.

Special Note
Kahului Airport is rebuilding. Over the next few years there will be some inconvenience with the commuter terminal. International and inter-island flights on the bigger carriers won't be affected. The commuter carrier terminal sits off by itself (follow signs). Eventually it will house helicopter companies, and the commuter airlines will move to the big terminal. But for now you must park at the lot at the main terminal, which can give you a 10-minute walk or more . . . tough with heavy luggage. Drop luggage off, and re-

Hawaiian Air's Dash Transit

turn to the lot. When you enter keep going straight ahead as far as you can to park, and this will put you closer to the commuter terminal.

Direct Mainland Flights

Until recently, **United Airlines** was the only carrier that offered nonstop flights from the Mainland to Maui. United, tel. (800) 241-6522, flies daily nonstop to Maui from San Francisco (two flights), and Los Angeles (one). Denver, Portland, and Seattle passengers fly via San Francisco or Los Angeles. Now, **Delta Airlines**, tel. (800) 221-1212, flies daily direct from Los Angeles with their other gateway city flights connecting through Los Angeles, while San Francisco flights go through Honolulu at no extra charge. **Hawaiian Air**, tel. (800) 367-5320, offers daily flights via San Francisco and Los Angeles through Honolulu.

Inter-island Carriers

Hawaiian Air, tel. (800) 367-5320, Maui 244-9111, offers more flights to Maui than any other inter-island carrier. The majority of flights are to and from Honolulu (average flight time 30 minutes), with over 30 per day in each direction. Hawaiian Air flights to Maui from Honolulu begin at 5:30 a.m., with flights thereafter about every 30 minutes until 8:35 p.m. Flights from Maui to Honolulu begin at 6:30 a.m. and go all day until 9:30 p.m. Hawaiian Air flights to and from Kauai (over 25 per day in each direction, about 35 minutes)

begin at 7 a.m. and go until 7 p.m. There are two flights to/from Hilo daily, one in the morning and one in mid-afternoon. Kona, on the Big Island, is serviced with three daily flights. Flights from Maui begin at 9:00 a.m. with the last at 4:35 p.m.; from Kona at 9:50 a.m. with the last at 4:55 p.m. There are three flights from Molokai, at 7 a.m, 12:30 p.m., and 3 p.m.

Aloha Airlines, tel. (800) 367-5250, Maui 244-9071, with an all-jet fleet of 737s, flies from Honolulu to Maui over 25 times per day beginning at 5:40 a.m., with the last flight at 8:10 p.m.; to Honolulu at 6:35 a.m., last at 9 p.m. Multiple flights throughout the day from Kauai begin at 6:35 a.m. until 7:15 p.m.; to Kauai at 6:35 a.m. and throughout the day until 7:10 p.m. From Hilo, three flights in mid-morning and the last at 7:15 p.m.; to Hilo three flights interspersed from 8:25 a.m. until 6:20 p.m. From Kona one flight leaves at 9:45 a.m. and three leave in the afternoon (the last at 6:55 p.m.); to Kona five flights from 7:10 a.m. until 4:35 p.m.

Commuter Airlines: Aloha Island Air, formerly Princeville Airlines, tel. (800) 323-3345 Mainland, (800) 652-6541 statewide, 833-3219 Oahu, offers daily flights connecting Maui with Oahu, Kauai, Hawaii, Lanai, and Molokai. Along with the state's main airports (Kona and Hilo excepted), they service the smaller and sometimes more convenient airports of Kapalua and Hana on Maui, Princeville on Kauai, Kalaupapa on Molokai, and Kamuela on the Big Island. Aloha Island Air is headquartered at the commuter terminal at Honolulu International Airport.

Reeves Air, tel. Oahu 833-9555, Maui 871-4624, has regularly scheduled flights between Honolulu, Maui, and Molokai on a daily basis as well as charter service to get you there when you want to go. Their prices are higher, but it's like hiring your own private air taxi.

Whenever you fly any of the commuter airlines, try to get as many stops as possible. Because they fly so low, it's like getting a free flightseeing tour. As always the costs are a bit more than the larger airlines, but it's more fun.

GETTING AROUND

If it's your intention to *see* Maui when you visit, and not just to lie on the beach in front of your hotel, the only efficient way is to rent a car. Limited public transportation, a few free shuttles, taxis, and the good old thumb are available, but all these are flawed in one way or another. Other unique and fun-filled ways to tour the island include renting a bike or moped, or hopping on a helicopter, but these conveyances are highly specialized and are more in the realm of sports than touring.

Public Transportation

The **Grayline Airporter,** tel. 877-5507, makes scheduled runs from the Kahului Airport (reservations to the airport are a must). First departure from the airport is at 10:15 a.m. and then once every hour and a half until the last departure at 4:15 p.m. It services all the popular destinations in Lahaina/Kaanapali, stopping at many of the major hotels and at Lahaina Harbor. It's a slightly expensive but no-hassle way to deal with arrival and departure, but out of the question for every-day transportation.

A *free* shuttle runs between the Kapalua-West Maui Airport (see p. 373) and all major hotels in and around the Kaanapali area. The first bus departs at 8:15 a.m. and then once every 45 minutes until 5:15 p.m.

Kaanapali Jitney, which runs up and down the Kaanapali Beach area from 8 a.m. to 10:30 p.m., costs $2 for an all-day pass. The run, every half hour, goes from the Royal Lahaina Hotel to the Wharf Mall on Front Street. The **Kaanapali Shuttle** is a free open-air bus running on the hour from 7 a.m. to 11 p.m., stopping at all hotels and condos, and terminating at Banyan Square in Lahaina. **Kapalua Shuttle** services all of the hotels and condos in Kapalua from 7 a.m. to 11 p.m. on an "on call" basis. Your hotel desk will make arrangements for you. The **Wailea Resorts Shuttle** is free and stops at all Wailea Beach hotels and condos from 6:30 a.m. until 10:30 p.m.

Taxis

About 10 taxi companies on Maui more or less operate in a fixed area. Most, besides providing normal taxi service, also run tours all over the island. Taxis are expensive. For example, a ride from Kahului Airport to Kaanapali is $30 for about six people (about half this much to Kihei). Try Mita Taxi, at the airport, tel. 871-4622; Kahului Taxi at tel. 242-6404; Red and White Cabs in Lahaina at tel. 661-3684; Lahaina Taxi, tel. 661-4147; Wailea Taxi, tel. 879-1059; and Kihei Taxi, tel. 879-3000.

Hitchhiking

The old tried-and-true method of hitchhiking—with thumb out, facing traffic, a smile on your interesting face—is "out" on Maui! It's illegal, and if a policeman sees you, you'll be hassled, if not arrested outright. You've got to play the game. Simply stand on the side of the road facing traffic with a smile on your interesting face, but put away the old thumb. In other words, you can't actively solicit a ride. People know what you're doing; just stand there. You can get around quite well by thumb, if you're not on a schedule. The success rate of getting a ride to the number of cars that go by isn't that great, but you will get picked up. Locals and the average tourist with family will generally pass you by. Recent residents and single tourists will most often pick you up, and 90% of the time these will be white males. Hitching short hops along the resort beaches is easy. People can tell by the way you're dressed that you're not going far and will give you a lift. Catching longer rides to Hana or up to Haleakala can be done, but it'll be tougher because the driver will know that you'll be with him or her for the duration of the ride. Women, under no circumstances, should hitch alone.

RENTAL CARS

Maui has over 30 car rental agencies that can put you behind the wheel of anything from a Mercedes convertible to a used station wagon with chipped paint and torn upholstery. There are national companies, inter-island firms, good local companies and a few fly-by-nights that'll rent you a clunker. More than a dozen companies are clustered in little booths at the Kahului Airport, a few at Kaanapali, and none at Hana Airport, but your Hana hotel can arrange a car for you. The rest are scattered around the island with a heavy concentration on Dairy Road near Kahului Airport. Those without an airport booth

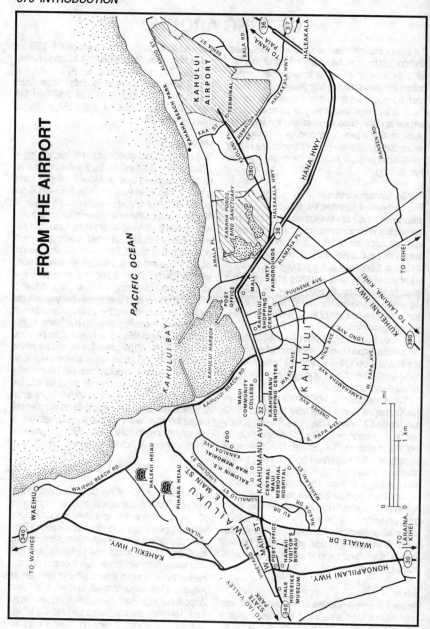

FROM THE AIRPORT

either have a courtesy phone or a number to call; they'll pick you up.

Stiff competition tends to keep the prices more or less reasonable. Good deals are offered off-season, with price wars flaring at anytime and making for real savings, but these unfortunately can't be predicted. Even with all these companies, it's best to book ahead. You might not save money, but you can save yourself headaches.

Tips
The best cars to rent on Maui happen to be the cheapest: subcompacts with standard shift. (If you can drive a standard!) Maui's main highways are broad and well paved, just like major roads on the Mainland, but the back roads where all the fun is are narrow twisty affairs. You'll appreciate the downshifting ability of standard transmissions on curves and steep inclines. If you get a big fatso luxury car, it'll be great for "puttin' on the ritz" at the resort areas, but you'll feel like a hippopotamus in the backcountry. If you've got that much money to burn, rent two cars! Try to get a car with cloth seats. Vinyl is too sticky, but sitting on your towel will help. Air-conditioning is nice especially if you plan on being in Lahaina a lot. The mile markers on back roads are great for pinpointing sites and beaches, and the lower number on these signs is the highway number, so you can always make sure that you're on the right road. The car rental agencies prohibit travel past Seven Sacred Pools on the other side of Hana, or around the top of the head of Maui. These roads are indeed rugged, but passable; the locals do it all the time. The car companies will warn you that your insurance "might" not cover you on these roads. They're really protecting their cars from being banged around. Traveling these roads is not recommended . . . for the fainthearted. Be careful, drive slowly, and have fun!

Nationally Known Companies
The following are major firms that have booths at Kahului Airport. **National Car Rental** (Kaanapali office services the Kaanapali area and Kapalua-West Maui Airport with a free shuttle), is one of the best of the nationally known firms. They have GMs, Nissans, Toyotas, Datsuns, vans, jeeps, and station wagons. National offers excellent weekly rates, especially on standard subcom-

pacts. All major credit cards are accepted. On Maui, call 871-8851. **Avis** is also located in Kaanapali. They feature late-model GM cars as well as most imports and convertibles. Call Avis at 871-7575 or in Kaanapali at 661-4588. **Budget** offers competitive rates on a variety of late-model cars. At Kahului call 871-8811, in Kaanapali 661-8721. **Hertz**, perhaps the best-known company, offers a wide variety of vehicles with some special weekly rates. Hertz has locations at Kaanapali and Wailea. Call 661-3195 and request the location nearest you. **Dollar** rents all kinds of cars, as well as jeeps and convertibles. At Kahului, call 877-6526; Kaanapali, 661-3037. **Alamo** has good weekly rates. Call (800) 327-9633.

Island Companies
The following companies are based in Hawaii and either have a booth at the airport or pickup service through courtesy phones. The biggest, and best, **Tropical Rent a Car**, has a good reputation for service and prices. Also located at Kaanapali, call 877-0002, 661-0061, or toll-free (800) 367-5140 Mainland, (800) 352-3923 in Hawaii. **Word of Mouth Rent a Used Car,** at 607 Haleakala Hwy., tel. 877-2436, pickup van provided, offers some fantastic deals on their used but not abused cars. All cars are four door automatics and rent for $80 per week, $90 with a/c. Office open 8-5, but they will leave a car at the airport at earlier or later hours with prior arrangement. **Roberts** has a good reputation, tel. 871-6226. Others include: **Trans Maui,** tel. 877-5222; **Andres,** tel. 877-5378; **Klunkers,** with variable rates at tel. 877-3197.

Four-wheel Drive
Though much more expensive than cars, some people might feel safer in them for completely circling Maui. Also unlike cars, the rental companies offering 4WDs put no restrictions on driving past the Seven Sacred Pools or around the head of West Maui. (Roads subject to closure, so check!) 4WDs can be had from **Maui Rent a Jeep,** tel. 877-6626 or **Hertz,** tel. 877-5167. Variable rates from company to company depend on availability and length of rental.

Camper Rentals
A good alternative to staying in hotels or condos. You might also want to rent a camper for an overnight trip to Hana. The convenience will offset

the extra cost, and might even save money over staying in a hotel. Unlike cars, campers carry a per-mile charge. The only outfit renting campers is **Hawaiian Custom Campers,** tel. 877-4522, at 180 D E. Wakea Ave., Kahului, HI 96732.

Mopeds

Just for running around town or to the beach mopeds are great. Expect to pay about $25 for the day or up to $125 for the week. For mopeds: **Go Go Bikes** at the Kaanapali Transportation Center, call 661-3063 or 669-6669; **A&B Mopeds** at Honokowai, tel. 669-0027. Mopeds are rented by the hour, day, or week.

BICYCLES

Bicycle enthusiasts should be thrilled with Maui, but the few flaws might flatten your spirits as well as your tires. The countryside is great, the weather is perfect, but the roads are heavily trafficked and the most interesting ones are narrow and have bad shoulders. Peddling to Hana will give you an up-close personal experience, but for bicycle safety this road is one of the worst. Haleakala is stupendous, but with a rise of more than 10,000 feet in less than 40 miles it is considered one of the most grueling rides in the world. A paved bike path runs from Lahaina to Kaanapali that's tame enough for everyone, and you can even arrange a bicycle tour of Lahaina. In short, cycling on Maui as your primary means of transportation is not for the neophyte; because of safety considerations and the tough rides, only experienced riders should consider it.

Getting your bike to Maui from one of the Neighbor Islands is no problem. All of the inter-island and commuter carriers will fly it for you for approximately $20, "space available," which means most likely it will be on the plane with you, but not guaranteed. If you plan ahead, you can send your bike the previous day by air freight and save yourself $10. Aloha Airlines has an excellent system promising 24-hour delivery. You don't have to box or disassemble your bike, but you must sign a damage waiver. This is usually OK because the awkwardness of a bike almost ensures that it will be placed on the top of the baggage out of harm's way. The freight terminal at Kahului is just a few minutes' walk from the passenger terminal, and opens at 7 a.m. You

can also take your bike free on the inter-island ferry, the *Maui Princess* (see p. 126).

For bike rentals, try: **Aloha Funway Rentals** in Lahaina at tel. 661-8702; **Go Go Bikes Hawaii** in Kaanapali at 661-3063; **Fun Rentals,** at 193 Lahainaluna Rd., Lahaina, tel. 661-3053, open daily 8 a.m. to 6 p.m., is a semi-benign bike and bike rental shop. Semi-benign because their prices are high, but they could be higher, and they have the best selection. This full-service bike shop sells and rents everything from clunkers for around town, up to world-class Tomasso racing bikes ($200 per week). Prices vary considerably but a good mid-range example is a 15-speed mountain bike that rents from $20 for eight hours, $25 for 24 hours, $35 for two days, and up by about $10 per day to $85 for one week. They'll tell you that the Park Service does not allow you to take your bike up to Haleakala National Park—bull droppings! You *cannot* ride the bike on the hiking paths, but going up the road (40 miles uphill) is OK if you have the steam. You are given this misinformation because they don't want the wear and tear on their bikes, but for the prices they charge, they shouldn't squawk.

Bicycle Tours

An adventure on Maui that's become famous is riding a specially equipped bike from the summit of Mt. Haleakala for 40 miles to the bottom. A pioneer in this field is **Maui Downhill,** 199 Dairy Rd., Kahului, tel. 871-2155. Included in the bike ride at $93 are two meals (continental breakfast and breakfast on the sunrise run, or lunch on the later picnic run), and windbreakers and helmets. To drench yourself in the beauty of a Haleakala sunrise, you have to pay your dues. You arrive at the base yard in Kahului at about 3:30 a.m. after being picked up at your condo by the courtesy van. Here, you'll muster with other bleary-eyed but hopeful adventurers and munch donuts and coffee, which at this time of the morning is more like a transfusion. Up the mountain through the chilly night air takes about 1½ hours, with singing and storytelling along the way. Once atop find your spot for the *best* natural light show in the world, as the sun goes wild with colors as it paints the sky and drips into Haleakala Crater (see p. 469). This is your first reward. Next comes your bicycle *environmental cruise* down the mountain with vistas and thrills every inch of the way. **Cruiser Bob's**, at 505 Front St., Lahaina, tel. 667-7717, offers a variation on the same theme. Essentially you get the same experience for about the same amount of money, but Maui Downhill is slightly cheaper, and their breakfast is an all-you-can-eat buffet.

For downhilling you have to be a fair rider; those under 16 require parental release. These outfits offer tamer tours of Lahaina and the beach resorts, with admissions into historical sites and museums included. There's no gripe with the Haleakala experience; it's guaranteed thrills, and since they have you for eight hours with two meals and pick-up service, the price isn't too hard to take.

SIGHTSEEING TOURS

Tours are offered that will literally let you cover Maui from head to foot; you can walk it, drive it, sail around it, fly over it, or see it from below the water. Almost every major hotel has a tour desk from which you can book.

Booking Agencies
The biggest, **Ocean Activities Center**, happens to be the best agency for booking any and all kinds of activities on Maui. For much of the fun events like snorkel/scuba, whalewatching, and sunset cruises, they have their own facilities and equipment, which means they cannot only provide you with an excellent outing, but offer very competitive prices. Ocean Activities can also book you on helicopters, parasails, land tours, and rent and sell boogie boards, snorkel equipment, sailboards, and surfboards. They have sun and surf stores/booking agencies in the Wailea Shopping Village, tel. 879- 4485, the Lahaina Cannery Mall, tel. 661-5309, in Kihei, tel. 879-0083, and service booths at Stouffer's Hotel, tel. 879-0181, and the InterContinental Hotel, tel. 879-7466. Ocean Activities also runs a boat from the beach at the Maui Prince Hotel to the underwater fantasy of Molokini Crater. Prices on all of their activities are very reasonable, and the service is excellent. If you had to choose one agency for all your fun needs, this would be your best bet!

One of the easiest ways to book an activity and sightsee at the same time is to walk along the Lahaina Wharf. Check it out first, and then plan to be there when the tour boats return. Asking the passengers, right on the spot, if they've had a good time is about the best you can do. You can also check out the boats and do some comparative pricing of your own. In Lahaina along Front Street try **Visitor Info and Ticket Center** in the Wharf Shopping Complex at tel. 661-5151.

Maui Beach Center, at 505 Front St., tel. 667-4395, open daily 8:30 a.m. to 5 p.m., does it all. Rentals for 24 hours are: surfboards $28, snorkel equipment $6, boogie boards $5. Featuring the *best* surf lessons on Maui, with guaranteed results, they can also arrange a wide variety of activities like parasailing and a Zodiac trip.

For boats and a full range of activities out of quiet Maalaea Harbor, contact **Maalaea Activities**, tel. 242-6982. They do it all from helicopters to horseback. They specialize in the boats berthed at Maalaea. And for some personalized attention by a very knowledgeable Maui resident, check out **Donya** at the Maui Hill Condominium, tel. 879-0180. She's got the inside scoop on many of the activities, and can book you on the best and save you some money at the same time.

Land Tours
It's easy to book tours to Maui's famous areas such as Lahaina, Hana, Kula, Iao Valley, and Haleakala. Normally they're run on either half- or full-day schedules (Hana is always a full day) and range anywhere from $20 to $60 with hotel pickup included. Big bus tours are run by **Grayline**, tel. 877-5507, and **Roberts**, tel. 877-5038. These tours are quite antiseptic, as you sit behind tinted glass in an air-conditioned bus. You get more personalized tours in the smaller vans, such as **Holo Holo Tours**, tel. 661-4858. Among other destinations they'll take you to Hana with a continental breakfast for $50. **Personalized Small Group Tours**, tel. 871-9551, goes to Hana for $40, or to Haleakala for $30. **No Kai Oi Tours** hits all the high spots and has competitive prices, tel. 871-9008; **Trans Hawaii Maui** specializes in all-day trips to Hana for $40, bring your own lunch, tel. 877-7308. **Polynesian Adventure Tours**, tel. 877-4242, offers tours to Hana, $35, or Haleakala $39. For a truly won-

derful hiking tour with Maui's foremost naturalist, see "Hike Maui" p. 388.

Air Tours

Maui is a spectacular sight from the air. A small charter airline and a handful of helicopter companies swoop you around the island. These joy rides are literally the highlight of many people's experiences on Maui, but they are expensive. The excursions vary, but expect to spend at least $100 for a basic half-hour tour. The most spectacular ones take you into Haleakala crater, or perhaps to the remote West Maui Mountains, where inaccessible gorges lie at your feet. Other tours are civilized; expect a champagne brunch after you visit Hana. Still others take you to nearby Lanai or Molokai to view some of the world's most spectacular sea cliffs and remote beaches. Know, however, that many hikers and trekkers have a beef with the air tours: after they've spent hours, or maybe days, hiking into remote valleys in search of peace and quiet, out of the sky comes the mechanical whir of a chopper to spoil the solitude.

Helicopters

Kenai Helicopter, tel. 871-6463, is one of the better and more experienced companies. All their rides are smoothly professional, leaving from Kahului Airport. **Papillon Helicopters,** tel. 669-4994, (800) 562-5641 Hawaii, (800) 367-7095 Mainland, flies from the Kahului Airport and is also one of the larger and more experienced firms. However, you'll be perfectly safe and can make some better deals with local Maui companies. **Maui Helicopter,** tel. 879-1601 or (800) 367-8003, has an excellent reputation as a locally owned outfit, and they offer preferred seating. The chopper is purely utilitarian, but with only four passengers, two front and two rear, everyone is assured of a good view. **Hawaii Helicopter,** tel. 877-3900, has plush interiors for your comfort, but they squeeze four people in the back, so the two middle ones don't get a good view. **Sunshine Helicopter,** tel. 871-0722, is another local, family-run outfit with one chopper. The inside is bare-bones, but the seating is two by two, and they go out of their way to give you a good ride. They sometimes offer a 20-minute "special" for only $49. For all, tours are narrated over specially designed earphones, and most companies will make special arrange-

ments to drop off and pick up campers in remote areas, or design a package especially for you. Most chopper companies are competitively priced with tours of West or East Maui at around $100. Circle-island tours are approximately $175, but the best would be to include a trip to Molokai in order to experience the world's tallest sea cliffs along the isolated windward coast, at approximately $200. For a slightly different thrill, experience a Maui joy ride out of Kahului Airport with **Paragon Airlines**, tel. 244-3356.

OCEAN TOURS

You haven't really seen Maui unless you've seen it from the sea. Tour boats operating out of Maui's Lahaina and Maalaea harbors take you fishing, sailing, whalewatching, dining, diving, and snorkeling. You can find boats that offer all of these or just sail you around for pure pleasure. Many take day trips to Lanai or to Molokai, with a visit to Kalaupapa Leper Colony included. Many visit Molokini, a submerged volcano with only half the crater rim above water that's been designated as a Marinelife Conservation District. The vast majority of Maui's pleasure boats are berthed in Lahaina Harbor and most have a booth right there on the wharf where you can sign up. Other boats come out of Maalaea, with a few companies based in Kihei. The following are basically limited to sailing/dining/touring activities, with snorkeling often part of the experience. If you're interested in other ocean activities such as snorkeling, scuba, and fishing, see "Sports And Recreation." That section also includes activities such as water- or jet-skiing, parasailing, sailboarding, and surfing.

Excursions/Dinner Sails

Sunset cruises are very romantic, and very popular. They last for about two hours and cost $25-35 for the basic cruise. A cocktail sail can be as little as $20, but for a dinner sail expect to spend $40-50. Remember, too, that the larger established companies are usually on Maui to stay, but that smaller companies come and go with the tide! The following are general tour boats that offer a variety of cruises.

Trilogy Excursions, tel. 661-4743, or (800) 874-2666, was founded and is operated by the Coon Family. A success in many ways, their Lanai Cruise is *the* best on Maui. Although the hand-picked crews have made the journey countless times, they never forget that it's *your* first time. They make the trip special by always being enthusiastic and helpful. They run two trimarans: the 50-foot *Trilogy,* and the 40-foot *Kailana,* which carries up to 35 passengers to Lanai. Once aboard you're served a mug of steaming Kona coffee, fresh juice, and Mama Coon's famous cinnamon buns. After anchoring in Manele Bay, a tour van picks you up and you're driven to Lanai City. Along the way, the driver, a Lanai resident, tells stories, history, and anecdotes concerning the Pineapple Island. After the tour, you return to frolic at Hulopoe Bay, which is beautiful for swimming, boogie boarding, and renowned as an excellent snorkeling area. All gear is provided. While you play, the crew is busy at work preparing a barbecue at the picnic facilities at Manele Harbor. The meal is delicious. You're served marinated chicken, rice, vegetable stir-fry, fresh fruit, and drinks. An all-day affair, you couldn't have a more memorable or enjoyable experience than sailing with Trilogy.

Captain Nemo's Emporium, tel. 661-5555, located on Front Street, sails *Seasmoke,* a 58-foot catamaran (built for James Arness and reported to be the fastest "cat" on the island) to Lanai on a snorkel and diving run. They leave at 8 a.m. and return at 2 p.m. and serve breakfast and lunch. Capt. Nemo's is one of the finest outfits operating on Maui, and has a well deserved reputation for an outing filled with fun, safety, and excitement. You can't go wrong! **Windjammer Cruises,** tel. 667-6834, offers trips aboard their 65-foot, three-masted schooner. They pack in over 100 passengers and on weekends feature a lunch at the Hotel Lanai in place of the barbecue. **Scotch Mist,** tel. 661-0386, has two racing yachts, *Scotch Mist I* and *II.* They are the oldest sailing charters on Maui (1970) and claim to be the fastest sailboats in the harbor, boasting the lightest boat, the biggest sail, and the best crew. They'll cruise, snorkel ($39-45 for three hours), or take their 19 passengers on a sunset sail complete with champagne for $33 or $25, depending on the boat.

The **Lin Wa** is a glass-bottom boat that's a facsimile of a Chinese junk. One of the tamest and least expensive tours out of Lahaina Harbor, it departs six times a day from slip #3 and charges $12.50 adults and $6.25 children. It gives you a tour just off Maui's shore and even goes for a whalewatch in season. It's little more than a seagoing carnival ride. Call the *Lin Wa* at 661-3392, and remember that it's very popular. **The Coral Sea,** tel. 661-8600, is more of the same only it's a bit larger and offers a snorkel-/picnic tour. For $39 (children half price) it provides equipment, lunch, and an open bar. It's in slip #1 at Lahaina Harbor.

One of the least expensive cruises ($15) is a cocktail sail aboard the 44-foot catamaran **Frogman,** tel. 667-7622. It departs from Maalaea Harbor and serves *pu pu,* mai tais, and beer on its tradewind sail. **Kaulana Cruises,** tel. 667-2518, offers a dinner sail for $32 and a cocktail sail for $20 (children half price) on its 70-foot catamaran. They also sail a picnic/snorkel to Lanai.

Out of Kihei you might try the **Maui Sailing Center,** tel. 879-5935, which takes six passengers on its Cal 27 for a full-day snorkel sail to Molokini, departing from Maalaea Harbor. Out of Maalaea Harbor is the **Mahana Maia,** tel. 871-8636, a 58-foot cat that'll carry 50 passengers out to Molokini. Also from Maalaea you can board the 65-foot **Wailea Kai** catamaran along with 90 others for a picnic/snorkel outing to Molokini. They also offer a popular dinner sail; contact **Ocean Activities Center,** tel. 879-4485. From Kaanapali the **Sea Sails** makes an evening dinner sail from its anchorage at the Sheraton Beach. Contact **Sea Sport Activities Center,** tel. 667-2759. **Aloha Voyages,** tel. 667-6284, offers a sunset dinner sail aboard the *Machias* that includes mai tais, champagne, and dinner cooked on board for $42.

Some of the above companies offer a variety of cocktail sails and whale watches for much cheaper prices, but many tend to pack people in so tightly that they're known derisively as "cattle boats." Don't expect the personal attention you'd receive on smaller boats (always check number of passengers when booking). However, all the boats going to Molokai or Lanai will take passengers for the one-way trip. You won't participate in the snorkeling or the food, but the prices (negotiable) are considerably cheaper. This extra service is offered only if there's room. Talk to the individual captains.

Unique Ocean Tours

For a totally different experience try **Captain Zodiac,** located at 115 Dickenson St., Lahaina, tel. 667-5351. A Zodiac is a highly maneuverable, totally seaworthy high-tech motorized raft. Its main features are speed and an ability to get intimate with the sea as its supple form bends with the undulations of the water. Simply, it can go where other craft cannot. Captain Zodiac pioneered the field starting as a one-man operation on Kauai. They've now come to Maui and offer their unique experience daily. Schedules change, but basically they offer a full day (7:30 a.m. to 2:30 p.m.) and half day (9 a.m. to 12:30 p.m., and again in the afternoon) for $95 and $53 respectively, children less; snacks, drinks, lunch (full day only), and snorkel gear included. A whale watch during the season is also offered. Departing from Mala Wharf, they cross the Lahaina Roads heading for the hidden spots of Lanai. En route, the knowledgeable crew tells tales, legends, and the natural history of the area. Once Lanai is reached, you snorkel along its amazing coastline in pristine spots like Five Needles, a virtually untouched wonderland of tropical fish and underwater grottoes. For something totally different and totally enjoyable try the Zodiac.

Two other companies that offer similar experiences in their oceangoing rafts are: **Blue Water Rafting**, tel. 879-7238, P.O. Box 10172, Lahaina, HI 96761. They depart from the Kihei Boat Ramp and primarily offer snorkel trips to Molokini (whalewatching in season).

If you've had enough of Front Street Lahaina, **Club Lanai**, tel. 871-1144, is a Maui-based company that runs day excursions to its developed facilities on Lanai (see p. 514). You board one of two catamarans at Lahaina Harbor, leaving at 7:30 a.m. En route you're served a continental breakfast of Danish pastry, juices and coffee. The boats cruise to Club Lanai's private beach just near old Halepaloa Landing, between the deserted villages of Keomoku and Naha, on Lanai's very secluded eastern shore. Awaiting you is an oasis of green landscaped beach. Palm trees provided shade over manmade lagoons, and hammocks wait for true relaxation. The club provides you with snorkel gear, boogie boards, kayaks with instruction, a glass-bottom boat, bicycles for your personal exploration of the area, horseshoes, volleyball, and even a guided tour. On the grounds are a gift shop and a Hawaiian village where you can learn handicrafts from a sparkling Lanai *kapuna,* Auntie Elaine. She keeps alive the oral traditions of sto-

rytelling and will be happy to tell you about the history, legends, and myths of Lanai. Clayton, the manager, is also a longtime Lanai resident and goes out of his way to ensure that you have a good time. The bar serves exotic drinks and is open all day. Lunch is a delicious buffet featuring Korean short ribs, barbecued chicken, *mahi mahi,* juices, fresh fruit, and salads. The entire day including sail, meals, and use of facilities is reasonably priced under $95. Club Lanai is the type of experience in which you set your own pace . . . do it all, or do nothing at all!

Whalewatching

Anyone on Maui from November, to April gets the added treat of watching humpback whales as they frolic in their feeding grounds just off Lahaina, one of the world's major wintering areas for the humpback. Almost every boat in the harbor runs a special whale watch during this time of year. A highly educational whale watch is sponsored by the **Pacific Whale Foundation,** located at Kealia Beach Plaza, Suite 25, 101 N. Kihei Rd., Kihei, HI 96753, tel. 879-8811, open daily 9 to 5. A nonprofit organization founded in 1980, it is dedicated to research, education, and conservation, and is one of the only research organizations that has been able to survive by generating their own funds through membership, donations, and their excellent whale watch cruises. They have the best whale watch on the island aboard their own two ships, the *Whale I* and *II,* because actual scientists and researchers make up the crew. They rotate and come out on the whale watch when they're not out in the Lahaina Roads getting up close to identify and study the whales. Most of the information that the other whale watches dispense to the tourists is generated by the Pacific Whale Foundation. Departures from Maalaea Harbor are four times daily from 7 a.m. to 4:30 p.m., adults $34. The foundation also offers an "Adopt-a-Whale Program" and various reef and snorkel cruises that run throughout the year.

Since Lahaina Harbor is an attraction in itself, just go there and stroll along to hand-pick your own boat. Many times the whale watch is combined with a snorkel and picnic sail so prices vary accordingly. Two of the cheapest are aboard the *Lin Wa* and the *Coral See*. Others include the *Mareva* and *The Kamehameha*. The *Mareva,* tel. 661-4522, is berthed in slip #63. This 38-foot sloop will take you out for a half-day whale watch for $30. *The Kamehameha* is a 15-foot catamaran for snorkeling or whalewatching at $17, in slip #67, tel. 661-4522. **Ocean Activities Center,** tel. 879-4485, can book you on a variety of whale watch sails. Call for competitive prices.

If Lahaina is too frenetic for your tastes, head for Kihei where you can get a boat out of Maalaea. Try booking through **The Dive Shop,** tel. 879-5172. For further information on whales, see "Flora and Fauna."

The Sugar Cane Train

The old steam engine puffs along from Lahaina to Kaanapali, a 25-minute ride each way, and costs $4.50 OW and $7.50 RT adults, $2.25 OW

and $3.75 RT children to age 12. A free bus shuttles between Lahaina Station and the waterfront to accommodate the most popular tour on Maui. The train runs throughout the day from 8:55 a.m. to 4:40 p.m. It's very popular so book in advance. All rides are narrated and there may even be a singing conductor. All kinds of tours are offered as well: some feature lunch, a tour of Lahaina with admission into the Baldwin House and the *Carthiginian,* and even a cruise on a glass-bottom boat. They're tame, touristy, and fun. The price is right: the deluxe tour including RT train ride, lunch, Lahaina tour, and an all-day Kaanapali Jitney pass is for $19. Call the Lahaina Kaanapali and Pacific Railroad at tel. 661-0089.

ACCOMMODATIONS

With over 12,000 rooms available, and more being built every day, Maui is second only to Oahu in the number of visitors it can accommodate. There's a tremendous concentration of condos on Maui, plenty of hotels, and a growing number of bed and breakfast inns. Camping is limited to a handful of parks, but what it lacks in number it easily makes up for in quality.

Tips

Maui has an **off-season,** like all of Hawaii, which runs from after Easter to just before Christmas, with the fall months being particularly beautiful. During this period you can save 25% or more on accommodations. If you'll be staying for over a week, get a condo with cooking facilities or a room with at least a refrigerator; you can save a bundle on food costs. You'll pay more for an ocean view, but along Maui's entire south shore from Kapalua to Wailea, you'll have a cheaper and cooler room if you're mountainside, away from the sun.

Your Choices

Over 80 hotels and condos have sprouted on West Maui, from Kapalua to Lahaina. The most expensive are in **Kaanapali** and include the Hyatt Regency, Marriott, and Maui Surf and Sheraton, strung along some of Maui's best beaches. The older condos just west in Honokawai are cheaper, with a mixture of expensive

and moderate as you head toward Kapalua. **Lahaina** itself offers only a handful of places to stay: condos at both ends of town, and the famous non-luxury Pioneer Inn. Most people find the pace a little too hectic, but you couldn't get more in the middle of "it" if you tried. **Maalaea Bay,** between Lahaina and Kihei, has over 20 quiet condos and a few hotels. Prices are reasonable, the beaches are fair, and you're in striking distance of the action in either direction.

Kihei is "condo row," with over 50 of them along the six miles of Kihei Ave., plus a few hotels. This is where you'll find top-notch beaches and the best deals on Maui. **Wailea** just up the road is expensive, but the hotels here are world class and the secluded beaches are gorgeous. **Kahului** often takes the rap for being an unattractive place to stay on Maui. It isn't all that bad. You're smack in the middle of striking out to the best of Maui's sights, and the airport is minutes away for people staying only a short time. Prices are cheaper, and Kanaha Beach is a sleeper, with great sand, surf, and few visitors. **Hana** is an experience in itself. You can camp, rent a cabin, or stay at an exclusive hotel. Always reserve in advance and consider splitting your stay on Maui, spending your last few nights in Hana. You can really soak up this wonderful area, and you won't have to worry about rushing back along the Hana Highway. Bed and Breakfast Inns are available on Maui (see p. 147).

CAMPING AND HIKING

A major aspect of the "Maui experience" is found in the simple beauty of nature and the outdoors. Visitors come to Maui to luxuriate at resorts and dine in fine restaurants, but everyone heads for the sand and surf, and most are captivated by the lush mountainous interior. What better way to savor this natural beauty than by hiking slowly through it or pitching a tent in the middle of it? Maui offers a full range of hiking and camping, and what's more, most of it is easily accessible and free. Camping facilities are located near many choice beaches and amid the most scenic areas of the island. They range in amenities from full-housekeeping cabins to primitive "hike-in" sites. Some restrictions to hiking apply because much of the land is privately owned, so you may require advance permission to hike. But plenty of public access trails along the coast and deep into the interior would fill the itineraries of even the most intrepid trekkers. If you enjoy the great outdoors on the Mainland, you'll be thrilled by these "mini-continents," where in one day you can go from the frosty summits of alpine wonderlands down into baking cactus-covered deserts and emerge through jungle foliage onto a sun-soaked subtropical shore.

Note: Descriptions of individual state parks, county beach parks, and Haleakala National Park, along with directions on how to get there, are given under "Sights" in the respective travel chapters.

HALEAKALA NATIONAL PARK

Camping at Haleakala National Park is free, but there is an automobile entrance fee of $3, with a senior citizen discount. Permits are not needed to camp at Hosmer Grove, just a short drive from Park Headquarters, or at Oheo Stream Campground (formerly Seven Sacred Pools) near Kipahulu, along the coastal road 10 miles south of Hana. Camping is on a first-come, first-served basis, and there's an official three-day stay limit, but it's a loose count, especially at Oheo, which is almost always empty.

The case is much different at the campsites located inside Haleakala Crater proper. On the floor of the crater are two primitive tenting campsites, one at Paliku on the east side and the other

at Holua on the north rim. For these you'll need a wilderness permit from Park Headquarters. Because of ecological considerations, only 25 campers per night can stay at each site, and a three-night, four-day maximum stay is strictly enforced, with tenting allowed at any one site for only two nights. However, because of the strenuous hike involved, campsites are open most of the time. You must be totally self-sufficient, and equipped for cold-weather camping to be comfortable at these two sites.

Also, Paliku, Holua, and another site at Kapalaoa on the south rim offer cabins. Fully self-contained with stoves, water, and nearby pit toilets, they can handle a maximum of 12 campers each. Cots are provided, but you must have your own warm bedding. The same maximum-stay limits apply as in the campgrounds. Staying at these cabins is at a premium—they're popular with visitors and residents alike. They're geared toward the group with rates at $2 per person, but there is a $6 minimum for a single. To have a chance at getting a cabin you must make reservations, so write well in advance for complete information to: Haleakala National Park, Box 537, Makawao, HI 96768, tel. 572-9306. For general information write: National Park Service, 300 Ala Moana Blvd., Honolulu, HI 96850, tel. 546-7584.

STATE PARKS

There are 10 state parks on Maui, managed by the Department of Land and Natural Resources through their Division of State Parks. These facilities include everything from historical sites to wildland parks accessible only by trail. Some are only for looking at, some are restricted to day use, and three of them offer overnight camping. Poli Poli and Wainapanapa offer free tenting, or self-contained cabins are available on a sliding fee; reservations necessary. At the other, Kaumahina, tent camping is free. Permits are required at all, and RVs technically are not allowed.

Park Rules

Tent camping permits are free and good for a maximum stay of five nights at any one park. A permit to the same person for the same park is again available only after 30 days have elapsed. Campgrounds are open every day. You can arrive after 2 p.m. and you should check out by 11 a.m. The minimum age for park permits is 18, and anyone under that age must be accompanied by an adult. Alcoholic beverages are prohibited, as is nude sunbathing. Plants and wildlife are protected, but reasonable amounts of fruits and seeds may be gathered for personal consumption. Fires on cookstoves or in designated pits only. Dogs and other pets must be under control at all times and are not permitted to run around unleashed. Hunting and freshwater fishing are allowed in season and only with a license, but ocean fishing is permitted, except when posted as prohibited. Permits are required for certain trails, so check at the State Parks office.

Cabins And Shelters
Housekeeping cabins are available as indicated on the accompanying chart. As with camping, permits are required with the same five-day maximum stay. Reservations are absolutely necessary, especially at Wainapanapa, and a 50% deposit at time of confirmation is required. There's a three-day cancellation requirement for refunds, and payment is to be made in cash, money order, certified check, or personal check, the latter only if it's received 30 days before arrival so that cashing procedures are possible. The balance is due on date of arrival. Cabins are on a sliding scale of $10 single, $14 double, and about $5 for each person thereafter. These are completely furnished down to the utensils, with heaters for cold weather and private baths.

Permit-issuing Office
Permits can be reserved two months in advance by writing a letter including your name, address, phone number, number of persons expected in your party, type of permit requested, and duration of your stay. They can be picked up on arrival with proof of identification. Office hours are 8 a.m. to 4:15 p.m., Monday through Friday. Usually, tent camping permits are no problem to secure on the day you arrive, but reserving ensures you a space and alleviates anxiety. The permits are available from the Maui (Molokai also) Division of State Parks, 54 High St., Wailuku, HI 96793, tel. 244-4354; or write Box 1049 Wailuku, HI 96793.

COUNTY PARKS

There are 15 county parks scattered primarily along Maui's coastline, and because of their locations, they're generally referred to as **beach parks**. Most are for day use only, where visitors fish, swim, snorkel, surf, picnic, and sunbathe, but two have overnight camping. The rules governing use of these parks are just about the same as those for state parks. The main difference is that along with a use permit, county beach parks charge a fee for overnight use. Again, the differences between individual parks are too numerous to mention, but the majority have a central pavilion for cooking, restrooms and cold-water showers, individual fire pits and picnic tables, with electricity usually only at the central pavilion. RVs are allowed to park in appropriate spaces. One safety point to consider is that beach parks are open to the general public and most are used with regularity. This means that quite a few people pass through, and your chances of encountering a hassle or running into a rip-off are slightly higher in beach parks.

Fees And Permits
The fees are quite reasonable at $1 per night per person, children $.50. To get a permit and pay your fees for use of a county beach park, either write in advance or visit the following issuing office, open 9 a.m. to 5 p.m., Mon. through Friday: Dept. of Parks and Recreation, Recreation Division, 1580 Kaahumanu Ave., (in War Memorial Gym) Wailuku, HI 96793, tel. 243-7389.

HIKING

The hiking on Maui is excellent; most times you have the trails to yourself, and the wide possibility of hikes range from a family saunter to a strenuous trek. The trails are mostly on public lands, though some cross private property. With the latter, the more established routes cause no problem, but for others you'll need special permission.

Haleakala Hikes
The most spectacular hikes on Maui are through Haleakala Crater's 30 miles of trail. **Halemauu Trail** is 10 miles long, beginning three miles up the mountain from Park Headquarters. It quickly winds down a switchback descending 1,400 feet

STATE AND COUNTY PARKS

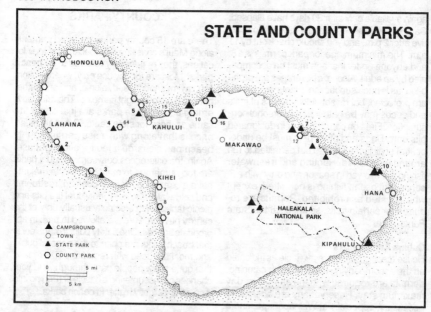

to the crater floor. It passes Holua Cabin and goes six more miles to Paliku Cabin, offering expansive views of Koolau Gap along the way. A spur leads to Sliding Sands Trail with a short walk to the visitors center. This trail passes Silversword Loop and the Bottomless Pit, two attractions in the crater. **Sliding Sands Trail** might be considered the main trail, beginning from the visitors center at the summit and leading 10 miles over the crater floor to Paliku Cabin. It passes Kapaloa Cabin en route and offers the best walk through the crater, with up-close views of cinder cones, lava flows, and unique vegetation. **Kaupo Gap Trail** begins at Paliku Cabin and descends rapidly through the Kaupo Gap, depositing you in the semi-ghost town of Kaupo. Below 4,000 feet the lava is rough and the vegetation thick. You pass through the private lands of the Kaupo Ranch along well-marked trails. Without a pick up arranged at the end, this is a tough one because the hitching is scanty.

West Maui Trails

The most frequented trails on West Maui are at Iao Needle. From the parking area you can follow the **Tableland Trail** for two miles, giving you beautiful panoramas of Iao Valley as you steadily climb to the tableland above, or you can descend to the valley floor and follow Iao Stream for a series of small but secluded swimming holes. **Waihee Ridge Trail** is a three-mile trek leading up the windward slopes of the West Maui Mountains. Follow Route 34 around the backside to Maluhia Road and turn up it to the Boy Scout camp. From here the trail rises swiftly to 2,560 feet. The views of Waihee Gorge are spectacular. **Kahakuloa Valley Trail** begins from this tiny forgotten fishing village on Maui's backside along Route 34. Start from the schoolhouse, passing burial caves and old terraced agricultural sites. Fruit trees line the way to trail's end two miles above the town.

Kula And Upcountry Trails

Most of these trails form a network through and around Poli Poli State Park. **Redwood Trail,** 1.7 miles, passes through a magnificent stand of redwoods, past the ranger station and down to an old CCC camp where there's a rough old shelter. **Tie Trail,** one-half mile, joins Redwood Trail with **Plum Trail,** so named because of its numerous plum trees, which bear during the summer. **Skyline Trail,** 6½ miles, starts atop Haleakala at 9,750 feet, passing through the

STATE PARKS

CODE NUMBER	PARK NAME	RESTROOMS	OVERLOOKS	PICNIC TABLES	OUTDOOR STOVES	DRINKING WATER	SWIMMING	SHELTERS	TENT CAMPING	CABINS	SHOWERS
1.	Wahikuli State Wayside	•		•	•	•	•	•			•
2.	Launiupoko State Wayside	•		•	•	•					•
3.	Ukumehame State Wayside			•			•				
4.	Iao Valley	•	•			•	•	•	•		
5.	Halekii-Pihana Heiau		•								
6.	Polipoli Spring Recreation Area	•		•	•	•			•		
7.	Kaumahina State Wayside	•	•	•	•	•			•		
8.	Keanae-Wailua Lookout		•								
9.	Puaa Kaa State Wayside	•		•	•	•	•	•			
10.	Waianapanapa	•	•	•	•	•	•		•		

COUNTY PARKS

		RESTROOMS	OVERLOOKS	PICNIC TABLES	OUTDOOR STOVES	DRINKING WATER	SWIMMING	SHELTERS	TENT CAMPING	CABINS	SHOWERS
1.	D.T. Fleming						•				•
2.	Honokowai	•		•		•					•
3.	Ukumehame	•		•	•	•					•
4.	Waihee	•		•	•	•					•
5.	Waiehu	•			•	•	•		•		•
6.	Kepaniwai	•	•	•	•	•	•	•			
7.	Mai Poina Oe Iau	•		•	•	•	•	•	•		•
8.	Kaiama	•		•	•	•	•	•	•		•
9.	Kamaole	•		•	•	•					•
10.	H.A. Baldwin	•	•	•			•	•	•	•	•
11.	Hookipai	•		•	•	•			•		•
12.	Honomanu Bay										
13.	Hana	•			•	•		•			•
14.	Paunau	•		•							•
15.	Kanaha Beach	•		•	•	•	•				•
16.	Rainbow	•							•		

southwest rift and eventually joining the **Halea-kala Ridge Trail,** 1.6 miles, at the 6,500-foot level, then descending through a series of switchbacks. You can join with the Plum Trail or continue to the shelter at the end. Both the Sky-line and Ridge trails offer superb vistas of Maui. Others throughout the area include: **Poli Poli,** one-half mile, passing through the famous forests of the area; **Boundary Trail,** four miles, leading from the Kula Forest Reserve to the ranger's cabin, passing numerous gulches still bearing native trees and shrubs; **Waiohuli Trail** which descends the mountain to join Boundary Trail and overlooks Keokea and Kihei with a shelter at the end; and **Waiakoa Trail,** seven miles, which begins at the Kula Forest Reserve Access Road. It ascends Haleakala to the 7,800-foot level and then descends through a series of switchbacks. It covers rugged territory and passes a natural cave shelter, eventually meeting up with **Waiakoa Loop Trail,** three miles. All of these trails offer intimate views of forests of native and introduced trees, and breathtaking views of the Maui coastline far below.

Coastal Trails

Along Maui's southernmost tip the **King's Highway Coastal Trail,** 5½ miles, leads from La Perouse Bay through the rugged and desolate lava flow of 1790, the time of Maui's last volcanic eruption. Kihei Road leading to the trail gets extremely rugged past La Perouse and should not be attempted by car, but is easy on foot. It leads over smooth stepping stones that were at one time trudged by royal tax collectors. The trail heads inland and passes many ancient Hawaiian stone walls and stone foundation sites. Spur trails lead down to the sea, including an overview of Cape Hanamanioa and its Coast Guard lighthouse. The trail eventually ends at private land. **Hana Wainapanapa Coastal Trail,** three miles, is at the opposite side of East Maui. You start from Wainapanapa State Park or from a gravel road near Hana Bay and again you follow the flat, laid stones of the "King's Highway." The trail is well maintained but fairly rugged due to lava and cinders. You pass natural arches, a string of *heiau,* blowholes, and caves. The vegetation is lush and long fingers of black lava stretch out into cobalt-blue waters.

Hiking Tour

This special Maui tour is a one-man show operated by an extraordinary man. It's called **Hike Maui,** and as its name implies, it offers walking tours to Maui's best scenic areas accompanied by Ken Schmitt, a professional nature guide. Ken has dedicated years to hiking Maui and has accumulated an unbelievable amount of knowledge about this awesome island. He's proficient in Maui's archaeology, botany, geology, anthropology, zoology, history, oceanography, and ancient Hawaiian cosmology. Moreover, he is a man of dynamic and gracious spirit who has tuned in to the soul of Maui. He hikes every day and is superbly fit, but will tailor his hikes for anyone, though good physical conditioning is essential.

Ken's hikes are actually workshops in Maui's natural history. As you walk along, Ken imparts his knowledge but he never seems to intrude on the beauty of the site itself.

His hikes require a minimum of two people and a maximum of six. He offers roundtrip transportation from your hotel, gourmet breakfasts, lunches, and snacks with an emphasis on natural health foods. All special equipment, including snorkel gear and camping gear for overnighters, is provided. His hikes take in sights from Hana to West Maui and to the summit of Haleakala, and range from the moderate to the hardy ability level. Half-day hikes last about five hours and all-day hikes go for at least twelve hours. The rates vary from $60 (about half for children) to $100. A day with Ken Schmitt is a classic outdoor experience. Don't miss it! Contact Hike Maui at tel. 879-5270, P.O. Box 330969, Kahului, Maui, HI 96733.

Guidebook

For a well-written and detailed hiking guide, comnplete with maps, check out *Hiking Maui* by Robert Smith, published by Wilderness Press, 2440 Bancroft Way, Berkeley, CA 94704.

FOOD AND RESTAURANTS

If you love to eat you'll love Maui. Besides great fish, there's fresh beef from Maui's ranches and fresh vegetables from Kula. The cuisines offered are as cosmopolitan as the people: Polynesian, Hawaiian, Italian, French, Mexican, Filipino, and Oriental. The following are just hors d'oeuvres; check the "Food" sections of the travel chapters for full descriptions.

Classy Dining

Five-star restaurants on Maui Include: **Raffles** at Stouffer's Wailea Resort, **The Planatation Veranda** at the Kapalua Bay Hotel, **The Swan Court** at the Hyatt Regency, **La Perouse** at the Maui Intercontinental Wailea, and the **Prince Court** at the Maui Prince Hotel. You won't be able to afford these every day, but for that one-time blowout, take your choice.

Fill 'Er Up

For more moderate fare, try these no-atmosphere restaurants that'll fill you up with good food for "at home" prices: **Ma Chan's** in the Kaahumanu Shopping Center; **Kitada's** in Makawao for the best bowl of saimin on the island; and both restaurants at the **Silversword** and **Makena golf courses**. For great sandwiches try the snack bars at all of the island's health food stores, especially **Paradise Fruit Co.** in Kihei, and **Picnics** in Paia. The best inexpensive dining is in Kahului OR Wailuku. Look in the "Food" sections of those chapters for a complete list.

Can't Go Wrong

There's great Mexican food (some vegetarian, no lard) at **Polli's Restaurant** in Kihei and Makawao, and **La Famiglia's** in Kihei has a great happy hour, complete with free chips and salsa. **Longhi's** in Lahaina is well established as a gourmet cosmopolitan/Italian restaurant. Also do yourself a flavor and dine in Lahaina at **Avalon**, or **Gerard's**—both out of this world! **Mama's Fish House** in Paia receives the highest compliment of being a favorite with the locals, and **The Grill and Bar** at the Kapalua Golf Course is extraordinarily good and always consistent. **Erik's Seafood Grotto** in Kahana is good value, and **Leilani's** is an up-and-comer in the Whaler's Village. The Sunday brunches at **Raffles Restaurant** at Stouffer's in Wailea and the **Maui Prince** in Makena are legendary. If you had to choose just one blowout, any of these would make an excellent choice.

Luaus And Buffets

The luau is an island institution. For a fixed price of about $30-40, you get to gorge yourself on a tremendous variety of island food, and enjoy a night of entertainment as well. On your luau day, eat a light breakfast, skip lunch, and do belly-stretching exercises!

Old Lahaina Luau has an excellent reputation because it is as close to authentic as you can get. Seating is Tuesday through Saturday, from 5:30 to 8:30 p.m., but reserve at least three days in advance to avoid disappointment. It's held on the beach at Lahaina's south end fronting 505 Front Street Mall. All-you-can-eat buffet and all-you-can-drink bar, tel. 667-1998, $37 adults, childen under 12, $16. The hula dancers use *ti*-leaf skirts, and the music is *fo' real*. A favorite with local people.

Jesse's Luau Polynesia at 1945 S. Kihei Rd., tel. 879-7227, is not a beachside luau but an excellent one. Jesse was with the Maui Lu Resort for many years and recently went on his own. The luau begins at 5 p.m. every Wed., Fri., and Sun., $37 adults, $20 children under 12. The *imu* ceremony (free) is on luau days at 10:30 a.m. Another local favorite.

Stouffer's Wailea Beach Resort, tel. 879-4900, recounts tales of old Hawaii with its very authentic and professional hula show and luau every Tuesday at 6 p.m. Host Rod Guerrero spins yarns and tales of Maui's past, and then bursts into song with his intriguing falsetto voice. Dramatically, a fire dancer appears, and the show moves on into the evening as you dine on a wonderful assortment of foods expertly prepared by Stouffer's chefs. Price includes open bar for, $38 adults, $21 children 12 and under.

The Aloha Luau, tel. 667-9564, every night at the Sheraton Maui, is a fun time of feasting and entertainment on one of the most beautiful sunset beaches on Maui. Prices, including full buffet, bar, and entertainment, are $36, children under 12, $19.

The **Royal Lahaina Resort,** tel. 661-3611, has been offering a nightly luau and entertainment for years in their Luau Gardens. The show is still spectacular and the food offered is authentic and good. Prices are $37 adults, children $18, reservations suggested.

For something a little different try the **Hawaiian Country BBQ** at Maui Tropical Plantation, tel. 244-7643, in Waikapu near Wailuku (see p. 406). Here you get a *yippee yai yo kai yeah* good time, complete with hula and square dancing! The grill is fired up and sizzles with savory steaks, and there's a big pot of chili and all the fixins. Price is $38, and the fun happens every Mon. and Wed. from 5:30 p.m. Host is Uncle Buddy Fo, who lassoes everyone into the good time with his singing, dancing, and drumming.

Markets

If you're shopping for general food supplies and are not interested in gourmet and specialty items, or organic foods, you'll save money by shopping at the big-name supermarkets, located in Lahaina, Kahului, and Kihei, often in malls. Smaller towns have general stores which are adequate but a bit more expensive. You can also find convenience items at commissaries in many condos and hotels, but these should be used only for snack foods or when absolutely necessary, because the prices are just too high.

Kahului

The greatest number of supermarkets is found in Kahului. They're all conveniently located along Route 32 (Kaahumanu Avenue) in three malls, one right after the other. **Foodland**, open daily 8:30 a.m. to 10 p.m., is in the **Kaahumanu Shopping Center**. Just down the road in the **Kahului Shopping Center** is the ethnic **Ah Fooks** (open seven days, 8 a.m. to 7 p.m., closes early Sat. and Sun.), specializing in Japanese, Chinese, and Hawaiian foods. Farther along is the **Maui Mall** is **Star Market**, open seven days, 8:30 a.m. to 9 p.m., till 7 p.m. Sunday. Just behind the Maui Mall on E. Kamehameha Ave. is a **Safeway**. Wailuku doesn't have shopping malls, but if you're taking an excursion around the top of West Maui, make a "last chance" stop at **T.K. Supermarket** at the end of N. Market St. in the Happy Valley area. They're open daily but close early on Sunday afternoons.

Kihei

In Kihei you've got a choice of three markets, all strung along S. Kihei Road., the main drag. **Foodland** in the Kihei Town Center, and **Star Market** just down the road, offer standard shopping. The most interesting is **Azeka's Market** in Azeka Plaza. This market is an institution and is very famous for its specially prepared (uncooked) ribs, perfect for a barbecue. In Wailea you'll find **Wailea Pantry** in the Wailea Shopping Village, open daily 8 a.m. to 7 p.m., but it's an exclusive area and the prices will make you sob.

Lahaina And Vicinity

In Lahaina you can shop at **Foodland** in Lahaina Square, just off Route 30. More interesting is **Nagasako's** in the Lahaina Shopping Center, just off Front Street. They've got all you need, plus a huge selection of Chinese and Japanese items. Nagasako's is open seven days, 8 a.m to 8 p.m., till 9 p.m. Fri. and 5 p.m. Saturday. If you're staying at a condo and doing your own cooking the largest and generally least expensive supermarket on West Maui is the **Safeway**, open daily, 24 hours, in the Cannery Shopping Mall. Just west of Lahaina in Honokowai you'll find the **Food Pantry**. Although there are a few sundry stores in various hotels in Kaanapali, this is the only real place to shop. It's open everyday 8 a.m. to 9 p.m. In Napili, pick up supplies at **Napili Village Store,** a bit expensive, but well stocked and convenient. In Olowalu, east of Lahaina, you can pick up some limited items at the **Olowalu General Store.**

Hana

In Hana you have the legendary **Hasegawa's General Store**. They have just about everything, and are geared toward standard American selections. Hasegawa's is open seven days, 7:30 a.m. to 6 p.m., 9 a.m. to 3:30 p.m. on Sunday. Also in Hana is the **Hana Store,** which actually has a better selection of health foods and imported beers. Open every day 7:30 a.m. to 6 p.m.

Around And About

Other stores where you might pick up supplies are: **Komoda's** in Makawao. They're famous throughout Hawaii for their cream buns, which are sold out by 8 a.m. At **Pukalani Superette** in Pukalani, open seven days, you can pick up supplies and food to go, including sushi. In Paia try **Nagata's** or **Paia General Store** on the main drag. In Kaupakulua you have **Hanzawa's**, a "last chance" store on the back road (Route 365) from Hana to Haleakala.

HEALTH FOOD

Those into organic foods, fresh vegetables, natural vitamins, and takeout snack bars have it made on Maui. At many fine health food stores you can have most of your needs met. Try the following: in Wailuku, **Down to Earth** is an excellent health food store complete with vitamins, bulk foods, and a snack bar. This Krishna-oriented market, on the corner of Central and Vineyard, is open daily 8 a.m. to 6 p.m., till 5 p.m. Sat., 4 p.m. Sunday. Formerly Lahaina Natural Foods, **Westside Natural Food** is now relocated on Dickenson Street. Open seven days, they're a full-service health food store, featuring baked goods and Herbalife vitamins. **Paradise Fruit Company** on S. Kihei Rd. is terrific. It's not strictly a health food store, but does have plenty of wholesome items. Their food bar is the best. They're open 24 hours every day. You can't go wrong! In Paia is **Mana Natural Foods,** open

daily 8 a.m. to 8 p.m., possibly the best health food store on Maui. You can pick up whatever you need for your trip to Hana. **Maui Natural Foods,** tel. 877-3018, in the Maui Mall in Kahului is open seven days and has a fair selection of fresh foods with a big emphasis on vitamins.

Fresh Fruit And Fish

What's Hawaii without its fruits, both from the vine and from the sea? For fresh fish try the Fish Market at **Maalaea Harbor**. They get their fish right from the boats, but they do have a retail counter. In Kihei along S. Kihei Road (just west of Azeka Place), some enterprising fishermen set up a roadside stand whenever they have a good day. Look for their coolers propping up a sign. For the best and freshest fruits, vegies, cheese, and breads search out **The Farmers' Market**. Gardeners bring their fresh Kula vegetables to roadside stands on Mon. and Thurs. 8 a.m. to 1:30 p.m. in Kahana near Fat Boy's Restaurant, and every Tues. and Fri. in N. Kihei by Suda's Store. Be early for the best selections. All along the road to Hana are little fruit stands tucked away. Many times no one is in attendance and the very reasonably priced fruit is paid for on the honor system.

SPORTS AND RECREATION

Maui won't let you down when you want to go outside and play. More than just a giant sandbox for big kids, its beaches and surf are warm and inviting, and there are all sorts of water sports from scuba diving to parasailing. You can fish, hunt, camp, or indulge yourself in golf or tennis to your heart's content. The hiking is marvelous and the horseback riding along beaches and on Haleakala is some of the most exciting in the world. The information offered in this chapter is merely an overview to let you know what's available. Specific areas are covered in the travel sections. Have fun!

Note

You can book most of the following through "activity centers." Please see "Sightseeing Tours" p. 379, and also check p. 380 for sailing boats and charters that may also offer other activities such as snorkeling and scuba.

Since your island is blessed with 150 miles of coastline, over 32 of which are wonderful beach-

es, your biggest problem is to choose which one you'll grace with your presence. The following should help you choose just where you'd like to romp about.

BEACHES

Southwest Maui Beaches

The most and best beaches for swimming and sunbathing are on the south coast of West Maui, strung along 18 glorious miles from Kapalua to Olowalu. For an all-purpose beach you can't beat **Kapalua Beach** (Fleming Beach) on Maui's western tip. It has everything: safe surf (except in winter), great swimming, snorkeling, and bodysurfing in a first-class, family-oriented area. Then comes the Kaanapali beaches along Route 30, bordered by the hotels and condos. All are open to the public and "rights of way" pass just along hotel grounds. **Black Rock** at the Sheraton is the best for snorkeling. Just east and west of Lahaina are **Lahaina Beach,** convenient but not private; **Launiupoko and Puamana waysides** have only fair swimming, but great views and grassy beaches. **Olowalu** has very good swimming beaches just across from the General Store, and **Papalaua Wayside** offers seclusion on a narrow beach fringed by *kiawe* trees that surround tiny patches of white sand.

Kihei And Wailea Beaches

The 10 miles stretching from the west end of Kihei to Wailea are dotted with beaches that range from poor to excellent. **Kihei Beach** extends for miles from Maalaea to Kihei. Excellent for walking and enjoying the view, but little else. **Kamaole Beach Parks I, II,** and **III** are at the east end of Kihei. Top-notch beaches, they have it all—swimming, snorkeling, and safety. **Keawakapu** is more of the same. Then come the great little beaches of Wailea that get more secluded as you head east: Mokapu, Ulua, Wailea, and Polo. All are surrounded by the picture-perfect hotels of Wailea and all have public access. Makena Beach, down an unpaved road east from Wailea, is very special. It's one of the island's best beaches. At one time, alternative people made Makena a haven and it still attracts free-spirited souls. There's nude bathing here in secluded coves, unofficial camping, and freedom. It gets the highest compliment with locals, and those staying at hotels and condos around Maui, come here to enjoy themselves.

Wailuku And Kahului

Poor ugly ducklings! There are shallow, unattractive beaches in both towns and no one spends any time there. However, **Kanaha Beach** between Kahului and the airport isn't bad at all. **Baldwin Beach Park** has a reputation for hostile locals protecting their turf, but the beach is good and you won't be hassled if you "live and let live." **Hookipa Beach** just west of Paia isn't good for the average swimmer but it is the "sailboarding capital" of Hawaii, and you should visit here just to see the exciting, colorful spectacle of people skipping over the ocean with bright sails.

Hana Beaches

Everything about Hana is heavenly, including its beaches. There's **Red Sand Beach,** almost too pretty to be real. **Wainapanapa** is surrounded by the state park and good for swimming and snorkeling, even providing a legendary cave

whose waters turn blood red. **Hana Bay** is well protected and safe for swimming. Farther along at **Oheo Stream** (Seven Sacred Pools) you'll find the paradise you've been searching for—gorgeous freshwater pools at the base of wispy waterfalls and fronted by a tremendous sea of pounding surf only a few yards away.

Freshwater Swimming

The best place for swimming is in various stream pools on the road to Hana. One of the very best is **Twin Falls,** up a short trail from Hoolawa Bridge. **Helio's Grave** is another good swimming spot between Hana and Oheo streams, which are excellent themselves, especially the upper pools. Also, you can take a refreshing dip at Iao Valley stream when you visit Iao Needle.

SNORKELING AND SCUBA

Maui is as beautiful from under the waves as it is above. There is world-class snorkeling and diving at many coral reefs and beds surrounding the island. You'll find the best, coincidentally, just where the best beaches are: mainly from Kihei to Makena, up around Napili Bay, and especially from Olowalu to Lahaina. Backside Maui is great (but mostly for experts), and for a total thrill, try diving Molokini, the submerged volcano, just peeking above the waves and designated a Marine Life Conservation District.

Great Underwater Spots

These are some of the best on Maui, but there are plenty more (see "Sights" in individual chapters). Use the same caution when scuba diving or snorkeling as when swimming. Be mindful of currents. It's generally safer to enter the water in the center of a bay than at the sides where rips are more likely to occur. The following sites are suitable for beginners to intermediates: on Maui's western tip **Honolua Bay,** a Marine Life Conservation District; nearby **Mokuleia Bay,** known as "Slaughterhouse," but gentle; Napili Bay for usually good, and safe conditions; in Kaanapali you'll enjoy **Black Rock** at the Sheraton Hotel; **Olowalu** is very gentle with plenty to see; also try **Kamaole Parks II** and **III** in Kihei and **Ulua,** and **Polo** and **Wailea beaches** in Wailea. On the windward side **Baldwin Beach Park** in Paia, and **Wainapanapa State Park** near Hana are both generally good. Under no circumstances should you miss taking a boat out to Molokini. It's worth every penny!

For **scuba divers,** there are underwater caves at **Nahuna** ("Five Graves") **Point** between Wailea and Makena, great diving at Molokini, magnificent caves out at the **Lanai Cathedrals,** and a sunken Navy sub, the USS *Bluegill,* to explore. Advanced divers *only* should attempt the backside of West Maui, the Seven Sacred Pools, and beyond Pu'uiki Island in Hana Bay.

Equipment

Sometimes condos and hotels have snorkeling equipment free for their guests, but if you have to rent it, don't do it from a hotel or condo but go to a dive shop where it's much cheaper. Expect to spend $7 a day for mask, fins, and snorkel. One of the best snorkel deals is through **Snorkel Bob's,** tel. 879-7449 Kihei, or 669-9603 Napili. Old Snorkel Bob will dispense info and full snorkel gear for only $15 weekly (see pp. 442 and 450). Scuba divers can rent gear for about $30 from most shops. In Lahaina rent from: **Lahaina Divers,** tel. 667-7496, at 710 Front St., one of the best all-around shops/schools on Maui; **American Dive Maui,** 628 Front, tel. 661-4885; **Central Pacific Divers,** 780 Front, tel. 661-8718; **Hawaii Reef Divers,** 129 Lahainaluna, tel. 667-7647, charge only $2.50 for the day, offer good instruction, and can arrange a reasonably priced snorkel/sail to Lanai; **Scuba Schools,** 1000 Limahana, tel. 661-8036. In Kihei an excellent all-around shop is **The Dive Shop,** 2411 S. Kihei Rd., Suite 2-A, tel. 879-5172; there's also a **Maui Dive Shop,** Azeka Pl., tel. 879-3388; and **Maui Sailing Center,** at the Kealia Beach Center, tel. 879-6260. You might also consider renting an underwater camera. Expect to spend $15-20, including film.

Scuba Certification

A number of Maui companies take you from your first dive to PADI, NAUI, or NASDS certification. Prices range from $50 for a quickie refresher dive up to around $300 for a four- to five-day certification course. Courses or arrangements can be made with any of the dive shops listed above or following: **Ocean Activities Center,** tel. 879-4485; **Destination Pacific,** tel. 874-0305; **Aquatic Charters,** tel. 879-0976.

Snorkel And Scuba Excursions

Many boats will take you out snorkeling or diving. Prices range from $30 (half day, four hours) to $60 (full day, eight hours) for a snorkeling adventure, and from $50 to $80 for scuba diving. Check "Getting Around—Ocean Tours" for many of the boats that do it all, from deep-sea fishing to moonlight cruises. All of the "activities centers" (p. 379) can arrange these excursions for no extra charge; check "Getting Around—Sightseeing Tours" for names and numbers.

The best all-around snorkel/scuba excursions/lessons are offered by a cooperative of dive shops that have joined to become part of **Dive Hawaii,** tel. 922-0975, P.O. Box 90295, Honolulu, HI 96835. All operators associated with Dive Hawaii have been thoroughly checked by their peers for safety, fair prices, reliable service, and know-how. Send $3 for the association's 24-page full-color *Dive Hawaii Guide* by writing or phoning the above address. Most of the shops/operations listed above are members. Dive Hawaii is a self-regulatory body interested in giving you a safe and worthwhile diving experience. Simply, they're the best!

Others that you might try are **Sea Safari Travel,** 2770 Highland Ave., Manhattan Beach, CA 90266, which offers a seven-night package for scuba divers to Maui; **Mike Severns,** tel. 879-6596, is one of the most experienced and respected divers on Maui. As a marine scientist/explorer, he is extremely knowledgeable about Maui both above and below the waves. Mike has his own boat and accepts both beginning and advanced divers. Diving with Mike is an extraordinary educational experience.

With a name like **Chuck Thorne,** what else can you expect but a world-class athlete of some kind? Well, Chuck is a diver who lives on Maui. He's written *The Divers' Guide to Maui,* the definitive book on all the best dive/snorkel spots on Maui. Chuck has a one-man operation, so unfortunately, he must limit his leadership and instruction to advanced divers only. People have been known to cancel flights home to dive with Chuck, and he receives the highest accolades from other divers. Some people feel that Chuck is Maui's "Rambo" diver. He's a no-nonsense kind of guy who's out to show you some great spots, but never forgets about safety first. He'll arrive in a pickup truck, oftentimes with ladders on the roof. These might come in handy later when he drives you to a remote area and you've got to climb down the cliff to get to the dive spot. No pencil-necked wimps! You can buy his book at many outlets or write: Maui Dive Guide, P.O. Box 1461, Kahului, HI 96732. You can contact Chuck through **The Dive Shop**, tel. 879-5172, or at 879-7068.

For a purely snorkeling adventure besides those offered by the dive shops and tour boats above, try **Snorkel Maui**, tel. 572-8437, with Ann Fielding, the naturalist author of *Hawaiian Reefs and Tide Pools*. Ms. Fielding will instruct you in snorkeling and in the natural history and biology of what you'll be seeing below the waves. She tailors the dive to fit the participants, and does scuba as well.

Snuba

No, that's not a typo. **Snuba**, tel. 874-0019, P.O. Box 1359, Kihei, HI 96753, is half snorkeling and half scuba diving. You have a regulator, and a weight belt, mask, and flippers, and you're tethered to scuba tanks that float 20 feet above you on a sea-sled. The idea is that many people become anxious diving under the waves encumbered by tanks and all the scuba apparatus. Snuba frees you. You would think that being tethered to the sled would slow you down, but actually you're sleeker and can make better time than a normal scuba diver. If you would like to try diving, this is a wonderful and easy way to start.

MORE WATER SPORTS

Bodysurfing

All you need are the right waves, conditions, and ocean bottom to have a ball bodysurfing. Always check conditions first as bodysurfing has led to some very serious neck and back injuries for the ill prepared. The following are some decent areas: Ulua, Wailea, Polo, or Makena beaches; the north end of Kamaole Beach Park I in Kihei; Napili Bay; and Baldwin Park.

Surfing

For good surfing beaches try: Lower Paia Park, Napili Bay, Baldwin Park, or Maalaea and Hookipa beaches. For surfing lessons: **Maui Beach Center**, tel. 661-4941, open daily 8:30 a.m. to 5:30 p.m., does it all from rental of surfboards to

sailboards at Kealia Beach

boogie boards. Rentals for 24 hours: surfboards $28, snorkel equipment $6, boogie boards $5, and they feature the *best* surfing lessons on Maui with guaranteed results. The owner is a local Maui waterman named Eric. He takes a hand in all the activities and most times will personally take you on a surfing safari. **Kaanapali Windsurfing** in Kaanapali, tel. 667-1964, also offers lessons.

Sailboarding

This is one of the world's newest sports, and unlike surfing, which tends to be male-dominated, women, too, are excellent at sailboarding. Hookipa Beach, just east of Paia, is the "sailboarding capital of the world," and the **O'Neill International Championship** is held here every year in March and April. Kanaha Beach Park, in nearby Kahului, is perfect with gentle winds and waves for learning the sport. To rent boards and to take instructions, try: **Maui Sailing Center** at Kealia Beach Center, N. Kihei Rd., tel. 879-5935. You can rent here for $15 an hour; lessons are extra.

TENNIS COURTS OF MAUI

COUNTY COURTS

Under jurisdiction of the Department of Parks & Recreation
200 High St., Wailuku, Maui. Phone: 244-7750
Courts listed are in or near visitor areas. there are
Three additional locations around the island.
* = Courts on state land, under state jurisdiction

Name	Location	No. of Courts	Lighted
Hana	Hana Ball Park	2	Yes
Kahului	Kahului Community Center	2	Yes
Kihei	Kalami Park	2	Yes
* Kihei	Fronting Maui Pacific Shores	2	No
Lahaina	Lahaina Civic Center	5	Yes
Lahaina	Malu-ulu-olele Park	4	Yes
Makawao	Eddie Tam Memorial Center	2	Yes
Pukalani	Pukalani community Center	2	Yes
Wailuku	Maui Community College Tel. 244-9181 Courts available after school hours	4	No
Wailuku	Wailuku Community Center	7	Yes
Wailuku	Wailuku War Memorial	4	Yes

HOTEL AND PRIVATE COURTS OPEN TO THE PUBLIC

Lahaina	Maui Marriott Resort	5	No
Kihei	Maui Sunset	2	No
Kaanapali	Maui Westin	3	No
Napili Bay	Napili Kai Beach Club	2	No
Kaanapali	Royal Lahaina Hotel	11	6 are
Kaanapali	Sheraton Maui Hotel	3	Yes
Kapalua	Tennis Garden	10	No
Wailea	Wailea Tennis Center	14	3 are
Makena	Makena Alanui Rd.	6	No

Sailboards Maui, 430 Alamaha, Suite 103, Kahului, tel. 871-7954, $25 half day, $35 full. **Kaanapali Windsurfing School,** tel. 667-1964. Remember—start with a big board and a small sail! Take lessons to save time and energy.

Note
A recent controversy has focused on what has been called "thrill craft." Usually this refers to jet skis, water-skiing boats, speed boats, and even by some to sailboards. The feeling among con-

GOLF COURSES OF MAUI

* = Weekday and special twilight rates in effect. Call for details.

Course	Holes	Par	Yards	Rates	Cart
* Kapalua Golf Club, Bay Course	18	71	6,145	$75	$15
Villa Course	18	73	6,194	$75	$15
Kapalua, HI 96791 669-8044					
Makena Golf Course	18	72	6,798	$65	Incl.
Kinei, HI 96753 879-3344					
Maui Country Club, Front Course	9	37	3,148	$35	Incl.
Back Course	9	37	3,247	$35	Incl.
Paia, HI 96779 877-0606 (Monday only for visitors)					
Pukalani Country Club	9	36	3,000	$10	$10
Pukalani, HI 96788 572-1314	9	36	3,200	$10	$10
Royal Kaanapali North Course	18	70	7,179	$90	Incl.
South Course	18	72	6,758	$90	Incl.
Kaanapali, HI 96761 661-3691					
* Waiehu Municipal Golf Course	18	72	6,367	$25	$12.50
Waiehu, HI 96793 244-5433					
Wailea Golf, Blue Course	18	72	6,327	$65	$15
Orange Course	18	72	6,405	$65	$15
Wailea, HI 96753 879-2966					
* Silversword Golf Course	18	71	6,200	$40-60	Incl.
Kihei, HI 96753 874-0777					

servationists is that these craft disturb others, and during whale season disturb the whales that come to nest in the rather small Lahaina Roads. As of yet, nothing has been resolved, but there are suggestions afoot to ban, restrict, or somehow control the use of thrill craft. This is definitely a case of "one man's pleasure is another man's poison."

Parasailing

If you've ever wanted to soar like an eagle, here's your chance with no prior experience necessary. Basically a parasail is a parachute tethered to a speed boat. And away we go! **Lahaina Parasail,** tel. 661-4887, located in downtown Lahaina on the south end of the breakwater, is a family-run business that was the first of its kind on Maui. These folks know what they're doing and have taken tens of thousands of people aloft on their thrill-of-a-lifetime ride. The most dangerous part, according to the crew, is getting in and

out of the shuttle boat that takes you to the floating platform about 1,000 yards offshore, from where you take off. Awaiting you is a power boat with special harness attached to a parachute. You're put in a life vest and strapped to the harness that forms a cradle upon which you sit while aloft. Make sure, once you're up, to pull the cradle as far under your thighs as you can. It's much more comfortable. Don't be afraid to loosen your steel grip on the guide ropes because that's not what's holding you anyway. In the air, you are as free as a bird and the unique view is phenomenal. You don't have time to fret about going up. The boat revs and you're airborne almost immediately. Once up, the feeling is very secure. The technology is simple, straightforward, and safe. Relax and have a ball. Cost is $42 for this joy ride.

Other companies include **West Maui Parasail,** tel. 661-4060; **UFO Parasail,** tel. 661-7UFO.

Jet Skis

To try this exciting sport, contact: **Kaanapali Jet Ski,** at Whaler's Village, tel. 667-7851; **Jammin Jet Skis,** in Kihei at 879-6662, from $30 to $60, seasonal prices on Kawasakis and Yamaha Wave Runners.

Water-skiing

Kaanapali Water Skiing, tel. 661-3324, can arrange an outing with lessons. Another is **Lahaina Water Ski,** tel. 661-5988, with professional instructors and a wide range of equipment.

Sailing/Boating

The most popular day sails are from Maui to Molokai or Lanai (fully discussed in "Getting Around—Ocean Tours"). Your basic half-day snorkel and swim sail will be $50. For serious sailors, some top-notch boats in Lahaina Harbor are open for lengthy charters. Try: **Alihilani Yacht Charters,** at Lahaina Harbor; **Scotch Mist,** tel. 661-0368.

For **kayaking** see p. 116. And see "Ocean Tours" for more alternatives, p. 380.

HORSEBACK RIDING

Those who love sightseeing from the back of a horse are in for a big treat on Maui. Stables dot the island, so you have a choice of terrain for your trail ride: a breathtaking ride through Haleakala Crater, or a backwoods ride out at the Seven Sacred Pools. Unfortunately, none of this comes cheap. In comparison, a bale of alfalfa, which goes for under $5 on the Mainland, fetches $18-22 on Maui. If you plan to do some serious riding, it's advisable to bring jeans (jogging suit bottoms will do) and a pair of boots, or at least jogging shoes.

The Rainbow Ranch

The Rainbow Ranch is operated by Kimo Harlacher and his top hands. You'll have your choice of rides: beginners ride daily at 9 a.m., for $20, on gentle horses; a beach and mountain-ride, through pineapple fields, an extended ride for experienced riders, $55; The West Maui Adventure, $35 for two hours, runs through the foothills of the mountains; picnic rides (bring your own) depart at 10 to 1 p.m., $45; No dress code, but long pants and close-toed shoes required. Rainbow Ranch, P.O. Box 10066, Lahaina 96761, tel. 669-4991, is located at mile marker 29 along Route 30 toward Kapalua.

Holo Lio Stables

Recently opened, these stables provide unique overnight camping at La Perouse Bay. It's located just past Polo Beach in Wailea on the road to Makena. You can't go wrong with these local cowpokes who have an old-fashioned love and respect for the land, tel. 879-1085.

Makena Stables, tel. 879-0244, is nearby, where Helaine and Pat Borge will take you on a 2½ hour ride along the mountains of Ulupalakua Ranch.

Haleakala And Environs

A few upcountry companies offer trail rides through the crater or over the mountain. Wear *warm* clothes! Here are some of the best: **Charley's Trailride and Pack Trips** takes you overnight camping in Haleakala, arranging for cabins and supplying all meals. Run by Charles Aki, c/o Kaupo Store, Hana, HI 96713, tel. 248-8209. **Pony Express Tours** offers rides through Haleakala with very experienced guides who give a full narration of the area. Lunch provided. Full day $120, partial day $90. Write Pony Express P.O. Box 535, Kula, HI 96790, tel. 667-2200. **Thompson Riding Stables** guides you over the slopes of Haleakala on one of Maui's oldest cattle ranches. Write Thompson Stables, Thompson Rd., Kula, HI 96790, tel. 878-1910.

Adventures On Horseback offers waterfall rides from Hana, $125, tel. 242-7445.

Kau Lio Stables

Just near Lahaina, they offer two-hour rides leaving at 8:30 and 11:30 a.m. and at 2:30 p.m., $33 including snack. They're located on private land, so they'll pick you up in Kaanapali. Write P.O. Box 16056, Kaanapali Beach, HI 96761, tel. 667-7896.

Hotel Hana-Maui Stables

The hotel guests are given priority for use of the horses, but you can call ahead to arrange a trail ride on this truly magnificent end of the island. For information call 248-7238.

MAUI INFORMATION

Emergency

To summon the police, fire department, or ambulance to any part of Maui, dial 911. **Helpline,** the island's crisis center, is tel. 244-7407. **Maui Memorial Hospital,** Kaahumanu Ave., Kahului, tel. 244-9056. **Pharmacies:** Kahului, tel. 877-0041; Kihei, tel. 879-1951; Lahaina, tel. 661-3119; Pukalani, tel. 572-8244.

Information

The state operates a **visitors kiosk** at Kahului Airport. Open seven days, 6 a.m. to 9 p.m., tel. 877-6413, plenty of practical brochures. **Hawaii Visitor's Bureau,** 26 N. Puunene Ave., Kahului, tel. 877-7822 is open Mon. to Fri., 8 a.m. to 4:30 p.m. The **Chamber of Commerce,** is in the Kahului Shopping Center, tel. 871-7711; for **Consumer Complaints,** call 244-7756. For **time,** call 242-0212.

Reading Material

For bookstores try: **Waldenbooks,** at Maui Mall, Kahului, tel. 877-0181, Kaahumanu Mall, tel. 871-6112, Lahaina Cannery Mall, tel. 667-6172, and at Whaler's Village, tel. 661-8638. Also the **Whalers' Book Shoppe** at The Wharf, Front St., Lahaina, tel. 667-9544.

Libraries: main branch at 251 High St., Wailuku, tel. 244-3945, other branches in Kahului, Lahaina, Makawao, and Hana. Open during a hodgepodge of hours through the week, usually closed Fri. or Saturday.

Free tourist literature is well done and loaded with tips, discounts, maps, happenings, etc. Found everywhere, in hotels, restaurants, and street stands. They include: *This Week Maui,* every Friday; *Guide to Maui* on Thursdays; *Maui Beach Press,* newspaper format and in-depth articles, every Friday; *Maui Gold,* one for each season; *Drive Guide,* excellent

maps and tips, given out free by all car rental agencies, bi monthly; *The Bulletin,* a TV guide with feature articles and local events; *Maui News,* a local newspaper for 25 cents, with a good "Datebook" listing of local events, Mon. to Fri., tel. 244-3981.

Parks And Recreation

State Parks in Wailuku, tel. 244-4354; County Parks in Wailuku, tel. 243-7389; Haleakala National Park HQ, tel. 527-7749.

Weather And Whales

For all-Maui weather, call 877-5111; for recreational areas, call 877-5124; for Haleakala, call 572-7749; for marine weather, call 877-3477; for whale sighting and reports in season, call 661-8527.

Post Offices

In Wailuku, tel. 244-4815; in Kahului, tel. 871-4710; in Kihei, tel. 879-2403; in Lahaina, tel. 667-6611. Other branch offices are scattered around the island.

Legal Help

For any legal problems, or advice while on Maui, contact **Padgett and Henry,** at 2099 Wells St., Wailuku, tel. 244-5514. They specialize in personal injury, and are well versed in the special problems that a tourist can have if they're involved in an accident. Husband-and-wife team Matthew and Elizabeth have a good and solid reputation.

Maui Facts

Maui is the second youngest and second largest Hawaiian island after Hawaii. Its nickname is the Valley Island. Its color is pink and its flower is the *lokelani,* a small rose.

1. banner butterfly fish (Dr. Greg Leo)　**2.** moray eel (Dr. Greg Leo)
3. Hawaiian gallinule (R.J. Shallenberger)

1. Kalalau Valley (D. Stanley) **2.** Haleakala, magical moments (Dr. Janos Balogh)

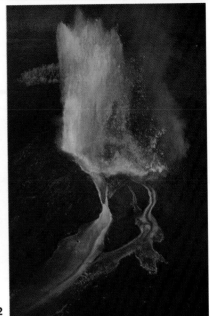

1. lava pool (J.D. Bisignani)   **2.** and **3.** awesome volcanic power,
1989 eruption (U.S. Geological Survey, J.D. Griggs)

1. Waikiki skyline (J.D. Bisignani)   **2.** Pololu Valley meets the sea (J.D. Bisignani)
3. Wailua Falls (Robert Nilsen)

1. Captain Dave Ventura and friend (J.D. Bisignani)
2. aloha, *paniolo* style (J.D. Bisignani) **3.** motorcycle madonna (J.D. Bisignani)

the *pali* from the Haiku Restaurant (J.D. Bisignani)

CENTRAL MAUI: THE ISTHMUS

KAHULUI

It is generally believed that Kahului means "The Winning," but perhaps it should be "The Survivor." Kahului suffered attack by Kamehameha I in the 1790s, when he landed his war canoes here in preparation for battle at Iao Valley. In 1900 it was purposely burned to thwart the plague, then rebuilt. Combined with Wailuku, the county seat just down the road, this area is home to 22,000 Mauians, over one-third of the island population. Here's where the people live. It's a practical, homey town, the only deep-water port from which Maui's sugar and pineapples are shipped. Although Kahului was an established sugar town by 1880, it's really only grown up in the last 20 years. In the 1960s, Hawaiian Commercial and Sugar Co. began building low-cost housing for its workers which became a model development for the whole of the U.S. Most people land at the airport, blast through for Lahaina or Kihei, and never give Kahului a second look. It's in no way a resort community, but it has the best general-purpose shopping on the island, a few noteworthy sites, and a convenient location to the airport.

SIGHTS

Kanaha Pond Wildlife Sanctuary
This one-time royal fishpond is 1½ miles southwest of the airport at the junctions of Routes 36 and 37. It's on the migratory route of various ducks and Canada geese, but most importantly it is home to the endangered Hawaiian stilt *(ae'o)* and the Hawaiian coot *(alae ke'oke'o)*. The stilt is a slender, 16-inch bird with a black back, white belly, and stick-like pink legs. The coot is a gray-black duck-like bird, which builds large floating nests. An observation shelter is maintained along Route 396 (just off Rt. 36). Kanaha Pond is always open and free of charge. Bring binoculars.

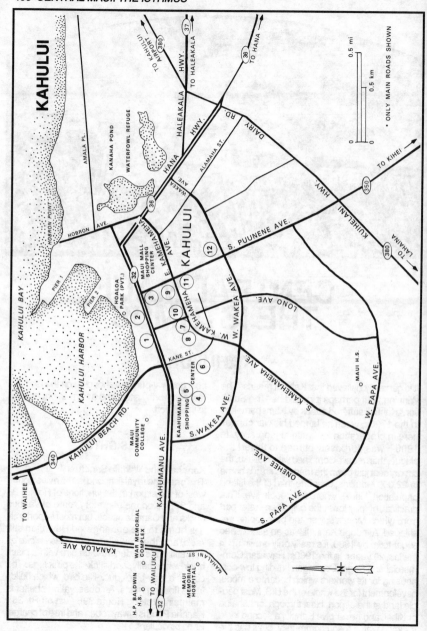

KAHULUI

1. Maui Palms Hotel
2. Maui Hukilau Hotel
3. bank
4. movie theater
5. bank
6. Foodland
7. laundromat
8. library
9. movie theater
10. bank
11. post office
12. fairgrounds

Maui Community College

Just across the street from the Kaahumanu Shopping Center on Route 32, this is a good place to check out the many bulletin boards for various activities, items for sale, and cheaper long-term housing. The **Student Center** is conspicuous as you drive in, and is a good place to get most information. The library is adequate.

Maui Zoo And Botanical Gardens

These grounds are more aptly described as a children's park. Plenty of young families enjoy themselves in this fenced-in area. The zoo houses various colorful birds such as cockatoos, peacocks, and macaws, as well as monkeys, baboons, and a giant tortoise that looks like a slow-moving boulder. The chickens, ducks, and swans are run-of-the-mill, but the ostriches, over seven feet tall, are excellent specimens. With pygmy goats and plenty of sheep, the atmosphere is like a kiddies' petting zoo. It's open daily 9 a.m. to 4 p.m., free. Turn at the red light onto Kanaloa Avenue off Route 32 about midway between Kahului and Wailuku. At this turn is also **Wailuku War Memorial Stadium.** Here, too, is a gymnasium, swimming pool, and free hot showers, and to the left, at the entrance to the gym, you can pick up county camping permits (see p. 385).

Alexander And Baldwin Sugar Mill Museum

The museum is located at the intersection of Puunene Ave. (Rt. 350) and Hanson Rd., about one-half mile from Dairy Rd. (Rt. 380), tel. 871-8058, open Mon.-Sat. 9:30 a.m. to 4 p.m., admission $2 adults, children $1, five and under free. (Avoid the area around 3 p.m. when the still-working mill changes shifts.) This small but highly informative museum could easily be your first stop after arriving at Kahului Airport only 15 minutes away (especially if you're heading to Kihei). Once you get off the plane, you'll realize that you're in the midst of sugar cane fields, and if you want to know the history of this crop and the people who worked and developed it, visit the museum. The vintage building was the home of the sugar mill supervisor, who literally lived surrounded by his work. Inside is a small but well-stocked bookstore and shop featuring Hawaiiana and handmade clothing and artifacts, with goodies like passionfruit syrup and raw sugar. One of the unique items for sale is *waraji,* Japanese sandals fashioned from bulrushes by a 92-year-old *sensei,* Kinichi Tasaka from Kauai. These sandals are traditional in Japan, often used by pilgrims to the 88 Sacred Temples of Shikoku, and for making the climb up Mt. Fuji. This is a dying handicraft even in Japan, so take the opportunity to see and to buy these distinctive gifts from days gone by.

As you begin your tour, notice the ancient refrigerator in the corner that the staff still uses. In the first room, you are given a brief description of the natural history of Maui, along with a rendition of the legends of the demigod Maui. Display cases explain Maui's rainfall and use of irrigation for a productive sugar cane yield. There is an old-fashioned copper rain gauge, along with pragmatic artifacts from the building of the Haiku Ditch. A collection of vintage photos feature the Baldwin and Alexander families, while a historical plaque recalls when workers lived in ethnic camps, each with its own euphemistic name (Chinese at Ah Fong, Japanese at Nashiwa, Portuguese at Cod Fish). This setup was designed to discourage competition (or cooperation) between the ethnic groups during labor disputes, and to ease the transition to the new land. These people are represented by everything from stuffed fighting cocks to baseball mitts from the '30s. The museum is in the shadow of the still-working mill, and you can hear the wheels turning and the mill grinding. It's not an antiseptic remembrance, but a real one where the history actually occurred.

Kanaha Beach Park

This is the only beach worth visiting in the area. Good for a swim and a picnic. Follow Route 380 toward the airport. Turn left on Keolani Place and left again on Kaa Street. Alternately, from Kaahumanu Avenue, turn left onto Hebron Avenue, and then an immediate right onto Amala

Street, and follow the signs to the park. It's also *the* best place to begin learning sailboarding. The wind is steady but not too strong, and the wave action is gentle.

ACCOMMODATIONS

Kahului features motel/hotels because most people are short-term visitors, heading to or from the airport. These accommodations are all bunched together across from the Kahului Shopping Center on the harbor side of Kaahumanu Avenue (Rt. 32). The best are the **Maui Beach Hotel,** tel. 877-0051, and just across a parking lot, its sister hotel, **The Maui Palms,** tel. 877- 0071. The Maui Beach has a pool on the second floor, and its daily buffet is good value. The central courtyard, tastefully landscaped, is off the main foyer, which has a Polynesian flavor. The Red Dragon Room provides the only disco (weekends mostly) on this part of the island. For reservations, call (800) 367-5004, inter-island (800) 272-5275. The two other hotels, within 100 yards, are the **Maui Hukilau,** tel. 877-3311, and **Maui Seaside,** tel. 877-3311. Both are part of the Sand and Seaside Hotels, an island-owned chain. For reservations, call (800) 367-7000. Except for the Maui Palms, which is about $10 cheaper, all of the above hotels are in the same price range, $48-55 s or d.

FOOD

The Kahului area has some elegant dining spots as well as an assortment of inexpensive yet good eating establishments. Many are found in the shopping malls. Here are some of the best.

Inexpensive

Ma Chan's, tel. 877-7818, is a terrific little "no atmosphere" restaurant in the **Kaahumanu Shopping Center** (Kaahumanu Ave.) offering Hawaiian, American, and Asian food—breakfast, lunch, or dinner. Order the specials, such as the shrimp dinner, and for under $5 you get soup, salad, grilled shrimp, rice, and garnish. No credit cards, but friendly island waitresses, and good quality. **The Coffee Store,** tel. 871-6860, is open daily 7:30 a.m. to 6 p.m., till 9 p.m. on Thurs. and Friday. Follow your nose to the delightful smell of coffee and you'll find a bright and airy new shop.

Light lunch includes savories like a hot croissant at $1.40 to a spinach roll pastry puff for $3.95. Coffees by the cup under $2.25, refills 35 cents. The coffees, roasted on the premises, are from 40 gourmet varieties hand-picked in Africa, South America, Indonesia, and include exotic beans like Jamaican Blue Mountain. Gifts and clothing too!

Across from the Maui Mall is **Aurelio's,** tel. 871-7656, that presents a selection of Italian dishes, with most pasta priced around $4.50, plate lunches like shrimp marinade, $6.75, hamburger steak, $4.50. Early bird specials Mon.- Sat. from 5 to 6:30 p.m. offer New York steak at $9.95, or chicken teriyaki, $8.95.

The **Maui Mall** has a terrific selection of inexpensive eateries. **Matsu Restaurant,** tel. 877- 0822, is a quick-food Japanese restaurant with an assortment of daily specials for under $4, or a steaming bowl of various types of saimin for $3.80. Very authentic, like a *soba ya* in Japan, nothing great but downhome. Japanese standards include *katsu don buri,* tempura, or curry rice, all for under $5. Adjacent is **Siu's Chinese Kitchen**: most of their typical Chinese dishes are under $4. **Sir Wilfred's,** tel. 877-3711, is another gourmet coffee shop that offers a commodious setting for sipping a hot brew and eating their gourmet sandwiches, like hot pastrami for under $5. A good place for an inexpensive lunch with some atmosphere. **Luigi's Pizza Factory** serves up decent pizza.

At counter seating in the back of **Toda Drugs,** locals go to enjoy daily specials of Hawaiian and other ethnic foods. Better than you'd think! Daily special under $5. In the Kahului Mall, open daily 8:30 a.m. to 4 p.m., tel. 877-4550. Next door you'll find **Ichiban,** another authentic and inexpensive Japanese restaurant.

Others worth trying include **Shirley's** and **Dairy Queen,** near each other on Lono Avenue. Both serve good and inexpensive plate lunches and sandwiches, and Shirley's is open early mornings.

Finally, for those who need their weekly fix of something fried and wrapped in styrofoam, Kahului's main streets are dotted with McDonald's (Puunene Ave.), Pizza Hut (Kamehameha Ave.), Burger King (Kaahumanu Ave.), and Kentucky Fried Chicken (Wakea St.); there are more at Maui and Kaahumanu malls.

Moderate

The **Maui Beach Hotel's** Rainbow Dining Room serves food in the second-floor dining room. You can fill up here at their lunch buffet from 11 a.m to 2 p.m., $6.50 ($5.50 salad bar only), or come for dinner from 6 to 9 p.m. (except Mon.) for their "Cantonese Buffet Dinner ," offered for a very reasonable $9.95 ($5.25 children under 11). Prime rib and seafood dinners are also served. Breakfast (from 7 a.m.) features fresh-baked goods from $5.75. For reservations, call 877-0051.

Maui Palms Hotel's East-West Dining Room, offers an "Imperial Tepanyaki Japanese Buffet," every day from 5:30 to 8:30 p.m. for $15. The food, although plentiful, is prepared for the undiscerning conventioneer and is either fried to death or a generic mish-mash of Japanese cuisine. All-you-can-eat salad bar daily for lunch, 11 a.m to 1 p.m., $6, tel. 877-0071.

At **Ming Yuen**, for under $10 you can dine on Chinese treats such as oysters with ginger and scallions. The hot-and-sour soup ($5.25) is almost a meal in itself. Inexpensive lunch from 11 a.m to 5 p.m. except Sun., dinner 5 to 9 p.m. daily. Behind the Maui Mall at 162 Alamaha St., off E. Kamehameha Avenue. Cantonese and Sichuan specialties. Reservations suggested, tel. 871-7787.

Vi's Restaurant is at the Maui Seaside Hotel. Breakfast from 7 to 9:30 a.m., dinner 6 to 8 p.m. Vi's offers over 20 dinners for under $10. Breakfast includes omelettes, hot cakes, and other island favorites, tel. 877-3311.

Expensive

The Chart House, on Kahului Bay at 500 N. Puunene Ave. (also in Lahaina), is a steak and seafood house that's not really expensive. This is a favorite with businessmen and travelers in transit to or from the airport. The quality is good and the atmosphere is soothing. Open for dinner daily 5:30 to 10 p.m., tel. 877-2476.

Mickey's is the only really elegant restaurant in Kahului. In the Kahului Building at 33 Lono Ave., tel. 871-7555, they specialize in island fish, prepared seven different ways. Open for lunch with slightly cheaper prices. Expect to spend $17 and up per person for dinner.

Liquor

Maui Wine and Liquor at 333 Dairy Road (out near the airport) is an excellent liquor store. They have an enormous wine selection, over 80 different types of imported beer, and even delivery service, tel. 871-7006. For a quick stop at a basic bottle shop try **Party Pantry** on Dairy Rd. or at the Maui Beach Hotel.

ENTERTAINMENT

The **Red Dragon Disco** at the Maui Beach Hotel is the only disco and dance spot on this side of the island. Open Fri. and Sat. from 10 p.m. to 2 a.m. With a reasonable dress code and cover charge, it's favorite with local people under 25.

The **Maui Palms Hotel** hosts the "Sakuras" every weekend (no cover). They specialize in "oldies," and their large repertoire includes Top 40, country, and even Hawaiian and Japanese ballads. Good for listening and dancing! A favorite with local people, whose children might be partying at the Red Dragon.

Holiday Cinema, tel. 877-6622, is at the Kaahumanu Mall, and **The Maui Theater,** tel. 877-3560, is at the Kahului Mall. In addition, legitimate theater is offered by the **Maui Community Theater,** tel. 242-6969, at 68 N. Market St., Wailuku. Major productions occur four times a year.

SERVICES AND INFORMATION

Shopping

Because of the three malls right in a row along Kaahumanu Avenue, Kahului has the best all-around shopping on the island. Here you can find absolutely everything you might need (see "Shopping" in the Introduction). Don't miss the **Maui Swap Meet,** tel. 877-3100, at the fairgrounds on Puunene Street every Saturday. You can also shop almost the minute you arrive or just before you leave at three touristy but good shops along Airport Road. At the **Little Airport Shopping Center** at the first stop sign from the airport are **Factory Tees and Things** and **Airport Flower and Fruit.** Almost next door is the **Pink and Black Coral Factory.** When Airport Road turns into Dairy Road you'll find **Floral Hawaii.** Both floral and fruit shops can provide you with produce that's pre-inspected and admissible to the Mainland. They also have a large selection of leis which can be packed to go. The T-shirt stores offer original Maui designs and custom shirts, and the Coral Factory makes distinctive Maui jewelry on the premises.

The **Kaahumanu Mall**, along Kaahumanu Avenue, is the largest and has the widest selection of stores. You'll find **Liberty House, Sears, Ben Franklin's,** apparel stores, shoe stores, computer centers, art shops, music stores, and **Waldenbooks,** tel. 871-6112, open 9 a.m. to mall closing at 5:30 p.m. Mon.-Sat. for the best selection of books on Maui. (See "Food" for inexpensive mall dining.)

At the **Maui Mall** just up the road is **Longs** for everything from aspirin to film, **Woolworth's,** and another **Waldenbooks,** tel. 877-0181, open Mon.- Thurs. 9 a.m. to 6 p.m., Fri. 9 a.m. to 9 p.m., Sat. 9-5:30, Sun. 10 a.m. to 4 p.m. Also, **Wow! of Hawaii** has a full selection of action and resortwear, and a **Postal Center,** open Mon.-Fri., 9-5, offers full mailing services. A great new store for a relaxing cup of coffee or light lunch is **The Coffee Store.**

The **Old Kahului Store Mall** is just that, an old building that held a bank and a series of shops that has been partially modernized and brought back to life, at 55 Kaahumanu Ave., just across from the Maui Mall. Some shops include **Lightning Bolt,** tel. 877-3484, specializing in surfboards and surf attire by Instinct and Billy Long; women's apparel stores, **Tiger Lily, Jazzed; Tropica,** another surf store; **Freedom Boards,** a purveyor of used, slightly used, beat up, and new sailboards; and **Tester's Shoe Repair,** which repairs Birkenstocks ($21.50!).

Services
There is a **Bank of Hawaii,** tel. 871-8250, on Puunene Street. **City Bank,** tel. 871-7761, is at Kaahumanu Mall. And find **First Hawaiian Bank,** tel. 877-2311, at 20 W. Kaahumanu Avenue.

Post Offices: The Kahului P.O. is on Puunene Ave. (Rt. 350) just across the street from the fairgrounds, tel. 871-4710.

The library, at 90 School St., has irregular hours, tel. 877-5048.

Laundromats: W & F Washerette features video games to wile away the time, 125 S. Wakea, tel. 877-0353.

WAILUKU

Often, historical towns maintain a certain aura long after their time of importance has passed. Wailuku is one of these. Today Maui's county seat, the town has the feel of one that has been important for a long time. Wailuku earned its name, which means "Bloody Waters," from a ferocious battle fought by Kamehameha I against Maui warriors just up the road in Iao Valley. The slaughter was so intense that over four miles of the local stream literally ran red with blood. Last century the missionaries settled in Wailuku, and their architectural influences, such as a white-steepled church and the courthouse at the top of the main street, give an impression of a New England town.

Wailuku is a pretty town, especially in the back streets. Built on the rolling foothills of the West Maui Mountains, this adds some character—unlike the often flat layout of many other Hawaiian towns. You can "do" Wailuku in only an hour, though most people don't even give it this much time. They just pass through on their way to Iao Needle, where everyone goes, or to Happy Valley and on to Kahakuloa, around the backside, where the car companies hope that no one goes. You *can* see Wailuku's sights from the window of your car, but don't short-change yourself this way. Definitely visit the Bailey House, now called **Hale Hoikeike,** and while you're out, walk the grounds of **Kaahumanu Church.** Market Street, just off Main, has a clutch of intriguing shops that you can peek into while you're at it.

SIGHTS

Kaahumanu Church
It's fitting that Maui's oldest existing stone church is named after the resolute but loving Queen Kaahumanu. This rock-willed woman is the "Saint Peter" of Hawaii, upon whom Christianity in the islands was built. She was the most important early convert, often attending services in Kahului's humble grass hut chapel. In 1832 an adobe church was built on the same spot and named in her honor. Rain and time washed it away, to be replaced by the island's first stone structure in 1837. In 1876 the church was reduced to about half its original size, and what remained is the white and green structure we know today. Oddly enough, the steeple was repaired in 1984 by the Skyline Engineers who hail from Massachusetts, the same place from which the

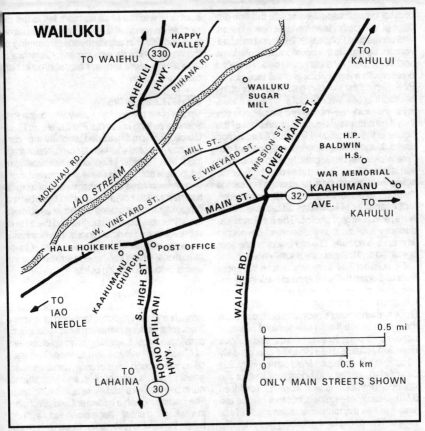

WAILUKU

TO WAIEHU

KAHEKILI HWY.

(330)

HAPPY VALLEY

PIIHANA RD.

WAILUKU SUGAR MILL

MOKUHAU RD.

MILL ST.

E. VINEYARD ST.

MISSION ST.

LOWER MAIN ST.

IAO STREAM

MAIN ST.

(32')

W. VINEYARD ST.

HALE HOIKEIKE

POST OFFICE

KAAHUMANU CHURCH

S. HIGH ST.

HONOAPIILANI HWY.

WAIALE RD.

TO IAO NEEDLE

TO LAHAINA

(30)

TO KAHULUI

H.P. BALDWIN H.S.

WAR MEMORIAL

KAAHUMANU AVE.

TO KAHULUI

0   0.5 mi

0   0.5 km

ONLY MAIN STREETS SHOWN

missionaries came 150 years earlier! You can see the church sitting there on High Street (Rt. 30), but it's usually closed during the week. Sunday services are at 9 a.m., when the Hawaiian congregation sings the Lord's praise in their native language. An excellent cultural and religious event to attend!

Hale Hoikeike

This is the old **Bailey House,** built from 1833-50, with various rooms added throughout the years. In the 1840s it housed the "Wailuku Female Seminary," of which Edward Bailey was principal until it closed in 1849. Bailey then went on to manage the Wailuku Sugar Company. More important for posterity, he became a prolific landscape painter of various areas around the is-

land. Most of his paintings record the period from 1866 through 1896. These paintings are now displayed in the "annex," known as the Bailey Gallery. This one-time seminary dining room was his actual studio. In July 1957 this old missionary homestead formally became the Maui Historical Society Museum, at which time it acquired its new name of Hale Hoikeike, "House of Display." It closed in 1973, then was refurbished and reopened in July 1975.

You'll be amazed at the two-feet-thick walls the missionaries taught the Hawaiians to build, using goat hair as the binding agent. Years of whitewashing make them resemble new-fallen snow. The rooms inside are given various themes. **The Hawaiian Room** houses excellent examples of the often practical artifacts of pre-contact Hawaii; especially notice the fine displays of tapa cloth. Hawaiian tapa, now a lost art, was considered Polynesia's finest and most advanced. Upstairs is the bedroom. It's quite large and dominated by a canopied bed. There's a dresser with a jewelry box and fine lace gloves. Peek behind the wooden gate in the rear of the bedroom to see swords, dolls, walking canes, toys, and muskets—now only a jumble, one day they'll be a display. Upstairs at the front of the house is the old office. Here you'll find rolltop desks, ledgers, and excellent examples of old-time wicker furniture, prototypes of examples you still see today. Downstairs you'll discover the sitting room and kitchen, heart of the house: the "feelings" are strongest here. There are excellent examples of Hawaiian adzes, old silverware, and plenty of photos. The lintel over the doorway is as stout as the spirits of the people who once lived here. The stonework on the floor is well laid and the fireplace is totally homey.

Go outside! The lanai runs across the entire front and down the side. Around back is the canoe shed, housing accurate replicas of Hawaiian-sewn sennit outrigger canoes, as well as Duke Kahanamoku's redwood surfboard. On the grounds you'll also see exhibits of sugar cane, sugar pots, konane boards, and various Hawaiian artifacts. Hale Hoikeike is open daily 10 a.m. to 4:30 p.m., on Main Street (Hwy. 32) on your left, just as you begin heading for Iao Valley. Admission is well worth $2 (children $.50). Usually self-guided, but tour guides are available free if arrangements are made in advance. The bookstore/gift shop has a terrific selection of souvenirs and Hawaiiana at better-than-average prices.

Kepaniwai Park

As you head up Route 32 to Iao Valley, you're in for a real treat. Two miles after leaving Wailuku, you come across Kepaniwai Park and Heritage Gardens. Here the architect, Richard C. Tongg, envisioned and created a park dedicated to all of Hawaii's people. See the Portuguese villa and garden complete with an outdoor oven, a thatch-roofed Hawaiian grass shack, a New England "salt box," a Chinese pagoda, a Japanese teahouse with authentic garden, and a bamboo house, the little "sugar shack" that songs and dreams are made of. Admission is free and there are pavilions with picnic tables. This now tranquil

spot is where the Maui warriors fell to the invincible Kamehameha and his merciless patron war-god, Ku. Kepaniwai means "Damming of the Waters"—literally with corpses. Kepaniwai is now a monument to man's higher nature: harmony and beauty.

John F. Kennedy Profile

Up the road toward Iao Valley you come to a scenic area long known as Pali Ele'ele, or Black Gorge. This stream-eroded amphitheater canyon has attracted attention for centuries. Amazingly, after President Kennedy was assassinated, people noticed his likeness portrayed there by a series of large boulders; mention of a profile had never been noted or recorded there before. A pipe stuck in the ground serves as a rudimentary telescope. Squint through it and there he is, with eyes closed in deep repose. The likeness is uncanny, and easily seen, unlike most of these formations, where you have to stretch your imagination to the breaking point.

Maui Tropical Plantation

This new attraction is somewhat out of the ordinary. The Maui Tropical Plantation presents a model of a working plantation which you tour by small train. Most interesting is an up-close look at Maui's agricultural abundance. The train takes you through fields of cane, bananas, mangoes, papayas, pineapples, and macadamia nuts; flowers here and there add exotic color. The plantation, with a restaurant and gift shop is in Waikapu, a small village along Route 30 between Lahaina and Wailuku. Open daily 9 a.m. to 5 p.m., tel. 244-7643. (See "Luaus" in the General Introduction for more information.)

IAO VALLEY STATE PARK

This valley has been a sacred spot and a place of pilgrimage since ancient times. Before Westerners arrived, the people of Maui, who came here to pay homage to the "Eternal Creator," named this valley Iao, "Supreme Light." In the center of this velvety green valley is a pillar of stone rising over 1,200 feet (actual height above sea level is 2,250 feet), that was at one time a natural altar. Now commonly called "The Needle", it's a tough basaltic core that remained after water swirled away the weaker stone surrounding it. Iao Valley is actually the remnant of the

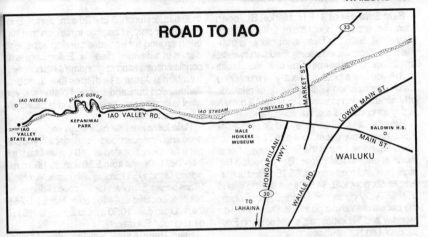

ROAD TO IAO

IAO NEEDLE
BLACK GORGE
KEPANIWAI PARK
IAO VALLEY STATE PARK
IAO VALLEY RD.
IAO STREAM
VINEYARD ST.
MARKET ST.
LOWER MAIN ST.
HALE HOIKEKE MUSEUM
HONOAPIILANI HWY.
BALDWIN H.S.
MAIN ST.
WAILUKU
WAIALE RD.
TO LAHAINA

volcanic caldera of the West Maui Mountains, whose grooved walls have been smoothed and enlarged by the restlessness of mountain streams. Robert Louis Stevenson had to stretch poetic license to create a word for Iao when he called it "viridescent."

The road here ends in a parking lot, where signs point you to a myriad of paths that crisscross the valley. The paths are tame and well maintained, some even paved, with plenty of vantage points for photographers. If you take the lower path to the river below, you'll find a good-sized and popular swimming hole; but remember, these are the West Maui Mountains, and it can rain at any time! You can escape the crowds even in this heavily touristed area by following the path toward The Needle until you come to the pavilion at the top. As you head back, take the paved path that bears to the right. It soon becomes dirt, skirting the river, and the tourists magically disappear. Here are a number of pint-sized pools where you can take a refreshing dip. Iao is for day use only. On your way back to Wailuku you might take a five-minute side excursion up to Wailuku Heights. Look for the road on your right. There's little here besides a housing development, but the view of the bay below is tops!

PRACTICALITIES

Accommodations

Visitors to Wailuku mostly stay elsewhere on Maui because there really isn't any place to lodge in town except for two very specialized and very humble hotels. The **Happy Valley Inn** is at 310 N. Market St., Wailuku, HI 96793 (in Happy Valley across from Aki's Restaurant), tel. 244-4786, and costs $20 s, $28 d, ($120 s or $168 d weekly). Until very recently, it was a flophouse for locals who were down on their luck. Now, it's an upbeat, clean hotel that is a mecca for avid sailboarders, cyclists, and students. Typically, you're liable to hear languages from a dozen countries, and if you're into sailboarding or just after a cross-cultural experience, this is the spot. The Happy Valley Inn offers basic accommodations, and if you care more about wind and surf conditions than what your bedroom looks like, it's the place for you. It's full every night, so call to reserve. The office hours are only 4 to 6 p.m. If you leave a message, they will return your call anywhere in the world. Make sure to give international area codes, etc.

Molina's Bar and Rooms, at 197 Market St., offers utilitarian rooms at $350/month, $25/night, $125/week, with private bath and room service. Bogart playing a character with a five-day-old beard and a hangover would be comfortable waking up at this basic, clean, and friendly fleabag.

Food

The establishments listed below are all in the bargain or reasonable range. The decor in most is basic and homey, with the emphasis placed on the food. Wailuku has the best and the most inexpensive restaurants on Maui.

Sam Sato's is at 318 N. Market St., open Mon.-Sat. (closed Thurs.) 8 a.m. to 4 p.m. (Happy Valley). Sato's is famous for *manju,* a puff-like pastry from Japan usually filled with sweets, meats, or *adzuki* beans. One of those places that, if you are a local resident, you *must* bring Sato's *manju* when visiting friends or relatives off-island. Lunch is served only until 2 p.m. A highly specialized place, but worth the effort.

Hazel's Cafe, 2080 Vineyard St., tel. 244-7278, open daily 6 a.m. to 9 p.m., 8 p.m. Sat., closed Sunday. One of the finest arrays of local foods at unbeatable prices. Daily specials like roast beef and mushrooms, $5.75, grilled butterfish, $5.50, pork tofu, $4.50. It's difficult to spend over $5. Very clean and friendly. This is where the *people* of Wailuku go to eat. Oxtail soup on Monday and Thursday, pig's feet soup on Friday. Bright and airy with ceiling fans.

Maui Boy Restaurant, tel. 244-7243, open daily 6:30 a.m. to 9 p.m., is just up the street from Hazel's at 2102 Vineyard Street. Another downhome place with excellent local foods for under $6. Sandwiches, *miso,* and Portuguese bean soup, Maui omelettes, $4.50. Dishes like teri-beef and *katsu don* are under $5, but the real specialties are Hawaiian foods like *kalua* pork or *lau lau* under $9. Good island food at reasonable prices.

If you get off the main highway and take Mill Street and Lower Main, the beachside roads connecting Kahului and Wailuku, you'll be rewarded with some the *most* local and *least* expensive restaurants on West Maui. They are totally unpretentious, and serve hefty portions of tasty, homemade local foods. If your aim is to *eat,* search out one of these. **Tasty Crust Restaurant,** at 1770 Mill St., tel. 244-0845, opens daily from 5:30 a.m. to 1:30 p.m., and again from 5-10 p.m., closed Monday night. If you have to carbo-load for a full day of sailing, snorkeling, or windsurfing, order their famous giant homemade hotcakes for only $.80. Or try **Nazo's Restaurant,** at 1063 Lower Main St., second floor of the Puuone Plaza, an older yellowish two-story building, tel. 244-0529. Park underneath and walk upstairs. Daily specials under $6, but they're renowned for their oxtail soup, $5.50, a clear consommé broth with peanuts and water chestnuts floating around, a delicious combination of East and West. **Tokyo Tei,** in the same complex, tel. 242-9630, open daily 11 a.m. to

1:30 p.m. for lunch, 5 to 8:30 p.m. dinner, Sunday dinner only, is another institution that has been around for decades serving Japanese dishes to a devoted clientele. Eating here is as consistent as eating at grandma's kitchen, with traditional Japanese dishes like tempura, various *don buri,* and seafood platters. If you want to sample real Japanese food at affordable prices, come here!

Hale Lava is a little cafe/lodge serving Japanese and American food. For under $7, you can get a full meal. Located at 740 Lower Main, tel. 244-0871, Opens from 5:30 a.m. to 1:30 p.m., closed Monday. A favorite with locals, **Archie's Place** serves full meals for $6, specializing in Japanese. Located at 1440 Lower Main, tel. 244-9401. Open daily 10:30 a.m. to 2 p.m., and 5 to 8 p.m., closed Sunday.

Siam Thai is a small restaurant painted black and white at 123 N. Market, tel. 244-3817. Excellent Thai food with an emphasis on vegetarian cuisine. Maybe the best deal in Wailuku! Open Mon.-Fri. 11 a.m. to 2:30 p.m., and again from 5-10 p.m., Sat. and Sun. dinner only.

Almost next door to Siam Thai at 133 N. Market is **Fujiya's,** tel. 244-0216, offering a full range of Japanese food and sushi. Open 11 a.m. to 5 p.m. The *miso* soup and tempura are inexpensive and quite good.

Moon Hoe Seafood Restaurant at 752 Lower Main St., tel. 242-7778, offers delicacies from the sea at a fair price. They're open on Sunday when many other places are closed, daily 11 a.m. to 2 p.m., and again from 5-9 p.m.

Down To Earth sells natural and health foods and has an excellent snack bar—basically a little window around back with a few tables available. Really filling! Located at 1910 Vineyard, tel. 242-6821. Open daily 8 a.m. to 6 p.m., till 5 Sat., till 4 Sunday.

And, for a different taste treat, try the *mochi* made fresh daily at Wailuku's **Shishido Bakery,** next door to the Moon Hoe Restaurant.

Shopping

Most shopping here is done in Kahului at the three big malls. But for an interesting diversion try one of these, all on or around Main or Market Street. **T-Shirt Factory Outlet** to save money on T-shirts that you'll see all over the island. **St. Anthony's Thrift Shop** on lower Main is open Wed. and Fri. from 8 a.m. to 1 p.m., where you'll find used articles from irons to aloha shirts. **Maui Wholesale Gold,** selling gold, jewelry, and eel skin items; **Treasure Imports,** selling just about the same type of articles; **New Maui Fishing Supply,** with all you need to land the big ones.

Wailuku's attic closets are overflowing. Three discovery shops in a row hang like prom-night tuxedos, limp with old memories. Each has its own style. Look for the aloha Santa Claus waving to you on the elevated portion of N. Market as you head toward Happy Valley. Here, you'll find **Things From The Past,** tel. 244-8177, with antiques, collectibles and jewelry, old mirrors, contemporary paintings, carvings, glass floats, old china, crystal, and Oriental curios. Next door is **Ali'i Antiques,** tel. 244-8012, open daily 9 a.m. to 8 p.m., offering Depression glass, dolls, china, photos, chandeliers, 200-year-old kimonos, and a menagerie of teddy bears. **Traders of the Lost Art** specializes in carvings from the Pacific, especially from New Guinea.

Services

There's a **Bank of Hawaii,** at 2105 Main, tel. 871-8200; **First Interstate,** 2005 Main, tel. 244-3951. The post office is at High St., tel. 244-4815, and the **library** is at 251 High St., tel. 244-3945. For **laundry,** try Happy Valley Wash-o-matic, 300 block of N. Market.

For conventional health care, go to **Maui Memorial Hospital,** Route 32, tel. 244-9056. **Camping permits** for county parks are available at War Memorial Gym, Room 102, Route 32, tel. 244-9018, $3 adult, $.50 children, per person, per night. State park permits can be had at the State Building, High St., tel. 244-4354 (see p. 384).

KAHAKULOA—WEST MAUI'S BACKSIDE

To get around to the backside of West Maui you can head northeast from Kaanapali, but the majority of those few who defy the car companies and brave the bad road strike out northwest from Wailuku. (Note: The dirt road portion of Route 340 is rugged and a sign warns that it is closed to all but local residents. Although the ordinance is not enforced, be extremely cautious on this road, especially during or just after bad weather.) Before you start this rugged 18-mile stretch, make sure you have adequate gas, water, and food. It'll take you a full three hours to go from Wailuku to Kapalua. Start heading north on Market Street, down toward the area of Wailuku called **Happy Valley** (good restaurants—see "Food," above). At the end of Market Street (Rt. 330) you'll find **T.K. Supermarket,** your best place to buy supplies (open seven days). At mile 2, Route 330 turns into Route 340, which you'll follow toward Kahakuloa Bay and all the way around. In a few minutes, just when you come to the bridge over Iao Stream, will be Kuhio Place on your left. Turn here to **Halekii and Pihana Heiau.** Although uninspiring, this area is historical and totally unvisited.

Back on Route 340 you come shortly to **Waihee** ("Slippery Water"). There's a little store here, but even if it's open it's probably understocked. On the right, a sign points you to **Waiehu Golf Course.** Mostly local people golf here; fees during the week are $10, $15 weekends. The fairways, strung along the sea, are beautiful to play. **Par Five Restaurant** is an adequate little eatery at the golf course. Also here are two county beach parks: **Waiehu** and **Waihee.** They're secluded and frequented mostly by local people. Although for day use only, they'd probably be OK for an unofficial overnight stay. For Waiehu go left just before the golf course parking lot along the fence; for Waihee go left instead of right at the intersection leading to the golf course.

At mile 7 the pavement begins to deteriorate. The road hugs the coastline and gains elevation quickly; the undisturbed valleys are resplendent. At mile 11, just past the Boy Scout camp, you'll see a metal gate and two enormous carved tikis. No explanation, just sitting there. You next enter the fishing village of **Kahakuloa** ("Tall Hill") with its dozen weatherworn houses and tiny white church. Here the road is at its absolute roughest and narrowest! The valley is very steep-sided and beautiful. Supposedly, great Maui himself loved this area. Two miles past Kahakuloa, you come to **Pohaku Kani,** the bell stone. It's about six feet tall and the same in diameter, but graffiti spoil it. Here the seascapes are tremendous. The surf pounds along the coast below and sends spumes skyward, roaring through a natural blowhole. The road once again becomes wide and well paved and you're soon at **Fleming Beach Park.** Civilization comes again too quickly.

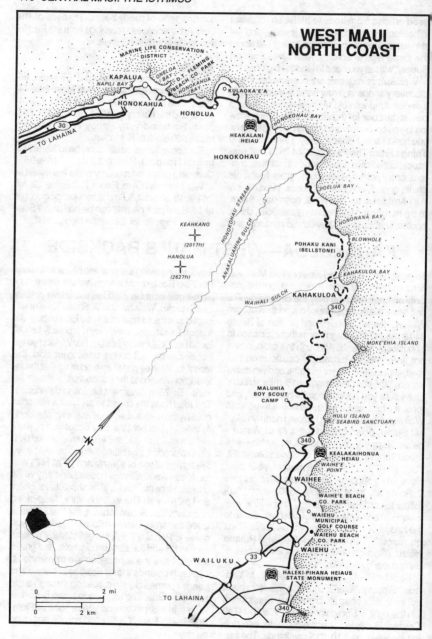

WEST MAUI
NORTH COAST

MARINE LIFE CONSERVATION DISTRICT

ONELOA BAY

D. FLEMING BEACH CO. PARK

HONOKAHUA BAY

KAPALUA
NAPILI BAY

HONOKAHUA

O KULAOKA'E'A

HONOLUA

HONOKOHAU BAY

TO LAHAINA

30

HEAKALANI HEIAU

HONOKOHAU

POELUA BAY

HONONANA BAY

KEAHKANO
+ (2017ft)

HANOLUA
+ (2627ft)

POHAKU KANI
(BELLSTONE)

BLOWHOLE

KAHAKULOA BAY

HONOKOHAU STREAM

ANAKALUAHINE GULCH

WAIHALI GULCH

KAHAKULOA

340

MOKE'EHIA ISLAND

MALUHIA BOY SCOUT CAMP

HULU ISLAND SEABIRD SANCTUARY

340

KEALAKAIHONUA HEIAU

WAIHE'E POINT

WAIHEE

WAIHE'E BEACH CO. PARK

WAIEHU MUNICIPAL GOLF COURSE

WAIEHU BEACH CO. PARK

WAIEHU

WAILUKU

33

HALEKI-PIHANA HEIAUS STATE MONUMENT

TO LAHAINA

340

0   2 mi

0   2 km

WEST MAUI

LAHAINA

Lahaina ("Merciless Sun") is and always has been the premier town on Maui. It's the most energized town on the island as well, and you can feel it from the first moment you walk down Front Street. Maui's famed warrior-king Kahekili lived here and ruled until Kamehameha, with the help of new-found cannon power, subdued Kahekili's son in Iao Valley at the turn at the 19th century. When Kamehameha I consolidated the Island Kingdom, he chose Lahaina as his seat of power. It served as such until Kamehameha III moved to Honolulu in the 1840s. Lahaina is where the modern world of the West and the old world of Hawaii collided, for better or worse. The *ali'i* of Hawaii loved to be entertained here; the **royal surf spot**, mentioned numerous times as an area of revelry in old missionary diaries, is just south of the Small Boat Harbor. Kamehameha I built in Lahaina the islands' first Western structure in 1801, known as the **Brick Palace**; a small ruin still remains. Queens Keopuolani and Kaahumanu, the two most powerful wives of the great Kamehameha's harem of over 20, were local Maui women who remained after their husband's death and helped to usher in the new order.

The whalers came preying for "sperms and humpbacks" in 1819 and set old Lahaina Town a-reelin'. Island girls, naked and willing, swam out to meet the ships, trading their favors for baubles from the modern world. Grog shops flourished, and drunken sailors with their brown-skinned doxies owned the debauched town. The missionaries, invited by Queen Keopuolani, came praying for souls in 1823. Led by the Reverends Stuart and Richards, they tried to harpoon moral chaos. In short order, there was a curfew, a *kapu* placed on the ships by wise but ineffectual old Governor Hoapili, and a jail and a fort to discourage the strong-arm tactics of unruly captains. The pagan Hawaiians transformed like willing children to the new order, but the Christian sailors damned the meddling missionaries. They even whistled a few cannonballs into the Lahaina homestead of Rev. Richards, hoping to send him speedily to his eternal reward. Time, a new breed of sailor, and the slow death of the whaling industry eased the tension.

Meanwhile, the missionaries built the first school and printing press west of the Rockies at **Lahainaluna,** in the mountains just above the town, along with downtown's **Wainee Church,** the first stone church on the island. Lahaina's glory days slipped by and it became a sleepy sugar town dominated by the Pioneer Sugar Mill that has operated since the 1860s. In 1901, the **Pioneer Inn** was built to accommodate inter-island ferry passengers, but no one *came* to Lahaina. In the 1960s, AMFAC had a brilliant idea. They turned Kaanapali, a magnificent stretch of beach just west, into one of the most beautifully planned and executed resorts in the world. The Pioneer Sugar Mill had long used the area as a refuse heap, but now the ugly duckling became a swan, and Lahaina flushed with new life. With superb farsightedness, the **Lahaina Restoration Society** was begun in those years and almost the entire town was made a national historical landmark. Lahaina, subdued but never tamed, throbs with its special energy once again.

SIGHTS

In short, strolling around Lahaina is the best of both worlds. It's busy, but it's bite-sized. It's engrossing enough, but you can "see" it in half a day. The main attractions are mainly downtown within a few blocks of each other. Lahaina technically stretches, long and narrow, along the coast for about four miles, but you'll only be interested in the central core, a mere mile or so. All along Front Street, the main drag, and the side streets running off it are innumerable shops, restaurants, and hide aways where you can browse, recoup your energy, or just wistfully watch the sun set. Go slow and savor, and you'll feel the dynamism of Lahaina past and present all around you. Enjoy!

Parking

Traffic congestion is a problem that needs to be addressed. Stay away from town from 4:30 to 5:30 p.m., when traffic is heaviest. The other thing to know to make your visit carefree is where to stash your car. The parking lot on the corner of Wainee and Dickenson street charges only $5.00 all day. There's another large lot on Prison Street, just up from Front (free three-hour limit), and two smallish lots along Luakini Street. The Lahaina Shopping Center has three-hour

parking. Most of the meters in town are a mere one hour, and the most efficient people on Maui are the "meter patrol!" Your car will wind up in the pound if you're not careful! The best place to find a spot is down at the end of Front Street past the Kamehameha School and along Shaw. You'll have to walk a few minutes, but it's worth it. For those staying in Napili or Kaanapali, leave your car at your hotel and take the Lahaina Express for the day. See "Getting Around" in the main Introduction for details.

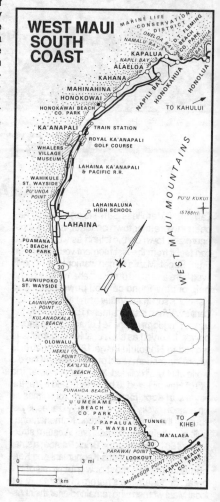

WEST MAUI SOUTH COAST

The Banyan Tree

The best place to start your tour of Lahaina is at this magnificent tree at the corner of Hotel and Front. You can't miss it as it spreads its shading boughs over almost an entire acre. Use the benches to sit and reconnoiter while the sun, for which Lahaina is infamous, is kept at bay. Children love it, and it seems to bring out the Tarzan in everyone. Old-timers sit here chatting, and you might be lucky enough to hear Ben Victorino, a tour guide who comes here frequently, entertain people with his ukulele and endless repertoire of Hawaiian tunes. The tree was planted in April 1873 by Sheriff Bill Smith in commemoration of the Congregationalist Missions' golden anniversary. One hundred years later, a ceremony was held here and over 500 people were accommodated under this natural canopy. Just left of the banyan, down the lane toward the harbor, was a canal and the Government Market. All kinds of commodities, manufactured and human, were sold here during the whaling days, and it was given the apt name of "Rotten Row."

The Courthouse

Behind the banyan on Wharf Street is the Courthouse. Built in the 1850s from coral blocks recycled from Kamehameha III's ill-fated palace, Hale Piula ("House of Iron"), also served as the police station, complete with a jail in the basement. Today, the jail is home to the **Lahaina Art Society,** where paintings and artifacts are kept behind bars, waiting for patrons to liberate them. Adjacent is **The Fort,** built in the 1830s to show the sailors that they couldn't run amok in Lahaina. It was more for show than for force, though. When it was torn down, the blocks were hauled over to Prison Street to build the real jail, **Hale Pa'ahao.** A corner battlement of the fort was restored, but that's it, because restoring the entire structure means mutilating the banyan.

Small Boat Harbor

Walking along the harbor stimulates the imagination and the senses. The boats waiting at anchor sway in confused syncopation. Hawser ropes groan and there's a feeling of anticipation and adventure in the air. Here you can board for all kinds of seagoing excursions. In the days of whaling there was no harbor; the boats tied up one to the other in the "roads," at times forming an impromptu floating bridge. The whalers came ashore in their chase boats; with the winds always up, departure could be made at a moment's notice. The activity here is still dominated by the sea.

The *Carthaginian II*

The masts and square rigging of this replica of the enterprising freighters that braved the Pacific tower over Lahaina Harbor. You'll be drawn to it . . . go! It's the only truly square-rigged ship left afloat on the seas. It replaced the *Carthaginian I* when that ship went aground in 1972 while being hauled to Honolulu for repairs. The Lahaina Restoration Foundation found this steel-hulled ship in Denmark; built in Germany in 1920 as a two-masted schooner, it tramped around the Baltic under converted diesel power. The foundation had it sailed 12,000 miles to Lahaina, where it underwent extensive conversion until it became the beautiful replica that you see today. The sails have yet to be made for lack of funds.

The *Carthaginian* is a floating museum dedicated to whaling and to whales. Richard Widmark, the actor, narrates a superb film documenting the life of humpbacks. Belowdecks is the museum containing artifacts and implements from the whaling days. There's even a whaling boat which was found intact in Alaska in the 1970s. The light belowdecks is subdued, and while you sit in the little "captains' chairs" the humpbacks chant their peaceful hymns in the background. Flip Nicklin's sensitive photos adorn the bulkheads. It's open daily 9:30 a.m. to 4:30 p.m., but arrive no later than 3:45 to see all the exhibits and videos. Admission $3.

Pioneer Inn

This vintage inn, situated at the corner of Hotel and Wharf streets, is just exactly where it belongs. Stand on its veranda with the honky-tonk piano playing in the open bar behind you and gaze at the *Carthaginian*. Presto . . . it's magic time! You'll see. It was even a favorite spot for actors like Errol Flynn and later Spencer Tracy, when he was in Lahaina filming *Devil at Four O'Clock.* The green and white inn was built in 1901 to accommodate inter-island ferry passengers, but its style seems much older. If ironwork had been used on the veranda, you'd think you were in New Orleans. A new wing was built

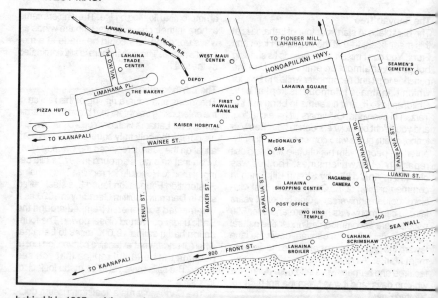

behind it in 1965 and the two form a courtyard. Make sure to read the hilarious rules governing behavior that are posted in the main lobby. The inn is still functional. The rooms in the old wing are colorfully seedy—spotlessly clean, but with character and atmosphere. The wooden stairway, painted red, leads upstairs to an uneven hallway lined with a threadbare carpet. The interior smells like the sea. There's no luxury here, but you might consider one night just for the experience. (See "Accommodations" below for details.) Downstairs the **Harpooner's Lanai Terrace** serves dinner, and you can't find a better place to watch life go by with a beautiful sunset backdrop than in the **Old Whaler's Saloon**.

The Brick Palace

This rude structure was commissioned by Kamehameha I in 1801 and slapped together by two forgotten Australian ex-convicts. It was the first Western structure in Hawaii, but unfortunately the substandard materials have for the most part disintegrated. Kamehameha never lived in it, but it was occupied and used as a storehouse until the 1850s. Just to the right of the Brick Palace, as you face the harbor, is **Hauola Stone**, marked by an HVB Warrior. Formed like a chair, it was believed by the Hawaiians to have curative powers if you sat on it and let the ocean bathe you. Best view at low tide.

Baldwin Home

One of the best attractions in Lahaina is the Baldwin Home, on the corner of Front and Dickenson. It was occupied by Doctor/Reverend Dwight Baldwin, his wife Charlotte, and their eight children. He was a trained teacher, as well as the first doctor/dentist in Hawaii. The building served from the 1830s to 1868 as a dispensary, meeting room, and boarding home for anyone in need. The two-foot-thick walls are of cut lava, and the mortar made of crushed coral, over which plaster was applied. As you enter, notice how low the doorway is, and that the doors inside are "Christian doors"—with a cross forming the upper panels and an open Bible at the bottom. The Steinway piano that dominates the entrance was built in 1859. In the bedroom to the right, along with all of the period furniture, is a wooden commode. Also notice the lack of closets; all items were kept in chests. Upstairs was a large dormitory where guests slept.

The doctor's fees are posted and are hilarious. Payment was by "size" of sickness: very big $50, diagnosis $3, refusal to pay $10! The Rev. Baldwin was 41 when he arrived in Hawaii

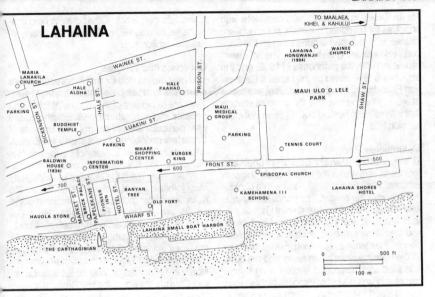

LAHAINA

from New England and his wife was 25. She was supposedly sickly (eight children!) and he had heart trouble, so they moved to Honolulu in 1868 to receive better health care. The home became a community center, housing the library and meeting rooms. Today, the Baldwin Home is a showcase museum of the Lahaina Restoration Society. It's open daily 9:30 a.m. to 5 p.m., admission $2, kids free accompanied by a parent.

Master's Reading Room

Originally a missionaries' store room, the Master's Reading Room was converted to an officers' club in 1834. Located next door to the Baldwin Home, these two venerable buildings constitute the oldest Western structures on Maui, and fittingly, this uniquely constructed coral stone building is home to the Lahaina Restoration Foundation. The building is not really open to the public, but you can visit to pick up maps, brochures, and information about Lahaina.

The **Lahaina Restoration Foundation,** begun in 1962, is headed by Jim Luckey, a historian in his own right who knows a great deal about Lahaina and the whaling era. The main purpose of the foundation is to preserve the flavor and authenticity of Lahaina without stifling progress—especially tourism. The Foundation

is privately funded and has managed to purchase many of the important historical sites in Lahaina. They own the two buildings mentioned, the restored Wo Hing Temple, the land under the U.S. Seamen's Hospital, and they'll own the plantation house next door in 18 years. The 42 people on the board of directors come from all socioeconomic backgrounds. You don't get on the board by how much money you give but by how much effort and time you are willing to invest in the foundation; the members are extremely dedicated. Merchants approach the foundation with new ideas for business and ask how they can best comply with the building codes. The townspeople know that their future is best served if they preserve the feeling of old Lahaina rather than rush headlong into frenzied growth. The historic village of Williamsburg, Virginia, is often cited as Lahaina's model, except that Lahaina wishes to remain a "real" living, working town.

Hale Pa'ahao

This is Lahaina's old prison, located mid-block on Prison Street, and it's name literally means "stuck-in-irons house." It was constructed by prisoners in the 1850s from blocks of stone salvaged from the old defunct fort. It had a catwalk for an armed guard, and cells complete with shackles for hardened criminals, but most were drunks who yahooed around town on the Sabbath, wildly spurring their horses. The cells were rebuilt in 1959, the gatehouse in 1988, and the structure is maintained by the Lahaina Restoration Foundation. The cells, curiously, are made of wood, which shows that the inmates weren't that interested in busting out. It's open daily, admission free.

Maluuluolele Park

This nondescript area at the corner of Shaw and Front was at one time the most important spot in Lahaina. Here was a small pond with a diminutive island in the center. The pond, Mokuhinia, was home to a *moo*, a lizard spirit. The tiny island, Mokuula, was the home of the Maui chiefs, and the Kamehamehas, when they were in residence. It became a royal mausoleum, but later all the remains were taken away and the pond was filled and the ground leveled. King Kamehameha III and his sister Princess Nahienaena were raised together in Lahaina. They fell in love, but the new ways caused turmoil and tragedy. Instead of marrying and producing royal children, a favored practice only 20 years earlier, they were wrenched apart by the new religion. He, for a time, numbed himself with alcohol, while she died woefully from a broken heart. She was buried here, and for many years Kamehameha III could frequently be found at her grave, quietly sitting and meditating.

Wainee Church And Cemetery

The church itself is not impressive, but its history is. This is the spot where the first Christian services were held in Hawaii, in 1823. A church was built here in 1832 which could hold 3,000 people, but it was razed by a freak hurricane in 1858. Rebuilt, it survived until 1894, when it was deliberately burned by an angry mob, upset with the abolition of the monarchy in Hawaii and the islands' annexation by the U.S. Another church was built, but it too was hit not only by a hurricane but by fire as well. The present structure was built in 1953. In the cemetery is a large part of Maui's history: buried here are Hawaiian royalty. Lying near each other are Queen Keopuolani, her star-crossed daughter, Princess Nahienaena, and old Governor Hoapili, their royal tomb marked by two large headstones surrounded by a wrought-iron fence. Other graves hold missionaries such as William Richards and many infants and children.

Churches And Temples

You may wish to stop for a moment at Lahaina's churches and temples dotted around town. They are reminders of the mixture of faiths and peoples that populated this village and added their particular style of energy. **The Episcopal Cemetery** on Wainee Street shows the English influence in the islands. Many of the royal family, including King Kalakaua, became Anglicans. This cemetery holds the remains of many early Maui families, and of Walter Murray Gibson, the notorious settler, politician, and firebrand of the 1880s. Just behind is **Hale Aloha,** "House of Love," a small structure built by Maui residents in thanksgiving for being saved from a terrible smallpox epidemic that ravaged Oahu but bypassed Maui in 1858. The structure was restored in 1974. Also on Wainee is **Maria Lanakila Church,** the site of the first Roman Catholic Mass in Lahaina, celebrated in 1841. The present structure dates from 1928. Next to the church's cemetery is the **Seamen's Cemetery** where many infirm from the ships that came to Lahaina were buried. Most stones have been obliterated by time and only a few remain. Herman Melville came here to pay his last respects to a cousin buried in this yard. **Hongwanjii Temple** is also on Wainee, between Prison and Shaw. It's a Buddhist temple with the largest congregation in Lahaina and dates from 1910, though the present structure was raised in 1927.

The **Wo Hing Temple** on Front Street is the Lahaina Restoration Foundation's newest reconstruction. It was opened to the public in 1984 and shows the Chinese influence in Lahaina. It's open 9 a.m. to 4 p.m. daily, from 10 a.m. Sunday, admission $1.00. **Holy Innocents Episcopal Church,** built in 1927, is also on Front Street, near Kamehameha III school. Known for its "Hawaiian Madonna," its altar is resplendent with fruits, plants, and birds of the islands.

The **Lahaina Jodo Mission** is at the opposite end of Front Street, near Mala Wharf on Ala Moana Street. When heading west, you'll leave the main section of town and keep going until you see a sign over a building that reads Jesus Is Coming Soon. Turn left toward the beach and you'll immediately spot the three-storied pagoda. Here the giant bronze Buddha sits exposed to the elements. The largest outside of Asia, it was dedicated in 1968 in commemoration of the centennial of the arrival of Japanese workers in Hawaii. The grounds are impeccable and serenely quiet. You may stroll around, but the buildings are closed to the public. If you climb the steps to peek into the temple, kindly remove your shoes. A striking cemetery is across the street along the beach. It seems incongruous to see tombstones set in sand. The entire area is quiet and a perfect spot for lunch or solitary meditation if you've had enough of frenetic Lahaina.

U.S. Seamen's Hospital

This notorious hospital was reconstructed by the Lahaina Restoration Foundation in 1982. Here is where sick seamen were cared for under the auspices of the U.S. State Department. Allegations during the late 1850s claimed that the care here extended past the grave! Unscrupulous medicos supposedly charged the U.S. government for care of seamen who had long since died. The hospital is located at Front and Baker, heading toward Kaanapali, near the Jodo Mission. The hospital now houses a Lahaina Printsellers Shop, specializing in vintage art of Hawaii and the Pacific. (See p. 371.)

Lahainaluna

Head up the mountain behind Lahaina on Lahainaluna Road for approximately two miles. On your left you'll pass the **Pioneer Sugar Mill,** in operation since 1860. Once at Lahainaluna ("Above Lahaina") you'll find the oldest school west of the Rockies, opened by the Congregationalist missionaries in 1831. Children from all over the islands, and many from California, came here to school if their parents could afford to send them away to boarding school. Today, the school is West Maui's public high school, but many children still come here to board. The first students were not only given a top-notch academic education, but a practical one as well. They built the school buildings, and many were also apprentices in the famous **Hale Pa'i** ("Printing House") that turned out Hawaii's first newspaper and made Lahaina famous as a printing center.

One look at Hale Pa'i and you think of New England. It's a white stucco building with blue trim and a wood-shake roof. It was restored in 1982 and is open by appointment only. If you

visit the campus when school is in session, you may go to Hale Pa'i, but if you want to walk around, please sign in at the vice-principal's office. Lahainaluna High School is still dedicated to the preservation of Hawaiian culture. Every year, in April, they celebrate the anniversary of one of their most famous students, David Malo. Considered Hawaii's first scholar, he authored the definitive *Hawaiian Antiquities*. His final wish was to be buried "high above the tide of foreign invasion" and his grave is close to the giant "L" atop Mount Ball, behind Lahainaluna. On the way back down to Lahaina, you get a wide, impressive panorama of the port and the sea.

Heading East

Five miles east of Lahaina along the coastal road (Rt. 30) is the little village of Olowalu. Today, little more than a general store and a French restaurant are here. This was the place of the Olowalu Massacre perpetrated by Capt. Metcalf. Its results were far-reaching, greatly influencing Hawaiian history. Two seamen, Young and Davis, were connected with this incident, and with their help Kamehameha I subdued all of Hawaii. Behind the store are petroglyphs. Follow the dirt track behind the store for about one-half mile; make sure you pass a water tower within the first few hundred yards because there are three similar roads here. You'll come to the remains of a wooden stairway going up a hill. There once was an HVB Warrior here, but he might be gone. Claw your way up the hill to the petroglyphs, which are believed to be 300 years old. If you continue east on Route 30, you'll pass **Papawai** and **McGregor points,** both noted for their vistas and as excellent locations to spot migrating whales in season. The road sign merely says "Scenic Lookout."

BEACHES

The best beaches around Lahaina are just west of town in Kaanapali, or just east toward Olowalu. A couple of adequate places to spread your towel are right in Lahaina, but they're not quite on a par with the beaches just a few miles away.

Maluulu O Lele Park

"The Breadfruit Shelter of Lele" is in town and basically parallels Front Street. It's crowded at times and there's plenty of "wash up" on this beach. It's cleaner and quieter at the east end down by Lahaina Shores, a one-time favorite with the *ali'i*. There are restrooms, the swimming is fair, and the snorkeling acceptable past the reef. **Lahaina Beach** is at the west end of town near Mala Wharf. Follow Front to Puunoa Place and turn down to the beach. This is a good place for families with tots because the water is clear, safe, and shallow.

Puamana Beach County Park

About two miles before you enter Lahaina from the east along Route 30, you'll see signs for this beach park. A narrow strip between the road and the sea, the swimming and snorkeling are only fair. The setting, however, is quite nice with picnic tables shaded by ironwood trees. The views are terrific and this is a great spot to eat your plate lunch only minutes from town. **Launiupoko State Park**, a mile farther east, has restrooms and showers, but no beach. This is more of a pit stop than anything else.

Wahikuli State Wayside

Along Route 30 between Lahaina and Kaanapali, the park is a favorite with local people and excellent for a picnic and swim. Restrooms and tennis courts are just across the street. The park is very clean and well maintained.

ACCOMMODATIONS

Lodging in Lahaina is limited, surprisingly inexpensive, and an experience . . . of sorts. Most visitors head for Kaanapali, because Lahaina tends to be hot and hot to trot, especially at night. But you can find good bargains here, and if you want to be in the thick of the "action," you're in the right spot.

Pioneer Inn

This is oldest hotel on Maui still accommodating guests. At 658 Wharf St., Lahaina, HI 96764, tel. 661-3636, or (800) 657-7890. Absolutely no luxury whatsoever, but a double scoop of atmosphere: this is the place to come if you want to save money, and be the star of your own movie with the Pioneer Inn as the stage set. Enter the tiny lobby full of memorabilia, and follow the creaking stairway up to a wooden hallway painted green on green. This is the old wing. Screen doors cover inner doors to clean but basic rooms which open out onto the building-long lanai overlooking the harbor. All rooms have ceiling fans. Rates are about $25 with shared bath, private bath (showers) a few dollars extra. Music and the sounds of life from the bar below late in the evening at no extra charge. The "new wing," basic modern, circa 1966, is attached. Starting at $60, it's no bargain. It offers a private lanai, bath, a/c, and overlooks the central courtyard. The old section is fun; the new section is only adequate.

The Plantation Inn

If Agatha Christie were seeking inspiration for *the* perfect setting for one of her novels, this is where she would come. The neo-Victorian building is appointed with posted verandas, hardwood floors, natural wood trim around windows and doors, and counterpointed by floral wall coverings and bedspreads. Rays of sunlight are diffused through stained-glass windows and wide double doors. Each room is comfortable, with overstuffed couches, four-poster beds, and private tiled baths with bold brass fixtures. The complete illusion is turn of the century, but the modern amenities of a/c, remote TV and VCR, a hidden fridge, daily maid service, and a soothing spa and pool are included. Prices are a reasonable $95 deluxe, $109 double, $129 suite, and all include breakfast at Gerard's, the fine French restaurant on the first floor (see following). The Plantation Inn also has money-saving options for dinner at Gerard's, and car package deals. For full information contact the inn at 174 Lahainaluna Rd., Lahaina, HI 96761, tel. 667-9225 or (800) 433- 6815. Set on a side street away from the bustle, it's simply the best and newest accommodation that Lahaina has to offer.

Lahaina Hotel

Is nothing sacred? Will Birkenstocks be on *every* foot, quiche on *every* table, and a sensible Volvo in *every* driveway? The old, down-at-the-heels, traveler's classic, Lahainaluna Hotel, is going *yuppie*. Gone from this cockroach paradise are the weather-beaten linoleum floors, bare-bulbed musty rooms, and rusted dripping faucets. In their place will be modern neo-Victorian, color-coordinated, tastefully appointed, bright and cheery rooms that would warm the cockles of every networking, upwardly mobile heart. You can still peer from the balcony of this vintage hotel, or observe the huddled masses below from behind lace curtains while drinking your designer morning coffee. Prices from $110-170, at 127 Lahainaluna Rd., Lahaina, HI 96761, tel. 661-0577, or (800) 669- 3444. Bar/restaurant on premises.

Maui Islander

Located a few blocks away from the hubbub, at 660 Wainee St., Lahaina, HI 96761, tel. 667-9766, (800) 367-5226. A very adequate hotel offering rooms with kitchenettes, studios, and suites of up to three bedrooms for seven guests or more. All with a/c and TV, plus pool and tennis courts. Homey atmosphere with daily planned activities. Basic hotel rooms start at $72, studios $85, $96 for one bedroom.

Lahaina Shores

This six-story condo was built before the Lahaina building code limited the height of new construction. Located at the east end of town, at 475 Front St., Lahaina, HI 96761, tel. 661-4835, (800) 367-2972. The tallest structure in town, it's become a landmark for incoming craft. It offers a swimming pool and spa and is located on the only beach in town. From a distance, the Southern mansion facade is striking: up close, though, it becomes painted cement blocks and false colonnades. The rooms, however, are a good value for the money. The basic contains a full bathroom, powder room, large color TV, and equipped kitchen. They're all light and airy, and the backside views of the harbor or frontside of the mountains are the best in town. Studios begin at $90, one bedroom suites $119, penthouse $150, $9 for additional guests.

Lahaina Roads

This condo/apartment is at the far west end of town at 1403 Front St., Lahaina, HI 96761, tel. 661-3166, (800) 624-8203. Expect a three-night minimum stay with a one-week minimum during peak season. All units have fully equipped kitchens, TV, and maid service on request. One- bedroom units start at $65 to $85 (high season), $7 additional guests. No credit cards honored. Discounts are offered for more than one-week stays. There is no beach as it sits right along the seawall, but there is a pool, and you couldn't have a better view, with all the units being oceanview deluxe at a standard price.

Puamana

One-bedroom units (fully equipped) begin at $105 low season, up to four people, $140 garden, $170 ocean, $155-210 two bedroom, $260 three bedroom. This condo is located one mile southeast of town. Write Box 515, Lahaina, HI 96767, tel. 667-2551, (800) 367-5630. Check in at the clubhouse.

FOOD

Lahaina's menu of restaurants is gigantic; all palates and pocketbooks can easily be satisfied: there's fast food, sandwiches, sushi, happy hours, and elegant cosmopolitan restaurants. Because Lahaina is a dynamic tourist spot, restaurants and eateries come and go with regularity. The following is not an exhaustive list of Lahaina's food spots—it couldn't be. But there is plenty listed here to feed everyone at breakfast, lunch, and dinner. *Bon appetit!*

Inexpensive

Seaside Inn, 1307 Front St., tel. 661-7195, serves local plate lunches and Japanese *bento* during the day for under $5, hot-table style with teriyaki chicken, beef tomatoes, and chicken curry. The evening menu offers American and Asian selections like rib-eye steak for $7.50, tempura, *tonkatsu,* or various tofu dishes for under $5; for a complete dinner add $2 and receive *miso* soup, salad, and *tsukemono.* This is where local people and those in the know come for a very good but no-frills meal. If eating hearty without caring about the ambience (actually the sunset view couldn't be better) is your aim, come here.

The **Thai Chef** will please any Thai food lover who wants a savory meal at a good price. Search for this restaurant stuck in a corner at the Lahaina Shopping Center, open Mon.-Sat. 11:30 a.m. to 2 p.m. for lunch, dinner nightly 5 to 10 p.m., tel. 667-2814. As in most Thai restaurants vegetarians are well taken care of with plenty of spicy tofu and vegetable dishes. The extensive menu offers everything from scrumptious Thai soups with ginger and coconut for $7.25 (enough for two) to curries and seafood. Most entrees are under $8 with a good selection under $6. It's not fancy, but food-wise you won't be disappointed.

Zushi's is a hole-in-the-wall, very reasonably priced Japanese restaurant selling sushi and various other Japanese dishes at the Lahaina Business Plaza, across the street from McDonald's. It's stuck away in the corner, so look for it around the back. They serve lunch (takeout too) 11 a.m. to 2 p.m., and dinner 5 to 9 p.m. Authentic with most items under $5. Also in the plaza is a small takeout window with the imaginative name of **Local Food** which sells local food in the form of plate lunches. Basic, cheap, filling, and good.

Sunrise Cafe, open from 5:30 a.m. to 10 p.m. at 693 Front, tel. 661-3326, is the kind of place that locals keep secret. It's a tiny little place where you can have excellent coffee or a sandwich on whole wheat or pita bread. The food is provided by the excellent La Bretagne French restaurant. You get gourmet quality for downhome prices. Seafood chowder is only $2.95, Micronesian chicken only $5.95. The most scrumptious deals however are the pastries, which La Bretagne is known for. The fine coffee selections are always freshly brewed, and they're complemented by a good selection of herbal teas. The Sunrise Cafe is just down the side street from **Lappert's Ice Cream,** which not only has ice cream, shave ice, and cookies, but also serves "fat-free" yogurt, about the only thing on Maui that is fat-free!

A tiny "no name" **sushi bar** and plate lunch place is on Prison Street just after you turn toward the mountains off Front Street. Look for it across the street from the parking lot. Very reasonable prices.

Your sweet tooth will begin to sing the moment you walk into **The Bakery** at 911 Limahana, near the "Sugar Cane Train Depot" off Honoapiilani Road (Hwy. 30) as you head toward Kaanapali. You can't beat their stuffed croissants for under $2, or their sandwiches for under $4! Coffee is a mere $.40 and their pastries, breads, and pasta are gooooood! Open daily 7 a.m. to 5 p.m., until noon on Sun., tel. 667-9062.

Happy Days, tel. 661-3235, is a theme restaurant along Lahainaluna Road just a half block from Front Street. Inside they've done a good job with bent-back chairs and jukebox that make you feel like you're in a soda shop from the '50s. The menu has all-American offerings like hot dogs, burgers, hot roast beef, and full breakfast

selections. Actually Happy Days has good vibes, and good food if you want pure American.

Wiki Wiki Pizza across from the Cannery Mall, at 1275 Front, tel. 661-5686, has a takeout window featuring an eight-inch lunch pizza for only $3.95, 12-inch $8.95, 16-inch $11.95, toppings extra. A deck-patio on the premises gives you a quiet nook to eat in as you overlook Mala Wharf and the Lahaina Roads. If you're in a nearby condo, they'll deliver free.

The Wharf Shopping Center includes the inexpensive **Blue Lagoon Saloon,** selling steak and seafood on the ground floor. The offerings are hot-table counter style, but the surroundings in the courtyard are pleasant. Clam basket, $5.95, daily special of soup and sandwich for under $5, sandwiches under $4. **Orange Julius** dispenses its famous drinks, along with hot dogs and sandwiches, for a quick cheap meal. **Pancho and Lefty's** is a very passable Mexican restaurant stuck away in the corner where you can get a full meal for around $6.95. To the rear on the opposite side is **Song's Oriental Kitchen.** This unpretentious restaurant is of the precooked hot plate variety, but you can stuff yourself on meals like beef stew for $3.95 or barbecued chicken, $3.85, all with two-scoop rice and macaroni salad. **Lani's Pancake Cottage** will carbo-load you with pancakes, waffles, omelettes, or even burgers for under $5. **The Fisherman's Wharf** is a moderate-priced restaurant on the second floor of The Wharf Shopping Center. You can perch here and watch life go by on Front Street below. The menu presents *mahi mahi* for $6.50, deep-fried scallops, $8.50, or cold combination seafood plate for $9.75, with most entrees under $13.

Another good one is **Mr. Sub,** tel. 667-5683, at 129 Lahainaluna Road. They feature double-fisted sandwiches and packed picnic lunches.

Blackie's Bar is on Route 30 about one-half mile out of town toward Kaanapali. Look for the orange roof. Open daily 10 a.m. to 10 p.m., tel. 667-7979. An institution, sort of, selling Mexican food and hamburgers! It's also known for its jazz on Sun., Mon., Wed., and Fri. evenings from 5 to 8 p.m.

Fast Food

Fanatics can get their fix at: **Burger King,** on Front Sreet near the banyan tree, or **Pizza Hut** at 127 Hinau Street. The Lahaina Shopping

Center has **Jack in the Box, Chris's Smoke House, McDonald's, Kentucky Fried Chicken,** and **Denny's** across the street.

Moderate

Musahi's is a Japanese restaurant and sushi bar in the Lahaina Shopping Center, tel. 667-6207, open daily for lunch 11 a.m. to 2 p.m., dinner 5 to 9:45. p.m. A wonderful assortment of Japanese dishes for lunch, like *yakiniku, tonkatsu,* and sukiyaki, all cost under $9; for dinner add about $4. The best deal, however, is all-you-can-eat sushi at lunchtime for only $12.50, a mere pittance for true sushi fanatics. The interior is modern American with enough natural wood around and shoji screens to give a Japanese feel. This restaurant is tops for what it serves, and the prices are right.

Kobe Japanese Steak House is at 136 Dickenson and the corner of Luakini, tel. 667-5555, open daily for dinner from 5:30 p.m. Service is *teppan yaki* style, which means that the chef comes to you. His sharp blade flashes through the air and thumps the table, keeping the culinary beat as it slices, dices, and minces faster than any Veg-o-Matic you've ever seen. The delectables of marinated meat, chicken, and vegetables are then expertly flash-fried at your own grill, oftentimes with aplomb in a ball of sake-induced flame. The experience is fun, the food very good, and the interior authentic Japanese. *Teppan* meals come complete with soup, tea, and dessert. Expect to spend at least $15 for an entree, $10 for an appetizer, or have sake or beer while munching at the sushi bar.

The **Harbor Front Restaurant** on the second floor at The Wharf Shopping Center on Front Street, tel. 667-8212, has a logo that reads "established a long time ago." Lunch up to $6, $5 sandwiches, $15 dinners. A display case at the entrance holds the fresh catch-of-the-day. The interior is surprisingly well done with many hanging plants in distinctive planters, high-backed wicker chairs, and white tables and bright orange table settings.

Lahaina Steak 'n' Lobster is at 1312 Front St., way at the west end near the Cannery Shopping Center, tel. 667-5558. They offer $8.95 early-bird specials like *mahi mahi,* prime rib, or teriyaki chicken from 5 to 6:30 p.m. The bar opens at 3 p.m. Nothing fancy, but a straightforward filler-up at a good price.

The Oceanhouse is at 831 Front St., tel. 661-3359. Daily lunch 11 a.m. to 2:30 p.m., dinner 6 to 10 p.m. Happy hour with free munchies, cheap beer, and well drinks. The Oceanhouse is known for its extensive salad bar; lunch is available for under $6. Dinner begins at $10. A good selection is Cajun smoked ribs with BBQ sauce for $15, most seafood, meats, and poultry from $16. An "early-bird special" entices with a good discount from 5 to 6 p.m. Nice atmosphere and terrific sunset view.

The **Whale's Tail** is next door to The Wharf Shopping Plaza, second level at 666 Front St., tel. 661-3676. Daily lunch 11:30 a.m. to 2:30 p.m., dinner from 5 p.m. They usually offer a guitarist, or sometimes an entire band. Lobster and filet mignon, $17.95, fresh catch in mango and butter, $19.95, or *mahi mahi* tempura $15.95, lunch specials for only $3.95. It's a good place to go to with a good central location to *perve* on the action. Children's menu.

Harpooner's Lanai is in the Pionner Inn, tel. 661-3636. Daily breakfast from 7 a.m., lunch from 11:30 a.m. Basic but good foods including pancakes and Portuguese bean soup. Most dishes and sandwiches under $8.

Kimo's, 845 Front St., tel. 661-4811, is friendly and has great harbor and sunset views on the lower level. If you're in Lahaina around 6 p.m. and need a break, head here to relax with some "Kimo therapy." Popular, but no reservations taken. They offer seafood from $12, with most entrees between $15 and $25, and are known for their catch-of-the-day, usually the best offering on the menu; limited menu for children. The downstairs bar has top-notch well drinks featuring brand-name liquor.

Bettino's, 505 Front Street Mall, tel. 661-8810, is open daily from 7 a.m. It's off the beaten track and a favorite with locals. Italian food, including fettucine from $9.95. Also featured are steaks and seafood, and they're renowned for their enormous salads. Worth the trip, and when others are overcrowded you can usually find a good table here.

Sam's Beachside Grill, at 505 Front Street Mall, tel. 667-4341, is open daily for lunch 11 a.m. to 4 p.m., dinner 5 to 10 p.m., Sunday brunch 9 a.m. to 2 p.m. This is one of the newest additions to the Lahaina food scene. Away from the central action, it's a great bet for always finding a table. The sunset view and classic interior of Italian marble floors and triton shell chandelier as you mount the circular staircase add that special touch for a great evening. Prices on the full menu are moderate, from an assortment of *pu pu* for under $6 to full-course meals from $15-20. Sam's has the potential for being a great place, but it's still finding its culinary feet, and the meals, though never bad, are not yet outstanding. If they could match the view and the decor, Sam would have a winner.

Tree House Restaurant in the Maui Marketplace off Front Street serves dinners from 5 to 9 p.m. Keeping with their name, there is a second floor surrounded by trees where you can perch and eat. Most entrees are only $12.95, with appetizers around $7. An open-air restaurant away from the action and where you can always get a good seat, the Tree House has a full bar. Expect a reasonable meal, but not gourmet.

The **Chart House** at the far west end of Lahaina at 1450 Front St., tel. 661-0937, serves daily dinner 5 to 9:30 p.m. No reservations, and a wait is common. They have another, less crowded restaurant in Kahului; both offer a good selection of seafood and beef. It's reasonably priced with a decent salad bar, and though the food is usually very good, it can slip to mediocre, depending upon the daily chef. There's no way of telling, so you just have to take a chance.

Gourmet Dining

When you feel like putting a major dent in your budget and satisfying your desire for gourmet food, you should be pleased with one of the following.

Avalon: Whoever said "east is east and west is west" would have whistled a different tune if only they had had the pleasure of dining at this terrific restaurant first. Owner/chefs Andy Leeds and Mark Ellman have put together a uniquely blended menu that they've dubbed "Pacific Basin cusine." Here are dishes from Sausalito to Saigon, and from Mexico City to Tokyo, with a bit of Nebraska and Hong Kong thrown in for good measure. Moreover, they've spiced, herbed, and garnished their delectables by mixing and matching the finest and most refined tastes from all the geographical areas, creating a culinary extravaganza.

If you're tired of the same old appetizers, try Maui onion rings with tamarind-chipotle catsup, or don't resist the combination platter with a selection of the best appetizers for $11.95 (enough for two). Move on to mixed greens and crispy noodles, tempting in a ginger sesame dressing, or *gado-gado* on a bed of brown rice turned sumptuous by a Balinese peanut sauce. Drift the Pacific through their grill selections like wok-fried veal in a picante salsa, or savor the juices of succulent Asian prawns with *shitake* mushrooms, or served in a sun-dried tomato and basil cream sauce. If you need more convincing, try the house specialty of whole Dungeness crab and clams in a garlic black bean sauce ($50 for two), or the mouthwatering Asian pasta like mama san wished she could make. If only people could get along together as well as this food! Lunch or late nights are special too with sandwiches at the bar. The Avalon is at 844 Front St., Lahaina, HI 96761, tel. 667-5559, just below Moose McGuillicuddy's.

Gerard's: Everyone knows that to qualify as a *real* Frenchman you must be an artist. Gerard Reversade, trained in the finest French culinary tradition since age 14, creates masterpieces. He feels that eating is not *an* experience, but *the* experience of life, around which everything else that is enjoyable revolves. He is aided by his friend Pierre, the hospitable wine steward, who intimately understands the magical blend of wine and food, bringing out the best in both. The menu changes, but it's always gourmet. Breakfast and lunch are actually quite reasonable, with many portions being large enough for two to share. Some superb choices are the island greens with raspberry vinaigrette dressing, and crusty French bread. Appetizers feature mouthwatering choices like *shitake* and wild mushrooms in a puff pastry. Full entrees titillate the palate; try herbed rack of lamb, or savory veal in a light tomato sauce and a side of spinach-and-cheese-filled ravioli. Gerard also insists that the people working as waiters and waitresses share his philosophy, so along with the excellent food comes excellent service.

This elegant restaurant has recently relocated to the **Plantation Inn** (see above), the epitome of neo-Victorian charm. The comfortable, puff-pillowed wicker chairs, fine linen and table settings, along with the glass-topped tables on the dining veranda couldn't be more perfect. Fronting the building is a small dining garden, and inside, the interior is rich with hardwood floors and a full oak bar. If you want a truly memorable dining experience go to Gerard's, at 174 Lahain-aluna Rd., tel. 661-8939, open daily at 7:30 a.m. for dinner from 6 p.m., lunch on Friday only from 11:30-2:00, parking and validated free parking nearby.

Alex's Hole-in-the-Wall, down an alleyway at 834 Front, will put a small hole in your wallet and a big smile on your face. The food is Italian with delights like veal parmigiana for $20, and chicken marsala for $15.95. The pasta is locally made and fresh. Open daily except Sun., from 6 to 10 p.m., tel. 661-3197.

Longhi's, 888 Front St., tel. 667-2288, serves daily from 7:30 a.m. to 10 p.m. Longhi owns the joint and he's a character. He feels that his place has "healing vibes" and that man's basic food is air. Prices at Longhi's may seem expensive but the portions are enormous and can fill two. Better yet is ordering a half-order for half-price, which is really just a little less than a full order. With all meals and salads comes a wonderful basket of jalapeno and pizza breads which are delicious and filling in themselves. Sometimes people complain about the service. It is different! No written menu, so when you sit down and aren't handed one, you might feel ignored, especially when they're busy. Don't! The waiter or waitress will come around and explain the menu to you. This is an attempt to make the dining experience richer, and it does with the added benefit of personal attention if you just wait and relax. Mornings you can order *frittatas,* like spinach, ham, and bacon, $5.50, easily enough for two. A good lunch choice is pasta Siciliana with calamari, spicy with marinara sauce; for dinner, the prawns amaretto and shrimp Longhi are good. Save room for the fabulous desserts that circulate on a tray, from which you may choose. It's hard not to have a fine meal here; there's always a line, no reservations, no dress code, and complimentary valet parking! There's also entertainment in the upstairs bar, which is open nightly, but has live dancing music Fri. and Sat. from 10:30 p.m.

La Bretagne, at the east end town at 562 C Front St., is in a vintage historical house surrounded by a tamed jungle of greenery. Open daily for dinner from 6 p.m., tel. 661-8966. Reservations. French, and a touch pretentious? But of course, *ma chere!* Meals run $20 and up. Elegant dining with exemplary desserts. The menu

changes daily, but a great standby is bouillabaisse in puff pastry.

Chez Paul, five miles east of Lahaina in Olowalu, is secluded, romantic, very popular, and French—what else! Local folks into elegant dining give it two thumbs up. The wine list is tops, the desserts fantastic, and the food, *magnifique!* Prices start at $22. On Route 30, tel. 661-3843. There are two seatings daily at 6:30 and 8:30 p.m., reservations only, credit cards accepted.

ENTERTAINMENT

Lahaina is one of those places where the real entertainment is the town itself. The best thing to do here is to stroll along Front Street and people-watch. As you walk along, it feels like a block party with the action going on all around you. Some people duck into one of the many establishments along the south side of Front Street for a breather, a drink, or just to watch the sunset. It's all free, enjoyable, and safe.

Night Spots/Discos
All of the evening entertainment in Lahaina are in restaurants and lounges (see corresponding restaurants in "Food" for details). The following should provide you with a few laughs.

Jazz is featured at **Blackie's** Sun., Mon., Wed., and Fri. evenings from 5 to 8 p.m.; there's free Hawaiian music and dance at the **Wharf Shopping Mall** courtyard as announced in the free tourist literature, and jam sessions and popular combos at the **Whale's Tale.**

An old standby with yet another new name (formerly The Keg, Blue Max) is **The Tiger Den** at 730 Front St., tel. 667-7003. Besides all-day videos on their big-screen TV, they rock nightly with various bands, singers, and combos, and are in the process of opening an Asian fine-dining restaurant. Live music is performed from 9:30 p.m. to closing. Still a good place to groove.

You too can be a disco king or queen on Longhi's black-and-white chessboard dance floor every weekend (see "Food" above). **Moose McGuillicuddy's** (just listen for the loud music on Front Street) is still a happening place with nightly music though it's becoming more of a cruise joint for post-adolescents. Those that have been around Lahaina for a while usually give it a miss, but if you want to feast your eyes on prime American two-legged beef on the hoof, this place is for you.

Hawaii Experience Omni Theater at 824 Front has continuous showings on the hour from 10 a.m. to 10 p.m. (45-min. duration), adults $5.95, children 12 and under $3.95. The idea is to give you a total sensory experience by means of the giant, specially designed concave screen. You sit surrounded by it. You will tour the islands as if you were sitting in a helicopter or diving below the waves. And you'll be amazed at how well the illusion works. You'll soar over Kauai's Waimea Canyon, dip low to frolic with humpbacks, and rise with the sun over Haleakala. If you can't afford the real thing, this is about as close as you can get. The lobby of the theater doubles as a gift shop where you can pick up souvenirs like carved whales, T-shirts, and a variety of inexpensive mementos, including Maui chips.

Drugs

Like everywhere else in Hawaii, the main street drug is pakalolo. You might pass guys on Front Street, especially around the seawall, who'll make a distinctive "joint-sucking" sound or whisper, "Buds?" It's usually vacuum-packed in Seal-a-Meal plastic bags; the tendency is to push the crops out as fast as possible, creating plenty of immature smoke. Most growers save all the best buds for personal use and pawn off the inferior stuff on the tourists. Some even go to the trouble of wrapping leaf tightly with thread to make it look good. It's a gamble, but most deals are usually straight, although inflated, business transactions.

Hookers

Lahaina had more than its share last century, and thankfully they haven't had a great resurgence, as in Waikiki. In the words of one longtime resident, "There's no prostitution in Lahaina. People come as couples. For single people, there's so much free stuff around that the pros would go hungry." Skin merchants in Honolulu, operating under the thin guise of escort services or masseuses, will fly their practitioners to Maui, but anyone going to this length would be better off at home on their knees praying for any kind of a clue to life!

SHOPPING

Once learned, everybody loves to do the "Lahaina Stroll." It's easy. Just act cool, nonchalant, and give it your best strut as you walk the gauntlet of Front Street's exclusive shops and exotic boutiques. The fun is just in being here. If you begin in the evening, go to the east end of town and park down by Prison Street; it's much easier to find a spot and you walk westward, catching the sunset.

The Lahaina Stroll

On Prison, check out **Dan's Greenhouse**, specializing in birds, and *fukubonsai*. These miniatures were originated by David Fukumoto. They're mailable (except to Australia and Japan), and when you get them home, just plop them in water and presto . . . a great little plant, from $15-23. The **505 Front Street Mall** offers a barrelfull of shops, stores, and restaurants at the south end of Front Street, away from the heavier foot traffic. The mall is like a New England village, and the shopping is good and unhurried. Some shops include **High as a Kite**, selling airborne fun-filled kites, **Alford's** for fine resort wear, **Cruiser Bob's** for a Haleakala downhill experience, **Lahaina Beach Center** for all your surf and sand needs, and **Lace Secrets**, selling exotic and erotic lingerie, swimsuits, leather dress and underwear, and lots of pink, purple, and red little frilly things.

Heading west on Front **The Scentuous Shop** will make you swoon with its assortment of heady perfumes and oils that make great gifts. Don't miss the **Lahaina Scrimshaw Factory.** The staff here are not only knowledgeable on this old art, but also willing to chat. Pieces sell in all price ranges (at The Cannery Mall too). **Jade and Jewels** is a treasure chest laden with rubies, emeralds, and carvings from India and China. **Whale of a Shirt** sells T-shirts for under $12, and advertises silk screening while you watch. **Apparels by Pauline** are reasonably priced, and **Alexia** features natural clothing with supernatural price tags. Check out the outdoor gear and good prices at **Vagabond.**

The **Wharf Shopping Center** at 658 Front offers three floors of eateries and shops. Browse **Lahaina Galleries** for fine art. **Seeger People,** on the ground floor, tel. 661-1084, is a new shop with a new concept—you create your own photo souvenir of Maui. A series of photos is mounted on a quarter-inch acrylic backing, and then cut out to form a multiple-image sculpture of you and/or your family. Costs $150, prepaid, mailed to you within four weeks. **The Whaler's Book Shoppe** on the third floor is well stocked with books, everything from Hawaiiana to best-sellers. There's a coffee bar where you can relax and read. **Island Hawaiiana Coins and Stamps** is a shop as frayed as an old photo album on the second floor. They specialize in philatelic supplies.

More Front Street Shopping

Claire the Ring Lady, with rings for every finger and occasion, open 9:30 a.m. to 9:30 p.m., tel. 667-9288, ranges in price from 14-karat gold settings starting at $95. Featured are gems from all over the world that Claire collects herself. **Seabreeze Ltd.** is a souvenir store with junk, like fake leis or generic muumuus that are no better or worse than others you'll find along Front Street, but their prices are good, especially for film. **The South Seas Trading Post** is just across from the Wo Hing Temple, at 851 Front St., tel. 661-3168, open daily 8:30 a.m. to 10 p.m., and is the second oldest shop open in modern Lahaina, dating back to 1871. They indeed have artifacts from the South Pacific, like tapa cloth from Tonga, but also colorful rugs from India, primitive carvings from Papua New Guinea, and Burmese *kalaga* wall hangings with their beautiful and intricate stitching from $30 to $300. You can pick up a one-of-a-kind bead necklace for only a few dollars, or a real treasure that would adorn any home for a decent price. **Maui Clothing Co.** has racks of hand-screened men's, women's, and kids' apparel; nice stuff.

Get yourself a permanent memento of Maui by visiting the "pin and ink" artists at **Skin Deep Tattooing,** tel. 661-8531. They feature "new age primal, tribal tattoos," Japanese-style intricate beauties, with women artists for shy women clientele. The walls are hung with sample photos and Harley-Davidson T-shirts that say Maui or Hawaii. No wimps allowed!

Lee Sands Eelskins, at 780 Front St., daily 9:30 a.m. to 9:30 p.m., is filled with accessories, clothing, handbags, briefcases, purses, and belts made from reptile and other unique animal skins. If "you are what you wear," set your own standards by adorning yourself in something made from pig skin, cobra, shark, stingray, peacock, and even chicken skin.

The **Lahaina Shopping Center,** just behind Longhi's, has a few inexpensive shops, a drug store, and **Nagasako's Market,** known for its good selection of local and Oriental food. Across the street at the **Lahaina Square Shopping Center** is **Foodland.**

Golden Reef is at 695 Front St., tel. 667-6633, open daily 10 to 10. Inside is all manner of jewelry, from heirloom quality to costume baubles made from black, gold, red, and pink coral, malachite, lapis, and mother of pearl. All designs are created on the premises. Everyone will be happy shopping here because prices go from $1 to $1000, and more. Golden Reef is also very happy to do individual one-of-a-kind work for you and you alone.

In the **Old Poi Factory, Pacific Visions** has hand-painted local garments done at Haiku, and art-deco items from Los Angeles, San Francisco, and New York. Or pick up a plumeria lei fashioned by a local girl sitting in an old chair for only $3. **Fox Photo** one-hour lab is on Front Street just across the street.

Off The Main Drag

Just off Front Street and Lahainaluna is **The Lahaina Market Place,** a collection of semi open-air stalls, open daily 9-9. Most buskers have roll-up stands and sell trinkets and baubles like hanging crystals and ivory *netsuke*. It's junk, but it's neat junk. An interesting shop is **Donna's Designs,** where Donna has tie-dyed T-shirts and sweatshirts with wild colors. For only $15 they make distinctive beachwear that will dazzle the eyes. Stuck in a corner is a small booth called the **Tarot Patch,** tel. 572-6006, where you can come for psychic readings, $15. The owner/reader is Kutira, but when she is off getting psychically recharged your spiritual road map will be laid out by Willi Vasudeva (Devine Within) Wolff, or another practitioner who mans the booth.

Nagamine Camera at 139 Lahainaluna Rd., tel. 667-6255, open daily 8:30 a.m. to 8:30 p.m., is a full-service, one-hour-developing camera store. They're the best on West Maui for any specialized photo needs. Prices on film, however, could be better.

Kula Bay, nearby at 120 Lahainaluna Rd. across from the Lahainaluna Hotel, and just off the Maui Market Place, tel. 667-5852, open 9 to 9, sells distinctive, 100% cotton tropical clothing that has been fabric washed. Not ordinary tourist quality, with special prints exclusive to Kula Bay.

To save some money try **991 Limahana Place** just near the Sugar Cane Train Depot off Hwy. 30. Here you'll find: **The Coral and Gift Wholesale Outlet** for coral, jade, pearls, ivory, and gemstones, open 9 to 5; **Posters Maui** features a wide selection of posters that you'll spot on Front Street, but at a more reasonable price; **J.R.'s Music Shop** has a great selection of music from "Beyond the Reef" to new age, but the prices aren't much cheaper than elsewhere.

For more off-the-main-drag shopping visit the **Lahaina Business Plaza** at 888 Wainae St., just across the street from McDonald's.

Arts, Crafts, And Photos

At The Wharf Shopping Mall check out the **The Royal Art Gallery,** with distinctive paintings of island dream scenes of superimposed faces in the clouds. Make sure to visit the **Lahaina Art Society** in the basement of the old jail in the Courthouse. The artists here are up and coming, and the prices for sometimes remarkable works are reasonable. The **Waterfront Gallery and Gifts** will tickle big kids with their fine ships, models, and imported sheep skins.

The vintage open-beamed stone building of the Seamen's Hospital (see p. 417) is the perfect setting for **Lahaina Printsellers,** tel. 667-7843. It is much more poignant looking at the antique prints and charts hung on the plaster walls because the seamen who used them, or whose lives depended upon them, may have actually lain ill in these very rooms. The building itself is a monument to the days of the great explorations, and the great hardships involved in opening the Pacific.

Provenance Gallery of Hawaii, at 122 Lahainaluna Rd., tel. 667-6222, (800)367-8047, ext. 555, advertise themselves as world-class art, and they are. Inside is artwork by Dali, Picasso, and Chagall. Others include: Joseph Venus, an American Indian who has captured the breath of the Great Spirit in his distinctive works; Guillaume Azoulay, one of only three living artists displayed at the Louvre; a wonderful collection of seascapes, often in panels like Japanese paintings, by Gary Fenske; Robert Blue's *Vogue*-like high-fashion women that are the rage in Japan; Eyvind Earle, the genius, famous for illustrating the Disney movies *Sleeping Beauty, Fantasia,* and *Snow White*; Frederick Rem ington's cowboys and Indians are here locked in fluid bronze; and Brian Davis brightens the walls with his famous flowers.

Lahaina Cannery Shopping Center

As practical looking as its name on the outside, the bright and well-appointed interior features some of the best and most convenient shopping on West Maui, open daily 9:30 a.m. to 9:30 p.m. If you'll be staying at a condo and doing your own cooking, the largest and generally least expensive supermarket on West Maui is **Safeway,** open daily 24 hours. To book any activities, from a whale watch to a dinner cruise, you'll find the **Ocean Activities Center** offers the most activities on Maui for the right price. Quickies can be picked up at the **ABC Sundry Store,** and you can beat the sun's glare by stopping into **Shades of Hawaii.** Chocoholics will be happy to discover the **Rocky Mountain Chocolate Factory,** where they even have sugarless chocolates for diabetics. **Dolphin Galleries** is an art shop specializing in whales and other mammals of the sea. Fast food is available at **Orange Julius** and **Burger King.** Although the mall is new, don't let that fool you because some of Lahaina's oldest and best shops, like the **Scrimshaw Factory** and **Gem Creations,** are here. You can take care of all your needs with shops like **Superwhale** for the kids, or **The Maui Dive Shop, Crazy Shirtz,** and the **Footlocker. Waldenbooks** has one of its excellent, well-stocked stores in the mall. Open daily 9:30 a.m. to 9:30 p.m., tel. 667-6172. One of the most unusual shops is **The Kite Fantasy,** featuring kites, wind socks, and toys for kids of all ages. You can buy kites like a six-foot flexifoil for $105 or a simple triangular plastic kite for only $2.50. Cloth kites are made from nylon with nice designs for a reasonable $15.95.

If you're into designer coffees come to **Sir Wilfred's.** They also feature lunches like roast beef on a baguette for $4.25 and quiche for $2.50. Their great selection of roasted coffees also makes a terrific gift. **Longs Drugs** is one of the cheapest places to buy and develop film. You can also find a selection of everything from aspirin to boogie boards.

Local Motion, across from the Cannery Shopping Center, at 1295 Front, open Mon.-Sat. 9 to 9, Sun. 9 to 5, tel. 661-7873, specialize in cotton T-shirts and lycra sportswear, most bearing the "Local Motion" logo; T-shirts are priced around $12. They're beauties and make great souvenirs. Also surfboards, boogie boards, skateboards, and skim boards for sale.

All those dreams of past and present kids "wished upon a star" come to life in the **Maui Mouse House** across from the Cannery Shopping Center, at 1287 Front St., tel. 661-5758, open daily 9 to 9. Owner/dreamer Martha Hughes has collected amazing gifts of licensed Disney merchandise. All the characters are here—Donald Duck and the boys, Mickey, Minnie, Pluto, and those whacky, wild Looney Toons. The shop is a stuffed toy of apparel, jewelry, stationery, educational materials, T-shirts, sweatshirts, umbrellas, and more. "Tha-that's all, folks."

SERVICES AND INFORMATION

Emergency: For fire, police, or ambulance, dial 911 throughout the Lahaina area. **Banks:** In Lahaina during normal banking hours try: **Bank of Hawaii** in the Lahaina Shopping Center, tel. 661-8781; **First Interstate** at 135 Papalaua St., tel. 667-9714; **First Hawaiian,** Papalaua St., tel. 661-3655.

Post Office
The post office is on the west edge of town towards Kaanapali, well marked, tel. 667-6611; **Mail Home Maui** is a post office contract station located at The Wharf Shopping Plaza, 658 Front

St., tel. 667-6620. They're open seven days from 10 a.m. to 5 p.m. Along with the normal stamps, etc., they specialize in sending packages home. They've got mailing boxes, tape, and packaging materials. They also sell souvenir packs of coffee, nuts, candies, and teas which might serve as a last-minute purchase, but are expensive.

Medical Treatment
A concentration of all types of specialists is found at **Lahaina Medical Group,** located at Lahaina Square, tel. 667-2534. Alternatively, the **Lahaina Health Center,** 180 Dickenson St., at Dickenson Square, Suite 205, tel. 667-6268, offers acupuncture, chiropractic, therapeutic massage, and podiatry. Most practitioners charge approximately $30 for their services. Pharmacies in Lahaina include: **Craft's** at the Lahaina Shopping Center, tel. 661-3119, and **Valley Isle** at 130 Prison, tel. 661-4747.

Laundromat
Try **Maui Dry Cleaning,** Lahaina Shopping Center, tel. 667-2659.

Information
The following groups and organizations should prove helpful: **Lahaina Restoration Foundation,** Box 338, Lahaina, HI 96761, tel. 661-3262, or in the "Master's Reading Room" along Front Street. They are a storehouse of information about historical Maui, and make sure to pick up their brochure, *Lahaina, A Walking Tour of Historic and Cultural Sites.* **The library** is at 680 Wharf St., tel. 661- 0566; open Mon. through Thursday. Stop in at **Whaler's Book Shoppe** on the upper level of The Wharf Mall along Front Street. They have an excellent book selection as well as a gourmet coffee and sandwich shop if you get tired browsing.

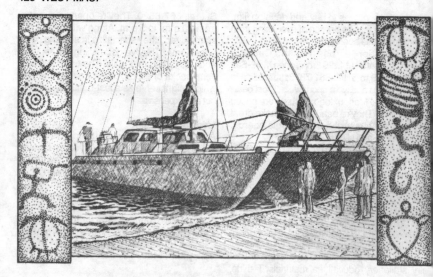

KAANAPALI AND VICINITY

Five lush valleys, nourished by streams from the West Maui Mountains, stretch luxuriously for 10 miles from Kaanapali northwest to Kapalua. All along the connecting **Honoapiilani Highway** (Rt. 30), the dazzle and glimmer of beaches is offset by black volcanic rock. Two sensitively planned and beautifully executed resorts are at each end of this drive. Kaanapali Resort is 500 acres of fun and relaxation at the east end. It houses six luxury hotels, six beautifully appointed condos, a shopping mall and museum, 36 holes of world-class golf, tennis courts galore, and epicurean dining in a chef's salad of cuisines. Two of the hotels, the **Hyatt Regency** and **Westin Maui**, are inspired architectural showcases that blend harmoniously with Maui's most beautiful seashore surroundings. At the western end is another gem, the **Kapalua Resort,** 750 of Maui's most beautifully sculpted acres with its own showcase, the **Kapalua Bay Hotel.** Here, too, is prime golf at **Fleming Beach,** perhaps the best on the island, plus exclusive shopping, horseback riding, and tennis aplenty.

Kaanapali, with its four miles of glorious beach, is Maui's westernmost point. In general, it begins where Lahaina ends, and continues west along jrh Route 30 until a mile or so before the village of Honokowai. Adjacent at the west end are the villages of Honokowai and Kahana, which service the condos tucked away here and there along the coast and mountainsides. Both are practical stops where you can buy food, gas, and all necessary supplies to keep your vacation rolling. The accommodations are not as grand, but the beaches and vistas are. Along this entire southwestern shore, Maui flashes its most captivating pearly white smile. The sights all along this coast are either natural or manmade, but not historical. This is where you come to gaze from mountain to sea and bathe yourself in natural beauty. Then, after a day of surf and sunshine, you repair to one of the gorgeous hotels or restaurants for a drink or dining, or just to promenade around the grounds.

History

Southwestern Maui was a mixture of scrub and precious *lo'i* land, reserved for taro, the highest life-sustaining plant given by the gods. The farms stretched to Kapalua, skirting the numerous bays all along the way. The area was important enough for a "royal highway" to be built by chief Piilani, and it still bears his name. Westerners used the lands surrounding Kaanapali to grow sugar cane, and the **Lahaina, Kaanapali**

and Pacific Railroad, known today as the "Sugar Cane Train," chugged to Kaanapali Beach to unburden itself onto barges that carried the cane to waiting ships. Kaanapali, until the 1960s, was a blemished beauty where the Pioneer Sugar Mill dumped its rubbish. Then AMFAC, one of the "Big Five," decided to put the land to better use. In creating Hawaii's first planned resort, they outdid themselves. Robert Trent Jones was hired to mold the golf course along this spectacular coast, while the Hyatt Regency and its grounds became an architectural marvel. The Sheraton-Maui was built atop, and integrated with, Puu Kekaa, "Black Rock." This area is a wave-eroded cinder cone, and the Sheraton architects used its sea cliffs as part of the walls of the resort. Here, on a deep underwater shelf, daring divers descend to harvest Maui's famous black coral trees. The Hawaiians believed that Puu Kekaa was a very holy place where the spirits of the dead left this earth and migrated into the spirit world. Kahekili, Maui's most famous 18th-century chief, often came here to leap into the sea below. This old-time daredevil was fond of the heart-stopping activity, and made famous "Kahekili's Leap," an even more treacherous sea cliff on nearby Lanai. Today, the Sheraton puts on a sunset show where this "leap" is re-enacted.

Unfortunately, developers picked up on AMFAC's great idea and built condos up the road starting in Honokowai. Interested in profit, not beauty, they earned that area the dubious title of "condo ghetto." Fortunately, the Maui Land and Pineapple Co. owned the land surrounding the idyllic Kapalua Bay, and Colin Cameron, one of the heirs to this holding, had visions of developing 750 acres of the plantation's 20,000 into the extraordinary **Kapalua Bay Resort.** He teamed up with Rockresort Management, headed by Laurence Rockefeller, and the complex was opened in 1979.

Transportation
The **Blue Shoreline Bus** runs all along the southwest coast from Kapalua to Lahaina and points east. Kaanapali is serviced by the **Kaanapali Trolley.** The Sugar Cane Train offers a day of fun for the entire family. For details see "Getting Around—Public Transportation" in the general Introduction.

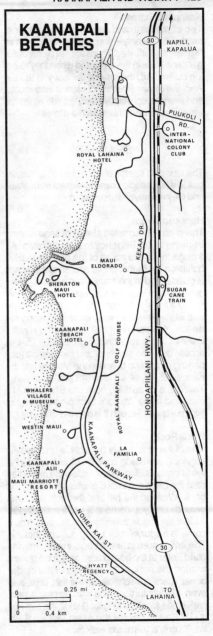

Kaanapali Extras

Two situations in and around Kaanapali mar its outstanding beauty—you might refer to them as "Kaanapali perfume." There are still plenty of sugar cane fields in the area, and when they're being burned off, the smoke is heavy in the air. Also, the sewage treatment plant is inadequate, and even the constantly blowing trade winds are insufficient to push this stench out to sea.

BEACHES

The four-mile stretch of pristine sand at Kaanapali is what people come to expect from Maui, and they are never disappointed.

Hanakoo Beach

This is an uninterrupted stretch of sand running from the Hyatt Regency to the Sheraton. Although these are some of the most exclusive hotels on the island, public access to the beach is guaranteed in the state's constitution. There are "rights of way," but parking your car is definitely a hassle. A good idea is to park at **Wahikuli State Park** and walk westward along the beach. You can park (10 cars) in the Hyatt's lower lot and enter along a right of way. There's access between the Hyatt and the Marriott (pay parking ramp) and between the Marriott and the Kaanapali Alii, which also has limited parking. There is also parking near the Sheraton (11 cars) and at the Whaler's Shopping Center, but you must pass through the gauntlet of shops.

Black Rock

One of the most easily accessible and visually engaging snorkeling spots on Maui is located at the Sheraton's Black Rock. Follow the main road past the Sheraton until it climbs the hill around back. Walk up the hill and through the hotel grounds until you come to a white metal fence. Follow the fence down toward the sea. You'll come to a spur of rock jutting out and that's it. The entire area is like an underwater marine park. Enter at the beach area and snorkel west around the rock, staying close to the cinder cone. There are schools of reef fish, rays, and even a lonely turtle. If you want to play it safe, park at the small parking lot (fee) at the far west end of Kaanapali near the Aston Kaanapali Villas. It's only a 10-minute walk away.

Sports

For a full listing of the sporting facilities and possibilities in the Kaanapali area, contact the Aloha Activity Center in the Whaler's Village, tel. 661-3815. **Golf** at the Royal Kaanapali North (par 70) and South (par 72) costs $90, tel. 661-3691. For **tennis,** the most famous is the Royal Lahaina Tennis Ranch with 11 courts, tennis clinics, and tournaments. The Sheraton has three courts, the Hyatt five, the Whaler three courts, one each at the Kaanapali Royal and Kaanapali Plantation and three at the Maui Surf. For **water sports**, catamarans are available twice a day from Kaanapali Beach. Contact any major hotel activities desk in the resort area, or **Kaanapali Jet Ski** at the Whaler's Village, tel. 667-7851.

ACCOMMODATIONS

The Kaanapali Resort offers accommodations ranging from "moderate deluxe" to "luxury." There are no budget accommodations here, but just northwest toward Honokowai are plenty of reasonably priced condos. As usual, they're more of a bargain the longer you stay, especially if you can share costs with a few people by renting a larger unit. And as always, you'll save money on food costs. The following should give you an idea of what's available.

Hyatt Regency

Located at Kaanapali's eastern extremity, at 200 Nohea Kai Drive, Lahaina, HI 96761. Reservations are made at tel. (800) 228-9000, or on Maui at tel. 661-1234. The least expensive room in this truly luxury hotel is $195 a day; they go as high as $2000 for the Presidential Suite. Of course, like many Hyatts, you don't have to stay there to appreciate its beauty. If you visit, valet parking is in front of the hotel. Cost is $4.50, or complimentary if you validate your ticket by dining at Spats or the Palm Court, or spend $25 in one of the shops. Around back is a self-parking lot with 160 spaces for guests (disregard numbered spaces; parking here is OK).

The moment you enter the main lobby the magic begins. A multi-tiered architectural extravaganza opens to the sky, birds fly freely, and magnificent potted plants and full-sized palm trees create the atmosphere of a modern Polynesian palace. Nooks and crannies abound where you can lounge in kingly wicker thrones. The walls are adorned with first-class artwork and tapestries, while glass showcases hold priceless ceramics. Peacocks strut their regal stuff amid impeccable Japanese gardens, and ducks and swans are floating alabaster on a symmetry of landscaped ponds. Around the swimming pool, guests luxuriate on huge blue hotel towels. The pool's architecture is inspired by the islands: grottoes, caves, waterfalls, and a huge slide are all built in. A swinging wood bridge connects the sections, and you can have an island drink at a sunken poolside bar. There are two five-star "Travel Holiday" award-winning restaurants, one doubling as a disco for human peacocking, and the "Elephant Walk," a covey of specialty shops and boutiques. The hotel offers half-hour scuba lessons in the pool for $10, beach dives for $59, and a four-day certification course, including all rental equipment and dives, for $395.

Sheraton-Maui

These 505 rooms are built around Kaanapali's most conspicuous natural phenomenon, Black Rock. For reservations, call (800) 325-3535, or on Maui, 661-0031. The prices are not as astronomical as the Hyatt's, with a basic room at $190, up to $400 for an oceanside suite. The snorkeling around Black Rock is the best in the area. There are two pools, and the view from the upper-level Sundowner Bar is worth the price of a drink. A catamaran is available to guests, and you can rent snorkeling equipment at a poolside kiosk, but the prices are triple what you pay at a dive shop.

The Westin Maui

The newest in luxury hotels to spring up along Kaanapali, at 2365 Kaanapali Pkwy., Lahaina, HI 96761, tel. 667-2525, (800) 228-3000, is actually a phoenix, risen from the old Maui Surf Hotel. True to the second life of that mythical bird, it is a beauty. Westin is known for its fabulous entranceways, lobbies, and quiet nooks, where superb artwork makes you feel as if you're in a living museum. A series of strolling paths take you through resplendent manicured grounds that surround an extensive pool area. Waterfalls, water slides, and natural rock formations all blend to create civilized paradise. To the left of the main lobby are a collection of exclusive

boutiques. The hotel's restaurant, **Cook's at the Beach,** is surprisingly reasonable (see "Food"). Standard rooms begin at $185, $20 extra person, $500 suite, and $350 Royal Beach Club. The price range, as usual, depends upon the view.

Royal Lahaina Resort

The largest acreage of all in Kaanapali, these 27 idyllic acres surround 521 luxurious rooms. The tropical landscaping leads directly to the sun-soaked beach. The property, one of the first to be developed, is divided into two categories: cottages and towers. Rates range from a standard room at $150 to a deluxe oceanfront at $225. The cottages rent from $175 to $225, with suites from $250 to $950. Reservations can be made at tel. (800) 733-777: Outrigger Hotels, Hawaii. There are no less than three restaurants and a nightly luau (see following), and three swimming pools on the well- maintained grounds. It's also home to the **Royal Lahaina Tennis Ranch,** boasting 10 courts and a stadium. Special tennis packages are offered.

Kaanapali Beach Hotel

For Kaanapali, this hotel is a bargain. Standard rooms from $135, a distinctive whale-shaped pool, and tennis privileges are some of the amenities at the Royal Lahaina, tel. (800) 367-5170, on Maui call 661-0011.

Condos

Generally less expensive than the hotels, condos begin at around $100 per night and offer full kitchens, some maid service, swimming pools, and often convenience stores and laundry facilities. Off-season rates and discounts for longer stays are usually offered. Combinations of the above are too numerous to mention, so it's best to ask all pertinent questions when booking. Not all condos accept credit cards, and a deposit is the norm when making reservations. The following should give you an idea of what to expect.

The Aston Kaanapali Shores: The green tranquility of this created oasis fronting Kaanapali Beach offers an unsurpassed view of sun-baked Lanai just across the channel. You enter a spacious and airy lobby open, and framing a living sculpture of palms and ferns. Water melts over a huge copper painting-sculpture of the moon, creating a smooth and soothing natural music. The grounds are a trimmed garden in large proportions dappled with sunlight and flowers. Soak away your cares in two whirlpools, one tucked away in a quiet corner of the central garden area for midnight romance, the other near the pool. Sundays offer a special warmth at the Kaanapali Shores, where you can enjoy old-fashioned family fun at "Sandcastle Sundays." Kids of all ages get a bucket and shovel, while sand-sculpture artists help you to build the castle of your dreams. Shop at **Beachside Casuals,** a special children's boutique of hand-picked toys, clothing, and games (big people's clothes, too) that will remind the little ones of their fabulous trip to Maui. Enjoy a romantic dinner at **The Beach Club,** a beautifully appointed restaurant serving delectables ranging from *pasta primavera* to the fresh catch-of-the-day (see "Food") All units have been recently refurbished with new drapes, carpets, and furniture, and include gourmet kitchens, sweeping lanais, TV, and a/c. Prices range from an affordable studio at $129, to $280 for a two-bedroom oceanfront suite. For reservations contact the Aston Kaanapali Shores at 3445 Lower Honoapiilani Hwy., tel. 667-2211, (800) 367-5124.

Mahana: The second that you walk into these reasonably priced condos and look through a large floor-to-ceiling window framing a swimming pool and the wide blue sea, your cares immediately begin to slip away. The condo sits on a point of beach at 110 Kaanapali Shore Pl., Lahaina, HI 96761, tel. 661-8751, (800) 922-7866, which allows all apartments to have an ocean view at no extra cost. Studios begin at $119, to $199 for a huge two-bedroom (up to two people). Enjoy a complete kitchen plus pool, sauna, tennis, maid service, and a money-saving family plan.

Aston Kaanapali Villas: Enjoy the surroundings of 11 sculpted acres at this affordably priced condo at 2805 Honoapiilani Hwy., Lahaina, HI 96761, tel. 661-8687, (800) 922-7866. The extensive grounds of cool swaying palms harbor three pools and expert tennis courts. Rates begin at $149 studio, $220 two-bedroom with a/c, cable TV, maid service, and a family plan. This property, located at the far west end of the Kaanapali development, has an added bonus of peace and quiet along with the best of the Kaanapali beaches, although you remain just

minutes from the *action.* You're just a few minutes walk from Black Rock, a superb snorkeling area. The units are very large with spacious bedrooms; even a one-bedroom is capable of handling four people.

Others in Kaanapali include **International Colony Club** on the *mauka* side of Route 30, tel. 661-4070; it offers individual cottages at $95, $10 extra person, four-day minimum. **Maui Eldorado,** tel. (800) 367-2967, on Maui tel. 661-0021, is surrounded by the golf course, rates from $125. **Kaanapali Plantation,** tel. 661-4446, offers accommodations from $85 with a $10 discount for 14 days or longer, plus maid service and most amenities. **Kaanapali Royal,** a golfer's dream right on the course, tel. (800) 367-5637, on Maui tel. 661-7133, has rooms from $125 with substantial low-season and long-term discounts.

FOOD

Every hotel in Kaanapali has at least one restaurant, with numerous others scattered throughout the area. Some of the most expensive and exquisite restaurants on Maui are found in these hotels, but surprisingly, at others you can dine very reasonably, even cheaply.

The Beach Club

Guest or not, a quiet and lovely restaurant in which to dine is **The Beach Club** at the Aston Kaanapali Shores. Centered in the garden area, the restaurant opens to the sea. Request a table in the terrace area overlooking the pool for an especially romantic setting. The interior is classy, with wrought-iron tables and chairs and crisp starched linens. Service is formal but friendly, and the prices are not as rich as the menu. A light appetite will be satiated with soup and Caesar salad for under $7. You can move on to sauté and broiler specialties like veal piccata for $16.95, pasta carbonara at $11.95, or the delicious catch-of-the-day for $17.95 *(opakapaka* sautéed in a marsala sauce is a standout). For reservations call 667-2211, ext. 43.

Nanatomi's

A newly opened Japanese restaurant in Kaanapali. At the first red light from Lahaina turn left, and it's on the right upstairs from the pro shop, tel. 667-7902. On Friday and Saturday night they have live entertainment. All other nights a sushi chef from Japan entertains with his dexterous hands at the 15-seat sushi bar. Open for breakfast, lunch, and dinner featuring an early-bird breakfast special from 7 to 8:30 a.m. for $1.99, or eggs Benedict, $5.75, or homemade buttermilk pancakes for $2.75. Lunch is from 11 a.m. to 3 p.m.—with a wide selection of sandwiches under $6, Korean ribs, $5.75, or a chef salad for $5.75. The dinner menu has a wide variety of *don buri,* meaning everything from fish to pork served in a bowl of rice. A holdover from when Nanatomi's was a Mexican restaurant is their happy hour, featuring large, stiff margaritas. You can come here to get bombed Mexican style, lounge Hawaiian style, and eat Japanese style.

Luigi's
This is one of three locations for Luigi's and used to be Apple Annie's. Located just off the Kaanapali Parkway as you turn into Kaanapali from the Honoapiilani Highway. Pizza prices start at $5.99 for a small one-item to $21.49 for a large smothered with toppings, or you can nibble a salad for only $2.99. Pasta ranges from $7.99 for a marinara sauce, to $10.99 for bolognese. Full-course meals include scallops Luigi for $14.99, and steak Luigi for $17.99. This is a family-oriented restaurant. Don't expect food like mama used to make, but is not bad for adopted Italians. For information and reservations call 661-3160.

Of special interest to those vacationing in condos who want to eat in but don't want to cook is **Chicken Express,** downstairs from Luigi's. They offer a takeout service with pizza, barbecued ribs, and chicken. Dinners are as little as $5.99 for three pieces of chicken, biscuits, potatoes, slaw, and salad, tel. 661-4500 (no delivery charge in the Kaanapali area).

Cook's At The Beach
You'll be surprised to find how reasonable this open-air restaurant at the deluxe Westin Maui can be, especially their evening barbecue buffet. Regular menu selections include various seafood platters for only $12.75, and a selection of pasta or tempura for under $10. The buffet is the best deal at $16.75, from which you can choose grilled steaks, chicken, and fresh catch-of-the-day. The salad bar is all you can eat, and live music soothes as the sun dips into the sea. The restaurant opens at 6:30 a.m. with a breakfast buffet for $13.75, lunch 11:30 a.m., and dinner from 6 to 9 p.m. For information call 667-2525, free valet parking.

Royal Lahaina Resort
You have no less than three establishments from which to choose, plus a luau. Follow your nose nightly to the Luau Gardens, where the biggest problem after the Polynesian Review is standing up after eating mountains of traditional food. Adults $39.95, children under 12 $19, reservations tel. 661-3611. **Moby Dick's** is a seafood restaurant open for dinner only, tel. 661-3611. Entrees are reasonably priced for around $15, but you pay for all the extras like soup and salad, which can push your bill to $20 or more. Royal Ocean Terrace is open daily for breakfast, lunch, and dinner, offering a breakfast buffet and better-than-average salad bar. Sunday brunch from 9 a.m. until 2 p.m. is a winner, tel. 661-3611. **Chopsticks** is a "dinner-hour only" restaurant that serves a variety of dishes, almost like dim sum, all under $6.95.

Swan Court
You don't come here to eat, you come here to dine, peasant! Anyone who has been enraptured by those old movies where couples regally glide down a central staircase to make their grand entrance will have his or her fantasies come true. Although expensive, you get your money's worth with attention to detail; prosciutto is served with papaya, ginger butter with the fresh catch-of-the-day, and pineapple chutney with the oysters. The wine list is a connoisseur's delight. The Swan Court offers a sumptuous breakfast/ brunch buffet daily from 6:30 a.m. It's $12.95 per person, and worth the price for the view alone. Save this one for a very special evening. Located in the Hyatt Regency, daily breakfast and dinner, tel. 667-7474.

Spats II is also at the Hyatt, tel. 667-7474, dinner only. They specialize in Italian food, with the average entree around $16. At night Spats becomes a disco, and fancy duds are in order.

Lahaina Provision Co., tel. 667-7474, could only survive with a name like that because it's at the Hyatt. Regular broiled fare, but you get a bowl of ice cream and are free to go hog-wild with chocolate toppings at their famous chocoholic bar. Guaranteed to make you repent all your sins!

Discovery Room

Located at the Sheraton, tel. 661-0031, open daily for breakfast and dinner. Basic American food like baked chicken, well prepared with all the trimmings, for $20. Entertainment is offered at dinner and at the 9:30 p.m. cocktail show. The **Aloha Luau** uncovers its *imu* daily at 5:30 p.m. beachside at the Sheraton, adults $36, children $19. The luau features Chief Faa, a fire/knife dancer, rum punch, Hawaiian arts and games, and a Polynesian review. For reservations call 667-9564.

Lokelani

At the Maui Marriott, tel. 667-1200, dinner only, from 6 p.m. Full dinners such as sautéed catch-of-the-day are served with all trimmings from $14. Also, here is **Nikko's Japanese Steak House,** tel. 667-1200, dinner from 6 p.m. No cheap imports here; prices are high, but the Japanese chef works right at your table slicing meats and vegetables quicker than you can say "samurai." An expensive but fun meal.

Kaanapali Beach Hotel Restaurant

The hotel might be fancy but the restaurant is down to earth. Good old cafeteria style American food. Dinner specials are only $5. Daily breakfast, lunch, and dinner, tel. 661-0011.

Whaler's Villge

This shopping mall has a half dozen or so dining establishments. You can find everything from pizza and frozen yogurt to lobster tail. Prices range from bargain to moderate. An up-and-comer is **Leilani's.** Their selections go from surf to turf. They offer famous Azeka ribs for $10.95, a sushi bar, and a daily dinner special from 5 to 6:30 p.m. for $8.50. This includes entree and soup or salad. Call 661-4495. **El Crab Catcher** is a well-established restaurant featuring seafood, with a variety of crab dishes, steaks, and chops. They have a sunken bar and swimming pool with the beach only a stride or two away. Desserts are special here from $10. Popular, so reserve at tel. 661-4423.

The **Rusty Harpoon,** previously a "do-it-yourself" broiler, has remodeled and changed its image. They offer a completly new menu and pleasing atmosphere. Piano music at night and popular with younger set. Lunch is from 11:30 a.m. to 3 p.m., dinner from 5-10 p.m. **Yami Yogurt** sells wholesome, well-made sandwiches for $3 and under. Salads, too, and yogurt, of course. No seating, but plenty of spots outside, tel. 661-8843. **Ricco's Deli** makes hefty sandwiches for under $4. Their mini-pizzas make a good inexpensive lunch, tel. 669-6811.

Chico's, tel. 667-2777, has a special happy hour from 4 to 6 p.m., when deluxe nachos, usually $5.95, are only $1, and all other menu items are $1 off; drinks are the same price. "Cinco de Chico's" is a special offered the 5th of every month, when you get all items at 50% off. Chico's offers a pleasant atmosphere in a cool stucco setting with plenty of cooling breezes to counterbalance the fiery-hot dishes.

ENTERTAINMENT

If you're out for a night of fun and frivolity, Kaanapali will keep you hopping. The dinner shows accompanying the luau at the Hyatt Regency feature pure island entertainment. "Drums of the Pacific" is a musical extravaganza that you would expect from the Hyatt. There are torch-lit processions and excitingly choreographed production numbers, with all the hula-skirted *wahines* and *malo*-clad *kanes* that you could imagine. Flames add drama to the setting and the grand finale is a fire dance. At both shows you're dined and entertained by mid-evening.

Those with dancing feet can boogie the night away at the Hyatt's **Spats II.** There is a dress code and plenty of room for those "big dippers" on this very large dance floor. Practice your waltzes for the outdoor **Pavilion Courtyard** at the Hyatt. The **Banana Moon** at the Marriott offers the best of both worlds—dance music and quiet, candlelit corners for romance. Most hotels, restaurants, and lounges offer some sort of music. Often it's a local combo singing Hawaiian favorites, or a pianist tinkling away in the background.

SHOPPING

Kaanapali provides a varied shopping scene: the **Whaler's Village Mall,** which is affordable; the **Maui Marriott** for some distinctive purchases; and the **Hyatt Regency,** where most people get financial jitters even window-shopping.

Whaler's Village Mall And Museum

This unique outdoor mall doubles as quite a passable museum, with showcases filled with items, mostly from the whaling days, accompanied by informative descriptions. You can easily find anything here that you might need. Some of the shops are: **Lahaina Scrimshaw Factory,** tel. 661-4034, for fine examples of scrimshaw and other art objects from affordable to expensive. **Liberty House,** tel. 661-4451, for the usual department store items. **Ka Honu Gift Gallery,** tel. 661-0137, for a large selection of arts and crafts inspired by the islands. Selections are wide and varied at **Waldenbooks** on the lower level of the mall, tel. 661-8638, open daily 9 a.m. to 9:30 p.m. The bookstore has it all from light mysteries to read on the beach to travel books to guide you happily around the island. **The Eyecatcher** will take care of your eyes with shades from $150 Revos to $5 cheapies. There are many other shops tucked away here and there. They come and go with regularity.

A fascinating new shop is **Lahaina Printsellers and Engravings,** tel. 667-7617, open daily 8:30 a.m. to 10:30 p.m. The shop features all original engravings, drawings, maps, charts, and naturalist sketches ranging in age from 150 to 400 years, each with an authenticity label. The collection comes from all over the world, but the Hawaiiana collection is amazing in its depth, with many works featuring a nautical theme; reminiscent of the amazing explorers who opened the Pacific. The Lahaina Printsellers, although new as a store, have been collecting for over 15 years, and are the largest purveyor of material relating to Captain Cook in the entire Pacific Basin. Prices range from $25 for the smallest antique print up to $15,000 for a rare museum-quality work.

The Hyatt Regency Mall

Off the main lobby and surrounding the gardens are a number of exclusive shops. They're high-priced, but their offerings are first class. Call 667-7421 and ask for the store of your choice. **Elephant Walk** specializes in primitive art such as tribal African masks and carved wooden statues. **Gold Point's** name says it all with baubles, trinkets, bracelets, and rings all in gold. **Sandal Tree** has footwear for men and women, with the emphasis on sandals. **Mark Christopher** is a series of shops selling jewelry, glassware, fabrics, and beachwear.

Maui Marriott Mall

The main store here is a **Liberty House,** tel. 667-6142, with the emphasis on clothing. The **Maui Sun and Surf,** tel. 667-9302, is a well-stocked dive and swimwear store where you'll find everything from visors to top-notch snorkeling equipment; **Friendship Store's** art objects, clothing, silks, and goods are all from the Republic of China. There are also women's stores and jewelry shops.

Center Art Galleries

In the Kaanapali area the Center Art Galleries have showrooms at the Hyatt, Westin, and Marriott. All are definitely worth a visit even if you only intend to browse. The art selections are superb and varied. Usually you'll find works by celebrity artists, like Tony Curtis portraying his fascination with Marilyn Monroe, Red Skelton's collection of the liquid faces of heart-melting clowns, and Anthony Quinn with his bold van Gogh style. Fine artists include original Rembrandt etchings, and a collection of Chagall's work. Some contemporary artists on display include Margaret Keene looking at the world with her distinctive "big eyes," Bill Mack with his bonded epoxy resins creating three-dimensional sculptures, and Maui's Chris Lassen with his fantastic suboceanic views of reality, capturing the emotions of the islands in his amazing use of color. Jan Parker, now living on Kauai, who does beautiful impressionism, almost like a macro-pointillism, is featured at the gallery. Most pieces are quite expensive, ranging from around $300, but you should go just to see the state of the arts in Hawaii.

Westin Maui Mall

Stroll a series of exclusive boutiques just left of the main lobby. Fine women's apparel is available at **Collections,** or you can purchase a superb diamond at **Edward Thomas Jewels.**

Beachside Casuals

You'll find a specialized boutique geared toward children located at the Kaanapali Shore. It's small, but jammed like a 12-year-old's closet. They feature hand-picked fashions, resortwear, toys, swimsuits, books, mementos, and even snorkel gear. Big people can choose from a few racks, rent a video, or have those special photos developed in 24 hours. Open daily from 9 a.m. to 9 p.m.

SERVICES AND INFORMATION

Banks

Most larger hotels can help with some banking needs, especially with the purchasing or cashing of traveler's checks.

Medical

Dr. Ben Azman maintains an office at the Whaler's Village, tel. 667-9721, or after hours tel. 244-3728.

Camera Needs

Shops are: **Makai Camera** in the Whaler's Village; **Hawaiian Vision** and **Sandy's Camera** in the Royal Lahaina complex; **Island Camera** in the Sheraton.

Laundromat

The Washerette Clinic is located in the Sheraton.

Information

For a complete source of information on all aspects of the Kaanapali area, contact Kaanapali Beach Operators Association, Box 616, Kaanapali, HI 96761, tel. 661-3271.

HONOKOWAI AND VICINITY

You head for Honokowai and Kahana if you want to enjoy Maui's west coast and not spend a bundle of money. They're not quite as pretty as Kaanapali or Kapalua, but proportionate to the money you'll save, you come out ahead. To get there, travel along the Honoapiilani Highway, take Lower Honoapiilani Highway through Honokowai, and continue on it to Kahana.

Beaches

Honokowai Beach Park is right in Honokowai town just across from the Food Pantry. Here you have a large lawn with palm trees and picnic tables, but a small beach. The water is shallow and tame—good for tots. The swimming is not as nice as at Kaanapali, but take a dip after shopping. Snorkeling is fair, and you can get through a break in the reef at the west end. **Kahana Beach** is near the Kahana Beach Resort; park across the street. Nothing spectacular, but the protected small beach is good for tots. There's a great view of Molokai and the beach is never crowded.

ACCOMMODATIONS

At last count there were well over three dozen condos and apartment complexes in the three

miles encompassing Honokowai and Kahana. There are plenty of private homes out here as well which give you a good cross-section of Hawaiian society. A multimillion-dollar spread may occupy a beach, while out in the bay is a local fisherman with his beat-up old boat trying to make a few bucks for the day. Many of the condos built out here were controversial. Locals refused to work on some because they were on holy ground, and a few actually experienced bad luck jinxes as they were being built. The smarter owners called in *kahuna* to bless the ground and the disturbances ceased.

Paki Maui Resort

Situated between Kaanapali and Kapalua at 3615 Lower Honoapiilani Hwy., Lahaina, HI 96761, tel. 669-8235, (800) 922-7866 Mainland, (800) 342-1551 Hawaii, this excellent-value condo presents airy and bright rooms with sweeping panoramas of the Lahaina Roads. Well-appointed studios begin at $109, to $160 for a two-bedroom apartment for up to four people, additional guests $10. Amenities include maid service, a/c, cable TV, pool with spa, and complete kitchens. Every unit has a private lanai overlooking a gem of a courtyard. You can save money by getting a garden-view studio without sacrificing that delightful feeling that you are in the tropics. Although the Paki Maui is in downtown Honokowai, it feels secluded the moment you walk onto this property, which forms a little oasis of tranquility. There is no sand beach fronting the condo, but the snorkeling along the reef is excellent.

Sands Of Kahana

Your pleasure begins when you spot the distinctive blue tile roofs of this gracious complex, which forms a central courtyard area at 4299 Honoapiilani Hwy., Lahaina, HI 96761, tel. 669-0400, (800) 367-6046 Mainland, (800) 663-1118 Canada. The condo boasts a tennis and pro shop and a **Beach Club Restaurant** (see same under "Kaanapali—Food"). The sandy-bottomed beach fronting the property is very safe and perfect for swimming and sunbathing. The Sands of Kahana gives you extraordinarily large units for the money, and to sweeten the pot, they're beautiful and well appointed. One-bedroom units from $189, two-bedroom units from $245 are massive with two lanais, two baths with a tub built for two, walk-in closets, and great ocean views. Each unit offers a gourmet kitchen, cable TV (free HBO), and daily maid service. The property, with pool, three tennis courts, putting green, and spa, exudes a sense of peace and quiet, and although there are plenty of guests, you never feel crowded. This is where you come when you want to get away from it all, but still be within reach of the *action*.

Honokawai Palms

At 3666 Lower Honoapiilani Hwy., Lahaina, HI 96761 (near Honokowai), tel. 669-6130, this condo is an old standby for budget travelers. The manager's office is just near the pool. Amenities include ping pong, BBQ grills, book exchange, color TVs. Older but not run-down, no tinsel and glitter, but neat and clean. A coin laundry is on the premises. Fully furnished with kitchen, full bath, and queen-size hide-a-bed. All units are recently upgraded with new carpets, drapes, bedspreads, and ceiling fans. Forget about the ocean-view rooms, which don't have a great view anyway. Save money by taking the standard rooms. You can get a one-bedroom ocean-view unit with lanai for $65, two-bedroom with lanai but no view $65, additional person after two

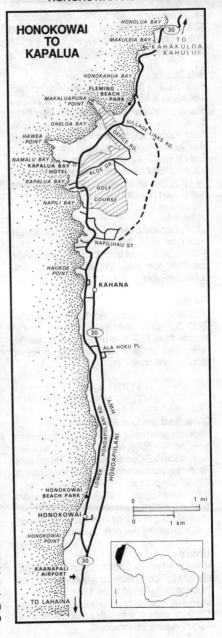

$6. There are weekly and monthly discounts, $200 deposit required, no credit cards accepted, three-night minimum; maid service is extra. This condo is clean and adequate.

Hale Ono Loa

Hale Ono Loa has peak- and low-season rates with about a $15 difference. Low-season one-bedroom, one to two days, garden-view $115, ocean-view $125, with prices rising as you ascend floors, reduction for longer stays. Offers stay, fly, and drive packages at varying rates; call Real Hawaii Condo vacations at (800) 367-5108. At 3823 Lower Honoapiilani Hwy., Lahaina, HI 96761, tel. 669-6362. Complete kitchens, partial maid service, pool.

Valley Isle

4327 Honoapiilani Hwy., (Kahana) Lahaina, HI 96761, tel. (800) 367-6092 Mainland, on Maui 669-4777. Rooms from $70 plus restaurant, cocktails, pool, shop, and maid service on request; five-night minimum.

Noelani

Located at 4095 Lower Honoapiilani Hwy., tel. (800) 367-6030, on Maui tel. 669-8374, it has studios from $77, one-bedroom $97, weekly rates. Two pools, BBQ area, fully equipped kitchens, and color TVs.

FOOD AND ENTERTAINMENT

China Boat Seafood Restaurant

Recently opened at 4474 Lower Honoapiilani Hwy., tel. 669-5089, open daily 5 to 10 p.m., just north of the A-Z Convenience Store on the right. Reasonably priced with deluxe dinners for two at $21.50 per person. House specialties range from *moo shu* pork at $9.50 to a wide assortment of appetizers and soups for under $5; with a typically large Chinese menu offering seafood, beef, vegetables, and pork, all can be satisfied.

Ricco's

At the **5-A Rent a Space Mall** in Kahana, tel. 669-6811, Ricco's features a good old-time deli featuring fresh-baked pizza. Large sandwiches for $4 and lunches to go, picnic supplies, spare ribs, beer, wine, and friendly service. A good inexpensive takeout restaurant.

Dollies

Located at 4310 Honoapiilani Hwy. (Kahana), tel. 669-0266, open from breakfast to late evening with sandwiches, pizza, and food to go. Deliveries to condos! Good food and fair prices, like turkey or roast beef with swiss and jack for $5.95.

Erik's Seafood Grotto

At 4242 Lower Honoapiilani Hwy., second floor of Kahana Villa, tel. 669- 4806. Open daily for dinner 5 to 10 p.m. Their very good fish selection, Sunset Special, is from 5-6 p.m., $11.95; menu changes daily. Dinners include chowder, bread basket, and potatoes or rice. Most dinners run $16-19 with a good selection of appetizers. Erik's is known to have *the* best selection of fresh fish on Maui. This is a quality restaurant with fair prices.

Kahana Keyes

Located at the Valley Isle Resort, tel. 669-8071. Dinner only. Music from 7:30 p.m. to 12:30 a.m. seven nights a week. Early-bird specials from 5 to 7 p.m. include whole lobster and prime rib, $13.95, steak and crab, $11.95, prime rib, $9.95, or *mahi mahi* for $9.95. They're well known for their salad bar and fresh fish. The Kahana Keyes Restaurant is the only show in town around here, and luckily it ain't bad! Local bands perform all types of music from rock to Hawaiian, and the intimate dance floor is hardly ever crowded.

SHOPPING AND SERVICES

Honokowai Food Pantry

The only real place west of Lahaina to shop for groceries and sundries. Located on Lower Honoapiilani Hwy. in Honokowai, tel. 669-6208, open daily from 8 a.m. to 9 p.m. The prices are just about right at this supermarket. Condo convenience stores in the area are good in a pinch but charge way too much. Stock up here; it's worth the drive.

The **Honokowai P.O.** is at the Honokowai Food Pantry. Never busy, this full-service post office accepts packages.

Convenience Stores

A to Z, next to the Hoolani Condominium in Kahana, is open 7 a.m. to 11 p.m. A quick-shop store with a good selection of groceries, liquors, and sundries at slightly inflated prices. Valley Isle Resort has the **Kahana Pantry,** a mini-mart and grocery store selling everything from beer to sunglasses. The **ABC Store,** in Honokowai, hours 6:30 a.m. to 11 p.m., tel. 669-0271, is a mini-market selling everything from resortwear to wine.

5-A Rent A Space Mall
A new mall has opened in Honokowai called 5-A Rent a Space. Here you'll find **Ricco's Pizza** (see above). The mall also includes **Maui Physicians,** a video store, and a one-hour photo.

The most interesting shop is **Posters Maui,** open 9 to 5 every day, tel. 669-5404, where you can get a vibrant visual memento of Maui, framed and ready for your wall back home. Well-known island artists include Robert Nelson, Anthony Casay, and photographer Robert Talbot, all with an oceanic feel. An upcoming new artist featured by Posters Maui is Richard Field, who has clued into the soul of Maui. He creates paintings turned to posters in the "realistic fantastic" mode, such as *Haleakala Sunrise.*

Annie And Bob's Rental
Located in Honokowai. tel. 669-0027, they rent on a 24-hour basis. Boogie boards and snorkel gear are $5 ($20 weekly), surfboards $10-15, mopeds for four hours, $15, eight hours $20, or $25 for 24 hours, insurance included.

KAPALUA AND NAPILI—THE WEST END

Kapalua sits like a crown atop Maui's head. One of the newest areas on Maui to be developed, it's been nicely done. Out here is the **Kapalua Bay Resort,** golf, horseback riding, and terrific beaches.

BEACHES AND SPORTS

Some of the very best beaches that Maui has to offer are clustered in this area. The following listing proceeds from south to north.

Napili Bay
There are rights of way to this perfect, but condo-lined, beach. Look for beach access signs along Napili Place near the Napili Shores, Napili Surf Beach Resort, and on Hui Drive near the Napili Sunset and Napili Bay condos. They're difficult to spot, but once on the beach there's better-than-average swimming, snorkeling, and a good place for beginning surfers.

Kapalua Beach
Along Lower Honoapiilani Road look for access just past the Napili Kai Beach Club. Park in the public lot and follow the path through the tunnel to the beach. Another beautiful crescent beach that's popular, though usually not overcrowded. The well-formed reef here has plenty of fish for snorkeling. Also here are restrooms, showers, and beach concessions.

D.T. Fleming Beach Park
One of Maui's best. Clearly marked just past mile marker #31 on Lower Honoapiilani along Route 30. Here you'll find parking, showers, and BBQ grills, and excellent swimming except in winter, when there's a pounding surf. Fair snorkeling and good surfing.

Oneloa Beach
Located a short mile past Fleming's, Oneloa is a small sandy beach down a steep path. Those who brave it can camp without a hassle from the officials.

Mokuleia Beach
Also known as "Slaughterhouse." You can spot it because the R.V. Deli, a lunch wagon, is usually parked here, about 200-300 yards after mile marker #32. This beach has great bodysurfing, but terribly dangerous currents in the winter when the surf is rough. Be careful. Follow the trail to the left for the beach. The path straight ahead takes you to a rocky lava flow. The entire area is a marinelife conservation district and the underwater life is fabulous.

Honolua Bay
Just past Mokuleia Bay heading north, look for a dirt road, then park. Some can try the road, but it's very rugged. The bay is good for swimming, snorkeling, and especially surfing. Many people stay the night without much problem.

Sports

The following are offered in the Kapalua area: **Kapalua Bay Golf Club,** Bay Course, par 72, $75 greens fee and a mandatory $15 cart; **Kapalua Bay Village Course,** par 71, $75 fee and a $15 cart. **Tennis** is found at the Napili Kai Beach Club, $9 guests; Kapalua Bay Hotel **Tennis Garden,** free to guests, $4 others, dress code, tel. 669-5677. There's **horseback riding** at the Rainbow Ranch; see "Sports" in the main Introduction for details.

ACCOMMODATIONS

Napili, just south of Kapalua Bay, sports a string of condos and a hotel or two. Almost all front the beach, which is hardly ever crowded in this still largely undeveloped area of Maui.

Napili Point Condominium

The Napili Point Condominium Apartments is one of the most beautifully situated complexes on Maui. The low-rise complex sits on its own promontory of black lava separating Kahana and Napili. Located at 5295 Honoapiilani Hwy., Napili, HI 96761, tel. 669-9222, (800) 922-

7866. The reef fronting the condo is home to a colorful display of reef fish and coral, providing some of the best snorkeling on the west end. Not graced with a sand beach (100 yards north along a path), nature however was generous in another way. Each room commands an unimpeded panorama with a breathtaking sunset view of Lanai and Molokai. You get a deluxe room for a standard price. Because of the unique setting, little development has occurred in the area, and the condo is very secluded though convenient to shops and stores. The two-story buildings offer fully furnished one- and two-bedroom units from a very affordable $129 to $185, with full kitchens, washers and dryers, walk-in closets, and large dressing and bath areas. Up to four people, extra person $10, and this includes maid service, two pools, and a family plan. Two-bedroom units on the second floor include a loft with its own sitting area. Floor-to-ceiling windows frame the living still life of sea and surf so you can enjoy the view from every part of the apartment.

Kapalua Bay Hotel And Villas

This, like other grand hotels, is more than a place to stay; it's an experience. The main lobby is partially open and accented with an enormous skylight. Plants trail from the ceiling. Below is a tropical terrace and restaurant and all colors are soothing and subdued. Although relaxing, this hotel is the kind of a place where if you don't wear an evening gown to go to the bathroom, you feel underdressed. In January 1988 renovations on this upscale hotel were completed to the tune of $20,000, per room which added ultra-luxury details like silk wallpaper in the already beautiful suites. The least expensive room in the hotel itself is one with a garden view at $185. The villas with a mountain view are $275, and climb rapidly to the $375-475 range. You can choose the "American plan," consisting of breakfast and dinner, for an extra $40. You must make a three-nights' deposit, refundable only with 14 days' notice. There are five restaurants in the complex and magnificent golf at the Kapalua Villa Club. Contact the hotel at One Bay Drive, Kapalua, HI 96761, tel. 669-5656, (800) 367-8000.

Napili Kai Beach Club

At 5900 Honoapiilani Rd., Lahaina, HI 96761, tel. (800) 367-5030, on Maui tel. 669-6271. The

Napili Kai Beach Club, the dream-come-true of now deceased Jack Millar, was built before regulations forced properties back from the beach. The setting couldn't be more idyllic, with the beach a crescent moon here with gentle wave action. The bay itself is slated to become a swim only area with no pleasure craft allowed. Jack Millar's ashes are buried near the restaurant under a flagpole bearing the U.S. and Canadian flags. It's expensive at $150 per studio to $475 for a luxury suite, but you do have a kitchenette, complimentary snorkel gear, putting green, jacuzzi, croquet, and daily tea party. There are five pools, putting greens, tennis courts, and the Kapalua Bay Golf Course just a nine-iron away. All rooms have Japanese touches and are complete with shoji screens. There's dancing and entertainment at their famous Restaurant of the Maui Moon, which has changed its name to the Sea House (see below).

Napili Bay

At 33 Hui Drive, Lahaina, HI 96761, tel. (800) 367-7042, on Maui 669-6044. For this neck of the woods, it's reasonably priced from $90 (four people) for a studio off the ocean. All have queen-size beds, lanai, full kitchens, maid service, and laundromat. No minimum stay.

Napili Surf Beach Resort

Located at 50 Napili Pl., Napili, HI 96761, tel. 669-8002, these are full condo units that operate as a hotel. Located at the south end of Napili Beach. Studios from $84, discount is 12% for 28 days or longer, 15% for 45 days. Preferred views and one-bedroom units from $128, $300 deposit. The grounds are not luxurious but nicely manicured with plenty of pride put into the property. Very clean rooms with full kitchens have their own lanai and open up onto the central grounds area with the sea in the background. Two pools, fantastic beach, maid service, and laundry. The adjacent **Napili Puamala** is a bit cheaper.

FOOD

The Grill And Bar

Don't underestimate this excellent restaurant (lunch and dinner), tel. 669-5653, at the Kapalua Golf Course, which is not nearly as utilitarian as

its name suggests. What's more, local people consider it one of the most consistently good and affordable restaurants in the area. The soothing main room is richly appointed with *koa* wood, and large windows frame a sweeping view of the super-green fairways of the golf course. The lunch menu offers a side of pasta for $8.95, or a large salad for only $3.50. Dinner entrees are tempting, with fettuccine pescatore from $16.95, to filet mignon and lobster for $24.95, and plenty of selections for around $20.95. To relax and soak up the scenery you can order dessert like amaretto creme caramel at $2.95, or sip wine selected from an extensive list. The best restaurant for the money in the area!

Kapalua Bay Resort Restaurants

There's a complete menu of restaurants, so you can choose from sandwich shops to elegant dining. **Market Cafe**, found in the "Shops" area, tel. 669-4888, has foods from around the world including wines, meats, cheeses, and pastries. All kinds of gourmet items, with delicious but expensive sandwiches cost from $7. **Bay Club,** at the resort entrance, tel. 669-8008, offers daily lunch 11:30 a.m. to 2 p.m., dinner 5:30 to 9:30 p.m. on a promontory overlooking the beach and Molokai in the distance. The pool is right here. Dress code; expect to spend $25 for a superbly prepared entree. **Plantation Veranda** offers daily dinner only, with varying hours, tel. 669-5656. The atmosphere is highlighted by natural woods, flowers everywhere, and original paintings. An extensive wine list complements magnificent entrees by Chef Randolph Pidd. Formal dining.

Napili Shores Resort

Two restaurants are located at this resort, at 5315 Honoapiilani Hwy. about one mile before Kapalua town. **Orient Express,** tel. 669-8077, is open daily except Mon. for dinner only from 5:30 to 10 p.m. Serving Thai and Chinese food with a flair for spices, duck salad and stuffed chicken wings are a specialty. Early-bird specials before 7 p.m., and take-out available.

The Sea House

At the Napili Kai Beach Club, 5900 Honoapiilani Rd., Lahaina, on Maui tel. 669-6271. The Restaurant of the Maui Moon, perhaps the nicest-sounding name for a restaurant on Maui, has changed to the The Sea House. On Sunday there is a breakfast lunch and you can order eggs Benedict or fresh blueberry pancakes. If you just want to soak up the rays and gorgeous view of Napili Bay, you can wear your swimwear and have a cool drink or light fare on the **Sea Breeze Terrace.** This newly opened addition was a stroke of luck after the federal government redid an old flood project ditch and allowed the hotel to build on the newly reclaimed land. Inside the semi-open-air restaurant appetizers range from sliced Maui onions and tomatoes from $3.95 or a bucket of little-neck clams for $8.95. Soups and salads from a reasonable $2.95 to $13.95 for a cold seafood salad with shrimp and scallops. Dinner choices are fresh catch (priced daily), beef teriyaki, $14.95, and fillet and lobster. A full wine list includes selections from California and France. Daily for breakfast 8 to 11 a.m., lunch 12 to 3 p.m., and dinner 6 to 9 p.m., reservations suggested. There is Hawaiian music nightly and a wonderful show put on by children who have studied their heritage under the guidance of the Napili Kai Foundation.

SHOPPING

Kapalua Resort And Shops

A cluster of exclusive shops service the resort. **Andrade,** tel. 669-5266, with fine apparel for men and women, has been an island tradition for 60 years; **Superwhale Children's Boutique,** tel. 669-5282, has clothes and distinctive quilts. At **Kapalua Shop,** tel. 669-4172, if you want to show off that you've at least been to the Kapalua Resort, all items of clothing sport the butterfly logo. **Mandalay Imports,** tel. 669-6170, has a potpourri of silks and cottons from the East, especially Thailand. Visit **La Perle,** tel. 669-8466, for pearls, diamonds, and other jewels; **Distant Drums,** tel. 669-5522, sports an amazing collection of offbeat artifacts from Asia.

Whaler's General Store

At Napili Bay, tel. 669-6773. A well-stocked little store and a known landmark, it's good for last-minute items, with fairly good prices for where it is. You can pick up picnic items and sandwiches. Next door is **Snorkel Bob's,** tel. 669-9603, where you can rent snorkel equipment (prescription masks available), and boogie boards for only $15 per week—one of the best prices on Maui (also in Kihei). **Napili Shores Condo Store** is mainly a convenience store for last-minute items.

oma'o

EAST MAUI

KIHEI

Kihei ("Shoulder Cloak") takes it on the chin whenever anti-development groups need an example to wag their finger at. For the last two decades, construction along both sides of Kihei Road, which runs the length of town, has continued unabated. Since there was no central planning for the development, mostly high-rise condos and a few hotels were built wherever they could be squeezed in: some are lovely, some are crass. There's hardly a spot left where you can get an unobstructed view of the beach as you drive along. That's the "slam" in a nutshell. The good news is that Kihei has so much to recommend it that if you refrain from becoming fixated on this one regrettable feature, you'll thoroughly enjoy yourself, and save money, too.

The developers went "hyper" here because it's perfect as a tourist area. The weather can be counted on to be the best on all of Maui. Haleakala, looming just behind the town, catches rainclouds before they drench Kihei. Days of blue skies and sunshine are taken for granted. On the other side of the condos and hotels are gorgeous beaches, every one open to the public. Once on the beachside, the condos don't matter anymore. The views out to sea are unobstructed vistas of Lanai, Kahoolawe, Molokini, and West Maui, which gives the illusion of being a separate island. The buildings are even a buffer to the traffic noise! Many islanders make Kihei their home, so there is a feeling of real community here. It's quieter than Lahaina, with fewer restaurants and not as much action, but for sun and surf activities, this place has it all.

Sights

The six-mile stretch bordered by beach and mountain that makes up Kihei has always been an important landing spot on Maui. Hawaiian war canoes moored here many times during countless skirmishes over the years; later, Western navigators such as Capt. George Vancouver found this stretch of beach to be a congenial anchorage. A totem pole across from the **Maui Lu Hotel** marks the spot where Vancouver landed. During WW II, when a Japanese invasion was feared, Kihei was considered a likely spot for an amphibious attack. Overgrown pillboxes and rusting tank traps are still found along the beaches. Many look like cement porcupines

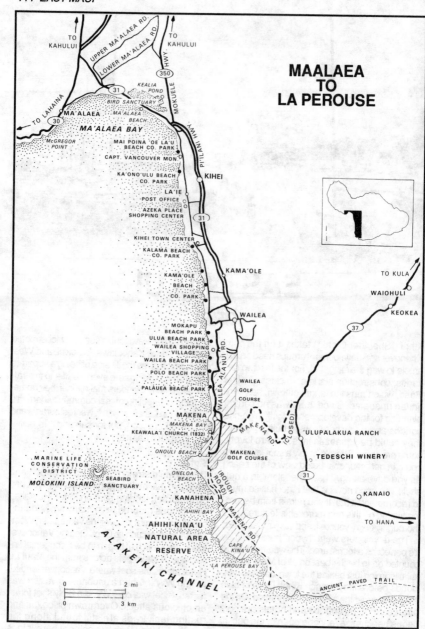

MAALAEA TO LA PEROUSE

TO KAHULUI

UPPER MA'ALAEA RD.

LOWER MA'ALAEA RD.

TO KAHULUI

350

MOKUELE HWY.

Kealia Pond

BIRD SANCTUARY

PI'ILANI HWY.

31

MA'ALAEA BEACH

TO LAHAINA

30

MA'ALAEA

MA'ALAEA BAY

McGregor Point

MAI POINA 'OE IA'U BEACH CO. PARK

CAPT. VANCOUVER MON.

KA'ONO'ULU BEACH CO. PARK

KIHEI

LA'IE

POST OFFICE

AZEKA PLACE SHOPPING CENTER

31

KIHEI TOWN CENTER

KALAMA BEACH CO. PARK

KAMA'OLE

KAMA'OLE BEACH CO. PARK

WAILEA

MOKAPU BEACH PARK

ULUA BEACH PARK

WAILEA SHOPPING VILLAGE

WAILEA BEACH PARK

POLO BEACH PARK

PALAUEA BEACH PARK

WAILEA ALA NUI RD.

WAILEA GOLF COURSE

TO KULA

WAIOHULI

KEOKEA

37

MAKENA

MAKENA BAY

KEAWALA'I CHURCH (1832)

ONOULI BEACH

MAKENA RD. (CLOSED)

MAKENA GOLF COURSE

'ULUPALAKUA RANCH

TEDESCHI WINERY

MARINE LIFE CONSERVATION DISTRICT

MOLOKINI ISLAND

SEABIRD SANCTUARY

ONELOA BEACH

KANAHENA

AHIHI-KINA'U NATURAL AREA RESERVE

AHIHI BAY

MAKENA RD. (ROUGH ROAD)

31

KANAIO

TO HANA

CAPE KINA'U

LA PEROUSE BAY

ALAEKIKI CHANNEL

ANCIENT PAVED TRAIL

0   2 mi

0   3 km

with iron quills. Kihei is a natural site with mountain and ocean vistas. It's great for beachcombing down toward Maalaea, but try to get there by morning because the afternoon wind is notorious for creating minor sandstorms.

BEACHES

Maalaea Beach
Three miles of windswept sand partially backed by Kealia Pond and a bird sanctuary. Many points of access between Maalaea and Kihei along Route 31. The strong winds make it undesirable for sunning and bathing, but it's a windsurfer's dream. Also the hard-packed sand is a natural track for joggers, who are profuse in the morning and afternoon. The beachcombing and strolling are quiet and productive.

Mai Poina Oe Lau Beach Park
On Kihei's western fringe, fronting Maui Lu Hotel, this beach offers only limited paved parking, or just along the road. Showers, tables, and restrooms front the long and narrow white-sand beach which has good safe swimming but is still plagued by strong winds by early afternoon. A windsurfer's delight.

Kaonouluulu Beach Park
You'll find parking, picnic tables, showers, and BBQs here, also very safe swimming and lesser winds. A small beach but not overcrowded.

Kalama Beach Park
Located about the middle of town. More for looking and outings than beach activities, Kalama has a large lawn ending in a breakwater with little beach in summer and none in winter. Thirty-six acres of pavilions, tables, BBQ pits, volleyball, basketball, tennis courts, baseball diamond, and soccer field. Great views of Molokai and Haleakala.

Kamaole I, II, And III
These beach parks are at the south end of town near Kihei Town Center. All three have beautiful white sand, picnic tables, and all the amenities. Shopping and dining are nearby. All have lifeguards. The swimming and bodysurfing are good. III has a kiddies' playground. Snorkeling is good for beginners on the reef between II and III, where much coral and colorful reef fish abound.

ACCOMMODATIONS

The emphasis in Kihei is on condos. With keen competition among them, you can save some money while having a more "homey" vacation. Close to 100 condos, plus a smattering of vacation apartments, cottages, and even a few hotel resorts are all strung along Kihei Road. As always, you pay more for ocean views. Don't shy away from accommodations on the *mauka* side of Kihei Road. You have total access to the beach, some superior views of Haleakala, and usually you pay less money.

Hotels
The Kihei area offers two hotels that are reasonably priced and well appointed. **Maui Lu Resort,** 575 S. Kihei Rd., Kihei, HI 96753, tel. (800) 367-5124 Mainland, (800) 423-8723, ext. 250, in Canada, (800) 342-1551 Hawaii, 879-5881 Maui. This hotel attempts to preserve the good-vibe feeling of old Hawaii with its Aloha Department and its emphasis on *ohana.* An abundance of activities here include a first-class luau, tennis, a Maui-shaped pool, and tiny private beaches strung along its 30 acres. Rooms from $73, $10 extra person, include refrigerators and hot drink unit. These are mostly in the new wing toward the mountains, which is also quieter. Cottages start at $93 and are separate units with gourmet kitchens. This full-service hotel pampers you in the old Hawaiian style.

Surf and Sand Hotel, at 2980 S. Kihei Rd., Kihei, HI 96753, tel. (800) 367-5004, on Maui 879-7744. This is a very affordable and well-maintained hotel just before you get to Wailea at the south end of town. Rates are $67 standard, $78 superior, and $88 deluxe, off-season even lower! It fronts a sandy beach, and offers "room and car" specials. There's also a jacuzzi. You can't go wrong at this terrific little hotel!

Condominiums
Kamaole Sands, at 2695 S. Kihei Rd., Kihei, HI 96753, tel. 879-0666, reservations tel. (800) 922-7866. All apartments come completely furnished with full baths and kitchen. Prices are: $110-125 one- bedroom, $145-185 two-bedroom, three-bedroom $205-215; 15% discount off-season, and rental car package available. The Kamaole Sands is a full-service resort offering much more than just a place to stay. It's a

family-oriented condo not only because of the wonderful activities, but because all units are spacious and geared toward making the entire family comfortable. One-bedroom units offer 900 square feet, and two bedrooms are 1,300 square feet. The **Sandpiper Grill** serves inexpensive breakfast, lunch, and dinner featuring fresh island fish—most dinners from $9.95. Enjoy a free Polynesian show called "Drums of the Islands," with complimentary mai tais. A marine biologist visits on Wednesday and presents a slide show of the flora and fauna of Maui, and Hawaiian ladies come on Thursday to sell their locally made crafts. One of the main features of the Kamaole Sands is its wonderful tennis courts, free to guests, with a tennis instructor to help you work on the fine points of your game. The Kamaole Sands is bright, cheerful, and gives you a lot for your money.

Maui Hill is at 2881 S. Kihei Rd., Kihei, HI 96753, tel. (800) 922-7866, (800) 342-1551 Hawaii, 879-6321 Maui. If you want to rise above it all in Kihei come to this upbeat condo with a Spanish motif that sits high on a hill and commands a sweeping view of the entire area. The one-, two-, or three-bedroom suites are spacious, bright, and airy. All have ceiling fans and a/c, cable TV, daily maid service, and gourmet kitchens. Monday evenings bring a complimentary mai tai party complete with games, singing, and door prizes. A concierge service helps with your every need and arranges all sun and surf activities. The grounds are secluded, beautifully maintained, and offer a pool, tennis courts, and spa. The Maui Hill sits between Kihei and Wailea, so you get a deluxe area at reasonable prices. One-bedroom from $115 up to four people, two-bedroom from $135 up to six people, three-bedroom from $175 up to seven people.

Lihi Kai, 2121 Ili'ili Rd., Kihei, HI 96753, tel. 879-2335. These cottages are such a bargain they're often booked out by returning guests. They're not plush, there's no pool, but they're homey and clean, with little touches like banana trees growing on the property; $59 s or d daily, $294 weekly, off-season cheaper, $465 monthly, deposit required, self-service laundromat. Write the manager at the above address well in advance.

Nona Lani Cottages, 455 S. Kihei Rd., Kihei, HI 96753, tel. 879-2497. Owned and operated by Dave and Nona Kong. Clean and neat units on the *mauka* side of Kihei Road. All units have full kitchen, queen beds, and day beds with full baths. Laundry facilities, public phones, and BBQs on premises. High season $65 d, small discount for longer stays, $10 additional person. Low season $46, three-night minimum.

Sunseeker Resort, 551 S. Kihei Rd., tel. 879-1261, write Box 276, Kihei, HI 96753. Studio with kitchenette $29, one-bedroom $39, two-bedroom $50, $6 additional person. Special rates off-season and long-term. Deposit required. Not bad at all.

Nani Kai Hale, 73 N. Kihei Rd., Kihei, HI 96753, tel. (800) 367-6032, on Maui tel. 879-9120. Very affordable at $32.50 for one bedroom with bath, $47.50 for studio with kitchenette, or two-bedroom, two-bath for $95. Substantial savings during off-season. Seven-day minimum, monthly rates, children under five free. There's a good beach plus sheltered parking, pool, laundry facilities, private lanai, and BBQs on premises. Good views.

Menehune Shores, 760 S. Kihei Rd., tel. 879-5828. Write Kihei Kona Rentals, Box 556, Kihei, HI 96753. This huge condo is on the beach overlooking an ancient fishpond. The building is highlighted with Hawaiian petroglyphs. All units have an ocean view; $85-102 one-bedroom, $112 two-bedroom, $122-140 three-bedroom, five-day minimum. No credit cards. Low-season savings of 30%. Full kitchens with dishwasher, washer and dryer, and disposals. Each unit is individually owned, so furnishings vary, but the majority are well furnished. A lot for the money.

Maui Sunset, 1032 S. Kihei Rd., Kihei, HI 96753, tel. (800) 843-5880. Two large buildings contain over 200 units; some are on a time-share basis and usually have nicer furnishings. Same rate year-round based on double occupancy at $65 one-bedroom, $85 two-bath/two-bedroom, $120 three-bath/three-bedroom. Full kitchens. Pitch and putt golf green, pool, beach front, and quality tennis courts are on the premises.

Hale Kai O Kihei, 1310 Uluniu Rd., Kihei, HI 96753, tel. 879-2757. Weekly rate based on double occupancy from $345-525 (high season) for one-bedroom, $495-695 (high season) for two-bedroom with up to four people, additional person $8.50. No children under six. Pool, parking, maid service on request.

Kauhale Makai, 930 S. Kihei Rd., write Condo and Home Realty, P.O. Box 1840 Kihei, HI 96753, tel. 879-5445. Rates from $60 studio, $70 one-bedroom, $85 two-bedroom, $7.50 additional person. Swimming pool, kiddie pool, BBQs, putting green, sauna, four-day minimum.

FOOD

Inexpensive

Azeka's Snacks, Azeka Place, S. Kihei Road, is open daily except Sun., 9:30 a.m. to 4 p.m. Basically takeout, featuring $1 hamburgers and a variety of plate lunches for $4.50. Azeka's is popular with locals and terrific for picnics. Also try **The Island Deli,** stuck away in a corner of the shopping plaza, open daily 7:30 a.m. to 9 p.m., tel. 874-1087. The deli features a full range of sandwiches, including bagels and lox. A good bargain is the salad bar for only $4.95 (salad bar usually closed by 8 p.m.).

International House of Pancakes is toward the rear of Azeka Place. Open daily from 6 a.m. to midnight, Fri. and Sat. until 2 a.m. Same American standards as on the Mainland with most sandwiches and plate lunches under $7, dinners under $10, and breakfasts anytime around $5. Not exotic, but basic and filling with a good reputation in the area for inexpensive but passable fresh fish and daily specials. Try **Luigi's Pasta and Pizzeria** for live entertainment, all-you-can-eat spaghetti on Saturday for $4.99, dancing from happy hour to 7 p.m., plus early-bird specials; inexpensive but mediocre food.

Paradise Fruit Co., 1913 S. Kihei Rd., across from McDonald's. Open hours 24 daily, tel. 879-1723. This fruit and vegetable market has a top-notch snack bar offering hearty, healthy sandwiches (under $4.50), vegetarian dishes, and a good selection of large, filling salads. Try the pita melt for $4.50, and any of the smoothies. A few tables out back and a community bulletin board, definitely worth a stop! It's the only place in Kihei open all night.

Moderate

Polli's Mexican Restaurant, 101 S. Kihei Rd., tel. 879-5275. Open daily 11 a.m. to midnight. Polli's has a well-deserved reputation for good food at fair prices. Formerly vegetarian, they now serve a variety of meat and chicken dishes, but still use the finest ingredients, cold-pressed oils, and no lard or bacon in preparing their bean dishes. The decor is classical Mexican with white stucco walls and tiled floors. There's an outdoor deck area with a great sunset view. Main dishes are under and up to $14, with a la carte tostadas for $7.75. Imported beers are $3. Polli's is meticulously clean, serves large portions, and has a friendly atmosphere. For a filling and inexpensive meal, try the daily (weekdays only) lunch special at only $4.95.

La Familia is an excellent and friendly Mexican restaurant at Kai Nani Village Plaza, 2511 S. Kihei Rd., tel. 879-8824, across from Kamaloe Park II. Many dishes are under $5, made with locally grown and organic ingredients when possible, and all soups are homemade. Pleasant waitresses, good service, and personal attention by Craig, the owner. Happy hour (2 to 6 p.m., and from 10 p.m. to midnight) features traditional margaritas at $1.99, only $.99 on Fridays. Free chips and salsa! Dishes are well prepared with large portions.

Upstairs is **Kihei Prime Rib House,** open from 5 p.m., tel. 879-1954. A touch expensive with most entrees from $15-20, but this includes a well-stocked salad bar. Scrumptious appetizers like sashimi, lobster, and mushrooms are under $10 and the salad bar is only $9.95. Early-bird specials under $10 are featured from 5 to 6 p.m. and include salad bar. Children's menu. Walls are adorned with carvings by Bruce Turnbull and paintings by Sigrid, two well-known local artists. One of the best choices is rack of lamb for $19.95. There's a good wine list with selections from California to France.

The **Island Fish House,** at 1945 S. Kihei Rd., tel. 879-7771, has a very good reputation and offers early-bird specials, $10.95, from 5 to 6 p.m., that include teri chicken, New York steak, and fresh fish. Entrees include seafood salad for $18.95, shrimp Polynesian at $17.95, with beef and chicken under $19. *Pu pu* range from escargot to a sample platter for two for $15.95, with most around $6. The house specialty is the King's Platter for Two, which is two types of fresh fish, sautéed lobster, deep-fried shrimp and scallops, New York steak, and scampi, all for $64.95.

Rainbow Lagoon, at the Rainbow Mall on S. Kihei Rd., open nightly for dinner from 5 to 10 p.m., is a steak, seafood, and prime rib house. Daily early bird specials from 5 to 7 p.m. include

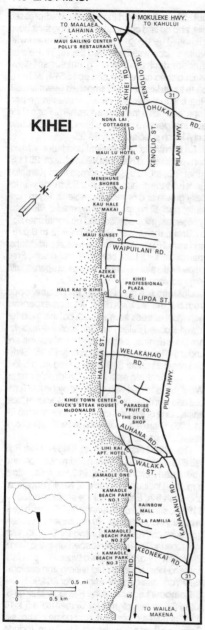

KIHEI

whole Maine lobster and prime rib for $18.95, prime rib, $18.95, and *mahi mahi*, $8.95. Try the regular selections like broiled lobster tail, $19.95, or teri steak for $16.95. They also have nightly entertainment and serve until 2 a.m., so this is a regular stop for many of the hotel and lounge workers in the area.

At the **The Kamaole Mall**, the larger mall just next door to the Rainbow Mall, you'll find three reasonably priced restaurants. **Denny's** serves food just like on the Mainland (but not open 24 hours), but with a few more island specialties. **Erik's Seafood**, tel. 879-8400, has a very good reputation for fresh fish (the biggest selection on Maui) and fair prices. The original restaurant is in Honokowai, and this is basically a clone. The **Canton Chef**, open 11 a.m. to 9:30 p.m., tel. 879-1988, is a moderately priced restaurant with the normal Chinese selections and features like Sichuan scallops with hot garlic sauce for $8.05, *kung pao* scallops, $8.05, noodles and rice dishes, $5, and chicken dishes from $5-7. Seafood is slightly more expensive, such as fresh fish with black bean sauce for $8.40.

The **Outrigger Restaurant** at the Surf and Sand has early-bird specials from $8.95. The food is acceptable, but the location is exceptional. You can have a romantic evening, or enjoy a sunset drink with a first-class view right on the water.

Silversword Golf Course Restaurant has opened at Maui's newest golf course, at 1345 Piilanai Hwy. (above and parallel to Kihei Rd.), daily for lunch 11 a.m. to 3:30 p.m., dinner from 6 to 9 p.m., with sandwiches served all day, tel. 879-0515. From the heights of the course, you get an extraordinary view, not only of the sweeping fairways, but of Kihei's coast below and the islands and mountains in the distance. The best news is that the food is very good, and the prices are unbeatable. You can order a hefty sandwich like pastrami or even lox and bagels for under $5, or a variety of salads from $4. But the best deals are the lunch entrees, like shrimp silversword, beef stroganoff, or hamburger steak for $5-6. The dinner menu is small, but again unbeatable. Choose from chicken cordon bleu $11, sautéed catfish $12.75, or choice cuts of beef under $13. Friday night brings a lobster special, and Saturday night it's rack of lamb, either for only $15 for the full meal. The dining room is basically a portico, and the elegance comes from the panoramic surroundings. A slightly different place to dine, but worth a try.

Expensive

Maui Lu Hotel, 575 S. Kihei Rd., tel. 879-5858. On Monday, Wednesday, and Friday a luau and Polynesian review are held in the hotel's Luau Garden, including limitless cocktails and a sumptuous buffet with all the specials— *imu* pork, poi, and a huge assortment of salads, entrees, and side dishes; $28, tax and gratuity included. Also, the **Aloha Mele Luncheon** is a tradition at the hotel. Again a laden buffet with cocktails from 11 a.m. to 1:30 p.m., Thursday only; $12.50 includes the luncheon, entertainment, tax, and tip.

Waterfront Restaurant, at the Milowai Condo in Maalaea Harbor, tel. 244-9028. Open daily from 5:30 to 10 p.m. features whole baked fish in oyster sauce for 2, $16.50, or lobster and crab, from $18. Scampi is $14.50. Great sunsets, tropical drinks.

Buzz's Wharf, at Maalaea Harbor, tel. 244-5426 is open daily 11 a.m. to 11 p.m. Seafood and fresh fish are the specialties. Most dishes are under $15. The waterfront atmosphere,enhances the great sunsets and views from the second story overlooking the harbor.

Chuck's Steak House, Kihei Town Center, tel. 879-4488. Lunch, Mon. to Fri. 11:30 a.m. to 2:30 p.m., dinner nightly from 5:30 p.m., no reservations necessary, but call to see how busy it is. Emphasis on steaks and ribs mostly under $15. The children's menu is under $8. Daily specials and "early birds" sometimes. Dirt pie and sandwiches cost under $5. Salad bar a la carte, $6.95. Standard American, with an island twist.

ENTERTAINMENT

Kihei isn't exactly a hotspot when it comes to evening entertainment. There is the **Polynesian Review** at the Maui Lu luau. The **Surf and Sand Hotel** offers Polynesian entertainment nightly, and there's dancing at **Polli's Mexican Restaurant** on weekends and dancing nightly at **Luigi's.** Many of the restaurants offer entertainment on a hit and miss basis, usually one artist with a guitar, a small dinner combo, or some

Hawaiian music. These are usually listed in the free tourist brochures.

SHOPPING

At the **Azeka Place Shopping Center,** along S. Kihei Rd., in about the center of town, you'll find all the practicalities. **Azeka's Market** is well stocked, and features famous Azeka ribs for barbecues. There's also a great community bulletin board listing apartments, yard sales, and all odds and ends. In the Plaza are **Ben Franklin** and a small **Liberty House.** A full range of books on Hawaiiana, along with distinctive cards and assorted gifts, are available from the **Silversword Book and Card Store,** tel. 879-4373, open daily 8:30 a.m. to 8 p.m., Sat. 8:30 a.m. to 5 p.m., and half day on Sunday. **Wow! of Hawaii,** tel. 879-1448, operated by Betty Olson, specializes in activewear, sportswear, and bathing suits. For the active person—everything from sea to gymnasium. In winter, selections include more resortwear. Open daily 9 a.m. to 9 p.m. (also in Kahului at the Maui Mall).

Rainbow Connection, open Mon.-Sat. 9 a.m. to 9 p.m., and Sun. 9 a.m. to 6 p.m., features personalized gifts. Look for painted reef fish sculptures, jewelry boxes, earrings, and cups, all with a Polynesian theme. The idea is to "connect" Polynesia and the world through the spirit in its art. **Leilani's** has towels, beachwear, hats, and postcards, and next door is **O'Rourke's Tourist Trap** where the junk ain't bad, and neither are the prices. One of the best shops is **Vagabonds,** stocking resortwear and a wide selection of luggage, especially backpacks, daypacks, and fanny packs, by Caribou Mountaineering. Quality merchandise at affordable prices.

Kihei Town Center

A small shopping center just south of Azeka offers a **Foodland, Kihei Drug Mart,** a bank, art gallery, McDonald's, and a few clothing stores.

Kamaole Shopping Center

This new mall at the east end of town features **Denny's, Erik's Seafood,** a Chinese takeout (see above), and various souvenir and sundries stores. Along its two floors you can buy a skimpy suit at a skimpy price at **Bikini Discount Store;** baubles, beads, and some nicer pieces at

Jewels and Gifts of Paradise; and clothes, luggage, and beachwear at the Vagabond Trading Co. The Wearhouse Outlet sells a tangle of beads, cups, and souvenirs. Lappert's Ice Cream sells island-made delights, plus fat-free yogurt so that you can bliss out but not balloon out.

Dolphin Shopping Plaza

This small, two story plaza along S. Kihei Road includes Island Kids, open daily 9 a.m. to 9 p.m., tel. 874-3040, with swimwear, beachwear, and toys for children (big people, too); Pro Photo and Gifts, featuring 40-minute processing; Baskin-Robbins Ice Cream, for ice cream treats; and the Fifth Avenue Mile for fancy alohawear. You can take care of your sweet tooth by visiting the Kihei Bakery, open daily 6 a.m. to 9 p.m., tel. 879-8666, where they make fresh bread, blueberry donuts, and even bagels daily.

Rainbow Mall

Yet another mall just up the road at 2439 S. Kihei Rd., with Lady Di's selling eel skin purses, stained glass, and accouterments for women; Maui Dive Shop, your complete diving store with rentals, swimwear, snorkels, cruises, and windsurfing lessons; and Tropical Trappings, an aloha store with resortwear.

Kukui Mall

The new Kukui Mall along S. Kihei Road is scheduled to open in early 1989. Stores will include Waldenbooks, a convenience store called Maui Minute Stop, Valley Isle Produce, with a cash-and-carry store, the first laundromat in Kihei, J.R.'s Music Store, apparel stores, eateries, and Maui Dive Shop.

Food/Liquor Stores

Azeka's Market is famous for its ribs and selections of exotic Asian foods and spices; buy health foods and more at Paradise Fruit Company, 1913 Kihei Rd. (see "Restaurants" above); Foodland at Kihei Town Center, and Star Market at 1310 S. Kihei Road. Rainbow Discount Liquor has a good sel ection of liquors, imported beers, and wine at the Rainbow Mall along S. Kihei Road.

Sporting Goods And Rentals

Swimwear and sportswear for the entire family are available from Wow! of Hawaii in the center, tel. 879-1448. You'll find all you need at Maui Sailing Center at 101 N. Kihei Rd., Kealia Beach Center, open daily 8 a.m. to 5 p.m. They offer windsurfing equipment and lessons, beach equipment, sailboats, snorkeling sets, jet-skis, and tours. The Dive Shop, 1975 S. Kihei Rd., tel. 879-5172, is owned and operated by John and Marilyn Phipps. This is your one-stop dive shop, and more—tours, excursions, snorkel and scuba equipment, with a branch opening in the new Kukui Mall. Maui Dive Shop in Azeka Place has a full range of equipment and rentals. Snorkel Bob's, tel. 879-8225, is along S. Kihei Rd. just near the McDonald's and behind Paradise Fruit Co. The weekly prices can't be beat at $15 for snorkel gear, or boogie boards (day rentals too). You also get snorkel tips, a fish I.D. card, and the semi-soggy underwater humor of Snorkel Bob. Sea Escape, tel. 879-3721, offers seagoing motorized rafts that you can use to go to all the snorkel, dive, and picturesque spots of the Lahaina Roads just offshore. The daily special is $135, two-hour minimum $80, and additional hours $25. Ocean Activities Center is at the Kamaole Shopping Center (look for the Denny's sign along S. Kihei); here you can book all fun activities on Maui, and purchase anything you'll need for sun and surf at this excellent one-stop store.

Practicalities And Services

At Azeka Place you'll find Bank of Hawaii, tel. 879-5844, the main post office at 1254 S. Kihei Rd., and a gas station. There's also Kihei Acupuncture Clinic, tel. 874-0544, with Dr. Nancy Macauley specializing in gentle needling techniques, and a full selection of Chinese herbs. If you're in desperate need of toggle bolts, you'll find Coast to Coast Hardware, and the Fox One Hour Lab does quick developing, and is a good place to buy film. This is where the "people" do their one-stop shopping. Kihei's first laundromat is at the new Kukui Mall, just down the road.

WAILEA AND BEYOND

Wailea ("Waters of Lea") isn't for the hoi polloi. It's a deluxe resort area custom-tailored to fit the egos of the upper class like a Bijan original. This section of southeastern Maui was barren and bleak until Alexander and Baldwin Co. decided to landscape it into an emerald 1,450-acre oasis of golf courses and world-class hotels. Every street light, palm tree, and potted plant is a deliberate accessory to the decor so that the overall feeling is soothing, pleasant, and in good taste. To dispel any notions of snootiness, the five sparkling beaches that front the resorts were left open to the public and even improved with better access, parking areas, showers, and picnic tables—a gracious gesture even if state law does require open access! You know when you leave Kihei and enter Wailea. The green, quiet, and wide tree-lined avenues give the impression of an upper-class residential area. Wailea is where you come when you're "putting on the Ritz," and with the prices you'll encounter it would be helpful if you *owned* the Ritz. At both the **Intercontinental Hotel** and **Stouffer's Resort** you'll find five-star dining, and there's exclusive shopping at the Wailea Shopping Center. Both hotels are first-rate architecturally and the grounds are exquisite. They're definitely worth a stroll, but remember your Gucci shoes.

Onward And Backward

If you turn your back to the sea and look toward Haleakala, you'll see its cool, green forests and peak wreathed in mysterious clouds. You'll want to run right over, but you can't get there from here! Outrageous as it may sound, you have to double back 18 miles to Kahului and then head down Route 37 for another 20 miles just to get to the exact same spot on Route 37 that you can easily see. On the map there's a neat little road called **Makena Road** that connects the Wailea-/Makena area with Upcountry in a mere two mile stretch, but it's closed! An ongoing fight over who's responsible for its maintenance keeps it that way. Once this appalling situation is rectified, you'll be able to travel easily to the **Tedeschi Winery,** and continue on the "wrong way" to Hana, or go left to Kula and Upcountry. For now, however, happy motoring!

BEACHES

If you're not fortunate enough to be staying in Wailea, the best reason for coming here are its beaches. These little beauties are crescent moons of white sand that usually end in lava outcroppings on both ends. This makes for sheltered swimmable waters and good snorkeling and scuba. Many of the hotel guests in Wailea seem to hang around the hotel pools, maybe peacocking or just trying to get their money's worth, so the beaches are surprisingly uncrowded. The following beaches are listed from west to east, toward Makena.

Keawakapu

The first Wailea beach, almost a buffer between Kihei and Wailea, is just past the Mana Kai Resort. Turn left onto Kamala Place, or proceed straight on S. Kihei Road until it dead ends. Plenty of parking at both accesses, but no amenities. Keawakapu is a lovely white-sand beach with a sandy bottom. Good swimming and fair snorkeling. There's also beginner's dive spot offshore where an underwater junkyard of a few hundred cars forms an artificial reef.

Mokapu And Ulua

These two beaches are shoulder to shoulder, separated only by a rock outcropping. Turn right off Wailea Alanui Drive at the first turn past the Intercontinental Hotel. The beach is clearly marked, and there's a parking area and showers. Being resort beaches, they're both particularly well-kept. Beautiful white sand, and protected waters are perfect for swimming. Good snorkeling at the outcropping separating the beaches, or swim out to the first reef just in front of the rocks for excellent snorkeling.

Wailea Beach

Travel one-half mile past the Wailea town center and turn right onto a clearly marked access road; at the beach there's good parking, also showers and toilets. A short but wide beach of pure white sand, Wailea offers good swimming and body-surfing, but the snorkeling is only fair.

Polo Beach

Follow Wailea Alanui Drive toward Makena. Turn right at the clearly marked sign near Polo Beach condo. Here also are paved parking, showers, and toilets. Polo Beach is good for swimming and sunbathing, with few tourists. There's excellent snorkeling in front of the rocks separating Polo from Wailea Beach—tremendous amounts of fish, and one of the easiest spots to get to.

ACCOMMODATIONS

Stouffer's Wailea Beach Resort

Always a beauty, and destined to be the best, Stouffer's, like a rich red cabernet, has mellowed with age. Under the direction of Don Takahashi, the general manager, it has not only maintained,

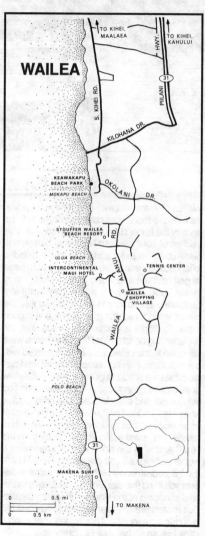

Stouffer's Wailea Beach Resort sets the standard of excellence in Wailea.

but surpassed, its excellent reputation for service. It's a superbly appointed resort with attention given to the most minute detail of comfort and luxury. When you drive to the main lobby, you're actually on the fifth floor, with the ones below terraced down the mountainside to the white-sand beach. The lobby has huge oak and brass doors, and original artwork adorn the walls, including an intricate tapestry made of natural fibers. The relaxing pool area has been recently renovated and expanded. A bubbling spa fashioned from lava rock is surrounded by vines and flowering trees, while another contains three little pools and a gurgling fountain, so that while the therapeutic waters soothe your muscles, the music of the fountain soothes your nerves. The hotel boasts the best beach in the area, long known as an excellent vantage point from which to view cavorting humpback whales in season. The impeccable grounds, originally landscaped to be lush, have grown, and are now an actual botanical garden, with all plants identified. And everywhere there is water, cascading over tiny waterfalls, tumbling in brooks, and reflecting the amazing green canopy in tranquil lagoons.

Stouffer's Wailea Beach Resort has been acclaimed as a five-diamond Resort by the AAA Motor Club for eight consecutive years, while Raffles' Restaurant has not only won official culinary awards but the praise of in-the-know local residents who highly recommend its mag-

nificent Sunday brunch (see description following). The most amazing feature about the resort is a permeating feeling of peace and tranquility. The rooms, whose color schemes are a soothing rose on blue and gray, are appointed with *koa* and rattan furniture. Thick carpeting meets a spacious lounge area of glazed ceramic flooring, while sliding doors lead to a lanai where you can relax or enjoy a quiet in-room meal. **Ocean Activities Center** maintains a desk at the hotel and they can book you into every kind of outdoor activity that Maui has to offer. Room rates are $165-360, with suites to $1200. Varying rates include a family plan, with children under 18 free in their parents' room, and a modified American plan. The hotel features the very private Mokapu Beach Club, a detached low-rise wing complete with its own pool and daily continental breakfast, and a variety of golf and tennis packages. Write Stouffer's Wailea Beach Resort, 3550 Wailea Alanui Dr., Wailea, HI 96753, tel. (800) 992-4532, tel. 879-4900 on Maui.

Maui Intercontinental Hotel

This hotel is a class act. Even the wrong way signs on the premises say *"Please, Do Not Enter."* The rooms are lavish with folding screens, original artwork, deep carpets and coordinated bedspreads, full baths, two lanais, refrigerators, and magnificent views no matter which way you're oriented. Rates run $185-350. Suites are available from $225-575. About a 20% reduction can be had from April 1 through December 23. The family plan includes no charge for children under 16 in their parents' room; during the off season they get their own adjoining room free. The American plan is $44 per day, modified at $35. The hotel offers room and car packages, golf and tennis specials, and honeymoon packages. There are three lovely pools, four restaurants, and the beach. For information write Box 779, Kihei-Wailea, HI 96753, tel. (800) 367-2960 Mainland, tel. (800) 537-5589 from Honolulu, tel. 879-1922 on Maui. This is living!

Independent from the hotel, but using its facilities, the **Waves of Wailea** presents Hawaii's first fitness vacation package. The program includes room, gourmet health-conscious meals, classes, equipment, and seminars. Rates begin around $1700, which will trim down your wallet at least. For information, call (800) 367-8047, ext. 217.

Destination Resorts
At 3750 Wailea Alanui, Wailea, HI 96753, tel. (800) 367-5246 Mainland, (800) 423-8773 ext. 310 Canada, and 879-1595 collect in Hawaii. This complex is made up of three separate villages: **Ekolu**, from $160, near the golf course; **Ekahi**, the least expensive, from $130 near the tennis courts; **Elua**, the most expensive, from $265 near the sea. All units are plush. Add $20 for additional people, monthly discounts; three-night minimum.

Polo Beach Club
At 20 Makena Rd., Wailea, HI 96753, tel. (800) 367-5246. Near Polo Beach toward Makena. Condo apartments fully furnished. From $215, six-person maximum. Low-season discounts. Pool, jacuzzi, and seclusion.

FOOD

Raffles' Restaurant
At Stouffer's Wailea Beach Resort, tel. 879-4900, reservations a must. Dinner daily from 6:30 to 10:30 p.m. Sunday brunch from 9 a.m. to 2 p.m., a prizewinner! You regally glide down the staircase from the main lobby and walk through enormous oak doors into the classy interior of this first-rate restaurant. You'd feel comfortable in a sport coat, but tasteful alohawear is fine. In-spired by the famed Raffles of Singapore, this restaurant lives up to the tradition. Sashimi, lobster and crab cocktail tantalize your taste buds, preparing them for the entrees. Salads galore, including mushroom, spinach, Manoa lettuce, and all in savory dressings, complement lobster bisque or Maui onion soup. Roast rack of lamb, *onaga* with baby spinach and caviar, or veal grenadine in whiskey cream, are just some of the delights prepared by the chefs. Wines are from the best vineyards around the world, and magnificent desserts make you pray for just a little more room. The Sunday brunch is legendary. For $25 you choose from the best island fruits and vegetables, and a table laden with rich and creamy desserts. Omelettes made to order are stuffed with seafood, crunchy vegetables, mushrooms, artichokes, or plump Portuguese sausages. The entree table groans with chops, steaks, fresh fish, caviar, prosciutto, crab, lobster, eggs Benedict, and more. Steaming pots of coffee are brought to every table while waiters constantly change all used table settings. Be smart, go slowly, and put only one or two items on your plate at a time. This is gourmet food that demands a gourmet attitude.

The **Palm Court** is Stouffer's main dining room. Walk though the lobby and look over the rail to the beautiful semi-open-air restaurant below. It's open for breakfast from 6-11 a.m., and for dinner nightly from 6 p.m. The menu offers sashimi or *carpaccio* to start. Entrees are delightful with ricotta ravioli and an outstanding selection and preparation of island fish. Sweet loonies can go crazy at the dessert buffet for only $2.50 with a prime rib dinner, or end the meal with dipped ice cream or freshly made yogurt. Besides menu selections, the Palm Court now features prime rib ($18.95 adults, $8.95 children) to order prepared by chefs before your eyes. The Palm Court is a first-rate restaurant with very reasonable prices. The best in its category in Wailea!

Stouffer's **Sunset Terrace** is a delightful perch on which to have a drink and survey the grounds and beach below. Every evening brings a dramatic torch-lighting ceremony. The drums reverberate, and the liquid melancholy of the conch trumpet sends a call for meditation at day's end. Drinks include the full complement of island specialties, and from 5 to 7 p.m. (not every day) you can get wonderful *pu pu* for only $1.

WAILEA AND BEYOND 455

These are gourmet quality, more like a mini-buffet with salads, dips, teri beef, Chinese spare ribs, Cajun-style chicken, and beautiful crunchy spring rolls. See **Lost Horizon,** the hotel's bar and disco, below under "Entertainment," and "Luaus" in the main Introduction for Stouffer's traditional Monday night feast.

The **Maui Onion** is a convenient snack-type restaurant at poolside. Burgers, sandwiches, salads, and Maui onion rings are on the limited menu. Prices are a bit steep, but if you don't want to budge from your poolside lounge chair it's worth it.

La Perouse Restaurant

At Maui Intercontinental Hotel, tel. 879-1922. Dinner nightly from 5:30 p.m., reservations a must. This elegant restaurant is gaining an international reputation. The surroundings themselves of rich *koa* wood and an immense ironwork gate at the entry set the theme. A dress code requires collared shirts, and most people dress up; no shorts. The callaloo crabmeat soup is a must. The bouillabaisse is out of this world. Breadfruit vichyssoise is unique. Wines from the private cellar are extremely well chosen but expensive, while the house wine is very palatable and affordable. The best selections are the seafood, but the chicken and lamb are also superb. Save room for dessert, offered on a pastry cart laden with exotic choices. This is no place for will power. Enjoy one of the best meals ever, and don't worry about the second mortgage tonight.

The **Kiawe Broiler** offers more moderately priced dinners at the hotel. Daily dinner 6 to 10 p.m, basically *kiawe*-broiled chops and steaks from $15, and a salad bar that's a deal. Informal setting with high-backed rattan decor. Other hotel restaurants include the **Lanai Terrace,** tel. 879- 1922, with a luau every Tue. and Thurs. from 5:30 p.m. (see "Luaus" in the Introduction); the **Inu Inu Lounge** for a nightly disco (no cover); **Makani's Coffee Shop** for reasonably priced American standards; and the **Wet Spot,** open 11 a.m. to 4 p.m. by the pool if you want to get soaked for an $8 sandwich.

Sandcastle Restaurant

At Wailea Shopping Village, tel. 879-0606, this restaurant is far enough out of the way so you can count on getting a table. Primarily they serve salad and sandwiches at lunch 11 a.m. to 3 p.m.

and dinner from 4 p.m. Early birds can peck from 4 to 6 p.m. for $11.95, which includes *mahi mahi,* prime rib, teriyaki chicken, and deep-fried shrimp, plus soup and salad bar. Most entrees are from $10-15, and they barbecue using mesquite imported from Mexico. The room is comfortable with high-backed cane chairs and even a little patio area.

Golf Ball Soup

The following restaurants are located at the golf links in the area. **Sakura,** tel. 879-1577, is open daily for lunch and dinner. It's surprisingly reasonable, both for being where it is and for serving Japanese fare. The traditional menu presents *yakitori,* or *yudofu* appetizers for under $4, sashimi plates for under $10, and traditional entrees like tempura, or *shabu shabu* for under $25. The menu describes all the dishes in English, so this is a good opportunity to sample some delectable Japanese food. Sunset is particularly striking, and small parties can request the tatami rooms.

Fairway, at Wailea Golf Course Club House, tel. 879-4060, is across the street from the entrance to Polo Beach; just follow the road to the clubhouse. Open from 7:30 a.m. for a full breakfast, like eggs Benedict for $5.95, to a simple omelette for $3.75 or buttermilk pancakes, all you can eat, for $2.99. Lunch offers burgers and sandwiches from $5-7. Selections from $15-20 include filet mignon, New York pepper steak, veal parmigiana, or salad bar for $11.95. Although the dining room isn't ultra fancy, there's a terrace, and the feeling is peaceful in an unhurried romantic setting. Good place to eat in an area not known for budget restaurants.

Makena Golf Course Restaurant, tel. 879- 1154. Open daily from 9:30 a.m. Nothing special, but well-prepared sandwiches, burgers, and fries, and it's convenient as the last stop on the way to Makena.

In the Wailea Shopping Center **Sandcastles,** tel. 926-1920, is worth trying. Their duck in Indonesian lime sauce is mouthwatering.

ENTERTAINMENT, SHOPPING, AND SERVICES

Entertainment

If you haven't had enough fun on the Wailea beaches during the day, you can show off your best dance steps at Stouffer's **Lost Horizon.** Rock to the sounds of Hau'ula from 9 p.m. to 1 a.m. Tues.-Thurs., and until 2 a.m. on Fri. and Saturday. The Intercontinental's **Inu Inu Room** swings with live music and disco dancing nightly.

Golf And Tennis
Two of the main attractions in Wailea are the fantastic golf and tennis opportunities. You have four magnificent golf courses that have been laid out on Haleakala's lower slopes, all open to the public. Tennis is great at the **Wailea Tennis Center,** tel. 879-1958, and many of the hotels and condos have their own championship courts and courses. Please see "Tennis" and "Golf" charts in the Introduction for rates and specifics.

Wailea Shopping Village
The only shopping in this area is **Wailea Shopping Center,** just east past the Intercontinental Hotel off Wailea Alanui Drive. It has the usual collection of boutiques and shops. **Superwhale** offers alohawear for chil dren. An **Ocean Activities Center** store provides you with all you'll need for sun and surf, and also bookings for all Maui outdoor activities from snorkeling to a helicopter ride. **Kiwina's** sells fine jewelry, while **Miki's** has racks of alohawear at very competitive prices that you wouldn't expect in this fancy neck of the woods. More exclusive fashions are at **Chapman's** for fine men's clothing, and **Sea and Shells** has a range of gifts from the islands. **Isle Style** is a fine arts gallery with works by local artists, and the most remarkable shop is **Lahaina Printsellers,** with their magnificent prints and maps (see p. 371). **Elephant Walk** is a shopping gallery of fine crafted items, and **For Your Eyes Only** sells sunglasses for every eye and lifestyle. Money needs are handled by the **First Hawaiian Bank, Island Camera** for film, accessories and processing, and **Whaler's General Store,** for food items and liquor, and **Ed and Don's** for fast foods, snacks, and gift items.

Transportation
Wailea Shuttle is a complimentary jitney constantly making trips up and down Wailea Alanui Drive, stopping at all major hotels and condos, the Wailea Shopping Center, and golf and tennis courts. It operates 6:30 a.m. to 10:30 p.m. With a little walking, this is a great way to hop from one beach to the next.

MAKENA TO LA PEROUSE

Just a skip down the road eastward is Makena Beach, but it's a world away from Wailea. Once the paved roads of Wailea give way to dirt, you know you're in Makena country. This was a hippie enclave during the '60s and early '70s, and the freewheeling spirit of the times still permeates the area. For one, "Little Makena" is a nude beach, but so what? You can skinny-dip in Connecticut. This fact gets too much attention. What's really important is that Makena is *the last* pristine coastal area of Maui that hasn't succumbed to development . . . yet. As you head down the road you'll notice Hawaii's unofficial bird, the building crane, arching its mechanical neck and lifting girders into place. The Japanese firm of Seibu Hawaii has built the Maui Prince Hotel, and three more luxury hotels are on the rise. Wailea Point, a promontory of land between Wailea and Makena, will be the site for two, and the other will be across the road near the tennis courts. Oceanside will be the Four Seasons and the Grand Hyatt. The hotels will open from mid-1989 to mid-1990.

In stark contrast, there's unofficial camping at Makena, with a few beach people who live here semi-permanently. There's nothing in the way of amenities past Wailea, so make sure to stock up on all supplies (for water see "Keawalai Church," below). The police come in and sweep the area now and again, but mostly it's mellow. They do arrest the nudists on Little Makena to make the point that Makena "ain't free no more" (see below). Rip-offs can be a problem, so lock your car, hide your camera, and don't leave anything of value in your tent. Be careful of the *kiawe* thorns when you park; they'll puncture a tire like a nail.

Makena is magnificent for bodysurfing and swimming. Whales frequent the area and come quite close to shore during the season. Turtles waddled on Makena until early in this century, where they came to lay their eggs in the warm sand. But too many people gathered the eggs and the turtles scrambled away forever. The

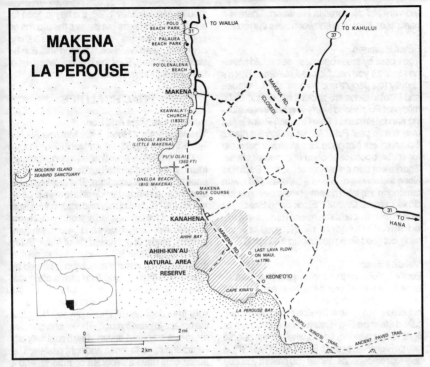

MAKENA
TO
LA PEROUSE

TO WAILUA

TO KAHULUI

POLO
BEACH PARK
PALAUEA
BEACH PARK

PO'OLENALENA BEACH

MAKENA

MAKENA RD.
(CLOSED)

KEAWALA'I
CHURCH
(1832)

ONOULI BEACH
(LITTLE MAKENA)

PU'U OLAI
(360 FT)

MOLOKINI ISLAND
SEABIRD SANCTUARY

ONELOA BEACH
(BIG MAKENA)

MAKENA
GOLF COURSE

TO
HANA

KANAHENA

AHIHI BAY

AHIHI-KIN'AU

NATURAL AREA

RESERVE

MAKENA RD.

LAST LAVA FLOW
ON MAUI,
ca.1790.

KEONE'O'IO

CAPE KINA'U

LA PEROUSE BAY

HOAPILI (KING'S) TRAIL

ANCIENT PAVED TRAIL

0   2 mi
0   2 km

sunsets from **Red Hill,** the cinder cone separating Makena from Little Makena, are among the best on Maui; watch it sink down between Lanai, Kahoolawe, and West Maui. The silhouettes of pastel and gleaming colors are awe-inspiring. Oranges, russets, and every shade of purple reflect off the clouds that are caught here. Makena attracts all kinds: gawkers, burn-outs, adventurers, tourists, and free spirits. It won't last long, so go and have a look now!

The Naked Truth
In a recent and extremely controversial episode the Maui police came down hard on the nudists. They arrested nine top-free women from various parts of the U.S. and from foreign countries. The police acted in defiance of a recent Hawaii Supreme Court ruling that states that a woman's breasts when uncovered in appropriate circumstances (i.e., isolated beaches) does *not* violate the state's "open lewdness" statute. The wo-

men, defended by attorney Anthony Ranken, are seeking compensation for malicious prosecution. Some point directly at Mayor Hannibal Tavares for running a personal crusade against the *au naturelle* sun-worshipers. To show the extent of the conflict, one hare-brained scheme that was actually proposed was to pave a walkway to **Puu Olai** ("Red Hill") so that Little Makena is no longer a "remote beach." The justification was to provide "wheelchair access" to Little Makena although a wheelchair would have to negotiate hundreds of yards of deep sand to get there. Imagine the consternation if the first wheelchair-bound sunbather just happened to be a nudist!

Keawalai Church
In Makena, you'll pass this Congregational church, established in 1832. It was restored in 1952 and services are held every Sunday at 9:30 a.m. Many of the hymns and part of the ser-

mon are still delivered in Hawaiian. There is a parking lot, toilet, and shower across the road.

Small Beaches

You'll pass by these beaches, via the Old Makena road, as you head toward Makena. There's usually few people and no amenities. Palauea and **Poolenalena** are about three-quarters of a mile past Polo. Good swimming and white, sloping sands. **Nahuna** ("Five Graves") **Point** is just over a mile past Polo. An old graveyard marks the entrance. Not good for swimming but great for scuba because of deep underwater caves. Snorkelers can enjoy this area, too. **Papipi** is along the road a mile and a half past Polo, with parking in the lot. The small sand beach is too close to road. **Oneuli** ("Black Sand Beach") is past Polo, not quite three miles. Turn down a rutted dirt road for a third of a mile. Not good for swimming, but good diving and unofficial camping.

Makena Beach

Bounce along for three miles past Polo Beach. Look for a wide dirt road that two cars can pass on. Turn right and follow the rutted road for a few hundred yards. This is **Oneloa Beach,** generally called **Makena Big Beach.** You can go left or right to find parking. Left is where most people camp. Right leads you to **Puu Olai** ("Red Hill"), a 360-foot cinder cone. When you cross it you'll be on **Little Makena,** a favorite nude beach. Both beaches are excellent for swimming (beware of currents in winter), bodysurfing, and superb snorkeling in front of Red Hill.

Ahihi-Kinau Natural Reserve

Look for the sign four miles past Polo Beach. Here you'll find a narrow beach and the remnants of a stone wall. It's an underwater reserve, so the scuba and snorkeling are first-rate. The best way to proceed is along the reef toward the left. Beware not to step on the many spiny urchins in the shallow waters. If you do, vinegar or urine will help with the stinging. The jutting thumb of lava to your left is **Cape Kinau.** This was Maui's last lava flow, occurring in 1790.

La Perouse Bay

Just shy of six miles from Polo Beach. After Ahihi-Kinau the road is rugged and cut along the lava flow. Named after the French navigator Jean de François La Perouse, first Westerner to land on Maui, in May 1786, the bay is good for snorkelers and divers but beware the urchins on entry. If you walk left you'll come across a string of pocket-sized beaches. The currents can be tricky along here. Past the bay are remnants of the Hoapili ("King's") Trail.

PRACTICALITIES

Accommodations And Food

The **Maui Prince Hotel,** 5400 Makena Ala Nui Rd., Kihei, HI 96753, tel. on Maui 874-1111, or (800) 321-6284, is a destination resort. You walk into a gleaming white building and face an enormous central courtyard. The architecture is simple and refined understatement. Lean across the hardwood rails and soak in the visual pleasure of the landscaped artwork below. From the balconies hang flowers and greenery in sympathetic mimic of the waterfalls of Maui. Every evening the water is turned off in the central courtyard. The natural melody is replaced by **Sterling Strings,** a duo that plays classical music that wafts upward for all to enjoy. All rooms have an alcove door so that you can open your front door and still have privacy, but allow the breeze to pass through. The least expensive room is a standard ocean view beautifully accentuated in earth tones and light pastels. The bathrooms have a separate commode, and a separate shower and tub. Ocean view and ocean front rooms range from $190-290, while one-bedroom suites are from $350-700, with a full giant living room, two lanais, a large-screen TV and VCR, and *yukata* to lounge in. The master bedroom has its own TV, listening center, and king-size bed. A nonsmoking wing is also available.

The Maui Prince faces a fantastic portion of Maluaka Beach, secluded and perfect for swimming and snorkeling. The beach is almost like a little bay, with two points of lava marking it as a safe spot for swimming. Seven sea turtles live on the south point and come up on the beach to nest and lay their eggs. To the left you can see Puu Olai, a red cinder cone that marks Makena. **Ocean Activities Center** comes in the morning with its catamaran, and will take you snorkeling to Molokini. The pool area is made up of two circular pools, one for adults, the other a wading pool for kids. There's volleyball, a children's program, croquet, seven tennis courts with a pro on the staff, and the golf course, the main attraction of the Maui Prince.

With the Prince being one of the newest luxury hotels in the area, head chef Roger Dikon is building an island-wide reputation for exquisite dining. He's succeeding admirably. The fanciest room is the **Prince Court**, featuring fine dining for dinner only, except for their truly exceptional Sunday brunch. The evening fare is gourmet and then some. Prepare with appetizers like smoked Alaskan salmon with dill cheesecake and salmon pearls, $11, or any of their copper kettle soups like black bean Creole for $5. Grilled pink snapper with avacado is $27, and most chicken, beef, and lamb entrees are under $28. The room is subdued-elegant and highlighted with snow-white tablecloths and sparkling crystal. The view is motionless facing the serene courtyard, or dramatic looking out to sea.

When chefs from the best restaurants on Maui want to impress visiting friends with a brunch, they come to the Maui Prince on Sunday. For only $27 you can surpass most of your dining fantasies. You start with a table laden with exotic fruits and fresh-squeezed juices. Nearby are plump and steaming rolls, croissants, and pastries rich in chocolates and creams. Then comes an omelette gauntlet, where you pick and choose your ingredients and an attendant chef creates it before your eyes. Hot entrees for the gastronomically timid are offered, from roast beef to fresh fish. But the real delights are the cornucopia of smoked seafood and shellfish. To the left pâté, to the right sushi, and *sashimi*

straight ahead, or choose cracked crab to nibble while you decide. Fat yellow rounds of imported cheeses squat on huge tables. Waiters and waitresses attend with fresh plates, champagne, and pots of coffee. You couldn't possibly eat like this every day, but *sacrifice* yourself at least once like this while on Maui.

Hakone is a Japanese restaurant and sushi bar with all chefs from Japan. They serve complete dinners like sukiyaki or tempura for under $29, but primarily they serve sushi and *sashimi*. In keeping with the tradition of Japan, the room is subdued and simple, with white shoji screens counterpointed by dark open beams. The floor is black slate atop packed sand, a style from old Japan.

The main dining room is **Cafe Kiowai**, which is open for breakfast lunch, and dinner. It is on the ground level, opening to the courtyard. Lunch choices are almost endless, beginning with appetizers like country pâté with papaya chutney, $6, steamed artichoke with herbed hollandaise, $6, or Maui onion soup or *saimin* for under $5; salads and sandwiches are under $8, seasonal salad with salami, prosciutto, turkey, and cheese, $7, mini-rolls with chicken salad, $6, and hot dishes under $15 like grilled *ahi* in *shoyu* with ginger and scallions are worthwhile. For now, food and accommodations in Makena means the Maui Prince.

Services: Except for the phones at the Maui Prince, Makena Golf Club, the sundries shop at the hotel, and the water at Keawalai Church, you won't find any amenities.

Commoners were required to lie face down when thay saw an approaching kahili, *a standard that resembled a huge feather duster. This was so the mana of an* ali'i *would not be defiled by their tounch, gaze, or even their shadow.*

UPCOUNTRY

Upcountry is much more than a geographical area to the people who live there: it's a way of life, a frame of mind. You can see Upcountry from anywhere on Maui by lifting your gaze to the slopes of Haleakala. There are no actual boundaries, but this area is usually considered as running from Makawao in the north all the way around to Kahikinui Ranch in the south, and from below the cloud cover up to about the 3,000-foot level. It encircles Haleakala like a large green floral bib patterned by pasture lands and festooned with wild and cultivated flowers. In this rich soil and cool to moderate temperatures, cattle ranching and truck farming thrive. Up here, *paniolo* ride herd on the range of the enormous 20,000-acre **Haleakala Ranch,** spread mostly around Makawao, and the even larger 30,000 acres of the **Ulupalakua Ranch,** which *is* the hills above Wailea. **Pukalani,** the largest town, is a way station for gas and sup-

plies. **Makawao** is a real cowboy town with saddleries, rodeos, and hitching posts. It's also sophisticated, with some exclusive shops and fine dining.

Kula is Maui's flower basket. This area is one enormous garden producing brilliant blooms and hearty vegetables. **Poli Poli State Park** is a forgotten wonderland of tall forests, a homogenized stand of trees from around the world. **Tedeschi Winery** in the south adds a classy touch to Upcountry; you can taste wine in a historic jailhouse. There are plenty of commercial greenhouses and flower farms to visit all over Upcountry, but the best is a free Sunday drive along the mountain roads and farm lanes, just soaking in the scenery. The purple mists of mountain jacaranda and the heady fragrance of eucalyptus encircling a mountain pasture manicured by herds of cattle is a portrait of the soul of Upcountry.

MAKAWAO

Makawao is proud of itself; it's not *like* a cowboy town, it *is* a cowboy town. Depending on the translation that you consult, it means "Eye of the

Dawn" or "Forest Beginning." Both are appropriate. Surrounding lowland fields of cane and pineapples give way to upland pastures rimmed

UPCOUNTRY

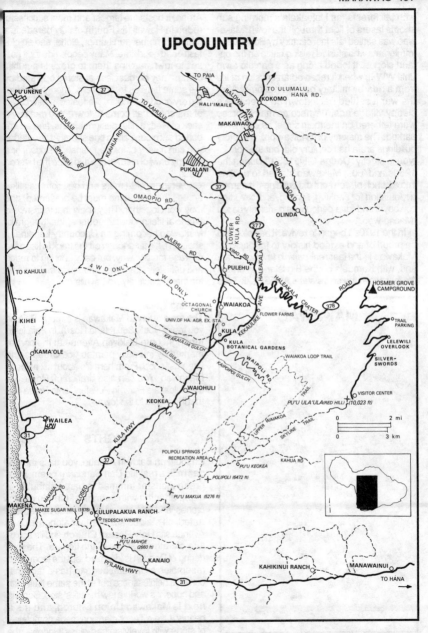

with tall forests, as Haleakala's morning sun shoots lasers of light through the town. Makawao was settled late last century by Portuguese immigrants who started raising cattle on the upland slopes. It loped along as a paniolo town until WW II, when it received an infusion of life from a nearby military base in Kokomo. After the war it settled back down and became a sleepy village again, where as many horses were tethered on the main street as cars were parked. The majority of its false-front, one-story buildings are a half century old, but their prototype is strictly "Dodge City, 1850." During the 1950s and '60s, Makawao started to decline into a bunch of worn-out old buildings. It earned a reputation for drinking, fighting, and cavorting cowboys, and for a period was derisively called "Macho-wao."

In the 1970s it began to revive. It had plenty to be proud of and a good history to fall back on. Makawao is *the* last real *paniolo* town on Maui and, with Kamuela on the Big Island, is one of the last two in the entire state. At the Oskie Rice Arena, it hosts the largest and most successful rodeo in Hawaii. Its Fourth of July parade is a marvel of homespun humor, aloha, and an old-fashioned good time. Many people ride their horses to town, leaving them to graze in a public corral. They do business at stores operated by the same families for 50 years. Though much of the dry goods are country-oriented, a new breed of merchant has come to town. You can buy a sack of feed, a rifle, designer jeans, and an imported silk blouse all on one street. At its eateries you can have lobster, vegetarian, Mexican, or a steamy bowl of saimin, reputed to be the best on Maui.

Everyone, old-timers and newcomers alike, agrees that Makawao must be preserved, and they work together. They know that tourism is a financial lifeline, but shudder at the thought of Makawao becoming an Upcountry Lahaina. It shouldn't. It's far enough off the track to keep the average tourist away, but easy enough to reach and definitely interesting enough to make a side trip there absolutely worthwhile.

Getting There

The main artery to Makawao is through Paia as you travel Route 360 (Hana Road). In Paia town turn right onto Baldwin Avenue at the corner marked by the gaily painted "Ice Creams and Dreams" shop. From here it's about six miles to Makawao. You can also branch off Route 37, the Haleakala Hwy., in Pukalani, onto Route 400 that'll lead you to the town.

SIGHTS

En route on Baldwin Avenue, you pass the **sugar mill,** a real-life Carl Sandburg poem. It's a green monster trimmed in bare lightbulbs at night, dripping with sounds of turning gears, cranes, and linkbelts, all surrounded by packed, rutted, oil-stained soil. Farther along Baldwin Avenue sits **Holy Rosary Church** and its sculpture of Father Damien of the Lepers. The rendering of Damien is idealized, but the leper, who resembles a Calcutta beggar, has a face that conveys helplessness but at the same time faith and hope. It's worth a few minutes' stop. Coming next is **Makawao Union Church,** and it's a beauty. Like a Tudor mansion made completely of stone with lovely stained-glass windows, the entrance is framed by two tall and stately royal palms.

The back way reaches Makawao by branching off Route 36 through Ulumalu and Kokomo. Just where Route 36 turns into Route 360, there's a road to the right. This is Kapakilui Road, or Route 365 (some maps show it as Rt. 400). Take it through backcountry Maui, where horses graze around neat little houses. Haleakala looms on the horizon; guavas, mangoes, and bananas grow wild. At the first Y, bear left to Kaupakulua. Pass a large junkyard and continue to Kokomo. There's a general store here. Notice the mixture of old and new houses—Maui's past and future in microcosm. Here, the neat little banana plantation on the outskirts of the diminutive town says it all. Pass St. Joseph's Church and you've arrived through Makawao's back door. This is an excellent off-track route to take on your way to or from Hana. You can also come over Route 365 through Pukalani, incorporating Makawao into your Haleakala trip.

Nearby Attractions

Take Olinda Road out of town. All along it custom houses have been built. Look for **Pookela Church,** a coral-block structure built in 1843. In four miles you pass **Rainbow Acres,** tel. 572-8020. Open Fri. and Sat. 10 a.m. to 4 p.m., they specialize in succulents. At the top of Olinda turn left onto Piiholo Road, which loops back down. Along it is **Aloha o ka Aina,** a nursery specializing in ferns. Open Wed. and Sun. 10 a.m. to 4 p.m. You'll also pass **Olinda Nursery,** offering general house plants. Open Fri. and Sat. 10 a.m. to 4 p.m.

PRACTICALITIES

Food

All the following establishments are on Makawao or Baldwin avenues. An excellent place to eat is **Polli's Mexican Restaurant.** Open daily 11:30 a.m. to 10:30 p.m., tel. 572-7808. This is the original restaurant; they now have a branch in Kihei. The meals are authentic Mexican, using the finest ingredients. Formerly vegetarian, they still use no lard or animal fat in their bean dishes. You can have a full meal for $6-7. Margaritas are large and tasty for $2, pitchers of domestic beer $5. The Sunday brunch is particularly good. One unfortunate policy is that they refuse to give free chips and salsa to a person dining alone, even when ordering a full meal, while couples dining get them free!

Makawao Steak House, tel. 572-8711, open daily for dinner from 5 p.m. Early-bird special until 6:30, Sunday brunch from 9:30 a.m. to 2 p.m. Casual, with wooden tables, salad bar, and good fish selections, dinners are from $8.95. The steak dishes, especially the prime rib, are the best. The Makawao Steak House has been around a long time and maintains a good, solid reputation. The best all-around restaurant in Makawao!

A surprising and delicious dining experience is found at **Casanova Italian Deli,** tel. 572-0220, located at Makawao Four Corners, open daily 8:30 a.m. to 8:30 p.m., Sun. 9:30 a.m. to 7 p.m. The interior is utilitarian. The deli case is loaded with salami, prosciutto, hams, cheeses, smoked salmon, and savory salads. Shelves are stocked with Italian delectables, designer chocolates, and ice cream, too. There's a counter for eating, with glossy high-society magazines provided for your reading pleasure. Specials are offered nightly, but the best dishes in the house are the fresh-made lasagna, ravioli, and spaghetti, all smothered in different sauces. Many of the best restaurants on Maui order their pasta from Casanova's. You order at the counter and are given a paper plate and plastic utensils. The best place to sit is on the front porch where you can perch above the street and watch Makawao life go by.

Kitada's makes the best saimin on Maui, according to all the locals. It's across from the Makawao Steak House. Open daily 6 a.m. to 1:30 p.m., tel. 572-7241. The 77-year-old owner, Takeshi Kitada, does all the prep work himself. Walk in, pour yourself a glass of water, and take a hardboard-topped table. The saimin is delicious and only $1.50. There are plate lunches, too. The walls have paintings of Upcountry by local artists; most show more heart than talent. Bus your own table while Kitada-san calculates your bill on an abacus. His birthday, May 26, has become a town event.

Komoda's is a corner general store that has been in business for over 50 years. They sell everything, but their bakery is renowned far and wide. They open at 6:30 a.m. with people already lined up outside to buy their cream buns and homemade cookies—all gone by 9 a.m.

Masa's Kitchen is an inexpensive place to eat along Makawao Avenue (on the rise on the left). They serve a variety of plate lunches under $4, Japanese dishes, and sushi. The sushi sells by the roll at $3.10. They offer it pre-made by the piece for only $.50, but if sushi ain't absolutely fresh *pardner san*, it ain't sushi.

At the corner of Makawao and Baldwin avenues is a new shop called **Your Just Desserts**, tel. 572-1101, open weekdays 10:30 a.m. to 10 p.m., Sunday shorter hours. It's one of those sweet shops where you can satisfy your cravings for goodies and not feel too guilty . . . kind of. Their menu includes frozen yogurt with all the trimmings, honey lemonade, home-baked cookies, and jams and jellies. Good stuff! The shelves also hold gift items, housewear, and children's toys. You can browse while you munch.

Mountainside Liquor and Deli, tel. 572-0204, can provide all the fixings for a lunch, or a full range of liquid refreshments. **Rodeo General Store** is a one-stop shop with a wide selection of natural foods, pastries, produce, and fresh fish. **Mountain Fresh Market**, open daily 9 a.m. to 7 p.m., till 6 p.m. on Sun., has an excellent community bulletin board out front. Upcountry's health food store, it's small, but jam-packed with juices, grains, vitamins, and organic fruits and vegies. **Upcountry Fishery**, open daily until 7 p.m., until 10 p.m. on Sat. and Sun., is on Makawao Avenue and also houses Dickey's Healthy Foods (just next to the library). The fish selections are excellent, being wide and varied, but the health food store is slightly understocked. However, the prices are good.

Shopping

Makawao is changing quickly, and nowhere is this more noticeable than in its local shops. The population is now made up of old guard *paniolo*, yuppies, and alternative people. What a combo! You can buy a bullwhip, a Gucci purse, a cold Bud, or sushi all within 100 feet of each other. Some unique and fascinating shops here can provide you with distinctive purchases. **Maui Moorea**, at 3639 Baldwin Ave., tel. 572-0801, sells expensive but highly fashionable clothing for women and children. Cindy, the owner, also has shelves of collectibles and handicrafts made on Maui. The rear of the shop is given over to handmade leather and suede clothing made by Carl, Cindy's husband. **Collections Boutique,** open daily till 9 p.m., imports items from throughout Asia: batik from Bali, clothes from India, jewelry and handicrafts from various countries. Operated by Pam Winans.

Silversword Stoves, tel. 572-4569, formerly Outdoor Sports, has the largest line of wood-burning stoves in Hawaii. That's right, stoves! Nights in the high country can get chilly, and on top of Haleakala downright cold. Also a good selection of cutlery, and a few residuals left over from when it was a great hardware and tack store. The owner, Gary Moore, is a relative newcomer who helped restore the integrity of Makawao and became a town historian in his own right. For fine art check out **David Warren's Studio** along Baldwin Avenue. David is one of the featured artists at the prestigious Maui Crafts Guild in Paia, but chose Upcountry for his studio. Next door is **Gecko Trading Co.,** a boutique bright with alohawear and T-shirts. **Coconut Classics** features Hawaiian collectibles in their semi-discovery shop, which has old and new merchandise. Close by is **Country Flowers** for leis or arranged flowers. **Hui Noeau** ("Club of Skills") is a local organization that features traditional and modern arts. Their member artisans produce everything from ceramics to *lau hala* (weaving). They are housed at Kaluanui, a mansion built in 1917 by the Baldwin family. They sponsor an annual Christmas Fair featuring their creations.

Events

Makawao has a tremendous rodeo season every year. Most meets are sponsored by the Maui Roping Club. They start in the spring and culminate in a massive rodeo on July 4th, with over $22,000 in prize money. These events attract the best cowboys from around the state. The organization of the event is headed by long-time resident Brendan Balthazar, who welcomes everyone to participate with only one rule, "Have fun, but maintain safety."

KULA

Kula could easily provide all of the ingredients for a full-course meal fit for a king. Its bounty is staggering: vegetables to make a splendid chef's salad, beef for the entree, flowers to brighten the spirits, and wine to set the mood. Up here, soil, sun, and moisture create a garden symphony. Sweet Maui onions, cabbages, potatoes, grapes, apples, pineapples, lettuce, and artichokes grow with abandon. Herefords and Black Anguses graze in knee-deep fields of sweet green grass. Flowers are everywhere: beds of proteas, camellias, carnations, roses, hydrangeas, and blooming peach and tangerine trees dot the countryside like daubs from van Gogh's brush. As you gain the heights along Kula's lanes, you look back on West Maui and a perfect view of the isthmus. You'll also enjoy wide-open spaces and rolling green hills fringed with trees like a lion's mane. Above, the sky changes from brooding gray to blazing blue, then back again. Kula is a different Maui—quiet and serene.

Getting There

The fastest way is the same route to Haleakala Crater. Take Route 37 through Pukalani, turn onto Route 377, and when you see Kimo Road on your left and right, you're in Kula country. If you have the time take the following scenic route. Back in Kahului start on Route 36 (Hana Hwy.), but as soon as you cross Dairy Road look for a sign on your left pointing to Pulehu-Omaopio Road. Take it! You'll wade through acres of sugar cane, and in six miles these two roads will split. You can take either, but Omaopio to the left is better because, at the top, it deposits you in the middle of things to see. Once the roads fork, you'll pass some excellent examples of flower and truck farms. You'll also go by the cooperative **Vacuum Cooling Plant** where many farmers store their produce. Then Omaopio Road comes again to Route 37 (Kula Hwy.). Don't take it yet. Cross and continue until Omaopio dead ends, in a few hundred yards. Turn right onto Lower Kula Road and watch for Kimo (Lower) Drive on your left, and take it straight uphill. This brings you through some absolutely beautiful countryside and in a few miles

crosses Route 377, where a right will take you to Haleakala Crater Road.

SIGHTS, FOOD, AND ACCOMMODATIONS

Pukalani

This way station town is uninteresting but a good place to get gas and supplies. There's a shopping mall where you can pick up just about anything. **Bullock's** restaurant just past the mall serves a wide assortment of good-value sandwiches. The moonburger is a tradition, but a full breakfast here for under $5 will give you all the energy you'll need for the day ahead. They also have plate lunches and some island-flavored shakes. The newest restaurant in the area is the **Pukalani Terrace,** open daily 10 a.m. to 9 p.m, tel. 572-1325, at the Pukalani Golf Course. They have a salad bar, sandwiches, but specialize in "local" and Hawaiian foods. Most patrons are local people so you know that they're doing something right.

Kula Lodge

The Kula Lodge is on Route 377 just past Kimo Drive and just before Haleakala Crater Road. The address is RR 1, Box 475, Kula, HI 96790, tel. 878-1535, (800) 233-1535. Lodging here is in $80-140 chalets. All have fireplaces with wood provided, and excellent views of lower Maui. The lobby and dining areas are impressively rustic. The walls are covered with high-quality photos of Maui: windsurfers, silverswords, sunsets, cowboys, and horses. The main dining room has a giant bay window with a superlative view. Breakfast is served daily from 6:30 a.m., lunch 11:30 a.m. to 5 p.m., dinner from 5 p.m. Entertainment in the evenings.

Hawaii Protea Corporation

Next door to the Kula Lodge, open Mon. through Fri. 9 a.m. to 4:30 p.m., tel. 878-6273, or (800) 367-8047. Don't miss seeing these amazing flowers. (For a full description see "Flora" in the main Introduction.) Here you can purchase a wide range of protea that can be shipped back home. Live or dried, these flowers are fantastic.

They start at $30, but are well worth the price. The salespeople are friendly and informative, and it's educational just to visit.

Upper Kimo Road

If you want to be intoxicated by some of the finest examples of Upcountry flower and vegetable farms, come up here. First, head back down Route 377 past thé Kula Lodge and turn on **Upper Kimo Road** on your right. At the very end is **Upcountry Protea Farm**, open daily 8 a.m. to 4:30 p.m., Box 485F, Kula, HI 96790, tel. 878-6015. They have over 50 varieties of protea and other flowers. You can walk the grounds or visit the gift shop where they offer gift packs and mail order.

Kula Botanical Gardens

Follow Route 377 south and look for the gardens on your left just before the road meets again with Route 37. The gardens are open daily from 9 a.m. to 4 p.m. Admission is $3, under 12 for $.50, tel. 878-1715. Here are five acres of identified plants on a self-guided tour. There are streams and ponds on the property, and plants include native *koa* and *kukui*, as well as many introduced species. The gardens are educational and will give names to many flowers and plants that you've observed around the island. It makes for a relaxing afternoon, with picnic tables provided.

Poli Poli State Park

If you want quietude and mountain walks, come here, because few others do. Just past the botanical gardens look for the park sign on your left leading up Waipoli Road. This 10-mile stretch is only partially paved, and the second half can be very rutted and muddy. As always, it's worth it. Poli Poli is an established forest of imported trees from around the world: eucalyptus, redwoods, cypress, and *sugi* pines. You can hike the **Redwood Trail** to a shelter at the end. Camping permits are required and are available from the Division of State Parks, Box 1049, Wailuku, HI 96793, tel. 244-4354. The cabin here is a spacious three bedroom affair with bunks for up to 10 people. It starts at $10 single and goes up about $5 per person. It's rustic, but all camping and cooking essentials are provided, including a woodburning stove. If you want to get away from it all, this is your spot.

Others

The University of Hawaii maintains an experimental station of 20 acres of flowers that they change with the seasons. Located on Copp Road off Route 37, open Mon. to Fri. 7:30 a.m. to 3:30 p.m. A self-guided tour map is available at the office, which is closed during lunch hour. **Holy Ghost Church** on Lower Kula Road, just past Kula Town, is an octagonal building raised in 1897 for the many Portuguese who worked the farms and ranches of Upcountry. There's a gas station in Kula Town.

Tedeschi Winery

Continue south on Route 37 through the town of Keokea, where you'll find gas, two general stores, and an excellent park for a picnic. Past Keokea you'll know you're in ranch country. The road narrows and herds of cattle graze in pastures that seem like manicured gardens highlighting *panini* (prickly pear) cactus. You'll pass Ulupalakua Ranch and then come to the Tedeschi Winery **tasting room** on the left. Open for tasting daily 9 a.m. to 5 p.m., tel. 878-6058. Here, Emil Tedeschi and his partner Pardee Erdman, who also owns the 30,000-acre Ulupalakua Ranch, offer samples of their wines. This is the only winery in all of Hawaii. When Erdman moved here in 1963 from California and noticed climatic similarities to the Napa Valley, he knew that this country could grow decent wine grapes. Tedeschi comes from California, where his family has a small winery near Calistoga. The partners have worked on making their dream of Maui wine a reality since 1973.

It takes time and patience to grow grapes and turn out a vintage wine. While they wait for their carnelian grapes to mature and be made into a sparkling wine, they ferment pineapple juice, which they call Maui Blanc. If you're expecting this to be a sickeningly sweet syrup, forget it. Maui Blanc is surprisingly dry and palatable. There's even an occasional pineapple sparkling wine called Maui Brut. Both are available in restaurants and stores around the island. In 1984 the first scheduled release of the winery's carnelian champagne celebrated the patience and craftsmanship of the vintners. You can taste the wines at the 100-year-old tasting room, which is a plaster and coral building. It served as the jailhouse of the old Rose Ranch owned by James Makee, a Maui pioneer sugar cane planter.

HALEAKALA

Haleakala ("House of the Sun") is spellbinding. Like seeing Niagara or the Grand Canyon for the first time, it makes no difference how many people have come before you; it's still an undiminished, powerful, personal experience. The mountain is a power spot, a natural conductor of cosmic energy. *Kahuna* brought their novitiates here to perform final rites of initiation. During the heyday of the *kahuna,* intense power struggles took place between the healing practitioners and "black" sorcerers atop the mountain. The "Bottomless Pit," a natural feature on the crater floor, held tremendous significance for both. Average Hawaiians did not live on Haleakala, but came now and again to quarry tool stones. Only *kahuna* and their apprentices lived here for any length of time, as a sort of spiritual preparation and testing ground. Today, students of higher consciousness from around the world are attracted to this natural cosmic empire because of the rarefied energy. They claim that it accelerates personal growth, and compare it to remote mountain and desert areas in the Holy Lands. Even the U.S. Air Force has a facility here, and their research indicates Haleakala is *the* strongest natural power point in America. Not only is there an energy configuration coming from the earth itself, but there is also a high focus of radiation coming from outside the atmos-

phere. No one is guaranteed a spiritual experience on Haleakala, but if you're at all sensitive, this is fertile ground.

Natural Features
Haleakala is the world's largest dormant volcano, composed of amazingly dense volcanic rock, almost like poured cement. Its 20,000 feet or so lying under the sea make it one of the tallest mountains on earth. Perhaps this mass accounts for the strange power of Haleakala as it sits like a mighty magnetic pyramid in the center of the North Pacific. The park's boundaries encompass 27,284 variable acres, which stretch from Hosmer Grove to Kipahulu, and include dry forests, rainforests, desert, and subtropical beaches. The most impressive feature is the crater itself. It's 3,000 feet deep, 7½ miles long, and 2½ miles wide, accounting for 19 square miles, with a circumference of 21 miles. A mini mountain range of nine cinder cones marches across the crater floor. They look deceptively tiny from the observation area, but the smallest is 600 feet, and the tallest, Puu O Maui, is 1,000 feet high. Haleakala was designated as a national park in 1961. Before that it was part of the Big Island's Volcanoes Park. The entire park is a nature preserve dedicated to Hawaii's quickly vanishing indigenous plants and ani-

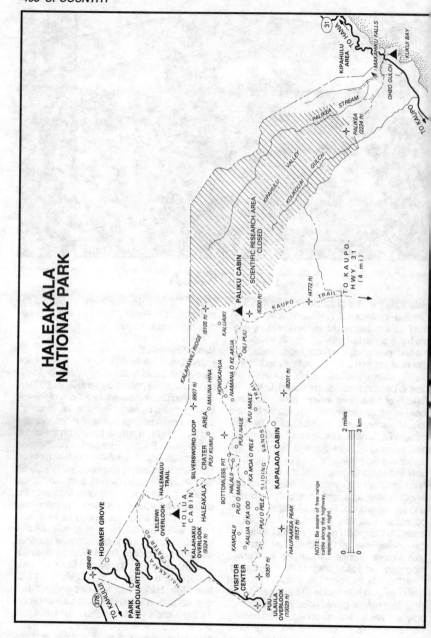

HALEAKALA
NATIONAL PARK

TO KAHULUI
(6849 ft)
378
TO KAHULUI
PARK HEADQUARTERS

HOSMER GROVE

HALEMAUU TRAIL

KALAPAWILI RIDGE (8105 ft)

SILVERSWORD LOOP (8907 ft)

HALEMAUU TRAIL

LELEIWI OVERLOOK

KALAHAKU OVERLOOK (9324 ft)

H O L U A

KALAHAKU CABIN

HALEAKALA

CRATER AREA

PUU KUMU

MAUNA HINA (8907 ft)

KALUAIKI

PALIKU CABIN

KALUAIKI

HONOKAHUA

NAMANA O KE AKUA

OILI PUU

BOTTOMLESS PIT

PUU O MAUI

HALALII

KAMOALII

PUU O KA OO

KA MOA O PELE

PUU NAUE

PUU MAILE TRAIL

KALUA O KA OO

KALUA O PELE

SLIDING SANDS

VISITOR CENTER

PUU ULAULA OVERLOOK (10023 ft)

HAUPAKEA PEAK (9157 ft)

(9357 ft)

KAPALAOA CABIN

(8201 ft)

(6300 ft)

KAUPO TRAIL

(4772 ft)

TO KAUPO HWY. 31 (4 mi)

SCIENTIFIC RESEARCH AREA CLOSED

KIPAHULU VALLEY

KOUKOUAI GULCH

PALIKEA STREAM

PALIKEA (2224 ft)

KIPAHULU AREA

MAKAHIKU FALLS

OHEO GULCH

KUKUI BAY

31

TO HANA

TO KAUPO

NOTE: Be aware of free range cattle along the highway, especially at night.

0   2 miles
0   3 km

mals. Only Volcanoes and Haleakala are home to the *nene,* the Hawaiian wild goose, and the silversword, a fantastically adapted plant. (For full descriptions, see "Flora and Fauna in the main Introduction.)

The Experience

If you're after *the* experience, you must see the sunrise or sunset. Both are magnificent, but both perform their stupendous light show with astonishing speed. Also, the weather must be cooperative. Misty, damp clouds can surround the crater, blocking out the sun, and then pour into the basin, obscuring even it from view. The *Maui News* prints the hours of sunrise and sunset on a daily basis that vary with the season, so make sure to check. The park provides an accurate daily weather recording at tel. 871-5054. For more specific information, you can call the Ranger Station at tel. 572-7749. Plan on taking a minimum of 1½ hours to arrive from Kahului, and to be safe, arrive at least 30 minutes before, because even one minute is critical. The sun, as it rises or sets, infuses the clouds with streaks, puffs, and bursts of dazzling pastels, at the same time backlighting and edging the crater in glorious golds and reds. Prepare for an emotional crescendo that will brim your eyes with tears at the majesty of it all. Engulfed by this magnificence, no one can remain unmoved.

Crater Facts

Haleakala was formed primarily from *pa'hoehoe* lava. This lava is the hottest natural substance on earth, and flows like swift fiery rivers. Because of its high viscosity, it forms classic shield volcanos. Plenty of *a'a'* is also found in the mountain's composition. This rock comes out partially solidified and filled with gases. It breaks apart and forms clinkers. You'll be hiking over both, but be especially careful on *a'a,'* because its jagged edges will cut you as quickly as coral. The crater is primarily formed from erosion, and not from caving in on itself. The erosion on Hawaii is quite accelerated due to carbonic acid build-up, a byproduct of the quick decomposition of abundant plant life. The rock breaks down into smaller particles of soil which is then washed off the mountain by rain, or blown off by wind. Natural drainage patterns form, and canyons begin to develop and slowly eat their way to the center. The two largest are Keanae Valley in the north

and Kaupo Gap in the south. These canyons, over time, moved their heads past each other to the center of the mountain, where they took several thousand feet off the summit, and formed a huge amphitheater-like crater.

Some stones that you encounter while hiking will be very light in weight. They once held water and gases that evaporated. If you knock two together, they'll sound like crystal. Also, be observant for Maui diamonds. They are garnet stones, a type of pyroxene, or crystal. The cinder cones in the crater are fascinating. They're volcanic vents with a high iron content and may form electromagnetic lines from the earth's center. Climbing them is not recommended, but many people have, even spending the night within. On top, they are like funnels, transmitters and receivers of energy, like natural pyramids. Notice the color of the compacted earth on the trails. It's obvious why you should remain on them. All the plants (silverswords, too) are shallow-rooted and live by condensing moisture on their leaves. Don't walk too close to them because you'll compact the earth around them and damage the roots. The ecosystem on Haleakala is very delicate, so please keep this in mind to preserve its beauty for future generations.

SIGHTS

You'll start enjoying Haleakala long before you reach the top. Don't make the mistake of simply bolting up the mountain without taking time to enjoy what you're passing. Route 37 from Kahului takes you through Pukalani, the last place to buy supplies. Here it branches to a clearly marked Route 377; in six miles it becomes the zigzag of Route 378 or Haleakala Crater Road. Along the way are forests of indigenous and introduced trees, including eucalyptus, beautifully flowering jacaranda, and stands of cactus. The vistas change rapidly from one vantage point to the next. Sometimes it's the green rolling hills of Ireland, and then instantly it's the tall, yellow grass of the plains. This is also cattle country, so don't be surprised to see all breeds, from Holsteins to Brahmas.

Headquarters

The first stopping point on the Crater Road is Hosmer Grove Campground (see below) on your left. Proceed past here a few minutes and you'll arrive at **Park Headquarters**. Campers can get their permits here and others will be happy to stop for all manner of brochures and information concerning the park. There are some silverswords outside and a cage for *nene* around back. After you pass Park HQ, there's trail parking on your left (see "Hikes," below). Following are two overlooks, **Leleiwi** and **Kalahaku**. Both offer tremendous views and different perspectives on the crater. They shouldn't be missed—especially Kalahaku, where there are silverswords and the remnants of a travelers' lodge from the days when an expedition to Haleakala took two days.

Visitors Center

At road's end is the Visitors Center, approximately 10 miles up the mountain from headquarters. It's open from sunrise to 3 p.m. and contains a clear and concise display featuring the geology of Haleakala. Maps are available, and the ranger talks, given every hour on the hour, are particularly informative (especially those by Ranger Jitsume Kunioke), delving into geology and the legends surrounding the great mountain.

Walks

One of the outside paths leads to **Pakaoao** ("White Hill"). An easy quarter-mile hike will take you to the summit, and along the way you'll pass stone shelters and sleeping platforms from the days when Hawaiians came here to quarry the special tool stone. It's a type of whitish slate that easily flakes and is so hard that when you strike two pieces together it rings almost like iron. Next comes **Puu'ulaula** ("Red Hill"), the highest point on Maui, at 10,023 feet. Atop is a glass-encased observation area (open 24 hours). This is where many people come to view the sunrise and sunset. From here, if the day is crystal clear, you can see all of the main Hawaiian islands except Kauai. The space colony on the crater floor below is **Science City**. This research facility is manned by the University of Hawaii and the Department of Defense. It is not open to the public.

Hikes

There are three trails in Haleakala Crater: Halemauu, Sliding Sands, and Kaupo. **Halemauu Trail** starts at the 8,000-foot level along the road

about four miles past HQ. It descends quickly to the 6,600-foot level on the crater floor. En route you'll pass Holua Cabin, Silversword Loop, the Bottomless Pit (a mere 65 feet deep), and then a portion of Sliding Sands Trail, and back to the Visitors Center. You shouldn't have any trouble hitching back to your car from here.

Sliding Sands begins at the summit of Haleakala near the Visitors Center. This is the main crater trail and gives you the best overall hike. It joins the Kaupo Trail at Paliku Cabin; alternatively, at Kapaloa Cabin you can turn left to the Bottomless Pit and exit via Halemauu Trial. This last choice is one of the best, but you'll have to hitch back to your car at the Visitors Center, which shouldn't be left for the dwindling late-evening traffic going up the mountain.

The **Kaupo Trail** is long and tough. It follows the Kaupo Gap to the park boundary at 3,800 feet. It then crosses private land, which is no problem, and deposits you in the semi-ghost town of Kaupo. This is the rugged part of the Hana loop that is forbidden by the rental car companies. You'll have to hitch west just to get to the scant traffic of Route 31, or head nine miles east to Oheo Gulch and its campground, and from there back along the Hana Road.

Along your walks, expect to see wild goats. These are often eradicated by park rangers, because they are considered an introduced pest. For those inclined, crater walks are conducted by the rangers during the summer months. These vary in length and difficulty so check at the ranger station. There are also horseback tours of the crater (see "Sports" in the main Introduction). Hikers should also consider a day with the professional guide, Ken Schmitt. His in-depth knowledge and commentary will make your trip not only more fulfilling, but enjoyably informative as well. (See "Getting Around" in the Introduction.)

PRACTICALITIES

Making "Do"

If you've come to Hawaii for sun and surf, and you aren't prepared for alpine temperatures, you can still enjoy Haleakala. For a day trip, wear your jogging suit or a sweater, if you've brought one. Make sure to wear socks, and even bring an extra pair as makeshift mittens. Use your *dry* beach towel to wrap around inside your sweater as extra insulation, and even consider taking your hotel blanket, which you can use Indian-fashion. Make rain gear from a large plastic garbage bag. Cut holes for head and arms, and this is also a good windbreaker. Take your beach hat, too. Don't worry about looking ridiculous in this get-up—you will! But you'll also keep warm! Remember that for every thousand feet you climb, the temperature drops three °F, so the summit is about 30 degrees cooler than at sea level. As the sun reaches its zenith, if there are no rain clouds, the crater floor will go from about 50 to 80 degrees. It can flip-flop from blazing hot to dismal and rainy a number of times in the same day. The nights will drop below freezing, with the coldest recorded temperature a bone-chilling 14°. Dawn and dusk are notorious for being bitter. Because of the altitude, be aware that the oxygen level will drop, and those with any impairing conditions should take precautions. The sun is ultra-strong atop the mountain and even those with deep tans are subject to burning. Noses are particularly susceptible.

Trekkers

Any serious hikers or campers must have sturdy shoes, good warm clothes, rain gear, canteens, down bag, and a serviceable tent. Hats and sunglasses are needed. Compasses are useless because of the high magnetism in the rock, but binoculars are particularly rewarding. No cook fires are allowed in the crater, so you'll need a stove. Don't burn any dead wood—the soil needs all the decomposing nutrients it can get. Drinking water is available at all of the cabins within the crater. This environment is particularly delicate. Stay on the established trails so that you don't cause undue erosion. Leave rocks and especially plants alone. Don't walk too close to silverswords or any other plants because you'll

compact the soil. Leave your pets at home; ground-nesting birds here are easily disturbed. If nature "calls," dig a very shallow hole, off the trail, and cover your toilet paper and all with the dirt. Urinating on it will hasten the decomposition process.

Camping

Admission to the park is $3, unless you arrive before the ranger, but camping is free with a necessary camping permit from Park headquarters. The **Hosmer Grove** campground is at the 6,800-foot level, just before Park headquarters; the free camping here is limited to 25 people, but there's generally room for all. There's water, pit toilets, grills, and a pavilion. It was named after Ralph Hosmer, who tried to save the watershed by planting fast-growing foreign trees like cedars, pines, and junipers. He succeeded, but this destroyed any chance of the native Hawaiian trees making a comeback.

Oheo Campground is a primitive camping area over at the Seven Pools. It's part of the park, but unless you're an intrepid hiker and descend all the way down the Kaupo Trail, you'll come to it via Hana (see "Hana and Beyond"). There are campsites in the crater at **Holua, Paliku,** and **Kapalaoa.** All three offer cabins, and tent camping is allowed at the first two. Camping at any of these is extremely popular, and reservations for the cabins must be made months in advance. A lottery of the applicants chosen for sites keeps it fair for all. Environmental impact studies limit the number of campers to 25 per area per day. Camping is limited to a total of three days, with no more than two days at each spot. For complete details write: Haleakala National Park, Box 369, Makawao, HI 96768, tel. 572-7749. Also, see the camping chart in the main Introduction.

The Hawaiians were the finest adz makers in Polynesia. One of the best stone quarries was atop Haleakala.

NORTHEAST MAUI

THE HANA ROAD

On the long and winding road to Hana's door, most people's daydreams of "paradise" come true. A trip to Maui without a visit to Hana is like ordering a sundae without a cherry on top. The 50 miles that it takes to get there from Kahului are some of the most remarkable in the world. The Hana Road (Rt. 36) starts out innocently enough, passing **Paia town.** The inspiration for Paia's gaily painted storefronts looks like it came from a jar of jelly beans. Next come some north-shore surfing beaches where windsurfers fly, doing amazing aquabatics. Soon there are a string of "rooster towns," so named because that's about all that seems to be stirring. Then Route 36 becomes Route 360 and at the three-mile marker the *real* Hana Road begins.

The semi-official count tallies over 600 rollicking turns and more than 50 one-lane bridges, inducing everyone to slow down and soak up the sights of this glorious road. It's like passing through a tunnel cut from trees. The ocean winks with azure blue through sudden openings on your left. To the right, streams, waterfalls, and pools sit wreathed with jungle and wildflowers. Coconuts, guavas, mangoes, and bananas grow everywhere on the mountainside. Fruit stands pop up regularly as you creep along. Then comes **Keanae** with its arboretum, and taro farms indicate that many ethnic Hawaiians still live along the road. There are places to camp, picnic, and swim, both in the ocean and in freshwater streams.

Then you reach **Hana** itself, a remarkable town. The great queen Kaahumanu was born here, and many celebrities live in the surrounding hills seeking peace and solitude. Past Hana, the road becomes even more rugged and besieged by jungle. It opens up again around **Oheo Stream** (or Seven Pools). Here waterfalls cascade over stupendous cataracts, forming a series of pools until they reach the sea. Beyond is a rental car's no-man's land, where the passable road toughens and Haleakala shows its barren volcanic face scarred by lava flows.

LOWER PAIA

Paia ("Noisy") was a bustling sugar town that took a nap. When it awoke, it had a set of whiskers and its vitality had flown away. At the turn of the century, many groups of ethnic field workers lived here, segregated in housing clusters called "camps" that stretched up Baldwin Avenue. Paia was the main gateway for sugar on East Maui, and even a railroad functioned here until 20 years ago. During the 1930s, its population, at over 10,000, was the largest on the island. Then fortunes shifted toward Kahului, and Paia lost its dynamism, until recently. Paia was resuscitated in the 1970s by an influx of paradise-seeking hippies, and then again in the '80s came another shot in the arm from windsurfers. These two groups have metamorphosed into townsfolk, and have pumped new life into its old muscles. The practical shops catering to the pragmatic needs of a "plantation town" were replaced. The storefronts were painted and spruced up. A new breed of merchants with their eye on passing tourists has taken over. Now Paia (Lower) focuses on boutiques, crafts, and artwork. Since you've got to pass through on your way to Hana, it serves as a great place not only to top off your gas tank, but also to stop for a bite and a browse. The prices are good for just about everything, and it boasts one of the island's best fish restaurants and art shops. Paia, under its heavy makeup, is still a vintage example of what it always was—a homey, serviceable, working town.

Sights

A mile or so before you enter Paia on the left is **Rinzai Buddhist Temple.** The grounds are pleasant and worth a look. **Mantokuji Buddhist Temple** in Paia heralds the sun's rising and setting by ringing its huge gong 18 times at dawn and dusk.

Baldwin County Park is on your left about seven miles past Kahului on Route 36; this spacious park is good for swimming, shell collecting, and decent winter surf. There's tent and trailer camping (county permit required) and full amenities. Unfortunately, Baldwin has a bad reputation. It's one of those places that locals have staked out with the attitude of "us against them." Hassles and robberies have been known to occur. Be nice, calm, and respectful. For the timid, to be on the safe side, be gone.

Hookipa Beach Park is about 10 minutes past Paia. There's a high, grassy sand dune along the road and the park is down below, where you'll enjoy full amenities and camping

with a county permit. Swimming is advisable only on calm days, as there are wicked currents. Primarily a surfing beach that is now regarded as one of the best sailboarding areas in Hawaii, this is home to the O'Neill International Windsurfing Championship, held yearly during early spring. The world's best sailboarders come here, trying to win the $10,000 prize. A colorful spectacle. Bring binoculars.

Food

Picnic's, along Baldwin Ave., tel. 579-8021, is open daily 7:30 a.m. to 3:30 p.m. Breakfast and lunch offer a great combination of food with everything from roast beef to vegetarian sandwiches like a scrumptious spinach nut burger and cheese or tofu burger, all under $5. The best news are boxed picnic lunches that add a special touch if you're heading to Hana (few restaurants there). They start from the basic "Countryside," which includes sandwiches and sides at $7.95 per person, to the "Executive" with sandwiches, *kiawe*-broiled chicken, sides, nut bread, condiments, cheeses, and even a tablecloth all in a foam ice chest for $42.50 (says it'll feed two, but with extra buns will feed four!). One of the best stops along the Hana Road even for a quick espresso, cappuccino, or frozen yogurt. Or treat yourself with the fresh-baked pastries like macadamia nut sticky buns, and the apple and papaya turnovers: worth the guilt!

Kihata Restaurant is a small Japanese restaurant and sushi bar that you can easily pass by. Don't! It's just where Baldwin Avenue meets Route 36 along the main road. Open Mon.-Sat. 10 a.m. to 2 p.m., 5 to 9 p.m., closed Sunday. The traditional Japanese menu offers *bento* and sushi, with all entrees under $8, mostly from $5-6, like *donburi, soba,* and *udon.* The best deal is the Kihata *teishoku,* a full meal of steak, shrimp, vegetables, and *miso* soup for under $12.

Dillon's, Hana Rd., Paia, tel. 579-9113, open daily for breakfast, lunch, and dinner. From the outside you'd expect Marshal Dillon and Kitty to come sashaying through the swinging doors, but inside it's Polynesian with a sort of German beer garden out back. The food is well prepared and the portions large. Mostly steaks, chops, and fish with a Hawaiian twist. Moderate to expensive. Dillon's is famous for it's eggs Benedict special from 7 to 8 a.m. for $5.95. After Mama's (below), the best place in Paia!

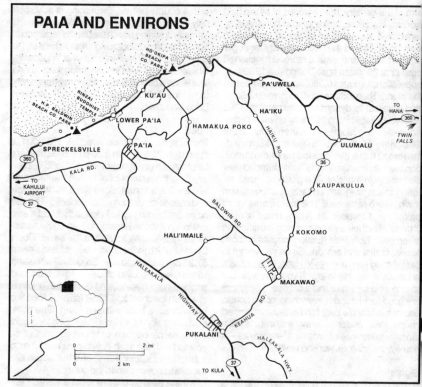

PAIA AND ENVIRONS

Mama's Fish House is just past Paia on the left, but look hard for the turnoff near the blinking yellow light, where you'll see a vintage car with a sign for Mama's. Turn left at the ship's flagpole and follow the "angel fish" sign down to Kuau Cove. Daily dinner only, reservations recommended, tel. 579-9672. Mama's has the best reputation possible—it gets thumbs up from local people. The fish is fresh daily, with some broiled over kiawe. Vegetables come from local gardens and the herbs are Mama's own. Special Hawaiian touches with every meal. Expensive, but worth it. Make reservations for the evening's return trip from Hana. One of the best restaurants on Maui!

For a quick bite you have **Charlie P. Woofers,** a saloon and restaurant with pool tables, selling food and beer. Choices include eggs Benedict, $6.25, huevos rancheros, $6.25,

lunch chili burger, $4.50, pasta around $6, and dinner lasagna for $7.50 including salad. The **Garden Cafe** offers inexpensive breakfasts under $5 like fruit-filled pancakes, or lunch spinach salad for $4.25, and house sandwiches like "tropical amnesia" for $4.95. **Ice Cream and Dreams** has frosty yummies and sandwiches at the corner of Baldwin Avenue.

For health food try **Mana Natural Foods,** at 49 Baldwin Ave., tel. 579- 8078, open daily 8 a.m. to 8 p.m., Sun. 9 a.m. to 7 p.m. Much expanded over the old Tradewinds, it's a well-stocked health-food store, maybe the best on Maui. Inside the old building you'll find local organic produce, and vitamins, grains, juices, bulk foods, and more. Outside, check out the great community bulletin board for what's selling and happening around Paia.

Shopping

Maui Crafts Guild is on the left just before entering Paia, at 43 Hana Rd., Box 609, Paia, HI 96779, tel. 579-9693. Open daily from 9 a.m. to 6 p.m. The Crafts Guild is one of the best art outlets in Hawaii. It's owned and operated by the artists themselves, all of whom must pass a thorough "jurying" by present members. All artists must be islanders, and they must use natural materials found in Hawaii to create their work except for some specialized clay, fabrics, and printmaking paper which must be imported. Items are tastefully displayed and it's an experience just to look. You'll find a wide variety of artwork and crafts including pottery, furniture, beadwork, woodcarving, bamboowork, stained glass, batik, and jewelry. Different artists man the shop on different days, but phone numbers are available if you want to see more of something you like. Prices on smaller items are reasonable, and this is an excellent place to make that one "big" purchase.

In downtown Paia (two blocks along the highway) is **Tropical Emporium** with resortwear, and the **Paia Trading Co.,** a discovery shop, open Mon.-Fri. 9 a.m. to 5 p.m., that has a rack of antique Hawaiian shirts, real collector's items. The **Tee Shirt Factory** sells T-shirts that are more expensive elsewhere. **Paia Gallery and Gifts,** tel. 579-8185, daily 8 a.m. to 7 p.m., displays art by local Maui artists, including fantastic woodcarvings by Bruce Whitaker, and watercolors by Eona that have captured the fantastic colors of Maui, from windsurfers to humpback whales. The porcelains are by Roman Hubble, basketry with feathers and reeds by Fiama.

Across the street **Exotic Maui Woods,** tel. 572-2993, open daily 9 a.m. to 6 p.m., is a treasure of amazing wood sculptures from birds on the wing to mermaids emerging from a wooden wave. Displayed are trays with inlaid fish and wooden eggs, and even a beautifully fashioned but practical picnic table is for sale. In the rear is the shop of **Eddie Flotte,** one of the finest and most highly acclaimed artists living on Maui today. His work has been compared with Norman Rockwell's, but he is an artistic genius who has his own style, and needs no comparison to elevate his work. Fame has made his simple, sensitive work very expensive, but you can purchase mounted, signed photos of the originals from only $55. Eddie Flotte is able to capture the essence of Maui. His subject matter is the "every day" that everyone else overlooks . . . a rusted-out surfer's VW, or some old-timers sitting in the shade of a tree. If you want to appreciate the soul of Maui on canvas, check out this studio. Next door is **Second Chance,** a discovery shop whose proceeds go to fund a self-help refuge for women and children who are victims of domestic violence. They sell a great selection of old photos, especially of Hawaiiana and classic movie actors like Clark Gable.

Walk along Baldwin Avenue for a half block and you'll find a drawerfull of boutiques and fashion shops. **Nuage Bleu,** a boutique open daily from 10 a.m. to 5 p.m., feaures distinctive fashions and gift items, mostly for women. **Ikeda's** is a tired old department store where the *people* shop so the goods are reasonably priced. **Rona Gale,** 27 Baldwin Ave., tel. 579-9984, open daily 10 a.m. to 5 p.m., specializes in natural fabrics and handmade Maui clothing, and woodcrafted items from Indonesia along with batik shirts, jackets, and cover-ups. **Yoki's Boutique,** tel. 572-9003, open daily 10 a.m. to 5 p.m., has jewelry, gifts, and apparel from all over the world. Yoki is an artist and she hand paints the one-of-a-kind fashions that adorn the walls. The **Clothes Addict** has antique aloha shirts, and sexy, new-wave bikinis.

Unocal 76 is the last place to fill your tank before reaching Hana. Next door is **Paia General Store** for supplies and sundries, with a takeout snack window called the **Paia Drive Inn.** Across the street is the **Paia Mercantile Shopping Complex,** a collection of shops ranging from surfing equipment to **North Shore Silks,** with silk clothing for women, and **Tropical Blossoms,** a wholesale outlet for gift items.

Heading down the road to Hana you'll see the **Maui Community Center** on your left, and soon, just past mile marker 12, look for W. Kuiaha Road and make a right heading for the old Pauwela Cannery, which is less than five minutes up the road. This huge tin can of a building has been divided into a honeycomb of studios and workshops housing fine artists, woodworkers, cabinetmakers, potters, and sailboard makers. All welcome guests to come and browse, and buy. In the rear is **Resta Studio,** the workshop of Piero Resta. He, along with his son Luigi, graciously welcomes visitors (call first, 575-2203), and with Italian hospitality makes you feel at home with a cup of cappuccino. To qualify as a *real* Italian gentleman you must have imagination! Without it you're like pasta with no sauce, or pesto with no basil. You must possess, and be willing to share, opinions on life, politics, religion, philosophy, and moreover you must be a lover . . . of art, women, music, and food, preferably all in the same evening! Piero Resta *is* an Italian gentleman. His studio with loft (necessary to be a real artist) is a vision of dynamism. His works are bold, colorful, neo- Renaissance personal statements of semi-abstract reality. Broad-hipped women with classical Greek faces pose or stride nonchalantly across a surrealistic collage of vibrant Maui colors. Carved wooden pillars wait to adorn a modern portico, while a mythical yellow tiger on a bold red background opens its mouth in anticipation of eating its own tail. The studio and the artwork surround you like a colorful wave. Soul surf with Piero. You'll be glad you did!

THE ROAD BEGINS

The road to Hana holds many spectacles and surprises, but one of the best is the road itself . . . it's a marvel! The road was hacked out from the coastline in 1927, every inch by hand using pick and shovel. An ancient Hawaiian trail followed the same route for part of the way, but mostly people moved up and down this coastline by boat. What makes the scenery so special is that the road snakes along Maui's windward side. There's abundant vegetation and countless streams flowing from Haleakala, carving gorgeous valleys. There are a few scattered villages with a house or two that you hardly notice, and the beaches, although few, are empty. Mostly, however, it's the "feeling" that you get along this road. Nature is close and accessible, and it's so incredibly "South Sea island" that it almost seems artificial. But it isn't.

Driving Tips

You've got 30 miles of turns ahead when Route 36 (mile marker 22) becomes Route 360 (mile marker 0) and the fun begins. The Hana Road has the reputation of being "bad road," but this isn't true. It's narrow, with plenty of hairpin turns, but it's well banked, has clearly marked bridges, and there's always maintenance going on (which can slow you up). Years back, it was a

harrowing experience. When mudslides blocked the road, drivers were known to swap their cars with those on the opposite side and carry on to where they were going. The road's reputation sets people up to expect an ordeal, so they make it one, and unfortunately, drive accordingly. Sometimes it seems as though tourists demand the road to be rugged, so that they can tell the folks back home that they, too, "survived the road to Hana." This popular slogan appears on T-shirts, copyrighted and sold by Hasegawa's famous store in Hana, and perpetuates this belief. You'll have no problem, and you'll see much more if you just take it easy.

Your speed will often drop below 10 miles per hour, and will rarely exceed 25. Standard-shift cars are better for the turns. Cloudbursts occur at any time so be ready for slick roads. A heavy fall of fruit from roadside mango trees can also coat the road with slippery slime. Look as far up the road as possible and don't allow yourself to be mesmerized by the 10 feet in front of your hood. If your tire dips off a rough shoulder, don't risk losing control by jerking the wheels back on immediately. Ride it for a while and either stop or wait for an even shoulder to come back on. Local people trying to make time will often ride your rear bumper, but generally they won't honk. Pull over and let them by when possible.

Driving from Kahului to Hana will take three hours, not counting some recommended stops. The greatest traffic flow is from 10 a.m. to noon; returning "car trains" start by 3 p.m. and are heaviest around 5 p.m. Many white-knuckled drivers head for Hana as if it were a prized goal, without stopping along the way. This is ridiculous. The best sights are *before* and *after* Hana; the town itself is hardly worth the effort. Expect to spend a long day exploring the Hana Road. To go all the way to Oheo Stream and take in some sights, you'll have to leave your hotel at sunup and won't get back until sundown. If your budget can afford it, think of staying the night in Hana (reservations definitely) and return the next day. This is a particularly good alternative if you have an afternoon departing flight from Kahului Airport. Also, most tourists seem terrified of driving the road at night. Actually it's easier. There is far less traffic, road reflectors mark the center and sides like a runway, and you're warned of oncoming cars by their headlights. Those in the know make much better time after dark!

HANA ROAD

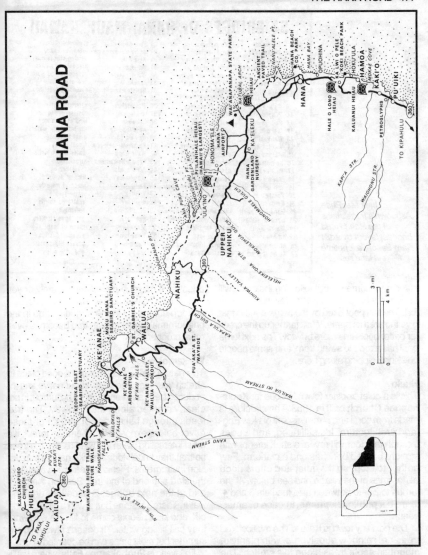

SIGHTS

Twin Falls

This is one of the first places to stop and enjoy. Park just before Hoolawa Bridge, coming up after mile marker 2 on Route 360. Go over the red gate in the center of the parking area and follow the jeep trail. Stay on the trail for about 15 minutes, ignoring the little cattle trails left and right. Plenty of guavas along here are free for the picking. Once you've reached the top of the hill, bear left toward the creek. The area *feels* like private property, but access is allowed. The falls can be tough to locate because of a lack of any out-

54 BRIDGES OF HANA, MAUI, HAWAII

#	Name	Translation	#	Name	Translation
1	O'o-pu-ola	life maturing	28	Pu-a-pa-pe	baptismal
2	Ma-ka-na-le	bright vision	29	Ka-ha-wai-ha-pa-pa	extensive valley
3	Ka-ai-ea	breathtaking view	30	Ke-a-a-iki	burning star (sirius)
4	Wai-a-ka-mo'i	waters of the king	31	Wai-oni (Akahi)	first ruffled waters
5	Pu-oho-ka-moa	sudden awakening	32	Wai-oni (Elua)	second ruffled waters
6	Hai-pue-na	glowing hearts	33	Lani-ke-le	heavenly mist
7	Ko-le'a	windborne joy	34	He-lele-i-ke-oha	extending greetings
8	Hono-manu	bird valley	35	Ula-i-no	intense sorrow
9	Nu'a-'ai-lua	large abundance	36	Moku-lehua	solemn feast
10	Pi-na-ao	kind hearted	37	'O-i-lo-wai	first sprouting
11	Pa-lauhulu	leaf sheltered	38	Hono-ma-'e-le	land of deep love
12	Wai-o-ka-milo	whirling waters	39	Ka-wai-pa-pa	the forbidden waters
13	Wai-kani	sounding waters	40	Ko-hoio-po	night traveling
14	Wai-lua-nui	increasing waters	41	Ka-ha-wai-'oka-pi-a	frugal valley
15	Wai-lua-iki	diminishing waters	42	Wai-o-honu	water of the turtle
16	Ko-pi-li-ula	sacred ceremony	43	Papa'a-hawa-hawa	stronghold
17	Pu'a-aka-a	open laughter	44	Ala-ala-'ula	reawakening
18	Wai-o-hu-e	deceptive waters	45	Wai-i-ka-ko'i	time of demand
19	Wai-o-hu-e-'lua	second deceptive water	46	Pa-'ihi	place of majesty
20	Pa-akea	spacious enclosure	47	Wai-lua	water spirits
21	Ka-pa-'ula	to hold sacred	48	Wa-'i-lua	scattered spirits
22	Hana-wi (Akahi)	first whistling wind	49	Pu'u-ha-o-a	burning hill
23	Hana-wi (Elua)	second whistling wind	50	Pae-hala	pandanus clusters
24	Ma-ka-pi-pi	desire for blessings	51	Maha-lawa	place of rest
25	Ku-hiwa	precious love	52	Hana-lawe	proud deduction
26	Ku-pu-koi	claiming tribute	53	Pua-a-lu-'u	prayer blossoms
27	Ka-ha-la-o-wa-ka	lightning flash	54	O'he'o	enduring pride

Interpretations Inez MacPhee Ashdown

Inez MacPhee Ashdown's translations of the Hana Road bridges; layout by artist Sam Eason, a longtime Hana resident

standing landmarks, but following the creek will ensure success, and they're well worth the effort. The first pool is fed by the two waterfalls that give the area its name. Walk farther up the creek for better pools and more privacy. The next large pool has a rope to swing from, and some people go skinny-dipping along here.

Huelo

This is a quiet "rooster town" famous for **Kaulanapueo Church** built in 1853. The structure is made from coral and is reminiscent of New England architecture. It's still used, and a peek through the door will reveal a stark interior with straight-backed benches and a platform. Few bother to stop, so it's quiet and offers good panoramas of the village and sea below. At the turnoff to Huelo between mile markers 3 and 4, there's a **public telephone,** in case of emergency.

The next tiny town is Kailua. The multicolored trees are rainbow eucalyptus, with plenty of mountain apple trees along this stretch. The rainbow eucalyptus, introduced late last century from Australia, are some of the most beautiful trees in Hawaii. Close by is a cousin, *Eucalyptus robusta,* which produces great timber, especially flooring, from its reddish-brown heartwood. This tree, due to its resins, gets extremely hard once it

dries, so it must be milled immediately or you can do nothing with it. In a few minutes, notice a sudden difference in the humidity, and in the phenomenal jungle growth that becomes even more pronounced.

Waikamoi Ridge

This nature walk (mosquitos!) is a good place to stretch your legs and learn about native and introduced trees and vegetation. The turnout is not clearly marked along the highway. The trail leads through tall stands of trees. For those never before exposed to a bamboo forest, it's most interesting when the wind rustles the trees so that they knock together like natural percussion instruments. Picnic tables are available at the start and end of the trail. Back on the road, and at the next bridge, is excellent drinking water. There's a stone barrel with a pipe coming out, and local people come to fill jugs with what they call "living water." It doesn't always run in summer but most times can be counted upon.

Following is **Puohokamoa Falls,** where you'll find a nice pool and picnic table. A short stroll will take you to the pool and its 30-foot cliff from where local kids jump off. You'll also find a trail near the falls, and if you go upstream about 100 yards you'll discover another invigorating pool with yet another waterfall. Swimming is great here, and the small crowd is gone. If you hike downstream about one-half mile through the stream (no trail), you come to the top of a 200-foot falls from where you can peer over the edge.

Beach Parks

Less than two miles past Waikamoi Ridge is **Kaumahina State Wayside** along the road, and **Honomanu County Park,** down at Honomanu Bay. Permits are required for camping. There are no amenities at Honomanu, but Kaumahina has them all. Camping here is in a rainforest with splendid views out to sea overlooking the rugged coastline and the black-sand beach of Honomanu Bay. Puohokamoa Falls are just a short walk away. Honomanu is not good for swimming because of strong currents, but is good for surfing.

Keanae

Honomanu Valley, just before the Kaenae Arboretum, is the largest valley on the north side of Haleakala. Most of the big valleys that once existed, especially on East Maui, were filled in by lava flows, greatly reducing their original size. But Honomanu goes back about five miles towards the center of the mountain, and has 3,000-foot cliffs and 1,000-foot waterfalls. Unfortunately, the trails are both quite difficult to find and to negotiate. Clearly marked on the right will be **Keanae Arboretum.** A hike through this facility will exemplify Hawaiian plant life in microcosm. There are three sections: native forest, introduced forest, and traditional Hawaiian plants and foodstuffs. You can picnic and swim along Piinaau Stream. Hardier hikers can continue for another mile through typical (identified) rainforest. **Camp Keanae YMCA** is just before the arboretum. It looks exactly as its name implies, set in a gorgeous natural pasture. There are various bunkhouses for men and women. Arrival time between 4 and 6 p.m., $8. For more information call the camp at tel. 248-8355.

The first bridge past the camp offers a good and easily accessible swimming hole. **Keanae Peninsula** is a thumb-like appendage of land formed by a lava flow that came down the hollowed-out valley of Haleakala Crater. A fantastic lookout is here, but is poorly marked. Look for a telephone pole with a tsunami loudspeaker atop, and pull off just there. Below you'll see neat little farms, mostly raising taro. Most people living on the peninsula are native Hawaiians. They still make poi the old-fashioned way: listen for the distinctive thud of poi-pounding in the background. Though *kapu* signs abound, the majority of people are friendly. A public road circles the peninsula, but fences across it give it a private vibration. If you visit, realize that this is one of the last patches of ground owned by Hawaiians and tended in the old way. Be respectful, please. Notice the lava-rock missionary church. Next comes the lonely Wailua Peninsula. It, too, is covered in taro, and is a picturesque spot. Realize that only 3,000 people live along the entire north coast of East Maui leading to and including Hana.

Fruit Stands

Do yourself a favor and look for **Uncle Harry's Fruit Stand**, clearly marked on the left just past the Keanae Peninsula. If he's there stop and talk. He's a medical kahuna who knows a great deal of the natural pharmacology of old Hawaii, and is a living encyclopedia on herbs and all their healing properties. Past Kaenae between mile markers 17 and 18 is a roadside stand where you can buy hot dogs, shave ice, and some fruit. Notice the picture-perfect, idyllic watercress farm on your left. Past mile marker 18 on the right is a fruit stand operated by a fellow named Joseph. He not only has coconuts and papayas, but also little-tasted exotic fruits like mountain apples, star fruit, pineapple, strawberry guavas, and Tahitian lemons. An authentic fruit stand worth a stop. Another one, operated by a Hawaiian woman, is only 50 yards on the left. If you have a hankering for fruit, this is the spot.

Wailua

At mile marker 18, you come to Wailua. Turn left here on Wailua Road, following signs for **Coral Miracle Church.** Here, too, you'll find the **Miracle of Fatima Shrine,** so named because a freak storm in the 1860s washed up enough coral onto Wailua Beach that the church could be constructed by the Hawaiian congregation. There is a lovely and relatively easy-access waterfall nearby. Pass the church, turn right, and park by the large field. Look for a worn path (may be private, but no signs or hassle) that leads down to the falls.

Puaa Kaa State Wayside

This lovely spot is about 14 miles before Hana. There's no camping, but there are picnic tables, grills, and restrooms. Nearby are Kopiliula and Waikani falls. A stream provides some smaller falls and pools suitable for swimming.

Nahiku

The village, named after the Hawaiian Pleiades, is reached by a three mile road, and has the dubious distinction of being one of the wettest spots along the coast. At one time Nahiku was a thriving Hawaiian village with thousands of inhabitants. Today it's home to only about 70 people, the best known being George Harrison. A few inhabitants are Hawaiian families, but mostly the people are wealthy Mainlanders seeking isolation. After a few large and attractive homes went up, the real estate agents changed the description from "desolate" to "secluded." What's the difference? About $500,000 per house! At the turn of the century it was the site of the Nahiku Rubber Co., the only commercial rubber plantation in the United States. Many rubber trees still line the road, although the venture collapsed in 1912 because the rubber was poor due to the overabundance of rainfall, and the village once again lost its vitality. Some people have augmented their incomes by growing *pakalolo* in the rainforest of this area. However, the alternative people who first came here and have settled in have discovered that there is just as much money to be made by raising ornamental tropical flowers ($5,000-10,000 per acre), and have become real "flower children."

Hana Airport

Pass **Hana Gardenland Nursery,** where you're free to browse and picnic. They have fresh-cut flowers daily, and the prices are some of the best on Maui. Past the Gardenland is a road leading left. This rough track will take you to Ulaino and **Piilanihale Heiau,** Hawaii's largest, with massive walls that rise over 50 feet. It's on private land, but accessible. In less than a mile past here, a sign points left to **Hana Airport,** where **Aloha Island Air,** tel. (800) 323-3345, operates daily flights servicing Hana.

Waianapanapa State Park

Only three miles outside Hana, this state park offers not only tent camping, but cabins sleeping up to six on a sliding scale, at $10 single up to $30 for six. The cabins offer hot water, a full kitchen, electricity, and bedding. A deposit is required. They're very popular so book far in advance by writing Division of State Parks (see "Camping" in the main Introduction). Even for those not camping, Waianapanapa is a "must stop." Pass the office to the beach park and its black-sand beach. The swimming is dangerous during heavy surf because the bottom drops off quickly, but on calm days it's mellow. The snorkeling is excellent. Just offshore is a clearly visible natural stone bridge. Write Box 1049, Wailuku, HI 96753, tel. 244-4354.

A well-marked trail leads to **Waianapanapa Caves.** The tunnel-like trail passes through a thicket of vines and *hao*, a bush used by the Hawaiians to mark an area as *kapu*. The caves are like huge smooth tubs formed from lava. The water trapped inside is crystal clear. These caves mark the site of a Hawaiian legend, in which a lovely princess named Popoalaea fled from her cruel husband, Kakae. He found her hiding here and killed her. During certain times of the year millions of tiny red shrimp invade the caves, turning the waters red, which the Hawaiians say is a reminder of the poor slain princess. Along the coastline here are remnants of the ancient Hawaiian **paved trail** that you can follow for a short distance.

Helani Gardens

Your last stop before Hana town, clearly marked on the right, these gardens are a labor of love begun 30 years ago and opened to the public in 1975. Howard Cooper, founder and longtime Hana resident, still tends them. The gardens are open daily 10 a.m to 4 p.m., adults $2, children $1, seniors $1, picnic tables and restrooms. Mr. Cooper's philosophy on life graces a bulletin board just before you cross the six bridges to heaven. In brief he says, "Don't hurry, don't worry, don't forget to smell the flowers." It's a self-guided tour with something for everyone. The "lower gardens" are five acres formally manicured, but the 65 acres of "upper garden" are much more wild and open to anyone wishing to stroll around. The lower gardens have flowering trees and shrubs, vines, fruit trees, and flowers and potted plants everywhere. People see many of these plants in nurseries around the country, and may even have grown some varieties at home, but these specimens are huge. There are baobab trees, ginger plants, carp ponds, even papyrus. The fruit trees alone could supply a supermarket. The upper gardens are actually a nursery where plants from around the world are raised. Some of the most popular are heliconia and ginger, and orchids galore. In one giant tree, Mr. Cooper's grandchildren have built a tree house, complete with picture windows, electricity, and plumbing! The entire operation is family run, with Howard himself conducting some tours and his grandson, Matthew, running the admission office. In Mr. Cooper's own words, "Helani Garden is where heaven touches the earth." Be one of the saved!

HANA TOWN

Hana is about as pretty a town as you'll find anywhere in Hawaii, but if you're expecting anything stupendous you'll be sadly disappointed. For most it will only be a quick stopover at a store or beach en route to Oheo Stream: the townsfolk refer to these people as "rent-a-car tourists." The lucky who stay in Hana, or those not worried about time, will find plenty to explore throughout the area. The town is built on rolling hills that descend to Hana Bay; much of the surrounding lands are given over to pasture, while trim cottages wearing flower corsages line the town's little lanes. Before the white man arrived, Hana was a stronghold that was conquered and reconquered by the kings of Maui and those of the north coast of the Big Island. The most strategic and historically laden spot is Kauiki Hill, the remnant of a cinder cone that dominates Hana Bay. This area is steeped in Hawaiian legend, and old stories relate that it was the demigod Maui's favorite spot. It's said that he transformed his daughter's lover into Kauiki Hill and turned her into the gentle rains that bathe it to this day.

Changing History
Hana was already a plantation town in the mid-1800s when a hard-boiled sea captain named George Wilfong started producing sugar on his 60 acres. Over the years the laborers came from the standard mixture of Hawaiian, Japanese, Chinese, Portuguese, Filipino, and even Puerto Rican stock. The luna were Scottish, German, or American. All have combined to become the people of Hana. Sugar production faded out by the 1940s and Hana began to die, its population dipping below 500. Just then, San Francisco industrialist Paul Fagan purchased 14,000 acres of what was to become the **Hana Ranch.** Realizing that sugar was *pau,* he replanted his lands in *pangola* range grass and imported Hereford cattle from another holding on Molokai. Their white faces staring back at you as you drive past are now a standard part of Hana's scenery. Fagan loved Hana and felt an obligation to and affection for its people. He also decided to retire here, and with enough money to materialze just about anything, he decided that Hana could best survive through limited tourism. He built the **Hotel Hana-Maui,** which catered to millionaires, mostly his friends, and began operation in 1946. Fagan owned a baseball team, the San Francisco Seals, and brought them to Hana in 1946 for spring training. This was a brilliant publicity move because sportswriters came along; becoming enchanted with Hana, they gave it a great deal of copy and were probably the first to publicize the phrase "Heavenly Hana." It wasn't long before tourists began arriving.

Unfortunately, the greatest heartbreak in modern Hana history occurred at just about the same time, on April 1, 1946. An earthquake in Alaska's Aleutian Islands sent huge tidal waves that raked the Hana coast. These destroyed hundreds of homes, wiping out entire villages and tragically sweeping away many people in their watery arms of death. Hana recovered, but never forgot. Life went on, and the menfolk began working as *paniolo* on Fagan's spread, and during round-up would drive the cattle through town and down to Hana Bay where they were forced to swim to waiting barges. Other entire families went to work at the resort, and so Hana lived again. It's this legacy of quietude and old-fashioned aloha that attracted people to Hana over the years. Everyone knows that Hana's future lies in its uniqueness and remoteness, and no one wants it to change. The people as well as the tourists know what they have here. What really makes Hana "heavenly" is similar to what's

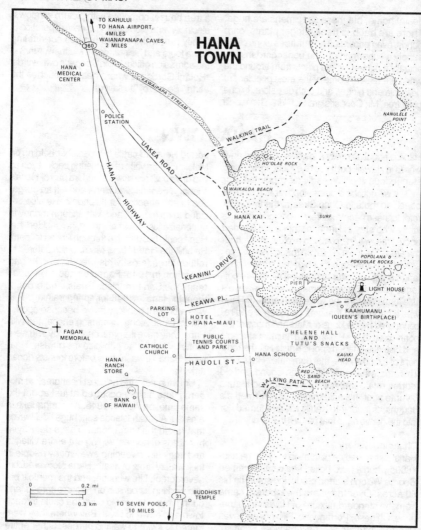

HANA TOWN

TO KAHULUI
TO HANA AIRPORT,
4 MILES
WAIANAPANAPA CAVES,
2 MILES

360

HANA MEDICAL CENTER

POLICE STATION

KAWAIPAPA STREAM

WALKING TRAIL

NANULELE POINT

UAKEA ROAD

HANA HIGHWAY

HO'OLAE ROCK

WAIKALOA BEACH

HANA KAI

SURF

KEANINI DRIVE

POPOLANA & POKUOLAE ROCKS

PIER

LIGHT HOUSE

KEAWA PL.

PARKING LOT

HOTEL HANA-MAUI

KAAHUMANU (QUEEN'S BIRTHPLACE)

FAGAN MEMORIAL

PUBLIC TENNIS COURTS AND PARK

HELENE HALL AND TUTU'S SNACKS

CATHOLIC CHURCH

HANA SCHOOL

KAUIKI HEAD

HANA RANCH STORE

HAUOLI ST.

RED SAND BEACH

BANK OF HAWAII

WALKING PATH

0   0.2 mi
0   0.3 km

31

BUDDHIST TEMPLE

TO SEVEN POOLS,
10 MILES

preached in Sunday school: everyone wants to go there, but not everyone makes it.

SIGHTS

Hana Bay
Dominating the bay is the red-faced Kauiki Hill. Fierce battles raged here, especially between Maui chief Kahekili and Kalaniopuu of Hawaii,

just before the islands were united under Kamehameha. Kalaniopuu held the natural fortress until Kahekili forced a capitulation by cutting off the water supply. It's believed that Kamehameha himself boarded Capt. James Cook's ship after a lookout spotted it from this hill. More importantly, Queen Kaahumanu, Kamehameha's favorite and the Hawaiian *ali'i* most responsible for ending the old *kapu* system and leading Hawaii into the "new age," was born in a cave here in 1768. Until very recent times fish spotters sat atop the hill looking for telltale signs of large schools of fish.

To get there, simply follow Uakea Road to its end, where it splits from the Hana Road at the police station at the edge of town. Take it right down to the pier and park. Hana Beach has full amenities and the swimming is good. It's been a surfing spot for centuries, although the best breakers occur in the middle of the bay. To explore Kauiki look for a pathway on your right and follow it. Hana disappears immediately; few tourists come out this way. Walk for five minutes until the lighthouse comes clearly into view. The footing is slightly difficult but there are plenty of ironwoods to hang onto as the path hugs the mountainside. A few pockets of red-sand beach eroded from the cinder cone are below. A copper plaque erected in 1928 commemorates the spot of Kaahumanu's birth. This entire area is a great spot for a secluded picnic only minutes from town. Proceed straight ahead to the lighthouse sitting on a small island. To cross, you'll have to leap from one jagged rock to another. If this doesn't suit you, take your bathing suit and swim across a narrow sandy-bottomed channel. Stop for a few moments and check the wave action to avoid being hurled against the rocks. When you've got it timed, go for it! The view from up top is great.

Fagan Memorial

Across from the Hotel Hana-Maui, atop Lyon's hill, is a lava-stone cross erected to the memory of Paul I. Fagan, who died in 1960. The land is privately owned, but it's OK to go up there if the gate is open. If not, inquire at the hotel. From atop the hill you get the most panoramic view of the entire Hana area. After a rain, magic mushrooms have been known to pop up in the "cow pies" in the pasture surrounding the cross. Near the hotel is the **Wananalua Church,** built from coral blocks in 1838. The missionaries deliberately and symbolically built it on top of an old heiau, where the pagan gods had been worshipped for centuries. It was the custom of chiefs to build heiau before entering battle. Since Hana was always contested ground, dozens of minor heiau can be found throughout the region.

Hana Cultural Center

Located along Uakea Road on the right just a few hundred yards after it splits from the Hana Road, open daily 10 a.m. to 4 p.m., $2 donation. The Cultural Center was founded in 1971 by Babes Hanchett, who is on the board of directors. It occupies an unpretentious building (notice the beautifully carved doors, however) on the grounds of the old courthouse and jail. The center houses fine examples of quiltwork: one, entitled "Aloha Kuu Hae," was done by Rosaline Kelinoi, a Hana resident and the first woman voted into the State Legislature. There are pre-contact stone implements, tapa cloth, and an extensive shell collection. Your $2 entitles you to visit the courthouse and jail. Simple but functional, with bench and witness stand, it makes "Andy of Mayberry" look like big time. The jail was used from 1871 to 1978, and the townsfolk knew whenever it held an inmate because he became the groundskeeper and the grass would suddenly be mowed.

BEACHES

Red Sand Beach

This is a fascinating and secluded beach area, but unfortunately the walk down is absolutely treacherous. The path, after a while, skirts the side of a cliff, and the footing is made tougher because of unstable and crumbly cinders. Grave accidents have occurred, and even locals won't make the trip. Follow Uakea Road past the turn-off to Hana Bay. Proceed ahead until you pass the public tennis courts on your right and Hana School on your left. The road dead ends in a grassy field. Look left for the worn path and follow it unless it has been posted *closed* by the Hana Ranch. Ahead is a Japanese cemetery with its distinctive headstones. Below are pockets of red sand amidst fingers of black lava washed by sky-blue water. There are many tidepools here. Keep walking until you are obviously in the hollowed-out amphitheater of the red cinder cone. Pat the walls to feel how crumbly they are— the red "sand" is eroded cinder. The water in the cove is fantastically blue against the redness.

Across the mouth of the bay are little pillars of stone, like castle parapets from a fairy kingdom, that keep the water safe for swimming. This is a favorite fishing spot for local people and the snorkeling is good, too. The beach is best in the morning before 11 a.m.; afterwards it can get hot if there's no wind. The coarse red sand massages your feet, and there's a natural jacuzzi area in foamy pools of water along the shore.

Koki Beach Park

The beach park is a mile or so out of town heading toward the Seven Pools. Look for the first road to your left with a sign directing you to Hamoa Village/Beach. Koki is only a few hundred yards on the left. The riptides are fierce in here so don't swim unless it's absolutely calm. The winds can whip along here, too, while at Hamoa Beach, less than a mile away, it can be dead calm. Koki is excellent for beachcombing and for a one-night's unofficial bivouac.

A very special person named Smitty lived in a cave on the north side of the beach. Hike left to the end of the beach and you'll find a rope ladder leading up to his platform. A distinguished older man, he "dropped out" a few years back and came here to live a simple monk's existence. He kept the beach clean and saved a number of people from the riptide. He was a long-distance runner who would tack up a "thought for the day" on Hana's public bulletin board. People loved him and he loved them in return. In 1984 the roof of his cave collapsed and he was killed.

Hamoa Beach

Follow Hamoa Road a few minutes past Koki Beach until you see the sign for Hamoa. Between Hamoa and Koki are the remnants of an extensive Hawaiian fishpond, part of which is still discernible. This entire area is an eroding cinder cone known as **Kaiwi o Pele** ("The Bones of Pele"). This is the spot where the swinish piggod, Kama pua'a, ravished her. Pele also fought a bitter battle with her sister here, who dashed her on the rocks, giving them their anatomical name. Out to sea is the diminutive Alau Island, a remnant left over by Maui after he fished up the Hawaiian Islands. You can tell that Hamoa is no ordinary beach the minute you start walking down the paved, torch-lined walkway. This is the semi-private beach of the Hotel Hana-Maui. But don't be intimidated, because no one can own the beach in Hawaii. Hamoa is terrific for swimming and bodysurfing. The hotel guests are shuttled here by a bus that arrives at 10 a.m. and

departs by 4 p.m. That means that you have this lovely beach to yourself before and after. There is a pavilion that the hotel uses for its Friday night luau, as well as restrooms and showers.

ACCOMMODATIONS

Hotel Hana-Maui

The hotel is the legacy of Paul Fagan, who built it in the late '40s, and operates as close to a family-run hotel as you can get. Most personnel have either been there from the beginning, or their jobs have passed to their family members. Guests love it that way, proven by an astonishing 80% in repeat visitors, most of whom feel like they're staying with old friends. The hotel has had only four managers in the last 40 years. In 1985 the hotel was sold to the Rosewood Corporation of Dallas, Texas, which has had the good sense to leave well enough alone. What they have changed has been for the better. All rooms have been extensively renovated and the hotel can now proudly take its place among the truly luxury hotels of Hawaii. Rooms, all with their own lanai, surround the beautifully appointed grounds where flowers add a splash of color to the green-on-green blanket of ferns and gently sloping lawn. Inside the colors are subdued shades of white and tan. Morning light, with the sun filtering through the louvered windows, is especially tranquil. All suites have a wet bar and large comfortable lounge area with rattan furniture covered in billowy white pillows. A glass-topped table is resplendent with a floral display, and a tray of fresh fruit greets all guests. Refrigerators are stocked with a full choice of drinks, and there's even fresh Kona coffee that you grind and brew yourself. The floors are a deep rich natural wood counterpointed by a light reed mat in the central area. The beds, all queen-size, are covered with a distinctive handmade Rosewood quilt, while Casablanca fans provide all the cooling necessary. Each room has a large free-standing pine closet, along with two walk-ins. The bathrooms, as large as most sitting rooms, are tiled with earth-tone ceramic. You climb a step to immerse yourself in the huge tub, then open eye-level windows that frame a private mini-garden like an expressionist's still life.

The hotel staff adds an intangible quality of friendliness and aloha that sets the hotel apart from all others. Housekeepers visit twice a day, leaving snow-white terrycloth robes, and orchids on every pillow. There is a pool, tennis courts, superb horseback riding, outdoor campouts, golf, and a famous luau held at the hotel's facilities on Hamoa Beach. All activities are easily arranged by visiting Lovey at the activities desk, who throughout the day can be counted on to keep family and children happy with Hawaiian language lessons, lei-making, or swaying hula lessons. Meals become a long-remembered sumptuous event. Follow Francine, the hostess, to your table in the new dining room. Here, breakfasts are all manner of fresh exotic fruits and juices, hot pastries, eggs Benedict poached or herbed into omelettes with petite steaks, fresh fish, or smoked Maui pork. Lunches, which upon request are prepared as very civilized picnics in wicker baskets with all fine linens and accouterments, include chilled seafood chowder, Oriental sesame chicken salad, mango-smoked turkey, *kiawe*-grilled fish, and a potpourri of vegetables. Special dinner menus are prepared daily, but you can begin with a *sashimi* plate, *sateh* chicken, and then move on to an assortment of grilled and roasted fowl, seafood, or locally grown beef, all basted in a variety of gourmet sauces. Vietnamese whole fish for two is especially tantalizing. Desserts are too tempting to resist, and if you can somehow save the room try lime or macadamia nut pie, banana cream cake, coconut mousse, or a rainbow of rich and creamy ice creams and sherbets.

Rates start at $338 s, $416 d, up to $701. This, however, includes three meals under the full American plan. Write Hotel Hana-Maui, Hana, HI 96713, tel. (800) 321-4262. The entire scene isn't stiff or fancy, but it is a memorable first-class experience!

Heavenly Hana Inn

The second most famous Hana hotel, the heavenly Hana resembles a Japanese *ryokan* (inn). Walk through the formal garden and remove your shoes on entering the open-beamed main dining hall. The four suites seem like little apartments broken up into sections by shoji screens. Rates are from $65-100 for up to four guests. The present owner is Alfreda Worst, who purchased it from a Japanese family about 16 years ago. The inn is homey and delightful. Write Box 146, Hana, HI 96713, tel. 248-8442.

Aloha Cottages

These are owned and operated by Zenzo and Fusae Nakamura, and the best bargain in town. The cottages are meticulously clean, well built, and well appointed. For $55-88 d, $10 per additional guest, you get two bedrooms, a full kitchen, living room, deck, and outdoor grills. Mrs. Nakamura is very friendly and provides daily maid service. The fruit trees on the property provide free fruit to guests. Box 205, Hana, HI 96713, tel. 248-8420.

Hana Kai

These resort apartments are at Box 38, Hana, HI 96713, tel. 248-8435. All are well maintained and offer a lot for the money. Studios from $50, deluxe one-bedrooms from $60. All have private lanai with exemplary views of Hana Bay. Maid service, laundry facilities, and barbecues.

Hana Bay Vacation Rentals

Stan and Suzanne Collins offer nine private cottages and houses in and around Hana for rent on a daily and long-term (discounted) basis. They start at $65 and go up to $170. Their rentals include everything from a rustic cabin to a beachfront three-bedroom home with banana and breadfruit trees in your own front yard. This small company has an excellent reputation for quality and service. Write Box 318, Hana, HI 96713, tel. 248-7727, or (800) 657-7970.

Hana Plantation Houses

This is a unique concept where you can rent a private house on the lush, tropical Hana coast. You have five homes to choose from and they range from the "Plantation House," a deluxe cedar one-bedroom, sleeping four complete with lanai, VCR, BBQ, and your own private waterfall for $130, to the "Lanai Makaalae Studio," a Japanese-style studio for two at $75. There's even a little one-room beachhouse for $45. For information contact Hana Plantation Houses, at P.O. Box 489, Hana, HI 96713, tel. 248-7248, or (800) 657-7723.

FOOD AND SHOPPING

As far as dining out goes, there's little to choose from in Hana. The **Hotel Hana-Maui** offers breakfast, lunch, and dinner buffets. Prices vary according to your choice of options, but expect to spend $10 for breakfast, $14 for lunch, and $40 for dinner. There's also a self-serve coffee shop, at the hotel. The **Hana Ranch Restaurant** serves very tasty family-style meals, but they can be stampeded by ravenous tourists heading up or down the Hana Road. **Tu Tu's Snack Shop** is at the community center building at Hana Bay; window service with tables available. Full breakfast, $4, plate lunches, and saimin. This building was donated by Mrs. Fagan to the community.

Hana Store

Take the Hana Road into town. Make the first right past St. Mary's Church and go up to the top of the hill. Open daily 7:30 a.m. to 6:30 p.m., tel. 248-8261. It's a general store with the emphasis on foodstuffs. Not as well stocked as it could be, but they do carry a good supply of imported beers and food items.

Wakiu Originals

You'll find this shop along the Hana Road on the right about one mile before entering town.

Everything sold here is handmade in Hana; prints, cards, wall hangings, and original T-shirts. Owned and operated by Bill and Anita. Not heavily stocked, but some good choices.

SERVICES AND INFORMATION

Hana Medical Center

Along the Hana Road, clearly marked on the right just as you enter town, tel. 248-8294. Open weekdays 8 a.m. to 5 p.m., Sat. 8-12, closed Sunday.

Police Station

At the Y between Hana and Uakea roads, just as you enter town. For emergencie call 911.

Services

The Bank of Hawaii, tel. 248-8015, is open Mon. to Thurs. 3 to 4:30 p.m., Fri. 3 to 6 p.m.; the **Post Office** is open weekdays 8 a.m. to 4:30 p.m. Both are next door to Hana Store (see above). The **Library** is at Hana School, open Mon. to Fri. 8 a.m. to 5 p.m.

heleconia

BEYOND HANA

Now you're getting into adventure. The first sign is that the road gets steadily worse after Hana. It begins to narrow, then the twists and turns begin again, and it's potholed. Signs warn, "Caution: Pig Crossing." There are no phones, no gas, and only a fruit stand or two and one store that can be counted on only to be closed. The fainthearted should turn back, but those with gumption are in for a treat. There are roadside waterfalls, cascading streams filling a series of pools, a hero's grave, and some forgotten towns. If you persevere all the way, you pop out at the Tedeschi Winery, where you can reward yourself with a glass of bubbly before returning to civilization.

Wailua Falls

About seven miles after leaving Hana, Wailua and Kanahualui falls tumble over steep lava *pali*, filling the air with a watery mist and filling their pools below. They're just outside your car door, and a five minute effort will take you to the mossy grotto at the base. There's plenty of room to park. If not for Oheo up ahead, this would be a great picnic spot, but wait! Sometimes roadside artists park here. In a few minutes you pass a

little shrine cut into the mountain. This is the **Virgin By The Roadside.** It's usually draped with a fresh lei.

OHEO GULCH

This is where the enormous **Kipahulu Valley** meets the sea. Palikea Stream starts way up on Haleakala and steps its way through the valley, leaving footprints of waterfalls and pools until it spends itself in the sea. The area was named the **Seven Sacred Pools** by white men. They made a mistake, but an honest one. The area should have been held sacred, but it wasn't. Everything was right here. You can feel the tremendous power of nature: bubbling waters, Haleakala red and regal in the background, and the sea pounding away. Hawaiians lived here but the *heiau* that you would surely expect are missing. Besides that there aren't seven pools; there are more like 24!

Getting There

Head straight on Rt. 31 for 10 miles out of Hana. You'll come to a large cement arched bridge (excellent view) and then a sign that says "Camp-

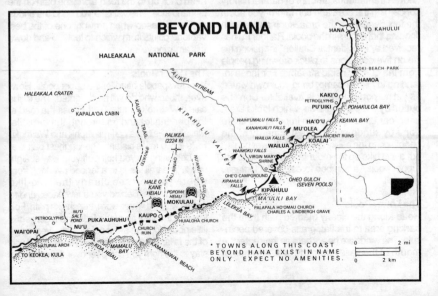

BEYOND HANA

HALEAKALA NATIONAL PARK

HALEAKALA CRATER

KAPALA'OA CABIN

PALIKEA STREAM

KAUPO TRAIL

KIPAHULU VALLEY

PALIKEA (2224 ft)

NU'UANU/OA GULCH

PALI/INIANU

WAIHI'UMALU FALLS
KANAHUALII FALLS
WAILUA FALLS
WAIMOKU FALLS
VIRGIN MARY SHRINE

PETROGLYPHS
PU'UIKI
KAKI'O
POHAKULOA BAY
HA'O'U
KEAWA BAY
MU'OLEA
KOALAI
ANCIENT RUINS

HANA
TO KAHULUI
KOKI BEACH PARK
HAMOA
HAMOA

HALE O KANE HEIAU
POPOIWI HEIAU
MOKULAU

OHE'O CAMPGROUND
KIPAHULU FALLS
KIPAHULU

OHEO GULCH (SEVEN POOLS)
MA'ULILI BAY
PALAPALA HO'OMAU CHURCH
CHARLES A. LINDBERGH GRAVE

PETROGLYPHS
NU'U SALT POND
WAI'OPAI
NU'U
PUKA'AUHUHU
KAUPO
CHURCH RUIN
HUIALOHA CHURCH
LELEKEA BAY

NATURAL ARCH
TO KEOKEA, KULA
KOA HEIAU
MAMALU BAY
KAMANAWAI BEACH

* TOWNS ALONG THIS COAST BEYOND HANA EXIST IN NAME ONLY. EXPECT NO AMENITIES.

0   2 mi
0   2 km

ing." Park here in the large grassy lot where you'll also find clean, well-built outhouses for your convenience.

Warnings And Tips

Before doing any exploring, try to talk to one of the rangers, Eddie Pu and Perry Bednorse, generally found around the parking area. They know a tremendous amount of natural history concerning the area and can inform you about the few dangers in the area, such as the flash flooding that occurs in the pools. Ranger Pu has received a "Presidential Citation" for risking his life on five occasions to pluck drowning people from the quickly rising streams. For those intending to hike or camp, bring your own water; as yet no potable water is available. Don't be put off by the parking area, which looks like a used-car lot for Japanese imports; 99% are gone by sundown. The vast majority of the people go to the easily accessible "lower pools," but a stiff hike up the mountain takes you to the "upper pools," a bamboo forest, and a fantastic waterfall.

The Lower Pools

Head along the clearly marked path from the parking area to the flat, grass-covered peninsula. The winds are heavy here as they enter the mouth of the valley from the sea. A series of pools to choose from are off to your left. It's delightful to lie in the last one and look out to the sea crunching the shore just a few yards away. Move upstream for the best swimming in the largest of the lower pools. Be careful, because you'll have to do some fairly difficult rock climbing. The best route is along the right-hand side as you face up the valley. Once you're satiated, head back up to the road along the path on the lefthand side. This will take you up to the bridge that you crossed when arriving, one of the best vantage points from which to look up and down this amazing valley.

The Upper Pools

Very few people head for the upper pools. However, those who do will be delighted. The trail is called **Waimoku Falls Trail.** Cross the road at the parking lot and go through the turnstile. Makahiku Falls is a half-mile uphill and Waimoku Falls is two miles distant. The toughest part is at the beginning as you huff-puff your way straight uphill. The trail leads to a fenced overlook from where you can see clearly the lace-like Makahiku Falls. Behind you a few paces and to the left will be a water-worn, trench-like path. Follow it to the very lip of the falls and a gorgeous little pool. You can swim safely to the very edge of the falls. The current is gentle here, and if you stay to the right you can peer over the edge and remain safe behind encircling boulders. Be extremely conscious of the water rising, and get out immediately if it does!

After refreshing yourself, continue on the path through a grassy area. Here you'll cross the creek where there's a wading pool, and then zigzag up the opposite bank. After some enormous mango trees, you start going through a high jungle area. Suddenly you're in an extremely dense bamboo forest. The trail is well cut as you pass through the green darkness of this stand. If the wind is blowing, the bamboo will sing a mournful song for you. Emerge into more mangoes and thimbleberries and there's the creek again. Turn left and follow the creek, without crossing yet, and the trail will become distinct again. There's a wooden walkway, and then, eureka! . . . Waimoku Falls. It cascades over the *pali* and is so high that you have to strain your neck back as far as it will go. It's more than a waterfall; it's silver filigree. You can stand in the shallow pool below surrounded by a sheer rock amphitheater. The sunlight dances in this area and tiny rainbows appear and disappear. There is a ranger-led hike to the falls on Saturdays. Horseback rides are also available from the nearby Oheo Riding Stables, tel. 248-7722.

Camping

This is part of Haleakala National Park. It's free to camp for a three-day limit (no one counts too closely) and no permit is necessary. The campgrounds are primitive and always empty. From the parking lot follow the sign that says "Camping" and proceed straight ahead on the dirt track. Bear right to a large grassy area overlooking the sea, where signs warn not to disturb an archaeological area. Notice how spongy the grass seems to be here. You'll see a very strange palm tree that bends and twists up and down from the ground like a serpent. Move to the trees just behind it to escape the wind.

BEYOND OHEO

Route 31 beyond Oheo is genuinely rugged and makes the car companies cry. It can be done, however, with even the tourist vans making it part of their regular route. Be aware, however, that after rough weather that has brought landslides in the past, the road can be closed by a

locked gate with access available only for official business and local residents. Check! In 1½ miles you come to **Palapala Hoomau Church** (St. Paul's) and its tiny cemetery where Charles Lindbergh is buried. People, especially those who are old enough to remember the "Lone Eagle's" historic flight, are drawn here like pilgrims. The public is not really encouraged to visit, but the human tide cannot be stopped. If you go, please follow all of the directions posted. Up ahead a sign reads, Samuel F. Pryor, Kipahulu Ranch. Mr. Pryor was a vice-president of Pan Am and a close chum of Lindbergh's. It was he who encouraged Lindbergh to spend his last years in Hana. Sam Pryor raises gibbons and lives quietly with his wife.

Kipahulu Ranch has seen other amazing men. Last century a Japanese samurai named Sentaro Ishii lived here. He was enormous, especially for a Japanese of that day, over six feet tall. He came in search of work, and at the age of 61 married Kehele, a local girl. He lived in Kipahulu until he died at the age of 102.

Past Sam Pryor's place is B.B. Smith's fruit stand (which isn't always open,) and another follows shortly. Here the road really begins to get rugged. The vistas open up at the beginning of the Kaupo Gap just when you pass **Huialoha Church,** built in 1859.

Kaupo Store

The village of **Kaupo** and the Kaupo Store follow Huialoha Church. A sign reads "This store is usually open Mon. to Fri., around 7:30 to 4:30. Don't be surprised if it's not open yet. It soon will be unless otherwise posted. Closed Saturday and Sunday and when necessary." Only a few families live in Kaupo, old ones and new ones trying to live independently. Kaupo is the last of a chain of stores that stretched all the way from Keanae and were owned by the Soon Family. Nick Soon was kind of a modern-day wizard. He lived in Kaupo, and among his exploits he assembled a car and truck brought piecemeal on a barge, built the first electric generator in the area, and even made a model airplane from scratch that flew. He was the son of an indentured Chinese laborer. After Kaupo you'll be in the heart of the Kaupo Gap. Enjoy it because in a few minutes the pavement will pick up again and you'll be back in the civilized world.

KAHOOLAWE

OVERVIEW

The island of Kahoolawe is clearly visible from many points along Maui's south shore, especially when it's lit up like a firecracker during heavy bombardment by the U.S. Navy. Kahoolawe is a target island, uninhabited except for a band of wild goats that refuse to be killed off. Kahoolawe was a sacred island born to Wakea and Papa, the two great mythical progenitors of Hawaii. The birth went badly and almost killed Papa, and it hasn't been any easier for her ill-omened child ever since. Kahoolawe became synonymous with Kanaloa, the man-god. Kanaloa was especially revered by the *kahuna ana'-ana*, the "black sorcerers" of old Hawaii. Kanaloa, much like Lucifer, was driven from heaven by Kane, the god of light. Kanaloa held dominion over all poisonous things and ruled in the land of the dead from his power spot here on Kahoolawe. There are scores of archaeological sites and remnants of *heiau* all over the bomb-cratered face of Kahoolawe. A long, bitter feud has raged between the U.S. Navy, which wishes to keep the island as a bombing range, and Protect Kahoolawe Ohana, a Hawaiian native-rights organization that wants the sacred island returned to the people.

The Land
Kahoolawe is 11 miles long and six miles wide, with 29 miles of coastline. The tallest hill is **Lua Makika** in the northeast section at 1,477 feet. There are no natural lakes or ponds on the island, but it does get some rain and there is a stream running through Ahupu Gulch.

MODERN HISTORY

It's perfectly clear that small families of Hawaiians lived on Kahoolawe for countless generations and that religious rites were carried out by many visiting *kahuna* over the centuries, but mostly Kahoolawe was left alone. In 1917 Angus MacPhee, a cattleman, leased Kahoolawe from the territorial government for $200 per year. The lease would run until 1954 with a renewal option, if by 1921 MacPhee could show reasonable pro-

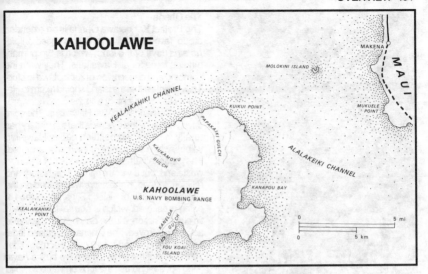

gress in taming the island. Harry Baldwin bought into the **Kahoolawe Ranch** in 1922, and with his money and MacPhee's know-how, Kahoolawe turned a neat profit. The island then supported indigenous vegetation such as *ohia,* mountain apple, and even Hawaiian cotton and tobacco. MacPhee planted eucalyptus and range grass from Australia, which caught on well and stopped much of the erosion. Gardens were planted around the homestead and the soil proved to be clean and fertile. Within a few years Kahoolawe Ranch cattle were being shipped regularly to markets on Maui.

The Navy Arrives
In 1939, with the threat of war on the horizon, MacPhee and Baldwin, stimulated by patriotism, offered a small tip of Kahoolawe's southern shore to the U.S. Army as an artillery range. One day after the attack on Pearl Harbor, the U.S. Navy seized all of Kahoolawe to further the "the war effort" and evicted MacPhee, immediately disenfranchising the Kahoolawe Ranch. Kahoolawe has since become the most bombarded piece of real estate on the face of the earth. During WW II the Navy praised Kahoolawe as being *the* most important factor in winning the Pacific War, and it has held Kahoolawe to the present day.

The Book On Kahoolawe
Inez MacPhee Ashdown lived on the island with her father and was a driving force in establishing the homestead. She has written a book, *Recollections of Kahoolawe,* available from Topgallant Publishing Co., Honolulu. This book chronicles the events from 1917 until the military takeover, and is rife with myths, legends, and historical facts about Kahoolawe. Mrs. Ashdown is in her late eighties, going blind and in failing health, but her mind remains brilliant. She resides on Maui.

The Problem
Hawaii has the dubious distinction of being the most militarized state in the Union. All five services are represented, and it's the headquarters of CINCPAC (Commander in Chief, Pacific), which controls 70% of the earth's surface, from California to Africa's east coast, and to both poles. Kahoolawe is the epitome of this military dominance, with every inch of its 73 square miles owned by the federal government. The Protect Kahoolawe Ohana is opposed to this dominance and wants the Navy to return the island to native Hawaiian control. The Navy says that Kahoolawe is still very important to national security and that it is a barren and lifeless island, anyway.

The Protect Kahoolawe Ohana resolutely builds a long house, pitting traditional Hawaiian beliefs against naval artillery.

The Ohana

The Protect Kahoolawe Ohana is an extended group, favoring traditional values based on *aloha aina* (love of the land) which is the primary binding force for all Hawaiians. They want the bombing and desecration of Kahoolawe to stop. They maintain that the island should return to Hawaiian Lands inventory with the *kahu* (stewardship) in the hands of native Hawaiians. The point driven home by the Ohana is that the military has totally ignored and belittled native Hawaiian values, which are now beginning to be asserted. They maintain that Kahoolawe is not a barren wasteland, but a vibrant part of their history and religion. Indeed, Kahoolawe was placed on the National Register of Historic Sites, but instead of being preserved, which is normal for this prestigious distinction, it is the only historic site that is actively destroyed. The Ohana has gained legal access to the island for 10 days per month, for 10 months of the year. They have built a *halau* (long house) and use the time on Kahoolawe to dedicate themselves to religious, cultural, and social pursuits. The Ohana look to Kahoolawe as their *pu'uhonua* (refuge), where they gain strength and knowledge from each other and the *aina*. The question is basic: Is Kahoolawe's future that of target island or sacred island?

LANAI

INTRODUCTION

Lanai, in the long dark past of Hawaiian legend-history, was a sad and desolate place inhabited by man-eating spirits and fiendish bloodcurdling ghouls. It was redeemed by spoiled but tough Prince Kaululaau, exiled there by his kingly father, Kakaalaneo of Maui. Kaululaau proved to be not only brave, but wily too; he cleared Lanai of its spirits through trickery, and opened the way for human habitation. Lanai was for many generations a burial ground for the *ali'i* and therefore filled with sacred mana and *kapu* to commoners. Later, reports of its inhospitable shores filled the logs of old sailing vessels. In foul weather, captains navigated desperately to avoid its infamously treacherous waters, whose melancholy whitecaps still outline "Shipwreck Beach" and give credence to its name.

The vast majority of people visiting the Hawaiian Islands view Lanai from Lahaina on West Maui, but never actually set foot upon this lovely quiet island. For two centuries, first hunters, and then lovers of the humpback whale, have come to peer across the waters of the Auau Channel, better known as the "Lahaina Roads," in search of these magnificent giants. Lanai in Hawaiian means "Hump," and it's as if nature built its own island-shrine to the whale in the exact spot where they are most plentiful. Lanai is a victim of its own reputation. Nicknamed the "Pineapple Island," most visitors are informed by even long-time residents that Lanai is a dull place covered in one large pineapple plantation. It's true that Lanai has the largest pineapple plantation in the world, 16,000 cultivated acres, which account for about 90% of U.S. production. But the island has 74,000 acres that remain untouched and perfect for exceptional outdoor experiences. Besides, the pineapple fields are themselves interesting: endless rows of the porcupine plants, sliced and organized by a labyrinth of roads,

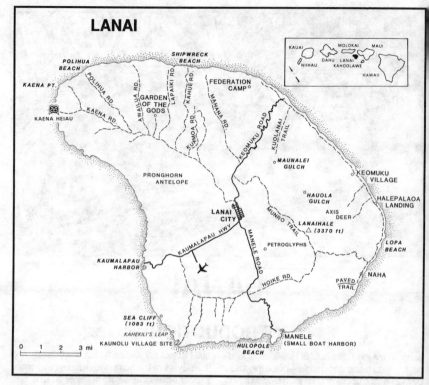

LANAI

SHIPWRECK BEACH

POLIHUA BEACH

KAENA PT.

POLIHUA RD.

KAENA HEIAU

KAENA RD.

AWALUA RD.

KUMOA RD.

GARDEN OF THE GODS

LAPAIKI RD.

KAHUE RD.

MAHANA RD.

FEDERATION CAMP

KEOMUKU ROAD

KUOLANAI TRAIL

MAUNALEI GULCH

KEOMUKU VILLAGE

HALEPALAOA LANDING

PRONGHORN ANTELOPE

LANAI CITY

HAUOLA GULCH

AXIS DEER

MUNRO TRAIL

LANAIHALE △ (3370 ft)

KAUMALAPAU HWY

MANELE ROAD

PETROGLYPHS

LOPA BEACH

KAUMALAPAU HARBOR

HOIKE RD.

PAVED TRAIL

NAHA

SEA CLIFF (1083 ft)

KAHEKILI'S LEAP

KAUNOLU VILLAGE SITE

HULOPOE BEACH

MANELE (SMALL BOAT HARBOR)

0 1 2 3 mi

KAUAI OAHU MOLOKAI MAUI
NIIHAU LANAI KAHOOLAWE
HAWAII

contoured and planted by improbable-looking machines, and tended by mostly Filipino workers in wide-brimmed hats and goggles.

Around And About

The people of Lanai live in one of the most fortuitously chosen spots for a working village in the world: Lanai City. All but about two dozen of the island's 2,600 permanent residents make their homes here. (See "Changing Lanai" below.) Nestled near the ridge of mountains in the northeast corner of the Palawai Basin, Lanai City is sheltered, cooled, and characterized by a mature and extensive grove of Norfolk pines planted in the early 1900s by the practical New Zealand naturalist, George Munro. This evergreen canopy creates a park-like atmosphere about town, while reaching tall green fingers to the clouds. A mountainous spine tickles drizzle from the water-bloated bellies of passing clouds

for the thirsty, red, sunburned plains of Lanai below. The trees, like the bristled hair of an annoyed cat, line the **Munro Trail** as it climbs Lanaihale, the highest spot on the island (3,370 feet). The Munro Trail's magnificent panoramas encompass sweeping views of no less than five of the eight major islands as it snakes along the mountain ridge, narrowing at times to less than 30 yards across. Here are limitless paths for trekking and four-wheel driving. Maunalei Gulch, a vast precipitous valley, visible from "The Trail," was the site of a last-ditch effort of Lanai warriors to repel an invasion by the warrior king of the Big Island at the turn of the 18th century. Now its craggy arms provide refuge to mouflon sheep as they execute death-defying leaps from one rocky ripple to the next. On the valley floors roam axis deer, and on the northwest grasslands are the remnants of an experimental herd of pronghorn antelope brought from Montana in 1959.

After saturating yourself with the glories of Lanai from the heights, descend and follow a well-paved road from Lanai City to the southern tip of the island. Here, **Manele** and **Hulopoe** bays sit side by side. Manele is a favorite spot of small sailing craft that have braved the channel from Lahaina. With its virtually untouched Underwater Marine Park, Manele is regarded as one of the premier snorkeling spots in the entire island chain. Hulopoe Bay, just next door, is as salubrious a spot as you can hope to find. It offers camping and all that's expected of a warm, sandy, palm-lined beach.

Changing Lanai

Most are amazed that George Munro's pines still shelter a tight-knit community that has remained untouched for so long. But all that's changing, and changing quickly. Two new hideaway luxury hotels have been built, and they're beauties. Both are Rock Resorts! **The Lodge at Koele**, with 102 rooms, is just a five-minute walk from downtown Lanai City. An upland hotel befitting this area of trees and cool summers, it's like a grand country home of the landed gentry, in neo-Victorian style. Amenities will include lawn bowling, an orchid house for pure visual pleasure, swimming pools, tennis courts, stables, and horseback riding. The other hotel, the **Manele Bay** (scheduled opening late 1990), houses 250 villa suites. The architecture is a blend, both classical and island inspired, a *kama aina* Mediterranean masonry style with tiled roofs. Outdoor features will include the unobstructed natural beauty of Manele/Hulope with 99% of the rooms having a view, a Jack Nicklaus-designed golf course (open to guests from The Lodge), tennis courts, and swimming pools.

These resorts have brought the most profound changes to Lanai since James Dole arrived at the turn of the century. Castle and Cooke, practically speaking, owns the island. David Murdoch is the CEO of Castle and Cooke and the hotels are his babies. He's developing them through a newly formed company called Lanai Resort Partners. The hotels employ a staff of 600 or so, more than all the workers needed to tend the pineapple fields, which today is just over 500 people. This brings an alternative job market, new life to the downtown area, and a housing spurt. One fact was undeniable concerning Lanai: if you wanted to make a living you either had to work the pineapple fields, or leave. Now that will change. To stop the disenfranchisement of the local people, which was generally the case with rapid development, Castle and Cooke is building three new housing projects, and they come with a promise! Local people, according to seniority with the company and length of residence on Lanai, have first choice. One group of houses will be multiple-family, geared to the entry-level buyer. The second are single-family homes selling at around $70,000, and the third are for middle-management types at around $100,000. The future also calls for million-dollar homes that will line the fairways of the new golf courses, for people like David Murdoch and his associates. This isn't all heart on the part of Castle and Cooke. They want to ensure that the hotels will have a steady and contented workforce to keep them running without a hitch.

Downtown Lanai is inadequate. It couldn't possibly handle the hotel guests and all the new workers and their families who will move to Lanai. Old buildings will be refurbished, some torn down and replaced, with more upscale businesses taking their place. The tired little shops in town are on Castle and Cooke property, most with month-to-month leases. Castle and Cooke again promises to be fair, but like the rest of Lanai, they'll have a choice: progress or perish. Most islanders are optimistic, keeping an open mind and adopting a "wait and see" attitude concerning the inevitable changes and the promises that have been made for a better life.

Adventure

You can hike or 4WD to Kaunolu Bay, one of the best-preserved ancient Hawaiian village sites. Kamehameha the Great came to this ruggedly masculine shore to fish and frolic his summers away with his favorite cronies. Here, a retainer named Kahekili leaped from a sea cliff to the ice-blue waters below, and challenged all other warriors to prove their loyalty to Kamehameha by following his example and hurtling themselves off what today is known as **Kahekili's Leap.**

You can quickly span a century by heading for the southeast corner of Lanai and its three abandoned villages of Lopa, Naha, and Keomuku. Here legends abound. *Kahuna* curses still guard a grove of coconut trees which are purported to refuse to let you down if you climb for their nuts without offering the proper prayers. Here also are the remnants of a sugar train believed to have caused its cane enterprise to fail because the rocks of a nearby *heiau* were disturbed and used in its track bed. An enchanting abandoned Hawaiian church in Keomuku insists on being photographed.

You can head north along the east shore to **Shipwreck Beach,** where the rusting hulk of a liberty ship, along with timbers and planks from the great wooden square-riggers of days gone by, lie along the beach, attesting to the authenticity of its name. Shipwreck Beach is a shore stroller's paradise, a real beachcomber's boutique. Also along here are some thought-provoking petroglyphs. Other petroglyphs are found on a hillside overlooking the "pine" fields of the Palawai Basin.

If you hunger for a totally private beach, head north for the Polihua Trail. En route, just to keep you from being bored, you'll pass through a fantastic area of ancient cataclysm aptly called **The Garden of the Gods.** This raw, baked area of monolithic rocks and tortured earth turns incredible shades of purple, red, magenta, and yellow as the sun plays upon it from different angles. You have a junction of trails here. You can bear left to lonely **Kaena Iki Point,** where you'll find Lanai's largest *heiau,* a brooding setting full of weird power vibrations. If you're hot and dusty and aching for a dip, continue due north to trail's end where the desolation of the Garden suddenly gives way to the gleaming brightness of virtually unvisited Polihua Beach.

After these daily excursions, return to the green serenity of Lanai City. Even if you're only spending a few days, you'll be made to feel like you're staying with old friends. You won't have to worry about bringing your dancing shoes, but if you've had enough hustle and bustle and yearn to stroll in quietude, sit by a crackling fire, and look up at a crystal-clear sky, head for Lanai. Your jangled nerves and ruffled spirit will be glad you did.

THE LAND

The sunburned face of Lanai seems parched but relaxed as it rises in a gentle, steady arc from sea level. When viewed from the air it looks like an irregularly shaped kidney bean. The sixth largest of the eight main islands, Lanai is roughly 140 square miles, measuring 18 miles north to south and 13 miles east to west at its longest points. A classic single-shield volcano, at one time Lanai was probably connected to Maui and Molokai as a single huge island. Marine fossils found at the 1,000-foot mark and even higher in the mountains indicate its slow rise from the sea. Its rounded features appear more benign than the violent creases of its closest island neighbors; this characteristic earned it the unflattering Hawaiian name of "Hump." More lyrical scholars, however, have refuted this translation, and claim the real meaning has been lost to the ages, but Lanai does look like a hump when viewed from a distance at sea.

Its topography is simple. A ridge of rugged mountains runs north to south along the eastern half of the island and their entire length is traversed by the Munro Trail. The highest peak is Lanaihale (3,370 feet). This area is creased by precipitous gulches: the two deepest are Maunalei and Hauola at more than 2,000 feet. The topography tapers off steadily as it reaches the sea to the east. A variety of beaches stretch from the white sands of Polihua in the north, along the salt-and-pepper sands of Naha on the east, and end with the beautiful rainbow arches of Manele and Hulopoe in the south. Palawai, Lanai's central basin, is completely cultivated in manicured, whorled fields of pineapple. Early this century, Palawai was covered in cactus. The west coast has phenomenal sea cliffs accessible only by boat. Some of the most majestic are the Kaholo Pali which run south from Kaumalapu Harbor, reaching their most amazing ruggedness at Kaunolu Bay. At many spots along this area the sea lies more than 1,500 feet below. Starting at Lanai City in the center, a half hour of driving in any direction presents a choice of this varied and fascinating geography.

Climate
The daily temperatures are quite balmy, especially at sea level, but it can get blisteringly hot in the basins and on the leeward side, so be sure to carry plenty of water when hiking or four-wheel driving. Lanai City gets refreshingly cool in the evenings and early mornings, but a light jacket or sweater is adequate, although thin-blooded residents bundle up.

AVERAGE MAXIMUM/MINIMUM TEMPERATURE AND RAINFALL

Island	Town		Jan.	March	May	June	Sept.	Nov.
Lanai	Lanai City	high	70	71	75	80	80	72
		low	60	60	62	65	65	62
		rain	3	3	2	0	2	4

N.B. Rainfall in inches; temperature in °F

Rainfall

Lying in the rain shadow of the West Maui Mountains, even Lanai's windward side receives only 40 inches of rainfall a year. The central basins and leeward shores taper off to a scant 12 inches, not bad for pineapples and sun worshippers. Lanai has always been short of water. Its scruffy vegetation and red-baked earth are responsible for its inhospitable reputation. There are no real rivers; the few year-round streams are found only in the gulches of the windward mountains. Most ventures at colonizing Lanai, both in ancient and modern times, were kept to a minimum because of this water shortage. The famous Norfolk pines of Lanai City, along with other introduced greenery, greatly helped the barrenness of the landscape and provided a watershed. The rust-red earth remains unchanged, and if you get it onto your clothes, it'll remain there as a permanent souvenir.

FLORA AND FAUNA

Most of Lanai's flora and fauna have been introduced. In fact, the Norfolk pine and the regal mouflon sheep were a manmade attempt to improve the natural, often barren habitat. These species have adapted so well that they now symbolize Lanai, along with, of course, the ubiquitous pineapple. Besides the mouflon, Lanai boasts pronghorns, axis deer, and a few feral goats. A wide variety of introduced game birds include the Rio Grande turkey, ring-necked pheasant, and an assortment of quail, francolins, and doves. Like the other Hawaiian islands, Lanai, unfortunately, is home to native birds that are headed for extinction. Along the Munro Trail and on the windward coast you pass through forests of Norfolk and Cook Island pines, tall eucalyptus stands, shaggy ironwoods, native *koa,* and silver oaks. Everywhere, dazzling colors and fragrances are provided by Lanai's flowers.

Flowers

Although Lanai's official flower is the *kaunaoa,* it's not really a flower, but an airplant that grows wild. It's easily found along the beach at Keomuku. It grows in conjunction with *pohuehue,* a pinkish-red, perennial seashore morning glory. Native to Hawaii, the *pohuehue* grows in large numbers along Lanai's seashore. It's easy to spot, and when you see a yellow-orange vinelike airplant growing with it, you've found Lanai's *kaunaoa,* which is traditionally fashioned into leis. The medicinal *ilima,* used to help asthma sufferers, is found in large numbers in Lanai's open fields. Its flat, open, yellow flower is about one inch in diameter and grows on a waist-high shrub. Two other flowers considered by some to be pests are the purple *koali* morning glory and the miniature red and yellow flowering lantana, known for its unpleasant odor. Both are abundant on the trail to the Garden of the Gods.

Norfolk Pine

These pines were discovered by Capt. Cook and named after Norfolk Island in the South Pacific, on which they were found. Imported in great numbers by George Munro, they adapted well to Lanai and helped considerably to attract moisture and provide a firm watershed. Exquisitely ornamental, they can also be grown in containers. Their perfect cone shape makes them a natural Christmas tree, used as such in Hawaii; some are even shipped to the Mainland for this purpose.

Endemic Birds

The list of native birds still found on Lanai gets smaller every year, and those still on the list are rarely seen. The *amakahi* is about five inches long with yellowish-green plumage. The males deliver a high-sounding tweet and a trilling call. Vegetarians, these birds live mostly on grasses and lichens, building their nests in the uppermost branches of tall trees. Some people believe that the *amakahi* is already extinct on Lanai. The *ua'u* or Hawaiian petrel is a large bird with a 36-inch wingspan. Its head and back are shades of black with a white underbelly. This "fisherbird" lives on squid and crustaceans that it regurgitates to its chicks. Unfortunately, the Hawaiian petrel nests on the ground, sometimes laying its eggs under rocks or in burrows, which makes it an easy prey for predators. Its call is reported to sound like a small yapping dog. The *apapane* is abundant on the other main islands, but dwindling rapidly on Lanai. It's a chubby red-bodied bird about five inches long with a black bill, legs, wingtips, and tail feathers. It's quick, flitty, and has a wide variety of calls and songs, from beautiful warbles to mechanical buzzes. Its feathers were sought by Hawaiians to produce distinctive ornate featherwork.

Axis Deer

This shy and beautiful creature came to Lanai via Molokai, where the first specimens arrived in 1868 as a gift from the Hawaiian consul in Hong Kong. Its native home is the parkland forests of India and Sri Lanka. The coats of most axis deer are golden tan with rows of round lifetime spots, along with a black stripe down the back and a white belly. They stand three to four feet at the shoulder, with bucks weighing an average of 160 pounds and does about 110. The bucks have an exquisite set of symmetrical antlers that always form a perfect three points. The antlers can stand 30 inches high and more than 20 inches across, making them coveted trophies. Does are antlerless and give birth to one fawn, usually from November to February, but Hawaii's congenial weather makes for good fawn survival anytime of year. Axis deer on Lanai can be spotted anywhere from the lowland *kiawe* forest to the higher rainforests along the Munro Trail. Careful and proper hunting management should keep the population stable for many generations. The meat from axis deer is reported to have a unique flavor, different from Mainland venison—one of the finest tasting of all wild game.

Mouflon Sheep

Another name for these wild mountain sheep is Mediterranean or European bighorn. One of only six species of wild sheep in the world, mouflon are native to the islands of Sardinia and Corsica, whose climates are quite similar to Hawaii's. They have been introduced throughout Europe, Africa, and North America. Although genetically similar to domestic sheep, they are much more shy, lack a woolly coat, and only infrequently give birth to twins. Both rams and ewes are a similar tannish brown, with a snow-white rump which is all that most people get to see of these always-alert creatures as they quickly and expertly head for cover. Rams weigh about 125 pounds (ewes a bit less) and produce a spectacular set of recurved horns. They need little water to survive, going for long periods only on the moisture in green plants. On Lanai they are found along the northwest coast in the grasslands and in the dry *kiawe* forest.

Pronghorns

Not a true antelope, this animal is a native to the Western states of North America. Both males and females produce short black antlers that curve inward at the tip. Males average 125 pounds (females about 90). Pronghorns are a reddish tan with two distinct white bands across

pronghorn antelope

he neck and a black patch under the ear. They can also flare the hair on their rumps to produce a white flag when alarmed. In 1959, 38 pronghorns were brought to Lanai in an attempt to introduce another big game animal. Lanai's upper grasslands seemed perfectly suited to the pronghorn, closely resembling the animal's natural habitat in Montana, and hopes ran high for survival. At first the herd increased, but then the numbers began to slowly and irreversibly dwindle. Experts felt that the animals were confused by the nearby salt water and those that drank it quickly died. Also, the new grasses of Lanai caused digestion problems. Poaching added even more problems to the troubled pronghorns. It's tough to spot the few that remain, but with good field glasses and perseverance you might catch some browsing on haole koa in the northcentral grasslands of Lanai. The fact that even a few pronghorns remain decades after introduction gives some hope that these noble animals can still beat the odds of extinction and make a permanent home for themselves in Hawaii.

HISTORY

Kakaalaneo peered across the mist-shrouded channel between West Maui and Lanai, and couldn't believe his eyes. Night after night, the campfire of his son Kaululaau burned, sending its faint but miraculous signal. Could it be that the boy was still alive? Kaululaau had been given every advantage of his noble birth, but still the prince had proved to be unmanageable. King Kakaalaneo had even ordered all children born on the same day as his son to be sent to Lahaina, where they would grow up as his son's friends and playmates. Spoiled rotten, young Kaululaau had terrorized Lahaina with his pranks and one day went too far: he destroyed a new planting of breadfruit. Even the chief's son could not trample the social order and endanger the livelihood of the people. So finally the old kahuna had to step in. Justice was hard and swift: Kaululaau must be banished to the terrible island of Lanai, where the man-eating spirits dwelled. There he would meet his fate, and no one expected him to live. But weeks had passed and Kalulaau's nightly fires still burned. Could it be some ghoulish trick? Kakaalaneo sent a canoe to investigate. It returned with incredible news. The boy was fine! All the spirits were

banished! Kaululaau had cleansed the island of its evil fiends and opened it up for the people to come and settle.

Oral History
In fact, it's recorded in the Hawaiian oral genealogical tradition that a young Kaululaau did open Lanai to significant numbers of inhabitants in approximately A.D. 1400. Lanai passed through the next few hundred years as a satellite of Maui, accepting the larger island's social, religious, and political dictates. During this period, Lanai supported about 3,000 people who lived by growing taro and fishing. Most inhabited the eastern shore facing Maui, but old home sites show that the population became established well enough to homestead the entire island. Lanai was caught up in the Hawaiian wars that raged in the last two decades of the 1700s, and was ravaged and pillaged in 1778 by the warriors of Kalaniopuu, aging king of the Big Island. These hard times marked a decline in Lanai's population; accounts by Western sea captains who passed even a few years later noted that the island looked desolate, with no large villages evident. Lanai began to recover and saw a small boost in population when Kamehameha the Great established his summer residence at Kaunolu on the southern shore. This kept Lanai vibrant for a few years at the turn of the 19th century but it began to fade soon thereafter. The decline continued until only a handful of Hawaiians remained by the 20th century. The old order ended completely when one of the last traditional kanaka, named Ohua, hid the traditional fish-god, Hunihi, and died shortly thereafter in his grass hut in the year 1900.

Early Foreign Influences
No one knows his name, but all historians agree that a Chinese man tried his luck at raising sugar cane on Lanai in 1802. He brought boiling pots and rollers to Naha on the east coast, but after a few years of hard luck gave up and moved on. About 100 years later a large commercial sugar enterprise was attempted in the same area. This time the sugar company even built a narrow-gauge railroad to carry the cane. A story goes that after disrupting a local heiau to make ballast for the rail line, the water in the area, never in great abundance to begin with, went brackish. Again sugar was foiled.

In 1854 a small band of Mormon elders tried to colonize Lanai by starting a "City of Joseph" at Palawai Basin. This began the career of one of Hawaii's strangest, most unfathomable, yet charismatic early leaders. Walter Murray Gibson came to Palawai to start an idyllic settlement for the Latter-day Saints. He energetically set to work improving the land with funds from Utah and hard work of the other Mormon settlers. The only fly in Gibson's grand ointment occurred when the Mormon Church discovered that the acres of Palawai were not registered to the church at all but to Walter Murray Gibson himself! He was excommunicated and the bilked settlers relocated. Gibson went on to have one of the strangest political careers in Hawaiian history, including championing native rights, and enjoying unbelievable influence at the royal Hawaiian court. His land at Palawai passed on to his daughter who became possessed by the one evil spirit Kaululaau failed to eradicate: she tried to raise sugar cane, but was fated, like the rest, to fail.

A few attempts at cattle raising proved uneconomical, and Lanai languished. The last big attempt at cattle raising produced The Ranch, part of whose lands make up the Cavendish Golf Course in Lanai City. This enterprise did have one bright note. A New Zealander named George Munro was hired as the manager. He imported all manner of seeds and cuttings in his attempt to foliate the island and create a watershed. The Ranch failed, but Munro's legacy of Norfolk pines stands as a proud testament to this amateur horticulturalist.

The Coming Of Pineapples

The purchase of Lanai in 1922 was one of the niftiest real estate deals in modern history. James D. Dole, the most enterprising of the pineapple pioneers, bought the island—lock, stock, and barrel—from the Baldwins, an old missionary family, for $1.1 million. That comes to only $12 per acre, though many of those acres were fairly scruffy, not to mention Lanai's bad economical track record. Dole had come from Boston at the turn of the century to figure out how to can pineapple profitably. Dole did such a remarkable job of marketing the "golden fruit" on the Mainland that in a few short years, Midwestern Americans who'd never even heard of pineapples before were buying cans of it regularly from the shelves of country grocery stores. In 1922, Jim Dole needed more land for his expanding pineapple fields, and the arid basin of Palawai seemed perfect.

Lanai Plantation was an oligarchy during the early years with the plantation manager as king. One of the most famous of these characters was H. Broomfield Brown, who ran Lanai Plantation in the '30s. He kept watch over the fields from his house through a telescope. If anyone loafed, he'd ride out into the fields to confront the offender. Mr. Brown personally "eyeballed" every new visitor to Lanai: all prostitutes, gamblers and deadbeats were turned back at the pier. An anti-litter fanatic, he'd even reprimand anyone who trashed the streets of Lanai City. During the labor strikes of the 1960s, workers' grievances were voiced and Lanai began to function as a more normal enterprise. With pineapple well established on the world market, Lanai finally had a firm economic base. From a few thousand fruits in the early days, the flow today can reach a million fruits per day during the height of the season. They're shipped from the manmade port at Kaumalapau which was specially built to accommodate Lanai's "pines."

ECONOMY

Pineapples! Lanai's 16,000 acres of them make up the largest single pineapple plantation in the world, producing 90% of the U.S. yearly total. The entire island is owned by Castle and Cooke and operated by its subsidary, The Dole Co., whose name has become synonymous with pineapples. A handful of tiny hereditary plots are still held by Hawaiian families and oddly enough, nearly half the working families own their homes, purchased from Dole. In one way or another, everyone on Lanai owed his livelihood to pineapples, from the worker who twisted his ankle in a "pine" field to the technician at the community hospital who X-rayed it. Now all that has changed with the opening of the two new Rock Resorts (see p. 495). Workers come and go all day long from equipment depots in Lanai City. Most field hands are Filipinos, some very recent arrivals to the U.S. Unskilled workers start at minimum wage, a union member who's worked for Dole for a few years can make a decent living. Japanese and *haole* hold most of the foreman and middle management jobs, although Dole is an equal opportunity employer.

Competition And Technology

Today foreign production, especially in the Philippines, has greatly increased and gives the Hawaiian pineapple industry some competitive headaches—though Dole feels its claim to fame is secure. They are after a premium-pack pineapple, according to Jim Parker, the plantation manager, who states, "Nobody gets more money for their pineapple than Dole does, because nobody ever matches Dole for quality." Pineapple cultivation is as tough as any other business and all competitors are after the very best technology. Dole is a leader in technology, and though they've been cutting down on the number of acres under cultivation, they have at the same time increased yield through intensified methods such as irrigation, which they pioneered. The new hotel development on Lanai will not greatly affect the pineapple industry. Presently there are 12,000 acres under cultivation, but Dole sees a future in which this will be streamlined to 10,000 acres. This is in keeping with Dole's view of producing a premium, more expensive pineapple that would reduce its total market share.

A recent furor involved a chemical called heptaclore used to kill ants on pineapples. All the pineapple producers use heptaclore, and though believed to be a carcinogen, it carries a federal label of approval. If guidelines are followed, it's considered safe, and according to testing, no heptaclore is found in the actual fruit itself. But in this case, pineapple stalks and leaves were chopped and sold to dairy farmers as feed. The milk produced had intolerable amounts of heptaclore. Health food stores on Oahu refused to sell milk outright and the dairies involved recalled their milk until it was once again considered safe. Dole was not involved, but all the producers felt the heat from consumers. Still, the port at Kaumalapau is very busy sending off the fruits of Lanai's labor. There is work on Lanai for any islander who wants it, and almost all do. The standard of living is working class: decent, hopeful, and proud.

THE PEOPLE

Lanai is characterized by the incredible mix of racial strains so common in Hawaii—Filipino, Japanese, Hawaiian, Chinese, and Caucasian. It is unique, however, in that 50-60% of its people are Filipino. The Filipinos, many recent immigrants, were solicited by Castle and Cooke to work as laborers on the pineapple plantation. Mostly 18-to 25-year-old men, the majority speak Ilocano and may have come to join relatives already on Lanai. Most arrive on their own; they learn English and from Lanai they spread out. As workers they're perfect: industrious and quiet. At night you wonder where they all are. Due to the tremendous shortage of eligible women, most workers stay home or fish or have a beer in the backyard with buddies. And on Sundays, there is the illegal (officially nonexistent) cockfight. For high living, everyone heads for Maui or Oahu.

The next largest racial groups are Japanese (18%) and whites (12%). The Japanese started as the field workers before the Filipinos, but now, along with the whites, are Lanai's professionals and middle management. The races coexist, but there are still unseen social strata. There's even a small Chinese population (1%) who fulfill their traditional role as shopkeepers. A good 10% of Lanaians are Hawaiians. Finally, almost 10% fall into the "mixed" category, with many of these Filipino-Hawaiian.

Community

Lanai has a strong sense of community and uniqueness that keeps the people close. For example, during a bitter three-month strike in 1964,

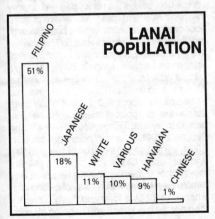

LANAI POPULATION

FILIPINO 51%
JAPANESE 18%
WHITE 11%
VARIOUS 10%
HAWAIIAN 9%
CHINESE 1%

the entire community rallied and all suffered equally: laborers, shopkeepers, and management. All who remember say that it brought out the best in the island tradition of aloha. If you really want to meet Lanaians, just sit in the park in the center of Lanai City for an hour or two. You'll notice a lot of old-timers, who seem to be very healthy. You could easily strike up a conversation with some of them.

Other Faces

It should strike you that most of the people you see around Lanai are men. That in itself is a social comment about Lanai. Where are the women? They're in the traditional roles at home, nurturing and trying to add the pleasantries of life. Some are field workers too. You might notice that there are no famous crafts of Lanai and no artists working commercially. This is not to say there is no art on Lanai, but the visitor rarely sees it. One reason that Lanai produces so little commercial art is that it's a workers' island with virtually no unemployment, so everyone is busy making a living. Old-timers are known to make superb fishing poles, nets, and even their own horseshoes. The island ladies are excellent seamstresses and with the rising interest in hula, make lovely leis from the beautiful *kunaoa*, Lanai's flower. If you turn your attention to the young people of Lanai, you'll see the statewide problem of babies having babies. Teenage pregnancy is rampant, and teenage parents are common. Young guys customize their 4WDs although there's no place to go, and Taka's Snack Shop is now exclusively given over to video games. If as a young person you wish to remain on Lanai, then in almost every case your future will be tied to Dole. If you have other aspirations, it's "goodbai to Lanai." These islanders are some of the most easygoing and relaxed people you'll encounter in Hawaii, but with the electronic age extending its long arms of communication, even here they're not nearly as "backwater" as you might think.

GETTING THERE

By Air

Hawaiian Air, tel. (800) 367-5320 Mainland, or 565-6429 Lanai, flies DC-9s and turbo-prop Dash Transits to Lanai. They have one flight on Fri. and Sun. from Kauai, Oahu, Molokai, Maui,

and Hawaii, with another flight on Mon. from Oahu only. Flights originating on the Big Island and Kauai are on DC-9s; those from Honolulu, Molokai, and Maui are on Dash Transits. If you get the "jitters" on small aircraft and want the security and comfort of a larger plane, fly Hawaiian Air. Daily flights are available to and from Lanai by **Aloha Island Air,** tel. 833-3219 Oahu, (800) 652-6541 Neighbor Islands, (800) 323-3345 Mainland. They fly to and from Honolulu seven times daily, with one flight to Molokai at 4:45 p.m. All three of Maui's airports (Kahului, Hana, Kapalua) are serviced, with the majority to and from Kahului Airport. The longest route is to Princeville on Kauai with two flights in the morning, and two in the afternoon.

Lanai Airport is a practical but dusty little strip out in the pineapple fields about four miles southwest of Lanai City. The one-room terminal offers no shops, car rental booths, lockers, public transportation, or even access to a toilet, unless there's a scheduled flight. A bulletin board near the door has all the practical information and phone numbers you'll need to get to Lanai City.

By Boat

One other possibility for getting to Lanai is going by pleasure boat from Maui. Many Lanai and Maui residents travel by this route and even receive special *kamaaina* rates. These are basically tour boats specializing in snorkeling, dinner cruising, whalewatching, and the like, but they're also willing to drop you off and pick you up at a later date. It's an enjoyable and actually inexpensive way of going. You'll have to make your own arrangements with the boat captains, mostly berthed at Lahaina Harbor. This alternative is particularly attractive to campers, as they anchor on Lanai at Manele Bay, just a five minute walk from the campsites at Hulopoe. There are no fixed rates for this service, but kamaaina pay about $20. Expect to pay more but use this as a point of reference. Some companies to try are: Trilogy, tel. 661-4743; Sea Bird, tel. 661-3643; and Windjammer, tel. 661-8384, all at Lahaina Harbor (see p. 380). Another outfit is Club Lanai, tel. 871-1144, but they anchor at their own private beach on very remote East Lanai, with no way of getting anywhere except by a long and dusty hike. Remember that, in effect, you're going standby with all of these companies, but there is generally room for one more.

GETTING AROUND

Public Transportation

No public transportation operates on Lanai, but Lanai City Service will pick you up at the airport if you're renting a car/jeep from them. Oshiro's Service Station will pick you up at the airport; if you're renting a vehicle from them, they'll charge $6 RT. The Hotel Lanai, tel. 565-7211, will pick you up if the van's available and you're intending to stay there, but you must arrange this in advance.

Car Rental

For a car, or better yet, a jeep, try **Lanai City Service**, Lanai City, HI 96763, tel. 565-6780. You'll be outfitted with wheels and given information on where to go and especially about road conditions. Pay heed! Make sure to tell them your plans, especially if you're heading for a remote area. That way, if you have problems and don't return, they'll know where to send the rescue party! Lanai City Service is now a subsidiary of Trilogy Excursions and rents Toyotas for $40/day, jeeps $89/day (insurance compulsory). **Oshiro Service and U-Drive,** Box 516, Lanai City, HI 96763, tel. 565-6952, rents modern Japanese compacts for $25-35/day plus gas, and jeeps for around $85.

4WD Rental

With only 22 miles of paved road on Lanai and rental cars firmly restricted to these, there is no real reason to rent one. The *real* adventure spots of Lanai require a 4WD vehicle. Mind-boggling spots on Lanai are reachable only on foot or by 4WD. Unfortunately, even the inveterate hiker will have a tough time because the best trailheads are quite a distance from town, and you'll spend as much time getting to them as hiking the actual trails.

Many people who have little or no experience driving 4WDs are under the slap-happy belief that they are unstoppable. Oh, that it were true! They do indeed get stuck, and it's usually miserable getting them unstuck. Both rental agencies will give you up-to-the-minute info on the road conditions, and a fairly accurate map for navigation. They tend to be a bit conservative on where they advise you to take "their" vehicles, but they

also live on the island and are accustomed to driving off-road, which balances out their conservative estimates. Also, remember road conditions change rapidly: a hard rain on the Munro Trail can change it from a flower-lined path to a nasty quagmire, or wind might lay a tree across a beach road. Keep your eye on the weather and if in doubt, don't push your luck. If you get stuck, you'll not only ruin your outing and have to hike back to town, but you'll also be charged for a service call which can be astronomical, especially if it's deemed to be due to your negligence. Most of your off-road driving will be in *compound* 4WD, first gear, low range.

Hitchhiking

Like everywhere else in Hawaii, hitching is technically illegal, but the islanders are friendly and are quite good about giving you a lift. Lanai, however, is a workers' island and the traffic is really skimpy during the day. You can only reasonably expect to get a ride from Lanai City to the airport or to Manele Bay since both are on paved roads and frequented by normal island traffic. There is a very slim chance of picking up a ride out through the "pine" fields toward the Garden of the Gods or Kaunolu, for example, so definitely don't count on it.

ACCOMMODATIONS

The two new luxury hotels that are rising will increase Lanai's available rooms a thousand-fold. Since these are in the ultra-luxury class and quite expensive, they won't, however, ease the demand for reasonably priced accommodations. If anything, they'll draw the spotlight to Lanai, and will most probably make getting a room tougher. So, if you're contemplating a trip to the island, make doubly sure to book in advance.

Hotel Lanai

Being the only hotel on the island (until 1990), you'd think the lack of competition would make it arrogant, indifferent, and expensive. Instead, it is a delight. The hotel has gone through very few cosmetic changes since it was built in 1923 as a guest lodge primarily for visiting executives of Dole Pineapple, which still owns it. Its architecture is simple Hawaiiana, and its setting among the tall pines fronted by a large lawn is refreshingly rustic. With a corrugated iron roof and two

the Hotel Lanai

wings connected by a long enclosed veranda, it looks like the main building at a Boy Scout camp. But don't be fooled. The hotel is managed by Castle and Cooke. The 10 remodeled rooms may not be plush, but they are cozy as can be. All have been painted in lively colors, and are clean with private baths, but no phones or TVs. Room rates are $51 s, $58 d, and $66 for three. The hotel has the only bar in town on its enclosed veranda, where guests and at times a few islanders have a quiet beer and twilight chat before retiring at the ungodly hour of nine o'clock. The main dining room (and only real restaurant on Lanai) is large, and lined with hunting trophies. So if you're lured by the quiet simplicity of Lanai and wish to avail yourself of one of the last family-style inns of Hawaii, write for reservations to Hotel Lanai, Lanai City, HI 96763, tel. 565-7211 or (800) 624-8849. With only 10 rooms, reservations are a must.

The Lodge at Koele

This magnificent luxury lodge has recently opened its doors to guests. Amenities include a swimming pool, restaurant, cocktail lounge and tennis courts. Rates begin at $275 for a standard room to $425 for a suite. For reservations contact Rock Resorts Inc. P.O. Box 774, Lanai City, Lanai, HI 96763, tel: 565-7245.

Lanai Realty

Lanai's first house rental agency recently opened for business. All houses are completely furnished including linens, kitchen utensils, washer/dryer, and TV. They rent three bedroom homes for $95-110/day, $550-700/week, $1800-2100/month, up to six people; four bedroom homes are, $225/day (more on weekends), $1300/week, $4000/month (eight people). Check-in is at 2 p.m., check-out 11 a.m., 50% deposit required, no credit cards, checks OK, two day minimum. Write Kathy Oshiro, Lanai Realty, Box 67, Lanai City, HI 96763, tel. 565-6597 or 565-6960.

Lanai Bucks Hunting Lodge

This lodge is an anomaly even to longtime island residents, many of whom claim they've never heard of it. It seems impossible on such a small island, but when contacted by mail the lodge does answer. Word is that Bucks Lodge provides small, unadorned, barrack-type rooms with kitchen privileges for $25. If interested write to: Gwendolyn Kaniho, Lanai Bucks Hunting Lodge, Box 879, Lanai City, Lanai, HI 96763. No phone number available.

Camping

The only official camping permitted to non-residents is located at Hulopoe Bay, administered by the Koele Company. Reservations for one of the six official campsites here are a must, although unbelievably there's usually a good chance of getting a space. Koele Co. officials state that they try to accommodate any "overflow" unreserved visitors, but don't count on it. Since Lanai is by and large privately owned by Castle and Cooke Inc., the parent company of

Koele, you really have no recourse but to play by their rules. It seems they want to hold visitors to a minimum and keep strict tabs on the ones that do arrive. Nonetheless, the campsites at Hulopoe Bay are great. Lining the idyllic beach, they're far enough apart to afford some privacy. The showers are designed so that the pipes, just below the surface, are solar heated. This means a good hot shower during daylight and early evening. Campsite use is limited to seven nights. The fee includes a one-time $5 registration and are $4.50 pp. For reservations write to the Koele Co., Box L, Lanai City, Lanai, HI 96763, tel. 565-6661. Permits, if not mailed in advance, are picked up at the Koele office. If visiting on the spur of the moment from a neighboring island, it's advisable to call ahead.

Note

While hiking or four-wheel driving the back roads of Lanai, especially along Naha, Shipwreck, and Polihua beaches, a multitude of picture-perfect camping spots will present themselves, but they can be used only by Lanai residents, although there's little supervision. A one-night bivouac would probably go undetected. No other island allows unofficial camping and unless it can be statistically shown that potential visitors are being turned away, it seems unlikely that the Koele Co. will change its policies. If you're one of the unlucky ones who have been turned down, write your letter of protest to parent company Castle and Cooke, 965 N. Nimitz Hwy., Honolulu, HI 96817, tel. 548-6611.

RESTAURANTS

Lanai City is the only place on the island where you can dine, shop, and take care of business. The food situation on Lanai is discouraging. Everything has to be brought in by barge. There's very little fresh produce, hardly any fresh fish, and even chicken is at a premium, which seems impossible given the huge Filipino population. People surely eat differently at home, but in the two tiny restaurants (Dahang's and S.T. Property) open to the traveler, the fare is restricted to the "two scoop rice and teri beef" variety, with fried noodles and spam as the pièce de résistance. Salad to most islanders meanss a potato-macaroni combination sure to stick to your ribs and anything else on the way. Vegetables are usually a tablespoon of grated cabbage and soy sauce.

Until recently, the best restaurant in town was at the **Hotel Lanai,** tel. 565-7211. The meals that come out of this kitchen are not gourmet, but are wholesome home cooking. The hotel bakes pies, and provides fresh fish and vegetables whenever possible. Budgeters can order a large stuffed potato, salad, soup of the day, and drink for under $8. Restaurant hours are breakfast 7 a.m. to 9:30 a.m., lunch 11:30 a.m. to 1:30 p.m., dinner 6:30 to 8:30 p.m. The best dish is the fresh fish when available, and all go for under $15 except for a steak dinner.

But if you're looking for a breakfast or snack with a true island flavor, try one of the following. **Dahang's Bakery** has recently remodeled and can even be called chic for Lanai. Their tasty pastries are sold out by early morning, and the breakfasts of eggs, bacon, potatoes, and the like cost about $3.50. They also have good plate lunches for about $4.50. Open every day 5:30 a.m. to 1:30 p.m., closed Sunday. Just up the road is an authentic workers' restaurant and sundries store called **S.T. Property.** No one should visit Lanai without at least stopping in here for morning coffee. It's totally run-down, but it's a pure cultural experience. Arrive before 7 a.m. when the company whistle calls most of the workers to the fields. All you have to do is look around at the faces of the people to see the spirit of Lanai. The restaurant at **The Lodge** is first-rate and open to non-guests.

OUTDOOR SPORTS

No question that Lanai's forte is its natural unspoiled setting and great outdoors. You can really get away from it all on Lanai. Traffic jams, neon lights, blaring discos, shopping boutiques, and all that jazz just don't exist here. The action is swimming, hiking, snorkeling, fishing, and some hunting. Two tennis courts and a nifty golf course set among the island's Norfolk pines round off the activities. Lanai is the place to revitalize your spirits—you want to get up with the birds, greet the sun, stretch, and soak up the good life.

Snorkeling, Scuba, And Swimming

Lanai, especially around Manele/Hulopoe Bay, has some of the best snorkeling and scuba in Hawaii. If you don't have your own equipment, try renting it from the tour boats that come over from Maui. The *Trilogy,* operated by the Coon family, often does this. Their van is parked at Manele Bay, and if someone is around he might rent you some gear. Lanai City Service, a subsidiary of Trilogy, rents snorkeling equipment and underwater cameras. Your other choice is to buy it from Pine Isle or Richards markets, but their prices are quite high. If you're the adventurous sort, you can dive for spiny lobsters off Shipwreck or Polihua, but make absolutely sure to check the surf conditions as it can be super treacherous. It would be best to go with a local.

Lanai City has a brand-new swimming pool. Located in town near the high school, it's open to the public daily during summer, and on a limited schedule during other seasons.

Tennis And Golf

You can play tennis at two lighted courts at the Lanai School. They have rubberized surfaces called "royal duck" and are fairly well maintained—definitely OK for a fun game. Golfers will be delighted to follow their balls around Cavendish Golf Course on the outskirts of Lanai City. This nine hole, 3,100-yard, par-36 course is set among Norfolk pines. It's free to islanders; guests are requested to pay $5 on the honor system. Just drop your money in the box provided. Come on, pay up! It's definitely worth it!

Hunting

The first cliché you hear about Lanai is that it's one big pineapple plantation. The second is that it's a hunter's paradise. Both are true. The big game action is provided by mouflon sheep and axis deer. Also spotted are the protected yet failing population of pronghorns which, thankfully, can only be shot with a camera. Various days are open for the hunting of game birds, which include: ring-necked and green pheasant; Gambel, Japanese, and California quail; wild turkey and a variety of doves, francolins, and partridges. Hunting of mouflon sheep and axis deer is open to the public only in the northwest of the island, which is leased to the state of Hawaii by the Koele Company. Brochures detailing all necessary information can be obtained free of charge by writing to Dept. of Land and Natural Resources, 1151 Punchbowl St., Honolulu, HI 96813. The Lanai regional office is at 338 8th St. Lanai City, HI 96763. Licenses are required ($7.50 resident, $15 nonresident) and can be purchased by mail from Dept. of Land and Natural Resources or picked up in person at their office on Lanai.

Public archery hunting of mouflon sheep is restricted to the first and second Sundays of August and rifle season occurs on the third and fourth Sundays, but hunters are restricted by public drawing. Axis deer regular season (rifle, shotgun, and bows) opens on the nine consecutive Sundays up to and including the last Sunday in April; it's also restricted by public drawing. Archery season for axis deer is the two Sundays preceding the regular season. Bag limits are one mouflon ram and one deer. Axis deer are hunted year-round on the private game reserves of the Koele Co., although the best trophy season is May through November. The rates are $180 per

GOLF AND TENNIS LANAI

Course	Par	Yards	Fees	Cart
Cavendish Golf Course* • Koele Company, P.O. Box L, Lanai City, HI 96763 tel. 565-9993	36	3071	$5.00	

N.B.* = 9 hole course • = no club rentals

This tennis court is open to the public. Call ahead to check availability.

Location	Name of Court	No. of Courts	Lighted
Near Lanai School	Lanai City	2	Yes

day for a hunting permit. Guide service is not officially mandatory, but you must prove that you have hunted Lanai before and are intimately knowledgeable about its terrain, hunting areas, and procedures. If not, you must acquire the services of either Kazu Ohara or Gary Onuma, two excellent rangers on Lanai. Guide service is $150 a day and an additional $50 per hunter/per party. This service includes all necessities, from airport pick-up to shipping the trophy. A box lunch and all ground transport to and from the hunt are also provided. For full details write to Chief Ranger, Koele Co., Box L, Lanai City, HI 96763, tel. 565-6661.

Fishing

No commercial or charter fishing boats operate out of Lanai, but that's not to say there are no fish. On the contrary, one of the island's greatest pastimes is this relaxing sport. Any day in Lanai City Park, you'll find plenty of old-timers to ask where the fish are biting. If you have the right approach and use the right smile, they just might tell you. Generally, the best fishing and easiest access on the island is at Shipwreck Beach running north toward Polihua. Near the lighthouse ruins is good for *papio* and *ulua,* the latter running to 50 pounds. Many of the local fishermen use throw nets to catch the smaller fish such as *manini,* preferred especially by Lanai's elders. Throw netting takes skill usually learned from childhood, but don't be afraid to try even if you throw what the locals call a "banana" or one that looks like Maui (a little head and a big body). They might snicker, but if you laugh too, you'll make a friend.

Mostly you'll fish with rod and reel using frozen squid or crab, available at Lanai's general stores. Bring a net bag or suitable container. This is the best beachcombing on the island and it's also excellent diving for spiny lobster. There is good shore fishing (especially for *awa*) and easy accessibility at Kaumalapau Harbor, from where the pineapples are shipped. It's best to go after 5 p.m. when wharf activity has slowed down. There is also superb offshore fishing at Kaunolu, Kamehameha's favorite angling spot on the south shore. You can catch *aku* and *kawa*

kawa, but to be really successful you'll need a boat. Finally, Manele Hulopoe Marine Life Conservation Park has limited fishing, but as the name implies, it's a conservation district so be sure to follow the rules prominently posted at Manele Bay.

PRACTICALITIES

Shopping

The two grocery stores in town are fairly well stocked with basics, but anyone into health foods or vegetarianism should carry supplies and use the markets for staples only. The markets are almost next door to each other: **Pine Isle Market,** run by Kerry Honda, and **Richards Shopping Center,** both open Mon. to Sat. 8 a.m. to 5:30 p.m. They supply all your basic camping, fishing, and general merchandise needs.

Money

Try full-service **First Hawaiian Bank** in Lanai City for all your banking needs. All major businesses accept traveler's checks. The *only* credit cards accepted on Lanai are MasterCard and Visa. None of the others, including venerable American Express, is accepted. Open Mon.-Thur., 8:30 a.m. to 3 p.m., and until 6 p.m. on Friday.

Post Office

The Lanai P.O., tel. 565-6517, is across the street from the Dole offices on Lanai Avenue. Open daily from 8 a.m. to 4:30 p.m., it's full service, but they do not sell boxes or padded mailers to send home beachcombing treasures; you can get these at the two stores in town.

Useful Phone Numbers

Oshiro Service Station, tel. 565-6952; Lanai City Service, tel. 565-6780; Hotel Lanai, tel. 565-7211; Koele Co. (camping and hiking info), tel. 565-6661; Dept. of Land and Natural Resources, tel. 565-6688; Lanai Airport, tel. 565-6757; Lanai Community Library, tel. 565-6996; police, tel. 565-6525.

EXPLORING LANAI

LANAI CITY

Lanai City (pop. 2,600) would be more aptly described and sound more appealing if it were called Lanai Village. A utilitarian town, it was built in the 1920s by Dole Pineapple. The architecture, field-worker plain, has definitely gained "character" in the last 60 years. It's an excellent spot for a town, sitting at 1,600 feet in the shadow of Lanaihale, the island's tallest mountain. George Munro's Norfolk pines have matured and now give the entire town a green, shaded, parklike atmosphere. It's cool and breezy—a great place to launch off from in the morning and a welcome spot to return to at night. Most visitors head out of town to the more spectacular sights and never take the chance to explore the back streets.

Houses

As you'd expect, most houses are square boxes with corrugated roofs, but each has its own personality. Painted every color of the rainbow, they'd be garish in any other place, but here they break the monotony and seem to work. The people of Lanai make their living from the land and can work wonders with it. Around many homes are colorful flower beds, green gardens bursting with vegetables, fruit trees, and flower-ing shrubs. When you look down the half-dirt, broken-pavement roads at a line of these houses, you can't help feeling that a certain nobility exists here. The houses are mud-spattered where the rain splashes red earth against them, but inside you know they're sparkling clean. Even some modern suburban homes sprawl on the south end of town. Most of these belong to Lanai's miniature middle class and would fit unnoticed in any up-and-coming neighborhood on the Mainland.

Downtown

If you sit on the steps of Hotel Lanai and peer across its huge front yard, you can scrutinize the heart of downtown Lanai City. Off to your right are the offices of the Dole Co. sitting squat and solid. In front of them, forming a type of town square, is Dole Park, where old-timers come to sit and young mothers bring their kids for some fresh air. No one in Lanai City rushes to do anything. Look around and you'll discover a real fountain of youth: many octagenarians with a spring in their step. Years of hard work without being hyper or anxious is why they say they're still around. The park is surrounded by commercial Lanai. There's nowhere to *go* except over to the schoolyard to play some tennis or to Cavendish Golf Course for a round of nine holes. Lanai

City had a movie theater, but it screened its last picture show a while back. You can plop yourself at Dahang's Pastry Shop or S.T. Properties for coffee, or stay in the park if you're in the mood to strike up a conversation—it won't take long. Go over to Taka's Snack Shop. Anywhere else, this building would seem abandoned—inside are a few video games and maybe a bag of potato chips to buy if they're not all gone.

Meander down Lanai Avenue past a complex of agricultural buildings and shops. Heavy equipment leaks grease in their rutted dirt lots, where Lanai shows its raw plantation muscle. Just down the street is a complex of log buildings with shake-shingled roofs. These rustic barracks are for the summer help that come to pick the pineapples—often Mormon kids from Utah out to make some money and see a bit of the world. They're known to be clean-living and quiet, and it's ironic that Lanai was once a failed Mormon colony. Do yourself a favor—get out of your rental car and walk around town for at least 30 minutes. You'll experience one of the most unique villages in America.

MUNRO TRAIL

The highlight of visiting Lanai is climbing the Munro Trail to its highest point, Lanaihale (3,370 feet), locally called **The Hale.** As soon as you set foot on Lanai the silhouette of this razor-back ridge with its bristling coat of Norfolk pines demands your attention. Set off for The Hale and you're soon engulfed in its cool stands of pines, eucalyptus, and ironwoods, all colored with ferns and wildflowers. George Munro, a New Zealander hired as the manager of the Lanai Ranch a short time before Jim Dole's arrival, is responsible. With a pouch full of seeds and clippings from his native New Zealand, he trudged all over Lanai planting, in an attempt to foliate the island and create a permanent watershed. Driven by that basic and primordial human desire to see things grow, he climbed The Hale time and again to renew and nurture his leafy progeny. Now, all benefit from his labors.

Getting There
There are two ways to go to The Hale, by foot or 4WD. Some local people go on horseback, but horses aren't generally for hire. Head out of town

on Route 44 toward Shipwreck Beach. Make sure to start before 8 a.m.; cloud cover is common by early afternoon. After less than two miles, still on the Lanai City side of the mountains, take the first major gravel road to the right. In about one-quarter mile the road comes to a Y—go left. You immediately start climbing and pass through a forested area past a series of gulches (see below). Continue and the road forks; again bear left. Always stay on the more obviously traveled road. The side roads look muddy and overgrown and it's obvious which is the main one. Robert Frost would be disappointed.

The Trail
As you climb, you pass a profusion of gulches, great red wounds cut into Lanai's windward side. First comes deep and brooding **Maunalei** ("Mountain Lei") **Gulch,** from where Lanai draws its water through a series of tunnels bored through the mountains. It's flanked by **Kuolanai Trail,** a rugged and dangerous footpath leading all the way to the coast. Next is **Hookio Gulch,** a battleground where Lanai's warriors were vanquished in 1778 by Kalaniopuu and his ferocious fighters from the Big Island. All that remains are a few room-sized notches cut into the walls where the warriors slept and piled stones to be hurled at the invaders. After Hookio Gulch, a trail bears left, bringing you to the gaping mouth of **Hauola Gulch,** over 2,000 feet deep. Keep your eyes peeled for axis deer, which seem to defy gravity and manage to cling and forage along the most unlikely and precipitous cliffs. Be very careful of your footing—even skilled Lanai hunters have fallen to their deaths in this area.

The jeep trail narrows on the ridge to little more than 100 feet across. On one side are the wild gulches, on the other the bucolic green, whorling fingerprints of the pineapple fields. Along the trail you can munch strawberries, common guavas, and as many thimbleberries as you can handle. At the crest of The Hale, let your eyes pan the horizon to see all the main islands of Hawaii (except for Kauai). Rising from the height-caused mirage of a still sea is the hazy specter of Oahu to the north, with Molokai and Maui clearly visible just 10 miles distant. Haleakala, Maui's magical mountain, has a dominant presence viewed from The Hale.

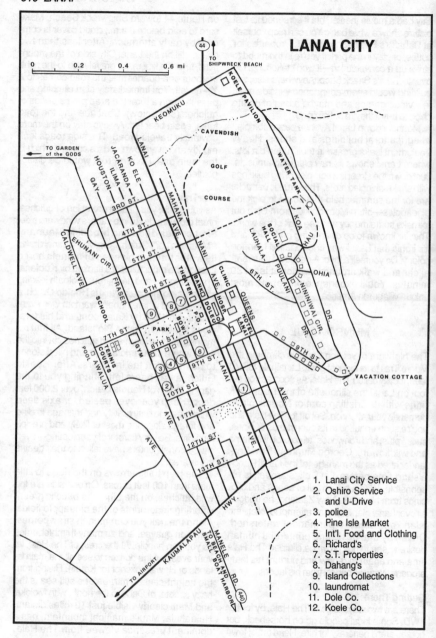

LANAI CITY

0   0.2   0.4   0.6 mi

TO SHIPWRECK BEACH

44

TO GARDEN of the GODS

KEOMUKU

KOELE PAVILION

CAVENDISH

GOLF COURSE

WATER TANK

KO ELE
LANAI
MAHANA AVE.
NANI
HOUSTON
GAY
JACARANDA
ILIMA
3RD ST.
CALDWELL AVE.
EHUNANI CIR.
4TH ST.
5TH ST.
6TH ST.
FRASER
THEATER
BANK
CLINIC AVE.
HOSP.
QUEENS
SOCIAL HALL
LAUHALA
PUULANI
OHIA
KOA
HAU
NININIWAI CIR.
OHIA DR.
6TH ST.
SCHOOL ST
7TH ST
PARK
8TH ST.
POOL
AWALUA
TENNIS COURTS
GYM
P.O.
DOLE CO.
BOWL
HOTEL LANAI
9TH ST.
9TH ST.
VACATION COTTAGE
3
4
5
9
8
7
6
2
1
9TH ST.
10TH ST.
11TH ST.
12TH ST.
13TH ST.
LANAI AVE.
KAUMALAPAU HWY.
TO BEACH AND SMALL BOAT HARBOR
TO AIRPORT
MANELE RD.
440

1. Lanai City Service
2. Oshiro Service and U-Drive
3. police
4. Pine Isle Market
5. Int'l. Food and Clothing
6. Richard's
7. S.T. Properties
8. Dahang's
9. Island Collections
10. laundromat
11. Dole Co.
12. Koele Co.

Sweep right to see Kahoolawe, bleak and barren, its body shattered by the bombs of the U.S. Navy, a victim of their controversial war games. Eighty miles south of Kahoolawe is the Big Island, its mammoth peaks, Mauna Loa and Mauna Kea, looming like ethereal islands floating in the clouds.

Just past the final lookout is a sign for **Awehi Trail**, which leads left to Naha on the beach. It's extremely rough and you'll definitely need a 4WD in compound low to get down. Most people continue straight ahead and join up with Hoike Road that flattens out and takes you through the pineapple fields until it joins with Route 44 just south of Lanai City. If you have time for only one outing on Lanai or funds budgeted for only one day of 4WD rental, make sure to treat yourself to the unforgettable Munro Trail.

HEADING SOUTH

Joseph Kaliihananui was the last of the free Hawaiian farmers to work the land of Lanai. His great-grandson, Lloyd Cockett, still lives in Lanai City. Joseph made his home in the arid but fertile Palawai Basin that was later bought by Jim Dole and turned into the heart of the pineapple plantation. Just south of Lanai City on Route 440 (Manele Road), the Palawai Basin is the crater of the extinct single volcano of which Lanai is formed. Joseph farmed sweet potatoes, which he traded for fish. He gathered his water in barrels from the dew that formed on his roof and from a trickling spring. His lands supported a few cattle among its now-extinct heavy stands of cactus. Here too Walter Murray Gibson attempted to begin a Mormon colony which he later aborted, supposedly because of his outrage over the idea of polygamy. Nothing noteworthy remains of this colony, but high on a hillside overlooking Palawai are the Luahiwa Petroglyphs, considered to be some of the best-preserved rock hieroglyphics in Hawaii.

Luahiwa Petroglyphs

The route through the maze of pineapple roads that lead to the petroglyphs is tough to follow, but the best recipe for success is being pointed in the right direction and adding a large dollop of perseverance. Heading south on Manele Road, look to your left for the back side of a triangular yield sign at Hoike Road, the main pineapple road. Hoike Road was once paved but has now disintegrated into gravel. After turning left onto Hoike, head straight toward a large water tank on the hill. You pass two round-bottomed irrigation ditches, easily spotted as they're always green with grass due to the water they carry. At the second ditch turn left and follow the road, keeping the ditch on your right. Proceed until you come to a silver water pipe about 12 inches in diameter. Follow this pipe as it runs along a hedgerow until you reach the third power pole. At the No Trespassing sign, bear left.

Follow this overgrown trail up the hill to the boulders on which appear the petroglyphs. The boulders are brownish-black and covered in lichens. Their natural arrangement resembles an oversized Japanese rock garden. Dotted on the hillside are sisal plants that look like bouquets of giant green swords. As you climb to the rocks be very careful of your footing—the ground is crumbly and the vegetation slippery. The boulders cover a three acre area; most of the petroglyphs are found on the south faces of the rocks. Some are hieroglyphics of symbolic circles, others are picture stories complete with canoes gliding under unfurled sails. Dogs snarl with their jaws agape, while enigmatic triangular stick-men try to tell their stories from the past. Equestrians gallop, showing that these stone picture-books were done even after the coming of the white man. The Luahiwa Petroglyphs are a very special spot where the ancient Hawaiians still sing their tales across the gulf of time.

Hulopoe And Manele Bays

Proceed south on Route 440 to Lanai's most salubrious spots, the twin bays of Manele and Hulopoe. At the crest of the hill, just past the milepost, you can look down on the white, inviting sands of Hulopoe to the right, and the rockier small boat harbor of Manele on the left. The island straight ahead is Kahoolawe, and on very clear days you might be able to glimpse the peaks of Hawaii's Mauna Loa and Mauna Kea. Manele Bay is a picture-perfect anchorage where a dozen or so small boats and yachts are tied up on any given day. Tour boats from Maui also tie up here, but according to local sailors the tourists don't seem to come on the weekends. Manele and Hulopoe are a Marine Life Conservation District with the rules for fishing and diving prominently displayed on a large bulletin board at the entrance to Manele. Because of this, the area is superb for snorkeling.

Hulopoe Bay offers very gentle waves and soothing, crystal-clear water. The beach is a beautiful expanse of white sand fringed by palms with a mingling of large boulders that really set it off. This is Lanai's offical camping area, and six sites are available. All are well spaced, each with a picnic table and fire pit. A series of shower stalls made of brown plywood provides just enough privacy, allowing your head and legs to protrude. The water is surprisingly warm—the pipes feeding the showers are laid close to the surface so that the water is solar heated. After refreshing yourself you can fish from the rock promontories on both sides of the bay. It's difficult to find a more wholesome and gentle spot anywhere in Hawaii.

Kaumalapau Harbor

A side trip to Kaumalapau Harbor is worth it. This manmade facility, which ships more than a million pineapples a day during peak harvest, is the only one of its kind in the world. Besides, you've probably already rented a vehicle and you might as well cover these few paved miles from Lanai City on Route 44 just to have a quick look. En route you pass Lanai's odoriferous garbage dump, which is a real eyesore. Hold your nose and try not to notice. The harbor facility itself is no-nonsense commercial, but the coastline is reasonably spectacular, with a glimpse of the island's dramatic sea cliffs. Also, this area has super-easy access to some decent fishing, right off the pier area. An added bonus for making the trek to this lonely area is that it is one of the best places on Lanai from which to view the sunset, and you usually have it all to yourself.

KAUNOLU: KAMEHAMEHA'S GETAWAY

At the southwestern tip of Lanai is Kaunolu Bay. At one time, this vibrant fishing village surrounded Halulu Heiau, a sacred refuge where the downtrodden were protected by the temple priests who could intercede with the benevolent gods. Kamehameha the Great would escape Lahaina's blistering summers and come to these very fertile fishing waters with his loyal

warriors. Some proved their valor to their great chief by diving from Ka hikili's Leap, a manmade opening in the rocks 60 feet above the sea. The remains of over 80 house sites and a smattering of petroglyphs dot the area. The last inhabitant was Ohua, elder brother of Joseph Kaliihananui, who lived in a grass hut just east of Kaunolu in Mamaki Bay. Ohua was entrusted by Kamehameha V to hide the heiau's fish-god, Kuniki; old accounts by the area's natives say that he died because of mishandling this stone god. The natural power still emanating from Kaunolu is obvious, and you can't help feeling the energy that drew the Hawaiians to this sacred spot.

Getting There

Proceed south on Manele Road from Lanai City through Palawai Basin until it makes a hard bend to the left. Here, a sign points you to Manele Bay. Do not go left to Manele, but proceed straight and stay on the once-paved pineapple road. At a dip by a huge silver water pipe, go straight through the pineapple fields until another obvious dip at two orange pipes (like fire hydrants) on the left and right. Turn left here onto a rather small road—pineapples on your left and tall grass along the irrigation ditch on your right. Follow the road left to a weatherworn sign that actually says "Kaunolu Road." This dirt track starts off innocently enough as it begins its plunge toward the sea. Only two miles long, the local folks consider it the roughest road on the island. It is a bone-cruncher, but if you take it super slow, you should have no real problem. Plot your progress against the lighthouse on the coast. This area is excellent for spotting axis deer. The deer are nourished by haole koa, a green bush with a brown seed pod that you see growing along the road. This natural feed also supports cattle, but is not good for horses, causing the hair on their tails to fall out.

Kaunolu

The village site lies at the end of a long dry gulch which terminates at a rocky beach, suitable in times past as a canoe anchorage. This entire area is a mecca for archaeologists and anthropologists. The most famous was the eminent Dr. Kenneth Emory of the Bishop Museum; he filed an extensive research report on the area. At its terminus, the road splits left and right. Go right to reach a large *kiawe* tree with a rudimentary picnic table under it. Just in front of you is a large pile of nondescript rocks purported to be the ruined foundation of Kamehameha's house. Unbelievably, this sacred area has been trashed out by disrespectful and ignorant picnickers. Hurricane Iwa also had a hand in changing the face of Kaunolu, as its tremendous force hit this area head on and even drove large boulders from the sea onto the land. As you look around, the ones that have a whitish appearance were washed up on the shore by the fury of Iwa.

The villagers of Kaunolu lived mostly on the east bank and had to keep an ever-watchful eye on nature because the bone-dry gulch could suddenly be engulfed by flash floods. In the center of the gulch, about 100 yards inland, was *Paao*, the area's freshwater well. *Paao* was *kapu* to menstruating women, and it was believed that if the *kapu* was broken, the well would dry up. It served the village for centuries. It's totally obliterated now; in 1895 a Mr. Hayselden tried to erect a windmill over it, destroying the native caulking and causing the well to turn brackish—an example of Lanai's precious water being tampered with by outsiders, causing disastrous results.

The Sites

Climb down the east bank and cross the rocky beach. The first well-laid wall close to the beach on the west bank is the remains of a canoe shed. Proceed inland and climb the rocky bank to the remains of **Halulu Heiau.** Just below in the undergrowth is where the well was located. The *heiau* site has a commanding view of the area, best described by the words of Dr. Emory himself: "The point on which it is located is surrounded on three sides by cliffs and on the north rises the magnificent cliff of Palikaholo, terminating in Kahilikalani crag, a thousand feet above the sea. The ocean swell entering Kolokolo Cave causes a rumbling like thunder, as if under the *heiau*. From every point in the village the *heiau* dominates the landscape." As you climb the west bank, notice that the mortarless walls are laid up for over 30 feet. If you have a keen eye you'll notice a perfectly square firepit right in the center of the *heiau*.

This area still has treasures that have never been catalogued. For example, you might chance upon a Hawaiian lamp, as big and perfectly round as a basketball, with an orange-sized hole in the middle where *kukui* nut oil was burned. Old records indicate that Kuniki, the temple idol itself, is still lying here face down no more than a few hundred yards away. If you happen to discover an artifact, do not remove it under any circumstance. Follow the advice of the late Lloyd Cockett, a *kapuna* of Lanai, who said, "I wouldn't take the rock because we Hawaiians don't steal from the land. Special rocks you don't touch."

Kahikili's Leap

Once you've explored the *heiau*, you'll be drawn toward the sea cliff. **Kaneapua Rock,** a giant tower-like chunk, sits perhaps 100 feet offshore. Below in the tidepool are basin-like carvings in the rock-salt evaporation pools, the bottoms still showing some white residue. Follow the cliff face along the natural wall obstructing your view to the south. You'll see a break in the wall about 15 feet wide with a very flat rock platform. From here, **Shark Island,** which closely resembles a shark fin, is perfectly framed. This opening is **Kahikili's Leap,** named after a Lanai chief, not the famous chief of Maui. Here, Kamehameha's warriors proved their courage by executing death-defying leaps into only 12 feet of water, and clearing a 15-foot protruding rock shelf. Scholars also believe that Kamehameha punished his warriors for petty offenses by sentencing them to make the jump. Kahikili's Leap is a perfect background for a photo. Below, the sea surges in unreal aquamarine colors. Off to the right is Kolokolo Cave above which is another, even more daring leap at 90 feet. Evidence suggests that Kolokolo is linked to Kaunolu Gulch by a lava tube that has been sealed and lost. On the beach below Kahikili's Leap the vacationing chiefs played *konane*, and many stone boards can still be found from this game of Hawaiian checkers.

Petroglyphs

To find them, walk directly inland from Kaneapua Rock, using it as your point of reference. On a large pile of rocks are stick figures, mostly with a bird-head motif. Some heads even look like a mason's hammer. This entire area has a masculine feeling to it. There aren't the usual swaying palms and gentle sandy beaches. With the stones and rugged sea cliffs, you get the feeling that a warrior king would enjoy this spot. Throughout the area is *pili* grass, used by the Hawaiians to thatch their homes. Children would pick one blade and hold it in their fingers while reciting *"E pili e, e pili e, au hea kuu hale."* The *pili* grass would then spin around in their fingers and point in the direction of home. Pick some *pili* and try it yourself before leaving this wondrous, powerful area.

THE EAST COAST: KEOMUKU AND NAHA

Until the turn of this century, most of Lanai's inhabitants lived in the villages of the now-deserted east coast. Before the coming of Westerners, 2,000 or so Hawaiians lived along these shores, fishing and raising taro. It was as if they wanted to keep Maui in sight so that they didn't feel so isolated. Numerous *heiau* from this period still mark the ancient sites. The first white men also tried to make a go of Lanai along this stretch. The Mauanalei Sugar Co. tried to raise sugar cane on the flat plains of Naha but failed and pulled up stakes in 1901—the last time that this entire coastline was populated to any extent. Today, the ancient *heiau* and a decaying church in Keomuku are the last vestiges of habitation, holding out against the ever-encroaching jungle. You can follow a jeep trail along this coast and get a fleeting glimpse of times past.

Getting There

Approach Keomuku and Naha from one of two directions. The most straightforward is from north to south. Follow Route 440 (Keomuku Road) from Lanai City until it turns to dirt and branches right (south) at the coast. This road meanders for about 15 miles all the way to Naha. Though the road is partial gravel and packed sand and not that rugged, you definitely need a 4WD. It's paralleled by a much smoother road that runs along the beach, but it can only be used at low tide. Many small roads connect the two, so you can hop back and forth between them every 200-300 yards. Consider two tips: first, if you take the beach road, you can make good time and have a smooth ride, but could sail past most of the sights since you won't know when to hop back on the inland road; second, be careful of the *kiawe* trees—the tough, inch-thick thorns

ahu, *a traveler's wish for happy trails*

can puncture tires as easily as nails. The other alternative is to take Awehi Trail, a rugged jeep track about halfway between Lopa and Naha. This trail leads up the mountain to the Munro Trail, but because of its ruggedness it's best to take it down from The Hale instead of up. A good long day of rattling in a jeep would take you along the Munro Trail, down Awehi Trail, then north along the coast back to Route 44. If you came south along the coast from Route 44, it would be better to retrace your steps instead of heading up Awehi. When you think you've suffered enough and have been bounced into submission by your jeep, remember that many of these trails were carved out by Juan Torqueza. He trailblazed alone on his bulldozer, unsupervised, and without benefit of survey. Now well into his 70s, he can be found in Dole Park in Lanai City, except when he's out here fishing.

A new island venture based on Maui, called **Club Lanai,** tel. 871-1144, has recently opened the remote east coast of Lanai to visitors. Basically they transport tourists from Maui aboard their boats to their private facility for a day of fun, games, and feasting. For full information see p. 382.

Keomuku Village

There isn't much to see in Keomuku ("Stretch of White") Village other than an abandoned Hawaiian church. Though this was the site of the Mauanalei Sugar Co., almost all the decaying buildings were razed in the early 1970s. A few hundred yards north and south of the town site are examples of some original fishponds. They're tough to see (overgrown with mangrove), but a close observation gives you an idea of how extensive they once were. The **Hawaiian church,** now being refurbished, is definitely worth a stop—it almost pleads to be photographed. From outside, you can see how frail it is, so if you go in tread lightly—both walls of the church are caving in and the floor is humped in the middle. The altar area, a podium with a little bench, remains. A banner on the fading blue-green walls reads *"Ualanaano Iehova Kalanakila Malmalama,* October 4, 1903." Only the soft wind sounds where once strong voices sang vibrant hymns of praise.

A few hundred yards south of the church is a walking trail. Follow it inland to **Kahea Heiau** and a smattering of petroglyphs. This is the *heiau* disturbed by the sugar cane train; its desecration was believed to have caused the sweet water of Keomuku to turn brackish. (See p. 499.) The people of Keomuku learned to survive on the brackish water and kept a special jug of fresh water for visitors.

Heading South

Farther south a Japanese cemetery and monument were erected for the deceased workers who built **Halepaloa Landing,** from where the cane was shipped. Today, only rotting timbers and stonework remain, but the pier offers an excellent vantage point for viewing Maui, and a good spot to fish. The next landmark is a semi-used getaway called "Whale's Tale." A boat sits in the front yard. This is a great place to find a coconut and have a free roadside refreshment. Also, a very fruitful *kamani* nut tree sits right at the entrance. The nut looks like an oversized bean. Place your knife in the center and drive it

down. The *kamani,* which tastes like a roasted almond, is 99% husk and 1% nut.

The road continues past **Lopa,** ending at **Naha.** You pass a few coconut groves on the way. Legend says that one of these was cursed by a *kahuna*—if you climb a tree to get a coconut you will not be able to come down. Luckily, most tourists have already been cursed by "midrift bulge" and can't climb the tree in the first place. When you get to Naha check out the remnants of the paved Hawaiian walking trail before slowly heading back from this decaying historical area.

SHIPWRECK BEACH

Heading over the mountains from Lanai City to Shipwreck Beach offers you a rewarding scenario: an intriguing destination point with fantastic scenery and splendid panoramas on the way. Head north from Lanai City on Route 440 (Keomuku Road). In less that 10 minutes you crest the mountains, and if you're lucky the sky will be clear and you'll be able to see the phenomenon that guided ancient navigators to land: the halo of dark brooding clouds over Maui and Molokai, a sure sign of landfall. Shorten your gaze and look at the terrain in the immediate vicinity. Here are the famous precipitous gulches of Lanai. The wounded earth bleeds red while offering patches of swaying grass and wildflowers. It looks like the canyons of Arizona have been dragged to the rim of the sea. As you wiggle your way down Keomuku Road, look left to see the rusting hull of a WW II Liberty Ship sitting on the shallow reef almost completely out of the water. For most, this derelict is the destination point on Shipwreck Beach.

The Beach

As you continue down the road, little piles of stones, usually three, sit atop a boulder. Although most are from modern times, these are called *ahu,* a traditional Hawaiian offering to ensure good fortune while traveling. If you have the right feeling in your heart and you're moved to erect your own *ahu* it's OK, but under no circumstances disturb the ones already there. Farther down, the lush grasses of the mountain slope disappear, and the scrub bush takes over. The pavement ends and the dirt road forks left (north) to Shipwreck Beach, or straight ahead (south) toward the abandoned town of Naha. If you turn left you'll be on an adequate sandy road, flanked on both sides by thorny, tire-puncturing *kiawe* trees. In less than a mile is a large open area to your right. If you're into unofficial camping, this isn't a bad spot for a one-night bivouac—the trees here provide privacy and an excellent windbreak against the constant strong ocean breezes. About two miles down the road is Federation Camp, actually a tiny village of unpretentious beach shacks built by Lanai's workers as "getaways" and fishing cabins. Charming in their humbleness and simplicity, they're made mostly from recycled timbers and boards that have washed ashore. Some have been worked on quite diligently and skillfully and are actual little homes, but somehow the rougher ones are more attractive. You can drive past the cabins for a few hundred yards, but to be on the safe side, park just past them and begin your walk.

Petroglyphs

At the very end of the road is a cabin that a local comedian has named the "Lanai Hilton." Just off to your left *(mauka)* are the ruins of a lighthouse. Look for a cement slab where two graffiti artists of bygone days carved their names: John Kupau and Kam Chee, Nov. 28, 1929. Behind the lighthouse ruins an arrow points you to "The Bird Man of Lanai Petroglyphs." Of all the petroglyphs on Lanai these are the easiest to find; trail-marking rocks have been painted white by Lanai's Boy Scouts. Follow them to a large rock that has the admonition Do Not Deface. Climb down the path with a keen eye—the rock carvings are small, most only about 10 inches tall. Little childlike stick figures, they have intriguing bird head whose symbolic meaning has been lost.

Hiking Trail

The trail along the beach goes for eight long hot miles to Polihua Beach. This trip leads through the Garden of the Gods and should be done separately, but at least walk as far as the Liberty Ship, about a mile from the cabins. The area has some of the best beachcombing in Hawaii; no telling what you might find. The most sought-after treasures are glass floats that have bobbed for thousands of miles across the Pacific, strays from Japanese fishnets. You might even see a modern ship washed onto the reef, like the

Canadian yacht that went aground in the spring of 1984. Navigational equipment has improved, but Shipwreck Beach can *still* be a nightmare to any captain caught in its turbulent whitecaps and long ragged coral fingers. This area is particularly good for lobsters and shore fishing. And you can swim in shallow sandy-bottom pools to refresh yourself as you hike.

Try to time your return car trip over the mountain for sundown. The tortuous terrain, stark in black and white shadows, is awe-inspiring. The larger rocks are giant sentinels: it's easy to feel the power and attraction they held for the ancient Hawaiians. As you climb the road on the windward side with its barren and beaten terrain, the feelings of mystery and mystique attributed to spiritual Lanai are obvious. You come over the top and suddenly see the valley—manicured, rolling, soft and verdant with pineapples and the few lights of Lanai City beckoning.

THE GARDEN OF THE GODS AND POLIHUA

The most ruggedly beautiful, barren, and inhospitable section of Lanai is out at the north end. After passing through a confusing maze of pineapple fields, you come to the appropriately named Garden of the Gods. Waiting is a fantasia of otherworldly landscapes—barren red earth, convulsed ancient lava flows, tortured pinnacles of stone, and psychedelic striations of vibrating colors, especially moving at sunrise and sunset. Little-traveled trails lead to Kaena Point, a wasteland dominated by sea cliffs where adulterous Hawaiian wives were sent into exile for a short time in 1837. Close by is Lanai's largest *heiau*, dubbed Kaenaiki, so isolated and forgotten that its real name and function were lost even to Hawaiian natives by the middle of the 19th century. After a blistering, sun-baked, 4WD drubbing, you emerge at the coast on Polihau, a totally secluded, pure-white beach where sea turtles once came to bury their eggs in the natural incubator of its soft warm sands.

Getting There

Lanai doesn't hand over its treasures easily, but they're worth pursuing. To get to the Garden of the Gods you have to tangle with the pineapple roads. Head north out of Lanai City on Fraser

Avenue. At the fields, it turns to dirt and splits in four directions. Two roads bear right, one goes left, and the main road (which you follow) goes straight ahead. This road proceeds north and then bears left, heading west. Stay on it and ignore all minor pineapple roads. In less than 10 minutes you come to a major crossroad. Turn right heading north again, keeping the ridge of Lanai's mountains on your right. This road gets smaller, then comes to a point where it splits in four again! Two roads bear left, one bears right, and the one you want goes straight ahead, more or less. Follow it, and in five minutes if you pass through an area that is very thick with spindly pine trees on both sides of the road, you know you're heading in the right direction. The road opens up in spots; watch for fields of wildflowers. Shortly, a marker points you off to the right on Lapaiki Road. This is a bit out of the way, but if followed you'll get a good view of the Garden, and eventually wind up at Shipwreck Beach. It's better, however, to proceed straight ahead to another marker pointing you down Awailua Trail to the right and Polihua straight ahead. Follow Polihua Trail, and soon you finally come to the Garden and another marker for Kaena Road, which leads to magnificent sea cliffs and Kaena-iki Heiau.

Hiking

Anyone wishing to hike this area should drive to the end of the pineapple fields. It's at least half the distance and the scenery is quite ordinary. Make sure to bring plenty of water and a windbreaker because the heavy winds blow almost continuously. Sturdy shoes and a sun hat are also needed. There is no official camping at Polihua Beach, but again, anyone doing so overnight probably wouldn't meet with any hassles.

Those with super-keen eyes might even pick out one of the scarce pronghorn that live in the fringe of surrounding grasslands.

The Garden Of The Gods

There, a shocking assault on your senses, is the bleak, red, burnt earth, devoid of vegetation, heralding the beginning of the Garden. The flowers here are made of rock, the shrubs are the twisted crusts of lava, and trees are baked minarets of stone, all subtle shades of orange, purple, and sulfurous yellow. The jeep trail has been sucked down by erosion and the Garden surrounds you. Stop many times to climb a likely outcropping and get a sweeping view. The wind rakes these badlands and the silence penetrates to your soul. Although eons have passed, you can feel the cataclysmic violence that created this haunting and delicate beauty.

Polihua Beach

Abruptly the road becomes smooth and flat. Straight ahead, like a mirage too bright for your eyes, an arch is cut into the green jungle, framing white sand and moving blue ocean. As you face the beach, to the right it's flat, expansive, and the sands are white, but the winds are heavy; if you hiked eight miles, you'd reach Shipwreck Beach. More interesting is the view to the left, which has a series of lonely little coves. The sand is brown and coarse and large black lava boulders are marbled with purplish-gray rock embedded in long, faulted seams. Polihua is not just a destination point where you come for a quick look. It takes so much effort coming and going that you should plan on having a picnic and a relaxing afternoon before heading back through the Garden of the Gods and its perfectly scheduled sunset light show.

MOLOKAI

INTRODUCTION

Molokai is a sanctuary, a human time capsule where the pendulum swings inexorably forward, but more slowly than in the rest of Hawaii. It has always been so. In ancient times, Molokai was known as *Pule-oo,* "Powerful Prayer," where its supreme chiefs protected their small underpopulated refuge, not through legions of warriors but through the chants of their *kahuna.* This powerful, ancient mysticism, handed down directly from the goddess Pahulu, was known and respected throughout the archipelago. Its mana was the oldest and strongest in Hawaii, and its practitioners were venerated by nobility and commoners alike—they had the ability to "pray you to death." The entire island was a haven, a refuge for the vanquished and *kapu*-breakers of all the islands. It's still so today, beckoning to determined escapees from the rat race!

The blazing lights of super-modern Honolulu can easily be seen from western Molokai, while Molokai as viewed from Oahu is fleeting and ephemeral, appearing and disappearing on the horizon. The island is home to the largest concentration of Hawaiians in the state. In effect it is a tribal homeland: over 2,500 of the island's 6,000 inhabitants have more than 50% Hawaiian blood and, except for Niihau, it's the only island where they are the majority. The 1920s Hawaiian Homes Act allowed *kuleana* of 40 acres to anyone with more than 50% Hawaiian ancestry. *Kuleana* owners form the grass-roots organizations that fight for Hawaiian rights and battle the colossal forces of rabid developers who have threatened Molokai for decades.

AN OVERVIEW

Kaunakakai And West
Kaunakakai, the island's main town, is like a Hollywood sound stage where Jesse James or Wyatt Earp would feel right at home. The town is flat, treeless, and three blocks long. Ala Malama, its main shopping street, is lined with false-front stores; pickup trucks are parked in front where horses and buggies ought to be. To the west are

the prairie-like plains of Molokai. The northern section of the island contains **Pala'au State Park,** where a campsite is always easily found, and **Phallic Rock,** a natural shrine where island women came to pray for fertility. Most of the west end is owned by the mammoth 70,000-acre **Molokai Ranch.** Part of its lands supports 6,000 head of cattle, **Wildlife Safari Park,** and herds of axis deer imported from India in 1867.

The 40-acre *kuleana* are here, as well as abandoned Dole and Del Monte pineapple fields. The once thriving pineapple company towns of **Maunaloa** and **Kualapuu** are now semi-ghost towns since the pineapple companies pulled up stakes in the last few years. Maunaloa is trying to hold on as an embryonic artists' colony, and the Kualapuu area attracts its scattered Filipino workers mostly on weekends, when they come to unofficially test their best cocks in the pit.

On the western shore is the Kaluakoi Resort and a handful of condos perched above the island's best beaches. Here, 7,000 acres sold by the Molokai Ranch to the Louisiana Land and Exploration Company is slated for development. This area, rich with the finest archaeological sites on the island, is a hotbed of contention between developers and preservationists. The Kaluakoi, however, is often pointed to as a well-planned development, a kind of model compromise between the factions. Its first-rate architecture, in low Polynesian style, blends well with the surroundings and is not a high-rise blight on the horizon.

The East Coastal Road
Highway 450 is a magnificent coastal road running east from Kaunakakai to Halawa Valley. A slow drive along this writhing country thoroughfare rewards you with easily accessible beach parks, glimpses of fishponds, *heiau,* wildlife sanctuaries, and small one-room churches strung along the road like rosary beads. Almost every mile has a historical marker pointing to such spots as the **Smith and Bronte Landing Site,** where two pioneers of trans-Pacific flight ignominiously alighted in a mangrove swamp, and **Paikalani Taro Patch,** the only one from which Kamehameha V would eat poi.

On Molokai's eastern tip is **Halawa Valley,** a real gem accessible by car. This pristine gorge has a just-right walk to a series of invigorating waterfalls and their pools, and a beach park where the valley meets the sea. The majority of the population of Halawa moved out in 1946 when a 30-foot tsunami washed their homes away and mangled their taro fields, leaving a thick salty residue. Today only a handful of mostly alternative lifestylers live in the valley among the overgrown stone walls that once marked the boundaries of manicured and prosperous family gardens. Just south on the grounds of Puu o Hoku Ranch is **Kalanikaula,** the sacred *kukui* grove of Lanikaula, Molokai's most powerful *kahuna* of the classic period. This grove was planted at his death and became the most sacred spot on Molokai. Today the trees are dying.

The Windward Coast
Kalaupapa leper colony, a lonely peninsula completely separated from the world by a hostile pounding surf and a precipitous 1,500-foot *pali,* is a modern story of human dignity. Kalaupapa was a howling charnel house where the unfortunate victims of leprosy were banished to die. Here humanity reached its lowest ebb of hopelessness, violence, and depravity, until one tiny flicker of light arrived in 1873 —Joseph de Veuster, a Belgian priest known throughout Hawaii as Father Damien. In the greatest example of pure aloha yet established on Hawaii, he became his brothers' keeper. Tours of Kalaupapa operated by well-informed former patients are enlightening and educational.

East of Kalaupapa along the windward (northeast) coast is a series of amazingly steep and isolated valleys. The inhabitants moved out at the beginning of this century except for one pioneering family that returned a few years ago to carve out a home. Well beyond the farthest reaches of the last road, this emerald-green primeval world awaits. The *pali* here mark the tallest sea cliffs in the world, and diving headfirst is **Kahiwa** ("Sacred One") **Falls,** the highest in Hawaii, at 1,750 feet. You get here only by helicopter excursion, by boat in the calmer summer months, or by foot over dangerous and unkempt mountain trails. For now, Molokai remains a

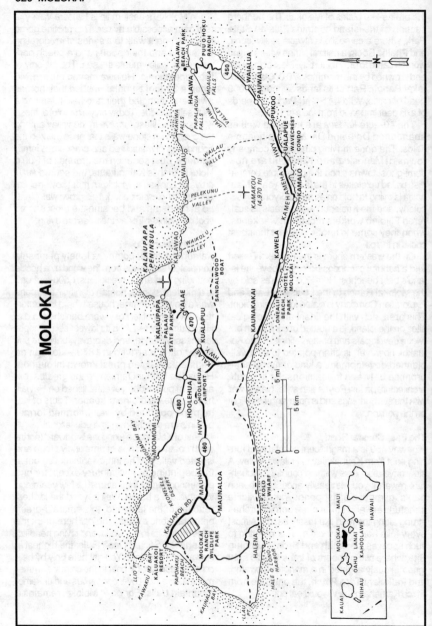

MOLOKAI

KAUAI
NIIHAU OAHU KAHOOLAWE

MOLOKAI
MAUI
LANAI
HAWAII

sanctuary, reminiscent of the Hawaii of simpler times. Around it the storm of modernity rages, but still the "Friendly Island" awaits those willing to venture off the beaten track.

THE LAND

Molokai is the fifth largest Hawaiian island. Its western tip, at Ilio Point, is a mere 22 miles from Oahu's eastern tip, Makapuu Point. Resembling a jogging shoe, Molokai is about 38 miles from heel to toe and 10 miles from laces to sole, totaling 165,760 acres, with just over 88 miles of coastline. Most of the arable land on the island is owned by the 70,000-acre Molokai Ranch, primarily on the western end, and the 14,000- acre Puu o Hoku Ranch on the eastern end. Molokai was formed by three distinct shield volcanos. Two linked together to form Molokai proper, and a later eruption formed the flat Kalaupapa Peninsula.

Physical Features

Although Molokai is rather small, it has a great deal of geographical diversity. Western Molokai is dry with rolling hills, natural pastures, and a maximum elevation of only 1,381 feet. The eastern sector of the island has heavy rainfall, the tallest sea cliffs in the world, and craggy narrow valleys perpetually covered in a velvet cloak of green mosses. Viewed from the sea it looks like a 2,000-foot vertical wall from surf to clouds, with tortuously deep chasms along the coastline. Mount Kamakou is the highest peak on Molokai, at 4,970 feet. The southcentral area is relatively swampy, while the west and especially northwest coasts around Moomomi have rolling sand dunes. Papohaku Beach, just below the Kaluakoi Resort on western Molokai, is one of the most massive white-sand beaches in Hawaii. A controversy was raised when it was discovered that huge amounts of sand were dredged from this area and hauled to Oahu; the Molokai Ranch was pressured and the dredgings ceased. The newly formed and very political Office of Hawaiian Affairs (OHA) became involved, and a court case on behalf of native Hawaiian rights is pending. A hefty section of land in the northcentral area is a state forest where new species of trees are planted on an experimental basis. The 240-acre Pala'au State Park is in this cool upland forested area.

Manmade Marvels

Two manmade features on Molokai are engineering marvels. One is the series of ancient fishponds along the south shore. Dozens still exist, but the most amazing is the enormous Keawanui Pond, covering 54 acres and surrounded by a three-foot-tall, 2,000-foot-long wall. The other is the modern Kualapuu Reservoir completed in 1969. The world's largest rubber-lined reservoir, it can hold 1.4 billion gallons of water. Part of its engineering dramatics is the Molokai Tunnel, which feeds it with water from the eastern valleys. The tunnel is eight feet tall, eight feet wide and almost 27,000 feet (five miles) long.

Climate

The average island temperature is 75-85° F (24° C). The yearly average rainfall is 30 inches; the east receives a much greater percentage than the west.

AVERAGE MAXIMUM/MINIMUM TEMPERATURE AND RAINFALL

Island	Town		Jan.	March	May	June	Sept.	Nov.
Molokai	Kaunakakai	high	79	79	81	82	82	80
		low	61	63	68	70	68	63
		rain	4	3	0	0	0	2
N.B. Rainfall in inches; temperature in °F								

FLORA AND FAUNA

The land animals on Molokai were brought by man. The island is unique in that it offers **Molokai Ranch Wildlife Safari** on the grounds of Molokai Ranch in the western sector, with more than 400 animals mostly imported from the savannahs of Africa (see p. 552). And who knows? Perhaps in a few hundred years after some specimens have escaped there might be such a thing as a "Molokai giraffe" that will look like any other giraffe except that its markings resemble flowers.

Birdlife
A few of Hawaii's endemic birds can be spotted by a determined observer at various locales around Molokai. They include: the Hawaiian petrel *(ua'u)*; Hawaiian coot *(alae ke'oke'o)*, prominent in Hawaiian mythology; Hawaiian stilt *(ae'o)*, a wading bird with ridiculous stick legs that protects its young by feigning wing injury and luring predators away from the nest; and the Hawaiian owl *(pueo)*, a bird that helps in its own demise by being easily approached. Molokai has a substantial number of introduced game birds that attract hunters throughout the year (see p. 530).

Flora
The *kukui* or candlenut tree is common to all the Hawaiian islands; along with being the official state tree, its tiny white blossom is Molokai's flower. The *kukui*, introduced centuries ago by the early Polynesians, grows on lower mountain slopes and can easily be distinguished by its pale green leaves.

HISTORY

The oral chant *"Molokai nui a Hina . . . "* ("Great Molokai, child of Hina") refers to Molokai as the island-child of the goddess Hina and the god Wakea, male progenitor of all the islands; Papa, Wakea's first wife, left him in anger as a result of this unfaithfulness. Hina's cave, just east of Kaluaaha on the southeast coast, can still be visited and has been revered as a sacred spot for countless centuries. Another ancient spot, Halawa Valley, on the eastern tip of Molokai, is considered one of the oldest settle-ments in Hawaii. As research continues, settlement dates are pushed further back, but for now scholars agree that early wayfarers from the Marquesas Islands settled Halawa in the mid-seventh century.

Molokai, from earliest times, was revered and feared as a center for mysticism and sorcery. **Ili'ili'opae Heiau** was renowned for its powerful priests whose incantations were mingled with the screams of human sacrifice. Commoners avoided Ili'ili'opae, and even powerful *kahuna* could not escape its terrible power. One, Kamalo, lost his sons as sacrifices at the *heiau* for their desecration of the temple drum. Kamalo sought revenge by invoking the help of his personal god, the terrible shark deity, Kauhuhu. After the proper prayers and offerings, Kauhuhu sent a flash flood to wipe out Mapulehu Valley where Ili'ili'opae was located. All perished except for Kamalo and his family, who were protected by a sacred fence around their home.

This tradition of mysticism reached its apex with the famous Lanikaula, "prophet of Molokai." During the 16th century, Lanikaula lived near Halawa Valley and practiced his arts, handed down by the goddess Pahulu, who even predated Pele. Pahulu was the goddess responsible for the "old ocean highway," which passed between Molokai and Lanai and led to Kahiki, lost homeland of all the islanders. Lanikaula practiced his sorcery in the utmost secrecy and even buried his excrement on an offshore island so that a rival *kahuna* could not find and burn it, which would surely cause his death. Hawaiian oral history does not say why Kawelo, a sorcerer from Lanai and a friend of Lanikaula, came to spy on Lanikaula and observed him hiding his excrement. Kawelo burned it in the sacred fires, and Lanikaula knew that his end was near. Lanikaula ordered his sons to bury him in a hidden grave so that his enemies could not find his bones and use their mana to control his spirit. To further hide his remains, he had a *kukui* grove planted over his body. **Kalanikaula** ("Sacred Grove of Lanikaula") is still visible today, though most of the trees appear to be dying (see p. 539).

Western Contacts
Captain James Cook first spotted Molokai on November 26, 1778, but because it looked bleak and uninhabited he decided to bypass it. It

wasn't until eight years later that Capt. George Dixon sighted the island and decided to land. Very little was recorded in his ship's log about this first encounter, and Molokai slipped from the attention of the Western world until Protestant missionaries arrived at Kaluaaha in 1832 and reported the native population at approximately 6,000.

In 1790 Kamehameha the Great came from the Big Island as a suitor seeking the hand of Keopuolani, a chieftess of Molokai. Within five years he returned again, but this time there was no merrymaking: he came as a conquering emperor on his thrust westward to Oahu. His warring canoes landed at Pakuhiwa Battleground, a bay just a few miles east of Kaunakakai; it's said that warriors lined the shores for more than four miles. The grossly outnumbered warriors of Molokai fought desperately, but even the incantations of their *kahuna* were no match for Kamehameha and his warriors. Inflamed with recent victory and infused with the power of their horrible war-god Ku ("of the Maggot-dripping Mouth"), they slaughtered the Molokai warriors and threw their broken bodies into a sea so filled with sharks that their feeding frenzy made the water appear to boil. Thus subdued, Molokai slipped into obscurity once again as its people turned to a quiet life of farming and fishing.

Molokai Ranch

Molokai remained almost unchanged until the 1850s. The Great Mahele of 1848 provided for private ownership of land, and giant tracts were formed into the Molokai Ranch. About 1850, German immigrant Rudolph Meyer came to Molokai and married a high chieftess named Dorcas Kalama Waha. Together they had 11 children, with whose aid he turned the vast lands of the Molokai Ranch into productive pastureland. A man of indomitable spirit, Meyer held public office on Molokai and became the island's unofficial patriarch. He managed Molokai Ranch for the original owner, Kamehameha V, and remained manager until his death in 1898, by which time the ranch was owned by the Bishop Estate. In 1875, Charles Bishop had bought half of the 70,000 acres of Molokai Ranch and his wife Bernice, a Kamehameha descendant, inherited the remainder. In 1898, the Molokai Ranch was sold to businessmen in Honolulu for $251,000. This consortium formed the American Sugar Co., but after a few plantings the available water on Molokai turned brackish and once again Molokai Ranch was sold. Charles Cooke bought controlling interest from the other businessmen in 1908, and Molokai Ranch remains in the Cooke family to this day.

Changing Times

Very little happened for a decade after Charles Cooke bought the Molokai Ranch from his partners. Molokai did become famous for its honey production, supplying a huge amount to the world up until WW I. During the 1920s, political and economic forces greatly changed Molokai. In 1921, Congress passed the Hawaiian Homes Act, which set aside 43,000 acres on the island for people who had at least 50% Hawaiian blood. By this time, however, all agriculturally productive land in Hawaii had already been claimed. The land given to the Hawaiians was very poor and lacked adequate water. Many Hawaiians had long since left the land, and were raised in towns and cities. Now out of touch with the simple life of the taro patch, they found it very difficult to readjust. To prevent the Hawaiians from selling their claims and losing the land forever, the Hawaiian Homes Act provided that the land be leased to them for 99 years. Making a go of these 40-acre parcels *(kuleana)* was so difficult that successful homesteaders were called "Molokai Miracles."

In 1923 Libby Corporation leased land from Molokai Ranch at Kaluakoi and went into pineapple production; Del Monte followed suit in 1927 at Kualapuu. Both built company towns and imported Japanese and Filipino field laborers, swelling Molokai's population and stabilizing the economy. Many of the native Hawaiians subleased their tracts to the pineapple growers, and the Hawaiian Homes Act seemed to backfire. Instead of the homesteaders working their own farms, they were given monthly checks and lured into a life of complacency. Those who grew little more than family plots became, in effect, permanent tenants on their own property. Much more importantly, they lost the psychological advantage of controlling their own future and regaining their pride as envisioned in the Hawaiian Homes Act.

Modern Times

For the next 50 years life was quiet. The pineapples grew, providing security. Another large ranch, **Puu O Hoku** ("Hill of Stars") was formed on the eastern tip of the island. It was originally owned by Paul Fagan, the amazing San Francisco entrepreneur who also developed Hana, Maui. In 1955, Fagan sold Puu O Hoku to George Murphy, a Canadian industrialist, for a meager $300,000, about 5% of its present worth. The ranch, under Murphy, became famous for beautiful white Charolais cattle, a breed originating in France.

In the late 1960s "things" started quietly happening on Molokai. The Molokai Ranch sold about 7,000 acres to the Kaluakoi Corp., which they controlled along with the Louisiana Land and Exploration Company. In 1969 the long-awaited Molokai reservoir was completed at Kualapuu; finally west Molokai had plenty of water. Shortly after Molokai's water problem appeared to be finally under control, Dole Corp. bought out Libby in 1972, lost millions in the next few years, and shut down its pineapple production at Maunaloa in 1975. By 1977 the 7,000 acres sold to the Kaluakoi Corp. was developed, and the Molokai Sheraton (now the Kaluakoi Resort) opened along with low-rise condominiums and home sites selling for a minimum of $150,000. Lo and behold, sleepy old Molokai with the tiny Hawaiian Homes farms was now prime real estate and worth a fortune. To complicate the picture even further, Del Monte shut down its operations in 1982, throwing more people out of work. In 1986 they did resume planting 250-acre tracts, but now all the pineapple is gone. Today Molokai is in a period of flux. There is great tension between developers, who are viewed as "carpetbaggers" interested only in a fast buck, and those who consider themselves the last remnants of a lost race holding on desperately to what little they have left.

ECONOMY

If it weren't for a pitifully bad economy, Molokai would have no economy at all. At one time the workers on the pineapple plantations had good steady incomes and the high hopes of the working class. Now with all the jobs gone, Molokai has been transformed from an island with virtually no unemployment to a hard-luck community where a whopping 80-90% of the people are on welfare. Inexplicably, Molokai also has the highest utility rates in Hawaii. Some say this is due to the fact that the utility company built a modern biomass plant, and didn't have enough biomass to keep it operating—the people were stuck with the fuel tab. The present situation is even more ludicrous when you consider that politically Molokai is part of Maui County. It is lumped together with Kaanapali on Maui's southern coast, one of Hawaii's most posh and wealthy areas, where the vast majority of people are recent arrivals from the Mainland. This amounts to almost no political-economic voice for grass-roots Molokai.

Agriculture

The word that is now bandied about is "diversified" agriculture. What this means is not pinning all hope to one crop like the ill-fated pineapple, but planting a potpourri of crops. Attempts at diversification are evident as you travel

Small private enterprises like gathering coconuts help bolster Molokai's flagging economy.

around Molokai. Fields of corn and wheat are just west of Kaunakakai; many small farmers are trying truck farming by raising a variety of garden vegetables that they hope to sell to the massive hotel food industry in Honolulu. The problem is not in production, but transportation. Molokai raises excellent crops, but little established transport exists for the perishable vegetables. A barge service, running on a loose twice-weekly schedule, is their only link to the market. No storage facilities on Molokai make it tough to compete in the hotel food business which requires the freshest produce. Unfortunately, vegetables don't wait well for late barges.

Development

A debate rages between those in favor of tourist development, which they say will save Molokai, and grass-roots organizations championed by OHA (Office of Hawaiian Affairs), which insist unchecked tourism development will despoil Molokai and give no real benefit to the people. A main character in the debate is the Kaluakoi Corp., which wants to build condos and sell lots for $500,000 each. They claim that this, coupled with a few more resorts, will bring in jobs. The people know that they will be relegated to service jobs (maids and waiters), while all the management jobs go to outsiders. Most islanders feel that only rich people from the Mainland can afford million-dollar condos, and that eventually they will become disenfranchised on their own island. Claims are that outsiders have no feeling for the *aina* (land), and will destroy important cultural sites whenever growth dictates.

A few years back the Kaluakoi Corp. hired an "independent" research team to investigate Kawakiu Bay, known to be an ancient adz quarry. After weeks of study, this Maui-based research team reported that Kawakiu was of "minor importance." Hawaii's academic sector went wild. The Society of Hawaiian Archaeology dispatched it's own team under Dr. Patrick Kirch, who stated that Kawakiu was one of the richest archaeological areas in Hawaii. In one day they discoverd six sites missed by the "independent" research team, and stated that a rank amateur could find artifacts by merely scraping away some of the surface. Reasonable voices call for moderation. Both sides agree Molokai must grow, but the growth must be controlled, and the people of Molokai must be represented and included as beneficiaries.

THE PEOPLE

Molokai is obviously experiencing a class struggle. The social problems hinge on the economy—the collapse of pineapple cultivation and the move toward tourism. The average income on Molokai is quite low and the people are not consumer-oriented. Tourism, especially "getaway condos," brings in the affluent. This creates friction; the "have-nots" don't know their situation until the "haves" come in and remind them. Today, most people hunt a little, fish, and have small gardens. Some are small-time *pakalolo* growers who get over the hard spots by making a few dollars from some backyard plants. There is no organized crime on Molokai. The worst you might run into is a group of local kids drinking on a weekend in one of their favorite spots. It's a territorial thing. If you come into their vicinity they might feel their turf is being invaded, and you could be in for some hassles. All this could add up to a bitter situation except that the true nature of most of the people is to be helpful and friendly. Just be sensitive to smiles and frowns and give people their space.

Ethnic Identity

An underground link exists between Molokai and other Hawaiian communities such as Waianae on Oahu. Molokai is unusual in that it is still Hawaiian in population and influence, with con-

MOLOKAI POPULATION

HAWAIIAN 44%
FILIPINO 25%
WHITE 14%
JAPANESE 9%
VARIOUS 7%
CHINESE 1%

tinuing culturally based outlooks which remain unacceptable to Western views. Ethnic Hawaiians are again becoming proud of their culture and heritage, as well as politically aware and sophisticated, and are just now entering the political arena. Few are lawyers, doctors, politicians, or executives; with ethnic identity returning, there is beginning to be a majority backlash against these professions. Among non-Hawaiian residents, it's put down, or unacknowledged as a real occurrence.

Social problems on Molokai relate directly to teenage boredom and hostility in the schools, fueled by a heavy drinking scene. A disproportionate rate of teen pregnancy is a direct byproduct. Teachers unofficially admit that they prefer a student who has smoked *pakalolo* to one who's been drinking. It mellows them out. The traditional educational approach is failing.

Ho'opono'opono is a fascinating family problem-solving technique still very much employed on Molokai. The process is like "peeling the onion" where a mediator, usually a respected *kapuna*, tries to get to the heart of a problem. Similar to group therapy, it's a closed family ordeal, never open to outsiders, and lasts until all emotions are out in the open and all concerned feel "clean."

GETTING THERE

Hawaiian Air has regularly scheduled flights throughout the day and early evening arriving from all the major islands. Depending on the flight, the planes are either DC-9s or four-engine turbo-prop Dash's. Five of seven flights originating in Honolulu are direct and take about 20 minutes in the air. Also, two 18-minute direct flights come from Maui. Flights originating on Kauai stop at Honolulu; those from Kona and Hilo on the Big Island stop en route at Maui.

Aloha Island Air, tel. 833-3219 Oahu, (800) 652-6541 Neighbor Islands, (800) 323-3345 Mainland, offers flights connecting Molokai with Oahu, Kauai, Maui, Lanai, and the Big Island. There is only one flight daily to Lanai and the Big Island but the other destinations have flights throughout the day.

Molokai Airport

At Hoolehua Airport you'll find a lunch counter with not too bad prices, but avoid the ham-

burgers, which are made from mystery meat. Pick up a loaf of excellent Molokai bread, the best souvenir available, or a lei from the small stand. Tropical, Avis, and Dollar have rental cars here. If you rent a car make sure to top off in Kaunakakai before returning it. The price is double at the car companies' pumps.

GETTING AROUND

Public Transportation

No public transportation services Molokai. Only one limited shuttle goes between Hoolehua Airport and the Kaluakoi Hotel complex on the west end. Operated by Rare Adventures Ltd., they run a van every hour on the hour from 8 a.m. to 5 p.m.; the fare is a stiff $6 OW for the 10-mile ride, tel. 552-2622.

Rental Cars

Molokai offers a limited choice of car rental agencies—make reservations to avoid being disappointed. You should arrive before 6 p.m., when most companies close. Special arrangements can be made to pick up your car at a later time. All rental car companies on Molokai are uptight about their cars being used on dirt roads (there are plenty), and strongly warn against it. No jeeps are available on Molokai at this time, but it's always in the air that one of the car companies will make them available sometime in the future. All companies are at the airport.

Tropical Rent a Car, tel. 567-6118 in Molokai, (800) 367-5140 Mainland, (800) 352-3923 Hawaii, is an island company with the best cars, deals, and reputation for service on Molokai. Ask for their free drive guide and bonus coupons, too. Other companies include **Dollar Rent a Car** at Hoolehua Airport, tel. 567-6156; **Avis,** tel. 553-3866, offers a free shuttle to their cars, which are kept in Kaunakakai. They have higher rates than the other companies and offer no weekly discounts.

Hitchhiking

The old thumb gives fair to good results on Molokai. Most islanders say they prefer to pick up hitchers who are making an effort by walking along, instead of lounging by the side of the road. It shows that you don't have a car, but do have some pride. Getting a ride to or from Kaunakakai and the airport is usually easy.

GUIDED TOURS

A few limited tours are offered on Molokai, but they only hit the highlights. If you rent a car, you can get to them just as easily on your own. **Roberts Hawaii,** tel. 552-2988, offers similar tours, but must be booked 48 hours in advance. These appeal more to day-trippers from Honolulu.

The newest and one of the most fun-filled cultural experiences that you can have is to spend an afternoon on the **Molokai Wagon Ride,** tel. 558-8380 or 567-6773, cost $25, open daily from 11:30 a.m. to 2:30 p.m. (departure time depends upon the arrival of the inter-island ferry, the *Maui Princess,* as its passengers often take the ride). The experience starts and ends from a hidden beach just past mile marker 15 on the east end of the island along Route 46. As you drive, look on the right for a sign to Mapulehu Mango Grove; you'll follow the road to a small white house and a picnic area prepared on the beach. The wonderful aspect of this venture is that it is a totally local operation completely devoid of glitz, glamor, and hype. It's run by three local guys: Junior Rawlins the wagonmaster, Kalele Logan who prepares some delicious island dishes and keeps the home fires burning; and Larry Helm, master of ceremonies, guitar player, and all-around funtime merry-maker.

After loading, the wagon leaves the beach and rolls through the **Mapulehu Mango Grove,** one of the largest in the world, with over 2,000 trees. Planted by the Hawaiian Sugar Co. in the 1930s in an attempt to diversify, trees came from all over the world, including Brazil, India, and Formosa. Unfortunately, most of the U.S. was not educated about eating exotic fruits, so the mangos rotted on the tree unpicked, and the grove became overgrown. The ride proceeds down a tree-shrouded lane with Larry Helm playing guitar, singing, and telling anecdotes along the way. In about 20 minutes you arrive at **Ili'ili'opae Heiau,** among the largest Hawaiian places of worship in the islands (see p. 539). Again Larry takes over, telling you about the history of the *heiau,* pointing out exotic fruits and plants in the area, and leading you atop the *heiau* for a photo session. You then return to the beach for a demonstration of coconut husking, throw netting, one of the oldest and most fascinating ways of catching fish, and a hula lesson.

You can also count on the Hawaiian tradition of hospitality. After a day in the sun, you won't have to worry about going away hungry. There's always something delicious, like a fish caught from the bay in front of you that Kalele has grilled, along with plenty of fruits and salads, and a fridge full of ice-cold beer and other drinks. The guys know how to treat you, but remember that this is the *real McCoy.* It's a day spent hanging out on their turf, so don't expect anything fancy or pretentious.

Helicopter Flights

An amazing way to see Molokai is by helicopter. This method is admittedly expensive, but dollar for dollar it is *the* most exciting way of touring and can get you places that no other means can. A handful of companies operate mostly from Maui and include overflights of Molokai. One of the best is **Papillon Helicopters** on Maui, tel. 669-4884. Flights start at $160 and often include champagne and a picnic lunch. Though they'll put a big hole in your budget, most agree they are among the most memorable experiences of their trip.

SHOPPING

Coming to Molokai in order to shop is like going to Waikiki and hoping to find a grass shack on a deserted beach. Molokai has only a handful of shops where you can buy locally produced crafts and Hawaiiana. Far and away, most of Molokai's shopping is centered along Ala Malama Street in downtown Kaunakakai. All three blocks of it! Here you'll find the island's only health-food store, three very good food markets, a drugstore that sells just about everything, and a clutch of souvenir shops. Away from Kaunakakai the pickins get mighty slim. Heading west you'll find the Kualapuu General Store off Route 470 on the way to Kalaupapa, and a sundries store along with a Liberty House at the Kaluakoi Resort on the far west end. The Maunaloa Hwy. (Rt. 460) basically ends in Maunaloa town. Go there! The best and most interesting shop, The Big Wind Kite Factory, is in town and is worth a visit in its own right. Also, in Maunaloa you'll find a market and a small homey restaurant. Heading east from Kaunakakai is another shoppers' wasteland with a few almost dry oases. The Hotel Molokai has one souvenir shop, then comes a convenience store at the Wavecrest Condominium; the last place to spend some money is at the Neighborhood Store, for groceries and snacks, at mile marker 16 on your way to Halawa. That's about it! For a full description see "Shopping" listings in the following travel sections.

OUTDOORS AND SPORTS

Since Molokai is a great place to get away from it all, you would expect an outdoor extravaganza. In fact, Molokai is a "good news, bad news" island when it comes to sports, especially in the water. Molokai has few excellent beaches with the two best, Halawa and Papohoku, on opposite sides of the island; **Papohoku Beach** on the west end is treacherous during the winter months. Surfers, windsurfers, and Hobie Cat enthusiasts will be disappointed with Molokai except at a few locales at the right time of year, while bathers, sun worshippers, and families will love the small secluded beaches with gentle waves located around the island.

Molokai has a small population and plenty of undeveloped "outback" land. This *should* add up to great trekking and camping, but the land is mostly privately owned and the tough trails are poorly maintained. However, permission is usually granted to trek across private land, and those bold enough to venture into the outback will virtually have it to themselves. Day-hiking trails and lightly used camping areas with good facilities are no problem. Molokai has tame, family-oriented beach parks along its southern shores, superb hunting and fishing, two excellent golf courses, and fine tennis courts. Couple this with clean air, no industrial pollution, no city noise, and a deliciously casual atmosphere, and you wind up with the epitome of relaxation.

BEACHES

Eastern Beaches
The beaches of Molokai have their own temperament, ranging from moody and rebellious to sweet and docile. Heading east from Kaunakakai along Route 450 takes you past a string of beaches that varies from poor to excellent. Much of this underbelly of Molokai is fringed by a protective coral reef that keeps the water flat, shallow, and at some spots murky. This area

was ideal for fishponds but leaves a lot to be desired as far as beaches are concerned. The farther east you go, the better the beaches become. The first one you come to is **One Ali'i Park,** about four miles east of Kaunakakai. Here you'll find a picnic area, campsites, good fishing, and family-class swimming where the kids can frolic with no danger from the sea. Next you pass **Kakahaia Beach Park** and **Kumimi Beach,** one of a series of lovely sandy crescents where the swimming is fine. Just before you reach Puko'o town, a small dirt road on your right goes to a hidden beach perfect for a secluded swim (see p. 539).

Halawa Bay, on Molokai's far east end, is the best all-around beach on the island. It's swimmable year-round, but be extra careful during the winter months. The bay protects the beach for a good distance; beyond its reach the breakers are excellent for surfing. The snorkeling and fishing are good to very good.

West End Beaches
The people of Molokai favor the beaches on the northwest section of the island. **Moomomi Beach** is one of the best and features good swimming, fair surfing, and pleasurable snorkeling along its sandy, rocky bottom. You have to drive over a dirt road to get there. Although car rental agencies are against it, the only problem is the dust. From Moomomi you can walk west along the beach and find your own secluded spot.

Very few visitors go south from Maunaloa town, but it is possible and rewarding for those seeking a totally secluded area. As you enter Maunaloa town a dirt track goes off to your right. Follow it through the Molokai Ranch gate (make sure to close it behind you). Follow the rugged but passable track down to the coast, the ghost town of Halena, and **Hale O Lono Harbor,** start of the Aloha Week Outrigger Canoe Race. A tough jeep track also proceeds east to collapsing **Kolo Wharf** and very secluded areas. The swimming is only fair because of murky water but the fantasy of a deserted island is pervasive.

Papohaku and **Kepuhi** beaches just below the Kaluakoi Resort are excellent, renowned for their vast expanses of sand. Unfortunately, they're treacherous in the winter with giant swells and heavy rips which make them a favorite for surfers. Anyone not accustomed to

MOLOKAI: GOLF AND TENNIS

Course	Par	Yards	Fees	Cart
Ironwood Hills Golf * ¤ • Course Del Monte, Molokai, HI 96757 tel. 567-6121	34	6148	$10-9 hole $12-18 hole	—
Kaluakoi Golf Course P.O. Box 26, Mounalo, HI 96770 tel. 552-2739	72	6618	$30	$15

N.B. * = 9 hole course • = no club rentals ¤ = guests only

These tennis courts are open to the public; call ahead to check availability.

Location	Name of Court	No. of Courts	Lighted
Kepuhi Beach	Kaluakoi Resort	4	Yes
Kaunakakai	Community Center	2	Yes
Molokai High	Hoolehua	2	Yes
Star Route	Wavecrest	2	Yes

strong sea conditions should limit themselves to sunning and wading only to the ankles. During the rest of the year this area is great for swimming, becoming like a lake in the summer months. North of Kepuhi Bay is an ideal beach named **Kawakiu**. Although it's less than a mile up the coast, it's more than 15 miles away by road. You have to branch off Route 46 and follow it north well before it forks towards the Kaluakoi Resort. A sign reading Right of Way to Beach points you down a seven mile dirt track. This area is well established as an archaeological site and access to the beach was a hardfought controversy between the people of Molokai and the Molokai Ranch. Good swimming depending upon tide conditions, and free camping on weekends.

Snorkeling

Some charter fishing boats arrange scuba and snorkeling excursions, but scuba and snorkeling on Molokai is just offshore and you don't need a boat to get to it. **Molokai Fish and Dive** in Kaunakakai, tel. 553-5926, is a full-service snorkel shop. They have very good rental rates, can give you directions to the best spots, and arrange excursions. Beginners will feel safe at **One Ali'i Park**, where the sea conditions are

mild, though the snorkeling is mediocre. The best underwater area is the string of beaches heading east past mile marker 18 on Route 45. You'll wind up at Halawa Bay, which is tops. Moomomi Beach on the northwest shore is very good, and Kawakiu Beach out on the west end is good around the rocks, but stay away during winter. Unfortunately, there are no air compressors available on Molokai, so scuba divers will have to bring their full tanks from off island.

Surfing

The best surfing is out on the east end past mile marker 20. Pohakuloa Point has excellent breaks, which continue eastward to Halawa Bay. Moomomi Beach has decent breaks; Kawakiu's huge waves are suitable only for experts during the winter months.

GOLF AND TENNIS

Molokai's two golf courses are as different as custom-made and rental clubs. The **Kaluakoi Golf Course,** tel. 552-2739, is a picture-perfect beauty that would challenge any top pro. Laid out by master links designer Ted Robinson, it's located out at the Kaluakoi Resort. The 6,618-yard, par-72 course winds through an absolutely beautiful setting including five holes strung right along the beach. There's a complete pro shop, driving range, and practice greens. Guests at the Kaluakoi receive reduced rates. The PGA head pro is Marty Keiter, the director Ben Neeley.

Molokai's other golf course is the homey **Ironwood Hills Golf Club.** This rarely used but well-maintained fun course is nine holes. Pay the affordable greens fee to a groundskeeper who will come around as you play. The course is close to town and you'll get directions by calling tel. 567-9097. The Ironwood golf course is turning from a frog to a prince. Plans are to completely rebuild it, making it an exclusive course for members only. As of now, it's still open but it won't last long.

Tennis

The best courts are at the **Kaluakoi Resort**: four lighted Lakloyd courts. They offer a free tennis clinic Fri. at 4 p.m.; call 552-2555, ext. 548, to reserve. Two courts are available at the **Ke Nani Kai Condos** out near the Kaluakoi, which are free to guests. Two courts at the **Wavecrest Condo** east of Kaunakakai on Route#45 are also free to guests. Public courts are available at Molokai High School and at the Community Center in Kaunakakai.

FISHING

The Penguin Banks of Molokai are some of the most fertile waters in Hawaii. Private boats as well as the commercial fishing fleet out of Oahu come here to try their luck. Trolling produces excellent game fish such as marlin, *mahi mahi, ahi,* a favorite with *sashimi* lovers, and *ono,* with its reputation of being the best-tasting fish in Hawaii. Bottom fishing, usually with live bait, yields *onaga* and *uku,* a gray snapper favored by local people. Molokai's shoreline, especially along the south and west, offers great bait casting for *ulua* and *ama ama. Ulua* is an excellent eating fish, and with a variance in weight from 15 to 110 pounds, can be a real whopper to catch from shore. Squidding, *limu* gathering, and torch fishing are all quite popular and productive along the south shore, especially around the old fishpond sites. These remnants of Hawaii's onetime vibrant aquaculture still produce mullet, the *ali'i's* favorite, an occasional Samoan crab, the

less desirable introduced tilapia, and the better-left-alone barracuda.

Fishing Boats: The *Welakaho* is a 24-footer specializing in deep-sea fishing, snorkeling, and excursions. Write George Peabody, Box 179, Kaunakakai 96748, tel. 558-8253. The *Alele II* is a twin-diesel, 35-foot, fully equipped fishing boat. It also offers whalewatching tours and sightseeing cruises to Molokai's north shore. The **Molokai Fish and Dive Co.** arranges deep-sea charters as well as excursions and shoreline sailing. Contact them at Box 576, Ala Malama St., Kaunakakai 96748, tel. 553-5926.

HUNTING

The best hunting on Molokai is on the private lands of the 44,000-acre **Molokai Ranch,** open to hunting year-round. However, the enormous fees charged by the Ranch have effectively stopped hunting on their lands to all but the very determined or very wealthy. A permit to hunt game animals (axis deer) costs $400 per day with an additional $600 preparation fee if you bag a trophy animal. The Molokai Ranch also offers year-round bird hunting for a mere one-time yearly fee of $200. For info contact Molokai ranch, tel. 553-5115.

Public hunting lands on Molokai are open to anyone with a valid state hunting license. Wild goats and pigs can be hunted in various hunting units year-round on weekends and state holidays. Bag limits are two animals per day. Axis deer hunting is limited to licenses drawn on a state public lottery with a one-buck bag limit per season, which extends for nine consecutive weekends up to and including the last Sunday in April. Hunting game birds (ring-necked pheasants, various quails, wild turkeys, partridges, and francolins) is open on public lands from the first Saturday in November to the third Sunday in January. A special dove season opens in January. For full info contact the Division of Forestry and Wildlife, Puu Kapeelua Ave., Hoolehua, Molokai, HI 96729, tel. 553-5415.

Game Animals

The earliest arrival still extant in the wild is the *pua'a* (pig). Molokai's pigs live in the upper wetland forests of the northeast, but they can actually thrive anywhere. Hunters say the meat from pigs that have lived in the lower dry forest is superior to those that acquire the muddy taste of ferns from the wetter upland areas. Pigs on Molokai are hunted mostly with the use of dogs who pin them by the ears and snout while the hunter approaches on foot and skewers them with a long knife.

A pair of **goats** left by Capt. Cook on the island of Niihau spread to all the islands, and were very well adapted to life on Molokai. Originally from the arid Mediterranean, goats could live well without any surface water, a condition quite prevalent over most of Molokai. They're found primarily in the mountainous area of the northeast.

The last free-roaming arrival to Molokai were **axis deer.** Molokai's deer came from the upper reaches of the Ganges River, sent to Kamehameha V by Dr. William Hillebrand while on a botanical trip to India in 1867. Kamehameha V sent some of the first specimens to Molokai, where they prospered. Today they are found mostly on western Molokai, though some travel the south coast to the east.

CAMPING AND HIKING

The best camping on Molokai is at **Pala'au State Park** off Route 470, in the cool mountains overlooking Kalaupapa Peninsula. It's also the site of Molokai's famous Phallic Rock. Here you'll find pavilions, grills, picnic tables, and fresh water. What you won't find is crowds; in fact, most likely you'll have the entire area to yourself. The camping here is free, but you need a permit, good for seven days, from the Dept. of Land and Natural Resouces in Hoolehua, tel. 567-6618. Camping is permitted free of charge at **Waikolu Lookout** in the Molokai Forest Reserve, but you'll have to follow a tough dirt road (Main Forest Road) for 10 miles to get to it. A free permit must be obtained from the Division of Forestry in Hoolehua, tel. 553-5019.

Seaside camping is allowed at **One Ali'i Park** just east of Kaunakakai, and at **Papohaku Beach Park** west of Kaunakakai. These parks have full facilities but due to their beach location and easy access just off Route 450 are often crowded, noisy, and bustling. Also, you are a target here for any rip-off artists. A county permit ($3/day) is required and available from County Parks and Recreation in Kaunakakai, tel. 553-5141. The Hawaiian Homelands Dept. in Hoole-

hua, tel. 567-6104, offers camping at **Kioea Park,** one mile west of Kaunakakai. The permit to this historical coconut grove is $5/day. One of the most amazing royal coconut groves in Hawaii, it's a treat to visit, but camping here, though quiet, can be hazardous. Make sure to pitch your tent away from any coconut-laden trees if possible, and vacate the premises if the winds come up.

Camping is allowed at Halena, Moomomi Beach, Hale O Lono, and Puulakima, for $5 per day for access, and an additional $55 per person for the spot. You can also camp free at **Moomomi Beach** on the island's northwest shore on a grassy plot where the pavilion used to be. You can't officially camp at Halawa Bay Beach Park but if you continue along the north side of the bay you'll come to a well-used but unofficial campground fringed by ironwoods and recognizable by old fire pits. This area does attract down-and-outers so don't leave your gear unattended.

Trekking
Molokai should be a hiker's paradise and there are exciting, well-maintained, easily accessible trails, but others cross private land, skirt guarded *pakololo* patches, are poorly maintained, and tough to follow. This section provides a general overview of the trekking possibilities available on Molokai. Full info is given in the respective "Sights" sections.

One of the most exciting hassle-free trails descends the *pali* to the **Kalaupapa Peninsula.** You follow the well-maintained mule trail down, and except for some "road apples" left by the mules, it's a totally enjoyable experience suitable for an in-shape family. You *must* have a reservation with the guide company to tour the former leper colony (see p. 547).

Another excellent trail is at Halawa Valley, which follows **Halawa Stream** to cascading Moaula Falls where you can take a refreshing dip if the famous *moo,* a mythical lizard said to live in the pool, is in the right mood. This trail is strenuous enough to be worthwhile and thrilling enough to be memorable. (See p. 540)

Molokai Forest Reserve, which you can reach by driving about 10 miles over the rugged Main Forest Road (passable by 4WD only in the dry season), has fine hiking. At road's end you'll find the Sandalwood Measuring Pit. The hale and hearty who push on will find themselves overlooking Waikolu and Pelekunu, two fabulous and enchanted valleys of the north coast. (See p. 543)

The most formidable trail on Molokai is the one that completely crosses the island from south to north and leads into **Wailau Valley**. It starts innocently enough at Ili'ili'opae Heiau about 15 miles east of Kaunakakai, but as you gain elevation it gets increasingly tougher to follow. After you've trekked all day, the trail comes to an abrupt halt over Wailau. From here you have to pick your way down an unmarked, slippery, and treacherous 3,000-foot *pali*. Don't attempt this trail alone. It's best to go with the Sierra Club, which organizes a yearly hike, or with a local person who knows the terrain. Wailan Valley is one of the last untouched valleys of bygone days. Here are bananas, papayas, and guavas left over from the last major inhabitants that left early in this century. The local people who summer here, and the one family that lives here year-round, are generous and friendly, but also very aware and rightfully protective of the last of old Hawaii in which they live. If you hike into Wailau Valley remember that in effect you are a guest. Be courteous and respectful and you'll come away with a unique and meaningful island experience.

MOLOKAI: INFORMATION PLEASE

Telephone numbers of service agencies that you might find useful: ambulance 553-5911; police 553-5355; hospital, 553-5331; County Parks and Recreation, 553-5141; Dept. of Land and Natural Resouces, 567-6083; Division of Forestry, 553-5019; Fire Department, 553-5401; Hawaiian Homelands, 567-6104; Library, 553-5483; Office of Hawaiian Affairs (OHA), 553-3611; pharmacy, 553-5790; post office, 553-5845.

KAUNAKAKAI

No matter where you're headed on the island you have to pass through Kaunakakai ("Beach Landing"), the tiny port town that is Molokai's hub. An hour spent walking the three blocks of Ala Malama Street, the main drag, gives you a good feeling for what's happening. As you walk along you might hear a mechanical whir and bump in the background—Molokai's generating plant almost in the middle of town! If you need to do any banking, mailing, or shopping for staples, Kaunakakai's the place. Hikers, campers, and even day-trippers should get all they need here since shops, both east and west, are few and far between, and understocked. Evenings are quiet with no bars or night spots in town, but a cup of coffee or lunch at either the Hop Inn or the Mid-Nite Inn should yield some small talk and camaraderie.

SIGHTS

Head toward the lagoon and you'll see Kaunakakai's pineapple wharf stretching out into the shallow harbor for over a half mile. Townsfolk like to drive their cars onto it, but it's much better to walk out. The fishing from the wharf isn't great but it's handy and you never can tell. If you decide to stroll out here, look for the remains of Lot Kamehameha's summer house near the canoe shed on the shore.

Kapuaiwa Coconut Grove

A three-minute drive or a 10-minute walk west brings you to this royal coconut grove planted in the 1860s for Kamehameha V (Lot Kamehameha), or Kapuaiwa to his friends. Kapuaiwa Coconut Grove was originally built because there were seven pools in which the *ali'i* would bathe, and the grove was planted to provide shade and seclusion. The grove also symbolically provided the king with food for the duration of his life. The grove has diminished from the 1,000 trees originally planted, but more than enough remain to give a sense of grandeur to the spot. Royal coconut palms are some of the tallest of the species, and besides providing nuts, they served as natural beacons pinpointing the spot inhabited by royalty. Now the grove has a park-like atmosphere and mostly you'll have it to yourself. Pay heed to the signs warning of falling coconuts. An aerial bombardment of hefty five-pounders will rudely customize the hood of your rental car. Definitely do not walk around under the palms if the wind is up. Just next to the grove is Kioea Park, where camping is permitted for $5/day through the Hawaiian Homelands Department (see p. 531).

Church Row

Sin has no chance against this formidable defensive line of churches standing altar to altar along the road across from Kapuaiwa Coconut Grove. A grant from Hawaiian Homelands provides that a church can be built on this stretch of land to any congregation that includes a minimum number of Hawaiian-blooded parishioners. The churches are basically one-room affairs that wait quietly until Sunday morning when worshippers come from all over the island. Let there be no doubt: old Satan would find no customers around here as all spiritual loopholes are covered by one denomination or another. Visitors are always welcome, so come join in. Be wary of this stretch of road—all services seem to let out at the same time on Sunday morning, causing a miniscule traffic jam.

Classic Fishponds

Molokai is known for its fishponds, which were a unique and highly advanced form of aquaculture prevalent from at least the early 13th century. Molokai, because of an abundance of shallow, flat waters along its southeastern shore, was able to support a network of these ponds numbering over five dozen during their heyday. Built and tended by the commoners for the royal *ali'i*, they provided succulent fish that could easily be rounded up at any time for a meal or impromptu feast. The ponds were formed in a likely spot by erecting a wall of stone or coral. It was necessary to choose an area that had just the right tides to keep the water circulating, but not so strong as to destroy the encircling walls. Openings were left in the wall for this purpose. **Kalokoeli Pond** is about two miles east of Kaunakakai along Route 450. Easily seen from the road, it's an excellent example of the classic fishpond. You can proceed a few more minutes east until you come to a large coconut grove just a half mile before One Ali'i Beach Park. Stop here for a sweeping view of **Ali'i Fishpond,** another fine example.

ACCOMMODATIONS

Besides camping, Kaunakakai has only three other places to stay. The only other place to lodge on the entire island is way out on the west end at the exclusive Kaluakoi Resort or the two condos that surround it, and at the Wavecrest

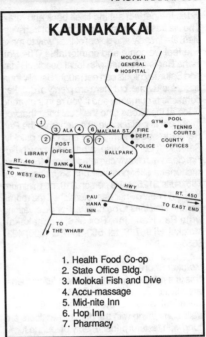

KAUNAKAKAI

1. Health Food Co-op
2. State Office Bldg.
3. Molokai Fish and Dive
4. Accu-massage
5. Mid-nite Inn
6. Hop Inn
7. Pharmacy

Condo east of Kaunakakai along the south coast. Head for Kauna kakai and its limited but adequate accommodations if you want to save money. The choices are all along the *makai* side of Route 450 as you head east from town.

Pau Hana Inn

For years the Pau Hana ("Work's Done") Inn had the reputation for being *the* budget place to stay on Molokai. Now all that's left is the reputation, although it's still cheap. The main reason for the decline of this otherwise character-laden hotel is that the owners live on Oahu, and the Pau Hana shows the lack of that special caring touch. But, they are starting to make improvements! All the character of the Pau Hana could still be brought out if someone had the inclination. Special touches still remain though, like leaving the windows of the dining room open so that birds can fly in to peck crumbs off the floor. A fireplace is lit in the morning to take the chill off the place; hanging over it is a noble stag with wide perfect antlers and tearful eyes. Outside, in the courtyard bar, a magnificent Bengalese banyan provides the perfect setting to sit back and relax. The waitresses, mostly a phantasm of transvestites, are friendly and go out of their way to make you feel welcome and comfortable. The Pau Hana Bar is a favorite with local people. Friday and Saturday nights can get rough. Usually tourists are left alone, but there are plenty of drunken domestic arguments, and if you're in the wrong place at the wrong time the local color that you might get is a black eye. It's clear that the Pau Hana Inn needs some love and care, quickly. Rates are: Long House, a barracks-type building, clean with newly carpeted floors $45; deluxe kitchenette $85; poolside unit $69, oceanfront $85, suite $125, extra person $10, no minimum stay. The new owner has refurnished the rooms and the staff tries to be helpful. For reservations write Pau Hana Inn, Box 546, Kaunakakai, Molokai, HI 96748, tel. 553-5347 or (800) 423-6656.

Molokai Shores

This is a relatively new condo with full kitchens, large living rooms, and separate bedrooms, a few minutes east of the Pau Hana. The white walls contrasting with the dark brown floors are hung with tasteful prints. Plenty of lounge furniture is provided along with a table for outside dining and barbecues. The upper floor of the three-story buildings offers an open-beam ceiling including a full loft. Some units have an extra bedroom built into the loft. The grounds are very well kept, quiet, and restful. The swimming pool fronts the gentle but unswimmable beach, and nearby is a classic fishpond. The only drawback with the Molokai Shores is that the architecture resembles a housing project. It's pragmatic and neat, but not beautiful. Rates are $70-80, one-bedroom deluxe; $100-105 two bedroom deluxe, two baths; $10 for each additional person. For information write Hawaiian Islands Resorts, Box 212, Honolulu, HI 96810, tel. 531-7595, or (800) 367-7042, or write Molokai Shores, P.O. Box 1037, Kaunakakai, Molokai, HI 96748, tel. 553-5945 or (800) 367-7042.

Hotel Molokai

The hotel was built in 1966 by an architect (Mr. Roberts) enamored with the South Seas, and who wanted to give his hotel a Polynesian village atmosphere. He succeeded. The buildings are two story, semi A-frames with sway-backed roofs covered with split wood shingles. Outside staircases lead to the large, airy studios that feature a lanai with swing. No cooking facilities, but a refrigerator in every room is handy. Although the Hotel Molokai is a semi-condo, there are hotel amenities like full maid service, a friendly staff, great dining, weekend entertainment, a well-appointed gift shop, and a swimming pool. The rates vary from $55 standard, $69 garden, $85 deluxe, and $99 oceanfront; add $10 for each additional person. For information write Hotel Molokai, Box 546, Kaunakakai, HI 96748, tel. 553-5347 or (800) 423-6656, on Oahu tel. 531-4004.

Also see **Wavecrest Resort Condominium,** pg. 538, for the only other accommodation on this end of the island.

FOOD AND ENTERTAINMENT

Like the hotel scene, Molokai has only a handful of places to eat, but among these are veritable institutions that if missed make your trip to Molokai incomplete. The following are all located on Kaunakakai's main street. Just ask anyone where they are.

Inexpensive

The 45-year-old **Mid-Nite Inn,** tel. 553-5302, was started as a saimin stand by Mrs. Kikukawa, the present owner's mother. People would come here to slurp noodles while waiting for the midnight inter-island steamer to take them to Honolulu. The steamers are gone but the restaurant remains. The Mid-Nite is clean, smells delicious, and looks dingy, which is relative because all of Kaunakakai looks run-down. Large, with Naugahyde atmosphere, it's open for breakfast 5:30-10:30 a.m., lunch 10:30 a.m. to 1:30 p.m., dinner 5:30 to 9 p.m., closed Sunday. Breakfasts start at $3.50 for a cheese omelette, and all include hot coffee, tea, or cocoa. Sandwiches are extremely reasonable, with the Mid-Nite burger, a double two-handed burger with the works and a smile face painted in ketchup, the most expensive at $3. Entrees are inexpensive, like hamburger steak, $4.25, or breaded *mahi mahi*, $7.90. The Mid-Nite has the *only* fresh pizza available on Molokai. Daily specials, like breaded shrimp, cost under $7, and the menu features veal cutlets, teri steak, and flank steak for around $5. No credit cards accepted, out smiles and small talk from travelers are greatly appreciated.

The **Kanemitsu Bakery** has been in business for almost 70 years, and is still run by the same family! The bakery is renowned for its Molokai breads, boasting cheese and onion among its best. Small inter-island airlines even hold up their planes to get their shipment from the bakery. It's open in the morning for breakfast and serves coffee. Mrs. Kanemitsu's cookies are scrumptious, and anyone contemplating a picnic or a day hike should load up.

The **Hop-Inn**, tel. 553-5465, is a Chinese restaurant across from the Mid-Nite Inn where you can fill up for $5. The menu is large, but don't let that fool you. Next to many listings is a penciled-in "out," especially the fish dishes. The funky building at one time housed the Kaunakakai Hotel. The Hop-Inn recently changed hands, but that's about all that changed. They did redecorate, which meant taking down some bad local art that was strung around the place hanging by clothes pins. Some were so dusty that you couldn't make them out. It was better that way. Now the walls have been painted, so there's nothing much of interest to look at while you wait for your chop suey.

Oviedo's Filipino Restaurant is the last building on the left along Ala Malama, where every item on the menu is $6. Choose from ethnic selections like pork *adobo*, chicken papaya, tripe stew, sweet and sour ribs, pig's feet, mongo beans, and a good selection of ice cream for dessert. Oviedo's is small, run-down, but clean. The decor is worn linoleum floors and Formica tables, and the cooling is provided by breezes that readily pass through large cracks in the walls.

Rabang's Filipino Restaurant looks like a great find, located in a tiny corner shop on the main drag, but the place seems never to be open, and locals say the food is mediocre to awful on any given day. A peek through the greasy window reveals an inexpensive ethnic menu thumb-tacked to the wall. Another tattered sign reads, Rooms for Rent tel. 553-3769, but they're probably no better than the food.

Hotel Restaurants/Entertainment

The **Pau Hana Inn** offers a full menu with most dinners being under $15. Start with breakfast for under $4.50, or carbo-load with French toast with meat for $5.25, made from famous Molokai bread dipped in a banana egg batter, coffee and tea included. Lunches are from $5-6, with offerings like chef salad, *mahi mahi,* French dip (sounds contagious!). Full dinners include chicken or shrimp tempura. The Pau Hana Bar has a daily happy hour from 4 to 6 p.m., when beer is only $1.75, and well drinks $2.25. Here you can relax under the famous banyan tree for an early evening cocktail. On the weekends, the crowds get rowdy, and there is an annoying cover charge, even for hotel guests who only want a quiet drink (see p. 533).

The **Hotel Molokai** has a salad bar including *soupe du jour* that ranges from mediocre to woeful on any given night. If you hit it lucky, you can combine it with an entree, such as fresh *mahi mahi* (grilled, not deep-fried) for around $15. The best lunch selection is honey-dipped chicken or a French-dipped steak sandwich with cheese and onion. The hotel's bar, mostly frequented by local *haole,* has happy hour from 4 to 6 p.m. In the dining room, host Butch Dudoit goes out of his way to make you feel welcome, and island music is provided by the talented Kimo Paleka Thursday through Saturday during the dinner hours. If Kimo looks familiar, you might have seen him at the airport handling bags for Hawaiian Air. With a pair of strong arms by day and gentle guitar fingerings at night, Kimo typifies the Hawaiian man of today.

Grocery Stores And Shopping

For those into wholesome health food **Outpost Natural Foods** is at 70 Makaena Place near Kalama's Gas Station. It's the only store of its kind on Molokai, but it's excellent. They're open Sun.-Thur. 9-6, Friday 9-3, closed Saturday, tel. 553-3377. The fruits and vegetables are locally and organically grown as much as possible. They also have huge sandwiches from $3, along with fresh juice and smoothies. The jam-packed shelves hold rennetless cheese, fresh yogurt, non-dairy ice cream, vitamins, minerals, supplements, and a good selection of herbs, oils, and spices. If you can't find what you need, ask Dennis, the general manager.

For general shopping along Ala Malama Street, the **Friendly Market,** the biggest and best on Molokai, combined with **Takes Variety Store** down the street, and **Misaki's Groceries and Dry Goods** a few steps farther along, sell just about everything in food and general merchandise that you'll require. For that special evening try **Molokai Wines and Spirits**, which has a small but good selection of vintage wines as well as gourmet treats. Also see Wavecrest Condo (p. 538) and the Neighborhood Store (p. 539) for shopping at the far east end of Molokai.

Molokai Fish and Dive sounds very practical, and it is, but it has a good selection of souvenirs, T-shirts, and fashions, along with its fishing equipment. The **Molokai Gallery,** tel. 553-3392, open daily 9 a.m. to 6 p.m., started out as an art shop but has metamorphosed into a clothing store. Inside are millinery, resortwear, T-shirts, jewelry, baubles and beads.

Molokai Sight and Sound, tel. 553-3600, open daily 9 a.m. to 8:30 p.m, Sunday 9 to 5, is a video store with records and tapes. There is no theater on Molokai, so if you want a movie only the VCR in your condo will serve. They rent camcorders from $19.95 for 24 hours. A few shops up is **Island Photo Processing,** tel. 553-9938, open daily 9:30 a.m. to 4:30 p.m., closed Sun., offering film and one-hour print developing. The **Molokai Hotel Gift Shop** has a good selection of resortwear, sundries, and gift items.

Molokai Drug Store, tel. 553-5790, is open daily 8:45 a.m. to 5:45 p.m., closed Sunday. Don't let the name fool you because they sell much more than potions and drugs. You can buy anything from sunglasses to film, watches, small appliances, and garden supplies. They have the *best* selection of film on Molokai, with a very good selection of books (the only one!), especially on Hawaiiana. Film processing, including slides, takes 48 hours.

For fresh fish check out the Chevron gas station at the light at the crossroads in Kaunakakai. Local fishermen bring their catch here, where it's sold from an ice chest. You'll have to take pot luck on their being any catch that day.

Services And Information

The following phone numbers may be of use in Kaunakakai: Bank of Hawaii, tel. 553-3273; Fire Department, tel. 553-5401; Maui Community College, tel. 553-5518; Molokai Clinic, tel. 553-5353; Molokai Drug Store, tel. 553-5790; Molokai Hospital tel. 553-5331. The Friendly Market has a community bulletin board outside. It might list cars for sale, Hawaiian genealogies, or fundraising sushi sales. Have a look!

EAST TO HALAWA VALLEY

The east end of Molokai, from Kaunakakai to Halawa Valley, was at one time the most densely populated area of the island. At almost every milepost is a historical site or point of interest, many dating from pre-contact times. A string of tiny churches attests to the coming of the missionaries in the mid-1800s, and a crash-landing site was an inauspicious harbinger of the deluge of Mainlanders bound for Hawaii in this century. This entire stretch of Route 450 is almost entirely undeveloped, and the classical sites such as *heiau,* listening stones, and old battlegrounds are difficult to find, although just a stone's throw from the road. The local people like it this way, as most would rather see the south shore of Molokai remain unchanged. A determined traveler might locate the sites, but unless you have local help, it will mean hours tramping around in marshes or on hillsides with no guarantee of satisfaction. Some sites such as **Ili'ili'opae Heiau** are on private land and require permission to visit. It's as if the spirits of the ancient *kahuna* protect this area.

SIGHTS

It's a toss-up whether the best part about heading out to the east end is the road itself or the reward of Halawa Valley at the end. Only 30 miles long, it takes 90 minutes to drive. The road slips and slides around corners, bends around huge boulders, and dips down here and there into coves and inlets. The cliff face and protruding stones have been painted white so that you can avoid an accident, especially at night. Sometimes the ocean and road are so close that spray splatters your windshield. Suddenly you'll round a bend to see an idyllic house surrounded by palm trees with a gaily painted boat gently rocking in a protected miniature cove. Behind is a valley or verdant hills with colors so vibrant they shimmer. You negotiate a hairpin curve and there's Lanai and Maui, black on the horizon, contrasted against the waves as they come crashing in foamy white and blue. Down the road chugs a pickup truck full of local people. They wave you a "hang loose" as their sincere smiles light up your already glorious day. Out in one of the innumerable bays are snorkelers, while beyond the reef, surfers glide in exhilarating solitude.

The local people think of the road as "their road." Why not? They use it as a sidewalk, playground, and extension of their back yards. Dogs snooze on it, while the rumps of grazing stock are only inches away from your fender. The speed limit is 35, but go slower and enjoy it more. The mile markers stop at mile 17, then four miles farther you come to the best part. Here, the well-tended two lane highway with the yellow stripe plays out. The road gets old and bumpy, but the scenery gets much more spectacular. It's about nine miles from where the bumpy part begins until you reach the overlook at Halawa Valley. Come with a full tank of gas, plenty of drinking water, a picnic lunch, and your sense of wonder.

One Ali'i Beach Park

Five minutes past the Hotel Molokai brings you to a stand of perhaps 80 coconut palms. Here is a little-used, unnamed beach park with an excellent view of one of the string of fishponds that are famous in this area. One Ali'i Beach Park, only a few minutes farther along, is open for camping. It's too close to the road, not well shaded, and a bit too overused to be comfortable. The swimming here is only fair for those who like a challenging surf, but excellent for families with little children who want calm waters. Clean restrooms and showers are available and the grounds are generally in good shape. Those not camping here would find it pleasant enough for a day excursion, but it's nothing compared with what's farther east along the road.

About two minutes past One Ali'i, Makanui Road leads up the hillside on the *mauka* side of the road. A two-minute ride up this road exposes the beginnings of a development. Only the roads and street lights are in place at this time, but the condos won't be far behind. As you gain the heights (one of the only roads that allows you to do so) you'll have an excellent view of the coastline with a panorama of the fishponds below and Lanai and Maui out to sea. Beyond this road is

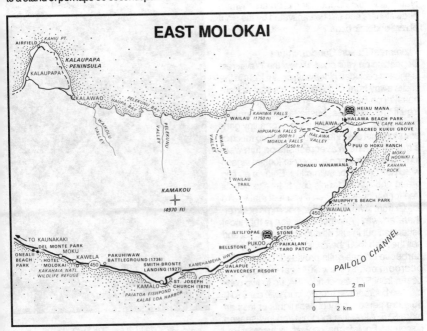

another just like it, leading into a future subdivision with much the same overview.

Kawela

The Kawela area was a scene of tragedy and triumph in Molokai's history. Here was Pakuhiwa, the battleground where Kamehameha I totally vanquished the warriors of Molokai on his way to conquering Oahu. In nearby Kawela Gulch was Pu'u Kaua, the fortress that Kamehameha overran. The fortress oddly doubled as a *pu'uhonua,* a temple of refuge, where the defeated could find sanctuary. Once the battle had been joined, and the outcome inevitable, the vanquished could find peace and solace in the very area that they had so recently defended.

Today the area offers refuge as **Kakahai'a Beach Park and National Wildlife Sanctuary.** The beach park is not used heavily: it too is close to the road. The fishpond here is still used though, and it's not uncommon to see people in it gathering *limu.* This is also an excellent area for coconut trees, with many nuts lying on the ground for the taking. Kakahai'a, designated a National Wildlife Sanctuary, is an area where birdwatchers can still be captivated by the sight of rare endemic birds.

Wavecrest Resort Condominium

Depending on your point of view the Wavecrest is either a secluded hideaway, or stuck out in the sticks away from all the action. It's east of Kaunakakai on Route 450 just at mile marker 13. You'll find *no* hustle, bustle, anxiety, nightlife, restaurants, or shopping except for a tiny general store that sells the basics for not too much of a mark-up. The Wavecrest sits on five well-tended acres fronting a lovely-to-look-at lagoon which isn't good for swimming. Enjoy a putting green and lighted tennis courts free to guests (fee for nonguests). Even if you feel that you're too far from town, remember, nothing is going on there anyway. Another attraction is that local fishermen put in just next to the Wavecrest and sell their fish for unbeatable prices. Guests can barbecue on gas grills provided. Rates: one-bedroom ocean-view $61; car-condo $84; ocean-front $71; car-condo $94, up to two people; two bedroom $81 (up to four) with car $104, $5 extra person, stay of two nights or less an extra $15. Attractive monthly and low-season discounts. For information write Wavecrest Resort, Star Route, Kaunakakai, HI 96748, tel. 558-8101 or (800) 367-2980.

The **Wavecrest Condo Store** is at the entrance of the Wavecrest. They have a small selection of staples and a good selection of beer and wine. More importantly, local fishermen put in at the Wavecrest beach—it's your best chance to get fresh fish at a very reasonable price.

Kamalo To Pukoo

This six mile stretch is loaded with historical sites. Kamalo is one of Molokai's natural harbors and was used for centuries before most of the island commerce moved to Kaunakakai. **Kamalo Wharf** (turn right down the dirt road at mile marker 10) still accommodates large sailboats from throughout the islands. It's a great place to meet local fishermen and inquire about crewing on island-cruising boats. A daily boat for Maui will give you a lift for $10.

Larry Helm of Molokai Wagon Ride

Saint Joseph Church, next in line, was built in 1876 by Father Damien. It's small, no more than 16 by 30 feet, and very basic. Inside is a small wooden altar adorned with flowers in a canning jar. A picture of Father Damien and one of St. Joseph adorn the walls. Outside is a black metal sculpture of Damien.

One mile or so past St. Joseph's, an HVB warrior points out the **Smith and Bronte Landing Site.** These two aviators safely crash-landed their plane here on July 14, 1927, completing the first trans-Pacific civilian flight in just over 25 hours. All you can see is a mangrove swamp, but it's not hard to imagine the relief of the men as they set foot even on soggy land after crossing the Pacific. They started a trend that would bring over four million people a year to the islands. The Wavecrest Condo is nearby at mile marker 13, and if you're not staying there, it's your next-to-last chance to pick up supplies, water, or food before proceeding east.

Before Pukoo are two noteworthy sites. **Kalua'aha Church** looks like a fortress with its tiny slit windows and three-foot-thick plastered walls and buttresses. It was the first Christian church on Molokai, built in 1844 by the Protestant missionaries Rev. and Mrs. Hitchcock. Used for worship until the 1940s, it has since fallen into disuse. The roof is caving in, but the parishioners have repair plans.

Then comes **Ili'ili'opae Heiau,** one of Hawaii's most famous human-sacrifice temples, and a university of sorcery, as it were, where *kahuna* from other islands are tutored. (For a unique tour of this area, along with nearby Mapulehu Mango Grove, see **Molokai Wagon Ride,** p. 527.) All of the wooden structures on the 267-foot stone platform have long since disappeared. Legend holds that all of the stone was carried across the island from Wailau Valley and perfectly fitted in one night of amazing work. Legend also holds that the sorcerers of Ili'ili'opae once sacrificed nine sons of a local *kahuna*. Outraged, he appealed to a powerful shark-god for justice. The god sent a flash flood to wipe out the evil sorcerers, washing them into the sea where the shark-god waited to devour them. The trailhead for Wailau Valley begins at Ili'ili'opae, but since the temple is now on private land it is necessary to receive permission to visit it. The easiest way to go about this is to stop at the "activities desk" of any of the island hotels or condos. They have the right telephone numbers and procedures.

Our Lady of Sorrows Church, another built by Father Damien in 1874 and rebuilt by the parishioners in 1966, is next. Inside are beautiful pen-and-ink drawings of the Stations of the Cross imported from Holland. Just past Our Lady of Sorrows are the **bell stones,** but they're almost impossible to locate.

Before you get to Pukoo, near mile marker 16, is the **Neighborhood Store.** It has changed dramatically from an understocked shack to a modern convenience store. You can buy most picnic items, as well as ice cream, or just pick up a plate lunch at their new snack bar for under $6, a bowl of chili for $4, and a full range of burgers for under $2.50. You can even have breakfast for around $3. Fortunately, Stacy, the young man running the store, is as friendly as ever, and will point you in the right direction . . . there's only one: one road in one road out. This is positively the last place to buy anything if you're headed out to the east end.

Just past Pukoo is the **octopus stone,** a large stone painted white next to the road. It is believed that this is the remainder of a cave inhabited by a mythical octopus, and that the stone still has magical powers.

On To Halawa Valley

Past Pukoo, the road gets very spectacular. Many blow-your-horn turns pop up as you weedle around the cliff face following the natural roll of the coastline. Coming in rapid succession are incredibly beautiful bays and tiny one-blanket beaches, where solitude and sunbathing are perfect. Be careful of surf conditions! Some of the fruitful valleys behind them are still cultivated for taro, and traditional community life beckons young people from throughout the islands to come and learn the old ways. Offshore is the crescent of **Moku Ho'oniki Island,** and Kanaha Rock in front. The road swerves inland, climbing the hills to the 14,000 acres of **Puu O Hoku** ("Hill of Stars") **Ranch.** People often mistake one of the ranch buildings along the road for a store. It's a print shop, but the people inside can direct you to an overlook where you can see the famous and sacred *kukui* grove where Lanikaula, one of the most powerful sorcerers of Molokai, is buried. The different-looking cattle grazing these hilly pastures are French Charolais, imported by Puu O Hoku Ranch and now flourishing on these choice pasture lands. The road comes to a hairpin turn where it feels like you'll be airborne. Before you is the magnificent chasm of Halawa Valley with its famous waterfalls sparkling against the green of the valley's jungle walls. Hundreds of feet below, frothy aquamarine breakers roll into the bay.

Halawa Valley And Bay

This choice valley, rich in soil and watered by Halawa Stream, is believed to be the first permanent settlement on Molokai, dating from the early seventh century. Your first glimpse is from the road's overlook from which you get a spectacular panorama across the half-mile valley to Lamaloa Head forming its north wall, and eastward, deep into its four mile cleft, where lies Moaula Falls. Many people are so overwhelmed when they gaze from the overlook into Halawa that they don't really look around. Turn to your right and walk only 15 yards directly away from Halawa. This view gives a totally different perspective of a deep V valley and the pounding surf of its rugged beach—so different from the gently arching haven of Halawa Bay. For centuries, Halawa's farmers carved geometric terraces for taro fields until a tidal wave of gigantic proportions inundated the valley in 1946, and left a plant-killing deposit of salt. Most people pulled out and left their homes and gardens to be reclaimed by the jungle.

Follow the paved road into the valley until you see a house that was obviously a church at one time. Cross Halawa Stream and follow the road as far as you can. Here you have a choice of bathing in the cool freshwater stream or in the surf of the protected bay. Don't go out past the mouth of the bay because the currents can be treacherous. This area is great for snorkeling and fishing, one of the only good surfing beaches on Molokai.

Halawa Bay is a beach park, but it's not well maintained. There are toilet facilities and a few dilapidated picnic tables, but no official overnight camping, and the water is not potable. You can bivouac for a night on Puu O Hoku Ranch land at the far north end of Halawa Bay under a canopy of ironwood trees, but be aware that this area attracts rip-offs and it's not safe to leave your gear unattended. Living just near the mouth of the bay is an island fisherman named Glenn and his wife Cathy. Glenn is an expert seaman and knowledgeable about the waters on this side of Molokai. He is willing to take people to Wailau Valley for $30 OW. The only problem is he has no phone, so you'll have to catch him at home or leave a note where he can contact you. Things are less efficient at Halawa Bay, and that's the beauty of it.

Parking

If you're going to the Moaula Falls, when you come to the end of the road you'll see a parking lot where a gentleman named Dupre Dudoit sells sodas, chips, etc. He'll promise to watch your car for only $5! You can park free, just as long as it's not in his lot. If you have no valuables to lose, forget it. For the $5, this stalwart watchman is just as likely to take a nap or go swimming or fishing as he is to actually watch your car.

Moaula Falls

One of *the* best walks on Molokai (mosquitos!) is to the famous 250-foot Moaula ("Red Chicken") Falls. Depending on recent rainfall it can be very difficult to get there, and although Moaula Falls is quite famous, the trail to it is very poorly maintained. Valley residents claim that a full 50% of the people headed for Moaula never get there. They start out wrong! After parking at the turnout at the bottom of the road, follow the dirt road past the little church and the group of houses for about 10 minutes (one-half mile) until it turns into a footpath. Pass a few houses and head toward Halawa Stream, keeping the stone wall on your left. This is where most people go wrong. You must cross the stream to the right-hand bank! If you stay on the left bank, you'll get into thick underbrush and miss the falls completely. *Sometimes* an arrow points across the stream, but it comes and goes at the whim of vandals.

Halawa Stream can be a trickle or torrent, depending upon recent rains. If the stream's hard to cross, Moaula will be spectacular. A minute after crossing, the trail continues under a thick canopy of giant mango trees. The luscious fruits are ripe from early spring to early fall. The trail goes up a rise until it forks at a trail paralleling the stream. Take the left fork and follow the water pipe until it crosses the stream once again. This entire area shows the remains of countless taro patches and home sites. Groves of *kemani* trees mark the sites where *ali'i* were buried, their tall trunks at one time used by Hawaiian fishermen and later by sailors as a landmark. Start listening for the falls and let your ears guide you.

Legend recalls that a female lizard, a *moo,* lives in the gorgeous pool at the bottom of the falls. Sometimes she craves a body and will drag a swimmer down to her watery lair. The only way to determine her mood is to place a *ti* leaf (abundant in the area) in the pool. If it floats you're safe, but if it sinks the lady lizard wants company—permanently! Minor gods who live in the rocks above Moaula Falls pool want to get into the act too. They'll drop tiny rocks on your head unless you make an offering (a penny under a *ti* leaf will do).

After you've crossed Moaula Stream and are heading the last 100 yards or so to the falls, a branch trail leads to the right up the cliff where it divides again in about 150 yards. If you take the left fork you come to another pool at the bottom of **Upper Moaula Falls,** but you have to scale the almost vertical cliff face aided only by a wire cable attached to the rock wall. The right fork leads you into heavy brush, but if you persevere for 500 yards or so you come to the cascading brilliance of 500-foot **Hipuapua Falls** and its smaller but totally refreshing swimming hole.

mourning gecko, natural flycatcher

SMILE IT NO BROKE YOUR FACE!

MIDDLE MOLOKAI AND KALAUPAPA

As you head west from Kaunakakai on Route 460 toward Molokai Airport you pass fields planted in various crops. These are Molokai's attempt at diversified agriculture since the demise of pineapple a few years ago. Iowa-like corn fields make it obvious that the experiment is working well and has a chance, if the large corporations and the state government get behind it. The cultivated fields give way to hundreds of acres filled with skeletons of dead trees. It's as if some eerie specter stalked the land and devoured their spirits. Farther along, the **Main Forest Road** intersects, posted for 4WD vehicles but navigable in a standard car during dry weather. This track leads to the Sandalwood Measuring Pit, a depression in the ground which is a permanent reminder of the furious and foolhardy trading of last century. Here too along little-used trails are spectacular views of the lost valleys of Molokai's inaccessible northeast shore.

West on Route 460, another branch road, Route 470, heads due north through Kualapuu, Del Monte's diminished pineapple town, to road's end at Palaau State Park, Molokai's best camping area and home to the famous Phallic Rock. Nearby is the lookout for Kalaupapa Peninsula and the beginning of the mule trail which switchbacks down over 1,600 feet to the humbling and uplifting experience of Kalaupapa.

Kualapuu
Kualapuu was a vibrant town when pineapples were king and Del Monte was headquartered here, but the vibrancy has flown away. Still, it is the only town where you can find basic services on the way to Kalaupapa. Turn left off Route 470 onto Route 480 and in a minute you'll come to the **Kualapuu Market,** open daily except Sun. from 8:30 a.m. to 6 p.m. Next door is a small restaurant that serves country-cooked foods.

Molokai Sugar Mill Museum
Along Route 470, two miles past Kualapuu in the village of Kalae, you'll discover the old R.W. Meyer Sugar Mill (see "History—Molokai Ranch"), entrance fee $2.50 adults, $1 students, open daily, call 567-6436 for hours. A functioning mill, it will show all the stages of creating sugar from cane. Within the next few years, a museum and cultural center will be added, which will focus on preserving and demonstrating Hawaiian arts and handicrafts like

quilting, lau hala weaving, woodcarving, plus demonstrations of lei-making and hula. The idea is to share and revive the arts of Hawaii, especially those of Molokai, in this interpretive center.

Main Forest Road

After mile marker 3, west on Route 460 from Kaunakakai, is a bridge (just past the Seventh-day Adventist church) with a white fence on both sides. There, heading into the mountains, is a red dirt road called Main Forest or Maunahui Road. Your car rental agency will tell you that this road is impassable except in a 4WD, and they're right—if it's raining! Follow the rutted road up into the hills and you'll soon be in a deep forest of *ohia*, pine, eucalyptus, and giant ferns thriving since their planting early this century. The cool, pleasant air mixes with rich earthy smells of the forest. In just under six miles a sign says Main Forest Road. If you miss this sign look for a Boy Scout camp (also under six miles) that'll let you know that you're on the right road. Ignore many small roads branching off.

After 10 miles, look for a road sign, Kamiloloa; park 100 yards past in a turnout and walk five minutes to the **Sandalwood Measuring Pit** *(Lua Na Moku Iliahi)*. It's not very spectacular, and this is a long way to go to see a shallow hole in the ground, but the Sandalwood Pit is a permanent reminder of the days of mindless exploitation in Hawaii when money and possessions were more important than the land or the people. Hawaiian chiefs had the pit dug to measure the amount of sandalwood necessary to fill the hold of a ship. They traded the aromatic wood to Yankee captains for baubles, whiskey, guns, manufactured goods, and tools. The traders carried the wood to China where they made huge profits. The trading was so lucrative that the men of entire villages were forced into the hills to collect it, even to the point where the taro fields were neglected and famine gnawed at the door. It only took a few years to denude the mountains of their copious stands of sandalwood, even more incredible when you consider that all the work was done by hand and all the wood was carried to the waiting ships on the coast using the *makaainana* as beasts of burden.

Travel past the Sandalwood Pit for about one mile and you'll come to **Waikolu** ("Three Waters" **Overlook**). From here you can peer down

into this pristine valley 3,700 feet below. If rains have been recent, hundreds of waterfalls spread their lace as they fall to the green jungle. The water here seeps into the ground, which soaks it up like a huge dripping sponge. A water tunnel, bored into the valley, collects the water and conducts it for more than five miles until it reaches the 1.4-billion gallon Kualapuu Reservoir. Only drive to this area on a clear day, because the rain will not only get you stuck in mud, but also obscure your view with heavy cloud cover.

Hiking trails through this area are poorly marked, poorly maintained, and strenuous—great qualifications for those who crave solitude and adventure. Up-to-the-minute information and maps are available from the Dept. of Land and Natural Resources in Kaunakakai, tel. 567-6618. **Hanalilolilo Trail** begins not far from Waikolu Lookout and winds through high mountain forests of *ohia* until it comes to a breathtaking view of **Pelekunu** ("Foul Smelling, No Sunshine") **Valley**. Don't let the name fool you. Hawaiians lived happily and well in this remote,

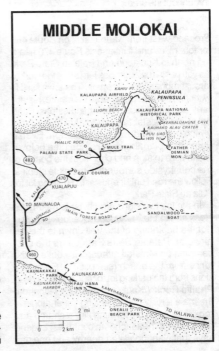

MIDDLE MOLOKAI

north shore valley for centuries. Time, aided by wind and rain, has turned the 4,000-foot sea cliffs of Pelekunu into the tallest in the world. Today, Pelekunu is more remote and isolated than ever. No permanent residents, although islanders come sporadically to camp in the summer, when the waters are calm enough to land.

East from this area is the 2,774-acre **Kamakou Preserve,** established by the Nature Conservancy of Hawaii in 1982, Which seeks to preserve this unique forest area, home to five species of endangered Hawaiian birds, two of which are endemic only to Molokai. There are 250 species of Hawaiian plants and ferns, 219 of which grow nowhere else in the world. Even a few clusters of sandalwoods tenaciously try to make a comeback. The land was donated by the Molokai Ranch, but they kept control of the water rights. Two officials of the ranch are on the Conservancy board, which causes some people to look suspiciously at their motives. The Kamakou Preserve manager is Ed Misaki. Most trails have been mapped and hunting is encouraged throughout the area.

Pala'au State Park

Proceed west from Kaunakakai on Route 460 for four miles until it intersects Route 470 heading north to Kualapuu and Pala'au State Park. As you pass Kualapuu look left to see the world's largest rubber-lined reservoir. The town itself is withering but holding on, and has a store, restaurant, and post office. A few minutes past Kualapuu are the stables for Molokai Mule Rides which take you down to Kalaupapa. Even if you're not planning a mule ride (see below), make sure to stop and check out the beauty of the countryside surrounding the mule stables. Follow the road until it ends at the parking lot for Pala'au State Park.

In the lot, two signs direct you to the Phallic Rock and to the Kalaupapa Overlook (which is not the beginning of the trail down to the peninsula). Pala'au State Park offers the best camping on Molokai although it's quite a distance from the beach (see p. 531). Follow the signs from the parking lot for about 200 yards to **Phallic Rock** ("Kauleomamahoa"). Nanahoa, the male fertility god inhabiting the anatomical rock, has been performing like a champ and hasn't had a "headache" in centuries! Legend says that Nanahoa lived nearby and one day

sat to admire a beautiful young girl who was looking at her reflection in a pool. Kawahuna, Nanahoa's wife, became so jealous when she saw her husband leering that she attacked the young girl by yanking on her hair. Nanahoa became outraged in turn, and struck his wife who rolled over a nearby cliff and turned to stone. Nanahoa also turned to stone in the shape of an erect penis and there he sits pointing skyward to this day. Barren women have come here to spend the night and pray for fertility. At the base of the rock is a tiny pool the size of a small bowl that collects rain water. The women would sit here hoping to absorb the child-giving mana of the rock. You can still see offerings, and of course graffiti. One says "Zap"—parents thankful for twins maybe.

Return to the parking lot and follow the signs to **Kalaupapa** ("Flat Leaf") **Overlook.** Jutting 1,600 feet below, almost like an afterthought, is the peninsula of Kalaupapa, which was the home of the lost lepers of Hawaii picked for its remoteness and inaccessibility. The almost vertical *pali* served as a natural barrier to the outside world. If you look to your right you'll see the mule trail weedling back and forth down the cliff. Look to the southeast sector of the peninsula to see the almost perfectly round **Kauhako Crater,** the remnant of the separate volcano that formed Kalaupapa.

THE KALAUPAPA EXPERIENCE

No one knew how the dreaded disease came to the Hawaiian Islands, but they did know that if you were contaminated by it your life would be misery. Leprosy has caused fear in the hearts of man since biblical times, and last century King Kamehameha V and his advisors were no exception. All they knew was that lepers had to be isolated. Kalawao Cove, on the southeast shore of Kalaupapa Peninsula, was regarded as the most isolated spot in the entire kingdom. So it was to Kalawao that the lepers of Hawaii were sent to die. Through crude diagnostic testing, anyone who had a suspicious skin discoloration, ulcer, or even bad sunburn was rounded up and sent to Kalawao. The islanders soon learned that once sent, there was no return. So the afflicted hid. Bounty hunters roamed the countryside. Babies, toddlers, teenagers, wives, grandfathers—none were immune to the bounty hunters. They hounded, captured, and sometimes killed anyone that had any sort of skin ailment. The captives were ripped from their villages and loaded on a ship. No one would come near the suspected lepers on board and they sat open to the elements in a cage. They were allowed only one small tin box of possessions. As the ship anchored in the always choppy bay at Kalawao, the cage was opened and the victims were tossed overboard. Their contaminated cage was followed by a few sealed barrels of food and clothing that had been collected by merciful Christians. Those too weak or sick or young drowned; the unlucky made it to shore. The crew waited nervously with loaded muskets in case any of the howling, walking nightmares on shore attempted in their delirium to board the ship.

Father Damien just weeks before his death from Hansen's Disease

Hell On Earth

Waiting for the newcomers were the forsaken. Abandoned by king, country, family, friends, and apparently the Lord himself, they became animals—beasts of prey. Young girls with hardly a blemish were raped by reeking deformed men in rags. Old men were bludgeoned, their tin boxes ripped from their hands. Children and babies cried and begged for food, turning instinctively to the demented women who had lost all motherly feelings. Finally too weak even to whimper, they died of starvation. Those victims that could made rude dwellings of sticks and stones, while others lived in caves or on the beach open to the elements. Finally, the conscience of the kingdom was stirred in 1866: the old dumping ground of Kalawao was abandoned and the lepers were exiled to the more hospitable Kalaupapa Peninsula, just a few hundred yards to the west.

The Move To Kalaupapa

The people of the sleepy village of Kalaupapa couldn't believe their eyes when they saw the ravaged ones. But these lepers now sent to Kalaupapa were treated more mercifully. Missionary groups and *kokua* ("helpers") provided food and rudimentary clothing. An end was put to the lawlessness and depravity. Still, the lepers were kept separate. For the most part they lived outdoors or in very rude huts. They never could come in direct contact with the *kokua*. If they met a healthy person walking along a path, they had

to grovel at the side. Most fell to the ground, hiding their faces and attempting to crawl like beaten dogs under a bush. Many *kokua*, horrified by Kalaupapa, left on the next available boat. With no medical attention, death was still the only release from Kalaupapa.

Light In Hell

It was by accident or miracle that **Joseph Damien de Veuster,** a Catholic priest, came from Belgium to Hawaii. His brother, also a priest, was supposed to come but he became ill and Father Damien came in his place. Damien spent a few years in Hawaii, building churches and learning the language and ways of the people, before he came to Kalaupapa in 1873. What he saw touched his heart. He was different from the rest, having come with a sense of mission to help the lepers and bring them hope and dignity. The other missionaries saw Kalaupapa not as a place to live, but to die. Damien saw the lepers as children of God, who had the right to live and be comforted. When they hid under a bush at his approach, he picked them up and stood them on their feet. He carried water all day long to the sick and dying. He bathed their wounds and built them shelters with his own two hands. When clothes or food or materials ran short, he walked topside and begged for more. Other church groups were against him and the government gave him little aid, but he persevered. Damien scraped together some lumber and fashioned a

the simple interior of St. Philomena's Church

flume pipe to carry water to his people, who were still dying mainly from pneumonia and tuberculosis brought on by neglect. Damien worked long days alone, until he dropped exhausted at night.

Father Damien built **St. Philomena Church** and invited the lepers inside. Those grossly afflicted could not control their mouths, so spittle would drip to the floor. They were ashamed to soil the church, so Damien cut squares in the floor through which they could spit onto the ground. Slowly a light began to shine in the hearts of the lepers and the authorities began to take notice. Conditions began to improve, but there were those who resented Damien. Robert Louis Stevenson visited the settlement, and after meeting Damien wrote an open letter that ended " . . . he is my father." Damien contracted leprosy, but by the time he died in 1889 at age 49, he knew his people would be cared for. In 1936, Damien's native Belgium asked that his remains be returned. He was exhumed and his remains sent home, but a memorial still stands where he was interred at Kalaupapa.

The Light Grows Brighter

Mother Mary Ann Cope, a Franciscan nun from Syracuse, New York, arrived in 1888 to carry on Damien's work. In addition, many missionary groups sent volunteers to help at the colony. Thereafter the people of Kalaupapa were treated with dignity and given a sense of hope. In 1873, the same year that Damien arrived at Kalaupapa, Norwegian physician Gerhard Hansen

isolated the bacteria that causes leprosy, and shortly thereafter the official name of the malady became Hansen's disease. By the turn of this century, adequate medical care and good living conditions were provided to the patients at Kalaupapa. Still, many died, mostly from complications such as TB or pneumonia. Families could not visit members confined to Kalaupapa unless they were near death, and any children born to the patients—who were now starting to marry—were whisked away at birth and adopted, or given to family members on the outside. Even until the 1940s people were still sent to Kalaupapa because of skin ailments that were never really diagnosed as leprosy. Many of these indeed did show signs of the disease, but there is always the haunting thought that they may have contracted it after arrival at the colony. Jimmy, one of the guides for Damien Tours, was one of these. He had some white spots as a child that his Hawaiian grandmother would treat with herbs. As soon as she stopped applying the herbs, the spots would return. A public health nurse at school saw the spots, and Jimmy was sent to Kalaupapa. At the time he was given only 10 years to live.

In the mid-1940s sulfa drugs were found to arrest most cases of Hansen's disease, and the prognosis for a normal life improved. By the 1960s further breakthroughs made Hansen's disease noncontagious, and the patients at Kalaupapa were free to leave and return to their homes. No new patients were admitted, but most, already living in the only home they'd ever known, opted to stay. The community of resident patients is less than 100 today, and the average age is about 60. Kalaupapa will be turned into a national park soon, but the residents are assured a lifetime occupancy.

Getting There

It shouldn't be a matter of *if* you go to Kalaupapa, but *how* you go. You have choices. You can fly, ride a mule, walk, or walk and fly. No matter how you go, you **cannot** walk around Kalaupapa unescorted. You must take an official tour, and children under 16 are not allowed. If you're going by mule or air, arrangements are made for you by the companies, but if you're walking you have to call ahead to one of the following, who will make arrangements to meet you at the entrance to the community. Contact **Damien Tours,** tel. 567-6171, or **Ike's Scenic Tours,** tel. 567-6437. Both tour companies charge $15 for a fascinating, four-hour tour conducted by one of the residents. Definitely worth the money; the insight you get from the resident-tour guide is priceless and unique. No food or beverages, except water, are available to visitors, so make sure to bring your own.

Molokai Mule Rides, tel. 526-0888, rents mules to take you down the 1,600-foot *pali* for $85 including lunch and the tour of Kalaupapa. The mules are sure-footed, well-trained animals which expertly negotiate 26 hairpin switchbacks

on the trail to the bottom. Restrictions say riders must weigh under 225 pounds and be in generally good physical condition. The stables are clearly marked on Route 470.

If you're walking to Kalaupapa, follow the mule trail, cut by Manuel Farinha in 1886. Go past the stables and look for a road to the right. At the trailhead is a small metal building with an odd sign that reads Advance Technology Center Hawaii USA. The mules leave by 9 a.m., so make sure you go ahead of them! The trail is well maintained and only mildly strenuous. It could be muddy in spots but you'll notice gravel all the way down that is carried by the bagful by the mules and deposited daily. While on the subject, be careful of *other* mule deposits as you walk along. It takes just about an hour and a half to make the descent. Once down, wait at the grassy clearing. Your tour guide will pick you up there.

You can fly in and out, or out only, which is a good alternative and relatively cheap. Aloha Island Air charges $40 RT, or $20 OW. They operate two flights to Kalaupapa at 8:50 a.m. and 9:55 a.m. The only return flight out is at 2:40 p.m. Papillon Helicopters, tel. 669-4884, flies over Kalaupapa from Maui but don't land; they charge $185 per person. If you decide to fly notice the breakers at the end of the runway sending spray 90 feet into the air. The pilots time their take-off to miss the spray!

bamboo

MOLOKAI'S WEST END

Long before contact with the Europeans, the west end of Molokai was famous throughout the Hawaiian Islands. The culture centered on Maunaloa, the ancient volcanic mountain that formed the land. On its slopes the goddess Laka learned the hula from her sister and spread its joyous undulations to all the other islands. Not far from the birthplace of the hula is Kaluakoi, one of the two most important adz quarries in old Hawaii. Without these stone tools, no canoes, bowls, or everyday items could have been fashioned. Voyagers came from every major island to trade for this perfect stone of Kaluakoi. With all this coming and going, the always small population of Molokai needed godly protection. Not far away at Kalai-pahoa, the "poison wood" sorcery gods of Molokai lived in a grove that supposedly sprouted to maturity in one night. With talismans made from this magical grove, Molokai kept invading warriors at bay for centuries.

Most of the island's arable land is out here. The thrust west began with the founding of the Molokai Ranch, whose 70,000 acres make up 50% of the good farmland on the island. The ranch was owned last century by Kamehameha V, and after his death was sold to private interests who began the successful raising of Santa Gertrudis cattle imported from the famous Texas King Ranch. The ranch still employs *paniolo*, with the life of riding the range and rodeo still strong.

The Northwest

The northwest section of Molokai, centered at **Hoolehua,** is where the Hawaiian Homes parcels are located. The entire area has a feeling of heartland America, and if you ignore the coastline in the background you could easily imagine yourself in the rolling hills of Missouri. Don't expect a town at Hoolehua. All that's there is a little post office and a building or two.

The real destination is **Moomomi** ("Jewelled Reptile") **Beach**. Follow Route 460 until it branches north at Route 480 a mile east of the airport. Follow Route 480 until it turns left onto Farrington Highway in Hoolehua, and contine for about four miles until it turns into a red dirt road. Go for about five minutes, bearing right at the main intersection until you come to an area

where a foundation remains of a burned bathhouse. Below you is Moomomi. This area is a favorite with local people who come here to swim, fish, and surf. The swells are good only in winter, but the beach becomes rocky at this time of year. The tides bring the sand in by April and the swimming until November is good.

Moomomi Beach goes back in Hawaiian legend. Besides the mythical lizards that inhabited this area, a great shark god was born here. The mother was a woman who became impregnated by the gods. Her husband was angry that her child would be from the spirit world, so he directed her to come and sit on a large rock down by the beach. She went into labor and began to cry. A tear, holding a tiny fish, rolled down her cheek and fell into the sea. He became a powerful shark-god and the rock upon which his mother sat is the large black one just to the right of the beach.

If you feel adventurous you can head west along the beach. Every 10 minutes or so you come to a tiny beach that you have entirely to yourself. Being so isolated, be extremely careful of surf conditions. About two miles west of Moomomi is **Keonelele,** a miniature desert of sand dunes. The wind whips through this region and carries the sand to the southwest shore. Geologists haunt this area trying to piece together Molokai's geological history. The Hawaiians used Keonelele as a burial site, and strange footprints found in the soft sandstone supposedly foretold the coming of white men. Today, Keonelele is totally deserted; although small, it gives the impression of a vast wasteland. Camping (no permit necessary) is allowed on the grassy area overlooking Moomomi Beach, but since a fire claimed the bathhouse, there are no showers or toilets. Water is available from a tap near the old foundation. You will be personally safe camping here, but if you leave gear unattended it could walk off.

Kawakiu Beach

This secluded and pristine beach on the far northwestern corner of Molokai was an item of controversy between the developers of the Kaluakoi Corporation and the grass-roots activists of Molokai. For years access to the beach was restricted, and the Kaluakoi Corp. planned to develop the area. It was known that the area was very important during pre-contact times, and rich in unexplored archaeological sites. The Kaluakoi Corp. hired a supposed team of "experts" that studied the site for months, and finally claimed that the area had no significant archaeological importance. Their findings were hooted at by local people and by scholars from various institutions who knew better. This controversy resulted in the Kawakiu Beach being opened to the public with plans of turning it into a beach park; the archaeological sites will be preserved.

The swimming here is excellent with the sandy bottom tapering off slowly. Camping is permitted in the large grove of trees with permission from the Molokai Ranch. To get there, keep your eyes peeled as you follow Route 460 past the airport for about four miles. The seven miles of dirt road from here are dusty and not well maintained, but passable at most times. Just before you reach Kawakiu the road branches—go right to the beach.

Maunaloa Town

Most people heading east-west between Kaunakakai and the Kaluakoi Resort never make it into Maunaloa town. That's because Route 460 splits just east of Maunaloa, and Kaluakoi Road heads north toward the Kaluakoi Resort and away from the town. With the pineapple gone and few visitors coming, the town is barely hanging on. Maunaloa is a wonderful example of a plantation town. As you pull in, there's a little patch of humble but well-kept workers' houses carved into a field. In front you're likely to see a tethered horse, a boat, or glass fishing floats hanging from the lanai. Overhead you may see a kite flying—that's your beacon that you've arrived in Maunaloa town. The townsfolk are friendly and if you're looking for conversation or a taste of Hawaiian history, the old-timers hanging around under the shaded lean-to near the post office are just the ticket.

A good reason to make the trek to Maunaloa is to visit the **Big Wind Kite Factory,** tel. 552-2364, owned and operated by Jonathan Sosher and his wife Daphane. It's amazing to note that the handcrafted kites from this downhome cottage industry are the same ones that sell at Honolulu's slick Ala Moana Mall, the Royal Hawaiian Shopping Arcade, and at the Cannery Shopping Center on Maui. All are made on the

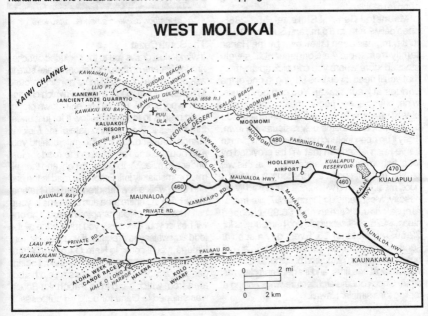

premises by Jonathan and Daphane, who come up with designs like panda bears, rainbow stegosauruses, and hula girls in ti-leaf skirts. Jonathan will give you a lesson in the park next door on any of the kites, including the two string controllable ones. Prices range from $10 to $200 for a rip-stop nylon kite; they make beautiful, easily transportable gifts that'll last for years. The shop itself is ablaze with beautiful colors, as if you've walked into the heart of a flower. This is a happy store. Part of it, **The Plantation Gallery**, sells a variety of crafts by local artists—tapa cloth, Hawaiian quilt pillow cases, Pacific isle shell jewelry, scrimshaw (on deerhorn), black coral necklaces, and earrings. Island cypress, Japanese *sugi* from a local tree, and *milo* have been carved by a local artist named Robin. **Bali Hale,** part of the boutique, has batiks, Balinese masks, woodcarvings, and sarongs; especially nice are carved mirror frames of storks, birds, and flowers. And if you just can't live without a blow gun from Irian Jaya, this is the place. After you've run through a million tourist shops and are sick of the shell leis, come here to find something truly unique. The Big Wind Kite Factory is the most interesting shop on Molokai.

Maunaloa General Store, tel. 552-2868, open daily 9 a.m. to 8 p.m., and Sunday 10 a.m. to 8 p.m., has been taken over by the Hansa family from India via Connecticut. It's well-stocked store where you can pick up anything that you'll need if you'll be staying in one of the condos at Kaunakakai. You can buy liquor, wine, beer, canned goods, meats, and vegetables. The same family has also purchased **Jo Jo's,** tel. 552-2803, the only restaurant in town. They'll be open for lunch and dinner and plan to serve fresh island fish that will be provided by local fishermen. The Hansas feel that this will benefit the community, and the tourists will find a good meal. Open on weekends, but closed Wednesday. Most items go for under $7, like macaroni salad and Korean ribs, $6.99, chopped steak, $4.75, cheeseburgers and hamburgers for $2.50, teri-plate for $5. Every day a special sandwich costs under $3. The cafe is in an old board-and-batten plantation building. The inside was a bar at one time, and it's neat and clean as a pin. Check out the architecture while getting a feeling for a simpler Hawaii.

Jonathon displays a hand-crafted kite.

The South Coast

If wanderlust draws you to the secluded beaches around **Halena** on the south shore, make sure to ask one of the local old-timers hanging around Maunaloa about road conditions (which change with every storm). Before you enter town proper a dirt road is to the right. Follow it for just under three miles to the unlocked gate of the Molokai Ranch. Proceed, closing the gate behind you, and bounce and rattle down the road for just under two miles. At the fork, go right and then almost immediately left. Follow the road to the end and then walk a few hundred yards to Halena. You'll have the entire area and shoreline to yourself. There's no official camping here, but no one will bother you. Obviously you must bring all the food and water you'll require. If you go west from Halena, you'll come to **Hale O Lono** in about one mile, the launch point for the annual outrigger canoe race to Oahu. There's an old harbor area from which sand from Papohaku Beach was shipped to Oahu for building purposes. If you go east back at the fork to Halena, you'll come to the dilapidated **Kolo Wharf** (two miles), from which Molokai once shipped its pineapples. The road is even more remote and rougher, so getting stuck will mean a long hike out and an astronomical towing charge. It's best to walk from Halena along the coast.

The Kaluakoi Resort And West End

This entire west end of Molokai is designated as the Kaluakoi Resort, owned by the Louisiana Land and Exploration Company. The complex includes the Kaluakoi Resort, Ke Nai Kai Condominiums, world-famous Kalua Koi Golf course, private home sites, and Papohaku, Hawaii's largest white-sand beach. (It's illegal even to mention the word "budget" in this area. If you do, you'll be pilloried in stocks made from melted credit cards and lashed with a Gucci whip!)

Accommodations And Restaurants

The **Kaluakoi Hotel and Golf Course,** Box 1977, Maunaloa, HI 96770, tel. 552-2555 or (800) 367-6046, is a showcase hotel and the destination point for most of the people coming to Molokai. The low-rise buildings are made primarily of wood. The architecture is superb and blends harmoniously with the surrounding countryside. The grounds are impeccable and all the trees and shrubbery are labeled to provide a miniature botanical tour. All rooms have color TVs, refrigerators, and those on the second floor have open-beam construction. Most rooms sit along the fairways of the golf course and have at least a partial ocean view. Because of the constant cool breezes, no air-conditioning is necessary, but there are ceiling fans. The entire hotel has been refurbished with wallpaper, carpeting, drapes, bedspreads, and dressers. The rooms are done in light pastels and earth colors, all very harmonious and pleasing to the senses. Dynamic color is provided by the large windows that open onto the fairways and the sea beyond. Actually, for a first-class hotel the rates aren't bad. The least expensive room is $85 d, and includes greens fee at the Kaluakoi Golf Course. The rates go up to $200 for an ocean cottage suite, but many hotels on the other islands change a lot more for a lot less. The best deal at the Kaluakoi is the **Colony Club.** This package includes rooms, daily cocktails, full American plan, and all activities. Make sure to avail yourself of the in-house activities. You can have a ball playing volleyball, taking nature walks, riding very good bicycles, or taking lei-making and hula lessons. In the evenings there are top-rated movies with free popcorn. The bar offers daily specials, usually exotic drinks at great prices.

Lighted tennis courts are free to guests (free clinics Tues., Fri., Sat.), and a small Liberty House provides limited shopping along with a sundries store selling snacks, magazines, and liquor. Past the tenth hole, which would basically be the far north end of the property, you'll overlook a very private beach. No rules or prying eyes here, so if you would like to swim *au naturel* this is the place.

The Kaluakoi's **Ohia Lodge** (reservations a must, and long pants and collared shirt required!) is the *best* restaurant on the island. The gourmet food is prepared by Tim and Hillary, a husband-and-wife team who specialize in making all the pastries, jams, and jellies on property. You'll be delighted by the range of culinary delights, but don't overlook a simple and light meal of salad bar and bread. The fresh-baked Molokai bread from Kanemitsu's bakery is scrumptious with crisp greens topped with the hot mustard-honey dressing. For a great dining experience, choose the fresh catch cooked to your liking. The most delectable, *opakapaka,* is pan-fried in drawn butter and topped with chopped macadamia nuts. The rack of lamb is so delicious that even in this fancy room people will understand if you run your bread around your plate to soak up the last of the savory juices. You'll pray to have a little extra room for the desserts. "Cappuccino Krunch," a light fluffy coffee-flavored pie, is one that will make your taste buds chuckle with glee. The snack bar is open daily and sells sandwiches and burgers at surprisingly reasonable prices.

Ke Nani Kai Condos are *mauka* of the road leading to the Kaluakoi Resort and they charge from $105-115 for one of their fully furnished studios; two bedrooms cost from $125-135. The complex is new so all studios are in excellent condition. Write Ke Nani Kai, Box 126, Molokai, HI 96770, tel. 552-2761 or (800) 888-2791.

Paniolo Hale is another condo complex nearby. Studios start at $75 d, $95 for one bedroom,

$115 two bedroom. Two bedroom units have a hot tub and enclosed lanai. Guests of the Paniolo Hale can use the Kaluakoi Resort's tennis courts for a small fee. Write Paniolo Hale, Box 146, Molokai, HI 96770, tel. 552-3731 or (800) 367-2984.

Excursions And Attractions

The **Molokai Ranch Wildlife Park** is a one-square-mile preserve on the ranch lands, open to the public, which houses over 400 grazing animals from Africa and India. Among the exotic occupants are giraffes, kudu, ibex, antelopes, and ostriches that have lost their fear of man and can be seen at very close quarters. The environment and grazing of west Molokai is almost identical to the animals' home in East Africa; because of this and the exemplary care afforded by the caretaker, Pilipo Solotario, the Wildlife Park has one of the best reputations in the world. Tours depart from the Kaluakoi Resort, daily approximately every two hours beginning at 8 a.m. with the last at 3 p.m. The tour costs $25 for adults and $10 for children under 12. For information call 552-2555 or 552-2767.

Papohaku Beach, the best attraction in the area, doesn't have a price tag. Papohaku Beach is the giant expanse of white sand in front of and running south from the Kaluakoi Resort. The sands here are so expansive that they were dredged and taken to Oahu in the 1950s. During the winter months a great deal of sand is stripped away and large lava boulders and outcroppings are exposed. Every spring and summer the tides carry the sand back and deposit it on the enormous beach.

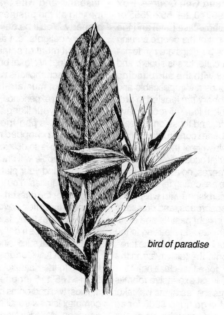

bird of paradise

THE BIG ISLAND

"*In what other land save this one is the commonest form of greeting not 'Good Day,' . . . but 'Love?' . . . Aloha . . . It is the positive affirmation of one's own heart giving.*"

—Jack London, 1916

INTRODUCTION

The island of Hawaii is grand in so many ways. Nicknamed The "Orchid Island" and The "Volcano Island," both are excellent choices: it produces more of these delicate blooms than anywhere else on earth and Pele, the fire goddess, makes her mythological home here, where she regularly sends rivers of lava from the world's largest and most active volcanoes. But Hawaii has only one real nickname to the people who live there, the "Big Island." Big isn't necessarily better, but when you combine it with beautiful, uncrowded, traditional, and inexpensive, it's hard to beat.

The Big Island was first inhabited by the Polynesian settlers, yet it's geologically the youngest of the Hawaiian Islands at barely a million years old. Like all the islands in the Hawaiian chain, it's a mini-continent whose geographical demarcations are made much more apparent because of its size. There are parched deserts, steaming fissures, jet-black sand beaches, raw semi-cooled lava flows, snow-covered mountains, entire forests encased in hardened stone, and lush valleys where countless waterfalls break through the rock faces of 1,000-foot-tall chasms. There are small working villages that time has passed by, the state's most tropical city, and an entire arid coast stretching over 90 miles where the sun is guaranteed to shine. You'll find some of the islands' least expensive accommodations as well as the world's most exclusive resorts.

Historically, the Big Island is loaded with religious upheavals, the births and deaths of great men, vintage missionary homes and churches, reconstructed *heiau,* and even a royal palace. Here is the country's largest privately owned ranch, where cowboy life is the norm, America's only coffee plantations, and enclaves of the counterculture, where alternative people are still trying to keep the faith of the '60s. Sportspeople love it here, too. The Big Island is a mecca for triathletes and offers snow skiing in season, plenty of camping and hiking, and the best marlin waters of all the oceans of the world. There are direct flights to the Big Island, where the fascination of perhaps not "old" Hawaii, but definitely "simple" Hawaii, still lingers.

OVERVIEW

Hilo on the east coast and Kailua-Kona on the west are the two ports of entry to the Big Island. At opposite ends of the island as well as the cul-

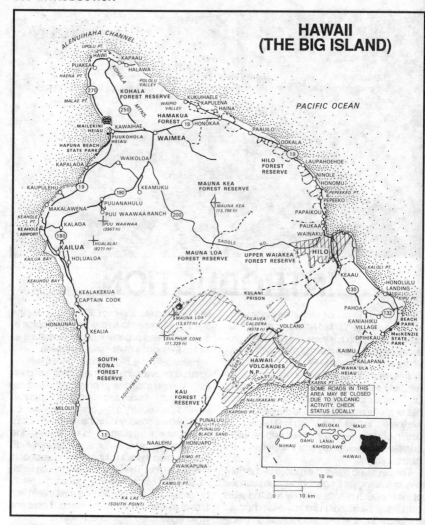

HAWAII (THE BIG ISLAND)

ALENUIHAHA CHANNEL

UPOLU PT.

PUAKEA · HAWI · KAPAAU

HAENA PT. · HALAWA

POLOLU VALLEY

270 · KOHALA FOREST RESERVE

250 · KOHALA MTNS

MAILEKINI HEIAU · KAWAIHAE

MALAE PT.

HAMAKUA FOREST

KUKUIHAELE · KAPULENA

WAIPIO VALLEY · HAINA

PUUKOHOLA HEIAU · WAIMEA

19 HONOKAA

PAAUILO

19 OOKALA

HAPUNA BEACH STATE PARK

KAPALAOA · WAIKOLOA

KAUPULEHU

19

PACIFIC OCEAN

LAUPAHOEHOE

HILO FOREST RESERVE

NINOLE

HONOMU

190 · KEAMUKU

PUUANAHULU

PUU WAAWAA RANCH

MAKALAWENA

KEAHOLE PT.

KE AHOLE AIRPORT

KALAOA

180

MAUNA KEA FOREST RESERVE

MAUNA KEA (13,796 ft)

PEPEEKEO PT.

PEPEEKEO

PAPAIKOU

PUU WAAWAA (3967 ft)

200

SADDLE RD.

PAUKAA

WAINAKU

KAILUA

HUALALAI (8271 ft)

HOLUALOA

KAILUA BAY

MAUNA LOA FOREST RESERVE

UPPER WAIAKEA FOREST RESERVE

HILO

KEAUHOU BAY

KEALAKEKUA CAPTAIN COOK

KEAAU

KALOLI PT.

HONOLULU LANDING

130 · SKIPU PT.

KULANI PRISON

HONAUNAU

KEALIA

MAUNA LOA (13,677 ft)

SULPHUR CONE (11,329 ft)

KILAUEA CALDERA (4078 ft)

VOLCANO

PAHOA

132 · BEACH PARK

KANIAHIKU VILLAGE

OPIHIKAU

MacKENZIE STATE PARK

SOUTH KONA FOREST RESERVE

DESERT TRAIL

HAWAII VOLCANOES N.P.

CHAIN OF CRATERS RD.

PUNA COAST TRAIL

KAIMU

WAHA'ULA HEIAU

KALAPANA

SOUTHWEST RIFT ZONE

KAU FOREST RESERVE

NALIIKAKANI PT.

KAPOHO PT.

SOME ROADS IN THIS AREA MAY BE CLOSED DUE TO VOLCANIC ACTIVITY. CHECK STATUS LOCALLY.

MILOLII

11

PUNALUU BLACK SAND

NAALEHU · HONUAPO

KIMO PT.

WAIKAPUNA

KAMILO PT.

KA LAE (SOUTH POINT)

KAUAI · MOLOKAI · MAUI

NIIHAU · OAHU · LANAI

KAHOOLAWE

HAWAII

0   10 mi

0   10 km

---

tural spectrum, a friendly rivalry exists between the two. It doesn't matter at which one you arrive, because a trip to the Big Island without visiting both is unthinkable. Better yet, split your stay and use each as a base while you tour. The Big Island is the only Hawaiian island big enough that you can't drive around it comfortably in one day, nor should you even try. Split into six districts,

each is interesting enough to spend at least one day exploring.

Hilo And Vicinity

Hilo is the oldest port of entry, the most tropical town in Hawaii, and the only major city built on the island's windward coast. The city is one tremendous greenhouse where exotic flowers and tropical plants are a normal part of the landscape, and entire blocks canopied by adjoining banyans are taken for granted. The town, which hosts the yearly Merry Monarch Festival, boasts an early-morning fish market, Japanese gardens, the Lyman House Museum, and a profusion of natural phenomena, including Rainbow Falls and Boiling Pots. Plenty of rooms in Hilo are generally easily available, and its variety of restaurants will titillate anyone's taste buds. Both go easy on the pocketbook while maintaining high standards.

Saddle Road begins just outside of Hilo. It slices directly across the island through a most astonishing high valley or "saddle" separating the mountains of Mauna Loa and Mauna Kea. A passable road, the bane of car rental companies, heads 13,796 feet straight to the top of Mauna Kea, where a series of astronomical observatories peer into the heavens through the clearest air on Earth.

Northeast

Hamakua refers to the entire northeast coast where streams, wind, and pounding surf have chiseled the lava into towering cliffs and precipitous valleys known locally by the unromantic name of "gulches." All the flat lands here are awash in a green sea of sugar cane. A spur road from the forgotten town of Honomu leads to Akaka Falls, whose waters tumble over a 442-foot cliff, making them the highest sheer drop of water in Hawaii. North along the coastal road is Honokaa, a one-street town of stores, restaurants, and craft shops. The main road bears left here to the cowboy town of Waimea, but a smaller road inches farther north. It dead ends at the top of Waipio Valley, cradled by cliffs on three sides with its mouth wide open to the sea. The valley is reachable only by foot, 4WD vehicle, or on horseback. On its verdant floor a handful of families live simply by raising taro, a few head of cattle, and some horses. Waipio was a burial ground of Hawaiian *ali'i*, where *kahuna* traditionally came to commune with spirits. The enchantment of this "power spot" remains.

Southeast

Puna lies south of Hilo and makes up the majority of the southeast coast. Here are the greatest lava fields that have spewed from Kilauea, the heart of Volcanoes National Park. An ancient flow embraced a forest in its fiery grasp, entombing trees that stand like sentinels in Lava Tree State Monument. Cape Kumukahi, a pointed lava flow that reached the ocean in 1868, is officially the easternmost point in Hawaii. Just below is a string of beaches featuring ebony-black sand.

Past the small village of Kalapana, the road skirts the coast before it dead ends where it has been covered over by lava. Chain of Craters Road is now passable only *from* Hawaii Volcanoes National Park. Wahaula Visitor Center has been torched by lava, but the **Wahaula Heiau,** where human sacrifice was introduced to the islands, survived and can be reached on foot if conditions permit. Chain of Craters Road spills off the mountain through a forbiddding, yet vibrant wasteland of old lava flows until it comes to the sea, where this living volcano fumes and throbs. Atop the volcano, miles of hiking trails crisscross the park and lead to the very summit of Mauna Loa. You can view the natural phenomena of steaming fissures, boiling mud, Devastation Trail, and the Thurston Lava Tube, large enough to accommodate a subway train. Here, too, you can lodge or dine at Volcano House, a venerable inn carved into the rim of the crater.

Kau, the southern tip of the island, is primarily a desert. On well-marked trails leading left and right from the main road you'll discover ancient petroglyphs and an eerie set of footprints, the remnants of an ill-fated band of warriors smothered under the moist ash of a volcanic eruption; their demise marked the ascendancy of Kamehameha the Great. Here are some lovely beaches and state parks you'll have virtually to yourself. A tiny road leads to Ka Lae ("South Point"), the most southerly piece of ground in the United States.

Kona

Kona, the west coast, is in every way the opposite of Hilo. It's dry, sunny, and brilliant, with large expanses of old barren lava flows. When watered, the rich soil blossoms, as in South Kona, renowned for its diminutive coffee plantations. The town of Captain Cook, named after the intrepid Pacific explorer, lies just above the very beach where he was slain because of a terrible miscommunication two centuries ago.

Ironically, nearby is the restored **Puuhonua O Honaunau Heiau,** where mercy and forgiveness were rendered to any *kapu*-breaker or vanquished warrior who made it into the confines of this temple of refuge.

Kailua-Kona is the center of Kona. The airport is just north and in town is a concentration of condos and hotels; the town also boasts an array of art and designer shops. World-class triathletes come here to train, and charter boats depart in search of marlin. Within Kailua is Mokuaikuaa Church, a legacy of the very first packet of missionaries to arrive in the islands, and Hulihee Palace, vacation home of the Kamehameha line of kings.

Northward, the Kona District offers a string of beaches. Just outside Kailua is a nudist beach, one of a very few in Hawaii, and farther up the coast in South Kohala is Hapuna Beach, best on the island. In 1965, Lawrence Rockefeller opened the Mauna Kea Resort here. For the last three decades this resort, along with its sculptured coast-hugging golf course, has been considered one of the finest in the world. Just south is the Kona Village Resort, whose guests can arrive at a private airstrip to spend the night in a "simple" grass shack on the beach. Its serenity is broken only by the soothing music of the surf, and the not-so-melodious singing of "Kona nightingales," a pampered herd of wild donkeys that frequents this area. The Hyatt Regency Waikoloa is here, billed as the most fabulous resort on earth, and just down the road is the Mauna Lani, another first-rate hotel.

North

North Kohala is primarily the peninsular thumb on the northern extremity of the island, although the area does dip south along the coast and eastward into rolling hills. At its base is Waimea (Kamuela), center of the enormous Parker Ranch. Here in the cool mountains, cattle graze in chest-high grass and *paniolo,* astride their sturdy mounts, ride herd in time-honored tradition. Hunters range the slopes of Mauna Kea in search of wild goats and boars, and the Fourth of July is boisterously acknowledged by the wild whoops of cowboys at the world-class Parker Ranch Rodeo. Along the coast are beach parks, empty except for an occasional local family picnic. A series of *heiau* dot the coast, and on the northernmost tip a broad plain, overlooking a sweeping panorama, marks the birthplace of Kamehameha the Great. The main town up here is Hawi, holding on after the sugar companies pulled out a few years ago. Down the road is Kapaau, where Kamehameha's statue resides in fulfillment of a *kahuna* prophecy. Along this little traveled road, a handful of artists offer their crafts in little shops. At road's end is the overlook of Pololu Valley. Here a steep descent takes you to secluded beaches and camping in an area once frequented by some of the most powerful sorcerers in the land.

THE LAND

Science and the oral history of the Kumulipo differ sharply on the age of the Big Island. Scientists say that Hawaii is the youngest of the islands, being a little over one million years old; the chanters claim that it was the first "island-child" of Wakea and Papa. It is, irrefutably, closest to the "hot spot" on the Pacific floor, evidenced by Kilauea's frequent eruptions and by **Loihi Seamount,** located 30 miles off the southeast coast, which is even now steadily growing about 3,000 feet below the waves. The geology, geography, and location of the Hawaiian Islands, and their ongoing drifting and building in the middle of the Pacific, make them among the most unique pieces of real estate on Earth, and the Big Island is the most unique of them all.

Size

The Big Island dwarfs all the others in the Hawaiian chain at 4,038 square miles and growing. This makes up about 63% of the state's total land mass; all the others could fit within it two times over. With 266 miles of coastline, the island stretches about 95 miles from north to south and 80 miles from east to west. Cape Kumukahi is the easternmost point in the state, and Ka Lae ("South Point") is the most southern point in the country.

THE MOUNTAINS

The tremendous volcanic peak of **Mauna Kea** ("White Mountain"), located in north-central Hawaii, has been extinct for over 4,000 years. Its seasonal snowcap earns Mauna Kea its name and reputation as a good skiing area in winter. Over 18,000 feet of mountain below the surface rises straight up from the ocean floor—making Mauna Kea actually 31,796 feet tall, a substantial 2,768 feet taller than Mt. Everest. Some consider it the tallest mountain in the world, but at 13,796 feet above sea level, there is no doubt that it is the tallest peak in the Pacific. Almost on top, at 13,020 feet, is **Lake Waiau,** the highest lake in the state and third highest in the U.S. Mauna Kea was obviously a sacred mountain to the Hawaiians, and its white dome was a welcome beacon to seafarers. On its slope is the largest adz quarry in Polynesia, whose first-class basalt was fashioned into prized tools. The atmosphere atop the mountain, as it sits in mid-Pacific so far from any pollutants, is the most rarefied and cleanest on Earth. Its clarity makes it a natural for astronomical observatories, and the complex of telescopes on its summit is internationally manned, providing data to scientists around the world.

The **Kohala Mountains** to the northwest are the oldest. This section looks more like the other Hawaiian islands, with deep gorges and valleys along the coast and a green forested interior. As you head east toward Waimea from Kawaihae on Route 19, for every mile that you travel you pick up about 10 inches of rainfall per year. This becomes obvious as you begin to pass little streams and rivulets running from the mountains.

Mount Hualalai at 8,271 feet is the backdrop to Kailua-Kona. It's home to many of the Big Island's endangered birds and supports many of the region's newest housing developments. Just a few years ago, Mt. Hualalai was thought to be extinct, since the last time it erupted was in 1801. Recently, volcanologists using infrared technology have discovered the mountain to be red-hot again. The U.S. Geological Service has listed this sleeper as the fourth most dangerous volcano in the U.S., because when it does erupt, it's expected to produce a tremendous amount of lava that will pour rapidly down its steep sides. The scientists, seconded by the opinion of local Hawaiians, say that the mountain will blow within the next ten years. The housing developers don't say anything.

Even though **Mauna Loa** ("Long Mountain") measures up at a respectable 13,677 feet, its height isn't its claim to fame. This active volcano, 60 miles long by 30 miles wide, is comprised of 10,000 cubic miles of iron-hard lava, making it the densest and most massive mountain on Earth. In 1950 a tremendous lava flow belched from Mauna Loa's summit, reaching an astonishing rate of 6,750,000 cubic yards per hour. Seven lava rivers flowed for 23 days emitting over 600 million cubic yards of lava that covered 35 square miles. There were no injuries, but the villages of Kaapuna and Honokua were partially destroyed along with the Magoo Ranch.

Kilauea, whose pragmatic name means "The Spewing," is the world's most active volcano. In the last hundred years, it has erupted on the average once every 11 months. The Hawaiians believed that the goddess Pele inhabited every volcano in the Hawaiian chain, and her home is now Halemaumau Crater in Kilauea Caldera. Kilauea is the most scientifically watched volcano in the world, with a permanent observatory

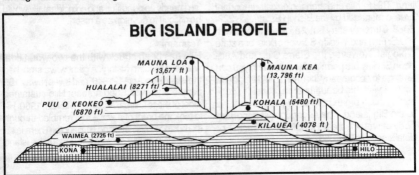

BIG ISLAND PROFILE

MAUNA LOA (13,677 ft)

MAUNA KEA (13,796 ft)

HUALALAI (8271 ft)

PUU O KEOKEO (6870 ft)

KOHALA (5480 ft)

KILAUEA (4078 ft)

WAIMEA (2725 ft)

KONA

HILO

built right into the crater rim. When it erupts, the flows are so predictable that observers run toward the mountain, not away from it! The flows, however, can burst out from fissures far from the center of the crater in areas that don't seem "active." Mostly, this occurs in the Puna District. In 1959, Kilauea Iki Crater came to life after 91 years, and although the flow wasn't as massive as others, it did send blazing fountains of lava 1,900 feet into the air. Kilauea has been very active within the last few years, with eruptions occurring at least once a month and expected to continue. Most activity has been from a yet unnamed vent below Pu'uo. You might be lucky enough to see this phenomenon while visiting.

BEACHES, PONDS, AND THE COAST

The Big Island takes the rap for having poor beaches—this isn't true! They are certainly few and far between, but they are spectacular. Hawaii is big and young, so distances are greater than on other islands and the wave action hasn't had enough time to grind the new lava into sand. The Kona and Kohala coast beaches, along with a few nooks and crannies around Hilo, are gorgeous. Puna's beaches are incredible black sand, and the southern part of the island has a string of hidden beaches enjoyed only by those intrepid enough to get to them. Full listings are found in the various travel chapters under "Beaches".

Makalawena, just north of the airport on a rough coastal trail, has a beautiful white-sand beach. Inland is its associated wetland pond, probably the most important one on the Big Island. This fragile and archaeologically important area is managed by the Bishop Estate, tel. 322-6088. Currently entry is not allowed, except with a U.S. Fish and Wildlife Service official or a state biologist. However, the Sierra Club and Audubon Society are permitted to enter, and you can arrange to accompany them on a field trip. If you wish to visit this beautiful area, consider contacting these organizations long before your trip to the Big Island. The second most important body of water is near Honokohau Beach. For details see pp. 657-658.

Currently controversy is raging over an attempt to place anchoring pins in the hard lava rock just off the Kailua-Kona Coast. Boats could latch onto them, and by doing so would not drag their anchors across the fragile coral reef, as is now the case. The Dive Council in Kona isn't known for agreeing on many issues because they represent so many different factions, but on this issue they agree unanimously that the pins should be put in place. So, they collectively decided to make a move in favor of the pins, which have been used successfully all over the world. The process is enviornmentally sound, and in fact the technology specifically needed for drilling in lava rock was worked out at the University of Hawaii.

After three years elapsed, during which the Department of Land and Natural Resources debated whether it was their responsibility or that of the Hawaii Department of Transportation to implement the program, the Dive Council went ahead and put in the pins, without the moorings. Upstaged, the Department of Land and Natural Resources was furious and at recent meetings tried to find a scapegoat at which they could throw their bureaucratic book. They would be better served spending their energies protecting the reef.

In a separate issue, the Department of Land and Natural Resources is attempting to trade 450 acres of state land surrounding Kua Bay (just north of the airport in Kona). This magnificent area has a secluded beach that is very popular with local people, and is well documented as having significant archaeological sites. In return, from international land developers, they will receive 340 acres of rocky coastal land that isn't nearly as beautiful, and coincidentally would be difficult to develop as a resort.

Tsunami

Hilo has been struck with the two worst tidal waves in modern history. A giant wave smashed the islands on April 1, 1946, and swept away 159 people and over 1,300 homes; Hilo sustained most of these losses. Again, on May 23, 1960, Hilo took the brunt of a wave that rumbled through the business district killing 61 people. There is an elaborate warning system throughout the island

AVERAGE MAXIMUM/MINIMUM TEMPERATURE AND RAINFALL

Island	Town		Jan.	Mar.	May	June	Sept.	Nov.
Hawaii	Hilo	high	79	79	80	82	82	80
		low	62	62	61	70	70	65
		rain	11	15	7	10	10	15
	Kona	high	80	81	81	82	82	81
		low	62	64	65	68	68	63
		rain	4	3	2	0	2	1

N.B. Rainfall in inches; temperature in F°

with warning procedures and Inundation Maps listed in the front of the telephone directory.

CLIMATE

The average temperature around the island varies between 72° and 78°. Summers raise the temperature to the mid-80s and winters cool off to the low 70s. Both Kona and Hilo seem to maintain a year-round average of about 80°. As usual, it's cooler in the higher elevations, and Waimea (Kamuela) sees most days in the mid 60s to low 70s, while Volcanoes maintain a steady 60°. Atop Mauna Kea, the temperature rarely climbs above 50° or dips below 30, while the summit of Mauna Loa is about 10° warmer.

Rainfall

Weatherwise the Big Island's climate varies not so much in temperature, but precipitation. Hawaii has some of the wettest and driest coastal (tourist) areas in the islands. The line separating wet from dry can be dramatic. Waimea, for example, has an actual dry and wet side of town, as if a boundary line split the town in two! Houses on the dry side are at a premium. Kona and Hilo are opposites. The Kona Coast is almost guaranteed to be sunny and bright, receiving as little as 15 inches of rainfall per year. Both Kona and the Kau Desert to the south are in the rainshadow of Mauna Loa, and most rain clouds coming from east to west are pierced by its summit before they ever reach Kona. Hilo is wet, with predictable afternoon and evening showers—they make the entire town blossom. Though this reputation keeps many tourists away, the rain's predictability makes it easy to avoid a drenching while exploring the town. Hilo does get as much as 150 inches of rainfall per year, with a record of 153.93 inches set in 1971. It also holds the dubious honor for the most rainfall recorded by the National Weather Service to fall in a town in a 24-hour period, a drenching 22.3 inches in February 1979.

FLORA AND FAUNA

The indigenous plants and birds of the Big Island have suffered the same fate as those of the other Hawaiian Islands: they're among the most endangered species on Earth and are disappearing at an alarming rate. There are some sanctuaries on the Big Island where native species still live, but they must be vigorously protected. Do your bit to save them; enjoy but do not disturb.

COMMON FLORA

The Hawaiians called the **prickly pear cactus** *panini,* which translates as "very unfriendly," undoubtedly because of the sharp spines covering the flat thick leaves. These cacti are typical of those found in Mexico and the southwestern United States. They were introduced to Hawaii before 1810 and established themselves coincidentally in conjunction with the cattle brought in at the time; *panini* are very common in North Kohala especially on the Parker Ranch lands. It is assumed that Don Marin, a Spanish advisor to Kamehameha I, was responsible for importing them. Perhaps the early *paniolo* ("cowboy") felt lonely without them. The *panini* can grow to heights of 15 feet and are now considered a pest, but nonetheless look as if they belong. They develop small delicious pear-shaped fruits. Hikers who decide to pick them should be careful of small yellowish bristles that can burrow under the skin and irritate. The fruit turns into beautiful three-inch yellow and orange flowers. An attempt is being made to control the cactus in *paniolo* country. *El cosano rojo,* the red worm found in the bottom of Mexican tequila, has been introduced to destroy these plants. It burrows into the cactus and eats the hardwood center, causing the plant to wither and die.

Lobelia is a common garden flower elsewhere. In Hawaii it has more species than anywhere else in the world, and it grows to tree height. You'll see some very unique species, ones covered with hairs, or with spikes all over them. Lobelia flowers are tiny, resembling a mini-orchid with curved and pointed ends, like the beak of the native i'iwi. This bird feeds on the flower's nectar, and it's obvious that they both evolved in Hawaii together and exhibit the strange phenomenon of nature mimicking nature.

The Big Island has more species of gesneriads, the African violet family, than anywhere on earth. Many don't have the showy flowers that you normally associate with African violets but have evolved into strange species with huge fuzzy leaves.

The *puahanui,* meaning "many flowers," is Hawaii's native hydrangea; they are common in the upland forests of the Big Island.

Ferns

If you travel to Volcanoes National Park you will find yourself deep in an amazing high-altitude tropical rainforest. This unique forest exists because of the 120 inches of annual rainfall, which turns the raw lava into a lush woodland. Besides stands of *ohia* and *koa* you'll be treated to a primordial display of ferns. All new fronds on

Fiddlehead ferns are prevalent along trails where the lava has weathered.

ferns are called fiddleheads because of the way they unfurl and resemble the scroll of a violin head. Fiddleheads were eaten by Hawaiians during times of famine. The most common ferns are *hapuu,* which are rather large tree ferns, and a smaller type with a more simple frond called *amauamau.* A soft furry growth around the base of the stalks is called *pulu.* At one time *pulu* was collected for stuffing mattresses, and a factory was located atop Volcanoes. But *pulu* breaks down and forms a very fine dust after a few years, so it never really became generally accepted for mattresses.

At high altitudes young ferns and other plants will often produce new growth that turns a bright red as protection against the sun's ultraviolet rays. You'll see it on new foliage before it hardens. Hawaiians called this new growth *liko.* Still today, people will make lei from *liko* because it has so many subtle and beautiful colors. *Ohia liko* is a favorite for leis because it is so striking.

BIRDS

You'll spot birds all over the Big Island, from the coastal areas to the high mountain slopes. Some are found on other islands as well, but the ones listed below are found only or mainly on the Big Island. Every bird listed is either threatened or endangered.

Hawaii's Own

The *nene,* or Hawaiian goose, is Hawaii's state bird and is making a comeback from the edge of extinction. The *nene* is found only on the slopes of Mauna Loa, Hualalai, and Mauna Kea on the Big Island, and in Haleakala Crater on Maui. It was extinct on Maui until a few birds were returned there in 1957, but some experts maintain that *nene* lived naturally only on the Big Island. *Nene* are raised at the Wildfowl Trust in Slimbridge, England, which placed the first birds at Haleakala, and at the Hawaiian Fish and Game Station at Pohakuloa, along the Saddle Road on Hawaii. Good places to view *nene* are in Volcanoes Park at Kipuka Nene Campground (see p. 647), and at Volcanoes Golf Course, at dawn and dusk, where they gather because they love to feed on grasses. The places to view them on the Kona side is at Puulani, a housing development north of Kailua-Kona, or you can drive up the slopes of Mt.Hualalai, where you'll find Kaloka Mauka, another housing development. At the top of the road is a trail, a good place to see *nene.* Unfortunately, as the housing developments proliferate and the residents invariably acquire dogs and cats, the *nene* will disappear. The *nene* is a perfect symbol for Hawaii: let it be, and it will live.

The **Hawaiian crow,** or *alala,* is reduced to less than 200 birds living on the slopes of Hualalai and Mauna Loa above the 3,000-foot level. They look like a common raven, but they have a more melodious voice and sometimes dull brown feathers. They breed in early spring and the greenish-blue, black-flecked eggs hatch from April to June. They are extremely nervous while nesting and any disturbance will cause them to abandon their young.

The **Hawaiian hawk** (*'io*) primarily lives on the slopes of Mauna Loa and Mauna Kea below 9,000 feet. It travels from there to other parts of the island and can often be seen kiting in the skies over Volcanoes National Park, upland

'io

from Kailua-Kona, and in remote spots like Waimanu Valley. These noble birds, the royalty of the skies, symbolized the ali'i. The 'io population was dwindling, and it was feared by many scientists that they were headed for extinction. The hawk exists only on the Big Island for reasons that are not entirely clear. The good news is that the 'io is making a dramatic comeback, also for reasons that are still unclear. Speculation has it that they may be gaining resistance to some diseases, including malaria, or they may have learned how to prey on the introduced rats, or even that they may be adapting to life in macadamia nut groves and other alternate habitats.

The *akiapola'au* is a five-inch yellow bird hardly bigger than its name. It lives mainly on the eastern slopes of *ohia* and *koa* forests above 3,500 feet. It has a long curved upper beak for probing and a smaller lower beak that it uses woodpecker-fashion. *Akiapola'au* open their mouths quite wide, strike the wood with their lower beak,and then use the upper beak to scrape out any larvae or insects. Listen for the distinctive rapping sound to spot this melodious singer. The *akiapola'au* can be spotted at the Hakelau Fish and Wildlife preserve, also south of Power Line Road off the Saddle Road, and along the Puu O'o Volcano Trail from Volcanoes Park.

Marine Birds

Two coastal birds that breed on the high slopes of Hawaii's volcanoes and feed on the coast are the **Hawaiian petrel** ('ua'u) and the **Newell shearwater** ('a'o). The 'ua'u lives on the barren high slopes and craters, where it nests in burrows or under stones. Breeding season lasts from mid-March to mid-October. Only one chick is born and nurtured on regurgitated squid and fish. Ua'u suffer heavily from predation. The 'a'o prefers the forested slopes of the interior. They breed from April to November, and spend their days at sea and nights inland. Feral cats and dogs reduce their numbers considerably.

Forest Birds

The following birds are found in the upland forests of the Big Island. The **elepaio** is found on other islands but is also spotted in Volcanoes Park. This long-tailed (often held upright), five-inch brown bird (appearance can vary considerably), can be coaxed to come within touching distance of the observer. Sometimes it will sit on lower branches above your head and scold you. The elepaio was the special aumakua of canoe builders in ancient lore. They're fairly common in the rainforest, and are basically a flycatcher.

The **i'iwi** is an endemic bird not endangered at the moment. This bright red bird with a salmon-colored hooked bill is found on Hawaii in the forests above 2,000 feet. The i'iwi can be spotted at the top of Kaloka Mauka, a housing development north of Kailua-Kona, at the Power Line Road, which goes south off the Saddle Road, and at Puu'Oo Trail in Volcanoes Park. Just listen for its harsh squeaking-hinge voice.

The **apapane** is abundant on Hawaii, especially atop Volcanoes, and being the most common native bird, is the easiest to see. It's a chubby red-bodied bird about five inches long with a black bill, legs, wingtips, and tail feathers. It's quick, flitty, and has a wide variety of calls and songs, from beautiful warbles to mechanical buzzes. Its feathers were sought by Hawaiians for fashioning into distinctive capes and helmets for the ali'i.

The **Hawaiian thrush** (oma'o) is a fairly common bird found above 3,000 feet in the windward forests of Hawaii. This eight-inch gray bird is a good singer, often seen perching with distinctive drooping wings and a shivering body.

The oma'o, is probably descended from the Townsend's Solitaire. The best place to look for them is at the Thurston Lava Tube (see p. 643) where you can see them doing their baby-bird shivering and shaking act. They are great mimics, and can sound like a cat, or even like an old-fashioned radio with stations changing as you turn the dial. Another good place to see them is along Power Line Road, off the Saddle Road.

The **akepa** is a four- to five-inch bird. The male is a brilliant orange to red, the female a drab green and yellow. They're found mainly on Hualalai and in windward forests.

The six-inch bright yellow **palila** is found only on Hawaii in the forests of Mauna Kea above 6,000 feet. They depend exclusively upon mamane trees for survival, eating the pods, buds, and flowers. However, mamane seedlings are destroyed by feral sheep. The Department of Land and Natural Resources for some inexplicable reason attempted to introduce sheep on the land that is the main refuge for the palilia, which greatly endangered the bird's survival (see p. 644 for details).

The **po'ouli**, is a dark brown, five-inch bird with a black mask and dark brown feet. Its tail is short and it sports a conical bill. It was saved from extinction through efforts of the Sierra Club and Audubon Society, who successfully had it listed as the newest addition to the Federal List of Endangered Species. The bird has one remaining stronghold on Puu Ula ula, a peak just off the Saddle Road that rises to 7,421 feet. The best way to get there is to follow a dirt road from the hunter's check-in cabin, which is near the Kilohana Girl Scout Camp. The dirt road is suitable for walking or 4WD only. It's a long strenuous walk, covering three to four miles with a stiff elevation gain all along the way.

MAMMALS AND OTHERS

Hawaii had only two indigenous land mammals, the monk seal and the hoary bat. The latter is found only on Hawaii in any great numbers. The remainder of the Big Island's mammals are transplants. But like anything else, including people, that have been in the islands long enough, they take on characteristics that make them "local."

Drosophila, the Hawaiian Fly

Most people pay little attention to a fly unless it pesters them by landing on their plate lunch. But geneticists from throughout the world, and especially from the Univeristy of Hawaii, make a special pilgrimage to the Volcano area of the Big Island and to Maui just to study the native Hawaiian *drosophila*. These critters are related to fruit flies and house flies, but there are hundreds of native species that are unique. The Hawaiian ecosystem is very simple and straightforward, so geneticists can trace the evolutionary changes from species to subspecies through mating behavior. The scientists compare the species between the two islands, and chart the differences. Major discoveries in evolutionary genetics have been made through these studies.

Hawaii's Animals

The following animals are found primarily on the Big Island. The **Hawaiian hoary bats** *(ope 'ape'a)* are cousins to Mainland bats, strong fliers that made it to Hawaii eons ago, where they developed their own species. Their tails have a whitish coloration, hence their name. They are found on Maui and Kauai, but mostly on the Big Island, where they have been spotted even on the upper slopes of Mauna Loa and Mauna Kea. They have a 13-inch wingspan, and unlike other bats, are solitary creatures, roosting in trees. They give birth to twins in early summer and can often be spotted over Hilo and Kealakekua bays just around sundown.

Feral dogs *(ilio)* are found on all the islands, but especially on the slopes of Mauna Kea, where packs chase feral sheep. Poisoned and shot by local ranchers, their numbers are diminishing. Black dogs, thought to be more tender, are still eaten in some Hawaiian and Filipino communities.

Feral sheep are escaped descendants of animals first brought to the islands by Capt. Vancouver in the 1790s and merinos, brought to the island later and raised for their exceptional woolly fleece. They exist only on the Big Island, on the upper slopes of Mauna Loa, Mauna Kea, and Hualalai; by the 1930s their numbers topped 40,000. The fleece is a buff brown, and their two-foot-wide recurved horns are often sought as hunting trophies. Feral sheep are responsible for the overgrazing of young *mamane*

trees, necessary to the endangered bird, *palila*. In 1979, a law was passed to exterminate or remove the sheep from Mauna Kea, so that the native *palila* could survive.

Mouflon sheep were introduced to Lanai and Hawaii to cut down on overgrazing and serve as trophy animals. These Mediterranean sheep can interbreed with the feral sheep and produce a hybrid. They live on the upper slopes of Mauna Loa and Mauna Kea. Unfortunately, their introduction has not been a success. No evidence concludes that the smaller family groups of mouflon cause less damage than the herding feral sheep, and hunters reportedly don't like the meat as much as feral mutton.

Feral donkeys, better known as "Kona nightingales," came to Hawaii as beasts of burden. Domesticated ones are found on all islands, but a few wild herds still roam the Big Island along the Kona coast, especially near the exclusive Kona Village Resort at Kaupulehu.

Feral cattle were introduced by Captain Vancouver, who gave a few domesticated head to Kamehameha; immediately a *kapu* against killing them went into effect for 10 years. The lush grasses of Hawaii were perfect, and the cattle flourished; by the early 1800s they were out of control and were hunted and exterminated. Finally, Mexican cowboys were brought to Hawaii to teach the local men how to be range hands. From this legacy sprang the Hawaiian *paniolo*.

Humpback whales migrate to Hawaiian waters yearly, arriving in late December and departing by mid-March. The best places to view them are along the South Kona coast, especially at Kealakekua Bay and Ka Lae ("South Point"), with many sightings off the Puna coast around Isaac Hale Beach Park.

BILLFISH

Although these magnificent game fish occur in various South Sea and Hawaiian waters, catching them is easiest in the clear, smooth waters off the Kona Coast. Billfish are commonly called swordfish, sailfish, marlin, and *a'u.* Their distinctive features are the long, spear-like or swordlike snout and prominent dorsal fin. The three main billfishes caught are the blue, striped, and black marlin. Of these the **blue marlin** is the leading game fish in Kona waters. The blue has tipped the scales at well over 1,000 pounds, but the average fish weighs in at 300 to 400 pounds. When alive this fish is a striking cobalt blue, but death brings on a color change to slate blue. They feed on skipjack tuna; throughout the summer, fishing boats look for schools of tuna as a tip-off to blues in the area. The **black marlin** is the largest and most coveted catch for blue-water anglers. This solitary fish is infrequently found in the banks off Kona. Granddaddies can weigh 1,800 pounds, but the average is a mere 200. The **striped marlin** is the most common commercial billfish, a highly prized food served in finer restaurants and often sliced into sashimi. Their coloration is a remarkable royal blue, and their spectacular leaps when caught give them a great reputation as fighters. Smaller than the other marlins, a 100-pounder is a very good catch. For more information see p. 647.

THE HAKALAU FOREST NATIONAL WILDLIFE REFUGE

The Hakalau Forest National Wildlife Refuge, tel. 969-9909, is a joint effort of the Nature Conservancy and the U.S. Fish and Wildlife Service who have acquired a large tract of rainforest off the Saddle Road that goes all the way up to the Parker Ranch lands. The topography is comprised of upland forest and scrub that drifts down into solid rainforest. These two agencies are working hand-in-hand to reconvert this area into natural habitat. Efforts include fencing, ridding

the area of cattle, pigs, feral dogs, and cats, and replanting with *koa* while removing introduced and exotic foliage. It's a tremendous task that's mainly being shouldered by Dick Watts and his helper, John Emig, rangers with the U.S. Fish and Wildlife Service. The refuge is not adequately staffed to accept visits by the general public at this time. Exceptions are made for working scientists or people who would like to volunteer for an ongoing project. If you *truly* have a dedication to help and aren't afraid to get your hands dirty, contact Dick for a very rewarding experience. The logistics of setting up your visit require that you be willing to work for at least an entire day in physically demanding conditions. The refuge is very beautiful, a diamond in the rough, and encompasses an incredible rainforest unlike any on the Big Island.

HISTORY OF THE ANTHURIUM

It was originally a native of Central America. Introduced into Hawaii in 1889 by Samuel M. Damon, an English missionary who discovered that Hawaii's climate and volcanic soil was an ideal environment for this exotic flower. Over the years since then, anthurium production has turned into a million-dollar export industry with all the major growers located on the Big Island.

HISTORY

The Big Island plays a significant role in Hawaii's history. A long list of "firsts" have occurred here. Historians generally believe (backed up by oral tradition) that the Big Island was first to be settled by the Polynesians. The dates now used are from A.D. 600 to 700. Hawaii is geographically the closest island to Polynesia; Mauna Loa and especially Mauna Kea, with its white summit, present an easily spotted landmark. Psychologically, the Polynesian wayfarers would have been very attracted to Hawaii as a lost homeland. Compared to Tahiti and most other South Sea Islands (except for Fiji), it's huge. It *looked* like the "promised land." Some may wonder why

the Polynesians chose to live atop an obviously active volcano, and not bypass it for a more congenial island. The volcanism of the Big Island is comparatively gentle, and the lava flows follow predictable routes and rarely turn killer. The animistic Hawaiians would have been drawn to live where the godly forces of nature were so apparent. The mana would be exceptionally strong, and therefore the *ali'i* would be great. Tahitians eclipsed this power and introduced human sacrifice to Hawaii at Wahaula Heiau in the Puna District in the 13th century, and from there *luakini* (human sacrifice temples) spread throughout the islands.

The Great One

The greatest native son of Hawaii, Kamehameha, was born under mysterious circumstances in the Kohala District, probably in 1753. He was royal born to Keoua Kupuapaikalaninui, the chief of Kohala, and Kekuiapoiwa, a chieftess from Kona. Accounts vary, but one claims that before his birth, a *kahuna* prophesized that this child would grow to be a "killer of chiefs." Because of this, the local chiefs conspired to murder the infant. When Kekuiapoiwa's time came, she secretly went to the royal birthing stones near Mookini Heiau and delivered Kamehameha. She entrusted her baby to a manservant, and instructed him to hide the child. He headed for the rugged and remote coast around Kapaau. Here Kamehameha was raised in the mountains, mostly by men. Always alone, he earned the nickname "The Lonely One."

Regardless of the circumstances surrounding his birth, Kamehameha did become a renowned warrior and a loyal retainer to his uncle, Kalaniopuu, the *moi* of Hawaii. With Kalaniopuu, he boarded Capt. Cook's ship and sailed from Maui to Hawaii, and speculation has it that he was with his uncle when Cook was killed at Kealakekua Bay. Before Kalaniopuu died, he called a council at Waipio Valley and there named his weak and ineffectual son Kiwalao king. He also made Kamehameha the keeper of the feathered family war-god, Kukailimoku, or Ku the Land Snatcher. Kiwalao and his half-brother Keoua engaged in a civil war over land rights. Kamehameha, aided by disgruntled chiefs from Kona, waged war on both, and at Mokuohai Kiwalao was killed. Kamehameha went on to fight on Maui. By this time he had acquired a small ship, the *Fair American,* and with the help of cannon manned by two white sailors, Isaac Davis and John Young, he defeated the Maui warriors at Iao Valley. If he could defeat Keoua at home, he would be king of all Hawaii.

The Gods Speak

A great oracle from Kauai announced that war would end on Hawaii only after a great *heiau* was built at Puukohala, dedicated by the corpse of a great chief. Kamehameha instantly set about building this *heiau,* and through cunning, wisdom, and true belief placed the conquest of Hawaii in the hands of the gods. Meanwhile, a great fleet of war canoes belonging to Kahekili of

Maui attacked Kamehameha's forces at Waimanu, near Waipio. Aided again by the *Fair American* and Davis and Young, Kamehameha won a decisive battle and subdued Kahekili once and for all. Keoua seized this opportunity to ravage Kamehameha's lands all the way from Waipio to Hilo. He sent his armies south through Kau, but when the middle legions were passing the foot of Kilauea, it erupted and suffocated them with poisonous gas and a heavy deposit of ash. Footprints, encased in the cement-like ash, still mark their last steps.

Kamehameha and Keoua both took this as a direct sign from the gods. Kamehameha returned to Puukohala and finished the *heiau.* Upon completion he summoned Keoua, who came by canoe with a small band of warriors resplendent in feather helmet and cape. He knew the fate that awaited him, and when he stepped ashore he was slaughtered by Keeaumoku. Keoua's body was laid on the altar, and at that moment the islands of Hawaii were united under one supreme ruler, Kamehameha, The Lonely One. He ruled until his death in 1819, and his passing marked the beginning of the end for old Hawaii.

Great Changes

The great navigator and explorer, Captain Cook, was killed at Kealakekua Bay on February 14, 1779. Kalaniopuu was still alive at the time and Kamehameha was only a minor chief, although Cook had previously written about him in the ship's log when he came aboard off Maui. During Kamehameha's reign ships from America, England, and various European countries came to trade. Americans monopolized the lucrative sandalwood business with China, and New England whalers discovered the rich whaling waters. The Englishman, Captain Vancouver, became a trusted advisor of Kamehameha and told him about the white man's form of worship, while introducing plants and animals such as oranges, grapes, cows, goats, and sheep. He even interceded for Kamehameha with his headstrong queen, Kaahumanu, and coaxed her out from her hiding place under a rock, when she sought refuge at Pu'uhonua o Honaunau.

When Kamehameha died in 1819, Hawaii was ripe for change. His two great queens, Kaahumanu and Keopuolani, realized that the old ways were coming to an end. They en-

SENATORIAL DISTRICTS

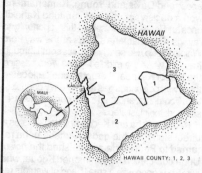

HAWAII COUNTY: 1, 2, 3

HOUSE DISTRICTS

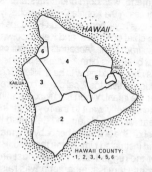

HAWAII COUNTY: 1, 2, 3, 4, 5, 6

couraged Liholiho (Kamehameha II) to end the *kapu* system. Men and women were forbidden to eat together, and those that violated this principal *kapu* were immediately killed to placate the gods before they retaliated with grave destruction. Keopuolani defied this belief when she sat down with Kauikeaouli, the seven-year-old brother of Liholiho. The gods remained quiet. Encouraged, Liholiho called for a great luau at Kailua, and openly sat down to eat with his chiefs and chieftesses. Symbolically, the impotent gods were toppled with every bite, and *heiau* and idols were razed throughout the land.

Into this spiritual vortex sailed the **Brig Thaddeus** on April 4, 1820. They had set sail from Boston on October 23, 1819, lured to the Big Island by Henry Opukahaia, a local boy born at Napoopoo in 1792. Coming ashore at Kailua, the first missionary packet convinced Liholiho to give them a one-year trial period. Hawaii changed forever in those brief months. By 1824 the new faith had such a foothold that Chieftess Keopuolani climbed to the firepit atop Kilauea and defied Pele. This was even more striking than the previous breaking of the food *kapu* because the strength of Pele could actually be seen. Keopuolani ate forbidden *ohelo* berries and cried out "Jehovah is my God." Over the next decades the governing of Hawaii slipped

away from the Big Island and moved to the new port cities of Lahaina, and later, Honolulu. In 1847, the Parker Ranch began with a two-acre grant given to John Parker. He coupled this with 360 acres given to his *ali'i* wife Kipikane by the land division known as the Great *Mahele*.

GOVERNMENT

The county of Hawaii is almost entirely Democratic with a token Republican state senator or representative here and there. Of the 25 State Senatorial Districts, Hawaii County is represented by three. The First District is the whole southern part of the island, from Puna to Kailua; its representative is one of the few Republicans holding office on the island. The Second District is mainly Hilo, and the Third District takes in the whole northern section and is a shared district with East Maui. The combination of these two areas has been traditional, even from old Hawaiian times.

Of 51 seats in the State House of Representatives, Hawaii County has six. The Sixth District is again shared with East Maui and takes in most of South Kohala. At this time, all representatives are Democrats, except for a Republican representing Kailua-Kona, Fifth District.

ECONOMY

The Big Island's economy is the most agriculturally based county in the state. Over 6,000 farmhands, horticultural workers and *paniolo* work the land, producing over half of the state's vegetables and melons, and over 75% of the fruit, leading all other islands especially in papayas. The Big Island also produces 33 million pounds of macadamia nuts, all the state's production, except for a small farm here and there on the other islands. The Big Island is also awash in color and fragrance as 300 or more horticultural farms produce the largest number of orchids and anthuriums in the state.

Sugar

Hawaii is the state's largest sugar cane grower with over 90,000 acres in cane. These produce four million tons of refined sugar, 40% of the state's output. The majority of sugar land is along the Hamakua Coast, long known for its abundant water supply. At one time, the cane was even transported to the mills by water flumes. Another large pocket of cane fields is in the southern part of the island, mostly in Puna.

Coffee

The Kona District is a splendid area for raising coffee; it gives the beans a beautiful tan. Lying in Mauna Loa's rain shadow, it gets dewy mornings followed by sunshine, and an afternoon cloud shadow. Kona coffee has long been accepted as gourmet quality, and is sold in the better restaurants throughout Hawaii and in fine coffee shops around the world. It's a dark full-bodied coffee with a rich aroma. Approximately 650 small farms produce nearly $4 million dollars a year in coffee revenue. Few however make it a full-time business.

Cattle

Hawaii's cattle ranches produce over 18 million pounds of beef per year, 65% of the state's total. More than 360 independant ranches are on the island, but they are dwarfed both in size and pro-

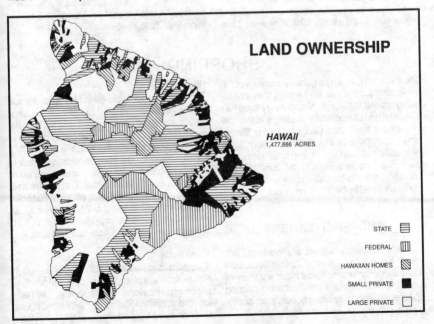

LAND OWNERSHIP

HAWAII
1,477,886 ACRES

STATE

FEDERAL

HAWAIIAN HOMES

SMALL PRIVATE

LARGE PRIVATE

duction by the massive Parker Ranch, which alone is three-quarters the size of Oahu.

The Military
There are just under 200 Army personnel on the island, with about the same number of dependants. Most of these people are attached to the enormous Pohakuloa Military Reserve in the center of the island. There are also a few minor installations around Hilo and at Kilauea.

Tourism
Over 3,000 island residents are directly employed by the hotel industry, and many more indirectly serve the tourists. There are slightly more than 7,000 hotel rooms, with the greatest concentration in Kona. They have the lowest occupancy rate in the state, which rarely rises above 60%. Of the major islands, Hawaii receives the fewest tourists annually, only about 7,000 on any given day.

PEOPLE

With 93,000 people, the Big Island has the second largest island population in Hawaii, just under 10% of the state's total. However, it has

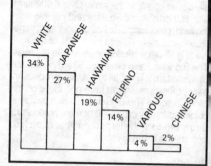

HAWAII POPULATION

WHITE 34%
JAPANESE 27%
HAWAIIAN 19%
FILIPINO 14%
VARIOUS 4%
CHINESE 2%

the smallest population density of the main islands, with only 23 people per square mile. Hilo has the largest population with 36,000 residents, followed by Kailua with barely 5,000, and Captain Cook with 2,000 or so. The ethnic breakdown of the 93,000 people is as follows: 34% white, 27% Japanese, 19% Hawaiian, 14% Filipino, 2% Chinese, 4% other.

SHOPPING

The following is merely a general overview of the main shopping areas and where they are located around the island. Almost every town has at least a gas station and a market, and they will be listed in the Travel Chapters under "Shopping." Look there for directions and descriptions of specific malls, art shops, and boutiques in the area. Supermarkets, health food stores, and local markets are in the individual travel chapters, generally listed in the "Food and Drink" section.

SHOPPING CENTERS

General shopping centers are found in Hilo, Kailua-Kona, Waimea, and Captain Cook. Like most shopping malls, these have a variety of stores with usually one establishment offering apparel, dry goods, sporting goods, food, photography supplies, or outdoor rentals.

Hilo Malls
The main shopping center in Hilo is the **Prince Kuhio Plaza,** at 111 E. Puainako. This shoppers' paradise is Hilo's newest and the island's largest shopping mall. An older but still full-service shopping center is the **Kaiko'o Mall** at 777 Kilauea Avenue. The **Hilo Shopping Center** is about one-half mile south on Kilauea Avenue at the corner of Kekuanoa Street. This smaller mall has only a handful of local shops. **Puainako Town Center** is located at 2100 Kanoelehua Avenue. **Waiakea Shopping Plaza** at 100 Kanoelehua Ave. has a small clutch of stores.

Kona Malls
Two commodities that you're guaranteed in Kailua-Kona are plenty of sunshine and plenty of shopping. The **Kona Inn Shopping Village** is located in central Kailua at 75-5744 Alii Drive and has more than 40 shops selling everything

from fabrics to fruits. The **World Square** is smaller and just across the road. The **Kona Banyan Court,** also in central Kailua, has a dozen shops with a medley of goods and services. The **Kailua Bay Inn Plaza** is along Alii Drive, the **Akona Kai Mall** is across from Kailua Pier, while the **Kona Coast Shopping Plaza** and the **Kona Shopping Center** are both along Palani Road. The **Lanihau Center,** at 75-5595 Palani Rd., tel. 329-9333, is one of Kailua-Kona's newest shopping additions. The **Hotel Kamehameha Mall** is an exclusive shopping haven on the first floor of the hotel, while the **Rawson Plaza,** at 74-5563 Kaiwi St., is in the industrial area and offers bargains. **Waterfront Row** is a new shopping and food complex at the south end of downtown Kailua-Kona that's done in period architecture with rough-cut lumber.

The **Keauhou Shopping Village** is conveniently located at the corner of Alii Dr. and Kamehameha III Road at the far end of Kailua-Kona. Here you'll find everything from a P.O. to a supermarket. Continuing south on Route 11 you'll spot the **Kainaliu Village Mall** along the main drag.

The **Kealakekua Ranch Center,** in Captain Cook, is a two-story mall with fashions, and general supplies.

Waimea (Kamuela) Malls

After the diversity of shopping malls in Kailua and Hilo, it's like a breath of fresh air to have only one choice. In Waimea try the **Parker Ranch Shopping Center** which has over 30 shops, including a pharmacy, grocery and general merchandise. A small herd of shops in this center also feature ranch and western-wear with a Hawaiian twist. **Parker Square Shopping Mall,** along Route 19 heading west, has a collection of fine boutiques and shops. The **Opelo Plaza** also along Route 19 heading west is one of Waimea's newest shopping malls.

BOOKSTORES

Two aspects of a quality vacation are knowing what you're doing and thoroughly relaxing while doing it. Nothing helps you do this better than a good book. The following stores offer a full selection.

Hilo has excellent bookstores. **Basically Books** downtown at 169 Keawe St., tel. 961-0144, is a print shop-plus with a good selection of Hawaiiana and an unbeatable selection of maps. The **Book Gallery** is a full-selection bookstore featuring Hawaiiana, hardcover, and paperbacks. They're at the Kaikoo Mall, open daily, tel. 935-2447. At **Serendipity Bookstore** you might stumble over some interesting discoveries, as the name implies. Look for this complete bookstore at the Puainako Town Center. Open daily, tel. 959-5841. **Bookfinders of Hawaii,** at 150 Haili St., tel. 961-5055, specializes in hard-to-find and out-of-print books. If you want it, they'll get it. Hilo has excellent bookstores.

Kailua Kona bookstores include **Waldenbooks,** in the Lanihau Center on Palani Rd., tel. 329-0015; **Middle Earth Bookshop** at 75-5719 Alii Ave., in the Kona Plaza Shopping Arcade, tel. 329-2123; the **Keauhou Village Bookshop** at the Keauhou Shopping Village, tel. 322-8111, open 9-9 Mon.-Fri., 9-6 Sat., 9-5 Sunday.

Waimea offers books at the **Waimea General Store,** located at the **Parker Square Shopping Mall,** open daily 9 a.m. to 5 p.m., Sun. 10 a.m. to 4 p.m., tel. 885-4479.

SPECIALTY SHOPS, ART, AND NEAT THINGS

You can stroll in and out of flower shops, T-shirt factories, and a panoply of boutiques offering ceramics, paintings, carvings and all manner of island handicrafts. Art and Craft shops are always a part of the Big Island's shopping malls, and in even the smallest village you can count on at least one local artist displaying his or her creations. The following list of artists and shops is by no means exhaustive, but for the most part, they are in out-of-the-way places and worth a visit. Art shops and boutiques in particular areas will be covered in the travel sections under "Shopping."

In Hilo **Kamaaina Crafts,** 1477 Kalanianaole Ave., tel. 935-4957, sells handmade crafts from the Big Island. **Hawaiian Handicrafts** at 760 Kilauea Ave., tel. 935-5587, specializes in woodcarvings. **Halemanu Crafts** is a shop at 195 Kinole St. where senior citizens from the Hilo

ipu, *a drum used to accompany hula*

area display their fine *lau hala* weavings. **Sugawara Lauhala and Gift Shop,** at 59 Kalakaua St., is a virtually unknown Hilo institution making genuine *lau hala* weavings. **Sig Zane Design,** at 140 Kilauea Ave., tel. 935-7077, is one of the most distinctive shops on the island, where owner and designer Sig Zane creates unique island wearables. **The Potter's Gallery,** at 95 Waianuenue Ave., tel. 935-4069, is a fascinating shop featuring contemporary works by Hawaiian artists and craftspeople.

While heading up the Hamakua Coast make sure to visit the **The Crystal Grotto** in Honomu which sells new age gifts, jewelry, metaphysical books, minerals, crystals, and rock specimens. If you are at all interested in the history of Hawaii, stop at **The Hawaiian Artifacts Shop** along the main drag in downtown Honokaa. **Waipio Woodworks** in Kukuihaele, tel. 775-0958, showcases exclusive artworks of distinguished island artists.

Pahoa Arts and Crafts Guild, in Pahoa Village, is an artists' co-op that has recently opened. They display paintings, scarves, sculptures, and jewelry, all made on the island.

If you are after an exquisite piece of art, a unique memento, or an inexpensive but distinctive souvenir, make sure to visit the **Volcano Art Center** in Volcano National Park.

In Kailua-Kona's Hotel King Kamehameha the **Tribal Arts Gallery** sells carvings, jewelry, and fabrics from exotic lands throughout the Pacific Basin. In the World Square Shopping Center visit the **Showcase Gallery** with its offerings of glasswork, beadwork, featherwork, enameling, and shell leis from the islands, mostly from the Big Island. Across the way the **Coral Isle Art Shop** presents modern versions of traditional Hawaiian carvings. **Collectors Fine Art** in the Kona Inn Shopping Village is a perfect labyrinth of rooms and hallways showcasing fine art from around the world. Here too, **Crystal Visions** has incense, perfume, metaphysical books, and the channelling of personal and cosmic vibrations through its large selection of crystals, crystal balls, and pyramids. **Kona Inn Jewelry,** for world treasures, is one of the oldest and best-known shops for a square deal in Kona. **Alapaki's,** at Waterfront Row, sells traditional island arts and crafts. **The Glass Blower,** across from the seawall along Likana Lane, is a very interesting shop where you can watch the artist actually blowing the glass.

The mountain village of Holualoa has become an artists' haven. As you enter the village you'll spot **Kimura's Lauhala Shop,** that has been selling and producing their famous *lau hala* hats ever since local weavers began bartering their creations for groceries in 1915. In town you'll find a converted coffee mill, gaily painted and decorated, that's the home of the **Kona Art Center,** a community art-cooperative run by Robert and Carol Rogers since 1965. The premier shop in town, **Studio 7,** is owned and operated by Hiroki Morinoue, who studied at the Kona Art Gallery as a young man. The shop showcases Hiroki's work along with that of about 35 Big Island artists, including famous *raku* potter Chiu Leong. A separate shop in the same building is **Goldsmithing by Sam Rosen,** with unusual one-of-a-kind works mostly in gold, silver, and precious stones.

In the nearby villages of Kainalu look for **The Blue Ginger Gallery,** tel. 322-3898, that displays the art of owners Jill and David Bever, as well as artists' works from all over the island. **Elizabeth Harris and Co.** in Kealakekua, tel. 323-2447, displays shirts, T-shirts, and dresses that are made by 13 local seamstresses and artists. The **Kahanahou Hawaiian Foundation,** tel. 322-3901, is along the road in Kealakekua. They deal in ancient Hawaiian handicrafts, including masks, hula drums, and hula accouterments.

The Little Grass Shack is an institution in Kealakekua. It looks like a tourist trap, but don't let that stop you from going in and finding some authentic souvenirs, most of which come from the surrounding area. **Tropical Temptations,** tel. 326-2007, in Kealakekua turns the best available grade of local fruits, nuts, and coffee beans into delicious candies. **Country Store Antiques** is next door to the Manago Hotel, just as you're entering Captain Cook. Owned and operated by E.L. Mahre, it's filled to the brim with kerosene lamps, dolls, glassware, old bottles, and Hawaiian antique jewelry.

Along the north shore in Kapaau across from the Kamehameha statue is **Ackerman Gallery,** where you'll find the work of artist Gary Ackerman along with displays of local pottery, carvings, and one-of-a-kind jewelry.

Hana Koa is a woodworking shop owned by artist Don Wilkinson. Don, a friendly storehouse of information, lives along Route 250 heading into Hawi from Waimea. Another local artist is **David Gomes,** a guitar and ukulele maker who works in koa. His small shop is located about a half mile on the Kapaau side of the junction of Routes 270 and 250.

In the *paniolo* town of Waimea you can pick up downhome cowboy items or sophisticated artwork at the following shops. At the **Parker Ranch Center,** the **Paddock Shop** sells boots, cowboy hats, shirts, skirts, and buckles and bows. **Nikko Natural Fabrics,** in the Kamuela Country Plaza, will dress you in cottons, woollens, and silks, and adorn your walls with batiks and fine fiber arts, tel. 885-7661. In the **Parker Square Center,** along Route 19, the **Gallery of Great Things,** tel. 885-7706, really is loaded with great things—everything from a carousel horse to *koa* hair sticks. Here too, **Gifts in Mind** has novelty items, and a very good selection of aloha shirts and dresses; **Mango Ranch** sells duds for cowpokes, including bow ties, fancy shirts, and cowboy hats. Across the road **Kamaaina Woods** sells locally created wood-handicrafts.

GETTING THERE

Almost all travelers to the Big Island arrive by air. A few lucky ones come by private yacht, and in season the cruise ship SS *Constitution* docks in Hilo on Sunday mornings, then sails around the island to Kailua. For the rest, the island's two major airports are at Hilo and Kailua-Kona, with a few secondary strips here and there. Almost every flight to the Big Island has a stopover, mostly in Honolulu, but it's efficient and at no extra cost. The following should help you plan your arrival.

THE AIRPORTS

The largest and only international airport on the Big Island is **Hilo International Airport,** tel. 935-0809, which services Hilo and the eastern half of the island. It's a modern facility with full amenities and its runways can handle all jumbo jets. The two-story terminal has an information center, restaurant, a number of vendors, including lei shops, and lockers. Most major car rental agen-

cies have a booth outside the terminal; a taxi for the three-mile ride to town costs about $6.50. This airport features 20 acres of landscaped flowers and an assortment of fountains and waterfalls supplied by rainwater collected on the terminal's roof.

Keahole Airport, tel. 329-2484, is nine miles north of Kailua-Kona and handles the air traffic for Kona. The terminal is designed as a series of open-sided Polynesian-style buildings. Here too are lockers, food, visitor information, various vendors, and most car rental agencies. The Gray Line limousine can take you to Kailua for under $10, while a private cab to your hotel is $15 or more.

Waimea-Kohala Airport, tel. 885-4520, is just outside Waimea (Kamuela). There are few amenities and no public transportation to town. **Upolu Airport,** tel. 889-9958, is a lonely strip on the extreme northern tip of the island, with no facilities whatsoever. Both are serviced only on request by small charter airlines.

Nonstop Flights

United Airlines operates the only nonstop flight to the Big Island from the Mainland. The San Francisco flight departs daily at 8:50 a.m. and arrives at Keahole Airport on the Kona Coast at 11:16 a.m. In the past during peak season, United has run a flight to Hilo International Airport, but it's an on-and-off affair depending on the number of travelers. It's also interesting to note that most island flights landed at Hilo International Airport in the past. Now, with the Kona Coast gaining popularity, the flights have shifted to that side of the island.

Stopover Flights

All the major carriers have arrangements for getting you to the Big Island. American carriers such as Hawaiian Air, Western, Continental, and American, along with foreign carriers like Canadian Pacific, Qantas, and Japan Airlines land at Honolulu. There they have an inter-line agreement with island carriers, including Hawaiian Air, and Aloha Airlines, which then take you to the Big Island. This sometimes involves a plane change, but your baggage can be booked straight through. Hawaiian Air has expanded to Mainland flights from San Francisco and Los Angeles, with connecting flights in Honolulu to Kona. They offer the added convenience of dealing with just one airline.

Inter-island Carriers

Getting to and from the Big Island from the other islands is easy and convenient. **Hawaiian Air,** tel. (800) 367-5320 nationwide, (800) 882- 8811 statewide, offers the most flights. From Honolulu to Kona, 17 flights are spread throughout the day from 6 a.m. to 6:40 p.m. The same scheduling applies to Hilo, except that there are slightly fewer flights, the last departing Honolulu at 6:55 p.m. Hawaiian Air also offers daily flights from Kauai, Molokai, Lanai, and Maui to both Hilo and

Kona. Most are aboard DC-9 jet aircraft, with some on the four-prop Dash Transits.

Aloha Airlines, tel. (800) 367-5250, 935-5771 Big Island, has the second largest number of flights to Hawaii from the other islands. Their 18 daily Honolulu-Kona runs start at 5:40 a.m. with the last at 7 p.m.; Hilo flights go throughout the day from 5:50 a.m. to 7:15 p.m. They fly from Kauai to Hilo and Kona with a dozen or so flights to each from approximately 6:30 a.m. to 6:30 p.m. Maui flights to Hilo and Kona are much fewer, with usually only four flights per day, two in the morning and two in the afternoon.

Aloha Island Air, tel. (800) 323-3345 nationwide, (800) 652-6541 statewide, offers limited service to Kamuela (Waimea) Airport. Daily scheduled flights are to and from Honolulu, Princeville on Kauai, Kahului, Kapalua, and Hana airports on Maui, and from Molokai, and Lanai. There are three flights from Honolulu, with the first at 6:10 a.m. and the last at 5 p.m. Flights to and from the other destinations are scheduled at one or two per day and often involve a stopover.

Big Island Air, tel. 329-4868, or (800) 367-8047, ext. 207, operates out of Kailua-Kona and has a regularly scheduled flight between Kona and Hilo on the Big Island only. The roundtrip flight leaves and returns daily between 11 a.m. and 12 noon. Check for specifics. Big Island Air also features jet charter service, and flight/see tours around the Big Island.

GETTING AROUND

CAR RENTALS

The first thing to remember when traveling on the Big Island is that it *is* big, over four times larger than Rhode Island. A complete range of vehicles is available for getting around, everything from helicopters to mopeds. Hawaii, like Oahu, has good public transportation. Choose the conveyance that fits your style, and you should have no trouble touring the Big Island.

Car Rental Tips

Renting a car is the best way to tour the island, but keep these few special tips in mind. Most car companies charge you a fee if you rent the car in Hilo and drop it off in Kona, and vice versa. This is usually less than $15, so check. The agencies are prejudiced against the Saddle Road and the spur road leading to South Point, both of which offer some of the *most* spectacular scenery on the island. Their prejudice is unfounded because both roads are paved, generally well-maintained, and no problem if you take your time. They'll claim the insurance will not cover you if you have a mishap on these roads. A good automobile policy at home will cover you in a rental car, but definitely check this before you take off. It's even possible, but not recommended, to drive to the top of Mauna Kea if there is no snow. Plenty of signs to the summit say "4WD Only;" heed them, not so much for going up but for needed braking power coming down. Don't even hint of these intentions to the car rental agencies, or they won't rent you a car.

No way whatsoever should you attempt to drive down to Waipio Valley in a car! The grade is unbelievably steep, and only a 4WD compound first gear can make it. Simply, you have a good chance of being killed if you try it in a car.

Gas stations are farther apart than on the other islands, and sometimes they close very early. As a rule, fill up whenever the gauge reads half full. Both General Lyman Field and Keahole Airport have a gauntlet of car rental booths and courtesy phones outside the terminal.

National Companies

The following are national firms represented at both airports. Kona numbers begin with "3," Hilo with "9." Among the best are **National Car Rent-**al, featuring GM cars, tel. 329-1674 or 935-0891; **Hertz,** tel. 329-3566 or 935-2896; **Dollar,** tel. 329-2744 or 961-6059; **Avis,** tel. 329-1745 or 935-1290; **Budget,** tel. 329- 3581 or 935-9678; and **American International,** tel. 329-2926 or 935-1108.

Local Companies

The following companies have a booth or courtesy phone at the airport. Sometimes, if business is slow, they'll deal on their prices. A local company with an excellent reputation is **Tropical Rent a Car,** tel. (800) 367-5140 nationwide, (800) 352-3923 from the Neighbor Islands, 329-2437 Kona, 935-3385 Hilo. Being based in Hawaii, they can take care of any problem on the spot without hassle. Tropical's personnel go out of their way to make your rental go smoothly by adding that " aloha touch." Prices are very competitive, and they can put you into anything from an economy car with no a/c, to a convertible, Cadillac, or European sports car. Other firms include **Wiki Wiki,** tel. 329-1752 or 935-6861; **Gray Line,** tel. 329-3161 or 935-1654; **Robert's,** tel. 329-1688 or 935-2858; **Phillip's,** tel. 329-1730 or 935-1936; **Marquez,** tel. 329-3411 or 935-2115; **Liberato's,** tel. 329-3035 or 935-8089.

4WD Rentals

To get off the beaten track try: **Hilo Motors,** in Hilo only at tel. 961-1225, for jeeps; **Wiki Wiki,** tel. 329-1752 or 935-5201, for Toyota Land Cruisers, available in Hilo only; **Hawaiian Rent a Jeep,** in Kona only at tel. 329-5077. Most 4WDs rent for approximately $45 per day including mileage.

OTHER ALTERNATIVES

Public Transportation

The county of Hawaii maintains the Mass Transportation System (MTS), known throughout the island as the **Hele-On Bus.** For information, schedules and fares contact the MTS at 25 Aupuni St., Hilo 96720, tel. 961-6722 or 935-8241. The main bus terminal is in downtown Hilo at Mooheau Park, just at the corner of Kamehameha Avenue and Mamo Street. Recently, it's been completely rebuilt and modernized. Like bus terminals everywhere, it has a local franchise of derelicts and down-and-outers, but they leave you alone. What the Hele-On Bus lacks in class, it more than makes up for in *color* and affordability. The Hele-On operates Mon. through Sat. from approximately 6 a.m. to 6 p.m., depending on the run. It goes just about everywhere on the island—sooner or later, but recently many of the routes have been curtailed. If you're in a hurry definitely forget about taking it, but if you want to meet the people of Hawaii, there's no better way. The base fare is $.50, which increases whenever you go into another zone. You can also be charged an extra $1 for a large backpack or suitcase. Don't worry about that—the Hele-On is one of the best bargains in the country. The routes are far too numerous to mention, but one goes from Kealia, south of Captain Cook, through Kailua, and all the way to Hilo on the east coast via Waimea, Honokaa, and Honomu. This sojurn covers 110 miles in just over four hours and costs $6.50, the most expensive fare in the system. You can take the southern route through Kau, passing through Naalehu, Volcanoes, and on to Hilo. This trip takes just over two hours and costs $4.

The county also maintains the **Banyan Shuttle** in Hilo. This bus does five runs Mon. through Fri. from 9 a.m. to 2:55 p.m. The Shuttle costs $.50, but you can buy a $2 pass for one-day unlimited use. The Shuttle runs from the Hukilau Hotel at the end of Banyan Drive to the Mooheau Bus Terminal in downtown Hilo. En route it stops at the better hotels, Puainako Town Center, Hilo, and Kaikoo Malls, Lyman Museum, and Rainbow Falls, where you're allowed 10 minutes for a look.

Kailua-Kona has the **Kailua Kona Shuttle** that cruises Alii Drive. This open-air bus will give you a free shuttle ride from the Kailua Pier to the Hilton Hotel. It runs every half hour from 11:30 a.m. to 8 p.m. from Thurs.-Sat., and from 9 a.m. to 8 p.m. Mon.-Wednesday. (See p. 653)

Taxis
General Lyman Field in Hilo and Keahole Airport north of Kailua always have taxis waiting for fares. From Hilo's airport to downtown costs about $8, and from Keahole to most hotels along Alii Drive in Kailua is $17. Obviously, a taxi is no way to get around if you're trying to save money. Most taxi companies, both in Kona and Hilo, run sightseeing services for a fixed price. In **Kona**

try: Kona Airport Taxi, tel. 329-7779; Paradise Taxi, tel. 329-1234; Marina Taxi, tel. 329-2481. In **Hilo** try: Hilo Harry's, tel. 935-7091; Bob's Taxi, tel. 935-5247; BIA Taxi, tel. 935-8303.

Hitchhiking
The old thumb works on the Big Island about as well as anywhere else. Some people hitchhike rather than take the Hele-On Bus not so much to save money but to save time! It's a good idea to check the bus schedule (and routes), and set out about 30 minutes before the scheduled departure. If you don't have good luck, just wait for the bus to come along and hail it down. It'll stop.

Bicycles
Pedaling around the Big Island can be both fascinating and frustrating. The roads are well paved, but the shoulders are often torn up. With all the triathletes coming to Hawaii, and all the fabulous little-trafficked roads, you'd think Hawaii would be great for a biker! It is, but only if you bring your own. If you intend on renting a bike, your choices are meager. Instead of a delicate road bike, you're better off renting a "cruiser" or "mountain bike" which can handle the sometimes poor road conditions as well as open up the possibilities of off-road biking. Even experienced mountain bikers should be careful on trails, which are often extremely muddy and rutted.

For rentals try the following: **Triple A Mopeds,** tel. 329-0112, in the parking lot near the Kona Hilton in front of Huggo's Restaurant. Prices are $10 all day for a one-speed cruiser. **Hawaiian Pedals** in the Kona Inn Shopping Plaza offers tours, and mountain bikes at $8.50 per day for four-seven days, $10 per day for two-three days, $15 for 24 hours, tandems at $25 per day; **Pacific United Rental,** at 1080 Kilauea Ave., Hilo, tel. 935-2974, with rentals limited to the Hilo area; **Bicycle Warehouse,** 74-5539 Kaiwi Bay 5, Kailua-Kona, tel. 329-9424; **Island Cycle Rentals,** at Jack's Diving Locker at the Kona Inn Plaza, tel. 329-7585.

For info on biking in Hawaii, contact **Hawaii Bicycling League,** Box 4403, Honolulu, HI 96813. This nonprofit corporation publishes a monthly newsletter, *Spoke-n-Words,* filled with tips and suggested rides. For those interested in **bicycle touring,** contact one of the following for their specialized bike trips. **Island Bicycle Ad-**

ventures, 569 Kapahulu Ave., Honolulu, HI 96815, tel. 734-0700, or (800) 233-2226. The owners and tour leaders are intimately familiar with bicycle touring and are members of the Hawaii Bicycling league. They offer tours to Maui, the Big Island, and Kauai. **Backroads Bicycle Touring,** Box 1626, San Leandro, CA 94577, tel. (415) 895-1738 are also experts in the field of bike touring, but at this time only tours of the Big Island are offered.

SIGHTSEEING TOURS

Tours are offered that will literally let you cover the Big Island from top to bottom. You can drive it, fly it, dive below it, or sail around it. For snorkel/scuba, deep sea fishing, and horseback riding tours, see the "Sports And Recreation" chapter.

Booking Agencies
Almost every major hotel has a tour desk that can book you on just the right tour. **Kona Coast Activities,** at the Kona Inn Shopping Village in downtown Kailua, tel. 329-2971, is a general-purpose activity center that can book you on just about anything from sightseeing to sport fishing. **Ohana Activities Desk** at the World Square in downtown Kailua-Kona, tel. 329-0531, is another well-known agency that can help book a tour. In Hilo try **All Around Travel,** tel. 935-2210, for all your touring needs.

Van And Bus Tours
Narrated and fairly tame island tours are operated by **Grayline,** tel. 329-9337 or 935-2835, and **Akamai Tours,** tel. 329-7324. Their small window vans are available for anything from a half-hour tour of Kona for $14 to an all-day circle-island tour for $38.

4WD tours include: **Hawaii Natural History Tours,** tel. 966-7044, whose professional guides take you on coastal, volcanic, or botanical tours; **Paradise Valley,** tel. 329-9282, will take you off-road to just about anywhere you want to go; **Waipio Valley Shuttle,** tel. 775-7121, offers a two-hour tour down to Waipio Valley for $15 (see p. 621).

Paradise Safaris, tel. 329-9282, Box A-D, Kailua-Kona, 96745, owned and operated by Pat Wright, has been taking visitors on high adventure trips around the Big Island for the last

Waipio Valley Shuttle

seven years. Pat, originally from New Mexico, is a professional guide who's plied his trade from the Rockies to New Zealand, and has taken people on trips ranging from mountaineering to white water rafting. Your comfort and safety, as you roam the Big Island, are assured as you ride in sturdy 4WD air-conditioned GMC High Sierra vans. The premier trip offered by Paradise Safaris is an eight-hour sojurn to the top of Mauna Kea. Pat not only fills your trip with stories, anecdotes, and fascinating facts during the ride, but tops off the safari by setting up an eight-inch telescope so you can get a personal view of the heavens through the rarefied atmosphere atop the great mountain. Pat will pick you up at your hotel in Kailua-Kona at about 4 p.m., and if you're staying on the Hilo side will meet you at a predetermined spot along the Saddle Road. The price is $80, with hot savory drinks and good warm parkas included. Paradise Safaris also runs trips to Waipio Valley, Green Sands Beach, and will tailor-fit special trips for photography, hiking, astronomy, and shore fishing.

Helicopter And Air Tours
Air tours are a great way to see the Big Island, but they are expensive especially when the volcano is putting on a mighty display. Expect to

spend a minimum of $135-275 for a front row seat to watch the amazing light show from the air. Kilauea Volcano erupting is like winning the lottery for these small companies, and many will charge whatever the market will bear.

Tip: to get the best view of the volcanic activity, schedule your flight for the morning, and no later than 2 p.m. Later, clouds and fog can set in to obstruct your view.

Volcano Helitours, tel. 967-7578, owned and operated by David Okita, is intimately familiar with the Volcano area. Their heliport sits atop Kilauea and is located just off a fairway of the Volcano Golf and Country Club. Rates are an extremely competitive $105, and because your flight originates atop the volcano, you waste no air time going to or from the eruption sites. The helicoptor is a four passenger (all have windows) Hughes 500D.

Helicopter flights from Hilo International Airport are very competively priced, with savings over the companies operating out of Kailua-Kona. Two good companies include **Hilo Bay Air,** tel. 969-1545, and **Io Aviation,** tel. 935-3031. Also try **Lacy Helicopter,** tel. 885-7272, and **Mauna Kea Helicopters,** tel. 885-6400, which both fly from the small Kamuela Airport in Waimea.

At mile marker 75 along Rt. 19 heading north from Kailu-Kona is the turnoff to Waikaloa Village. Just here is a heliport that services the helicopter companies on the Kona side. One of the major island firms, **Papillon Helicopters,** tel. 329-0551, not only flies from here, but maintains its office here. Prices range from a 45- to 50-minute flight along the Kohala Coast for $130 to a "Pele Spectacular" for $275 that flies over the volcano, dips low over Waipio Valley, and then runs along the Kohala Coast. All seats cost the same price, but the premier seats are up front with the pilot.

Kenai Helicopters, tel. 329-7424, are in direct, but friendly, competition with Papillon. Their prices are about the same, but they do have the advantage of being one of the oldest and most knowledgeable helicopter companies on the Big Island. A ride with Kenai is a once-in-a-lifetime thrill.

For fixed-wing air tours try one of the following: **Big Island Air** offers small plane flights from Keahole Airport, two-person minimum, tel. 329-4868. They fly a circle-island tour that runs two

hours for $135 in a Cessna 402 which holds eight passengers. This tour passes over the volcanic activity. **Hawaii Adventures,** tel. 329-0014, offers sightseeing and photographic tours from Keahole Airport. **Hawaii Pacific Aviation,** tel. 961-5591, will take you topside from Hilo International Airport.

Ocean Tours
Captain Zodiac, tel. 329-3199, P.O. Box 5612, Kailua-Kona, 96745, owned and operated by Capt. Ted Muhlert, will take you on a fantastic ocean odyssey beginning at Honokohau Small Boat Harbor just north of Kailua-Kona. From here you'll skirt the coast south all the way to Pu'uhonua O Honaunau City of Refuge. A Zodiac is a very tough motorized rubber raft. It looks like a big, horseshoe-shaped innertube that bends itself and undulates with the waves like a floating waterbed. These seaworthy craft, powered by twin Mercury 280s, have five separate air chambers for unsinkable safety. They'll take you for a thrilling ride down the Kona Coast, pausing along the way to whisk you into sea caves, grottos, and caverns. The Kona coast is also marked with ancient ruins and the remains of villages, which the captains point out, and characterize with historical anecdotes as you pass by. On the return run you stop at Kealakekua Bay, where you can swim and snorkel in this underwater conservation park. Roundtrips departing at 8 a.m. and again at 12 noon take about five hours and cost $50 adults, $40 children under 11. Captain Zodiac also provides a light tropical lunch of fresh exotic fruit, taro chips, fruit juice, ice tea, and sodas. All you need is a bathing suit, sun hat, towel, lotion, your camera, and a sense of adventure.

Atlantis Submarine, tel. 329-6626, allows everyone to live out the fantasy of Captain Nemo as it slips silently under the waves off Kailua-Kona. After checking in at their office in the Hotel King Kamehameha Mall, you board a launch at Kailua Pier that takes you on a 10-minute cruise to the waiting submarine tethered offshore. You're given all of your safety tips on the way there. As you descend, notice that everything white including teeth, turns pink because the ultraviolet rays are filtered out. The only colors that you can see clearly beneath the waves are blues and greens because water, 800 times denser than air, filters out the reds and oranges.

Everyone has an excellent seat with a viewing port; there's not a bad seat in the submarine, so you don't have to rush to get on. Don't worry about being claustrophobic either—it's amazingly airy and bright, with white space-age plastic on the inside walls and aircraft-quality air blowers over your seat. Prices are $58 adult, half price for children four to 12, children under four not permitted.

For more conventional sailing and boating adventures try: **Hawaii Sailing Academy,** in Kailua-Kona, tel. 329-9201, or (800) 367-8047 ext. 306, that offers tailor-made diving, sailing, and snorkeling charters; **Captain Beans',** tel. 329-2955, daily at 1:30 p.m., $7 adults, a Kona institution that'll take you aboard its glass-bottomed boat to enjoy a very tame cruise spotting fish while listening to island music; *Capt. Cook VII,* tel. 329-6411, also a glass-bottomed boat, but for $25 adults, the tour includes snorkeling and lunch; **The Party Boat,** tel. 329-2177 sets sail nightly and sways with classic rock-and-roll music, volleyball, snorkeiling, a BBQ, and open bar.

Whalewatch cruises in season are provided by **Hawaiian Cruises,** tel. 329-6411, and **Tri Sea,** tel. 329-3556. Cruises usually last about three hours and cost $25: For a day of snorkeling and sailing contact **Kamanu Charters,** tel. 329-2021, or **Intuition,** tel. 329-8171.

ACCOMMODATIONS

Finding suitable accommodations on Hawaii is never a problem. The 7,000-plus rooms available have the lowest annual occupancy rate of any in the islands at only 65%. Except for the height of the high seasons and during the Merry Monarch Festival in Hilo, you can count on finding a room at a bargain. Many places offer kitchenettes and long-term discounts as a matter of course. The highest concentration of rooms is strung along Alii Drive in Kailua-Kona—over 4,500 in condos, apartment hotels, and standard hotels. Hilo has almost 2,000 rooms, and many of its hotels have "gone condo," and you can get some great deals. The rest are scattered around the island in small villages from Naalehu in the south to Hawi in the north, where you can almost count on being the only off-island guest. You can comfortably stay in the cowboy town of Waimea, or perch above Kilauea Crater at one of the oldest hotel sites in the islands. There are bed and breakfasts, and the camping is superb, with a campsite almost guaranteed at anytime.

The Range
The Big Island has a tremendous range of accommodations. A concentration of the world's greatest luxury resorts are within minutes of each other on the Kohala coast: The Mauna Kea Beach Hotel, Mauna Lani, Hyatt Regency Wai-

Kona Hilton Beach and Tennis Resort

KONA HILTON BEACH AND TENNIS RESORT

koloa, and Kona Village Resort. The Mauna Kea, built by Lawrence Rockefeller, has everything the name implies. The others are just as superb with hideaway "grass shacks," exquisite art collections as an integral part of the grounds, world-ranked golf courses, and perfect crescent beaches.

Kona has fine hotels like the King Kamehameha and Kona Hilton in downtown Kailua. Just south towards Keahou are a string of reasonably priced yet luxury hotels like the Kona Lagoon. Interspersed among the big hotels are little places with homey atmospheres and great rates. Hilo offers the best accommodations bargains. Luxury hotels such as the Hilo Hawaiian and Naniloa Surf are priced like mid-range hotels on the other islands. There are also semifleabags in town that pass the basic cleanliness test and go for as little as $18 per day, along with gems like the Dolphin Bay Hotel that gives you so much for your money it's embarrassing. And for a real treat, head to Volcanoes National Park and stay at tucked away bed and breakfasts, or at Volcano House where raw nature

has thrilled kings, queens, and luminaries like humorist Mark Twain for over a century.

If you want to get away from everybody else, no problem, and you don't have to be rich to do it. Pass-through towns like Captain Cook and Waimea offer accommodations at very reasonable prices. You can try a self-growth retreat in Puna at Kalani Honua Culture Center or at the Wood Valley Buddhist Temple above Pahala. Want ultimate seclusion? Head down to Tom Araki's Hotel in Waipio Valley, or spend the night at a defunct century-old girl's boarding school in Kapaau.

The Big Island is also blessed with a profusion of bed and breakfast homes in extremely unique settings. You can find these lodgings in places like Volcano Village, along South Point Road, or in Kukuihaele overlooking the amazing Waipio Valley.

For specific recommendations see "Accommodations" in the Travel Chapters, and for **B&B booking agencies** see p. 147 in the general Introduction.

CAMPING AND HIKING

The Big Island has the best camping in the state, with more facilities and less competition for campsites than on the other islands. Over three dozen parks fringe the coastline and sit deep in the interior; almost half offer camping. The others boast a combination of rugged hikes, easy strolls, self-guided nature walks, swimming, historical sites, and natural phenomena. The ones with campgrounds are state-, county-, and nationally operated, ranging from remote walk-in sites to housekeeping cabins. All, except the national park, require inexpensive camping permits, and although there is usually no problem obtaining sites, always write for reservations well in advance, allowing a minimum of one month for letters to go back and forth.

GENERAL INFORMATION

Most campgrounds have pavilions, fireplaces, toilets (sometimes pit), running water, but usually no individual electrical hookups. Pavilions often have electric lights, but sometimes campers appropriate the bulbs, so it's wise to carry your own. Drinking water is available, but at

times brackish water is used for flushing toilets and for showers, so read all signs regarding water. Backcountry shelters have catchment water, but never hike without an adequate supply of your own. Cooking fires are allowed in established firepits, but no wood is provided. Charcoal is a good idea. When camping in the mountains, be prepared for cold and rainy weather. Women, especially, should never hike or camp alone, and everyone should exercise precaution against theft, though it's not as prevalent as on the other islands. Camping equipment is available from: **Pacific United Rent All,** 1080 Kilauea Ave., Hilo, tel. 935-2974; **Kona Rent All,** 74- 5602 Alapaa St., Kailua-Kona, tel. 329-1644.

County Parks

The county-maintained parks are open to the public for day use, and permits are required only for camping (tents or RVs). For information write: Dept. of Parks and Recreation, County of Hawaii, Hilo, HI 96720, tel. 961-8311. The main office is located behind the Kaikoo Mall at 25 Aupuni Street. You can pick up your permits here, but only during business hours Mon. through Friday. If you'll be arriving after hours or on a weekend, have the permits mailed to you. Branch offices are located at Hale Halawai in Kailua-Kona, tel. 329-1989, and at Captain Cook, tel. 323-3046. Fees are $1 per adult, per day; children 13 to 17, $.50; youngsters free. Pavilions for exclusive use are $5 p/d with kitchen, $2 without.

State Parks

Day use of state parks is free, with no permit required, but you will need one for tent camping and for cabins. If you want a cabin, at least one week's notice is required regardless of availability. You can pick up your permit if you arrive during normal business hours, but again it saves time if you do it all by mail. Write: Dept. of Land and Natural Resources, Div. of State Parks, Box

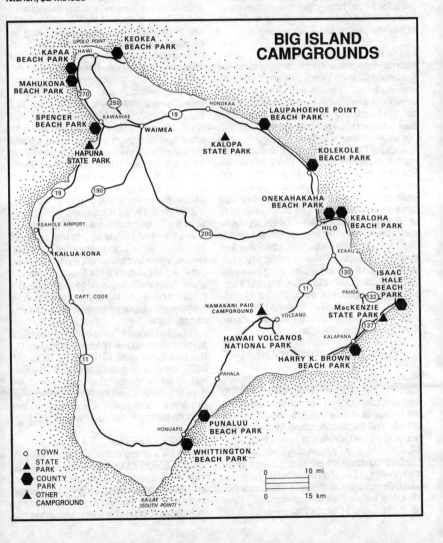

BIG ISLAND CAMPGROUNDS

O TOWN
▲ STATE PARK
⬢ COUNTY PARK
▲ OTHER CAMPGROUND

0 10 mi
0 15 km

936, Hilo, HI 96720, tel. 961-7200. The main office is at 75 Aupuni Street. Cabins or A-frames are offered at Mauna Kea's Pohakuloa Camp, tel. 935-7237; Hapuna, tel. 882-7995; Kalopa, tel. 775-7114; and Niaulani Cabin at Kilauea State Park. Fees and regulations vary slightly so specify exactly which facility you require, for how long, and for how many people when writing for permit. For example, the A-frames at Hapuna are a flat $7 per night with a four-person maximum; Niaulani Cabin is on a sliding scale from $10 for one person, to $30 for six people.

Hawaii Volcanoes National Park

Both day use and overnight camping at Hawaii Volcanoes National Park is free and no permits are required. The drive-in campgrounds throughout the park can be reserved, but usually operate on a first-come first-served basis. Your stay is limited to seven days per campground per year. A-frame cabins are provided at Namakani Paio Campgrounds, and arrangements are made through Volcano House, Hawaii Volcanoes National Park, HI 96718, tel. 967-7321. There are walk-in trail cabins and shelters throughout the park; they are free, you can't reserve them and you should expect to share them with other hikers. Coleman stoves and lanterns are sometimes provided (check), but you provide the fuel. Basic bedding and cooking utensils are also there for your convenience. Shelters, in the park along the coast, are three-sided open affairs that only offer a partial covering against the elements. For information on camping and hiking in the park, write Hawaii Volcanoes National Park, Information Services, Volcano, HI 96718.

HIKING THE BIG ISLAND

Hiking on the Big Island is stupendous. There's something for everyone, from civilized walks to the breathtaking Akaka Falls to huff-puff treks to the summit of Mauna Loa. The largest number of trails, and the most outstanding according to many, are laced across Volcanoes Park. After all, this is the world's most active volcano. You can hike across the crater floor, spurred on by the knowledge that it can shake to life at any moment. Or dip down off the mountain and amble the lonely trails in the Kau desert or along remnants of the King's Coastal Trail in Puna.

The most important thing to do, before heading out in Volcanoes, is to stop at the Ranger HQ and inquire about trail conditions. Make absolutely sure to register, giving the rangers your hiking itinerary. In the event of an eruption, they will be able to locate you and send a helicopter if necessary. Follow this advice; your life may depend upon it! Everyone can enjoy vistas on Devastation Trail, at the Sulphur Banks, or at the Thurston Lava Tube without any danger whatsoever. In the north you'll find Waipio, Waimanu, and Pololu valleys. All offer secluded hiking and camping, where you can play Robinson Crusoe on your own beach and gather a variety of island fruits from once cultivated trees gone wild.

Camping/Hiking Tours

Hawaiian Island Adventures, P.O. Box 726, Pahoa, HI 96778, tel. 965-8925, or (800) 726-HIKE, offers adventure hiking tours from a 14-day deluxe tour covering the Big Island, Molokai, Maui and Kauai, to a three-day Waimanu Valley escape to this pristine area along the Big Island's north coast. The tours are designed for a great deal of personal attention, with a maximum of 16 people per group allowed. Tour leaders, intimately versed in the flora, fauna, geology, history, and ancient cosmology of the islands, share their knowledge as you trek along. All inter-island flights along with accommodations ranging from a tent to a condo, and all meals, are provided at the daily $104 fixed rate (special group rates available). A deposit is required to confirm a place on a tour and to receive a packet containing necessary information to make your tour enjoyable.

An organization offering camping and hiking trips to the Big Island is **Wilderness Hawaii** P.O. Box 61692, Honolulu, HI 96839, tel. (808) 737-4697. Lead by Sheena Sandler, Wilderness Hawaii offers courses that range from a few days of overnight backpacking to a 21-day sojurn where the experiential journey takes place as much within yourself as on the hiking trail.

Precautions And Tips

Always tell a ranger or official of your hiking intentions. Supply an itinerary and your expected route, then stick to it. Be aware of current lava flows, and heed all posted advice. If lost, walk on ridges and avoid the gulches, which have more obstacles and make it harder for rescuers to spot you. Be careful of elevation sickness, especially on Mauna Loa and Mauna Kea. The best cure is to head down as soon as possible.

Hilo's **Basically Books,** downtown at 169 Keawe St., tel. 961-0144, has an unbeatable se-

lection of maps. You can get anywhere you want to go with their nautical charts, road maps, topographical maps, and sectionals for serious hikers and trekkers. Their collection covers most of the Pacific.

SPORTS AND RECREATION

You'll have no problem having fun on the Big Island. Everybody goes outside to play. You can drive golf balls over lagoons, smack tennis balls at over 50 private and public courts, ski, snorkel, windsurf, gallop a horse, bag a wild turkey, or latch on to a marlin that'll tail-walk across a windowpane sea. Choose your sport and have a ball.

FISHING

Deep-sea Fishing
The fishing around the Big Island's Kona Coast ranges from excellent to outstanding! It's legendary for marlin fishing, but there are other fish in the sea. A large fleet of charter boats with skilled captains and tested crews is ready, willing, and competent to take you out. The vast majority are berthed at Honokohau Small Boat Harbor just north of Kailua-Kona (see p. 656). The best times of year for marlin are July through September, and again from January to March when the generally larger females arrive. August is the optimum month. Rough seas can keep most boats in during December and early January; many venture out by February.

You can hire a boat for a private or share charter, staying out for a full day or half day. Boat size varies, but four anglers per mid-size boat is about average. Approximate rates are: private, full day $400-$600; half day $250-$350; share, full day $65-$110; half day $60-$75. Full days are eight hours, half days four, with three-quarter days available too! No licenses are required and all gear is provided. Bring your own lunch, beverages, and camera.

To charter a boat, contact the individual captains directly, check at your hotel activities desk, or book through one of the following agencies. **Kona Fuel Dock Sportfishing Center,** at Honokohau Harbor, tel. 329- 7529 or (800) 648-7529, is owned by Jim Dahlberg, who was born and raised on the Big Island. This is the main

booking facility in the area. If you're after a company that's knowledgeable about getting you to waters where you'll have the opportunity to catch one of the twirling and gigantic "big blues," this is the place to come. For general booking agencies try: **Kona Activities Center,** Box 1035, Kailua-Kona, HI 96740, tel. 329-3171; **Kona Coast Activities,** Box 5397, Kailua-Kona, HI 96740, tel. 329-2971; **Kona Charter Skippers Assoc.,** Box 806, Kailua-Kona, HI 96740, tel. 329-3600; **Mauna Kea Beach Hotel,** Travel Desk, Box 218, Kamuela, HI 96743, tel. 882-7222.

weigh-in at Honokohau Harbor

Most boats are berthed at Honokohau Harbor off Rt. 19, about midway between downtown Kailua and Keahole Airport. Big fish are sometimes still weighed in at Kailua Pier, in front of the Hotel King Kamehameha for the benefit of the tourists. But Honokohau Harbor has eclipsed Kailua Pier which is now tamed and primarily for swimmers, triathletes, body boarders, and children swimming in the water. It's become congested and difficult for the charter boats to get in and out of there, so the majority of the trade has moved up to Honokohau (see p. 656). An excellent publication listing boats and general deepsea fishing information is *Hawaii Fishing Charter Guide.* This tabloid is available free at newsstands or hotel/condo lobbies and is filled with descriptions of boats, phone numbers, captains' names, maps, and photos of recent catches. For subscription rates, call 325-6171, or write to Box P, Kailua-Kona, HI 96745.

Coastal And Freshwater Fishing

You don't have to hire a boat to catch fish! The coastline is productive too. *Ulua* are caught all along the coast south of Hilo, and at South Point and Kealakekua Point. *Papio* and *hahalalu* are caught in bays all around the island, while *manini* and *ama'ama* hit from Kawaihai to Puako. Hilo Bay is easily accessible to anyone, and the fishing is very exciting, especially at the mouth of the Wailuku River.

Freshwater fishing is limited to the **Waiakea Public Fishing Area,** a state-operated facility in downtown Hilo. This 26-acre pond offers a variety of saltwater and brackish fish. A license is required. You can pick one up at sporting goods stores or at the Division of Conservation and Resources Enforcement Office, 75 Aupuni St., Hilo, HI 96720, tel. 961-7291.

WATER SPORTS

Scuba and Snorkeling

Those in the know consider the **deep diving** along the steep drop-offs of Hawaii's geologically young coastline some of the best in the state. The ocean surrounding the Big Island has not had a chance to turn the rather new lava to sand, which makes the visibility absolutely perfect, even to depths of 150 feet or more. There's also 60-70 miles of coral belt around the Big Is-

land, which adds up to a magnificent diving experience. Only advanced divers should attempt deep-water dives, but beginners and snorkelers will have many visual thrills inside the protected bays and coves. (See "Beaches" in the travel sections.)

One of the best outfits to dive with on the Big Island is **Dive Makai** in Kona, tel. 329-2025, operated by Tom Shockley and Lisa Choquette. These very experienced divers have run this service for years and have many dedicated customers. Both Tom and Lisa are conservationists who help to preserve the fragile reef. They've worked very hard with the Diver's Council to protect dive sites from fish collectors, and to protect the reef from destruction by anchors. Their motto, "We care," is not a trite saying, as they continue to preserve the reef for you and your children.

Another excellent diving outfit is **Jack's Diving Locker,** tel. 329-7585, in the Kona Inn Shopping Village. They are a responsible outfit that does a good job of watching out for their customers and taking care of the reef. Jack's also specializes in snorkel sales and rentals ($6.50 for 24 hours), scuba rentals, certification classes, and dive classes. You can do a three-hour snorkel/sail on the *Double Eagle,* which departs at 8:30 a.m. and again at 12 p.m. daily.

King Kamehameha Divers in the Hotel King Kamehameha, Kailua, tel. 329-5662, offers a daily boat charter where you get a two-tank certified dive with your own gear for $65, or $75 with their gear. An introductory dive is $95 and snorkeling is $35. This includes continental breakfast, lunch, and soft drinks. Rental rates for snorkeling gear run $7.50 for 24 hours, boogie boards $15.

Big Island Divers, tel. 329-6068, in the Kona Market Place, offer a scuba certification course for only $90 that's given on five consecutive Saturdays, so you must intend to stay on the Big Island for that length of time. The normal four-day course costs $365. They also rent complete snorkel gear for only $5 for 24 hours, and boogie boards for $5-8 for 24 hours.

Kona Kai Diving, in Kona at tel. 329-0695, is owned and operated by Kate Tearnan. Kate was a former diver with Scripps Institute of Oceanography and tailors all of her dives to enable her guests to learn and appreciate the unique ocean ecosystem of the Big Island.

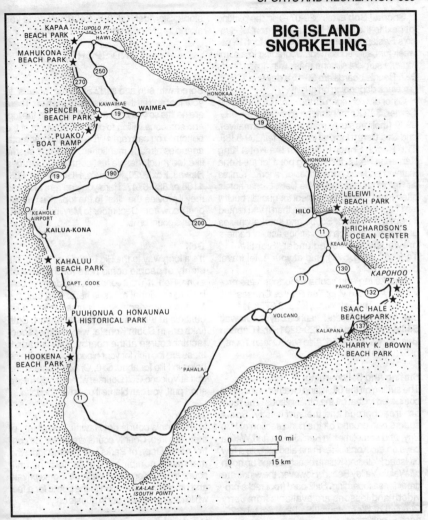

BIG ISLAND SNORKELING

Kohala Divers, in Kawaihae (see p. 700), tel. 882-7774, have an open-water class and certification for $250. Snorkeling gear is $10 for 24 hours, and a scuba rental is $22.

Mauna Loa Diving Service, in Hilo at 97 Haili St., tel. 935-3299, is owned by Phil Snowden and Alys Wall. They offer PADI open-water courses for only $116, but it takes two weeks to complete. They certify people right off Richard-

son's Beach or Leleiwi Beach Park in the Hilo area.

An alternative to boat dives is shore diving. *Shore Diving in Kona* is a great book listing sites, equipment, regulations, and suggestions for successful and safe dives. If your budget is limited, and you're an experienced shore diver, it's a way to have a great outing at a reasonable price.

Snorkel Bob's, tel. 329-0770, in the parking lot next to the Kona Hilton right in front of Huggo's Restaurant, offers snorkel gear for $15 per week for basic equipment. Upgrading to a comfortable surgical silicone mask with Italian fins is $27. Boogie boards are $9-15 a day and $22-35 per week depending on quality.

Other dive companies include: **Nautilus Dive Center,** 382 Kamehameha Ave., Hilo, tel. 935-6939 (their free dive map is quite informative), and **Sea Camp Hawaii** in Kailua, tel. 329-3388. The **Beach Shack** in front of the Hotel King Kamehameha is the starting point for the Kona triathlon and has good prices on snorkel rentals as well as kayaks and Hobie Cats. Larger hotels often have snorkel equipment for guests, but if it isn't free, it always costs more than if you rented it from a dive shop. Scuba and snorkel cruises are booked through the various activity centers previously mentioned under "Sightseeing Tours," (see p. 577), and at your hotel travel desk.

Snorkeling and scuba excursions are provided by the following: **Sea Breeze Cruises,** tel. 326-1311; The **Fair Wind,** tel. 322-2788, leaving daily from magnificent Keauhou Bay; the **Hawaii Sailing Academy,** tel. 329-9201; and **Captain Beans',** tel. 329-2955. Also see "Ocean Tours," p. 578.

Surfing And Sailboarding

The surfing off the Big Island is rather uninspiring compared to that off the other islands. The reefs are treacherous and the surf is lazy. Some surfers bob around off the north section of Hilo Bay, and sometimes in Kealakekua and Wailua bays on the Kona side. Puna also attracts a few off Isaac Hale and Kaimu beaches, and up north off Waipio Valley Beach. However, the winds are great for sailboarding. Sailboard (roof racks provided) and lessons are available from Jerry Classen of **West Hawaii Sailboards,** tel. 329-3669 or 885-7744.

Jet-skiing, Parasailing, Et Cetera

If you are interested in thrill rides contact: **Hawaii Speed Sports,** tel. 326-1419, which rents jet skis for rides along the Kona Coast at $30 for a half-hour and $45 for a full hour. They also rent skateboards and sailboarding equipment. **Kona Water Sports,** tel. 329-1593, rents jet skis and conducts water-skiing and parasailing excursions; **Skyrider,** tel. 326-2426, will send you aloft in its patented parasailing "arm chair."

LAND SPORTS

Skiing

Bored with sun and surf? Strap the "boards" to your feet and hit the slopes of Mauna Kea. There are no lifts so you'll need a 4WD to get to the top, and someone willing to pick you up again at the bottom. You can rent 4WDs from the car rental agencies already mentioned, but if that seems like too much hassle just contact **Ski Guides Hawaii,** Box 2020, Kamuela, HI 96743, tel. 885-4188 or 889-6747. Here you can rent skis and they'll provide the "lifts" to the top. You can expect snow from December to May, but you can't always count on it.

Golf

It's a long way to the Big Island just to golf, but plenty of people come here for that reason alone. Robert Trent Jones Sr. and Jr. have both built exceptional courses here. Dad built the Mauna Kea Beach Hotel course, while the kid built his at the Waikoloa Beach Resort. Both links are in South Kohala, with another spectacular course at the nearby Mauna Lani. If these are too rich for your blood, you can hit nine holes in Hilo for about $10. Or how about some golf at Volcano Golf Course, where, if you miss a short putt, you can blame it on an earthquake.

Tennis

Many tennis courts dot Hawaii, and plenty of them are free. County courts are under the control of the Dept. of Parks and Recreation, who maintain a combination of lighted and unlit courts in Hilo, Kona, and Waimea. Some private and hotel courts are open to the public for a fee, while others restrict play to guests only.

Hunting

Huge unpopulated expanses of grasslands, forests, and scrubby mountainsides are very good for hunting. The Big Island's game includes feral pig, sheep, and goats, plus pheasants, quails, doves, and wild turkeys. Mauna Kea Beach Hotel guests can hunt on the Parker Ranch, while the **McCandless Ranch** near Captain Cook supplies guides for its 30,000 acres. For information contact Steve Arrington, Box 63 G,

TENNIS COURTS OF HAWAII

COUNTY COURTS

Under jursidiction of the Department of Parks and Recreation,
25 Aupuni St. Hilo, HI 96720. Tel. 961-8311. Courts listed are in the Hilo, Waimea,
and Kailua-Kona areas. There are nine additional locations around the island.

Location	Name of Court	No. of Courts	Lighted
Hilo	Hoolulu Park	8	Yes
Hilo	Lincoln Park	4	Yes
Hilo	Mohouli Park	2	No
Hilo	University of Hawaii-Hilo College	2	No
Kona	Kailua Park	4	Yes
Kona	Kailua Playground	1	Yes
Kona	Keauhou Park	1	No
Waimea	Waimea Park	2	Yes

HOTEL AND PRIVATE COURTS THAT ARE OPEN TO THE PUBLIC

Location	Name of Court	No. Of Courts	Lighted
Hilo	Sheraton-Walakea Village Hotel (fee)	2	No
Kailua-Kona	Hotel King Kamehameha (fee)	2	Yes
Kailua-Kona	Kona Hilton Beach and Tennis Resort (fee)	4	Yes
Kailua-Kona	Kona Lagoon (fee for non-guests)	2	Yes
Kamuela	Waimea Park	2	Yes
Keauhou-Kona	Keauhou Beach Hotel (fee)	6	Yes
Keauhou-Kona	Kona Surf Hotel Racket Club (fee)	7	Yes
Pahala	Seamountain Tennis Center (fee)	4	No
Waikoloa	Waikoloa village (fee)	2	Yes

Captain Cook, HI 96704, tel. 328- 2349/2389. Public game lands are situated all over the island and a license is required to take birds and game. For full information, write Division of Forestry and Wildlife, 1643 Kilauea Ave., Box 4849, Hilo, HI 96720, tel. 961-7221.

Horseback riding

A classic way to see an island known for its cattle and cowboys is from the back of a horse. Excel-

lent trail rides through *paniolo* country are offered by **Ironwood Outfitters,** Box 832, Kamuela, HI 96743, tel. 885-4941. These stables, run by a lady wrangler, Judy Ellis, and her top hand, Charlie, are located along Rt. 250 between Kamuela and Hawi near mile marker 11. Judy's a farm girl from Iowa who's spent all her life around horses. She came to the Big Island in the early '70s and made her living breaking rough stock. Now she offers a variety of trail

GOLF COURSES OF HAWAII

Course	Par	Yards	Fees	Cart
Discovery Harbor Kau District, HI 96772 tel. 929-7353	72	6640	$5	$10
Hamakua Country Club * ¤ P.O. Box 344 Honokaa, HI 96727 tel. 775-7244	33	2520	$5	—
Hilo Country Club * 120 Banyon Br., Hilo HI 96720 tel. 935-7388	70	6100	$3	$1
Hilo Municipal Golf course 340 Haihai St., Hilo HI 96720 tel. 959-7711	72	6210	Wkday $3 Wkend $4	$10.40
Keauhou-Kona Golf Course 78-7000 Alii Br. Kailua-Kona, HI 96740 tel. 322-2595	72	6329	$25	$9.50
Mauna Kea Beach Hotel Golf Course P.O. Box 218, Kamuela, HI 96743 tel. 882-7222	72	6455	$30	$9.50
Mauna Lani Resort, Frances H. I'l Brown Golf Course P.O. Box 4959, Kawaihae, HI 96743 tel. 885-6655	72	6259	$32	$9.50
Seamountain Golf Course P.O. Box 85, Pahala, HI 96777 tel. 928-8000	72	6106	$17	$16
Volcano Golf and Country Club P.O. Box 46, Colcano National Park, HI 96718 tel. 967-7331	72	5936	$11	$8
Waikoloa Beach Golf Course P.O. Box 5100, Waikoloa, HI 96743 tel. 883-6060	71	6003	$27	$8
Waikoloa Village Golf Course P.O. Box 3068, Waikoloa, HI 96743 tel. 883-9621	72	6316	$27	$8

N.B. * = 9 hole course • = no club rental ¤ = guests only

rides over the spectacular 30,000 acres of the Kahua Ranch. Her well-adapted "mountain horses" cost $18 p/h and the most popular ride is a three-hour "mountain ride" for $40. Judy tailors rides to suit just about any situation. Her rides are popular, so book in advance.

Waipio Naalapa Trail Rides, operated by Sherri Hannum, tel. 775- 0419, offer the most unique rides on Hawaii. Sherri and her family have lived in Waipio Valley for 15 years and know its history, geology, and legends intimately. She offers pickup service from Kukuihaele for the half-day ($55) and full-day ($100) rides. Sherri treats guests like family, offering tasty local treats and a refreshing dip either off Waipio's Black Sand Beach or at the myth-shrouded Nanaue Falls. If you have time, don't miss this adventure. For full information see p. 621.

Waipio Valley Wagon Tour, tel. 775-9518, owned and operated by Peter Tolin, is a mule-drawn tour of the magnificent Waipio Valley. The two-hour tours leave four times daily at 10 a.m., 11:30 a.m., 1:30 p.m., and 3 p.m. The cost is $25, children under 12 half price, children two and under free. For full information see p. 621.

Enjoyable rides are offered by the **Mauna Kea Beach Hotel** (non- guests too!), tel. 882-7222. They have an arrangement with the Parker Ranch which will supply a *paniolo* to guide you over the quarter-million acres of open range on the slopes of Mauna Kea. The stables are at Parker Ranch HQ in Waimea. Rates are $24 p/h. The **Waikoloa Paniolos,** Box 3006, Waikoloa Village, HI 96743, tel. 883-9335, have 10,000 acres to gallop over. They offer a variety of rides, but the specialty is a sunset two-hour ride. **Waikoloa Village Stables,** tel. 883-9335, has a good reputation and will also take you on rides throughout the Waikoloa area. **Waiono Meadows Trail Rides,** tel. 329-0888, offers a chance to view the Kona Coast from the slopes of Mt. Hualalai. They feature a breakfast, lunch, and sunset ride. **King's Trail Rides,** tel. 323-2388, have offices along Route 11 high above the Kona Coast on the outskirts of Kealakekua. Prices are $30/hour, $75 for two hours. The ride covers portions of the Kealakekua Ranch lands, a 20,000 acre working spread. You're driven to the 4,200-foot level, where you get your mount. All rides, except the one-hour, includes lunch.

INFORMATION AND SERVICES

Emergency

Police phone numbers vary by community so check the inside front cover of the local telephone directory for a complete list. For **Ambulance and fire** all island, call 961-6022. **Hospitals:** Kealakekua, tel. 322-9311; Hilo, tel. 961-4211; Honokaa, tel. 775-7211; Kohala, tel. 889-6211; Kau, tel. 928-8331. **Drugstores:** Longs Drugs, 555 Kilauea Ave., Hilo, tel. 935-3357; Kona Coast Drugs, Kailua, tel. 329-8886; Village Pharmacy, Waimea, tel. 885-4418.

Information

The best information is dispensed by the **Hawaii Visitors Bureau,** 180 Kinoole St., Suite 104, Hilo, tel. 935-5271, also at the Wailoa Center just near the State Building in Hilo at tel. 961-7360. In Kailua-Kona the HVB is located downtown in the Hilo Plaza, tel. 329-1782. The State Visitor Information centers at the airports, Hilo tel. 935-1018, and Kona tel. 329-3423, are good sources of information on arrival. The **Chamber of Commerce,** in Hilo, tel. 935-7178, is at 180 Kinoole Street.

Disabled Services

At Hilo Airport there are no facilities for deplaning non-ambulatory people from propeller planes, only from jets and on the jetways. Inter-island flights should be arranged only on jets. Ramps and a special elevator provide access in the bi-level terminal. Parking is convenient in designated areas. At Kona airport, boarding and deplaning is possible for the handicapped. Ramps make the terminal accessible. To get around, **Handi-Vans** are available in Hilo, tel. 961-6722. **Kamealoha Unlimited** has specially equipped vans, tel. 966-7244. **Parking permits** are avialable from Dept. of Finance, tel. 961-8231. Medical help, nurses, and companions can be arranged through **Big Island Center for Independent Living,** tel. 935-3777. Doctors are referred by **Hilo Hospital,** tel. 961-4211, and **Kona Hospital,** tel. 322-9311. Medical equipment is available from **Kamealoha Unlimited,** tel. 966-7244; **Medi-Home,** tel. 969-1123; **Pacific Rentall,** tel. 935-2974.

Alternative Health Care

The Big Island is blessed with some of the finest natural healers and practitioners in the state. For a holistic healing experience of body, mind, and soul, the following are highly recommended. For hospitals, drugstores, and medical doctors see "Emergency And Medical Care," p. 136.

School of Hawaiian Lomi Lomi, Box 221, Captain Cook, HI 96704, tel. 323-2416 or 328-2472. Here, Margaret Machado, assisted by her husband Daniel, provides the finest *lomi lomi* and traditional Hawaiian herbal cures in the islands. Both are renowned *kapuna* who dispense a heavy dose of love and concern with every remedy prescribed.

Acupuncture and Herbs is the domain of Angela Longo. This remarkable woman is not only a superbly trained, licensed practitioner of traditional Chinese medicine and acupuncture, but she covers all bases by holding a Ph.D. in biochemistry from U.C. Berkeley. For a totally holistic health experience, contact Angela at her Waimea/Kamuela office, tel. 885-7886.

The **Hawaiian Islands School of Body Therapy,** tel. 322-0048, owned and operated by Peter Wind and Lynn Filkins-Wind, offers state-certified massage courses and mini-courses for the beginning or experienced therapist. A full range of massage, anatomy, and physiology are part of the coursework preparing the student for a Hawaii State License. Programs include a basic massage program taking 150 hours, an advanced massage program of 450 hours, and a third-level course designed for the professional that takes a minimum of one year's intensive study to complete. Under Peter and Lynn's tutelage you'll learn *lomi lomi,* reflexology, hydrotherapy, aroma therapy, trigger point therapy, and treatment therapy. Lynn specializes in treatment therapy, which she teaches by the European, hands-on approach, while Peter is a hydrotherapist and colonics therapist. They are assisted by Gigi Goochey, the anatomy and physiology instructor. Lynn and Peter are dedicated professionals that have clued in, body and soul, to the art of healing.

To revitalize those aching muscles and to put a spring in your step the following massage practitioners have magic in their hands: **Kiauhou Massage and Spa** at the Kiauhou Beach Hotel, tel. 322-3441, room 227. Open Tues., Thurs., and Sat. 10 a.m. to 5 p.m., and Mon., Wed., and Fri. 5 p.m. to 8 p.m.

To get that just-right chiropractic adjustment try **Rodgers Chiropractic Arts** with Howard Rodgers, D.C., in the WOW Building, Kailua, tel. 329-2271, or **Kohala Chiropractic** with Dr. Bob Abdy, Kamuela, tel. 885-6847. Also in Waimea is **Kohala Coast Massage,** tel. 885-5442, and

the **Chiropractic Clinic** of Dr. Kenneth C. Williams, tel. 885-7719, emergency tel. 885-6812.

A wonderful healing center is **Halemana,** in Pahoa at tel. 965-7783, where they'll soothe you with acupuncture and massage. For full details see p. 630.

Reading Material

Make sure to pick up copies of the following free literature. Besides maps and general information, they often include money-saving coupons. Available at most hotels/condos and at all tourist areas, published weekly, they include: *Guide to Hawaii, Big Island Beach Press,* and *This Week Big Island.* Harry Lyons' *Kona Coast* is a monthly tabloid offering topical island editorials, restaurant critiques, humorous anecdotes and jokes, and an advertisers' bulletin board. Island newspapers include: *Hawaii-Tribune Herald,* a Hilo publication, and *West Hawaii Today,* published in Kona. **Libraries** are located in towns and schools all over the island. The main branch is at 300 Waianuenue Ave., Hilo, tel. 935-5407. They provide all information regarding libraries; in Kailua-Kona, the library is at 75-140 Hualalai Rd., tel. 329-2196. Please refer to the "Shopping" chapter for bookstores.

Weather Information

Receive 24-hour recorded information regarding volcanic activity by calling 967-7977; weather information, tel. 961-5582; Coast Guard tide conditions, tel. 935-6370.

Post Office

Branch post offices are found in most major towns. The following are the main ones: Hilo, tel. 935-2821; Kailua, tel. 329-2927; Captain Cook, tel. 323-3663; Waimea/Kamuela, tel. 885-4026.

Island Facts

Hawaii has three fitting nicknames: the Big Island, the Volcano Island, and the Orchid Island. It's the youngest, most southerly, and largest (4,038 square miles) island in the Hawaiian chain. Its color is red, and the island lei is fashioned from the *lehua,* an *ohia* blossom.

HILO

Hilo is a blind date. Everyone tells you what a beautiful personality she has, but . . . But? . . . It rains: 133 inches a year. Mostly the rains come in winter, and are limited to predictable afternoon showers, but they do scare some tourists away, keeping Hilo reasonably priced and lowkeyed. In spite of, and because of, the rain, Hilo is gorgeous. It's one of the oldest permanently settled towns in Hawaii, and the largest on the windward coast of the island. Hilo's weather makes it a natural greenhouse. Twenty acres of exotic orchids and flowers line the runways at the airport! Botanical gardens and flower farms surround Hilo like a giant lei, and shoulder-to-shoulder banyans canopy entire city blocks. To counterpoint this tropical explosion, Mauna Kea's winter snows backdrop the town. The crescent of Hilo Bay blazes gold at sunrise, while a sculpted lagoon, Oriental pagodas, rock gardens, and even a tiny island connected by footbridge line its shores. Downtown's waterfront has the perfect false-front buildings that always need a paint job. They lean on each other like "old salts" that've had one too many. Don't make the mistake of underestimating Hilo, or counting it out because of its rainy reputation. For most, the blind date with this exotic beauty turns into a fun-filled love affair.

SIGHTS AND BEACHES

SIGHTS

Hilo is one of the most unique towns in the most unique state in America. You can walk down streets with names like Puueo and Keawe, and they could be streets in *Anywhere, U.S.A.* with neatly painted houses surrounded by a white picket fence. Families live here. There are roots, and traditions, but the town is changing. Fishermen still come for the nightly ritual of soul-fishing and story-swapping from the bridge spanning the Wailuku River, while just down the street newly arrived chefs prepare Cajun blackened fish at a yuppie restaurant while midnight philosophers sip gourmet coffee and munch sweets next door. Hilo is a classic tropical town. Some preserved buildings, proud again after new face lifts, are a few stories tall and date from the turn of the century when Hilo was a major port of entry to Hawaii. Sidewalks in older sections are covered with awnings because of the rains and add a turn-of-the-century gentility. Because Hilo

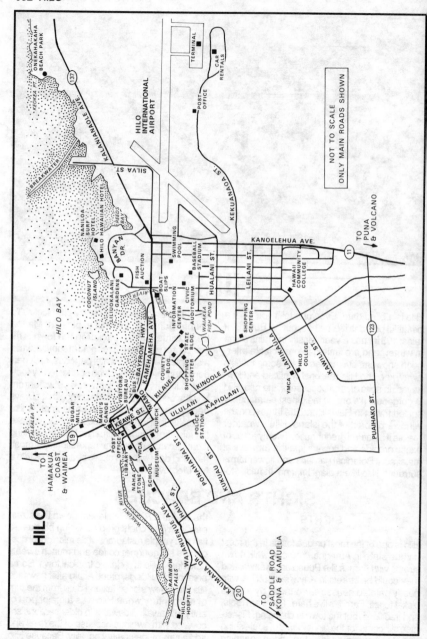

HILO

NOT TO SCALE
ONLY MAIN ROADS SHOWN

s a town, most Americans can relate to it: it's big enough to have one-way streets and malls, but not so big that it's a metropolis like Honolulu, or so small that it's a village like Hana. You can walk the central area comfortably in an afternoon, but the town does sprawl, and it's happening. Teenagers in "boom box" cars cruise the main strip which is lined with fine restaurants, high-tech discos, and mom-and-pop shops. There's even a down-and-out section where guys hunker down in alleyways, smoking cigarettes and peering into the night. But in the still night, there's the deep-throated sound of a ship's foghorn, almost like a specter of times past when Hilo was a vibrant port. Hilo is the opposite of Kailua-Kona both spiritually and physically. There, everything is running super fast, a clone of Honolulu. In Hilo the old beat, the old music, that feeling of a tropical place where rhythms are slow and sensual still exists. Hilo nights are alive with sounds of the tropics and the heady smell of fruits and flowering trees wafting on the breeze. Hilo still remains what it always was—a town, a place where people live.

Hilo is the eastern hub of the island. Choose a direction, and an hour's driving puts you in a time-lost valley, deep into *paniolo* country, sitting on the blackness of a recent lava flow, or surveying the steaming fumaroles of Volcanoes Park. In and around town are museums, riverbank fishing, cultural centers, plenty of gardens, waterfalls, a potholed riverbed, and lava caves. Hilo's beaches are small, rocky, and hard to find—perfect for keeping crowds away. Hilo is bite-sized, but you'll need a rental car or the Banyan Shuttle to visit most of the sights around town.

The main thoroughfares through town are Kilauea Street, which merges into Keawe Street and runs one-way toward the Wailuku River, and Kinoole Street, which runs one-way away from the river. Basically they feed into each other and make a big loop through the downtown area. Kamehameha Avenue fronts the town area and runs along the bay.

Lyman Mission House And Museum

At 276 Haili Street, Hilo 96720, tel. 835-5021. Open daily except Sun. 9 a.m. to 4 p.m. Admission $3.50 adults, $2.50 children (six to 18 years). This admission allows you into both the original Lyman House and the museum, the large new building just next door.

This well-preserved New England-style frame house was the homestead of the Lymans, a Congregationalist missionary family. It's the oldest frame building on Hawaii, built by David and Sarah Lyman in 1839. In 1856, a second story was added, which provided more room and a perfect view of the harbor. In 1926, Haili Street was extended past the home, and at that time the Wilcox and Lyman families had the house turned parallel to the street so that it would front the entrance. Lyman House was opened as a museum in 1932. The furniture is authentic "Sandwich Isles" circa 1850, the best pieces fashioned from *ohia*. Much of it has come from other missionary homes although many pieces belonged to the original occupants.

The floors, mantles, and doors are deep, luxurious *koa*. The main door is a "Christian door," built by the Hilo Boys Boarding School. The top panels form a cross and the bottom depicts an open Bible. Many of the artifacts on the deep windowsills are tacked down because of earthquakes. One room was used as a schoolroom/dayroom where Mrs. Lyman taught arithmetic, map-making, and proper manners. The dining room holds an original family rocking chair and table that would be set with "blue willow" china seen in a nearby hutch. Some of the most interesting exhibits are small personal items like a music box that still plays, and a collection of New England autumn leaves that Mrs. Lyman had sent over to show her children what that season was like. Upstairs are bedrooms that were occupied by the parents and the eight children (six boys). Their portraits hang in a row. Emma, youngest of the eight, kept a diary and faithfully recorded eruptions, earthquakes, and tsunamis. Scientists still refer to it for some of the earliest recorded data on these natural disturbances. The master bedroom has a large *koa* bed with pineapples carved into the bedposts, handmade by a sea captain who lived in Hilo. The bedroom mirror is an original, in which many Hawaiians received their first surprised look at themselves. Connected to the master bedroom is the nursery that holds a cradle used by all eight children. It's obvious that the Lymans did not live luxuriously, but they were comfortable in their new island home.

Next door to the Lyman House, in a modern two-story building, is the museum. As you enter, you are greeted by a bust of King David Kalakaua, the Merry Monarch, who reigned from 1874 until 1891. The first floor is designated as the **Island Heritage Gallery.** On entering is a replica of a Hawaiian grass house, complete with thatched roof and floor mats. Nearby are Hawaiian tools: hammers of clinkstone, chisels of basalt, and state-of-the-art "stone age" polishing stones with varying textures used to rub bowls and canoes to a smooth finish. Hawaiian fiberwork, the best in Polynesia, is next. As well as coconut and pandanus, the Hawaiians used the pliable air root of the ie'ie. The material, dyed brown or black, was woven into intricate designs. There are fishhooks, stone lamps, mortars and pestles, lomi lomi sticks, even a display on kahunas, with a fine text on the kapu system. Pre-contact displays give way to kimonos from Japan, a Chinese herbal medicine display, and a nook dedicated to Filipino heritage. Saying good-bye is a bust of Mark Twain, carved from a piece of the very monkeypod tree that he planted in Waiohinu in 1866.

Upstairs is the **Earth Heritage Gallery.** The mineral and rock collection here is rated one of the top 10 in the entire country, and by far the best in Polynesia. Marvel at thunder eggs, agates, jaspers, India blue mezolite, aquamarine lazerite from Afghanistan, and hunks of weirdly shaped lava. These displays are the lifelong collection of the great-grandson of the original Rev. Lyman. Anything coming from the earth can be exhibited here: shells named and categorized from around the world, petrified wood, cases of glass paperweights, crystals, Chinese artifacts, and Japanese screens. Scientific works from Kilauea and Mauna Kea are explained, and an entire section is dedicated to the vanishing flora and fauna of Hawaii. The museum is an educational delight.

Natural Sites And Walking Tour

Start your tour of Hilo by picking up a pamphlet/map entitled Discover Downtown Hilo, A Walking Tour of Historic Sites, free at most restaurants, hotels, and shops. This self-guiding pamphlet takes you down the main streets and back lanes where you discover the unique architecture of Hilo's glory days. The majority of the vintage buildings have been restored and the architecture varies from the continental style of the Hawaiian Telephone Building, to the Zen Buddhist Taishoji Shoto Mission.

A remarkable building is the old police station just across from Kalakaua Park. Behind in a classic plantation building is the home of the **East Hawaii Culture Center,** a nonprofit organization which supports local arts and hosts varying festivals, performances, and workshops throughout the year (see p. 90).

After leaving the Lyman Museum, it's a short walk over to Hilo's library, 300 Waianuenue Ave. Sitting at the entrance are two large stones. The larger is called **Naha Stone,** known for its ability to detect any offspring of the ruling Naha clan. The test was simple: place a baby on it, and if it remained silent, it was Naha; if it cried, it wasn't. It is believed that this 7,000-pound monolith was brought from Kauai by canoe and placed near P-inao Temple in the immediate vicinity of what is now Wailuku Drive and Keawe Street. Kamehameha the Great supposedly fulfilled a prophecy of "moving a mountain" by budging this stone. The smaller stone is thought to be an entrance pillar of the Pinao Temple. Just behind the library is the Wailuku River. Pick any of its bridges for a panoramic view down to the sea. Often, local fishermen try their luck from the Wailuku's grassy banks. The massive boulder sitting in the mouth of the river is known as Maui's Canoe.

A few miles out of town, heading west on Waianuenue Avenue, are two natural spectacles definitely worth a look. Just past Hilo High School a sign directs you to Wailuku River State Park. Here is **Rainbow Falls,** a most spectacular yet easily visited natural wonder. You'll overlook a circular pool in the river below that's almost 100 feet in diameter, and cascading into it is a lovely waterfall. The falls deserve their name because as they hit the water below, their mists throw flocks of rainbows into the air. Underneath the falls is a huge cavern. Most people are content to look from the vantage point near the parking lot, but if you walk to the left a stone stairway leads to a private viewing area directly over the falls. Here the river, strewn with volcanic boulders, pours over the edge. Follow the path for a minute or so along the bank to come to a gigantic banyan tree and a different vantage point.

Follow Waianuenue Street for two more miles past Hilo Hospital to the heights above town. A

ign to turn right onto Pee Pee Falls Street points
[to] the **Boiling Pots.** Usually no one is here. At
[t]he parking lot is an emergency phone and toi-
[l]ets. Follow the path past No Swimming signs to
[a]n overlook. Indented into the riverbed below
[a]re a series of irregularly shaped holes that look
[li]ke a peg-legged giant left his "peg prints" in the
[h]ot lava. Seven or eight are like naturally bub-
[b]ling jacuzzis. Turn your head upriver to see Pee
[P]ee Falls, a gorgeous five-spouted waterfall.
[Y]ou'll have this area to yourself, and it's great for
[a] quiet picnic lunch.

Around Banyan Drive

[I]f your Hilo hotel isn't situated along Banyan
[D]rive, go there. This bucolic road skirts the edge
[o]f the Waiakea Peninsula sticking out into Hilo
[B]ay. Lining the drive is an almost uninterrupted
[s]eries of banyans forming a giant hedgerow,
[w]hile the fairways and greens of the Banyan
Golf Course take up the center of the tiny peninsula. Park your car at one end and take a 15-
minute stroll through this park-like atmosphere;
the banyans have been named for well-known
American luminaries. Boutiques and a variety of
restaurants sit coolly under the trees.

 Liliuokalani Gardens are formal Japanese-
style gardens located along the west end of
Banyan Drive. Meditatively quiet, they offer a
beautiful view of the bay. **Coconut Island** just
offshore is connected by a footbridge leading
from the gardens. Along the footpaths are pagodas designed for relaxing, *torii* gates, stone lanterns, and half-moon bridges spanning a series
of ponds and streams. Few people visit, and if it
weren't for the striking fingers of black lava and
coconut trees, you could easily be in Japan.

 Suisan Fish Market is at the corner of
Banyan Drive and Lihiwai Street which crosses
Kamehameha Avenue. This fish auction draws
island fishermen of every nationality. The auc-
tioneer's staccato is pure pidgin. Restaurateurs,
housewives, and a smattering of tourists gather
by 7:30 a.m. to eyeball the catch of the day.
Boats tie up and fishermen talk quietly about the
prices. Next door a small snack shop sells sandwiches and piping hot coffee. Grab a cup and
walk over to the gardens through a nearby entrance—you'll have them to yourself.

 Cross Lihiwai Street heading south. **Waiakea
Pond,** a brackish lagoon where people often
fish, is on your right. To the left are **Hoolulu**

Rainbow Falls

County Park, Civic Center Auditorium, and a
city nursery brimming with orchids. The **Culture
Center Nihon** is also here, at 123 Lihiwai
Street, which displays artwork and cultural exhibits from Japan. The center is also a restaurant
and sushi bar, with a special room set aside for
the "tea ceremony." (For more details see
"Food" below.)

 On the opposite side of Waiakea Fish Pond
(drive down Kamehameha Avenue and make a
left onto Pauahi Street since no bridges cross),
you'll find **Wailoa Information Center** dispensing all manner of brochures and pamphlets
on Hilo's and the Big Island's activities. The walls
of this 10- sided building are used to display
works of local artists and cultural/historic exhibits,
changed on a monthly basis. Across the parking
lot in a grassy area is the **Tsunami Memorial,**
dedicated to those who lost their lives in the devastating tidal waves that raked the island. Volcanic stone, inlaid with blue and green tile, has
been laid to form a circular wall that undulates
and peaks like a wave. It's worth a look.

Hilo's Gardens

Hilo's greatest asset is its flowers. Its biggest cash crops are orchids and anthuriums. Flowers grow everywhere, but to see them in a more formalized view, visit one of the following nurseries in and around town. Most have excellent prices for floral arrangements sent back to the Mainland. They'll do a Hawaiian bouquet with heliconia, anthuriums, and orchids, for around $25 including shipping. The flowers arrive neatly packaged but unassembled, with a picture of the arrangement so that you can put them together yourself. These hearty cut flowers will look fresh and vibrant for as long as two weeks, so a few days in the mail won't hurt them. (Also see "Hawaii Tropical Botanical Gardens," p. 598.)

Hilo Tropical Gardens, (formerly Kong's Floraleigh), 1477 Kalanianaole Ave., Hilo, HI 96720, tel. 935-4957, is open daily 9 to 5. Go on a free self-guided tour through the gardens; all plants have been labeled. Everything's here: plumeria, lipstick trees, anthuriums, orchids, birds of paradise, even pineapples, coconuts, and papayas. You can purchase all manner of dried and fresh-cut flowers, seeds, packaged plants, seedlings, and corsages. A boutique offers handmade Hawaiian products. The "no-pressure" sales people are courteous and friendly. Shipping purchases is no problem.

Along Kilauea Avenue, between Lanikaula and Kawili Street, the Department of Natural Resources, Division of Forestry maintains the **Hilo Arboretum,** open 7:45 a.m.-4:30 p.m. Mon.-Fri., closed Sat., Sun., and holidays; free admission. This tree nursery contains most of the trees present in Hawaii including indigenous and imported specimens. Enter the office, where they'll provide you with a mimeographed sheet entitled "Hilo Nursery Arboretum". It's basically a self-guided tour, but the clerks will warn you that it's not very good. It attempts to name the trees by matching them to points on the map as you pass by instead of having little plaques or signs on each speciman. However, the trees are magnificent and you will virtually have this quiet area to yourself. Originally the site was an animal quarantine station operated by the Territory of Hawaii; the 19.4 acres of the arboretum was established in 1920 by Brother Mathias Newell. Brother Newell was a nurseryman employed by the Catholic boys' school in

Hilo. At that time the board of forestry was already actively introducing plant species from all over the world. For 40 years from 1921-1961 the department was engaged in the developmen and maintenance of arboretums consisting primarily of plant species from Australia and Africa Arboretum sites ranged from sea level to Mauna Kea. Plant materials were exchanged and thou sands of breadfruit cuttings were exported. Over 1,000 different tree species and 500 different fruit trees were field tested. Here at the Hilo Ar boretum over 1,000 trees were planted. A few trees such as the paper bark and and a few pines are more than 50 years old. Presently a small number of timber species are grown for re forestation purposes. Essentially the Hilo site is utilized for the propagation of rare and en dangered plant species, research, and experi mental pursuits.

Rainbow Tropicals is just past mile marker 4 on Route 11 heading toward Volcanoes, where you make a right on Mamaki Street, heading towards the zoo. Rainbow Tropicals is open daily 8:30 a.m.-5 p.m. They're friendly and a self-guided tour takes you under the huge nets of shade canopies that cover the flowers. It's like being under a titanic mosquito net that covers four-five acres. Prices for their flowers are excellent.

Nanimau Gardens are some of the largest in and around Hilo, and touring these spectacular displays is well worth an afternoon. Located at 421 Makalika Street, (off Route 11) Hilo, HI 96720, tel. 959-3541, open daily 8:30 a.m. to 5 p.m., admission $5, golf cart for touring $6. The gardens consist of 20 sculpted acres with 33 more being developed. More than just a botanical garden, Nani Mau is a "floral theme park" designed as a tourist attraction. Walks throughout the garden are very tame, but very beautiful; umbrellas are provided during rainy weather which adds it own dripping crystalline charm to the experience. Plants are labeled in English, Latin, and Japanese. The gardens are a huge but ordered display of flowers, flowering trees, and shrubbery, with tropical birds here and there competing with their wild plummage against the exotic blooms. The gardens are broken off into separate areas: fruit orchards, heliconia garden, ginger garden, anthurium garden, orchid garden, orchid pavilion, gardenia garden, and bromeliad garden. The newest addition on the

3 acres is an annual garden, a white-sand each, a little volcano, a picture garden for photos, and orchids and more orchids. The new section also features floral sculptures, a small reflective pond, and an assortment of flowers and shrubs laid out in geometric patterns, hearts, mountains, and even *aloha,* and *Hilo Hawaii* spelled out with flowers. The tourist shop and snack area is exactly like a Japanese *omiyagi* (souvenir) shop. No wonder, since it's owned by Japanese, and the tour buses coming in here are all filled with Japanese. If you enjoy a clean, outdoor experience, surrounded by magnificent flowers, this is the place.

Hirose Nursery is even closer to town on Route 11. Spot the Puainako Town Center and look across the street for a big *Visitors Welcome* sign inviting you into the nursery located at 2212 Kanoelehua Ave., tel. 959-4561, open Mon.-Sat. 8 a.m. to 4 p.m., admission free. Enter through a little souvenir shop, and the retail flower shop which leads to a greenhouse. Then go out back following a garden path. Here, you enter a jungle of tall bamboo, huge green leaves, and hanging vines. It's almost like being in someone's private backyard, and takes only 20 minutes for a complete tour.

Tanaka's is an excellent nursery from which to buy and to send flowers. They call themselves Jewel Box Orchids, and also The Orchidarium, Hawaii Inc., at 524 Manono Street, Hilo, HI. It's off the main track. Follow Route 11 toward Volcano, make a right on Kekuanaoa Street, and go down four blocks to Manono. Make a right and they're a few hundred yards down on the left. Beautiful orchids for unbeatable prices. Search them out.

While in the neighborhood visit **Paradise Plants,** at 575 Hinano Street, tel. 935-4043, a complete garden center specializing in indoor-outdoor plants and tropical fruit trees. They send orchids and other live flowers to the Mainland. Also featured is a large gift area with gifts from around the world. While browsing check out their free orchid garden, which ranks as Hilo's oldest.

Kualoa Farms is at the corner of Mamaki (off Route 11) and Kealakai streets, tel. 959-4565, open daily 8 a.m. to 4 p.m. A guided tour takes you over some of the 62 acres planted in anthuriums, *ti* plants, torch gingers, and macadamia and papaya orchards.

Mauna Loa Macadamia Nut Factory is located along Mauna Loa Road, eight miles out of Hilo on Route 11 heading towards Volcanoes. Head down the drive until you come to the visitors center. Inside will be a free video explaining the development and processing of macadamia nuts in Hawaii. Take a self-guided tour through the orchards with all trees and plants identified. Then return to the snack shop for mac-nut goodies like ice cream and cookies. The gift shop has a wide assortment of mac-nut items at considerably lower prices than anywhere else on the island.

Panaewa Rainforest Zoo

Not many travelers can visit a zoo in such a unique setting where the animals virtually live in paradise. The road leading to the zoo is a trip in itself, getting you back into the country. Follow Route 11 toward Volcanoes for a few miles until you see the sign pointing down Mamaki Street leading to the zoo. On a typical weekday, you'll have the place to yourself. The zoo, operated by the Dept. of Parks and Recreation, is open Mon.-Fri. 9-4, Sat. 11-2, gates locked at 4:15 p.m., closed Christmas and New Year's Day, admission free.

Here you have more of a feeling of being fenced out, than the animals being fenced in. The collection includes ordinary and exotic animals from around the world. You'll see a giant anteater from Costa Rica, pygmy hippos from Africa, and a wide assortment of birds like pheasants and peacocks. The zoo is also a botanical garden with many of the trees, shrubs, and ferns labeled. The zoo hosts many endangered animals indigenous to Hawaii like the Laysan duck, the Hawaiian coot, the *pueo,* Hawaiian galllinule, and even a feral pig in his own stone mini-condo. There are some great iguanas and mongooses, lemurs, and an aviary section with different and exotic birds like yellow-fronted parrots and blue and gold macaws. The central area is a tigers' playground; a tall fence marks this rather large area where tigers still rule in their little domain. It's got its own pond, and tall grasses which make the tigers feel at home, but also make them hard to spot.

A touching spot is the **Astronaut Grove,** in memory of the astronauts who were killed on the regrettable explosion of the space shuttle, *Challenger.* All are remembered, especially Ellison

Onizuka, a native son of the Big Island. The zoo makes a perfect side trip for families, or anyone wishing to get off the beaten track.

Scenic Drive

Route 19 heading north from Hilo toward Honokaa is a must, with magnificent inland and coastal views one after another. (See "Hamakua Coast," p. 615 for full coverage of the northern section leading to Waipio). Only five minutes from Hilo, you'll come to Papaikou town. Look for a small convenience store on the right. Just here is a road posted as a scenic drive which dips down towards the coast. Take it! Almost immediately a sign says Narrow Winding Road, 20 MPH, letting you know what kind of an area you're coming into. Start down this lane past some very modest homes, and into the jungle that covers the road like a green living tunnel. Prepare for tiny bridges crossing tiny valleys. Stop, and you can almost hear the jungle growing.

In a few minutes you'll come to **Hawaii Tropical Botanical Gardens,** tel. 964-5233, open daily 8:30 a.m. to 5:30 p.m., with the last shuttle van departing for the garden from the registration area at 4:30 p.m., admission is $10, children under 16 are free. Remember that the $10 entrance fee not only allows you to walk through the best tamed tropical rainforest available on the Big Island, but helps preserve the area as a tropical rainforest and a bird sanctuary in perpetuity. The gardens were established in 1978 when Dan and Pauline Lutkenhouse purchased the property in order to educate the public to the beauty of tropical plants in their natural setting. The gardens have been open for viewing since 1984. Mr. Lutkenhouse, a retired San Francisco businessman, purchased the 25-acre valley and personally performed the work that transformed it into one of the most exotic spots in all of Hawaii. The locality was amazingly beautiful but inaccessible because it was so rugged. Through a personal investment of nearly $1 million, and six painstaking years of toil aided only by two helpers, he hand-cleared the land, built trails and bridges, developed an irrigation system, acquired more than 1,600 different species of trees and plants, and established one mile of scenic trails and a large water lily lake stocked with *koi* and tropical fish. A shuttle van takes you on a five-minute ride down to Onomea Bay where the

gardens are located. Onomea was a favorite spot with the Hawaiians, who came to fish and camp for the night. The valley was a fishing village called Pahalii in the early 1800s. Later on it became a rough-water seaport used for shipping sugar cane and other tropical products. Recently, a remake of *Lord of the Flies* was filmed here, and it's easy to see why the area made the perfect movie set.

The van drops you off at a staging area in the garden where you'll find self-guiding maps, drinking water, restrooms, umbrellas for your convenience, and *jungle perfume*—better known as mosquito repellent! The very informative booklet provided, lists plants from the four corners of the globe including ones from Iran, Central China, Japan, tropical Africa, native plants from Hawaii, India, Borneo, Brazil, East Indies, South Pacific Islands, tropical America, and the Philippines. All plants are named and numbered with a full botanical description. Also listed are birds that you may encounter: the white-tailed tropic bird, black-crowned heron, Pacific golden plover, Hawaiian hawk, Japanese white eye, common mynah, and northern cardinal. Choose one of the aptly named trails like Ocean Trail, or Waterfall Trail and lose yourself in the beauty of the surroundings. You are in the middle of a tamed jungle, walking along manicured paths. Stroll the Ocean Trail down to the sea, where the rugged coastline is dramaticaly pummeled by frothy waves. You can hear the waves entering submerged lava caves where they blow in and out like a giant bellows. Away from the sea you'll encounter cages filled with exotic birds like cockatoos from Indonesia and blue-fronted Amazon parrots. Walk the inland trails past waterfalls, streams, a bamboo grove, and innumerable flowers. For at least a brief time you get to feel the power and beauty of a living Garden of Eden.

Hawaiian Artifacts, just a minute down Scenic Drive past the gardens, is a shop owned and operated by Paul Gephart, tel. 964-1729, open Mon.-Sat. 9-5. Paul creates wood sculptures, mainly from *koa* and *ohia* that he turns into whales, dolphins, birds, and poi bowls. Here's also a small but tasteful collection of jewelry and seashells, all at very decent prices.

Continue for another two-three miles, and you'll come to a wooden bridge with a white railing overlooking a cascading mountain stream with a big swimming hole. Great for a freshwater

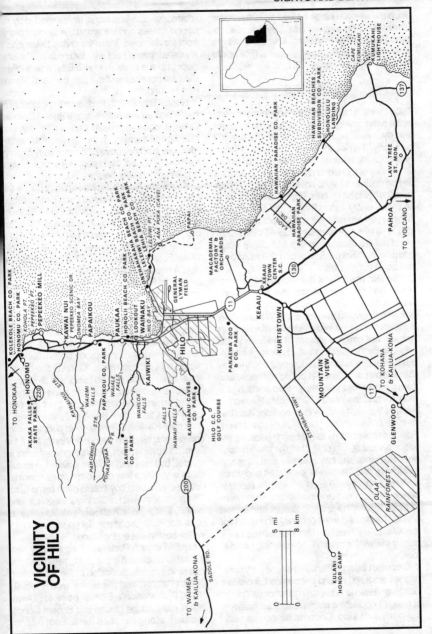

VICINITY OF HILO

0 5 mi
0 8 km

TO WAIMEA & KAILUA-KONA

SADDLE RD.

KULANI HONOR CAMP

OLAA RAINFOREST

GLENWOOD

(11)

MOUNTAIN VIEW

TO KOHANA & KAILUA-KONA

KURTISTOWN

STAINBACK HWY.

HILO C.C. GOLF COURSE

KAUMANA CAVES CO. PARK

PANAEWA ZOO & CO. PARK

HAWAII FALLS

WAHILOA FALLS

WHALE FALLS

WAIEMI FALLS

PAPAIKOU CO. PARK

PAHOEHOE STR.

POHAKUPAA STR.

KAWAINUI STR.

KAIWIKI CO. PARK

KAIWIKI

WAINAKU

PAUKAA

PAPAIKOU

KAWAI NUI

HONOMU

AKAKA FALLS STATE PARK

TO HONOKAA

(220)

KOLEKOLE BEACH CO. PARK

HONOMU CO. PARK

PEPEEKEO PT.

KOHOLA PT.

PEPEEKEO MILL

PEPEEKEO SCENIC DR.

ONOMEA BAY

HONOLII BEACH CO. PARK

LOOKOUT

HILO BAY

HILO

GENERAL LYMAN FIELD

LELEIWI PT.

ONE LELEIWI BEACH CO. PARK

JAHAKHA BEACH CO. PARK

JAHAKHA BEACH CO. PARK

ANA PUKA (CAVE)

PAPAI

MACADEMIA FACTORY & ORCHARDS

KEAAU TOWN CENTER S.C.

KEAAU

(11)

KAOHI

HAWAIIAN PARADISE PARK

KAOHI DR.

(130)

HAWAIIAN BEACHES SUBDIVISION CO. PARK

HONOLULU LANDING

LAVA TREE ST. MON.

PAHOA

TO VOLCANO

(137)

CAPE KUMUKAHI

KUMUKAHI LIGHTHOUSE

dip, but always be careful: these streams can be torrential during a heavy rain. The side road rejoins Route 19 at Papeeko, a workers' village where you can get gas or supplies. (For points north see "Hamakua Coast", p. 615.)

BEACHES

If you define a beach as a long open expanse of white sand covered by a thousand sunbathers and their beach umbrellas, then Hilo doesn't have any. If a beach, to you, can be a smaller, more intimate affair where a good but not gigantic number of tourists and families can spend the day on pockets of sand between fingers of black lava, then Hilo has plenty. Hilo's best beaches all lie to the east of the city along Kalanianaole Avenue, which runs six miles from downtown Hilo to where it dead ends at Lelei Point. Not all beaches are clearly marked, but all are easily spotted by cars parked along the road or in makeshift parking lots.

Hilo Bayfront Park is a thousand yards of black sand that narrows considerably as it runs west from the Wailuku River toward downtown. At one time it went all the way to the Wailuku River and was renowned throughout the islands for its beauty, but commercialism of the harbor has ruined it. By the 1960s, so much sewage and industrial waste had been pumped into the bay that it was considered a public menace, and then the great tsunami came. Reclamation projects created the Wailoa River State Recreation Area at the east end, and shorefront land became a buffer zone against future inundation. Few swimmers come to the beach because the water is cloudy and chilly, but the sharks don't seem to mind! The bay is terrific for fishing and picnicking, and the sails of small craft and windsurfers can always be seen. It's a perfect spot for canoe races, and many local teams come here to train. Notice the judging towers and canoe sheds. Toward the west end, near the mouth of the Wailuku River, surfers catch long rides during the winter months, entertaining spectators.

Coconut Island Park is reached by footbridge from a spit of land just outside Liliuokalani Gardens. It was at one time a *pu'uhonua* ("place of refuge") opposite a human sacrificial *heiau* on the peninsula side. Coconut Island has restrooms, pavilion, and picnic tables shaded by tall coconut trees and ironwoods. A favorite picnic spot for decades, there's a diving tower and a sheltered natural pool area for children. The only decent place to swim in Hilo Bay, it also offers the best panorama of the city, bay, and Mauna Kea beyond.

Reeds Bay Beach Park is on the east side of the Waiakea Peninsula at the end of Banyan Drive. It too is technically part of Hilo Bay, and offers good swimming, though the water is notoriously cold because of a constantly flowing freshwater spring. Most people just picnic here, and fishermen frequent the area.

Keaukaha Beach, located on Puhi Bay, is the first in a series of beaches as you head east on Kalanianaole Avenue. Look for Baker Avenue, and pull off left into a parking area just near an old pavilion. Not an official beach park, it is a favorite spot with local people who swim at "Cold Water Pond," a spring-fed inlet at the head of the bay. A sewage treatment plant fronts the western side of Puhi Bay. Much nicer areas await just up Kalanianaole Avenue.

Onekahakaha Beach Park has it all: safe swimming, white-sand beach, lifeguards, all amenities, and camping. Turn left onto Machida Lane and park in the lot of Hilo's favorite "family" beach. Swim in the large sandy-bottom pool protected by the breakwater. Outside the breakwater the currents can be fierce and drownings have been recorded. Walk east along the shore to find an undeveloped area of the park with many small tidal pools. Beware of sea urchins.

James Kealoha Park is next; people swim, snorkel, and fish, and during winter months it's a favorite surfing spot. A large grassy area is shaded by trees and a picnic pavilion. Just offshore is Mahikea Island, also known as Scout Island because local boy scouts often camp here. This entire area was known for its fishponds, and inland, just across Kalanianaole Avenue, is Loko'aka Pond, a commercial operation providing the best mullet on the island.

Leleiwi Beach Park lies along a lovely residential area carved into the rugged coastline. Part of the park is dedicated to the Richardson Ocean Center, and the entire area is locally called **Richardson's Beach.** Look for Uwau Street, just past the Mauna Loa Shores Condo, and park along the road here. Spot a fancy house surrounded by tall coconut trees and follow the pathway through the grove. Use a shower that's coming out of the retaining wall surrounding the house. Keep walking until you come to a sea wall. A tiny cove and black-sand beach is the first in a series. This is a terrific area for snorkeling, with plenty of marinelife. Walk east to a natural lava breakwater. Behind it pools are filled and flushed by the surging tide. The water breaks over the top of the lava and rushes into the pools, making a natural jacuzzi. This is one of the most picturesque swimming areas on the island. At Leleiwi Beach Park proper (three pavilions), the shore is open to the ocean and there are strong currents; it's best to head directly to Richardson's.

Lehia Park is the end of the road. When the pavement stops follow the dirt track until you come to a large grassy field shaded by a variety of trees. This unofficial camping area has no amenities whatsoever. A series of pools like those at Richardson's are small, sandy-bottomed, and safe. Outside of the natural lava breakwater currents are treacherous. Wintertime often sends tides surging inland here, making Lehia unusable. This area is about as far away as you can get and still be within a few minutes of downtown Hilo.

PRACTICALITIES

ACCOMMODATIONS

Accommodations in Hilo are hardly ever booked out, and they're reasonably priced. Sounds great, but many hotels have "gone condo" to survive, while others have simply shut their doors, so there aren't as many as there once were. During the Merry Monarch Festival (late April), the entire town is booked solid! The best hotels are clustered along Banyan Drive, with a few gems tucked away on the city streets.

Banyan Drive Hotels
The following hotels all lie along Banyan Drive. They range from moderate to deluxe; all are serviced by the Banyan Shuttle (see p. 576).

Hilo Hawaiian Hotel, 71 Banyan Dr., Hilo, HI 96720, tel. 935-9361 or (800) 272-5725. This classy hotel's prices start at $83-104; all rooms have a/c, phone, and TV, plus there's a pool. The Hilo Hawaiian occupies the most beautiful grounds of any hotel in Hilo. From the vantage of the hotel's colonnaded veranda, you overlook formal gardens, Coconut Island, and Hilo Bay. The hotel buffet, especially seafood on Friday, is absolutely out of this world (see below). Built like a huge arc, its architecture blends well with its surroundings and expresses the theme set by Hilo Bay, that of a long sweeping crescent. As a deluxe hotel, the Hilo Hawaiian is the best that Hilo has to offer.

Hawaii Naniloa Hotel, 93 Banyan Dr., Hilo, HI 96720, tel. 935-0831, or (800) 367-5360. This massive 386-room hotel offers deluxe accommodations starting at $80 to $130 for a deluxe room with private balcony. They offer a/c, TV, hotel pool, parking, and tennis. The pool setting, just above the lava, is the nicest in Hilo. Headquarters of the Merry Monarch Festival, the original hotel dates back over 60 years, and has built up a fine reputation for value and service. The Hawaii Naniloa has recently undergone extensive renovations, and is now as beautiful as ever.

Hilo Bay Hotel is sandwiched between the above deluxe hotels at 87 Banyan Dr., Hilo, HI 96720, tel. 935-0861 or (800) 442-5841. Rooms here begin at $49 double, with the most expensive under $80. The Hilo Bay offers good value, but it's a bit of "mutton dressed as lamb." The building is yellow stucco, with a wood-shingled lanai running around the outside. There is parking, pool, and all rooms are clean, have TV, a/c, and phones. Uncle Billy's Polynesian Marketplace is part of the complex.

You can't miss the orange and black **Hilo Hukilau Hotel,** 126 Banyan Drive, tel. 935-0821 or (800) 367-7000. This is the budget hotel on Banyan Drive. It's island-owned by the Kimi family, and like the others in this small chain, it's clean, well-kept, and has Polynesian-inspired decor. Room prices vary according to the amount of business happening at the time, and can dip as low as $40 s, but expect to pay about $50. The grounds are laid out around a central courtyard and the pool is secluded away from the street.

This family-style hotel has a motel atmosphere, where the friendly staff go out of their way to make you feel welcome.

Downtown Hotels

The following hotels are found along Hilo's downtown streets. Some are in quiet residential areas, while others are along busy thoroughfares. They are moderately to inexpensively priced.

Dolphin Bay Hotel is a sparkling little gem—simply the best hotel bargain in Hilo, one of those places where you get more than what you pay for. It sits on a side street in the Puueo section of town at the north end of Hilo Bay: 333 Iliahi St., Hilo 96720, tel. 935-1466. John Alexander, the owner/manager, is available at the front desk every day. He's a font of information about the Big Island, and will happily dispense advice on how to make your day trips fulfilling. The hotel was built by his father who spent years in Japan, and you'll be happy to discover this influence when you sink deep into the *ofuro*-type tubs in every room. The 18 units all have full modern kitchens, and you can rent from a $29 single studio apartment, to a two-bedroom, fully furnished unit for $69. Deluxe units upstairs have open-beam ceilings and a lanai, and with three spacious rooms feel like an apartment. No swimming pool or a/c, but there are color TVs and fans with excellent cross ventilation. The grounds and housekeeping are immaculate, and bananas, papayas, and other exotic fruits are found in hanging baskets free for guests. Weekly rates range from $156 for a studio to $300 for a two-bedroom deluxe. Make reservations, because everyone who has found the Dolphin Bay comes back again and again.

The **Lanikai** (formerly Hotel Palm Terrace) is just down the street from the Dolphin Bay at 100 Puueo St., tel. 935-5556. The hotel has just been sold and is being renovated and cleaned. After years of decline the hotel is attempting a comeback. You can't beat the prices at $19.95 s, $27.95 d, weekly $95 s, $120 d, with even greater monthly discounts. For this you'll get a small, adequately furnished room that may have a refrigerator and hot plate. The views from the walkway along the upper floors are spectacular.

The **Hilo Hotel** is downtown at 142 Kinoole St., Hilo 96720, tel. 961-3733. This vintage hotel originally opened in 1888 and was managed by Uncle George Lycurgus, who was more famous as manager of Volcano House. The present buildings date from 1971, but a sense of nostalgia still lingers under the huge rubber tree that fronts the hotel. Additions have been added over the years, but basic rooms in both old and new wings are under $35. Old-wing rooms have phones; new-wing rooms are quieter and have a/c, and all rooms have a fridge. A big front porch holds rocking chairs, and a complimentary continental breakfast is served at the pool every morning. The Hilo Hotel is also home to the Fuji Restaurant, one of the best in Hilo (see p. 606). Mr. Maeda, the manager for 15 years, takes a personal hand in the running of the hotel. He's made two-bedrooms units, renting for $68, in the rear of the property that are nestled away from the noise of the street and are complete with sitting rooms, full baths, and a kitchenette. The Hilo Hotel is a classic hotel where you get full value for your money, and where the staff takes pride in doing things the right way.

The **Iolani Hotel,** 193 Kinoole St., Hilo 96720, tel. 961-9863, and the **Kamaaina Hotel** at 110 Haili St., tel. 961-9860, are your basic flea-bag dives. You can get a room at both for about $85 a week if you can ever find anyone to check you in.

The **Hilo Bay Inn and Hostel** is the newest addition to Hilo's accommodations, opening in the summer of 1990, and one of the most unique in all of Hawaii. Fully accredited by the American Youth Hostel Asociation, it offers clean and decent accommodations. The philosophy adopted by founder and director David Larson, and implemented by his staff, is "to provide the opportunity to experience hospitality from a perspective of love, health, cooperation and ecology, while persuing a profit as a business." Simply, they put people first. The hostel is located on the grounds of the old Kuhio Gardens, at 311 Kalanianaole St., Hilo, HI 96720, tel. 935-1383. Just outside the doors of the hostel is a beautiful lagoon dotted with tidepools, and opening to Reed's Bay. Guests can fish or rent a kayak from the hostel for an afternoon of exploration. Special attention will also be paid to traveling cyclists, with bicycles available for rental. Dorm-style bunkbeds are $12 AYH member, or $15 non-members. In addition, nine private rooms will accommodate two to three people per night, for

$30 members, and $3 per person, per room, extra for non-members. A communal kitchen is provided for self-prepared meals, but there is also the **Garden Cafe,** where you can dine on natural and vegetarian fare, herbal teas, coffees, juices, smoothies, and sandwiches. The cafe will uses organic vegetables from its own garden. **Island Treasures Gift Shoppe,** also on the premises features island crafts in a country atmosphere. The Hilo Bay Inn and Hostel is an excellent choice not only for the budget traveler, but also for anyone seeking a *real* travel experience.

FOOD

Inexpensive Dining

Mun Cheong Lau is a cheap Chinese joint in downtown Hilo at 172 Kilauea Ave., Hilo 96720. tel. 935-3040 (take out too), open daily 11 a.m.-11 p.m., closed Tuesdays. If you want to eat with the "people," this is the spot. Soups on the front of the menu are $3.50; those on the back are $2.50, and are about the same except that they don't contain noodles. The bowls are generous. Entrees like crispy chicken in oyster sauce for under $5 are delicious at any price. Seafoods offered include abalone with vegies for $3.40, abalone with black mushrooms, $4.50, and shrimp with corn, $3.75. A variety of pork or beef dishes are all under $3.50, while pineapple spare ribs are $2.70, and boneless chicken with mushrooms is $3.75. These are full plates served with steamed rice, $.60 extra if you want fried rice. For under $4 you can still fill up in this place. It's clean, service is friendly, and the dining experience is certainly not fancy, but is definitely authentic.

Ting Hao Mandarin Kitchen is a family affair run by Alice Chang and her sister. Located at Puainako Town Center Mall, just south of town on Route 11, tel. 959-6288, open weekdays 11 a.m. to 8:30 p.m., weekends 5- 8:30 p.m. Seek them out for a mouthwatering, home-cooked meal. The two most expensive items on the menu are Seafood Treasure for $6, and half a tea-smoked duck for $7; all others are under $5. Service is slow due to individual-order cooking, and those in the know pick up a handout menu and call to place their orders 30 minutes before arriving.

Bear's Coffee Shop, at 910 Keawe, tel. 935-0708, next to Roussel's, is an upscale coffee shop that is renowned for breakfast. It features Belgian waffles (made from malted flour) and an assortment of egg dishes from 7-11:30 a.m. for $2.75. Lunch is hearty sandwiches of turkey, pastrami, chicken fillet, tuna, or ham for under $4, along with a small but zesty selection of Mexican food, and salads. Beverages include Italian sodas, homemade lemonade, and a large selection of coffee, cappuccino, and cafe latte. All perfect with desserts like carrot cake, Bear's cookies, cheesecake, and pies. A great place to relax, read the morning paper, and watch Hilo life go by.

Kay's Family Restaurant, at 684 Kilauea Ave., tel. 969-1776, open from Tues.-Sun. 5 a.m.-2 p.m., and again from 5-9 p.m., can't be beat for a good square meal of either Asian, Hawaiian, or American standards. Sandwich favorites like hamburgers, fish burgers, grilled cheese, and tuna are all under $3. Large bowls of *saimin* and wonton soups are under $4. Any of their grilled plates like Korean BBQ beef, or *kolbi* (short ribs) are all done over an open wood fire, and are delicious. Combo plates of their grilled offerings are $5.95 for one choice, two choices for $6.95, and three choices for $7.95, and include rice, *miso* soup, four kinds of *kimchi,* and vegetables. Kay's isn't much to look at, with leatherette booths and formica tables, but it's a winner.

Satsuki's, along the 200 block of Keawe St., receives the highest recommendation because when local people want a good meal at an inexpensive price they head here. Open for lunch 10 a.m-2 p.m., dinner 4:30-9 p.m., closed Tuesday. Specialties are oxtail soup, the lunch special for $4.25, and the Okinawa *soba* plate lunch for only $3.95. Dinner specials are beef teriyaki for $5.70, *tonkatsu,* $5.65, and fish teriyaki $7.50. Plenty of traditional favorites like *donburi* and *nabemono.* All meals come with *miso* soup, Japanese pickles and condiments, rice, and tea. No decor, but spotlessly clean and friendly. Excellent food at excellent value.

Sachi's Gourmet, only a few seconds away at 250 Keawe St., open Mon. 8 a.m.-2 p.m. only, Tues.-Sat. 8 a.m.-2 p.m., and dinner 5-9 p.m., Sun. dinner only 5-9 p.m., is the same type of restaurant as Satsuki's, with its own loyal local clentele. The food is excellent here, too, and the prices are unbeatable. You'll walk away stuffed on traditional Japanese food for about $8 for a full meal.

Dick's Coffee House in the Hilo Shopping Center, tel. 935-2769, is American standard with a Hawaiian twist. Open daily 7 a.m. to p.m., Sun. 7 to 10:30 a.m. This place could be Smalltown, U.S.A., with the walls covered in pennants, except that the waitresses wear outrageously colorful Hawaiian-style uniforms. Excellent prices for decent food—full meals with soup, salad, dessert, and coffee for $4.50.

Hukilau Restaurant at the Hukilau Hotel, 136 Banyan Way, is open daily 7 a.m. to 9 p.m. Along with passable breakfasts and dinners, the Hukilau Restaurant unfortunately offers an all-you-can-eat daily lunch special for $2.45 that's popular with senior citizens. "How can I go wrong?" you ask. Everything is mercilessly deep-fried with enough grease to plug the Alaska pipeline, and the rest is out of a can.

Tomi Zushi, a hole-in-the-wall Japanese restaurant, is a favorite with local people. It's at 68 Mamo St., tel. 961-6100. More of the same is Jimmy's at 362 Kinoole, tel. 935-5571, where you can fill up for under $6.

A small, rather new, no-name Chinese restaurant is at 510 Kilauea Ave., tel. 961-5677, open daily 10 a.m.-10 p.m., serving basic Chinese combo plates of chicken, duck, pork, beef, and seafood. The most expensive seafood on the menu is $7 for abalone and Chinese mushrooms. There's special plates like steamed chicken with ginger, onion sauce, and steamed rice for $3.80, beef broccoli and crispy chicken for $2.80. Not much class, almost like a McDonald's of Chinese food, it's bright, shiny, and sparkly.

Moderately Priced

Restaurant Miwa, at Hilo Shopping Center, 1261 Kilauea Ave. tel. 961-4454, is open daily 10 a.m.-9 p.m., sometimes until 10 p.m. It's very beautifully appointed, which will be a surprise, especially since it's stuck back in the corner of the shopping center. Enter to find traditional *shoji* screens and wooden tables adorned with fine linens. The waitresses wear kimonos, though most are local girls, and not necessarily Japanese. The menu is excellent. They have appetizers like sake-flavored steamed clams for $4.95,

and crab *sunomono* (seaweed, cucumber slices, and crab meat) for $4.25. A specialty is *nabemono*, which is a hearty and zesty soup/-stew, prepared at your table, with a two-order minimum. Traditional favorites popular with Westerners include beef sukiyaki and *shabu shabu* (both $14), and there's also a variety of combination dinners which give you a wider sampling of the menu at good value. Restaurant Miwa is an absolutely excellent choice for a gourmet meal, at reasonable prices in a congenial setting.

J.D's Banyan Broiler is next door to the Neolani Hotel at 111 Banyan Drive, tel. 961-5802. You save money here by being your own chef. Sirloin steak is $10.75, lobster $17.50, and the catch-of-the-day $8.50. All trimmings are included. The atmosphere is very casual in this airy Polynesian-style restaurant.

Uncle Billy's at the Hilo Bay Hotel along Banyan Dr., tel. 935- 0861, is open for breakfast featuring a $1.99 "aloha special" from 6:30 to 9 a.m., dinner from 5 to 8:30 p.m. Enjoy the free nightly hula show from 6:30 to 7:30 p.m. The interior is neo-Polynesian with a Model T Ford as part of the decor. Basically a fish and steak restaurant serving up shrimp scampi for $9.95, steaks at $11, and catch-of-the-day from $7.75—a good, fun place to dine.

Ken's Pancake House is one of a chain but you can have a good meal for a good price (cocktails too). Open 24 hours, it's conveniently located on the way to the airport at 1730 Kamehameha Ave., tel. 935-8711.

Nihon Culture Center, 123 Lihiwai St., tel. 969-1133 (reservations required), presents authentic Japanese meals and an excellent sushi bar, and combination dinners along with cultural and artistic displays. Open daily for breakfast, lunch, and dinner until 9 p.m., sushi bar until 10 p.m.

Reuben's Mexican Restaurant will enliven your palate with its zesty dishes. The food is well prepared and the atmosphere is homey. Beer, wine, and margaritas are available. Open daily 10 a.m. to 11 p.m., Sun. 4 to 9 p.m., 336 Kamehameha Ave., tel. 961-2552. Olé!

Expensive Restaurants

Queen's Court Restaurant at the Hilo Hawaiian Hotel on Banyan Drive, tel. 935-9361, offers a nightly buffet that is *the* best on Hawaii. Connoisseurs usually don't consider buffets to be gourmet quality, but the Queen's Court proves them wrong. Each night has a different food theme but the Friday evening "Seafood Buffet" would give the finest restaurants anywhere a run for their money. The dining room is grand with large archways and windows overlooking Hilo Bay. A massive table is laden with fresh island vegetables and 15 different salads. Next, on seafood night, comes clams steamed and on the half shell, oysters, shrimp, crab, sushi, and *sashimi*. Then the chefs take over. Resplendent in white uniforms and chef's hats they stand ready to sauté or broil your choice of fish, which always includes best cuts like swordfish or *ono*. Beverages include white, rose, and rich red wines, plus fresh-squeezed guava and orange juice. The dessert table entices with fresh fruits and imported cheeses, and dares you to save room for cream pies, fresh-baked cookies, and eclairs. The price is an unbelievable $14.95. Sunday morning champagne brunch is more of the same quality at $10.75. Make reservations especially on seafood night, because the Hilo Hawaiian attracts many Hilo residents who love great food.

Roussel's, at 60 Keawe St., tel. 935-5111, open for lunch Mon.-Fri., dinner Mon.-Sat, with service all day in the lounge 11:30 a.m.-10 p.m., closed Sun., is one of the newest additions to Hilo's upscale dining. The building housing the restaurant dates from the 1920s, a former bank in a section of the Bishop Trust Building. Roussels is owned by two brother chefs, Spencer and Andrew Oliver, who joined with a Louisiana friend, Herbert Roussel to create the restaurant. They changed the facade of the building to evoke a New Orleans French Quarter style, but preserved the original hardwood floor and hand-molded plaster walls and ceilings. Also, the vault has been converted to a private dining room, brightened by black-and-white checkered floors, mirrors, track lighting, and drumhead tables and chairs. Roussel's specializes in spicy Cajun food. The shrimp and oyster gumbo are outstanding, as are the blackened fish, crisp on the outside and succulent on the inside. Complete dinners such as trout amandine and shrimp creole include rice, a fresh vegetable, and Roussel's fresh-baked bread, and range from $9.95 to $14.95. Distinctive appetizers like soft shell crab and avocado romanoff are under $6, while a selection of gumbo, soup, and salads are under $4. Roussel's is the place to see and be seen. It's upscale Cajun cooking, down on the bayou here in Hilo.

Caper's Bar and Restaurant, at 235 Keawe St., tel. 935-8801, open for lunch and dinner, is a partnership of Ron Cohen and Ron Morris, who are assisted in this family-run business by their wives. They call themselves "Hilo's newest fine dining experience," and with their hands-on approach, are on to something. The restaurant building is part of the *Main St. U.S.A. Restoration Project* so evident in downtown Hilo. The building has had multiple uses over the years. As part of its colorful past, it served as a house of ill repute. Now it's "dishes" come on fine china instead of rumpled beds! Completely redone, it has been transformed into a cheery and bright room done in pastels of blue on pink, contrasted with *koa* trim and room dividers of etched glass. The mood is set by baby spotlights in the ceiling, and you're cooled by a bank of Casablanca fans. Lunch brings soups and salads like soup de jour, $3, house vegetable minestrone, $2.50, and garden salad, $4. Sandwich selections include turkey clubs, char-grilled burgers, and chicken parmigiana for $6-7. The best are the char-grilled *ahi* on whole wheat with Maui onions for $6.25, and the raspberry chicken breast. Pasta is another specialty made fresh daily. Choose from various linguini to fettuccine for $7-10. For dinner begin with antipasto such as spicy marinated scampi for $7, or Caesar salad, $4, then move on to the excellent entrees all priced around $12. All recipes are by Chef Lon Weisman who trained in the French and Italian traditions, and who even studied under the White House Chef. President Bush may be eating these same entrees, but don't hold that against the place. The extensive wine list includes varietals from Italy, France, California, and Germany plus a good selection of champagne as well. Finish with homemade desserts like chocolate truffle or amaretto bread pudding.

Lehua's Bar and Restaurant, at 11 Waianuenue Ave., tel. 935-8055, is another upscale restaurant in a restored building. The mood is set with track lighting, Casablanca fans, and an excellent sound system. The decor is gray on gray with cane chairs and art deco silverware. They display a different local artist's work every two months in connection with the Potter's Gallery, just up the street. Owners Mark and Larry, transplanted from Oahu where they had spent years in the nightclub business, have joined with Chef Kelvin Roo to create a restaurant inspired by *island-style cuisine.* Lunch offerings feature Lehua's clam chowder at $1.50, Caesar salad, $3.25, and shrimp Lehua for $6.75. Also charbroiled burgers, $5.95, club sandwiches, $6.25, charbroiled chicken, $6.50, and BBQ ribs for $7.95. Evenings, dine on appetizers like jumbo prawns, $5.25, shrimp Lehua salad, $7.25, catch of the day, $14.50, and a mixed grill of prawns, chicken, and teriyaki steak for $14.95. Specialties of the house include spinach lasagne, $8.50, and shrimp scampi, $13.95. Friday and Saturday nights bring live entertainment, mostly jazz and Hawaiian music, and occasionally a comedy night, not counting what the owners do every day. Lehua's is upbeat, with delicious food, and fun thrown in for free.

Sandalwood Room is the main restaurant of the Naniloa Surf Hotel on Banyan Drive, tel. 935-0831. Here, in an elegant room overlooking the bay and lined with aromatic sandalwood, you can feast on a selection of recipes from around the world. Zesty curries, rich French sauces, chops done in wine, and Polynesian-inspired dishes are offered on this full and expensive menu.

Fuji Restaurant, as its name implies, is a fine Japanese restaurant at the Hilo Hotel, 142 Kinoole St., tel. 961-3733. Specialties are *teppenyaki* (beef cut thinly and cooked right at your table), or *uminoko* (seafood cooked at your table). Tempura and various *teishoku* (full meals) are part of the menu, and most dinners cost from $12 to $20. For lunch, choose the assortment of *teishoku* (a fixed plate) over the *donburi* because for only $1-2 more, you get a much more substantial meal. All the chefs are from Japan, and the food is authentic.

KK Tei Restaurant, 1550 Kamehameha Ave., tel. 961-3791, is a favored restaurant of many local people. The centerpiece is a *bonsai* garden complete with pagodas and arched moon bridges. Cook your own beef, chicken, or fish at your tableside hibachi and dip them into an array of savory sauces, or the chefs will prepare your selection from their full menu of Japanese dishes. Entrees cost about $10 in this

unique Oriental setting. This restaurant, for those in the know, achieves gourmet status.

Harrington's, at 135 Kalanianaole St., tel. 961-4966, is open nightly for dinner from 5:30-10 p.m., Sun. 5:30-9 p.m., lounge open 5:30-closing. The setting couldn't be more brilliant as the restaurant sits overlooking the bay. A sunset cocktail or dinner is even more romantic with the melodic strains of live jazz, contemporary, or Hawaiin music playing softly in the background. The continentail cuisine features appetizers like shrimp cocktail at $6.50, seafood chowder for $3.25, and a variety of salads. Special vegetarian dishes like eggplant parmigiana are $11.50, while seafood selctions of prawns scampi are $17.95, and seafood brochette $14.25. Meat and fowl dishes are tempting with Slavic steak for $12.25, prime rib au jus, $16.25, and chicken Marsala $12.95. If you are after an evening of good food, romance, and relaxation head for Harrington's at the bay.

Reflections, at the Hilo Lagoon Condominiums, 101 Aupuni St., tel. 935-8501, is an elegant restaurant, open for lunch, dinner, and Sunday brunch. They also feature a prime rib buffet and an extensive salad bar. The interior is intimate with floor-to-ceiling mirrors, etched glass, velveteen booths with soft, comfy chairs. Weekday evenings from 4-8 p.m. brings "attitude adjustment hour" in the lounge, with well drinks priced at $2, and draft beer and wine for $1.50. Sample finger foods like mini-pizza or hot sausage for $2, and free *pu pu* Monday nights, especially popular during football season because of the giant 10-foot picture screen TV. Daily lunch includes French dip, $5.95, club triple decker, $5.50, and chef selections like teri beef for $6.25. For dinner start with appetizers like escargot, $5.50, or soups of the day at $3 and $4. Entrees are blackened rib eye steak, $15.95, rack of lamb, $19.95, and the specialty prime rib au jus, petite cut for $11.95, large cut $15.95. Reflections swings nightly with a listening and dance band. No strict dress code, but you'll feel more comfortable in slacks, casual alohawear, and close-toed shoes. A fancy place at affordable prices.

Fast Foods And Snacks
OK! For those that must, **McDonald's** is at 88 Kanoelehua Ave. and 177 Ululani Street. **Wendy's** is at 438 Kilauea Ave., and **Pizza Hut,**

which actually has a decent salad bar, is at 326 Kilauea Avenue. On Banyan Drive just outside of the Naniloa Surf Hotel, get delicious scoops of ice cream featuring island flavors like macadamia nut, at the **Ice Cream Factory,** and nearby is the **Banyan Snack Shop** which dispenses whopping plate sandwiches like a *loco moko*— two scoops of rice and a hamburger covered in a fried egg and gravy—for only $2.75. The breakfast specials here are very cheap too. **The Chocolate Bar,** next door to the Potter's Gallery at 98 Keawe St., will tempt you with fine candies and ice cream. Everything's homemade, from gummi bears to rolled chocolates. **Sophie's Place,** at 207 Kilauea, tel. 935-7300, is a cheap, downhome, beat up, but clean local counter restaurant that serves Filipino and American food, both available for takeout. **Hilo Seeds and Snacks** next to Lehua's Restaurant at 15 Waianuenue Ave. sells sandwiches and authentic crackseed. The **Kilauea Preserve Center,** at the corner of Kilauea and Ponahawai Streets, also sells authentic crackseed.

ENTERTAINMENT

Hilo doesn't have a lot of nightlife, but it's not a morgue either. You can dance, disco, or listen to a quiet piano at a few lounges and hotels around town. **Note:** Since most of these entertainment spots are also restaurants, their addresses and phone numbers can be found above in "Food."

In a classic plantation building behind the old police station on Kalakaua between Keawe and Kinoole Streets is the **East Hawaii Culture Center,** a nonprofit organization that supports local art by showcasing the works of different artists monthly on a revolving basis in the large entrance hall of the old police station. They also host **Shakespeare in the Park,** a local repetorie of performers who stage, direct, design, and act Shakesperean plays under the large banyan in Kalakaua Park during the month of July. If you're in Hilo at this time, it shouldn't be missed. The Big Island Arts Guild and Dance Council also meet here, and there is always a bulletin board filled with announcements about happenings with the local art scene.

J.D's Banyan Broiler along Banyan Drive transforms from a restaurant into a nightspot at about 10 p.m. The music cranks up and it's usu-ally rock 'n' roll. There's no dance floor, but don't let that hold you back if you really have "dancin' feet." It's a younger crowd with plenty of enthusiasm, and keeps rolling until about 2 a.m.

Lehua's Bar and Restaurant, 11 Wainuenue Ave., (see p. 179) offers a mixed bag of jazz, Hawaiian, or contemporary music on weekends. Occasionally there is a comedy night. Upbeat vibes with good food as well.

The **New Wave Room** at the Naniloa Surf Hotel becomes a disco on the weekends and stays open until 3 a.m.

If you're looking for quiet listening in a "piano bar" atmosphere, you can't beat the **Menehune Lounge** at the Hilo Hawaiian Hotel. **Uncle Billy's** at the Hilo Bay Hotel has two dinner hula shows nightly at 6:30 and 7:30 p.m. **Reflections,** (see p. 180) at the Hilo Lagoon Condominium on Aupuni St., offers casual listening and dancing nightly. **Harrington's** (see p. 179), one of Hilo's most romantic night spots, offers live jazz, contemporary, or Hawaiian music nightly. Perfect for dinner or just for relaxing.

Others

To catch a flick try the **Waiakea Theaters** I, II and III at the Waiakea Mall on Kanoelehua Ave., tel. 935-9747; downtown, the **Palace Theater** is on Haili Street. You'll enjoy great listening on **KIPA Rainbow Radio.** This AM station at 620 on your dial plays an excellent selection of contemporary music with few commercial interruptions. It sounds the way FM used to be. K-BIG FM 98 is worth listening too, and KAOI FM 95 from Maui puts out some really good tunes.

SHOPPING

Shopping Malls

Hilo has the best general-purpose shopping on the island. Stock up on film and food before you do any touring or camping. **Prince Kuhio Plaza,** at 111 E. Puainako, is Hilo's newest and the island's largest shopping mall. Restaurants, jewelry shops, shoe stores, supermarkets, and large department stores like Sears and Liberty House make it a one-stop shopper's paradise. Here too you'll find Longs Drugs for film, and Waldenbooks for an extensive selection of reading material. An older but still full-service shopping center is the **Kaiko'o Mall** at 777 Kilauea Ave. which includes a J.C. Penney's, Ben Fran-

vintage building housing the Potter's Gallery

klin's, Mall Foods, The Book Gallery, and Longs Drugs. The **Hilo Shopping Center** is about one-half mile south on Kilauea Avenue at the corner of Kekuanoa Street. This smaller mall has only a handful of local shops. **Puainako Town Center** is located at 2100 Kanoelehua Ave. (Rt. 11 south toward Volcanoes), with lots of shops, Foodland, and Serendipity Bookstore. **Waiakea Shopping Plaza** at 100 Kanoelehua Ave. has a small clutch of stores.

For Hilo's real treasures see "Hilo's Gardens" p. 596, where you'll find listings for the wonderful commercial flower gardens that surround the city. They are experts at preparing and shipping vibrant and colorful floral arrangements. Prices are reasonable and no other gift says Hawaii like a magnificent bouquet of exotic flowers.

Food Markets

For groceries and supplies try: **Food Fair,** 194 Kilauea Ave.; **Safeway,** 333 Kilauea Ave.; **Foodland** at Puainako Shopping Center; **Mall Foods** in the Kaiko'o Mall; **Pick and Pay**, Hilo Shopping Center; and **Da Store** which offers groceries and sundries, open 24 hours, at 776 Kilauea Ave. For a real treat visit the early morning (over by 8 a.m.) **Suisan Fish Auction** at 85 Lihiwai Street. A retail fresh fish market is next door (see p. 595). Also see "Fast Foods And Snacks," p. 606.

Health Food And Fruit Stores

Abundant Life Natural Foods is in downtown Hilo at 90 Kamehameha Hwy. at the corner of Waianuinui Street. Open daily 8:30 a.m. to 6 p.m., Sun. 10 a.m. to 3 p.m., tel. 935-7411. Unfortunately, they no longer have a snack bar, but they do have a good selection of fresh fruits and vegies, bulk foods, cosmetics, vitamins, and herbs. The bookshelves cosmically vibrate with a selection of tomes on metaphysics and new age literature. **Edesu's** along Keawe St. is a combination flower and fruit store. It's a beat-up old joint, with nothing new about it except for the sign. On Saturday morning, check out the **farmer's market** along Kamehameha Avenue fronting the bay in the center of the downtown area. Great for bargains and local color.

Bookstores

Hilo has excellent bookstores (also see shopping malls above). **Basically Books** downtown at 169 Keawe St., tel. 961-0144, is a print shop-plus with a good selection of Hawaiiana and an unbeatable selection of maps. You can get anywhere you want to go with their nautical charts, road maps, and topographical maps, including sectionals for serious hikers and trekkers. Their collection covers most of the Pacific. They also feature a very good selection of travel books, and flags from countries throughout the world. The **Book Gallery** is a full-selection bookstore featuring Hawaiiana, hardcover, and paperbacks. They're at the Kaiko'o Mall, open daily, tel. 935-2447. At **Serendipity Bookstore,** you too might stumble over some interesting discoveries, as the name implies. Look for this complete bookstore at the Puainako Town Center. Open daily, tel. 959-5841. **Bookfinders of Hawaii** at 150 Haili St., tel. 961-5055, specializes in hard-to-find and out-of-print books. If you want it, they'll get it.

Gifts And Crafts

If you're looking for that special island memento or souvenirs to bring home to family and friends, Uncle Billy covers all the bases and along with everything else offers the **Polynesian Market Place** adjacent to the Hilo Bay Hotel. Open daily 8 a.m. to p.m., the marketplace sells a lot of good junk, liquor, resortwear, and fancy food items. **Hilo Hattie** has a store in front of the Hilo Hawaiian Hotel on Banyan Drive, but for a huge selection of alohawear, visit their outlet at 933 Kanoelehua St. (Rt. 11). This fashion factory has all you need in island clothing. Open daily 8:30 a.m. to 5 p.m., free tour and hotel pick-up. **Kamaaina Crafts,** 1477 Kalanianaole Ave., tel. 935-4957, sells handmade crafts from the Big Island. They have an excellent and varied selection of *lau hala* weavings, carvings, macrame, and flowers. **Hawaiian Handcrafts** at 760 Kilauea Ave., tel. 935-5587, specializes in woodcarvings. Here, Dan DeLuz uses exotic woods to turn out bowls, boxes, and vases, and sells shells from around the Pacific.

Halemanu Crafts is a delightful shop at 195 Kinole St. where senior citizens from the Hilo area display their fine *lau hala* weavings. A great purchase is a woven hat. It's flexible, airy, and will last for years. The woman operating the shop shows you around and gives you some background on the weaving process. They're open daily 8:30 a.m. to 4:30 p.m. with few visitors and plenty of time to spend on you.

Sugawara Lauhala and Gift Shop, at 59 Kalakaua St., is a virtually unknown Hilo institution operated by the Sugawara sisters, who have been in the business for most of their 70-plus years. They make genuine *lau hala* weavings right on the premises of their character-laden shop. Their best hats sell from $75 up, and they also have baskets from $15. If you are after the genuine article made to last a lifetime, you'll find it here.

Sig Zane Design, at 140 Kilauea Ave., tel. 935-7077, open Mon.-Sat. 9:30 a.m.-4:30 p.m., is one of the most unique and distinctive shops on the island. Here, owner and designer Sig Zane creates distinctive island wearables all in 100% cotton. All designs are not only Hawaiian/tropical, but also chronicle useful and medicinal Hawaiian plants and implements from the past. Sig was a well-known hula dancer, and his wife, who helps him in the shop, is a *kumu hula*. Many hula implements and instruments are also integrated into his fabric designs. You can get shirts for $45, dresses around $50, *pareu* $22, and affordable house slippers, sweatshirts, T-shirts, *hapi* coats, and even futon covers. Outfit yourself from head to toe at Sig's shop and be totally in style and comfort.

The Potter's Gallery, at 95 Waianuenue Ave., tel. 935-4069, open Mon.-Sat. 9-5, is a fascinating shop featuring contemporary works by Hawaiian artists and craftspeople. It's located in the vintage, redwood frame Burns Building built in 1911. Scheduled to be torn down six years ago, it was saved by the Historical Society under the *Main St. U.S.A. Restoration Project.* As the name implies, the gallery specializes in pottery by Randy Morehouse, the owner, who along with his wife also sells a selection of oil paintings, batiks, and silk paintings. Randy has been producing his art on Hawaii for 14 years, and knows most of the artists, whose hand-picked works are displayed in the shop, personally. There was no outlet for their work so the shop developed, and now over 40 island artists are represented, among them Chu Leong, a famous potter from Volcano, woodworker Thomas Stout, furniture maker Marcus Casting, posters and original paintings by Miles Mason, and Kathy Long's pencil drawings. Also check out the 100% cotton hammocks in all the colors of the rainbow. The Potter's Gallery also carries a wide variety of T-shirts, including the distinctive logo, *Madame Pele's Hot Sauce.* If you want your memento of Hawaii to be a real work of art, check out the Potter's Gallery.

Almost next door, but a galaxy away artwise is **Da Ceramics Shop.** Stop in to see amateurish but heartfelt precast ceramic lions with their tongues sticking out, French poodles, Santa Claus, little ducks, and merry-go-rounds. So overly cute that it deserves a quick look.

The 100 block of Keawe Avenue, between Shipman and Kalakaua streets., is Hilo's **yuppie row.** Designer shoulder to designer shoulder are the **Chocolate Bar** with fine handmade temptations, **The Futon Connection,** with baskets, futons, and futon furniture, the **Picture**

Frame Shop and Cunningham Gallery for fine arts, and The Most Irresistible Shop in Hilo, with Ciao backpacks and bags. Here too is The Fire Place Store, featuring coffeepots, Mexican *piñatas,* children's toys, greeting cards, *pareu,* T-shirts, and a good selection of cosmetics.

The other side of yuppie row is downhome Hilo. Some downtown shops along Keawe Street selling basic items include Tokunaga Store with fishing supplies, Kodani's Florist for fresh cut flowers and leis, and Hawaii Sales and Surplus, featuring raincoats, hats, military supplies, knives, backpacks, rubber rafts, and plenty of old and new military uniforms.

Big Island Estate Jewelry and Pawn Shop, at 164 Kilauea St., open Sun.-Thur. 10 a.m.-3 p.m., is a must-stop. Inside are the expected cameras and guitars, but you'll also find Japanese miniature dolls, glassware, and hula supplies. Northern Lights Antiques, diagonally across on Ponahawai St., is another treasure chest overflowing with antiques, curios, lamps, beads, and oriental antiques.

The Modern Camera Center, at 165 Kiawe St., tel. 935-3279/3150, is one of the few full-service camera shops in Hilo.

SERVICES AND INFORMATION

Emergencies
When in need call: Police 935-3311; Fire-Ambulance tel. 961-6022; Hilo Hospital at 1190 Waianuenue St., tel. 961-4211. Keiko Gido has an office at 140 Kinoole St., where she practices the ancient healing arts of acupuncture, *shiatsu,* and various theraputic massages.

Information
The following will be helpful: Hawaii Visitors Bureau, 180 Kinoole St., tel. 935-5271, downstairs in the Hilo Plaza; Chamber of Commerce, (next door) 180 Kinoole St., tel. 935-7178, both good sources of maps and helpful brochures; Hilo Public Library, 300 Waianuenue St., tel. 935-5407; University of Hawaii in Hilo at 1400 Kapiolani St., tel. 961-9311.

Banks
For your money needs try the following: City Bank at the Kaiko'o Mall, tel. 935-6844; First Interstate at 100 Waianuenue Ave., tel. 935-2826; Central Pacific, 525 Kilauea Ave., tel. 935-5251; First Hawaiian, 1205 Kilauea Ave., tel. 969-2211.

Laundromats
Self-service laundries include: Kaikoo Coin Laundry, Kaiko'o Mall, tel. 961-6490, open daily 6 a.m. to 9 p.m.; Mitchell Wash-O-Matic in the Hilo Shopping Center, tel. 935-1970, open daily 6 a.m. to 10 p.m.

Anthurium
obake variety

THE SADDLE ROAD

Slicing west across the Hilo District with a north-ward list is Route 200, the Saddle Road. Everyone with a sense of adventure loves this bold cut across the Big Island along a high valley separating the two great mountains, Mauna Loa and Mauna Kea. Along it you pass explorable caves, a *nene* sanctuary, camping areas, and a spur road leading to the very top of Mauna Kea. Besides, it's a great adventure for anyone traveling between Hilo and Kona. Keep your eyes peeled for convoys of tanks and armored personnel carriers as they sometimes sally forth from Pohakuloa Military Camp.

Getting There

The car rental companies cringe when you mention the Saddle Road. Some even intimidate you by saying that their insurance won't cover you on this road. They're terrified you'll rattle their cars to death. For the most part these fears are groundless. For a few miles the Saddle Road is corrugated because of heavy use by the military, but, by and large, it's a good road, no worse than many others around the island, but it *is* isolated, and there are no facilities along the way. If you bypass it, you'll miss some of the best scenery

on the Big Island. From Hilo, follow Waianuenue Avenue west past Rainbow Falls. Saddle Road (Route 200) splits left within a mile or two and is clearly marked. If you follow it across the island, you'll intersect Route 190 on which you can turn north to Waimea, or south to Kona. For professional guide service to the top of Mauna Kea see p. 577. For skiing expeditions see p. 586.

KAUMANA CAVES

In 1881 Mauna Loa's tremendous eruption created a huge flow of lava. The lava became rivers that crusted over, forming a tube through which molten lava continued to flow. Once the eruption ceased, the lava inside siphoned out, leaving the tube that we now call Kaumana Caves. The caves are only five miles out of Hilo along Route 200, clearly marked next to the road. Oddly enough, they are posted as a fallout shelter. Follow a staircase down into a gray hole draped with green ferns and brightened by wildflowers. You can walk about 50 yards into the cave before you'll need a flashlight. It's a thrill to turn around and look at the entranceway with blazing sunlight shooting through the ferns and wildflowers. The floor of the cave is cemented over for easy walking. Another cave visible across the way is undeveloped and more rugged to explore.

Two miles past Kaumana Caves is **Hilo Municipal Golf Course,** a 5,991-yard, par-72 course where you can golf for under $10.

MAUNA KEA

The lava along both sides of the road is old as you approach Mauna Kea ("White Mountain"). The lowlands are covered with grass, ferns, small trees, and mossy rocks. Twenty-seven miles out of Hilo, a clearly marked road to your right leads to the summit of 13,796-foot Mauna Kea. A sign warns you this road is rough, unpaved, and narrow, with no water, food, fuel, restrooms, or shelters. Moreover, you can expect winds, rain, fog, hail, snow, and altitude sickness. Intrigued? Proceed: it's not as bad as it sounds. A 4WD vehicle is highly advised, and if there's snow it's impossible without one. A normal rental car isn't powerful enough, mainly because you're gaining more than 8,000 feet of elevation in 15 miles, which plays havoc with carburetors. But the real problem is coming down. For a small car with not very good gearing you're going to be riding your brakes for 15 miles. If they fail, you'll stand a very good chance of becoming a resident spirit of the mountain!

Four miles up you pass **Hale Pohaku** ("House of Stone") which looks like a ski resort; many of the scientists from the observatory atop

the mountain live here. A sign says you need a permit from the Dept. of Land and Natural Resources (in Hilo) and a 4WD vehicle to proceed. Actually, the road is graded, banked, and well maintained, with the upper four miles paved so that dust is kept to a minimum to protect the sensitive "eyes" of the telescopes. As you climb, you pass through the clouds to a barren world, devoid of all vegetation. The earth is red and rolling in a series of volcanic cones. You get an incredible vista of Mauna Loa peeking through the clouds and what seems like the entire island lying at your feet. In the distance the lights of Maui flicker. **Lake Waiau,** which unbelievably translates as "Swim Water," is almost at the top at 13,020 feet, making it the third-highest lake in the U.S. If the vistas aren't enough, bring a kite along and watch it soar in the winds of the Earth's upper atmosphere. Off to your right is Puu Kahinahina, a small hill whose name means "hill of the silversword." It's one of the only places on the Big Island where you'll actually see this very rare plant. The mountaintop was at one time federal land, and funds were made availa-

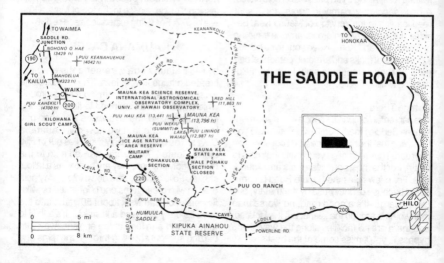

THE SADDLE ROAD

ble to eradicate feral goats, one of the worst destroyers of the silversword and many other native Hawaiian plants.

Mauna Kea is the only spot in the tropical Pacific that was glaciated. The entire summit of the mountain was covered in 500 feet of ice. Toward the summit, you may notice piles of rock which are the terminal moraines of these ancient glaciers. The snows atop Mauna Kea are unpredictable. Some years it is merely a dusting, while in other years, as in 1982, there was enough snow to ski from late November to late July. The ski run comes all the way down from the summit, giving you about a four-mile trail. For skiing adventures and expeditions see p. 586. Here and there around the summit are small caves, remnants of ancient quarries where Hawaiians came to dig a special kind of fired rock which is the hardest in all Hawaii. They hauled the roughed-out tools down to the lowlands where they refined them into excellent implements that became coveted trade items. A natural phenomenon is the strange thermal properties manifested by the cinder cones that dot the top of the mountain. Only 10 feet or so under their surface is permafrost which dates back 10,000 years to the Pleistocene Epoch. If you drill into the cones for only 10-20 feet and put a pipe in, during daylight hours air will go into the pipe, forming a suction. At night warm air comes out of the pipe strong enough to keep a hat levitating in thin air. Evening brings an incredibly clean and cool breeze that flows down the mountain. The Hawaiians called it the Keihau Wind, whose source, according to ancient legend, is the burning heart of the mountain. To the Hawaiians, this inspiring heavenly summit was the home of Poliahu, The Goddess of Snow and Ice, who vied with the fiery Pele across the way on Mauna Loa for the love of a man. He could throw himself into the never-ending embrace of a mythical *ice queen,* or a *red-hot mama.* Tough choice, poor fellow!

Mauna Kea Observatory Complex

Atop the mountain is a mushroom grove of astronomical observatories, as incongruously striking as a futuristic Earth colony on a remote planet of a distant galaxy. The crystal-clear air and lack of dust and light pollution rank the Mauna Kea Observatory Complex as *the* best in the world. At close to 14,000 feet, it is above 40 per-

cent of the Earth's atmosphere. Although temperatures generally hover around freezing, there's only 9-11 inches of precipitation annually, mostly in the form of snow. The astronomers have come to expect an average of 325 crystal-clear nights per year, perfect for observation. The state of Hawaii leases the tops of the cinder cones to various institutions from all over the world, upon which they construct telescopes. These institutions in turn give the University of Hawaii 15% of their viewing time. The university sells the excess viewing time for $5000-10,000 a night, which supports the entire astronomy program and makes a little money on the side. Those who work up here must come down every four days because the thin air seems to make them forgetful and susceptible to making minor calculation errors.

Scientists from around the world book months in advance for a squint through one of these phenomenal telescopes which hold almost every record for the world's largest in one dimension or another. The first telescope that you see on your left is the **James Clark Maxwell Telescope,** the largest reflecting telescope in the world, with a primary mirror over 15 meters in diameter. It was dedicated by Britain's Prince Philip, who rode all the way to the top in a Rolls Royce. The most expensive telescope to date is the **France, Canada, and Hawaii Telescope** built in 1977 for $33 million. It was the first to spot Halley's comet in 1983, and still can see it. Then there's the **Royal British Telescope,** which can be operated by remote control from the World Observatory in Scotland. Another is the U.K.'s infrared telescope, which is the world's largest infrared telescope as well as largest glass-mirrored telescope, with a 150-inch primary mirror. The Keck Foundation (Standard Oil) from Los Angeles is currently building the world's largest and most expensive telescope, at a cost of almost $100 million. This titanic eyeball should start winking at the heavens by 1991. **The W.M. Keck Observatory** will have an aperture of 400 inches and will employ entirely new and unique types of technology. The primary reflector, an incredibly huge mirror, is fashioned from a mosaic of 36 hectagonal mirrors, each only three inches thick and six feet in diameter that have been very carefully joined together to form an "unrigid" light reflector surface. To take control of that undulating reflector surface the backs of each of the mirrors will be controlled by several electronic devices that will flex them up to 100 times a minute to make the heavenly objects absolutely perfect.

Visitors are welcome to tour the complex and to have a look through the telescopes on special weekends from May through September. Reservations are a must, and arrangements can be made by calling the **Mauna Kea Support Services** in Hilo at tel. 935-3371. You must provide your own transportation to the summit. Photographers, using fast film, get some of the most dazzling shots *after* sunset. During the gloaming, the light show begins. Look down upon the clouds to see them filled with fire. This heavenly light is reflected off the mountain to the clouds and then back up like a celestial mirror in which you get a fleeting glimpse of the soul of the universe.

MAUNA KEA STATE PARK

This area, known as Pohakuloa ("Long Stone"), is five miles west from the Mauna Kea Observatory Road (33 miles from Hilo). The altitude is 6,500 feet and the land begins to change into the rolling grasslands for which this *paniolo* country is famous. Here you'll find a cluster of seven cabins that can be rented (arrange in advance) from the Dept. of Land and Natural Resources, Division of State Parks, 75 Aupuni St., Hilo, HI 96720, tel. 961-7200. The cabins are completely furnished with cooking facilities and hot showers. You'll need warm clothing, but the days and nights are unusually clear and dry with very little rain. The park is within the Pohakuloa Game Management Area, so expect hunting and shooting in season. A few minutes west is the Pohakuloa Military Camp, whose manuevers can sometimes disturb the peace in this high mountain area. Follow the Saddle Road about 20 miles west to intersect Route 190 on which you can turn right (north) to Waimea in seven miles, or left (south) to Kailua in 33 miles.

Birdwatchers or nature enthusiasts should turn into Koa Kipuka, a bite-sized hill just near mile marker 28. (A *kipuka* is a very special area, usually a hill or gully, in the middle of a lava flow that was never inundated by lava and therefore provides an old, original, and established ecosystem.) Look for Powerline Road, and Puu O'o Volcano Trail. Follow either for a chance to see the very rare *akiapola'au,* or *apapane,* and even some wild turkeys. For descriptions see p. 564. For the Hakalau Forest National Wildlife Refuge see p 566.

norfolk pine

HAMAKUA COAST

Inland the Hamakua Coast is awash in a green rolling sea of sugar cane, while along the shore cobalt waves foam into razor-sharp valleys where cold mountain streams meet the sea at lonely pebbled beaches. For 50 miles, from Hilo to Waipio along the Belt Road (Route 19), the Big Island has grown its cane for 100 years or more. Water is needed for sugar, a ton to produce a pound, and this coast has plenty. Huge flumes once carried the cut cane to the mills. Last century so many Scots worked the plantations hereabouts that Hamakua was called the "Scotch Coast." Now most residents are a mixture of Scottish, Japanese, Filipino, and Portuguese ancestry. Side roads dip off Route 19 into one-family valleys where a modest weather-beaten home of a plantation worker sits surrounded by garden plots on tiny hand-hewn terraces. These valleys, as they march up the coast, are unromantically referred to as "gulches." From the Belt Road's many bridges, you can trace silvery-ribboned streams that mark the valley floors as they open to the sea. Each is jungle-lush with wildflowers and fruit trees transforming the steep sides to emerald green velvet.

SIGHTS

The ride alone, as you head north on the Belt Road, is gorgeous enough to be considered a sight. But there's more! You can pull off the road into sleepy one-horse towns where dogs are safe sleeping in the middle of the road. You can visit a plantation store in Honomu on your way to Akaka Falls, or take a cautious dip at one of the seaside beach parks. If you want solitude, you can go inland to a forest reserve and miles of trails. The largest town on the coast is Honokaa, with supplies, handmade mementos, and a macadamia nut factory. You can veer west to Waimea from Honokaa, but don't. Take the spur road, Route 240, to Waipio Valley, known as the "Valley of Kings," one of the most beautiful in all of Hawaii.

HONOMU AND VICINITY

During its heyday Honomu ("Silent Bay") was a bustling center of the sugar industry boasting saloons, a hotel/bordello, and a church or two for repentance. Now, Honomu is only a stop as you head somewhere else. It's 10 miles north of Hilo and a mile or so inland on Route 220 which leads to Akaka Falls. As you enter Honomu

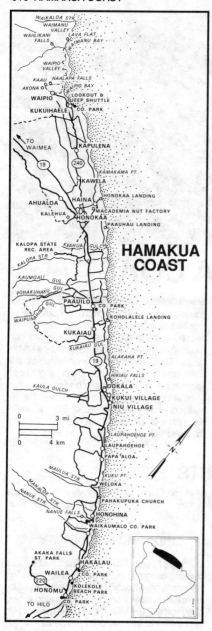

there's a string of false-front buildings that are doing a good but unofficial rendition of a living history museum. It's as if the entire town has taken a nap and is about to wake up at any moment. At the south end of town, just at the turn to Akaka Falls, notice the **Odaishasan,** a beautifully preserved Buddhist Temple. Honomu is definitely worth a stop. It takes only five minutes to walk the main street, but those five minutes can give you a glimpse of history that will take you back 100 years.

Practicalities

Before entering town proper you'll spot **Jan's,** a convenience store selling cold beer and groceries. As you enter town look for **The Plate Lunch,** offering sushi, shave ice, sub sandwiches, and frozen bananas, about as downhome as you can get. Along the row is **The Crystal Grotto** selling new age gifts, jewelry, metaphysical books, minerals, crystals, crystal balls, and rock specimens. Their sign, instead of "Closed," reads "To Be Continued." For your view into the past, present, or future here in Honomu visit the Crystal Grotto. Next door to the Crystal Grotto is the **Akaka Falls Flea Market.** The merchandise changes, so you never know what to expect, but they claim "all new quality merchandise at reduced prices." And, in case you're suddenly struck by an irresistible urge for a permanent memento of Honomu, there's even a **tattoo parlor** in town.

As you walk the main street of Honomu, make sure to stop into **Ishigo's General Store,** tel. 963-6128, open Mon.-Fri. 7 a.m.-6 p.m., Sat. and Sun. 7 a.m.-5:30 p.m., to see a real plantation store still in operation. Owned and operated by Hideo Ishigo, the original store began in 1910 when his forebears, Inokichi Ishigo and his wife Maki, immigrated from Fukuoka Japan to begin a new life in Hawaii. They began with a bakery, employing recipies that they learned from all the ethnic groups in Hawaii. They passed their knowledge down to their children, who still use the same recipies in the bakery section of the store. The general store section has food, ice cream, sandwiches, and pizza, but the real treats are in the bakery. Here, in a case from which you help yourself, are familiar munchies like blueberry, pineapple, and coconut turnovers along with *taro* bread, but according to Mr. Ishigo

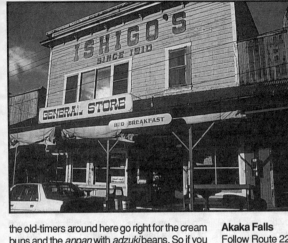

Ishigo's General Store

the old-timers around here go right for the cream buns and the *anpan* with *adzuki* beans. So if you want to get some *real* local flavor, pick one of these and sit out front sipping a cup of Kona coffee. Mr. Ishigo is very friendly and will "talk story" about Honomu, and may even invite you to a relative's orchid farm in the nearby area. If he's around, it's an added treat, but you can give yourself a small history course of Honomu by checking out the antiques, mementos, and vintage photos that have been placed around the store. Most photos are of Japanese couples who immigrated to the area. Check out the bottles of *okolehau,* local moonshine, that could easily fuel the space shuttle, and an old HVB roadside warrior that's made of wood. The vintage building also houses a few rooms that can be rented out as a **bed and breakfast** at $30 deluxe with double bed and private bath, and $25 for a shared bath. Upstairs in the B&B you overlook downtown Honomu, all 12 houses of it, with the corrugated iron roofs staring at you. The rooms are basic, but clean, and there's a ceiling fan for cooling, and a small desk. The decor is landlord yellow carpet and a Sears Roebuck-inspired foldout couch in stripes and browns, with a big overstuffed old chair. There's a full kitchen area available to guests that overlooks the backyard, which is an incredible jumble of pipes like a surrealistic garden of homespun industrialization. Breakfast (included) is a pastry from the bakery and a cup of Kona coffee. Don't expect a gingerbread, cutsie-pie setting, but a night at Ishigo's is a night in Hawaii the way it was.

Akaka Falls

Follow Route 220 from Honomu past dense sugar cane fields for 3½ miles to the parking lot of Akaka Falls. From here, walk counterclockwise along a paved "circle route" that takes you through everybody's idea of a pristine Hawaiian valley. For 40 minutes you're surrounded by heliconia, gingers, orchids, ferns, and bamboo groves as you cross bubbling streams on wooden footbridges. Many varieties of plants that would be in window pots anywhere else are giants here, almost like trees. An overlook views Kahuna Falls as it spills into a lush green valley below. The trail becomes an enchanted tunnel through hanging orchids and bougainvillea. In a few moments you arrive at Akaka Falls. The mountain cooperates with the perfect setting, a semicircle for the falls to tumble 420 feet in one sheer drop. After heavy rains expect a mad torrent of power; during dry periods marvel at liquid-silver thread forming mist and rainbows. The area, maintained by the Division of State Parks, is one of the most easily accessible forays into Hawaii's beautiful interior.

Kolekole Beach Park

Look for the first tall bridge (100 feet high) a few minutes past Honomu, where a sign points to a small road that snakes its way down the valley to the beach park below. Amenities include showers, restrooms, grills, electricity, picnic tables, and a camping area (county permit). Kolekole is very popular with local people who use its five pavilions for all manner of special occasions, usually on weekends. A black-sand beach fronts an extremely treacherous ocean. The entire valley was inundated with over 30 feet of water during the great 1946 tsunami. The stream running through Kolekole comes from Akaka Falls, four miles inland. It forms a pool complete with waterfall that is safe for swimming but quite cold.

Laupahoehoe Point

This wave-lashed peninsula is a finger of smooth *pahoehoe* lava that juts into the bay. Located about halfway between Honomu and Honokaa, at one time the valley supported farmers and fishermen who specialized in catching turtles. Laupahoehoe was the best boat landing along the coast, and for years canoes and, later, schooners would stop here. A plaque commemorates the tragic loss of 20 schoolchildren and their teacher who were taken by the great tsunami of 1946. Afterwards, the village was moved to the high ground overlooking the point. Laupahoehoe Beach Park now occupies the low peninsula: picnic tables, showers, electricity, and a county camping area. The sea is too rough to swim, but many fishermen still come here, along with some daring surfers. Laupahoehoe makes a beautiful rest stop along the Belt Road.

Ten miles inland from Laupahoehoe Point along a very rugged jeep trail is **David Douglas Historical Monument.** This marks the spot where the naturalist, after whom the Douglas fir is named, lost his life under mysterious circumstances. Douglas, on a fact-gathering expedition on the rugged slopes of Mauna Kea, never returned. His body was found at the bottom of a deep pit that was used at the time to catch feral cattle. Douglas had spent the previous night at a cabin occupied by an Australian who had been a convict. Many suspected that the Austalian had murdered Douglas in a robbery attempt and thrown his body into the pit as an alibi. No hard evidence of murder could be found, and the death was officially termed accidental.

HONOKAA AND VICINITY

With a population of nearly 2,000, Honokaa ("Crumbling Bay") is the major town on the Hamakua Coast. Here you can continue on Route 19 to Waimea, or take Route 240 through Honokaa and north to Waipio, which you should

not miss. First, however, stroll the main street of Honokaa, where a number of shops specialize in locally produced handicrafts. It's also the best place to stock up on supplies or gasoline. The surrounding area is the center of the macadamia nut industry. If you are proceeding north along Route 240, the coastal route heading to Waipio Valley, just past mile marker 6 on the left, keep an eye peeled for a lava tube cave right along the roadway. This is just a tease of the amazing natural sights that follow. (See Waipio, p. 620.)

Kalopa State Park

This spacious natural area is 12 miles north of Laupahoehoe (two miles south of Honokaa), and two miles inland on a well-marked secondary road. Little used by tourists, it's a great place to get away from it all. Hiking is terrific throughout the park on a series of nature trails where much of the flora has been identified. All trails are well marked and vary widely in difficulty. The park provides an excellent opportunity to explore some of the lush gulches of the Hamakua Coast, as well as tent camping (state permit) and furnished cabins that can house up to eight people (see p. 581).

Hawaiian Holiday Macadamia Nut Factory

This factory, open 9 a.m.-5. p.m., is on a side road that leads from the middle of town down a steep hill toward the sea. A self-guided tour explains how John MacAdams discovered the delicious qualities of these nuts, and how they were named after him. The macadamia nut industry was started in Honokaa, when W.H. Purvis, a British agriculturalist who had been working in Australia, brought the first trees to Honokaa in 1881, one of which is still bearing! Then in 1924, W. Pierre Naquin, then manager of the Honokaa Sugar Co., started the first commercial nut farm in the area. You can buy a large variety of macadamia items, from butters to candies. A delicious and nutritious munchy is a five-oz. vacuum-packed can of nuts that make a great souvenir, or add a special touch to a picnic lunch.

Practicalities

Centrally located along Route 24 is the **Hotel Honokaa Club.** Contact Henry Morita, Manager, Box 185, Honokaa, tel. 775-0533. What it lacks in elegance it makes up for in cleanliness and friendliness. The hotel, mostly used by local people, is old and appears run-down. Upstairs rooms (view and TV) are $29 s, $32 d. The more spartan downstairs rooms go for $24 s, $27 d. The hotel dining room serves the best meals in town. Breakfasts are served daily from 6:30 to 11 a.m., lunch from 11 a.m. to 2 p.m., and dinner nightly from 5:30 to 8 p.m. The cooking is home-style with a different dinner special daily, such as a seafood platter for $5.75, *mahi mahi* special, $6, or lobster and steak, $16.75. Specials include rice, potatoes, salad, and coffee. Weekends rock with **live entertainment** and dancing.

Along the main street the **Tourist Cocktail Lounge** has live music on Sat. from 8:30 p.m. until after midnight. To save money, get a filling plate lunch at the local **Dairy Queen.** Pick up supplies and even a few health food items at **T. Kaneshiro Store** and **K.K. Market** in town.

Honokaa Pizza and Subs, in downtown Honokaa, open 11 a.m. to 9 p.m., Mon.-Sat., tel. 775-9966, serves sit-down and takeout pizzas for $5.50 to $10.50. They also make hefty subs like meatball with tomato sauce for $3.95, steak and onions with cheese for $3.95. A more formal dinner from 4 p.m. brings simple but savory fare like spaghetti and meatballs for $4.95. The desserts are homemade and include pastries like chocolate eclairs, and cream puffs with real cream filling, and chocolate fudge with walnuts. Terrific for a picnic lunch.

Herb's Place, next to the 76 Gas Station, is open for breakfast, lunch, and dinner from 5:30 a.m. Mon.-Fri., 8:30 a.m. Sat., closed Sunday. Basic meals and cocktails in this little roadside joint.

C.C. Jon's is a plate lunch, local fast-food stand just as you enter town. Most of their dishes are under $4.50.

If you are at all interested in the history of Hawaii, make sure to stop by the **The Hawaiian Artifacts Shop** along the main drag in downtown Honokaa. Just look for a carved mermaid and a strobe light blinking you into the shop. This amazing curio and art shop is owned and operated by James and Lokikamakahiki "Loki" Rice. The Rices, both elderly and in failing health, keep no set hours, opening when they feel like, but they're usually there for a few hours in the morning and in the afternoon. At first glance the shop may look unauthentic, but once inside that impression quickly melts away. Loki, a full-blooded Hawaiian, was born and raised in

Waipio Valley, and James has traveled the Pacific for years. Between the two, the stories from the old days are almost endless. Notice a tiki that serves as a main beam, and two giant shields against the back wall. They belong to Loki's father, a giant of a man over seven feet tall and over 450 pounds who had to have a special coffin made when he was buried on the island of Niihau. Local people bring in their carvings and handicrafts to sell, many of which are hula implements and instruments like drums and rattles. Some of the bric-a-brac is from the Philippines or other south sea islands, but Jim will identify them for you. Mingled in with what seems to be junk are some real artifacts like poi pounders, adzes, and really good drums. Many have come from Loki's family, while others have been collected by the Rices over the years. But the real treasures inside the shop are Jim and Loki, who will share their aloha as long as time permits.

About two shops down from Hawaiian Artifacts is a **clockmaker.** There's no sign directing you to this shop that time has passed by, but the craftsman inside not only repairs clocks, but makes them as well.

On the right, just near the Hotel Honokaa Club is the **Honokaa Trading Co.,** selling new and used goods, antiques, and collectibles.

KUKUIHAELE

For all of you looking for the "light at the end of the tunnel," Kukuihaele ("Traveling Light") is it. On the main road, the **Last Chance** grocery and gas station, open 9 a.m.-6 p.m. daily, stocks basic supplies plus a small assortment of handicrafts and gift items.

Waipio Woodworks, tel. 775-0958, open daily 9 a.m.-5 p.m., is an excellent shop in which to pick up an art object. There are plenty of offerings in wood including carvings and bowls, but they also showcase various Hawaii-based artists working in different mediums. Definitely check out inspired prints by Sue Sweardlow, who has tuned in to the soul of Hawaii, and paintings by Steve Grossman and Kim Starr. You'll also find tikis, earrings, quiltwork, and basketry made from natural fibers, yarns, and strings. Waipio Woodworks is also the meeting place for **Waipio Valley Shuttle,** tel. 775-7121, which will take you down to Waipio Valley (see p. 621).

Accommodations

Waipio Wayside, P.O. Box 840, Honokaa, HI 96727, tel. 775-0275, is a vintage plantation manager's home that is now owned and operated by Jackie Horne as a congenial B&B. You enter through double French doors, onto a rich wooden floor shining with a well-waxed patina. The walls are hand-laid vertical paneling, the prototype of what modern paneling tries to emulate. The home contains five double bedrooms ranging in price from $45 for one of two small front rooms, $55 for a larger room with half bath, to $65 for the master bedroom, with $10 pp extra. The master bedroom is in its own little space out back, but attached to the house. The room, rich with knotty pine, is spacious and airy with plenty of windows. Every bedroom has beautiful curtains that are hand-painted originals by Jackie's friend, Laura Lewis, a local Island artist. The back yard swimming pool is on manicured grounds that gently descend, affording a panoramic view of the coast. Here, a one-time playhouse has been converted into a tranquil meditation nook. Jackie hosts weekly meditation classes, and *kiatsu* (thumb massage) on Monday evenings, given by a local Japanese *sensei* to which guests are cordially invited. Jackie, whose meticulous and tastefully appointed home is straight from the pages of *Ladies' Home Journal,* is also a gourmet cook. Breakfast is sometimes waffles with strawberries and whipped cream, or omelettes and biscuits, with fresh fruit from the property. Beverages are pure kona coffee, juices, and an assortment of 24 gourmet teas from around the world. A stay at Waipio Wayside is guaranteed to be civilized, relaxing, and affordable.

Enjoy the privacy of **Hamakua Hideaway,** Box 5104, Kukuihaele, HI 96727, tel. 775-7425. A B&B only 15 minutes walk from Waipio Overlook, they offer the entire home, s/d, for $60 daily, with reduced weekly and monthly rates available.

WAIPIO VALLEY

Waipio is the way the Lord would have liked to fashion the Garden of Eden, if he hadn't been on such a tight schedule. You can read about this incredible valley, but you really can't believe it until you see it for yourself. Route 24 ends a minute outside of Kukuihaele at an overlook, and 1,000 feet below is Waipio ("Arching Water"). The valley is a mile across where it fronts the sea at a series of high sand dunes. It's vibrantly green, always watered by Waipio Stream and lesser ones that sprout as waterfalls from the *pali* at the rear of the valley. The green is offset by a wide band of black-sand beach. The far side of the valley ends abruptly at a steep *pali* that is higher than the one on which you're standing. A six-mile trail leads over it to Waimanu Valley, smaller, more remote, and more luxuriant.

Travelers have long extolled the amazing abundance of Waipio. From the overlook you can make out the overgrown outlines of garden terraces, *taro* patches, and fishponds in what was Hawaii's largest cultivated valley. Every foodstuff known to the Hawaiians flourished here; even Waipio pigs were said to be bigger than anywhere else. In times of famine, the produce from Waipio could sustain the populace of the entire island (estimated at 100,000 people).

On the valley floor and alongside the streams you'll still find avocados, bananas, coconuts, passionfruit, mountain apples, guavas, breadfruit, tapioca, lemons, limes, coffee, grapefruit, and pumpkins. The old fishponds and streams are alive with prawns, wild pigs roam the interior, and there are abundant fish in the sea. The lovingly tended order, most homes, and the lifestyle were washed away in the tsunami of 1946. Now Waipio is unkempt, a wild jungle of mutated abundance. The valley is a neglected maiden with a dirty face and disheveled, windblown hair. Only love and nurturing can refresh her lingering beauty.

Getting There

The road leading down to Waipio is outrageously steep and narrow. If you attempt it in a regular car, it'll eat you up and spit out your bones. Over 20 fatalities have occurred since people started driving it, and it has only been paved since the early 1970s. You'll definitely need 4WD, low range, to make it; downhill vehicles yield to those coming up. There is very little traffic on the road except for when there are good surfing conditions. Sometimes, Waipio Beach has the first good waves of the season and this brings out the surfers en masse. **Waipio Valley Shuttle,** tel. 775-7121, has their office at Waipio Woodworks in Kukuihaele. They still have a few super-tough and adventurous open Landrovers for their 90-minute descent and tour, but mostly you'll ride in air-conditioned comfort in 4WD vans. The tour costs $20.80. Buy your ticket at Waipio Woodworks and then proceed to the Waipio Overlook from where the vans leave every hour on the hour. This is the tamest, but safest, way to enjoy the valley. If you decide to hike down or stay overnight, you can make arrangements for the van to pick you up or drop you off for an added cost. The same company also offers a trip to the top of Mauna Kea.

If you have the energy, the hike down the paved section of the road is only just over one mile, but it's a tough mile coming back up! Expect to take three to four hours down and back, adding more time to swim or look around. (For details see "Camping And Hiking" below.)

ACTIVITIES

For a fun-filled experience guaranteed to please, try horseback riding with **Waipio Naalapa Trail Rides,** tel. 775-0419. Sherri Hannum, a young mother of three who moved to Waipio from Missouri almost 15 years ago, and her husband Mark, own and operate the trail rides. Both are enamored with the valley, and as fate would have it, have become the *old-timers* of Waipio. They gladly accept the charge of keeping the ancient accounts and oral traditions alive. The adventure begins when Mark picks you up at 9:30 a.m. at the Last Chance Store in Kukuihaele. You begin a 40-minute 4WD ride down to the ranch, which gives you an excellent tour of the valley in and of itself, since their spread is even deeper into the valley than the end of the line of the commercial valley tour! En route you cross three or four streams, as Mark tells you some of the history and lore of Waipio. When you arrive, Sherri has the horses ready to go. Sherri knows the trails of Waipio intimately. She mounts you on a sure-footed Waipio pony and spends all day telling you legends and stories while leading you to waterfalls, gravesites, *heiau,* and finally a beach ride with a refreshing dip if you desire. The horses of Waipio date from the late 1700s. They were gifts to the *ali'i* from Capt. George Vancouver. Waipio was especially chosen because the

horses were easy to corral and could not escape. Today, over 150 semi-wild head still roam the valley floor as progeny from this original stock. Technically, you should bring your own lunch for the ride, since you can't always count on the fruits of Waipio to be happening. But if they are, Sherri will point them out and you can munch to your heart's delight. Half-day tours cost $55, and run from 9 a.m. to 1 p.m. and again from 1:30 p.m. to 5:30 p.m. Full-day tours cost $100 and go from 9 a.m. to 5:30 p.m. (minimum of two and a maximum of four riders required). Sorry, but no children under 12. Go prepared with long pants, shoes, and a swimsuit. A ride with Sherri isn't just an adventure; it's an experience with memories that'll last a lifetime.

Waipio Valley Wagon Tour, P.O. Box 1340, Honokaa, HI 96727, tel. 775-9518, owned and operated by Peter Tolin, is the newest and one of the most fun-filled ways of exploring Waipio. This surrey-type wagon, which can hold about a dozen people, is drawn by two Tennessee mules. Tours, lasting two hours, depart four times per day at 10 a.m., 11:30 a.m., 1:30 p.m., and 3 p.m., and cost $25, children under 12 half price, children two and under free. To participate, make reservations 24 hours in advance, and then check in 30 minutes before departure at the ticket office which is located next door to the Last Chance Store in Kukuihaele. A four-wheel-drive will pick you up and bring you down to the start of the wagon ride. Lunch is not included, but if you bring your own they do offer a lunch special where you can spend an extra hour down at the beach. The original wagon was built by Peter himself from parts that he ordered from the Mainland. Unfortunately, every part that he ordered broke down over a nine-month trial period. Peter had all new parts made at a local machine shop, only three times thicker than the originals! Now that the wagon has been *Waipionized,* the problems have ceased. The only high-tech aspect of the wagon ride is a set of small loudspeakers through which Peter narrates the history, biology, and the myths of Waipio as you roll along.

HISTORY

Legend And Oral History
Waipio is a mystical place. Inhabited for over 1,000 years, it figures prominently in old Ha-

waiian lore. In the primordial past, Wakea, progenitor of all the islands, favored the valley, and oral tradition holds that the great gods Kane and Kanaloa dallied in Waipio intoxicating themselves on awa. One oral chant relates that the demigod Maui, that wild prankster, met his untimely end here by trying to steal baked bananas from these two drunken heavyweights. Lono, god of the Makahiki, came to Waipio in search of a bride. He found Kaikilani, a beautiful maiden who lived in a breadfruit tree near **Hiilawe Waterfall,** which tumbles 1,300 feet to the valley below and is Hawaii's highest free-falling falls.

Nenewe, a shark-man, lived near a pool at the bottom of another waterfall on the west side of Waipio. The pool was connected to the sea by an underwater tunnel. All went well for Nenewe until his grandfather disobeyed a warning never to feed his grandson meat. Once Nenewe tasted meat he began eating Waipio residents after first warning them about sharks as they passed his sea-connected pool on their way to fish. His constant warnings roused suspicions. Finally, a cape he always wore was ripped from his shoulders, and there on his back was a shark's mouth! He dove into his pool and left Waipio to hunt the waters of the other islands.

Pupualenalena, a *kupua* (nature spirit), takes the form of a yellow dog who can change his size from tiny to huge. He was sent by the chiefs of Waipio to steal a conch shell that was constantly blown by mischievous water sprites, just to irritate the people. The shell was inherited by Kamehameha and is now in the Bishop Museum. Another dog-spirit lives in a rock embedded in the hillside halfway down the road to Waipio. In times of danger, he comes out of his rock to stand in the middle of the road as a warning that bad things are about to happen.

Finally, a secret section of Waipio beach is called **Lua O Milu,** the legendary doorway to the land of the dead. At certain times, it is believed, ghosts of great *ali'i* come back to Earth as "Marchers of the Night," and their strong chants and torch-lit processions fill the darkness in Waipio. Many great kings were buried in Waipio, and it's felt that because of their mana, no harm will come to the people that live here. Oddly enough, the horrible tsunami of 1946 and a raging flood in 1979 filled the valley with wild torrents of water. In both cases, the devastation to homes and the land was tremendous, but not one life was lost. Everyone who still lives in Waipio will tell you that somehow, they feel protected.

The remains of **Paka'alana Heiau** is in a grove of trees on the right-hand side of the beach as you face the sea. It dates from the 12th century and was a "temple of refuge" where *kapu* breakers, vanquished warriors, and the weak and infirm could find sanctuary. The other restored and more famous temple of this type is Pu'uhonua O Honaunau in Kona (see p. 678). Paka'alana was a huge *heiau* with tremendous walls that were mostly intact until the tsunami of 1946. The tidal wave sounded like an explosion when the waters hit the walls of Paka'alana, according to first-hand accounts. The rocks were scattered, and all was turned to ruins. Nearby, **Hanua'aloa** is another *heiau* that is in ruins. Archaeologists know even less about this *heiau,* but all agree that both were healing temples of body and spirit, and the local people feel that their positive mana is part of the protection in Waipio.

Recorded History

Great chiefs have dwelt in Waipio. King Umialiloa planted *taro* just like a commoner, and fished with his own hands. He went on to unite the island into one kingdom in the 15th century. Waipio was the traditional lands of Kamehameha the Great, and in many ways was the basis of his earthly and spiritual power. He came here to rest after heavy battles, and offshore was the scene of the first modern naval battle in Hawaii. Here, Kamehameha's war canoes faced those of his nemesis, Keoua. Both had recently acquired cannon bartered from passing sea captains. Kamehameha's artillery was manned by two white sailors, Davis and Young, who became trusted advisors. Kamehameha's forces won the engagement in what became known as the "Battle of the Red-Mouthed Gun."

When Capt. Cook came to Hawaii, 4,000 natives lived in Waipio; a century later only 600 remained. At the turn of this century many Chinese and Japanese moved to Waipio and began raising rice and *taro*. People moved in and out of the valley by horse and mule and there were schools and a strong community spirit. Waipio was painstakingly tended. The undergrowth was kept trimmed and you could see clearly from the back of the valley all the way to the sea.

WW II arrived and many people were lured away from the remoteness of the valley by a changing lifestyle and a desire for modernity. The tidal wave in 1946 swept away most of the homes, and the majority of the people pulled up stakes and moved away. For 25 years the valley lay virtually abandoned. The Peace Corps considered it a perfect place to build a compound in which to train volunteers headed for Southeast Asia. This too was abandoned. Then in the late '60s and early '70s a few "back to nature" hippies started trickling in. Most only played "Tarzan and Jane" and moved on, especially after Waipio served them a "reality sandwich" in the form of the flood of 1979.

Waipio is still very unpredictable. In a three-week period from late March to early April of 1989, 47 inches of rain drenched the valley. Roads were turned to quagmires, houses washed away, and more people left. Part of the problem is the imported trees in Waipio. Until the 1940s, the valley was a manicured garden, but now it's very heavily forested. All of the trees that you will see are new; the oldest are mangroves and coconuts. The trees are both a boon and a blight. They give shade and fruit, but when there are floods, they fall into the river, creating log jams that increases the flooding dramatically. Waipio takes care of itself best when man does not interfere. Now the *taro* farmers are having problems because the irrigation system for their crops was washed away in the last flood. But, with hope and a prayer to Waipio's spirits, they'll rebuild, knowing full well that there will be a next time. And so it goes.

Waipio Now

Waipio is at a crossroads. Many of the old people are dying off, or moving topside with relatives. Those who live here learn to accept life in Waipio and genuinely come to love the valley, while others come only to exploit its beauty. Fortunately, the latter underestimate the raw power of Waipio. Developers have eyed the area for years as a magnificent spot in which to build a luxury resort. But even they are wise enough to realize that nature rules Waipio, not man. For now the valley is secure. A few gutsy families with a real commitment have stayed on and continue to revitalize Waipio. The valley now supports perhaps 50 residents. A handful of elderly Filipino bachelors who worked for the sugar plantation continue to live here. About 50 more people live topside, but come down to Waipio to tend their gardens. On entering the valley, you'll see a lotus-flower pond, and if you're lucky enough to be there in December, it will be in bloom. It's tended by an 80- year-old Chinese gentleman, Mr. Nelson Chun, who wades in chest-deep water, harvesting the sausage-linked lotus roots by clipping them with his toes! Margaret Loo comes to harvest wild ferns served at the exclusive banquets at the Mauna Kea Beach Resort. Fannie and Ramuldo Dulduloa tend their *taro* patch, and Seiko Tanashiro is perhaps the most famous *taro* farmer because of his poi factory that produces "Ono Ono Waipio Brand Taro." Another old-timer is Charlie Kawashima who still grows *taro* the old-fashioned way, as an art form passed from father to son. He harvests the *taro* with an *o'o* ("digging stick") and after it's harvested cuts off the corm and sticks the *huli* ("stalk") back into the ground, where it begins to sprout again in a week or so.

Harrison Kanakoa mostly lives topside because of failing health. He was born in a house built in 1881 near Kauiki Heiau, one of the biggest and most powerful in the valley. If he's around, he loves to "talk story", relating tales of when his family was the keeper of the *heiau*. As a small boy his grandfather took him to the *heiau* where he rolled away an entrance stone to reveal a small tunnel that went deep inside. He followed his grandfather in a ways, but his child's courage failed, and he turned away and ran out. He said his grandfather yelled after him something in Hawaiian like "You coward," and refused to show him that place again. In 1952, C.H. Brewer, a very powerful sugar cane company in this area, bulldozed the *heiau* and planted macadamia nuts on top. The trees still bear nuts, but the *heiau* was obliterated.

Camping in Waipio

For camping in Waipio Valley you must get a permit from the Hamakua Sugar Co., tel. 776-1511. The office is located about 15 minutes from the overlook in Paauilo and you must pick up the permit in person. Camping is allowed in designated areas only on the east side of Waipio Stream. Many hikers and campers have stayed in Waipio overnight without a permit and have had no problem. Remember, however, that most of the land, except for the beach, *is* privately owned.

Waipio Beach, stretching over a mile, is the longest black-sand beach on the island. The surf here can be very dangerous and there are many riptides. During the summer, the sands drift to the western side of the valley and in winter they drift back east. If there is strong wave action, swimming is not advised. It is, however, a good place for surfing and fishing.

WAIMANU VALLEY, CAMPING AND HIKING

Hiking down to Waipio and continuing over the *pali* to Waimanu Valley 12 miles away is one of the top three treks in Hawaii. You must be fully prepared for camping and in excellent condition to attept this hike. Also, drinking water from the streams and falls is not always good due to irrigation and cattle grazing topside; bring purification tablets or boil it to be safe. To get to Waimanu Valley, a switchback trail leads over the *pali* about 100 yards inland from the Waipio Beach. The beginning of the switchback trail has a yellow post and a green marker. Waimanu was bought by the State of Hawaii about 12 years ago, and they are responsible for trail maintenance. The trail ahead is rough, as you go up and down about 14 gulches before reaching Waimanu. At the ninth gulch is a trail shelter. Finally, below is Waimau Valley, half the size of Waipio but more verdant, and even wilder because it has been uninhabited for a longer time. Cross Waimanu Stream in the shallows where it meets the sea. Pick your own beachfront camping spot and relax. For drinking water (remember to treat it), walk along the west side of the *pali* until you find a likely waterfall.

Early this century, because of economic necessity brought on by the valley's remoteness, Waimanu was known for its *okolehau* (moonshine). Solomon, one of the elders of the community at the time, decided that Waimanu had to diversify for the good of its people. He decided to raise domesticated pigs introduced by the Chinese, who roasted them in rock ovens with spices as a great delicacy. Solomon began to raise and sell the pigs commercially, but when he died, out of respect, no one wanted to handle his pigs, so they let them run loose. They began to interbreed with feral pigs, and after a while there were so many pigs in Waimanu, that they ate all the *taro,* bananas, and breadfruit. The porkers' voracious appetites caused a famine which forced the last remaining families of Waimanu to leave in the late 1940s. Most of the trails that you will encounter are made by wild-pig hunters who still regularly go after Solomon's legacy. According to oral tradition the first *kahuna lapaau* (healing doctor) of Hawaii was from Waimanu Valley. His disciples crossed and recrossed Waipio Valley, greatly influencing the development of the area. Some of the *heiau* in Waipio are specifically dedicated to the healing of the human torso and their origins are traced to the healing *kahuna* of Waimanu.

Accommodations

Waipio has a hotel! Owned and operated by Tom Araki, it was built by his dad to serve as a residence for the officers of a nearby, now defunct Peace Corps training camp. You'll find eight basic but clean rooms. Light is provided by kerosene lamp, and you must bring your own food to prepare in a communal kitchen. Tom, at 75, is a treasure house of information about Waipio, and a "character." He's more interested in tending his *taro* patch, telling stories, and drinking wine than he is in running a hotel. His philosophy, which has enabled him to get along with everyone from millionaires to hippies, is a simple "live and let live." The Waipio Hotel has become known and it's even fashionable to stay there. For reservations, write Tom Araki, 25 Malama Pl., Hilo, HI 96720, or call Tom down in Waipio Valley at tel. 775-0368.

PUNA

The Puna District was formed from rivers of lava spilling from Mauna Loa and Kilauea again and again over the last million years or so. The molten rivers stopped only when they hit the sea, where they fizzled and cooled, forming a chunk of semi-raw land that bulges into the Pacific—marking the state's easternmost point at **Cape Kumukahi.** These titanic lava flows have left phenomenal reminders of their power. **Lava Tree State Monument** was once a rainforest whose giant trees were covered with lava like hot dogs dipped in batter. The encased wood burned, leaving a hollow stone skeleton. You can stroll through this lichen-green rock forest before you head farther east into the brilliant sunshine of the coast. Little-traveled side roads take you past a multitude of orchid, anthurium, and papaya farms, oases of color in a desert of solid black lava. A lighthouse sits atop Cape Kumukahi, and to the north an ancient paved trail passes beaches where no one ever goes.

Southward is a string of popular beaches—some white, some black. You can camp, swim, surf, or just play in the water to your heart's delight. Villages have gas and food, and all along the coast you can visit natural areas where the sea tortured the hot lava into caves, tubes, arches, and even a natural bathtub whose waters are flushed and replenished by the sea. There are historical sites where petroglyphs tell vague stories from the past, and where generations of families placed the umbilical cords of their newborn into manmade holes in the rock. On Puna's south coast are remains of ancient villages, including Kamoamoa where you can camp. The park **visitors center,** that used to stand just before the beginning of Chain of Craters Road, burned down in the summer of 1989 when lava surged across the road, severing this eastern gateway to Volcanoes Park. (The road is still closed, with no opening scheduled for the near future. See p. 645.) The **Hawaiian Belt Road** (Route 11) is a corridor cutting through the center of Puna. It goes through the highlands to Volcanoes Park, passing well-established villages and scattered

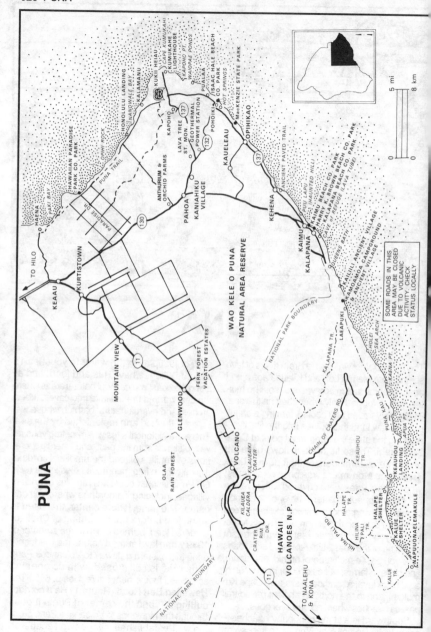

PUNA

housing developments as new as the lava on which they precariously sit. Back in these hills new-wave gardeners grow "Puna Butter" *pakalolo,* as wild and raunchy as its name. On the border of Puna and the Kau District to the south is **Volcanoes National Park.** Here the goddess Pele resides at Kilauea Caldera, center of one of the world's most active volcanoes.

HAWAII BELT ROAD—HILO TO VOLCANOES

If you're heading for Volcanoes Park, Route 11 (Hawaii Belt Road) splits in Keaau and passes through the high mountain villages of Mountain View, Glenwood, Volcano, and then enters the park. If "making time" is your main consideration, this is the way to go. However, if you want much more exciting scenery and a host of natural and historic sites, head south on Route 130 toward Pahoa and the east coast. It takes a full day and then some to see and appreciate Volcanoes Park, so if you're returning to Hilo in the evening, plan on taking the Belt Road back; Route 130 shouldn't be traveled at night. The Belt Road, although only two lanes, is straight, well surfaced, and scrupulously maintained. In short, if time is on your side, take one day to visit Volcanoes, using the Belt Road for convenience, and another to "Sunday drive" Route 130 along the coast.

KEAAU

Keaau is the first town south of Hilo (10 miles) on Route 11, and although pleasant enough, is little more than a Y in the road. At the junction of Route 11 and Route 130 is **Keaau Town Center,** a small shopping mall with a handful of variety stores, a laundromat, a P.O., restaurants, and a sizable Ben Franklin's, where you can pick up supplies. Here, the **Sure Save Supermarket** not only has groceries, but plenty of sundries and a decent camera department, along with a public fax service.

Food
Mama Lani's in the mall, open Mon.-Fri. 11:30 a.m.-9 p.m., Sat. and Sun. 12-9 p.m., tel. 966-7525, is a basic Mexican restaurant. They feature fresh *ahi* sauté, $14, fish and chips, $7, chili relleno and avocado burrito for $5.30, plus quesadillas, taco salad, and sandwiches. **Snappy's Pizza,** open Mon.-Sat. 11 a.m.-10 p.m., besides serving all sizes of pizzas from a mini for $3.50 to a large with all the toppings for about $20, also have takeout plate specials for $3.49 with a choice of chicken, spaghetti, or sub

sandwich. The local **Dairy Queen** not only makes malts and sundaes, but also serves breakfast, lunch, and dinner. Plate specials, burgers, and sandwiches like a Reuben with french fries go for $3.95.

Across the street, a few hundred yards down Route 130, is **Keaau Natural Foods** with a large stock of organic food items, herbs, and grains but no juice or snack bar. However, pre-made sandwiches like *tempeh* burgers with all the trimmings are $4, and fresh-baked goods are always available. **Tonya's Cafe** is a tiny place next door to Keaau Natural Foods; hours are 11 a.m.-7 p.m. Mon.-Fri., closed Sat. and Sunday. She has surfer specials, sandwiches, and side orders like nachos and tostadas, but the main cuisine is vegetarian. Tonya's is a mix of funk and yuppy in moderate but tasteful decor where you can read the latest metaphysical tome while eating a frozen yogurt. Her hours can be irregular, but when she's there she serves up some of the best vegetarian food on this side of the island.

A few hundred yards down Route 130 heading toward Pahoa, you'll see **Verna's Drive-In.** Behind is a small mall with a **Wiki Wiki Mini-Mart.** This is the location of **Papa Aldo's Italian Restaurant,** tel. 966-8066, open Tues.-Sat. 10 a.m.-10 p.m., Sun. 10 a.m.-9 p.m., closed Mon., that has been serving zesty and hearty Italian food and pizza for over 15 years. The pizzas, ranging from $4 to $10, have a delicious thick crust. For lunch, you can have a plump calzone, or a daily special from 11 a.m.-2 p.m. For dinner choose spaghetti marinara, or with a meat sauce for $5, or go light with minestrone and salad for $4.50. Daily dinner specials can be chicken cacciatore and pasta for $8.95. Papa Aldo's is basically a pizzeria with a few tables, but the food is very good.

Accommodations
Banyan House B&B, built in grand-elegant style in 1898, tel. 966-8598, P.O. Box 432, Keaau, HI 96749, is one of the finest examples

of Victorian architecture still extant in the entire state. Owned, operated, and lovingly cared for by Alice "Boo" Beach, it was the one-time home of the manager of the Puna Sugar Plantation. The home fell into disrepair until it was purchased by the Beach family in 1985. Now, the entire family including Boo, her mother, two daughters, granddaughter, and grandson, are restoring the house inch by inch, piece by piece. Everything about this home is grand. The interior has over 14,000 square feet of living space, with another 3,000 square feet that was never finished, ready to be added. The drawing room is dominated by an enormous lava fireplace and a bank of windows opening onto a huge colonnaded front porch that looks directly out to sea. Boo has furnished the home with antiques, mostly from Bavaria, that she has collected over the years. There are filigreed mirrors, intricately carved chairs, candelabra, and a century-old cane rocker by the fireplace. Underneath layers of paint and inferior panelling lie the original *koa* and mahogany walls which are being restored. The formal dining room is magnificent with formidable table and chairs over 500 years old, a rosewood and ebony sideboard from England, and German umbrella stands that are used as serving tables.

The front lawn leading to the house covers over two acres and is lined with royal palms. The grounds, festooned with a myriad of flowers, trees and shrubs, could easily be a substantial botanical park. In residence is what is believed to be *the* largest banyan tree in Hawaii, along with plants and shrubs from all over the world. There's a Java plum, giant avocado trees, bananas, and birds of paradise.

Shampoo ginger, shaped like a small red hand grenade and whose milky juice was used by Hawaiian women to lend a sheen to their hair, is everywhere, along with every other kind of ginger that you could imagine—blue, yellow, white, red, crepe, wax, and torch. Palm trees galore, mangos, plumeria, Chinese grapefruit, tangerines, oranges, lemons, limes, loquats, and lichi all flourish as part of a semi-tamed jungle. The most amazing feature of the extensive grounds is an old mound that local Hawaiians believe was a *heiau*. Preliminary investigation shows it to be a very extensive area, and obviously a very important *heiau*. Upon entering the ruins, realize that the four corners corre-

spond exactly with the four cardinal points of the compass! Inside is an intricate pile of stone that *feels* like an altar. *Ti* plants, whose leaves were used to wrap offerings, are everywhere. At sunset, the rays of the sun fall directly upon the altar

By the time Banyan House is completely restored there will be approximately five suites in addition to a guest cottage with two bedrooms, two bathrooms, a communal front room, and kitchenette. There will also be a restored 18- by 36-foot swimming pool. The main house has a variety of rooms with private and shared bath that are ready for occupancy. The bathrooms are very civilized, with pedestal sinks, separate showers, and baths that are large enough to stretch out in. Future plans call for a restoration of the carriage house and stable, which will become part of a cultural and historical museum. Rates for a large room with private bath are $55, room with shared bath $45, and a small single runs $35, which includes breakfast of homemade tropical branola, fresh fruit, juice, milk, coffee, and popovers. Staying at the Banyan House is a unique treat where you can share in the history of island gentility as lived by turn-of-the century royalty, the sugar planters of Hawaii.

MOUNTAIN VILLAGES

Heading south on Route 11, at approximately 10-mile intervals, are Mountain View, Glenwood, and Volcano. **Mountain View** is a village of nurseries specializing in anthuriums. Many sport signs inviting you to a free tour. Along Route 11 is a mini-mart and **Roger and Ira's Mountain View Snack Shop** serving plate lunches, burgers, and shakes. As you pass through, take a minute to explore the short side road into the village itself. Every house has a garden of ferns, flowers, and native trees. In the village is **Mt. View Bakery,** home of the very famous stone cookies, and the **Mt. View Village Store** which is fairly well supplied.

Look for a vintage plantation house painted blue between mile marker 12 and 13. This is **Tinny Fisher's Antique Shop,** owned and operated by Charles and Dorothy Wittig. What started as "yard sale treasures" about 10 years ago has turned into a unique curio, antique, and collectibles shop. Open everyday 10 a.m.-5 p.m., Sun. 12-5 p.m., the shop has all kinds of antiques and collectibles from Asia and Hawaii, including glass balls, Asian furniture, jewelry, and glassware galore. Tinny's also features a good Hawaiiana collection, with artifacts from the ancient days like *kukui* nut lamps, poi pounders, and stone knives.

There are no facilities in **Glenwood,** but a few minutes down the road you pass **Akatsuka**

Tropical Orchids and Flower Gardens, open daily 8:30 a.m. to 5 p.m. If tour buses don't overflow the parking lot, stop in for a look at how orchids are grown or to use the clean restrooms. They offer a complimentary orchid to all visitors. Just before entering Volcanoes Park, a sign points to the right down a short side road to **Volcano village** (see p. 642).

ROUTE 130 AND THE SOUTHEAST COAST

The most enjoyable area in the Puna District is the southeast coast, with its beaches and most of the points of natural and historical interest. If you take Route 130 south from Keaau, in about 12 miles you pass **Pahoa.** As in Keaau, Pahoa is primarily a crossroad. You can continue due south on Route 130 to the seaside villages of **Kaimu** and **Kalapana** where Route 130 joins coastal Route 137, feeding into Chain of Craters Road which has been buried by recent lava flows and is impassable. (For more information on Chain of Craters Road see p. 229.) Along Route 130, about halfway between Pahoa and Kaimu, look for a small unobtrusive sign that reads, "Scenic Overlook." Pull off and walk toward the sea until you find four hot steam vents. Many local people use them as a natural sauna bath. You might go directly east from Pahoa along Route 132. This lovely tree-lined country road takes you past **Lava Tree State Monument,** which shouldn't be missed, and then branches northeast, intersecting Route 137 and terminating at **Cape Kumukahi.** If this seems just *too* far out of the way, head down **Pohoiki Road,** just past Lava Tree. You bypass a controversial geothermal power station, then reach the coast at **Isaac Hale Beach Park.** From there, Route 137 heads directly south to Kalapana, passing the best Puna beaches en route. Fortunately for you, this area of Puna is one of those places that no matter which way you decide to go, you really can't go wrong.

PAHOA AND VICINITY

You can breeze through this "one-street" town, but you won't regret stopping if even for a few minutes. A raised wooden sidewalk passing false-front shops is fun to walk along to get a feeling of last century. Most of the shops lining it

are family-run fruit and vegetable stands supplied by local gardeners. Selections depend upon whether the old pickup truck started and made it to town that day. At one time Pahoa boasted *the* largest saw mill in America. Its buzz saw ripped *ohia* railway ties for the Santa Fe and other railroads. It was into one of these ties that the *golden spike,* uniting east and west, was driven. Many local people earned their livelihood from *ohia* charcoal that they made and sold all over the island until it was made obsolete by the widespread use of kerosene and gas introduced in the early 1950s. Pahoa's commercial heart went up in flames in 1955. Along the main street was a *tofu* factory that had a wood-fired furnace. The old fellow who owned the factory banked his fires as usual before he went home for the night. Somehow, they got out of control and burned all the way down to the main alley dividing the commercial district. The only reason the fire didn't jump the alley was because a papaya farmer happened to be around and had a load of water on the back of his truck, which he used to douse the buildings and save the town. Pahoa is attempting to become part of the *Main Street U.S.A. Project* which will protect and revitalize its commercial center and bring new life to vintage buildings like the Akebono Theater, where classic movies will be shown. Pahoa has one of the highest concentrations of old buildings still standing in Hawaii that are easily accessible. Many other towns have been bypassed, ripped down, or renovated. Unfortunately, there's talk about putting a bypass around Pahoa. Before this ill-advised catastrophe occurs, take a stroll along Pahoa's tiny back roads. The town is attempting to become the anthurium capital of the world, and they have a good start on it. In virtually every garden, surrounded by distinctive lava-rock walls, you'll see black shade mesh under which are magnificent specimens of the normal red flowers, plenty of white ones, a few green, and even black anthuriums.

Lava Tree State Monument

In 1790, slick, fast-flowing *pahoehoe* lava surged through this *ohia* forest, covering the tree trunks from the ground to about a 12- foot level. The moisture inside the trees cooled the lava, forming a hardened shell. At the same time tremors and huge fissures, cracked the earth in the area. When the eruption ended, the still-hot lava drained away through the fissures leaving the encased tree trunks standing like sentinels. The floor of the forest is so smooth in some areas that the lava seems like asphalt. Each lava tree has its own personality; some resemble totem poles, and it doesn't take much imagination to see old craggy faces staring back at you. The most spectacular part of the park is just as you enter. Immense trees loom over cavernous cracks *(puka)* in the earth and send their roots, like stilled waterfalls, tumbling down into them. To get there take Route 132 east from Pahoa for three miles and look for the well-marked entrance on the left. Brochures are available as you enter.

Cape Kumakahi

It's fitting that Kumakahi means "First Beginning" since it is the easternmost point of Hawaii and was recognized as such by the original Polynesian settlers. Follow Route 132 past Lava Tree for about 10 miles until it hits the coast, where a lighthouse sits like an exclamation point. Along the way, get an instant course in volcanology: you can easily chart the destructive and regenerative forces at work on Hawaii. At the five-mile marker a HVB Warrior points out the lava flow of 1955. Tiny plants give the lava a greenish cast and shrubs are already eating into it, turning it to soil. An extensive flat basin with papaya orchards grows in the raw lava. The contrast of the black lifeless earth and the vibrant green of the trees is startling. In the center of the flatland rises a cinder cone, a caldera of a much older mini-volcano unscathed by the modern flows; it is gorgeous with lush vegetation. An HVB Warrior points out the lava flow of 1960, and you can see at a glance how different it was from the flow of five years earlier. When Route 132 intersects Route 137, go straight ahead down a paved road for two miles to the Cape Kumukahi Lighthouse. People in these parts swear that on the fateful night in 1960, when the nearby village of Kapoho was consumed by the lava flow, an old woman (a favorite guise of Madame Pele) came to town begging for food and was turned away by everyone. She next went to the lighthouse asking for help, and was cordially treated by the lighthouse keeper. When the flow was at its strongest, it came within yards of the lighthouse and then miraculously split, completely encircling the structure but leaving it unharmed as it continued out to sea for a considerable distance.

Practicalities

When you pull into Pahoa Town you are greeted by **Pahoa Cash and Carry,** a grocery store, a **7-eleven,** and the **Pahoa Casherette,** which are enough for any supplies or incidentals that you may need. Close by is **Pagoda Chop Suey,** a downhome restaurant where you can eat cheaply. Also, the local **Dairy Queen** serves plate lunches, and down the street is **Luguin's Place,** a reasonably priced Mexican restaurant that offers a combination of tasty platters for under $6.

Pahoa Natural Groceries, specializing in organic fruits and juices, is one of the finest health food stores on the Big Island. They have an excellent selection of fresh vegies, organic grains, herbs and minerals, deli items, and a very good bakery selection. Out front is the best bulletin board in town with ads for everything from used cars to astrological charts.

Halemana, tel. 965-7783, open 9-5 Mon.-Fri. or by appointment, adjacent to the health food store, is an acupuncture and massage clinic. The acupuncturists are Françoise Hesselink, Jocelyn Mayeux, and Rhonda Ashby. The massage therapist, Gary Grubb, has healing magic in his hands. Relax as you lie on the table as breezes blow through the vintage rooms. Let one of these fine practitioners energize and revitalize your spirit and put spring back into your aching muscles.

The Puna Sands Restaurant, a block away, makes luscious banana, papaya, or passionfruit smoothies for $2. Sandwiches, all under $5, include roast beef with peppers sautéed in olive oil on a french roll, BBQ ham with homemade sauce, and Italian sausage and peppers with spaghetti sauce: there's also a breakfast special for $1.95. The Pahoa **Coffee Shop** along the main drag specializes in breakfast, but is open for lunch and dinner too. Next door is the **Pahoa Lounge** that rocks with live music every Friday and Saturday night.

Along the elevated boardwalk, you'll spot shops like the **T-shirt Boutique, Ernie's Produce,** and a laundromat. Stop in at **Franco's Second Chance Store,** open 9-5 Mon.-Fri., for everything from T-shirts to guitars. There's leather jackets, books, instruments, wallets, and tools, even some *raku* pottery.

By far the best place to eat in Pahoa is **Paradise West,** tel. 965-8334, open 7 a.m.-9 p.m. daily, breakfast until noon, owned and operated by Dave and Carrie Marry. Dave is the unofficial mayor of Pahoa, and has a remarkable knowledge of Pahoa's history which he is willing to share if time permits. Breakfast is served with hash browns, rice, and multigrained bread, and includes eggs with bacon, $3.95, two eggs with 5 oz. pork chop, $4.95, build-your-own-omelette, or two eggs with cheese and onions, $3.60. One of the best deals is *huevos rancheros* with tortillas, beans, and salsa for $2.95. The lunch menu is basic cheeseburgers, *tempeh* burgers, and tuna melt, all under $4.50. The dinner menu changes daily, but you can count on fresh fish and tender steaks. They also take care of the vegetarians with a vegie special every night. Some selections from the enormous menu are clam chowder or tomato vegetable soup for $2.50, rib-eye steak and fresh *ahi,* $11.95, chicken marsala $9.95, papaya-ginger sauce over chicken, $8.95, and BBQ pork ribs for $9.95. Desserts include banana cheese pie, $2.25, oatmeal cookies, and strawberry cheesecake. There's a full-service bar with select wines and spirits.

Out behind the restaurant is the **Marry Whales Hotel,** a one-time house of ill repute. Japanese entertainment troupes used to lodge here when they performed at one of three major theaters in town. The hotel has 14 rooms and a quiet courtyard filled with flowers, cacti, and a Japanese *ofuro* which is now an outside bath painted by a local artist to look like the inside of an aquarium. The classically designed redwood structure is in remarkably good shape. Rates are $15 per night, with a shared bath. The rooms are clean, newly painted, but basic. No reservations accepted because of the limited amount of rooms, but always check with Dave because he knows of other people in the area willing to rent a room. The rooms have cable TV, and there's a swing under the lanai area.

Pahoa Arts and Crafts Guild, open 11 a.m.-9 p.m. daily, is an artists' co-op that has recently opened. They display paintings, scarves, sculptures, and jewelry, all made on the island. Out behind in the sculpture garden you can sip coffee or herbal teas while munching on homemade pastries.

KAIMU AND KALAPANA

These two seaside villages lie along coastal Route 137, a spur of Route 130, and a few minutes beyond them the road ends where it has been buried under recent lava flows. The portion of the road connecting these two routes is famous for **Puu Lapu** ("Haunted Hill"), a natural curiosity where cars appear to defy gravity by rolling uphill. Kaimu, little more than a wide spot in the road, is famous for Kaimu Beach Park, better known as Black Sand Beach. Kalapana is an actual town with a beach park of its own (see "Beaches, Parks, and Campgrounds" below).

Special Note: As of this writing Kalapana is severely threatened with annihilation from an advancing lava flow. Volcano watchers and local residents, accustomed to the unbridled power of the volcano, hold little hope for the town's survival. An effort to save the historic "Painted Church" has been mounted, and it is being moved. Whether or not the town will still exist when you arrive is in the hands of Madame Pele. For a full description of **Chain Of Craters Road** see p. 645. Parts of the road are still open, but only *from* Volcanoes National Park.

Sights
Star of the Sea Catholic Church, in Kalapana, is a small but famous structure better known as **The Painted Church.** A brief history of the area asserts that Kalapana was a spiritual magnet for Roman Catholic priests. Old Spanish documents support evidence that a Spanish priest, crossing the Pacific from Mexico, actually landed very near here in 1555! Father Damien,

the painted church

End Of The Road

A mile or two past Kalapana Routes 130 and 137 come to an abrupt halt where Madame Pele has repaved the road with lava. At the end of the line you come to a barricaded area with a bulletin board informing you about the current volcanic activity that has continued virtually unabated since January 1983. Dramatically, lava fountains soared 1500 feet into the sky, and produced a cone over 800 feet tall. The initial lava flow was localized at Puu O'o vent, but after dozens of eruptive episodes it shifted to Kupaianaha, which has continuously produced about half a million cubic yards of lava per day. The lava flows eight miles to the sea, mostly through lava tubes. It has inundated almost 20,000 acres, caused $25 million worth of property damage, and has added more than 100 acres of new land to the Puna Coast. (For more information see p.638-639.)

A sign strongly warns against walking out onto the lava. Some hazards that you may encounter are brush fires, smoke, ash, and methane gas, which is extremely explosive. You can also fall through the thin crusted lava into a tube which will immediately reduce you to a burnt offering to Pele, and unceremoniously deposit your ashes into the sea! New lava can cut like broken glass, and molten lava can be flung through the air by steam explosions, especially near the coastline. Sea cliffs collapse frequently, and huge boulders can be tossed several hundred feet into the air. The steam clouds contain minerals that can cause burning eyes, throat and skin irritations, and difficulty in breathing.

If you are still intrigued, realize that you are on the most unstable piece of real estate on the face of the Earth. For those maniacs, fools, adventurers, and thrill-seekers who just can't stay away, the walk to the sea takes about 25-minutes. Give yourself up for dead, and proceed. Follow the old roadbed, up and down, over the lava. When you can no longer discern the road, look off to your left and you'll see a large steam cloud rising. Pick your way to it, but don't get too close. Observers say that every day huge chunks fall off into the sea in this area. As you look back at the mountain you can see heat waves rising from the land upon which you are standing. A camera with a zoom lens, or a pair of binoculars, accentuates this phenomenon even

famous priest of the Molokai Leper Colony, established a grass church about two miles north and conducted a school when he first arrived in the islands in 1864. The present church dates from 1928 when Father Everest Gielen began its construction. Like an inspired but much less talented Michelangelo, this priest painted the ceiling of the church, working mostly at night by oil lamp. Father Everest was transferred to Lanai in 1941, and it wasn't until 1964 when Mr. George Heidler, an artist from Atlanta, Georgia, came to Kalapana and decided to paint the unfinished lower panels in the altar section. The artwork itself can only be described as gaudy but sincere. The colors are wild blues, purples, and oranges. The ceiling is adorned with symbols, portraits of Christ, the angel Gabriel, and scenes from the Nativity. Behind the altar a painted perspective gives the impression that you're looking down a long hallway at an altar that hangs suspended in air. The church is definitely worth a few minutes at least.

more. The whole mountain waves in front of you. As you walk closer to the sea, the lava cools and you can see every type there is: rope lava, lava toes, lava fingers. The tortured flow, that crinkles as you walk over it, has created many imaginative shapes: gargoyles, medieval faces, dolphins, and mythical creatures. At the coast, the lava pours into the sea, creating a white spume of steam lifting 200-300 feet into the air. No other place in the world gives you the opportunity to be the first person to tread upon the Earth's newest land.

Practicalities

Keoki's Mart, open 7:30 a.m.-5 p.m. daily, at Kaimu Black Sand Beach offers a drive-in and gift shop where you can get breakfast, plate lunches under $5, snacks, and supplies. For a real island treat, try an ice-cold drinking coconut for $2.50 that they'll open fresh right in front of you.

Kalani Honua, Box 4500, Kalapana, HI 96778, tel. 965-7828, is an international conference and retreat center, a haven where people come when they truly want to get away from it all. The entrance is located a few miles north of Kalapana on Route 137 between mile 17 and 18. Look for a large pink Visitors Welcome sign and proceed until you see the office area and a gift and sundries shop. Depending upon the yearly schedule, they offer a variety of activities that include holistic massage, meditation, yoga, hula, lei-making, language classes, computers, woodworking, music of all kinds, and general crafts. You'll have to contact them to find out what's happening when you'll be on the Big Island. The grounds have a commune-type atmosphere, with a rain-fed swimming pool, hot tub, jacuzzi, assembly studios, classrooms, and cedar lodges with kitchen facilities. It's the only place along the Puna Coast that offers lodging and vegetarian fare. Rates are $18 s for a bunk with shared bath, $22 d, group rates cheaper, $45 for a private room with private bath. A conch shell calls you to breakfast at 8 a.m., and to dinner at 6 p.m. (nonguests welcome). Cost is $5 and $10 respectively with a meal ticket pre-purchased at the office. Lights out at 10:30 p.m., but candles are provided for night owls. Kalani Honua is not for everyone, but if you are looking for unpretentious peace and quiet, there's no better place on the island.

Hale Kipa O Kiana, tel. 965-8661, is a modern guesthouse, owned and operated by Diana Allegra. It's located along Route 137 very close to Harry K. Brown Park. Diana is a wonderful cook and loves to do breakfast, which is complimentary. It consists of home-baked bread, fresh locally grown fruit, homemade jams, and coffee. The rooms (there are only two) have a full communal kitchen where you can prepare your own lunch and dinner. One room is suitable for one or two people. It's an open-beam design, fully carpeted, with knotty pine panelling, and tasteful artwork on the walls. This room features louvered wooden doors, an extra-large closet, desk, private sink, and private bath. The other room is like a small efficiency apartment with a double and single bed. You have direct access to the kitchen, which actually adjoins the room. The small knotty pine room rents for $40 s, $50 d, $10 per additional person, futons available. The small apartment is $60 (up to three people), $300 weekly, $1050 monthly. The entire area rents for $550 weekly (up to six people), and would include both bedrooms, kitchen, two private baths, and massage room (Diana is a masseuse). The house is styled in a beautiful neo-Hawaiian classical design. The upstairs, where Diana resides, has a huge porch which extends over the downstairs area, so you have your own lanai with wrought iron furniture, and a chaise lounge. You are sitting right on the sea, so the melody in your little paradise is the rolling surf, unbeatable for pure relaxation.

BEACHES, PARKS, AND CAMPGROUNDS

All of Puna's beaches, parks, and campgrounds lie along coastal Route 137 stretching for 20 miles from Pohoiki to Kamoamoa. Surfers, families, transients, even nudists have their favorite beaches along this southeast coast. For the most part, swimming is possible, but be cautious during high tide. There is plenty of sun, snorkeling sites, good fishing, and the campgrounds are almost always available.

Isaac Hale County Beach Park

You can't miss this beach park located on Pohoiki Bay, at the junction of Route 137 and Pohoiki Road. Just look for a jumble of boats and trailers parked under the palms. At one time Pohoiki

the Puna coast

Bay served the Hawaiians as a canoe landing, then later became the site of a commercial wharf for the Puna Sugar Company. It remains the only boat launching area for the entire Puna Coast, used by pleasure boaters and commercial fishermen. Due to this dual role, it's often very crowded. Full amenities include pavilions, restrooms, and showers (county permit). Experienced surfers dodge the rip-current in the center of the bay, and swimming is generally good when the sea is calm. Pohoiki Bay is also one of the best scuba sites on the island. Within walking distance of the salt and pepper beach are hot springs that bubble into lava sinks surrounded by lush vegetation. They're popular with tourists and residents, and provide a unique and relaxing way to wash away sand and salt. To find them, face away from the sea and turn left, then look for a small but well-worn path that leads through the jungle. The pools are warm, small, and tranquil. Harmless, tiny brine shrimp nibble at your toes while you soak.

MacKenzie State Recreation Area

This popular state park was named for Forest Ranger A.J. MacKenzie, highly regarded throughout the Puna District and killed in the area in 1938. The park's 13 acres sit among a cool grove of ironwoods originally planted by MacKenzie. A portion of the old King's Highway, scratched out by prisoners last century as a form of community service, bisects the area. Many people who first arrive on the Big Island hang out at MacKenzie until they can get their start. Con-

sequently, the park receives its share of hardcore types, which has earned it a reputation for rip-offs. Mostly it's safe, but if you're camping, take precautions with your valuables. The entire coastline along MacKenzie is bordered by rugged black lava sea cliffs. Swimming is dangerous, but the fishing is excellent. Be extremely careful when beach-walking, especially out on the fingers of lava; over the years, people have been swept away by freak waves. MacKenzie Park is located along Route 137, two miles south of Isaac Hale—full amenities and state permits for overnight camping.

Kehena

Kehena is actually two pockets of black-sand beach below a low sea cliff. Entrance to the beach is marked only by a scenic pulloff on Route 137, about five miles south of MacKenzie; usually a half-dozen cars are parked there. At one time Kehena was very popular, and a stone staircase led down to the beach. In 1975 a strong earthquake jolted the area, breaking up the stairway and lowering the beach by three feet. Now access is via a well-worn path, but make sure to wear sneakers because the lava is rough. The ocean here is dangerous, and often pebbles and rocks whisked along by the surf can injure legs. Once down on the beach head north for the smaller patch of sand, because the larger patch is open to the sea and can often be awash in waves. The black sand is hot, but a row of coconut palms provides shade. The inaccessibility of Kehena makes it a favorite "no-hassle" nudist beach with many "full" sunbathers congregating here.

Kaimu Beach County Park

When people refer to **Black Sand Beach** they actually mean Kaimu Beach Park. This is one of the major scenic attractions along the Puna Coast, and most travelers stop here at least long enough for a photo. There are no amenities except for a few picnic tables, but there is Black Sands Beach Drive-In just across the road, where you can pick up sandwiches and soft drinks. The coconut palms run right down to the water's edge whose white foam is in striking contrast to the coal-black sands. An earthquake in 1975 dropped the beach three feet, severely diminishing it and bringing the waters in to undermine the shoreline palms. The swimming here is extremely dangerous, and the lifeguard tower is there not to signify safe swimming but to protect unsuspecting tourists. Don't swim in the area called Drain Pipe, which is for experienced surfers only! Kaimu was the best surfing spot on the Puna Coast, but the earthquake changed the ocean floor enough to dramatically affect the break. Surfers still congregate here, but those in the know maintain that Kaimu isn't what it used to be. Signs along the beach warn against removing the black sand as souvenirs. Please obey them, as the natural erosion process is already drastically reducing the volume of sand. Kaimu Beach Park is in the tiny village of Kaimu, along Route 137 just after it splits from Route 130 heading south.

Harry K. Brown Beach Park

Located in the village of Kalapana a mile south of Kaimu is this county beach park which is also famous for its black-sand beach. Harry K. Brown Beach Park is the most popular surfside spot in Puna. It offers some of the only safe swimming in the area as well as full amenities and camping (county permit). In the park proper, across from the beach, are remnants of a local *heiau* and a collection of important cultural stones from around the district. These were brought here in 1934 in an attempt to protect them from vandalism. At one time, signs told their history, but now one can only guess what the slab-like and round stones were used for. Swimming offshore from the beach is very dangerous because it's unprotected from the open ocean and there are strong rips. A safe protected ocean pond at the southwest end of the beach once served as a canoe landing. Families enjoy this area, but be careful of the hot black sand, especially on children's tender feet. You can always spot newcomers to the area. They're the ones walking barefoot who get halfway across the beach and start an impromptu version of the Mexican hat dance! Kalapana is the best surfing in Puna. The choice spot is called "Drain Pipe," for expert surfers only. An annual contest attracts the best island surfers to Kalapana.

HAWAII VOLCANOES NATIONAL PARK

INTRODUCTION

Hawaii Volcanoes National Park (HVNP) is an unparalleled experience in geological grandeur. The western end of the park is the summit of stupendous **Mauna Loa,** the most massive mountain on Earth. The park's heart is **Kilauea Caldera,** encircled by 11 miles of **Crater Rim Drive.** Starting out you pass the park and visitor's center where you can give yourself a crash course in geology while picking up park maps and information. Nearby is **Volcano House,** Hawaii's oldest hotel, which has hosted a steady stream of adventurers, luminaries, royalty, and heads of state ever since it opened its doors in the 1860s. Amidst all the natural wonders is a golf course—for those who want to boast they've done it all after hitting a sand wedge from a volcanic fissure. Just down the road is one of Hawaii's last remaining indigenous forests, providing the perfect setting for a bird sanctuary. Mauna Loa Road branches off and quickly deteriorates to a 4WD track, then becomes a foot trail for the hale and hardy trekking to the 13,677-foot summit.

The rim drive continues past steam vents, sulphur springs, and tortured fault lines that always seem on the verge of gaping wide and swallowing. You can peer into the maw of **Halemaumau Crater,** home of the fire goddess, Pele. For those unromantic enough to think that gods and goddesses don't rule the world, **Hawaiian Volcano Observatory** (not open to public) has been monitoring geologic activity since the turn of the century. Nearby is the **Thomas A. Jaggar Museum,** an excellent facility where you can educate yourself on the past and present volcanology of the park. A fantastic walk is along **Devastation Trail,** an elevated boardwalk across a desolate black lava field where gray lifeless trunks of a suffocated forest lean like old gravestones. Within minutes is **Thurston Lava Tube,** a magnificent natural tunnel *leid* by amazingly vibrant fern grottoes at the entrance and exit. The indomitable power of Volcanoes Park is apparent to all who come here. Mark Twain, enchanted by his sojourn through Vol-

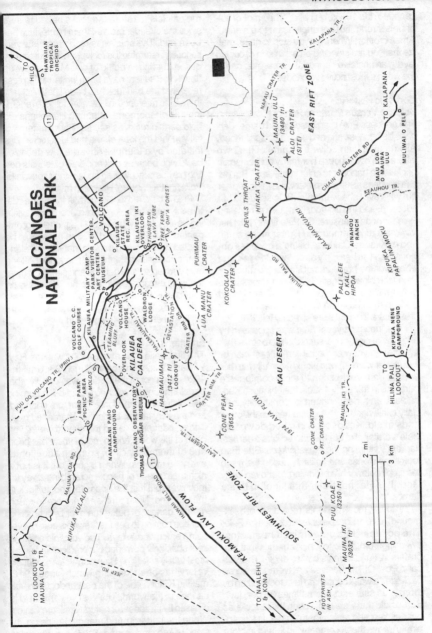

VOLCANOES NATIONAL PARK

canoes in the 1860s, quipped, "The smell of sulphur is strong, but not unpleasant to a sinner." Amen brother! Wherever you stop to gaze, realize that you are standing on a thin skin of cooled lava in an unstable earthquake zone atop one of the world's most active volcanoes.

Geologic History:
Science Versus Madame Pele

The goddess Pele is an irascible old dame. Perhaps it's because she had such a bad childhood. All she ever wanted was a home of her own where she could house her family and entertain her lover, a handsome chief from Kauai. But her sea goddess sister, Namakaokaha'i, flooded her out wherever she went after Pele seduced her husband, and the pig god, Kama Pu'a, ravished Pele for good measure. So Pele finally built her love nest at Halemaumau Crater at the south end of Kilauea Caldera. Being a goddess obviously isn't as heavenly as one would think, and whenever the pressures of life get too much for Pele, she blows her stack. These tempestuous outbursts made Pele one of the most revered gods in the Hawaiian pantheon because her presence and might were so easily felt.

For a thousand years Pele was appeased by offerings of pigs, dogs, sacred *ohelo* berries (her favorite) and now and again an outcast man or two (never women) who would hopefully turn her energy from destruction to more comfortable pursuits. In the early 1820s, the chieftess Keopuolani, an ardent convert to Christianity, officially challenged Pele, topping her like the other gods of old. Keopuolani climbed down into Pele's crater and ate the sacred *ohelo* berries, flagrantly violating the ageless *kapu*. She then took large stones and defiantly hurled them into the firepit below while bellowing, "Jehovah is my God. It is He, not Pele, that kindled these flames."

Yet today, most residents, regardless of background, have an inexplicable reverence for Pele. The goddess has modernized her tastes, switching from *ohelo* to juniper berries that she prefers in liquid form as bottles of gin! The Volcano Post Office receives an average of three packages a week containing lava rocks taken by tourists as souvenirs (sometimes 30 per day). Some hold that Pele looks upon these rocks as her children and taking them, to her, is kidnapping. Always the accompanying letters implore the officials to return the rocks because ever since the offender brought them home, luck has been bad. The officials take the requests very seriously, returning the rocks with the customary peace offering: a bottle of gin. Many follow-up "thank you" letters have been written to express relief that the bad luck has been lifted. Actually there is no reference in Hawaiian folklore regarding this phenomena, although Hawaiians did hold certain rocks as sacred. Park rangers will tell you that the idea of "the bad luck rocks" was initiated by a tour bus driver, a few decades back, who became sick and tired of tourists getting his bus dirty by piling aboard their souvenirs. *Voilà* another ancient Hawaiian myth!

Pele is believed to take human form. She customarily appears before an eruption as a ravishing beauty or a withered old hag, often accompanied by a little white dog. She expects to be treated cordially, and it's said that she will stand by the roadside at night hitching a ride. After a brief encounter, she departs and seems to mysteriously evaporate into the ether. Kindness on your part is the key, and if you come across a strange woman at night treat her well—it might not help, but it definitely won't hurt.

Eruptions

The first white man atop Kilauea was the Rev. William Ellis, who scaled it in 1823. Until the 1920s, the floor of the caldera was exactly what people thought a volcano would be, a burning lake of fire. Then the forces of nature changed, and the fiery lava subsided and hardened over. Today, Kilauea is called the only "drive-in" volcano in the world, and in recent years has been one of the most active, erupting about once every 10 months. When it goes off, it is not a nightmare scene of people scrambling away for their lives, but just the opposite; people flock *to* the volcano. Most thrill-seekers are in much greater danger of being run over by a hustling tour bus coming to see the fireworks than of ever being entombed in lava. The volcanic action is soul-shakingly powerful, but predictable and almost totally safe. The Hawaiian Volcano Observatory has been keeping watch since 1912, making Kilauea one of the best understood volcanoes in the world. The vast volcanic field is creased by rift zones, or natural pressure valves. When the underground magma builds up, instead of *kaboom!* as in Mt. St. Helens, it bubbles to the surface like a spring and gushes out as a river of lava. Naturally, anyone or anything in its path would be burned to a cinder, but scientists routinely walk within a few feet of the still-flowing lava to take readings. The lava establishes a course that it follows much like an impromptu mountain stream caused by heavy rains.

This does not mean that the lava flows are entirely benign, or that anyone should visit the area during an eruption without prior approval by the Park Service. When anything is happening, the local radio stations give up-to-the-minute news, and the Park Service provides a recorded message at tel. 967-7977. In 1790 a puff of noxious gases was emitted from Kilauea and descended on the Kau Desert, asphyxiating a rival army of Kamehameha's that just happened to be in the area. Eighty people died in their tracks. In 1881 a flow of lava spilled toward undeveloped Hilo and engulfed an area within today's city limits. In 1942, a heavy flow came within 12 miles of the city. Still, this was child's play in comparison with the unbelievable flow of 1950. Luckily, this went down the western rift zone where only scattered homes were in its path. It took no lives as it disgorged well over 600 million cubic yards of magma that covered 35 square miles! The flow continued for 23 days and produced seven huge torrents of lava that sliced across the Belt Road in three different areas. At its height, the flow traveled six miles per hour and put out enough material to pave an eight-lane freeway twice around the world. In 1960, a flow swallowed the town of Kapoho on the east coast. In 1975 Hawaii's strongest earthquake since 1868 caused a tsunami to hit the southeast coast, killing two campers, and sinking almost the entire Puna Coast by three feet.

The newest, and very dramatic, series of eruptions that spectacularly began on Jan. 3, 1983, have continued virtually unabated ever since. Magma bubbled to the surface about two miles back from Puu O'o. The gigantic fissure fountained lava and formed Puu O'o Cinder Cone that is now 830 feet high and almost 1,000 feet across. Over a 3½-year period, there were 47 eruptions from this vent. On July 20, 1986 a new fissure, comprised of approximately two miles of fountaining lava, broke upon the surface at Kupaianaha, and has since formed a lava lake about one acre in size and 180 feet deep. At the end of April 1987 all activity suddenly stopped,

and all of the lava drained from the lake and the tube system, allowing scientists to accurately gauge the depth. About a week later, it all started up again when lava poured back into the lake, went through the tube system, and flowed back down to the ocean. The output is estimated at 650,000 cubic yards per day, which is equal to 55,000 truckloads of cement, enough to cover a football field 38 miles high.

From that point, the flow turned destructive and started taking homes. It moved to the coast in tubes, wiping out Kapaahu, parts of Kalapana, and most of the Royal Gardens Subdivision, with over 70 homes incinerated. In May, 1989 it moved into the national park proper, and on June 22, it swallowed the park visitor center at Waha'ula. But so far it has spared Waha'ula Heiau (see p. 646-647). The destruction has caused over $25 million worth of damage. Many of the homesteaders in the worst areas of the flow were rugged individualists and back-to-nature alternative types who lived in homes that generally had no electricity, running water, or telephones. They were wiped out. Some disreputable insurance companies, with legitimate policy holders, tried to wiggle out of paying premiums for lost homes although the policies specifically stipulated loss by lava flow. The insurance companies whined that the 2,000 degree lava never really touched some of the homes, and therefore, they were exonerated from paying the coverage. Their claims were resoundingly repudiated in the courts, and people were paid for their losses. One gentleman, however, has been forced to continue living in the middle of the lava flow. He's been there from the beginning because his insurance company will not pay if he leaves, claiming that the house was abandoned and therefore not covered. He sits in the middle of the lava plain with the flows all around him. For the last seven years, he's ridden a bicycle out from his house to the road. From there he goes to work and goes about his business, then goes back in on his bicycle. Sometimes in the middle of the night, or while he's gone, a lava flow occurrs and he has to wait a couple of days for it to crust over before he can get in and out. Makes you want to rush right out and pay your premium to your caring friends in the insurance business. A prayer to Pele would easily be more effective. There is only one way to treat the power of Hawaii's magnificent volcanoes: not with fear, but with the utmost respect.

Mauna Loa

At 13,677 feet, this magnificent mountain is a mere 117 feet shorter than its neighbor Mauna Kea, which is the tallest peak in the Pacific, and by some accounts, tallest in the world. Measured from its base, 18,000 feet under the sea, it would top even Mt. Everest. Mauna Loa is the most massive mountain on Earth, displacing 10,000 cubic miles of solid iron-hard lava. This titan weighs more than California's entire Sierra Nevada range! In fact, Mauna Loa ("Long Mountain"), at 60 miles long and 30 wide, occupies the whole southern half of the Big Island, with Volcanoes Park merely a section of its great expanse.

KILAUEA CALDERA

The sights of Hawaii Volcanoes National Park are arranged one after another along **Crater Rim Drive.** A side road now and again takes you to places of special interest such as **Tree Molds** or **Bird Park,** 10-minute detours. **Mauna Loa Road** is also off the beaten track but worth a look, along with the **Kau Desert Footprints,** six miles south from the visitors center on the Hawaiian Belt Road. Most of the sights are the "drive-up" variety, but plenty of major and minor trails lead off here and there.

Admission to the park is $5 per vehicle; good for multiple entry over a seven-day period, $15 for an annual permit, $2 for bicycle traffic, and free for those 62 and over with a *golden age permit.*

Tips

Expect to spend a long full day atop Kilauea to take in all the sights. Try to arrive by 9 a.m. with a picnic lunch to save time and hassles. Kilauea Caldera, at 4,000 feet, is about 10 degrees cooler than the coast. Oftentimes it's overcast and there can be showers. Wear your walking shoes and bring a sweater and/ or windbreaker. Binoculars, sunglasses, and a hat will also come in handy. Those with respiratory ailments should note that the fumes from the volcano can cause added problems. Just stay away from areas of steam vents and don't overdo it, and you should be fine. Crater Rim Drive is a circular route; it matters little which way you proceed. Take your choice, but the following sights are listed counterclockwise beginning from Kilauea Visitors Center. Your biggest problem will be timing your arrival at the "drive-in" sights to avoid the steady stream of tour buses.

A very dramatic way to experience the awesome power of the volcano is to take a **helicopter tour.** The choppers are perfectly suited for the up-close maneuverability necessary to get an intimate bird's-eye view. The pilots will fly you over the areas offering the most activity, often dipping low over lava pools, skimming still glowing flows, and circling the towering steam clouds rising from where lava meets the sea. When activity is really happening, tours are jammed, and prices, like lava fountains, go sky-high. Still, this is a once-in-a-lifetime experience, and if available shouldn't be missed. (For full details see p. 577.)

SIGHTS

Kilauea Visitors Center

The best place to start is at the Visitors Center/-Park HQ. The turnoff is clearly marked off Belt Road (Route 11). By midmorning it's jammed so try to be an early bird. The center is well run by the National Park Service. They offer a free lecture and film about geology and volcanism, with tremendous highlights of past eruptions. It runs every hour on the hour starting at 9 a.m. Also, a self-guided natural history museum gives more information about the geology of the area, with plenty of exhibits of the flora and fauna. You will greatly enrich your visit if you take a half-hour tour of the museum. Actually the visitors center has been eclipsed by the state-of-the-art information available at the **Thomas A. Jaggar Museum** a few minutes up the road (see p. 643).

For safety's sake, anyone trekking to the backcountry *must* inform the rangers at the center, especially during times of eruption. Do not be foolhardy! There is no charge for camping (see p. 647) and the rangers can give you up-to-the-minute information on trails, backcountry shelters, and cabins. Trails routinely close due to lava flows, tremors, and rock slides. The rangers cannot help you if they don't know where you are.

Many day trails leading into the caldera from the Rim Road are easy walks that need no special preparation. The backcountry trails can be very challenging, and detailed maps (highly recommended) are sold at the center along with special-interest geology and natural history publications prepared by the Hawaii Natural History Association. The visitors center is open daily 9 a.m. to 5 p.m.; call 967-7311 for trail and camping information, or 967-7977 for a recorded message concerning the latest news on any volcanic activity.

Volcano House

Have you ever dreamed of sleeping with a goddess? Well, you can cuddle up with Pele by staying at Volcano House (for details see p. 648). If your plans don't include an overnight stop, go in for a look. Sometimes this is impossible, because not only tour buses from the Big Island disgorge here, but tour groups are flown in from Honolulu. Stopping at the bar provides refreshments and a tremendous view of the crater. Volcano House still has the feel of a country inn, although in reality it's a Sheraton Inn. This particular building dates from the 1940s, but the site has remained the same since a grass hut was perched on the rim of the crater by a sugar planter in 1846. He charged $1 a night. A steady stream of notable visitors has come ever since: almost all of Hawaii's kings and queens dating from the middle of last century, as well as royalty from Europe. Mark Twain was a guest, followed by Franklin Roosevelt, and most recently, a contigent of astronauts lodged here and used the crater floor to prepare for walking on the moon. In 1866 a large grass hut replaced the first, and in 1877 a wooden Victorian-style hotel was built. It is now the Volcano Art Center, and has been moved just across the road. The longest owner/operator of Volcano House was Mr. George Lycurgus, who took over management of the hotel in the 1890s. His son, Nick, followed him and managed the hotel until the 1960s.

Volcano Art Center

Art and history buffs should walk across the street to the Volcano Art Center, tel. 967-7511, which is the original 1877 Volcano House, Hawaii's oldest hotel. You not only get to see some fine arts and crafts but you can take a self-guided tour of this mini-museum. The center is open 9 a.m.-5 p.m. Sept.-May, and 9 a.m.-6 p.m. during the summer months. A new show, featuring one of the many superlative island artists on display, is presented monthly. Some prominent artists represented are John Wisnosky, who teaches at the University of Hawaii; Harry Wishard from Waimea, who does oil on linen; Chiu Leong, who has a studio nearby where he turns out inspired *raku* pottery; Richard Nelson, a Maui artist renowned for his tri-hue watercolors; Rick Mills, the best young glass artist in the state; Deitrich Varez, who makes affordable and distinctive wood-block prints; Garron Alexander who does *raku* marine life; Wilford Yamazawa, another amazing glassworker; Marin Burger, a young artist who lives in Volcano, known as one of the best naturalist painters around; Kathy Long, creator of insightful pencil drawings of local people; Pam Barton, who does whimsical fiber arts; woodworker Jack Straka, famous for his rich turned bowls; and Boone Morrison, the founder of the center, a photog-

friendly and knowledgeable salesperson at the Volcano Art Center

rapher and architect who apprenticed under Ansel Adams. There are also a profusion of less expensive but distinctive items like posters, cards, and earthy basketry made from natural fibers collected locally. One of the functions of the art center is to provide an interpretive function for the national park. All of the 250- plus artists that exhibit here do works that in some way relates to Hawaii's environment. Volcano Art Center is one of the finest art shops in the entire state, boasting works from the best that the islands have to offer.

Volcano Village

You shouldn't miss taking a ride through Volcano Village. It's a beautiful settlement with truly charming houses and cottages that are outlined in ferns. Tiny gravel roads lace the development, which virtually sits atop one of the world's undeniable "power spots." The area is so green and so vibrant that it appears surrealistic. With flowers, ferns, and trees everywhere, it is hard to imagine a more picturesque village in all of America.

Volcano Golf And Country Club

What's most amazing about this course is where it is. Imagine! You're teeing off atop an active volcano surrounded by one of the last pristine forests in the state. At the right time of year, the surrounding *ohia* turn scarlet when they are in bloom. The fairways are carved from lava, while in the distance Mauna Loa looms. A poor shot, and you can watch your ball disappear down a steam vent. The course began about 70 years ago when a group of local golfers hand-cleared three "greens," placing stakes that served as holes. Later this was improved to sand greens with tin cans for holes, and after an eruption in 1924 blanketed the area with volcanic ash that served as excellent fertilizer, the grass grew and the course became a lush green. After WW II the course was extended to 18 holes, and a clubhouse was added. Finally, Jack Snyder, a well known course architect redesigned the course to its present par-72, 6,119-yard layout. Rates are $30 with shared cart.

CRATER RIM DRIVE

So many intriguing nooks and crannies run along Crater Rim Drive where you can stop for a look, that you'll have to force yourself to be picky if you intend to cover the park in one day. Actually, you can easily walk to **Sulphur Banks** from Volcano Art Center along a 10-minute trail. If driving, signs along the Rim Drive direct you, and your nose will tell you when you're close. As you approach these fumaroles, the earth surrounding them turns a deep reddish-brown, covered over in yellowish-green sulphur. The rising steam is caused by surface water leaking into the cracks where it becomes heated and rises as vapor. Kelauea releases hundreds of tons of sulphur gases every day, with Sulphur Banks being merely an obvious example. This gaseous activity stunts the growth of vegetation, and when atmospheric conditions create a low ceiling, they sometimes cause the eyes and nose to water. The area is best avoided by those with heart and lung conditions.

Steam Vents comes next, also fumaroles, but without sulphur. The entire field behind the partitioned area is steaming. The feeling is like being in a sauna. There are no strong fumes to contend with here, just the tour buses. **Kilauea Military Camp** follows—not open to the public. The camp serves as an R&R facility for military personnel.

Hawaii Volcano Observatory

This observatory has been keeping tabs on the volcanic activity in the area since the turn of the century. The actual observatory is filled with delicate seismic equipment and is closed to the public, but a lookout nearby gives you a dentist's view into the mouth of Halemaumau Crater ("House of Ferns"), Pele's home. Steam rises and you can feel the power, but until 1924 it was an even more phenomenally spectacular view: a lake of molten lava. The lava has since sunk below the surface, which is now crusted over. Scientists do not predict a recurrence in the near future, but no one knows Pele's mind. This is a major stop for the tour buses, but a two-minute saunter along the hiking trail gives you the view to yourself. Information plaques in the immediate area tell of the history and volcanology of the park. One points out a spot to observe the perfect shield volcano form of Mauna Loa—most times too cloudy to see. Another reminds you that you're in the middle of the Pacific, an incredible detail you tend to forget when atop these mountains. Here too is Uwekahuna

("Wailing Priest") Bluff, where the *kahuna* made offerings of appeasement to Pele. A Hawaiian prayer commemorates their religious rites.

Thomas A. Jaggar Museum

This newest addition to the national park is located next door to the Hawaiian Volcano Observatory, and offers a fantastic multimedia display of the amazing geology and volcanology of the area. The state-of-the-art museum complete with a miniseries of spectacular photos on moveable walls, topographical maps, inspired paintings, and TV videos, is open 8:30 a.m.-5 p.m. daily, admission free. The expert staff is constantly upgrading the displays to keep the public informed on the newest eruptions. The 30-45 minutes that it takes to explore the teaching museum will enhance your understanding of the volcanic area immesurably. Do yourself a favor and visit this museum before setting out on any explorations.

Moon Walks

A string of interesting stops follows the observatory. One points out the **Kau Desert,** an inhospitable site of red-earth plains studded with a few scraggly plants (see p. 648). Next comes the **Southwest Rift,** a series of cracks running from Kilauea's summit to the sea. You can observe at a glance that you are standing directly over a major earthquake fault. Dated lava flows follow in rapid succession until you arrive at **Halemaumau Trail.** The well-maintained trail is only one-quarter mile long and gives an up-close view of the crater. The area is rife with fumaroles and should be avoided by those with respiratory problems. At the end you're treated to a full explanation of Halemaumau. Farther along the road a roped-off area was once an observation point that caved in. You won't take the ground under your feet for granted! Close by is **Keanakakoi,** a prehistory quarry from which superior stone was gathered to make tools. It was destroyed by a flow in 1877. If that seems to be in the remote past, realize that you are now on a section of road that was naturally paved over with lava from a "quickie" eruption in 1982!

Most visitors hike along **Devastation Trail.** The half mile it covers is fascinating, one of the most photographed areas in the park. It leads across a field devastated by a tremendous eruption from **Kilauea Iki** ("Little Kilauea") in 1959, when fountains of lava shot 1,900 feet into the air. The area was once an *ohia* forest that was denuded of limbs and leaves, then choked by black pumice and ash. The vegetation has regenerated since then, and the recuperative powers of the flora is part of an ongoing study. Blackberries, not indigenous to Hawaii, are slowly taking over. The good news is that you'll be able to pick and eat blackberries as you hike. The trail begins as a cinder path, then becomes an elevated boardwalk. Notice that many of the trees have sprouted aerial roots trailing down from the branches: this is total adaptation to the situation, as these roots don't normally appear. As you move farther along the trail little tufts of grass and bushes peek out of the pumice. But then the surroundings become totally barren and look like the nightmare of a nuclear holocaust.

Thurston Lava Tubes

If the Devastation Trail produced a sense of melancholy, the Thurston Lava Tubes make you feel like Alice walking through the looking glass. Inside is a fairy kingdom. As you approach, the expected billboard gives you the lowdown on the geology and flora and fauna of the area. Take the five minutes to educate yourself. The paved trail starts as a steep incline which quickly enters a fern forest. All about you are fern trees, vibrantly green, with native birds flitting here and there. As you approach the lava tube, it seems almost man-made, like a perfectly formed tunnel leading into a mine. At the entrance, ferns and moss hang down, and if you stand just inside the entrance looking out, it's as if the very air is tinged with green. If there were such things as elves and gnomes, they would surely live here. The walk through takes about 10 minutes, and the tube rolls and undulates through narrow passages and into large "rooms." At the other end, the fantasy world of ferns and moss reappears.

Small Detours

Less than one mile past Kilauea Military Camp, a road branches from the Rim Drive, on Route 11, and links up with Mauna Loa Road. If you're interested in golf, natural phenomena, or trekking to the summit of Mauna Loa, take it. As an added incentive, a minute down this road leaves 90% of the tourists behind. **Volcano Golf and Country Club** is an 18-hole, 6,119-yard, par-72 course. Green fees are $14, and carts are available; tel. 967-7550. To beat the heavy lunch crowd at Volcano House, try the restaurant at the course, tel. 967-7331 (see p. 650). When the road crosses Route 11 turn right, and follow it east for one mile to the entrance of the course.

Tree Molds is an ordinary name for an extraordinary place. Off Route 11 follow the signs for five minutes to a cul-de-sac. At the entrance, a billboard tries hard to dramatically explain what occurred here. In a moment, you realize that you're standing atop a lava flow, and that the scattered potholes are entombed tree trunks. Unlike Lava Tree State Monument, where the magma encased the tree and flowed away, the opposite action happened here. The lava stayed put while the tree trunk burned away, leaving 15- to 18-foot-deep holes.

Off Route 11 close to Volcano village, turn on Wright Road (or County Rd. 148) heading toward Mauna Loa (on a clear morning you can see Mauna Kea). Continue for approximately three miles until you see a barbed wire fence. The fence is distinctive because along it you'll see a profusion of *hapu'u* ferns which are in sharp contrast to the adjacent property. There's no designated trail, but just climb over the fence. Here is an *ola'a* rainforest, part of the national park and open to the public, although park scientists like to keep it quiet. Be aware that the area is laced with lava tubes. Most are small ankle twisters, but others can open up under you like a glacial cravass. In here is a true example of a quickly disappearing native forest. What's beautiful about an endemic forest is that virtually all species coexist wonderfully. The ground cover is a rich mulch of decomposing ferns and leaves, both fragrant and amazingly soft. This walk is more for the intrepid hiker or naturalist who is fascinated by Hawaii's unique foliage.

Bird Sanctuary
Kipuka Puaulu is a sanctuary for birds and nature lovers who want to leave the crowds behind, just under two miles down Mauna Loa Road from the park's entrance. The sanctuary is an island atop an island. A *kipuka* is a piece of land that is surrounded by lava, but has not been inundated by it, leaving the original vegetation and land contour intact. A few hundred yards away small scrub vegetation struggles, but in the sanctuary the trees form a towering canopy a

apapane

hundred feet tall. The first sign for Bird Park takes you to an ideal picnic area; the second, 100 yards beyond, takes you to Kipuka Puaulu Loop Trail. As you enter the trail, a bulletin board describes the birds and plants, some of the last remaining indigenous fauna and flora in Hawaii. Please follow all rules. The trail is self-guided, and pamphlets describing the stations along the way are dispensed from a box 50 feet down the path. The loop is only one mile long, but to really assimilate the area, especially if you plan to do any birdwatching, expect to spend an hour minimum. It doesn't take long to realize that you are privileged to see some of the world's rarest plants, such as a small nondescript bush called aalii. In the branches of the towering ohia trees you might see an elepaio, or an apapane, two birds native to Hawaii. Common finches and Japanese white eyes are imported birds that are here to stay. There's a fine example of a lava tube, and an explanation of how ash from eruptions provided the soil and nutrients for the forest to grow. Orange nasturtiums and blue morning glories, beautiful but deadly, have taken over acres of the hillside, wiping out all the natural vegetation. This is a microcosm of the demise of Hawaii's flora and fauna. When you do come across a native Hawaiian plant, it seems somehow older, almost prehistoric. If a pre-contact Hawaiian could be materialized, even here in this preserve, he would recognize only a few plants and trees. More than four times as many plants and animals have become extinct in Hawaii in the last 200 years than on all of the North American continent. As you leave, listen for the melodies coming from the treetops, and hope the day never comes when no birds sing.

Further Afield
Mauna Loa Road continues westward and gains elevation for approximately 10 miles. At the end of the pavement, at 6,662 feet, you find a parking area and lookout. A trail leads from here to the summit of Mauna Loa. (See "Camping and Hiking" following.) It takes three to four days to hike, under no circumstances by novice hikers or those unprepared for cold alpine conditions. At 6,000 feet, altitude is already a concern.

The **Kau Desert Footprints** are six miles south along Route 11 from the visitors center between mile markers 37 and 38, designated as the Kau Desert Trail Head. People going to or from Kailua-Kona can see them en route, but those staying in Hilo should take the time to visit the footprints. The trek across the small section of desert is fascinating, and the history of the footprints makes the experience more evocative. The trail is only 1.6 miles RT and can be hustled along in less than 30 minutes, but allow

at least an hour, mostly for observation. The predominant foliage is a red bottlebrush that contrasts with the bleak surroundings—the feeling throughout the area is one of foreboding. You pass a wasteland of *a'a* and *pahoehoe* lava flows to arrive at the footprints. A metal fence in a sturdy pavilion surrounds them. They look like they're cast in cement. Actually they're formed from pisolites: particles of ash stuck together with moisture, which formed mud that hardened like plaster. In 1790 Kamehameha was waging war with Keoua over the control of the Big Island. One of Keoua's warrior parties of approximately 80 people attempted to cross the desert while Kilauea was erupting. Toxic gases descended upon them and the warriors and their families were enveloped and suffocated. They literally died in their tracks, which remain as the Footprints. This unfortunate occurrence was regarded by the Hawaiians as a direct message from the gods proclaiming their support for Kamehameha. Keoua, who could not deny the sacred signs, felt abandoned and shortly thereafter became a human sacrifice at Puukohala Heiau built by Kamehameha to honor his war-god, Kukailimoku.

CHAIN OF CRATERS ROAD

The Chain of Craters Road that once linked Volcanoes with Kalapana village on the east coast has been severed by an enormous lava flow and can only be driven from Volcanoes down to road's end near Kamoamoa Campground. Remember that the volcanic activity in this area is unpredictable, and that the road can be closed at a moments notice. Flying volcanic ash, mixed with the frequent drizzle, can be as slippery as ice. Heading down, every bend in the road—and they are uncountable—offers a panoramic vista. There are dozens of pulloffs, many of which are named, like Naulu ("Sea Orchards"), where plaques provide geological information about past eruptions and lava flows. The grandeur, power, and immensity of the forces that have been creating the Earth from the beginning of time are right before your eyes. The lower part of the road is spectacular. Here, blacker-than-black sea cliffs, covered by a thin layer of green, abruptly stop at the sea. The surf rolls in sending up spumes of seawater. In the distance, steam billows into the air from where the lava flows into

the sea. At road's end you will find a barricade that is manned by park rangers. Heed their warnings. The drive from atop the volcano to the barricade takes about 30 minutes. If you are going in the evening, when the spectacle is more apparent, bring a flashlight. A ranger will escort you onto the flow, giving an interpretive talk as you walk along. To experience the lava flow from the Kalapana side, see p. 632.

When the road almost reaches the coast look for a roadside marker that indicates the **Kau Puna Trail,** and just across the road is the **Pu'u Loa Petroglyph Field.** The Kau Puna Trail leads along the coast where you can find shelters at Keauhou and Halape. Rain catchment tanks provide drinking water. All campers must register at the Kilauea Visitors Center. In 1975 an earthquake rocked the area, generating a tidal wave that killed two campers; more than 30 others had to be helicoptered to safety. Only registering will alert authorities of your whereabouts in case of a disaster. A number of trails cross in this area and you can take them back up to

Chain of Craters Road or continue on a real expedition through the Kau Desert. The Kau Puna Trail requires full trekking and camping gear.

Pu'u Loa Petroglyphs

The walk out to Pu'u Loa Petroglyphs is delightful, highly educational, and only takes one hour. The trail, although it traverses solid lava, is discernible. The tread of feet over the centuries has discolored the rock. As you walk along, note the ahu, traditional trail markers that are piles of stone shaped like little Christmas trees. Most of the lava field leading to the petroglyphs is undulating pa'hoehoe and looks like a frozen sea. You can climb bumps of lava, from eight to ten feet high, to scout the immediate territory. Mountainside, the pali is quite visible and you can pick out the most recent lava flows—the blackest and least vegetated. As you approach the site, the lava changes dramatically and looks like long strands of braided rope. The petroglyphs are in an area about the size of a soccer field. A wooden walkway encircles them and ensures their protection. A common motif is a circle with a hole in the middle, like a donut. There are men with triangular-shaped heads, and some rocks are entirely covered with designs while others have only a symbolic scratch or two. If you stand upon the walkway and trek off at the two o'clock position you'll see a small hill. Go over and down it and you will discover even better petroglyphs that include a sailing canoe about two feet high. At the back end of the walkway a sign proclaims that Pu'u Loa meant "Long Hill," which the Hawaiians euphemised into "Long Life." For countless generations, fathers would come here to place pieces of their infants' umbilical cords into small holes as an offering to the gods to grant long life to their children. Concentric circles surrounded by the holes held the umbilical cords. The entire area, an obvious power spot, screams in utter silence, and the still-strong mana is easily felt.

Kamoamoa Village And Campground is just before the end of the line. The free, lightly used campground is more than adequate with large separated camping sites, flush toilets, and shaded picnic grove. A pavilion houses an ingenious cookstove: a cement culvert rigged as an efficient wood-burner. A half-mile trail begins here that takes you through native and exotic lowland forest along the coast to Kamoamoa village and the remains of a heiau. Plaques along the trail give historical, cultural, and botanical facts concerning the area. As you walk along, you come to old burial sites, low round humps about 15 feet in diameter that resemble upside-down bowls. The pathway continues along the coast to a low flat stone that marked the floor of a canoe shed. Following are the remains of a heiau and, just off the coast, a clearly visible natural stone bridge. The path ends at the remains of Kamoamoa village. Look for a grove of coconut trees, a short variety that are easily picked. Grass houses once sat atop the low stone platforms within the compound area. No camping is allowed in this area, but tenters have been known to make it a one-night bivouac just for the experience. Just here along the coast is the world's newest, and largest, black-sand beach that formed only in 1988. At over two miles long, it makes the other black-sand beaches on the island look like miniatures. It's not safe for swimming because of the turbulence in the water created by the lava, and also because of the sheer dropoff just a few yards from shore. Fishing boats used to moor here, but now even these seaworthy craft can't approach the awesome creation of an active volcano.

Waha'ula Heiau

A few minutes' walk from the campground is Waha'ula Heiau, "Temple of the Red Mouth," that radically changed the rituals and practices of the relatively benign Hawaiian religion by introducing the idea of human sacrifice. The 13th century marked the end of the frequent comings and goings between Hawaii and the "Lands to the South" (Tahiti), and began the isolation which would last 500 years until Capt. Cook arrived. Unfortunately, this last influx of Polynesians brought a rash of conquering warriors carrying ferocious gods who lusted for human blood before they would be appeased. Paao, a powerful Tahitian priest, supervised the building of Waha'ula and brought in a new chief, Pili, to strengthen the diminished mana of the Hawaiian chiefs due to their commonplace practice of intermarriage with commoners. Waha'ula became the foremost luakini (human sacrifice) temple in the island kingdom and held this position until the demise of the old ways in the 1820s. The heiau is not at all grandiose, merely an elevated rock platform smoothed over with pebbles. Inside a self-guided tour reveals the nature of the old practices and where and how they were carried out. It's easy for modern people to condemn the old ways, but a sensitive historical account at the *heiau* makes one realize that within the context of Hawaiian beliefs, these practices were not considered barbaric. This entire area is now inaccessible by car due to the recent lava flows. The restored temple is completely surrounded by lava, but has so far escaped destruction. Only a benevolent blessing from Madame Pele can save it.

PRACTICALITIES

CAMPING AND HIKING

Campgrounds And Cabins

The main campground in Volcanoes is **Namakani Paio**, down a short service road behind Hawaii Volcano Observatory. There is no charge for tent camping and no reservations are required, but you must get a permit (limited to seven days) from Park HQ. A cooking pavilion has fireplaces but no wood is provided. **Cabins** are available through Volcano House. Each accommodates four people and costs $18. A $10 key deposit gives access to the shower and toilet; linens are an optional extra. Check in at Volcano House at 3:00 p.m. and check out by 12 p.m. For information and reservations write Volcano House at the address below. For Kamoamoa Campground along the coast, see p. 646.

Kipuka Nene is another campground, approximately 10 miles south of Park HQ down Hilina Pali Road. Much fewer people camp here and it too is free. You must get a seven-day permit from HQ, and you'll find a cooking pavilion, fireplaces, but no firewood.

Niaulani Cabin is operated by the Division of State Parks. The cabin is outside the park along Old Volcano Road, about a half mile south of the Village General Store in Volcano Village. The cabin is completely furnished with full kitchen and bathroom facilities. It accommodates up to six people, and the rates are on a sliding scale determined by number of people and length of stay: one person for one day is $10, two people are $14, and six people are $30. Reservations and a deposit are required. For full details write Dept. of Land and Natural Resources, Div. of State Parks, Box 936, Hilo, HI 96720, tel. 961-7200. Upon arrival the key is picked up from the Div. of State Parks office at 75 Aupuni St., Hilo, between 7:45 a.m. and 4:30 p.m. Holidays and weekends the key is left at the Hilo Airport information booth.

HIKING

The slopes of Mauna Loa and HVNP are a trekker's paradise. You'll find trails that last for days or just an hour or two. Many have shelters, and those trails that require an overnight stay provide cabins. Because of the possibility of an eruption or earthquake, it is *imperative* to check in at Park HQ, where you can also pick up current trail info and maps (see p. 640).

The hike to the summit of **Mauna Loa** (13,679 feet) is the most grueling. The trailhead is at the lookout at the end of the pavement of Mauna Loa Road. Hikers in excellent condition can make the summit (RT) in three days, but four would be more comfortable. There is a considerable height gain so expect chilly weather even in summer, and snow in winter. Altitude sickness is also a problem. En route you pass through *nene* country, with a good chance to spot these lava-adapted geese. Fences keep out feral goats, so remember to close gates after you. The first cabin is at Red Hill (10,092 feet) and the second is at the summit. Water is from roof catchment and should be boiled. The summit treats you to a sweeping panorama that includes Haleakala. Mauna Loa's Mokuaweoweo Caldera is over three miles long and has vertical walls towering 600 feet. From November to May, if there is snow, steam rises from the caldera. The trail cabin is down inside.

The **Crater Rim Loop Trail** begins at Park HQ and follows the Crater Rim Road, crossing back and forth a number of times. Hiking the entire 11 miles takes a full day, but you can take it in sections as time and energy permit. It's a well-marked and maintained trail, and all you need is warm clothing, water, and determination. For your efforts, you'll get an up-close view of all of the sights outlined along Crater Rim Drive.

Kilauea Iki Trail begins at the Thurston Lava Tube, or at Park HQ via the Byron Ledge Trail.

This five-mile trail generally takes three to four hours, as it passes through the center of Kilauea Iki Caldera. It's easy to link up with the Byron Ledge Trail or with the Halemaumau Trail. You can return north to Park HQ or continue on either of these two trails to Halemaumau Parking Area directly south of Park Headquarters.

Halemaumau Trail provides the best scenery for the effort. It begins at Park HQ and descends into Kilauea Caldera, covering six miles (five hours). If possible, arrange to be picked up at Halemaumau Parking area due south of Park Headquarters.

ACCOMMODATIONS, FOOD, AND SHOPPING

If you intend to spend the night atop Kilauea, your choices of accommodations are few and simple. Volcano House provides the only hotel, but cabins are available at the campgrounds, there are plenty of tenting sites, and there is a wonderful assortment of bed and breakfast homes.

Kilauea Lodge

This superb and recent addition to the Volcano area, tel. 967-7366, owned and operated by Lorna Larsen-Jeyte and Albert Jeyte, is the premier restaurant and lodge atop Volcano as well as being one of the very best on the island. The solid stone and timber structure was built in 1938 as a YMCA camp and functioned as such until 1962, when it became a "mom and pop operation," often failing and changing ownership periodically. It faded into the ferns until Lorna and Albert revitalized it in 1987, opening in 1988. The lodge is a classic with a vaulted open-beamed *koa* ceiling. There's a warm and cozy *international fireplace* dating from the days of the YMCA camp that's embedded with stones and plaques from all over the world, along with coins from countries such as Malaysia, Japan, Singapore, Australia, New Zealand, Finland, Germany, and Italy, to name a few.

The **Kilauea Lodge Restaurant,** open for dinner 5:30-9 p.m. daily, reservations a must, lunch 10:30 a.m.-2:30 p.m. with champagne brunch served on Sunday, Jan.-Sept., closed off-season, is an extraordinary restaurant serving gourmet continental cuisine at reasonable prices. Choose a seat below the neo-Victorian windows or at a table from which you can view the vibrant green ferns and manicured trees of the grounds. A very friendly and professional staff serves the excellent food prepared by Albert, and starts you off with a fresh "loafette" studded like their fireplace, but with sunflowers and sesame seeds. Dinner features a special such as rack of lamb in papaya sauce, along with a daily catch-of-the-day that's baked, broiled, or sautéed with a savory sauce. Entrees are under $20, which includes soup, salad, and vegetables. Sunday brunch ranges from $5.50 for sweet bread French toast to $9.95 for steak and eggs. At lunch try the seafood combo sandwich, the German sausage plate (Albert is from Germany), or the beef papate of rib with meat and mushroom stuffing cooked in a tempura style.

The Kilauea Lodge is also an exquisite inn with an assortment of rooms ranging from $75-110, including a complete breakfast for all guests. The architect, Virginia McDonald, a Volcano resident, worked magic in transforming the old brooding rooms into bright, comfortable, and romantic suites. Each bathroom, with vaulted 18-foot ceilings, has a skylight. The sink and grooming area is one piece of Corianne with a light built into it, so that the entire sink area glows. The rooms, all differently appointed, range from neo-calico with balloon curtains, or Oriental with a motif of Japanese fans. All have a working fireplace, queen-size beds, and a swivel rocking chair. At present, there are five rooms and a private cottage, with seven more rooms being added. The Kilauea Lodge is excellent, providing one of the most *civilized* atmospheres in Hawaii.

Volcano House

If you decide to lodge at Volcano House, tel. 967-7321 or (800) 325-3535, Box 53, Hawaii Volcanoes National Park, HI 96718, don't be frightened away by the daytime crowds. They disappear with the sun. Then Volcano House metamorphoses into what it has always been: a quiet country inn. The 37 rooms are comfy but old-fashioned. Who needs a pool or TV when you can look out your window into a volcano caldera? Unfortunately, the management of this venerable hotel has been in a state of flux lately, and there have been reports of indifferent service. Be advised! Volcano House charges $57 to

$102 for a room with a crater view, $10 for each additional person.

Volcano House offers a full menu for breakfast, lunch, and dinner. The quality is fair and the prices reasonable; however, the lunchtime buffet is overwhelmingly crowded and should be avoided if possible.

Bonnie Goodell's Guest House

This very friendly hideaway, tel. 967-7775, Volcano HI 96785, is on the back roads of Volcano Village. The fully furnished house is designed as a self-sufficient unit where the guests are guaranteed peace and quiet on this lovely six acre homesite. Bonnie grew up in Hawaii and was for many years the education director for the Honolulu Botanic Gardens. She *knows* her plants and is willing to chat with her guests. The place is particularly good for families. Children have plenty of room to play, while the parents can roam the orchards on the property. The two-story guest home is bright and airy. Enter into a combo living room, kitchen, and dining area with a large bathroom off to the right. Upstairs is a sleeping area with two twin beds and a queen-size foldout bed; downstairs is another foldout bed. Futons can sleep even more. Another cottage, smaller but more luxurious (wheelchair-accessible) is nearing completion. Plans call for a fireplace, and the romantic mood is designed for honeymoon couples who want to be alone. The price range is $50 d, $5 for each additional person, off-season $40, minimum stay two nights. Sometimes Bonnie will allow an emergency one-night stay if the house is not booked, but she charges $10 extra because the entire house has to be cleaned.

Volcano B&B

This gingerbread house, Hawaiian style, tel. 967-7779, P.O. Box 22, Volcano, HI 96785, is owned and operated by Jim and Sandy Pedersen. The home is actually in the old Volcano village, and was originally built in 1912 as a vacation getaway for a local Hawaiian family. Additions and improvements followed over the years until it was purchased by the Pedersens, who have transformed it into a serene mountain bungalow. All windows are original, and along with the vaulted ceilings give the common rooms an open and airy feel. One of the finest features is a lovely sun porch, bedecked in white with blue-trimmed wicker furniture. Morning on the porch is especially beautiful to greet the sunshine, and to overlook a garden of ferns, flowers, and trees. Breakfast fills the house with the homey smell of fresh muffins baking in the oven, which you will enjoy with a large bowl of fresh fruit, yogurt-fruit sauce, and 100-percent pure organic Kona coffee. The B&B has three very comfortable guest rooms. They're small, but rich with the feeling of absolute hominess and relaxation built around a theme with differing furniture and color. All are immaculate. The second and third floors of the house are dedicated to the guests, with the exception of the kitchen. The Pedersens live below. The common area and the sun porch are separated from the living room by two sets of French doors. The living room, equipped with a TV and VCR, also serves as a reading room and a piano room. The hosts provide bicycles for touring and also help with small items like coolers, water bottles, and flashlights to view the volcano after dark.

Other Lodging

A B&B with an excellent reputation is **My Island,** tel. 967-7216, Box 100, Volcano, HI 96785. Rates begin at a very reasonable $25 single with shared bath to $50 for a double with private bath, and there's even a private studio.

Bonnie Goodell (see above) recommends a similar cottage owned by her friend Beverly Jackon, tel. 967-7986. The setup is just about the same as Bonnie's, except that Beverly's cottage is closer to the road, which makes it more convenient, but a bit less secluded.

Volcano Vacation, Box 608, Kailua-Kona, HI 96745, tel. 325-7708, offers a fully furnished, two-bedroom luxury cabin complete with sauna and fireplace for $80, with special weekly and monthly rates, deposit required. When you visit look for a Hawaiian hawk that loves to take a daily bath in their catchment basin.

For inexpensive rooms call **Village House** in Volcano at tel. 967-7470. The atmosphere is like a student hostel and might not be to everyone's liking, but the rates are unbeatable at $17.50 s, $35 d.

Other reasonably priced cabins and housekeeping units in the Volcano area that you might try are Kay Fuller's guest house at tel. 967-8172, and a few housekeeping cabins next to the park that rent for $300 p/w at tel. 967-7775.

Other Food and Shopping

If you are after an exquisite piece of art, a unique memento, or an inexpensive but distinctive souvenir, be sure to visit the **Volcano Art Center** (see p. 224).

You can get away from the crowds and have a satisfying meal at **Volcano Country Club Restaurant** at Volcano Golf Course. The cuisine is quite good, with a full lunch menu daily 11 a.m.-3 p.m., open weekends for breakfast at 6:30 a.m. Selections include hearty sandwiches for $4 and under, burgers with trimmings, luncheon N.Y. steak smothered in onions for $6, and a seafood plate with shrimp, fish, and onion rings for $5.75. Next to the Kilauea Lodge it's the best place for lunch in the area.

A **farmer's market** opens on the first and third Sunday of the month and sells local produce, baked goods, and used books. It's located at the Community Center at the corner of Wright Road (the north entrance to the village) and Route 11, between mile markers 26 and 27.

Volcano Store, tel. 967-7210, open 6 a.m.-7 p.m. daily, is in the middle of Volcano village and sells gasoline, film, and a good selection of basic foods. Next door is a mediocre plate lunch window where you can get most of their offerings for about $5.

Just down the road, **Kilauea General Store,** open 6 a.m.-7 p.m., Sun. 6:30 a.m.-6:30 p.m., also sells gas but is not as well stocked.

tree fern

KONA

Kona is long and lean, and takes its suntanned body for granted. This district is the west coast of the Big Island and lies in the rain shadows of both Mauna Loa and Mauna Kea. You can come here expecting brilliant sunny days and glorious sunsets, and you won't be disappointed; this reliable sunshine has earned Kona the nickname of "The Gold Coast." Offshore, the fishing grounds are legendary, especially for marlin that lure game-fishing enthusiasts from around the world. There are actually two Konas, north and south, and both enjoy an upland interior of forests, ranches, and homesteads while most of the coastline is low, broad, and flat. If you've been fantasizing about swaying palms and tropical jungles dripping with wild orchids, you might be in for "Kona shock," especially if you fly directly into Keahole Airport. Around the airport the land is raw black lava that can appear as forbidding as the tailings from an old mining operation. Don't despair. Just north is one of the premier resorts in Hawaii, with a gorgeous white beach lined with dancing coconut palms, and throughout Kona the lava has been transformed into beautiful gardens with just a little love and care.

Kailua-Kona is the heart of North Kona, by far the most developed area in the district. Its **Ali'i Drive** is lined with shops, hotels, and condos, but for the most part the shoreline vista remains intact because the majority are low-rise. To show just how fertile lava can be when tended, miles of multihued bougainvillea and poinsettias line Ali'i Drive like a lei that leads to the flower pot of the **Kona Gardens.** East of town is **Mt. Hualalai** (8,271 feet), where local people still earn a living growing vegetables and *taro* on small truck farms high in the mountain coolness. **South Kona** begins in the town of **Captain Cook.** Southward is a region of diminutive coffee plantations, the only ones in the U.S. The bushes grow to the shoulder of the road and the air is heady with the rich aroma of roasting coffee. Farther south, rough but passable roads branch from the main highway and tumble toward hidden beaches and tiny fishing villages where time just slips away. From north to south Kona is awash in brilliant sunshine, where the rumble of surf and the plaintive cry of seabirds create the music of peace.

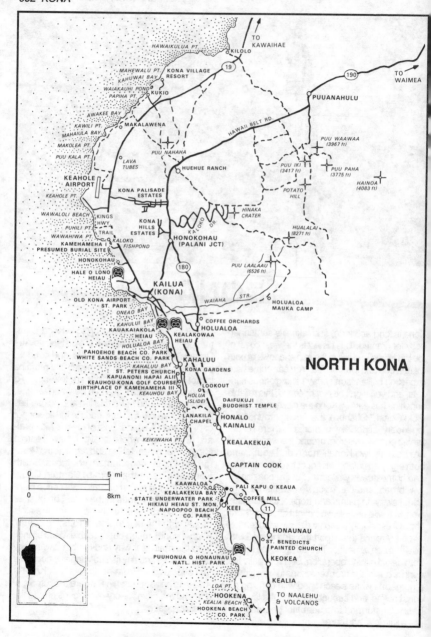

NORTH KONA

KAILUA-KONA AND VICINITY

SIGHTS

The entire Kona District is both old and historic. This was the land of Lono, god of fertility and patron of the Makahiki Festival. It was also the spot where the first missionary packet landed and changed Hawaii forever, and it's been a resort ever since the 19th century. In and around **Kailua** are restored *heiau*, a landmark lava church, and a royal palace where the monarchs of Hawaii came to relax. The coastline is rife with historical sites of lesser *heiau*, petroglyph fields, and curious amusement rides dating from the days of the Makahiki. Below the town of Captain Cook is **Kealakekua Bay,** the first and main *haole* anchorage in the islands until the development of Honolulu Harbor. This bay overwhelms with historical significance, alternately being a place of life, death, and hope from where the spirit of Hawaii was changed for all time. Here on the southern coast is a Hawaiian "temple of refuge," restored and made into a National Historical Park. The majority of Kona's sights are strung along Route 11. Except for Kailua-Kona, where a walking tour is perfect, you need a rental car to visit the sights; the Big Island's Hele-On Bus is too infrequent to be feasible. The sights listed below are arranged from Kailua heading south.

If you want to concentrate on the scenery and not the driving, at least along Alii Drive, take the **Kailua Kona Shuttle.** This open-air bus, gaily decorated with pink curtains and aloha seats, will give you a free shuttle ride from the Kailua Pier to the Hilton Hotel. Operated by William May, it runs every half hour from 11:30 a.m. to 8 p.m. from Thurs.- Sat., and from 9 a.m. to 8 p.m. Mon.-Wednesday. When you see the bus coming, just flag it down.

Mokuaikaua Church

Kailua is one of those towns that would love to contemplate its own navel if it could only find it. It really doesn't have a center, and if you had to pick one, it would have to be the 112-foot steeple of Mokuaikaua ("The trees are felled, now let us eat") Church. This highest structure in town has been a landmark for travelers and seafarers ever since the church was completed in January

1838. The church claims to be the oldest house of Christian worship in Hawaii. The site was given by King Liholiho to the first Congregationalist missionaries who arrived on the brig *Thaddeus* in 1820. The actual construction was undertaken in 1836 by the Hawaiian congregation under the direction of Rev. Asa Thurston. Much thought was given to the orientation of the structure, designed so the prevailing winds blow through the entire length of the church keeping it cool and comfortable. The walls of the church are fashioned from massive rough-hewn lava stone, mortared with plaster made from crushed and burned coral that was bound with *kukui* nut oil. The huge cornerstones are believed to have been salvaged from a *heiau* built in the 15th C. by King Umi. The masonry is crude but effective—still sound after 150 years.

Inside, the church is extremely soothing, expressing a feeling of strength and simplicity. The resolute beams are native *ohia,* pegged together and closely resembling the fine beam work used in barns throughout 19th-century New England. The pews, railings, pulpit, and trim are all fashioned from *koa,* a rich brown lustrous wood that just begs to be stroked. Although the church is still used as a house of worship, it also has the air of a museum, housing paintings of historical personages instrumental in Hawaii's Christian past. The crowning touch is an excellent model of the brig *Thaddeus,* painstakingly built by the men of the Pacific Fleet Command and presented to the church in 1934. The church is open daily from sunrise to sunset, and volunteer hostesses answer your questions from 10 a.m. to noon, and 1 p.m. to 3:30 p.m. Mokuaikaua Church is a few hundred yards south of Kailua Pier on the *mauka* side of Ali'i Drive.

Hulihee Palace

Go from the spiritual to the temporal by walking across the street from Mokuaikaua Church and entering Hulihee ("Flight") Palace. This two-story Victorian structure commissioned by Hawaii's first governor, John Kuakini, also dates from 1838. A favorite summer getaway for all the Hawaiian monarchs that followed, especially King Kalakaua, it was used as such until 1916. At first glance, the outside is unimpressive, but the more you look the more you realize how

KAILUA-KONA

FIRE STATION
190
TO HONOKOHAU & WAIMEA
TO AIRPORT, KAWAIHAE
182
TO CAPT. COOK
KONA COAST SHOPPING CENTER
PALANI RD.
KALANI KAI CONDO
KONA LAUNDRY
MORMON CHURCH
LIBRARY
HUALALAI RD.
KONA PLANTATION HOTEL
KAMAAINE HALE
BANK OF HAWAII
MacDONALD'S
GAS
ISLANDER INN
KUAKINI
ROYAL KAILUAN
THE DOLPHIN
CHAMBER OF COMMERCE
KAILUA VILLAGE
11 HWY.
KONA SHOPPING CENTER
MOKUAIKAUA CHURCH
CATHOLIC CHURCH
KONA ALII
KONA SUNSET
KALANI ST.
KALANI BAY INN
PARKING
ALII DR.
TO CAPT. COOK & VOLCANO
KONA HUKILAU
MARKET PLACE
BILLFISHER
MALIA KAI
KONA SEASIDE
HULIHEE PALACE
KONA BANYAN COURT
HALE HALAWAI
JOLLY ROGER WATERFRONT ROW
HUGGOS
WALUA RD.
TO KEAUHOU
GAS
KING KAMEHAMEHA HOTEL
HILO HATTIE
KONA HILTON
HALE KONA KAI
PARKING
HISTORICAL SITE
HEIAU
CAPT. BEANS
FISH WEIGH SCALES
KAILUA BAY
NOT TO SCALE ONLY MAIN ROADS SHOWN
PARKING

simple and grand it is. The architectural lines are those of an English country manor, and indeed Great Britain was held in high esteem by the Hawaiian royalty. Inside, the palace is bright and airy. Most of the massive carved furniture is made from *koa*. The most magnificent pieces include a huge formal dining table, 70 inches in diameter, fashioned from one solid *koa* log. Upstairs is a tremendous four-poster bed that belonged to Queen Kapiolani, and two magnificent cabinets that were built by a Chinese convict who was serving a life sentence for smuggling opium. King Kalakaua heard of his talents and commissioned him to build the cabinets. They proved to be so wonderfully crafted that after they were completed the king pardoned the craftsman. Prince Kuhio, who inherited the palace from his uncle, King Kalakaua, was the first Hawaiian delegate to Congress. He decided to auction off all the furniture and artifacts to raise money, supposedly for the benefit of the Hawaiian people. Providentially, the night before the auction each piece was painstakingly numbered by the royal ladies of the palace, and the name of the person bidding for the piece was dutifully recorded. In the years that followed the **Daughters of Hawaii,** who now operate the palace as a museum, tracked down the owners and convinced many to return the items for display. Most of the pieces are privately owned, and because each is unique, the owners wish no du-

plicates to be made. It is for this reason, coupled with the fact that flash bulbs can fade the wood, that a strict *no photography* policy is enforced. Delicate and priceless heirlooms include a tiger-claw necklace belonging to Kapiolani, and there's a portrait gallery of Hawaiian monarchs. Personal and mundane items are also displayed, like old report cards showing a 68 in philosophy for King Kalakaua, and lining the stairs is a collection of spears reputedly belonging to the great Kamehameha himself. Hulihee Palace, tel. 329-1877, is on the *makai* side of Ali'i Drive, open daily from 9 a.m. to 4 p.m., last tour at 3:30, and on Sat. from 9 a.m. until 4 p.m., admission $4. A hostess is usually on duty who is very knowledgeable in Hawaiiana, and who can answer most questions.

The **Palace Gift Shop,** small but with quality items, is on the grounds next door to the palace. It offers a fine selection of *koa* sculptures of fish, sharks, and even a turtle, along with Hawaiiana books and postcards. Just outside is a saltwater pond with tropical fish.

Ahuena Heiau

Directly behind the King Kamehameha Hotel, at the north end of "downtown" Kailua, is the restored Ahuena Heiau. Built around Kamakahonu ("Eye of the Turtle") Beach, it's in a very important historical area. Kamehameha I, the great conqueror, came here to spend the last years of

Ahuena Heiau

his life, settling down to a peaceful existence after so many years of war and strife. The king, like all Hawaiians, reaffirmed his own love of the *aina* and tended his own royal *taro* patch on the slopes of Mt. Hualalai. After he died his bones were prepared according to ancient ritual on a stone platform within the temple, then taken to a secret burial place just north of town which is believed to be somewhere near Wawahiwa Point. It was Kamehameha who initiated the first re-building of Ahuena Heiau, a temple of peace and prosperity dedicated to Lono, god of fertility. The rituals held here were a far cry from the bloody human sacrifices dedicated to the god of war, Kukailimoku, that were held at Puukohola Heiau, which Kamehameha had built a few leagues north and a few decades earlier. At Ahuena, Kamehameha gathered the sage *kahuna* of the land to discourse in the Hale Mana (main prayer house) on topics concerning wise government and statesmanship. It was here that Liholiho, Kamehameha's son and heir, was educated, and as a grown man, it was here that Liholiho sat down with the great queens, Keopuolani and Kaahumanu, and broke the ancient *kapu* of eating with women, thereby destroying the old order.

The tallest structure on the grounds of the temple is the anuu (oracle tower) where the chief priest, in deep trance, received messages from the gods. Throughout the grounds are superbly carved kia akua (temple images) in the distinctive Kona style, considered some of the finest of all Polynesian art forms. The spiritual focus of the heiau was to man's higher nature, and the tallest figure, crowned with an image of the golden plover, was that of Koleamoku, a god of healing. Another interesting structure is a small thatched hut of sugar cane leaves, Hale Nana Mahina, which means "house from which to watch the farmland." Kamehameha would come here to meditate while a guard kept watch from a nearby shelter. The commanding view from the doorway affords a sweeping panorama from the sea to the king's plantations on the slopes of Mt. Hualalai. Though the reconstructed temple grounds are impressive, done under the auspices of the Bishop Museum, they are only one-third of the original. The heiau is open daily from 9 a.m. to 4 p.m., and admission is free. You can wander around following a self-guided tour, or the King Kamehameha Hotel, tel. 329-2911, offers free tours of the temple and their own hotel grounds. This includes a walk through the lobby, where various artifacts are displayed, and an extremely informative botanical tour that highlights the medicinal herbs of old Hawaii. The hotel tours begin 10 a.m. and again at 1:30 p.m. Don't miss this excellent educational opportunity, well worth the time and effort!

While in the area make sure to visit the **Kailua Pier,** across the street from the *heiau.* Fishing boats are in and out all day, with most charters returning around 5 p.m. You'll have a chance to see some of the marlin that Kona is noted for, but if you have a sympathetic heart or weak stomach it might not be for you. This area is frantic with energy during the various "Billfish Tournaments" (see "Events") held throughout the year.

Honokohau Marina

Honokohau Harbor, three miles north of Kailua-Kona, is a new boat harbor and deep-sea fishing facility that has eclipsed the old Kailua Pier. The shops here are fishing-oriented and it's also home to **Captain Zodiac Cruises** (p. 578) and **Atilla's Bar and Grill** (p. 662), where you can have a yarn with Kona's old salts. Primarily, this is where you come to see huge marlin caught that day, and to talk to the skippers of the deep-sea fishing boats that go after them. (For a description of deep-sea fishing see p. 583). Be at the harbor at 4 p.m. when all the boats come in every day like clockwork. When you pull into the marina there's a road that goes off to the left. Head that way toward the tan building with a Texaco sign to where the pier and the weigh-station are located. The huge fish will be hoisted, measured, and photographed, while the skippers and their crew clean and prepare the boat for the next day's outing. If you're into deep-sea fishing, this is your chance to pick a likely boat and to get acquainted with the crew.

The Natural Energy Labs

These amazing facilities, tel. 329-7341, offer tours on Thursdays at 2 p.m. The Natural Energy Labs are located just south of the airport where you'll find a turnoff heading toward the sea. Incredible things are being done here. For example, cold water, from several thousand feet below the surface of the ocean, is being placed in a turbine with warm surface water. This would potentially generate electricity and also provide desalinated water. In addition, the cold water is being used for growing very un-Hawaiian things such as giant strawberries, lobsters, abalone, and kelp. Make sure you call ahead to ensure a place on a tour.

Along Ali'i Drive

Ali'i Drive heads south from Kailua, passing the majority of Kona's resorts. On the mountain side of the road, a continuous flow of flowers drapes the shoulder like a *femme fatale's* seductive boa, while seaside the coastline slips along, rugged and bright, making Ali'i Drive a soothing sight.

For your first stop, look for signs to Kahaluu Beach Park; pull in and park here. On the rocky northern shore of this bay is St. Peter's Catholic Church. Its diminutive size, capped by a blue tin roof that winks at you from amidst the lava like a bright morning glory in an ebony vase, has earned it the nickname **Little Blue Church.** Built in 1889 on the site of an old partially reclaimed *heiau,* the church is a favorite spot to take a snapshot. Inside the epitome of simplicity reigns with bare wood walls and a simple crucifix. The only splash of color is a bouquet of fresh flowers on the altar.

Do yourself a favor and visit the grounds of the **Kona Surf Hotel,** which have graciously been opened to the public. You're free to stroll around on your own, and non-guests can take a tour on Wed. and Fri. at 9 a.m. Here are 14 acres of ponds and gardens glorious with the perfumes and blooms of over 30,000 plants, flowers, fruits, and shrubs gathered from throughout Polynesia. To complement the natural setting of the grounds, a profusion of Oriental and Hawaiian artwork has been placed here and there. Inside, the main hallways of the hotel's four wings are resplendent with over $1,000,000 worth of wall hangings and tapestries. For a special treat, visit in the evening, when the hotel shines spotlights on the water and attracts a flock of manta rays.

A short stroll or a minute's drive south brings you to **Keauhou Bay.** Here you'll find a cluster of historical sites, and the pier for the Fair Winds Snorkel Dive and Charter. Look for a monument marking the birthplace of Kamehameha III in 1814. Local people come to fish from the pier around 5 p.m. for *halalu,* a tough little fish to catch. Ask for a free area map available at the Keauhou Bay Hotel. Along the shoreline are a number of partially developed *heiau* sites. You'll also find a *holua,* grass-covered rocks that were slicked with water to form a slide. Hawaiians rode it on wooden sleds especially during the Makahiki Festival. A small home stuck on a point of land on the edge of the bay is where John Wayne married his wife Pilar in 1954, and marks the site of the first modern house built on the bay.

For those itching to buy a souvenir or original artwork, make sure to visit the **Kona Flea Market,** just outside the Kona Gardens, every Sat. from 7:30 a.m. to 2:30 p.m. Vendors come from around the island, and the offerings are always different. Admission is free and it's a good place to browse for that "just right" memento.

BEACHES AND PARKS

If Kona is short on anything, it is beaches. The ones that it has are adequate and quite striking in their own way, but they tend to be small, few, and far between. Most people expecting a huge expanse of white sands will be disappointed. These beaches do exist on the Big Island's west coast, but they are north of Kailua-Kona in the Kohala District. Kona does, however, have beaches alive with marinelife, providing excellent and safe snorkeling and top-notch tidepooling.

Note: The following are the main beaches in Kailua-Kona and South Kona. (For more descriptions of out-of-the-way beaches, refer to Milolii, Hookena, and Keei, pp. 678-680.)

Kamakahonu Beach

You couldn't be more centrally located than at "Eye of the Turtle" Beach. Find it in downtown Kailua-Kona near Kailua Pier and the King Kamehameha Hotel. Local people refer to it as "Kids' Beach" because it is so gentle and perfect for a refreshing dip. Big kids come here to play too, when every year world-class athletes churn the gentle waters into a fury at the start of the Ironman Triathlon. Rent snorkel gear, kayaks, and Hobie Cats for a reasonable price from the **Beach Shack,** located on the beach itself. Restrooms are on the pier.

Old Kona Airport State Recreation Area

In 1970 the old Kona Airport closed and the state of Hawaii turned it into a beach park. To get there simply walk along the shoreline for a few hundred yards north of the King Kamehameha Hotel. If driving, follow Alii Drive to the junction just before the North Kona Shopping Center and turn left on the Kuakini Highway Extension. Facilities include showers, restrooms, and picnic area. Parking is unlimited along the old runway. The white-sand beach is sandwiched between water's edge and the runway. You can enter the water at some shallow inlets, but the bottom is often rocky and the waters can be treacherous during high surf. The safest spot is a little sandy cove at the southern end of the beach. Snorkeling is good at the northern end of the beach, and

offshore a break makes Old Airport popular with Kona surfers. There is no official camping at the park, but people often do at the north end. A heated controversy erupted when a developer purchased the land adjacent to the north end of the park, then closed it to camping. Local fishermen had camped here for years. Protesting in 1981, they raised a tent village named Kukai-li-moku, which disbanded when the leaders were arrested for trespassing. It's also disputed whether the developer has claimed eight acres that actually belong to the state. The controversy goes on.

Honokohau Beach

All types of people come to Honokohau Beach, including fishermen, surfers, and snorkelers, but primarily it's known as a nudist beach. Follow Route 19 north from Kailua-Kona for three miles and turn left on the marked road leading to the Honokohau Small Boat Harbor. Stay to the right and park almost at the end of the access road in a dirt pulloff. Look for a blue painted rock with a sign that says "Beach." Follow the well-worn path into the vegetation past a garbage pit and keep walking for a few minutes to the beach. Honokohau is a well-established nudist beach with no hassles. This area was populated during old Hawaiian days and plenty of archaeological sites can be explored along the shoreline. The swimming is safe but shallow. There are no facilities. People often camp here overnight, but you have to backpack everything in. After a swim, walk to the north end of the beach, where a trail leads inland through thick vegetation. Follow it to the "Queen's Bath," a brackish pond surrounded by rock cairns holding spring-fed sweetwater which is great for rinsing off. The entire Honokohau area has actually been designated as a National Historic Site. There's even a ranger back in here, but it's not officially opened. Along with extensive fishponds, you may find a few petroglyphs. On the way out pause at the active small-boat harbor. Although there are shark signs, snorkelers frequent the bay.

One of the main local proponents of nudism is longtime Kona resident, Dr. Bruno Keith. He approaches nudism almost like a religion: if people were free enough to be naked together, the world would be a better place. After all, *desperados* and the like would have a tough time hiding their guns! Mr. Keith, when not at the beach, is often found around Kailua Pier—a bronzed, spry old gent who favors aloha shirts and a floppy hat. He often carries a brown paper bag full of exotic fruits picked off his property, and gives them away to tourists. His background is amazing, and he's fond of telling stories, especially about nudism. He claims that he's gone skinny-dipping with both John Kennedy and Lyndon Johnson, among others. He's been a doctor, journalist, and school teacher, all while traveling the world. He landed in Kona about 30 years ago, fell in love, and stayed on. Bruno is a man of good spirit, and although not a native Hawaiian, he definitely knows the meaning of aloha.

Alii Drive Beaches

The following beaches are strung one after the other along Kailua-Kona's Alii Drive. The first is **Pahoehoe Beach County Park,** about three miles south of town center. It's not very much of a swimming beach, with only one small pocket of white sand next to a low seawall, but it's a handy spot to pull off to view the coastline or have a picnic.

White Sands Beach County Park (a.k.a **Magic Sands** or **Disappearing Sands,**) is an excellent spot for a dip . . . if the sand is there. Every year, usually in March and April, the sands are stripped away by heavy seas and currents, exposing rough coral and making the area rugged for the average swimmer. But people still come during those months, because it's a good vantage point for observing migrating humpback whales. The sands always come back, though, and when they do it's terrific for all kinds of water sports, including bodysurfing and snorkeling. The annual **Magic Sands Bodysurfing Contest** is held during the winter months. The best board surfing is just north of the beach in a break the locals call "Banyans." White Sands' amenities include picnic pavilions, showers, and restrooms, making the beach a favorite spot with local people and tourists.

Kahaluu Beach Park on Kahaluu Bay has always been a productive fishing area. Even today, fishermen come to "throw net," and large family parties surround their favorite fish with a huge *hukilau* net, and then all participants share in the bounty. Because of this age-old tradition, the area has not been designated a marine conservation district. Kahuluu became a beach park in 1966. This ensured that the people of Kona would always have access to this favorite spot which quickly became surrounded by commercial development. Amenities include picnic tables, showers, restrooms, even a basketball court. The swimming is very good, but the real attraction is snorkeling. The waters are very gentle and Kahaluu is a perfect place for families or beginning snorkelers. However, stay *within* the bay because a powerful and dangerous rip current lurks outside, and more rescues are made on this beach than any other in Kona. The shoreline waters are alive with tropical fish: angelfish, parrotfish, the works. Bring bread or cheese with you, and in a minute you'll be surrounded by a live rainbow of colors. Some fish are even bold enough to nip your fingers. It's very curious that when these semi-tame fish spot a swimmer with a spear gun, they'll completely avoid him. They know the difference! Unfortunately, Kahaluu is often crowded, but it is still much worth a visit.

ACCOMMODATIONS

Almost all of Kona's accommodations lie along the six miles of Alii Drive from Kailua-Kona to Keauhou. A super-luxury hotel is just north of Kailua-Kona, while most hotels/condos fall in the moderate to expensive range. A few inexpensive hotels are scattered here and there along Alii Drive, and back up in the hills are a "sleeper" or two that are cheap but decent (see p. 680.) The following list should provide you with a good cross section.

Camping Note

It's sad but true: except for the limited beach park in the village of Milolii, 25 miles south of Kailua-Kona, there is *no* official camping in all of the Kona District. Campers wishing to enjoy the Kona Coast must go north to the Kohala District to find a campground, or south to Kau. Some unofficial camping does exist in Kona (see "Beaches And Parks" above), but as always, this generates certain insecurities. Bivouacking for a night or two in any of the unofficial camp spots should be hassle-free. Good luck!

Inexpensive

For a reasonable and homey hotel try the **Kona Tiki,** Box 1567, Kailua-Kona, HI 96745, tel. 329-

425, along Alii Drive. Featuring refrigerators in all rooms (some kitchen units) and complimentary coffee and donuts daily, also free island fruits and fishing poles lying around for guests. The hotel is close to the road so it's a bit noisy in the day but quiets down at night. Rooms are clean, with ceiling fans, but a touch gaudy with green-and-white paneling. All units face the ocean so everyone gets a view. There's a lovely lanai, a pool, and a trim little garden of raked sand. Prices are $35 s/d, $5 extra person, and a nominal charge for kitchen facilities. Minimum three days, a/c, but no phones in rooms.

The **Kona Bay Hotel,** at 75-5739 Alii Drive, Kailua-Kona, HI 96740, tel. 329-1393 or 800-367-5102, is a locally owned downtown hotel run by Uncle Billy and his Kona family. Its best feature is the friendly and warm staff. The hotel is a remaining wing of the old Kona Inn, torn down to accommodate the shopping center across the road. The Kona Bay is built around a central courtyard and garden containing the Banana Cafe, a pool, and bar. Like Uncle Billy's Hilo Bay Hotel, the motif is "cellophane Polynesian," highlighted by some artificial palms. The rooms are a combination of basic and superior with a/c, TV, green carpeting, one wall papered and the other bare cinder block. All rooms have a mini-fridge, and some can be outfitted with a kitchenette. Rates begin at $59 s, to $74 d, add $10 for a kitchenette; car rental package available.

Kona White Sands apartment hotel is a two-story building just across from the famous White (Disappearing) Sands Beach. All units are fully furnished, with electric kitchens, lanai, and cross ventilated; prices run $40-50 s/d, $6 extra person, three-day minimum. For information write Kona White Sands Apartments, Box 594, Kailua-Kona, HI 96745, tel. 329-3210, or (800) 553-5035.

Kona Magic Sands condominium is next door to Dorian's Restaurant at 77-6452 Alii Dr., Kailua-Kona, HI 96740, tel. 329-9177. The resident manager is Lee Gilbert. Amenities include TV, parking, cocktail lounge, pool, and maid service on request. Rates on studios are from $55 to $62 d, $10 extra person, four-night minimum. There's a 15% off-season discount and monthly and weekly rates. This condo is acceptable for the money, but nothing special.

Kona Hukilau Hotel is another downtown hotel at 75-5646 Palani Rd., Kailua-Kona, HI 96740, tel. 367-7000 or (800) 367-7000. It's part of the island-owned Sands, Seaside, and Hukilau chain. Its sister hotel, the Kona Seaside, is just up the road; they share pools and other facilities. Most rooms have a/c, cross ventilation, lanai, but no TV. There's a sun deck and central area with enclosed courtyard and lobby. Prices range from $55 standard to $76 deluxe, double. A car package adds $10 daily.

Moderate Hotels And Condos
Kona by the Sea, tel. 329-0200, (800) 922-7866, 75-6106 Alii Dr., Kailua-Kona, HI 96740, is a rather new and beautifully situated condominium with extraordinary coastal views. Like many of Kona's properties, there is no beach, but there are both a fresh and salt water pool for your enjoyment. From the balcony of your suite overlook a central courtyard, and watch the aqua blue surf crash onto the black lava rocks below. Spacious one- and two-bedroom units have two bathrooms, a tiled lanai, modern kitchen complete with dishwasher and garbage disposal, living room with foldout couch, dining room, color cable TV, and central air. Furniture differs slightly from unit to unit, but is always tasteful and often includes rattan with plush cushions, with mauve and earth-toned rugs and walls. Prices are a very reasonable $140-175 for one bedroom, and $160-195 for a two-bedroom unit. The **Beach Club Restaurant,** (see p. 666 for details) just off the courtyard, is an intimate dining room that opens to an outside patio for fair-weather dining. You don't have to go any further to find a table for the evening with a romantic and sweeping sunset view. Kona by the Sea offers excellent value for a peaceful Kona vacation.

Kanaloa at Kona, tel. 322-2272 or (800) 657-7872, 78-261 Manukai St., Kailua-Kona, HI 96740, is situated in an upscale residential area at the southern end of Kailua-Kona and is one of those special places where you feel that you get more than what you pay for. The one- to three-bedroom units are enormous. Big isn't always better, but in this case it is. Each unit comes equipped with a complete and modern kitchen, two baths, a lanai with comfortable outdoor furniture, and a wet bar for entertaining. Rates range from $125 for a one bedroom to $205 for a three bedroom; the rooms can accommodate four and six people respectively at no extra charge. A security officer is on duty, and on the grounds you'll find three pools, lighted tennis courts, jacuzzis, gas BBQs, an activities desk with free morning coffee, and even a restaurant and cocktail lounge overlooking the black-sand beach. Units are tastefully furnished, and the complex is made up of low-rise units around a central courtyard. If you would like to escape the hustle and bustle but stay near the action, the Kanaloa at Kona is the place.

Just down the road from the Kona Surf is the **Kona Lagoon Hotel.** Most rooms feature a lanai that overlooks a tranquil lagoon, and all have a/c, color TV, and phones. There is a swimming pool, tennis courts, and the nearby Kailua-Keauhou Golf Course. Dining and cocktails are provided at the Tonga Room and the Wharf Restaurant, and the Polynesian Long House meeting facility accommodates up to 700 people. Rates begin at a reasonable $58 d, $8 additional person. For information write Kona Lagoon Hotel, 78-6780 Alii Dr., Kailua-Kona, HI 96740, tel. 322-2727 or (800) 367-5004.

The **Keauhou Beach Hotel,** tel. 322-3441, (800) 367-6025, 78-6740 Alii Dr., Kailua-Kona, HI 96745, is built on a historic site that includes the remains of a *heiau* and a reconstruction of King Kamehameha III's summer cottage. The hotel is famous for its bougainvillea that plummets over the seven-story face of the hotel. Kahaluu Beach Park is adjacent, and the entire area is known for fantastic tidepools. This famous Kona hotel has been undergoing extensive renovation over the past year, but is open to receive guests. Standard rooms begin at $77 and all have a/c, TV, phone, private lanai, and small refrigerators.

The **Casa De Emdeko** is a condominium that receives the best possible praise: people that have lodged there once always return. It's a quiet, low-rise condo surrounding a central courtyard. There's a freshwater and a saltwater pool, maid service every three days, and a sauna. All units have a/c, full kitchens, and lanai. Prices start at $70 d, $8 extra person, for a garden-view apartment with every seventh night free. Contact Casa De Emdeko at 75-6082 Alii Dr., Kailua-Kona, HI 96745, tel. 329-2160, (resident manager), or through the booking agent of Kona Vacation Resort, tel. 329-6488 or (800) 367-5168.

Kona Islander Inn condominium apartment are well appointed for a reasonable price. Conveniently located within walking distance o downtown Kailua-Kona, they're just next door t the Spindrifter Restaurant. The style is "turn-o the-century plantation," shaded by tall palms. A 100 units have phone, off-road parking, a/c, an TV. For information write Kona Islander Inn, 75 5776 Kuakini Hwy., Kailua-Kona, HI 96740, te 329-3181. Also, Aston Resorts, tel. (800) 367 5124, in Hawaii (800) 342-1551.

A few reasonably priced and attractive condo minium apartments include: **Kona Mansion,** quarter mile from downtown, offering one-bed room suites for up to four persons from $55-60 There's a swimming pool, parking, TV, and mai service on request, with a minimum stay of fiv nights. Contact Hawaiian Apartment Leasing 1240 Cliff Drive, Laguna Beach, CA 92651, te (714) 497-4253 or (800) 854-8843, in California tel. (800) 472-8449. Also available throug Clyde M. Crawfoot Realty, see following fo address. **Alii Villas,** oceanside just a half mile from Kailua-Kona, offers full kitchens, lanai, TV parking, pool, and BBQs. Rates vary from one bedroom units at $45 daily to $252 weekly fo two to three guests, two bedrooms (all units wa terfront) from $60 daily to $380 weekly for fou guests. Additional guests extra. There is a 20%monthly discount, and every seventh nigh is free. **Kona Billfisher** near downtown offers full kitchens, pool, BBQs, limited maid service, and gazebo. One-bedroom units rent from $40 daily for up to four persons, two-bedrooms from $60 up to six guests. Weekly and monthly rates and discounts. **Kona Plaza** downtown has a swimming pool, sundecks, wheelchair-accessible. Daily rates are $40 d, $50 up to four. Weekly, monthly, and off-season rates available. For all of the above, contact Clyde M. Crawfoot Realty, Box 263, Kailua-Kona, HI 96740, tel. 329-0154.

Expensive

The **Kona Hilton Beach and Tennis Resort,** tel. 329-3111 or (800) 452- 4411, Box 1179, Kailua-Kona, HI 96745, has figuratively and literally become a Kona landmark. The rooms are spacious and all include a lanai, (so protected from view that it easily serves as an outdoor room). The tennis facilities are superb, and an ocean-fed pool is sheltered from the force of the waves by huge black lava boulders. Rates run from $99 for a standard room to $200. The hotel, built like rising steps with the floor below larger than the one above, commands a magnificent view from its perch atop a beautiful promontory of black lava. On the property, you can dine in the **Hele Mai,** the main dining room open for dinner only, or have breakfast and lunch in the Lanai Coffee Shop, which has a beautiful veranda with a magnificent view of the surrounding coastline (for details see p. 665). At both you'll be treated to the wonderful creations of executive chef Sam Choy. The hotel also boasts a mini shopping mall complete with a sundries store and Liberty House outlet. The **Windjammer,** an open-air bar with nightly entertainment, features a live band Sunday-Tuesday, with *karaoke* on the other evenings. The hotel pool, completely refurbished, has an upper kiddies pool and the lower retiled main pool adjacent to the rolling surf. Between the main building and the beach tower, is the coconut grove. The *imu* is fired up every Monday, Wednesday, and Friday, and the luau comes complete with island entertainment that fills the grounds with music and laughter. The tennis courts, attended by hotel pro Adrian Canencia, are lighted for nighttime play, and are open to the public. Costs are a reasonable $5 per hour per court, or $6 for all day; non-guests pay $6 and $8 respectively. Other full-service ammenities include a laundry, free parking, beauty salon, babysitters, and children stay there free regardless of age if they share a room with their parents. The Kona Hilton keeps alive the tradition of quality service at a quality hotel.

The **Aston Royal Sea Cliff Resort** offers first-rate condo apartments. They run from studios at $115-135 per day, to two-bedroom suites ranging from $150-425, extra person $10. There's free tennis, daily maid service, two swimming pools, and cable color TV. Package deals are available. Contact Royal Sea Cliff Resort, 75-6040 Alii Dr., Kailua-Kona, HI 96740, tel. 329-8020 or (800) 367-5124.

Hotel King Kamehameha is located in downtown Kailua-Kona at 75-5660 Palani Rd., Kailua-Kona, HI 96740, tel. 329-2911 or (800) 227-4700, on a spot favored by Hawaiian royalty; Kamehameha the Great spent the last days of his life here. It's one of the only Kona hotels

that has its own beach, adjacent to the restored Ahuena Heiau. The walls of the lobby are lined with artifacts of ancient battles, and a hotel staff member gives historical and botanical tours of the grounds. Rooms all have a/c, TV, and phones, appointed in shades of blue with rattan, and all feature lanai with sweeping panoramas of the bay and Mt. Hualalai. Prices begin at $92 for a standard room, up to $265 for a three-bedroom suite. The hotel has a variety of restaurants, cocktail lounges, tennis courts, shops, and a pool.

The **Kona Surf Resort,** 78-128 Ehukai St., Kailua-Kona, HI 96740, tel. 322-3411, (800) 367-8011, is located at Keauhou Bay, six miles south of Kailua-Kona. The building, comprised of four wings and lined with over $1 million worth of art, are architecturally superb. The impeccable hotel grounds are a magnificent match and open to the public (see p. 656). The hotel features the **S.S. *James Makee*** restaurant and nightly entertainment in their Puka and Poi Pounder Rooms. All 535 rooms have a/c, phones, and TVs. Prices begin at $99 to $365 for a suite. There are two swimming pools, lighted tennis courts, and the Keauhou-Kona Golf course just next door, with special rates and starting times for hotel guests.

FOOD

Inexpensive

"So, budget traveler," you've been asking yourself, "which is the best restaurant in town, with the most food at lowest prices, with that down-home atmosphere?" **The Ocean View Inn,** tel. 329-9998, is it! The gigantic menu of Chinese, American, Japanese, and Hawaiian food is like a mini-directory. Lunch and dinner range from $5 to $9, and a huge breakfast goes for about $3.50. The most expensive dinner is T-bone steak at $10.95. They're open daily except Monday from 6:30 a.m. to 2:45 p.m., and from 5:30-9:00 p.m. Located across from the seawall near the King Kamehameha Hotel, they're always crowded with local people, a sure sign that the food is good.

Stan's Restaurant, tel. 329-1655, is an open-air establishment one notch up in both price and atmosphere from the Ocean View Inn,

Many of Kailua-Kona's restaurants are found in shopping plazas like the newly built "Waterfront Row."

which is just next door. Here you have a cocktail lounge and a stab at atmosphere with some cozy lighting and rattan furniture. Breakfast is pleasing with an assortment of island-inspired hotcakes, and a special for $2.95; no lunch is served. Dinner specials, starting at 5 p.m., are prime rib $8.95, fresh island fish, $8.95, and steak and crab for $9.75. All include salad, rice, or whipped potatoes, fresh fruit, and dinner bread. The food is good, but not great, and you generally get a satisfying meal for a very reasonable price.

The **Royal Jade Garden,** tel. 326-7288, daily 10:30 a.m.-10:30 p.m., in the Lanihau Center, is a Chinese restaurant where you can get an amazing amount of well-prepared food for moderate prices. They have the normal run-of-the-mill chow meins for $5-6, noodle soups in the $3-5 range, and main dishes like chicken, duck, pork, and beef for $3.95 to $5.25. More expensive items include lobster with black bean sauce for $15.95, and a variety of fresh fish and seafoods for $7-8. But they have an unbeatable special every night, where you get to choose three entrees plus fried rice or fried noodles for only $4. It's pre-prepared and placed on a hot table, but it's not cooked to death. You wind up with so much food that the most difficult part is keeping it on your plate. In the Royal Jade, there's no decor, but if you are hungry and on a tight budget, this is one of the best values in town.

Tom Bombadill's food and drink take their inspiration from Tolkien's Middle Earth, but its lo-cation is a lot noisier perched over Alii Drive and overlooking the Hilton's tennis courts. They talk about the view, but your neck will have to stretch like the mozzarella on their pizza to see it. The bar pours domestic beers at $1.65, imports $2.50, pitchers $5.50, plus a free "Bud Lite" bumper with every shot. Watch out! The menu includes hamburgers, $4, soups, $1.75, Mexican pizza appetizers, $3.75, and a variety of chicken, fish, and shrimp platters from $5. All of these meals are good, but the real specialty is pizza, from $8 up depending upon size and toppings. Open daily 11 a.m. to 10 p.m., tel. 329-1292.

Attilla's Bar and Grill, tel. 326-BEER, open daily except Sunday from 10:30 a.m.-8:30 p.m., features Kona's longest bar at the Honokohau Small Boat Harbor. Atilla's is more or less an open-air pavilion, but it is actually quite picturesque as it overlooks the harbor. If you are interested in a charter fishing boat, this is the best place to come to spin a "yarn" with the local skippers who congregate here nightly at about 4:30 p.m. The food is actually quite good and includes burgers and sandwiches for under $5, plate lunch/dinners like teri steak or marinated sirloin for about $9.50, and chili and soups around $5. Bottled beer is $2.25 for domestic, $3 for imported, and schooners on tap for $2.25. Try their delicious macadamia nut pie for $2.50. Attila's is one of the truly *colorful* places in Kailua-Kona.

Poki's, in the Kailua Bay Shopping Plaza across from the seawall, serves up pasta. They eature daily specials like lasagna and ravioli, or ettuccine with onion sauce for $8.95. Poki's is a small place, but the smells are good, and prices are right.

Fast Foods And Snacks

In the Kona Inn Shopping Village try: **Mrs. Barry's Cookies,** homemade yummies including macadamia nut, chocolate chip, and peanut butter, gift boxed to send home; just follow your nose to the **Coffee Cantata** and drink a cup in the little courtyard; **Kona Kai Farms Coffee House** features a sampler cup of Kona coffee; **Be Happy Cafe** has plate lunches like beef stew, chicken garlic, a mixed plate of teri beef and shrimp, and chicken and fries all for around $5-6.

Around town, The **Bartender's Ocean Breeze** serves up 12 oz. mugs of ice-cold beer for $1, and grill-your-own burgers for $2.75. Other snacks are available on Alii Drive, near the Kona Hilton tennis courts, tel. 329-7622. **McGurk's** is a *fill-er-up* joint next door to Marty's Steak and Seafood in the Kailua Bay Inn Shopping Plaza in downtown Kailua-Kona. They serve an evening special like the Wednesday fish buffet for $5.95 that includes mac-nut cole slaw and french fries. Basically a takeout place with a limited sit-down menu. McGurk's isn't special, but the food is worth the money.

At the Kona Shopping Plaza there's **Subways,** a chain selling double-fisted sandwiches to go. On Kuakini Street next to **McDonald's** golden arches is a **7-eleven,** open 24 hours, and along Palani Road is **Taco Bell,** next door to **Pizza Hut,** which is across the road from **Burger King.**

In the **Lanihau Center** along Palani Road, you can snack at **Gifu Bento,** a sidewalk cafe where you'll find a Japanese-style plate lunch for under $5. **Buns In The Sun** is a bakery serving everything from croissants to apple turnovers. Also enjoy sandwiches from $3.75 to $4.50 at a few wrought-iron tables under their outdoor canopy. The center also houses **Kentucky Fried Chicken, Penguin's Frozen Yogurt,** where you can also order a smoothie, and **Rocky's Pizza,** where you can get a tray for $8.95-12.95, or a slice for $1.75.

The **Kona Coast Shopping Center,** also along Palani Road, holds a number of small local and ethnic restaurants where you can get an inexpensive but savory meal. **Kim's Place,** open daily 10 a.m.-8 p.m., closed Sunday, tel. 329-4677, features takeout and catering, and has a few tables with umbrellas; enjoy Korean items like *kalbi, pulgogi,* Korean chicken, and even tempura. Prices for most items are under $5. Next door is **Monster Burger,** featuring gigantic hamburgers with all the trimmings, ice cream, drinks, and sandwiches; open for breakfast, lunch, and dinner. For breakfast you can fill up with a three-egg omelette for $2.75 or one with the works, including a breakfast meat, for $5.75. Next to Monster Burger is **Betty's Chinese Kitchen** with specials every night. Items include beef broccoli, $3.55, chicken with oyster sauce, $3.70, dim sum, and snacks like Chinese donuts and a variety of **manapua** for $1 or so. For the health conscious **Kona Health Ways,** open Mon.-Fri. 9 a.m.-7 p.m., Sat. 9 a.m.-6 p.m., Sun. 9:30 a.m.-5 p.m. is a full-service health food store that makes up ready-to-eat sandwiches, salads, and soups geared toward the vegetarian.

The Kona Square Shopping Center is home to the very inexpensive **Stumble Inn.** They have breakfast specials for $1.99, and a lunch special. Unfortunately, there is little that's special about their food, but they are open from 5:30 a.m. for those off fishing who need a very early breakfast.

On your way to Pu'uhonua O Honaunau (see "Sights") you might consider stopping in at **Barry's Nut Farm** along Route 160. They'll give you a free tour of the gardens and nursery, or you can browse for pottery or buy sandwiches and drinks. Open daily 9 a.m. to 5 p.m., tel. 328-9930.

Moderate

Sibu Cafe, in the Kona Banyan Court Shopping Plaza, open daily except Sun. from 11:30 a.m.-10 p.m., tel. 329-1112, is an Indonesian restaurant serving savory marinated meats and vegetables spiced with zesty sauces and flame grilled. The restaurant, across from the seawall under the big banyan tree, has only a few outside tables, and no decor whatsoever. To make the menu even more varied, the Italian owner offers a daily pasta dish using recipes over 100 years old that have been handed down by her grandmother. *Delisioso!* If you're hungry go for the *gado gado* for $6.50, an Indonesian salad layered with spices and peanut sauce, which can be dinner for one, or a salad entree for two or three. Stir-fry vegetables with chicken or tofu are $6.25, chicken and vegetable curries are $7 and $6.50 respectively, and Balinese chicken, marinated in tarragon, garlic, and spices, is $7. The combination plates are the best deals: you get a stir-fry, chicken curry, and choice of sauté for $7.75. Cafe Sibu serves *the* best and *the* most interesting moderately priced food in Kailua-Kona.

Poo Ping Thai Cuisine, in the Kona Inn Shopping Village, tel. 329-2677, open daily for lunch 11 a.m.-3 p.m. and dinner 5-10 p.m., is located on the upper level and is open and cool with windows all around. The view overlooks the street below, and the decor is simple with white tablecloths and blue plastic chairs. The large metal cups on every table are water pitchers, not finger bowls. Appetizers start at $3.75 for spring rolls to $5.75 for mouthwatering *sate*. There's rich coconut-based soups, enough for two, while main dishes feature an assortment of Thai curries and seafood dishes like charcoal shrimp with lemon grass, all under $8. A couple could eat dinner, and even have a Thai beer, for around $20. The food is very good and worth the money, but not extraordinary.

The **Jolly Roger,** walking distance from downtown at 75-5776 Alii Dr., tel. 329-1344 (formerly the Spindrifter), is another Kona restaurant with a remarkable seaside setting. The gently rolling surf lapping at the shore is like free dessert. Full breakfasts are served from 6:30 a.m. to 12 p.m. and start at $4, with waffles and pancakes cheaper. Lunch is from 11 a.m. to 4 p.m., dinner from 5:30 p.m. to 10 p.m. Sandwiches start at $3, an assortment of salads are $5, full salad bar $5.95, and entrees of fresh fish, seafood, and beef are from $10. Happy hour daily from 11 a.m. to 6 p.m. features an assortment of *pu pu*. A daily special of steak and eggs Benedict costs $4.75 and runs from 6:30 a.m.-noon. The decor is bent bamboo with puffy cushions, and the tile-floored veranda has marble-top tables and white wrought-iron chairs.

Cousin Kimo's Restaurant, tel. 329-1393, is located in the courtyard of Uncle Billy's downtown Kona Bay Hotel. Following in the semi-plastic Polynesian tradition of Uncle Billy, they serve fair to passable food at reasonable prices: a delicious well-prepared catch of the day, cut of

savory beef, or fried-to-death frozen *mahi mahi*. The all-you-can-eat salad bar comes with full meals and displays crisp island vegetables and fruits right next to items fresh from the can! A stuffed marlin, seemingly too huge and colorful to be real, gazes down at everyone from the wall. Free hula shows are part of the bargain every night at 6:30 and 7:30 p.m. Open daily from 6:30 a.m. (breakfast specials $1.99), this restaurant could be an "old reliable" with just a touch more care in the food preparation.

Reuben's Mexican Cafe, open daily 11 a.m. to 11 p.m., Sun. 3-11 p.m., tel. 329-7031, is tucked away in the downtown Kona Plaza and serves up hefty portions of south-of-the-border fare at good prices. There's a full menu from chili rellenos to huevos rancheros all between $5 and $7, and the only "slam" against Reuben's is that the dishes are a bit too tame. Reuben's does have the best prices on imported beers—offering Dos Equis, Corona, and Heineken for only $2.

Marty's Steak and Seafood House, open daily for lunch 11 a.m. to 3 p.m., dinner 5-10 p.m., tel. 329-1571, was a former Buzz's Steak House. They serve hefty orders of chops, steaks, fresh fish, and Korean-style BBQ ribs for under $15. Fresh hot bread and the salad bar are filling and priced reasonably. A nightly buffet special of BBQ beef back ribs is $12.95, while crab is $21.95. Sunday nights bring a special of prime rib for $10.95, or larger cut at $13.95. Marty's has reliable quality and is located upstairs in the Kailua Bay Inn Shopping Plaza. The atmosphere in this open and airy perch overlooking the bay is congenial.

Don Drysdale's Club 53, open daily 10-2 a.m. tel. 329-6651, is owned by the famous Dodger pitcher, and in the good sense of the word can best be described as a saloon. The amiable bar and grill serves reasonably priced beer, drinks, and sandwiches until 1 a.m. Sports fans away from home can always catch their favorite events on the bar's TV. Soup and salads from $2.50, a wide variety of pu pu from $4, sandwiches from $3 to $5, plus the special peanut butter cream pie at $2.35. Drysdale's is one of the most relaxing and casual bars in town, overlooking the bay at the Kona Inn Shopping Village.

The Kona Galley, along Alii Drive just near the pier, is a well-established Kona favorite serving fresh fish and combination platters in its soothing open-air dining room. It also specializes in seafood and is known for its Saturday night prime rib. Reasonably priced lunch, with the dinner menu more expensive. Open daily 11 a.m. to 10 p.m., tel. 329-3777.

Quinn's seems to be Kona's yuppie bar. The local in-crowd comes here to the patio for sandwiches, vegetarian specialties, seafood, beef, and football games in season. Daily from lunch until 1 a.m. for late-night dining, Sun. until 10 p.m. Across from the King Kamehameha Hotel, tel. 329-3822.

The **Rusty Harpoon,** perched above Alii Drive at the Kona Market place, tel. 329-8881, open daily from 7:30 a.m. to 10:00 p.m., is a perfect place to people-watch and to have a cup of coffee. Breakfast brings waffles with a variety of syrups, fruit toppings, and nuts for $5.50, or you can chow down with a *loco moco,* a whopper of a breakfast that includes two scoops of rice, broiled hamburger patty and two eggs with a rich beef gravy for $4.95. Have that for breakfast and don't go swimming for at least a week! Lunch fromn 11:30 a.m.-3 p.m. features bay shrimp parfait, $5.95, cheeseicles, like cheese pizza without the crust served with marinara sauce for dunking at $4.50, and prawn cocktail, $6.95. Soups and salads range from $7.95 for an *ahi* salad to $2.95 for soup du jour. Sandwiches from chicken salad to a club are under $7. Dinner, served from 5 p.m., offers fresh fish for $12.95, combination dinners like shrimp tempura and sirloin for $16.95, and Korean ribs for $10.95. The Rusty Harpoon has well-prepared, if not memorable, food at reasonable prices. Generally good value.

Expensive

The **Hele Mai** dining room at the Kona Hilton Hotel, tel. 329-3111, offers premier dining from 5-9:30 p.m. in a magnificent setting. Executive chef Sam Choy said, "I went to the best cooking school in Hawaii . . . my parent's kitchen! My dad owned a catering business and I grew up helping to cook for 10 to 200 people." If you dine at the Hilton, you can become one of those lucky people. Sam and his assistant chefs start you off with Thai chicken *sate,* or shrimp scampi for $7.95. Soups are Tahitian crabmeat for $4.95, or soup du jour for $3.95, which you can combine with the gourmet salad bar for an excellent yet moderately priced meal. Seafood from sautéed *mahi mahi* to sizzling lobster tail come with rice pilaf and fresh vegetables. Entrees include curried chicken pineapple for $16.95, sautéed pork loin at $17.95, and veal piccatta at $22.95. The phenomenally hungry, Sam's favorite people, can order the Alii Platter at $38, which comes laden with *sashimi,* shrimp, crab claws, sirloin steak, chicken macadamia, *kalua* pig, chicken *sate,* sliced lobster, and a personal beach boy or two to help lift you from your chair. Choose a table in the richly appointed dining room, or perch on the veranda for an outdoor setting. A remodeling done in 1985 lifted the floor 12 inches so that everyone is assured a spectacular view through the wraparound windows. The Hilton's Sunday champagne brunch, at $18.95 adults, $9.95 children, is considered the best in Kailua-Kona by local people. Seatings are from 9 a.m. to 12:30 p.m., with reservations strongly recommended. The Kona Hilton's Hele Mai Room offers truly fine dining in an elegant hotel. If you're into something simpler in a casual setting, try the hotel's **Lanai Coffee Shop,** open daily for breakfast, lunch, and dinner. This serves full breakfast from steak and eggs for $9.85 to Belgian waffles smothered in nuts, berries, and fresh fruits for $7.25. Lunch can be an assortment of burgers and sandwiches all priced under $8, or a crisp chef's salad laden with ham, roast beef, and turkey for $7.75. Dinner, simple but tasty, brings fish and chips, lemon chicken, or an oriental stir-fry all for under $10.

Oui oui monsieur, but of course we have zee restaurant *Français.* It is **La Bourgogne,** tel. 329-6711, located five minutes from downtown on Route 11 (Kuakini Hwy.), open Tuesday to Friday 11:30 a.m. to 2 p.m., Monday to Saturday 6-10 p.m., with master chef Guy Chatelard. For those who just can't live without escargots, shrimp Provençal, or pheasant, you've been saved. How much? Plenty, *mon petit!* Cold and hot appetizers include *pâté du chef* for $5, jumbo shrimp cocktail at $9.50, and mussels baked in garlic butter for $5. Soups of the day are scrumptious with French onion at $3.50, and homemade lobster soup when available at $4.75. For salads order greens with Roquefort dressing at $2.75, or Caesar salad for two at $7. Titillating seafood and poultry entrees feature fresh catch of the day $17, jumbo shrimp in butter, parsley, and garlic sauce for $19.50, and sliced breast of roast duck with lemon-orange sauce, $13.50. Meat courses are delectable roast saddle of lamb with creamy mustard sauce, $24.50, or veal in creamy white wine and mushroom sauce for $23. Top off your gourmet meal with fresh in-house desserts. This restaurant, slightly out of the way, is definitely worth a visit for those who enjoy exceptional food.

The Pottery, tel. 329-2277, open daily for dinner, located a few minutes from town at 75-5995 Kuakini Hwy., is a small privately owned chain out of Honolulu where art and dining become one. The decor in this romantic hideaway, including your table setting, is accented by ceramics made on the premises; there are even some pots that you can take home. Specialties include steaks, Cornish game hens, prawns, and fresh fish. Expect to spend $15 for an entree.

Jameson's-by-the Sea (formerly Dorian's), tel. 329-3195, open daily for lunch 110 a.m. to 2:30 p.m., dinner from 6 p.m., Sunday champagne brunch from 10 a.m. to 2 p.m., is located along Alii Drive next to White Sands Beach. It's an elegant restaurant with high-back wicker chairs, crystal everywhere, and white linen table settings. The quality of the food is excellent, but falls short of gourmet. Sit on the veranda next to the sea, $4 minimum order per person—better than inside. The bar serves domestic beer for $2, imported beer, $2.50, well drinks, $2, and exotics, $4, happy hour daily 3-6 p.m. The lunch menu is less expensive, offering French onion soup, $4, shrimp cocktail, $8.50, clams and pasta, $9.75, fettuccine $10, plus a variety of sandwiches, vegetarian to steak, from $4 to $10. Jameson's is one of the only places in town offering oysters on the half shell, $6 a half dozen. At dinner expect to spend $60-70 for two with wine. Featured are 48-inch platters, two-person minimum, entrees, such as the Continental, with lamb and chops, steak, and baby lobster tails; the best is the Chef's Silver Platter. All come with baked potato parmigiana, vegetables, house salad, and freshly baked bread.

The **Beach Club Restaurant,** tel. 329-3743, dinner only, at Aston Kona by the Sea Condominium (see p. 659), is an intimate restaurant with a dozen tables overlooking the panoramic coastline. Moreover, this secluded restaurant has French-trained chefs serving a limited but

gourmet menu. Start with cha-cha chicken and salsa for $4.75, or chilies stuffed with goat cheese for $4.50. Salads are special with Waimea watercress in raspberry vinaigrette dressing for $5.50, or a spicy Thai salad for $6.95. Pasta ranges from seafood fettuccine to rigatoni marinara, all priced under $15. Specially prepared entrees include tequilla-marinated game hen for $16.75, bouillabaisse for $15.75, and coconut scampi with sweet peppers for $17.50. When other restaurants are crowded you can count on getting a table with a beautiful sunset view thrown into the bargain.

At **Huggo's Restaurant,** tel. 329-1493, on Alii Drive next door to the Kona Hilton, it's difficult to concentrate on the food because the setting is so spectacular. If you were any closer to the sea, you'd be in it, and of course the sunset is great. Huggo's swings with live music nightly and is open daily 11 a.m. to 2 p.m. for lunch, and from 5:30 for dinner. Waiters and waitresses are outfitted in alohawear, and each table features various inlaid maps of the Pacific. The salad bar is exceptional and lunch reasonable, with tasties like tostada, shrimp cocktail, and Reuben sandwiches for under $8. A specialty is the seafood chowder at $2 a cup, $4 a bowl, made with clams and fresh fish and seasoned with sherry, cream, and butter. Chowder and salad is $6.50. The dinner menu includes steak scampi, Kona chicken, and prime rib from $10 to $20. Tuesday and Thursday lunch is special and crowded when Huggo's serves BBQ ribs and beans for $6.95, with more on your plate than you can eat. If you're not hungry for a full meal, enjoy free *pu pu* daily from 4:30-5:30 p.m. while sipping a cocktail as the Kona sun goes down.

S.S. *James Makee* is a fancy continental restaurant at the Kona Surf Hotel. The nautical decor is commemorative of the restaurant's namesake, an old island steamer. The limited menu includes shrimp Kamehameha, teriyaki steak, various veals, and filet mignon. Fresh fish of the day is always well prepared and a good choice. A major part of the minimum $20 per person dining experience is the atmosphere. Open daily for dinner from 6 p.m. by reservation only—of course, matey! tel. 322-3411.

The Kona Inn Restaurant, open daily for lunch and dinner, plus Sunday brunch, at the Kona Inn Shopping Village, tel. 329-4455, is a lovely but lonely carry-over from the venerable old Kona Inn. Part of the deal for tearing down the Kona Inn and putting up the sterile Kona Inn Shopping Village was giving the restaurant a prime location. On entering, notice the marlin over the doorway and a huge piece of hung glass through which the sunset sometimes beams. The bar and dining area are richly appointed in native *koa* and made more elegant with a mixture of turn-of-the-century wooden chairs, highbacked peacock thrones, polished hardwood floors, and sturdy open-beam ceilings. If you want to enjoy the view, try a cocktail and a *sashimi* plate at $5.95, jumbo shrimp cocktail, $7.95, pasta and chicken salad for $6.95, or New England clam chowder and garlic bread for under $5. The evening bill of fare is rich with the fresh catch, market price usually under $20, stir-fry shrimp, $15.95, calamari only $11.95, chicken cordon bleu $12.95, or steak and lobster for $23.95. The Kona Inn Restaurant epitomizes Kona beachside dining.

Adjacent is **Fisherman's Landing,** open daily, lunch 11:30 a.m. to 2 p.m., dinner 5:30-10 p.m., tel. 326-2555, with excellent food and an even better location, being closer to the shore. You walk down a cobblestone pathway to find five Hawaiian dining huts separated by *koi* ponds and wooden bridges. A bronze cannon sits in a reflecting pool, while a gigantic blue marlin is a still-life marquee promising fresh seafood within. The tasteful decor is accentuated with glass fishing floats, bronze lanterns, and bamboo tables and chairs. Entrees by chef Curtis Masuda feature Kona-caught fish delicately broiled over a *kiawe* fire. Lunch specials can be a *sashimi* burger for $6.95, fish and chips for $7.95, chicken Hawaiian $8.95, or crab Louie, $8.95. The extensive dinner menu starts with appetizers like shrimp scampi for $7.75 or fresh oysters in the half shell, $6.95, and moves on to entrees like shrimp tempura and teriyaki beef for $17.95, shrimp or chicken with Oriental vegies for $14.95, filet mignon $18.95, and shellfish sauté, $19.95. Create your own entertainment every Wednesday from 9-midnight with *karaoke,* or dance to the live music of Sugar Sugar Sunday through Thursday from 7:30-11:30 p.m. Fisherman's Landing is a perfect Kona restaurant for a relaxing and romantic evening.

Philip Paolo's, in Waterfront Row, run by Tim O'Higgin—a true Italian if there ever was one— is open for lunch daily 11 a.m.-2 p.m., and for dinner from 5:30 p.m. Savory selections include antipasto for two at $9.95, minestrone soup for $3.95, and specialty salads that could make a meal, like scallops, crab, and shrimp marinated in olive oil, garlic, and fresh herbs for $8.95. For lunch, cold sandwiches are stuffed with roast beef, ham, or turkey for $7.95, or try linguini with clam sauce for $10.95. Dinners are served with pasta sautéed in garlic, olive oil, and fresh herbs. The menu suggests soft-shell crab for $24.95, veal parmigiana for $21.95, chicken parmisan $15.95, or the house specialties like fettuccine Giuseppe, meat sautéed in creamy garlic butter and onions for $18.95. The extensive wine list offers varietals from Italy, France, Australia, and California. The large room is appointed with open-beam ceilings, joined by distinctive copper couplings, and Casablanca fans.

The **Kona Ranch House** is a delightful restaurant with something for everyone. It has two rooms: the family-oriented Paniolo Room, where hearty appetites are filled family style, and the elegant Plantation Lanai, where both palate and sense of beauty are satiated. This restaurant, highlighted by copper drainpipes, brass ceiling fans, wicker furniture, and lattice work all against a natural wood and brick background, epitomizes plantation dining. The Kona Ranch House is a classy establishment where you get more than what you pay for. Prices range from reasonable to expensive, and the menus in the two separate rooms reflect this. Open daily from 6:30 a.m. to 10 p.m., Sunday brunch, reservations needed for the Plantation Lanai. Located two minutes from downtown at the corner of Kuakini Highway and Palani Road, tel. 329-7061.

Eclipse Restaurant is one of Kona's newest continental restaurants. Offerings range from the simple to complex and include oysters Rockefeller, mustard and brandy cream sauce served over pepper steak, plus seafood, veal, and prawns. The owner/chef prepares a specialty nightly. Lunch daily, and dinner from 5-9 p.m. At night the chrome deco restaurant transforms into a disco. On Kuakini Hwy., across from Foodland, tel. 329-4686.

Kanazawa-tei, tel. 326-1881, open daily for lunch 11:30-2 p.m., dinner 6-9:30 p.m., at 75-5845 Alii Dr., across from Kona Hilton, is a Japanese restaurant and sushi bar that boasts chefs directly from Japan. Specialties include sukiyaki, teriyaki, and tempura. The lunch menu offers tempura and chicken *bentos* (box lunch) for $12, and includes miso soup and rice. The dinner menu lists appetizers like *age* tofu, $3.45, small tempura for $7.45, and butterfish *misoyaki* for $9.95. Evening *bentos* are extensive and include the *Kanazawa-tei bento* with tempura, *sashimi, yakimoto, nimono*, rice, miso soup and *sukemono* for $18.50. Also, a variety of sushi dinners are offered. Kanazawa-tei is an authentic and gourmet Japanese restaurant.

Luaus, Buffets, And Such

The **Keauhou Beach Hotel Buffet**, tel. 322-3441, at the hotel's Ocean Terrace, is legendary. People in the know flock here especially for the *Seafood Buffet* for $16.95, served from 5-9 p.m. Friday-Sunday. Fill your plate again and again with Alaskan snow crab legs, prime rib (excellent), seafood Newberg, sautéed mahi mahi, fresh teriyaki marlin, deep-fried oysters, New England clam chowder, sashimi, poki and boiled shrimp. They also have a great dessert bar with Boston cream pies, strawberry shortcake, rich double-chocolate carrot cake, and banana cream pie. A Chinese buffet is offered Monday-Thursday for $9.95 and features roast duck, dim sum, Mandarin salad, and a medley of Cantonese and Sichuan selections. The restaurant has a beautiful view of the coast, and dinner is rounded off with live nightly entertainment.

The **Kona Hilton Luau**, tel. 329-3111, held every Monday, Wednesday, and Friday at the hotel's Coconut Grove, offers an authentic evening of entertainment and feasting, Hawaiian style. The *imu* ceremony begins at 6 p.m. and is followed by an open bar, lavish buffet, and thrilling entertainment for three fun-filled hours. Many supposedly authentic luaus play-act with the *imu*-baked pig, but here it is carved and served to the guests. Prices are adults $36, children under 12, $20, with reservations strongly recommended.

A sumptuous feast is held at the **Kona Village Resort**, just north of Kailua-Kona (see p. 294). It's worth attending this luau just to visit and be pampered at this private hotel beach. Adults pay around $40, children under 12 half-price. Held every Friday, by reservation only, tel. 325-5555. The *imu* ceremony is at 6 p.m., followed by no-host cocktails; the luau and Hawaiian entertainment begin at 8 p.m. Also, limited reservations are accepted during the week for lunch, dinner, and special dinners and buffets.

Hotel King Kamehameha has a long-standing luau every Sun., Tues., Wed., and Friday. The *imu* ceremony begins at 6:15 p.m., cocktails from 6-7 p.m.; the luau begins at 7 p.m. and is followed by entertainment. Adults $36, children under 12, $20. Reservations required; call 329-2911.

Captain Beans' Dinner Cruise departs Kailua Pier daily at 5 p.m. and returns at 8 p.m. You are entertained while the bar dispenses liberal drinks and the deck groans with all-you-can-eat food. Besides, you get a terrific panorama of the Kona Coast from the sea. You can't help having a good time on this cruise, and if the boat sinks with all that food and booze in your belly, you're a goner . . . but what a way to go! Minimum age 18 years, $30 includes tax and tip. Reservations suggested, tel. 329-2955.

Kona Chuckwagon Buffet, open daily, at Casa De Emdeko on Alii Dr., tel. 329-2818, gives you all-you-can-eat, or more precisely all you care to eat. Breakfast is $3.50, 7-10 a.m., lunch $5, 11 a.m. to 5 p.m., dinner $6.50, 5-9 p.m. Expect a lot of fried food, heavy on the gravies, instant potatoes, white breads, and canned vegetables. You can go "hog belly" here, so it's hard to complain, but don't expect anything beyond cafeteria food.

ENTERTAINMENT AND ACTIVITIES

Kona nights come alive mostly in its restaurants and the dining rooms of the big hotels. The most memorable experience for most is free: watching the sunset from Kailua Pier, and taking a leisurely stroll along Alii Drive. All of the luaus previously mentioned have "Polynesian Revues" of one sort or another, which are generally good, clean, sexy fun, but of course these shows are limited only to the luau guests. "For those who have "dancin' feet," or wish to spend the evening listening to live music, there's a small but varied selection from which to choose. **Note:** All the hotels and restaurants listed below have been previously mentioned in either the "Accommodations" or "Food" sections, so please refer there for addresses and directions.

Free

Cousin Kimo's Restaurant at the Kona Bay Hotel presents two free dinner shows of hula and a medley of Hawaiian tunes nightly at 6:30 and 7:30 p.m. If you're not interested in dining, you can order a drink and watch the fun.

Around Town

Huggo's Restaurant with its romantic waterfront setting along Alii Drive features live music nightly from 8:30 p.m. until 12:30 a.m. Tuesday through Thursday the place swings with the cool rhythms of the Doug Johnson Jazz Trio. Weekends bring more jazz, or contemporary easy listening with a touch of rock now and again.

The **Windjammer**, at the Kona Hilton, is an open-air bar with nightly entertainment featuring Silk and Steal, a live band from Sunday-Tuesday, with *karaoke* offered on the other evenings.

The **Keauhou Beach Hotel** soothes you with easy listening, Hawaiian style, nightly at the Sunset Rib Lanai from 9:30 p.m. until midnight, or rocks you in Don The Beachcomber's Disco in the transformed main dining room.

At the **Kona Surf Resort** a quiet piano tinkles in the S.S. *James Makee* Restaurant from 6-11 p.m., or you can glide around the dance floor in the Puka Bar to live music from 9 p.m. until closing. More yet!! Tuesday through Saturday, the Poi Pounder Nightclub beats out "top 40" dancin' tunes from 9 p.m. until the wee hours.

At the **Kona Hilton** piano bar you can enjoy happy hour from 4:30- 6 p.m. with free *pu pu* while listening to the mellow piano which begins at 4:30 p.m. and goes until closing. The Windjammer Lounge has dancing music nightly except Monday from 8:30 p.m. until closing.

In downtown Kailua-Kona you can pick your fun at the **Hotel King Kamehameha**. The Billfish Bar has happy hour from 5-7 p.m. and nightly entertainment from 5-10 p.m. You'll hear everything from country to contemporary with Hawaiian tunes thrown in so you won't forget where you are. Weekends bring easy listening, contemporary, and Hawaiian music to Moby Dick's in the hotel.

Around town, the **Eclipse Restaurant** has dance music from 10 p.m. until 1:30 a.m. every night; the **Jolly Roger Restaurant** offers a variety of live music throughout the week beginning at 8:30 p.m.; at the **Keauhou-Kona Golf Course Restaurant** you can enjoy live contemporary Hawaiian music performed by local artists every evening from 7 p.m.; on weekends the **Pottery Steak House** offers piano music for listening and dancing enjoyment; for a quiet beer, sports talk, or just hanging out with the local people try **Quinn's, Drysdale's,** or the **Ocean View Inn** all in downtown Kailua-Kona.

At **Fisherman's Landing Restaurant,** *karaoke* is presented every Wednesday from 9 p.m.-12 midnight. They also have live music and dancing nightly to the tunes of Sugar Sugar, a local dance band, and on Friday-Saturday from 6-9 p.m., a solo musician plays a mixed bag of country, classic rock and roll, and Hawaiian music.

The **Tech**, one of Kailua-Kona's newest discos and hangouts, is open nightly on the premises of the Poo Ping Restaurant II. The restaurant is located at Kamehameha Square, a small shopping mall a few minutes from town along the Kuakini Highway leading to the arirport. It draws a younger, local crowd, but is friendly and what's happening now.

For movies try the **World Square Theater** in the Market Place Shopping Plaza or the **Hualalai Theater** in Kailua-Kona.

SHOPPING

Kona Malls

The Kailua-Kona area has an abundance of two commodities near and dear to a tourist's heart: sunshine and plenty of shopping malls. The following merely lists the malls in the Kailua-Kona area. For particular listings of the unique shops found in these malls, look in the following specific category breakdowns.

One of the largest malls in Kailua is the **Kona Inn Shopping Village** at 75-5744 Alii Drive. This shopping village boasts more than 40 shops selling fabrics, fashions, art, fruits, gems and jewelry, photo and music needs, food, and even exotic skins.

The **Market Place** is in central Kailua-Kona, offering a variety of shops selling everything from burgers to bathing suits. The **Kona Banyan Court,** also in central Kailua-Kona, has a dozen shops with a medley of goods and services. Distinctive shops include: **Kona Fine Woods** for souvenir-quality woodcarvings; **Unison,** a surfing shop with T-shirts, sandals, hats,

Kona's best treats are available from roadside stands.

and boogie boards; **Goldsmith's Big Island Jewelers** for fine jewelry; **South Sea Silver Company,** whose name says it all.

You'll also find the **Kailua Bay Inn Plaza** along Alii Drive, and the **Akona Kai Mall** across from Kailua Pier. The **Hotel King Kamehameha Mall,** fully air-conditioned, features a cluster of specialty shops and a Liberty House. One excellent shop is **Myna Bird Fabrics,** for original fabric designs that are inspired by Balinese *batik* and Japanese prints. **Gifts For All Seasons** sells jewelry, **Jafar** presents high fashions, and **Tots and Teens** sells clothes for children.

The **Lanihau Center,** tel. 329-9333, at 75-5595 Palani Road, is one of Kailua-Kona's newest shopping additions. This shopping mecca offers **Longs Drugs,** for sundries and photo supplies, an assortment of restaurants (see "Food"), apparel and shoe stores, **Waldenbooks,** and **Zack's Photo,** a very friendly and professional photo store (see following).

Waterfront Row is a new shopping and food complex at the south end of downtown Kailua-Kona that's built of rough-cut lumber and done in period architecture, reminiscent of an outdoor promenade perhaps in a Boston shipyard at the turn of the century. **Pleasant Hawaiian Holidays** maintains a booth here that can book you on tours, from the *Atlantis* submarine to volcano helicopter flights. **Pacific Vibrations,** a surf shop, sells everything from postcards to hats, backpacks, and aloha shirts. **Alapaki's** features items "made in Hawaii" (see "Art Shops" following), while **Kona Jack's** offers distinctive unisex apparel featuring its logo.

The **Rawson Plaza,** at 74-5563 Kaiwi St., is just past the Kamehameha Hotel in the industrial area. This practical, no-frills area abounds in "no-name" shops selling everything you'll find in town but at substantial savings.

The **Kona Coast Shopping Center,** along Palani Road, features **Pay 'n' Save** for sundries and everything from scuba gear to styrofoam coolers; **K. Taniguchi Market** (see below), the **Undercover Shop,** with fine lingerie, **Hallmark Cards,** and a smattering of clothing, accessory, and shoe stores.

South Kona Malls

If, god forbid, you haven't found what you need in Kailua, or if you suddenly need a "shopping fix," even more malls are south on Route 11. The **Keauhou Shopping Village** is at the corner of Alii Drive and Kamehameha III Road. This mall houses apparel shops, restaurants, a P.O., and photo processing booths. You can find all your food and prescription needs at **KTA Supermarket,** the largest in the area. The **Bookshop** is a full-service bookstore, and **Henri's Fine Candies and Coffee** will take care of your sweet tooth; you can also buy there a pound or two of the freshest Kona coffee. Other shops include: **Lady L,** with accoutrements and high fashions for women; the **Showcase Gallery,** for glassware, paintings, ceramics, and local crafts; **Collectors Cottage,** offering an assortment of miniatures, posters, and *koa* bowls; **Lane-Ke,** with racks of fine apparel for women; and **Possible Dreams,** a small art shop selling paints, cards, gifts, and prints.

Continuing south on Route 11 you'll spot the **Kainaliu Village Mall** along the main drag.

Food Markets

K. Tanaguchi Market is generally the cheapest market in town and is located at the Kona Coast Shopping Center along Palani Road. They're well stocked with sundries, an excellent selection of oriental foods, fresh vegies, fish, fruit, and a smattering of health food that's mixed in with the normal food items. Sugar Pops and *kimchi,* anyone?!

Across the road, **Food for Less,** in the Lanihau Center, open 24 hours, is one of the main supermarkets in town.

The **Casa De Emdeko Liquor and Deli** is south of town center at 75-6082 Alii Drive. It's well stocked with liquor and groceries, but at convenience-store prices. Others include the **King Kamehameha Pantry,** tel. 329-9191, selling liquors, groceries, and sundries, and the **Keauhou Pantry,** tel. 322-3066, in Keauhou along Alii Drive, selling more of the same.

KTA Supermarket, open Mon.-Sat. 8 a.m.-10 p.m., Sun. 8 a.m.-9 p.m., is at the Keauhou Village Mall, at the extreme south end of Alii Drive and the junction of Kamehameha III Road. You can save time and traffic hassles by shopping here, and the market also offers a full-service pharmacy.

Health Food Stores

Kona keeps you healthy with **Kona Healthways** in the Kona Coast Shopping Center, tel. 329-2296, open Mon.-Fri. 9 a.m.-7 p.m., Sat. 9 a.m.-6 p.m., Sun. 9:30 a.m.-5 p.m. Besides a neat assortment of health foods, they have cosmetics, books, and dietary supplements. Vegetarians will like their ready-to-eat sandwiches, salads, and soups. Shelves are lined with teas and organic vitamins. They also have a cooler with organic juices, cheeses, and soy milk. A refrigerator holds organic produce, while bins are filled with bulk grains.

Bookstores

Waldenbooks, in the Lanihau Center on Palani Road, tel. 329-0015, open Mon.-Thurs. 9:30 a.m.-6 p.m., Fri. 9:30 a.m.-9 p.m., Sun. 10 a.m.-5 p.m., not only has the well-stocked and far-ranging selection that this national chain has become famous for, but also features an in-depth Hawaiiana collection and even some Hawaiian music tapes

In Kailua-Kona be sure to venture into the **Middle Earth Bookshop** at 75-5719 Alii Ave., in the Kona Plaza Shopping Arcade, tel. 329-2123. This jam-packed bookstore has shelves laden with fiction, nonfiction, paperbacks, hardbacks, travel books, maps, and Hawaiiana. A great place to browse.

The **Keauhou Village Bookshop** at the Keauhou Shopping Village, tel. 322-8111, open 9-9 Mon.-Fri., 9-6 Sat., 9-5 Sun., is a full-service bookstore, with plenty of Hawaiiana selections, general reading material, and a good travel guide section.

Art, Photo, And Specialty Shops

Zack's Photo, in the Lanihau Center, tel. 329-0006, open 7 a.m.-9 p.m. every day, develops prints in one hour and slides in two days. Zack, a native of Belgium, will even make minor camera repairs free of charge. Prices are very competitive and you can save more by clipping two-for-one and 20-percent discount coupons from the free tourist brochure, *This Week, Big Island.* **Longs Drugs,** in the same mall, also has excellent prices on film and camera supplies.

Alii Photo Hut, in the parking lot in front of Huggo's Restaurant along Alii Drive, open daily 7:30 a.m.-5:30 p.m., develops prints and rents underwater cameras. Rates are $17.95 for camera plus a roll of 36 exposures. A 20-percent discount on developing is offered when you rent the camera.

The **Kona Photo Center** in the North Kona Shopping Plaza, at the corner of Palani Road and the Kuakini Highway, tel. 329-3676, open Mon.- Sat. 8 a.m.-6 p.m., is a *real* photography store where you can get lenses, cameras, filters, and even telescopes and binoculars. They're processing is competitive, and they also offer custom developing.

In the Hotel King Kamehameha the **Tribal Arts Gallery** sells carvings, jewelry, and fabrics from exotic lands throughout the Pacific Basin, while **The Shellery** lives up to its name giving you baubles, bangles, and beads all made from shells.

The Seaside Mall across from the Kamehameha Hotel features the **Butterfly Boutique,** selling locally designed and made beachwear and casual wear, and the smaller **Kona Botik** specializing in bikinis. A minute away is **Hilo Hattie's,** an island institution along Palani Road, next door to Burger King. They have a huge assortment of alohawear, but much of the fabric used is synthetic. Still, it's fun to visit and you're given a free lei greeting, refreshments, and even bus service to and from your hotel.

In the World Square Shopping Center visit the **Showcase Gallery** operated by Jean Hamilton. All the talented offerings of glasswork, beadwork, featherwork, enameling, and shell leis come from the islands, mostly from the Big Island. Across the way the **Coral Isle Art Shop** presents modern versions of traditional Hawaiian carvings. You'll find everything from tikis to scrimshaw, with exceptionally good carvings of sharks and whales for a pricy $75 or so. The **Smuggler's Loft** bills itself as a "man's store" and sells a wide variety of nautical items with objets d'art, mostly in brass, bronze, or ceramics.

At the **Kona Inn Shopping Village** you can buy eel-skin accoutrements at **Exotic Skins,** custom jewelry at **Jim Bill's Gemfire,** hand-painted one-of-a-kind original clothing at **Noa Noa,** and distinctive Hawaiian black-coral jewelry and scrimshaw at **Original Maui Divers.** Also **Collectors Fine Art** is a perfect labyrinth of rooms and hallways showcasing the acclaimed works of international artists. Not a shop to buy trinkets, prices range from $300 to $250,000 for some of the finer paintings. One of the best shops is **Collector's Fine Art,** featuring paintings and sculptures from internationally acclaimed artists. Another distinctive shop is **Crystal Visions** for incense, perfume, metaphysical books, and channeling personal and cosmic vibrations through its large selection of crystals, crystal balls, and pyramids. A sign proclaims, "shoplifting is bad karma," and a shop assistant claims that the owner looked at her *aura,* not her resume, when she was hired. Crystal Visions also stocks essential oils and small handmade bags with beads for carrying your precious items. A unique item of interest to travelers might be the azurite spheres for expansion of consciousness and astral travel—in case you have lost your airline tickets or your flight has been delayed. If you're feeling low, and your cosmic vibrations need a boost, come in to Crystal Visions.

At **Kona Inn Flower and Lei** you can pick up flowers to add that perfect touch to a romantic evening. Nearby **Chrestel's Collectibles** has stuffed toys, stuffed pillows, and even some clothing. **Kona Inn Jewelry,** for world-wide treasures, is one of the oldest and best known shops for a square deal in Kona. Owned and operated by Joe Goldscharek and his family, they take time to help you choose just the right gift. Inside you'll find stained glass hangings, jewelry, fine gemstones, and a collection of hand-painted fish. The family tries to pick unique items from around the world that can be found in no other Kona shop. Be aware that the shop is protected by Mama Cat, a sleeping ball of fur honored with her own post card, who if you're not careful will purr you to death.

Other shops in the center include: **Flamingo's** for contemporary island clothing, and evening wear mainly for women; **Big Island Hat Co.,** for headgear ranging from a pith helmet to a sombrero; **The Treasury,** specializing in jewelry, T-shirts, and beachwear; **Bags and Bears,** with hats, sunglasses, backpacks, shoulder bags, and postcards; **Elizabeth Harris and Co.,** presenting distinctive, beautifully fashioned T-shirts; **Tahiti Fabrics,** offering bolts of cloth and a nice collection of Hawaiian shirts; **Alley Gecko's,** showcasing colorful gifts from around the world; **Sky's the Limit,** a specialty kite shop where you can get a high flyer to take advantage of the wonderful Kona winds; **Glyn Woodroger's,** brimming with hand-painted, original T-shirts; and the **Old Hawaiian Gold Co.,** which can bedeck you in gold chains, and pearl and coral jewelry.

At the **Kona Marketplace** in the downtown area, look for **Sunshine Sports Ltd.** which sells T-shirts, aloha wear, and beachwear. Across the way is the **Kona Jewelery** specializing in fine jewelry and ceramics. One shop good for trinkets is the **Kona Bazaar Affordables,** or pick up a pair of eel-skin cowboy boots at **Lee San's Eelskin.** The jam-packed **Aloha From Kona** specializes in baubles, bangles, postcards, handbags, and purses. In contrast is **Alii Nexus,** for fine jewelry, one of the nicest and most low-keyed shops in town. The **Kona Flea Market** stuck to the rear of the mall sells inexpensive travel bags, shells, beach mats, suntan lotion, and all the junk that you could want. **Island Salsa** features original silk-screened T-shirts, especially football jerseys and long-sleeved sweatsuits in distinctive colors. They also have ladies' evening wear, and dinner clothes. Finally, the **Chocolate Orchid Gallery** showcases paintings, especially R.K. McGuire's distinctive paintings of Japan, featuring samurai and kabuki actors. Another favored artist is Phan N. Barker, who does *batik* on silk.

Alapaki's, at Waterfront Row, sells distinctive island arts and crafts. Inside you'll find pink, gold, and black coral jewelry, leis from shells and seeds, and *tu tu* dolls bedecked in colorful muumuus. Distinctive items include *koa* bowls, all signed by the artist, and a replica of a Hawaiian double-hulled canoe made from coconut and cloth with traditional crab-claw sails. Original paintings by R.K. McGuire feature Hawaiian animals, and there's basketry, fans, and jewelry made from ironwood needles by local artist Barb Walls. Some of the finest artwork displayed are feather leis by Eloise Deshea.

For some practical purchases at wholesale prices check out **Kona Jeans** for shirts, tops, footwear, and jeans, at 74-5576 Kaiwi Street. **Liberty House Penthouse** at the Keauhou Beach Hotel will appeal to bargain hunters. This outlet store sells items that have been cleared and reduced from the famous Liberty House stores. You can save on everything from alohawear to formal dresses.

In the parking lot in front of Huggo's Restaurant, along Alii Drive, a little truck sells **Hawaii Mountain Gold,** coffee grown by the Ferrari family at their nearby coffee plantation between Palani Junction and Halualoa, on Route 180. You'll notice the plantation by a big pink coffee cup, and visitors are welcome.

Two shops along Alii Drive, across from Hulihee Palace, are the **Sandal Basket,** for a pair of just-right thongs or even Birkenstocks, and **Hawaiian Wear Unlimited** next door where you can pick up alohawear for a very reasonable price. Just up the road **The Glass Blower,** across from the seawall along Likana Lane, is a very interesting shop where you can watch the artist actually blowing the glass. This is a perfect shop to purchase a distinctive treasure. Next door is **Ululani Fresh Cut Flowers,** a reasonably priced lei stand. **Goodies** just up the alley has gift boxes of jams and jellies, Maui onion mustard, macadamia nuts, an assortment of coffees, and different perfumes and scents.

Real treasure hunters will love the **Kona Gardens Flea Market** held every Wed. and Sat. 8 a.m. to 2 p.m. at the Kona Botanical Gardens along Alii Drive, tel. 322-2751. Unfortunately, this formerly huge flea market is now only a shadow of its former self.

SERVICES AND INFORMATION

Emergencies
For **Ambulance and Fire** call 961-6022; for **Police** in Kona communities, call 323-2645; the **Kona Hospital** is in Kealakekua, tel. 322-9311; the most convenient **pharmacies** are Kona Coast Drugs in Kailua, tel. 329-8886, or Pay 'n' Save Drugs, tel. 329-3577. For **alternative health care services and massage,** both well established in Kailua-Kona, see p. 136.

Information And Services
An **information gazebo** is open daily 7 a.m. to 9 p.m. along the boardwalk in the Kona Inn Shopping Village. They can handle all your questions from dining to diving. The **Hawaii Visitors Bureau** maintains an office in the Kona Plaza, at 75-5719 Alii Drive, tel. 329-7787. Information officer, Ms. Ami Gay, is friendly, helpful, and extremely knowledgeable about touring the Big Island. The **library** is at 75-140 Hualalai Road, tel. 329-2196. The Hele Mai Laundromat is at the North Kona Shopping Center, at the corner of Alii Drive and Palani Road, tel. 329-3494. For more services and info see p. 173.

Banks, Post Office, Et Cetera
First Interstate Bank, tel. 329-4481, is at 75-5722 Kuakini Hwy.; **First Hawaiian Bank,** Kona office, can be reached at tel. 329-2461; **Bank of Hawaii** maintains two area offices, one in Kailua at tel. 329-7033, the other in Kealakekua at tel. 322-9377. The main **post office** is on Palani Road, tel. 329-1927, just past the Lanihau Center. There is also mail service at the **General Store,** a market along Alii Drive in central Kailua-Kona. **Mail Boxes U.S.A.,** at the Lanihau Center, Palani Road, provides Western Union, a notary public, typing service, money orders, gift wrapping, and the boxing and shipping of parcels.

CENTRAL TO SOUTH KONA

Kailua-Kona's Ali'i Drive eventually turns up the mountainside and joins Route 11, which in its central section is called the **Kuakini Highway.** This road quickly passes the towns of **Honalo, Kainaliu** ("Bail the Bilge"), **Kealakekua,** and **Captain Cook.** You'll have ample opportunity to stop along the way for gas, picnic supplies, or to just browse. These towns have some terrific restaurants, specialty shops, and boutiques. Dip down to the coast and visit a working coffee mill, or continue to **Pu'uhonua O Honaunau,** a reconstructed temple of refuge, the best in the state. Little-traveled side roads take you to the sleepy seaside villages of **Hookena,** and **Milolii,** where traditional lifestyles are still the norm. Or, travel Route 180, a high mountain road that parallells Route11 and takes you to the artist community of **Holualoa** from where you get an expansive view of the coastline below.

HOLUALOA

Holualoa ("The Sledding Course") is an undisturbed mountain community perched high above the Kailua-Kona Coast. Get there by taking the spur Route 182 off Route 11 from Kailua-Kona, or by taking Route 180 from Honalo in the south or from Honokohau in the north. Climbing Route 182 affords glorious views of the coast

below. Notice the immediate contrast of lush foliage compared to the lowland area. On the mountainside are tall forest trees interspersed with banana, papaya, and a variety of flowering trees. If you want to get away from the Kona heat, and from barren volcanic land, head up to Holualoa.

Practicalities

After Route 182 winds its way up through this verdant jungle area you suddenly enter the village where you are greeted by **Kimura's Lauhala Shop,** open daily 9 a.m.-5 p.m., closed Sunday. The shop, still tended by Mrs. Kimura and her daughter, Alfreda, has been in existence since 1915. In the beginning, Kimura's was a general store, but they always sold *lau hala* and became famous for their hats that local people would barter for groceries. Only *Kona-side* hats have a distinctive pull-string that makes the hat larger or smaller. All *lau hala* weavings are done on the premises, while some of the other gift items are brought in. Choose from authentic baskets, floor mats, handbags, slippers, and of course an assortment of the classic sun hats that start at $25.

After Kimura's follow the road for a minute or so to enter the actual village, where you'll see the **post office,** and a cross atop a white steeple welcoming you to town. The tiny village, complete with its own elementary school, is well kept, with an obvious double helping of pride put into this artists' community by its citizens. Numerous art shops line the main street. Look for **Kim Starr's Gallery,** open 10-5 Wed.-Sat., across from the post office, and nearby **Sigel Pottery,** open 9-5 Tues.-Sat., that features distinctive locally made pottery. Just here is **Paul's Place,** a well-stocked country store, open 7 a.m.-8 p.m.

Along the main road is a converted coffee mill, gaily painted and decorated. This is the home of the **Kona Art Center,** open Tue.-Sat. 10 a.m.-4 p.m., run by Robert and Carol Rogers. Uncle Bob and Aunt Carol, as they are affectionately known to many, have extensive backgrounds in art teaching. They moved from San Francisco to Holualoa in 1965 and began offering community workshop classes. Carol says, "I love Kona because we share, care, and love with our people here." Across the road is another restored building, a one-time country church and now the Kona Art Center, that was rescued from the ravages of weather and termites and now proudly displays the works of the center's members. In here you will find everything from hobby crafts to serious renderings that might include paintings, basketry, sculptures, and even tie-dyed shirts. The center is very friendly and welcomes guests with a cup of Kona coffee. The building is rickety and old, but it's obviously filled with good vibrations and with love.

Across from the Kona Art Center is the **Country Frame Shop,** open Mon.-Fri. 9:30 a.m.-4:30 p.m., Sat. 9:30 a.m.-1:30 p.m., which specializes in framing, but also has prints by famous local artists. Check out the distinctive *koa* wood frames that add a special island touch to any artwork. The owner, Chuck Hart, accepts credit cards and will ship anywhere.

The premier shop in town, **Studio 7,** open Tue.-Sat., 10 a.m.-4 p.m., is owned and operated by Hiroki Morinoue, who studied at the Kona Art Center as a young man. The shop showcases Hiroki's work along with that of about 35 Big Island artists. Hiroki works in multimedia, but primarily he does large watercolors or woodblock prints. Setsuko, Hiroki's wife, is a ceramist and displays her work with about six other potters including the famous Chiu Leong. Check out the "neoclassical" silkscreen by contemporary Japanese artist, Hideo Takeda, one of seven contemporary Japanese printmakers carried in the shop. Affordable items include wooden bracelets, and free-form bowls for nuts or candy that have been signed by the artist. To the rear of the shop is a wooden walkway over gray lava gravel that looks out onto a Japanese-style garden. It's worth the trip to Holualoa just to visit Studio 7.

A separate shop in the same building is **Goldsmithing by Sam Rosen.** Sam works mostly in gold, silver, and precious stones, but will work in coral if it's unusual. He can supply the stones as well, from his collection that includes amazing specimens like malachite, and polyhedroid, a quartz from Brazil. All works have a distinctive island theme and are destined to become heirlooms.

The **Kona Hotel,** along Holualoa's main street, tel. 324-1155 primarily rents its 11 units to local people who spend the work-week in Kailua-Kona's seaside resorts and then go home on weekends. $12-24 will get you a clean room with a bed and dresser and a shared bath down the hall. No reservations are taken and your best bet for getting a room is on weekends.

HONALO TO CAPTAIN COOK AND VICINITY

These mountainside communities all lie along a five-mile strip of Route 11, and if it weren't for the road signs, it would be difficult for the itinerant traveler to know where one village ends and the next begins. However, if you are after budget accommodations, unique boutique shopping, inexpensive island cuisine, and some off-the-beaten-track sightseeing, you won't be disappointed.

Honalo

This dot on the map is at the junction of Route 11 and Route 180. Not much changes here, and the town is primarily known for **Dai Fukuji Buddhist Temple** along the road. It's open daily 9 a.m. to 4:30 p.m., free. Inside are two ornate altars; feel free to take photos but please remember to remove your shoes. There's a **Circle K** for sundries, food, and gasoline, and the **Teshima Inn and Restaurant,** an old budget traveler's standby (see following).

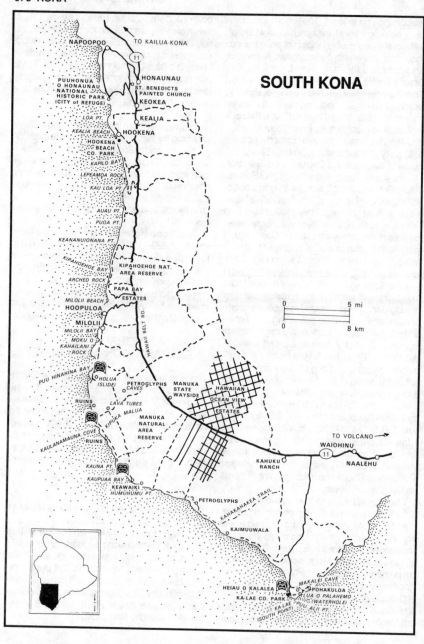

SOUTH KONA

TO KAILUA-KONA

11

NAPOOPOO

HONAUNAU
ST. BENEDICTS
PAINTED CHURCH
PUUHONUA
O HONAUNAU
NATIONAL
HISTORIC PARK
(CITY of REFUGE)   KEOKEA

LOA PT.   KEALIA

KEALIA BEACH   HOOKENA

HOOKENA
BEACH
CO. PARK

KAPILO BAY

LEPEAMOA ROCK

KAU LOA PT.

AUAU PT.
PUOA PT.

KEANANUIONANA PT.

KIPAHOEHOE BAY   KIPAHOEHOE NAT.
ARCHED ROCK   AREA RESERVE

MILOLII BEACH   PAPA BAY
HOOPULOA   ESTATES

MILOLII

MILOLII BAY
MOKU O
KAHAILANI
ROCK

0   5 mi

0   8 km

PUU HINAHINA BAY

HOLUA
(SLIDE)   PETROGLYPHS
CAVES   MANUKA
STATE   HAWAIIAN
WAYSIDE   OCEAN VIEW
RUINS   ESTATES
LAVA TUBES

KIPUKA MALUA   MANUKA
NATURAL
KAULANAMAUNA COVE   AREA
RESERVE
RUINS

HAWAII BELT RD.

TO VOLCANO →

KAUNA PT.   WAIOHINU

KAUPUAA BAY   KAHUKU   NAALEHU
KEAWAIKI   RANCH
HUMUHUMU PT.

PETROGLYPHS

KAHAKAHAKEA TRAIL

KAIMUUWALA

11

HEIAU O KALALEA   MAKALEI CAVE
POHAKULOA
KA-LAE CO. PARK   LUA O PALAHEMO
(WATERHOLE)
(SOUTH POINT)   PUU ALI PT.
KA-LAE

Royal Kona Coffee Mill and Museum

In the town of Captain Cook, **Napoopoo Road** branches off Route 11 and begins a roller-coaster ride down to the sea, where it ends at Kealakekua Bay. En route it passes the well-marked Royal Kona Coffee Mill. Along the way you can't help noticing the trim coffee bushes planted along the hillside. Many counterculture types have taken up residence in semi-abandoned "coffee shacks" throughout this hard-pressed economic area, but this cheap, idyllic, and convenience-free life isn't as easy to arrange as it once was. The area is being "rediscovered" and getting more popular. For those just visiting, the tantalizing smell of roasting coffee and the lure of a "free cup" are more than enough stimulus to make you stop. Mark Twain did! The museum is small, of the non-touchable variety with most exhibits behind glass. Mostly they're old black and white prints of the way Kona coffee country used to be. Some heavy machinery is displayed out on the back porch. The most interesting is a homemade husker built from an old automobile. While walking around be careful not to step on a couple of lazy old cats so lethargic they might as well be stuffed. Perhaps a cup of the local "java" in their milk bowl would put a spring in their feline step! Inside, more or less integrated into the museum, is a small gift shop. You can pick up the usual souvenirs, but the real treats are gourmet honeys, jellies, jams, candies, and of course coffee. Buy a pound of Royal Kona Blend for about $4, but for 100-percent Royal Kona it's around $7. Actually, it's cheaper at other retail outlets and supermarkets around the island, but you can't beat the freshness of getting it right from the source. Refill anyone? The museum is open daily 8 a.m. to 4:30 p.m., tel. 328-2511. Mailing address: Mauna Kea Coffee Co., Box 829, Captain Cook, HI 96704.

Kealakekua Bay

Continue down Napoopoo Road through the once-thriving fishing village of Napoopoo ("Holes"), now just a circle on the map with a few houses fronted by neat gardens. At road's end, you arrive at Kealakekua ("Road of the God") Bay. Relax a minute and tune in all your sensors because you're in for a treat. The bay is not only a **Marine Life Conservation District** with a fine beach and top-notch snorkeling (see Napoopoo Beach Park following), but it drips with history. *Mauka,* just at the parking lot, is the well-preserved **Hikiau Heiau,** dedicated to the god Lono, who had long been prophecied to return from the heavens to this very bay, and whose coming would usher in a "new order." Perhaps the soothsaying *kahuna* were a bit vague on the points of the "new order," but it is undeniable that at this spot of initial contact between Europeans and Hawaiians, great changes occurred whose ramifications radically altered the course of Hawaiian history.

The *heiau* is carved into the steep *pali* forming a well-engineered wall. From these heights the temple priests had a panoramic view of the ocean to mark the approach of Lono's "floating island," heralded by tall white tapa banners. The platform formed by the *heiau* was meticulously backfilled with smooth small stones; a series of stone footings, once the bases of grass and thatch houses used in the religious rites, is still very much intact. The *pali* above the bay is pocked with numerous burial caves that still hold the bones of the ancients.

Captain James Cook, leading his ships *Resolution* and *Discovery* under billowing white sails, entered the bay on the morning of January 17, 1778, during the height of the Makahiki Festival, and the awestruck natives were sure that Lono had returned. Immediately, traditional ways were challenged. An old crewman, William Watman, had just died, and Cook went ashore to perform a Christian burial atop the *heiau.* This was, of course, the first Christian ceremony in the islands, and a plaque at the *heiau* entrance commemorates the event. Another plaque is dedicated to Henry Opukahaia, a young native boy taken to New England where he was educated and converted to Christianity. Through impassioned speeches begging salvation for his pagan countrymen, he convinced the first Congregationalist missionaries to come to the islands in 1820. But long before these events, on the fateful day of February 4, 1778, a few weeks after open-armed welcome, the goodwill camaraderie that had developed between the English voyagers and their island hosts turned sour, due to terrible cultural misunderstandings. The sad result was the death of Capt. Cook. This magnificent man, who had resolutely sailed and explored the greatest sea on Earth, stood helplessly in knee-deep water, unable to swim to rescue-boats sent from his waiting ships. Hawaiians, provoked to a furious frenzy because of an unintentioned insult, beat, stabbed and clubbed the great captain and four of his marines to death. (For a full accounting of these events, see p. 25.) A 27-foot, white marble obelisk erected to Cook's memory in 1874 "by some of his fellow countrymen" is at the far northern end of the bay. The land around the monument is actually under British rule, somewhat like the grounds of a foreign consulate. Once a year, an Australian ship comes to tend it, and sometimes local people are hired to clear the weeds. The monument fence is fashioned from old cannons with cannon balls atop. Here too is a bronze plaque often awash by the waves that marks the exact spot where Cook fell. You can see the marble obelisk from the heiau, but actually getting to it is tough. Expert snorkelers have braved the mile swim to the point, but be advised it's through open ocean, and Kealakekua Bay is known for sharks that come in during the evening to feed. A rugged jeep/foot trail leads down the *pali* to the monument, but it's poorly marked and starts way back near the town of Captain Cook, almost immediately after Napoopoo Road branches off from Route 11. If you opt for this route, you'll have to backtrack to visit the coffee museum and the *heiau* side of the bay.

Napoopoo Beach Park

Kealakekua Bay since long before the arrival of Captain Cook has been known as a safe anchorage and draws boats of all descriptions. The area, designated a **Marine Life Conservation District,** lives up to its title by being an excellent scuba and snorkeling site. Organized tours from Kailua-Kona often flood the area with boats and divers, but the ocean expanse is vast and you can generally find your own secluded spot to enjoy the underwater show. If you've just come for a quick dip or to enjoy the sunset, look for beautiful yellow-tailed tropic birds that frequent the bay. Napoopoo Beach Park has full amenities including showers, picnic tables, and restrooms.

Heading For Pu'uhonua O Honaunau

This historical park, the main attraction in the area, shouldn't be missed. Once known as City of Refuge Park, in keeping with the emergence of "Hawaiian heritage," the official name is com-

ing into more use. The best way to get there is to bounce along the four miles of coastal road from Kealakekua Bay. En route, you pass a smaller, more rugged road to **Keei;** this side trip ends at a black-sand canoe launch area, and a cozy white-sand beach that's good for swimming. A channel has been sliced through the coral that leads to an underwater grotto. On the shore are remains of Kamaiko Heiau, where humans were once sacrificed.

The other, more direct way to Pu'uhonua O Honaunau is to take Route 160 at Keokea where it branches off Route 11 at mile marker 104. Either going or coming this way, make sure to take a five-minute side trip off Route 160 to **St. Benedict's Painted Church.** This small house of worship is fronted by latticework, and with its gothic-style belfry looks like a little castle. Inside, a Belgian priest, John Berchman Velghe, took house paint and with a fair measure of talent and religious fervor painted biblical scenes on the walls. His masterpiece is a painted illusion behind the altar that gives you the impression of being in the famous Spanish cathedral in Burgos. Father John was pastor here from 1899 until 1904, when he did these paintings, similar to others that he did in small churches throughout Polynesia. Before leaving, visit the cemetery with its petroglyphs and homemade pipe crosses.

Pu'uhonua O Honaunau National Historical Park

The setting of Pu'uhonua O Honaunau couldn't be more idyllic. It's a picture-perfect cove with many paths leading out onto the sea-washed lava flow. The tall royal palms surrounding this compound shimmer like neon against the black lava so prevalent in this part of Kona. Planted for the purpose, these beacons promised safety and salvation to the vanquished, weak, war-tossed, and *kapu*-breakers of old Hawaii. If you made it to this "temple of refuge," scurrying frantically before avenging warriors or leaping into the sea to swim the last desperate miles, the attendant *kahuna,* under pain of their own death, had to offer you sanctuary. *Kapu* breakers were particularly pursued because their misdeeds could anger the always moody gods, who might send a lava flow or tidal wave to punish all. Only the *kahuna* could perform the rituals that would bathe you in the sacred mana, and thus absolve you from all wrongdoing. This *pu'uhonua* ("temple of refuge") was the largest in all of Hawaii, and be it fact or fancy, you can feel its power to this day.

The temple complex sits on a 20-acre finger of lava bordered by the sea on all sides. A massive 1,000-foot mortarless wall, measuring 10 feet high and 17 feet thick, borders the site on the landward side and marks it as a temple of refuge. Archaeological evidence dates the use of the temple from the mid-16th C., and some scholars argue that it was a well-known sacred spot as much as 200 years earlier. Actually, three separate *heiau* are within the enclosure. In the mid-16th C., Keawe, a great chief of Kona and the great-grandfather of Kamehameha, ruled here. After his death, he was entombed in *Hale O Keawe Heiau* at the end of the great wall, and his *mana* reinfused the temple with cleansing powers. For 250 years the *ali'i* of Kona continued to be buried here, making the spot more and more powerful. Even the great Queen Kaahumanu came here seeking sanctuary. As a 16-year-old bride, she refused to submit to the will of her husband, Kamehameha, and defied him openly, often wantonly giving herself to lesser chiefs. To escape Kamehameha's rampage, she made for the temple. Kaahumanu chose a large rock to hide under, and she couldn't be found until her pet dog barked and gave her away. Kaahumanu was coaxed out only after a lengthy intercession by Captain George Vancouver, who had become a friend of the king. The last royal personage buried here was a son of Kamehameha who died in 1818. Soon afterwards, the "old religion" of Hawaii died and the temple grounds were abandoned but not entirely destroyed. The foundations were left intact of this largest city of refuge in the Hawaiian Islands.

In 1961, the National Park Service opened Pu'uhonua O Honaunau after a complete and faithful restoration was carried out. Careful consultation of old records and vintage sketches from early ships' artists gave the restoration a true sense of authenticity. Local artists used traditional tools and techniques to carve giant *ohia* logs into faithful renditions of the temple gods. They now stand again, protecting the *heiau* from evil. One of the most curious is a god-figure, with his maleness erect, glaring out to sea as if looking for some voluptuous mermaid. All the buildings are painstakingly lashed together in the Hawaiian fashion, but instead of using traditional cordage, which would have added the perfect touch, nylon rope was substituted. Entrance to the park is $1, children under 16 free. Stop at the visitors center where you can pick up a map and brochure for a self-guided tour. Exhibits line a wall, complete with murals done in heroic style. Push a button and the recorded messages give you a brief history of Hawaiian beliefs and the system governing daily life. Educate yourself; the visitors center, tel. 328-2326, is open daily 7:30 a.m. to 5:30 p.m., with rangers giving tours from 10 a.m. to 3:30 p.m. The beach park section (see below) is open 6 a.m. to midnight. Follow the refuge wall toward the northwest to a large flat rock perfect for lying back and watching the sun set.

Hookena

If you want to see how the people of Kona still live, visit Hookena. A mile or two south of the Pu'uhonua O Honaunau turnoff, or 20 miles south of Kailua-Kona, take a well-marked spur road *makai* off Route 11 and follow it to the sea. The village is in a state of disrepair, but a number of homey cottages and some semi-permanent tents are used mostly on weekends by local fishermen. Hookena also boasts a beach park with showers, picnic tables, but no potable water or camping. For drinking water, a tap is attached to the telephone pole when you begin your descent down the spur road. The black-sand (actually gray) beach is broad, long, probably *the* best in South Kona for both swimming and body surfing. If the sun gets too hot, plenty of palms lining the beach provide not only shade but a picture-perfect setting. Until the road connecting Kona to Hilo was finally finished in the 1930s, Hookena shipped the produce of the surrounding area from its bustling wharf. At one time, Hookena was the main port in South Kona and even hosted Robert Louis Stevenson when he passed through the islands in 1889. Part of the wharf still remains, and nearby a fleet of outrigger fishing canoes is pulled up on shore. The surrounding cliffs are honeycombed with burial caves, and if you walk a half mile north, you'll find the crumpled walls and steeple of Maria Lanakila Church, leveled in an earthquake in 1950. The church was another "painted church," done by Father John Velghe in the same style as St. Benedict's.

Milolii

This active fishing village is approximately 15 miles south of Pu'uhonua O Honaunau. Again, look for signs to a spur road off Route 11 heading *makai*. The road, leading through bleak lava flows, is extremely narrow but worth the detour. Milolii means "Fine Twist," and earned its name from times past when it was famous for producing *'aha*, a sennit made from coconut-husk fibers, and *olona*, a twine made from the *olona* plant and best for fish nets. The people of Milolii supplement their fishing income by growing ferns and anthuriums on soil that they truck in. This is one of the last villages in Hawaii where traditional fishing is the major source of income, and where old-timers are heard speaking Hawaiian. Fishermen still use small outrigger canoes, now powered by outboards, to catch *opelu*, a type of mackerel that schools in these waters. The method of catching the *opelu* has remained unchanged for centuries. Boats gather and drop packets of chum made primarily from poi, sweet potatoes, or rice. No meat is used so sharks won't be attracted. In the village, a little understocked store is operated by old-timer Eugene Kaupiko, though the whole family pitches in. Mr. Kaupiko has lived in Milolii all his life, and is the unofficial mayor. He's seen a lot in his 78 years. He met actor Jimmy Stewart, who bought land nearby, and what he remembers most about meeting Elvis Presley who came here in the 1960s, was looking off his porch and seeing nothing but "girls, girls, girls." Milolii has a **beach park** that is a favorite with local people on the weekends. Technically, it's a county park (permit), but no one checks. Tents are pitched in and around the parking lot, just under the ironwoods at road's end. Notice that a number of them appear to be semi-permanent. There are pit toilets, a basketball court, but no water, so bring some. Swimming is safe inside the reef and the tidepooling in the area is some of the best on the south coast.

PRACTICALITIES

Accommodations

So you came to Kona for the sun, surf, and scenery and couldn't care less about your room so long as it's clean and the people running the hotel are friendly? Well, you can't go wrong with any of the following out-of-the-mainstream

hotels. They're all basic, but none are fleabags. At all of these inexpensive hotels, it is very important to get your rooms first thing in the morning, if you don't have reservations. They are very, very, tough to get into. People know about them, and the rooms are at a premium.

Manago Hotel in Captain Cook has been in the Manago family for 70 years, and anyone who puts his name on a place and keeps it there that long is doing something right. The old section of the hotel along the road is clean but a little worse for wear, and doesn't impress much because it looks like a storefront. Walk in to find a bridgeway into a garden area that's open, bright, and secluded away from the road. The rates with common bath are single $17, double $20, triple $22. Rooms with private bath and lanai run single first floor $26, double first floor $29, triple first floor $32. For $40-43, extra person $3, you're accommodated in the new wing where you have a lanai, private bath, and can train your eyes to catch the brilliance of the Kona sunset by practicing looking at the orange floor and pink furniture. Psychedelic! The views from the hotel grounds of the Kona Coast are terrific. You can dine in a restaurant in the old section, open for breakfast 7-9 a.m., lunch 11 a.m.-2 p.m., dinner 5-7:30 p.m., closed Monday. For information, write to: Herald Manago, c/o Manago Hotel, Box 145, Captain Cook, Kona, HI 96704, tel. 323-2642.

Teshima's Inn, tel. 322-9140, is a small, clean, family-run hotel in the mountain village of Honalo at the junction of Routes 180 and 11. Operated by septuagenarians Mr. and Mrs. Harry Teshima, it's somewhat like a Japanese *minshuku* with all rooms fronting a Japanese garden. To be sure of getting a room, call three days to a week in advance. Don't just turn up. Check in is at the restaurant section, between 2-5 p.m. The rooms at $17 s, $30 d, $200 monthly, are spartan but very clean.

Kona Lodge and Hostel, located in Honalo, mailing address Box 645, Kealakekua, HI 96750, tel. 322-9056 is a downhome lodge where Dave and Mary Jo McJunkin welcome families, travelers, and athletes to stay on their acre of land that's abundant with organic fruits and produce. In season, you can gorge on mangos, avocados, bananas, papayas, and macadamia nuts. Dave and Mary Jo have succeeded in creating an atmosphere conducive to health and relaxation. There's no smoking/drinking allowed on the premises. You can choose a bunk bed or private room, and use the hot tub or open kitchen when you desire. Besides the rooms, there's tenting on the grounds at $45 weekly or $7 per night. You can also rent a tent for $2/night and a bedroll for $1. A dormitory bunk is $14, $12 YH member, $90 weekly, $80 YH member. A double room is $35, $5 extra person, weekly $200, $15 extra person. A single room is $24, two people in single room $29, weekly $140, two people $160. Group and off-season rates available, though the lodge is usually booked solid during the Iron Man Triathalon. Notice that even when it's blazing hot outside, the rooms are cool because of the thick canopy of trees that shade them. A huge avocado tree that drops its fruits like grenades on the tin roof lets you know who the newcomers to the lodge are when they jump out of their chairs. The vibes at the Kona Lodge are friendly, fun, and helpful. It's common to find travelers here from many foreign nations.

Howard and Marge Abert's B&B in Kealakekua tel. 322-2405, is friendly with the entire bottom floor of the home given over to the guests. Both former Peace Corps volunteers, they are now retired and have taken up tropical gardening, as well as opening their home to travelers.

Food

All of the restaurants in this section happen to fall in the inexpensive range. None merits a special trip, but all are worth stopping at if you're hungry when you go by. Actually, some are great, especially for breakfast and brunch. For markets and health food stores, see "Shopping" following.

Teshima's Restaurant, tel. 322-9140, open Mon.-Sun. 6:30 a.m.-2 p.m., and 5-10 p.m. at the junction of Routes 11 and 180 in the mountain village of Honalo, is just like the small, clean, and homey Teshima Inn that adjoins it. Here, amongst unpretentious surroundings, you can enjoy a full lunch for $5, sandwiches under $3, or dinner, including various Japanese dishes, for $5-6. If you're interested in a good square meal, you can't go wrong.

The **Aloha Theater Cafe,** open daily from 7:30 a.m. to around 8 p.m., tel. 322-3383, is part of the lobby of the Aloha Theater in Kainaliu. The enormous breakfasts ($3-7) feature locally grown eggs, homemade muffins, and potatoes. Lunchtime sandwiches ($4-7) are super-stuffed with varied morsels from tofu and avocado to eggplant sesame cheeseburgers. There's also a variety of soups and salads and Mexican dishes like a burrito *especial* for $5.75. Full dinners like fresh *ahi* and *ono* are $11.95, filet mignon goes for $15.95, and pasta and shells are $8.95. For a snack choose from an assortment of homemade baked goods that you'll enjoy with an espresso or cappuccino. Order at the counter first (table service for dinner), and then sit on the lanai that overlooks a bucolic scene of cows at a watering trough, with the coast below. This is an excellent stop for breakfast or to pick up a picnic lunch on your way south. Also, check out the bulletin board for local happenings, sales, services, and the like.

Ignore if you can **McDonald's** golden arches as you enter Kealakekua. Just beyond look for the **Canaan Deli.** This full-service deli has an Italian flair. The owner, Tom Butler, from New York City, doesn't sound Italian, but a few lucky people are let into the club! He brings along the "Big Apple's" deli tradition of a lot of food for little money. You can't go wrong with spaghetti and meatballs for $4.25, eggplant parmigiana or fettuccine for $5.75. The pizza special of two slices and a soft drink for $1.99 is great value. They also serve a full assortment of herbal and English teas.

There are very few places in Captain Cook where you can get a meal. On the right just as you enter town is a take-out restaurant with BBQ ribs, chicken, hot biscuits, coleslaw, and salad. You can also try **Hong Kong Chop Suey** in the Ranch Center, which is as basic as can be with most items at $5.

Shopping

The **Aloha Village Store,** just next door to the Aloha Cafe in Kainaliu, sells gifts, sundries, and natural foods. It's a well-stocked health food store with a good selection of powders, herbs, spices, fresh produce, and a dairy case with organic foodstuffs. The bulletin board is great for letting you know what's happening, especially alternatively, in the area. Also in town is **Oshima's General Store, Ben Franklin's, Ace Hardware,** and **Kimura's Market,** a well-stocked grocery store.

The **Kamigaki Store** is in Kealakekua, and **Sure Save** is in Kealakekua Shopping Center. The **Shimizu Market** is south on Route 11 in Honaunau. Farther south between mile markers 77 and 78 you'll find the very well-stocked **Ocean View General Store,** tel. 929-9966, which sells groceries, snacks, and gas. It's the last place to stock up before Naalehu, at the southern tip of the island.

Crystal Star Gallery, in Kainaliu, specializes in cosmic vibrations and how to get in tune with them. You can feel the *vibes* as soon as you walk into this lavender and purple shop stocked with alluring crystals for channeling and massage, plus crystal balls and two full bookracks with new age books.

The Blue Ginger Gallery, in Kainaliu, tel. 322-3898, open 9 a.m.-5 p.m. Mon.-Sat., showcases the art of owners Jill and David Bever, as well as artists' works from all over the island. David creates art pieces in stained glass, fused glass, and wood. The small but well-appointed shop brims over with paintings, ceramics, sculptures, woodworking, and jewelry. A rack holds one-of-a-kind clothing items like sarongs and aloha shirts. Jill paints on silk, creating fantasy works in strong primary colors. The Blue Ginger Gallery is a perfect stop to find a memorable souvenir of Hawaii.

Elizabeth Harris and Co. in Kealakekua, tel. 323-2447, open Mon.- Fri. 9 a.m.-5 p.m. displays shirts, T-shirts, and dresses that are made by 13 local seamstresses and artists who come in to showcase their works. You'll be greeted by the manager, Mary Harper, who'll be sitting behind a Singer sewing machine, or hand-painting shirts. Take a look at the ceramics and glasswork as well. A great stop for truly distinctive clothing.

The **Kahanahou Hawaiian Foundation,** tel. 322-3901, is along the road in Kealakekua. They deal in ancient Hawaiian handicrafts, including masks, hula drums, and hula accoutrements. This nonprofit organization serves as an apprenticeship school for native Hawaiians who are trying to revitalize all traditional arts. Unfortunately, no one seems to be in attendance in the shop, and you are instructed to ring the buzzer. A sign says "If you're just here to browse and to kill time don't kill ours; we can't afford the luxury." That sets the tone of your greeting when someone finally appears to scowl at you. Obviously the foundation is not into preserving aloha.

In Kealakekua look for a big yellow building, mountainside, that houses the **Ohana O Ka Aina Food Co-op,** open 9 a.m.-6 p.m. weekdays, 10 a.m.-5 p.m. Saturdays. This full-range health food store and snack bar serves fresh-made sandwiches daily but opens its cafe only seasonally, mostly in the winter months. You can buy fresh orange and carrot juice made on the premises. It not only has the largest herb supply in Hawaii, but it's the last *real* food co-op left in the state. Keep the faith, brother.

The Little Grass Shack, open 9 a.m.-5 p.m. Mon.-Sat., usually 12-5 p.m. on Sunday, is an institution in Kealakekua. It looks like a tourist trap, but don't let that stop you from going in and finding some authentic souvenirs, most of which come from the area, the workshop next door, or from rehabilitation centers around the island. The items *not* from Hawaii are clearly marked with a big orange sign that says "Sorry These Items Were Not Made In Hawaii." But the price is right. There are plenty of trinkets and souvenir items, but there is also a fine assortment of artistic pieces, especially wooden bowls, hula items, and Hawaiian masks. A shop specialty are items made from curly *koa.* Each piece is signed with the craftsperson's name and the type of wood used. One of the craftsmen displayed here is master woodworker, Jack Straka. Items are also made from Norfolk pine and milo. A showcase holds jewelry and tapa cloth imported from Fiji. The shop is famous for its distinctive *lau hala* hats, the best hat for the tropics.

Tropical Temptations, tel. 326-2007, open 10 a.m.-5 p.m. Mon.- Sat., is housed in Kealakekua in a gaily painted yellow and green building. Climb the steps to the porch, where you'll find a service buzzer that will summon owner and chief tempter, Lance Dassance, who will smile a welcome into his candy kitchen. Lance turns the best available grade of local fruits, nuts, and coffee beans into delicious candies. The fresh-fruit process uses no preservatives, additives, waxes, extenders, and no sugars except in the chocolate which is the best grade possible. The drying process used is slow-drying, so as little nutrients as possible are lost. A shop specialty is candies made from rare white pineapple, which grows for only eight weeks per year. Lance, if not too busy, will be happy to

Lance of Tropical Temptations

take you on a tour of the facility. He takes a personal pride in making the best candy possible and stresses that he only uses fruit ripened in the last 24 hours. Tropical Temptations, the healthiest candy store in Hawaii, has an outlet booth in Kailua-Kona at the Kona Inn Shopping Village.

Konakai Coffee Farms has a tasting room and restaurant at the south end of Kealakekua. They serve produce and cups of Kona coffee plain, as espresso, cappuccino, and caffe latte. Check the racks of fresh-roasted pure Kona coffee at about $12/pound.

Country Store Antiques is next door to the Manago Hotel, just as you're entering Captain Cook. Owned and operated by E.L. Mahre,

open Mon.- Fri. 9 a.m.-3 p.m., it's filled to the brim from back to front. Inside you'll find kerosene lamps, dolls, glassware, old bottles, and Hawaiian antique jewelry. The shop is more like a museum than an antique store. There are plenty of purse and suitcase-size items that will travel well and make a lasting memento of your trip. On the other side of the Manago Hotel is the **Manaloa Gallery and Thrift Store,** another bric-a-brac shop filled with art objects and curiosities.

The **Kealakekua Ranch Center,** in Captain Cook, is a two-story mall with fashions and general supplies. Here you'll find a TruValue Hardware Store, Ben Franklin's, and Sure Save Supermarket. The most interesting shop is **Mauna Loa Nutrition,** tel. 323-3955, a "health store" not a "health food store." Although you can refresh yourself with snacks and drinks, the store stocks herbs, crystals, an extensive collection of body-care products, and the largest and lowest-priced selection of Birkenstock footwear in the islands. Owned and operated by two seasoned world travelers, Wayne and Mars Stier, it's well worth stopping, if just to chat. Wayne has authored three fine and insightful travel books which Mars distributes through their own company, Meru Publishing.

A row of international flags waving along the roadside might lure you into the **Kona Country Fair,** an upscale tourist trap. They offer free coffee from 8 a.m.-6 p.m., and the prices on the souvenir-quality items are cheaper than in Kailua-Kona. Peer from the elevated platforms to the coast below before entering. Inside you'll find Kona coffee, T-shirts, carved coconuts, towels, beads, and paper leis. The grounds just below hold blue- roofed gazebo-type buildings where a flea market is held from 8 a.m.-3 p.m. every **Wednesday, Friday,** and **Saturday.** Downstairs in the main building is a deli.

Bong Brothers, about a mile past the Kona Country Fair, is an authentic fruit store. Check it out just for the atmosphere, and also for the fresh local fruit.

KAU

The **Kau District** is simple and straightforward like the broad open face of a country gentleman. It's not boring, and it does hold pleasant surprises for those willing to look. Formed entirely from the massive slopes of Mauna Loa, the district presents some of the most ecologically diverse land in the islands. The bulk of it stretches 50 miles from north to south and almost 40 miles from east to west, tumbling from the snowcapped mountain through the cool green canopy of highland forests. Lower it becomes pasturelands of belly-deep grass ending in blistering hot black sands along the coast, encircled by a necklace of foamy white sea. At the bottom of Kau is **Ka Lae** ("South Point"), the southernmost tip of Hawaii and the southernmost point in the U.S. Latitudinally it lies 500 miles south of Miami and twice that below Los Angeles. Ka Lae was probably the first landfall made by the Polynesian explorers on the islands. A variety of archaeological remains support this belief.

Most people dash through Kau on the Hawaii Belt Road, heading to or from Volcanoes National Park. Its main towns, **Naalehu** and **Pahala,** are little more than pit stops. The Belt Road follows the old Mamalahoa Trail, where, for centuries, nothing moved faster than a contented man's stroll. Kau's beauties, mostly tucked away down secondary roads, are hardly given a look by most unknowing visitors. If you take the time and get off the beaten track, you'll discover black- and green-sand beaches, the world's largest macadamia nut farm, Wild West rodeos, and an electricity farm sprouting windmill generators. The upper slopes and broad pasturelands are the domain of hunters, hikers, and *paniolo,* who still ride the range on sure-footed horses. In Kau are sleepy plantation towns that don't even know how quaint they are, and beach parks where you can count on finding a secluded spot to pitch a tent. Time in Kau moves slowly, and aloha still forms the basis of day-to-day life.

SIGHTS AND BEACHES

The following sights are listed from west to east along Route 11, with detours down secondary roads indicated whenever necessary. The majority of Kau's pleasures are accessible by a

standard rental car, but many secluded coastal spots can be reached only by 4WD. For example, **Kailiki,** just west of Ka Lae, was an important fishing village in times past. A few archaeological remains are found here, and the beach has a green cast due to the lava's high olivine content. Few tourists ever visit; only hardy fishermen come here to angle the coastal waters. Spots of this type abound, especially in Kau's remote sections. But civilization has found Kau as well: when you pass mile marker 63, look down to the coast and notice a stand of royal palms and a large brackish pond. This is Luahinivai Beach, one of the finest on the island, where country and western star Loretta Lynn has built a fabulous home. Those willing to abandon their cars, and to hike the sparsley populated coast or interior of Kau, are rewarded with areas unchanged and untouched for generations.

Manuka State Wayside

If hoofing it or 4WDing isn't your pleasure, consider a stop at Manuka State Wayside, 12 miles before you get to South Point Road just inside the Kau District. This civilized scene has restrooms, pavilions, and trails through manicured gardens surrounded by an arboretum. Shelter camping (no tents) is allowed on the grounds. All plants are identified, and this is an excellent rest or picnic stop. The forested slopes above Manuka provide ample habitat for introduced, and now totally successful, colonies of wild pigs, pheasants, and turkeys. Some popular hiking areas are covered in the Volcanoes Park section (see p. 647). Be advised that the entire district is subject to volcanic activity and, except where indicated, has no water, food, shelter, or amenities.

South Point

The Hawaiians simply called this Ka Lae, "The Point." Some scholars believe Polynesian sailors made landfall here as early as A.D. 150, and that their amazing exploits became navigating legend long before true colonization began. A paved, narrow, but passable road branches off from Route 11 approximately six miles west of Naalehu, and drops directly south for 12 miles to land's end. Luckily the shoulders are firm, and you can pull over to let another car go by. The car rental agencies warn against using this road, but their fears are unfounded. You proceed through a flat treeless area trimmed by free-ranging herds of cattle and horses: more road obstacles to be aware of. Suddenly, incongru-

ously, huge mechanical windmills appear, beating their arms against the sky. This is the **Kamoa Wind Farm.** Notice that this futuristic experiment at America's most southern point uses windmills made in Japan by Mitsubishi! The trees here are bent over by the prevailing wind, demonstrating the obviously excellent wind-power potential of the area. Farther along, a road sign informs that the surrounding countryside is controlled by the **Hawaiian Homeland Agency,** and that you are forbidden to enter. That means that you are not welcome on the land, but you do have right-of-way on the road.

Here the road splits left and right. Go right until the road ends, where you'll find a parking area usually filled with the pickup trucks of local fishermen. Walk to the cliff and notice attached ladders that plummet straight down to where the fishing boats are anchored. Local skippers moor their boats here and bring supplies and their catch up and down the ladders. Proceed south along the coast for only five minutes and you'll see a tall white structure with a big square sign on it turned sideways like a diamond. It marks the true *South Point,* the southernmost tip of the United States. Proceed to the sea and notice the tidepools, a warning that the swells can come high onto the rocks, and that you can be swept away if you turn your back on *moana.* Usually, a few people are line fishing for Crevalle or pampano. The rocks are covered with Hawaiian dental floss, monofilament fishing line that has been snapped. Survey the mighty Pacific and realize that the closest continental landfall is Antarctica, 7,500 miles to the south.

Back at the Hawaiian Homes sign, follow the road left and pass a series of WW II barracks being reclaimed by nature. This road, too, leads to a parking area and a boat ramp where a few seaworthy craft are bobbing away at their moorings. Walk toward the the navigational marker and you may notice small holes drilled into the stone. These were used by Hawaiian fishermen to secure their canoes by long ropes to land while the current carried them a short way offshore. In this manner, they could fish without being swept away. Today fishermen still use these holes, but instead of manned canoes they use floats or tiny boats to carry their lines out to sea. The *ulua,* tuna, and *ahi* fishing is renowned throughout this area. When the *kona* winds blow out of the South Pacific, South Point takes it on

the chin. The weather should always be a consideration when you visit. In times past, any canoe caught in the wicked currents was considered lost. Even today, only experienced boatmen brave South Point, and only during fine weather. The fishing grounds were extremely fertile, and thousands of shell and bone fish-hooks have been found throughout the area. Scuba divers say that the rocks off South Point are covered with broken fishing line that the currents have woven into wild macrame. There is no official camping or facilities of any kind at South Point, but plenty of boat owners bivouac for a night to get an early start in the morning. The lava flow in this area is quite old and grass-covered, and the constant winds act like a natural lawn mower.

Green Sand Beach

From the boat ramp, a footpath leads east toward Kaulana Bay, and all along here are remnants of pre-contact habitation, including the remains of a *heiau* foundation. If you walk for three miles, you'll come to Papakolea, better known as Green Sand Beach. The lava in this area contains olivine, a green semiprecious stone that weathered into sand-like particles distributed along the beach. The road heading down to Green Sand Beach is incredible. It begins as a very rugged jeep trail, and disintegrates from there. Do not attempt this walk unless you have close-toed shoes. Thongs will not make it. You're walking into the wind going down, but it's not a rough go—there's no elevation gain to speak of. The lava in the area is *a'a,* weathered and overlayed by a rather thick ground cover. Follow the road, and after 10 minutes, the lava ends and rich, green pasture-land begins. An ancient eruption deposited 15-18 feet of ash right here, and the grasses grew. Continue for approximately 35 minutes, until you see what is obviously an eroded cinder cone at the edge of the sea. (About 15 minutes back, you'll have noticed an area where many 4WDs have pulled off at an overlook. That isn't it!) Peer over the edge to see the beach with its definite green tinge. This is the only *beach* along the way, so it's hard to mistake. Getting down to it is absolutely treacherous. You'll be scrambling over tough lava rock, and you'll have to make drops of four-five feet in certain spots. The best approach to follow is to go over the edge as soon as you come to the cinder cone area; don't walk around to what would be the south point of the caldera where the sand is. Once you get over the lip of heavy-duty rock, the trail down is not so bad. When you begin your descent, notice overhangs, almost like caves, where rocks have been piled up to extend them. These rocked-in areas make great shelters, and you can see remnants of recent campfires in spots perfect for a night's bivouac.

Green Sand Beach definitely lives up to its name, but don't expect emerald green. It's more like an army green, a dullish khaki green. Down at the beach, be very aware of the wave action. Watch for at least 15 minutes to be sure breakers are not inundating the entire beach. Then you can walk across it, but stay close to the lava rock wall. The currents can be wicked here and you should only enter the water on very calm days. No one is around to save you, and you don't want to wind up as flotsam in Antarctica.

Waiohinu

As you head east toward Naalehu, you pass through the tiny town of Waiohinu. A tall church steeple welcomes you to town just after you wiggle your way down a long hill to the coast. There's nothing remarkable about this village, except that as you pass through you'll be seeing an example of the real Hawaiian lifestyle as it exists today. Just past the well-marked Shirakawa Motel (see following) on the *mauka* side of the road is the **Mark Twain Monkeypod Tree.** Unfortunately, Waiohinu's only claim to fame except for its undisturbed peace and quiet blew down in a heavy windstorm in 1957. Part of the original trunk, carved into a bust of Twain, is on display at the Lyman House Museum in Hilo. Now, a few shoots have begun sprouting from the original trunk and in years to come the Monkeypod Tree will be an attraction again.

Naalehu

Next you come to sizable Naalehu, the largest town in the area and the most southern town in the U.S. Naalehu is lush. Check out the overhanging monkey pod trees. They form a magnificent living tunnel as you go down Route 11 through the center of town. Between Naalehu and Punaluu, the coastal area is majestic. You've left the mountains behind and stretching out into the sea is a tableland of black lava with the aqua blue sea crashing against it, creating a surrealistic seascape that seems to go on forever.

Whittington Beach Park

Three miles north of Naalehu, just past mile marker 61, is a county park with full amenities and camping. This park is tough to spot from the road because it's not clearly marked. As you're coming down a steep hill from Naalehu you'll see a bridge at the bottom. Turn right and you're there. The park is a bit run down, but never crowded. If you follow the dirt roads to its undeveloped sections you encounter many old ruins from the turn of the century when Honuapo Bay was an important sugar port.

Ninole And Punaluu

Just east of Naalehu is Whittington Beach Park, followed by Ninole, where you'll find Punaluu Beach Park (mile marker 56) which is famous for its black-sand beach (see below). Punaluu was an important port during the sugar boom of the 1880s and even had a railroad. Notice the tall coconut palms in the vicinity, unusual for Kau. Punaluu means "Diving Spring," so named because freshwater springs can be found on the floor of the bay. Native divers once paddled out to sea, then dove with calabashes that they filled with fresh water from the underwater springs. This was the main source of drinking water for the region.

Ninole is also home to the **Seamountain Resort and Golf Course,** built in the early 1970s by a branch of the C. Brewer Company. The string of flat-topped hills in the background are the remains of volcanoes that became dormant about 100,000 years ago. In sharp contrast with them is **Loihi Seamount,** 20 miles offshore and about 3,000 feet below the surface of the sea. This very active submarine volcano is steadily building, and should reach the surface in the next thousand years or so. Near Ninole is **Hokuloa Church,** which houses a memorial to Henry Opukahaia, the Hawaiian most responsible for encouraging the first missionaries to go to Hawaii to save his people from damnation.

Punaluu Beach Park

Between Pahala and Naalehu is Punaluu Beach Park, a county park (permit) with full amenities. Here you'll find a pavilion, bathrooms, telephone, and an open camping area. During the day there are plenty of tourists around, but at night the beach park empties, and you virtually have it to yourself. Punaluu boasts some of the only safe swimming on the south coast, but that doesn't mean that it can't have its treacherous moments. Head for the northeast section of the beach near the boat ramp. Stay close to shore because a prevailing rip current lurks just outside the bay. Just near the beach is **Joe and Pauline's Curio Shop.** If you have time stop in; these people have a reputation for being more interested in offering aloha than in selling you a trinket. **Ninole Cove Park,** part of the Seamountain Resort, is within walking distance and open to the public. For day use, you might consider parking near the pro shop. As you walk to the beach from here you pass a freshwater pond, quite cold but good for swimming.

Pahala

Eight miles east of Ninole and 22 miles from Volcanoes is Pahala, clearly marked off Route 11. The Hawaii Belt Road flashes past this town, but if you drive into it, heading for the tall stack of the Kau Sugar Co., you'll find one of the best preserved examples of a classic sugar town in the islands. It was once gospel that sugar would be "king" in these parts forever, but the huge stone stack of the sugarmill puffs erratically, while in the background the whir of a modern macadamia nut processing plant breaks the stillness. Another half hour or so of driving from Pahala puts you in Volcanoes National Park (for Kau Desert Footprints, see p. 228).

Wood Valley Temple

Also known as Nechung Drayang Ling, "Island of Melodious Sound," tel. 928-8539, P.O. Box 250, Pahala, HI 96777, is true to its name. This Tibetan Buddhist temple sits like a sparkling jewel surrounded by the emerald-green velvet of its manicured grounds. To get there, enter Pahala Village, proceed to the stop sign in the village center, and turn right. The road will open up into a very wide cane road where you should be aware of monstrous cane trucks that can lumber down it at any moment. Proceed for five miles until you come to a Y where you go left. Follow this small road for a few hundred yards through an aromatic stand of majestic eucalyptus trees and look for two tall prayer poles on the

right; pull into the parking lot and you'll see the temple, gaily painted red, yellow, orange, and green, glistening on top of the hill. Here Marya and Miguel, the caretakers and administrators, will greet you if they are not off on to one of their frequent trips to Asia.

Buddha gave the world essentially 84,000 different teachings to pacify, purify, and develop the mind. In Tibetan Buddhism there are four major lineages, and this temple, founded by Tibetan master Nechung Drayang Rampuche, is a classic synthesis of all four. Monks and scholars from different schools of Buddhism are periodically invited to come and lecture as resident teachers. The Dalai Lama came in 1980 to dedicate the temple, and many *lama* have come since then. Two affiliate temples are located in Dansala, India and in Lawson, Tibet. Programs vary, but people genuinely interested in Buddhism come here for meditation, soul searching, and for peace, quiet, relaxation, and direction. Morning and evening services at 7 a.m. and 7 p.m. are lead by Debula, the Tibetan monk in residence. Formal classes depend upon which invited teacher is in residence (write ahead for a schedule of programs).

The retreat facility is called the Tara Temple and at one time housed a Japanese Shingon Temple in Pahala. When the Shingon sect moved to a new facility in Kona, this building was abandoned and given to Wood Valley Temple. A local contractor moved it to its present location, cranked it up one story, and built the dormitories underneath. The grounds, hallowed and consecrated for decades, already held a Nichiren temple, the main temple here today, that was dismantled in 1919 and rebuilt on its present site to protect it from lowland flooding. Rates at the retreat facility are private room $15 single, $90 weekly, $25 double, $150 weekly. A bunk in the dorm is $10 with use of a large communal kitchen and shared bath.

The majority of the flowering and fruit trees on the premises are imports. Plenty of parishioners are into agriculture, and there is a strong movement by the temple members to slowly replant the grounds with native vegetation which they collect from various sites in and around Pahala. The grounds, like a botanical garden, vibrate with life and energy. Buddhism strives for its followers to become wise and compassionate people. The focus of the temple is to bring together all meditation and church groups in the community. Plenty of local Christian and Buddhist groups use the nonsectarian facilities. Any group that is spiritually, socially, and community oriented and that has a positive outlook is welcome. Wood Valley Temple can't promise *nirvana,* but they can point you to the path.

PRACTICALITIES

One thing you won't be hassled with in the Kau District is deciding on where to eat or spend the night. The list is short and sweet.

ACCOMMODATIONS

The **Shirakawa Motel,** Box 467 Naalehu, HI 96772, tel. 929-7462, is a small, clean, comfortable hotel where your peace and quiet is guaranteed. Open since 1928, the Japanese family that runs it is as quiet and unobtrusive as *ninja.* Prices are a reasonable $22 s, $25 s with kitchen, $30 d with kitchen, a 10% discount for a one-week stay, 15% for longer. You'll be greeted by two doberman pincers, Rex and Max, who have both given up their authoritarian Germanic heritage and opted for the "hang loose, no worries" island lifestyle.

Seamountain Resort at Punaluu, tel. 928-8301 or (800) 367-8047, Box 340, Pahala, HI 96777, is a condominium/hotel complex. Prices range from a studio at $67 to a two-bedroom apartment for $114 (two-day minimum stay). Because of its rural location, Seamountain can offer deluxe accommodations for moderate prices. Your condo unit will be a low-rise, Polynesian-inspired bungalow with a shake roof. Outside your door are the resort's fairways and greens, backdropped by the spectacular coast. If you're after peace and quiet, Seamountain is hard to beat. Besides golf, amenities include a nearby restaurant, tennis courts, pool, and weekly maid service.

Maluhia Acres is Beverly and Walt Ahnert's hideaway that they have recently opened as a bed and breakfast. It sits on a picture-perfect site along South Point Road, and in Walt's words "only about six people live further south in the U.S. than us." The grounds, complete with a swimming pool, couldn't be more peaceful and serene, like a concentrated oasis of paradise in the middle of paradise. Walt, a retired Boeing engineer, is an urbane gentleman in the truest sense of the word who, along with his son, built the home. Beverly is a bubbly and gracious hostess who goes out of her way to make you feel at home. Both welcome you heartily, often opening a bottle of vintage wine to help pass the evening in civilized conversation. Both Walt and Beverly are happy to share their years of experience in Hawaii, often giving advice on restaurants, sights, and hikes in the area. Beverly offers a gourmet breakfast that often includes homemade biscuits, jams, fresh fruits, and steaming pots of coffee. Rates are a very reasonable $55 d, $50 s, with private bath. For further information and reservations contact B&B Hawaii, P.O. Box 449, Kapaa HI, 96746, tel. 822-7771, or (800) 657-7832.

For a unique and distinctive accommodation see **Wood Valley Temple,** p. 688.

FOOD AND SHOPPING

The Kau Drive-in Restaurant is open for breakfast, lunch, and dinner. You pass it on the left between mile marker 78 and 77, just near a Texaco gas station. The food is simple, but good, and makes a perfect lunch.

A mile further south is **South Point Bar and Restaurant** that has been changing owners regularly but making a valiant effort to stay open. The bar is open till 2 a.m., while the restaurant opens for dinner at 5 p.m., and for Sunday brunch from 11 a.m.-3 p.m. The new chefs specialize in fresh local seafood. South Point is the only restaurant until you get to Naalehu.

Kau Ice and Fishing Center in Waiohinu offers fresh local fish that make a perfect self-prepared meal for anyone heading back to a condo in Kailua-Kona. Just down the road, you can pick up supplies at **Wong Yuen General Store and Gas Station,** open 8:30 a.m. to 5 p.m., Sun. to 3 p.m., tel. 929-7223.

The **Naalehu Shopping Center** is along the road at the west end of town. In the small complex you'll find Food Mart, Ed's Laundromat, and **Greensan's Shop,** where you can pick up sandwiches and plate lunches.

In **Naalehu** you can gas yourself or your car at the **Luzon Liquor Store,** open Mon. to Sat. 7 a.m. to 7:30 p.m., Sun. till 6 p.m., closed Tues., tel. 929-7103. For a quick sandwich or full meal try the **Naalehu Coffee Shop,** open daily, tel. 929-7238. Many of the local people call this restaurant Roy's, after the owner's first name. The menu is typical island cuisine, with a Japanese flavor, but the best item is the fresh fish that comes from local waters. The restautrant is basic and clean, with most meals on the menu around $7. They also have a wide assortment of souvenirs and tourist junk, and a large *koi* pond outside. Look for the big yellow building just near the shopping center as you enter town.

The **Naalehu Fruit Stand,** tel. 929-9009, open Mon.-Thurs. 9 a.m.- 6:30 p.m., Fri. and Sat. till 7 p.m., Sun. till 5 p.m., is a favorite with local people, always a tip-off that the food is great. Along with fresh fruit, they sell submarines, hot dogs, chili, pizza, salads, sodas, teas, coffee, and a good selection of grains, minerals, vitamins, and health foods. The owners, John and Dorene Santangelo, are very friendly and willing to give advice about touring the Kau area. This is the best place on the south coast for a light meal or picnic lunch.

Across the road from the Naalehu Fruit Stand notice the baseball park. Here **Lilly's Plate Lunch** serves hearty sandwiches and island favorites ready to go.

The only real "dining" in the area is at the **Punaluu Black Sands Restaurant,** tel. 928-8344, open daily for breakfast, lunch, and dinner. The setting couldn't be more lovely, as the restaurant sits just off the Seamountain Golf Course overlooking the black-sand beach. Unfortunately, all those pesky tourists dieseling by in their tour buses think so, too. The special is a daily buffet at $8.95 offered from 10:30 a.m.-2 p.m, with a la carte items until 5 p.m., and dinner from 5:30-8:30 p.m. Two double-hulled canoes serve as the buffet table and hold a variety of fresh tropical fruit, salad greens and dressings, pickled vegies, an assortment of fish, meat, and poultry entrees, steamed rice, buttered potatoes, sweet bread, homemade desserts, and a choice of island-grown coffee, hot mint or ice tea, and fruit juice. Lighter fare includes sandwiches and burgers with trimmings for around $6. Dinner brings teriyaki chicken, pork chops, N.Y. steak with bearnaise sauce, *mahi mahi* florentine, and crab imperial with prices ranging from $11-$15. The lava stone buildings are Polynesian-inspired with a bright and airy feeling because of wraparound windows that are usually open to the ocean breezes. The **19th Hole** at the Seamountain Resort Pro Shop has a selection of sandwiches, soups, and salads for a quick lunch.

Just across from the entrance to Whittington Beach Park, three miles east of Naalehu and just past mile marker 61, look for **Big Island Expressions.** This shop is really a downhome place and features locally made arts and crafts.

In **Pahala village** (see p. 688) you'll find the basics like a gas station, small shopping center, P.O., Bank of Hawaii, Mizumo's Superette, and a takeout plate lunch restaurant.

SPORTS AND ACTIVITIES

Besides the great outdoors and the sea, the only organized sporting facility in Kau is at the Seamountain Resort. Here you'll find four unlit tennis courts and a 6,106-yard, 18-hole, par-72 course. Green fees are $30, cart $16, and clubs $10.

The **Southern Star Theater** is a large building on the left as soon as you drive into Naalehu. It's a classic old-time theater usually open on weekends, adults $3.25, children $1.75.

The best **sailboarding** in the area is at Kaulana Bay. Head down South Point Road (see p. 685.), and about a half mile before you get to the windmills is a passable dirt road to the left. You can only see about half a mile down it when you first start out, but keep going. Pass through cattle gates and make absolutely sure to close them behind you. When you get to the bay, go to the left-hand side for the best entry. Remember that down here, there is no help available, and you are totally on your own!

Kau Windsurfing in Naalehu, next to the Naalehu Fruit Stand, rents and sells sailboards, fins, snorkels, and masks.

SOUTH KOHALA

The Kohala District is the peninsular thumb in the northwestern portion of the Big Island. At its tip is **Upolo Point,** only 40 miles from Maui across the **Alenuihaha Channel.** Kohala was the first section of the Big Island to rise from beneath the sea. The long-extinct volcanoes of the Kohala Mountains running down its spine have been reduced by time and the elements from lofty ragged peaks to rounded domes of 5,000 feet or so. Kohala is divided into North and South Kohala. **South Kohala** boasts *the* most beautiful swimming beaches on the Big Island, along with good camping and world-class hotels. Inland is **Waimea** (Kamuela), the *paniolo* town and center of the massive Parker Ranch. Founded last century by John Parker, its 200,000 acres on the western slopes of Mauna Kea now make it the largest privately owned ranch in America.

Getting There From Hilo

If you're approaching Kohala from Hilo or the east side of the island, you can take two routes. **The Saddle Road** (Route 200) comes directly west from Hilo and bypasses Mauna Kea and the Observatory Road. This very scenic road has the alluring distinction of being the least favorite route of the car rental agencies. The Saddle Road intersects Route 190, where you can turn north for six miles to Waimea, or south for 32 miles to Kailua-Kona (see p. 651). **Route 19,** the main artery connecting Hilo with the west coast, changes its "locally known" name quite often, but it's always posted as Route 19. Directly north from Hilo as it hugs the Hamakua coast it's called the "Hawaiian Belt Road." When it turns west in Honokaa, heading for Waimea, it's called the "Mamalahoa Highway." From Waimea directly west to Waikui on the coast Route 19 becomes "Kawaihae Road," and when it turns due south along the coast heading for Kailua-Kona its moniker changes again to "Queen Kaahumanu Highway." The routes heading to Kohala from Kailua-Kona are discussed in the following sections. Many are "sights" in and of themselves, with lovely panoramas and leisurely back-lane rides.

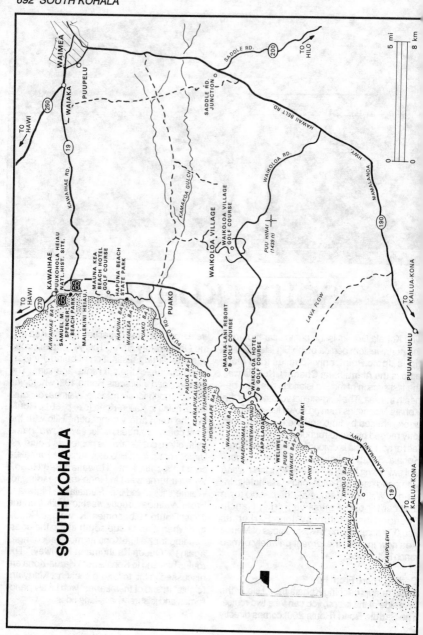

THE COAST

The shoreline of South Kohala, from Anaehoomalu Bay north to Kawaihae Bay, is rich in perhaps the finest super-deluxe resorts in the state. This coast's fabulous beaches are known not only for swimming and surf, but for tidepooling and awe-inspiring sunsets as well. Also, the two main beaches offer camping and even rental cabins. There are little-disturbed and rarely visited archaeological sites, expressive petroglyph fields well off the beaten track, the educational **Puukohola Heiau,** and even a rodeo. No "towns" lie along the coast, in the sense of a laid-out community with a main street and attendant businesses and services. The closest facsimile is Kawaihae, with a small cluster of restaurants, shops, and a gas station. Waikoloa Village also provides some services, with exclusive boutique shopping in the resorts.

Route 19,
The Queen Kaahumanu Highway

As you begin heading north from Kailua-Kona on coastal Route 19 (Queen Kaahumanu Hwy.), you leave civilization behind. There won't be a house or any structures at all, and you'll understand why they call it the "Big Island." Perhaps to soften the shock of what's ahead, magnificent bushes loaded with pink and purple flowers line the roadway . . . for a while. Notice too that friends and lovers have gathered and placed white coral rocks on the black lava, forming pleasant graffiti messages such as "Aloha Mary," and "Love Kevin."

Suddenly you're in the midst of enormous flows of old a'a and pa'hoehoe as you pass through a huge and desolate lava desert. At first it appears ugly and uninviting, but the subtle beauty begins to grow. On clear days you can see Maui floating on the horizon, and mauka looms the formidable presence of Mauna Kea streaked by sunlight filtering through its crown of clouds. Along the roadside, little wisps of grass have broken through the lava. Their color, a shade of pinkish gold, is quite extraordinary, and made more striking juxtaposed against the inky-black lava. Caught by your headlights at night, or especially in the magical light of dusk, the grass wisps come alive, giving the illusion of wild-haired gnomes rising from the earth. In actuality, it's fountain grass imported from Africa.

Around mile marker 70, the land softens and changes. The lava is older, carpeted in rich green grass appearing as rolling hills of pastureland. No cows are in evidence, but be aware of "Kona nightingales," wild jackasses that roam throughout this area and can be road hazards. Also, these long flat stretches can give you "lead foot." Be careful! The police patrol this strip heavily, using unmarked cars (high-performance Trans Ams and the likes are favorites) and look for unsuspecting tourists that have been "road hypnotized." From Kailua-Kona to the Royal Waikoloa Hotel at Anaehoomalu is about 30 miles, with another 10 miles to the Mauna Kea Beach Hotel near Kawaihae. If you're day-tripping to the beaches, expect to spend an hour each way.

SIGHTS AND NEARBY COMMUNITIES

The following sights, beaches, and accommodations are listed from south to north. Since most of the accommodations of South Kohala are themselves sights, and lie on the best beaches, make sure to cross-reference the following sections. All, except for Waikoloa Village, lie along coastal Route 19 which is posted with mile markers, so finding the spots where you want to stop is easy.

Waikoloa Road

If you're interested in visiting Waimea (Kamuela) and still seeing the South Kohala coast, you might consider turning right off Route 19 between mile markers 74 and 75 onto Waikoloa Road. This is a great deal of territory to cover in one day! This route cuts inland for 13 miles, connecting coastal Route 19 with inland Route 190 which leads to Waimea. About halfway, you pass the planned and quickly growing community of **Waikoloa village.** The village has a gas station, market, and a few restaurants and shops. This is also the home of **Waikoloa Stables,** tel. 883-9335, that hosts a number of rodeos and Wild West shows (see p. 587) along with saddle horses and a variety of trail rides for the visitor. Here too is the **Waikoloa Village Golf Course,** tel. 883-9621, a private course open to the public. You can chase that little white ball for par 72 over 6,316 yards for about $40 including cart.

In the village you'll find **Waikoloa Villas,** Box 3066, Waikoloa Village Station, Kamuela, HI 96743, tel. (800) 367-7042, on the Big Island tel. 883-9588. Rates are one-bedroom for $65-80 d, two-bedrooms $85-95 d, three-bedrooms (loft) $105-115 d, $8 extra person, two-night minimum stay. Amenities include swimming pool, nearby golf, and weekly maid service. All units are fully furnished with complete kitchens. The condo offers a money-saving condo/car package.

Puako

This alluring area is located *makai* on a side road off Route 19 about four miles south of Kawaihae. Hawaiians lived here in times past, but a modern community has been building along the three miles of Puako Bay since the 1950s. A thin ribbon of white sand runs the length of the beach that provides fair swimming, good fishing and snorkeling, and terrific tidepooling. Sunsets here are also magnificent and you'll usually have a large stretch of beach to yourself, but remember your flashlight for the walk back because there's no lighting. Near-shore scuba diving is excellent, with huge caverns and caves to explore, and a colorful concentration of coral and marinelife. Along Puako Road is **Hokuloa Church,** built by Rev. Lorenzo Lyons in 1859. This musically talented reverend mastered the Hawaiian language and composed lovely ballads such as "Hawaii Aloha," which has become the unofficial anthem of the islands. Follow the road through the village to where it ends at a green gate; this is the beginning of the extensive field of **Puako Petroglyphs.** The entrance is marked by an HVB Warrior; the path leading to the rock carvings takes about 20 minutes each way. (Access info and brochures are also available from the nearby Sheraton Hotel's front desk.) These markings are considered some of the finest and oldest in Hawaii, but carvings of horses and cattle signify ongoing art that happened long after Westerners appeared. Circles outlined by a series of small holes belonged to families who placed the umbilical cords of their infants into these indentations to tie them to the *aina* and give them strength for a long and good life. State archaeologists and anthropologists have reported a deterioration of the site due to vandalism, so please look but don't deface and stay on all established paths.

Pu'ukohola Heiau

Don't miss this completely restored Hawaiian temple, a National Historical Site located one mile south of Kawaihae where coastal Route 19 turns into Route 270 heading into North Kohala. This site, covering 77 acres, includes **Mailekini Heiau** and the nearby **John Young House** site. It is administered by the National Park Service, open daily 7:30 a.m. to 4 p.m., admission free. As you enter, pick up a map highlighting the main points of interest, and it's worthwhile checking out the visitors center where Ranger Benjamin Saldua and others provide excellent information. Puukohola ("Whale Hill") received its name either because the hill itself resembles a whale, or because migrating whales pass very close offshore every year. It was fated to become a hill of destiny.

Kamehameha I built this heiau in 1790 on the advice of Kapoukahi, a prophet from Kauai who said that Kamehameha would unify all the islands only after he built a temple to his war-god Kukailimoku. Kamehameha complied, building this last of the great Hawaiian *heiau* from mortarless stone that when finished measured 100 by 224 feet. The dedication ceremony of the heiau is fascinating history. Kamehameha's last rival was his cousin, Keoua Kuahuula. This warlike chief, through prophecy and advice from his own *kahuna,* realized that it was Kamehameha who would rise to be sovereign of all the islands. Kamehameha invited him to the dedication ceremony, but en route Keoua, in preparation for the inevitable outcome, performed a death purification ceremony by circumcizing his own penis. When his canoes came into view, they were met by a hail of spears and musket balls. Keoua's body was carried to Kukailimoku's altar and Kamehameha was the unopposed sovereign of the Big Island, and within a few years, of all of Hawaii.

Near the heiau is the house site of John Young, an English seaman who became a close adviser to Kamehameha, who dubbed him Olohana, "All Hands." Young taught the Hawaiians how to use cannon and musket and fought alongside Kamehameha in many battles. He turned Mailekini Heiau into a fort, and over a century later it was used during WW II by the Army as an observation area. Young became a respected

Hawaiian chief, and grandfather of Queen Emma. He's one of only two white men buried at the Royal Mausoleum in Nuuanu Valley on Oahu.

Kawaihae Town

The port marks the northern end of the South Kohala coast. Here Route 19 turns eastward toward Waimea, or turns into Route 270 heading up the coast into North Kohala. Kawaihae town is basically utilitarian, with wharfs and fuel tanks. A service cluster has a shop or two and the Harbor Hut, a reasonably priced restaurant in the vicinity (see p. 700).

BEACHES, PARKS, AND CAMPGROUNDS

Anaehoomalu Bay

After becoming transfixed by the monochrome blackness of Kohala's lava flows for almost 30 miles, a standout green of palm trees beckons in the distance. Between mile markers 76 and 77, a well-marked access road heads *makai* to the Royal Waikoloa Hotel and historic **Anaehoomalu Bay.** The bay area, with its freshwater springs, coconut trees, blue lagoon, and white-sand beach, is a picture-perfect seaside oasis. Between the large coconut grove and the beach are two well-preserved fishponds where mullet was raised *only* for consumption by the royalty that lived nearby, or those happening by in seagoing canoes. Throughout the area along well-marked trails are **petroglyphs,** a segment of the cobblestoned **King's Highway,** and numerous archaeological sites including house sites and some hard-to-find burial caves. The white-sand beach is open to the public with access, parking, picnic tables, and showers at the south end. Although the sand is a bit grainy, the swimming, snorkeling, scuba, and windsurfing are fine. Walking north along the bay brings you to an area of excellent tidepools and waters heavily populated by marinelife. The next beach north is at Puako Bay (see p. 694).

Hapuna Beach State Park

Approximately 12 miles north of Anaehoomalu is the second-best, but most accessible white-sand beach on the island. (The best, Kauna'oa, is listed next.) **Camping** is available in six A-frame screened shelters that rent for $7 per night and accommodate up to four. Provided are sleeping platforms (no bedding), electric outlets, cold-water showers, and toilets in separate comfort stations, plus a shared range and refrigerator in a central pavilion. Check in at 2 p.m., check out at 10 a.m. Very popular so reservations and deposit required. Receive full information by contacting the Division of State Parks, Box 936 (75 Aupuni St. to pick up key on arrival), Hilo, HI 96720, tel. 961-7200. There is unofficial camping south along **Waialea Bay** that you can get to by walking or taking the turnoff at mile marker 69. Hapuna Beach is wide and spacious, almost 700 yards long by 70 wide in summer, with a reduction by heavy surf in winter. A lava finger divides the beach into almost equal halves. During good weather the swimming is excellent, but a controversy rages because there is no lifeguard there. During heavy weather, usually in winter, the rips are fierce, and Hapuna has claimed more lives than any other beach park on all of Hawaii! At the north end is a small cove almost forming a pool that is always safe, a favorite with families and children. Many classes in beginning scuba and snorkeling are held in this area, and shore fishing is good throughout. At the south end good breaks make for tremendous bodysurfing (no boards allowed), and those familiar with the area make spectacular leaps from the sea cliffs.

Kauna'oa Beach

Better known as **Mauna Kea Beach** because of the nearby luxury hotel of the same name, Kauna'oa is less than a mile north of Hapuna Beach and is considered to be the best beach on the Big Island. In times past, it was a nesting and mating ground for green sea turtles, and although these activities no longer occur because of human pressure on the habitat, turtles still visit the south end of the beach. Mauna Kea Beach is long and wide, and the sandy bottom makes for excellent swimming. It is more sheltered than Hapuna, but can still be dangerous. Hotel beach boys, always in attendance, are unofficial lifeguards who have saved many unsuspecting tourists. During high surf, the shoreline is a favorite with surfers. All beaches in Hawaii are public, but *access* to this beach was won only by a lawsuit against the Mauna Kea Beach Hotel in 1973. The ruling forced the hotel to open the beach to the public, which they did in the form of

10 parking spaces, a right of way, public shower, and toilet facilities. To keep the number of non-guests down, only 10 parking passes are handed out each day on a first-come first-served basis. Pick them up at the guardhouse as you enter the hotel grounds. These entitle you to spend the day on the beach, but on weekends they're gone by 9:30 a.m. You can wait for someone to leave and then get the pass, but that's unreliable. The hotel also issues a pass for a one-hour visit to the hotel grounds (overstaying results in a $10 fine). You can use this pass to drop off family, friends, beach paraphernalia, and picnic supplies, then return via an easy mile-long **nature trail** connecting Hapuna and Mauna Kea beaches, the route used by the majority of people unable to get a pass. Also, the hotel issues a "food and drink" pass that entitles you to stay as long as you wish, if you get it validated at one of the restaurants or snack bars. So as long as you're in there, you might as well use the beach for the price of a soft drink. In time the hotel will catch on, so test the waters before winding up with a fine.

Spencer County Beach Park

Look for the entrance a minute or two past Pu■ kohola Heiau on Route 19 just before enterin■ Kawaihae. Trails lead from the beach park up ■ the *heiau*, so you can combine a day at th■ beach with a cultural education. The park i■ named after Samuel Mahuka Spencer, a long time island resident who was born in Waime■ served as county mayor for 20 years, and died i■ 1960 at Honokaa. The park provides pavilions■ restrooms, cold-water showers, electricity, pic■ nic facilities, and even tennis courts. Day use i■ free, but tent and trailer **camping** is by count■ permit only, at $1 per day (see p. 580). Spence■ Beach is protected from wind and heavy wave■ action by an offshore reef and by breakwater■ built around Kawaihae Bay. These make it the■ safest and best swimming beach along South Kohala's shore and a favorite with local families with small children. The wide shallow reef is home to a wide spectrum of marinelife, making the snorkeling easy and excellent. The shoreline fishing is also excellent.

PRACTICALITIES

RESORTS AND ACCOMMODATIONS

Except for a few community-oriented restaurants in Waikoloa Village, and a few reasonably priced roadside restaurants in Kawaihae, all of the food in South Kohala is served in the elegant but expensive restaurants of the luxury hotels. These hotels also provide the **entertainment** along the coast, mostly in the form of quiet musical combos and dinner shows. The **shopping**, too, is in the exclusive boutiques found in the hotel lobbies and mini-malls. The following hotels lie along coastal Route 19 and are listed from south to north.

Kona Village Resort

So you want to go "native," and you're dreaming of a "little grass shack" along a secluded beach? No problem! The Kona Village Resort is a once-in-a-lifetime dream experience. Located on Kaupulehu Bay, a picture-perfect cove of white sand dotted with coconut palms, the village lies 15 miles north of Kailua-Kona, surrounded by 12,000 open acres promising seclusion. The accommodations, called "beachcomber hales,"

are individual renditions of thatch-roofed huts found throughout Polynesia. They are simple but luxurious, and in keeping with the idea of getting away from it all have no TVs, radios, or telephones. All, however, do have ceiling fans and louverd windows to let the tropical breezes blow through. Beds are covered with distinctive quilts and pillows, and all huts feature a wet bar, fridge, coffee-making machine, and an extra-large bathroom. Your "do not disturb" sign is a coconut that you place upon your private lanai, and messages are hand delivered and placed in a basket, also on the lanai. At one time you had to fly into the hotel's private airstrip, but today you can arrive by car. You enter by way of an access road that leads through the tortured black lava fields of South Kohala. Don't despair! Down by the sea you can see the shimmering green palm trees as they beckon you to the resort. Kona Village gives you your money's worth, with tennis, ping pong, lei greetings, water sports, and a variety of cocktail parties and luaus. Guided tours are also offered to the many historic sites in the area. Rates start at $255 s, $310 d, which includes a full American plan (three meals). There is a strict reservations and refund policy, so

hale at Kona
Village Resort

check. For information, contact Kona Village Resort, Box 1299, Kailua-Kona, HI 96740, tel. 325-5555 or (800) 367-5290.

Meals are served in the Hale Moana, the main dining room, and at the Halemoana Terrace, where a luncheon buffet is served daily from 12:30-2 p.m. (reservations recommended for dinner). At Hale Ookipa, "House of Hospitality" a luau is held on Friday nights, and a steak-fry every Wednesday. The restaurant facilities are open to non-hotel guests, and cost $20 per person for a buffet lunch.

A public tour is offered weekdays from 11 a.m. that includes a 15-acre petroglyph field on the property that you can inspect if you make prior arrangements. Just show up at the main gate at about 10:50 a.m. and you will be met by a tour guide. The Kona Village has special deals for Hawaii residents that include a 20% discount for senior citizens. The hotel manager is Fred Dewar, who's been at the facility since 1966, along with most of his highly professional and seasoned personnel. They take pride in the hotel, and do everything to help you have a rewarding, enjoyable, and relaxing stay at this premier resort. The Kona Village is a Hawaiian classic that deserves its well-earned reputation for excellence.

The Royal Waikoloan Hotel

The Sheraton chain wanted to enter the luxury hotel market with a splash, so in 1981 they opened the $70-million, 543-room Sheraton Royal Waikoloa Hotel. They found the perfect spot at Anaehoomalu Bay (between mile marker 77-78), and produced a class act. The hotel lobby is a spacious open-air affair, beautifully appointed in koa and objects d'art. All rooms are tastefully decorated and provide a/c, color TV, king-size beds, and a private lanai. Rates begin at $100-155 s/d for a standard, to $250 for a cabana, and $550 for a suite, $15 additional person. For reservations, write: Royal Waikoloan, Box 5000, Waikoloa, HI 96743, tel. 885-6789, Mainland tel. (800) 537-9800. On the superbly kept grounds are six tennis courts, numerous ponds, and a swimming pool. Special features include a small shopping arcade with a dozen or so choice shops, horseback riding, and free shuttle service to Kailua-Kona. There's even a helicopter pad. The focal points, however, are two marvelous golf courses designed by Robert Trent Jones Jr. He learned his trade from his dad, whose masterpiece is just up the road at the Mauna Kea Resort.

You have a choice of dining facilities. The **Garden Room** features American cuisine, open daily for breakfast, lunch, and dinner. The atmosphere is relaxed and the prices are affordable for such a hotel. **The Tiare** offers elegant dining in elegant surroundings for elegant prices. The continental cuisine includes shrimp nouvelle, rack of lamb, lobster, and roast duckling served to the melodious notes of a jazz trio. Open Wed. to Sun. 6:30-10 p.m., tel. 885-6789, reservations recommended. The **Royal Terrace** opens its doors to the sea and provides island or Western entertainment with dinner daily from 6:30-10:30 p.m. Featured are seafood, catch-of-the-day, and prime rib. Expensive.

Hyatt Regency Waikoloa

This newest South Kohala hotel, at tel. 885-1234, or (800) 228-9000, 1 Waikoloa Beach Resort, Waikoloa, HI 96743, bills itself as the "most spectacular resort on Earth." Why limit it to Earth? The idea was to create a reality, so beautiful and naturally harmonious, that anyone who came here, sinner and saint alike, would be guaranteed at least one glimpse of paradise. The architecture, subdued and understated, is linked by salubrious walkways, canals navigated by hotel launches, or by a space-age tram that whispers about the grounds. Sculptures, art treasures, and brilliant flowers soothe the visual senses. Songs of rare tropical birds, and the wind whispering through a bamboo forest create the natural melody that surrounds you. You can swim in a private lagoon accompanied by dolphins, dine in magnificent restaurants, explore surrounding ranchlands, or just let your cares slip away as you lounge in perfect tranquility.

To get there travel north on Route 19 about 15 minutes past the airport. Look for mile marker 76, and turn beachside towards Waikoloa. Follow the roadway through the lava fields until you arrive at the hotel. Valets will park your car. Developer Chris Hemmeter's signature is obvious. The architecture is "fantasy grand," and attention to the smallest detail is immediately apparent. Elevators are done in rich woods and burnished brass. Cigarette receptacles, which are actually large pots from Asia or ceramic dolphins with mouths agape, are filled with black sand. An alcove may hold a dozen superbly hand-carved puppets from Indonesia. Halls are bedecked with chandeliers, marble-topped tables, and immense floral displays. Rooms are luxurious, and pampering is complete. In the evening a silver plate arrives. On it are three truffles rolled in nuts, and a small conch shell made of white chocolate. Two mini bottles hold macadamia and coffee liqueur. Turn-down service brings more chocolate, flowers, and a Hawaiian legend card. Fluffy robes, and Japanese *yukata* are provided in every room.

The three main buildings, the Lagoon, Palace, and Ocean towers, are spread over the grounds almost a mile apart. Each encloses a central courtyard that's a miniature botanical garden filled with ferns and populated by exotic birds. A bubbling fountain with sculpted mermaids and frolicking children is the centerpiece. Walkways, if you opt not to ride the launches or tram, are pink flagstone, and here and there are matching flocks of pink flamingos. At every main junction, and in every nook and cranny, is statuary, mostly of a Buddhist theme. The beach fronting the property offers excellent snorkeling, while three gigantic pools complete with waterslides, and a series of lagoons are perfect for water activities and sunbathing.

A museum promenade joins the main towers. Walk slowly to savor the artwork as one theme flows into the next. Start with the Hawaiiana collection of carved *koa* bowls and feather leis. Next comes carvings from Thailand, paintings from Japan, and porcelains from China. Fantastic pots, taller than a man, are topped with two handles of gold elephant faces and tusks. Look through archways at perfectly framed grottoes harboring *koi* ponds and waterfalls. Sit on royal thrones and benches next to intricately carved credenzas and tables and simply delight at the beauty.

The hotel's restaurants are culinary extravaganzas. **Waters Edge** is formal, serving continental cuisine; **Donatello's** features classic Italian; **Cascades** is a Polynesian buffet; **Imari** serves traditional Japanese fare; **Kona Provision Co.** specializes in steak and seafood and then there's the hotel's bars, lounges, and casual poolside dining options which are all amazingly moderately priced. Every taste is accounted for.

Take the amazing "Behind the House" tour of this facility (free). You are led below ground, deep into the heart of the hotel, where you get to see how everything works. An underground service roadway, complete with stop signs and traffic cops, runs for a over a mile and is traveled by employees on bicycles and motorized utility carts. As you pass offices with signs that read Wildlife Director, Curator of Art, Astronomer, you come to realize how distinctive an undertaking the hotel really is. Next come the florist shop, the butcher, the baker, and the laundry with more output than any other laundry in the state of Hawaii (22 pounds of linen go in each Hyatt room). There's Wardrobe, responsible for outfitting the myriad employees: *lava lava* for bellmen, brocaded white uniforms for the launch skippers, evening wear for hosts and hostesses, and uniforms for everyone from the spa's masseuses to airport greeters. The hotel's 2,000 employee's arrive from their own parking lot on a bus equipped with a video that tells "what's happening" at the hotel on that day. You're given staggering figures: 750,000 gallons of fresh water is needed for the pools; over 18 million gallons of seawater is pumped through the canals on a daily basis; each motor launch costs $300,000; the 41 chandeliers weigh over 24 tons; the hotel's 300 computers are linked by over 28 miles of cable. On and on, the statistics match the magnificence of what you see.

With all this splendor, still the most talked-about activity at the hotel is **Dolphin Quest.** A specially constructed saltwater pond, 65 times larger than federal regulations require, contains 2½ million gallons of naturally filtered sea water. The pond, home to Atlantic bottlenose dolphins, is 22 feet deep in the center and 350 feet from end to end. Daily, on a lottery basis, guests are chosen to "interact with the dolphins." The program was founded by two highly respected marine veterinarians, Dr. Jay Sweeney and Dr. Rae Stone, both prominent in their field for protecting and preserving marine mammals. It was their idea to bring a new experience to the public in which the interaction was from the dolphin's point of view rather than a stadium-type setting where dolphins were performers and the people spectators. They wanted to create something more natural so that the dolphins would enjoy the experience as much as the people. The dolphins come from Florida's Gulf Coast panhandle, where they're found in bays and lagoons living most of their lives in water six to 20 feet deep. Much of the proceeds from the program goes toward marine research. Recently, a team from the University of Santa Cruz was housed, funded, and provided with boats to investigate a way to save the more than 100,000 spinner dolphins that are caught in tuna nets every year. At the facility, there's no riding dolphins, and they don't do tricks for people. Dolphin Quest is trying to steer the program away from the concept of "swimming with dolphins," and more toward an educational experience. In the half-hour session, typically 10 minutes are spent in the free pool, where people wade in chest-deep water with the dolphins gliding by. If they want to be petted they stop, if not they move past like a torpedo. The rest of the time is spent on the dock, where you are given information concerning not only dolphins, but all marinelife and man's interdependence with it. The experience is voluntary on the dolphins' part, and in actuality they choose to swim with you as a guest in their domain.

This futuristic and fantastic hotel complex has set a new standard against which all future resorts will be measured. Like a beautiful young debutante, it has all the graces necessary to be not only a raving beauty, but a complete and actualized woman. Experience and time is an ally that will surely mature the Hyatt Regency Waikoloa into one of the finest resorts on Earth.

Mauna Lani Resort And Golf Club

Marvel at this exclusive hotel in the center of the gorgeous **Francis I'i Brown Golf Course,** whose artistically laid out fairways, greens, and sand traps make it a modern landscape sculpture. The course is carved from lava, with striking ocean views in every direction. It's not a tough course, though it measures 6,813 yards, par 72. Green fees are expensive, with preferred starting times given to hotel guests. (Call the Pro Shop at tel. 882-7255 for more information.) As soon as you turn off Route 19, the entrance road, trimmed in purple bougainvillea, begins to set the mood for this 70-million dollar, 350-room hotel that opened in 1983. The emphasis was placed on relaxation and luxury, as each oversized room, the majority with an ocean view, cost an average of $200,000 each, the most ever spent per unit in Hawaii. The hotel has a tennis garden with 10 courts, a lovely beach and lagoon area, a health spa, exclusive shops, and swimming pools. The Mauna Lani's rooms begin at $260. For full information, contact: Mauna Lani Bay Hotel, Box 4000, Kawaihae HI, 96743, tel. 885-6622 or (800) 367-2323, in Hawaii tel. (800) 992-7987.

The **Third Floor Restaurant** (actually on the ground floor) is patterned after the gourmet restaurant of the same name in Waikiki, and its imaginative French cuisine is *magnifique,* along with the prices. You can dine from a noteworthy menu at slightly lower prices at the **Bay Terrace.** A superb bistro owned by Herman Miller, named **HFM,** is just off the main lobby. Mr. Miller has been a collector of Chinese art since the '30s, and displayed here are museum-quality pieces from his personal collection. Mr. Miller also showcases the woodwork of Billy Parks, a former pro football player who has turned his hand to creating exquisite Oriental furniture. All pieces are handmade and connected by traditional intricate joinery.

The Mauna Kea Beach Resort

This hotel has set the standard of excellence along Kohala's coast ever since former Hawaii Governor William Quinn interested Lawrence Rockefeller in the lucrative possibilities of building a luxury hideaway for the rich and famous. Beautiful coastal land was leased from the Parker Ranch, and the resort opened in 1965. The Mauna Kea was the only one of its kind for a few years until the other luxury hotels were built along this coast. It's getting a bit older, and getting stiff competition from newer nearby luxury resorts, but class is always class and the Mauna Kea receives very high accolades as a fine resort.

The hotel's classic, trendsetting **golf course** designed by the master, Robert Trent Jones, has been voted among America's 100 greatest courses and as Hawaii's finest. Also, *Tennis Magazine* includes the hotel among the "50 greatest U.S. tennis resorts." The hotel itself is an eight-story terraced complex of simple, clean-cut design. The grounds and lobbies showcase over 1,000 museum-quality art pieces from throughout the Pacific, and over a half-million plants add greenery and beauty to the surroundings. The landings and lobbies, open and large enough to hold full-grown palm trees, also display beautiful tapestries, bird cages with their singing captives, and huge copper pots on polished brick floors. The Mauna Kea offers a modified American plan (breakfast and dinner), the best beach on the island, and its own catamaran for seagoing adventure. The hotel has become such a landmark that tour buses visit its grounds daily. There's no charge for looking around. Million-dollar condos grace the grounds, and guests tend to come back year after year. The beautifully appointed rooms, starting at $230 s, $300 d, $75 extra person, are free of TVs and phones, but feature an extra-large lanai and specially made wicker furniture. For full information contact Mauna Kea Beach Hotel, Box 218, Kamuela, HI 96743, tel. 882-7222 or (800) 228-3000.

Sumptuous dining is presented in the three-level **Dining Pavilion,** and in the **Batik Room,** where French, Italian, German, and Island delicacies create an international gastronomical symphony. There's also a weekly luau in the North Garden.

Puako Beach Apartments

Puako village has the only reasonably priced accommodations in this diamond-studded neck of the woods. The 38 modern units start from $50 to $120 (four bedrooms), $5 extra person. All units have a kitchen, laundry facilities, lanai, and twice-weekly maid service. There is ample parking, TV, and a swimming pool. Write Puako Beach Apartments, 3 Puako Beach Dr., Kamuela, HI 96743, tel. 882-7711.

FOOD AND SHOPPING

Kawaihae Center

The Kawaihae Shopping Center can take care of your rudimentary shopping needs. It sits at the Y-junction of Routes 19 and 270 and is so situated that the upper floors face Route 19 and the lower floors are along Route 270. There's a **7-eleven** convenience store, an ice cream store, and restaurants on the lower level (see following).

Across the road is a **Chevron gas station,** and **Kawaihae General Store,** open 7 a.m.-9 p.m. Mon.-Sat., and 7 a.m.-6 p.m. Sunday, that sells groceries, dry goods, beer, fishing supplies, beachwear, and also serves breakfast and lunch. Next door is the **Harbor Gallery,** filled with antiques and arts of Hawaii.

Kohala Divers, along Route 270 in Kawaihae, open daily 8 a.m.-5 p.m., tel. 882-7774, offers scuba certification for $250, snorkel rentals for $10 (24 hours), and scuba rentals for $22. They do two-tank dives for $65, and will take snorkelers along if they have room on the boat. It's a bit far to go from Kailua-Kona but it's a big savings, and the only dive company along the Kohala coast.

Harbor Hut Restaurant

This downhome restaurant, open for breakfast Saturday and Sunday only 7:30-11 a.m., lunch 11 a.m.-2:30 p.m., lounge open from 2:30 p.m.-closing, dinner from 5:30-9 p.m., tel. 882-7783, is located in Kawaihae, on the right-hand side of Route 270 heading north. This restaurant serves everything from takeout sandwiches for a few dollars to sit-down dinners for not much more. The garden out back, with umbrella-covered picnic tables, offers a relaxing place to dine, especially after a sunny day on the beach. The service is friendly but slow. Notice a shelf with "99 bottles of beer on the wall" from which you can choose. The beers come from the U.S., Samoa, China, Japan, the Philippines, Australia, Czechoslovakia, Belgium, Holland, Norway, Italy, France, Ireland, Scotland, and Germany. They even have some beers like Samuel Smith Oatmeal Stout from England for $5.95. Luncheon sandwiches (daily specials $4) include blue water *mahi* burgers for $6.95, seaman's club sandwich at $4.95, and a shrimp boat for $7.50. Happy hour daily from 3-6 p.m. features *pupu* and $.99 draft beer. The evening menu is complete with items like shrimp cocktail for $8.95, fresh catch market price, *mahi mahi* sauté for $10.95, deep-fried shrimp, $13.95, N.Y. steak, $10.95, and a few basic Chinese meals for under $12.

Jinho's

This plate-lunch restaurant, in Kawaihae along Route 270, open Mon.-Fri. 6 a.m.-5 p.m., Sat. 7 a.m.-5 p.m., closed Sun., is an old plantation house where you're welcome to sit on the front porch and eat your meal, all for under $5. It's funky, but real, as the local scene slowly strolls by.

Cafe Pesto/We're Talkin' Pizza

Who'd expect a yuppy upscale restaurant, open 11 a.m.-9 p.m. Sun.-Thurs., 11 a.m.-10 p.m. Fri. and Sat., in the sleepy village of Kawaihae? Cafe Pesto's interior design is chic with black-and-white checkerboard flooring and black-and-white tables. The bold gourmet menu tantalizes with Cajun shrimp and sausage sandwich for $4.95, Greek pasta salad, and *ceviche* pasta with cilantro pesto for $4.50. Cafe Pesto also serves gourmet pizza with the crust and sauces made fresh daily. Among their best pizzas are *shitake* mushrooms and artichokes with rosemary and garganzola sauce, seafood pesto pizza, or pizza luau, all ranging in price from $5.95 for a small to $16.95 for a large (also served by the slice for $2). Cafe Pesto is *the* perfect place to stop for a civilized lunch as you explore the Kohala coast.

Almost next door is **Polihale Bar and Nightclub,** which is a local hangout where you can order a cold beer and listen to live music on most weekends.

screw pine

WAIMEA (KAMUELA)

Boundary-wise, **Waimea** is in South Kohala. Because of its inland topography of high mountain pasture, mostly covering Mauna Kea's western slopes, Waimea could be considered a district in its own right. Also, it has a unique culture inspired by the range-riding *paniolo* of the expansive **Parker Ranch.** This spread, founded early last century by John Palmer Parker, dominates the heart and soul of the region. Waimea revolves around ranch life and livestock. A herd of rodeos and "Wild West shows" are scheduled throughout the year. But a visit here isn't one-dimensional. In town are home accommodations and inspired country dining. For fun and relaxation there's a visitors and ranch center; Puuopelu, the Parker mansion and art collection; a wonderful museum operated by John Parker's great-great grandaughter and her husband; a litany of historic shrines and churches; and a fresh-air abundance of wide-open spaces not so easily found in the islands.

The town is split almost directly down the center—the east side is the wet side, and the west is the dry side. Houses on the east side are easy to find and reasonable to rent; houses on the dry side are expensive and usually unavailable. You can literally walk from verdant green fields and tall trees to dry desert in a matter of minutes. This imaginary line also demarcates the local twofold social order: upper-class ranch managers (dry), and working class *paniolo* (wet). However, the air of Waimea, refreshed and cooled by fine mists *(kipuupuu),* combines with only 20 inches of rainfall a year into the best mountain weather in Hawaii. Waimea is equally known as **Kamuela,** the Hawaiianized version of Samuel, after one of John Parker's grandsons. Kamuela is used as the post office address, so as not to confuse Waimea with a town of the same name on the island of Kauai. The village is experiencing a growth spurt. In 1980 it had no traffic lights and was home to about 2,000 people. Now the population has grown fivefold and there are traffic jams. Waimea is modernizing, and it's cowboy backwoods character is rapidly changing.

Getting There
The main artery connecting Waimea and Kailua-Kona is Route 190, also known as the Hawaiian Belt Road. This stretch is locally called the Mamalahoa Highway. From Kailua-Kona, head out Palani Road until it turns into Route 190. As you gain elevation heading into the interior, look left to see the broad and flat coastal lava flows.

Seven miles before reaching Waimea, Saddle Road (Route 200) intersects from the right, and now the highlands, with grazing cattle amidst fields of cactus, look much more like Marlboro Country than the land of aloha. The Saddle Road and Route 19, connecting Waimea with Hilo and points east, have been fully described on p. 611 and p. 691. The **Waimea-Kohala Airport,** tel. 885-4520, is along Route 190 just a mile or so before entering town. Facilities amount to a basic restroom and waiting area with a few car-rental windows. Unless a flight is scheduled, even these are closed. For a description of Route 250 leading to Kapaau and Hawi on the coast, see p. 712.

SIGHTS

HISTORIC HOMES AND ART COLLECTION AT PUUOPELU

Richard Smart, heir to the fantastic Parker Ranch, has opened Puuopelu, his century-old mansion, to the public. Inside this living museum over 100 prominent artists are displayed, including works by Degas, Renoir, and Chagall. On the grounds, original and reconstructed Parker Ranch homes are also open to visitors. Puuopelu is located along Route 190 a few minutes south of town and is open daily from 9:30 a.m.-4:30 p.m., admission $5 adults, $2.50 children.

A formal drive lined with stately eucalyptus leads to the mansion. Enter an elegant sitting room illuminated by a crystal chandelier to begin your tour. The home was begun in 1852 by John Palmer Parker II. In 1910 Richard Smart's grandmother, Aunt Tootsie, added the living room, kitchen, and fireplace. In 1969 Richard Smart, who inherited the ranch lands and home from Aunt Tootsie, gutted it and raised the ceiling to 19 feet to accommodate his art collection. He added elegant French doors and skylights. Part of the kitchen was converted into a dining room, the Gold Room was created, and the *koa* doorways were raised to match. Richard Smart became a well-known actor. He studied at the Pasadena Playhouse in the late '20s, and appeared on Broadway with famous names such as Carol Channing and Nannette Fabray. Mr. Smart has performed in plays all over the U.S., and to top it off sings in Italian, French, and Spanish, with renditions of songs in these languages providing the background music as you tour the art collection. You've heard of actors becoming ranchers; well, he was a rancher that became an actor. The tour is self-guided with all art pieces named. Besides works of famous artists, there are magnificent pieces like a tall wooden cabinet with carved yellow Chinese Peiping glass from the 19th century, silver tea sets, decanters for pouring wine at elegant functions, large cut crystal punch bowls, and the skylights overhead hung with magnificent chandeliers. Make sure to see the little side bedroom, called the Venetian Room, aptly decorated with paintings of gondolas and appointed with treasures all from Venice. Lighting the room are two chandeliers, one pink and the other torquoise. Here, the filigreed art-deco mirrors are also fabulous. The feeling is one of genteel elegance, but notice that the walls are rather rough board and battten covered with beautiful art works. You get a feeling of class, but it's obvious that you are on a ranch. In the emerald green kingdom that is the Parker Ranch, Puuopelu is the crowning jewel.

Just outside Puuopelu is the reconstructed **Mana Home** (admission included), the original Parker Ranch homestead. A knowledgeable tour guide, Mr. Ed, leads you through and provides historical anecdotes about the Parker family. The home was built in 1847 by family patriarch John Palmer Parker from the durable native *koa* found at high elevations on the ranch lands. The exterior of the original home, covered by a heavy slate roof, was too brittle to move from it's original site 12 miles away, but the interior was removed, numbered, and put back together again like a giant jigsaw puzzle in the reconstructed home. A photo in the living room shows you what the original site looked like back in the 1800s. To preserve the rich wood interior of the home, all that's required is to wipe it down once a year with lemon oil. A collection of fine calabashes handed down over the generations is on display. At first the home seems like a small cabin, just what you'd expect from the 1850s, but in actuality it's a two-story home with one bedroom downstairs and three upstairs.

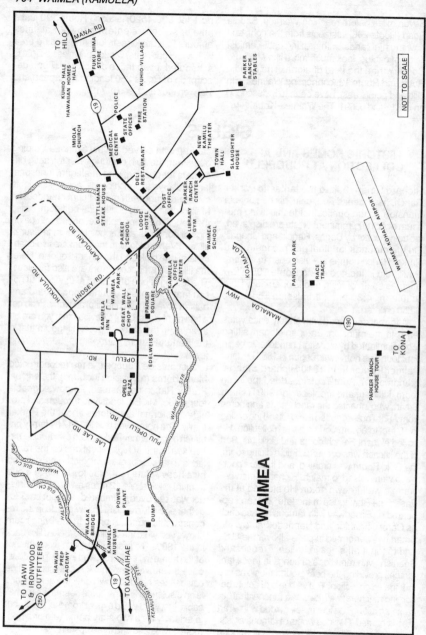

NOT TO SCALE

WAIMEA

The Parker dynasty began (see Parker Ranch Visitor Center following for more information) when John Palmer Parker jumped ship and married Kipikani, the granddaughter of Kamehameha. They bought two acres of land for $10, and Parker with his two sons built the Mana Home. In later years Kipikani, being the granddaughter of the king, received 640 acres. The two sons, John Palmer Parker II and Ebenezer, who were by then married, built two homes on it, and as children came, added more rooms in the sprawling New England tradition. They also built one large community kitchen, at which the entire family cooked and dined. A replica shows how the home grew over the years, and it is a good indicator of how the Parker fortunes grew along with it. As the children's children got older, they needed a schoolhouse, so they built one at the corner of the original site. It still stands and is maintained by a *paniolo* and his family who live there. Unfortunately, many members of the Parker Family died young. The first-born, John Palmer Parker II, married Hanai. His brother, Ebenezer, married Kilea, a woman from Maui, who bore him four children. One of their boys was Samuel Parker, known in Hawaiian as Kamuela, the co-name of Waimea. Samuel married Napela, and together they had nine children. Samuel's father Ebenezer died at age 26 after swallowing a flubber bone (a little bird the size of a pigeon) that punctured his intestine. Kilea could never get over his death and visited his grave daily. Finally, she decided that she wanted to return to her family on Maui. She was advised by the people of the island not to go because of rough seas. Kilea did not heed the advice, and along with her entourage was lost at sea. Meanwhile, John Palmer Parker II and Hanai gave birth to only one boy who died within 12 months. Childless, they adopted one of their nephew Samuel's nine children as a *hanai* child, a practice that continues to this day. He was the fifth child, John, who became John Palmer Parker III and who later married Elizabeth Dowsick, known as Aunt Tootsie. They had one girl, Thelma Parker, before John III died of pneumonia at age 19. Aunt Tootsie raised Thelma as a single parent, and somehow managed to purchase Samuel Parker's and his eight children's half of the ranch. Thelma Parker married Gillian Smart. They had one boy, Mr. Richard Smart, the present owner, before his mother Thelma

died at age 20 of tuberculosis. Aunt Tootsie, literally and figuratively, took the bull by the horns, kept the ranch going, and when she passed away in 1943 left everything to her grandson Richard. The ranch prospered under his ownership and spread to its present 225,000 acres with 50,000 head of cattle that supplies fully one-third of the beef in all the Hawaiian Islands.

Ranch Tours
The Parker Ranch also offers a variety of tours throughout the ranch lands in comfortable vans. The grand tour is the **Paniolo Country Tour,** two departures daily 9 a.m. to 1 p.m., and noon to 4 p.m., allow four hours, lunch included, reservations recommended, $38 adult, $19 children (rough road so heavy rains cancel the tour), which includes admission to the visitors center and Puuopelu. The tour takes you 12 miles up the mountain to the original two-acre home site where the ranch actually began. Here you'll see the outside structure of the Mana Home, outbuildings, the old school house, and the Parker family graveyard. There's a **Paniolo Shuttle Tour,** daily every 20 minutes from 9 a.m. to 3 p.m., allow one-two hours, for $15 adults, $7.50 children, visitors center and Puuopelu included, that provides an overview of the Parker Ranch. The ranch also offers horseback riding through the Mauna Kea Stables at $25 per hour, and helicopter tours through Mauna Kea Helicopters. Information and reservations for all of the above can be made by calling **Parker Ranch Tours** at tel. 885-7655.

SIGHTS IN TOWN

Parker Ranch
Visitors Center And Museum
This is the first place to stop while in town. The center is open daily from 9 a.m. until 5 p.m., tel. 885-7655, adults $4, children $2 (joint admission to Puuopelu available, see above). After spending an hour at the center's two museums and taking in the slide presentation, you'll have a good overview of the history of the Parker Ranch, and by extension, Waimea. The **John Palmer Parker Museum**'s exhibits depict the history and genealogy of the six generations of Parkers who have owned the ranch. At the entrance is a photo of the founder, John Parker, a seaman who left Newton, Massachusetts, on a

trading vessel in 1809 and landed in Keala-kekua, becoming a fast friend of Kamehameha the Great. Parker, then only 19, continued his voyages, returning in 1814 and marrying Kipi-kane, a chieftess and close relative of Kameha-meha. In the interim, domesticated cattle, a present from Capt. Vancouver to Kamehameha, had gone wild due to neglect and were becoming a dangerous nuisance all over the Big Island. Parker was hired to round up the best of them and to exterminate the rest. While doing so, he chose the finest head for his own herd. In 1847 King Kamehameha III divided the land by what was known as the Great *Mahele,* and John Parker was granted Royal Deed No. 7, for a two-acre parcel on the northeast slopes of Mauna Kea. His wife, being noble born, was entitled to 640 acres, and with these lands and tough determination, the mighty 225,000-acre Parker Ranch began. It remains the largest privately owned ranch in the U.S., and on its fertile pastures over 50,000 cattle and 1,000 horses are raised.

In the museum old family photos include one of Rev. Elias Bond who presided over a Christian marriage for Parker and his Hawaiian wife in 1820. Preserved also are old Bibles, clothing from the era, and an entire *koa* hut once occupied by woodcutters and range riders. There are fine examples of quilting, stuffed animals, an arsenal of old weapons, and even a vintage printing press. A separate room is dedicated to **Duke Kahanamoku,** the great Hawaiian Olympian and "Father of Modern Surfing." Inside are paddles he used, his bed and dresser, legions of medals, cups, and trophies he won, and even Duke's walking sticks. The 15-minute video in the comfortable **Thelma Parker Theater** begins whenever enough people have assembled after going through the museum. The video presents a thorough and professional rendition of the Parker Ranch history, along with sensitive glimpses of ranch life of the still very active *pani-olo.* It is narrated by Richard Smart, professional actor and heir to the Parker Ranch. The last lines of the narration conclude, "Over the better part of two centuries the main ingredient of the Parker Ranch success story is people. An open road lies ahead in the future progress and development of this ranch. Together we strive to fulfill my great-great-great-grandfather's vigil

and dream, and perpetuate the traditions of Hawaii for a long time to come."

Imiola Church

Head east on Route 19 to "church row," a cluster of New England-style structures on the left, a few minutes past the Parker Ranch Center. Most famous among them is Imiola ("Seeking Life") Church. It was built in 1857 by the Rev. Lorenzo Lyons, who mastered the Hawaiian language and translated some of the great old Christian hymns into Hawaiian, as well as melodic Hawaiian chants into English. The current minister is a friendly and urbane man, Rev. Bill Hawk, a new arrival who is assisted by his wife Sandra. The yellow clapboard church with white trim would be at home along any New England village green. When you enter, there is an oddity: the pulpit is at the near side and you walk around it to face the rear of the church. The walls and ceilings are of rich brown *koa,* but the pews, supposedly of the same lustrous wood, have been painted pink! The hymnals contain many of the songs translated by Father Lyons. Outside is a simple monument to Rev. Lyons, along with a number of gravesites of his children. A tour of the church is free, and definitely worth the time.

Kamuela Museum

The Kamuela Museum, largest privately owned museum in Hawaii, is a fantastic labor of love. For the septuagenarian owners, founders, and curators, Albert and Harriet Solomon, it's a vocation that began in 1968 and fulfilled a prophecy of Albert's grandmother, who was pure Hawaiian and a renowned *kahuna* from Pololu Valley. When Albert was only eight years old, his grandmother foretold that he would build "a great longhouse near three mountains and that he would become famous, visited by people from all over the world." This prediction struck him so much that he wrote it down and kept it throughout his life. When grown, he married Harriet, the great-great granddaughter of John Palmer Parker, and the two lived in Honolulu for most of their adult lives, where Albert was a policeman. For 50 years the Solomon's collected, collected, and collected! Also Harriet, being a Parker, inherited many family heirlooms from the Ranch, while other family members gave her items to exhibit. The museum is west of town center on Route 19—50 yards after the junction with Route 250 heading toward Hawi. An HVB Warrior, facing in the wrong direction, marks the spot. The museum, dedicated to Mary Ann Parker, John Parker's only daughter, is open every day of the year from 8 a.m. to 5 p.m., tel. 885-4724, admission $2, children under 12, $1.00.

As you enter, the screen door purposefully bangs like a shot to signal Albert and Harriet that another visitor has arrived. Mrs. Solomon directs you through the museum, almost like a stern "schoolmarm" who knows what's best for you, but actually she's a sweetheart who has plenty of time for her guests and is willing to "talk story." Inside it's easy to become overwhelmed as you're confronted with everything from sombreros to a stuffed albatross, moose head, and South American lizard. An extensive weapons collection includes Khyber rifles, Japanese machine guns, swords, and knives. If you enjoy Hawaiiana, there's *kahili* and *konane* boards, poi pounders, stone sinkers and hooks, wooden surfboards, and heavy stones, like bowling balls, used to test strength. Antiques of every description include Japanese and Hawaiian feathered fans, carved Chinese furniture, an antique brass diving helmet, and even buffalo robes used by the pioneers. And everywhere are old photos commemorating the lives of the Parkers down through the years. Before you leave go into the back room, where the view through a huge picture window perfectly frames a pond and a remarkable slice of *paniolo* country.

PRACTICALITIES

ACCOMMODATIONS

As far as staying in Waimea is concerned, you won't be plagued with indecision. Of the two hotels in town, both are basic and clean, one inexpensive and the other upscale.

Kamuela Inn is your basic cinderblock, 19-unit motel located down a small cul-de-sac on Route 19 just before Opelu Road. Quiet clean rooms with a large bath go for $44, $55 with kitchenette. If no one is at the office, go to room eight. There is usually no problem finding a vacancy. Write Kamuela Inn, Box 1994, Kamuela, HI 96743, tel. 885-4516.

The Parker Ranch Lodge is located along Linsey Road in "downtown" Waimea, but don't let "downtown" fool you because it's very quiet. The rooms are called junior suites, and all have kitchenettes, vaulted ceilings, and full baths. The suites are well-appointed with rich brown carpeting, large writing desks, two easy chairs, phones, and TVs. The brown board-and-batten inn sits off by itself and lives up to being in paniolo country by giving the impression of being a gentleman's bunkhouse. Rates are $57 standard, $70 deluxe, $8 additional person with some kitchenettes available. For information write Parker Ranch Lodge, Box 458, Kamuela, HI 96743, tel. 885-4100.

FOOD

Inexpensive/Moderate

One of the cheapest places in Waimea to get good standard American food is the **Kamuela Drive-In Deli.** This no-nonsense eatery, frequented by local people, is next door to the Parker Ranch Center. They get the folks in these parts started at 5 a.m. with a hearty breakfast for a few dollars. Plate lunches of teriyaki beef and the like sell for $3-5. If you're into food and not atmosphere, this is the place.

Kamuela Deli is on Route 19 just past the Parker Visitors Center on the right. They too serve basic American/Oriental/Hawaiian plate lunches and sandwiches from $2-5.

To get to the **Cramped Quarters Cafe,** continue on Route 19 toward Hilo, passing church row. You'll see a blinking light and a Dairy Queen on the left. On the right is the cafe, tel. 885-5066, serving pizza and a good selection of Mexican food.

Auntie Alice's is a small restuarant in the Parker Ranch Shopping Center serving homemade pies and breakfast for under $4, with hefty sandwiches around $5.

Massayo's is another basic eatery open daily 5 a.m. to 3 p.m., where you can get hearty breakfasts and plate lunches with an Oriental twist for $4-5. It's in the Hayashi Building near the Kamuela Inn along Route 19 heading west out of town.

For mid-range fare try **Great Wall Chop Suey** near the Kamuela Inn on Route 19. Its appealing selection of standard Chinese dishes range from $4 to $6. This restaurant is open Tues. to Thurs. 11 a.m. to 8:30 p.m., Fri. to Sun. 11 a.m. to 9 p.m., closed Mon., tel. 885-7252.

The **Cattleman's Steakhouse,** tel. 885-4077, along Route 19 heading east, is a terrific place to soak up the local scene and to enjoy basic but hearty food. Recently renovated, the menu is steak and more steak, all from the Parker Ranch. Daily from Tuesday through Saturday, they have the *Pau Hana* Relaxer, happy hour, live music, and *pu pu* from 7 p.m.-closing. A great place to go native.

Fine Dining

One of the best benefits of Waimea's coming of age is a number of excellent restaurants that have recently opened. The competition is stiff, so all try to find their culinary niche in preparing gourmet foods.

The **Edelweiss** on Route 19 across from the Kamuela Inn is Waimea's established gourmet restaurant, where chef Hans-Peter Hager, formerly of the super-exclusive Mauna Kea Beach Hotel, serves gourmet food in rustic but elegant surroundings. The Edelweiss is open daily except Mon. from 11:30 a.m. to 2 p.m., and for dinner from 5:30 p.m., tel. 885-6800. Inside, heavy posts and beams exude that "country feeling," but fine crystal and pure-white tablecloths let you know you're in for some superb dining. The wine cellar is quite extensive, with selections of domestic, French, Italian, and German wines. Affordable lunches include offerings like soup, turkey sandwiches, and chicken salad in papaya for under $7. Dinner starts with melon with prosciutto at $4.75, escargot for $5.75, onion soup at $3.75, and Caesar salad for $3.75. Some Edelweiss specialties are sautéed veal, lamb, beef, and bacon with pfefferling for $13.75, roast duck braised with a light orange sauce at $14.50, half spring chicken diablo, $12.50, and of course German favorites like Wiener schnitzel at $13.50, and roast pork and sauerkraut for $12.50. The cooking is rich and delicious, proved by a loyal clientele who returns again and again.

Gentlemen ranchers love **The Parker Ranch Restaurant,** open daily for lunch and dinner, tel. 885-7366, in the Parker Ranch Center. Put on your best duds and sashay into the cushy red velvet saloon, or into the tasteful *koa*-panelled main dining area. The chef, Al Salvador, chooses the best cuts of Parker Ranch beef to create a variety of savory meat dishes starting from $12. There's also clam chowder for $2.75, steak sandwiches for $7.50, *Paniolo* burgers, $3.95, Korean short ribs, $4.95, grilled cheese sandwich, $2.45, and spinach salad for $3.95. Even if you don't dine here, it's worth a trip to the bar just for the atmosphere.

To arrive at the newly opened **Bree Garden Restaurant,** reminiscent of a 1930s roadhouse, head east on Route 19 and look for the Circle-K convenience store with the restaurant just behind, open 4:30-9:30 p.m., tel. 885-5888, reservations recommended. Outside a small courtyard filled with cactus frames an East Indian banyan. Inside are glass covered pillars, pink tablecloths under formal settings, and chairs of bent bamboo and wicker with nice comfy fat cushions. The unique leather menu, made by Chef Bree's brother, a well-known leather craftsman from his native Germany, includes *sashimi* for $5.50, angel hair pasta marinara $6, and Korean wonton soup with chicken broth at $3.50. Salads are $4, with a large fresh salad platter available as a main course for $9.50. Chef Bree specializes in fresh fish and pasta with sauces and garnishes made daily from scratch. Entrees are fresh catch $19, prawns amaretto $19.75, chicken breast curry $17, and roast prime rib for $20. The food is complemented by an extensive wine list including varietals from California, France, Germany, and Italy.

Merriman's, tel. 885-6822, open for Sunday brunch 10:30 a.m.-1:30 p.m., lunch daily from 11:30 a.m.-1:30 p.m., dinner 5:30-9 p.m., in the Opelo Shopping Center along Route 19, has been receiving a great deal of praise from travelers and residents alike for its excellent food. The restaurant, like a small house from the outside, is stylish with pink and gray tablecloths, multicolored Fiestaware settings, and black- or pink-cushioned chairs of bent bamboo. Chef Peter Merriman creates classical European and American haute cuisine from local ingredients like Kohala lamb, Parker Ranch beef, Waimea lettuce, Puna goat cheese, and vine-ripened tomatoes. The menu changes every few months, but perennial lunch favorites are onion soup for $3.50, grilled *mahi mahi* with lemon butter for $6.75, turkey sandwich on a croissant for $4.25, and Caesar salad priced at $4.75. Dinner selections offer appetizers like smoked salmon linguini for $5.75, and entrees of veal medallions in mushroom and marsala sauce for $19.50, shepherd's pie, $12.50, seafood sausage, chicken, fish, and shellfish in a saffron sauce at $18.50, and Thai-style shrimp curry for $18.50. Merriman's is destined to become a Big Island classic. Enjoy!

SHOPPING

Shops And Boutiques

Waimea's accelerated growth can be measured by the shopping centers that are springing up around town. One new center, still under construction across from the Parker Ranch Center, has some people concerned, as it will surround the Spencer House, a classical home from the ranch period. People were not thrilled when this area was denuded of its stately trees to accommodate the shopping center.

There is shopping in and around town, but the greatest concentration of shops is at the **Parker Ranch Center,** with over 30 specialty stores selling shoes, apparel, sporting goods, toys, and food. The **Paddock Shop** sells boots, cowboy hats, shirts, skirts, and buckles and bows. There are many handcrafted items made on the premises. Open daily, tel. 885-4977. **Setay,** a unique fine jewelry shop, sells china, crystal, silver, and gold, tel. 885-4127. Here too you'll find **Ben Franklin's,** for sundries, **Value Right Pharmacy,** for prescriptions and toiletries, **Keep In Touch,** with books and stationary, and **Honolulu Sporting Goods,** to name a just a few.

Around town try: **Waimea Design Center** along Route 19, tel. 885- 6171, offering Oriental handicrafts and Hawaiian *koa* bowls and furniture; **Waimea Sand Box,** where you'll find books, handmade baskets, *koa* artifacts, and maps, tel. 885-4737, on Route 19; **Suzumi,** selling fine women's apparel from around the world, at the Ironwood Center, Route 19, tel. 885-6422. **The Warehouse** is a small shopping complex whose specialty shops sell books, coffees, spices, flowers, and alohawear, tel. 885-7905. **Nikko Natural Fabrics** will dress you in cottons, woolens, and silks, and adorn your walls with batiks and fine fiber arts, tel. 885-7661, in the Kamuela Country Plaza.

Parker Square Shopping Mall, along Route 19 heading west, has a collection of fine boutiques and shops. Here, the **Gallery of Great Things,** tel. 885-7706, open 9 a.m.-5 p.m., Mon.-Sat., really is loaded with grest things. Inside you'll find novelty items like a carousel horse, silk dresses—pricey at $200—straw hats, *koa* paddles for $700, a Persian *kris* for $425, vintage kimonos, an antique water jar from the Ching Mai area of northern Thailand for $925, Japanese woodblock prints, enormous bronze fish that once fit the entranceway of a palatial estate, and less expensive items like shell earrings for $8, and *koa* hair sticks for $4. The Gallery of Great Things, with its museum quality items, is definitely worth a browse. Also in the mall, **Crystal's Collectibles** overflows with knickknacks, pillows, toys, and even lingerie. The **Waimea Body Works** features swimsuits and outdoor gear for the active traveler. **Gifts in Mind** has novelty items and a very good selection of aloha shirts and dresses. **Mango Ranch** sells duds for cowpokes, including bow ties, fancy shirts, and cowboy hats. **Bentley's** specializes in ceramics and tableware. **Noa Noa** imports its fashions from Indonesia, offering beautiful *batik* creations mostly for women, but there are some items for men. Don't let the name **Waimea General Store** fool you. It mostly sells sundries with plenty of stationery, children's games, stuffed toys, and books on Hawaiiana.

The **Opelo Plaza,** also along Route 19 heading east, is one of Waimea's newest shopping malls. It features **Ross Sutherland,** a fine men's clothing store. **Kamaaina Woods** produces locally created wood art, and the small **Gift Shop** sells just that, small mementos, sundries, and souvenirs.

Food And Sundries

For **food shopping** at the Parker Ranch Center there's the **Sure Save Supermarket,** the **Kamuela Meat Market,** featuring fine cuts of Parker Ranch beef, and **Big Island Natural Foods,** selling snacks, sundries, lotions, potions, notions, and coffee.

The **Circle K** convenience store, with food items and gasoline, is located along Route 19 heading west out of town.

SERVICES AND INFORMATION

Entertainment

There ain't much happening around the old town entertainment-wise, but **free hula lessons** are given at the Parker Ranch center on Mon. afternoons. Enjoy live music and dancing nightly at the **Cattleman's Steakhouse** (see above).

Emergency/Health

Police can be be reached at tel. 885-7334, **ambulance and fire** at tel. 961-6022.

Physicians are available at Lucy Henriques Medical Center, tel. 885-7921.

Chiropractic care is available from **Kohala Chiropractic,** tel. 885-6847, open Mon., Wed., Fri. 9 a.m.-12 p.m., and 2-5 p.m.; Tues. and Thurs. 9 a.m.-1 p.m. with Dr. Bob Abdy; his office is in a small shopping center across from the Edelweiss Restaurant, west of town on Route 19. Doctor Abdy has an excellent reputation. In the Ironwood Center, east of town on Route 19 (across from the Circle K) is **Hamakua Kohala Coast Massage,** tel. 885-5442, and the **Chiropractic Clinic** of Dr. Kenneth C. Williams, tel. 885-7719.

Angela Longo Ph.D., tel. 885-7886, located in the Kamuela Office Center, is a practitioner of acupuncture and a Chinese herbalist. Angela, who graduated from U.C. Berkely with a Ph.D. in biochemistry, combines principles from both East and West into a holistic approach to health and well-being. Besides attending to her demanding practice, Angela is a devoted single parent and a classical Indian dancer who performs at special functions around the island. She is one of the most amazing health practitioners in the entire state.

Dr. Richard Leibman is a **naturopathic physician,** in town at tel. 885-4611.

Information/Services

The **Paniola Press** is a free paper with local feature stories and ads, available around town.

The **Post Office** is located in the Parker Ranch Center Mall. Mailing address for Waimea is Kamuela, so as not to confuse it with the *Waimeas* on Oahu and Kauai.

The **Waimea Visitors Center** is west of town along Route 19, almost directly across from the Opelo Shopping Center. They hand out free maps and brochures of the area and provide public restrooms.

The **Chock Inn Launderette** is west on Route 19 at tel. 885-4655.

NORTH KOHALA

Jungle trees with crocheted shawls of hanging vines stand in shadowed silence as tiny stores and humble homes abandoned by time melt slowly back into the muted North Kohala earth. This secluded region changes very little, and very slowly. You can count on it being more or less the same. It also has an eastward list toward the wetter side of the island, so if you're suffering from "Kona shock" and want to see flowers, palms, banana trees, and Hawaiian jungle, head for the north coast. Here the island of Hawaii lives up to its reputation of being not only big, but bold and beautiful as well.

North Kohala was the home of Kamehameha the Great. From this fiefdom he launched his conquest of all the islands. The shores and lands of North Kohala are rife with historical significance, and with beach parks where no one but a few local people ever go. Here cattle were introduced to the islands in the 1790s by Capt. Vancouver, an early explorer and friend of Kamehameha. Among North Kohala's cultural treasures are **Lapakahi State Historical Park,** a must stop that offers "touchable" exhibits which allow you to become actively involved in

Hawaii's traditional past and **Pu'u Koha Heiau,** one of the last great traditional temples built in Hawaii. Northward is the very place of **Kamehameha's birth,** and within walking distance is **Mookini Heiau,** one of the oldest in Hawaii and still actively ministered by the current generation of a long line of *kahuna.*

Hawi comes next, a sugar town whose economy recently turned sour when the sugar company drastically cut back its local operations. Hawi is making a comeback, along with this entire northern shore, which has seen an influx of small boutique-like businesses and art shops. In **Kapaau** a statue of Kamehameha I peering over the chief's ancestral dominions fulfills an old *kahuna* prophecy. On a nearby side road stands historic **Kalahikiola Church,** established in 1855 by Rev. Elias Bond. On the same side road is the old **Bond Homestead,** the most authentic yet virtually unvisited missionary home in all of Hawaii. Financially strapped, but lovingly tended by the remaining members of the Bond family, it's on the National Historical Record, and even rents *the* cheapest rooms on all of the Big Island. The main coastal road ends at **Pololu Valley**

Lookout, a premier *taro* valley of old Hawaii. A walk down the steep *pali* into this valley is a walk into timelessness with civilization disappearing like an ebbing tide.

Getting There

In Kawaihae, at the base of the North Kohala peninsula, Route 19 turns east and coastal Route 270, known as the Akoni Pule Highway, heads north along the coast. It passes through both of North Kohala's two major towns, Hawi and Kapaau, and ends at the *pali* overlooking Pololu Valley. All the historical sites, beach parks, and towns in the following sections are along this route, listed from south to north.

Route 250, the back road to Hawi, is a delightful country lane that winds through glorious green grazing lands for almost 20 miles along the leeward side of the Kohala Mountains. It begins in the western outskirts of Waimea and ends in Hawi on the far north coast. One of the most picturesque roads on the island, it's dotted with mood-setting cactus and small "line shacks." Suddenly vistas open to your left, and far below are expansive panoramas of rolling hills tumbling to the sea. At mile marker 8 is **Von Holt Memorial Park,** a scenic overlook perfect for a high mountain picnic. Past here at mile marker 13 is **Ironwood Outfitters,** a horse ranch and riding stable owned and operated by Judy

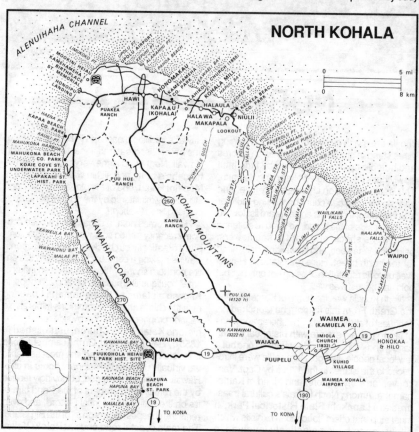

Ellis. Trail rides with Ms. Ellis through this upland *paniolo* country are among the best that you can find on the island (see pp. 587-588. Around mile marker 19, keep your eyes peeled for a herd of llamas on the left. At the coast, Route 250 splits. Right takes you to Kapaau, and left to Hawi. If you're coming along the coastal Route 270 between Kapaau and Hawi look for K. Naito's store, and make a left there to go back over

Route 250 to Waimea; you don't have to go all the way to Hawi to catch Route 250.

Upolu Airport, tel. 889-9958, is a lonely strip at Upolu Point, the closest spot to Maui. A sign points the way at mile marker 20 along coastal Route 270. Here, you'll find only a bench and a public telephone. The strip is serviced only on request by the small propeller planes of charter and commuter airlines.

SIGHTS, BEACHES, AND TOWNS

KAWAIHAE COAST

Lapakahi State Historical Park

This 600-year-old reconstructed Hawaiian fishing village, combined with adjacent **Koai'e Cove Marine Conservation District,** is a standout hunk of coastline 12 miles north of Kawaihae. Gates are open daily from 8 a.m. to 4 p.m., when park guides are in attendance. Sometimes, especially on weekends, they take the day off, and it's OK to park outside the gate and take the self-guided tour, although the knowlegeable anecdotes of the guides make the tour much more educational. As you enter, the small grass shack near some *lau hala* trees stocks annotated brochures and yellow water jugs. As you walk counterclockwise around the numbered stations, you pass canoe sheds and a fish shrine dedicated to *Ku'ula,* to whom the fishermen always dedicated a portion of their catch. A salt-making area demonstrates how the Hawaiians evaporated sea water by moving it into progressively smaller "pans" carved in the rock. There are numerous home sites along the wood-chip trail. Particularly interesting to children are exhibits of games like *konane* (Hawaiian checkers), and *ulimika,* a form of bowling using stones that the children are encouraged to try. Throughout the area, all trees, flowers, and shrubs are identified, and as an extra treat, migrating whales come close to shore from December through April. Don't leave without finding a shady spot and taking the time to look out to sea. For information write Lapakahi State Park, Box 100, Kapaau, HI 96755, tel. 889-5566.

Mahukona And Kapaa Beach Parks

Mahukona Beach County Park is a few minutes north of Lapakahi down a well-marked side

road. As you approach, notice a number of abandoned buildings and warehouses left standing from when Mahukona was an important port from which the Kohala Sugar Co. shipped its goods. Still existing is a pier with a hoist used by local fishermen to launch their boats. The harbor is filled with industrial debris which makes for some good underwater exploring, and snorkeling the offshore reef is rewarded with an abundance of sea life. Swimming off the pier is also good, but all water activities are dangerous during winter months and high surf. Picnic facilities include a large pavilion and tables, with a large green tank holding the drinking water. There are also cold-water showers and restrooms, with electricity available in the pavilion. Although numerous signs close to the pavilion say "No Camping," both tent and trailer camping is allowed with a county permit near the parking lot.

Kapaa Beach Park is five minutes farther north. Turn *makai* on a side road and cross a cattle grate as you head toward the sea. This park is even less visited than Mahukona. The rocky beach makes water entry difficult. It's primarily for day use and fishing, but there are showers, a restroom, and a pavilion. Camping is allowed with a county permit. Neither of these two beaches is spectacular, but they are secluded and accessible. If you're interested in a very quiet spot to contemplate a lovely panorama of Maui in the distance, this is it.

Mookini Luakini Heiau And Kamehameha's Birthplace

At mile marker 20 turn down a one-lane road to Upolu Airport. Follow it until it reaches the dead end at the runway. Turn left here on a tough dirt road for two miles to Mookini Luakini Heiau. This entire area is one of the most rugged and isolated on the Big Island, with wide windswept fields, steep sea cliffs, and pounding surf. Only *ali'i* came here to purify themselves and worship, sometimes offering human sacrifices. In 1963, Mookini Heiau was the first Hawaiian site to be listed in the National Historical Sites Registry. Legend says that the very first temple at Mookini was built as early as 480 A.D. This incredible date implies that Mookini must have been built immediately upon the arrival of the first Polynesian explorers, who many scholars maintain arrived in large numbers a full two centuries later. More believable oral history relates that the still-standing foundation of the temple was built by the Tahitian high priest Paao, who came with conquering warriors from the south in the 12th C., bringing the powerful mana of the fierce war-god Kukailimoku. The oral tale relates that the stones for the temple were fitted in a single night, passed hand to hand by a human chain of 18,000 warriors for a distance of 14 miles from Pololu Valley. They created an irregular rectangle measuring 125 by 250 feet, with 30-foot-high and 15-foot-thick walls all around.

When you visit the *heiau*, pick up a small brochure from a box at the entrance (oftentimes empty); if none are available a signboard nearby gives general information. Notice that the leeward stones are covered in lichens, giving them a greenish cast and testifying to the age of the *heiau*. Notice a huge flat stone near another embedded in the ground which gives off the menacing feeling of a preparation altar, and another nearby, a clone of the famous "Phallic Rock" on Molokai. Please be respectful as you walk around as this temple is still in use, and stay on the designated paths that are cordoned off by woven rope. To the rear is an altar area where recent offerings are often seen; the floor of the temple is carpeted with well-placed stones and tiny green plants that give a natural mosaic effect. For at least eight and perhaps 15 centuries, members of the Mookini family have been the priests and priestesses of the temple. Today, the inherited title of *kahuna nui* rests with Leimomi Mookini Lum, a nearby resident. The entire *heiau* is surrounded by a wave-like hump, perhaps the remnant of an earlier structure, that resembles a castle moat. Be sure to visit the nearby "little grass shack," one of the best examples of

this traditional Hawaiian architecture in the islands. Check how sturdy the walls are, and what excellent protection is provided by the grass-shingled roof. Also, be aware of the integration of its stone platform and how perfectly suited it is to provide comfort against the elements in Hawaii. Look through the door at a timeless panorama of the sea and surf.

A minute from the *heiau* along the dirt road, an HVB Warrior points to Kamehameha's birthplace, **Kamehameha Akahi Aina Hanau.** The entrance to the area is at the backside, away from the sea. Inside the low stone wall are some large boulders, believed to be the actual "birthing stones" where the high chieftess Kekuiapoiwa, wife of the warrior *ali'i* Keoua, gave birth to Kamehameha sometime around 1752. It is fitting that this male child, born as his father prepared a battle fleet to invade Maui, would grow to be the greatest of the Hawaiian chiefs—a brave, powerful, but lonely man, just like the flat plateau upon which he drew his first breath. In the background, the temple's ritual drums and haunting chants dedicated to Ku were the infants first lullabies. He would grow to accept Ku as his god, and together they would subjugate all of Hawaii. In this expansive North Kohala area Kamehameha was confronted with unencumbered vistas, sweeping views of neighboring islands, unlike most Hawaiians, whose outlooks were held in check by the narrow, confining, but secure walls of steep-sided valleys. Only this man with this background could rise to become "The Lonely One," high chief of a unified kingdom.

HAWI, KAPAAU, AND VICINITY

Hawi

Coming into Hawi, strung along Route 270 for a few blocks are a line of false-front buildings, leaning shoulder to shoulder like patient old men knowing that something *will* happen. In the middle of town Route 250, crossing the Kohala Mountains from Waimea, intersects the main road. Hawi was a bustling sugar town that boasted four movie theaters in its heyday. In the early 1970s, the Kohala Sugar Company pulled up stakes, leaving the one-industry town high and dry. Still standing is the monumental stack of the sugar works, a dormant reminder of what once was. The people of Hawi have always had grit, and instead of moving away they're hanging in and doing a good job of revitalizing their town. Spirit, elbow grease, and paint are their chief allies. Toughing it out are a handful of local shops selling food and household goods, an information center, a hotel (the only functional one in North Kohala), a restaurant or two, a pizza parlor, and some remarkable craft shops and boutiques (see below).

Kapaau

Kapaau is a sleepy community, the last town for any amenities on Route 270 before you reach the end of the line at Pololu Overlook. There's a gas station, grocery store, library, bank, and police station. Most young people have moved away seeking economic opportunity, but the old folks remain, and macadamia nuts are bringing some vitality back into the area. Here too, but on a smaller scale than in Hawi, local artists and some new folks are starting shops and businesses catering to tourists. The main attraction in town is **Kamehameha's Statue,** in front of the Kapaau Courthouse. The statue was commissioned by King Kalakaua in 1878, at which time an old *kahuna* said that the statue would feel at home only in the lands of Kamehameha's birth. Thomas Gould, an American sculptor living in Italy, was hired to do the statue, and he used John Baker, a part Hawaiian and close friend of Kalakaua as the model. Gould was paid $10,000 and he produced a remarkable and heroic sculpture that was sent to Paris to be bronzed. It was freighted to Hawaii, but the ship carrying the original statue sank just off Port Stanley in the Falkland Islands, and the nine-ton statue was thought lost forever. With the insurance money, Gould was recommissioned and he produced another statue that arrived in Honolulu in 1883, where it still stands in front of the Judiciary Building. Within a few weeks, however, a British ship arrived in Honolulu, carrying the original statue that had somehow been salvaged and unceremoniously dumped in a Port Stanley junk yard. The English captain bought it there and sold it to King Kalakaua for $850. There was only one place for the statue to be sent: to the then-thriving town of Kapaau in the heart of Kamehameha's ancestral homelands. Every year on the night before Kamehameha Day, the statue is

original Kamehameha statue

freshly painted with a new coat of house paint, but underneath the bronze remains as lustrous and strong as the great king's will.

Kamehameha County Park, down a marked side road, has a full recreation area, including an Olympic pool open to the public, basketball courts, and weight rooms in the main building along with outside tennis courts with night lighting. There is a kiddie area, restrooms, and picnic tables, all free.

Kalahikiola Church

A few minutes east of town an HVB Warrior points to a county lane leading to Kalahikiola Congregational Church. The road is delightfully lined with palm trees, pines, and macadamias like the formal driveway which it once was. Pass the weathering buildings of the **Bond Estate** and follow the road to the church on the hill. This church was built by Rev. Elias Bond and his wife Ellen, who arrived at Kohala in 1841 and dedicated the church in 1855. Rev. Bond and his parishioners were determined to overcome many formidable obstacles in building Kalahikiloa ("Life from the Sun") Church, so that they could "sit in a dry and decent house in Jehovah's presence." They hauled timber for miles, quarried and carried stone from distant gulches, raised lime from the sea floor, and brought sand by the jarful all the way from Kawaiahae to mix their mortar. After two years of backbreaking work and $8,000, the church finally stood in God's praise, 85 feet long by 45 wide. The attached bell tower, oddly out of place, looks like a shoe box standing on end topped by four mean-looking spikes. Note that the doors don't swing but slide—some visitors leave because they think it's locked. Inside, the church is dark and cool, and inexplicably the same type of spikes on the belltower flank both sides of the altar. There is also a remarkable koa table, and pamphlets ($.25) describe the history of the church.

The Bond Estate

The most remarkable and undisturbed missionary estate still extant in Hawaii is the old Bond Homestead and its attendant buildings which include the now defunct, but renovated, Kohala Girls School. The estate is kept up by 10 surviving cousins of the Bond family, who have recently formed the nonprofit **Iole Mission Homestead Foundation.** Chaired by Mrs. Noreen Alexander of Honolulu, the Foundation is dedicated to preserving the home and opening it and the surrounding grounds to public tours in the very near future. It's already on the National Historical Register. But, age and the loss of that caring touch of a family actually living in the home have taken their toll. The Foundation is refurbishing the home and strengthening the basic structure so that this venerable old house can take the extra stress created by the traffic of future visitors. Until the renovations are completed, the Bond Estate is closed to the public; please remember this. They will begin admitting the public by first opening *the grounds only* to walking tours in early 1990, and tours of the home itself will hopefully begin in 1991. Mr. Walter Fruitiger, a North Kohala resident and board member of the Foundation, has graciously dedicated his time to answering questions concerning the future visitation of the Bond Estate. If you have any ques-

tions or interest in future developments please contact Mr. Fruitiger at tel. 889-5267. Note, however, that you can rent a room in the refurbished Kohala Girls school for the cheapest rates in Hawaii (see p. 719).

When you enter the grounds, the clock turns back 100 years. The first buildings were completed in 1841 by Rev. Isaac Bliss, who preceded Elias and Ellen Bond. The main buildings, connected in New England farm fashion, have steep-pitched roofs designed to keep off the "back East" snows. They worked equally well here to keep rainwater out, as they were originally covered in thatch. All of the original furniture and family possessions are still placed as if they were all just out for the afternoon, although the family has not lived in the house since 1925, when it was occupied by Dr. Benjamin Bond. In the majority of missionary homes and museums in Hawaii, suitable period furniture had to be purchased or replicas made to fill the house, but here it is all original! The homey dining and writing room is dominated by a large table that can take six leaves because the Bond's never knew how many there would be for dinner—four or 60 that might have landed by schooner in the middle of the afternoon. A full set of dishes waits undisturbed in the sideboard. A cozy little parlor has comfortable wicker rocking chairs and a settee under a photo of Elias Bond himself. The reverend built the settee and most of the furniture in the house. His furniture from New England arrived on a later ship than he, but being the Sabbath, the reverend refused to have it unloaded. Unfortunately, the ship caught fire and all the Bond's personal possessions were lost. In the kitchen area a refrigerator dating from the '20s looks like a bank vault. It ran on electricity from a generator on the homestead that was frequently used by local plantation owners to recharge their batteries. Off in a side room an old wooden bathtub is as sound as the day it was built. In Rev. Bond's bedroom is a crocheted "primer" dated 1817, made by his sister Eliza who died before he came to Hawaii; he brought it as a memento and it still hangs on the wall. Upstairs are two large rooms in disrepair, which contain a treasure trove of antiques. Notice too, the sturdy barn-style architecture of pegs and beams.

The small wing attached to the main house, called "The Cottage," was built when Dr. Ben-

Pololu Valley

jamin Bond was first married. The family ate together in the main house, so the cottage is only a totally Victorian bedroom and sitting room, abounding with photos and antiques. The attached bathroom was once a summerhouse that was dragged to the present location by a steam tractor, then plumbed. As you look around, you'll feel that everything is here except for the people.

Keokea Beach Park

Two miles past Kapaau toward Pololu you pass a small fruit stand and an access road heading *makai* to secluded Keokea Beach Park. The park, on the side of the hill going down to the sea, is very picturesque and luxuriant. It is a favorite spot of North Kohala residents, especially on weekends, but receives little use during the week. The rocky shoreline faces the open ocean, so swimming is not advised except during summer calm. There is a pavilion, restrooms, showers, and picnic tables. A county permit is required for tent and trailer camping.

POLOLU VALLEY AND BEYOND

Finally you come to Pololu Valley Overlook. Off to the right is a small home belonging to Bill Sproat, a man of mixed Hawaiian ancestry and a longtime resident of Pololu. Bill, whose vim and vigor belie his 81 years, was a mule skinner throughout the area for 50 years. He is a treasure house of knowledge and homespun wisdom, and still speaks fluent Hawaiian. His mother was a Hawaiian lady who became a school teacher down in Pololu, and his dad was an adventurer who came to Hawaii in the 1890s. Bill's grandmother was a *kahuna* who lived in the valley and never converted to Christianity. Most of the folks feared her dark powers, but not Bill who, although a strong Christian, learned much about Hawaii and its ways from his grandmother. If Bill is in his yard, perhaps tending a mule, make sure to stop and talk with him.

It's about 12 miles from Pololu to Waipio Valley, with five U-shaped valleys in between, including Honokea and Waimanu, two of the largest. From the lookout it takes about 15 minutes to walk down to the floor of Pololu. The trail is well maintained as you pass through a heavy growth of *lau hala,* but it can be slippery when wet. At the bottom is a gate that keeps grazing animals in; make sure to close it after you! The **Kohala Ditch,** a monument to labor-intensive engineering, is to the rear of these valleys. It carried precious water to the sugar plantations. Pololu and the other valleys were once all inhabited and were among the richest wet taro plantations of old Hawaii. Today, abandoned and neglected, introduced vegetation has taken them over. The black-sand beach fronting Pololu is lined with sand dunes, with a small sandbar offshore. The rip current here can be very dangerous, so enter the water only in summer months. The rip fortunately weakens not too far from shore; if caught go with it and ride the waves back in. Many people hike into Pololu for seclusion and back-to-nature camping. Make sure to boil the stream water before drinking. Plenty of wild fruits grow that can augment your food supply, and the shoreline fishing is excellent. The trails leading eastward to the other valleys are in disrepair and should not be attempted unless you are totally prepared, and better yet accompanied by someone who knows the terrain.

axis deer

PRACTICALITIES

ACCOMMODATIONS

You won't spend a lot of time wondering where you'll be staying in North Kohala. If you don't intend on camping, only one hotel welcomes you, another doesn't, and you can rent an old plantation manager's house, or a very modest room at the Bond Estate.

The Kohala Lodge, Box 521, Kapaau, HI 96755, tel. 889-5577, in Hawi was long known as Luke's Hotel. The hotel has always catered to local working people or island families visiting the area. It is basic, adequate, and clean. Located in central Hawi, it has a quiet little courtyard, restaurant, swimming pool, and TV. Rooms are a reasonable $37 per night, $95 per week, $325 per month, $6 additional person, discounts on long stays and for sharing a bathroom.

The Kohala Club Hotel, tel. 889-6793, is an odd-ball little country hotel along Route 270 in Kaapau. At one time, it was known as "The British Club," since many of the sugar company foremen who frequented it were British. In the dining room hangs a large painting of Queen Victoria that was supposedly saluted and toasted by her loyal subjects far from home. Now, the hotel is operated by a reclusive Japanese family that seems more surprised than pleased if you turn up looking for a room.

The **Hawaiian Plantation House** (Aha Hui Hale), Box 10, Hawi, HI 96719, tel. 889-5523, was once a plantation manager's house. The white clapboard structure sits on four lush acres, letting its two bedroom suites for $65 d, $10 extra person, communal kitchen.

Mr. David Winter, manager of the Iole Development Corp., tel. 889- 5217/6989, rents modest rooms in the old **Kohala Girls School** section of the Bond Estate (p. 716). These buildings are very old, but the conveniences and amenities have been upgraded. Basically, you'll have to take care of yourself as no housekeeping services are provided. Mr. Winter prefers renting these rooms to school and civic organizations, but he will rent to travelers . . . if they are the right sort, which translates as clean, quiet, and respectful! Rates are $275 per month, with shared bath, and kitchen. Daily rates made upon request.

RESTAURANTS

You can get a good inexpensive meal at the **Kohala Lodge Restaurant,** the "food wing" of the Kohala Hotel in downtown Hawi, open Mon.-Sat., breakfast 7 a.m-11 p.m., lunch 11 a.m.-2 p.m., dinner 5-8 p.m., cocktail lounge open 8 p.m.-12 a.m., closed Sunday. Omelettes with the works are under $4, cheeseburgers are $2, soup $1.85, and most sandwiches are under $2.50. More substantial meals like fried chicken and the trimmings are $4.75, hamburger steak $4, and *mahi mahi* $5.75. There is also a cocktail lounge at this no-frills, downhome restaurant.

The **Ohana Pizza & Beer Garden,** tel. 889-5888, also in downtown Hawi, features very good pizza from $5.50 to $10.75 depending upon size and toppings. This clean, friendly restaurant also offers hefty sandwiches for $2.95, and pasta dinners for $5.95 that include homemade lasagna, served with dinner salad and homemade garlic bread for $6. Salads are $1.50, and homemade garlic bread $1. You can order wine or a chilled domestic beer for $1.75, or an import for $2.50. The staff of local people are friendly and hospitable. A great place to pick up a picnic lunch.

Mits Drive-In, tel. 889-6474, is a small roadside restaurant in Kapaau where you can pick up a fast hamburger, hot dog, soft drink, or snack. Inexpensive.

Don's Family Deli, tel. 889-5822, open daily for breakfast, lunch, and dinner until 8 p.m., across the street from the Kamehameha Statue in Kapaau, is a taste of New York in North Kohala. How can a visit to tropical paradise be complete without bagels and lox, lasagna, or a thick slice of quiche? Don's features Dreyer's ice cream and homemade biscotti filled with nuts and that zesty anisette flavor. Don Rich, a longtime Koahala resident, will also fix you up with a tofu or *mahi* burger, and offers a wide selection of meats and breads if you prefer to make your own picnic lunch.

Tropical Dreams Gourmet Shop, in bustling downtown Kapaau, open 9 a.m.-5 p.m. Mon.-Fri., 10 a.m.-5 p.m. weekends, serves freshly made ice cream (macadamia is great), and fresh fruit sorbet in season.

Almost next door is **Cafe Kohala,** an unpretentious eatery serving sandwiches for around $3, and full meals like *kahlua* pig with cabbage, or *kiave*-broiled sirloin, T-bone, and hamburger, for $5-6. This basic but clean restaurant is open Tues. and Wed. 6 a.m.-9:30 p.m., Thurs. and Fri. 6 a.m.-8 p.m., Sat. 7 a.m.-8:30 p.m., and Sun. 7 a.m.-11:30 p.m. Just stand by the door to catch some of the delicious smells wafting from the kitchen.

SHOPPING

For **food shopping** try: **Union Market,** tel. 889-6450, along Route 270 coming into Kapaau, which sells not only general merchandise and meats, but also a hefty assortment of grains, nuts, fruits, and locally made pastries and breads; **H. Naito** is a general grocery, dry goods and fishing supplies store in Kapaau, tel. 889-6851; **K. Takata** is a well-stocked grocery store in Hawi, tel. 889-5261; **Kohala Market,** a small general store just north of Kawaihae on the right as you head up to the North Kohala peninsula, also sells sandwiches and drinks to go. For a special treat try **Tropical Dreams,** a locally owned company in Kohala that hand-makes gourmet macadamia nut butters. Some of their mouthwatering butters are flavored with Kona coffee, chocolate, and *lehua* honey. They also make a variety of jellies and jams, including passionfruit and papaya-coconut. Can't resist? Contact Tropical Dreams for their full brochure at Box 557, Kapaau, HI 96755, tel. 889-5386. Gift package assortments a specialty. In Kapaau, **Kohala Spirits,** open 10 a.m.-10 p.m. Mon.-Sat., sells a fairly wide range of liquor, beer, and wine.

In Kapaau, across from the Kamehameha statue, is **Ackerman Gallery,** open 9 a.m.-5:30 p.m. daily, tel. 889-5971, owned and operated by artist Gary Ackerman. Besides showcasing his own sensitive, island-inspired paintings, he displays local pottery, carvings, and one-of-a-kind jewelry. He also carries a smattering of artwork from throughout the Pacific. The selections are tasteful, but expensive. You can also choose a reasonably priced gift item, especially from the handmade jewelry section. Make sure to check out the beautiful hand-blown glass display made by a local artist named Yamazawa. The distinctive iridescent glaze is achieved by using volcanic cinders. You can bring home a true island memento that includes a bit of Madame Pele herself.

Almost next door is **Kohala Sporting,** with a selection of boogie boards, T-shirts, and hunting licenses.

Hana Koa is a woodworking shop owned by artist Don Wilkinson, who learned the trade of making fine antique furniture replicas from his father. His work is authentic and excellent. He works primarily in *koa* and focuses on the early 1900 period. He is also a friend of Mr. Phil Hooten, an old-timer in Kohala who fashions authentic carvings of old Hawaiian artifacts from ivory, turtleshell, and bone. Don, a friendly storehouse of information, lives along Route 250 heading in from Waimea, tel. 889-6444.

Another local artist is **David Gomes,** tel. 889-5100, a guitar and ukulele maker. He works in *koa* and other woods and does inlay in shell, abalone, and wood. His beautiful instruments take from four to six months to complete. His small shop is located about a half mile on the Kapaau side of the junction of Routes 270 and 250. Next door is a hobby and crafts store.

In Hawi, **Dawn's,** tel. 889-5112, sells sports clothes, T-shirts, and alohawear. The **Heritage Tree** is a specialty hula supply store in Kapaau across from the Kamehameha statue. If you're looking for a small variety of traditional arts and crafts, this shop is worth a stop.

SERVICES AND INFORMATION

The **Kohala Visitors Center** dispenses maps, information, and aloha. It's open daily and located just near the junction of Routes 270 and 250 in Hawi. Next door is the local **laundromat,** a semi open-aired affair that can be used just about all the time. **Police** can be reached at tel. 889-6225, emergency **fire** and **ambulance** at tel. 961-6022.

The area **post office** is on Route 270 between Hawi and Kapaau across the road from the H. Naito Store.

The full service **Kamehameha Pharmacy** is along Route 270 in downtown Kapaau.

KAUAI

KAUAI-BOUND TRAVELERS, PLEASE NOTE: At press time for this printing of *Hawaii Handbook,* Kauai was still recovering from the effects of Hurricane Iniki, which hit the island on September 11th, 1992. Many of the hotels were still closed or accommodating civil defense personnel. Hotels on Kauai are expected to reopen soon, but before arriving on Kauai, travelers are advised to call one of the following numbers for current information about the island's available services. The **Kauai Hotline,** tel. toll-free (800) 262-1400 or toll-free fax (800) 637-5762, will be in service through October 1993. Or call the **Hawaii Visitor's Bureau** on Kauai, tel. (808) 245-3971.

KAUAI

INTRODUCTION

Kauai is the oldest of the main Hawaiian Islands, and nature has had ample time to work, sculpting Kauai into a beauty among beauties. Flowers and fruits burst from its fertile soil, but the "Garden Island" is much more than greenery and flora, it's the poetry of land itself! Its mountains have become rounded and smooth, and its streams tumbling to the sea have cut deep and wide, giving Kauai the only navigable river in Hawaii. The interior is a dramatic series of mountains, valleys, and primordial swamp. The great gouge of Waimea Canyon, called the "Grand Canyon of the Pacific," is an enchanting layer of pastels where uncountable rainbows form prismatic necklaces from which waterfalls hang like silvery pendants. To the northwest are the seacliffs of Na Pali, mightiest in all of Oceania, looming 4,000 feet above the pounding surf.

Only 100 miles (25 minutes) by air from Honolulu, you land on Kauai just about the time you're finishing your in-flight cocktail. Everything seems quieter here, rural but upbeat, with the main town being just that, a town. The pursuit of carefree relaxation is unavoidable at five-star hotels, where you're treated like a visiting *ali'i,* or at campsites deep in interior valleys or along secluded beaches where reality *is* the fantasy of paradise.

Kauai is where Hollywood comes when the script calls for "paradise." The island has a dozen major films to its credit, everything from idyllic scenes in *South Pacific* to the lurking horror of Asian villages in *Uncommon Valor. King Kong* tore up this countryside in search of love, and Tattoo spotted "de plane, boss" in "Fantasy Island." In *Blue Hawaii,* Elvis's hips mimicked the swaying palms in a famous island grove, while torrid love scenes from *The Thorn Birds* were steamier than the jungle in the background. Perhaps its greatest compliment is that Kauai is where other islanders come to look at the scenery.

But the Garden Island is much more than just another pretty face: the island and its people have integrity. In November 1982, Hurricane Iwa ripped ashore and slapped Kauai around like the moll in a Bogart movie. Her people immediately set about rebuilding hotels and homes, while nature took care of the rest. In no time, her mussed hair was combed and her streaked makeup was daubed into shape. Now, the hurricane damage is mostly a memory and Kauai has emerged a

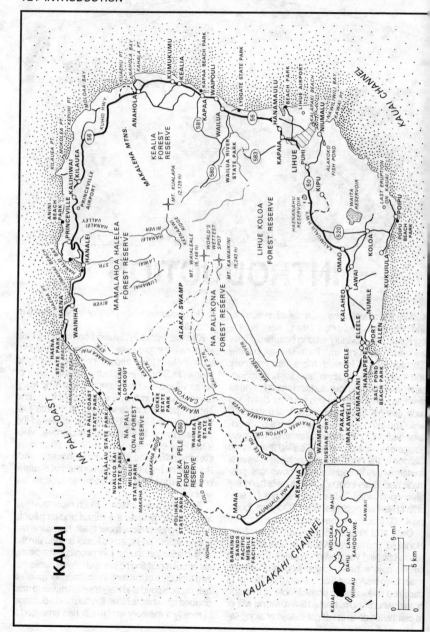

KAUAI

ouch more self-assured and as beautiful as
ever.

AN OVERVIEW

Kauai is the most regularly shaped of all the ma-
or islands, more or less round, like a partially de-
iated beach ball. The puckered skin around the
coast forms bays, beaches, and inlets, while the
center is a no man's land of mountains, canyon,
and swamp. Almost everyone arrives at the ma-
or airport in **Lihue**, although another small strip
n Princeville has limited service by commuter
aircraft. Lihue is the county seat and major town
supporting government agencies, full amenities,
and a wide array of restaurants and shopping.
For many years the town's only full-service resort was the Kauai Surf Hotel (now the **Westin
Kauai**), but the **Hilton** has recently opened a ho-
tel-condo on Kauai Beach Drive. Lihue also
boasts some of the cheapest accommodations
on the island, in small family-operated hotels;
however, most visitors head north for Wai-
lua/Kapaa or west to the fabulous Poipu Beach
area. Lihue's **Kauai Museum** is a must stop,
where you'll learn the geological and social history of the island, immensely enriching your visit.

On the outskirts of town is the oldest Lutheran
church in the islands and the remarkably preserved **Grove Farm Homestead**, a classic Hawaiian plantation that is so intact that all that
seems to be missing are the workers. At Nawiliwili Bay you can see firsthand the Menehunes'
handiwork at the **Menehune (Alakoko) Fish
Pond,** still in use. Just north are the two suburbs
of **Kapaia** and **Hanamaulu**. Here too you'll find
shops and restaurants and the junction of Route
583 leading inland through miles of sugar cane
fields and terminating at a breathtaking panorama of **Wailua Falls**.

East Coast

Heading northeast from Lihue along Route 56
takes you to **Wailua** and **Kapaa**. En route, you
pass Wailua Golf Course, beautiful, cheap, and
open to the public. Wailua town is built along the
Wailua River, the only navigable stream in
Hawaii. At the mouth of the river are two enchanting beach parks and a temple of refuge,
while upstream are more *heiau,* petroglyphs,
royal birth stones, the heavily touristed yet beautiful Fern Grotto, and the Kamokila Hawaiian folk

village, all within the **Wailua River State Park**.
Here too are remarkable views of the river below
and the cascading Opaekaa Waterfalls. **The
Coco Palms Resort** of Wailua is an island institution set in the heart of the most outstanding
coconut grove on Kauai. Its evening torch-lighting ceremony is the best authentic fake-Hawaii
on the island, and it's free even to non-guests.
Up Route 56 toward Kapaa you pass **The
Market Place**, an extensive mall that will satisfy
your every shopping need and then some. In the
vicinity, a clutch of first-rate yet affordable hotels
and condos line the beach. **Kapaa** is a workers'
town with more casual shopping and good, inexpensive restaurants. Heading north toward
Hanalei, you pass **Pohakuloa Point**, an excellent surfers' beach, **Anahola Beach Park**,
where the water and camping are fine, and
Moloa'a Bay, a secluded beach that you can
have mostly to yourself.

North Coast

Before entering **Kilauea**, the first town in Hanalei
District, unmarked side roads lead to secret
beaches and unofficial camp spots. A small
coastal road leads you to **Kilauea Lighthouse**,
a beacon of safety for passing ships and for a remarkable array of birds that come to this wildfowl
sanctuary. **Princeville** is next, largest planned
resort in Hawaii, featuring its own airstrip. Here
an entire modern village is built around a superb
golf course and the newest exclusive hotel on
Kauai.

Down the narrowing lane and over a single-
lane steel-strut bridge is **Hanalei**. Inland is a terraced valley planted in taro just like in the old
days. Oceanside is Hanalei Bay, a safe anchorage and haven to seagoing yachts that have
made it a port of call ever since Westerners began coming to Hawaii. On the outskirts is **Waioli
Mission House**, a preserved home and museum dating from 1837. Then comes a string of
beaches, uncrowded and safe for swimming
and snorkeling. You pass through the tiny village
of **Wainiha**, and then **Haena**, with the island's
"last resort." In quick succession come **Haena
Beach County Park**, the **wet and dry caves**,
and the end of the road at **Kee Beach** in **Haena
State Park**. Here are beach houses for those
who want to get away from it all, **Kaulu Paoa
Heiau** dedicated to hula, and the location where
the beach scenes from *The Thorn Birds* were

filmed. From here only your feet and love of adventure take you down the **Kalalau Trail** to back-to-nature camping. You pass along a narrow foot trail down the **Na Pali Coast**, skirting emerald valleys cut off from the world by impassable 4,000-foot seacliffs, mightiest in the Pacific. All along here are heiau, ancient village sites, caves, lava tubes, and the romantic yet true **Valley of the Lost Tribe** just beyond trail's end.

South Coast

From Lihue west is a different story. Route 50 takes you past the **Kukui Grove Center** and then through **Puhi,** home of Kauai Community College. As the coastal **Hoary Head Mountains** slip past your window, **Queen Victoria's Profile** squints down at you. **Maluhia Road,** famous for its tunnel-like line of eucalyptus, branches off toward **Koloa,** a sugar town now rejuvenated with shops, boutiques, and restaurants. Continuing to the coast is **Poipu Beach,** the best on Kauai with its bevy of beautiful hotels and resorts.

Westward are a string of sugar towns. First is **Kalaheo,** where an island philanthropist, Walter McBride, gave the munificent land gift that has become **Kukui O Lono Park.** Here you'll find a picture-perfect Japanese garden surrounded by an excellent yet little-played golf course. Farther west on Route 50 is **Hanapepe,** a good stop for supplies and famous for its restaurants. The road skirts the shore, passing **Olokele,** a perfect caricature of a sugar town with its neatly trimmed cottages, and **Pakala,** an excellent surfing beach. Quickly comes **Waimea,** where Captain Cook first came ashore, and on the outskirts is the **Russian Fort,** dating from 1817 when all the world powers were present in Hawaii, jockeying to influence this Pacific gem.

In Waimea and farther westward in **Kekaha** the road branches inland, leading along the rim of **Waimea Canyon.** This is what everyone comes to see, and none are disappointed. The wonderfully winding road serves up lookout after lookout and trail after trail. You end up at **Kokee State Park** and the **Kalalau Valley Lookout** where you're king of the mountain, and 4,000 feet below is your vast domain of Na Pali. Past Kekaha is a flat stretch of desert vast enough that the military has installed **Barking Sands Missile Range.** The pavement ends and a good tourist-intimidating "cane road" takes over, leading you to the seclusion of **Polihale State Park,** where you can swim, camp, and luxuriate in privacy. If Madame Pele had had her choice, she never would have moved.

THE LAND

One hundred miles northwest of Oahu, Kauai is the northernmost of the six major islands and fourth largest. It is approximately 33 miles long and 25 miles wide at its farthest points, with an area of 554 square miles and 90 miles of coastline. Kauai was built by one huge volcano that became extinct about six million years ago. Mount Waialeale in central Kauai is its eastern rim, and speculation holds that Niihau, 20 miles off the west coast, was at one time connected. The volcanic "hotspot" under Kauai was sealed by the weight of the island; as Kauai drifted northward the hot spot burst through again and again, building the string of islands from Oahu to Hawaii.

A simplified but chronologically accurate account of Kauai's emergence is found in a version of the Pele myth retold in *The Kumulipo.* It depicts the fire-goddess as a young, beautiful woman who visits Kauai during a hula festival and becomes enraptured with Lohiau, a handsome and mighty chief. She wants him as a husband and determines to dig a fire-pit home where they can reside in contented bliss. Unfortunately, her unrelenting and unforgiving sea-goddess sister pursues her, forcing Pele to abandon Kauai and Lohiau. Thus, she wandered and sparked volcanic eruptions on Oahu, Maui, and finally atop Kilauea Crater on Hawaii, where she now resides.

Phenomenal Features Of Kauai

Located almost smack-dab in the middle of the island are **Mount Kawaikini** (5,243 feet) and adjacent **Mount Waialeale** (5,148 feet), highest points on Kauai. Mount Waialeale is an unsurpassed "rain magnet," drawing an estimated 480 inches (40 feet) of precipitation per year and earning itself a dubious distinction as "the wettest spot on Earth." Don't be intimidated—this rain is amazingly localized, with only 20 inches per year falling just 20 miles away. Visitors can

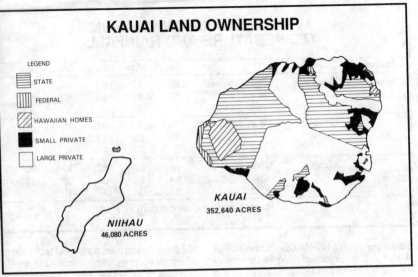

KAUAI LAND OWNERSHIP

LEGEND

▨ STATE

▥ FEDERAL

▨ HAWAIIAN HOMES

■ SMALL PRIVATE

☐ LARGE PRIVATE

KAUAI
352,640 ACRES

NIIHAU
46,080 ACRES

now enter this mist-shrouded world aboard helicopters which fly through countless rainbows and hover above a thousand waterfalls. Draining Waialeale is **Alakai Swamp**, a dripping sponge of earth covering about 30 square miles of trackless bog. This patch of mire contains flora and fauna found nowhere else. For example, *ohia* trees, mighty giants of upland forests, grow here as natural bonsais that could pass as potted plants. On the swamp's western border is **Waimea Canyon**, running north to south. Whipping winds, pelting rain, and the incessant grinding of streams and rivulets have chiseled the red bedrock to depths of 3,600 feet and expanses 10 miles wide. On the western slopes of Waimea Canyon is the **Na Pali Coast**, a scalloped, undulating vastness of cliffs and valleys forming a bulwark 4,000 feet high.

Other mountains and outcroppings around the island have formed curious natural formations. The **Hoary Head Mountains**, a diminutive range barely 2,000 feet tall south of Lihue, form a profile of Queen Victoria. A ridge just behind Wailua gives the impression of a man in repose and has been dubbed The Sleeping Giant. Another small range in the northeast, the **Anahola Mountains**, had until recently an odd series of boulders that formed "Hole in the Mountain," mythologically created when a giant

hurled his spear through sheer rock. Erosion has collapsed the formation but the tale lives on.

Land Ownership

Of Kauai's total usable land area (398,720 acres), 62% is privately owned. Of this, almost 90% is controlled by only half a dozen or so large landholders, mainly Gay & Robinson, AMFAC, Alexander & Baldwin, C. Brewer & Co., and Grove Farm. The remaining 38%, which includes a section of Hawaiian Homes lands, is primarily owned by the state, and a small portion is owned by the county of Kauai and the federal government. As everywhere in Hawaii, no one owns the beaches and public access to them is guaranteed.

Channels, Lakes, And Rivers

Kauai is separated from Oahu by the **Kauai Channel.** Reaching an incredible depth of 10,900 feet and a width of 72 miles, it is by far the state's deepest and widest channel. Inland, manmade **Waita Reservoir** north of Koloa is the largest body of fresh water in Hawaii, covering 424 acres with a three-mile shoreline. The **Waimea River**, running through the floor of the canyon, is the island's longest at just under 20 miles, while the **Hanalei River** moves the greatest amount of water, emptying 150 million

AVERAGE MAXIMUM/MINIMUM TEMPERATURE AND RAINFALL

Island	Town		Jan.	March	May	June	Sept.	Nov.
Kauai	Hanapepe	high	79	80	81	84	82	80
		low	60	60	61	65	62	61
		rain	5	2	0	0	2	3
	Lihue	high	79	79	79	82	82	80
		low	60	60	65	70	68	65
		rain	5	3	2	2	5	5
	Kilauea	high	79	79	80	82	82	80
		low	62	64	66	68	69	65
		rain	5	5	3	3	1	5

N.B. Rainfall in inches; temperature in °F

gallons per day into Hanalei Bay. But the **Wailua River** has the distinction of being the state's only navigable stream, although passage by boat is restricted to a scant three miles upstream. The flatlands around Kekaha were at one time Hawaii's largest body of inland water. They were brackish and drained last century when the Waimea Ditch was built to irrigate the cane fields.

CLIMATE

Kauai's climate will make you happy. Along the coastline the average temperature is 80° F in spring and summer, and about 75° during the remainder of the year. The warmest areas are along the south coast from Lihue westward, where the mercury can hit the 90s in midsummer. To escape the heat any time of year, head for Kokee atop Waimea Canyon, where the weather is always moderate.

In the areas most interesting to visitors, rain is not a problem. The driest section of Kauai is the southwestern desert, from Polihale to Poipu Beach (five inches per year) up to a mere 20 inches around the resorts. Lihue receives about 30 inches. As you head northeast toward Hanalei, rainfall becomes more frequent but is still a tolerable 45 inches per year. Cloudbursts in winter are frequent but short-lived.

Thanksgiving was not a very nice time on Kauai back in November 1982. Along with the stuffing and cranberries came an unwelcome guest who showed no aloha, **Hurricane Iwa**. What made this rude 80-mile-per-hour partycrasher so unforgettable was that she was only the fourth such storm to come ashore on Hawaii since records have been kept and the first since the late 1950s. All told, she caused $200 million dollars' worth of damage. A few beaches were washed away, perhaps forever, and great destruction was suffered by beach homes and resorts, especially around Poipu. Trees were twisted from the ground and bushes were flattened, but Kauai is strong and fertile and the damage was superficial and temporary. Like all the islands, Kauai has a very competent warning system in place, and, thank God, there was no loss of life. Chances of encountering another hurricane on Kauai in the foreseeable future are very rare indeed.

FLORA AND FAUNA

Kauai exceeds its reputation as the Garden Island. It has had a much longer time for soil building and rooting of a wide variety of plant life, so it's lusher than the other islands. Lying on a main bird migratory route, lands such as the **Hanalei National Wildlife Sanctuary** have long since been set aside for their benefit. Impenetrable inland regions surrounding Mount Waialeale and dominated by the Alakai Swamp have provided a natural sanctuary for Kauai's own bird and plant life. Because of this, Kauai is home to the largest number of indigenous birds extant in Hawaii, though even here they are tragically endangered. As on the other Hawaiian Islands, a large number of birds, plants, and mammals have been introduced in the past 200 years. Most have either aggressively competed for, or simply destroyed, the habitat of indigenous species. As the newcomers gain dominance, Kauai's own flora and fauna slide inevitably toward oblivion.

Introduced Fauna

One terribly destructive predator of native ground-nesting birds is the **mongoose**. Introduced to Hawaii last century as a cure for a rat infestation, the mongoose has only recently made it to Kauai, where a vigorous monitoring and extermination process is underway. More acceptable game mammals found in Kauai's forests include feral goats and pigs, although they too have caused destruction by uprooting seedlings and by overgrazing shrubs and grasses. Game fowl that have successfully acclimatized

the mongoose, an experiment gone bad

include francolins, ring-necked pheasants, and an assortment of quail and dove. All are hunted at certain times of year (see p. 754).

One game animal found in Hawaii only on Kauai is the **black-tailed deer.** Kauai's thriving herd of 700 started as a few orphaned fawns from Oregon in 1961. These handsome animals, a species of western mule deer, are at home on the hilly slopes west of Waimea Canyon. Although there is little noticeable change in seasons in Hawaii, bucks and does continue to operate on genetically transmitted biological time clocks. The males shed their antlers during late winter months and the females give birth in spring. Hunting of black-tails is allowed only by public lottery in October.

BIRDS

Common Birds

Kauai is rich in all manner of birds, from migratory marine birds to upland forest dwellers. Many live in areas you can visit; others you can see by taking a short stroll and remaining observant. Some, of course, are rare and very difficult to spot. The most easily spotted island birds frequent almost all areas, from the Kekaha Salt Ponds to Kalalau and the upland regions of Kokee, including the blazing red **northern cardinal**; the comedic, brash **common myna**; the operatic **western meadowlark**, introduced in 1930 and found in Hawaii only on Kauai; the ubiquitous **Japanese white-eye**; sudden fluttering flocks of **house finches**; that Arctic traveler the **golden plover**, found along mud flats everywhere; the **cattle egret**, a white, 20-inch-tall heron found anywhere from the backs of cattle to the lids of garbage cans (introduced from Florida in 1960 to control cattle pests, they have so proliferated that they are now considered a pest by some); and the **white-tailed tropic bird**, snow-white elegance with a three-foot wingspan and a long wispy kite-like tail.

Marine And Water Birds

Among the millions of birds that visit Kauai yearly, some of the most outstanding are its marine and water birds. Many beautiful individuals are seen at **Kilauea Point**, where they often nest in the trees on the cliff or on **Moku'ae'ae Islet.** The

Laysan albatross *(moli)* is a far-ranging Pacific flier whose 11-foot wingspan carries it in effortless flight. This bird has little fear of man, and while on the ground is easily approachable. It also nests along Barking Sands. The **wedge-tailed shearwater** *(ua'u kani)* is known as the "moaning bird" because of its doleful sounds. These birds have no fear of predators and often fall prey to feral dogs and cats. Also seen making spectacular dives for squid off Kilauea Point is the **red-footed booby**, a fluffy white bird with a blue bill and a three-foot wingspan. One of the most amazing is the **great frigate bird**, an awesome specimen with an eight-foot wingspan. Predominantly black, the males have a red throat pouch that they inflate like a balloon. These giants, the kings of the rookery, often steal food from lesser birds. They nest off Kilauea Point and are also seen along Kalalau Trail and even at Poipu Beach.

Many of Kauai's water birds are most easily found in the marshes and ponds of **Hanalei National Wildlife Refuge**, though they have also been spotted on some of the island's reservoirs, especially at **Menehune Fish Pond** in the **Huleia National Wildlife Refuge** and its vicinity. The **Hawaiian stilt** *(ae'o)* is a 1½-foot-tall wading bird with pink stick-like legs. The **Hawaiian coot** *(alae ke'oke'o)* is a gray-black duck-like bird with a white belly and face. The **Hawaiian gallinule** *(alae ula)*, an endemic Hawaiian bird often found in Hanalei's taro patches, has a duck-like body with a red face tipped in yellow. It uses its huge chicken-like feet to hop across floating vegetation. The **Hawaiian duck** *(koloa maoli)* looks like a mallard, and because of interbreeding with common ducks, is becoming rarer as a distinctive species.

Indigenous Forest Birds
Kauai's upland forests are still home to many Hawaiian birds; they're dwindling but holding on. You may be lucky enough to spot some of the following. The **Hawaiian owl** *(pueo)*, one of the friendliest *aumakua* (ancestral spirit) in ancient Hawaii, hunts both by day and night. The **elepaio** is an indigenous bird found around Kokee and so named because its song sounds like its name. A small brown bird with white rump feathers, it's very friendly and can even be prompted to come to an observer offering food. Found above 2,000 feet, feeding on a variety of insects

the friendly elepaio

and flowers, is the **iiwi**, a bright red bird with salmon-colored hooked bill. While most often sounding like a squeaking hinge, it can also produce a melodious song. **Anianiau** is a four-inch yellow-green bird found around Kokee. Its demise is due to a lack of fear of man. The **nukupu'u,** extinct on the other islands except for a few on Maui, is found in Kauai's upper forests and bordering the Alakai Swamp. It's a five-inch bird with a drab green back and a bright yellow chest.

Birds Of The Alakai Swamp
The following scarce birds are some of the last indigenous Hawaiian birds, saved only by the inhospitability of the Alakai Swamp. All are endangered species and under no circumstances should they be disturbed. The last survivors include: the **o'u**, a chubby seven-inch bird with a green body, yellow head, and lovely whistle ranging half an octave; the relatively common **Hawaiian creeper**, a hand-sized bird with a light green back and white belly, which travels in pairs and searches bark for insects; **puaiohi,** a dark brown, white-bellied seven-inch bird that is so rare that its nesting habits are unknown. The **o'o'a'a',** although its name may resemble the sounds you make getting into a steaming hot tub, is an eight-inch black bird which played a special role in Hawaiian history. Its blazing yellow leg feathers were used to fashion the spectacular capes and helmets of the *ali'i.* Even before the white man came, this bird was ruthlessly pursued by specially trained hunters that cap-

tured it and plucked its feathers. The *akialoa* is a seven-inch greenish-yellow bird with a long, slender, curved bill.

BOTANICAL GARDENS AND NATURAL HISTORY MUSEUM

For those interested in the flora of Kauai beyond what can be seen out of the car window, a visit to the following will be both educational and inspiring. **Kokee Natural History Museum**, just past the Kokee State Park HQ, has exhibits explaining the geology and plant and animal life of the park and the surrounding upper mountain and swamp regions of the island, tel. 335-9975. Free; open daily from 10 to 4.

Pacific Tropical Botanical Gardens in Lawai is the only research facility for tropical plants in the country and the premier botanical garden on Kauai (see p. 827). Lasting about 2½ hours and costing $15, tours are given twice daily during the week and once a day on weekends. The visitors center/museum/gift shop is open daily from 7:30 to 4 for walk-in visitors. Here you can take a short self-guided tour (map provided) of the plants around this building, but to go into the gardens you need reservations in advance. Call 332-7361 for information.

Nearby in Kalaheo is the **Olu Pua Gardens.** Formerly the manager's estate of the Kauai Pineapple Plantation, these gardens are open to the public for a limited time daily at 9:30 a.m., 11:30 a.m., and 1:30 p.m. The 12½-acre site includes *kaukau,* hibiscus, palm, and jungle gardens, as well as a front lawn of flowering shade trees. Tours are $10 and reservations may be made by calling 332-8182 (see p. 829).

The **Kiahuna Plantation Gardens** are located at the Kiahuna Plantation Resort in Poipu. Over a 27-year period during the mid-1900s, five acres of this former plantation site were cultivated with about 2,500 plants from Africa, the Americas, the Pacific, and India, and include cactus and aloe sections. Open daily during daylight hours, free guided tours of the property are given weekdays at 10 a.m.; call 742-6411 for more information (see p. 813).

In Lihue is the privately owned **Menehune Garden**, where all plants are labeled and many of their uses explained, tel. 245-2660. It is hoped that after current litigation, this garden will quickly reopen so as to enrich your experience of the island (see p. 763).

Smith's Tropical Paradise, a finely manicured and well-kept botanical and cultural garden with a bountiful, beautiful collection of ordinary and exotic plants (many labeled), is on 30 riverfront acres adjacent to the Wailua marina. Have a look here before heading upcountry. Open until 4:30 p.m., entrance rates are $4 for adults and $2 for children 2-11 (see p.775X). For information call 822-4654.

HISTORY

Kauai is *first* among the Hawaiian islands in many ways. Besides being the oldest main island geologically, it's believed that Kauai was the first island to be populated by Polynesian explorers. Theoretically, this colony was well established as early as A.D. 200, which predates the populating of the other islands by almost 500 years. Even Madame Pele chose Kauai as her first home and was content here until her sister drove her away. Her fires went out when she moved on, but she, like all visitors, never forgot Kauai.

Mu And Menehune
Hawaiian legends give accounts of dwarf-like aborigines on Kauai called the Mu and the Menehune. These two hirsute tribes of pixie-like creatures were said to have lived on the island before and after the arrival of the Polynesians. The Mu were fond of jokes and games, while the Menehune were dedicated workers, stonemasons par excellence, who could build monumental structures in just one night. Many stoneworks that can still be seen around the island are attributed to these hard-working nocturnal people, and a wonderfully educational exhibit concerning these pre-contact leprechauns is presented at the Kauai Museum.

Anthropological theory supports the legends that say that some non-Polynesian peoples actually did exist on Kauai. According to oral history, their chief felt that too much interplay and intermarriage was occurring with the Polynesians. He wished his race to remain pure so he ordered them to leave on a "triple-decker floating island," and they haven't been seen since, though if you ask a Kauaian if he or she believes in the Menehune, the answer is likely to be, "Of course not! But, they're there anyway." Speculation holds that they may have been an entirely different race of people or perhaps the remaining tribes of the first Polynesians. It's possible that they were cut off from their original culture for so long that they developed their own separate culture, and that the food supply was so diminished that their very stature was reduced in comparison to other Polynesians.

Written History

The written history of Hawaii began when Capt. James Cook sailed into Waimea Bay on Kauai's south shore on the afternoon of September 20, 1778, and opened Hawaii to the rest of the world. In the years just preceding Cook's discovery, Hawaii was undergoing a unique change. Kamehameha the Great, a chief of the Big Island, was in the process of conquering the islands and uniting them under his rule. King Kaumualii of Kauai was able to remain independent from Kamehameha's rule by his use of diplomacy, guile, and the large distances separating his island from the others. Finally, after all the other islands had been subjugated, Kaumualii joined Kamehameha through negotiations, not warfare; he retained control of Kauai by being made governor of the island by Kamehameha. After Kamehameha died, his successor, Kamehameha II, forced Kaumualii to go to Oahu, where arrangements were made for him to marry the great queen Kaahumanu, the favorite wife of Kamehameha, and the greatest surviving *ali'i* of the land. Kaumualii never returned to his native island.

Hawaii was in a great state of flux at the beginning of the 1800s. The missionaries were coming, along with adventurers and schemers from throughout Europe. One of the latter was George Scheffer, a Prussian in the service of Czar Nicholas of Russia. He convinced Kaumualii to build a Russian fort in Waimea in 1817, which Kaumualii saw as a means to discourage other Europeans from overrunning his lands. A loose alliance was made between Kaumualii and Scheffer. The adventurer eventually lost the czar's support, and Kaumualii ran him off the island, but the remains of **Fort Elizabeth** still

stand. Around the same time, George Kaumualii, the king's son who had been sent to Boston to be educated, was accompanying the first missionary packet to the islands. He came with Rev. Sam Whitney, whom Kaumualii invited to stay, and who planted the first sugar on the island and taught the natives to dig wells. **Wailoi Mission House**, just north of Hanalei, dates from 1836 and is still standing and preserved as a museum. Nearby, Hanalei Bay was a commercial harbor for trading and whaling. From here, produce such as oranges was shipped from Na Pali farms to California. In Koloa, on the opposite end of the island, a stack from the Koloa Sugar plantation, started in 1835, marks the site of the first successful sugar-refining operation in the islands. Another successful enterprise was **Lihue Plantation.** Founded by a German firm in 1850, it prospered until WW I, when anti-German sentiment forced the owners to sell out. In Lihue town, you can still see the Haleko Shops, a cluster of four two-story buildings that show a strong German influence. The **Lihue Lutheran Church** has an ornate altar very similar to ones found in old German churches.

During the 1870s and '80s, leprosy raged throughout the kingdom and strong measures were taken. Those believed to be afflicted were wrenched from their families and sent to the hideous colony of Kalaupapa on Molokai. One famous Kauaian leper, Koolau, born in 1862 in Kekaha, refused to be brought in and took his family to live in the mountain fortress of Na Pali. He fought the authorities for years and killed all those sent to take him in. He was made popular by Jack London in his short story, "Koolau, the Leper."

When WW II came to Hawaii, Nawiliwili Harbor was shelled on December 31, 1941, but there was little damage. The island remained much the same, quiet and rural until the late 1960s when development began in earnest. The first resort destination on the island was the Coco Palms Hotel in Wailua, followed by development in Poipu, and another in Princeville. Meanwhile, Hollywood had discovered Kauai and featured its haunting beauty as a "silent star" in dozens of major films. Today, development goes on, but the island remains quiet, serene, and beautiful.

GOVERNMENT, PEOPLE, AND ECONOMY

GOVERNMENT

Kauai County

Kauai County is comprised of the inhabited islands of Kauai and Niihau and the uninhabited islands of Kaula and Lehua. Lihue is the county seat. It's represented by two state senators elected from the 24th District, a split district including north Kauai and the Waianae Coast of Oahu, and the 25th District, which includes all of southern Kauai and Niihau. Kauai has three state congressmen, one from the 49th District, which is again a split district with north Kauai and the Waianae Coast, the other two from the 50th District around Lihue and the 51st District, which includes all of southwestern Kauai and Niihau. Elected in 1988, the present mayor of Kauai County is JoAnn Yukimura.

ECONOMY

The economy of Kauai, like that of the entire state, is based on agriculture, the military, and tourism, the fastest-growing sector.

Tourism

Kauai, third-most-visited island after Oahu and Maui, attracts about one million visitors annually, accounting for 17% of the state's total. Approximately 7,200 hotel and condo units are available, averaging about a 70% occupancy rate. At one time, Kauai was the most difficult island on which to build a resort because of a strong grass-roots antidevelopment faction. Recently, this trend has been changing due to the recession that hit everyone after Hurricane Iwa scared off many tourists. Island residents realized how much their livelihood was tied to tourism, and a recent ad campaign depicting tourists as visitors (rather than unwelcome invaders) has helped in their acceptance. Also, the resorts being built on Kauai are first rate, and the developers are savvy enough to create "destination areas" instead of more high-rise boxes of rooms. Three of the finest hotels in Hawaii include the recently completed Sheraton Princeville overlooking Hanalei Bay, the fabulous Waiohai Resort of Poipu Beach, and the gargantuan Westin Kauai in Li-hue. Also, Kauai's quality of room compared to price is the state's best.

Agriculture

Agriculture still accounts for a hefty portion of Kauai's income. **Sugar** has taken a recent downward trend from a yearly yield of $85 million in 1980 to about $50 million today. Kauai produces about 6% of the state's diversified agricultural crop, with a strong yield in papayas. But in 1982, California banned the importation of Kauai's papayas because they were sprayed with EDB. Hanalei Valley and many other smaller areas produce five million pounds of taro that is quickly turned into poi, and the county produces two million pounds of guavas, as well as pineapples, beef, and pork for its own use. A growing aquaculture industry produces prawns. Recently, large acreages near Kalaheo have been put into coffee, tea, and macadamia nut production.

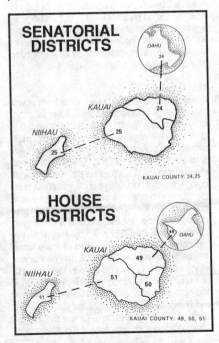

SENATORIAL DISTRICTS

OAHU
24
KAUAI
24
NIIHAU
25
25

KAUAI COUNTY: 24,25

HOUSE DISTRICTS

49 OAHU
KAUAI
49
NIIHAU
51
51
50

KAUAI COUNTY: 49, 50, 51

Military

The military influence on Kauai is small but vital. NASA's major tracking facilities in Kokee Park are now being turned over to the Navy and Air Force. At **Barking Sands**, the Navy operates BARSTUR, an underwater tactical range for training in antisubmarine warfare. Also along Barking Sands (a fitting name!) is the **Pacific Missile Range**, operated by the Navy but available to the Air Force, Department of Defense, NASA, and the Department of Energy. Civilian visitors to these facilities are few and far between, and as welcome as door-to-door encyclopedia salespeople.

POPULATION

Kauai County's 48,000 people, plus 230 relatively pure-blood Hawaiians living on Niihau, account for only 4% of the state's total population, making it the least populous county. Also, 325

KAUAI POPULATION	
White	28%
Filipino	26%
Japanese	25%
Hawaiian	15%
Various	5%
Chinese	1%

military personnel and their dependents live on the island. The largest town is Kapaa with 4,500 people, followed by Lihue with 4,000. Ethnically, there is no clear majority on Kauai. The people of Kauai include: 28% Caucasians, 26% Filipinos, 25% Japanese, 15% Hawaiians, including those of mixed blood, 1.3% Chinese, and the remaining 5% are Koreans, Samoans, and a smattering of Afro-Americans and American Indians.

GETTING THERE

Kauai's Lihue Airport is connected to all the Hawaiian Islands by direct flight, but no nonstop flights from the Mainland are currently operating. All Mainland and international passengers arrive via Honolulu, from which the three major inter-island carriers offer numerous daily flights.

The Airports

Lihue Airport, less than two miles from downtown Lihue, Lihue Airport receives the vast majority of Kauai's flights. No public transportation to or from the airport is available, so you must either rent a car, hitch (fairly good opportunities), or hire a taxi (about $3.50). The new terminal, long and low, has a restaurant and cocktail lounge, snack shop, flower shop, gift shop, restrooms, and a handful of suitcase-sized coin lockers ($1) in the lobby. The gift shop sells pre-inspected island fruit that's boxed and ready to transport; tel. 245-6273. All major car rental agencies and a good number of local firms maintain booths just outside the main entrance-way; other agencies send vans to the airport to pick up customers. Baggage pick-up is at either end of the building, Aloha and United to the left, and Hawaiian Air to the right, as you enter the terminal from the plane —follow the signs. Check-in counters are along the outside corri-

dor, Hawaiian Air on the left, and Aloha and United on the right, as you look at the terminal building. All non-carry-on baggage must go through an agricultural inspection at the terminal entrance; carry-on luggage is run through X-ray machines.

Princeville Airport is basically a strip servicing Princeville. Located along Route 56 just east of town, it is used only by Aloha Island Air and Papillon Helicopters. The terminal is a cute little building made inconspicuous by the immense beauty surrounding it, and there is a toilet, telephone, Amelia's Cafe and lounge, and Hertz and Avis car rental offices. Located on the second floor, with windows looking out onto the runway and open to the lobby below, Amelia's serves drinks, sandwiches, hot dogs, nachos, and chili—most for under $5. The rental car booths stay open until the last incoming flight has arrived.

Kauai's Lihue Airport is connected to all the Hawaiian Islands by direct flight, but no nonstop flights from the Mainland are currently operating. All Mainland and international passengers arrive via Honolulu, from which the three major inter-island carriers offer numerous daily flights.

Average flying times to Kauai are 35 minutes from Honolulu, one to two hours from the Big Is-

and depending upon stops, and just over one hour from Maui, including the stop in Honolulu. Outgoing and incoming flights are dispersed equally throughout the day.

The Airline Carriers

Hawaiian Air, on Kauai tel. 245-3671, (800) 367-5320 on the Mainland, offers the largest number of daily flights. From Honolulu, 26 nonstop flights depart from 5:40 a.m. to 8 p.m.; from Kahului, Maui, 17 flights run from 6:30 a.m. to 7:10 p.m., two nonstop; from Kapalua, West Maui, there are 14 flights from 7:15 a.m. to 5:15 p.m., all passing through Honolulu; from Kona, Hawaii, 10 flights from 6:55 a.m. to 5:05 p.m. stop in Maui or Honolulu; from Hilo, Hawaii, seven flights from 6:55 a.m. to 6:30 p.m. all stop in Maui or Honolulu; from Lanai, two afternoon flights run via Honolulu; and from Molokai, 10 flights from 7:55 a.m. to 6:40 p.m. all go via Honolulu.

Aloha Airlines, on Kauai tel. 245-3691 and (800) 367-5250 on the Mainland, connects Kauai to Honolulu, Maui, and both Kona and Hilo on Hawaii. Aloha's routes to Lihue are: from Honolulu, 22 nonstop flights from 5:40 a.m. until 6:10 p.m.; from Maui, 15 flights via Honolulu from 6:35 a.m. to 7 p.m., and two nonstop flights at 10:25 a.m. and 11:55 a.m.; from Kona, 13 flights via Honolulu and/or Maui from 6:45 a.m. to 5:35 p.m.; and from Hilo, nine flights from 7 a.m. to 6:30 p.m.

Aloha Island Air (formerly Princeville Airways), tel. (800) 652-6541 on Kauai and (800) 323-3345 on the Mainland, is a commuter airline operating flights to and from Princeville Airport on Kauai's north shore. Flying comfortable 18-passenger Twin Otter De Havilland aircraft, they connect the resort community of Princeville with airports on all the islands. There are seven daily nonstop flights from Honolulu starting at 6 a.m. and ending at 5:15 p.m.; the four flights (8:30 a.m. to 4:35 p.m.) from Molokai all stop in Honolulu. Flights from Kapalua, West Maui, arrive four times a day, 9:10 a.m. until 3:35 p.m., all with one stop; from Kahului, Maui, they run from 8:35 a.m. until 3:30 p.m., all with two stops; and from Hana, Maui, flights leave three times daily from 8:10 a.m. until 2:45 p.m., all with three stops. Additional flights come from Lanai at 9:05 a.m. and 4:10 p.m., and from Kamuela, Hawaii, at 7:30 a.m. and 1:40 p.m., all going through Honolulu.

GETTING AROUND

The most common way to get around Kauai is by rental car. Plenty of agencies keep prices competitive. As always, reserve during peak season, and take your chances by shopping around to score a good deal in the off-season. Kauai also has limited shuttle bus service, expensive taxis, bicycle, moped and scooter rentals, and the good old (legal) thumb.

RENTAL CARS

Many agencies maintain rental booths or courtesy phones at Lihue Airport. The larger companies offer all types of cars from compacts to luxury cars, many with convertibles and jeeps; the smaller companies deal more with the economical compacts. Local companies with reliable reputations are **Tropical**, tel. 245-6988, with free prompt pick-up service from Lihue and very reasonable prices; and **Robert's**, tel. 245-4008, which has new cars and reasonable rates, can supply mini vans, and has some fly/drive deals with Hawaiian Air. Also available are: **Thrifty**, tel. 245-7388 or (800) 426-2534; **Rent-a-Wreck**, tel. 245-4755, which offers great deals in late-model cars; and **Westside-U-Drive**, tel. 332-864.

Nationwide firms include **National Car Rental**, tel. 245-3502 or (800) 342-8431 in Hawaii and (800) 227-7368 on the Mainland, which features GM and Nissan cars and accepts all major credit cards. They rent without a credit card if you leave a $100/day deposit, less if you take full insurance coverage. **Budget**, tel. 245-1901 or (800) 527-0700, also maintains offices at the Coco Palms, the Waiohai Resort in Poipu, the Hilton, and the Kiahuna Plantation. They work extensively with major hotel/condos on fly-/drive/accommodation deals. **Hertz**, tel. 245-3356 or (800) 654-3131, is competitively priced with many fly/drive deals. They also maintain desks at the Sheration hotels in Poipu, Waipouli, and Princeville, at the Princeville Airport, and at the Westin Kauai. Others are **Alamo**, tel. 245-

8953 or (800) 327-9633, with a dubious reputation; **Avis**, tel. 245-3512, tel. 826-9773 in Princeville, or (800) 831-8000; and **Dollar**, tel. 245-3651 or (800) 342-7398.

Specialty rental agencies are: **Bad Cars**, which offers fast Maserati, Porsche, and Ferrari sports cars, with a $1000 deposit; and **Adventures Unlimited**, tel. 245-9622, for four-wheel-drive jeeps and mopeds.

Mopeds and **scooters** are also available from **South Shore Activities**, tel. 742-6873, at Poipu Beach, $22 for eight hours; for $10 a day from **Budget** rental car at Kiahuna Plantation in Poipu; and by the hour or $20 for eight hours from **Pedal and Paddle** in Hanalei, tel. 826-9069.

OTHER ALTERNATIVES

Buses And Taxis

There is no public transportation on Kauai. The **Shoppe Hopper Shuttle** is virtually the only company that services the resort and shopping areas on the east and south shores of the island. The eastside route runs from Kapaa to Kukui Grove Center, with scheduled stops at the Sheraton, Coco Palms, and Kauai Hilton hotels; "call for pick-up" stops are at Lihue Airport, Westin Kauai, Kukui Grove Center, and the Market Place shopping center. The southside route has scheduled stops at the Sheraton Kauai and Stouffer Waiohai Resort in Poipu, with "call for pick-up" stops at Koloa, Lihue Airport, Westin Kauai, and Kukui Grove Center. One-way fares vary from $1 (Kapaa to Wailua) to $9 (Poipu to Kapaa); children under 13 ride for half price. The shuttle runs from about 9 a.m. until 3 p.m.—no service on Sunday. Reservations are recommended, and group charter rates are available for $20 per hour. For reservations and information call 332-7272.

Taxis are all metered and charge a hefty price for their services; all have the same rates. Airport taxis have a monopoly on pick-ups at the airport, although others can drop off there. Sample fares are $3.50 from Lihue and $25 from Poipu to the airport, $22 from Lihue to Poipu, $52 from Lihue to Princeville, and $18 from Princeville to Kee Beach and the Kalalau trailhead. Reputable companies include: **Akiko's**, tel. 822-3613, in Wailua; **A-1**, tel. 742-7441, in Poipu; **Garden Isle**, tel. 245-6161, in Lihue; and **North Shore Taxi**, tel. 826-6189, in Hanalei.

Hitchhiking

Using your thumb to get around is legal on Kauai, but you must stay off the paved portion of the road. For short hops in and around the towns, like from Koloa to Poipu or from the airport to Lihue, thumbing isn't difficult. But getting out to the Kalalau Trail or to Polihale on the west end, when you're toting a backpack and appear to be going a longer distance, is tough. As on all the islands, your best chance of being picked up is by a visiting or local *haole*. Sometimes locals in pickup trucks will stop to give you a ride for short distances. Women *should not* hitch alone!

Bicycles

Riding a bike around Kauai is fairly easy, thanks to the lack of big hills, except for the road up to Kokee State Park. If you attempt this ride, you'll have to be in excellent condition. Going up, take Kokee Road, which has a relatively gradual climb and better surface as compared to Waimea Canyon Road. The latter, however, is great to zoom down. Island-wide, traffic is moderate, especially in the cool of early morning when it's best for making some distance. Peak seasons bring a dramatic increase in traffic and road congestion. Roads are generally good, but shoulders aren't wide and are sometimes nonexistent. Take care! Perhaps the best riding is by mountain bike on the cane haul roads that head into the interior. Rental bikes go for about $5 an hour, or $15-20 a day. Rental shops include: **Aquatics Kauai**, tel. 822-9213, in Kapaa; **Shore Activities**, tel. 742-6873, at Poipu Beach; and **Pedal and Paddle**, tel. 826-9069, in Hanalei. The best bike shop on the island for sales and repair is **Bicycle Kauai**, tel. 822-3315, at 1379 Kuhio Hwy. in Kapaa. Stop in, take a look at their huge topo map of Kauai, and talk to the guys; they can give you great advice on where to ride for your type of bike. Other shops include **Bicycle John**, tel. 245-7579; **Kawamoto's**, tel. 922-4771; **Dan's Sport Shop**, tel. 246-0151; and **Kauai Sports**, tel. 245-8052. Shipping your own bicycle inter-island costs about $20, and from the Mainland another $25 if it goes on a different airline. You must provide your own box and pack the bike yourself.

SIGHTSEEING TOURS

Magnificent Kauai is fascinating to explore by land, sea, or air. Looking around on your own is no problem, but some of the most outstanding areas are more expediently seen with a professional guide. Some options are discussed below.

Van And Bus Tours

On Kauai, most tour companies run vans, but some larger companies also use buses. Though cheaper, tours on a full-sized coach are generally less personalized. Wherever a bus can go, so can your rental car, but on a tour you can relax and enjoy the scenery without worrying about driving. Also, the drivers are very experienced with the area and know many stories and legends with which they annotate and enrich your trip. Coach tours vary, but typical trips go to Hanalei and the north coast, to Waimea Canyon and the south coast sights, or combine one of these tours with the Wailua River. Each agency has its own route and schedule, but all hit the major tourist sites. Rates sometimes include entrance fees and lunch. Half-day fares run about $25-35, while full-day fares run $45-60; children's fares are about one-quarter less. Fares also vary according to area of pick-up and route. Tours are usually run with a minimum number of people, but it is possible to join another group to fill a van. Often a tour to the Fern Grotto is considered the "highlight" . . . that should say it all! Companies offering these tours include **Trans Hawaiian**, tel. 245-5108; **Polynesian Adventure Tours**, tel. 246-0122; **Chandler's Kauai Tours**, tel. 245-9134; **Robert's Hawaii**, tel. 245-9558; and **Grayline-Kauai**, tel. 245-3344.

One unique tour company is **Kauai Mountain Tours, Inc.** It alone is licensed to operate tours in the Na Pali Kona Forest Reserve. Knowledgeable guides take you into the backcountry over dirt roads by four-wheel-drive GMC Suburbans, with an informed narrative on the way. They let you see a part of Kauai not reached by anyone that doesn't walk in. Traveling is rough but the sights are unsurpassed; truly, this is one of the few ways in Kauai to get off the beaten path. Their guides, like Anthony, a native Hawaiian, are excellent. Anthony has a tremendous amount of knowledge about the island's flora and fauna, and he has been known to bring in specimens of very rare plants and flowers so that local artists can sketch them for posterity. However, he won't tell where he found them! This seven-hour adventure costs $72 plus tax ($51.90 for children under 11), and includes a picnic lunch prepared by the Green Garden Restaurant. Tours start about 8 a.m. There is free pick-up in the Wailua and Poipu areas, but an extra $15 is charged for pick-up in Princeville. A shorter, 4½- to five-hour trip is also available, costing $55 plus tax with no lunch, but it is not as highly recommended as much less time is actually spent in the backcountry. For information and reservations call 245-7224 or (800) 222-7756, or write P.O. Box 3069, Lihue, Kauai, HI 96766.

Helicopter Tours

Flying in a chopper is a thrilling experience, like flying in a light plane . . . with a twist. They take you into all those otherwise inaccessible little nooks and crannies. Routes cover the entire island, but the highlights are flying through Waimea Canyon, into the Mount Waialeale crater, where it almost never stops raining, and over the Alakai Swamp, where you see thousands of waterfalls and even 360-degree rainbows floating in midair. Then, to top it off, you fly to the Na Pali Coast, swooping along its ruffled edge and dipping down for an up-close look at its caves and giant seacliffs. Earphones cut the noise of the aircraft and play soul-stirring music as a background to the pilot's narration. The basic one-hour around-the-island flight runs about $130 per person; other flights are 45-75 minutes in length. Some companies tailor your own flight, which might include a swim at a remote pool along with a champagne lunch, but these are more costly. Niihau Helicopters also flies periodically to points on Niihau. These flights are more expensive, but it's the only way to get to see this island up close. Discounts of up to 15% from some of the companies are always featured in the ubiquitous free tourist brochures, and are occasionally offered through tourist activity and information centers.

Outdoor purists disparage this mode of transport, saying, "If you can't hike in you shouldn't be there," but that's tunnel vision and not always appropriate. To go deep into the mist-shrouded interior, especially through the Alakai Swamp, the average traveler "can't get there from here" ... it's just too rugged and dangerous! The only reasonable way to see it is by helicopter, and except for the noise, choppers actually have less of an impact on the ecosystem than hikers.

Everyone has an opinion on which company offers the best ride, the best narration, or the best service. All the helicopter companies on Kauai are safe and reputable, and most fly Bell Jet Ranger equipment or Hughes 550-D models. Some helicopters accommodate only four passengers while others take five; some have two-way microphones so you can ask questions of the pilot. Make sure that everyone has a window seat or at least an unobstructed view out the front bubble window.

Of the nearly two dozen helicopter companies on Kauai, the majority operate from Lihue Airport, a handful from Burns Field in Hanapepe, and one flies from the Princeville airport. The following have top-notch reputations. **Ohana Helicopter Tours**, 3222 Kuhio Hwy., Suite #4, Lihue, Hi 96766, tel. 245-3995 or (800) 222-6989, is an owner-operated company that gives personalized service. Either "Mrs. Bogart" or Nancy (a talkative Texan with a big smile, strong hug, and a desire to make you feel as welcome as can be) greets you at the office and explains the flight procedure and what the ride will be like. They want you to have the time of your life—not hard with this experience. The pilot, Bogart Kealoha, has years of commercial and military experience, and *knows* this island of his birth. From smooth liftoff to gentle landing, you are in good hands.

The granddaddy of them all is **Jack Harter Helicopters**, Box 306, Lihue, HI 96766, tel. 245-3774. Jack, along with his wife Beverly, literally started the helicopter business on Kauai, and has been flying the island for over 20 years. Jack doesn't advertise but he is always booked up. He knows countless stories about Kauai and just about everywhere to go on the island. He gives you a full hour and a half in the air, and his logo, "Imitated by all, equalled by none," says it all.

The slickest and best of the new companies is **Papillon Helicopters**, Box 339, Hanalei, HI 96714, tel. 826-6591 or (800) 367-7095. They fly from their own heliport at Princeville, just past mile marker 26, with some flights leaving from Lihue Airport, and offer the largest variety of tours. Besides taking you around the island, one tour features a drop-off with gourmet picnic lunch at a secluded hideaway. At their facilities in Princeville, you are treated to a pre-flight video orientation, while hostesses offer munchies, juice, and wine.

Other companies with good reputations and competitive prices flying out of Lihue Airport are: **Mehehune Helicopters**, 3222 Kuhio Hwy., Suite #2, Lihue, HI 96766, tel. 245-7705; **Island Helicopters**, Box 3101, Lihue, HI 96766, tel. 245-8588, owned and piloted by Curt Lofstedt, who also hires Rudy Dela Cruz, a local instructor with the Air National Guard; **South Seas Helicopters**, P.O. Box 1445, Lihue, HI 96766, tel. 245-7781 or (800) 367- 2914; **Kenai Helicopters**, tel. 245-8591 or (800) 622-3144, which also operates on the Big Island; and **Will Squyre Helicopters**, tel. 245-8881, a one-man operation with personalized service from a man who loves his work.

Reputable companies that fly from Burns Field in Hanapepe are: **Inter-island Helicopters**, P.O. Box 156, Hanapepe, HI 96716, tel. 335-5009 or (800) 245-9696, which offers tailor-made group flights and aerial photography options in addition to its tourist flights; **Bruce Needham Helicopters**, tel. 335-3115; **Bali Hai**, tel. 332-7331; and **Niihau Helicopters**, P.O. Box 370, Makaweli, HI 96769, tel. 335-3500. The primary purpose of Niihau Helicopters is to provide medical and emergency treatment for the residents of Niihau. However, to defray costs, occasional, nonscheduled tourist charters are offered on its twin-engine Agusta 109A. Two of their flights last 90 and 110 minutes, each with 30-minute stops on secluded beaches on Niihau; fares are $185 and $235, respectively. Two other options are an overflight of Niihau for $135, and a tour of the Na Pali Coast with a Niihau overflight for $235. While they cannot compete with helicopter companies that regularly fly only over Kauai, Niihau Helicopters does offer you the only way to see Niihau up close. Let pilot Tom Mishler show you a bit of this Forbidden Island.

Glider Flights
Who says you can't fly without an engine? **Tradewinds Glider** proves that you can, enjoyably. Operating out of Port Allen Airport, this is the only glider outfit on the island. A tow plane

pulls the glider to about 4,000 feet before the release is pulled and you're set free. Not silent as many suspect, there is a constant not-so-muffled rush of air over the cockpit and wings. Heading for the nearest cloud, the glider swoops alongside to take advantage of lift. The pilot rides thermals of rising warm air to gain elevation and dips under clouds or soars across cloudless space to pick up speed and increase distance. In the right conditions, the constant elevation gain and speed of gliding can keep you going all day for great distances, as cross-country gliders do. The sailplanes here rarely go faster than 80 mph (unless in a dive) or over 5,000 feet in elevation. Although speed change is obvious, your change in elevation is almost imperceptible unless you check the altimeter on the control panel.

Glider pilots need visual references: land formations, the sea, clouds and their shadows, plus wind direction and thermals are all important in determining where, how, and for how long you can fly. Keep an eye out for the split-tailed, white tropic birds, for they have better instruments than your plane and know more intuitively than man how to take advantage of the air conditions. Watch also the constant change in cloud formation, for they seem to appear and disappear before your eyes. The great height lends fabulous perspective to land formations; waterfalls of the interior, mountain ridges and broad slopes, farm boundaries, and the coastline all take on an entirely different character.

Take along a hat (the glass bubble of the cockpit intensifies the sun's rays) and a plastic bag, even if you don't have a tendency to be affected by motion sickness.

Tradewinds Glider offers three flight options: the 20-minute Hanapepe scenic tour for $75 s, $90 d (you can ride two in the back seat, if you're slim), the 40-minute "Top Gun" flight for $125 s, $150 d, and the 20-minute thrill-seeker acrobatic flight for $175, where you do loops, spins, wingovers, and rolls in the sky. From takeoff to landing, any of these will be a memorable flight and great photo opportunity. All pilots are licensed and the planes are serviced and inspected on a regular schedule. Open 9 to 5 daily, the Tradewinds Glider office is near the Green Garden restaurant on Kuhio Highway in Hanapepe. For information, reservations, and directions to the airport call 335-5086.

Wailua River Cruises

You too can be one of the many cruising up the Wailua River on a large, canopied, motorized barge. The Fern Grotto, where the boat docks, is a natural amphitheater festooned with hanging ferns, and one of the most touristed spots in Hawaii. The oldest company is **Smith's Motor Boat Service**, tel. 822-4111, in operation since 1947. The extended Smith family still operates the business and members serve in every capacity. During the 20-minute ride upriver you're entertained with music and recounting of leg-

Tourist boat on the Wailua River cruising to the Fern Grotto

ends, and at the Fern Grotto a small but well-done medley of island songs is performed. Daily cruises depart every half hour from Wailua Marina from 9 a.m. till 4 p.m. Adults $9, children $4.50 Evening cruises are only done for large groups by special request. **Waialeale Boat Tours**, tel. 822-4908, is Smith's only competition. Also at the marina, they're a smaller operation with the same rates.

Zodiacs, Catamarans, And Kayaks

The exact opposite experience from the tame Wailua River trip is an adventurous ride down the Na Pali Coast in a motorized rubber raft, a specially built kayak, a Boston whaler, or catamaran.

A **Zodiac** is a very tough motorized rubber raft. It looks like a big, horseshoe-shaped inner-tube that bends itself and undulates with the waves like a floating waterbed. These seaworthy craft, powered by twin Mercury 280s, have five separate air chambers for unsinkable safety. They'll take you for a thrilling ride down the Na Pali Coast, pausing along the way to whisk you into caves and caverns. Once at Kalalau Valley, you can swim and snorkel before the return ride; the roundtrip, including the stop, takes about five hours. If you wish, you can stay overnight and be picked up the next day, or hike in or out and ride only one way; this service is $60 OW, $105 RT. You roll with the wind and sea going down the coast and head into it coming back. The wind generally picks up in the afternoon, so for a more comfortable ride, book the morning cruise.

Other Zodiac trips include a hike to an archaeological site at Nualolo Kai Beach, a whale-watching tour, and a trip to Kipu Kai or up little-visited rivers on the south coast. All are popular so make reservations. Rates vary with the season and particular expedition, but the ultimate once-in-a-lifetime ride is around $135. Shorter trips vary from $60-65. Bring bathing suit, snorkel gear (rental available), lunch, drinks (cooler provided), camera (in a plastic bag for protection), sneakers for exploring, and a windbreaker for the return ride. Summer weather permits excursions almost every day, but winter's swells are turbulent and these experienced seamen won't go if it's too rough. Take their word for it! Pregnant women and those with bad backs are not advised to ride.

Oldest and best known of the Zodiac companies is **Na Pali Zodiac**, Box 456, Hanalei, HI 96714, tel. 826-9371 or (800) 422-7824, owned and operated by "Captain Zodiac," Clancy Greff, and his wife Pam. They now operate on Maui and Hawaii, too. **Blue Odyssey Kauai**, tel. 826-9033, gives Zodiac rides in 28-foot craft, the largest on the coast. Their north coast trips last 4½ hours and cost $65-75. On their "Tandem Tour" you can go one way by Zodiac and return via cabin cruiser. Their south coast trip is slightly less expensive and combines whalewatching (in season) and a beach party. **Bali Hai Charters**, tel. 826-9787, and **Hanalei Sea Tours**, tel. 826-7254, also have Zodiacs.

For those who want or need a smoother ride, try a Boston whaler or catamaran. Boston whalers are stable flat-hulled ships, the fastest on the coast, and catamarans ride on two widely spaced hulls. Both provide smooth sailing down the coast and get you back in great comfort. Like the Zodiacs, each ventures into the sea caves (sea conditions permitting), stop for you to snorkel, and provide complimentary snacks after your swim. Tours vary, but typically are: half day for about $65; five hours, with a hike to an ancient fishing village site at Nualolo Kai, for $90; whalewatching trips on the north and south coasts for $45-65; and during the summer, sunset tours for $80. When calling be sure to ask about the particulars of each trip and what "extras" each company provides.

Paradise Adventure Cruises, Inc., P.O. Box 1379, Hanalei, HI 96714, tel. 826-9999, owned by Byron Fears, runs the most personalized charter boat trips on the island, taking a maximum of six passengers on his Boston whalers. All his captains know the coast well, and one may even take out his guitar and serenade you while you're scarfing down the crackers, cheese, and soft drinks provided. Byron is the only operator to provide free use of simple underwater cameras—bring ASA 400 film. Those companies that run catamarans are **Hanalei Sea Tours**, P.O. Box 1437, Hanalei, HI 96714, tel. 826-7254, owned and operated by Capt. Tom Hegarty; and **Na Pali Adventures**, P.O. Box 1017, Hanalei, HI 96714, tel. 826-6804. They offer approximately the same trip as Paradise Adventure Cruises.

Two companies with excellent reputations that rent kayaks on Kauai are Kayak Kauai and Island Adventures. **Kayak Kauai**, P.O. Box 508, Hanalei, HI 96714, tel. 826-9844, seems to have the most extensive experience. Its owners are world-class kayak experts and the staff includes sensitive people who provide good service while having a good time. Two-person Metzeler inflatable kayaks ($48 or $58) and one- and three-person hard-shell kayaks ($35-75) are available. From May to October they lead ocean tours up the Na Pali Coast for $95. They also rent and sell surf skis, boogie boards, masks, fins, *tabi,* tents, and other beach and camping gear. They will rig your car to carry an inflatable kayak and will provide drop-off and pick-up service at Kee Beach for $7, or at Polihale State Park for $35, when it's safe to be on the ocean. **Adventure Kayaking International** also runs kayaking expeditions on Kauai, in coordination with **Island Adventure Inc.,** P.O. Box 3370, Lihue, HI 96766, tel. 245-9662. During the summer, guided tours are taken along the Na Pali Coast, and when conditions are too harsh there, trips are run to Kipu Kai along the south coast or up the Huleia Stream in Nawiliwili. Other companies building solid reputations are **Kayak Jungle Outfitters,** P.O. Box 508, Hanalei, HI 96714, tel. 826-9844, and **Outfitters Kauai,** P.O. Box 1149, Poipu Beach, Kauai, HI 96756, tel. 742-9667. All of the above offer good family-style fun.

Cabin Cruisers And Sailing Ships

Blue Odyssey Kauai, tel. 826-9033, runs a 50-foot cabin cruiser on both the north and south coasts, half-day trips for $65, $70 when combined with a one-way Zodiac ride on the north coast. Their dinner cruise is $49.95. From Port Allen, the **Na Pali Cruise Line,** tel. 826-9696, operates the island's finest cruise ship. This 130-foot liner takes you from Port Allen around the west end of the island and up the Na Pali Coast in comfort and elegance for $85, or $110 if you combine it with a Zodiac ride partway along the coast. A sunset dinner cruise is also available—very romantic.

Running under sail is also possible around Kauai. Captain Andy of **Captain Andy's Sailing Adventures**, tel. 822-7833, lets the wind power his 40-foot trimaran along the south coast in winter and the north coast in summer. A real jolly fellow, he will take you for a half day of sailing, snorkeling, and beachcombing for $65, or a two-hour sunset cruise for $35. **Bluewater Sailing Kauai**, tel. 822-0525, runs a 33-foot sloop and a 42-foot ketch-rigged yacht, also on the south coast in winter and the north coast in summer. Half-day rates are $60, all day $100, and a sunset sail is $35. Hourly, daily, or weekly charters can be arranged.

ACCOMMODATIONS

Kauai is very lucky when it comes to places to stay, due to a combination of happenstance and planning. Kauai was not a major Hawaiian destination until the early '70s. By that time, all concerned had wised up to the fact that what you *didn't do* was build endless miles of high-rise hotels and condos that blotted out the sun and ruined the view of the coast. Besides that, a very strong grass-roots movement here insisted on tastefully done low-rise structures that blend into and complement the surrounding natural setting. This concept mandates "destination resorts," the kind of hotels and condos that lure visitors because of their superb architecture, artistic appointments, and luxurious grounds. There is room for growth on Kauai, but the message is clear: Kauai is the most beautiful island of them all and the preservation of this delicate beauty

benefits everyone. The good luck doesn't stop there. Kauai leads the other islands in offering the best quality rooms for the price.

Hotels And Condos

Approximately 75 properties have a total of 7,200 available rooms, of which 35% are condominium units. Almost all the available rooms on Kauai are split between four major destinations: Poipu Beach, Lihue, Wailua/Kapaa, and Princeville/Hanalei. Except for Kokee Lodge overlooking Waimea Canyon and Waimea Plantation Cottages in Waimea, little is available west of Poipu. Specialized and inexpensive accommodations are offered inland from Poipu at Kahili Mountain Park, but these very basic cottages are just a step up from what you'd find at a Boy Scout camp. Long stretches along the coast between the major centers have no lodgings whatsoever. The north shore past Hanalei has one resort, a few condos, and some scattered guest homes, but you won't find any large concentration of rooms. Aside from hotel/condo or cottage rooms, rental homes are peppered throughout the island.

Poipu, the best general-purpose beach and most popular destination on Kauai, has three major hotels (one under construction) and a host of condos. Prices are reasonable, and most of the condos offer long-term discounts. For years Lihue had only one luxury hotel, the Kauai Surf (now the Westin Kauai), which overlooks Nawiliwili Bay. Recently another deluxe resort, the Kauai Hilton, has opened its doors. In and around Lihue you'll also find most of Kauai's inexpensive hotels, guest cottages, and one mandatory "flea bag." Small hotels, and especially the guest cottages, are family run. They're moderately priced, very clean, and more than adequate. However, they are in town and you have to drive to the beach.

Wailua/Kapaa on the east coast has good beaches and a concentration of accommodations, mostly hotels. Here you'll find the Aston Kauai Resort, which traditionally has brought most of the big-name entertainment to Kauai. The Coco Palms in Wailua is a classic. Used many times as a Hollywood movie set, that's the vibe. It's terrific nonetheless, and has a very loyal clientele, the sure sign of a quality hotel. The Coconut Plantation is just east of Coco Palms and has an extensive shopping center, three large hotels, and a concentration of condos. Almost all sit right on the beach and offer superior rooms at a standard price.

Princeville is a planned "destination resort." It boasts a commuter airport, shopping center, 1,000 condo units, and the Sheraton Princeville Hotel, a showcase resort overlooking Hanalei Bay. From here to Haena are few accommodations until you get to the Hanalei Colony Resort, literally "the last resort." For **Bed and Breakfast Agencies** see p. 147 in the general Introduction.

Vacation Rental Agencies

Another way to find vacation or long-term rentals is through a rental/real estate agent. This can be handled either on Kauai or through the mail. If handled through the mail, the process may take considerably longer, and you'll have to chance getting the type of place that you want. Throughout the island, everything from simple beach homes to look-alike condominiums and luxurious hideaways are put into the hands of rental agents. They have descriptions of the properties and terms of the rental contracts, and many will furnish photographs. When contacting an agency, be as specific as possible about your needs, length of stay, desired location, and how much you're willing to spend. Write several months in advance. Be aware that during high-season rentals are at a premium, and if you're slow to inquire there may be slim pickings.

Some agencies that handle rental properties as a substantial part of their business are: **Na Pali Properties**, P.O. Box 475, Hanalei, HI 96714, tel. 826-7272; **Princeville Travel**, P.O. Box 990, Hanalei, HI 96714, tel. 826-9661; **North Shore Properties and Vacation Rentals**, Princeville Center, Princeville, HI 96714, tel. 826-9622; **Windward Properties**, 4-788 Kuhio Hwy., Kapaa, HI 96746, tel. 822-7700; **Grantham Resorts**, P.O. Box 983, Poipu, HI 96756, tel. 742-7220; **Kauai Vacation Rental and Real Estate**, 4480 Ahukini Rd., Lihue, HI 96766, tel. 245-8841; **R.R Realty and Rentals**, 2827 Poipu Rd., Koloa, HI 96756, tel. 742-7555.

CAMPING AND HIKING

Kauai is very hospitable to campers and hikers. More than a dozen state and county parks offer camping, and a network of trails leads into the interior. The various types of camping available will suit everyone: you can drive right up to your spot at a convenient beach park, or hike for a day through incredible country to build your campfire in total seclusion. A profusion of "secret beaches" have unofficial camping, and the State Division of Forestry even maintains free campsites along its many trails. Kokee State Park provides affordable self-contained cabins, but RV camping is permitted only at Kokee and Polihale state parks and at Haena, Hanamaulu, and Niumalu county parks. Hikers can take the Kalalau Trail, perhaps the premier hiking experience in Hawaii, or go topside to Kokee and follow numerous paths to breathtaking views over the bared-teeth cliffs of Na Pali. Hunting trails follow many of the streams into the interior; or, if you don't mind mud and rain, you can pluck your way across the Alakai Swamp. Wherever you go, enjoy but don't destroy, and leave the land as beautiful as you find it.

CAMPING

General Information
All the campgrounds, except for the state parks along Na Pali, provide grills, pavilions (some with electricity), picnic tables, cold-water showers, and drinking water. No one can camp "under the stars" at official caompgrounds; all must have a tent. Campsites are unattended, so be careful with your gear, especially radios, stereos, and cameras. Your tent and sleeping bag are generally OK. Always be prepared for wind and rain, especially along the north shore.

County Parks
A permit is required for camping at all county-maintained parks. The cost is $3 per person per day, children under 18 free if accompanied by parent or guardian. Permits are issued for four nights, with one renewal for a total of seven nights per campground. Camping is limited to 60 days total in any one-year period. The permit-issuing office is the Department of Finance, Parks Permit Section, 4280-A Rice St., Bldg. B, Lihue, HI 96766, tel. 245-1881. They're open Mon. to Fri. 7:45 a.m. to 4:30 p.m. At all other times, including weekends and holidays, you can pick up your permit at the Kauai Police Dept., Lihue Branch, 3060 Umi St., tel. 245-9711. Write in advance for information and reservations, but do not send money! They'll send you an application, and after returning it with the appropriate information, your request will be logged in the reservations book. You'll also receive brochures and maps of the campgrounds. When you arrive you must pick up and pay for your permit at the Parks and Recreation office, or at the police station.

State Parks
A camping permit is required at all state parks. Permits are free, and camping is restricted to five nights within a 30-day period per campground, with a two- and three-night maximum at some of the stopovers along the Kalalau Trail. You can pick up the permits at the Dept. of Land and Natural Resources, Division of State Parks, Rm. 306, or at the State Building on Umi St. in Lihue, tel. 245-4444. Permits can be picked up Mon. to Fri. 8 a.m. to 4 p.m. only. *No* permits will be issued without proper identification. You can write well in advance for permits which will be mailed to you, but you must include photocopies of identification for each camper over 18. Children under 18 will not be issued a permit, and they must be accompanied by an adult. Allow at least one month for the entire process; no reservations are guaranteed without at least a seven-day notice. Include name, dates, number of campers (with ID photocopy!) and tents. Mailing address: Dept. of Land and Natural Resources, Division of State Parks, P.O. Box 1671, Lihue, HI 96766.

Camping is allowed at Kokee State Park, and the **Kokee Lodge** also provides self-contained housekeeping cabins. They are furnished with stoves, refrigerators, hot showers, cooking and eating utensils, bedding, and linen; wood is available for the fireplaces. The cabins cost $35 and $45 per night (five-night maximum) and vary from one large room that accommodates three, to two-bedroom units that sleep seven. The cabins are tough to get on holidays, during trout fishing season (August and September), and during the wild plum harvest in June and July. For reservations write Kokee Lodge, Box 819, Waimea, Kauai, HI 96796, tel. 335-6061. Please include a SASE and specify number of people and preferred dates. One night's deposit is required for confirmation of reservation. Write well in advance. Check-in is from 2 p.m. (call if you will arrive after 5 p.m.), check-out is before noon. The lodge is open Mon. to Thurs. 8:30 a.m. to 5:30 p.m., until 10 p.m. Fri. and Saturday. Breakfast and lunch are served daily, while dinner is available from 6 p.m. to 9 p.m. Fri. and Sat. evenings only. The lodge also has a bar and small shop with sundries and snacks. The nearest town, Kekaha, is 15 miles down the mountain, on the coast.

Rental Equipment And Sales
A full range of backpacking and camping equipment is rented and sold by **Hanalei Camping and Backpacking**, Ching Young Village, Box 1245, Hanalei, HI 96714, tel. 826-6664. They rent everything from rain gear to tents and sleep-

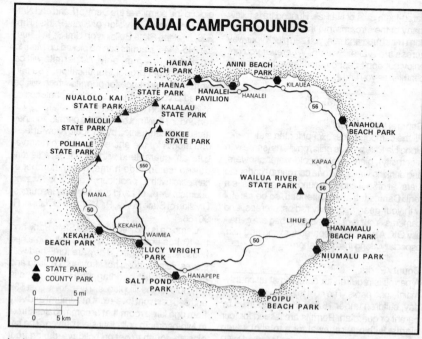

KAUAI CAMPGROUNDS

- ○ TOWN
- ▲ STATE PARK
- ⬡ COUNTY PARK

0   5 mi
0   5 km

ing bags on a daily, overnight, or weekly basis. They also provide backpack storage, hiking information, and sell books and maps. Other camping supply outlets are: **Dan's Sports Shop**, 4393 Rice St. in Lihue; **Kauai Sports**, in the Kukui Grove Center outside of town; and. **The Mandala Store**, at 3122 Kuhio Hwy. in Lihue, which carries mosquito nets and hammocks.

HIKING

Over 90% of Kauai is inaccessible by road, making it a backpackers' paradise. Treks range from overnighters requiring superb fitness and preparedness, to 10-minute nature loops just outside your car door. Most trails are well marked and maintained, and all reward you with either a swimming hole, waterfall, panoramic overlook, or botanical and historical information.

The Dept. of Natural Resources, Box 1671, Lihue, Kauai, HI 96766, provides free detailed maps and descriptions of most trails; contact the following departments. For state park trails (Ka-

lalau and Kokee) write the Divison of State Parks; for forest reserve trails, the Division of Forestry; for hunting trails, the Division of Fish and Game.

Tips And Warnings

Many trails are used by hunters after wild boar, deer, or game birds. Oftentimes these forest reserve trails, maintained by the State Division of Forestry, have a "check-in station" at the trailhead. Trekkers and hunters must sign a logbook, especially if they intend to use the camping areas along the trails. The comments by previous hikers are worth reading for up-to-the-minute information on trail conditions. Many roads leading to the trailheads are marked for 4WD only. Heed the warning, especially during rainy weather when roads are very slick and swollen streams can swallow your rental car. Also remember: going in may be fine, but a sudden storm can leave you stranded. Maps of the trails are usually *only* available in Lihue from the various agencies, not at trailheads. Water is unsafe to drink along the trails and should only be drunk from catchment barrels, or boiled. Expect wind and rain at anytime along the coast or in the interior. Exercise normal caution when entering the ocean, and never swim during periods of high surf. Make sure to check in at stations and leave your itinerary. A few minutes of filling in forms could save your life.

Kokee State Park Trails

Maps of Kokee's trails are available at the ranger's booth at Park HQ, and the Kokee Natural History Museum has additional maps and information. Never attempt to climb up or down the park's *pali* (cliffs). You *cannot* go from Kokee down to the valleys of Na Pali. Every now and again someone attempts it and is killed. The *pali* are impossibly steep and brittle, and your handholds and footholds will break from under you. Don't be foolish.

If you're going into the Alakai Swamp, remember that all the birds and flora you encounter are unique, most of them fighting extinction. Also, your clothes will become permanently stained with swamp mud, a wonderful memento of your trip. Before attempting any of the trails, please sign in at Park HQ.

A number of trails start along Kokee Drive or the dirt roads that lead off from it; most are marked and well maintained. The first you encounter heading up from the coast is **Cliff Trail**, only a few hundred yards long and leading to a spectacular overview of the canyon. Look for feral goats on the canyon ledges. **Canyon Trail** continues off Cliff Trail for 1½ miles. It's a strenuous trail that dips down to Waipoo Waterfall before climbing out of the canyon to Kumuwela Lookout. **Halemanu-Kokee Trail** begins off a secondary road, from the old ranger station just before the military installation. It travels just over a mile and is a self-guiding nature trail. With plenty of native plants and trees, it's a favorite area for indigenous birds.

One of the best trails off Kokee Road is the **Kukui Trail**. The well-marked trailhead is between mile markers 8 and 9. The trail starts with the **Iliau Nature Loop**, an easy, 10-minute, self-guided trail that's great for sunset lovers. Notice the pygmy palms among the many varieties of plants and flowers. The sign-in hut for the Kukui Trail is at the end of the Nature Loop. Read some of the comments before heading down. The trail descends 2,000 feet through a series of switchbacks in 2½ miles. It ends on the floor of the canyon at Wiliwili Campsite. From here the hale and hardy can head up the Waimea River for one-half mile to the beginning of the **Koaie Canyon Trail**. This three-mile trail takes you along the south side of Koaie Canyon, along which are plenty of pools and campsites. This trail *should not* be attempted during rainy weather because of flash flooding. You can also branch south from the Kukui Trail and link up with the **Waimea Canyon Trail**, which takes you eight miles to the town of Waimea. Because it crosses private land, you must have a special permit available at the trailhead. There is no camping south of Waialeale Stream.

At pole #320 near Park HQ, you find the beginning of **Mohihi Camp 10 Road**. This road is recommended for four-wheel drives, but can be crossed with a regular car *only* in dry weather. It leads to a number of trails, some heading into valleys, others out along ridges, and still others into the Alakai Swamp. **Berry Flat**, a one-mile trail, and **Puu Ka Ohelo**, under a half mile, are easy loops that give you an up-close look at a vibrant upland forest. Under the green canopy are specimens such as sugi pine, California redwood, eucalyptus from Australia, and native *koa*. Locals come here in June to harvest the methley plums, for which the area is famous. Off the Camp Road is the entrance to the Forest Reserve at **Sugi Grove**, where camping is limited to three days. **Kawaikoi Stream Trail** begins three-quarters of a mile past Sugi Grove. This 3½-mile trail is moderately strenuous and known for its scenic beauty. It follows the south side of the stream (trout), crosses over, and loops back on the north side. Avoid it if the stream is high.

The **Alakai Swamp Trail** is otherworldly, crossing one of the most unusual pieces of real estate in the world. It begins off Camp Road at a parking area one-quarter mile north of the Na Pali Forest Reserve entrance sign. The trails descends into the swamp for 3½ miles and is very strenuous. Because you cross a number of bogs, be prepared to get wet and muddy. Good hiking shoes that won't be sucked off your feet are a must! The trail follows abandoned telephone poles from WW II, and then a series of brown and white (keep an eye out) trail markers. Along the way, if you smell anise, that's the *mokihana* berry, fashioned with *maile* for wedding leis. The

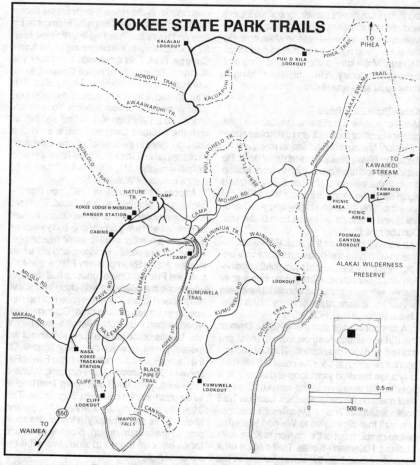

KOKEE STATE PARK TRAILS

KALALAU LOOKOUT

PUU O KILA LOOKOUT

TO PIHEA

PIHEA TRAIL

ALAKAI SWAMP TRAIL

HONOPU TRAIL

KALUAPUHI TR.

AWAAWAPUHI TR.

NUALOLO TRAIL

PUU KAOHELO TR.

KAUAIKINANA STR.

BERRY FLAT TR.

MOHIHI RD.

TO KAWAIKOI STREAM

KAWAIKOI CAMP

NATURE TR.

CAMP

KOKEE LODGE & MUSEUM RANGER STATION

CABINS

CAMP

WAININIUA TR.

WAININIUA RD.

PICNIC AREA

PICNIC AREA

POOMAU CANYON LOOKOUT

ALAKAI WILDERNESS PRESERVE

MILOLII RD.

FAYE RD.

HALEMANU RD.

HALEMANU-KOKEE TR.

CAMP

KUMUWELA TRAIL

KUMUWELA RD.

KAHALA RD.

LOOKOUT

DITCH TRAIL

POOMAU STREAM

MAKAHA RD.

NASA KOKEE TRACKING STATION

KOKEE STR.

BLACK PIPE TRAIL

KUMUWELA LOOKOUT

CLIFF TR.

CLIFF LOOKOUT

CANYON TR.

WAIPOO FALLS

(550)

TO WAIMEA

0   0.5 mi

0   500 m

trail ends at Kilohana, where there's an expansive vista of Wainiha and Hanalei Valley.

One of the most rewarding trails for the time and effort is **Awaawapuhi Trail**. The trailhead is after Park HQ, just past pole #152 at the crest of the hill. It's three miles long and takes you out onto a thin finger of *pali*, with the sea and an emerald valley 2,500 feet below. The sun dapples the upland forest that still bears the scars of Hurricane Iwa. Everywhere flowers and fiddlehead ferns delight the eyes, while wild thimbleberries and passion fruit delight the taste buds. The trail is well marked and slightly strenuous. At the three-mile marker the **Nualolo Trail**, which starts near Park HQ, connects with Awaawapuhi. It's the easiest trail to the *pali* with an overview of Nualolo Valley.

Pihea Trail begins at the end of the paved road near the Puu O Kila Overlook. It's a good general-interest trail because it gives you a great view of Kalalau Valley, then descends into the Alakai Swamp where it connects with the Alakai Swamp Trail. It also connects with the Kawaikoi Stream Trail, and from each you can return via Camp 10 Road for an amazing loop of the area.

East Kauai Trails

All these trails are in the mountains behind Wailua. Most start off Route 580, which parallels the Wailua River. Here are an arboretum and some fantastic vistas from Nonou Mountain, known as the "Sleeping Giant."

Nonou Mountain Trail, East Side, begins off Haleilio Road just north of the junction of Routes 56 and 580, at the Kinipopo Shopping Village. Follow Haleilio Road for 1.2 miles to pole #38. Park near a water pump. The trailhead is across the drainage ditch and leads to a series of switchbacks that scales the mountain for 1¾ miles. The trail climbs steadily through native and introduced forest, and ends at a picnic table and shelter. From here you can proceed south through a stand of monkeypod trees to a trail that leads to the Giant's face. The going gets tough, and unless you're very sure-footed, stop before the narrow ridge (500-foot drop) which you must cross. The views are extraordinary and you'll have them to yourself.

Nonou Mountain Trail, West Side, is found after turning onto Route 580 at the Coco Palms. Follow it a few miles to Route 581, turn right for just over a mile and park at pole #11. Follow the right of way until it joins the trail. This will lead you through a forest of introduced trees planted in the 1930s. The West Trail joins the East Trail at the 1½-mile marker and proceeds to the picnic table and shelter. This trail is slightly shorter and not as arduous. For both, bring water as there is none on the way.

Follow Route 580 until you come to the University of Hawaii Experimental Station. Keep going until the pavement ends and then follow the dirt road for almost a mile. A developed picnic and freshwater swimming area is at Keahua Stream. On the left is a trailhead for **Keahua Arboretum.** The moderate trail is one-half mile through a forest reserve maintained by the Division of Forestry, where marked posts identify the many varieties of plants and trees. The **Kuilau Trail** begins about 200 yards before the entrance to the arboretum, on the right. This trail climbs the ridge for 2½ miles, en route passing a picnic area and shelter. Here are some magnificent views of the mountains; continue through a gorgeous area complete with waterfalls. After you cross a footbridge and climb the ridge, you come to another picnic area. A few minutes down the trail from here you join the **Moalepe Trail**, which starts off Olohena Road 1½ miles down Route 581 after it branches off Route 580. Follow Olohena Road to the end and then take a dirt road for 1½ miles to the turnaround. The last part can be extremely rutted and slick in rainy weather. This trail is a popular horseback-riding trail. It gains the heights and offers some excellent panoramas before joining the Kuilau Trail.

The Kalalau Trail

The Kalalau Trail not only leads you physically along the Na Pali Coast, but back in time to classic romantic Hawaii. You leave the 20th century further and further behind with every step and reenter a time and place where you can come face to face with your *nature self*. This hike is *the* premier hike on Kauai and perhaps in the entire state. For a full description see p. 808.

SHOPPING

Kauai has plenty of shops of all varieties: food stores in every town, boutiques, and specialty stores here and there. Health food stores and farmers' markets, two extensive shopping malls, even a flea market rounds out the picture. The following is the overview; specific stores, with their hours and descriptions, are covered in the travel sections. For food markets, health food stores, farmers' markets, and fresh fish see p. 750.

Shopping Centers

The **Kukui Grove Center**, tel. 245-7784, is one of the two largest malls on Kauai. It's a few minutes west of Lihue along the Kaumuali'i Highway. (Rt. 50). Clustered around an open courtyard, its more than 50 shops sell everything from food to fashions, sports gear to artwork. Across Route 58 and toward the city from this complex is a cluster of offices and shops that includes fast-food restaurants, banks, the Kauai Athletic Club, Kauai Medical Group offices, Island Helicopter office, and the Kukui Grove Cinema.

Lihue has four small shopping centers off Rice Street. **Lihue Shopping Center**, tel. 245-3731, includes a small clutch of shops, a restaurant or two, a bank, supermarket, and discount store.

The **Rice Shopping Center**, tel. 245-2033, features variety stores, a natural food and nutrition center, and Kay's Pub karaoke bar. Down the road, on the opposite side, is Pay 'n Save with a row of shops, including Cameralab and Daylight Donuts. In Nawiliwili is the **Harbor Village Shopping Center**. Several restaurants and two of Lihue's hot nights spots, the Bull Shed lounge and the Park Palace nightclub, are found here near the harbor.

The Market Place, tel. 822-3641, Kauai's other extensive shopping mall, is along the Kuhio Highway (Rt. 56) in Waipouli between Wailua and Kapaa. The Market Place is even larger than Kukui Grove and offers over 70 shops in a very attractive open-air setting. Aside from the clothing and gift shops, there is a bookstore, a good activity and information center, over a dozen eateries, cinemas, and a Hawaiian Air office. In its courtyard is a huge banyan tree, a lookout tower, and colorful sculptures made of pipes, fittings, and machinery from old sugar mills. Along Kuhio Highway, in Wailua, Waipouli, and Kaapa, are six smaller shopping centers. Starting from the Route 580 turnoff, they are the **Coco Palms Arcade** at the Coco Palms Hotel, the **Kinipopo Shopping Center** just beyond the hotel, **Waipouli Town Center**, **Waipouli Plaza**, and **Waipouli Complex**, all on the north side of the highway in rapid succession. Finally, just before entering the main part of Kapaa is **Kapaa Shopping Center**, tel. 245-2033, the largest of these complexes with the greatest variety of stores.

Across the road from the Kiahuna Plantation Condominiums in Poipu is the **Kiahuna Shopping Village**, tel. 851-1200, an attractive cluster of shops and restaurants geared toward the tourist. The proletarian **Eleele Shopping Center**, tel. 245-2033, at the Route 541 turnoff to the Port Allen harbor is the only one farther to the west along the south shore.

The north coast has but two shopping centers. **Princeville Center**, tel. 826-3320, the newest and largest, provides the main shopping for the residents of this planned community. In Hanalei, you'll find limited shopping at the **Ching Young Shopping Center**, tel. 826-7222.

Specialty Shops And Boutiques

You can't go wrong in the following shops. The **Kauai Museum Shop** on Rice Street in Lihue,

tel. 245-6931, has perhaps the island's best selection of Kauaian arts and crafts at reasonable prices, as well as books on Hawaii. **Kapaia Stitchery**, tel. 245-2281, has beautiful handmade quilts, embroideries, and 100% cotton alohawear. Many shops can be found at **Kilohana**, tel. 245-5608, west of Lihue on the way to Puhi. Most rooms in this 1930 plantation estate of Gaylord Wilcox have been turned into upscale boutiques that feature gifts, artwork, clothing, jewelry, antiques, and plants. **Rehabilitation Unlimited of Kauai**, tel. 822-4975, in Wailua, is where some of Kauai's special citizens create well-crafted items at very reasonable prices. **Remember Kauai**, 4-734 Kuhio Hwy. between Wailua and Kapaa, tel. 822-0161, sells a very wide selection of coral and shell necklaces, featuring famous Niihau shellwork, bracelets, earrings, buckles, and chains.

A co-op of four goldsmiths displays its craftsmanship at **The Goldsmith's Gallery**, tel. 822-4653, in the Kikipopo Shopping Village, Waipouli. The **Only Show In Town**, tel. 822-1442, downtown Kapaa, is a must-stop curio and antique store where Paul Wroblewski has amassed the largest and most bizarre collection of priceless antiques, bric-a-brac, and junk in all of Hawaii.

Artisans International, tel. 828-1918, a new shop in Kilauea, stocks only handmade gifts and household items. The old standby there is **Kong Lung Store**, which prides itself on being an "exotic gift emporium" and offers such things as jewelry, Niihau shells, upscale gift items including gourmet food and drinks, children's clothes, and books. Nearly three dozen first-rate island artists display their artwork at the **Artisans' Guild of Kauai**, tel. 826-6441, in Hanalei. Excellent bargains are found at **Spouting Horn Flea Market** near Poipu Beach, where buskers set up stalls selling cut-rate merchandise.

Bookstores

The most extensive bookstores on Kauai are the two **Waldenbooks** shops, one at the Kukui Grove Shopping Center in Lihue, tel. 245-7162, and the other at The Market Place in Waipouli, tel. 822-9362. Perhaps the place with the widest selection of Hawaiiana, Kauaiana, and guidebooks is the **Kauai Museum Shop**; other stores to check for these books are the **Kokee Natural History Museum** in Kokee State Park, the **Ha-**

GALLERIES OF KAUAI

A Thing Of Beauty—The Gallery at Waiohai, at Stouffer Waiohai Beach Resort in Poipu, tel. 742-9211. Antiques, contemporary paintings, sculpture, and lithographs.

Artisan's Guild Of Kauai in Hanapepe, tel. 826-6441. On the second floor above Papagayo Azul Mexican restaurant. Co-op gallery displaying and selling paintings, prints, pottery, cloth, shellwork, metal, and other art and handicraft items of several dozen local artists.

D.S. Collection, 4-370 Kuhio Hwy., Waipouli, tel. 822-3341. Co-op venture of local jewelers.

Hanalei Wishing Well, 5-5183 Kuhio Hwy., Hanalei, tel. 826-7408. Located across from the Ching Young Shopping Village, it displays banana leaf paintings, painted T-shirts and more.

James Hoyle Gallery, 3900 Hanapepe Rd., Hanapepe, tel. 335-3582. Features impressionist paintings of James Hoyle.

Kahana Ki'i Gallery of Koloa. At the end of the Old Koloa town strip, across from the post office, tel. 742-1408.

Kahn Galleries. Two locations: Sheraton Princeville Hotel, tel. 826-6631, and at the Coconut Plantation Market Place, tel. 822-4277. High-class paintings by well-known Hawaiian artists. Also shell, wood, glass, ceramic, and woven items.

Kauai Museum, 4428 Rice St, Lihue, tel. 245-6931. Second floor of the museum has a changing exhibit by local artists, mostly paintings.

Kilohana Galleries, Kilohana, Puhi, tel. 245-9352.

Kiyoko's Art Gallery, 9936 Kaumualii Hwy., Waimea, tel. 338-1667.

Koloa Gallery. Gallery and gift shop in the Sheraton Kauai at Poipu, tel. 742-7118.

Lighthouse Gallery. Located behind the Kong Lung Store, Kilauea, tel. 828-1828. Mostly paintings and woodwork, emphasis is on local themes by state artists.

Port Of Kauai at the Coconut Plantation Market Place. Has mostly scrimshaw and nautical items.

Princeville Gallery. Princeville Center, Princeville, tel. 826-9151.

Stones at Kilohana, Kilohana, Puhi, tel. 245-9452. Wide selection of arts and crafts.

Stones Gallery at Kukui Grove Center, Lihue, tel. 245-6652. Mixed media, with paintings and prints of famous island artists. Espresso bar.

The Art Shop, 3196 Akahi St., Lihue, tel. 245-3810.

The Goldsmith's Gallery, Kinipopo Shopping Village, Waipouli, tel. 822-4653. Gold and jewelry.

The Island Heritage Collection, 5450 Koloa Rd., Koloa, tel. 742-7583. Photographs, lithographs, and serigraphs.

The Poster Shop. Two locations: Koloa, tel. 742-7447, and at the Coconut Plantation Market Place, tel. 822-3636. Prints, posters, paintings.

The Ship Store Gallery, Kiahuna Shopping Village, Poipu, tel. 742-7123. Paintings, scrimshaw, and nautical items.

Tideline Gallery, Kiahuna Shopping Village, tel. 742-1117.

Ye Old Ship Store, Coconut Plantation Market Place, tel. 822-1401. Paintings and the best selection of scrimshaw on the island.

waiian Art Museum and Bookstore and Kong Lung Store in Kilauea, Happy Talk and Hanalei Camping and Backpacking in Hanalei, and hotel gift shops. The Rosetta Stone in Kapaa specializes in books on metaphysics, spiritualism, and self-help, while books on health, cooking, and natural foods can be found at the Hanalei Health and Natural Foods store in Hanalei.

Food Stores And Supermarkets

Groceries and picnic supplies can be purchased in almost every town on the island. Many of the markets in the smaller towns also sell a limited selection of dry goods and gifts. The general rule is the smaller the store, the bigger the price. The largest and cheapest stores with the biggest selections are in Lihue and Kapaa. Big Save Value Centers sell groceries, produce, and liquors in Eleele, Hanalei, Kapaa, Koloa, Lihue, and Waimea. Most stores are open weekdays 8:30 a.m. to 9 p.m., weekends until 6 p.m. Foodland supermarkets operate large stores at the Waipouli Town Center and at the Princeville Center. The Princeville store is the largest and best-stocked market on the north shore. All open weekdays from 8:30 a.m. to 8 p.m., with earlier closings on weekends. Star Super Market is a well-stocked store in the Kukui Grove Center. Smaller but well stocked are the Menehune Food Marts found in Kekaha, Kalaheo, and Kilauea.

Smaller individual markets around the island include: Yoneji's Market at 4253 Rice St., Lihue, an overflowing market and dry-goods store where you can soak up the local color, and Kojima's and Pono Market in Kapaa. Heading north from Kapaa are Whalers General Store in Anahola, The Farmers Market in Kilauea, and the "last chance" limited-selection Wainiha Store in Wainiha. Along the south coast look for Sueoka Store in Koloa, the Kukuiula Store at the turnoff to Spouting Horn, Whalers General Store in the Kiahuna Shopping Village, Brennecke's Mini Mart across from Poipu Beach in Poipu, Matsuura Store in Lawai, Mariko's Mini Mart in Hanapepe, and the Ishihara Market in Waimea. There are 7-eleven shops in Lihue, Hanamaulu, and Wailua.

Health Food, Farmers' Markets, And Fresh Fish

If not the best, at least the most down-to-earth health food store on Kauai is Ambrose' Kapuna Natural Foods, tel. 822-7112, along the Kuhio Highway across from the Foodland Supermarket in Kapaa. Ambrose is a character worth visiting just for the fun of it. His shop is we stocked with yogurt, juices, nuts, grains, and is land fruits. When he has tamales in stock don wait—get down there right away for these homemade tasty treats. If he's not in the store just give a holler around the back. He's there General Nutrition Center, tel. 245-6657, in the Kukui Grove Center, is a full-service health food store. Hale O' Health, tel. 245-9053, in the Rice Center in Lihue, is a limited health food store featuring tonics and vitamins. On the north shore try Hanalei Health and Natural Foods in the Ching Young Shopping Village. Although cramped, this little store has a good vibe and a reasonable selection of bulk foods, fresh produce, hand-squeezed juices, vitamins, and books. Farmers' markets are also found on Kauai; each have at least 20 vendors. The Sunshine Market, featuring backyard produce from people's garden surplus, is held six days a week: Monday at the baseball field in Koloa at noon; Tuesday at 3 p.m. in Hanalei at Waipa, on the west side of Hanalei Bay; Wednesday at the beach park in Kapaa at 3 p.m.; Thursday on the lawn of the First United Church of Christ in Hanapepe at 4 p.m.; Friday at 3 p.m. in Lihue at Vidinha Stadium; and two on Saturday, both at noon, one at the Waldorf School in Kilauea and the other in Kekaha. Local gardeners bring their produce to town; a large selection of island produce is available at very good prices. The stories and local color are even more delicious than the fruit. Contact the county information and complaint office, tel. 245-3213, for exact times and places. An excellent fish store is Kuhio Fish Market in Kapaa, open Mon. through Sat. 9 a.m. to 8:30 p.m. and Sun. till 6 p.m. They have fresh fish daily and often offer specials. Fish can also be purchased at J & R Seafoods at 4361 Rice St., The Fish Express at 3343 Kuhio Hwy. in Lihue, and at Nishimura's Market in Hanapepe.

SPORTS AND RECREATION

Kauai is an exciting island for all types of sports enthusiasts, with golf, tennis, hunting, fresh- and saltwater fishing, and all manner of water sports. You can rent horses or simply relax on a cruise. The following should start the fun rolling.

BEACHES AND WATER SPORTS

With so many to choose from, the problem on Kauai is picking which beach to visit. If you venture farther than the immediate area of your hotel, the following will give you some help in deciding just where you'd like to romp about.

East Kauai Beaches

Kalapaki Beach in Lihue is one of the best on the island and convenient to the island's principal town center. Its gentle wave action is just right for learning bodysurfing or how to ride the boogie board; snorkeling is fair. Two small crescent beaches lie just below the lighthouse at the far end of this beach. Water is rougher there, with much exposed rock; snorkeling should be done on calm days only. Also accessible but less frequented is **Hanamaulu Beach**, just up the coast, with a lagoon, picnic spots, and camping with permit. Like its accommodations, the beaches of Wailua are few but very good. **Lydgate Beach** has two lava pools, and the beaches below Wailua Municipal Golf Course offer seclusion in sheltered coves where there's fine snorkeling. **Waipouli Beach** and **Kapaa Beach** flank the well-developed town of Kapaa, while out along a cane road near Pohakuloa is the little-frequented **Donkey Beach**, known for its good surfing and snorkeling.

The undertow is quite strong here so don't venture out too far if you don't swim well. **Anahola Beach**, at the south end of Anahola Bay, has safe swimming in a protected cove, freshwater swimming in the stream that empties into the bay, picnicking, and camping with permit. Snorkel a short distance up the shore where the reef comes in close—an area where locals come for shore fishing. Still farther north is **Moloa'a Beach**, a little-visited half-moon swath of sand.

North Kauai Beaches

Just south of Kilauea is **Secret Beach**, all that its name implies. At the end of a tiny dirt road, the start of which eludes many people, is a huge stretch of white sand. You're sure to find it nearly empty. Camping is good, and no one is around to bother you. North of town is **Kilihiwai Beach**, great for swimming and bodysurfing during the right conditions. People camp in the ironwood trees that line the beach. There is a park at **Anini Beach**, a great place to snorkel as it has the longest exposed reef in Kauai, and a wonderful place to learn windsurfing because of the shallow water inside the reef.

Hanalei Bay is a prime spot on the north coast. Swim at the mouth of the Hanalei River (but watch out for boats) or on the far side of the bay. Experienced surfers ride the waves below the Sheraton while others snorkel closer to the cliffs. West of Hanalei is **Lumahai Beach**, a beautiful curve of white sand backed by cliffs and thick jungle that was the silent star of the movie *South Pacific*. The inviting water here has a fierce riptide, so enter only when the water is calm. **Haena Beach** is a great swimming and snorkeling spot, while just east at "Tunnels," the waves roll in, making some of the best surfing on the island for experts.

At the end of the road is **Kee Beach**, a popular place with some amenities—good swimming in summer with adequate snorkeling. Many secluded beaches at the foot of the Na Pali cliffs dot the coast to the west along the Kalalau Trail. **Hanakapi'ai Beach** is reached after one hour on the trail and is fine for sunbathing; the water, especially in winter, can be torturous so stay out. **Kalalau Beach** is a full day's hike down this spectacular coast, while others can only be reached by boat.

South Kauai Beaches

The **Poipu Beach** area is the most developed on the island. Accommodating, tame, and relaxing, you can swim, snorkel, and bodysurf here to your heart's content. Down the coast are **Salt Pond Beach**, one of the island's best and good for swimming and windsurfing, and **Pakala Beach**, popular with surfers but also good for swimming and snorkeling. The golden strand of **Kekaha Beach** runs for miles with excellent swimming, snorkeling, and surfing, and stretches into Barking Sands Military Base, where you can go with permission for good views of Niihau when no military exercises are in progress. **Polihale Beach** is the end of the road. Swimming is not the best as the surf is high and the undertow strong, but walk along the shore for a view of the south end of the great Na Pali cliffs.

Scuba And Snorkeling

The best beaches for snorkeling and scuba are found along the northeast coast from Anahola to Kee. The reefs off Poipu, roughed up by Hurricane Iwa, are making a remarkable comeback. Those interested can buy or rent equipment in dive shops and department stores. Sometimes condos and hotels have snorkeling equipment free for their guests, but if you have to rent it, don't do it from a hotel or condo; go to a dive shop where it's much cheaper. Expect to spend $7 a day for mask, fins, and snorkel. Scuba divers can rent gear for about $25 from most shops. To get just what you need at the right price, be sure to call ahead and ask particulars about what each company offers. A complete array of snorkel equipment can be rented for $7-10 at the following: **South Shore Activities**, tel. 742-6873, in Poipu; **Pedal and Paddle**, tel. 826-9069, and **Hanalei Sailboards**, tel. 826-9733, in Hanalei; and at most of the island's dive shops. These shops and others also rent additional beach gear.

Get Wet Kauai, tel. 822-5113, runs a full-day snorkel/scuba complete with box lunch for $95, half day for $65, or snorkel group only for $25. Hotel pick-up available anywhere from Wailua to Poipu. This is one of the best companies for scuba instruction and certification. Local word has it that the most professional is **Aquatics Kauai**, tel. 822-9422. These guys rent snorkel and scuba equipment, and give instruction and certification courses. They also operate their own cabin cruiser, so you have a choice of diving from shore or from the boat. Introductory scuba courses are $65 from shore, and $75 from the boat. Boat dives for certified divers with all equipment and a guide are $85. Refresher and certification courses run from $130-395, depending on level of expertise.

There are other good companies in the Kapaa area. **Sea Sage**, tel. 822-3841, gives snorkeling and scuba lessons by Nikolas and Howard, who are very familiar with Kauaian waters, plus spear fishing and underwater photography. **Bubbles Below**, tel. 822-3483, runs the most unusual dives (and perhaps the most expensive) when they go to Lehua Island off Niihau—but dives there, where the water is clear to depths of over a hundred feet, are tops. **Dive Kauai**, tel. 822-0452, has established a fine reputation; they offer discounts. **Wet-n-Wonderful**, tel. 822-0211, has everything from snorkel to certification courses, and underwater photography and video.

The second concentration of dive shops is in Koloa. **Fathom Five Divers**, tel. 742-6991, also a well-respected professional group, offers diving charters with their own boat and certification courses at competitive prices. **Kauai Divers**, tel. 742-1580, goes shore diving for $55, with a three- or five-day certification course at $295. Others are **Sea Sports Divers**, tel. 742-7288; **The Poipu Dive Co.**, tel. 742-7661; and **Ocean Odyssey**, tel. 245-8661. The **Waiohai Hotel** offers an introductory scuba lesson in the hotel pool. Several other hotels also have instruction by local dive shop experts at their pools. Contact your hotel for information. For additional information about scuba diving and diving clubs in Hawaii, contact **Hawaii Council of Dive Clubs**, P.O. Box 298, Honolulu, HI 96809.

Surfing And Sailboarding

Surfing has long been the premier water sport in Hawaii. Locals, and now "surfies" from all over the world, know where the best waves are and when they come. While Anahola Beach was a traditional surfing spot for Hawaiians of yesterday, the north shore has the beaches of choice today. The east side of the Hanalei Bay provides a good roll in winter for experts, as does Tunnels. Quarry Beach, near Kilauea, and Donkey Beach, north of Kapaa, are used mostly by locals. On the south coast, the surfers' favorite is the area in front of the Waiohai Resort, or west of there near Pakala. Listen to local advice as to where and when to ride and why. The sea is unforgiving, and particularly unpredictable in winter. Surfing lessons are available. The most easonable is for $30 an hour by **Mike Smith International Surfing School**, tel. 245-3882. World champion Margo Oberg runs a school at the Kiahuna Plantation Resort on Poipu Beach, tel. 822-5113, for $35 an hour, and Nancy Palmer of **Garden Island Windsurfing**, tel. 826-9005, offers surfing lessons at the Lawai Beach Resort for $40 an hour. **Hanalei Surf Co.**, formerly Hanalei Sailboards, tel. 826-9733, just a few minutes from a great beginners' surfing area at Hanalei offer surfing lessons for $45 with a 24-hour board rental included. Daily board rentals without lessons are $12 for a soft surfboard, and $15 for a standard fiberglass board. Hanalei Bay goes completely flat in summer, so call ahead for surfing conditions.

Windsurfing has become very popular on Kauai in the last few years. The best spots for beginners are at Anini Beach on the north coast and Poipu Beach on the south. For the advanced only, Haena Beach on the north coast is preferred. Windsurfing lessons are given by Nancy Palmer of **Hanalei Surf Co.**, tel. 826-9733 at Aninini Beach, three hours for $55, and by **Kalapaki Beach Center**, tel. 245-5955, in Nawiliwili. For windsurfing rental gear and other beach rentals and sales, contact **Hanalei Surf Co.**; they're the best in the business. Also contact **Pedal And Paddle**, tel. 826-9069, and **Sand People**, tel. 826-6981, in Hanalei; **Kalapaki Beach Center**, tel. 245-5595, in Nawiliwili; **South Shore Activities,** tel. 742- 6873, in Poipu; or any of the sports shops on the island.

Water-skiing And Parasailing

When you think of recreation on Kauai, water-skiing and parasailing don't necessarily come to mind. In fact, neither are big sports on the island, but both are possible. **Kauai Water Ski and Sports** has established itself as the main ski company. Skimming placid Wailua River, freshwater skiers pass tour boats going to and from the Fern Grotto. Water-skiing fees include boat, driver, gas, skis, and other equipment, and instruction at all levels can be arranged. Their office is behind Kinipopo Shopping Village in Wailua, tel. 822-3574, where they also sell beach clothes and water sporting equipment. Inquire here about the Terheggen International Ski Club. For saltwater skiing on Hanamaulu Bay, or for a 15-minute glide through the sky by parasail, try **Adventures Unlimited, Inc.**, Lihue, tel. 245-8766.

If you've ever wanted to soar like an eagle, you can have your chance with no prior experience. Try parasailing. Basically a parasail is a parachute with a special harness tethered to a speed boat. You're put in a life vest and strapped to the harness that forms a cradle upon which you sit while aloft. Make sure, once you're up, to pull the cradle as far under your thighs as you can—it's much more comfortable. Don't be afraid to loosen your steel grip on the guide ropes because that's not what's holding you anyway. In the air, you are as free as a bird and the unique view is phenomenal. You don't have time to fret about going up. The boat revs and you're airborne almost immediately. Once up, the feeling is very secure. The technology is simple, straightforward, and safe. Relax and have a ball. The cost is about $40 for this joy ride.

Freshwater Fishing

Kauai has trout and bass. Rainbow trout were introduced in 1920 and thrive in 13 miles of fishable streams, ditches, and reservoirs in the Kokee Public Fishing Area. Large, small, and *tucanare* bass are also popular gamefish on Kauai. Introduced in 1908, they're hooked in reservoirs and in the Wailua River and its feeder streams. Bass are in season all year. **Bass Guides of Kauai**, tel. 822-1405, goes freshwater game-fishing for $85 per person or $125 for two people for a half-day. Their 17-foot aluminum boat takes two plus a guide. Licenses are required.

No license is needed for recreational saltwater fishing. A Freshwater Game Fishing License is needed, however, for certain freshwater fish during their seasons; licenses cost $7.50 for nonresidents, $3.50 for tourists (good for 30 days), $3.75 for residents and military personnel, $1.50 for children between nine and 15 years old, and they're free to senior citizens. Licenses and a digest of fishing laws and rules are available from the State Division of Conservation and Resources Enforcement or from most sporting goods stores. For free booklets and information, write Division of Aquatic Resources, Department of Land and Natural Resources, P.O. Box 1671, Lihue, HI 96744, or stop by Room 306 of the state office building in Lihue, tel. 245-4444. Nearly all gamefish may be taken year-round, except trout. Trout, found only in the Kokee Public Fishing Area on Kauai, may be taken for 16 days commencing on the first Saturday of August. Thereafter, for the remainder of August and September, trout can be taken only on Sat., Sun., and state holidays.

Deep-sea Fishing

Some excellent fishing grounds are off Kauai, especially around Niihau, and a few charter boats are for hire. Most are berthed at Nawiliwili Harbor, with some on the north coast. Deep-sea fishing is rather expensive, and the captain usually keeps some of the catch. Rates vary, as do the length of outings (usually four, six, or eight hours), and number of passengers allowed on the boats, so call for information before planning a trip. Some private yachts offer charters, but these come and go with the tides.

An excellent charter service is **Lady Ann Charters**, tel. 245-8538, at Nawiliwili. They run two boats, the *Lady Ann*, a 32-footer, and the *Island Voyager*. One of the captains was a researcher for Pacific Whale Foundation so you'll go with a knowledgeable guide. Fishing excursions run in the vicinity of $75 half-day, $125 full-day, a half-day exclusive for $350, and full-day for $500. **Lucky Lady**, tel. 822-7033, with Capt. John Teixeira, runs a 33-foot twin-diesel craft off Niihau for the big ones, for whalewatching in season, or bottom fishing "Hawaiian style."

Alana Lynn Too, tel. 245-7446, **Gent-Lee**, tel. 245-7504, **Coastal Charters**, tel. 822-7007, and others also leave from Nawiliwili small boat harbor. **Sea Breeze III**, tel. 828-1285, with skipper Bob Kutowski, specializes in bottom fishing. He and **Robert McReynolds**, tel. 828-1379, leave from Anini Beach. McReynolds uses medium tackle and fishes the area off Kilauea Lighthouse. Going with him is perhaps the best introduction to sport fishing in Kauai. Whalewatching cruises run from January through April. Many of the above charter companies, plus some of the companies listed on pp. 740-741 also run special whalewatching tours.

LAND SPORTS

Hunting

All game animals on Kauai have been introduced, including feral pigs and goats. Black-

tailed deer come from Oregon. Forty were released on Kauai in 1961; the herd is now stabilized at around 700 and they're hunted in October by public lottery. Because they thrive on island fruits, their meat is sweeter and less gamey than Mainland deer.

A number of game birds are found on Kauai. Bag limits and hunting seasons vary, so check with the Division of Forestry and Wildlife for details. Ring-necked pheasant are one of the best game birds. Francolins—gray, black, and Erkel's—from India and the Sudan are similar to partridges. They are hunted with dogs and are great roasted. There are also chukar from Tibet, found on rugged mountain slopes; a number of quail, including the Japanese and California varieties; and spotted and zebra doves.

Horseback riding

There are two stables on Kauai. You can hire mounts from **CJM Country Stables**, tel. 245-6666, two miles east of Poipu Kai Condominiums in Poipu. CJM offers three rides: a one-hour beach ride for $20; a two-hour ride through woods, sugar cane fields, and down along the beach for $40; and a three-hour beach breakfast ride for $55, where your meal is prepared by your "galloping gourmet guide." **Pooku Stables**, tel. 826-6777, along Route 56, Princeville, also has three rides. One is a one-hour valley ride across ranch land in Hanalei Valley. Another is a two-hour shoreline ride near Anini Beach. The most adventurous is a three-hour waterfall picnic ride where you can rest halfway, swim in a waterfall pool, and munch trail snacks before your return.

Golf And Tennis

The five courses on Kauai offer varied and exciting golf. Kukuiolono Golf Course, a mountaintop course in Kalaheo, is never crowded and is worth visiting just to see the gardens: Wailua Golf Course is a public course with reasonable greens fee, considered excellent by visitors and residents. Princeville boasts 36 magnificent holes sculpted around Hanalei Bay. The Westin Kauai Lagoons Course has been a favorite for years, and guests get a special price. The new 18-hole Kiele course was designed by Jack Nicklaus. Kiahuna Golf Village is the island's newest course, conveniently located in Poipu. See travel chapters for details.

The following chart lists private and public tennis courts. Many hotel tennis courts are open to non-guests, usually for a fee. Some, such as the Poipu Kai Resort, Waiohai Hotel, and Kiahuna Plantation Condominiums, have fine courts but charge even guests for their use. Both the Coco Palms Hotel and Mirage Princeville Tennis Club have a few clay courts for those who prefer that surface.

Fitness Centers

There are four health club/fitness centers on Kauai. The largest and best equipped is **Kauai Athletic Club**, tel. 245-5381, across from the Kukui Grove Center. Its sister club is **Hanalei Athletic Club**, tel. 826-7333, in the Princeville Golf Course clubhouse. Affordable and with convenient hours, both offer aerobic classes, free weights, Nautilus machines, a swimming pool, jacuzzi, steam room, sauna, and massage by appointment. Nutrition programs can be set up with the staff, who also have information about running courses. **Poipu Beach Fitness Center**, at Stouffer's Waiohai Hotel, tel. 742-9511, has about the same facilities but is a bit more pricey. It caters mostly to hotel and

TENNIS COURTS OF KAUAI

COUNTY COURTS

Under jurisdiction of the Department of Parks and Recreation, P.O. Box 111, Lihue, Kauai, HI 96766. Tel. 245-4751. Courts listed are in Lihue and near the Wailua and Poipu areas. There are additional locations around the island.

Location	Name of Court/Location	No. of Courts	Lighted
Hanapepe	Next to stadium	2	Yes
Kekaha	Next to Park	2	Yes
Kalahea	Kalawai Park	2	Yes
Kapaa	New Park	2	Yes
Koloa	Next to fire station	2	Yes
Lihue	Next to convention hall	2	Yes
Wailua	Wailua Park	4	Yes
Waimea	Next to High School	4	Yes

HOTEL & PRIVATE COURTS THAT ARE OPEN TO THE PUBLIC

Location	Name of Court/Location	No. of Courts	Lighted
Hanalei	Hanalei Bay Resort	11	Yes
Hanalei	Princeville at Hanalei (fee)	6	No
Kalapaki Beach	Westin Kauai (fee)	10	No
Kapaa	Holiday Inn Kauai Beach (fee)	3	No
Poipu	Poipu Kai Resort (fee for non-guests)	4	No
Poipu Beach	Kiahuna Beach & Tennis Resort (fee)	10	Yes
Poipu Beach	Waiohai & Poipu Beach Hotel (fee)	6	Yes
Wailua Beach	Coco Palms Hotel (fee)	9	Yes

condo guests in the Poipu area. With smaller exercise facilities and more emphasis on spas, massage, and wellness, the health club/spa at the Westin Kauai Hotel is used mostly by hotel guests. It is more expensive than the other fitness centers.

KAUAI'S GOLF COURSES

Course	Par	Yards	Fees	Cart
Kauai Surf Golf & Tennis Club 3500 Rice Street, Lihue, HI 96766 tel. 245-3631	72	6392	$17	$8
Kiahuna Plantation Golf Course Route 1, Box 37, Koloa, HI 96756 tel. 742-9595	70	5669	$30	Incl.
Kukuiolono Plantation Golf * Course P.O. Box 987, Lihue, HI 96766 tel. 332-9151	36	3173	$5	$5
**Princeville Makai Golf Course Ocean Course *** P.O. Box 3040, Lihue, HI 96722 tel. 826-9666	36	3051	$38	$20
Lake Course *	36	3171	$38	$20
Woods Course *	36	3113	$38	$20
Wailua Municipal Golf Course P.O. Box 1017, Kapaa, HI 96746 tel. 245-8092	72	6631	$10 Wkday $11 Wkend	$11.50

N.B. * = 9 hole course

INFORMATION AND SERVICES

Emergency
For the police, fire, and ambulance anywhere on Kauai dial 911.

Coast Guard Search And Rescue On Kauai: tel. 245-4521.

Civil Defense: In case of natural disaster such as hurricanes or tsunamis on Kauai call 245-4001.

Crisis Intervention Helpline: tel. 245-3411; **Rape Crisis Hotline,** tel. 245-4144; and **Kauai Hotline,** tel. 822-4114.

Hospitals: Wilcox Memorial, 3420 Kuhio Hwy., Lihue, tel. 245-1100; Kauai Veterans, in Waimea at tel. 338-9431; and Samuel Mahelona Hospital, in Kapaa at 822-4961.

Medical Clinics And Physicians:
Kauai Medical Group, 3420 B Kuhio Hwy., tel. 245-1500, after hours call 245-1831. Office hours are 8 a.m. to 5 p.m. weekdays and 8 a.m. to noon weekends. Offices also at Kapaa, Koloa, Kukui Grove Center, Kilauea, and Princeville. Garden Island Medical Group, Waimea, tel. 338-1645, after hours call 338-9431. Office hours are 8 a.m. to 5 p.m. weekdays and 8 a.m. to noon weekends. Offices also at Eleele and Koloa. Hawaiian Planned Parenthood, tel. 245-5678. Natural Health and Pain Relief Clinic, tel. 245-2277. A fine pediatrician with four young children of his own is Dr. Terry Carolan, at 4491 Rice St., Lihue, tel. 245-8566.

Pharmacies:

Southshore Pharmacy in Koloa, tel. 742-7511, with senior discounts; Westside Pharmacy in Hanapepe, tel. 335-5342; Shoreview Pharmacy in Kapaa, tel. 822-1447; Long's Drug in the Kukui Grove Center, tel. 245-7771; and Pay 'n Save in Lihue, tel. 245-8896. All the hospitals and medical groups also have their own pharmacies.

Weather And Time

For a recorded message 24 hours a day, call 245-6001. For marine weather call 245-3564. For time, call 245-0212.

Consumer Protection

If you encounter problems with accommodations, bad service, or downright rip-offs try the following, all on Kauai: Chamber of Commerce, tel. 245-7363; Hawaii Hotel Association, tel. 923-0407; Office of Consumer Protection, tel. 245-4365; and the Better Business Bureau of Hawaii on Oahu, tel. 942-2355.

Parks

For state parks on Kauai contact the Division of State Parks, State Bldg., 3060 Eiwa St., Box 1671, Lihue, HI 96766, tel. 245-4444. For lodging at Kokee State Park, write Kokee Lodge, Box 819, Waimea, HI 96796, tel. 335- 6061. For county parks: 4280-A Rice St., Lihue, HI 96766, tel. 245-1881, or during off hours at Lihue Police Station, 3060 Umi St., Lihue, HI 96766, tel. 245-6721.

Post Offices

Normal business hours are 8 a.m. until 4:30 p.m., Mon. through Fri., Sat. from 8 a.m. until noon. The central post office on Kauai is at 4441 Rice St., Lihue, tel. 245-4994. Main branches are located at Kapaa, tel. 822-5421, and Waimea, tel. 338-9973, with 13 others scattered throughout the island. Most larger hotels also offer limited postal services.

Reading Material

The central library is at 4344 Hardy St., Lihue, tel. 245-3617. Branch libraries are located in Hanapepe, Kapaa, Koloa, and Waimea. Check with the main library for times and services.

Free tourist literature, such as *This Week Kauai, Spotlight Kauai*, and *Kauai Beach Press,* is available at all hotels and most restaurants and shopping centers around the island. They come out every Monday and contain money-saving coupons and up-to-the-minute information on local events. *Kauai Drive Guide* is available from the car rental agencies and contains tips, coupons, and good maps. The AAA Hawaii *Tourbook* is also very useful.

There are two island newspapers, *The Garden Island,* published four times weekly, and the *Kauai Times,* appearing once a week. The bimonthly *The Source* is a free newspaper focused on healing, growth, self-help, and metaphysics. Hawaii's two main English-language dailies are *The Honolulu Star Bulletin,* and *The Honolulu Advertiser.* The Japanese-English *Hawaii Hochi* and the Chinese *United Chinese Press* are also available. The last four are published on Oahu but available on Kauai. Magazines to look for that deal on Kauai are *The Sandwich Islands Quarterly, The North Shore Quarterly, Kauai*, and *Kauai Dining*. Others of interest that feature ads, stories, and information, about all the islands include *Art to Onions,* a fine art and leisure magazine, and the inflight magazines of Aloha and Hawaiian airlines.

Banks

Banks on Kauai are Bank of Hawaii, Central Pacific Bank, First Hawaiian Bank, First Interstate Bank of Hawaii, and 1st Nationwide Bank.

Radio Stations

Stations at AM 570 and FM 93 and KAUI at AM 720 play contemporary, rock, and Hawaiian music.

Laundromats

Self-service laundromats are Lihue Washerette in the lower level of the Lihue Shopping Center and Kapaa Laundry Center in the Kapaa Shopping Center.

Island Facts

Nicknamed the "Garden Isle," Kauai is the oldest of the main Hawaiian Islands. Its lei is made from the *mokihana,* a small native citrus fruit of purple color.

LIHUE

The twin stacks of the **Lihue Sugar Company** let you know where you are: in a plantation town on one of the world's most gorgeous islands. Lihue ("Open to Chill") began growing cane in the 1840s, and its fields are still among Hawaii's most productive. The town has correspondingly flourished and boasts all the modern conveniences, complete with chrome-and-glass shopping centers, libraries, museums, and a hospital. But the feeling is still that of a sugar town. Lihue, the county seat, has 4,000 residents and two traffic lights. It isn't the geographical center of the island (Mt. Waialeale has that distinction), but it is halfway along the coastal road that encircles the island, making it a perfect jumping-off point for exploring the rest of Kauai. It has the island's largest concentration of restaurants, the most varied shopping, a major resort, and right-priced accommodations. If you're going to find any night life at all, beyond the lounges at the big resorts, it'll be here—but don't expect much. Good beaches are within a five-minute drive, and you can be out of town and exploring long before your shave ice begins to melt.

SIGHTS

KAUAI MUSEUM

If you really want to enrich your Kauai experience, this is the first place to visit. Spending an hour or two here infuses you with a wealth of information regarding Kauai's social and cultural history. The two-building complex is at 4428 Rice St. in downtown Lihue, tel. 245-6931, open Mon. to Fri. 9:30 a.m. to 4:30 p.m., and Sat. until 1 p.m., admission $3, under 18 free. The main building was dedicated in 1924 to Albert Spencer Wilcox, son of pioneer missionaries at H

analei. It has a Greco-Roman facade, and was the public library until 1970. Its two floors house the main gallery, dedicated to ethnic heritage and island art exhibits that are changed on a regular basis. The **Museum Shop** sells books, Hawaiiana prints, and a fine selection of detailed U.S. Geological Survey maps of the entire island. Some inexpensive but tasteful purchases include baskets, wooden bowls, and selections of tapa. (The tapa is made in Fiji, but native craftspeople are studying Fijian techniques and hope to re-create this lost art.) The main room contains an extensive and fascinating exhibit of calabashes, *koa* furniture, quilts, and feather leis. One large calabash belonged to Princess Ruth, who gave it to a local child. Its finish, hand rubbed with the original *kukui* nut oil, still shows a fine luster. The rear of the main floor is dedicated to the **Senda Gallery**, with its collection of vintage photos shot by W.J. Senda, a Japanese immigrant from Matsue who arrived in 1906. These black and whites are classics, opening a window onto old Kauai.

Kauai's fascinating natural and cultural history begins to unfold when you walk through the courtyard into the **William Hyde Rice Building.** Notice the large black iron pot used to cook sugar cane. The exhibits are self-explanatory, chronicling Kauai's development over the centuries. The windows of the **Natural History Tunnel** show the zones of cultivation on Kauai, along with its beaches and native forests. Farther on is an extensive collection of Kauai shells, old photos, and displays of classic muumuus. The central first floor area houses a model of a Hawaiian village with an extensive collection of weapons, some fine examples of adzes used to hollow canoes, and a model of HMS *Resolution* at anchor off Waimea. An excerpt from the ship's log records Capt. Cook's thoughts on the day that he discovered Hawaii for the rest of the world.

As you ascend the stairs to the second floor time moves on. Missionaries stare from old photos, their countenances the epitome of piety and zeal. Just looking at them makes you want to repent! Most old photos record the plantation era. Be sure to see the **Spalding Shell Collection,** gathered by Col. Spalding, an Ohio Civil War veteran who came to Kauai and married the daughter of Capt. James Makee, owner of the Makee Sugar Company. Besides shells from around the world are examples of magnificent *koa* furniture, table settings, children's toys, dolls, and photos of Niihau, about all that the outside world ever sees.

Follow the stairs to the ground floor and notice the resplendent examples of feather capes on the wall. On the main floor, in an alcove by the front door, push the button to begin a 15-minute aerial-view video of Kauai. This pictorial is a treat for the eyes; soothing Hawaiian chanting in the background sets the mood. Next, the final treat, a thorough, well-done exhibit teaches you about the legendary Menehune and Mu—their kings, work habits, beliefs, and why they disappeared from Kauai.

GROVE FARM HOMESTEAD

Grove Farm is a plantation started in 1864 by George Wilcox, the son of missionaries who preached at Hanalei. George earned his degree in engineering in Honolulu and returned to Kauai to work for the original owner of the surrounding acreage. The first owner saw no future in the parched land and sold 500 acres to Wilcox for $1000. Through a system of aqueducts, Wilcox brought water down from the mountains and began one of the most profitable sugar plantations in Hawaii. The homestead was a working plantation until the mid-1930s, when George died and operations were moved elsewhere. The remaining family continued to occupy the dwellings and care for the extensive grounds. In 1971, Mabel Wilcox, a niece of the founder, dedicated the family estate to posterity. Well advanced in years but spirited in mind, she created a nonprofit organization to preserve Grove Farm Homestead as a museum. We can now reap the benefits of her efforts by visiting this self-sufficient farm every Mon., Wed., and Thursday. Well-informed guides (such as Charlotte Duvel, who came to Kauai as a young bride in 1926 and became well acquainted with the Wilcoxes and plantation life) take you on a two-hour tour of the grounds and various buildings. Admission is $3 adults, $1 children under 12. Tours are by *reservation only!* Drop-in visitors will be turned away. Call 245-3202 at least 24 hours in advance to make arrangements. Mail reservations are accepted up to three months in advance; write: Grove Farm Homestead, P.O. Box 1631, Lihue, Kauai, HI 96766. The homestead is located off Nawiliwili Road; precise directions are given when you call. Group size is limited to give full attention to detail and minimize wear and tear on the buildings. Tours begin at 10 a.m. and 1 p.m. Be prompt please!

Living History

The first thing you notice when entering Grove Farm is the rumble of your tires crossing a narrow-gauge railroad track. The tracks meant sugar, and sugar meant prosperity and change

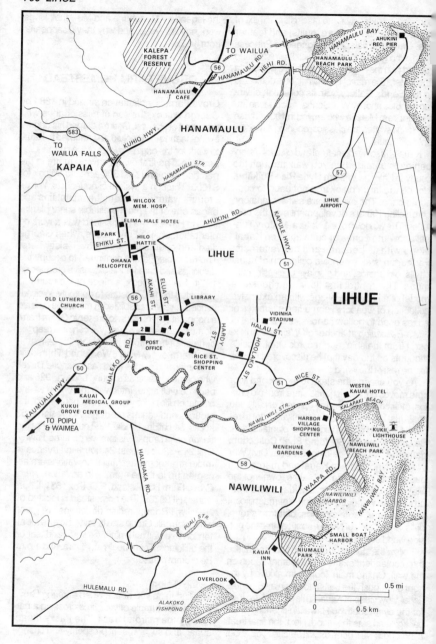

KALEPA FOREST RESERVE

TO WAILUA

HANAMAULU BAY

AHUKINI REC. PIER

HANAMAULU BEACH PARK

56 HANAMAULU RD.

HEHI RD.

HANAMAULU CAFE

583

TO WAILUA FALLS

KAPAIA

KUHIO HWY

HANAMAULU

HANAMAULU STR.

57

LIHUE AIRPORT

WILCOX MEM. HOSP.

ELIMA HALE HOTEL

AHUKINI RD.

KAPULE HWY

PARK

EHIKU ST.

HILO HATTIE

LIHUE

OHANA HELICOPTER

AKAHI ST.

ELUA ST.

56

OLD LUTHERN CHURCH

LIBRARY

LIHUE

51

VIDINHA STADIUM

HALAU ST.

1 3
2 4 5
6

HARDY ST.

HOOLAKO ST.

HALEKO RD.

POST OFFICE

7

RICE ST. SHOPPING CENTER

51

RICE ST.

WESTIN KAUAI HOTEL

50

KAUAI MEDICAL GROUP

KUKUI GROVE CENTER

KAUMUALII HWY

TO POIPU & WAIMEA

KALAPAKI BEACH

KUKII LIGHTHOUSE

NAWILIWILI STR.

HARBOR VILLAGE SHOPPING CENTER

NAWILIWILI BEACH PARK

HALEHAKA RD.

58

MENEHUNE GARDENS

WAAPA RD.

NAWILIWILI

NAWILIWILI HARBOR

NAWILIWILI BAY

PUALI STR.

SMALL BOAT HARBOR

HULEMALU RD.

OVERLOOK

KAUAI INN

NIUMALU PARK

ALAKOKO FISHPOND

0   0.5 mi

0   0.5 km

LIHUE

1. Lihue Shopping Center
2. Kauai Museum
3. State Building
4. County Building
5. Police Station
6. HVB
7. Pay 'n Save

for old Hawaii. The minute that you set foot upon Grove Farm Homestead you can feel this spirit permeating the place. This is no "glass-case" museum. It's a real place with living history, where people experienced the drama of changing Hawaii.

George Wilcox never married. In love once, he was jilted, and that ended that. In 1870 his brother Sam came to live on the homestead. In 1874 Sam married Emma, daughter of missionaries from the Big Island. She had been educated in Dearborn, Michigan, and had recently returned to Hawaii. The couple had six children, three boys and three girls. Two of the boys survived to manhood and managed the farm, but both met later with tragic deaths. Of the girls only Henrietta, the oldest, married. The two other sisters, Miss Elsie and Miss Mabel, remained single all their lives. Elsie became very involved in politics, while Mabel went to Johns Hopkins University and earned a degree as a registered nurse. Her parents wouldn't let her leave home until she was 25 years old, when they felt she could cope with the big, bad world. She returned in 1911 and opened a public health office on the grounds.

The Tour

The buildings, furnishings, orchards, and surrounding lands are part of the oldest intact sugar plantation in Hawaii. You meet your guide at the plantation office, which has a safe dating from 1880, when it was customary to pay for everything in cash. On top sits a cannonball that's been there as long as anyone can remember. Perhaps it was placed there by Mr. Pervis, the original bookkeeper. As time went on the safe's combination, which is in letters, not numbers, was lost. Recently a safecracker was hired to open it, and inside was the combination written in a big, bold hand . . . B-A-L-L.

You cross the grounds to a simple dwelling and enter the home of the Moriwakis. Mrs. Moriwaki came to Grove Farm as a "picture bride," though she was born in Hawaii and taken back to Japan as a child. She was the cook at the big house for almost 50 years; after the grounds opened to the public, and until her death in 1986, she returned on tour days to explain her role in running the homestead. Her home is meticulously clean and humble, a symbol of Japanese plantation workers' lives on Hawaii. Notice the food safe. There were no ice boxes for most workers in Hawaii and they kept vermin away by placing sardine cans filled with water or kerosene inside. A small print of Mt. Fuji and a geisha doll in a glass case are simple yet meaningful touches. Together they are a memory of the past and the hope of a brighter future that all plantation workers sought for their children.

As you walk around, notice how lush and fruitful the grounds are, with all sorts of trees and plants. At one time the workers were encouraged to have their own gardens. A highlight is a small latticework building half submerged in the ground. This is the **fernery,** at one time a status symbol of the good life in Hawaii. There was great competition among the ladies of Victorian Hawaii who were proud of their ferns, and you became an instant friend if you presented a new and unique variety while on a social visit. Behind the Wilcox Home is a small schoolhouse built in 1900. It later became Mabel Wilcox's public health office; now a depository for all sorts of artifacts and memorabilia, it's called the **Trunk Room.** A photo of Mabel shows her in a Red Cross uniform. By all accounts, Mabel was a serious but not humorless woman. Her dry and subtle wit was given away only by her sparkling eyes, which are obvious in the photo.

Wilcox Home

Shoes are removed before entering this grand mansion. The Wilcoxes were pleasant people given to quiet philanthropy, but their roots as New England missionaries made them frugal. The women always wore homemade cotton dresses and in the words of a tour guide, "nothing was ever thrown away by this family." The home is comfortable and smacks of culture, class, and money—in the old-fashioned way. As you enter, you'll be struck with the feeling of space. The archways were fashioned so they get smaller as you look through the house. This shrinking perspective gives an illusion of great length. The walls and staircase are of rich, brown *koa*. Much of the furniture was bought second-hand from families returning to the Mainland. This was done not out of a sense of frugality, but simply because it often was the only good furniture available.

A piano here belonged to Emma Wilcox; the profusion of artwork includes many original pieces, often done by visitors to the homestead. One longtime visitor, a sickly girl from the East Coast, did some amazing embroidery. Her finest piece on display took 10 years to complete. Portraits of the family include a good one of George Wilcox. Notice a Japanese chest that Miss Mabel won in a drawing while she was in Japan

with her sister Elsie and Uncle George in 1907 Notice too the extensive collection of Hawaiiana that the family accumulated over the decades. In the separate kitchen wing is a stove that is still functional after 100 years of hard use. A porch, so obviously homey during rainstorms, looks out onto a teahouse. Everything in the home is of fine quality and in good taste. It's a dwelling of peace and tranquility.

The Cottage

Finally you arrive at the private home of a private man, George Wilcox himself. It is the picture of simplicity. Only an old bachelor would have chosen these spartan surroundings. An inveterate cigar smoker along with his brother Sam, both were forbidden by the ladies to smoke in the main house. Here, he did as he pleased.

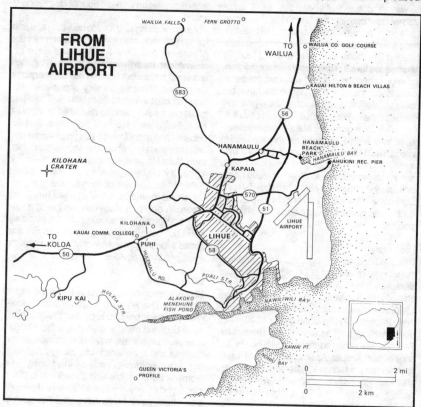

Maybe the women were right, George died of throat cancer . . . in 1933 at the age of 94!

The first room you enter is his office. George was a small man and a gentleman. Whenever he left the house, he donned a hat. You'll notice a collection of his favorites hanging on pegs in the hallway. One of his few comforts was a red-wood tub he'd soak in for hours. This self-made millionaire kept his soap in an old sardine tin, but he did use fine embroidered towels. His bed-room is simple, bright, and airy. The mattress is of extremely comfortable horsehair. Outside his window is a profusion of fruit trees, many of which George planted himself. As the tour ends you get the feeling that these trees are what Grove Farm is all about—a homestead where people lived, and worked, and dreamed.

OTHER SIGHTS

Lihue's Churches

When Route 56 becomes Route 50 just as you pass the Lihue Sugar Mill, look for the HVB Warrior pointing you to the **Old Lutheran Church.** Just before the bridge, follow Hoomana Road to the right through a well-kept residential area. Built in 1883, it has everything a church should have, including a bell tower and spire, but it's all miniature-sized. The church reflects a strong German influence that dominated Lihue and its plantation until WW I. The turn-of-the-century pastor was Hans Isenberg, brother of the plantation founder and husband to Dora Rice from the old *kamaaina* family. Pastor Rice was responsible for procuring the Lihue Horse Trough, an ornate marble work imported from Italy in 1909, now on display at the Haleko Shops' botanical gardens in downtown Lihue. The outside of the church is basic New England, but inside, the ornate altar is reminiscent of baroque Germany. Headstones in the yard to the side indicate just how old this congregation is.

On a nearby hill is **Lihue Union Church** that was mostly attended by the common people. Its Hawaiian cemetery is filled with simple tombstones, and plumeria trees eternally produce blossoms for the departed ones. If you follow the main road past the Lutheran church it dead-ends at an enormous cane field. This sea of green runs to the mountains and lets you know just how much sugar still dominates the way of life in Lihue and on Kauai in general.

Around Town

Across the street from Lihue Shopping Center, a stone's throw from the twin stacks of the sugar mill, are four solid-looking buildings known as the **Haleko Shops.** Once the homes of German plantation managers before they gave up their holdings during WW I, they're now occupied by restaurants and shops—part of the shopping center across the road. Around them is a botanical garden. Each plant carries a description of its traditional use and which ethnic group brought it to the island. (Look for the Lihue Horse Trough imported by Pastor Isenberg.)

Follow Umi Street off Rice to Hardy Street. At the corner is the **Kauai Library.** In the entrance is a batik wall hanging by Jerome Wallace, the largest painting of its type in the world.

Follow Rice Street toward Nawiliwili Harbor and it turns into Route 51, known as Waapa Road. Then come to the junction of Route 58 (known as Nawiliwili Road), where you turn right for the **Menehune Gardens.** While currently going through litigation and temporarily closed to the public, plans were to reopen the gardens in 1989 so call 245-2660 to find out if it's possible to visit. The owners, Mr. and Mrs. Kailikea, often served as guides and were more than happy to share with you their deep love and respect for the *aina* and its plants. Every plant is labeled, but the visitor's experience was enriched by a guide who described each plant and how it was used. On the grounds is an immense banyan tree with over 1,000 aerial shoots that covers more than an acre—one of the largest in the world. After the tour Auntie Sarah and her husband sing ancient Hawaiian chants for you, and for a brief glimmering moment you have a glimpse of old Hawaii. The peace and quiet alone are worth the admission charge.

Take Nawiliwili Road to Niumalu Road and turn left, following it to Hulemalu Road. You pass the predominantly Hawaiian settlement of Niumalu. Along Hulemalu Road is a lookout, below which is **Alakoko** ("Rippling Blood") **Pond**, commonly known as Menehune Fishpond. You have a sweeping view of Huleia Stream, the harbor, and the Hoary Head Mountains in the background. The 900-foot mullet-raising fishpond is said to be the handiwork of the Menehune. Legend says that they built this pond for a royal prince and princess, and that they made only one demand: that no one watch them in their labor. In one night, the indefatigable Menehune passed the stones needed for the construction from hand to hand in a double line that stretched for 25 miles. But, the royal prince and princess could not contain their curiosity, and climbed to a nearby ridge to watch the little people. They were spotted by the Menehune, who stopped building, leaving holes in the wall, and turned the royal pair into the twin pillars of stone still seen on the mountainside overlooking the pond.

Wailua Falls

In Kapaia, Route 583 branches from Route 56 and heads into the interior. As the road lifts up and away from the ocean, you realize that the rolling terrain surrounded by lofty mountain peaks is completely given over to sugar cane. To the left and right are small homes with the usual patch of tropical fruit trees. Route 583 ends at mile marker 3. Far below, Wailua Falls tumbles 80 feet over a severe *pali* into a large round pool. It's said that the *ali'i* would come here to dive from the cliff into the pool as a show of physical prowess; commoners were not considered to be infused with enough mana to perform this feat.

Many of the trees here are unwilling trellises for rampant morning glory. Pest or not, it's still beautiful as its blossoms climb the limbs. A trail down to the falls is particularly tough and steep. If you make it down, you'll have the falls to yourself, but you'll be like a goldfish in a bowl with the tourists, perhaps enviously, peering down at you. See the map on p. 762.

Wailua Falls

BEACHES AND PARKS

Lihue has very convenient beaches. You can sun yourself within 10 minutes from anywhere in town, with a choice of beaches on either Nawiliwili or Hanamaulu bays. Few tourists head to Hanamaulu Bay, while Nawiliwili Bay is a classic example of "beauty and the beast." There is hardly a more beautiful harbor than Nawiliwili's, with a stream flowing into it and verdant mountains all around. However, it is a working harbor complete with rusting barges, groaning cranes, and petrochemical tanks. Private yachts and catamarans bob at anchor with their bright colors reflecting off dappled waters, and as your eye sweeps the lovely panorama it runs into the dull gray wall of a warehouse where raw sugar is stored before being shipped to the Mainland to be processed. It's one of those places that separates perspectives: some see the "beauty" while others focus on the "beast."

Kalapaki Beach

This most beautiful beach at Nawiliwili fronts the lavish Westin Kauai. Just follow Rice Street until it becomes Route 51, where you'll soon see the bay and entrance to the hotel on your left. The hotel serves as a type of giant folding screen, blocking out most of the industrial area and leaving the lovely views of the bay. Park in the visitors' area at the hotel entrance, or to the rear of the hotel at the north end of Nawiliwili Beach Park, where a footbridge leads across the Nawiliwili Stream to the hotel property and the beach. Access to the beach is open to anyone, but if you want to use the hotel pool and showers, you'll have a lot less hassle if you order a light breakfast or lunch at one of the restaurants. The homemade ice cream at the hotel ice cream shop is delicious!

The wave action at Kalapaki is gentle at most times, with long swells combing the sandy-bottomed beach. Kalapaki is one of the best swimming beaches on the island, fair for snorkeling, and a great place to try either bodysurfing or beginning surfing. Two secluded beaches in this area are generally frequented by local people. Head through the hotel grounds following the road to the right past the few private homes that overlook this bay. From here you'll see a lighthouse on Ninini Point. Keep the lighthouse to your left as you walk across the golf course to the bay. Below are two small crescent beaches, both good for swimming and sunbathing. The right one has numerous springs that flow up into the sand. You can also head for **Nawiliwili County Beach Park** by following Route 51 downhill past the Westin Kauai until you come to the water; on the left is the beach park. Here are showers, picnic tables, and a pavilion along with some shady palm trees for a picnic. A seawall has been erected here, so for swimming and sunning it's much better to walk up to your left and spend the day at Kalapaki Beach.

Niumalu County Beach Park
This county-maintained beach park is along the Huleia Stream on the west end of Nawiliwili Harbor. Many small fishing and charter boats are berthed nearby and local men use the wharf area to fish and "talk story." There is no swimming and you are surrounded by the industrial area. However, you are very close to Lihue and there are pavilions, showers, toilets, and camping both for tents and RVs (permit required). To get there take Route 51 to Nawiliwili Harbor. Continue on Waapa Road along the harbor until you arrive at the beach park.

Ahukini Recreation Pier
As the name implies, this state park is simply a pier from which local people fish, and it's some of the best fishing around. Follow Route 57 to Lihue Airport. With the airport to your right keep going until the road ends at a large circular parking lot and fishing pier. The scenery is only fair, so if you're not into fishing give it a miss.

Hanamaulu County Beach Park
This is a wonderful beach, and although it is very accessible and good for swimming, very few tourists come here. There is not only a beach, but to the right is a lagoon area with pools formed by Hanamaulu Stream. Local families frequent this park, and it's particularly loved by children as they can play Tom Sawyer on the banks of the heavily forested stream. There are picnic tables, showers, toilets, a pavilion, and camping (county permit). In Hanamaulu, turn *makai* off Route 56 onto Hanamaulu Road, take the right fork onto Hehi Road, and follow it to the beach park.

PRACTICALITIES

ACCOMMODATIONS

If you like simple choices, you'll appreciate Lihue; only two fancy resorts are here, the rest are either family-run hotel/motels or apartment hotels. Prices are also best here because Lihue isn't considered a prime resort town. But it makes an ideal base, because from Lihue you can get there *anywhere* on the island in less than an hour. Although it's the county seat, the town is quiet, especially in the evenings, so you won't have to deal with noise or hustle and bustle.

Inexpensive Hotels, Motels, And Apartments
Motel Lani, owned and operated by Janet Naumu, offers clean, inexpensive rooms at the corner of Rice and Hardy streets. The lobby is actually an extension of Janet's home, where she and her children often watch TV. There are 10 Mexican-pink units, three of which offer cooking facilities, and although close to the road they're surprisingly quiet. All rooms have a small desk, dresser, bath, fan, refrigerator, and are cross-ventilated. No TVs. Janet usually doesn't allow children under three years old, especially if they misbehave, but she's reasonable and will make exceptions. A small courtyard with a BBQ is available to guests. Rates (two-night minimum) are $18 s, $24 up to three people, $7 additional person—slightly more for only one night. Rooms with cooking facilities (hard to get) are $28. For reservations write: Motel Lani, Box 1836, Lihue, HI 96766, tel. 245-2965.

Head down Rice Street toward Nawiliwili; at the corner of Wilcox Road is the **Ocean View**

Motel—no sign. The motel is across from Nawi-liwili Beach Park, and just a stroll from Kalapaki Beach. Its owner and manager, Spike Kanja, built the place. From this pink, three-story building you can scan the harbor, and you'll have an unobstructed view of the cement works! Spike's proud of his carp pond, about all there is to be proud of, although the basic rooms are clean. All rooms have refrigerators and are $20 s, $22 d, and $1 less a night for weekly rates. For reservations write: Ocean View Motel, 3445 Wilcox Rd., Nawiliwili, HI 96766, tel. 245-6345.

The **Kauai Inn**, formerly the Hale Niumalu Motel, is off the main drag near the boat harbor in Niumalu. The buildings were at one time overflow accommodations for a big hotel, but are now independently owned. The rooms are large and well kept but plain. The best feature is a screened lanai in the old building with a profusion of hanging plants. No longer the deal it used to be, rates are $42.50 for one night, $85 for two nights, and $297 for a week, for a one-bedroom efficiency with two to four beds. Across from Niumalu Park at the corner of Niumalu and Hulemalu roads, tel. 245-3316 or 245-2720.

The **Hale Lihue** is a quiet, clean, and basic motel (another one painted pink—there must have been a terrific sale!) on Kalena Street, a little side road off Rice. It was owned and operated for many years by a lovely Japanese couple, Mr. and Mrs. Morishige, whose hospitality made it an institution. They retired in 1984 and sold the hotel to a "man from Los Angeles," whose name Mrs. Morishige couldn't remember. She'd been assured, however, that he would keep "everything the same," news that past guests will be happy to hear. Rates are $18 s, $20 d, $24 t for a basic room with ceiling fan, $20 s, $24 d, $30 t for kitchenettes. For reservations write: Hale Lihue Motel, 2931 Kalena St., Lihue, HI 96766, tel. 245-3151.

The **Hale Pumehana Motel** is across the street from the Big Save in the Lihue Shopping Center, at 3083 Akahi Street. The sign welcoming you to the "house of warmth" reads "Hale Pumehana Motel-Liquor." Don't be put off. The place is a touch run-down, but OK, and the sign refers to a small liquor store/deli on the premises. The yellow and brown building has drab little rooms for $19.80 s, $24.20 d, $28.60 for three in a room. No phones, no TVs, but ceiling fans and private baths. For reservations write:

Hale Pumehana, Box 1828, Lihue, HI 96766, tel. 245-2106.

The **Tip Top Motel**, 3173 Akahi St., is a combination lounge, restaurant, and bakery popular with local folks. It's a functional two-story cinderblock building, and you guessed it . . . painted pink! The lobby/cafe/bakery is open 6:45 a.m. to 9 p.m. The rooms are antiseptic in every way, a plus as your feet stay cool on the bare linoleum floor. All are air-conditioned. Just to add that mixed-society touch, instead of a Gideon's Bible in the dresser drawer, you get *The Teachings of Buddha* placed by the Sudaka Society of Honolulu. Rates are $22 s, $28 d, $32 t, and $36 for four. For reservations: Tip Top Motel, Box 1231, Lihue, HI 96766, tel. 245-2333.

If you want to get out of town you can find basic accommodations at the **Elima Hale Hotel**, near the Wilcox Memorial Hospital, on Elima Street between Hanamaulu and Lihue. They offer rooms (some with private baths) with TVs, refrigerators, and use of a kitchen. Rates are $20 s, $24 d, with monthly and weekly rates. For information write: Elima Hale Hotel, 3360 Elima St., Lihue, HI 96766, tel. 245-9950.

Deluxe Accommodations

The **Kauai Hilton and Beach Villas** is one of Kauai's newest hotel/condos. On 25 landscaped acres overlooking Hanamaulu Beach, it offers 350 hotel rooms, all with mini-refrigerators, and 136 villas with full kitchens and laundry facilities. The hotel pool is in three sections connected by tiny waterfalls and cascades. Dining amenities include late-night room service, lobby lounge, pool bar and restaurant, **Gilligan's** for drinks and dancing, the casual **Jacaranda Terrace** main dining hall, and the **Midori** intercontinental dining restaurant. There are four tennis courts, two whirlpools, and water sports equipment. Prior to the nightly luau a torch lighting ceremony is performed, and a wide range of events is run by the activities desk. Rates are hotel $125-175, one-bedroom villa $140-200, two-bedroom villa (up to four people) $190-250. Special honeymoon, tennis, and golf packages are available. For information write: Kauai Hilton, 4331 Kauai Beach Dr., Lihue, HI 96766, tel. (800) 445-8667, on Kauai 245-1955.

Reopened in 1987 after having been totally refurbished and new construction done, the **Westin Kauai** at Kauai Lagoons is the island's fanciest and most modern resort complex. The core structures are unique: built before new building ordinances took effect, their 10 floors make them the tallest buildings on the island. This hotel was a prototype for the concept of a "destination resort" that provides all the activities a guest might require. Here are 500 acres of beautifully landscaped grounds, 11 restaurants and lounges, 60 shops in three arcades, eight plexipave tennis courts, 36 holes of golf designed by Jack Nicklaus, a spa and fitness center, one of Hawaii's largest and most opulent fountain pools, Kauai's largest swimming pool rimmed with four waterfalls and five jacuzzis, horsedrawn carriage rides, Venetian launch rides through the lagoons, and all insulated only minutes from town on Kalapaki, Lihue's finest beach.

All rooms have been redecorated. The predominant colors are pink, coral, light gray, and other soft pastels. The overall art motif is Oriental, with art objects and reproductions (over two million dollars' worth) from China and Japan. Fewer Korean, Thai, Indonesian, and Niuginian art pieces are on display, but there is a concerted effort to include more Hawaiiana and Polynesian art. A Chinese quarry was rented for two years to produce all the white stone statuary placed throughout the grounds. A free-standing boathouse near the beach houses the water activities center, the Royal Boathouse Restaurant, the Verandah Bar, and the Paddling Club discotheque. Built on five levels, with bars on the top and bottom floors, the disco is the newest hot spot in town. Dance the rather small hardwood dance floor or relax on the comfortable tiers and watch the music video as it plays on the wall.

Golfing fees run $75-95 for hotel guests and $100-125 for non-guests. Club rental and lessons are available for additional fees, and reservations are needed. Tennis court fees are $20 an hour per court; clinics, instruction, ball machines, and racquet rentals are available.

Standard room rates for single or double occupancy are Courtyard $185, Garden-view $225, Pool-view $255, Ocean-view $275, Beachfront $295, and Royal Beach Club $385; add $20 for an extra person. Suites range from $475-1500. All rooms have complimentary coffee-making machines, small refrigerators, and safes. Special honeymoon, spa, tennis, and

golf packages are offered. A 750-plus-room hotel is planned for the far side of the golf course. This multilevel affair will step down the hillside to the ocean, and will be used mostly for independent travelers while the present structure will serve conventions and group travelers. Planned also is a buggy ride from the airport to the lagoon, from where a launch will take you to the front entrance of the new hotel. For information and reservations contact: The Westin Kauai, Kalapaki Beach, Lihue, Kauai, HI 96766, tel. (800) 228-3000 or (808) 245-5050.

FOOD

Dining in Lihue is a treat. The menu of restaurants in and around town is the most extensive on the island. You can have savory snacks at saimin shops or at bargain-priced eateries frequented by local people. You'll find pizza parlors and fast-food chains. Stepping up in class, there are continental, Italian, and Japanese restaurants, while moderately priced establishments serve up hearty dishes of Mexican, Chinese, and good old American fare. Finally, fancier dining is found in some of the big hotels. The dining in Lihue is good to your palate and to your budget.

Inexpensive

If you ask anyone in Lihue where you can chow down for cheap, they'll send you to **Ma's Family Inc.** It's already an institution. Their building on Halenani Street, behind B.J. Furniture on Rice Street, is a bit run-down but clean. A few tourists find it, but mostly it's local working people. Lunches are good, but the super deals are breakfast and Hawaiian food. The coffee, which is free with breakfast, arrives hot in a large pot about as soon as your seat hits the chair. The menu is posted above the kitchen. You can start the day with a two-egg special for $1.55, or with "the works," which includes either potatoes or fried noodles with bacon or sausage and toast for $3. From the Hawaiian menu try *kalua* pork with two eggs and rice for $3.10, poi and *lomi* salmon for $2.65, Kauai sausage for $3.50, or a pound of *kalua* pork for $5.50. Don't bother the guy that orders this last item! Follow Rice Street until you see Kress Street, make a right and follow it to the corner, where you'll find Ma's at 4277

Halenani St., open daily 5 a.m. to 1:30 p.m., Sat., Sun., and holidays 5 a.m. to 10 a.m., tel. 245-3142.

Hamura Saimin Stand is just around the corner from Ma's. People flock to this old counter all day long for giant steaming bowls of saimin. But the real show is around 2 a.m. when all the bars and discos let loose their revelers. There is no decor, just good food. Your first time, try the Saimin Special which gives you noodles, slivers of meat and fish, vegetables, won ton, and eggs, all floating in a golden broth. Other items on the small menu are variations on the same theme with nothing over $3. Open daily at 2956 Kress St., tel. 245-3271. **Halo Halo Shave Ice** occupies a second counter in the same building—use the side entrance. Here you can get some of the best throat coolers on the island.

Yokozuna's Ramen has taken the place of Judy's Saimin, but keeps serving good food. This little shop is on the lower street level of the Lihue Shopping Center.

One of the best places for excellent Cantonese food at very reasonable prices is the cubbyhole **Ho's Garden** next to the Hawaiian Visitor's Bureau at Umi and Rice streets. Forget the surroundings and concentrate on the extensive menu. Open Mon. to Fri. 10:30 a.m. to 2 p.m. and 4:30 p.m. to 9 p.m., and Sat. 5 p.m. to 9 p.m., tel. 245-5255.

Garden Isle Kitchen has an odd location—it's in the grease bay of an old gas station that's made from lava rock and has a false grass-shack roof fashioned from cement. Open 8 a.m. to 5 p.m. Mon. to Fri. and until 2 p.m. Sat., they serve Hawaiian and Filipino food, including box lunches, plate lunches, *manapua, lumpia,* and *halohalo,* and run a catering service as well. In the Garden Island Plaza, tel. 246-9021.

Tip Top Restaurant/Bakery is the downstairs of the Tip Top Motel. A local favorite with unpretentious but clean surroundings, the food is wholesome but uninspired, just like the service. Breakfast is the best deal for around $2, and the macadamia nut pancakes are delish! Plate lunches are under $4 and dinners under $6. You can choose anything from pork chops to teriyaki chicken, and you get soup, salad, rice, and coffee. The *bento* (box lunches), either American style or Oriental, are a good deal at $3. Visit the bakery section and let your eyes tell your stomach what to do. The *malasadas* are fresh daily.

At 3173 Akahi St. between Rice and Route 57, open daily 6:45 a.m. to 9 p.m., tel. 245-2333.

Two cafeteria-style basic restaurants are **Kauai Kitchens,** tel. 245-4513, at the Rice Street Shopping Center, and **Kountry Kitchen Restaurant** at the Kukui Grove Center. At the latter, you can select such foods as sandwiches for $1.75, burgers $1.95, saimin $2-3, and plate lunches from $3.75-4.75. The breakfast menu runs $2-3.50 for pancakes, eggs, or omelettes. Hours are Mon. to Thurs. 8 a.m. to 5:30 p.m., Fri. 8 a.m. to 9 p.m., Sat. and Sun. 8 a.m. to 5 p.m.

Looking for a light lunch of pasta, salads, or sandwiches in countless varieties? Try **Paisanos** delicatessen for a complete line of gourmet fast foods—eat in or takeout. Located across Hardy St. from Big Save. Open Mon. to Fri. 11 a.m. to 3 p.m., tel. 245-5060.

Dani's is another favorite with local people. It's been around a while and has a good reputation for giving you a hearty meal for a reasonable price. The food is American-Hawaiian-Japanese. Most full meals range from $2.50 to $5 and you can choose from selections like *lomi* salmon, tripe stew, teri beef and chicken, and fried fish. Dani's is at 4201 Rice St. toward Nawiliwili near the fire department. Open Mon. to Sat. 5 a.m. to 2 p.m., Sun. 6 a.m. to 2 p.m., tel. 245-4991.

Kunja's Korean Restaurant opened recently and is the only place in town serving authentic Korean food. Sit down or takeout. Dishes include short ribs, marinated beef strips, mixed rice and vegetables, and various noodle soups, priced from $3.25 to $5.75. Many are made with the Hawaiian palate in mind, but for a real spicy dish try *O-jing-o Po Kum* for $4.50 or *kimchi* soup for $5.50. Clean and tidy, with only eight tables. Open from 9:30 a.m. to 8 p.m. Mon. to Sat., Kunja's is located at 4252 Rice St., across from N. Yoneji's Store, tel. 245-8792.

Moderate—In Lihue

The majority of restaurants in and around Lihue charge as little as $5, and average $10. Most of these restaurants advertise specials and discounts in the free tourist literature.

Casa Italian is in the Haleko Shops, just behind easily spotted Eggberts restaurant. Its husband-wife team from New York tries to make each dish special. The menu features manicotti, canelloni, and veal. The hefty salad bar has a special Italian twist, and the pasta is made fresh daily. An order of the homemade garlic and pepper bread and a bowl of minestrone soup for only $1.25 makes a delicious meal. The good wine list and espresso bar add to the continental patio atmosphere with tile floors and marble-topped tables accentuated with red settings. Open daily for dinner 5:30 to 10 p.m., reservations, tel. 245-9586.

The Eggberts, also in the Haleko Shops, specializes in all kinds of omelettes. Their specialty is Eggberts Benedict, regular, vegetarian, or with ham or turkey breast, with a special secret sauce. Prices range from $4.50 up to $7.95 for half or full orders. Lunch specialties are sandwiches, mostly $3.95 to $4.95, and dinners feature beef, chicken, and fish from $6 to $12. The service is friendly, the coffee hot and quick, and the atmosphere bright; 4483 Rice St., daily breakfast and lunch 7 a.m. to 2 p.m., dinner 5:30 p.m. to 9:30 p.m., and the lounge stays open until closing, tel. 245-6325.

Restaurant Kiibo serves authentic Japanese meals without a big price tag. Many Japanese around town come here to eat. The low stools at the counter are reminiscent of a Japanese *akachochin* or *sushiya*. In fact, the sushi bar is a recent addition. Savory offerings of *udon,* tempura, teriyaki, and a variety of *teishoku* (specials) all are accompanied by a picture showing you just what you'll get. The service is quick and friendly; most offerings are under $10. Restaurant Kiibo is *ichiban!* Located just off Rice Street, at 2991 Umi Street. Open for lunch from 11 a.m. to 1 p.m. (attracts many office workers) and for dinner from 5:30 to 9 p.m., closed Sunday and holidays, tel. 245-2650. Just around the corner is the **Lihue Cafe** for Japanese and Chinese food. Unpretentious setting, basic food. Open Mon. to Sat. 4:30 p.m. to 9 p.m. (to 10 pm. on Fri.), tel. 245-6471.

The Barbecue Inn has been in business for three decades, and if you want a testimonial, just observe the steady stream of local people, from car mechanics to doctors, heading for this restaurant. Word has it that it's better for lunch than dinner. The atmosphere is "leatherette and formica," but the service is homey, friendly, and prompt. Japanese and American servings are huge. Over 30 entrees range from a chicken platter to seafood and even prime rib. The Friday teriyaki platter is a good choice. The scampi is

perhaps the best for the price on the island. Most meals are complete with soup/salad, banana bread, vegetables, beverage, and dessert for around $6 and up. Breakfast goes for a reasonable $2, with lunch at bargain prices. The homemade pies are amazing for only $.50. Cocktails. No credit cards accepted; 2982 Kress St., open daily 7:30 a.m. to 8:45 p.m., tel. 245-2921.

The **Club Jetty** overlooks Nawiliwili Harbor. Follow the access road at the beach park to the end, where it sits with a commanding view of the bay. It's especially picturesque on the evenings when the USS *Independence,* a cruise ship silhouetted by deck lights, lies at anchor. The restaurant serves an American menu with steaks, seafood, and a salad bar, but their house specialty is extensive Cantonese cuisine. Sweet-and-sour spare ribs in fresh pineapple with a side of fried rice at $5.25 is about average. *Mahi mahi* or chicken dinners cost $8.95, and luscious soups like abalone and vegetable are $4.25. The club changes from a family place with local entertainment to a hotshot disco at night. Loyal customers liked the old beat better! From Wednesday to Saturday you can boogie to live bands and drink imported beers until 3 a.m. Dinner is served daily from 4:30 to 9:30 p.m., tel. 245-4970. Reservations, especially for a table with a view, are needed.

The **Bull Shed** in the Harbor Village has a reputation for serving the best prime rib on Kauai, and usually lives up to it. The salad bar is also praiseworthy, served in a loaded-down canoe, but it's best early on busy nights, before it's hit too hard. They serve lobster, tenderloin fillet, and teriyaki steak or chicken. Open daily for dinner from 5:30 p.m., tel. 245-4551. While in the Harbor Village also check out **Kauai Chop Suey,** a no-frills, reasonably priced Chinese restaurant. Relatively new, it already has a steady clientele. Most dishes are well prepared, under $5. Open Tues. to Sat. 11 a.m. to 2 p.m. for lunch, Tues. to Sun. 4:30 to 9 p.m. for dinner, takeout for picnics available, tel. 245-8790. Across the courtyard is **Denmar's Restaurant,** tel. 245-3917, serving American breakfasts and Mexican lunch and dinner.

Moderate—Around Lihue

Rosita's Mexican restaurant has recently moved from Nawiliwili to Kukui Grove Shopping

Center. The new decor of light stucco and wrought iron is upbeat and tasteful; you sit in semi-enclosed booths for privacy. The margaritas are large and tasty. Enjoy a full range of dinners, nearly all under $10.75. Their loyal clientele comes out from Lihue. Open daily for lunch from 11:30 a.m. to 3 p.m., dinner from 5:30 to 10 p.m., tel. 245-8561.

In Hanamaulu is the **Hanamaulu Restaurant & Tea House.** They must be doing something right to have lasted in the same location for over 65 years. The decor is basic but the menu, including sushi, *yakiniku,* and a variety of Japanese and Chinese dishes, is varied and priced right. Next door is **Ara's Sushi Bar** with a sushi bar that looks over a fishpond, and *tatami*-floored rooms that face a Japanese garden. Open daily except Mon. 9 a.m. to 1 p.m. for lunch, 4:30 to 9 p.m. for dinner, tel. 245-2511.

The Planter's also sits along Route 56 in Hanamaulu, tel. 245-1606. The menu is long and varied but the specialty is *kiawe*-broiled prime rib and steak. Most meals run in the $10-14 range. Open windows let in the breeze, but also the traffic noise along the highway. Open Mon. to Sat. for lunch and dinner—dinner only on Sunday. Happy hour at the bar runs 3:30-5 p.m., between meal times. In the large green building next door (built in 1908) are the post office, a few shops, and **Sampaquita's Saimin** for a quick bowl of noodles.

Expensive

If you want both classy dining and a choice of restaurants, head for the **Westin Kauai.** Prices vary from moderate to expensive in their varied restaurants, and each cuisine is specialized with an emphasis on American, Hawaiian, seafood, or Japanese. Nibble Kyoto-style sushi or *sashimi* at the **Tempura Garden** while looking out over the fishponds and sculpted garden. At the Kauai Lagoons Golf and Racquet Club, **The Terrace** serves exceptional breakfasts, including a light and fluffy waffle made the old-fashioned way. For seafood and pasta, take a carriage ride or launch to the **Inn on the Cliffs.** The most elegant restaurant (reservations and jackets required) is **The Masters** at the Kauai Lagoons Golf and Racquet Club, where continental cuisine is prepared by a French chef. For a more informal setting, try the dinner and show at **The Royal Boathouse**, steak and seafood

on the top floor of the Surf Tower at **Prince Bill's**, or the poolside **Cook's at the Beach.**

The **Kauai Hilton** offers two restaurants: The **Jacaranda Terrace** is known for casual breakfasts, lunches, and dinners, while the **Midori** combines Japanese decor with continental and Oriental cuisine. Tofu *cordon bleu,* anyone? Dinner only, tel. 245-1955.

The rear flagstone veranda and original dining room at Kilohana, the restored 1935 plantation estate of Gaylord Wilcox near Puhi, have been turned into the breezy **Gaylord's at Kilohana.** Light salads and sandwiches for $6.95-7.95 are the fare at lunch but dinners are more substantial. Try the Rainbow Duck with three sauces for $19.95, lamb with raspberry-mango chutney sauce for $21.95, or any of the daily specials and you can't go wrong.

Fast Foods

Yes, the smell of the Colonel's frying chicken overpowers the flower-scented air, and the Golden Arches glimmer in the bright Kauai sun. **Pizza Hut, Jack in the Box, McDonald's, Kentucky Fried Chicken, Zack's Frozen Yogurt,** and **Subway Sub Shop** are all located along Kuhio Highway. **Burger King** and **Taco Bell** are at the Kukui Grove Shopping Mall, and a **Dairy Queen** brazier can be found on Rice Street across from the Rice Street Shopping Center.

Farmers' Market

If you're making your own meals while visiting Kauai, remember that locally grown fresh fruit and vegetables are available from vendors at the farmers' market every Fri. at 3 p.m. at Vidinha Stadium in Lihue.

ENTERTAINMENT

Lihue is not the entertainment capital of the world, but if you have the itch to step out at night, there are a few places around town where you can scratch it.

Club Jetty Restaurant in Nawiliwili transforms from a family restaurant to a throbbing disco/live music dance bar Thurs. through Saturday. Bands are usually brought in from neighboring islands or the Mainland. The flashing lights crank up around 10 p.m. and continue until the early hours of the morning. There's a cover, but drinks aren't too inflated. The **Park Place**

Nightclub and Restaurant in the Harbor Village Shopping Center also has dancing until about 4 a.m.

The favorite hotspot for evening entertainment is the **Paddling Room** at the Westin Kauai Hotel. This multilevel disco has a bar on the top and bottom levels and seats along the stepped tiers below the DJ's box. Music videos are projected on a large screen over the small hardwood dance floor. Loud, boisterous, and busy. Here, hotel guests mingle with the local crowd. A dress code is enforced. Park in the lot across the stream near the Oar House Saloon (a watering hole with pool tables and shaded lights) and walk across the pedestrian footbridge.

The **Kauai Hilton** has dancing and entertainment at **Gilligan's.** Weekends are popular here with locals from Lihue and Kapaa who are looking for a night out on the town. The music seems to get louder as the night wears on and the dance floor is seldom empty. Open Sun. to Thurs. 8 p.m. to 2 a.m., Fri. and Sat. 8 p.m. to 4 a.m. Dress code.

If you desire slower dancing and quieter music, find your way to the Lihue Neighborhood Center (tel. 822-4836) any Friday evening from 7:30 to 9:30 for down-home square dancing. A $1 donation is asked for at the door. Records provide the music, and a caller helps even the novice become proficient by the end of the evening.

On Thursday and Friday evenings, contemporary Hawaiian music is played at **Rosita's** at the Kukui Grove Center. The surroundings are quite elegant with stained-glass lanterns, murals on white stucco walls, and plenty of plants. The atmosphere is more convivial after a few margaritas, which are the house specialty.

Sometimes the **Kukui Grove Center** presents free entertainment, usually of a Hawaiian nature. The schedule varies but these shows mainly occur on weekends. Check the free tourist literature to see if anything's going on—they're worth the effort!

The newest type of entertainment spot to hit Kauai is the *karoake* bar, of which **Kay's Pub** is *the* place in Lihue. For payment of $1, the customer is given the microphone and sings along with the music, the video and words to which are projected on a screen in the corner. A funky, dark little place with booths and formica tables, it's become a local hangout for crooners. Even if you're not an undiscovered Johnny Mathis, pay your buck and sing along. *Pu pus* are free, beer and drinks are reasonably priced. Open Mon. to Sat. 2 p.m. to 1 a.m. in the Rice Street Shopping Center.

Other possibilities for evening entertainment include the nightly luau and torchlighting ceremony at the Kauai Hilton, the Hawaiian dinner show at the Royal Boathouse, and afternoon and early evening soft music or piano bars in the Lobby Lounge at the Kauai Hilton, and at the Veranda Bar, Colonnade Bar, and the Inn on the Cliffs, all at the Westin Kauai.

Theater

For 17 years the **Kauai Community Players** have presented the island with virtually its only theatrical performances. Four times a year, beginning in Nov., Feb., April, and July, this non-professional, community theater group puts on well-known and experimental plays, usually in the Lihue Parish Hall across Nawiliwili Road from the Kukui Grove Shopping Center. Curtain time is 8 p.m., and ticket prices are $7 adults, $5 students and senior citizens—a dollar less with advance purchase. For information on what's currently showing call 822-7797.

SHOPPING

Lihue makes you reach for your wallet, with good cause. A stroll through one of its shopping centers (see pp. 747-750) is guaranteed to send you home with more in your luggage than you came with. Kauai's best selections and bargains are found here. It helps that Lihue is a *resort* town second to being a *living* town. Kauaians shop in Lihue, and the reasonable prices that local purchasing generates are passed on to you.

Clothing

Don't pass up **Hilo Hattie**, an institution on alohawear, at least to educate yourself on products and prices. Though their designs may not be one of a kind, their clothing is very serviceable and well made. Specials are always offered in the free tourist literature, along with clearance racks at the store itself. They also have a selection of gifts and souvenirs. Plenty of incentives to get you in include free hotel pick-up from Poipu to Kapaa, a tour of the factory, free refreshments while you look around, and free on-the-spot alterations. Look for them at 3252 Kuhio Hwy., at the intersection of Route 57. Open every day from 8:30 a.m. to 5 p.m., tel. 245-3404.

Kapaia Stitchery is where you find handmade and distinctive fashions. This shop is along Route 56 in Kapaia, a tiny village between Hanamaulu and Lihue. The owner is Julie Yukimura, who, along with her grandmother and a number of very experienced island seamstresses, creates fashions, quilts, and embroideries that are beautiful, painstakingly made, and priced right. You can choose a garment off the rack or have one tailor-made from the Stitchery's wide selection of cotton fabrics. You can't help being pleased with this fine shop!

Clothing at discount prices is found at **Garment Factory to You** in the Lihue Shopping Center. This store is as practical as its name. For more practical items try **Sears** or **L&M Jeans** for all shapes and sizes of jeans, and **Foot Locker** for athletic shoes, all at the Kukui Grove Center.

Also, you can't go wrong taking a promenade through the tasteful shops located on the ground floor of the Aston Kauai Hotel or the numerous boutiques at the Westin Kauai Hotel, where you'll find everything from artwork to clothing. Prices tend to be higher than at other shops, but selections are more distinctive.

Arts, Crafts, And Souvenirs

If you're after just filling a shopping basket with trinkets and gimjicks for family and friends back home, go to **Gem** in Lihue, or **Longs Drugstore** in the Kukui Grove Center. Their bargain counters are loaded with terrific junk for a buck or two. Try the **Nawiliwili Marketplace** near the Oar House Saloon for jewelry, trinkets, T-shirts, and gift items. For better-quality souvenirs, along with custom jewelry, try **Linda's Creation** at 4254 Rice Street. This shop, owned and operated by Joe and Linda Vito, is well stocked with items ranging from silk wallets for $2 to lovely vases for over $100. **Kauai Museum Shop** at the Kauai Museum has authentic souvenirs and items Hawaiian with competitive prices. **Mandala's** is a combination head shop and poster and T-shirt store on Route 56 in the Garden Island Plaza, a small complex across from McDonald's.

The walls of **Stone's Gallery** at the Kukui Grove Center are brightened by serigraphs by Pegge Hopper and lovely pieces by Carol Bennet and James Kay. Ceramics, photos, and prints round out the selections. To the rear of the gallery is a small espresso bar where you can relax and contemplate the island artwork over your shoulder. Also at the mall check out **See You In China**. A square-rigged "China trader" would sink if it had this store's large selection in its hold—plenty of *objects d'art* from the Orient along with jewelry, clothing, stationery, and gift items.

Photo Needs

For a full-line photo store go to **Don's Camera Center**, 4286 Rice St., tel. 245-6581. All you'll need from a wide selection of famous brands, plus camera repair, and one-day processing. **Longs Drug** and **Kauai 1-hour Photo** at the Kukui Grove Center have inexpensive film and processing. **Cameralab** near McDonald's on the Kuhio Hwy. develops film in one hour, and **Senda Studio** at 4450 Hardy St. is a studio and supply shop.

WAILUA

Wailua ("Two Waters") is heralded by the sway-ing fronds of extra tall royal palms, and when-ever you see these, like the *kahili* of old, you know you're entering a special place. The Ha-waiian *ali'i* knew a choice piece of real estate when they saw one, and they cultivated this prime area at the mouth of the Wailua River as their own. Through the centuries they built many *heiau* in the area, some where unfortunates were slaughtered to appease the gods, others where the weak and vanquished could find suc-cor and sanctuary. The road leading inland along the Wailua River was called the King's Highway. Commoners were confined to travel-ing only along this road and could approach the royal settlement by invitation only. The most ex-alted of the island's *ali'i* traced their proud lineage to Puna, a Tahitian priest who, accord-ing to the oral tradition, arrived in the earliest mi-grations and settled here.

Even before the Polynesians came, the area was purportedly settled by the semi-mythical Mu. This lost tribe may have been early Polyne-sians who were isolated for such a long time that they developed different physical characteristics from their original root stock. Or perhaps they were a unique people altogether, whom history never recorded. But like another island group, the Menehune, they were dwarfish creatures who shunned outsiders. Unlike the industrious Mene-hune, who helped the Polynesians, the Mu were fierce and brutal savages whose misanthropic characters confined them to solitary caves in the deep interior along the Wailua River, where they led unsuspecting victims to their deaths.

Wailua today has a population of over 1,500, but you'd never know it driving past, as most houses are scattered in the hills behind the coast. Though an older resort area, it's not at all overdeveloped. The natural charm is as vibrant as ever. Depending on conditions, the beaches can be excellent, and there're shops, restau-rants, and nightlife close at hand. With develop-ment increasing both to the east and west, per-haps now, as in days of old, the outstanding beauty of Wailua will beckon once again.

SIGHTS AND PRACTICALITIES

Wailua is primarily famous because of two attractions, one natural, the other manmade. People flock to these, but in the hills behind the settlement along King's Highway are deserted *heiau*, sacred birthing stones, old cemeteries, and meditative views of the river below.

Fern Grotto

Nature's foremost attraction is the Wailua River itself, Hawaii's only navigable stream, which meanders inland toward its headwaters atop forbidding Mt. Waialeale. Along this route is the **Fern Grotto**, a tourist institution of glitz, hype, and beauty rolled into one. Two local companies run sightseeing trips to the grotto on large motorized barges. As you head the two miles upriver, the crew tells legends of the area and serenades visitors with Hawaiian songs. A hula demonstration is given, where you are encouraged to get up and swing along. The grotto itself is a natural rock amphitheater, whose ever-misty walls create the perfect conditions for ferns to grow. And grow they do, wildly and with abandon, filling the cavern with their deep musty smell and penetrating green beauty. Partially denuded of its lush green coat by Hurricane Iwa, the grotto is slowly filling in and becoming the beauty it once was. Smaller than one might imagine, the resonating acoustics are wonderful from inside the grotto. Here in the natural cathedral, musicians break into the "Hawaiian Wedding Song," where over the years a steady stream of brides and grooms have come to exchange vows. The Fern Grotto trip is an amusement ride, but it's also the only way to get there. It's enjoyable and memorable, but you have to stay in the right frame of mind, otherwise it's too easily put down. For tours see p. 739.

The Coco Palms

The Coco Palms Resort is a classic Hawaiian hotel, one of the first tourist destinations built on the island. The Polynesian-inspired buildings are interspersed amidst a monumental coconut grove planted by a German immigrant in the early 1800s. His aspiration was to start a copra plantation, and although it failed, his plantings matured into one of the largest stands of coconut trees in the islands. Nightly, the hostelry's famous torch-lighting ceremony takes place under the palm canopy that encircles a royal lagoon, once used to fatten succulent fish for the exclusive use of the *ali'i*. Everyone is welcome to the ceremony, hotel guest or not, and you should definitely go if you're in the area around sundown. The Lagoon Terrace Lounge, with soft evening entertainment, and the Lagoon Dining Room have superb front-row seats. Some may put the performance down as "fake traditional," but it's the best fake traditional on the island, both dramatic and fun. It was started by the recently retired Grace Guslander, the congenial hostess famous for her cocktail parties.

The hotel grounds are inspiring, and often when Hollywood needed "paradise" they came here. Parts of past movie sets still remain. Notice the authentic-looking cement palm trees used to blend in the construction of some of the buildings. There's a small zoo, museum, and a chapel built by Columbia Pictures for Rita Hayworth in the movie *Sadie Thompson*. More than 2,000 marriages have been performed in this chapel since, and not all to Zsa Zsa Gabor and Liz Taylor! When Tattoo informs Mr. Rourk about "De plane, boss," in the once popular TV series "Fantasy Island," it is into the Coco Palms grove that he drives the jeep. Elvis came here to film *Blue Hawaii*, and segments of *South Pacific* were shot on the grounds. Frank Sinatra found out who the "chairman of the board" really was when one day he was swept out to sea from a nearby beach. "Old Blue Eyes" used his velvet voice to scream for help, and was rescued by local men from the fire department using a surfboard. After the rescue, Sinatra discovered that they had no boat; showing the class he's famous for, he bought them a spanking new CrisCraft. The hotel bought the beach house known as the "Sinatra House" and rented it out. Sinatra was later upstaged when John Kennedy visited a number of times, and the house was renamed the "President's House." The hotel divested itself of this property recently. As soon as you walk onto the grounds you feel romantic. You can't help it. No one's immune! The Coco Palms is a peaceful garden. Let it surround you.

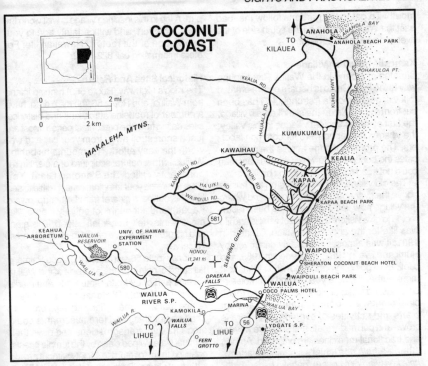

Smith's Tropical Paradise

Set along the Wailua River is this 30-acre botanical and cultural garden. A large entranceway welcomes you, and proclaims it a "tropical paradise." Inside, most plants are labeled; many are ordinary island foliage, others rare and exotic even for the Garden Island. The entire area is sheltered and well watered, and it's easy to imagine how idyllic life was for the original Hawaiians. Some of the buildings include a luau house and lagoon theater used in the evening for an international musical show. Peacocks and chickens pecking beneath the trees are natural groundskeepers, preventing insects and weeds from overpowering the gardens. The "villages"—Japanese-, Philippine-, and Polynesian-inspired settlements—are merely plywood facsimiles. However, the grounds themselves are beautifully kept and very impressive. For those who won't be trekking into the Kauaian backcountry, but especially for those who will,

this garden provides an excellent opportunity to familiarize yourself with Kauai's plants, flowers, and trees. You are welcome to walk where you will, but signs guide you down a recommended walk. Scheduled mini-trams carry tourists around the grounds for an additional fee. Entrance fees are $3 adults, $1.50 children two to 11; the tram tour is an additional $2 for adults, $1 for children. Enter anytime from 8:30 a.m. until 4:30 p.m., when the gardens are readied for the evening entertainment. The luau/musical show costs $36 for adults, $23 children two to 11, and $10 and $5, respectively, for the show only. Reservations are necessary for both. Rated the favorite luau show on the island, Hawaiian music, a fiery volcanic eruption, and dances from all over the Pacific are some examples of what awaits you at this spectacle. For information, call 822-4654, 822-9599, or 822-3467, or pick up tickets at Smith's booth across from the entrance to the Coco Palms on the north side of the river-mouth. To get to the gardens follow the road past the Wailua Marina on the south side of the river and park in the large lot.

Kamokila Hawaiian Village

Situated at a bend in the Wailua River on the way to the Fern Grotto is Kauai's only re-created folk village. Kamokila ("stronghold") has been cut from the jungle on the site of an *ali'i* village, the first of seven ancient villages in this valley; the villages farther up were for common laborers. The prominent ridge across the river indicates the boundary into which the ordinary man could not tread for fear of his losing his life.

The old village sat on terraces on the hillside above the river and fields were cultivated where the village now lies. Kamokila has been resurrected to give visitors a glimpse of what island life was like for the ancient Hawaiian. Created in 1981, it was almost immediately destroyed by Hurricane Iwa in 1982. Reopened in 1985, and continually going through renovation to make it more authentic, here you will find examples of buildings, agricultural plots, fruit trees and medicinal plants, and demonstrations of ancient crafts and activities of everyday life. Taro is grown and poi made, mats and skirts are woven, and traditional medicines are prepared. Among others, a *hale noa* (chief's sleeping quarters), *hale koa* (warrior's house), *pahoku hanau* (birthing house), *hale ali'i akoakoa* (assembly hall), *laola pa'au* (herbal medicine office), and *lana nu'u mamao* (oracle tower) have been erected. *Imu* pits for cooking are functional, an athletic ground is used for games at festive times of the year, and the tikis (spirit containers) and *aumakua* (gods) are set up at propitious spots around the village.

Lloyd, a real storehouse of knowledge, or one of the dozen other guides, will escort you around and explain the importance of each site, the methods of creating handicrafts and tools, the use of all ordinary and medicinal plants, and how the village operated on a daily basis. You may drive down to the village by following a steep one-lane track that skirts the ridge—the turnoff is just above the Opaekaa Falls overlook on Route 580. A free shuttle bus service is available from hotels in the Wailua and Kapaa area. Future plans include a ferry ride from the Wailua Marina to the village. The entrance fee is $5 for adults, $1.50 for children under 12; open Mon. to Sat. 9 a.m. to 4 p.m. A trip to this inspiring village is well worth the time and effort, and will certainly add to your knowledge of the roots of Hawaiian life. For more information call 822-1192.

Historical Sites And *Heiau*

The King's Highway (Route 580) running inland from Wailua, and Route 56, the main drag, have a number of roadside attractions and historical sites dating from the precontact period. Most are just a short stroll away from your car and well worth the easy effort. The mountains behind Wailua form a natural sculpture of a giant in repose, aptly called **The Sleeping Giant**. You have to stretch your imagination just a little to see him (his outline is clearer from farther up toward Kapaa), and although not entirely a bore, like most giants, he's better left asleep. This giant and his green cover are part of the Nonou Forest Reserve.

Along Route 56 just before the Coco Palms, a tall stand of palms on the east side of the Wailua River is part of Lydgate State Park, and marks the spot of **Hauola O' Honaunau**, a temple of refuge that welcomed offending *kapu* breakers of all social classes. Here miscreants could atone for their transgressions and have their spiritual slates wiped clean by the temple priests, enabling them to return to society without paying with their lives. Both the refuge and **Hikina Heiau** are marked by a low encircling wall. The area is extremely picturesque here, where the Wailua River meets the sea. Perhaps it's knowledge about the temple of refuge that creates the atmosphere, but here, as at all of these merciful temple sites, the atmosphere is calm and uplifting, as if some spiritual residue has permeated the centuries. It's a good spot to relax in the cool of the grove and there are picnic tables available.

As Route 580 meanders inland, you pass **Wailua River State Park.** Then immediately look for **Poaiahu Arboretum** and its convenient turnout. The arboretum is merely a stand of trees along the roadside. Across the road is **Holo Holo Ku Heiau**, where the unfortunate ones who didn't make it to the temple of refuge were sacrificed to the never-satisfied gods. This temple is one of Kauai's most ancient; the altar itself is the large slab of rock near the southwest corner. Behind the *heiau*, a silver guardrail leads up the hill to a small, neatly tended Japanese cemetery. The traditional tombstones chronicling the lives and deaths of those buried here turn green with lichens against the pale blue sky. As if to represent the universality of the life-death cycle, **Pohaku Hoo Hanau,** the "royal birthing stones," are within an infant's cry away. Royal mothers came here to deliver the future kings and queens of the island. The stones somehow look comfortable to lean against and perhaps their solidity reinforced the courage of the mother.

Back on Route 580 you start wending your way uphill. You can see how eroded and lush Kauai is from this upland perch. On your left is the lush Wailua Valley, watered by the river, and on your right, separated by a spit of land perhaps only 200 yards wide, is a relatively dry gulch. Notice, too, the dark green fresh water as it becomes engulfed by the royal blue of the ocean in the distance. As you climb look for an HVB Warrior pointing to **Opaekaa Falls.** The far side of the road has an overlook, below which is the Wailua River and the Kamokila Hawaiian Village. Take a look around to see how undeveloped Kauai is. Across the road and down a bit from the Opaekaa turnoff is **Poliahu Heiau,** supposedly built by the Menehune. Nothing is left but a square wall enclosure that is overgrown on the inside. Do not walk on the walls as it's believed that the spirits of the ancestors are contained in the rocks. Down the ridge, at the end of a gravel track, are the **bell stones;** pounded when a royal *wahine* gave birth, their peal could be heard for miles. From here there is a great view over the river and down to the coast.

Beaches, Parks, And Recreation

Wailua has few beaches, but they're excellent. **Wailua Municipal Golf Course** skirts the coast, fronting a secluded beach, and because of its idyllic setting is perhaps the most beautiful public links in Hawaii. Even if you're not an avid golfer, you can take a lovely stroll over the fairways as they stretch out along the coastline. The greens fee is a reasonable $10 weekdays, $11 weekends, with carts and clubs for rent. The driving range is open until 10 p.m. For the convenience of golfers, the clubhouse has a dining room and snack bar open daily. For information or link reservations call 245-2163. Below the links is a secluded beach. You can drive to it by following the paved road at the western end of the course until it becomes dirt and branches to the sea. The

swimming is good in sheltered coves and the snorkeling is better than average along the reef. Few ever come here, and plenty of nooks and crannies are good for one night's bivouac.

Lydgate State Park is a gem. It's clearly marked along Route 56 on the south side of the Wailua River, behind the Aston Kauai Resort complex. Two large lava pools make for great swimming even in high surf. The smaller pool is completely protected and perfect for tots, while the larger pool is great for swimming and snorkeling. Stay off the slippery volcanic rock barrier. This beach is never overcrowded, and you can find even more seclusion by walking along the coast away from the built-up area. If you head to the river, the brackish water is refreshing, but stay away from where it meets the ocean, creating tricky, wicked currents. Lydgate State Park also provides sheltered picnic tables under a cool canopy provided by a thick stand of ironwoods, plus grills, restrooms, and showers, but no camping. The beach across the river fronting the Coco Palms is very treacherous and should only be entered on calm days when lifeguards are in attendance.

ACCOMMODATIONS

The hotel scene in Wailua is like the beaches, few but good. Your choices include the famous Coco Palms or the Aston Kauai Resort, with its admirable location fronting Lydgate Park.

The **Coco Palms Resort** has recently changed hands, and now belongs to Park Lane International. The new owners have gone to great lengths to keep the friendly and cordial atmosphere that made the hotel memorable to all past visitors. While the 45 acres of grounds are as outstanding as ever, Park Lane has spent millions refurbishing the hotel and grounds. When you enter, the unusual lobby is a harmonious blend of Polynesian longhouse and European cathedral. The huge chandeliers hang like birds of paradise spreading subdued red and yellow light; a *koa* staircase leads to the upper levels. The front desk is a series of conga-like drums, and there is always a magnificent floral display of Kauai's most exotic blooms. There are nightly performances of the torch-lighting ceremony and the Larry Rivera Polynesian show, Grace Guslander-inspired cocktail parties several times a week, twice-weekly storytelling in the lobby with Auntie Sarah, and a small museum and library that house the personal belongings of Mrs. Guslander and tell an intimate tale of the island. The resort boasts tennis courts (three of clay and two nightlit), three swimming pools, two cocktail lounges, and two restaurants. The chapel has services every Sunday, and a hotel mini-mall sells gifts and a few necessities.

The resort's 390 rooms are in different wings with names like Top of the Palms, Ali'i Kai and Sea Building, and in 22 separate cottages that front the lagoon. For a terrific view of the lagoon and the torch-lighting ceremony, request a room in Top of the Palms. All rooms have a refrigerator, color TV, and air-conditioning, and bathroom basins are huge "killer" clamshells for which the Palms has become famous. The cottages have private, outdoor lava rock baths or jacuzzis. Even if you are after more modest accommodations for a long-term stay, a night or two at the Coco Palms is definitely worth it. Rates are $110-150 for rooms, $180 for a Queen's Cottage, $200 for a King's Cottage, $240 for Prince of Hawaii Cottages, and suites run to $370. Optional room and car, tennis, and wedding packages are available. For more information contact the Coco Palms Resort, Wailua, Kauai, HI 96746, tel. (800) 542-2626, on Kauai 822-4921.

The **Aston Kauai Resort** has a lovely setting above Lydgate Park, with the Hauola Temple of Refuge adjacent to the grounds. Incorporated into the architecture are a series of cascading pools and a koi (carp) pond that boils with frenzied color during feeding time. The main lobby is a huge affair with swooping beams in longhouse style. There is a Polynesian review five nights a week, a luau, and the hotel buffet receives the ultimate compliment of high attendance by local people. The hotel is one of the best places on Kauai for name entertainment—Mainland performers such as Jesse Colin Young, and Hawaii's own, like the Peter Moon Band. Every night except Monday the lobby lounge features music—often jazz—by local artists; a good place to people-watch and wind down after a hard day. Rooms are well appointed and most have ocean views. Rates are from $99 standard to $159 for a deluxe oceanfront, and $1699 for cabanas with kitchenettes, which are separate from the main facility and provide unobstructed views of the beach. For in-

formation contact Aston Hotels and Resorts, 3-5920 Kuhio Hwy., Kapaa, Kauai, HI 96746, tel. (800) 922-7866, on Kauai 245-3931.

FOOD

Not to break the pattern, the food scene is akin to Wailua's accommodations and beaches: not a smorgasbord to choose from, but a good range of prices and cuisine.

Inexpensive
Wailua Pizza Stop serves pizza, submarine sandwiches, pasta, and salads in the Kikipopo Shopping Village along Route 56 past the Coco Palms on the right as you head for Kapaa. Their hefty pizzas range from a small cheese at $5.70 to a huge pie with the works for $15.95. The subs are about $4,with cheaper sandwiches available. Salads run $3-6, and if they're anything like the pizzas and subs, they ought to be good. Open daily 10 a.m. to 10 p.m., tel. 822-9222. Also in this center is the clean but characterless **Chopstix Chinese Food** shop, open 9 a.m. to 9 p.m., where everything on the menu is under $5.

Some will be happy, and others sad, to hear that fast foods have arrived in Wailua. North of the Coco Palms is a **Sizzler Steakhouse**, where the aroma of barbecued beef wafts on the ocean breezes. Quick snacks and packaged foods can be bought at the **7-eleven** next door, or at **Tony's Minit Mart** or the Shell station mini-mart across the street.

Moderate
The **Wailua Marina Restaurant**, overlooking the Wailua River, offers inexpensive to moderately priced "local-style" food, and free hotel pick-up in the Wailua area for dinner. If you're going on a Fern Grotto boat trip consider eating here. Breakfast, 8:30 to 11 a.m., is under $3, lunches until 2 p.m. offer plates like a small tenderloin, fries, and a tossed green salad for $6.25; dinner entrees like Korean barbecue ribs or breaded veal cutlets in mushroom sauce are served for under $9 from 5 to 9 p.m. It's convenient, and there's never a wait after the last boat upriver. At the Wailua Marina, tel. 822-4311.

Perhaps the best moderately priced meals in Wailua are the buffets at the **Pacific Dining Room** in the Aston Kauai Resort. Generally, buffets are ho-hum, but the Saturday night prime rib buffet ($13.25) or the seafood extravaganza every Sun., Tues., and Fri. ($18.50) are terrific, with as many local people in attendance as hotel guests. The seafood includes the catch of the day, steamed shrimp, crab, clams, oysters, and sushi, plus fried chicken and roast beef along with tables laden with salads and desserts. Dinner is served from 6 to 8:30 p.m. For reservations call 245- 3931. The Aston Kauai also features a luau every night except Mon. and Fri., beginning with an *imu* ceremony at 6 p.m. Even with plenty of food, lei greeting, and Polynesian show, somehow this luau isn't quite as good as the buffet, especially since it costs almost double at $38. The Aston Kauai Resort provides free shuttle service to most area hotels. Reservations are suggested at tel. 245-3931.

The **Seashell Restaurant,** part of the Coco Palms Resort, has long been a favorite with visitors and residents. Well-prepared island fish entrees are from $14.95 to $19.95; chicken, meat, and a basic salad bar are also available. You'll never go wrong with the specials of the evening. Open 5:30 to 10 p.m., this oceanfront restaurant is popular, so make reservations and if possible sit at window tables both for a view and fresh ocean breezes, tel. 822-3632.

A more romantic setting is the open-air **Lagoon Dining Room**, the hotel's main restaurant. The menu is average, the service friendly, and the setting exceptional—overlooking the lagoon. They're open daily for breakfast, lunch, and dinner. Subdued candlelight and a free dinner show (seating from 8:15 p.m.) make the room more romantic in the evenings. Notice the remodeled decor of overlapping banana-leaf ceiling (reminiscent of a traditional canoe house) and woven pandanus-leaf light shades. For reservations call 822-4921.

Expensive

The Japanese legend of Kintaro, a pint-sized boy born to an old couple from inside a peach pit, is slightly less miraculous than this excellent and authentic Japanese restaurant owned and operated by a Korean gentleman, Don Kim. From the outside **Restaurant Kintaro** is nothing special, but inside it transforms to the simple and subtle beauty of Japan. Moreover, the true spirit of Japanese cooking is presented, with the food as pleasing to the eye as to the palate. The sushi bar alone, taking up an entire wall, is worth stopping in for. The dinners are expertly and authentically prepared, equaling those served in fine restaurants in Japan. If you have never sampled Japanese food before, Restaurant Kintaro is the best place to start. Those accustomed to the cuisine can choose from favorites like tempura, sukiyaki, a variety of *soba,* and the old standby teriyaki. Open daily for dinner only 5:30 to 9:30 p.m., along Route 56 just past the Coco Palms. Reservations often necessary; call 822-3341.

SHOPPING

If you're after an authentic island gift made with love, make sure to stop in at the **Kauai Closet Thrift Shop** behind Smith's information booth, across from the Coco Palms Resort. This store employs handicapped people who manufacture souvenirs and mementos from coconuts, shells, and palm fronds. They have a wide assortment of bric-a-brac and items like coconut wind chimes, with many items priced under $1.

The Coco Palms has a shopping arcade on two levels, with shops selling flowers, camera goods and gift items, drugs and sundries, jewelry, clothing, souvenirs, and ice cream. The Aston Kauai also has several shops at its entrance.

The Kinipopo Shopping Village has the bulk of shops in Wailua. Here you can find the **Goldsmith's Gallery** and **D.S. Collection** for fine jewelry and artwork. The Goldsmith's Gallery is among the finest shops in all of Hawaii. Four jewelers make all of the individual pieces, most with Hawaiian motifs. Diamonds, gold, and Australian opals add brilliance (and a hefty price tag) to the artwork. Much of the jewelry is commissioned, and some fine cloisonné boxes and a few stained-glass hangings are displayed. Beach rentals and some clothes are sold at **Wailua Surf and Beachware Co.** and at **Kauai Water Ski and Sports** shops. **Bachman's** also handles clothes, shells, and gift items. Directly across the street is **Kinipopo General Store.** This small market sells groceries, sundries, and liquors.

KAPAA AND VICINITY

Kapaa means "fixed," or "crystallized," as in "fixed course." In the old days when the canoes set out to sail to Oahu, they'd always stop first at Kapaa to get their bearings, then make a beeline directly across the channel to Oahu. Yachts still do the same today. Kapaa is a different kind of town, with unusual contrasts. At the south end is **Waipouli** ("Dark Water"), actually a separate municipality along the main drag, though you'd never know it. Clustered here are newish hotels, condos, a full-service shopping mall, restaurants, nightlife—a "live-in resort" atmosphere. The heart of Kapaa itself is a workers' settlement, with modest homes, pragmatic shops, some down-home eateries, and a funky hotel.

Actually, a few more people live here than in Lihue, and the vibe is a touch more local. There are no sights per se. You spend your time checking out the shops, scanning the color-mottled mountains of the interior, and combing the beaches, especially those to the north toward Hanalei. Two minutes upcoast you're in wide-open spaces. Cane roads cut from Route 56 and rumble along the coast. Small oceanside communities like **Anahola** and **Moloa'a Bay** pop up, their residents split between beachhouse vacationers and settled *kamaaina*. What distinguishes Kapaa is its unpretentiousness. This is "everyday paradise," where the visitor is made to feel welcome and then stands in line with everyone else at the supermarket. Generally the weather is cooperative throughout the area, prices on all commodities and services are good, beaches are fair to spectacular, and the pace unhurried. Kapaa isn't the choicest vacation spot on the island, but you can have a great time here while saving money too.

SIGHTS AND PRACTICALITIES

Beaches And Parks

Central Kapaa's beaches begin at **Waipouli Beach Park,** fronting the cluster of hotels just north of the Market Place Shopping Center, and end near the royal coconut grove by the Sheraton Hotel. The town interrupts the beach for a while this side of the Waikaea Canal, and then the beach picks up again as **Kapaa Beach**

ark, running north for almost a mile until it ends near a community swimming pool and the Ka-aa Library. A number of small roads lead from Route 56 to the nearby beach. Kapaa Beach Park has just over 15 acres, with a pavilion, pic-ic tables, showers, toilets, and grills. The beach is pretty to look at, but this section of town is run-lown. The feeling here is that it *belongs* to the lo-cals, although no undue hassles have been re-sorted.

As soon as you cross the Kapaa Stream on the north end of town you're in the one-store village of Kealia. Past mile marker #1, look for Ray's Auto Saloon, and turn off onto the cane road. At the junction is **Kealia Beach.** This wide white strand curves along the coast for a half mile. Not a beach park, so no facilities, but during calm weather the swimming is good, particularly at the north end, and few people are ever here ex-cept for some local fishermen and surfers.

Continue along the cane road (watch for on-coming trucks!) for just over two miles. The ride is much more picturesque than Route 56, as you skirt the coastline, heading for **Pohakuloa Point** and a surfing beach that the locals call **Donkey Beach.** Look for a tall stand of ironwoods, a makeshift rutted pulloff, and a wide sandy beach below. A footpath leads down to it. This area is very secluded and good for unofficial camping. Unfortunately, the undertow is severe, espe-cially during rough weather, and only ex-perienced surfers challenge the waves here. You can sunbathe and take dips, but remain in the shallows close to shore. Continue north on the cane road until it intersects Route 56 again. Be even more careful of the monolithic cane trucks because a sign here (which everyone ig-nores) points One Way in the *other* direction—and who are you to argue, in a subcompact whose only trace of extreme foolhardiness would be a grease spot in the road?

Nearby Villages And Beaches

Route 56 north from Kapaa is a visual treat. Out your window, the coastline glides along in an ever-changing panorama. Development is vir-tually nonexistent until you get to Kilauea in the Hanalei District. To your left are the **Anahola Mountains**, jagged, pointed, and intriguing.

The first village that you come to is **Anahola**. Here is the **Whaler's General Store,** open Mon. to Sat. 10 a.m. to 6 p.m., selling groceries, sou-

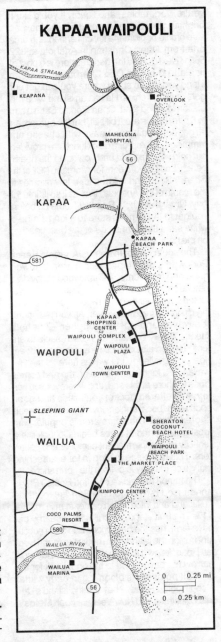

venirs, vegetables, and liquor. If you'd like to brighten your day or evening with an inexpensive orchid or plumeria lei, call ahead and order one from Albert Christian in Anahola at 822-5691. Next door to the general store is a post office and **Duane's Ono Charburger,** a clean, friendly roadside stand where you can get burgers or fish 'n' chips. He has an island-wide reputation for good food. Open Mon. to Sat. 10 a.m. to 6 p.m. Prices are a bit stiff, but the burgers are large, delicious, and heavy with cheese and trimmings. Tables for a quick lunch are provided, but hold your appetite until you get to the nearby beach. Look to your right for Aliomanu ("Oil of the Shark") Road and follow it for a few minutes to the mouth of the Anahola River as it spills into the bay. Or take Anahola Road off Route 56 before you get to the general store to a long strand of white sand that forms one of the best beaches on the north shore.

The south end of the bay is **Anahola Beach Park** with a developed picnic area, shower, grills, and restrooms. Tall ironwoods provide a natural canopy. The swimming is safe in the protected cove near the beach park, as is a refreshing dip in the freshwater river. As you walk north the waves and rips get tougher—Anahola means "Easily Broken." It's not advisable to enter the water, although some experienced board riders do challenge the waves here as the Hawaiians did long ago. However, the reef comes close to shore at this end, and wherever you can find a sheltered pocket you'll also find good snorkeling. Local anglers love this spot for nearshore fishing. The entire area is popular with local people, and at times begins to look like a tent-city of semipermanent campers and squatters. This is a place to stop in for a refreshing plunge on the way to or from the north shore.

The turnoff to Moloa'a ("Matted Roots") Bay is announced by the **Moloa'a Sunrise** roadside fruit stand and information center at mile marker #17. The fruit stand, an outlet for a nearby papaya farm, has the best prices and most succulent fruit on the island. Turn down the rough Koolau Road, follow it to Moloa'a Road, and take this narrow but paved road to the end. Look for the brilliant poinsettias blooming in early winter along Koolau Road—they are the island's clue that Christmas and New Year are near. **Moloa'a**

Bay is a magnificent but rarely visited beach. The road leading down is a luscious little thoroughfare, cutting over domed hillocks by means of a series of switchbacks. The jungle canopy is thick and then it opens into a series of glens and pastures. Off to the sides are vacation homes perched on stilts made from telephone poles. A short drive takes you to road's end and a small cluster of dwellings where there is limited space to put your vehicle. Park here and follow the "Right of way to the beach" signs. Here, a stream comes into the bay, providing a great place to wash off the ocean water after a dip. The beach is lovely, bright, and wide, forming a crescent moon. To the north the beach ends in a grassy hillock, and south it's confined by a steep *pali.* Swimming at all north shore beaches is advised only during calm weather, and is best at the south end of the beach. Snorkeling is good, but you'll have to swim the channel out to the base of the *pali* which is unadvisable if the waves are rough. Although a few homes are around, Moloa'a is a place of peaceful solitude. Sunsets are light shows of changing color, and you'll probably be a solitary spectator.

ACCOMMODATIONS

Inexpensive

Hotel Coral Reef is relatively inexpensive and definitely has character. Toward the north end of Kapaa between the main road and the beach, this humble hotel has a deluxe view of the bay. Although it closely resembles one, the Coral Reef isn't a fleabag, because it's clean, well tended, and attracts decent clientele. One of the first hotels in the area, this 33-year-old establishment is friendly, homey, and funky, and it has recently been refurbished. The lobby is small, not conducive to relaxing, adorned only by a fish tank and color TV. Rooms in the old wing, with limited views of the ocean, are clean and cheap at $25-32; two-bedroom suites for four or more run $45. Cleaner and brighter, the new wing has an A-plus view of the bay. Large and airy rooms with lanais, sliding glass doors, and refrigerators go for only $58. For reservations, write Hotel Coral Reef, 1516 Kuhio Hwy., Kapaa, Kauai, HI 96746, or call (800) 843-4659, 822-4481 in Kapaa.

An Alternative

For those visiting the island "who value their personal health, and who seek inner growth and the opening of creative potential," the **Keapana Center** may be the place for you. This bed and breakfast has rooms in a building with a huge dance floor, a secluded garden cottage with its own kitchen and bath, a solar jacuzzi, huge lanais, and good vistas over the lush hillside to the beach only five minutes away. Rooms with shared/private baths are $35/45 s, $50/60 d, and $300/350 a week; the cottage sleeps up to four and is $75 a night or $450 a week. All rates include a continental breakfast and use of the jacuzzi and dance floor. The owner is a dance and meditation instructor, and although there are no seminars or workshops currently being given, arrangements can be made for all sorts of massage and body work, naturopathic medicine, rebirthing, imaging and creative visualization, fasting, stress management, yoga, tai chi, the twelve-step program, and other healing and wellness programs. It is a nonsmoking environment. For more information write to Keapana Center, 5620 Keapana Rd., Kapaa, Kauai, HI 96746, or call (800) 822-7968.

Moderate

Part of the Hawaiian-owned Sand and Seaside Hotels, **Kauai Sands** is a better-than-average budget hotel with a convenient location, spacious grounds, accommodating staff, large relaxing lobby, budget restaurant, two pools, and beach access. Recently renovated, all rooms have two double beds, refrigerator, a/c, ceiling fan, TV, telephone, and a lanai. What it lacks in luster it makes up in price. Daily hotel rates are given for room only/car package: standard $58/70, superior $75/87, kitchenette $85/95. For a third person add $10. For reservations, write Sand and Seaside Hotels, 2222 Kalakaua Ave., Suite 714, Honolulu, HI 96815, tel. (800) 367-7000. You'll find the hotel just behind the Market Place Shopping Center, at 420 Papaloa Rd., Wailua, HI 96746, tel. 822-4951.

For a deluxe hotel at moderate prices, you can't go wrong with the **Kauai Beachboy Hotel**, located along the coastline at the Coconut Plantation. Cool and quiet, most rooms surround a central courtyard and pool. All rooms have a shower (no tub), color TV, a small fridge, and lanai. The decor is pleasant "Hawaiian style"; each unit has a powder room, large closet, and full mirror. The hotel also offers a poolside bar, shuffleboard, volleyball, tennis facilities, and free daily scuba lessons for guests. The hotel's Perry's Smorgy Restaurant is an all-you-can-eat place with reasonable prices. Rates for a double are: $78 for a garden room, $83 superior, and $93 for a deluxe oceanfront room, with $15 extra for each additional person; high-season rates, Dec. 20 to March 31 are $10 more. For reservations contact Kauai Beachboy, 4-484 Kuhio Hwy. #100, Kapaa, Kauai, HI 96746, tel. (800) 367-8047 or 822-0843 on Kauai.

Between the Beachboy and Kauai Sands hotels is the **Islander on the Beach Hotel**, a bright white hotel with a front veranda on all levels, giving it a Southern plantation look. The studio apartments have been changed to regular hotel rooms with amenities including wet bar, refrigerater, coffeemaker, color TV, and lanai. Set right on the beach, the hotel has a pool, beach activities center, and a gift shop. Room rates are: $78 for a standard room, $89 oceanview, $99 oceanfront, $115 junior suite, and $135 for an oceanfront suite; add $10 more for high season. Write Islander on the Beach, 484 Kuhio Hwy., Kapaa, Kauai, HI 96746, or call (800) 367-7052, 822-7417 on Kauai.

Kapaa also has several condos in the moderate price range. The **Kapaa Shore Condo** is along the main road just north of the Coconut Plantation. These one- and two-condo units offer a swimming pool, heated jacuzzi, tennis courts, and maid service on request. All units are bright and cheerful, with full kitchen and dishwashers. One-bedroom garden-view units accommodate up to four for $100; one-bedroom ocean-view units run $110; and two-bedroom ocean-view units house up to six for $130. For reservations contact Aston Hotels and Resorts, 2255 Kuhio Ave., Honolulu, HI 96815, tel. (800) 922-7866; on Kauai, 40-900 Kuhio Hwy., Kapaa, HI 96746, tel. 822-3055.

Other reasonably priced condominiums in the area include the **Kapaa Sands,** with pool and maid service. The oldest condo on the island—since 1968—Kapaa Sands is kept clean and up-to-date. The manager, Harriet Kaholokula, will make you feel like part of a big family. This condo is situated on an old Japanese ground that once was the site of a Shinto shrine. The Japanese motif is still reflected in the roofline of the units and the tori design above each door number. Each unit has a full kitchen, ceiling fan in all rooms, and lanai. Two-bedroom units are on two levels, and even the garden units have a limited view of the ocean. Room rates are $59 for garden studios, $69 for oceanfront studios, $79 for two-bedroom garden units, and $89 for two-bedroom oceanfront units. Monthly rates are available; minimum stay is three days, except during winter when it is seven days. For reservations write Kapaa Sands, 380 Papaloa Rd., Kapaa, Kauai, HI 96746, or call (800) 222-4901, 822-4901 on Kauai.

The **Pono Kai** condominium is a step up in class, offering one-bedroom units at $110-165, and two bedrooms at $149-195. All units have a full kitchen, color cable TV, and lanai. Available from Aston Hotel and Resorts located at 1250 Kuhio Hwy., Kapaa, Kauai, HI 96746. For reservations call (800) 922-7866, or 822-9831 on Kauai. The **Plantation Hale** is a condominium that also offers daily rates. It's across the street from Waipouli Beach Park just beyond the Market Place at Coconut Plantation. There are only one-bedroom units. Each is like a small apartment with full kitchen, bath, dining room, and living area. Rates for up to four people are $105 and $95, for high and low seasons respectively. At 484 Kuhio Hwy., Kapaa, Kauai, HI 96746. For reservations call (800) 367-6046, or 822-4911 on Kauai.

Expensive

Amidst a huge grove of swaying palms sits the **Sheraton Coconut Beach Hotel**, a transformed Holiday Inn that's now the fanciest hotel in Kapaa. The palm grove once belonged to the family of the famous swimmer and actor, Buster Crabbe of "Buck Rogers" fame. He and his twin brother, Bud, were born and raised right here, and Buster learned to swim along this very coast. The lobby is alive with trees, flowers, and vines trellised from the balconies. Wicker chairs, stained glass, a huge carpet sculpture, and a 40-foot waterfall add comfort and grandeur. The Voyage Room is an indoor/outdoor restaurant featuring original artwork. Have a drink and listen to nightly entertainment at Cook's Landing, or try the hotel luau, one of the best on the island. And there is no better authentic entertainment than the twice-weekly traditional Hawaiian music and dance of Na Kaholokula.

Make sure to check out the fine photos hanging along the main hall and the superb replica of a double-hulled sailing canoe. Also, the charts in the Chart Room that look like those nifty old ragged-edged maps of yore are the real McCoy. They belong to Mr. Rate Bowman, who displays at the hotel.

The Sheraton has just undergone a massive sprucing-up. The rooms, already beautiful, are even more so with matching decor like rose and lavender carpets, drapes, and bedspreads. Every room has its own refrigerator, small lanai, TV, and original artwork. Bathrooms and dressing rooms are spacious. The fourth floor offers enormous, high-ceilinged deluxe rooms and breathtaking views of the ironwoods and ocean below. The Sheraton is pricey at $105-175, with VIP suites for $300, but you do get all that you pay for. Write Sheraton Coconut Beach Hotel, P.O. Box 830, Coconut Plantation, Kapaa, Kauai, HI 96746, tel. (800) 325-3535, on Kauai 822-3455.

Colony Resorts manages two deluxe condos in and around the Coconut Plantation. A touch more classy than their Plantation Hale is the **Lae Nani**, offering one- and two-bedroom units on the beach. The rich decor varies by unit but all have a full kitchen, lanai, ceiling fans, and a full and half bath; most have an ocean view. There is a laundry room and daily maid service, a swimming pool, tennis courts, and barbecue grills on the lawn. A small *heiau* is on the property near the beach. One-bedroom units for up to four people are $150-179, and the two-bedroom units are $185-205, maximum six persons; rates are $20 cheaper during low season. At 410 Papaloa Rd., Kapaa, Kauai, HI 96746. For reservations call (800) 367-6046, or 822-4938 on Kauai. The **Lanikai** is next door at 390 Papaloa Rd., tel. 822-7456. Here there are only two-bedroom, two-bath units that rent for $200 a day, $20 cheaper during low season. Make all reservations through Colony Resorts, 32 Merchant St., Honolulu, HI 96813, tel. (800) 367-6046.

FOOD

From the Market Place at Coconut Plantation to the north edge of Kapaa, there are dozens of

Uncle Bill prepares the imu for the Sheraton's luau.

places at which to eat. The vast majority are either inexpensive diners or mid-priced restaurants, but there is one fine restaurant, several luaus and buffets, the ubiquitous fast-food chains, and several bakeries, fruits stands, markets, and grocery stores.

Inexpensive

Surrounded by hotels and condos, just north of the Coco Palms is the Market Place at Coconut Plantation, the island's largest shopping center. In this huge complex are more than a dozen eateries. For a quick, cool snack try **Farrell's of Kauai** or **Lappert's** for ice cream, or **Rainbow Frozen Yogurt** for the competition. For quick counter food try **The Fish Hut, Island Chicken,** or **JJ's Dog House**—JJ's has hot dogs for $1.95-2.70, serves beer, and looks out on one of the center's intriguing fountains. For more substantial food check out **Ramona's Mexican Food** (tacos, burritos, and tostadas in the $2-4 range, with combination plates up to $5.25), the **Banyan Tree Cafe,** or **Bella Rosa Pizza**. At **Don's Deli and Picnic Basket** you can get a large sandwich for $2.50- 4.50, subs, or a picnic basket for your day on the beach or trip to the north coast. One step up, try breakfast (from 7:30 a.m.), a cup of fine coffee and bakery goods, at **Cafe Espresso**. For your sweet tooth, step in to see what mouthwatering delicacies the **Rocky Mountain Chocolate Factory** and **Nut Cracker Sweet** shops have to offer. While at the Market Place, check out the **Kauai Visitor's Center**, tel. 245- 3882. This one-stop information source offers great advice about island activities, can make reservations for helicopter or boat tours, and has the lowdown on the best entertainment, luaus, and restaurants. Ask for Lance.

A short way up the highway, *mauka* from the road is the **Waipouili Town Center—McDonald's** and **Pizza Hut** indicate the spot. Near the yogurt shop is **Waipouli Restaurant**, a cafeteria-style eatery with breakfast specials, Mexican food, seafood, and saimin. Open Mon. 7 a.m to 3 p.m., and Tues.-Sun. 7 a.m. to 3 p.m. and 5 to 9 p.m. In the next two little complexes up, the Waipouli Plaza and Waipouli Complex, are four restaurants where you can get good hearty ethnic meals. The plaza has one of the best new restaurants on the island, **The King and I**, tel. 822-1642. This Thai restaurant serves wonderful food that will make your taste buds stand up and be counted. Most dinners are $5-8. Open 11 a.m. to 2 p.m. Mon., Tues., Thurs., and Fri., and 5 to 9 p.m. for dinner nightly. Also in the Plaza is the Chinese restaurant **Dragon Inn** that has a well-deserved reputation for filling meals at reasonable prices. There is a menu an arm long, and most dinners go for $5-7. Stop in for lunch Tues. to Sat. 11 a.m. to 2 p.m. and nightly for dinner from 4:30 to 9:30 p.m.

In the Waipouli Complex is the **Aloha Diner**, tel. 822-3851. Open daily except Sun. 11:30 a.m. to 3 p.m. and 5:30 to 9 p.m., this diner serves Hawaiian food. It offers a la carte selections like *kalua* pig, chicken luau, *lomi* salmon, rice and poi, *haupia,* and *kulolo.* Dinner specials run around $5-6, with full dinners from $7.50-9.50. Takeouts are available. There is no atmosphere, the service is slow and friendly, and most people eating here are residents. Next door is the Japanese **Restaurant Shiroma,** which serves Chinese standards as well. The daily lunch and dinner specials include items like shrimp tempura, pork tofu, teriyaki steak, or seafood combo. A money-saving lunch is a huge bowl of *wonton min* and a side of rice. And you must have a slice of the homemade pineapple or passion fruit chiffon pie for $1. Shiroma's is open Fri. to Sun. 7 a.m. to 9 p.m., and Mon., Wed., and Thurs. 7 a.m. to 2 p.m., closed Tuesday.

In the Kapaa Shopping Center, still farther up the highway, are the **Kauai Kitchens** snack shop in the Big Save grocery store and **Tropical Taco,** tel. 822-3622. Relax in the south-of-the-border atmosphere and have a taco, burrito, tostada, or enchilada; ask about their Apple Jack (deep-fried flour tortilla stuffed with apple pie filling and cheese and topped with ice cream) for dessert. Most meals are in the $4.50-6.50 range. The cafe is open daily 11 a.m. to 9:30 p.m.; the cantina stays open later.

In Kapaa proper are several more convenient restaurants. **Fast Freddy's Diner** serves no-nonsense food in no-nonsense surroundings, tel. 822-0488. Try their Deuces Wild breakfast special of two eggs, two pancakes, two sausage links, and two strips of bacon for $2.22. Dinner specials are scampi for $9.95 and *mahi mahi* for $5.95. Breakfast is served from 8 a.m., dinner from 5:30 p.m. except Wed.; closed on Sunday. The **Olympic Cafe,** tel. 822-5731, sounds as if it should serve Greek cuisine but actually serves Japanese and American food to a mostly local crowd. Breakfast and lunch from 6 a.m. to 2 p.m., and dinner from 5 to 9 p.m. daily. A diner with formica tables and a lunch counter, **T. Higashi Store** also caters mostly to local residents, tel. 822-5982. Serving everyday Japanese food, they are open 6 a.m. to 8 p.m.

The **Ono Family Restaurant** is a step up from the others mentioned here, but the prices are right. The atmosphere is "functional cozy," with nice touches like carpeted floors, ceiling fans, even a chandelier. Creative breakfasts include eggs Margo (a takeoff on eggs Benedict) with turkey, tomatoes, and hollandaise sauce over poached eggs and an English muffin, pancakes, and a variety of omelettes like a Local Boy, which combines Portuguese sausage and *kimchi.* Lunch salads run about $3.50, and the island's best burger is $5.25. For dinner you can't go wrong with a mushroom melt burger for $6.95, and from the broiler and grill try sirloin steak, barbecued ribs, teri chicken, and even a Mexican plate. For those with a taste for the exotic, you can even get a real buffalo burger here from American bison raised in Hanalei and Kansas. The daily fish special is always terrific, and depending upon the catch goes for about $12. The Ono Family Restaurant is located in downtown Kapaa, at 4-1292 Kuhio Hwy., open daily from 7 a.m., closed Sunday evenings, tel. 822-1710.

Moderate

When you don't want to fool around deciding where to get a good meal, head for the north end of Kapaa and the local favorite **Kountry Kitchen.** Open daily 6 a.m. to 9 p.m., the tables are usually packed with regulars during peak dining hours. Breakfasts are full meals of hefty omelettes for about $3-4 to a Hungryman Special for over $6. Lunches range from $4-6, and full dinners like country ribs, sesame shrimp, and baked ham served with soup, bread, potatoes/rice and vegies are from $7-9. The food is tasty, the service prompt and friendly, and the portions large. The Kountry Kitchen is at 1485 Kuhio Hwy., tel. 822-3511.

Nearby is the **Makai Restaurant,** tel. 822-3955, which serves Hawaiian, Mediterranean, and continental food. Try their fish and chips, gyros, or moussaka; you can get it to go. The open windows let in the breeze and morning sunlight, but as it is close to the road it also lets in the sounds of passing cars.

Norberto's El Cafe is a family-run Mexican restaurant from *sombrero* to *zapatos.* Then what's it doing on a side street on a Pacific island, you ask? Hey gringo, don't look a gift burro in the face! They serve nutritious, delicious, wholesome food, and they cater to vegetarians, as all dishes are prepared without lard or animal fats. The smell of food wafting out of the front door around dinnertime is this restaurants best advertisement. It serves the best Mexican food on the island. Full-course meals of burritos, enchiladas, and tostadas are $9-10, children's plates are $5, while a la carte dishes are from $4-5. The best deals are the chef's specials of burrito el cafe, Mexican salad, and chili relleno, all for under $6, or fajitas for $11.95. Other entrees are rellenos tampico, chimichangas, tacos, and quesadillas. Dinners are served with soup, beans, and rice; chips and salsa are complimentary. There's beer on tap, or if you really want to head south of the border (by way of sliding under the table), try a pitcher of margaritas. If you have room after stuffing yourself like a chimichanga try a slice of delicious chocolate cream pie or homemade rum cake. The cafe is extremely popular with local folks and tables fill as soon as they're empty. Look for Norberto's at the intersection of Kukui Street and Route 56 in downtown Kapaa, tel. 822-3362; open daily 5:30 to 9:30 p.m.

Jimmy's Grill is in downtown Kapaa in the refurbished Hee Fat Marketplace building. A casual, open-ceilinged cafe which extends out onto a balcony, its bright, airy interior is dominated by beach motif decorations with nautical flags, windsails, and surfboards. Like the interior the menu is light and casual with *pu pu* $4-7.95, soups and salads from $1.75-7.50, burgers, $4.75-5.75, and sandwiches, $6-6.75. Entrees, like barbecued ribs ($8.25,) New York steak ($13.50) and fresh island fish (daily quote) are more substantial. Downstairs in the sand-floored, open-front bar, beer, wine, and potent mixed drinks are served. How can you go wrong in a place that has a "groovy hour?" An electronic dart game sits in the corner for those who care to challenge someone for a bit of fun.

Across the side street from Jimmy's is **Captain and the Cook** New York pizzeria, tel. 822-7128, open Mon. to Sat. 10 a.m. to 10 p.m. For New York-style pizza by the slice, half, or whole, this is the place. If you're not into pizza but want a quick meal, try their broasted chicken, hero or sub sandwiches, meatballs, hot dogs, salads, or ice cream. They even make their own New York-style pretzels.

As soon as you enter the restaurant section of the **Kapaa Fish and Chowder House** (formerly Kauai Gardens) you'll know that they love growing things, and you might mistake it for a greenhouse. It's the epitome of a fern bar with plants everywhere. What makes it even more attractive is that the basic building was little more than a warehouse that love and creativity have turned into something beautiful. Open ceilings, louvered windows, Casablanca-style fans, sooth-ing colors, a nautical motif, and small stained-glass chandeliers make the perfect blend of casual elegance. But that's not all! The food happens to be terrific, too. At the front entrance is the bar, behind are the dining rooms. Doors open at 5 p.m.; dinner is served from 5:30. At that time you can choose from appetizers like *sashimi* (market price), Cajun seafood crepe $4.50, and shrimp remoulade $6.95, or New England, Manhattan, or the house chowder for $2- 3.50. Entrees include pepper steak at $17.95, calamari for $9.95, coconut shrimp, $12.75, sautéed clams $11.50, Alaskan crab legs $16.95, or seafood fettucini for $13.95. Aside from bar drinks, half a dozen after-dinner coffee drinks are available. The Kapaa Fish and Chowder House is one of those places that always seems right. You can drop in for a beer fresh off the beach, or put on your best for a romantic evening of fine dining. At the north end of Kapaa, 4-1639 Kuhio Hwy., call 822-7746 for reservations.

JJ's Boiler Room, tel. 822-4411, is in the Market Place Shopping Center. You can't go wrong here if you're after steak or beef, but chicken and fish are also available. Open daily for dinner and cocktails from 5 p.m., they offer beef kabobs at $9.75, steak and lobster, the famous Slavonic steak of thin-sliced meat broiled in wine and garlic for $11.95, and a salad bar for $6.95. Check out their early-bird specials from 5-6 p.m. or late evening specials from 9 to 10 p.m.

Also at the Market Place Shopping Center is **Buzz's Steak and Lobster** restaurant, tel. 922-7491. Lunch is 11 a.m. to 3 p.m., *pu pu* and happy hour from 3 to 5 p.m., and dinner from 5 to 10:30 p.m. Word on the street says the salad bar here is the best. Two of the many appetizers include deep-fried artichokes or calamari at $4.95. Various steaks run $10.95-16.95, 12-ounce prime rib $16.95, lobster trap combo $19.95, and other seafood $7.95-14.95. A light dining menu of *mahi mahi,* ginger chicken kabob, and seafood brochette is offered for the more health and nutrition conscious. As an added benefit, you can sit at the bar after dinner and listen to nightly entertainment from 9 p.m. to midnight.

Like Buzz's the **Jolly Roger Restaurant** also offers nightly entertainment. Open 6 a.m. to 2 a.m., Jolly Roger claims to have the longest happy hour on the island—6:30 a.m. to 7 p.m. Not known for exceptional food, but you always get hearty, substantial portions no matter what time of day you come to dine. You can find Jolly Roger behind the Market Place Shopping Center, near Islander on the Beach Hotel, tel. 822-3451.

Al and Don's Restaurant, in the Kauai Sands Hotel is open daily from 7 a.m., tel. 822-4221. The service and food are good but not memorable. However, the view from the spacious booths overlooking the seacoast is magnificent. Prices are reasonable for their numerous dinner and breakfast selections. Perhaps this is the problem: though you don't get the bum's rush, the place feels like one of those feeding troughs in Waikiki that caters to everyone and pleases no one. You can't complain about breakfast, like $3.85 for all-you-can-eat hot cakes, one egg, grilled ham, and coffee. And you won't be disappointed with their "build-your-own-omelette." Most breakfasts are under $4, and there are plenty of evening specials, with most dinners under $10. Dinner includes soup and salad bar with adequate entrees like *ahi* or swordfish, top sirloin, and chicken exotica. Their bar serves good drinks for reasonable prices. When you leave Al and Don's, you won't feel like complaining, but you won't rush back either.

Almost Expensive

The following restaurants are "in between," with prices that aren't really expensive, but have just enough class to fall into that category. You won't be out of place dressed in snazzy casual attire.

The **Bull Shed** is known for prime rib; its chicken and seafood dishes are also praised. The menu includes prime rib at $15.95, jumbo prawns at $13.95, and grilled teriyaki chicken for $9.95. Other entrees include lobster tail, $18.95, garlic tenderloin, $14.95, New Zealand lamb rack, $14.95, and various combination plates from $12.95-22.95. The wine list is better than average and includes Domaine Chandon champagne for $22.95. Insiders go for the extensive salad bar at only $6.95, but be warned that the pickings get all jumbled together as the night goes on, and the salad bar peaks out by 7:30. The Bull Shed is open daily for cocktails and dinner from 5:30 p.m. at 796 Kuhio Hwy., down the little lane across from McDonald's, tel. 822-3791.

The **Rib 'n' Tail** is in the same category as the Bull Shed: prime rib, steak, seafood, and salad

bar. Dessert specialties are homemade cheese cake and mud pie. Open daily from 5 p.m. there's a happy hour 4 to 6 p.m. Mon. to Fri. and entertainment and dancing on the weekends. In the small complex behind the Shell gas station at the Kapaa Shopping Center, tel. 822-9632.

Expensive, Luaus, And Buffets

The **Voyage Room** at the Sheraton Coconut Beach Hotel is the only real classy restaurant on this part of the island. The room is cheerful, spacious, and trimmed with classical island decor of high-backed rattan furniture. The service is first rate and you're made to feel "waited upon," an always welcome addition to every meal. The salad bar, exemplary for quality, quantity, and style, is a bargain, and includes soup. Entrees of beef, fish, roast duck, rack of lamb, and chicken rochambeau are $12-20. Meals are a la carte and buffet style; watch for their nightly specials. Open daily for breakfast, lunch, and dinner, tel. 822-4222.

The Sheraton Coconut Beach presents an all-you-can-eat prime rib buffet and dinner show every Tues. and Thurs. from 6 to 9:30 p.m. in the **Paddle Room**. Dinner starts at 6, cocktail seating at 7:30, and the show begins at 7:45. Traditional and contemporary Hawaiian music is performed by local island artists called Na Kaholokula and the hula is done by Puamohala. The gentle music and swaying dance will certainly conjure up images of this lush, enchanting garden isle. Adults $34, children $24 for dinner and the show, or $16 for the show only.

The real treat is the hotel luau, which everyone agrees is one of the best on the island. It's held every night except Monday in the special luau *halau* (long house) under a canopy of stars and palm trees. The luau master is Uncle Bill, who learned the art from his grandparents "just the other day in 1922!" His ethnic combination of Hawaiian-Italian gives him instant credibility as a fine cook. He starts the *imu,* with the aid of his grandchildren, every morning at 10:45—stop by and watch. He can lay in the hot stones and banana stalks so well that the underground oven maintains a perfect 400°. With one glance he can gauge the weight and fat content of a succulent porker and decide just how long it should be cooked. The water in the leaves covering the pig steams and roasts it at the same time so that the meat falls off the fork. Uncle Bill says about his luau, "All that you can't eat in the *imu* are the hot stones." You arrive at 7 p.m. to an open bar or come at 6:45 to see the torch-lighting ceremony). The *imu* ceremony is at 7:10, followed by cocktails. At 7:30 the luau begins with tables laden with pork, chicken, Oriental beef, salmon, fish, exotic fruits, salads, coconut cake, and *haupia*. Then at 8:30 you recline and watch the Victor Punua Polynesian review of local dancers and musicians. Adults $40, children under 12 $24, show only $17.50; reservations suggested, tel. 822-3455, ext. 651.

On a day of hearty appetite when you want to try a little bit of everything, but don't want to bust your wallet, stop in at **Perry's Smorgy.** At the Kauai Beachboy Hotel, this restaurant serves up long tables laden with food for all you care to eat. Breakfast at $3.95 is served from 7 to 10:30 a.m. Some of the selections are sausage and eggs, hotcakes, toast, fruit, and pastries. Lunch at $5.45 runs from 11 a.m. to 2:30 p.m., and offers such tasty morsels as fried chicken, stews, pasta, and salads. At $7.95 dinner can hardly be beat. The five main entrees are complemented by fruit and a salad bar. While not elegant dining, the surroundings are pleasant, and you can certainly get your money's worth.

ENTERTAINMENT

The night scene in Kapaa isn't very extensive, but there is enough to satisfy everyone. In the area you'll usually find one good disco, dinner show, easy-listening music, and Polynesian extravaganza.

The **Jolly Roger Restaurant** at the Market Place features Jimmy Limo and his one-man band performing rock and roll, reggae, blues, oldies, goodies, and more. You can listen and dance nightly from 9 p.m. to 1:30 a.m. The atmosphere is casual, the talk friendly.

Nearby **Buzz's** also has nightly entertainment, usually a small band playing contemporary, original, and country and western music. Sit at the bar and enjoy the casual Polynesian setting.

The **Sheraton Coconut Beach Hotel** offers a little of everything. You can enjoy free *pu pu* and entertainment at **Cook's Landing,** just off the gardens and pool deck—happy hour from 4 to 6 p.m. Every evening from 8 to 11 p.m. listen to pop, contemporary, and standard hits by local

musicians. The dinner show in the **Paddle Room** presents a full performance of Hawaiian dance and music. And swing, rock, and Hawaiian music, as well as hula from the Polynesian show, accompany the luau (see above).

Watering holes, other than Jimmy's Grill and Cook's Landing, where you can find cool drinks and conversation include the **Tradewind's Southsea Bar** at the Market Place Shopping Center and **Tropical Taco Cantina** at the Kapaa Shopping Center.

The Market Place shopping center hosts a free **Polynesian Hula Show** Thurs. through Sat. at 4 p.m. The young local dancers and musicians put as much effort into their routines as if this were the big time. Be warned that local sneak thieves have rifled cars in the parking lot, knowing that their owners are preoccupied watching the show. Also at the shopping center is the **Plantation Cinema 1 and 2** for moviegoers.

The old **Roxy Theater** in downtown Kapaa has been made into a music and dance hall that's open every Fri. and Sat. night from 8 to 11 p.m. Adults $4, students $3, under 12 $2—everyone is welcome. Outdoor posters advertise dance contests, fun, video, live DJ's, requests, and prizes.

SHOPPING

Kapaa teems with shopping opportunities. Lining Kuhio Highway is a major shopping mall, The Market Place, and several other smaller shopping plazas. All your needs are met in a variety of food stores, health stores, drugstores, a farmers' market, fish vendors, and some extraordinary shops and boutiques tucked away here and there. You can easily find photo supplies, sporting equipment, "treasures," and inexpensive leis to brighten your day.

The Market Place

The name doesn't lie about this cluster of over 70 shops, restaurants, galleries, and movie theaters. Prices are kept down because of the natural competition of so many shops, and each tries to "specialize," which usually means good choices for what strikes your fancy. As you walk around notice the blown-up photos that give you a glimpse into old Hawaii. **Ye Old Ship Store** displays the best collection of scrimshaw on Kauai and some sea paintings by local artists.

Any of the jewelry shops have enough stock on hand to drop even Mr. T to his knees. With so many apparel and footwear shops the job of finding just the right alohashirt, muumuu, or sports clothing shouldn't be a problem. **Walden-books** has the corner on books and magazines. **Pottery Tree** overflows with everything from junk to fine pieces. Select from stained-glass chandeliers, "I Love Hawaii" mugs, and some cheap yet nice shell mobiles. **High as a Kite** is great for high fliers that add fun to any beach outing. **Kahn Gallery** features the fine work of Hawaii's artists along with basketry, sculpture, woodcarvings, and superb jewelry. Expensive but once-in-a-lifetime purchases.

If your heart desires Hawaiian delicacies like Kona coffee, Maui onion mustard, macadamia nuts, island candy, Kauai Kookies, Kukui jams and jellies, and much more, head for **The Nut Cracker Sweet** shop and just see if you can pull yourself away. For the ordinary purchase head for **Whaler's General Store.** Aside from the shops, **Foto Freddie** will develop film, **Hawaiian Air** will confirm a plane reservation, and **Kauai Visitor's Center** can give you information about things to see, places to explore, and adventures to have.

The **Kapaa Shopping Center** is much smaller and more pragmatic. Here, you'll find a Big Save Value Center, Clic Photo for inexpensive film and fast developing, Kapaa Bakery, Kapaa Laundry (the nearest competition is Pono Cleaners in downtown Kapaa), Kapaa Sports Center, Kauai Video (rentals), and a restaurant and snack shop. Also in this shopping center are the Kapaa clinic of the Kauai Medical Group, the office of Bed and Breakfast Hawaii, and a Shell station.

Across the highway from another Shell station and the Dive Kauai office, in the **Waipouli Complex,** is Popo's Cookies. Closed Mon.-Wed., it is open at 8 a.m. the rest of the week but closes at 5 p.m. on Thurs. and Fri., 3 p.m. on Sat., and 2 p.m. on Sunday. Nearby in the **Waipouli Plaza** are several clothing shops and a shell merchant that sells retail and wholesale. Farther down the road in the **Waipouli Town Center** you'll find Foodland grocery store, Deja Vu clothing shop, Fun Factory arcade for games, and JM's jewelry store.

There are several markets and groceries in the Waipouli/Kapaa area where you can pick up your food needs if you're cooking for yourself. **Ambrose's Kapuna Natural Foods** (in a funky yellow building) serves the community's tofu, tamale, and bulk and health food needs. Ambrose and his friends are real storehouses of information about the island; they have the "poop" on what's happening and where it's at. If you have kids, check next door at the children's shop. Therre's a farmers' market every Wed. at 3 p.m. at the beach park. **Pono Market** is stuffed to the gills, **Kuhio Fish Market** always has the freshest seafood (also *kimchi* and poi), and the **Farm Fresh Fruit Stand** carries not only fruits but other island food products. All these are in downtown Kapaa, while **Kojima's** grocery, for produce, meat, liquor, beer, and picnic supplies, is beyond the Aloha Lumberyard at the north end of town.

The **Awapuhi Emporium** is a must-stop at 788 Kuhio Hwy., tel. 822-3581, in a tired little building across the street from Foodland. It specializes in handmade Hawaiiana. Inside the dusty glass cases are old maps, feather leis, tapa cloth, *koa* bowls, glass floats, and a varied selection of Oriental artwork. Prices are reasonable and the antiques, junk, and art pieces constantly change like the tides.

Next door is a tiny lei shop. It's open if Liz, the lei lady, puts out her sign that simply says **Leis,** which depends on her supply of fresh flowers. If she's open, rush in because they won't last long. She'll make you a lovely lei for $5, and what she calls "flower jewelry" of necklaces, hair adornments, and brooches for $4. Liz usually opens around 11 a.m., till as late as 7 p.m.

Remember Kauai, 4-734 Kuhio Hwy., tel. 822-0161, just past the Sheraton, specializes in unique Hawaiian jewelry, like necklaces made from shells, beads, wood, and gold. The counters shine with belt buckles, pins, and a large collection of gemstones from around the world. Niihau shellwork is available, and fine specimens run up to $1200. The scrimshaw, worked by Kauai artists on fossilized walrus ivory, adds rich texture to everything from knives to paperweights. Any place like this with a rainbow painted on its roof is worth a look.

Across the road from Remember Kauai is **Aquatics Kauai,** one of the top scuba shops on the island, tel. 822-9422. This shop also rents mountain bikes for $15 a day. Next door is **Cameralab,** tel. 822-7338, for all your photo-finishing eeds. In downtown Kapaa, **Pono Studio** also develops film, carries photographic equipment, and has a studio for portraits. At the Market Place Shopping Center, **Foto Freddie** and **Plantation Camera and Gifts** also do photo developing.

Downtown Kapaa has perhaps the best bicycle shop on Kauai. **Kapaa Bicycle**, next to Norberto's El Cafe, deals in sales and repair of bikes and skateboards. Unfortunately they don't rent any bikes. However, there is a big topo map of Kauai on the wall that shows all the island's roads and trails. Stop in and talk with these knowledgeable guys about where and how to bike the island, especially if you're on a mountain bike.

In the center of old Kapaa Town at 1495 Kuhio Hwy., tel. 822-1442, is an antique and curio shop named **The Only Show In Town**, and it's a mind bender. It's owned and operated by Paul Wroblewski, a tall handsome Polish fellow given to wearing white patent-leather shoes and enough jewelry to attract lightning from a clear sky. The shop is magnificent, more like a mad museum than anything else. The walls and showcases are covered with silk top hats, stuffed antelopes, glass balls, Catholic statuary, and a collection of dolls from around the world. There are toys, postcards, clothes, jewelry, instruments of all sorts, and old photos and movie posters. The antiques and collectibles come from all over the world, but the shop is heavy on Oriental items. Paul is now specializing in Hawaiian bottles, and he has the island's largest collection of cobalt-blue specimens, which sell for anywhere from $5 to $2,000. A separate section sells used clothing, like an upscale Salvation Army specializing in inexpensive alohawear—all $8 apiece.

Even if you don't buy, you'll be missing one of Kapaa's main "sights" if you don't stop in here.

INFORMATION

Aside from the hotel activity desks, there are four places in Waipouli/Kapaa where you can get tourist information. Very helpful is the **Kauai Visitor's Center** in the Market Place Shopping Center, tel. 245-3882. They have a complete range of free information on all the island's activities, are able to make reservations, and have an eye for the deals. **K.B.T.C.** also has the full range of information and sometimes gets discount deals. Stop in at their main booth at the Pono Kai Condo, at their cubbyhole office below Jimmy's Grill in downtown Kapaa, or call 822-7447. Across the street from Jimmy's is **Gilligan's Land of Bargains**, tel. 822- 0600. Gilligan's has information on island activities and also rents some beach equipment.

Information of another sort can be had at **The Rosetta Stone** on the north end of Kapaa near the Shiatsu International Massage Clinic and the Kapaa Chiropractic Clinic. The Rosetta Stone is a metaphysical resource center that is tapping into the spiritual elements on the island. Books, tapes, crystals, flower essences, gem elixirs, and more are sold, a reference library is being started, and a used-book shelf is also beginning. If you're interested in the mystic arts, spiritual and healing workshops, channeling, psychic guidance, homeopathic remedies, and various practitioner referrals, stop in at 1536 Kuhio Hwy. or call Susan at 822- 2745. For more information on healing, growth, and transformation, look for the free island newspaper, *The Source.*

THE NORTH SHORE

The north shore is a soulful song of wonder, a contented chant of dream-reality, where the Garden Island harmonizes gloriously. The refrain rises, falls, falling, and finally reaches a booming crescendo deep in the emerald green of Na Pali. In so many ways this region is a haven: tiny towns and villages that refused to crumble when sugar pulled out; a patchwork quilt of diminutive *kuleana* homesteads of native Hawaiians running deep into luxuriant valleys where ageless stone walls encircle fields of taro; a winter sanctuary for migrating birds, and gritty native species desperately holding on to life; and a haven for its myriad visitors, the adventuring, vacationing, life-tossed, or work-weary who come to its shores seeking the setting so conducive to finding peace of body and soul.

The north shore is only 30 miles long, but oh, what miles! Along its undulating mountains are one-lane roads and luminescent bays like landlocked caves still umbilically tied to the sea; historical sites, the remnants of peace or domination once so important and now reduced by time; and living "movie sets," some occupied by villas of stars or dignitaries, enough to bore even the worst name-dropper. Enduring, too, is the history of old Hawaii in this fabled homeland of the Menehune, overrun by the Polynesians who set up their elaborate kingdoms built on a strict social order. The usurpers' *heiau* remain, and from one came the hula, swaying, stirring, and spreading throughout the island kingdoms.

Starting in **Kilauea**, an old plantation town, you can search out the spiritual by visiting two intriguing churches, visit an "everything" general store, or marvel at the coastline from bold promontories pummelled by the sea. Then there are the north shore beaches, Oriental fans of white sand, some easily visited as official parks, others hidden, the domains of simplicity and free spirits. **Princeville** follows, a convenient but incongruous planned community flexing condo muscles and vibrant with its own shopping mall and airport. Over the rise is **Hanalei**, more poetic than its lovely name, a tiny town, a yachties' anchorage with good food, spirited, slow, a bay of beauty and enchantment. The cameras once rolled at neighboring **Lumahai Beach**, and an entire generation shared the dream of paradise when they saw this spot in *South Pacific*. Next in rapid succession are **Wainiha**, and **Haena** with its few amenities, the last available indoor lodgng, restaurant, bar, and a little of the world's most relaxed lifestyle. The road ends at **Kee Beach,** where adventure begins with the start of the Na Pali Coast Trail. The north shore remains for most visitors the perfect setting for seeking and maybe actually finding peace, solitude, the dream, yourself.

SIGHTS AND PRACTICALITIES

KILAUEA

There's no saying *exactly* where it begins, but Kilauea is generally considered the gateway to the north shore. The village was built on sugar, which melted away almost 20 years ago. Now the town holds on as a way station to some of the most intriguing scenery along this fabulous coast. Look for mile marker #23 and a Shell station on your right. A Menehune Food Mart is next door. This is where you turn onto Kolo Road, following the signs to Kilauea Lighthouse and National Wildlife Refuge. The promontory that it occupies, Kilauea Point, is the northernmost tip of the main Hawaiian Islands. Before heading out there, notice the bright, cheery, and well-kept homes as you pass through this community. The homeowners, perhaps short on cash, are nonetheless long on pride, and surround their dwellings with lovingly tended flower gardens. The bungalows, pictures of homey contentment, are ablaze with color. A second way into Kilauea is by turning off the highway at Pu'u Lani fruit and produce stand (a farmers' market is held every Saturday at noon in the Waldorf schoolyard next door). Go in one block and turn left. Pass St. Sylvester's Church, and proceed over a bridge past the Kilauea School into town.

Sights

As you head down Kolo Road from the gas station, you pass the post office. Where Kolo Road intersects Kilauea Road sits **Christ Memorial Episcopal Church** on the right. Hawaii seems to sprout as many churches as bamboo shoots but this one is special. The shrubbery and flowers immediately catch your eye, their vibrant colors matched by the stained-glass windows imported from England. The present church was built in 1941 from cut lava stone. Inside is a hand-hewn altar, and surrounding the church is a cemetery with some old tombstones for long-departed parishioners. Go in, have a look, and perhaps meditate for a moment.

Before turning on Kilauea Road have a look at **St. Sylvester's Catholic Church.** This church is octagonal with an odd roof. Inside are murals painted by Jean Charlot, a famous island artist. The church, built by Fr. John Macdonald, was an attempt to reintroduce art as one of the bulwarks of Catholicism.

Head down Kilauea Road past the Kong Lung Store, and keep going until Kilauea Road makes a hard swing to the left. Proceeding straight ahead up Mihi Road brings you to a little Japanese cemetery on your right. This road has been blocked as it's now privately owned and closed to the public, but it leads to Mokolea Point's **Crater Hill,** where 568 feet straight down is the Pacific, virtually unobstructed until it hits Asia. The seacliff is like a giant stack of pancakes, layered and jagged, with the edges eaten by age, and covered with a green syrup of lichen and mosses. The cliff is undercut and gives the sensation of floating in midair. There is a profusion of purple and yellow flowers all along the edge. The cliffs are a giant rookery for sea birds, and along with Mokolea Point to the east are now part of the **Kilauea National Wildlife Refuge** that also encompasses Kilauea Point.

For a more civilized experience of the same view with perhaps a touch less drama, head down Kilauea Road to the end and park at **Kilauea Lighthouse,** a designated national historical landmark. This facility, built in 1913 and at one time manned by the Coast Guard but now under the jurisdiction of the Department of the Interior's Fish and Wildlife Service, boasts the largest "clamshell lens" in the world, capable of sending a beacon 90 miles out to sea. The clamshell lens has not been used since the mid-'70s, and a small high-intensity light now shines as an important reference point for mariners.

The area is alive with resident and migrating birds. Keep your eyes peeled for the **great frigate bird** kiting on its eight-foot wingspan, or the **red-footed booby,** a white bird with black wingtips darting here and there, and always wearing

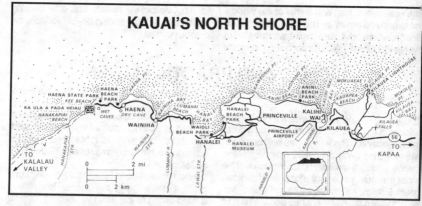

KAUAI'S NORTH SHORE

red dancing shoes. At certain times of the year **Hawaiian monk seals** and **green turtles** can be seen along the shore and around Mokuaeae Island just off Kilauea Point. Dolphins and whales are also spotted offshore. Information at the visitors center gives you a fast lesson on local birdlife and a pictorial history of the lighthouse—worth reading. A good selection of books on Hawaiian flora, fauna, history, and hiking, as well as maps of the islands, are available. The center also lends binoculars free (you must sign for them) for viewing the birds, and there are usually informative docents in the yard with monoculars trained on a particular bird or nesting site on the nearby cliffs.

A leisurely walk takes you out onto this amazingly narrow peninsula, where you'll learn more about the plant and birdlife in the area. Don't keep your eyes only in the air, however. Look for the coastal *naupaka* plants that surround the parking lot and line the walk to the lighthouse. Common along the seashore and able to grow even in arid regions, these plants have bunches of bright green, moisture-retaining, leathery leaves, at the center of which are white half flowers, the size of a fingernail, and small white seeds.

The refuge plans to establish a four-mile-long walking trail from Kilauea Point, around Crater Hill, to Mokolea Point that will be used strictly for tours led by refuge personnel. This facility is open Mon. to Fri. 10 a.m. to 4 p.m., closed weekends and federal holidays. The entrance fee is $2 adults, children under 16 free, and an annual refuge permit is $10; the Golden Eagle Pass, Golden Access Pass, Golden Age Pass, and Federal Duck Stamp are also honored for free entrance.

Beaches

The Kilauea area includes some fantastic beaches. One is a beach park with full amenities and camping, one is hidden and rarely visited, while others are for fishing or just looking.

Kauapea Beach, more commonly called **Secret Beach**, lives up to everything that its name implies. After passing through Kilauea look for Banana Joe's tropical fruit stand on the left. Almost directly across Route 56 from their driveway a rough dirt road goes up the bank and through some fields. Follow this tiny road for about one mile until it turns right at an iron gate. Continue down the hill to a parking area and a little homemade sign saying Beach Trail. Follow the signs that point you to the beach—if there are signs it can't be too secret. Even some local residents ruefully admit that the "secret" is out. However, if you venture to this beach, be conscious that there are private homes nearby and that it's a place locals come to enjoy away from the crowds of tourists.

Walk beside the barbed-wire fence and work your way down the slippery slope to the beach. You pass through some excellent jungle area before emerging at Secret Beach in less than 15 minutes. If you expect Secret Beach to be small, you're in for a shock. This white-sand strand is huge. Off to the right you can see Kilauea Lighthouse, dazzling white in the sun. Along the beach is a fine stand of trees providing shade and perfect for pitching a tent. A stream flowing into the beach when you come down the hill is OK for washing in but not drinking. For drinking water head south along the beach and keep your eyes peeled for a freshwater spring coming out of the mountain. What more can you ask for? The camping is terrific and free of hassles.

Kilauea Bay offers great fishing, unofficial camping, and beautiful scenery. Proceed through Kilauea along Kilauea Road and pass Kong Lung Store. Take the second dirt road to the right; it angles through cane fields, about 100 yards past the Martin Farm produce stand. Follow this rutted, gravel road 1½ miles down to what the local people call **Quarry Beach**, also called Kahili Beach. At the end of the road is the now-abandoned Kahili Quarry. Although easy to get to, this wide sandy beach is rarely visited. Characteristic of Kauai, Kilauea Stream runs into the bay. From the parking lot, you must wade across the stream to the beach. The swimming is good in the stream and along the beach, but only during calm periods. Some local residents come here to surf or use boogie boards; do this only if you have been on the bay before and are experienced with Hawaiian waters. Plenty of places along the streambank or on the beach are good for picnicking and camping. Many local fishermen come here to catch a transparent fish called *oio* that they use for bait. It's too bony to fry, but they have figured out an ingenious way to get the meat. They cut off the tail and roll a soda pop bottle over it, squeezing the meat out through the cut. They then mix it with some water, hot pepper, and bread crumbs to make delicious fish balls.

Kalihiwai Beach is just past Kilauea off Route 56 and down Kalihiwai Road. If you go over the Kalihiwai River you've gone too far, even though another section of the Kalihiwai Road also leads from there down to the coast. This road was once part of the coastal road, but the devastating tsunami of 1946 took out the lower bridge and the road is now divided by the river. As on many such rivers in Kauai, a ferry was used here to ease early transportation difficulties. In less than half a mile down the first Kalihiwai Road you come to an off-the-track white-sand beach lined by ironwoods. The swimming and bodysurfing are outstanding during the right conditions. The river behind the ironwoods has formed a freshwater pool for rinsing off but there are no amenities whatsoever. People camp among the ironwoods without a problem. The second Kalihiwai Road leads you to the beach on the west side of the river where some people come to fish.

Go over the bridge and turn right on the second Kalihiwai Road. Follow this to a Y, taking the left fork, Anini Road, which ends at the remarkable **Anini Beach County Park.**

The reef here is the longest exposed reef off Kauai; consequently the snorkeling is first-rate. It's amazing to snorkel out to the reef in no more than four feet of water and then to peer over the edge into waters that seem bottomless. Windsurfers also love this area, and their bright sails can be seen year-round. Those in the know say that this is the *best* spot on Kauai for beginning

great frigate bird

windsurfers as the winds are generally steady, the bottom shallow, and the beach protected. Several shops in Hanalei give lessons here.

Follow the road to the end where a shallow brackish lagoon and large sandbar make for good wading. This beach offers all amenities: toilets, picnic tables, grills, a pavilion, and camping (county permit). A polo ground is across the road from the open camping area, and several times a month matches are held. There are private homes at both ends of this beach, so be considerate when coming and going.

Shopping, Accommodations, And Food

An institution in this area is **Kong Lung Store**, which has been serving the needs of the north shore plantation towns for almost a century. But don't expect bulk rice and pipe fittings. It prides itself on being an "exotic gift emporium." On the shelves are gourmet cheeses, fine wines, and all the accouterments necessary for a very civilized picnic. Another section is a clothing boutique selling name-brand beach duds, casual clothes, and alohawear. Enter an adjoining room to find an art gallery specializing in carvings, pottery, jewelry, and Niihau shellwork. Notice too the old-fashioned rag carpets woven with modern pastel material. A children's section and shelves of cards and books of Kauaiana and Hawaiiana round out this unique store. Kong Lung is located along Kilauea Lighthouse Road at the intersection of Keneke Street, tel. 828-1822, open daily 9 to 5.

Next door to Kong Lung Store is **Casa di Amici**, the best Italian restaurant on the north shore. The staff makes you feel right at home in this "house of friends." Start with an antipasti like *insalata di pasta* (pasta of the day, $5) or *antipasto alla casalinga* (homestyle antipasto, $8), and move on to one of the many soups, salads, pasta or side dishes. Entrees are selected from all regions of Italy, and include *scallopine di vitello al marsala* (veal sautéed with marsala wine and mushrooms, $17), *pesce arrostito alla Siciliana* (fish suatéed Sicilian style with onions, vegetables, spices, and wine, $16), *pollo alla cacciatora* (chicken breasts with vegetables and marsala, $12), and fettuccine Alfredo (ribbon pasta, $11). The wine list is deliciously sufficient as well, and you can enjoy your meal inside, or out on the veranda. You will not come away disappointed. Open for lunch 11 a.m. to 4 p.m. and for dinner 5 to 9:45 p.m., tel. 828-1388.

Just behind this restaurant is **The Bread Also Rises** bakery, tel. 828-1537. Using natural ingredients, this bakery is open every day except Sun. and supplies some of the best restaurants along the north shore. The list of baked goods is long, but they have some dynamite *foccacia* and occasionally put out something a bit offbeat like pumpkin coconut muffins. As with the other shops in this little complex, The Bread Also Rises succeeds in offering something special. Coffee is also served, so you can sit down and have a snack rather than fumbling with it as you walk.

Directly behind Kong Lung Store is the **Lighthouse Gallery**, tel. 828-1828. Open every day except Sun., this shop carries paintings, prints, and some wood art by statewide artists. Concentrating on local themes, these items are in the moderate price range, and the object of the gallery is to offer something different from what is seen in the ordinary tourist shops.

Next door to Casa di Amici is the Kilauea neighborhood center and theater, and beyond that a deli/grocery store. Open 9 a.m. to 9 p.m., the deli carries food items and beverages, and makes homemade and filling (but not cheap) soup and sandwiches for those who care for something substantial but don't want a full sit-down meal. Behind the center is a small community park.

The Martin Farm produce stand is just beyond town. Open Mon. to Sat. 9 a.m. to 5 p.m., it operates on the self-service honor system. Select what you want, add up the cost marked on each item, and drop your payment in the box.

Do you find "paradise" incomplete without a slice of mouthwatering French pastry? Well, it's available at **Jacques French Bakery.** Before Kong Lung Store turn right on Oka Street and follow your nose to the large Quonset hut which houses the bakery. Jacques no longer lives on the island but his staff handmake every loaf using whole wheat, bran, and other all-natural ingredients. Baking is now done only three days a week. You can choose a butter-melting box of croissants, or a rich loaf of honey-bran bread. Munch your treats and wash them down with steaming hot cups of Kona coffee at a few tables outside. Their menu has been expanded to include a simple breakfast and lunch with a half dozen items. Nothing on the menu is over $4. Jacques is open 6 a.m. to 6 p.m. You can get breakfast from 6:30 to 10 a.m. and lunch until 1:30 p.m. It's a popular stop for the local townsfolk. At the corner of Oka Street is the Kilauea clinic of the Kauai Medical Group.

Across Lighthouse Road from Kong Lung Store is the Kilauea Plantation Center, a low lava-rock building. Recently remodeled, there are several shops, boutiques, and offices, one of which is **Artisan's International,** tel. 828-1918. Open Mon. to Sat. 10:30 a.m. to 5:30 p.m., this shop is chock-a-block with quality household items, fine furnishings, gifts, craft items, jewelry, clothes, and collectibles—not an inch is left bare. All items are handmade, and this helps create a real "feeling" store as Jeri, the owner, likes to say.

At the intersection of Kolo and Kilauea roads, across from the Episcopal church, is the **Hawaiian Art Museum.** A project of Aloha International, it seems more like a gift shop with books, tapes, gift items, postcards, and a few art and craft items for sale.

After visiting all these places, you need a rest. The perfect stop is just west of town at **Banana Joe's** fruit stand, *mauka* of the highway, tel. 828-1092. Run by Joe Halasey, his wife, and friends, this little yellow stand offers fresh fruit, smoothies and other drinks, packaged fruit baskets, baked goods with fruit, and other fruit products. They have more kinds of fruit than you've ever heard of—try something new. If you're into it and they have the time, you may be able to visit the farm behind the stand and talk to Banana Joe himself, but you'll have to ask first.

The **Mahi Ko Inn,** G.D., Kilauea, HI 96754, tel. 828-1103, or (800) 458-3444, is a restored plantation home that's hosted by Cathy and Doug Weber. Rates are from $75 to $135, with a continental breakfast included.

PRINCEVILLE

Princeville is 11,000 acres of planned luxury overlooking Hanalei Bay. Last century the surrounding countryside was a huge ranch, Kauai's oldest, established in 1853 by the Scotsman R.C. Wyllie. After an official royal vacation to the ranch by Kamehameha IV and Queen Emma in 1860, the name was changed to Princeville in honor of their son, Prince Albert. The young heir unfortunately died within two years and his heartbroken father soon followed.

Since 1969, Consolidated Gas and Oil of Honolulu has taken these same 11,000 acres and developed them into a prime vacation community dedicated to keeping the humdrum world far away. Now owned by Princeville Development Corp., a subsidiary of Quitex Australia, everything is provided: accommodations, shopping, dining, recreational facilities (especially golf and tennis), and even its own fire and police force and airport. First-rate condos are scattered around the property and a new multi-tiered Sheraton Mirage Hotel perches over the bay. The guests expect to stay put, except for an occasional day trip. Management and clientele are in league to provide and receive satisfaction, and without even trying, this is just about guaranteed.

Sights

The sights around Princeville are exactly that, beautiful sweeping vistas of **Hanalei Valley** and the sea, especially at sunset. People come just for the light show and are never disappointed. When you proceed past the Princeville turnoff keep your eyes peeled for the Hanalei Valley scenic overlook. Don't miss it! Drifting into the distance is the pastel living impressionism of Hanalei Valley—most dramatic in late afternoon when soft shadows from deeply slanting sunrays create depth in this quilt of fields. Down the center, the liquid silver Hanalei River flows until it meets the sea where the valley broadens into a wide flat fan. Along its banks impossible shades of green vibrate as the valley steps back for almost nine miles, all cradled in the protective arms of 3,500-foot *pali*. Turned on or off by rains, waterfalls tumble over the *pali* like lace curtains billowing in a gentle wind, or with the blasting power of a firehose. Local wisdom says that "When you can count 17 waterfalls it's time to get out of Hanalei." The valley has always been one of the most accommodating places in all of Hawaii in which to live, and its abundance was ever-blessed by the old gods. Madame Pele even sent a thunderbolt to split a boulder so that the Hawaiians could run an irrigation ditch through its center to their fields.

In the old days, Hanalei produced taro, and deep in the valley the outlines of the ancient fields can still be discerned. Then the white man came and planted coffee which failed, sugar which petered out, or ran cattle which grazed the valley away. During these times Hanalei had to *import* poi from Kalalau. Later, when Chinese plantation laborers moved in, the valley was terraced again, but this time the wet fields were given over to rice. This crop proved profitable for many years and was still grown as late as the 1930s. Then, amazingly, the valley began to slowly revert back to taro patches.

In 1972, 917 acres of this valley were designated **Hanalei National Wildlife Refuge**; native water birds such as the Hawaiian coot, stilt, duck, and gallinule loved it and reclaimed their ancient nesting grounds. Today, the large, green, heart-like leaves of taro carpet the valley, and the abundant crop supplies about 50% of Hawaii's poi. You can go into Hanalei Valley; however, you're not permitted in the designated wildlife areas except for fishing or hiking along the river. Never disturb any nesting birds. Look below to where a one-lane bridge crosses the river. Just there, Ohiki Road branches inland. Drive slowly along it to view the simple and quiet homesteads, old rice mill, nesting birds, wildflowers, and terraced fields of this enchanted land.

Golf, Tennis, And Other Activities

Those addicted to striking hard dimpled white balls or fuzzy soft ones have come to the right spot. In Princeville, golf and tennis are the royal couple. The **Princeville Makai Golf Course** offers 27 holes of magnificent golf designed by Robert Trent Jones, Jr. This course, chosen as one of America's top 100, hosted the 26th annual World Cup in 1978 and is where the LPGA Women's Kemper Open is played. There are three nine-hole par-36 courses you can use in any combination that radiate from the central clubhouse. They include the **Woods, Lake**, and **Ocean** courses, the names highlighting their special focus. Open to the public, golf costs $68 ($63 low season) per 18-hole round, including golf cart and greens fee, while guests staying on Mirage Princeville property are charged $53 and $43, respectively.

Opened in 1987, the nine-hole **Prince** course (to be expanded to 18 holes) is also open to the public. It's located off Highway 56 just east of the Woods course, and has its own clubhouse. For this course, accuracy and control are much more important than power and distance. Many expert golfers judge the Prince extremely difficult, perhaps the most challenging in Hawaii— one par-six hole, one hole with the tee 300 feet above the fairway, plus ravines and streams to play over, among other obstacles. Rates are $35 and $33 for high and low season, while Mirage guests pay $28 and $25, respectively.

Nine-hole twilight golf on any course is available on weekdays after 3 p.m. for $19.50. Extra carts and club rentals are $9 apiece for nine holes, and half-hour individual or group golf instruction is $35. The clubhouse has an extensive pro shop, a snack shop, and club storage; call 826-3580 for information and reservations for tee times. The driving range, open during daylight hours, charges $3.50 per basket of balls. Plenty of package deals to the resort include flights, accommodations, rental car, and unlimited golf. For example, for $250-300 you get two nights and three days of golf with confirmed tee times. One such company that offers these deals is The Hawaiian Islands Resorts, Inc. Get information by calling (808) 531-7595 or (800) 367-7042.

You can charge the net on 22 professional tennis courts, day or night at the **Princeville Tennis Club**. There are two pro shops, lessons of all sorts, racquet rental, ball machines, and even video playback so that you can burn yourself up a second time while reviewing your mistakes. Court use is $8 per hour, $7 for Princeville guests, and $5 for guests of the Sheraton Mirage Hotel and for *kamaaina*. Lessons with a pro are $35 an hour and a daily clinic is $12. Ball machines are $15, and racquet rental $5. Membership rates run $50-600 per year. For information call 826-3620. Several condos in Princeville, such as The Cliffs and the Hanalei Bay Resort, also have tennis courts, but these are for their guests only.

On the lower level of the Princeville Clubhouse is the **Hanalei Athletic Club**, open weekdays 7 a.m. to 8 p.m., Sat. 8 a.m. to 6 p.m., and Sun. 11 a.m. to 5 p.m., tel. 826-7333. This is a sister club of the Kauai Athletic Club in Lihue, so you can use both if you are a member. Available are aerobics classes, Nautilus machines, free weights, an outdoor pool, jacuzzi, and sauna. It also has designated running courses throughout the Princeville resort area. Daily, weekly, and monthly rates are $10, $35, and $65, respectively, with discounts for couples. There is a $5 pool charge and $7 charge for the aerobics classes only. For those with small children, a babysitting service at $5 an hour is available by appointment from 8:30 to 10 a.m. weekdays. For additional information call Melody, the manager. Operating through the health club is Hanalei Health and Sports Massage; call 826-1455 for an appointment. Licensed, professional staff give *lomi lomi*, shiatsu, Swedish, Esalen, and sports massages.

Two miles east of Princeville is the Princeville Airport. **Papillon Helicopters**, tel. 826-6591, operates its magical mystery tours deep into Kauai's interior from here. Once-in-a-lifetime, unforgettable experiences, the flights range anywhere from the Discover at 30 minutes for $85 to the Odyssey, which includes a complete view of the island and a two-hour picnic stop, for $225.

If flying isn't your pleasure, how about loping along on horseback? **Pooku Stables**, tel. 826-6777, is located a half mile east of Princeville Center. Open Mon. to Sat. 7:30 a.m. to 4 p.m., you can rent a mount here for one of three group rides that take you throughout the area's fascinating countryside. Prices are $20, $40, and $65 for the Hanalei Valley, shoreline, and waterfall picnic rides. Hanalei Stampede, Kauai's largest rodeo, is held at Pooku Stables in early August; adults $6, children $1. Call for details.

Accommodations

The condos and hotel rooms in Princeville all fall into the high-moderate to expensive range. The best deals naturally occur off-season (fall), especially if you plan on staying a week or more. One would think a project like Princeville should make booking one of its many condos an easy matter, but it's sadly lacking on this service. Lack of a centralized organization that handles reservations causes the confusion. Each condo building can have half a dozen booking agents, all with different phone numbers and widely differing rates! The units are privately owned and the owners simply choose one agency or another. If you're going through a travel agent at home, be aware of these discrepancies and insist on the least expensive rates. A situation which reduces the number of units available here is that many of the condos are switching to complete time-share programs while others still offer rental units with their time-share units, so check out the possibilities thoroughly.

Set high on the bluff overlooking the Pacific Ocean, having one of the nicest views in the area, is **The Cliffs at Princeville.** These one-bedroom condo units have full-size baths and a small wet bar in the room; a second full bath is off the entryway. At the far end of the L-shaped living and dining room is the fully equipped kitchen, so you can prepare everything from a fresh pot of morning coffee to a five-course meal at your leisure and in the comfort of your own living space. Two large lanais, one at each end of the unit, offer both an ocean view and mountain view. Carpets run throughout the unit and the furniture is of contemporary style. Fresh flowers, potted plants, Hawaiian prints, and artwork counter the pastel colors and the subdued floral patterns of the bedroom linen. The bedrooms have king-size beds and the cushy living-room couch pulls out to sleep two more. Units have a color TV, video and stereo systems, compact washer and drier, an iron and ironing board, a small safe for valuables, and daily maid service. Some units on the third floor have two bedrooms. These are basically the same as the one-bedroom units except that the second bedroom is in a loft and the living-room ceiling slants up to the second floor. One-bedroom garden units are $90, ocean-view $115; two-bedroom units run $135 for garden-view and $155 for ocean-view. The property also has a pool and tennis courts free to the guests, and a breezy common room off the pool with large-screen TV, reading material, and a laundry room. The Cliffs is managed by Colony Hotels and Resorts. For information and reservations call (800) 367-6046, or 826-6219 on Kauai.

The best deal in Princeville is offered by **Sandpiper Village** condominiums. By chance they stumbled onto a good thing. When they first opened they priced their units low to attract clientele. The response was so good, with so many repeat visitors, that they have decided to keep it that way . . . for the time being. For $70 per night, you get a roomy one-bedroom unit (one to two people), for $85 a two-bedroom, two-bath unit (one to four people), or for $100 a two-bedroom unit with a loft (up to six people). Minimum stay is two nights mid-April to mid-Dec., and three or seven days the rest of the year. A few unadvertised one-room studios with bath for $40 per night are also available on a limited basis, but you must specifically ask about these. All units have garden views. Each has a full kitchen with dishwasher, laundry facilities, color TV, and private lanai. Maid service is available every four days. On the grounds are a pool, jacuzzi, barbecue grills, and recreational building, all surrounding well-tended gardens. For reservations and information contact Sandpiper Village at tel. 826-1176 or (800) 525-1166, or book through Hawaiiana Resorts at tel. (800) 367-7040.

Other condos in the development are expensive, charging a minimum $100 per night. They're out to please and don't skimp on the luxuries. For example, the Ka'eo Kai, tel. (800) 367-8047, gives you a massive 2,300- square-foot unit with lanai, custom kitchen, fireplace, stereo, and big-screen TV. The units accommodate seven comfortably. The **Hanalei Bay Resort**, tel. (800) 367-7040, and **Hanalei Bay Villas** also offer reasonable accommodations. The Bay Resort has a bit more going for it with tennis courts, two swimming pools, a sauna, and a good restaurant on the premises. The **Pali Ke Kua** condos sit right on the cliffs. It, the **Pu'u Po'a**, and the **Hale Moi** condos are managed by Hawaiian Islands Resorts, tel. (800) 367- 7042, which offers many fly/drive/golf packages. One of the best restaurants on the north coast, the Beamreach, is at the Pali Ke Kua. More luxurious, the Pu'u Po'a is slightly more expensive than the Pali Ke Kua; overlooking the golf course, the Hale Moi is about half the price.

Other good units include the **Alii Kai II** (like the Sandpiper and Hanalei Bay Resort, managed by Hawaiiana Resorts), where all units are $100, and the **Paniolo** and weathered-grey Cape Cod-ish **Sealodge;** reservations for both can be made by writing or calling Hanalei Aloha Rental Management, Box 1109, Hanalei, HI 96714, tel. (800) 367-8047, on Kauai tel. 826-9833.

The **Sheraton Mirage Princeville** is in a class by itself. Not only is it a magnificent and dramatic architectural feat, built in tiers stepping down the point of the peninsula, but it is the only hotel in Princeville. There is not a bad view in the place, with most looking out over Hanalei Bay toward Bali Hai peak down the coast. Spectacular! All but 16 of the 300 rooms have either a bay or an ocean view—the others get a great view of the mountains. (On the other hand, local folks who hated to lose one of the premier views on the north shore say it looks like a prison of tiny concrete squares.) In the lobby, a collection of artifacts—antique quilts, missionary furniture, and an outrigger canoe suspended from the ceiling—tells the history of Hanalei.

A definite Hawaiian motif runs through all decorations and furnishings. Predominantly pineapple and breadfruit designs, these images turn up in rugs, wallpaper, and upholstery, stitched into quilts, and even punched into the copper doors of the "pie-plate" television cabinets in each room. Most rooms are navy blue or mauve. Each features a reproduction of a Hawaiian quilt, settee, and other old furniture, wet bar, refrigerator, TV, full bath and complimentary amenities, fresh flowers, and lanai. A sweet welcome awaits you on your first day, when a little jar of warm brownies will be placed in your room. In addition, there are three restaurants, two lounges, a swimming pool, gift shops, an art gallery, activities desk, and a white-sand beach on the bay. Free shuttle service is provided to and from the golf course, tennis courts, shopping center, and Princeville Airport.

Virtually all rooms are double occupancy. A standard mountain-view room is $240, superior oceanfront $450, and suites from $750-2100; third-person charge is $25. For information write Sheraton Mirage Princeville, P.O. Box 3069, Princeville, Kauai, HI 96722, or call (800) 325-3535, on Kauai 826-9644.

Food

The restaurants, many located within the condos, are expensive but good. The **Bali Hai**, an open-air restaurant in the Hanalei Bay Resort, enjoys an excellent reputation not only for its food but for its superb atmosphere and prize-winning view of the sunset. Bamboo, batik, and tapestries hung in this bilevel restaurant add an informal elegance. Breakfast and lunch are mainly eggs, omelettes, salads, and sandwiches, with dinner more outstanding and more pricey. The menu includes chicken, fish, and beef dishes, with none under $10. Children's platters are slightly less. Open daily, tel. 826-7670.

Beamreach is an intimate restaurant stowed away in the Pali Ke Kua Condominium. Open daily 6 to 10 p.m. for dinner and cocktails, it's a favorite with yachties, which is reflected in its nautical decor. Known for steak and lobster, its entrees range between $10.95-19.95. Two house specialties, the large salad with croutons and the strawberry daiquiri from the bar, are exceptional. Reservations are necessary, tel. 826-9131.

The **Lanai Restaurant** at the Princeville clubhouse is an open-air restaurant right on the fairways—great sunsets over the course. It gets the most consistent praise of any eatery in Princeville. The Lanai serves continental and American fare, with a touch of Oriental. Open at 4 p.m. for cocktails, sunset dinners start at 6 p.m. Light entertainment is provided nightly by local musicians. Call 826-6226.

The word is that the restaurants and snack bars in the Sheraton are overpriced for what you get . . . except for **Nobles.** This is the signature restaurant of the hotel and its decor is reminiscent of Victorian England, a favorite motif of Hawaii's last monarch. The gourmet food is pricey but well prepared and served with great civility. Others at the Sheraton are **Hale Kapa**, open for dinner and Sunday brunch, and the casual **Cafe Hanalei.** The **Lime Tree Lounge** is in the lobby, a perfect place to relax after a hard day before going out to eat. With its touch of 18th-century Japanese decor the **Ukiyo Lounge** is the place for music and dance, and **Pool Lanai** is good for snacks and cocktails.

At the Princeville Center you'll find **Chuck's Steak House**, **Iulani Isle Italian Restaurant**, and **Cafe Zelo's Deli & Espresso Bar.** Chuck's has a good reputation for meat dishes and has a loyal local clientele. The Iulani basically serves pasta and seafood but word is that if you want the best Italian food in this area, go to Kilauea. Both are open for lunch and dinner, and entrees are about $12-18. Zelo's is the place to go for breakfast. Definitely more casual and simpatico than the hotel restaurants, this little cafe is open Mon. to Sat. 8 a.m. to 6 p.m., until 3 p.m. on Sun., tel. 826-9700. Breakfasts include omelettes, crepes, and bagels, most for under $4.50; for lunch, various sandwiches and salads, most under $6. Pastries, desserts, fruit drinks, and coffee are served at any time. Sit inside under the high-arch ceiling or out on the patio and order coffee from the largest selection on the north coast. The sub-

dued grays and whites make the brighter colors in the wall hangings of tropical birds, fish, and vegetation stand out. On occasion, you'll be lucky to catch one of the local musicians strumming softly on his guitar in the corner.

Also at the Princeville Center, **Lappert's Ice Cream** will fill a cone for you, **Sweet Temptation Bakery** will tempt you to come in and try a mouthwatering treat, and you can order guess what at the **Pizza Burger.** Don't forget **Amelia's** at the Princeville Airport for sandwiches, snacks, and drinks on your way into or out of town.

Entertainment

There is little in the way of evening entertainment in Princeville, so you may have to be creative and make your own. However, the following are worth checking out. The **Lanai Restaurant** hosts live music nightly, ranging from Hawaiian to jazz to contemporary sounds. At the **Bali Hai Restaurant** you can listen to Hawaiian music five nights a week. Most nights the Iulani offers live country and western or rock 'n' roll and dancing until 2 a.m., and the **Ukiyo Lounge** at the Sheraton (dress code) is a disco that stays open until midnight Sun. through Thurs., and until 2 a.m. on Fri. and Saturday.

Shopping And Services

Aside from the few shops and the Sheraton, the clubhouse, and tennis pro shop, the shopping in Princeville is clustered in the Princeville Center complex. A few stores sell souvenirs and gifts, but since Princeville is a self-contained community, most are practical shops: bank, hardware store, sporting goods outlet, real estate offices, Kauai Medical Group clinic, post office, restaurants, and a **Foodland** supermarket. The latter is important because it offers the cheapest food prices on the north shore. Before it was built, the local people would drive to Kapaa to shop; now they come here. The last gas station on the north shore is **Princeville Chevron.** If your gauge is low make sure to tank up if you're driving back down the coast. They're open Mon. to Thurs. 7 a.m. to 7 p.m., Fri. and Sat. until 8 p.m., and Sun. until 6 p.m.

Note: Mileage markers on Highway 56 going west are renumbered from one (1) at Princeville. It is 10 miles from here to the end of the road at Kee Beach.

HANALEI

If Puff the Magic Dragon had resided in the sunshine of Hanalei instead of the mists of Hanalee, Little Jackie Paper would still be hangin' around. You know you're entering a magic land the minute you drop down from the heights and cross the Hanalei River. The narrow one-lane bridge is like a gateway to the enchanted coast, forcing you to slow down and take stock of where you are. To add to your amazement, as you look "up valley" over a sea of green taro, what else would you expect to find but a herd of buffalo? (They're imported by a local entrepreneur trying to crossbreed them with beef cattle.)

Hanalei ("Lei-making Town") compacts a lot into a little space. You're in and out of the town in two blinks, but you'll find a small shopping center, some terrific restaurants, beach and ocean activities, historical sites, and a cultural and art center. You also get two superlatives for the price of one: the epitome of a north shore laid-back village, and a truly magnificent bay. In fact, if one was forced to choose the most beautiful bay in all of Hawaii, Hanalei (and Lumahai, the silent star of the movie South Pacific, just north of town), would definitely be among the finalists.

Sights

Hanalei town and beach are sights in themselves. Don't make this sojourn up the north coast without getting out to stretch your legs; you'll do yourself a disservice. Overlooking the bay on a tall bluff are the remains of an old Russian fort (1816) from the days when Hawaii was lusted after by many European powers. It's too difficult to find, but knowing it's there adds a little spice. As you enter town look for the Hanalei Trader on your right. Just past is **Hanalei Museum**, on the left, one of Hawaii's funkiest museums. Often closed, and seemingly an addendum to a small stand selling plate lunches and saimin, it's great just because it is so unostentatious. Perhaps the most intriguing things in this two-room, rough-wood building are the photographs from the early years of the century. Go around back to the little outhouse-like shed holding a few items, rusty and muddy, like an old sink and a mirror. The experience is cultural, like being invited into someone's back yard.

Down the block, on the right next to Napali Zodiac, an old building (the old Ching Young Store) houses the **Native Hawaiian Trading and Cultural Center**. Don't get *too* excited because this good idea doesn't have its act together yet. Aside from a very small museum (open daily 10 a.m. to 5 p.m.), they have some authentic Hawaiian crafts, and some awful touristy junk, too. You can buy handmade jewelry, shells, clothes, and sweets, but some of the really worthwhile items are lovely fresh plumeria leis and flowers. Upstairs is the Artisans Guild of Kauai, a fine co-op where local artists display and sell their arts and crafts.

Waioli Mission House Museum

As you leave town, look to your left to see **Waioli Hui'ia Church**. If you're in Hanalei on Sunday do yourself a favor and go to the 10 a.m. service to be uplifted by a choir of rich voices singing enchanting hymns in Hawaiian. They do justice to the meaning of Waioli, which is "Healing or Singing Waters." The **Waioli Mission House** is a must-stop whenever you pass through. You know you're in for a treat as soon as you pull into the parking lot completely surrounded by trees, creeping vines, ferns, and even papayas. You walk over stepping stones through a formal garden with the jagged mountains framing a classical American homestead. Most mission homes are New England-style, and this one is too, inside. But outside it's Southern, because the missionary architect was a Kentuckian, Rev. William P. Alexander, who arrived with his wife Mary Ann in 1834 by double-hulled canoe from Waimea. Although a number of missionary families lived in the home in the first few years after it was built in 1837, in 1846 Abner and Lucy Wilcox arrived, and the home became synonymous with this family. Indeed, it was owned and occupied by the *kamaaina* Wilcox family until very recently. It was George, the son of Abner and Lucy, who founded Grove Homestead over by Lihue. Miss Mabel Wilcox, his niece who died in 1978, and her sister Miss Elsie, who was the first woman representative of Hawaii in the '30s, set up a nonprofit educational foundation that operates the home.

Your first treat will be meeting Joan, the lovely tour guide. A "fusspot" in the best sense of the word, she's like a proper old auntie who gives

Waioli Mission House

you the "hairy eyeball" if you muss up the doily on the coffee table. Joan knows an unbelievable amount of history and anecdotes, not only about the mission house, but about the entire area and Hawaii in general. The home is great, and she makes it better. The first thing she says, almost apologetically, to Mainlanders is, "Take off your shoes. It's an old Hawaiian custom and feels good to your feet."

You enter the parlor where Lucy Wilcox taught native girls who'd never seen a needle and thread before to sew. Within a few years, their nimble fingers were fashioning muumuus to cover their pre-Christian nakedness. In the background an old clock ticks. In 1866 a missionary coming to visit from Boston was given $8 to buy a clock; here it is keeping time more than 120 years later. The picture on it is of the St. Louis Courthouse. Paintings of the Wilcoxes line the walls. Lucy looks like a happy, sympathetic woman. Abner's books line the shelves. Notice an old copy of *Uncle Tom's Cabin,* and *God Against Slavery.* Mr. Wilcox, in addition to being a missionary, was a doctor, teacher, public official, and veterinarian. His preserved letters show that he was a very serious man, not given to humor. He and Lucy didn't want to come to Waioli at first, but they learned to love the place. He worried about his sons, and about being poor. He even wrote letters to the king urging that Hawaiian be retained as the first language, with English as a second. He and Lucy returned to

New England for a visit in 1869, where both took sick and died.

During the time that this was a mission household, nine children were born in the main bedroom, eight of them boys. Behind it is a nursery, the only room that has had a major change: Lucy and Mabel had a closet built and an indoor bathroom installed there in 1921. Upstairs is a guest bedroom that the Wilcoxes dubbed the "room of the travelling prophet," because it was invariably occupied by visiting missionaries. Also used by Abner Wilcox as a study, the books in the room are original primers printed on Oahu. The homestead served as a school for selected boys who were trained as teachers.

The house has been added to several times and is surprisingly spacious. It was also a self-sufficient farm where they raised chickens and cattle. Around the home are artifacts, dishes, and knickknacks from last century; notice candle molds, a food locker, a charcoal iron, and the old butter churn. Lucy Wilcox churned butter that she shipped to Honolulu in buckets, which brought in some good money. Most of the furniture is donated period pieces; only a few were actually used by the Wilcoxes. From the upstairs window you can still see the same view from last century, Hanalei Bay, beautifully serene and timeless. The Waioli Mission House is open Tues., Thurs., and Sat. 9 a.m. to 3 p.m., and is free! There is a bucket for donations; please be generous.

Beaches

Since the days of the migrating Polynesians, Hanalei Bay has been known as one of the Pacific's most perfect anchorages. Used as one of Kauai's three main ports until very recently, it's still a favorite port of call for world-class yachts. They start arriving in mid-May and stay throughout the summer, when 40 to 50 magnificent boats bob in the bay, making the most of the easy entrance and sandy bottom. They leave by October, when even this inviting bay becomes rough, with occasional 30-foot waves. When you drive to the bay, the section under the trees near the river is called Black Pot. It received this name from an earlier time when the people of Hanalei would greet the yachties with island aloha, which of course included food. A fire was always going with a large black pot hanging over it, into which everyone contributed and then shared in the meal. Across the road and upriver a few hundred yards is **Hanalei Canoe Club.** This small local club has produced a number of winning teams in statewide competitions, oftentimes appearing against much larger clubs.

The sweeping crescent bay is gorgeous. The Hanalei River (and three smaller streams) empties into it, and all around it's protected by embracing mountains. A long pier is in the center, and two reefs front the bay, **Queen** to the left and **King** to the right. The bay provides excellent sailing, surfing, and swimming, mostly in summer. The swimming is good near the river (but watch out for boats and Zodiac rafts which are launched from here!) and at the west end, but rip currents can appear anywhere, even around the pier area, so be careful. The best surf rolls in at the outside reef below Pu'u Po'a Point on the east side of the bay, but it's definitely recommended only for expert surfers. For beginners, try the middle of the bay during summer when the surf is smaller and gentler. The state maintains three parks on the bay: Black Pot at the Hanalei River mouth, Pine Trees in the middle of the bay, and Waipa on the west side. Black Pot and Pine Trees have picnic areas, restrooms, and showers. Camping is permitted only at Pine Trees. A small *kaukau* wagon sells plate lunches near the river; local fishermen launch their boats in the bay and are often amenable to selling their catch.

Lumahai Beach is a femme fatale, lovely to look at but treacherous. This hauntingly beautiful beach, meaning "Twist of Fingers," is what dreams are made of: white sand curving perfectly at the bottom of a dark lava cliff with tropical jungle in the background. The riptides here are fierce even with the reef, and the water should never be entered except in very calm conditions during the summer. Look for a vista point just past mile marker #4. Cars invariably park here. It's a sharp curve, so make sure to pull completely off the road or the police may ticket you. An extensive grove of *hala* trees appears just as you set off down a steep and often muddy footpath leading down to the east end of the beach. The best and easiest place to park is amongst the ironwood trees at the west end of the beach near the bridge that crosses the Lumahai River; an emergency phone is across the road from this parking area. From here you can walk to the south end if you want seclusion.

Accommodations

There is only one advertised place to stay in Hanalei. The inexpensive **Mahikoa's Hanalei Bay Inn** is on the west side of town across from the school, tucked in amongst flowering bushes and trees. With only six units, it's a quiet, relaxing place. Five units have a living/ bedroom area with a queen-size or two twin beds, an efficiency kitchen sufficient for preparing light meals, and a full bath; one of the units has an additional separate bedroom. The efficiency studios run $55 ($45 after two days) and the one-bedroom is $65 ($55 after two days). In addition, a bed-and-breakfast room maintained in the innkeeper's cottage goes for $50 plus tax. Maid service is available after four days. For more information call 826-9333 or write to Edmund Gardien, Innkeeper, Mahikoa's Hanalei Bay Inn, P.O. Box 122, Hanalei, Kauai, HI 96714.

Private rental homes, generally listed through property and rental agencies, are also available in town (and farther along the coast). For information contact **Na Pali Properties, Inc.**, P.O. Box 475, Hanalei, Kauai, HI 96714, tel. 826-7272; **North Shore Properties, Ltd.**, P.O. Box 607, Hanalei, Kauai, HI 96714, tel. 826-9622; or **Ironwood Rentals**, tel. 826-7533.

Food

Hanalei has a number of eating institutions, ranging from excellent restaurants to *kaukau* wagons. The food is great at any time of day, but those in the know time their arrival to coincide with sunset. They watch the free show and then go for a great meal.

The first restaurant you encounter is the **Hanalei Dolphin**, overlooking the Hanalei River. For years it has enjoyed a reputation as the north shore's premier seafood restaurant, although they also serve meat dishes. The restaurant was damaged by Hurricane Iwa and has since been remodeled, but its menu remains much the same. Don't mull over the menu, however; listen to the waiters instead. They'll tell you what's good that night—believe them. You can't go wrong starting with the clam chowder, however. They serve good plain food, nothing out of the ordinary. The Hanalei Dolphin is open daily for dinner from 6 to 10 p.m. No reservations are taken.

You've got to stop at the **Tahiti Nui**, if just to look around and have a cool drink. The original owner, Louise Marston, was dedicated to creating a friendly, family atmosphere and she succeeded admirably. The restaurant is now run by her daughter and son-in-law, but the tradition carries on. Inside, it's pure Pacific island. The decorations are modern Polynesian longhouse, with blowfish lanterns and stools carved from palm tree trunks. The bar, open from noon to 2 a.m., is center of the action. Old-timers drop in to "talk story" and someone is always willing to sing and play a Hawaiian tune. The mai tais are fabulous. Just sit out on the porch, kick back, and sip away. The lunch and dinner menu is limited and prices run $10-15. It includes fresh fish, beef, and chicken, all prepared with an island twist. You sit at long tables and eat family style. The Tahiti Nui is famous for its luau-style party, Wed. and Fri. at 6:30 p.m. There's singing, dancing, and good cheer all around, a perfect time to mingle with the local people. The food is real Hawaiian, and the show is no glitzy extravaganza or slick production. This luau is very down-to-earth, casual, Kauaian, and everybody has a good time. Adults $30, children $15. For reservations call 826-6277.

The **Hanalei Shell House** is deliciously funky and reasonably priced. Many local people come here to "talk story" in the evenings, oftentimes providing spontaneous entertainment. The tables on the veranda, open windows, wooden walls, and coziness give it atmosphere. It's just

down the road from Tahiti Nui at Aku Road, near the Na Pali Zodiac office. They're open for breakfast, lunch, and dinner, with music and drinks going to the wee hours. Breakfast includes omelettes, lunch is mainly salads and sandwiches, and dinner entrees focus on seafood—the clam chowder is raved about. What this restaurant has over the Hanalei Dolphin is that each item of this full and varied menu is prepared more creatively. What it lacks is the setting. The Shell House is set right on the main road through town, and even though there is relatively little traffic, cars pass only a few feet away. Phone 826-7977 for reservations.

Foong Wong specializes in Cantonese cuisine, located upstairs in the new Ching Young Village Shopping Center. Their extensive menu includes dishes like kung pao chicken at $7.60, shrimp with black bean sauce ($7.35), beef chow mein ($6.50), stir-fry garden vegetable chop suey ($5.75), chef's specials in the $10-12 range, and family-style dinners from $11.95-16.95. They also do takeouts. Unfortunately, Foong Wong's gets its fortune cookies crumbled. Portions are large but bland, and the atmosphere is plain, simple, and sterile, despite the requisite lanterns, scrolls, and embroidered wall hangings. Open noon to 9 p.m. daily, 5 to 9 p.m. on Mon., tel. 826-6996.

Hanalei has a great collection of fast, inexpensive, and downright delicious places at which to eat. The problem is which one to choose! **Papagayo Azul** serves hearty Mexican food from a takeout window, below the Artisan's Guild studio in the old Ching Young store. Their food is *muy bueno* and you can choose munchies like nachos for $1.90, or tacos, burritos, tostadas, and enchiladas for under $4. A filling Papagayo burrito, with all the extras, is $4.95. Charbroiled or barbecued chicken, and barbecued beef and pork ribs are also available. Open Mon. to Sat. 11 a.m. to 9 p.m., tel. 826-9442.

In the Ching Young Shopping Center, **Pizza Hanalei** serves the area's only pizza, and it's delicious. Made with thin, white or whole wheat crusts, these pizzas run from $5.85 to $17.95, more with additional toppings. There is pizza by the slice from 11 a.m. to 5 p.m. Green and pasta salads, garlic bread, lasagna, and pizzarittos (pizza filling rolled up in a pizza shell like a burrito) are also on the menu. Open daily 11 a.m. to 9 p.m., they also deliver in the Hanalei/Princeville area from 5 to 8:30 p.m., tel. 826-9494.

Next to Pizza Hanalei is the **Hanalei Natural Foods** store. Open daily 8:30 a.m. to 8:30 p.m., this shop carries bulk foods, fresh fruits and vegetables, a variety of baked breads, freshly squeezed juices, deli foods, and sandwiches, as well as books and vitamins. If you're into natural foods and healthful living, stop in, look around, and chat.

If the little food monster gets hold of you and a slab of tofu just won't do, walk across the courtyard to **The Village Snack And Bake Shop.** Open 6 a.m. to 6 p.m. daily, it serves just what its name implies. Next to Tahiti Nui, in the Kauhale Center, is the **West of the Moon Cafe**, the perfect breakfast place in Hanalei. Cubbyhole small, there are also a few tables out on the veranda. The cheery help and smell of freshly brewed cof fee and good home cookin' should help you start off your day on the right foot. Try a giant muffin for $2 and glass of fresh orange or pineapple juice. If you want something more filling ask for the scrambled eggs on a bagel ($2.50) or the special spuds ($3.50). For the hearty eater, go for the fritatas ($6.50), a quiche-like dish with home fries. West of the Moon Cafe opens 7 a.m. to 12:30 p.m. daily, tel. 826-7460. Just down the walkway in this group of shops is the **Black Pot Luau Hut** restaurant and bar, tel. 826-9871, serving mostly Hawaiian food.

For a mouthwatering burger with all the trimmings, a plate lunch, or an undisputedly luscious bowl of saimin (this last only in the evening), try the food stand at the **Hanalei Museum** on your left just as you enter town. Competing with Papagayo Azul's, the **Tropical Taco** *kaukau* wagon dispenses great food at cheap prices. He opens about noon and is usually parked next to the Hanalei Trader as you enter town.

If you're looking for something cooler and more refreshing try shave ice at the Bali Hai Charters office across Hwy. 56 from the Ching Young Shopping Center, or Lappert's ice cream in the Native Hawaiian Trading and Cultural Center. Every Tues. from 3 to 5 p.m. pick up some farm-fresh fruit and vegetables from the **Hawaiian Farmers of Hanalei** farmers' market located one-half mile west of town in Waipa, on the road to Haena. Look for the sign along the road on the left.

Shopping And Services

The **Ching Young Village** in the center of town is a small shopping center. Among its shops are **Big Save Supermarket**, a number of variety and gift stores, a few clothing shops, **Hanalei Camping And Backpacking** sports and rental store, **Pedal n' Paddle** ocean activities and bike rental shop, **Foto Freddie**, a **Bank of Hawaii** office, and the **See Kauai** activity and information booth; the post office is next door. If you are looking for arts and crafts, you're in luck. Check out the **Artisan's Guild of Kauai**, a co-op of local artists displaying and selling paintings, prints, pottery, cloth, shellwork, metalwork and items in other media. Friendly, with a good selection, the prices are not out of sight. Walk up the stairs above Papagayo Azul's or call 826-6441.

The **Hanalei Trader** is the first building as you enter town. Here you'll find **Ola's** hand-crafted novelty items, **Sand People** beach clothes and rentals, and **Hanalei Sailboards.** The **Hanalei Liquor Store** is on the right just up the road, and across the street, next to the Hanalei Museum, is the **Hanalei Sea Tours** office.

Up the road, across from Tahiti Nui, is a newly renovated school building, housing the new **Hanalei Sailboards** shop, clothing boutiques, and jewelry and gift shops. Across the alley from Tahiti Nui is **Happy Talk**, selling paperback books, music, and Hawaiiana and renting videotapes. Open Mon. to Wed. 1 to 6 p.m. and Thurs. to Sat. 1 to 7 p.m. Down the lanai is **Aku's Hawaiian Express** one-hour photo-finishing service. Next to Blue Odyssey boat charter company at the west end of town are massage and hair-cutting salons.

For luxury car rentals call **Bad Cars**, tel. 826-1138. The **North Shore Taxi** company not only runs a pick-up and delivery service, they also do tours ("South Pacific Discovery Tour"—two hours for $19.95). The ordinary fare from Hanalei to Princeville is just a few bucks, to the end of the road at Kee Beach is $18, and to Lihue Airport it's $50. Call 826-6189 for information and reservations.

Outdoor And Sporting Services

Hanalei is alive with outdoor activities. The following is merely a quick list of what's available. The services provided by the majority of the establishments listed here have been fully described in the Introduction either under "Sightseeing Tours," "Sports," or "Camping."

Na Pali Zodiac does stupendous rides up the Na Pali Coast in a seagoing rubber raft, hiking drop-off service too; tel. 826-9371. Other Zodiac companies are: **Blue Odyssey Kauai**, tel. 826-9033; **Hanalei Sea Tours**, tel. 826-7254; and **Bali Hai Charters**, tel. 826-9787. For boat rides up the coast contact **Paradise Adventure Cruises, Inc.**, tel. 826-9999; **Na Pali Adventures**, tel. 826-6804; **Hanalei Sea Tours**, tel. 826-7254; **Blue Odyssey Kauai**; and **Luana of Hawaii**, tel. 826-9195. *The* company to go to for a kayaking adventure up the Hanalei River or during summer along the coast is **Kayak Kauai**, tel. 826-9844. A variety of sailing and fishing adventures are available from **Hawaiian Z-boat Co.**, tel. 822-5113; **Robert McReynolds**, tel. 822-5113; and Captain Andy's **Blue Water Sailing**, tel. 822-0525. The sailboats run only during the summer.

For those who want to experience windsurfing contact either Nancy Palmer's **Garden Island Windsurfing**, tel. 826-9005, or **Hanalei Sailboards**, tel. 826-9732. An extensive range of backpacking and hiking equipment to rent or buy is available from **Hanalei Camping and Backpacking** in the Ching Young Center, tel. 826-6664. They are *the* camping and hiking information center on the island, and have a great selection of books. **Pedal n' Paddle**, also in the center, rents snorkel gear, bikes, boats, sailboats, surfboards, and sailboards, tel. 826-9069.

ROAD'S END

Past Hanalei you have six miles of pure magic until the road ends at Kee Beach. To thrill you further and make your ride even more enjoyable, you'll find historical sites, natural wonders, a resort, restaurant, grocery store, and the *heiau* where the hula was born, overlooking a lovely beach.

Sights, Accommodations, And Services

As you drive along you cross one-lane bridges, and pass little beaches and bays, one after another, invariably with a small stream flowing in. Try not to get jaded peering at "just another gorgeous north shore beach." Over a small white bridge is the village of **Wainiha**, ("Angry Water"). Here is the tiny **Wainiha Store**, where you can pick up a few supplies and sundries. Talk to Mary here if you're looking for a place to stay; people from around the area come to the store to post a flier if they have a room to rent. You can still get a shack on the beach or in amongst the banana trees! Attached to the store are **Wainiha Sandwiches** (they serve great island-inspired natural smoothies for $2, a meal in themselves) and a T-shirt/gift shop. Ask Linda at the gift shop about a hut she rents. It's not hard to find a bunch of local guys hanging around, perhaps listening to reggae music, who could brighten your day by selling you some of the local produce!

After the store you cross two bridges in a row, and they're dillies! Be careful. Soon a driveway turns off the highway to **Tunnels Beach**. It's superb for snorkeling and scuba, with a host of underwater caves off to the left as you face the sea. Both surfing and windsurfing are great, and the swimming is too if the sea is calm. Watch out for boats that come inside the reef to anchor. Off to the right and down a bit is a nude beach. Be careful not to sunburn delicate parts!

Next up look for signs to the **Hanalei Colony Resort**, literally the "last resort." You can rent very comfortable, spacious, two-bedroom condos here, each with a full kitchen, shower/tub, and lanai. The brown board and batten buildings blend into the surroundings. The resort has a jacuzzi and swimming pool, complimentary snorkel gear, barbecue grills, coin-operated washers and driers, and maid service every fourth day. The beach in front of the resort is great for a stroll at sunset, but is not good for swimming because of the strong currents. Based on single or double occupancy, oceanfront units are $145, oceanview $110, and mountainview $90, with $15 for each additional person, and $5 more per night from mid-December through early April. Car rental packages are available if arranged before arriving on Kauai. For information contact Hanalei Colony Resort, Box 206, Hanalei, HI 96714, tel. (800) 367-8047, ext. 148, on Kauai tel. 826-6235.

On the premises is **Charo's Restaurant**—yes, *that* Charo! It replaced the old Sandgroper. This predominantly forest-green restaurant serves lunch from 11:30 a.m. to 3 p.m., cocktails and *pu pu* 3 to 5:30 p.m., and dinner from 6 to 10 p.m., reservations 826-6422. The *pu pu* are great, the margaritas are mean, and the view is outstanding. The dinner menu features fresh fish and steaks in the $16.95-24.95 range, with lobster a steep $41.95. Every evening Charo's presents the Tropical Fiesta International Show, a Las Vegas-style Latin and Hawaiian music and dance show. This is pleasant entertainment with beautiful costumes, well-choreographed and performed, but not Hawaiiana. However, if you are on the island for pleasure and simply want an entertaining evening out, why not? Casual attire is OK; collared shirts and footwear are required. If Charo is around, she might come around after the show and sign autographs. There are plans to build a dinner theater above the restaurant, which now gets a little crowded for the evening show, so the Tropical Fiesta may soon be performed in a more convivial setting.

Just past Hanalei Resort, between mile markers 7 and 8 on the highway, look for the entrance to the **YMCA Camp Naue**. The turnoff is at the road entrance by the phone booth. Here, several buildings are filled with bunks and a separate toilet area and cooking facilities. The camp caters to large groups but is open to single travelers for the staggering sum of $10 per night. Kauai residents are $9, children half price, $8 for a tent and the first person plus $5 for each additional person in the tent. The bunk houses lie under beachside trees and campers stay in the yard. As with most YMCAs, there are many rules to be followed. You can get full information from YMCA headquarters in Lihue or by writing YMCA of Kauai, Box 1786, Lihue, HI 96766, tel. 246-9090, 742-1200, or 826-6419 in Haena.

Haena Beach County Park, just before road's end, is a large, flat, field-like area, where you carve out your own camping site. For your convenience the county provides tables, a pavilion, grills, and showers. Permit required. The sand on this long crescent beach is rather coarse, and the swimming is good only when the sea is gentle, but in summertime a reef offshore is great for snorkeling. Some Zodiac boats are launched a few hundred yards down the beach to the east. The cold stream running through the park is always good for a dip. Kuulei's kaukau wagon is usually parked in this lot every day from about 10 a.m.

Across the road is **Maniniholo dry cave**. Notice the gorgeous grotto of trees, and the jungle wild with vines. You walk in and it feels airy and very conducive for living quarters. Luckily, it hasn't been trashed. Up the road, just after entering **Haena State Park**, an HVB Warrior points the way to the **Waikapalae wet caves**; right along the road is Waikanaloa and 150 yards up the side of a hill is Waikapalae. Their wide openings are almost like a gaping frog's mouth, and the water is liquid crystal. Amazingly, the dry cave is down by the sea, while Waikapalae, subject to the tides, is inland uphill. Look around for ti leaves and a few scraggly guavas. Straight up, different lavas that have flowed over the eons create a stacked pancake effect. The best time to come is an hour before and after noon, when the sun shoots rays into the water. If azure could bleed, it would be this color.

Road ends at popular **Kee Beach**, with restrooms and showers. Here is the beginning of the Kalalau Trail. As always, the swimming is good mostly in summertime. A reef offshore is also great for snorkeling. If conditions are right and the tide is out, you can walk left around the point to get a dazzling view of the Na Pali cliffs. Don't attempt this when the sea is rough! This path takes you past some hidden beach homes. One was used as the setting for the famous love rendezvous in the *Thorn Birds*. Past the homes, another path takes you up the hill to the site of the ancient **Ka Ulu A Paoa Heiau**, birthplace of the hula. The views from up here are remarkable and worth the climb, especially during winter when the sun drops close to the cliffs backlighting Lehua Island, and sinks into its molten reflection. After the novitiate had graduated from the hula heiau, she had to jump into the sea below and swim around to Kee Beach as a sign of her dedication. Tourists aren't required to perform this act.

The Kalalau Trail

This is *the* trail on Kauai. The Kalalau is a destination in and of itself, and those who have walked these phenomenal 11 miles never forget it. (See p. 740 for alternative rides in or out of Kalalau.) The trail leads down the Na Pali Coast, as close as you can get to the Hawaiian paradise of old. Getting there is simple: follow Route 56 until it ends and then hike. But before you start be aware that the entire area falls under the jurisdiction of the Division of State Parks, and a ranger at Kalalau Valley oversees matters. The trailhead has a box where you sign in. Day-use per-

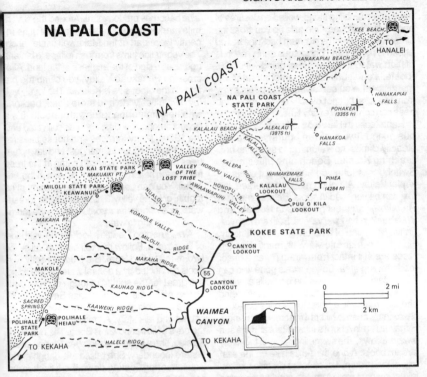

NA PALI COAST

mits are required beyond Hanakapiai (two miles in); camping permits are required to stay overnight at Hanakapiai, Hanakoa, and Kalalau. You can camp for five nights, but no two consecutive nights are allowed either at Hanakapiai or Hanakoa.

You need a good waterproof tent, sleeping bag, repellent (fierce mosquitos), first-aid kit, biodegradable soap, food, and toiletries. There are many streams along the trail, but the water can be biologically contaminated and cause horrible stomach distress. Boil it or use purification tablets. Little firewood is available, and you can't cut trees, so take a stove. Don't litter; carry out what you carried in.

The trail is well marked by countless centuries of use, so you won't get lost, but it's rutted, root strewn, and muddy. Remnants of mileage posts are all along the way. Streams become torrents during rains, but recede quickly. Just wait! Mountain climbing is dangerous because of the

crumbly soil, and the swimming along the coast is unpredictable, with many rips. Summers, when the wave action returns sand to the beach, are usually fine, but stay out from September to April. At Hanakapiai a grim reminder reads, "This life-saving equipment was donated by the family and friends of Dr. Rulf Fahleson, a strong swimmer, who drowned at Hanakapiai in March 1979." Pay heed! In keeping with the tradition of "Garden of Eden," many people go *au naturel* at Kalalau Beach. Private parts unaccustomed to sunshine can make you wish you hadn't.

Many people hike in as far as **Hanakapiai.** This is a fairly strenuous two-mile hike, the first mile uphill, the last down, ending at the beach. Camp at spots on the far side of the stream up from the beach. You can also camp in the caves at the beach, but only during summer at low tide. The unmaintained **Hanakapiai Trail** leads two miles up the valley to the splendid **Hanakapiai Falls,** taking you past some magnificent mango trees and crumbling stone-walled enclosures of ancient taro patches. One mile up you cross the stream. If the stream is high turn back; the trail up ahead is narrow and dangerous during periods of high water. If it's low, keep going—the 300-foot falls and surrounding amphitheater are magnificent. You can swim in the pools away from the falls, but not directly under: rocks and trees can come over at any time.

Hanakapiai to **Hanakoa** is two miles of serious hiking (two or three hours) as the trail steadily climbs, not returning to sea level until reaching Kalalau Beach nine miles away. Switchbacks take you 600 feet out of Hanakapiai Valley. Although heavily traversed, the trail can be very bad in spots. Before arriving at Hanakoa, you must go through **Hoolulu** and **Waiahuakua** hanging valleys. Both are lush with native flora, part of a nature preserve. Shortly, Hanakoa comes into view. Its many wide terraces are still intact from when it was a major food-growing area. Coffee plants gone wild can still be seen. You can use the old walls as windbreaks, or you can spend the night in the roofed shelter. Nearby is a Forestry Service trail-crew shack that's open to hikers if the crew isn't using it. Hanakoa is rainy, but it's intermittent and the sun always follows. The swimming is fine in the many stream pools. A one-third-mile hike up the east fork of the stream, just after the six-mile marker, takes you past more terraces good for camping before coming to Hanakoa Falls. The terraces are wonderful, but the trail is subject to erosion, and is treacherous with many steep sections.

Hanakoa to **Kalalau Beach** is under five miles and takes about three tough hours. Start early in the morning because it's hot, and although you're only traveling five miles, it gets noticeably drier and more open as you approach Kalalau. The views along the way are ample reward. The power and spirit of the incomparable *aina* becomes predominant. Around the seven-mile marker you enter lands that until quite recently were part of the Makaweli cattle ranch. The vegetation turns from lush foliage to lantana and sisal, a sign of the aridness of the land. After crossing Pohakuao Valley, you climb the *pali* and on the other side is Kalalau. The lovely valley, two miles wide and three deep, beckons with its glimmering freshwater pools. It's a beauty among beauties, and was cultivated until the 1920s. Many terraces and house sites remain. Plenty of guavas, mangos, and Java plum trees can be found. You can camp in the trees fronting the beach or in the caves west of the waterfall. You can't camp along the stream, at its mouth, or in the valley. The waterfall has a freshwater pool, where feral goats come in the morning and evening to water.

A *heiau* is atop the little hillock on the west side of the stream. Follow the trail here up-valley for two miles to **Big Pool.** Big Pool is really two pools connected by a natural water slide. Riding it is great for the spirit, but tough on your butt. Enjoy! Along the way you pass Smoke Rock, where *pakalolo* growers at one time came to smoke and talk story. A longtime resident from the days of flower power is Bobo. The nymph of Kalalau, she's been there forever. Stories about her are legendary. She raised two daughters in Kalalau, often floating down the treacherous coast with her babes on an inner tube or surfboard. Once, she paddled eight miles in to shore on a surfboard when a yacht she was crewing on foundered. Bobo then walked the Kalalau Trail for help at night, hiked back, and floated back out to the yacht. She's as brown as a bean and as free as they come. When she goes to town, she often forgets to take her clothes, and the way she parties is even wilder than the way she lives. Bobo probably knows more about Kalalau than anyone alive. You'll know her if you see her!

POIPU AND KOLOA

Poipu-Koloa is the most well-established and developed tourist area on Kauai, but it's now fielding competition from developments in Kapaa and Princeville. On the site of the island's oldest sugar mill—a stone chimney remains to mark the spot—Koloa has been transformed from a tumbledown sugar town to a thriving tourist community where shops, restaurants, and boutiques line its wooden sidewalks. Nearby is the site of Hawaii's first Catholic mission. At the sea in Poipu, luxury accommodations and fine restaurants front the wide, accommodating beach, the water beckons, and the surf is gentle. Flanking this resort community on the east is Pu'uhi Mount, where the last volcanic eruption occurred on the island; to the west, beyond Prince Kuhio's birthplace, is the Spouting Horn, a plume of water that jets up through an opening in the volcanic rock shore with every incoming wave. Whether exploring the sights, cultivating a tan on the beach, combing the shops for your gift list, or sampling island treats, Poipu-Koloa will not fail to provide.

SIGHTS, VILLAGES, AND BEACHES

KOLOA

Five miles west of Lihue, Maluhia Road (Rt. 520) dips south off Route 50 and heads for Koloa. But if you continue three minutes west on Route 50, a sign on the right directs you inland to **Kahili Mountain Park.** Keep this in mind because it's the least-expensive private accommodations available near Poipu (see p. 814). As you head down Maluhia Road, you pass through a fragrant tunnel of trees also called **Eucalyptus Avenue.** These trees are rough-bark *Eucalyptus robustus,* sometimes referred to as "swamp mahogany." Brought from Australia, they're now very well established, adding beauty and shade to over a mile of this narrow country lane.

Koloa town attracts a large number of tourists and packs them into a small area. There are plenty of shops, restaurants, and water sport equipment rentals in town. Nearly all the old shops are remodeled plantation buildings. Dressed in red paint and trimmed with white, they are festooned with strings of lights as if decorated for a perpetual Christmas festivity.

The traffic is hectic around 5:30 p.m. and parking is always a problem, but you can easily

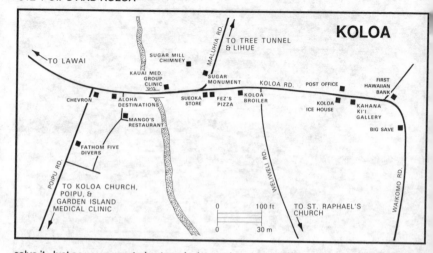

solve it. Just as you are entering town look to your right to see a weathered stone chimney standing alone in a little field. Park here and simply walk across the street, avoiding the hassles. This unmarked edifice is what's left of the **Koloa Sugar Plantation**, established in 1835, site of the first successful attempt at refining sugar in the islands. Although of major historical significance, the chimney is in a terrible state of disrepair—many broken beer bottles litter the inside. Notice, too, that shrubs are growing off the top and a nearby banyan has thrown off an aerial root and is engulfing the structure. Unless action is taken soon, this historical site will be lost forever.

On this overgrown corner lot is a circle of over a dozen varieties of sugar cane, each with a short explanation of its characteristics and where it was grown. A plaque and sculpture have recently been added to this site. Reading the plaque will give you an explanation of and appreciation for the sugar industry on Hawaii, the significance of the Koloa Sugar Plantation, and the people who worked the fields. The bronze sculpture portrays individuals of the seven ethnic groups that provided the greatest manpower for the sugar plantations of Hawaii: Hawaiians, Chinese, Japanese, Portuguese, Puerto Ricans, Koreans, and Filipinos. (From the 1830s to the first decade of this century, smaller numbers of Englishmen, Scots, Germans, Scandinavians, Poles, Spaniards, Afro-

Americans, and Russians also arrived to work. All in all, about 35,000 immigrants came to Hawaii to make the sugar industry the success it has been.) Koloa is the birthplace of the Hawaiian sugar industry, the strongest economic force in the state for over a century. More than anything else, it helped to shape the multi-ethnic mixture of Hawaii's population. While the original mill is gone, the fields surrounding Koloa still produce cane for the McBryde Sugar Co., Ltd., which has a mill to the east of town.

The tall steeple on the way to Poipu belongs to **Koloa Church**, locally known as the White Church. Dating from 1837, it was remodeled in 1929. For many years the steeple was an official landmark used in many land surveys. If you turn left on Koloa Road, right on Weliweli Road, and then follow Hapa Road to its end, you come to **St. Raphael's Catholic Church**, marking the spot of the first Roman Catholic mission permitted in the islands (in 1841). The stone church itself dates from 1856 when it was built by Fr. Robert Walsh. The roof of the church can be seen sticking above the trees from Kiahuna Golf Course in Poipu.

POIPU

Poipu Road continues south from Koloa for two miles until it reaches the coast. En route it passes a cane road (traffic signal) that takes you to Hanapepe via Numila, and a bit farther passes Lawai Road, which turns right along the coast and terminates at the Spouting Horn. Poipu Road itself bends left past a string of condos and hotels, into what might be considered the town, except nothing in particular makes it so. Both Hoonani and Hoowili roads lead to different sections of the beach. As you pass the mouth of Waikomo Stream (along Hoonani Road), you're at **Koloa Landing**, once the island's most important port. When whaling was king, dozens of ships anchored here to trade with the natives for provisions. Today nothing remains. Behind Poipu is **Pu'uhi Mount**, believed to be the site of the last eruption to have occurred on Kauai.

Along Poipu Road look for the driveway into the Kiahuna Plantation Resort on the right across from the Kiahuna Shopping Village. This is the site of the **Kiahuna Plantation Gardens**, formerly known as the Moir Gardens (the central area still maintains this name). The 35 lovely acres are adorned with over 3,000 varieties of tropical flowers, trees, and plants, and a lovely lagoon. The gardens were heavily battered by Hurricane Iwa, but the two dozen full-time gardeners have restored them to their former beauty. These grounds, originally part of the old sugar plantation, were a "cactus patch" started by the manager, Hector Moir, and his wife back in 1938. Over the years the gardens grew more and more lavish until they became a standard Poipu sight. The Kiahuna Plantation has greatly expanded the original gardens, opening them to the public during daylight hours, free of charge. Many plants are identified.

Poipu Beach Park

This is Kauai's best developed beach in the middle of the island's most developed area, so it can be crowded. The actual beach park is at the eastern end of Poipu, and if you walk west many half-moon crescents front the hotels and condos, from the Waiohai Resort to the Sheraton Kauai. Poipu Beach Park provides a pavilion, tables, showers, toilets, playground, and lifeguards. The swimming, snorkeling, and bodysurfing are great. A sheltered pool rimmed by lava boulders is gentle enough for anyone, and going just beyond it provides the more exciting wave action often used by local surfers. Follow the rocks out to Nukamai Point, where there are a number of tidepools. Following the shoreline around to the east you'll end up at Brennecke's Beach, a good spot to boogie board and watch locals shore fish.

On Poipu Road (it turns into a dirt road), continue east past the Poipu Kai Resort. In less than a mile is a wide sandy beach known as **Shipwreck Beach.** Construction is underway here for the new and, as reports have it, elegantly designed Hyatt Regency Kauai Hotel. Hurricane Iwa deposited sand here, making the beach wider and longer. The swimming and snorkeling are good, but as at all secluded beaches, use extra caution. There is no official camping here, but local people sometimes bivouac in the ironwoods at the east end, beyond which is a rocky bluff from where you have a fine view of the coastline east of here. The only people who regularly frequent the beach are fishermen and a few nude sunbathers; sometimes, since Brennecke's Beach was roughed up by Iwa, surfers come for the big swells. If you continue walking eastward, more hidden beaches follow.

West End

Turn onto Lawai Road to pass **Kuhio Park**, the birthplace of Prince Kuhio. Loved and respected, Prince Cupid, a nickname by which he was known, was Hawaii's delegate to Congress from the turn of the century until his death in 1922. He often returned to the shores of his birth whenever his duties permitted. With a statue and monument, lava terrace walls, palm trees, and a pool, this well-manicured acre faces the sea. Farther along is **Kukui'ula Bay.** Before Hurricane Iwa pummelled this shoreline, the bay was an attractive beach park where many small boats anchored. Today you can still launch a boat here, but the surrounding area is still recovering from the storm. Sailing cruises leave from this harbor in winter, shore fishermen come to try their luck, and scuba divers explore the coral reef offshore, but no swimming is allowed.

In a moment you arrive at the **Spouting Horn.** A large parking area has many stalls marked for tour buses. At the **flea market** here you can pick up trinkets and souvenirs. Don't make the mistake of looking just at the Spouting Horn. Have "big eyes" and look around at the full sweep of this remarkable coastline! The Spouting Horn is a lava tube that extends into the sea with its open mouth on the rocky shore. The wave action causes the spouting phenomenon, which can

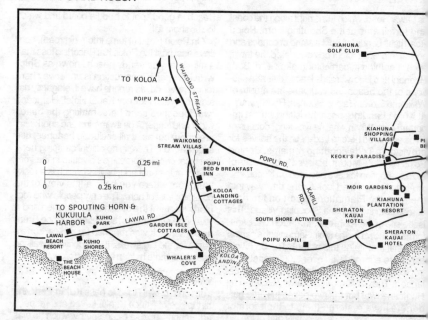

blow spumes quite high, depending on surf conditions. In the old days, they say it shot higher, but that the salt spray damaged the nearby cane fields. Supposedly, the plantation owners had the opening made larger so that the spray wouldn't carry as far. Photographers wishing to catch the Spouting Horn in action have an ally. Just before it shoots, a hole behind the spout makes a large belch, and a second later the spume flies. Be ready to click.

ACCOMMODATIONS

Lodging here is concentrated almost exclusively at Poipu. Most available rooms are in medium- to high-priced condos; however, there are two first- class hotels, a handful of cottages and bed and breakfasts, and a private mountain park.

Inexpensive
Kahili Mountain Park is a gem, *if* you enjoy what it has to offer: it's like a camp for big people. To get there follow Route 50 west about one-half mile past the turnoff to Koloa, and look for the sign pointing mountainside up a cane road. About one mile up is a gate made from an enor-

mous ship's anchor chain. The surroundings are absolutely beautiful, and the only noises, except for singing birds, are from an occasional helicopter flying into Waimea Canyon and the children attending the school on the premises. The high meadow is surrounded by mountains, with the coast visible and Poipu Beach about 15 minutes away. In the middle of the meadow is a cluster of rocks, a mini-replica of the mountains in the background. A spring-fed pond is chilly for swimming, but great for catching bass that make a tasty dinner.

There are two types of accommodations: cabinettes and cabins. The sparsely furnished cabinettes are the more rustic, with bare wood walls, open ceilings, and cement floors. They're in a cluster facing a meadow and each is surrounded by flower beds and trees. Inside these one-room units are double or twin beds; attached is a screened cooking lanai with a sink, running water, a two-burner stove, small refrigerator, and electricity. All dishes and utensils are provided, but you must do all your own housekeeping. Bathrooms and showers are in a central building, while laundry facilities are in a separate building; the relaxing Japanese *ofuro* (hot tub) is

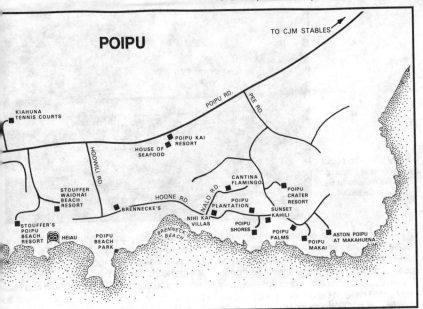

POIPU

TO CJM STABLES

KIAHUNA TENNIS COURTS

POIPU RD.

PEE RD.

HOOWILI RD.

POIPU KAI RESORT

HOUSE OF SEAFOOD

CANTINA FLAMINGO

NALO RD.

POIPU CRATER RESORT

STOUFFER WAIOHAI BEACH RESORT

HOONE RD.

POIPU PLANTATION

SUNSET KAHILI

BRENNECKE'S

NIHI KAI VILLAS

POIPU SHORES

POIPU PALMS

STOUFFER'S POIPU BEACH RESORT

HEIAU

POIPU BEACH PARK

BRENNECKE'S BEACH

POIPU MAKAI

ASTON POIPU AT MAKAHUENA

an added pleasure. Cabinettes rent for $18.50 d, $4 extra person. The cabins are raised wooden-floor houses with a full kitchen, bedrooms with chairs, tables, and dressers, private toilets, outdoor showers, priced reasonably at $32 d, $4 for an extra person. Daily rates only; 9% tax extra. The park has been open for about 20 years and has recently been purchased by the Seventh-day Adventist Church, which runs the school while retaining the rental units. The grounds and the facility are beautifully kept by the original caretakers, Smitty, Ralph, and Veronica. For full information, write Kahili Mountain Park, Box 298, Koloa, Kauai, HI 96756, tel. 742-9921.

Near Koloa Landing are two establishments. At 2749 Hoonani Rd. is **Koloa Landing Cottages.** These modern units, the cheapest in the Poipu area, are in a quiet residential area. Two-bedroom, two-bath units for up to five people are available. Each has a full kitchen with dishwasher, and a color television. Rates are $70 for one or two persons, $80 for three or four, and $5 for an additional person. Studios, also equipped with a kitchen and color TV, run $50 for one or two people. Laundry facilities are on the premises. Reservations are suggested; four nights'

deposit is required, 25% for stays longer than 14 days. Contact Sylvia or Hans at tel. 742-1470, or write to Koloa Landing Cottages, 2827 Poipu Rd., Koloa, Kauai, HI 96756.

Garden Isle Cottages are tucked away at the west end along Hoona Road between Poipu Beach and the Spouting Horn. They sit on the beach surrounded by lush foliage, offering privacy. The cottages are operated by artists Robert and Sharon Flynn, whose original works highlight each of the units. All the studios to two-bedroom apartments are self-contained and fully equipped. Prices range from $45-68 single or double for a studio with bath and lanai but no kitchen (refrigerator, coffee pot, and toaster only), to $130-135 for a two-bedroom, two-bath unit for up to four people; $6 per additional person in any unit. Weekly maid service is provided for the studios. Four nights' deposit is required, 25% if staying over 14 days. Phone 742-6717 any day 9 a.m. to noon, or write Garden Isle Cottages, 2666 Puuholo Rd., Koloa, Kauai, HI 96756.

Bed And Breakfasts

You will find no bedroom closer to the gentle surf than at **Gloria's Spouting Horn Bed and**

For peace and quiet, few places in Poipu can beat the Halemanu Bed and Breakfast Inn.

Breakfast. A remodeled plantation worker's house from the 1940s, its white wood walls make it bright and airy, and antique furniture and tasteful decorations make it feel like home. Three units are downstairs, two upstairs; only one doesn't have an ocean view, but it looks out on a koi pond. Overlooking a rocky beach, its stepped front lanai is about 40 feet from the water. Lie on the grass, swing in a hammock, or sit on the side lanai out of the sun; in the sitting room, TV, a piano, chess, and books on Hawaii are provided for your use. Rooms are not large but they're cozy and comfortable—just right for newlyweds. Each room has a TV, refrigerator, and ceiling fan. Two of the downstairs rooms have a shared bath. No children under 14, no pets, no smoking inside. Room rates, which include a daily continental breakfast, range from $50-80 a night; discounts can be arranged for stays of a week or more; add 20% for the Christmas season. Reservations are necessary. Call 742-6995 and talk with Gloria, or write Gloria's Spouting Horn Bed and Breakfast, 4464 Lawai Beach Rd., Poipu, Kauai, HI 96756. Though it's only a few steps from the Spouting Horn, near the end of this dead-end road, there is little traffic in the evening so it's quiet.

Poipu Bed And Breakfast Inn is also a renovated plantation house, but it's larger and more spacious than Gloria's. However, it doesn't have the fine seaside location. Stained in tropical colors, this wooden house has all the comforts of home, plus antiques, art, and crafts from the island. If you have that child-like affection for

carousel rides, you'll love this place because there are several carousel horses in the house. On either side of the large, central sitting room are the bedrooms. Each has a color TV, refrigerator, and private bath. The sitting room also has a TV, videotapes, books, and games. There is no smoking inside the house; sit out on the large, comfortable lanai or walk in the garden. Children are welcome. Daily room rates, including a continental breakfast, range $65-100. Rooms combined into two-bedroom, two-bath suites are $140 and $155; the entire house can be rented for $250. An extra $10 is charged for a child or additional person; $5 less for single occupancy. For information and reservations call 742-1146 or (800) 552-0095, or write to Poipu Bed and Breakfast Inn, 2720 Hoonani Rd., Koloa, Kauai, HI 96756.

More expensive, yet much more tranquil is **Halemanu Bed And Breakfast Inn.** Perched atop a hill overlooking Waita Reservoir, Halemanu ("House of Birds") Inn offers seclusion in a rustic setting, with nothing here but clean air and sweeping vistas of the ocean, cane fields, and mountains. Wooden buildings from the mid-1880s were moved to this site from other parts of the island and remodeled. There are four bedrooms, a spacious sitting room, and a breezy kitchen. Each room has simple period-piece furniture and a private bath; tastefully appointed, decorations are at a minimum. An English breakfast is provided daily. Room rates are $125 and $150. The first night's deposit is required for any reservation. For information and directions contact Valdemar or Karma Knutsen at 742-1288, or write Halemanu, P.O. Box 729, Koloa, Kauai, HI 96756.

Moderate

Although the prices in Poipu can be a bit higher than elsewhere on Kauai, you get a lot for your money. Over a dozen well-appointed modern condos are lined up along the beach and just off it, with thousands of units available. Most are a variation on the same theme: comfortably furnished, fully equipped, with a tennis court here and there, always a swimming pool, and maid service available. Most require a minimum stay of at least two nights, with discounts for long-term stays. The following condos have been chosen to give you a general idea of what to expect, and because of their locations. Prices average about $140 s or d for a one-bedroom apartment, up to $200 for a two- or three-bedroom, with extra persons ($10) charged only for groups of more than four and six people in the multiple-bedroom units. Rates during high season (mid-December through mid-April) are approximately 10% higher. You can get excellent brochures listing most Poipu area accommodations by writing to **Poipu Beach Resort Association**, Box 730, Koloa, Kauai, HI 96756, tel. 742-7444.

With 110 acres **Poipu Kai Resort** has the largest grounds in the area, one corner of which runs down to the ocean. Set amongst broad gardens, most units look out onto a swimming pool or the tennis courts. Light color schemes, bright and airy rooms, wickerwork furniture, ceiling fans, woven pandanus items that decorate walls and tables, and Hawaiian art prints typify room decorations. Most units have queen-size beds and a walk-in closet with a chest of drawers; bathrooms have a large shower/tub and double sinks. For your convenience, color TVs, an economy washer and dryer unit, iron and ironing board, and a floor safe are in each unit. Daily maid service is provided. Kitchens are fully equipped with electric utilities and sufficient cookware to prepare a full-course meal. Dining rooms adjoin spacious living rooms, which open onto broad lanais.

There are one- and two-bedroom units, in 15 different floor plans. Some are Hawaiian in theme, others in Spanish style with stucco and arched entryways. Modern units show more

glass and chrome, while a few may resemble your own Mainland home.

A handful of three-bedroom homes are also available in the adjacent housing estate. Room rates are (high/low season) $130-150/$115-135 for one-bedroom units, $175-240/$160-210 for two bedrooms and two baths, and $205/$180 for the homes. Facilities on the grounds include nine tennis courts (free for guests), a pro shop (open 8 a.m. to noon and 2 to 6 p.m.) with a resident tennis pro, five swimming pools, one outdoor jacuzzi, numerous barbecue grills. The activity center, open to everyone from 8 a.m. to 1 p.m. and 2:30 to 4 p.m., can arrange everything, from a towel for the beach to a helicopter tour of the island. Across the walkway from the resort office is the House of Seafood, the area's premier seafood restaurant; open only for dinner. For reservations write to Poipu Kai Resort, RR 1, Koloa, Kauai, HI 96756, or call (800) 367-6046, on Kauai 742-6464.

The **Kiahuna Plantation Resort** surrounds the lovely Kiahuna Gardens. Its front office, the main dining room, garden restaurant, and bar have been converted from the old plantation manager's house. The large, bright and airy units featuring cross ventilation through louvered windows, have full bathrooms, kitchens, and enormous lanais. Apartments overlook both the Kiahuna and Moir gardens, and the impeccable grounds of the Sheraton next door. You get a lot for your money at the Kiahuna Plantation, with up to five and seven people at no extra charge in the appropriate units. One-bedroom, one-bath units range from $125-280 ($115-265 during off-season) and two-bedroom, two-bath units go for $210-375 ($190-360, off-season); there is a two-night minimum stay. Housekeeping is available, laundry facilities are on the premises, and there is an activities director. Aside from enjoying the beach, other activities include scuba and surfing lessons, golf at the Kiahuna Golf Course, tennis, and swimming at the resort pool. Write Kiahuna Plantation Resort, RR 1, Box 73, Koloa, Kauai, HI 96756, tel. (800) 367-7052, on Kauai, tel. 742-6411.

The **Poipu Shores** Condo is at the east end of the beach, surrounded by other small condos. They're slightly less expensive than the rest, allowing up to six people at no extra charge for certain two- and three-bedroom units. Try their one-bedroom units for $110; a standard two-bedroom is $150, a deluxe two-bedroom is $160, and a three-bedroom unit runs $165. Rates are $10-20 cheaper off-season. There is a three-night minimum stay. Maid service is provided free every other day. All units are clean, spacious, and airy, with the area's best beaches a short stroll away. Write Poipu Shores, 1775 Pee Rd., Koloa, Kauai, HI 96756, tel. (800) 367-8047, 742-7700 on Kauai.

Poipu Kapili is a three-story condo that looks more like "back East" bungalows. Across the road from the beach, most units have ocean views. The pool is located in the center of the property, and lighted tennis courts are free, racquets and balls provided. The bedrooms are huge, with ceiling fans and wicker headboards; kitchens are spacious with full stoves and dishwashers; each unit has its own private lanai. Rates range from $175-225 for one bedroom and $225-300 for two. Monthly and weekly discounts available. Write Poipu Kapili, 2221 Kapili Rd., Koloa, Kauai, HI 96756, tel. (800) 443-7714, on Kauai tel. 742-6449.

The **Stouffer Poipu Beach Resort** is friendly, with a family atmosphere. On the beach, each room has a lanai overlooking the sea, money-saving kitchenette, color TV, and air-conditioning. There's a large courtyard with pool, barbecue grills, and tennis next door. Inside is a restaurant and cocktail lounge with nightly entertainment. Rates begin at a reasonable $85 single or double for a standard to $140 for a beachfront room, up to $280 for a two-bedroom suite; $10 charge for an additional person. Rooms have recently been renovated. Write Stouffer Poipu Beach Resort, 2251 Poipu Rd., Koloa, Kauai, HI 96756, tel. (800) 426-4122, on Kauai, tel. 742-1681.

Other condos also stretch along this wonderful shore. The smaller condos generally cluster at the east end of the beach; others are near Koloa Landing and Kuhio Park: **Aston Poipu At Makahuena** sits on Makahuena Cliff with the crashing waves below, tel. (800) 922-7866. **Poipu Crater Resort** snuggles inside a small seaside caldera, tel. (800) 367- 8020. **Poipu Makai**, tel. (800) 367-8022; **Poipu Palms**, tel. (800) 367-8022; **Sunset Kahili**, tel. (800) 367-8047, ext. 212; **Poipu Plantation**, tel. 742-6757; and **Nihi Kai Villas**, tel. (800) 367-2363, all run in quick succession across the cliff at the east end of Poipu Beach. On the west end **Grantham Resorts** and **Waikomo Stream Villas**, also managed by Grantham Resorts, are next door to each other along the stream, tel. (800) 325-5701. On the far side of Koloa Landing is **Whaler's Cove**, tel. (800) 367-7040; and at Lawai Beach are **Lawai Beach Resort**, tel. (800) 367-6046, and **Kuhio Shores**, tel. 367-8022.

Expensive

Plenty of expensive condos are available with every luxury imaginable, but the following are Poipu's premier hotels. The Sheraton Kauai is a deluxe hotel, while the Waiohai is world-class super-deluxe.

The original beachfront **Sheraton Kauai** was roughed up by that pesky wind Iwa, but the new wing across the road weathered the storm beautifully and is carrying on in the hospitable Sheraton tradition. The main lobby is soothing and airy, while the buildings are constructed around a freshwater lagoon. Koi ponds hold not only multicolored carp, but small nondescript fish that eat mosquito larvae. The rooms are done with plush tan carpets, with a green color scheme and tasteful prints on the walls. You either get a garden or ocean view, with the vistas and price rising as you move toward the beach. Prices range from a garden view for $160, to a luxury oceanfront $280, additional persons $15-25. There is a wide choice of restaurants, lounges, and snack bars in the hotel, and an excellent Polynesian Revue and dinner on Wed. and Sun. evenings. Write Sheraton Kauai, Poipu Beach, Koloa, Kauai, HI 96756, tel. (800) 325-3535, on Kauai, tel. 742-1661.

The **Stouffer Waiohai Beach Resort** is a first-rate luxury hotel. It's low-rise, with the wings aligned to form a W. No expense was spared to create a full-service hotel geared to your comfort. Each room comes with a refrigerator and stocked wet bar. You simply tick off your drinks and pay when you check out. The bathrooms and dressing rooms are ultra posh. The main hallways, all open and breezy, are adorned with silk hangings, marble, teak, and brass. There are three pools, spas, a health club, and various boutiques. At the beach activities center sailboards, surfboards, and catamarans can be rented, and snorkel equipment is available. For the very genteel, tea is served afternoons in the reading room, which has a superb collection of books on Hawaii. Various workshops and classes deal with Hawaiian arts and culture offered at the hotel, while its **Tamarind Room** provides an elegant dining experience. There's even a small lending library. A few steps toward the beach will tell you of the significance of the site, as there you will find a *heiau* on the lawn under the palm trees. Prices range from $135 for a standard room to $280 for one fronting the beach; suites start at $375 and rise to $1200. An extra person is an additional $20. For information write Stouffer's Waiohai Beach Resort, Box 174, Koloa, Kauai, HI 96756, tel. (800) 468-3571, tel. 742-9511 on Kauai.

FOOD

Inexpensive

A few places in and around Poipu-Koloa serve budget-priced meals, but mostly they sell snacks and takeouts. At the following restaurants and stands, you can fill up for under $5-6 with tasty and nutritious foods.

Koloa Ice House is on the right along Koloa Road as you enter town. It seems more like a deli than a restaurant, but you can have sit-down meals. They feature ice cream, shave ice, and mud pies. Tempting treats also include sandwiches, cheeses, fresh juices, fancy pastries, even lox and bagels! Open daily 10:30 a.m. to 9 p.m., tel. 742-6063. Also as you enter Koloa is **Fez's Pizza**, specializing in gourmet deep-dish pizza, sandwiches, and pasta. Open daily from lunch until 11 p.m., tel. 742-9096. Between these two is **Lappert's Aloha Ice Cream**, whose name is its menu. Next to Sueoka's Market is a small plate-lunch counter that dishes out hearty, wholesome food until early afternoon.

On your right as you approach Poipu is a small complex called the Poipu Plaza. There, at **Taqueria Nortenos**, you can fill up on Mexican fast food for under $4. They make their tacos and burritos a bit differently from most Mexican food stands: a taco is simply rice and beans in a taco shell. If you want the standard cheese, tomato, and lettuce, you have to ask for it at no extra charge. The flavorful food is homemade but precooked, waiting in heating trays. Vegetarian meals are also served. Order at the walkup window and take your tray to one of the picnic tables in the next room; they do takeout as well. Filling, good, but not special, the Taqueria Nortenos is open daily 11 a.m. to 11 p.m., until 5:30 p.m. on Wednesdays. **Brennecke's Snack Bar** is located just off Poipu Beach, below Brennecke's restaurant; open 10:30 a.m. to 4 p.m. The best deals are takeout hot dogs, burgers, and filling plate lunches. For a bit more sophistication, try one of the hotel's poolside grills and cafes for a light lunch.

The best place outside of the hotel restaurants for a breakfast of pastry and coffee is **Garden Isle Bake Shoppe** in the Kiahuna Shopping Village; tel. 742-6070. Every half-hour until 9 a.m. warm fresh pastries are brought out (all for under $1.50)—there should be a morning schedule posted outside. Donuts, Danishes, croissants, cinnamon rolls, breads, and pies are also available, as are coffee, tea, milk, and soft drinks. A short walk from the central Poipu area, sit and bring in the morning leisurely. For lunch or dinner try **Kino's Burgers** for (surprise!) various burgers, plate lunches ($4.25), sandwiches ($3.25), and other assorted dishes, some up to $5-6. Shops selling ice cream, yogurt, cookies, and hot dogs are also here for your midafternoon craving for sweets and snacks.

Moderate

If you want pampering, keep walking past the **Koloa Broiler**, but if you want a good meal at an unbeatable price, drop in. At the Koloa Broiler *you* are the chef. You order top sirloin ($9.45), beef kabob ($8.45), *mahi mahi* ($8.45), barbecued chicken ($8.45), or beef burger ($5.95), and your uncooked selection is brought to your table; you take it to a central grill where a large clock and a poster of cooking times tell you how long your self-made dinner will take. The feeling is like being at a potluck barbecue, and you can't help making friends with the other "chefs." There is a simple salad bar and a huge pot of baked beans from which you can help yourself. Waiters bring fresh-baked bread and a pitcher of ice water. Put your selection on the grill, fix and eat a salad, and it's just about time to turn your meat on the barbecue. Just before it's done, toast some bread on the grill. The small bar attracts a good mixture of tourists and local people in a neighborhood bar-type atmosphere. In fact, the Koloa Broiler Bar is in the next room. After dinner order a cup of coffee or one of their special drinks like Mighty Mai Tai, Passionate Margarita, and Forbidden Fruit. Centrally located on Koloa Road. Open daily for lunch and dinner, cocktails from 11 a.m to 10 p.m., tel. 742-9122.

Mango's Tropical Restaurant and Bar has a much larger selection than Koloa Broiler, but it has a casual atmosphere like the Broiler. Lunch items range from soup and salads to sandwiches, fish, and health foods. The dinner menu is a bit heavier. After an island appetizer, try a full meal of *kiawe*-broiled beef or pork, seafood and fish, or fettuccine, or eat light with a soup or salad. Most lunch items range from $6-10, while dinner prices go up to $17.25. Located near the corner of Koloa and Poipu roads, Mango's is open 11 a.m. to 3 p.m. for lunch, 3 to 5:30 for cocktails, and 5:30 to 10 p.m. for dinner, tel. 742-7377. Dress is casual, there's a children's menu, and takeout is available.

Three restaurants in Poipu specialize in seafood. They are Brennecke's Beach Broiler, Keoki's Paradise, and Tropical Garden Cafe. Located on the terrace of Kiahuna Plantation Resort (once the plantation manager's home) under towering trees and surrounded by lush greenery, the **Tropical Garden Cafe** emanates the most Hawaiian atmosphere. *Pu pu* run $3.95 to $6.95 and just whet your appetite for the meal to come. Try Hawaiian chicken, shrimp tempura, or the pasta special, all $9.95, seafood or vegetable salads, and sandwiches. After dinner have a mouthwatering dessert or walk across the lobby for a tropical drink in the lounge. **Brennecke's Beach Broiler** may have to take a back seat in the elegance department, but its view can't be beat. A large part of the restaurant is an open-air, second-story deck directly across from Poipu Beach Park. Seafood is the dinner specialty but *kiawe*-broiled beef and chicken and pasta are also served. Prices range from $8.95-16.50. All entrees are served with soup, salad, pasta primavera (instead of regular old potatoes), and garlic bread. Salads and sandwiches are served for lunch, and *pu pu* until dinner starts. There is a children's menu for both lunch and dinner. Lunch is from 11:30 a.m. to 3 p.m., happy hour 2 to 4 p.m., and dinner 5 to 10:30 p.m.; tel. 742-7588. Like the other restaurants, **Keoki's Paradise** serves the fresh fish of the day, plus steaks and ribs ($9.95-19.95). Evening specials at $7.95 are served from 5:30

to 6:15, and the house wine list is better than most. Keoki's has tables inside and under the stars next to the fishpond; have dinner by torchlight. Their seafood and taco bar (a good place for conversation for single travelers) is open 4:30 to midnight. Have an island drink before going into dinner, served 5:30 to 10 p.m. Keoki's is at the Kiahuna Shopping Village, tel. 742-7534.

Also at the Kiahuna Shopping Village is **Pizza Bella**, a real happening place with very good food. Black-and-white checkered tile floor, mirrored walls, glass blocks under the counter backlit by pink neon lights, ceiling fans, and lots of potted plants and trees give this eatery a contemporary feel. You can get medium or large combination pizzas from $9.95 to $19.95 on thick whole wheat or white crust. Pizza by the slice is available until 4:30 p.m. for $1.95. If you want something more unusual try one of the gourmet pizzas: quattro formaggi with homemade sauce of olive oil, crushed garlic, and spices, and four kinds of cheese; barbecued chicken with red onion; seafood; Mexican, with meat, beans, cheese, bell pepper, black olives, and jalapenos; or Cajun seafood. Sound great? Hot and cold sandwiches, salads, various pasta dishes, beer, and wine are also served. Pizza Bella has earned a good reputation. There always seem to be a lot of people here, and when it gets crowded the service is not as good as it could be. Open daily 11:30 a.m. to 10 p.m. They also do takeout. Pizzas are delivered in the Poipu-Koloa area, call 742-9571.

If you don't want Mexican pizza but still want south-of-the-border food, try the homey **Cantina Flamingo**, on Nalo Road in amongst the condos—follow the pink flamingos! Sizzling fajitas are the specialty of the house and a real treat; other items on the menu are enchiladas tasca, flamingo burritos, taquitos rancheros, flautas Kauai, appetizers, soups, and salads. Chips and salsa are free. Nothing on the menu is over $9.95. You can't go wrong here. How about deep-fried ice cream for dessert? If not, head to the next room, beyond the wall aquarium, for a cool-down drink at the cantina. There you can choose one of at least nine kinds of fruit margaritas. (Imagine what it's like to peer through the distortion of the aquarium divider after a few of these potent concoctions!) Food is served 3:30 to 9:30 daily, *pu pu* free from 3:30 to 5:30 p.m.;

takeout is available for some menu items. Hanging greenery, pink flamingos (of course!), and piñatas lend this eatery its distinctive touch. Call 742-9505.

You can find other mid-price restaurants in the hotels and clubhouses in Poipu. Sit in the breeze under the trees at seaside at Stouffer's **Waiohai Terrace** or try **Breakers, The Restaurant** at the Sheraton. A bit more informal are the clubhouse restaurant at the Kiahuna Golf Course and the cafe at the Kiahuna Tennis Club.

Expensive

Exquisite dining can be enjoyed at various restaurants that have perfect positions along Poipu's beaches for catching the setting sun. Prices are high, but the surroundings are elegant and the service impeccable.

The Sheraton Kauai's main dining facility, the **Outrigger Room**, features full breakfasts, midday buffets, and intimate dinners. Fridays are special, with seafood buffets. The Outrigger Room has long been known for its Polynesian Revue and the sumptuous feast that accompanies it on Sundays and Wednesdays. The Sheraton also houses the **Naniwa Japanese Restaurant**, serving elegant food next to the fish-filled lagoon, and the **Drum Lounge** for cocktails and dancing.

The **Tamarind Room** in the Waiohai Hotel is *the* most elegant restaurant on Kauai. The European chef does justice to the richly furnished formal dining room. Dining here is designed to be a total experience. No windows in the room, the beauty comes from the surroundings themselves. Enjoy tables set with silver and crystal on linen tablecloths with all meals arriving under silver pineapple domes. Start with papaya bisque in a carved ice bowl, exotically laced with creme de cacao, ginger, and cream. The duck in peppercorn sauce is a good entree, and passion fruit mousse is a fine dessert selection. The waiters are extremely attentive without being obtrusive. Each course is announced, and water glasses are replaced, not refilled. The wine list has almost 400 selections, most vintages coming from California's finest cellars. At meal's end, a cart filled with liqueurs arrives as the final touch. Your bill of at least $100 for two is sweetened with a complimentary box of fine chocolates, along with a red

rose for the lady. Definitely make reservations, tel. 742-9511. Dress code.

The **Plantation Gardens** at the Kiahuna Plantation Resort specializes in seafood. You're put in the mood with a walk through the lovely gardens into the waiting room—the original porch of the old plantation house—filled with parlor furniture and a brass-rail bar with corkscrew stools. The restaurant is richly appointed, and tables are set with crystal and silver. The menu offers appetizers such as escargot for $6.95, light suppers like linguini with baby clams for $12.95, and seafood dinners with a small selection of beef from $16.95. Children's dinners are $7.95. The vegetable selection is included with a basket of hot bread. Open daily. Call 742-1695 for reservations, especially for window tables.

As their names indicate, both the **The House of Seafood** and the **Beach House** specialize in seafoods. Set right on Lawai Beach, the Beach House has the nod for best location, especially for sunsets. Any table in the room is perfect as the large plate-glass windows give everyone a full view down the coast. Dinner is from 5:30 to 10 p.m., and the bar opens at 4:30. Steak and ribs are also served. Most meals are in the $16-25 range, with king crab legs and lobster above that. Call 742-7575 for reservations. The House of Seafood doesn't do as well in the location department, but windows that open onto palm fronds, gardens, and the distant ocean isn't bad. It consistently has the largest selection of fresh fish in the area, generally from eight to 12 varieties, and its dishes are very creative—baked in puff pastry, sautéed with macadamia nut sauce, marinated and broiled, steamed in a ginger sauce to name a few. Ask the waiter for the best choice of the day. Start your meal off with an appetizer, soup, or salad, and finish with a creamy island-fruit dessert or drink. Entrees run $15.50-35; a children's menu is $7-9. Located at Poipu Kai Resort, call 742-6433 for reservations.

Buffets And Brunches

Two Poipu feasts that have become deservedly famous are the Waiohai's Sunday champagne brunch, and the Sheraton's Polynesian Revue. On Sunday mornings, the Waiohai's chefs are set free to create culinary delights, and they outdo themselves. In the hotel's Terrace Room, huge banquet tables are laden with sushi, smoked salmon, seafoods galore, croissants, eggs, beef, chicken, fruits, juices, sweets, and mouthwatering pies. The presentation is spectacular. The chef-artists create vegetable flowers, ice sculptures, and geometric designs. The eyes are as satiated as the appetite. The very popular brunch starts at 10 a.m., but the line forms by 9 a.m. Free coffee helps with the wait, and reservations are not accepted for parties of less than 10 people, tel. 742-9511. This very reasonably priced brunch lasts until 2 p.m., and the lines start getting shorter after 1 p.m., but to do justice to all that's offered, allow yourself at least two hours to dine.

The Sheraton Kauai's Polynesian Revue is held in the Outrigger Room on Sunday and Wednesday evenings, with seating from 6 p.m. Dinner starts at 6:45 p.m., and the show starts at 8 p.m., when you'll be treated to dances and music from throughout the islands of Polynesia. The buffet is as varied as the people of Hawaii with dishes of *sashimi, kalua* pork, standing ribs of beef, Oriental favorites, and a full complement of fruits, salads, and pastries. The price for dinner and show is $42, $24 for children; for reservations call 742-1661. The Waiohai luau, at Stouffer's Waiohai Beach Resort, offers about the same deal. Every Monday at 6 p.m. cocktails are served, followed by a sumptuous luau buffet and the South Seas Reflections of Paradise Revue show. Call 742-9511 for reservations.

Two other notable buffets are the Sunday seafood buffet in the Outrigger Room at the Sheraton Hotel. From 6 to 9 p.m. every Friday, this splash has one of the best selections of food from the sea that you're likely to taste. Enjoy yourself while you watch the sun set. Perhaps less elegant but just as nourishing is the Sunday breakfast buffet at the Beach Club Restaurant at Stouffer's Poipu Beach Resort, tel. 742-1681.

ENTERTAINMENT

If, after a sunset dinner and a lovely stroll along the beach, you find yourself with "dancing feet," or a desire to hear the strains of your favorite tunes, Poipu won't let you down. Many restaurants in the area feature piano music or small combos, often with a Hawaiian flair.

You can ease into the night by listening to classical music in the Waiohai's **Terrace Restaurant**, from 6:30 to 10 p.m. Also, if you've dined in the hotel's Tamarind Lounge, tinkling softly along with the crystal is a piano from 7:30 p.m. to midnight. The Sheraton Kauai's **Drum Lounge** beats with the rhythms of Hawaiian tunes nightly from 5 to 6:30 p.m., while the dance floor sways nightly to live rock and roll from 8 to midnight, and a bit later on weekends. The Poipu Beach Hotel's **Beach Club Lounge** picks up the beat with soft Hawaiian dance music nearly every night. They're always listed in the local free tourist literature. The Sheraton and Waiohai Polynesian Revue shows provide some of the best family entertainment in the area, but the Kiahuna Shopping Village *keiki* hula and Polynesian show, provided free every Thurs. at 5:30 p.m., may be more exciting for kids. For those looking for an after-dinner watering hole aside from the bars and lounges already mentioned, try the sophisticated Winery at the Sheraton for wine or other drinks. More pedestrian is **The Hut** at the Poipu Shores Condominium, a bar that nearly hangs over the cliff to the east of Poipu Beach.

SHOPPING

In Koloa shops and boutiques are strung along the road like flowers on a lei. You can buy everything from original art to beach towels. Jewelry stores, surf shops, gourmet stores, even a specialty shop for sunglasses are just a few. Old Koloa town packs a lot of shopping into a little area. Besides, it's fun just walking the raised sidewalks of what looks very much like an old Western town. Shopping in Poipu is a bit more varied and extensive. The Kiahuna Shopping Village has the largest concentration of shops, but don't forget Poipu Plaza, the hotel arcades, and the Spouting Horn flea market.

Food Stores

In Koloa, a **Big Save Supermarket** is on Koloa Road, at the junction of Waikomo Road. **Sueoka's Store** downtown is a local grocery and produce market. Both carry virtually everything that you'll need for condo cooking. Poipu has the very well-stocked **Kukuiula Store**, at Poipu

Plaza. Open Mon. to Fri. 8 a.m. to 8:30 p.m., Sat. and Sun. 8 a.m. to 6:30 p.m., here you'll find groceries, produce, bakery goods, sundries, and liquor. **Whaler's General Store**, at Kiahuna Shopping Village, and **Brennecke's Mini Mart**, across from Poipu Beach Park, carry fewer items but are closer to most accommodations. If you're staying in a Poipu condo, you may save money by making the trip to a larger market in one of the nearby towns if you're buying large amounts of food.

If you are cooking for yourself, you may want to pick up fresh fruits and vegetables at the farmers' market, every Monday at noon at the baseball field in Koloa.

Boutiques, Gifts, And Apparel

Koloa town has some fine shops along the main street and for a few hundred yards down Poipu Road. Look for: **Crazy Shirts,** selling T-shirts and islandwear; **Koloa Gold,** and **Koloa Jewelry,** offering rings, necklaces, and scrimshaw; **Paradise Clothing** for alohawear; **Progressive Expressions** for surf boards, surf gear, and islandwear; **Kauai One Hour Photo**; and **Kahana Ki'i Art Gallery** if you're looking for quality island art.

In Poipu the **Koloa Gallery** in the Sheraton sells pearls, coral jewelry, and handcrafted tiles by local artists. **Foto Freddie** in the Poipu Plaza does processing and sells film of all kinds. The **Kiahuna Shopping Village** offers unique one-stop shopping in a number of shops, including: **The Ship Store Gallery** for all things nautical, including sea-inspired art; **The Black Pearl Collection** for pearls and jewelry; **Traders of Kauai,** featuring distinctive gifts, children's wear, and alohawear; **Tropical Shirts** for original airbrush designs on shirts; **For Your Eyes Only** for distinctive sunglasses; and **Poipu Fast Photo.**

Activity Centers, Sports, And Recreation

The Koloa-Poipu area has many surf and sailing shops that rent sports equipment, diving gear, and sponsor boating excursions. **South Shore Activities,** tel. 742-6873, offers just about all you'll need for sun and surf in Poipu. They feature all activities, from horseback riding to helicopter tours, rent all kinds of ocean equipment and provide lessons, and rent bicycles and mopeds. Call for exact rental rates and stipula-

tions; open 9 a.m. to 5 p.m. except Sundays. **Brennecke's Ocean Sports,** tel. 742-6570, specializes in snorkel and scuba lessons, and also rents surfboards, boogie boards, and windsurfers, and offers canoe rides and charter boats.

Other one-stop rental and/or tourist information centers are **Poipu Activities Center** at the Poipu Kai Resort, tel. 742-7431; **Aloha Destinations** in Koloa, tel. 742-7548; and the **Visitor Information Center** at Kiahuna Shopping Village, tel. 742-1223. If you're staying at one of the hotels, the hotel activity desk is a good source of information for things to do and can make arrangements for you, while their beach activity booths rent beach equipment.

Fathom Five Divers in Koloa, tel. 742-6991, is a complete diving center offering lessons, certification, and rentals. Other companies that offer similar activities are **Sea Sports Divers,** tel. 742-7288, **Kauai Divers,** tel. 742-1580, and **The Poipu Dive Co.,** tel. 742-7661. There are several possibilities for **surfing.** Nancy Palmer teaches surfing and windsurfing at Lawai Beach for $40 an hour; call 742-6155. Slightly less expensive, world surfing champion Margo Oberg teaches surfing at the Kiahuna Plantation Resort beach; call 742-6411. For the most reasonable prices, surfing is taught by Mike Smith at Lawai Beach; call 742-7051.

Captain Andy's Sailing Adventures runs a catamaran along the lovely, sculpted south coast during winter. Famous are the sunset trips with this jovial seaman; call 822-7833 for information. He also sails the north shore during the summer. **Bass Guides of Kauai,** tel. 822-1405, operates charter tours for two people in 17-foot aluminum boats on the reservoirs near Koloa. All equipment is provided. For deep-sea fishing, call **Sports Fishing Kauai** at 742-7013: four-, six-, and eight-hour trips, tackle provided.

If you're into horseback riding try **CJM Country Stables** for any of their three scheduled rides. The one-hour, easy beach ride leaves at 12:30 p.m. and costs $20. Departing at 2:30 p.m., the two-hour $40 ride is more extensive, wandering along the beach, into the ironwood trees and cane fields, and over sand dunes. Leaving at 8:30 a.m., the beach breakfast ride takes you to a secluded beach girdled by high mountains where you relax while breakfast is prepared for you; $55, three hours. CJM is located two miles past Poipu Kai Resort on the dirt road. For information and reservations, call 742-6096 or 245-6666.

Designed by Robert Trent Jones Jr., the **Kiahuna Golf Club** course is the best on the south shore. This 18-hole, par 70 course is up the road from Kiahuna Shopping Village. Open for play from 7 a.m. until sunset, the pro shop hours are 6:30 a.m. to 6:30 p.m. A round of 18 holes is $55, greens fee and cart fee included; after 2 p.m. in winter and 3 p.m. in summer it's $33; nine holes anytime is $28. Rental clubs are $16 for 18 holes, lessons $30 a half-hour, and $2 for a basket of balls for the driving range. Reservations are requested a week in advance if possible. The club restaurant serves breakfast (from 7 a.m.), lunch (until 3:30 p.m.), and dinner (to 9 p.m. except Mon. and Tues.); happy hour is 3:30 to 5 p.m. For information and tee time reservation, call 742-9595.

If hitting fuzzy yellow balls is more your style, stop by the **Kiahuna Tennis Club**. Courts are open 8 a.m. to 6 p.m., and run $9 a day or $5 an hour. Reservations are requested 24 hours in advance, lessons are given by the resident pro, and a round-robin is held every day at 4 p.m. There are lockers, a pool (8:30 a.m. to 10 p.m.), and a courtside cafe. Call 742-9533 for information or reservations. Other tennis courts open to the public for a fee are at the Waiohai Hotel and Poipu Kai Resort.

SERVICES AND INFORMATION

Medical, Emergency, And Health
At the Koloa Clinic, the **Kauai Medical Group**, tel. 742-1621, offers medical services Mon. to Fri. 8 a.m. to 5 p.m., Sat. 8 a.m. to noon, and after hours by arrangement at tel. 245-6810. This clinic is located by the stream, next to the Koloa Sugar Mill chimney. **Garden Island Medical Group, Inc.**, tel. 742-1677, has an office at 3176 Poipu Rd. in Koloa. Hours are the same as above; for after-hours appointments call 338-9431. The **South Shore Pharmacy**, tel. 742-7511, is next door in the same building; open Mon. to Fri. 9 a.m. to 5 p.m., and Sat. 9 a.m. to 1 p.m., closed Sunday. It not only has a prescrip-

tion service, but first-aid supplies, skin care, and health care products. (If they can't help, the Kauai Mortuary is right next door!) Whether you want to pump iron or have a gentle workout, see **Poipu Beach Fitness Center** at the Waiohai Hotel; tel. 742-9391. They have full workout, massage and spa facilities, and aerobic classes. The cost is $9.50 per day; hours: Mon. to Fri. 7 a.m. to 9 p.m., Sat. 8 a.m. to 7 p.m., Sun. 9 a.m. to 6 p.m.

The **American Educational Institute** has a unique way of mixing business with pleasure. They offer seminars in medical, dental, and legal malpractice, as well as a general course in financial planning and marketing. You put the course to work immediately by learning how to get a tax break on your tuition and vacation expenses. Seminars are held five days a week, from 8 a.m. to noon at the Plantation Garden Restaurant; on-site registration. Call 742-7244 for seminar times, costs, and other information.

General Information
Rental cars are available in Poipu from **Avis**, tel. 742-7633, and **Budget**, tel. 742-9511, through Stouffer's Waiohai Resort; **National**, tel. 742-9311; and from **Hertz**, tel. 742-6011, at the Sheraton Kauai. There are no gas stations in Poipu, but three in Koloa. The **Chevron station**, tel. 742-6868, at the corner of Koloa and Poipu roads, has the most thriving business. Across the street is another Chevron, and at the west edge of town, on the way to Lawai, is a **76 station**.

The **Shoppe Hopper** shuttle runs a regular route stopping at both the Sheraton and Waiohai hotels and Koloa town, on the way to Lihue Airport, Westin Kauai, and Kukui Grove Center. A second shuttle, also stopping at Lihue Airport, Westin Kauai, and Kukui Grove Center, runs east as far as Sheraton Coconut Grove Hotel. The first of five buses leaves Poipu at approximately 8:50 a.m., the last at about 2:50 p.m. From Poipu to Lihue is $5, while the highest fare is only $9. It is best to call first to confirm the routing and times, tel. 332-7272.

The **Koloa Post Office** is along Koloa Road, tel. 742-6565. At the end of Koloa Road is **First Hawaiian Bank**, the area's only bank.

SOUTHWEST KAUAI

The sometimes turbulent but forever enduring love affair between non-Polynesian travelers and the Hawaiian Islands began in southwest Kauai, when Capt. Cook hove to off Waimea Bay and a longboat full of wide-eyed sailors made the beach. Immediately, journals were filled with glowing descriptions of the loveliness of the newly found island and its people, and the liaison has continued unabated ever since.

The **Kaumuali'i Highway** (the "Royal Oven" road—Route 50) heads, wends, leads west from Lihue, with the **Hoary Head Mountains** adding a dash of beauty to the south and Queen Victoria's Profile winking down from the heights. Soon, **Maluhia** ("Peaceful") **Road** branches to the south through an open lei of fragrant eucalyptus trees lining the route to Koloa and Poipu. Quickly come the towns of **Omao, Lawai,** and **Kalaheo**, way stations on the road west. Hereabouts three separate botanical gardens create a living canvas of color in blooms.

After Kalaheo, the road dips south again and passes **Port Allen**, then goes on to **Hanapepe**, at the mouth of the Hanapepe River, whose basin has long been known as one of the best taro lands in the islands. Tiny "sugar towns" and hidden beaches follow until you enter **Waimea**, whose east flank was once dominated by a Russian fort. Captain Cook landed at Waimea in mid-afternoon of January 20, 1778, and a small monument in the town center commemorates the great event. A secondary road leading north from Waimea and another from Kekaha farther west converge inland, then meander along Waimea Canyon, the Pacific's most superlative gorge. **Kekaha**, with its belching sugar stacks, marks the end of civilization, and the hard road gives out just past the **Barking Sands Missile Range**. A "cane road" picks up and carries you to the wide sun-drenched beach of **Polihale** ("Protected Breast"), the end of the line, and the southern extremity of the Na Pali Coast.

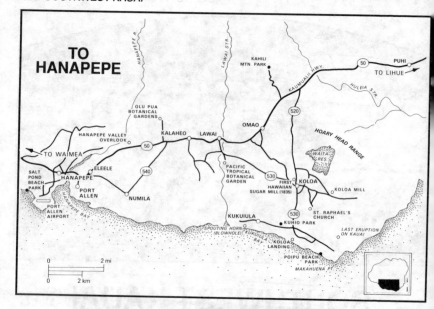

SIGHTS, VILLAGES, AND BEACHES

The **Koloa District** starts just west of the Hoary Head Mountains and ends on the east bank of the Hanapepe River. It mostly incorporates the ancient *ahuapua'a,* a land division shaped like a piece of pie with its pointed end deep in the Alakai Swamp and the broad end along the coast. *Koloa* means "duck," probably named because of the preponderance of ponds throughout the district that attract these water-loving fowl. Its villages are strung along Route 50, except for Koloa and Poipu, which lie south of the main road.

The adjoining *ahuapua'a* is the **Waimea District,** whose broad end continues from Hanapepe until it terminates about midway up the Na Pali Coast. Waimea means "Red Waters," named after the distinctive color of the Waimea River that bleeds from Mt. Waialeale, cutting through Waimea Canyon and depositing the rich red soil at its mouth.

Kauai's southwest underbelly has the best beaches on the island. They're not only lovely to look at, but at most the surf is inviting and cooperative, and they lie in the island's sunbelt.

At some you can camp, at all you can picnic, and a barefoot stroll is easy to come by just about anywhere along these 30 sun-drenched miles. Lodging in the southwest mostly means staying in the Poipu area (see pp. 814-819). Otherwise, avail yourself of facilities in the beach parks (for permits and general information on camping, see pp. 742-747), the Kokee Lodge cabins (see p. 835), the Waimea Plantation Cottages (see p. 833), and at Kahili Mountain Park (see p. 814), which sits at the foot of Mt. Kahili ("Tower of Silence") off Route 50.

PUHI

This village is technically in Lihue District, but since it's the first settlement you pass heading west, it's included here. Two signs tip you off that you're in Puhi, one for **Kauai Community College** and the other for **Queen Victoria's Profile** scenic overlook turnout. It's beneficial to keep abreast of what's happening at the college by reading the local newspaper and free tourist brochures. Oftentimes, workshops and seminars concerning Hawaiian culture, folk medicine, and various crafts are offered; most are open to the general public and free of charge. Queen Victoria's Profile isn't tremendously remarkable, but a definite resemblance to this double-chinned monarch has been fashioned by nature on the ridge of the Hoary Head Mountains to the south. More importantly, look for the **People's Market** across from the college. Here, you can pick up fruit and vegetables, and they offer excellent prices for freshly strung plumeria leis, an inexpensive way to brighten your day. Next door is the brown wooden **Puhi Store**, a small sundries shop that has the feel of bygone days (built in 1917). Also in Puhi is the Grove Farms Co., Inc. office, **Lappert's Ice Cream** shop, **Kauai Sausage** shop, the **Sea Star** store for windsurfing and ocean gear supplies, and a **Shell station**, with gas slightly cheaper than in either Lihue or Koloa.

LAWAI

This village is along Route 50 near the intersection of Route 530, which comes up from Koloa. In times past *ali'i* from throughout the kingdom came here to visit an ancient fishpond in the caldera of an extinct volcano. Legend says that this was the first attempt by Madame Pele to dig herself a fiery home. In town next to the post office are **Matsuura's Store**, and the **Lawai Restaurant** for a filling, reasonably priced breakfast, lunch, or dinner. Down in the valley below town is an abandoned pineapple factory. At the intersection of Routes 50 and 530 is the **Hawaiian Trader** gift shop and **Mustard's Last Stand** snack shop. Mustard's features over a dozen varieties of hot dogs and sausages ($2.95-3.85), sandwiches, and delicious scoops of island-flavor Lappert's ice cream. Picnic tables in a pleasant grove of coconut, breadfruit, orange African tulip, and purple Hong Kong orchid trees sit next to a miniature golf course ($1 as long as you want to play). The store, referred to by locals as "the tourist trap," sells a mind-boggling variety of handcrafted items as well as a large selection of souvenirs, treasures, and tourist junk. Featured are goods made from eel skin and other exotic leathers (chicken feet, python, lizard . . .). Other selections include T-shirts, jewelry, carvings, and an excellent display of shells that

should be featured but are stuck away on a back counter. For $10 or so, you can treat a lot of people back home with purchases from here.

The 186 acres of the **Pacific Tropical Botanical Gardens**—now part of the National Botanical Gardens—constitute the only tropical plant research facility in the country. Its primary aims are to preserve, propagate, and dispense knowledge about tropical plants, and this is becoming increasingly more important as large areas of the world's tropical forests are being destroyed. Chartered by Congress in 1964, this nonprofit botanical and horticultural research and educational organization is supported by private contributions.

Currently, the garden's living collection has over 6,000 species of tropical plants, and about 1,000 individual plants are added to their collection each year. The staggering variety of tropical plants flourishing here ranges from common bamboo to romantic orchids. The gardens are separated into individual sections that include plants of nutritional value, medicinal value, herbs and spices, and rare and endangered species in need of conservation; other groups include plants of special ethnobotanical interest, plants of unexploited potential, tropical fruits, and ornamentals. This garden also maintains two satellite gardens, one in the wetter Limahuli Valley on the north coast of Kauai (1,000 acres), and another at Hana, Maui (120 acres), which contains Piilanihale Heiau, the largest *heiau* in the islands.

These gardens are so enchanting that many visitors regard them as one of the real treats of their trip. The visitors center (with a small museum and gift shop) is open Mon. to Fri. 7:30 a.m. to 4 p.m., and from there you can take a self-guided walking tour of the lawn surrounding the center and its two dozen labeled plants. Organized tours at 9 a.m. and 1 p.m. on weekdays, Saturdays at 9 a.m., and Sundays at 1 p.m. (come at least 15 minutes early) take you by van into the gardens proper, and include a two-mile walk. The tour, led by knowledgeable horticultural staff or a Na Lima Kokua ("Helping Hands") volunteer, lasts for about 2½ hours and costs $15. The weekday tours include a walk into the Allerton Estate, while the weekend tours include only a partial tour of the estate and more time in the gardens. Wear good walking shoes, carry an umbrella if it looks like showers, and bring mosquito repellent! Reservations are needed and should be made four to five days in advance—longer during the Christmas and Thanksgiving seasons. Call the visitors center at 332-7361, or write well in advance to the reservations secretary at Box 340, Lawai, Kauai, HI 96765. Annual membership, from $35 and up, entitles you to many benefits not given casual visitors—write to the membership chairman at the address above.

Adjoining these gardens is the 100-acre Allerton Garden, started by John Allerton, a member of the Mainland cattle-raising family which founded the First National Bank of Chicago. This garden dates from the 1870s when Queen Emma made the first plantings here at one of her summer vacation homes. John Allerton (grandson of the original owner), assisting and carrying on the work of his father Robert, scoured the islands of the South Pacific to bring back their living treasures. Oftentimes, old *kamaaina* families would send cuttings of their rarest plants to be included in the collection. For 20 years, father and son, helped by a host of gardeners, cleared the jungle and planted. The Lawai River runs through the property, and pools and statuary help set the mood. To reach the gardens, go 2.8 miles north from Koloa (or turn onto Route 530 from Route 50 if coming from Lihue). Turn into Hailima Road (the third right if coming from Route 50) and follow the gravel driveway past the Dead End sign to the visitors center.

KALAHEO

This is the first sizable town between Lihue and Hanapepe where you can pick up anything you need to continue west. The area around Kalaheo is springing up with many new housing subdivisions, and large tracts of coffee, tea, and macadamia nut trees are tinting the hillsides in new shades of green. In town are three gas stations, a liquor store, post office, a medical clinic, two restaurants, a Menehune Food Mart, and a new office/ shopping plaza, all along Route 50. Those in condos or with cooking facilities might even stop in at Medeiro's Farm, just up the hill toward Kukui O Lono Park, for fresh poultry and eggs. If you're interested in a pizza or sandwich to go, stop in at **Brick Oven Pizza**. Not a place you come to for elegance, it's a local hangout.

Have a look at the odd paintings of food on the walls. Its reputation is well deserved; this easy-going, family-style eatery with red-and-white-checked tablecloths and linoleum floor offers over a dozen varieties of whole wheat (spread with garlic if you want) or white thin-crust pizzas that go from $5.75 to $17.95. The sandwiches are under $4. Beer, wine, and tossed salads are also available. Open Tues. to Sat. 11 a.m. to 11 p.m., Sun. 12 to 11, closed Monday. If you're heading to Waimea or Polihale, call ahead to have a pizza ready for you, tel. 332-8561. Another option for food is the blue and white **Camp House Grill**, specializing in burgers, Hawaiian-style barbecued chicken, and box lunches, tel. 332-9755. They're located across from the food mart.

Kukui O Lono Park is a personal gift from Walter D. McBryde, the well-known plantation owner who donated the land to the people of Kauai in 1919. Accept it! It's off the beaten track, but definitely worth the trip. Turn left in Kalaheo at the Menehune Food Mart and go up the hill following the road for one mile until you come to (the second) Puu Road (the first Puu Road skirts the hill below the park). A sharp right turn brings you through the large stone and metal-picket gate—gates open 6:30 a.m. and close 6:30 p.m. Inside the park is a golf course and Japanese-style garden. The entrance road leads through a tunnel of eucalyptus trees to a commemorative plaque to McBryde. A flock of green parrots that nest in the tall eucalyptus trees on the grounds can be heard in a symphony of sound in the early evening.

For the gardens and McBryde's memorial, head straight ahead to the parking lot; to get to the clubhouse follow the road to your right for about a half mile. At the clubhouse are a pro shop and snack bar run by a very accommodating man, Mr. Kajitani. He knows a lot about the park and the surrounding area and is willing to chat. A round of golf on the par-72 course is only $5 daily or $50 semi annually; carts and clubs are rented at a similarly reasonable rate. Lessons are $10 a half-hour and must be arranged with the pro.

This isn't a swanky resort, but it's great fun, and as it's set on top of a hill the sweeping views in all directions are striking. Unfortunately, perfectly placed in the center of one of the nicest views is a microwave antenna and dish! Set

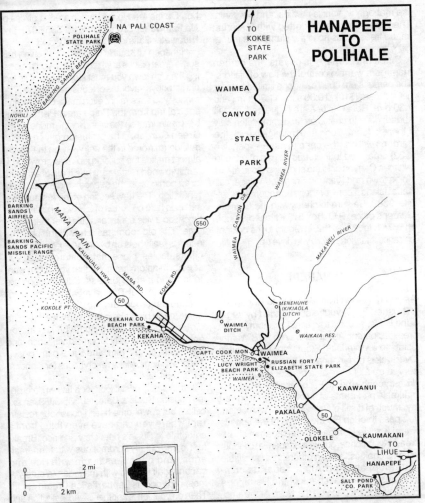

HANAPEPE
TO
POLIHALE

NA PALI COAST

POLIHALE STATE PARK

TO KOKEE STATE PARK

WAIMEA

CANYON

STATE

PARK

BARKING SANDS BEACH

NOHILI PT.

BARKING SANDS AIRFIELD

BARKING SANDS PACIFIC MISSILE RANGE

MANA PLAIN

KAUMUALII HWY

MANA RD

KOKEE RD

550

WAIMEA CANYON DR

WAIMEA RIVER

MAKAWELI RIVER

KOKOLE PT.

50

KEKAHA CO. BEACH PARK

KEKAHA

WAIMEA DITCH

MENEHUHE IKIKIAOLA DITCHI

WAIKAIA RES.

CAPT. COOK MON. WAIMEA

LUCY WRIGHT BEACH PARK

RUSSIAN FORT ELIZABETH STATE PARK

WAIMEA

KAAWANUI

PAKALA

50

OLOKELE

KAUMAKANI

TO LIHUE

HANAPEPE

SALT POND CO. PARK

0 2 mi
0 2 km

amidst a grove of towering trees, the Japanese garden offers peace and tranquility. A short stone bridge crosses a small pool, around which finely sculpted shrubs and small lanterns have been set; unusually, flowers line the adjoining walks. Many weddings are held here. The whole scene is conducive to Zen-like meditation. Enjoy it.

Olu Pua Gardens are the former formal gardens of the Kauai Pineapple Plantation that have been opened to the public. West of Kalaheo, just past the turnoff for Route 540, a sign on the right indicates the private drive to this 12-acre garden and plantation estate. Olu Pua ("Floral Serenity") typifies the atmosphere of these grounds. There are basically four gardens: the *kaukau* garden filled with fruit trees and other edible and exotic plants, a hibiscus garden, a palm garden that lives up to its name, and a jungle garden thick with tropical exotics like mahogany, vanilla orchids, and heliconia. The broad open lawn, dotted with flowering shade trees, leads up to the plantations manager's handsome house.

Since the property is private, the garden managers want to control the flow of visitors. The gardens are open daily for a limited time for guided tours ($10) at 9:30 a.m., 11:30 a.m., and 1:30 p.m. Reservations are requested, so call ahead; drive-in guests are accommodated *only* if there is room. Soon (the manager says), the gardens will only be open to more expensive ($22) organized tour groups as part of a trip to Waimea Canyon or to the shopping stops at Old Koloa town and Kiahuna Shopping Village; call Kauai Island Tours for these arrangements, tel. 245-9382. Be sure to check with the Olu Pua Gardens office, P.O. Box 518 Kalaheo, Kauai, HI 96741, tel. 332-8182, in regard to the present entrance situation *before* you drive up.

HANAPEPE

As you roll along from Kalaheo to Hanapepe ("Crushed Bay") you're surrounded by sugar cane fields, and the traditional economy of the area is apparent. About halfway an HVB Warrior points to an overlook. Stop! **Hanapepe Valley Overlook** is no farther away than your car door, served up as easily as a fast-food snack at a drive-through window. For no effort, you get a remarkable panorama of a classic Hawaiian valley, much of it still planted in taro. In a moment you pass through **Ele'ele** (home of the famous Kauai Kookie Kompany—macadamia shortbread, Kona coffee, guava macadamia, coconut krispies cookies, among others, now available statewide) and **Port Allen**, separate communities on the east bank of the Hanapepe River, with Hanapepe on the west. At the junction for Route 541 leading to Port Allen is the **Ele'ele Shopping Center.** Here, along with various eateries, is a post office, Big Save store, a laundromat, bank, Chevron station, the Bruce Needham helicopter office (tel. 335-3115), and a Garden Isle Medical Group clinic (tel. 335-3107). Serving lunch and dinner (breakfast on Saturday and Sunday, and no dinner on Sunday) and cool island drinks at reasonable prices, the **Past Pub** is one of the only places for fine food on Kauai's southwest coast. Port Allen is a small boat harbor. On the road to the launch are the offices of **Na Pali Coast Cruise Line,** tel. 335-5079, and **Bluewater Sailing,** tel. 335-6440.

Hanapepe ("Kauai's Biggest Little Town") has some great places at which to eat. If you're passing through town you must stop at one of its two old standbys, favorites of tourists and locals. The money you save might even make them worth a special trip from the Poipu area. Perhaps the best restaurant on the island for the money is the **Green Garden.** The profusion of vegetation outside (mirrored in the entryway on the inside) almost makes the building look overgrown. This family-owned restaurant has it all: great food, large portions, aloha service, and an excellent reputation. The new section of the restaurant is set up to hold busloads of tourists who arrive for lunch; go a little earlier or a little later than noontime. The old room has a few plants, but the name is really held up by the decor; green walls, chairs, tables, place mats, bathrooms. If you see anything on the menu that you might want to mix and match, just ask. Substitutions are cheerfully made! The full meal selections, including beverage, are mostly under $7. The homemade pies alone are worth the trip. The Green Garden is along Route 50 just as you enter town, open daily for breakfast, lunch, and dinner, 7 a.m. to 2 p.m. and 5 to 9 p.m., closed Tues. evenings. Make reservations for dinner at tel. 335-5422.

Immediately past it look for a tiny white building housing **Susie's Cafe,** tel. 335-3989, an excellent but downhome health-conscious restaurant where you can have everything from a smoothie to Susie's beef stew and rice. Breakfast is particularly scrumptious with farm-fresh eggs, and pancakes made with rice and bananas, all topped with macadamia nuts. Almost next door is **Lappert's Ice Cream** stand. Then on your left is another island institution and oddity, the combination **Conrad's** and **Wong's** restaurants. Although they occupy the same building, they are different restaurants with different menus. The one giant dining room accommodates both restaurants in an atmosphere reminiscent of a small-town banquet hall that caters to local bowling leagues. Both are very reasonably priced, but they too are a favorite with the tour buses, and can be crowded. When you go in to the cafeteria-style dining room, you're handed two separate menus. Feel free to order from each. Conrad's (formerly Mike's—his dad) has standard American fare with a Hawaiian twist. Most sandwiches are under $4, main course dinners under $6. Wong's specialties are Chinese and Japanese dishes, all under $8, with many around $5. The service is friendly, the portions large, but the cooking is mediocre, except for the pies. You won't complain, but you won't be impressed either. Open daily, for breakfast, lunch, and dinner, closed after 2 p.m. Mon.; tel. 335-5066. If that isn't enough, next door is **Omoide's Deli and Bakery**, and across the street, in a russet-colored building, is **Kauai Kitchen**, a local coffee shop. Both are open early in the morning for breakfast.

In the center of town, keep a lookout for the **Soto Zen Temple Zenshuji** on your left. It's quite large and interesting to people who haven't visited a temple before. Also along the highway in town are the Westside Pharmacy, tel. 335-5342; a library; **Pacific Aviation Inter-island Helicopters** office, tel. 335-5009; **Bali Hai Helicopter** offices, tel. 335-3166; the **Tradewinds glider** office, tel. 335-5086; **Mariko** mini mart; and several gas stations. At the eastern approach to town, as you turn off the highway, look up to your right and notice an entire hillside of bougainvilleas, ablaze with a multicolored patchwork of blossoms in early winter. Following this road into the center of the old town you pass by both the **James Hoyle Gallery** and **Lele Aka Studio Gallery**, a small white church that has a farmers' market on its lawn every Thurs. from 4 to 6 p.m., a bank, small arts and crafts shops, and food markets. While in town, stop at the **Shimonishi Orchid** nursery for a real treat. Here are hundreds of varieties of this tropical favorite, *the* place on the island to buy and ask about this flower. As you leave town, a small gift shop called **The Station** sits on the right. A friendly young woman sells yarn, crochet material, and Hawaiian-style needlepoint designs.

On the western outskirts of town, just past The Station, a sign points *makai* down Route 543 to the Kauai Humane Society and Hanapepe Refuse Disposal. Follow the sign to a small Japanese cemetery (there are several others nearby) where an HVB Warrior points to **Salt Pond County Beach Park**, the best beach and windsurfing spot on this end of the island. This beach is at the west end of the Port Allen Airport runway, once the major airport for the island but

now servicing only a few helicopters and the glider company. The local people from around Hanapepe enjoy this popular beach park. It was heavily damaged by Hurricane Iwa, and has recently undergone an extensive facelift, with pavilions, tables, toilets, showers, and camping (with county permit). The swimming and snorkeling are excellent, and a natural breakwater in front of the lifeguard makes a pool safe for tots. Surfers enjoy the breaks here, and a constant gentle breeze makes the area popular with windsurfers.

Along the road to Salt Pond Beach, you pass the actual salt ponds, evaporative basins cut into the red earth that have been used for hundreds of years. The sea salt here is still harvested but isn't considered *pure* enough for commercial use, but the local people know better. They make and harvest the salt in the spring and summer, and because of its so-called *impurities* that add a special flavor, it is a sought-after commodity and an appreciated gift for family and friends. If you see salt in the basins, it belongs to someone, but there won't be any hassles if you take a *small* pinch. Don't scrape it up with your fingers because the sharp crystals can cut you, and you'll rub salt into your own wounds in the process.

WAIMEA

The road hugs the coast after Hanapepe bypassing a series of still-working sugar towns until you arrive in Waimea. **Kaumakani**, a small cluster of homes with a few dirt lanes, has a post office, thrifty mart, and the **Niihau Helicopter** office, tel. 335-3500. Put to use mostly for medical emergencies and air-lifting supplies to the island, the helicopter is scheduled for occasional tours to Niihau. This company has the exclusive landing rights on Niihau, and it's the only way to get there without a special invitation. **Olokele** is another sugar town, and when you get here take a fast drive through, drawing your own conclusions on the quality of life. You'll find small homes that are kept up with obvious pride. The road dips down to the sugar refinery, the focus of the town, while the main street is lined with quaint lampposts lending an air of last century.

Next is **Pakala**, noted more for its surfing beach than for the town itself. At mile marker

#21, a bunch of cars pulled off the road means "surf's up." Follow the pathway to try the waves yourself, or just to watch the show. Popular with the surfers, this beach is not an official park. Walk down past the bridge to a well-worn pathway leading through a field. In a few minutes is the beach, a 500-yard-long horseshoe of white sand. Off to the left is a rocky promontory popular with local fishermen. The swimming is fair, and the reef provides good snorkeling, but the real go is the surf. The beach is also nicknamed "Infinity" because the waves last so long. They come rolling in graceful arcs to spill upon the beach, then recede in a regular, hypnotic pattern, causing the next wave to break and roll perfectly. Sunset is a wonderful time to come here for a romantic evening picnic.

The remains of the Russian fort still guard the eastern entrance to Waimea town. Turn left at the sign for **Fort Elizabeth State Park** and the crumbling foundation is right there. The fort, shaped like a six-pointed star, dates from 1817 when a German doctor, George Anton Scheffer, built it in the name of Czar Nicholas of Russia, naming it after the potentate's daughter. Scheffer, a self-styled adventurer and one-time Moscow policeman, saw great potential in the domination of Hawaii, and built other forts in Honolulu and along the Waioli River, which empties into Hanalei Bay on Kauai's north shore. Due to political maneuverings with other European nations, Czar Nicholas never warmed to Scheffer's enterprises and withdrew official support. For a time, Kauai's King Kaumuali'i continued to fly the Russian flag, perhaps in a subtle attempt to play one foreign power against another. The fort fell into disrepair and was virtually dismantled in 1864, when 38 guns of various sizes were removed. The stout walls, once 30 feet thick, are now mere rubble, humbled by time-encircling nondescript underbrush. However, if you climb onto the ramparts you'll still get a commanding view of Waimea Bay.

Just after you cross the Waimea River signs point to **Lucy Wright Beach County Park**, a five-acre park popular with the local folk. There's a picnic area, restrooms, showers, playground, and tent camping (with county permit). Pick up supplies in Waimea. The park is situated around the mouth of the river, which makes the water a bit murky. The swimming is fair if the water is clear, and the surfing is decent around the river mouth. A few hundred feet to the west of this park is a recreational pier. Good for fishing, reach it by walking along the beach or down a back street behind the Waimea Library.

Captain Cook's achievements were surely more deserving than the uninspiring commemorative markers around Waimea indicate. Whether you revere him as a great explorer or denigrate him as an opportunistic despoiler, his achievements in mapping the great Pacific were unparalleled, and changed the course of history. In his memory are **Captain Cook's Landing**, a modest marker near Lucy Wright Beach Park, commemorating his "discovery" of the Sandwich Islands at 3:30 p.m. on September 20, 1778, and **Captain Cook's Monument**, on a little median strip in downtown Waimea.

If you're fascinated by Kauai's half-legendary little people, you might want to take a look at the **Menehune Ditch**, a stone wall encasing an aqueduct curiously built in a fashion unused and apparently unknown to the Polynesian settlers of Hawaii. The oral tradition states that the ditch was built by order of Ola, high chief of Waimea, and that he paid his little workers in *opae*, a tiny shrimp that was their staple. On payday, they supposedly sent up such a great cheer that they were heard on Oahu. Today, the work is greatly reduced, as many of the distinctively hand-hewn boulders have been removed for use in buildings around the island, especially in the Protestant church in Waimea. Some steadfastly maintain that the Menehune never existed, but a census taken in the 1820s, at the request of capable King Kaumuali'i, officially listed 65 persons living in Wainiha Valley as Menehune!

Waimea itself has little of interest as far as sights go, but there is an unescorted walking tour that introduces you to the major historical sites in town. Ask at the library (tel. 338-1738) for the free map and description of each site. The walk should take about 1½ hours. Waimea does have some reasonably good restaurants and shopping. Along the main road, facing Capt. Cook's statue, is **Ishihara's Market**, where you'll find all the necessities. Down the street is **Wrangler's Restaurant**, a rustic place for Mexican food, fish, burgers, and plate lunches. In an adjacent building is a shop that sells donuts, coffee, sandwiches, and shave ice. Kitty-corner across the intersection is the police station; the street running inland from there goes to the Menehune Ditch. Across the street is a well-stocked **Big Save Supermarket.** Their lunch counter, believe it or not, features terrific local dishes at very reasonable prices. Next door to that is **Menehune Saimin**, a great little restaurant operated by local ladies, selling steaming bowls of homemade Oriental soups for "can't go wrong" prices. In town are three gas stations, a liquor store, laundromat, photography supply shop, bank, discount clothing shop, **Kiyoki's Art Gallery**, and **West Side Sporting Goods.** A **Dairy Queen** is at the west end of town, and one-half mile up Waimea Canyon Road is **Kauai Veterans Memorial Hospital**.

Aside from a few private rental homes, **Waimea Plantation Cottages** is virtually the only place to stay along the south shore west of Poipu, and what a place it is. Owned and operated by the Kikiaola Land Company, Ltd., this oceanfront property is set in a grove of over 750 coconut and a few huge banyan trees at the west end of Waimea. Not giving in to big bucks or modern resort development, worker and supervisor cottages and the manager's house from the former Waimea sugar plantation have been renovated and preserved, and the grounds maintained in an old-style way. Here you are treated to a touch from the past. While some modern amenities such as full kitchens, bathrooms, and color cable TVs have been added for comfort and convenience, an effort has been made to keep each unit as much in the original state as possible (1920-'30s period); period furniture and other furnishings add to the feel of that bygone era. Most buildings have bare wood floors and painted wood walls. Nearly all have ceiling fans and lanais. Weekly housekeeping and linen service are included. Complimentary washers and dryers are available on the premises. A swimming pool in the 1930s style has been constructed on the lawn, and a small oceanfront restaurant is being planned, which will be a perfect place for a sunset dinner. In accordance with this philosophy of preservation, some long-time employees of the plantation (no longer a functioning entity) still are offered low- or no-rent cottages behind the company office rather than being turned out to develop the land for profit.

Presently, there are 33 units. The one-, two-, and three-bedroom cottages run $60-120 a night, and the director's three-bedroom house is $150; weekly rates are available. The five-bedroom manager's house is only rented by the week, for $2100. The average length of stay is over 10 days, with a 35% return rate; make your reservations several months in advance. Low-key and unpretentious, this institution aims to please and offers a chance for seclusion and serenity. What better way than to relax and read a favorite book on your breezy lanai, watch the sunset through the coconut grove, or take a moonlight stroll along the gently lapping shore? Waimea Plantation Cottages also manages a six-bedroom house and a one-bedroom cottage on the beach in Hanalei. If you are going to the north coast and need a place to stay, check with the office here about these two accommodations. The manager, Mr. Raymond Blouin, or either of the very helpful office workers can provide additional information. Call (800) 992-4632, or 338-1625 on Kauai, Mon. to Fri. 8 to 5, or write Waimea Plantation Cottages, P.O. Box 367, Waimea, Kauai, HI 96796.

WAIMEA CANYON AND KOKEE STATE PARK

The "Grand Canyon of the Pacific" is an unforgettable part of your trip, and you shouldn't miss it for any reason. Waimea Canyon Drive begins on the outskirts of Waimea, heading inland past suger cane fields for six miles, where it joins Kokee Road coming up from Kekaha. Either route is worthwhile, and you can catch both by going in one leg and coming out the other. In about a mile you enter **Waimea Canyon State Park**, a ridgetop park that flanks the road to Kokee. This serpentine route runs along a good but narrow road into Kauai's cool interior with plenty of fascinating vistas and turnouts along the way. The passenger, going up, gets the better view. Behind you, the coastal towns and their tall refinery stacks fade into the pale blue sea, while the cultivated fields are a study of green on green.

Ever climbing, you feel as though you're entering a mountain fortress. The canyon yawns, devouring clouds washed down by draughts of sunlight. The colors are diffused, blended strata of grays, royal purples, vibrant reds, russets, jet blacks, and schoolgirl pink. You reach the thrilling spine, obviously different, where the trees on

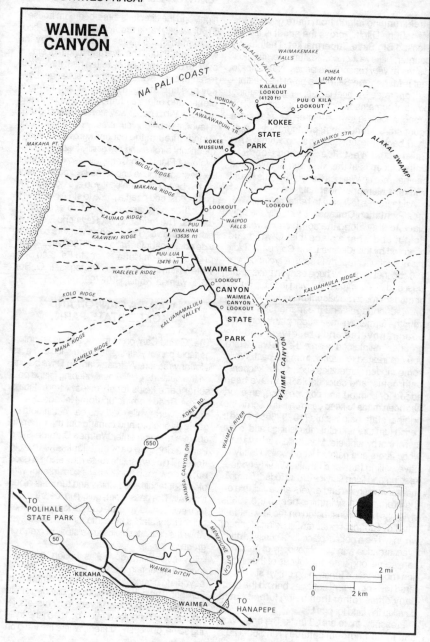

the red bare earth are gnarled and twisted. The road becomes a roller coaster whipping you past raw beauty, immense and powerful. Drink deeply, contemplate, and move on into the clouds at the 2,000-foot level where the trees get larger again. As you climb, every lookout demands a photo. At **Waimea Canyon Overlook** (3,400 feet) you have the most expansive view of the canyon across to valleys that slice down from the lofty peak. From here it's obvious why this canyon was given its nickname. Keep a watch out for soaring birds, mountain goats, and low-flying helicopters.

From **Po'okapele Overlook**, Waipoo Waterfall is seen tumbling forcefully off the hanging valley across the canyon. A small rest area with a few picnic tables lies across the road. **Po'ohinahina Overlook** (3,500 feet) provides the best views down the canyon toward the ocean. Walk up a short trail behind the restrooms and you have a good view of Niihau adrift in the ocean to the west. A little farther along is a NASA space flight and tracking station, and at the same turnoff is a track that leads into the valley, from which several trails start. From here, Kokee's trails come one after another.

After passing Po'ohinahina Overlook you enter **Kokee State Park**, soon reaching park headquarters, then the **Kokee Natural History Museum** and the **Kokee Lodge**. At the headquarters, helpful staff (when duties allow them to be present) can provide you with a map of walking trails in the park and some information about the region's flora and fauna. Open 10 a.m. to 4 p.m. daily, the museum is a better place for maps and additional information about the mountain environment of Kauai. Inside are displays of native birds, descriptions of plants and animals found in the park, books on Kauai and Hawaii, detailed hiking maps of the park and the surrounding national forests, and a relief map of the island. The lodge is open 8:30 a.m. to 5:30 p.m. Sun. to Thurs., until 10 p.m. on Fri. and Saturday. Its restaurant serves a full breakfast and lunch daily from 8:30 a.m. to 3:30 p.m., dinner on Fri. and Sat. evenings only from 6 to 9 p.m. The cool weather calls especially for a slice of homemade pie and a steaming pot of coffee. Drinks can be bought at the lounge. Prices for food and drink are on the expensive side, but after all, everything has to be trucked up the mountain.

The next nearest restaurant or bar is 15 miles down the road at Kekaha. Also in the lodge is a shop that sells postcards, T-shirts, snacks, sundries, and souvenirs.

Temperatures here are several degrees cooler than along the coast, and can be positively chilly at night, so bring a sweater or jacket. Wild boar hunting and trout fishing are permitted within the park at certain times of the year, but check with the Department of Land and Natural Resources in Lihue (third floor of the state office building) about licenses, limits, season, etc., *before* coming up the mountain. To see wildlife anywhere in the park, it's best early in the morning or late in the afternoon when they are out to feed.

Two spectacular lookouts await you farther up the road. At **Kalalau Valley Overlook** (4,000 feet) walk a minute and pray that the clouds are cooperative, allowing lasers of sunlight to illuminate the hump-backed, green-cloaked mountains, silent and tortured, plummeting straight down to the roiling sea far, far below. **Puu O Kila Lookout** (4,176 feet) is the end of the road. From here you not only get a wonderful view into the Kalalau Valley, the widest and largest valley along the Na Pali Coast, but also up across the Alakai Swamp to Mt. Waialeale—if the clouds are cooperative. One trail starts here and runs along an abandoned road construction project to Pihea, from where others run out to Alealau Point, high above the ocean and in to Alakai Swamp.

Tent camping is allowed at **Kokee State Park** with a permit, and the **Kokee Lodge** also provides a dozen self-contained cabins, furnished with stoves, refrigerators, hot showers, cooking and eating utensils, and bedding; wood is available for fireplaces. The cabins cost $35 or $45 per night (five-night maximum) and vary from one large room for three, to two-bedroom units that sleep seven. The cabins are tough to get on holidays, in trout-fishing season (August to September), and during the wild plum harvest in June and July. For reservations write well in advance to Kokee Lodge, Box 819, Waimea, Kauai, HI 96796, tel. 335-6061. Please include a SASE and specify number of people and dates requested. A $35 deposit is required for confirmation of reservation. Check-in is 2 p.m., check-out at noon.

Note: For a full description of **Kokee State Park Trails** see pp. 745-746 in the chapter Introduction "Camping and Hiking."

Kekaha

You enter Kekaha passing the homes of plantation workers trimmed in neat green lawns and shaded from the baking sun by palm and mango trees. Japanese gardens peek from behind fences. Along the main street are two gas stations—your last chance if heading west or up Waimea Canyon—plus **Kinipopo's Store, Kauai's Hidden Treasures** shop, **Traveler's Den** restaurant, and the post office. Cane trucks, like drones returning to the hive, carry their burdens into the ever-hungry jaws of the Kekaha Sugar Company, whose smokestack owns the skyline. Notice the sweet molasses smell in the air. The turnoff for Route 550 leading to Waimea Canyon, and Kokee 15 miles away, branches off in the center of town. At this intersection are a few other shops and **Menehune Food Market,** your last chance for snacks and sundries. Every Saturday at noon there is a farmers' market where you can pick up fresh produce. Ask around for the location. Kekaha isn't large, so it shouldn't be hard to navigate.

Route 50 proceeds along the coast. When still in town, you pass **H.P. Faye Park.** Then the golden sands of **Kekaha Beach Park** stretch for miles, widening as you head west, with pulloffs and shade-tree clusters now and again. The sun always shines, and the swimming and surfing are excellent. Pick your spot anywhere along the beach. The area is good for swimming and snorkeling during calm weather, and fair for surfing, although the reef can be quite shallow in spots. In town, across the road from H.P. Faye Park, are Kekaha Beach Park's pavilion, tables, toilets, and grills. Since there's no tourist development in the area, it's generally quite empty.

The sea sparkles, and the land flattens wide and long, with green cane billowing all around. Dry gulches and red buttes form an impromptu inland wall. In six miles are the gates of **Barking Sands Airfield and Pacific Missile Range.** Here howl the dogs of war, leashed but on guard. You can use its beach and even arrange to camp for a few days if maneuvers are not in progress by calling 335-4111. They're hot, shadeless, and pounded by unfriendly surf, but they afford the best view of **Niihau,** a purple Rorschach's blot on the horizon, and the closest that you're ever likely to get to the "Forbidden Island." The beach has the largest sand dunes on the island, due to the ocean's shallowness between the two islands. Supposedly, if you slide down the dunes, made from a mixture of sand and ground coral, the friction will cause a sound like a barking dog.

Route 50 curves to the right after you pass the missile range, and an HVB Warrior points left to **Polihale State Park.** You go in via five miles of well-graded dirt cane road. The earth is a definite buff color here, unlike the deep red that predominates throughout the rest of the island. At a stop sign at a crossroads, you're pointed to Polihale ("Home of the Spirits"). You can day-trip to soak up the sights and you'll find pavilions, showers, toilets, and grills. Both RV and tent camping are allowed with a state park permit. The camping area is on the top of the dune on the left before you get to the pavilions. There are generally no hassles, but the rangers do come around, and you should have a permit because it's a long way back to Lihue to get one.

From the parking area at the chain gate walk over the dune and down to the beach. The swimming can be dangerous but the hiking is grand. The powdery white-sand beach stretches for nearly three miles, pushing up against the Na Pali cliffs to the north and meeting the Mana Plain to the east. Literally at the end of the road, this beach takes you away from the crowds but you'll hardly ever be all by yourself. Here the cliffs come down to the sea, brawny and rugged with the Na Pali Coast beginning around the far bend. Where the cliffs meet the sea is the ruin of **Polihale Heiau.** This is a powerful spot, where the souls of the dead made their leap from land into infinity. The priests of this temple chanted special prayers to speed them on their way, as the waters of life flowed from a sacred spring in the mountainside.

NIIHAU

The only thing forbidding about Niihau is its nickname, "The Forbidden Island." Ironically, it's one of the last real havens of peace, tranquility, and tradition left on the face of the Earth. This privately owned island, operating as one large cattle and sheep ranch, is manned by the last remaining pure Hawaiians in the state. To go there, you must have a personal invitation by the owners or one of the residents. Some people find this situation strange, but it would be no stranger than walking up to an Iowa farmhouse unannounced and expecting to be invited in to dinner. The islanders are free to come and go as they wish, and are given the security of knowing that the last real Hawaiian place is not going to be engulfed by the modern world. Niihau is a reservation, but a *free-will* reservation, that anyone who has felt the world too much with them could easily envy.

OVERVIEW

The Land And Climate
The 17-mile **Kaulakahi Channel** separates Niihau from the western tip of Kauai. The island's maximum dimensions are 18 miles long by six miles wide, with a total area of 73 square miles. The highest point on the island, **Paniau** (1,281 feet), lies on the east-central coast. There are no port facilities on the island, but the occasional boats put in at **Kii** and **Lehua landings**, both on the northern tip. Since Niihau is so low and lies in the rainshadow of Kauai, it receives only 30 inches of precipitation per year, making it rather arid. Oddly enough, low-lying basins, eroded from the single shield volcano that made the island, act like a catchment system. In them are the state's largest naturally occurring lakes, **Halalii** and the slightly larger 182-acre **Lake Halulu.** Two uninhabited islets, **Lehua**, just off the northern tip and exceptional for scuba diving, and **Kaula**, a few miles off the southern tip, each barely cover one-half square mile and join Niihau as part of Kauai County.

HISTORY

After the goddess Papa returned from Tahiti and discovered that her husband, Wakea, was playing around, she left him. The great Wakea did some squirming, and after these island-parents reconciled, Papa became pregnant and gave

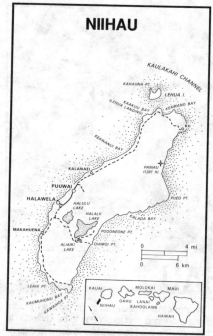

NIIHAU

birth to Kauai. According to the creation chants found in *The Kumulipo*, Niihau popped out as the afterbirth, along with Lehua and Kaula, the last of the low reef islands.

Niihau was never a very populous island because of the relatively poor soil, so the islanders had to rely on trade with nearby Kauai for many necessities, including poi. Luckily, the fishing grounds off the island's coastal waters are the richest in the area, and Niihauans could always trade fish. The islanders became famous for Niihau mats, a good trade item, made from *makaloa*, a sedge that's plentiful on the island. Craftsmen also fashioned *ipu pawehe*, a geometrically designed gourd highly prized in the old days. When Capt. Cook arrived and wished to provision his ships, he remarked that the Niihau natives were much more eager to trade than those on Kauai, and he secured potatoes and yams that seemed to be in abundant supply.

Kamehameha IV Sells

Along with Kauai, Niihau became part of the kingdom under Kamehameha. It passed down

to his successors, and in the 1860s, Kamehameha IV sold it to the Robinson family for $10,000. This Scottish family, which came to Hawaii via New Zealand, has been the sole proprietor of the island ever since, although they now live on Kauai. They began a sheep and cattle ranch, hiring the island's natives as workers. No one can say exactly why, but it's evident that this family felt a great sense of responsibility and purpose. Tradition passed down over the years dictated that islanders could live on Niihau as long as they pleased, but that visitors were not welcome without a personal invitation. With the native Hawaiian population decimated, the Robinsons felt that these proud people should have at least one place to call theirs and theirs alone. To keep the race pure, male visitors to the island were generally asked to leave by sundown.

Niihau Invaded

During WW II, Niihau was the only island of Hawaii to be occupied by the Japanese. A Zero pilot, after hitting Pearl Harbor, developed engine trouble and had to ditch on Niihau. At first the islanders took him prisoner, but he somehow managed to escape and commandeer the machine guns from his plane. He terrorized the island, and the residents headed for the hills. One old woman who refused to leave was like a Hawaiian Barbara Fritchie. She told the Japanese to shoot her if he wished, but to please stop making a nuisance of himself; it wasn't nice! He would have saved himself a lot of trouble if he had only listened. Fed up with hiding, one huge *kanaka*, Benehakaka Kanahele, decided to approach the pilot with aloha. He was convinced the intruder would see the error of his ways. This latter-day samurai shot Mr. Kanahele for his trouble. Ben persisted and was shot again. An expression of pain, disgust, and disbelief at the stranger's poor manners spread across Ben's face, but still he tried pleading with the Japanese, who shot him for the third time. Ben had had enough, and grabbed the astonished pilot and flung him headlong against a wall, cracking his skull and killing him instantly. This incident gave rise to two wartime ditties. One went, "Don't shoot a Hawaiian three times or you'll make him mad." The other, a song, was titled, "You can't conquer Niihau, No how." Mr. Kanahele lived out his life on Niihau, and died in the 1960s.

Life Today

The only reliable connection that the islanders have with the outside world is a WW II-vintage landing craft that they use to bring in supplies from Kauai and a new Agusta helicopter used for medical emergencies, supplies, and aerial tours. Until recently homing pigeons were used to send messages, but they have been replaced by two-way radios. There's no communal electricity on the island, but people do have generators to power refrigerators and TVs. Transistor radios are very popular, and most people get around either on horseback or in pickup trucks. The population numbers around 230 people, 95% of whom are Hawaiian, with the other 5% being Japanese. There is one elementary school, in which English is used, but most people speak Hawaiian at home. The children go off to Kauai for high school, but after they get a taste of what the world at large has to offer, a surprisingly large number return to Niihau.

After Hurricane Iwa battered the island a few years back, the state was very eager to offer aid. The people of Niihau thanked them for their concern, but told them not to bother, that they would take care of things themselves. Niihau was the only island to reject statehood in the plebiscite of 1959. In November 1988, when a group of environmentally conscious Kauaians took a boat to Niihau to try to clear some of the beaches of the floating sea junk that had washed up on shore, the Niihauans felt that the island was being trespassed—they didn't want such help in any case—and a few shots were fired, as if to say "back off." Still unsettled, the controversy focuses on the question of who owns the beach—all beaches in Hawaii are open to free access, yet the whole island of Niihau is privately owned.

Today, some people accuse the Robinson family of being greedy barons of a medieval fiefdom, holding the Niihauans as virtual slaves. This idea is utter nonsense. Besides the fact that the islanders have an open door, the Robinsons would make immeasurably more money selling the island off to resort developers than running it as a livestock ranch. As if the spirit of old Hawaii was trying to send a sign, it's interesting that Niihau's official lei is fashioned from the *pupu,* a rare shell found only on the island's beaches, and its island-color is white, the universal symbol of purity.

Niihau Shellwork

The finest shellwork made in Hawaii comes from Niihau, in a tradition passed down over the generations. The shells themselves—tiny and very rare *kahelelani* and *kamoa*—are abundant only in the deep waters off the windward coast. Sometimes, the tides and winds are just right and they are deposited on Niihau's beaches, but rarely more than three times per year. Islanders then stop everything and head for the shore to painstakingly collect them. The shells are sorted according to size and color, and only the finest are kept: 80% are discarded. The most prized are so tiny that a dozen fit on a thumbnail. Colors are white, yellow, blue, and the very rare gold. The best-quality shells are free from chips or cracks and, after sorting, the shells are drilled. Various pieces of jewelry are fashioned, but the traditional pieces are necklaces and leis. These can be short single-strand chokers, or the lovely *pikake* pattern, a heavy double strand. The *rice* motif is always popular, and these are usually multistranded with the main shells clipped on the ends with various colored shells strung in as highlights.

A necklace takes long painstaking hours, with every shell connected by intricate and minute knots. Usually the women of Niihau do this work. Clasps are made from cowrie shells found only on Niihau. No two necklaces are exactly alike. They sell by the inch, and the pure white and golden ones are very expensive, most handed down as priceless heirlooms. Although Niihau shellwork is available in fine stores all over the state, Kauai, because it's closest, gets the largest selection. If you're after a once-in-a-lifetime purchase, consider Niihau shellwork.

MUSEUMS, LIBRARIES, ZOOS, GALLERIES AND GARDENS

OAHU

Aloha Tower and Maritime Museum, at Ala Moana Blvd., and Bishop St., Honolulu, HI tel. 536-6373 or 548-5713. A landmark that said "Hawaii" to all who arrived by sea before planes took over. Great harbor and city views from top of tower. Visit *Hawaii Maritime Center* on 9th floor and famous double-hulled canoe *Hokule'a* and tall masted *Falls of Clyde,* berthed just next door at Pier 7.

USS *Arizona* Memorial and Submarine Museum , Arizona Memorial Dr., Pearl Harbor, 96818, tel. 422-2771. A free tour of the sleek 184-foot white concrete structure that spans the sunken USS *Arizona.* Free Navy launches take you on the tour of "Battleship Row." Open Tues. to Sun., 8 a.m. to 3 p.m. No reservations, first come first served. Launches every 15 minutes. Visitor center offers graphic materials and movie reflecting the events of Pearl Harbor attack.

Army Museum, Fort DeRussy, Box 8064, Honolulu HI 96815, tel. 543-2639. Official records, private papers, photos documenting activities of the U.S. Army in east Asia and the Pacific islands. Access to holdings is by appointment.

Bishop Museum and Planetarium, 1525 Bernice St., Honolulu, HI 96819, tel. 847-3511. Open daily 9 a.m. to 5 p.m., $4.75 for adults, $2.50 ages six to 17, under 6 free. The best collection in the world on Polynesia in general and Hawaii specifically. A true cultural treat. Should not be missed.

Children's Museum of Natural History, 1201 Ala Moana Blvd., Honolulu, Mon. to Fri. 9 a.m. to 4 p.m., Sat. 9 a.m. to 12 p.m. Natural history and science exhibits.

East-West Center, 1777 East-West Road, Univ. of Hawaii, Honolulu 96848, tel. 948-8006. Cultural institute bringing together the peoples, art, history, and ways of East and West.

Episcopal Church in Hawaii, Queen Emma Square, Honolulu, HI 96813, tel. 536-7776. Records and photos of church ministry in Hawaii from 1862.

Falls of Clyde Marine Museum, Pier 7, adjacent Aloha Tower, tel. 536-6373. Open daily 9:30 a.m. to 4 p.m. Full-rigged sailing ship from last century.

Foster Botanical Garden, 50 N. Vineyard Blvd. Open daily 9 a.m. to 4 p.m., tel. 531-1939. Nine-acre oasis of exotic trees and rare plants.

Hawaii Chinese Historical Center, 111 N. King St. Room 410, Honolulu, HI 96813, tel. 536-9302. Open 12 hours per week. Rare books, oral histories, and photos concerning the history of Chinese in Hawaii.

Hawaii Medical Library, Inc, 1221 Punchbowl St., Honolulu, HI 96813, tel. 536-9302. History of medicine in Hawaii.

Hawaii Pacific College Library. College information call 544-0200.

Hawaiian Historical Society, 560 Kawaiahao St. Honolulu, HI 96813, tel. 537-6271. Open Mon. to Fri., 10 a.m. to 4 p.m. Extensive collection of 19th century materials on Hawaiian Islands. 3,000 photos, 10,000 books, maps, microforms. Adjacent to Hawaiian Mission Children's Society. Should be seen together and should not be missed.

Hawaiian Mission Children's Society, 553 S. King St., Honolulu HI 96813. tel. 531-0481. Open Mon. to Fri., 10 a.m. to 4 p.m. Admission: $1.50 adults, $.75 children. Records, personal journals, letters and photos of early 19th century Congregational missionaries to the Hawaiian Islands; archieve of the Congregational Church in the Pacific. See Honolulu sights. Shouldn't be missed.

Hawaiian State Archives, Iolani Palace Grounds, Honolulu, HI 96813, tel. 547-2355. Open Mon. to Fri., 7:45 a.m. to 4:30 p.m. Archives of the government of Hawaii. Private papers of Hawaiian royalty and government officials, photos, illustrations, etchings recording Hawaiian history. For anyone seriously interested in Hawaii. Shouldn't be missed.

Honolulu Academy of Arts, 900 S. Beretania St., Honolulu, HI 96814, tel. 538-3693. Object is to collect, preserve, and exhibit works of art (to conduct a public art education program related to the collection). Permanent and special exhibitions. Tours, classes, lectures, films.

Honolulu Botanical Gardens, 50 N. Vine Yard Blvd., Honolulu, HI 96817, tel. 533-3406. See Foster Botanical Gardens.

Honolulu Zoo, 151 Kapahulu Ave., tel. 521-3487. Open daily 9 a.m. to 5 p.m. Quiet respite from hustle of Waikiki. Includes a collection of tropical birds as well as pandas, zebras, and gibbon apes. Great for kids of all ages.

Iolani Palace, Box 2259 Honolulu, HI 96804, tel. 536-3552. Iolani Palace Grounds. Perform all aspects of Historic research, restoration, and refurbishing of palace. The only royal palace in the U.S. Vintage artworks, antiques.

Kamehameha Schools, Kapalma Heights Road, Honolulu, HI 96813, tel. 842-8620. Open Mon. to Fri., 7:30 a.m. to 4 p.m. Traditional school for children of Hawaiian descent. Rare books, periodicals, slides on Hawaiiana.

Paradise Park, 3737 Manoa Rd., Honolulu, HI 96822, tel. 988-2141. Exotic birds displayed in a tropical forest setting, includes trained birds presenting a performance.

Punahou School, 1601 Punahou St., Honolulu, HI 96822, tel. 944-5823. Collection available by special arrangment. Institutional archives of the oldest private school in Hawaii.

Queen Emma Summer Palace, 2913 Pali Hwy., Honolulu, HI 96817, tel. 595-3167. Restored historic home, built about 1848. Furniture and mementos of Queen Emma and her family.

Some items belong to other members of royal family.

Sea Life Park, Makapuu Point, Waimanalo, HI 96795, tel. 259-7933. Varieties of Pacific marine plant and animal life, including several species of dolphins and whales. Feeding pool, Kaupa Village, turtle lagoon, restaurant, gift shop. See HNL sights.

Friends of Waipahu Cultural Garden Park, Box 103 Waipahu, HI 96797, tel. 677-0110. Recreation of a plantation village in the style of a living museum.

USS Bowfin, 11 Arizona Memorial Drive. Open daily from 9:30 a.m. to 4:30 p.m., tel. 423-1341. Fully restored WW II submarine. Insight into the underwater war. Self-guided tours. Fascinating. Next door to Arizona memorial. See HNL sights for more details.

Libraries. Oahu has more than a dozen libraries all over the island. The Central Administration number is 988-2194. Library for the Blind and physically handicapped is at 402 Kapahulu Ave., tel. 732-7767.

HAWAII

Bond Mission House, Hawi, HI 96719. Contact Lyman Bond at 889-5108 for an appointment. Original, unrestored, off-the-beaten-track missionary house. See North Kohala sights for more information.

Hawaiian Volcanoes National Park, Thomas A. Jaggar Memorial Museum. Open daily 7:30 a.m. to 5 p.m. Natural history exhibits emphasize volcanology, but includes ethnology, zoology, and botany. A must-see.

Hulihee Palace, Box 1838 Kailua, HI 96740, tel. 329-1877. Downtown Kailua-Kona. Exhibits of artifacts and furniture of 19th century Hawaii, particularly items connected with members of the royal family.

Kamuela Museum, Box 507 Kamuela, HI 96743. Mr. and Mrs. Solomon, owners, curators, tel. 885-4724. Open daily 8 a.m. to 5 p.m. Hawaiian artifacts from ancient Hawaii through the monarchy period, including ethnic groups arriving in the 19th century.

Kona Historical Society, Box 398, Captain Cook, HI 96704, tel. 323-3222. Small collection of materials on the Kona section of the island. Founded 1976.

Liliuokalani Gardens Park. See Hilo map for location. Peace and quiet, amidst surroundings of a classical Japanese-style park.

Lyman House Memorial Museum, 276 Haili St., Hilo, HI 96720, tel. 935-5021. By appointment Saturdays. 5,600 publications, 10,000 photos, 600 newspapers. Inventory in process on correspondence, diaries, business records. Church school records. Maps and photos of island of Hawaii. Collection dates to 1832. One of the best private rock and mineral collections in the world.

Panaewa Zoo and Equestrian Center, 25 Apuni St., Hilo, HI 96720, tel. 961- 8311. Exhibits of animal and plant specimens, educational and recreational facility.

Puuhonua O Honaunau National Historical Park, Box 129 Honaunali, HI 96726, tel. 328-2326. Preserved and interpretive sights associated with temple of refuge. Excellent, park-like atmosphere. Shouldn't be missed. See South Kona sights for more information.

Libraries. There are libraries located in the main communities all over Hawaii. The central number in Hilo is 935-5407.

MAUI

Alexander and Baldwin Sugar Museum, 3957 Hansen Road, tel. 871-8050.

Baldwin House, Front St., Lahaina, Maui 96761. Open daily 9:30 a.m. to 5 p.m., tel. 661-3262. Two-story home of medical missionary Dwight Baldwin. See Lahaina sights for details.

Brig Carthaginian Floating Museum, Lahaina Harbor, Lahaina. Open daily 9 a.m. to 5 p.m. Replica of a 19th century brig. Features whaling artifacts and exhibits of the humpback whale. See Lahaian sights for more information.

Hale Hoikeke Museum, 2375 A Main, Wailuku, tel. 244-3326. Hawaiian History Museum. Art Gallery featuring Kahoolawe artifacts and the renowned paintings of Edward Bailey.

Hale Pa'i Printshop Museum, Box 338, Lahaina, HI 96761, tel. 667-7040. Located on grounds of Lahainaluna school. See Lahaina sites. Operational relics of original printing press. Original Lahainaluna press publications, exhibit of Lahainaluna school past and present.

Hana Cultural Center, Box 27 Hana, HI 96713, tel. 248-8070. Preserves and restores historical sites, artifacts, photos, documents etc. Construction of museums facilities in Hana.

Kula Botanical Gardens, Highway 377 to Upper Kula Road, tel. 878-1715. Open daily 9 a.m. to 4 p.m. Excellent arrangments of tropical plants and flowers. Up-country Maui.

Lahaina Arts Society, Box 991, Lahaina, HI 96761, tel. 661-0111. To perpetuate Hawaiian culture, arts, crafts. Two galleries, annual scholarship, traveling exhibitions, help maintain Lahaina district courthouse.

Lahaina Restoration Foundation, Box 991 Lahaina, HI 96761, tel. 661-3262. James C. Luckey, director. Open Mon. to Fri., 10 a.m. to 4 p.m. Organization dedicated to the preservation of historical Lahaina. Sponsor restorations, archaeological digs and renovation of cultural and historical sites. Operate Baldwin Home, Brig Carthaginian, among others.

Maui Historical Society, Box 1018, Wailuku, HI 96793, tel. 244-3326. Same as or part of Hale Hoikeke Museum. Promotes interest in and knowledge of history of Hawaii and Maui county. Six free lectures per year.

Whaler's Village Museum, Whaler's Village Shopping Center, Kaanapali, tel. 667-9564. Whaling artifacts, 30-foot sperm whale skeleton set among gift shops. Self-guided learning experience while you shop.

Libraries. Maui's main library in Wailuku is at tel. 244-3945. Lanai Public Library, tel. 565-6996. Molokai Library at tel. 553-5483.

KAUAI

Coco Palms Zoo, Coco Palms Hotel, Box 631 Lihue, Hawaii 96766. The Coco Palms is a must-see in itself. See Coco Palms for more information.

Grove Farm Homestead, P.O. Box 1631, Lihue, Kauai 96766, tel. 245-3202. Open by appointment only. Records, business, and personal papers of early sugar planter George N. Wilcox. Definitely worth a visit. Personalized tours.

Hanalei Museum, Box 91, Hanalei, Kauai 96714, tel. 826-6783. Local history. Aquariums with exotic reef fish.

Kauai Mekehune Garden, tel. 245-2660. Historical ancient Hawaiian garden.

Kauai Museum, 4428 Rice, Lihue, Kauai 96766, tel. 245-6931. Open Mon. to Fri. 9:30 a.m. to 4:30 p.m. Two buildings. Story of Kauai. Art and ethnic exhibits. Hawaiiana books, maps, prints, available at museum shop.

Kookee Natural History Museum, Box NN Kekaha, Kauai 96752, tel. 335-9975. Free. Open daily 10 a.m. to 4 p.m. Exhibits interpreting the geology, unique plants and animals of Kauai's mountain wilderness. Great to visit while visiting Waimea canyon.

Olu Pua Botanical Gardens, Kalaheo, Kauai, tel. 332-8182. Open daily 8:30 a.m. to 5 p.m. Tours at 10:30 a.m. to 2:30 p.m. "Garden of a Thousand Flowers."

Paradise Pacifica Gardens, Wailua State Park, tel. 822-4911. Open daily. International dinner and evening show nightly.

Waioli Mission House, Contact Director Barnes Riznik at tel. 245-3202. Waioli Corporation, Box 1631, Lihue, Hawaii 96766.

Libraries. The central library is at 4344 Hardy St., Lihue, tel. 245-3617

HAWAII NATIONAL WILDLIFE REFUGES

Name & Address	Location
Pearl Harbor NWR (Oahu) c/o Hawaiian and Pacific Islands NWRs 300 Ala Moana Blvd., P.O. Box 50167 Honolulu, HI 96850; (808) 541-1201	Located within Pearl Harbor Naval Base
James C. Campbell NWR (Oahu) c/o Hawaiian and Pacific Islands NWRs 300 Ala Moana Blvd., P.O. Box 50167 Honolulu, HI 96850; (808) 541-1201	Near Kahuku on the northeastern shore of the island of Oahu
Kilauea Point NWR (Kauai) c/o P.O. Box 87 Kilauea, Kauai, HI 96754; (808) 541-1201	One mile N of Kilauea on a paved road. Headquarters and parking area on Kilauea Point.
Huleia NWR (Kauai) c/o P.O. Box 87 Kilauea, Kauai, HI 96754 (808) 541-1201	Viewing is best from the Menehune Fish Pond over-look along Hulemalu Rd. W of Puhi Rd.
Hanalei NWR (Kauai) c/o P.O. Box 87, Kilauea, Kauai, HI 96754 (808) 541-1201	1½ miles E of Hanalei on Hwy. 56. Observe wildlife from Ohiki Rd. which begins at the W end of Hanalei River bridge.
Hakalau Forest NWR (Hawaii) 300 Ala Moana Blvd., P.O. Box 50167 Honolulu, HI 96850; (808) 541-1201	Located between the 3,900 and 7,200 feet elevation on the windward slope of Mauna Kea. Take Saddle Rd. Turn R (N) on Keanakolu Rd., and continue for 6 miles. Keanakolu Rd. is the refuge's upper boundary.
Kakahaia NWR (Molokai) c/o Hawaiian and Pacific Islands NWRs 300 Ala Moana Blvd. P.O. Box 50167 Honolulu, HI 96850; (808) 541-1201	Five miles E of Kaunakakai along Hwy. 450.
Hawaiian Islands NWR c/o Hawaiian and Pacific Islands NWRs 300 Ala Moana Blvd., P.O. Box 50167 Honolulu, HI 96850; (808) 541-1201	Far flung islands and atolls strung 1,000 miles N of main Hawaiian Islands.
Baker, Howland, Jarvis and Johnston Island NWRs c/o Hawaiian and Pacific Islands NWR Complex 300 Ala Moana Blvd., P.O. Box 50167 Honolulu, HI 96850; (808) 541-1201	Near the equator. Lies about 1,600 miles SW of Honolulu. Jarvis is about 1,300 miles S of Honolulu. Johnston Atoll is located about 825 miles SW of Honolulu.

Wildlife	Habitat & Information
Hawaiian gallinule, Hawaiian coot, Hawaiian stilt, Koloa (Hawaiian duck) and black-crowned night herons.	61 acres of man-made wetlands. Contact manager for tours.
Hawaiian gallinule, Hawaiian coot, Hawaiian stilt, *Koloa* (Hawaiian duck), black-crowned night herons, introduced birds, migratory shorebirds and waterfowl	142 acres in two units: Punamano Pond is a natural spring-fed marsh; the Kii Unit is man-made ponds once used as sugar cane waste settling basins. Contact manager for tours.
Red-footed boobies, Shearwaters, Great frigate-birds, brown boobies, red-tailed & white-tailed tropic-birds and Laysan albatross, green sea turtles, humpback whales and dolphins.	31 acres of cliffs and headlands with native coastal plants. open 10 a.m.-4 p.m., Mon.-Fri. Binoculars are available.
Koloa (Hawaiian duck), Hawaiian coot, Hawaiian gallinule, and Hawaiian stilt	238 acres of seasonally flooded river bottom land, and wooded slopes of the Huleia River Valley. No general admittance. Contact manager for special permission.
Koloa (Hawaiian duck), Hawaiian coot, Hawaiian gallinule, and Hawaiian stilt	917 acres of river bottom land, taro farms and wooded slopes in the Hanalei River Valley on the N coast of Kauai. By special permit only. Contact manager.
Akiapolaau, the Hawaii *akepa,* Hawaii creeper, Hawaiian hawk, *ou,* the Hawaiian hoary bat, *amakihi,* Hawaiian thrush, *elepaio,* the iiwi and the *apapane*	11,000 acres of Koa-Ohia habitat. Instrumental in sustaining the naturally evolving mid-elevation rainforest. Entry is authorized only by special use permit. Contact manager.
Hawaiian coot and Hawaiian stilt	40 acres of freshwater pond and marsh with dense thickets of bullrush. Arrange visits with the refuge manager.
Seabirds, Laysan and black-footed albatrosses, sooty terns, white terns, brown and black noddies, shearwaters and petrels, red-tailed tropicbirds, frigatebirds and boobies.	A string of widely separated tiny islands and reefs. 1,000 miles long, reaching almost to Midway Island. Rugged volcanic remnants, sparsely vegetated low sandy islands in the NW. By charter or private boat only. Special permission from managers.
Seabird nesting rookeries. Sooty terns, gray-backed terns, shearwaters, red-footed boobies, brown boobies, masked boobies, lesser and great frigatebirds, red-tailed tropicbirds and brown noddies.	11,000 acres of Koa-Ohia habitat. Instrumental in sustaining the naturally evolving mid-elevation rainforest. Entry to refuge is authorized only by special use permit obtained from the refuge manager.

BOOKLIST

INTRODUCTORY

Aloha, The Magazine of Hawaii and the Pacific. Honolulu, HI.: Davick Publications. This excellent bi-monthly magazine is much more than just slick and glossy photography. Special features may focus on sports, the arts, history, flora and fauna, or just pure island adventure. *Aloha* is equally useful as a "dream book" for those who wish that they could visit Hawaii, and as a current resource for those actually going. One of the best for an overall view of Hawaii, and well worth the subscription price.

Barrow, Terrence. *Incredible Hawaii.* Rutland, Vt.: Tuttle, 1974. Illustrated by Ray Lanternman. A pocket-sized compilation of oddities, little-known facts, trivia, and superlatives regarding the Hawaiian Islands. Fun, easy reading, and informative.

Cohen, David, and Rick Smolan. *A Day in the Life of Hawaii.* New York: Workman, 1984. On December 2, 1983, 50 of the world's top photojournalists were invited to Hawaii to photograph a variety of normal life incidents occurring on that day. The photos are excellently reproduced, and are accompanied by a minimum of text.

Day, A.G., and C. Stroven. *A Hawaiian Reader.* New York: Appleton, Century, Crofts, 1959. A poignant compilation of essays, diary entries, and fictitious writings that takes you from the death of Captain Cook through the "statehood services."

Emphasis International. *On the Hana Coast.* Honolulu: Emphasis International Ltd., 1983. Text by Ron Youngblood. Sketches of the people, land, legends, and history of Maui's northeast coast. Beautifully illustrated with line drawings, vintage photos, and modern color work. Expresses true feeling and insight into people and things Hawaiian by letting them talk for themselves. An excellent book

capturing what's different and what's universal about the people of the Hana District.

Friends of the Earth. *Maui, The Last Hawaiian Place.* New York: Friends of the Earth, 1970. A pictorial capturing the spirit of Maui in 61 contemporary color plates along with a handful of historical illustrations. A highly informative as well as beautiful book printed in Italy.

Island Heritage Limited. *The Hawaiians.* Norfolk Island, Australia: Island Heritage Ltd., 1970. Text by Gavan Daws and Ed Sheehan. Primarily a "coffee table" picture book that lets the camera do the talking with limited yet informative text.

Hopkins, Jerry. *The Hula.* Edited by Rebecca Crockett-Hopkins. Hong Kong: APA Productions, 1982. Page after page of this beautifully illustrated book sways with the dynamic vibrancy of ancient Hawaii's surviving artform. Hopkins leads you from dances performed and remembered only through legends, to those of past and present masters captured in vintage and classic photos. For anyone interested in the history and the spirit of Hawaii portrayed in its own unique style of expressive motion.

Judd, Gerritt P., comp. *A Hawaiian Anthology.* New York: MacMillan, 1967. A potpourri of observations from literati such as Twain and Stevenson who have visited the islands over the years. Also, excerpts from ordinary people's journals and missionary letters from early times down to a gleeful report of the day that Hawaii became a state.

Krauss, Bob. *Here's Hawaii.* New York: Coward, McCann Inc., 1960. Social commentary in a series of humorous anecdotes excerpted from this newspaperman's column from the late '60s. Dated, but in essence still useful because people and values obviously change very little.

Lueras, Leonard. *Surfing, The Ultimate Pleasure.* New York: Workman Publishing, 1984. An absolutely outstanding pictorial account of Hawaii's own sport—surfing. Vintage and contemporary photos are surrounded by well-researched and written text. Bound to become a classic.

McBride, L.R. *Practical Folk Medicine of Hawaii.* Hilo, Hi.: Petroglyph Press, 1975. An illustrated guide to Hawaii's medicinal plants as used by the *kahuna lapa'au* (medical healers). Includes a thorough section on ailments, diagnosis, and the proper folk remedy to employ. Illustrated by the author, a renowned botanical researcher and former ranger at Volcanoes National Park.

Michener, James A. *Hawaii.* New York: Random House, 1959. Michener's fictionalized historical novel has done more to inform *and* misinform readers about Hawaii than any other book ever written. A great tale with plenty of local color and information that should be read for pleasure and not considered fact.

Piercy, LaRue. *Hawaii, This and That.* Hilo, Hi.: Petroglyph Press, 1981. Illustrated by Scot Ebanez. A 60-page book filled with one-sentence facts and oddities about all manner of things Hawaiian. Informative, amazing, and fun to read.

Rose, Roger G. *Hawaii: The Royal Isles.* Honolulu: Bishop Museum Press, 1980. Photographs, Seth Joel. A pictorial mixture of artifacts and luminaries from Hawaii's past. Includes a mixture of Hawaiian and Western art depicting island ways. Beautifully photographed with highly descriptive accompanying text.

Wilkerson, James A., M.D., ed. *Medicine for Mountaineering.* 3rd ed. Seattle: The Mountaineers, 1985. Don't let the title fool you. Although the book focuses on specific health problems that may be encountered while mountaineering, it is the best first-aid and general health guide available today. Written by doctors for the layman to use until help arrives, it is jam-packed with easily understandable techniques and procedures. For those intending extended treks, it is a must.

HISTORY/POLITICAL SCIENCE

Albertini, Jim, et al. *The Dark Side of Paradise, Hawaii in a Nuclear War.* Honolulu: cAtholic Action of Hawaii. Well-documented research outlining Hawaii's role and vulnerability in a nuclear world. This book presents the anti-nuclear and anti-military side of the political issue in Hawaii.

Apple, Russell A. *Trails: From Steppingstones to Kerbstones.* Honolulu: Bishop Museum Press, 1965. This "Special Publication #53" is a special-interest archaeological survey focusing on the trails, roadways, footpaths, and highways and how they were designed and maintained throughout the years. Many "royal highways" from pre-contact Hawaii are cited.

Ashdown, Inez MacPhee. *Old Lahaina.* Honolulu: Hawaiian Service Inc., 1976. A small pamphlet-type book listing most of the historical attractions of Lahaina Town, past and present. Ashdown is a life-long resident of Hawaii and gathered her information firsthand by listening to and recording stories of ethnic Hawaiians and old *kamaaina* families.

Ashdown, Inez MacPhee. *Ke Alaloa o Maui.* Wailuku, Hi.: Kamaaina Historians Inc., 1971. A compilation of the history and legends of sites on the island of Maui. Ashdown was at one time a "lady in waiting" for Queen Liliuokalani and has since been proclaimed Maui's "Historian Emeritus."

Bell, Roger. *Last Among Equals: Hawaiian Statehood and American Politics.* Honolulu: University of Hawaii, 1984. Documents Hawaii's long and rocky road to statehood, tracing political partisanship, racism, and social change.

Cameron, Roderick. *The Golden Haze*. New York: World Publishing, 1964. An account of Captain James Cook's voyages of discovery throughout the South Seas. Uses original diaries and journals for an "on the spot" reconstruction of this great seafaring adventure.

Daws, Gavan. *Shoal of Time, A History of the Hawaiian Islands*. Honolulu: University of Hawaii Press, 1968. A highly readable history of Hawaii dating from its "discovery" by the Western world down to its acceptance as the 50th state. Good insight into the psychological makeup of the influential characters that formed Hawaii's past.

Department of Geography, University of Hawaii. *Atlas of Hawaii*. 2nd ed. Honolulu: University of Hawaii Press, 1983. Much more than an atlas filled with reference maps, it also contains commentary on the natural environment, culture, sociology, a gazetteer, and statistical tables. Actually a mini encyclopedia.

Feher, Joseph. *Hawaii: A Pictorial History*. Honolulu: Bishop Museum Press, 1969. Text by Edward Joesting and O.A. Bushnell. An oversized tome laden with annotated historical and contemporary photos, prints, and paintings. Seems like a big "school book," but extremely well done. If you are going to read one survey about Hawaii's historical, social, and cultural past, this is the one.

Fuchs, Lawrence. *Hawaii Pono*. New York: Harcourt, Brace and World, 1961. A detailed, scholarly work presenting an overview of Hawaii's history, based upon psychological and sociological interpretations. Encompasses most socio-ethnological groups from native Hawaiians to modern entrepreneurs. A must for social historical background.

Handy, E.S., and Elizabeth Handy. *Native Planters in Old Hawaii*. Honolulu: Bishop Museum Press, 1972. A superbly written, easily understandable scholarly work on the intimate relationship of pre-contact Hawaiians and the *aina* (land). Much more than its title implies, should be read by anyone seriously interested in Polynesian Hawaii.

The Hawaii Book. Chicago: J.G. Ferguson, 1961. Insightful selections of short stories, essays, and historical and political commentaries by experts specializing in Hawaii. Good choice of photos and illustrations.

Hawaiian Children's Mission Society. *Missionary Album*. Honolulu: Mission Society, 1969. Firsthand accounts of the New England missionaries sent to Hawaii and instrumental in its conversion to Christianity. Down-home stories of daily life's ups and downs.

Heyerdahl, Thor. *American Indians in the Pacific*. London: Allen and Unwin Ltd., 1952. Theoretical and anthropological accounts of the influence on Polynesia of the Indians along the Pacific coast of North and South America. Fascinating reading, with unsubstantiated yet intriguing theories presented.

Ii, John Papa. *Fragments of Hawaiian History*. Honolulu: Bishop Museum, 1959. Hawaii's history under Kamehameha I as told by a Hawaiian who actually experienced it.

Joesting, Edward. *Hawaii: An Uncommon History*. New York: W.W. Norton Co., 1972. A truly uncommon history told in a series of vignettes relating to the lives and personalities of the first white men in Hawaii, Hawaiian nobility, sea captains, writers, and adventurers. Brings history to life. Absolutely excellent!

Lee, William S. *The Islands*. New York: Holt, Rinehart, 1966. A socio-historical set of stories concerning *malihini* (newcomers) and how they influenced and molded the Hawaii of today.

Liliuokalani. *Hawaii's Story By Hawaii's Queen*. Rutland, Vt.: Tuttle, 1964. A moving personal account of Hawaii's inevitable move from monarchy to U.S. Territory by its last queen, Liliuokalani. The facts can be found in other histories, but none provides the emotion or point of view as expressed by Hawaii's deposed monarch. A "must" read to get the whole picture.

Nickerson, Roy. *Lahaina, Royal Capital of Hawaii.* Honolulu: Hawaiian Service, 1978. The story of Lahaina from whaling days to present, spiced with ample photographs.

Smith, Richard A., et al., eds. *The Frontier States.* New York: Time-Life Books, 1968. Short and concise comparisons of the two newest states: Hawaii and Alaska. Dated information, but good social commentary and an excellent appendix suggesting tours, museums, and local festivals.

Takaki, Ronald. *Plantation Life and Labor in Hawaii, 1835-1920.* Honolulu: University of Hawaii Press, 1983. A perspective of plantation life in Hawaii from a multi-ethnic viewpoint. Written by a nationally known island scholar.

MYTHOLOGY AND LEGENDS

Beckwith, Martha. *Hawaiian Mythology.* Honolulu: University of Hawaii Press, 1970. Forty-five years after its original printing, this work remains *the* definitive text on Hawaiian mythology. Ms. Beckwith compiled this book from many sources, giving exhaustive cross-references to genealogies and legends expressed in the oral tradition. If you are going to read one book on Hawaii's folklore, this should be it.

Colum, Padraic. *Legends of Hawaii.* New Haven: Yale University Press, 1937. Selected legends of old Hawaii reinterpreted, but closely based upon the originals.

Elbert, S., comp. *Hawaiian Antiquities and Folklore.* Honolulu: Univerity of Hawaii Press, 1959. Illustrated by Jean Charlot. A selection of the main legends from Abraham Fornander's great work, *The Polynesian Race.*

Melville, Leinanai. *Children of the Rainbow.* Wheaton, Ill.: Theosophical Publishing, 1969. A book on higher spiritual consciousness attuned to nature, which was the basic belief of pre-Christian Hawaii. The appendix contains illustrations of mystical symbols used by the *kahuna.* An enlightening book in many ways.

Thrum, Thomas. *Hawaiian Folk Tales.* Chicago: McClurg and Co., 1907. A collection of Hawaiian tales from the oral tradition as told to the author from various sources.

Westervelt, W.D. *Hawaiian Legends of Volcanoes.* Boston: Ellis Press, 1916. A small book concerning the volcanic legends of Hawaii and how they related to the fledgling field of volcanism at the turn of the century. The vintage photos alone are worth a look.

NATURAL SCIENCES

Abbott, Agatin, Gordon MacDonald, and Frank Peterson. *Volcanoes in the Sea.* Honolulu: University of Hawaii Press, 1983. A simplified yet comprehensive text covering the geology and volcanism of the Hawaiian Islands. Focuses upon the forces of nature (wind, rain, and surf) that shape the islands.

Boom, Robert. *Hawaiian Seashells.* Honolulu: Waikiki Aquarium, 1972. Photos, Jerry Kringle. A collection of 137 seashells found in Hawaiian waters, featuring many found nowhere else on Earth. Broken into categories with accompanying text including common and scientific names, physical descriptions, and likely habitats. A must for shell collectors.

Brock, Vernon, and W.A. Gosline. *Handbook of Hawaiian Fishes.* Honolulu: University of Hawaii Press, 1960. A detailed guide to most of the fishes occurring in Hawaiian waters.

Carlquist, Sherwin. *Hawaii: A Natural History.* New York: Doubleday, 1970. Definitive account of Hawaii's natural history.

Carpenter, Blyth, and Russell Carpenter. *Fish Watching in Hawaii*. San Mateo, Ca.: Natural World Press, 1981. A color guide to many of the reef fish found in Hawaii and often spotted by snorkelers. If you're interested in the fish that you'll be looking at, this guide will be very helpful.

Fielding, Ann, and Ed Robinson. *An Underwater Guide to Hawaii*. Honolulu: University of Hawaii Press, 1987. If you've ever had a desire to snorkel/scuba the living reef waters of Hawaii and to be familiar with what you're seeing, get this small but fact-packed book. The amazing array of marine life found throughout the archipelago is captured in glossy photos with accompaning informative text. Both the scientific and common names of specimens are given. This book will enrich your underwater experience, and serve as an easily understood reference guide for many years.

Hamaishi, Amy, and Doug Wallin. *Flowers of Hawaii*. Honolulu: World Wide Distributors, 1975. Close-up color photos of many of the most common flowers spotted in Hawaii.

Hawaii Audubon Society. *Hawaii's Birds*. Honolulu: Hawaii Audubon Society, 1981. A field guide to Hawaii's birds, listing the endangered indigenous species, migrants, and introduced species that are now quite common. Color photos with text listing distribution, description, voice, and habits. Excellent field guide.

Hosaka, Edward. *Shore Fishing in Hawaii*. Hilo, Hi.: Petroglyph Press, 1984. Known as the best book on Hawaiian fishing since 1944. Receives the highest praise because it has born and bred many Hawaiian fishermen.

Hubbard, Douglass, and Gordon MacDonald. *Volcanoes of the National Parks of Hawaii*. Volcanoes, Hi.: Hawaii Natural History Assoc., 1982. The volcanology of Hawaii, documenting the major lava flows and their geological effect on the state.

Island Heritage Limited. *Hawaii's Flowering Trees*. Honolulu: Island Heritage Press. A concise field guide to many of Hawaii's most common flowering trees. All color photos with accompanying descriptive text.

Kay, E. Alison, comp. *A Natural History of the Hawaiian Islands*. Honolulu: University of Hawaii Press, 1972. A selection of concise articles by experts in the fields of volcanism, oceanography, meteorology, and biology. An excellent reference source.

Kuck, Lorraine, and Richard Togg. *Hawaiian Flowers and Flowering Trees*. Rutland, Vt.: Tuttle, 1960. A classic field guide to tropical and subtropical flora illustrated in watercolor. A "to the point" description of Hawaiian plants and flowers with a brief history of their places of origin and their introduction to Hawaii.

Merlin, Mark D. *Hawaiian Forest Plants, A Hiker's Guide*. Honolulu: Oriental Publishing, 1980. A companion guide to trekkers into Hawaii's interior. Full-color plates identify and describe the most common forest plants encountered.

Merlin, Mark D. *Hawaiian Coastal Plants*. Honolulu: Oriental Publishing, 1980. Color photos and botanical descriptions of many of the plants and flowers found growing along Hawaii's varied shorelines.

Merrill, Elmer. *Plant Life of the Pacific World*. Rutland, Vt.: Tuttle, 1983. The definitive book for anyone planning a botanical tour to the entire Pacific Basin. Originally published in the 1930s, it remains a tremendous work.

Nickerson, Roy. *Brother Whale, A Pacific Whalewatcher's Log*. San Francisco: Chronicle Books, 1977. Introduces the average person to the life of Earth's greatest mammals. Provides historical accounts, photos, and tips on whale-watching. Well written, descriptive, and the best "first time" book on whales.

Sohmer, S. H., and R. Gustafson. *Plants and Flowers of Hawaii*. Honolulu: University of Hawaii Press, 1987. Sohmer and Gustafson range the vegetation zones of Hawaii, from mountains to coast, introducing you to the wide and varied floral biology of the islands. They give a good introduction to the history, and the uniqueness of the evolution of Hawaiian plantlife. Beautiful color plates are accompanied by clear and concise plant descriptions, with the scientific and common Hawaiian names listed.

Stearns, Harold T. *Road Guide to Points of Geological Interest in the Hawaiian Islands*. Palo Alto, Ca.: Pacific Books, 1966. The title is almost as long as this handy little book that lets you know what forces of nature formed the scenery that you see in the islands.

van Riper, Charles, and Sandra van Riper. *A Field Guide to the Mammals of Hawaii*. Honolulu: Oriental Publishing. A guide to the surprising number of mammals introduced into Hawaii. Full-color pages document description, uses, tendencies, and habitat. Small and thin, makes a worthwhile addition to any serious trekker's backpack.

TRAVEL

Birnbaum, Stephen, et al., eds. *Hawaii 1984*. Boston: Houghton Mifflin, 1983. Well-researched, informative writing, with good background material. Focuses primarily on known tourist spots with only perfunctory coverage of out-of-the-way places. Lacking in full-coverage maps.

Bone, Robert W. *The Maverick Guide to Hawaii*. Gretna, La.: Pelican, 1983. Adequate, personalized writing style.

Fodor, Eugene, comp. *Fodor's Hawaii*. New York: Fodor's Guides, 1983. Great coverage on the cliches, but short on out-of-the-way places.

Hammel, Faye, and Sylvan Levy. *Frommer's Hawaii on $35 a Day*. New York: Frommer,

Pasmantier, 1984. Hammel and Levy are good writers, but the book is top-heavy with info on Honolulu and Oahu and skimps on the rest.

Riegert, Ray. *Hidden Hawaii*. Berkeley, Ca. : And/Or Press, 1982. Ray offers a "user friendly" guide to the islands.

Rizzuto, Shirley. *Hawaiian Camping*. Berkeley, Ca.: Wilderness Press, 1979. Adequate coverage of the "nuts and bolts" of camping in Hawaii. Slightly conservative in approach and geared toward the family.

Smith, Robert. *Hawaii's Best Hiking Trails*. Also, *Hiking Kauai, Hiking Maui, Hiking Oahu,* and *Hiking Hawaii*. Berkeley: Wilderness Press, 1977 to 1982. Smith's books are specialized, detailed trekker's guides to Hawaii's outdoors. Complete with useful maps, historical references, official procedures, and plants and animals encountered along the way. If you're focused on hiking, these are the best to take along.

Stanley, David. *South Pacific Handbook*. 3rd ed. Chico, Ca.: Moon Publications, 1986. The model upon which all travel guides should be based. Simply the best book in the world for travel throughout the South Pacific.

Sutton, Horace. *Aloha Hawaii*. New York: Doubleday, 1967. A dated but still excellent guide to Hawaii providing sociological, historical, and cultural insight. Horace Sutton's literary style is the best in the travel guide field. Entertaining reading.

Thorne, Chuck. *The Diver's Guide to Maui*. Kahului, Hi.: Maui Dive Guide, 1984. A nononsense snorkeler's and diver's guide to Maui waters. Extensive maps, descriptions, and "straight from the shoulder" advice by one of Maui's best and most experienced divers. A must for all levels of divers and snorkelers.

Thorne, Chuck, and Lou Zitnik. *A Divers' Guide to Hawaii*. Kihei, Hi.: Hawaii's Diver's

Guide, 1984. An expanded divers' and snorkelers' guide to the waters of the 6 main Hawaiian islands. Complete list of maps with full descriptions, tips, and ability levels. A must for all levels of snorkelers and divers.

Wurman, Richard. *Hawaii Access*. Los Angeles: Access Press, 1983. The "fast food" publishers of travel guides. The packaging is colorful and bright like a burger in a styrofoam box, but there's little of substance inside.

COOKING

Alexander, Agnes. *How to Use Hawaiian Fruit*. Hilo, Hi.: Petroglyph Press, 1984. A full range of recipes using delicious and different Hawaiian fruits.

Fitzgerald, Donald, et al., eds. *The Pacific House Hawaii Cookbook*. Pacific House, 1968. A full range of Hawaiian cuisine including recipes from traditional Chinese, Japanese, Portuguese, New England, and Filipino dishes.

Gibbons, Euell. *Beachcombers Handbook*. New York: McKay Co., 1967. An autobiographical account of this world-famous naturalist as a young man living "off the land" in Hawaii. Great tips on spotting and gathering naturally occurring foods, survival advice, and recipes. Unfortunately the lifestyle described is long outdated.

Margah, Irish, and Elvira Monroe. *Hawaii, Cooking with Aloha*. San Carlos, Ca.: Wide World, 1984. Island recipes including *kalua* pig, *lomi* salmon, and hints on decor.

LANGUAGE

Boom, Robert, and Chris Christensen. *Important Hawaiian Place Names*. Honolulu: Boom Enterprises, 1978. A handy pocket-sized book listing most of the major island place names and their translations.

Elbert, Samuel. *Spoken Hawaiian*. Honolulu: University of Hawaii Press, 1970. Progressive conversational lessons.

Elbert, Samuel, and Mary Pukui. *Hawaiian Dictionary*. Honolulu: University of Hawaii, 1971. The best dictionary available on the Hawaiian language. The *Pocket Hawaiian Dictionary* is a condensed version of this dictionary which is less expensive and adequate for most travelers with a general interest in the language.

GLOSSARY

Words marked with an asterisk (*) are used commonly throughout the islands.

*a'a**—rough clinker lava. *A'a* has become the correct geological term to describe this type of lava found anywhere in the world.

ahuapua—pie-shaped land divisions running from mountain to sea that were governed by *konohiki,* local *ali'i* who owed their allegiance to a reigning chief

aikane—friend; pal; buddy

aina—land; the binding spirit to all Hawaiians. Love of the land is paramount in traditional Hawaiian beliefs.

akamai—smart; clever; wise

akua—a god, or simply "divine." You'll hear people speak of their family or personal *aumakua* (ancestral spirit). A favorite is the shark or the *pueo* (Hawaiian owl).

ali'i—a Hawaiian chief or nobleman

*aloha**—the most common greeting in the islands. Can mean both hello or goodbye, welcome or farewell. It also can mean romantic love, affection, or best wishes.

aole—no

auwe—alas; ouch! When a great chief or loved one died, it was a traditional wail of mourning.

halakahiki—pineapple

*hale**—house or building; often combined with other words to name a specific place such as Haleakala ("House of the Sun") or Hale Pai ("printing house").

*hana**—work; combined with *pau* means end of work or quitting time

hanai—literally "to feed." Part of the true aloha spirit. A *hanai* is a permanent guest, or an adopted family member, usually an old person or a child. This is an enduring cultural phenomenon in Hawaii, in which a child from one family (perhaps that of a brother or sister, and quite often one's grandchild) is raised as one's own without formal adoption.

*haole**—a word that at one time meant foreigner, but which now means a white person or Caucasian. Many etymological definitions have been put forth, but none satisfies everyone. Some feel that it signified a person without a background, because the first white men could not chant their genealogies as was common to Hawaiians.

*hapa**—half, as in a mixed-blooded person being referred to as *hapa haole*

*hapai**—pregnant; used by all ethnic groups when a *keiki* is on the way

*haupia**—a coconut custard dessert often served at luau

*heiau**—a traditional Hawaiian temple. A platform made of skillfully fitted rocks, upon which structures were built and offerings made to the gods.

*holomuu**—an ankle-length dress that is much more fitted than a muumuu, and which is often worn on formal occasions

hono—bay, as in Honolulu ("Sheltered Bay")

ho'oilo—traditional Hawaiian winter that began in November

hoolaulea—any happy event, but especially a family outing or picnic

*hoomalimali**—sweet talk; flattery

*huhu**—angry; irritated

*hui**—a group; meeting; society. Often used to refer to Chinese businessmen or family members who pool their money to get businesses started.

hukilau—traditional shoreline fish-gathering in which everyone lends a hand to *huki* (pull) the huge net. Anyone taking part shares in the *lau* (food). It is much more like a party than hard work, and if you're lucky you'll be able to take part in one.

*hula**—a native Hawaiian dance in which the rhythm of the islands is captured by swaying hips and stories told by lyrically moving hands. A *halau* is a group or school of hula.

huli huli—barbecue, as in *huli huli* chicken

i'a—fish in general. *I'a maka* is raw fish.

imu—underground oven filled with hot rocks and used for baking. The main cooking feature at luaus, used to steam-bake the pork and other succulent dishes. Traditionally the tending of the *imu* was for men only.

ipo—sweetheart; lover; girlfriend or boyfriend

kahili—a tall pole topped with feathers, resembling a huge feather duster. It was used by an *ali'i* to announce his presence.

*kahuna**—priest; sorcerer; doctor; skillful person. *Kahuna* had tremendous power in old Hawaii which they used for both good and evil. The *kahuna 'ana'ana* was a feared individual because he practiced "black magic" and could pray a person to death, while the *kahuna lapa'au* was a medical practitioner bringing aid and comfort to the people.

kai—the sea. Many businesses and hotels employ *kai* as part of their name.

kalua—roasted underground in an *imu*. A favorite island food is *kalua* pork.

*kamaaina**—a child of the land; an old-timer; a longtime island resident of any ethnic background; a resident of Hawaii or native son. Oftentimes hotels and airlines offer discounts called "kamaaina rates" to anyone who can prove island residency.

kanaka—man or commoner; later used to distinguish a Hawaiian from other races. Tone of voice can make it a derisive expression.

*kane**—means man, but actually used to signify a relationship such as husband or boyfriend. Written on a door it means "Men's Room."

*kapu**—forbidden; taboo; keep out; do not touch

kapuna—a grandparent or old-timer; usually means someone who has gained wisdom. The statewide school system now invites *kapuna* to talk to the children about the old ways and methods.

*kaola**—any food that has been broiled or barbecued

*kaukau**—slang word meaning food or chow; grub. Some of the best food in Hawaii comes from the "kaukau wagons," trucks that sell plate lunches and other morsels.

kauwa—a landless, untouchable caste that was confined to living on reservations. Members of this caste were often used as human sacrifice at *heiau*. Calling someone *kauwa* is still considered a grave insult.

kava—a mildly intoxicating traditional drink made from the juice of chewed awaroot, spat into a bowl, and used in religious ceremonies.

*keiki**—child or children; used by all ethnic groups. "Have you hugged your *keiki* today?"

kiawe—an algaroba tree from S. America commonly found in Hawaii along the shore. It grows a nasty long thorn that can easily puncture a tire. Legend has it that the trees were introduced to the islands by a misguided missionary who hoped the thorns would coerce natives into wearing shoes. Actually, they are good for fuel, as fodder for hogs and cattle, and for reforestation, none of which you'll appreciate if you step on one of their thorns, or flatten a tire on your rental car!

kokua—help. As in "Your *kokua* is needed to keep Hawaii free from litter."

*kona wind**—a muggy subtropical wind that blows from the south and hits the leeward side of the islands. It usually brings sticky hot weather, and is one of the few times when air-conditioning will be appreciated.

konane—a traditional Hawaiian game, similar to checkers, played with pebbles on a large flat stone used as a board

koolau—windward side of the island

kukui—a candlenut tree whose pods are polished and then strung together to make a beautiful lei. Traditionally the oil-rich nuts were strung on the rib of a coconut leaf and used as a candle.

kuleana—homesite; the old homestead; small farms. Especially used to describe the small spreads on Hawaiian Homes Lands on Molokai.

*Kumulipo**—ancient Hawaiian genealogical chant that records the pantheon of gods, creation, and the beginning of mankind

la—the sun. Often combined with other words to be more descriptive, such as *La*-haina ("Merciless Sun") or Haleakal*a* ("House of the Sun").

lanai*—veranda or porch. You'll pay more for a hotel room if it has a lanai with an ocean view.

lani—sky or the heavens

lau hala*—traditional Hawaiian weaving of mats, hats, etc., from the prepared fronds of the pandanus (screw pine)

lei*—a traditional garland of flowers or vines. One of Hawaii's most beautiful customs. Given at any auspicious occasion, but especially when arriving or leaving Hawaii.

lele—the stone altar at a *heiau*

limu—edible seaweed of various types. Gathered from the shoreline, it makes an excellent salad. It's used to garnish many island dishes and is a favorite at luaus.

lomilomi—traditional Hawaiian massage; also, raw salmon made up into a vinegared salad with chopped onion and spices

lua*—the toilet; the head; the bathroom

luakini—a human sacrifice temple. Introduced to Hawaii in the 13th C. at Wahaula Heiau on the Big Island.

luau*—a Hawaiian feast featuring poi, *imu*-baked pork, and other traditional foods. Good ones provide some of the best gastronomical delights in the world.

luna—foreman or overseer in the plantation fields. They were often mounted on horseback and were renowned either for their fairness or cruelty. They represented the middle class, and served as a buffer between the plantation workers and the white plantation owners.

mahalo*—thank you. *Mahalo nui* means "big thanks" or "thank you very much."

mahele—division. The "Great Mahele" of 1848 changed Hawaii forever when the traditional common lands were broken up into privately owned plots.

mahu—a homosexual; often used derisively like "fag" or "queer"

mahi mahi*—a favorite eating fish. Often called a dolphin, but a *mahi mahi* is a true fish, not a cetacean.

maile—a fragrant vine used in a traditional leis. It looks ordinary but smells delightful.

makai*—toward the sea; used by most islanders when giving directions

makaainana—a commoner; a person "belonging" to the *aina* (land), who supported the *ali'i* by fishing, farming, and as warriors

make—dead; deceased

malihini*—newcomer; tenderfoot; a recent arrival

malo—the native Hawaiian loincloth. Never worn anymore except at festivals or pageants.

mana*—power from the spirit world; innate energy of all things animate or inanimate; the grace of god. Mana could be passed on from one person to another, or even stolen. Great care was taken to protect the *ali'i* from having their mana defiled. Commoners were required to lie flat on the ground and cover their faces whenever a great *ali'i* approached. *Kahuna* were often employed in the regaining or transference of mana.

manauahi—free; gratis; extra

manini—stingy; tight. A Hawaiianized word taken from the name of Don Francisco *Marin,* who was instrumental in bringing many fruits and plants to Hawaii. He was known for never sharing any of the bounty from his substantial gardens on Vineyard Street in Honolulu.

mauka*—toward the mountains; used by most islanders when giving directions

mele—a song or chant in the Hawaiian oral tradition that records the history and genealogies of the *ali'i*

mauna—mountain. Often combined with other words to be more descriptive, such as Mauna Kea ("White Mountain").

menehune—the legendary "little people" of Hawaii. Like leprechauns, they are said to have shunned mankind and possess magical powers. Stone walls said to have been completed in one night are often attributed to them. Some historians argue that they actually existed and were the aboriginals of Hawaii, inhabiting the islands before the coming of the Polynesians.

moa—chicken; fowl

moana*—the ocean; the sea. Many businesses and hotels as well as places have moana as part of their name.

moe—sleep

moolelo—ancient tales kept alive by the oral tradition and recited only by day

muumuu*—a "Mother Hubbard," an ankle-length dress with a high neckline introduced by the missionaries to cover the nakedness of the Hawaiians. It has become fashionable attire for almost any occasion in Hawaii.

nani—beautiful

nui—big; great; large; as in mahalo nui (thank you very much)

ohana—a family; the fundamental social division; extended family. Now used to denote a social organization with grass-roots overtones, as in the "Protect Kahoolawe Ohana."

okolehau—literally "iron bottom"; a traditional booze made from ti root; okole means your "rear end" and hau means "iron," which was descriptive of the huge blubber pots that it was made in. Also, if you drink too much it'll surely knock you on your okole.

ono*—delicious; delightful; the best. Ono ono means "extra or absolutely delicious."

opihi—a shellfish or limpet that clings to rocks and is gathered as one of the islands' favorite pu pu. Custom dictates that you never remove all of the opihi from a rock; some are always left to grow for future generations.

opu—belly; stomach

pa'hoehoe*—smooth ropey lava that looks like burnt pancake batter. Pa'hoehoe is now the correct geological term used to describe this type of lava found anywhere in the world.

pake—a Chinese person. Can be derisive depending on tone in which it is used. It is a bastardization of the Chinese word meaning "uncle."

pali*—a cliff; precipice. Hawaii's geology makes them quite common. The most famous are the pali of Oahu where a major battle was fought.

paniolo*—a Hawaiian cowboy. Derived from the Spanish espaniola. The first cowboys brought to Hawaii during the early 19th century were Mexicans from California.

papale—hat. Except for the feathered helmets of the ali'i warriors of old Hawaii, hats were generally not worn. However, once the islanders saw their practical uses and how fashionable they were, they began weaving them from various materials and quickly became experts at manufacture and design.

pau*—finished; done; completed. Often combined into pau hana, which means end of work or quitting time.

pa'u—long split skirt often worn by women when horseback riding. Last century, an island treat was when pa'u riders would turn out in their beautiful dresses at Kapiolani Park in Honolulu. The tradition is carried on today at many of Hawaii's rodeos.

pilau—stink; bad smell; stench

pilikia—trouble of any kind, big or small; bad times

poi*—a glutinous paste made from the pounded corn of taro which ferments slightly and has a light sour taste. Purplish in color, it's a staple at luaus, where it is called "one-, two-, or three-finger" poi, depending upon its thickness.

pono—righteous or excellent

pua—flower

puka*—a hole of any size. Puka is used by all island residents, whether talking about a pinhole in a rubber boat or a tunnel through a mountain.

punalua—the tradition of sharing mates in practice before the missionaries came. Western seamen took advantage of it, and this led to the spreading of contagious diseases and eventually to the ultimate demise of the Hawaiian people.

punee*—bed; narrow couch. Used by all ethnic groups. To recline on a *punee* on a breezy lanai is a true island treat.

pu pu*—an appetizer; a snack; hors d'oeuvres; can be anything from cheese and crackers to sushi. Oftentimes, bars or nightclubs offer them free.

pupule—crazy; nuts; out of your mind

pu'u—hill, as in Pu'u Ulaula ("Red Hill")

tapa*—a traditional paper cloth made from beaten bark. Intricate designs were stamped in using beaters, and natural dyes added color. The tradition was lost for many years, but is now making a comeback, and provides some of the most beautiful folk art in the islands.

taro*—the staple of old Hawaii. A plant with a distinctive broad leaf that produces a starchy root. It was brought by the first Polynesians and was grown on magnificently irrigated plantations. According to the oral tradition, the life-giving properties of taro hold mystical significance for Hawaiians, since it was created by the gods at about the same time as mankind.

ti—a broad green-leafed plant that was used for many purposes, from plates to hula skirts (never grass), and especially used to wrap religious offerings presented at the *heiau*.

tutu*—grandmother; granny; older woman. Used by all as a term of respect and endearment.

ukulele*—*uku* means "flea" and *lele* means "jumping," so literally "jumping flea"—the way the Hawaiians perceived the quick finger movements on the banjo-like Portuguese folk instrument called a *cavaquinho*. The ukulele quickly became synonymous with the islands.

wahine*—young woman; female; girl; wife. Used by all ethnic groups. When written on a door it means "Women's Room."

wai—fresh water; drinking water

wela—hot. *Wela kahao* is a "hot time" or "making whoopee."

wiki*—quickly; fast; in a hurry. Often seen as *wiki wiki* (very fast), as in "Wiki Wiki Messenger Service."

HOTEL INDEX

RESTAURANT INDEX

INDEX

Boldfaced page numbers indicate primary reference. Italicized page number indicate information in maps, illustrations, call-outs, or charts. For designated towns, beaches, special sights and listings: (H) = Hawaii Island; (K) = Kauai; (L) = Lanai; (M) = Maui; (MO) = Molokai; (N) = Niihau; (O) = Oahu

ABOUT THE AUTHOR

Joe Bisignani is a fortunate man because he makes his living doing the two things that he likes best: traveling and writing. Joe has been with Moon Publications since 1979 and is the author of *Japan Handbook, Kauai Handbook, Hawaii Handbook, Oahu Handbook, Maui Handbook,* and *Big Island Handbook.* When not traveling, he makes his home in Northern California.

ABOUT THE ILLUSTRATORS

Mary Ann Abel was born and raised in a small town in West Virginia. She uses this background to infuse her work with what she values most: family and nature. Mary Ann is a member of the Sunday Art Mart in Honolulu, where she sells her artwork. She also displays at various juried shows in and around Honolulu, and currently, her work can be seen at the Myonghee Art Gallery in Waikiki. Mary Ann lives in Honolulu with her husband Richard and her daughters Robin and Nicole. Her illustration appears on pages 364, and 505.

Brian C. Bardwell was born in Blythe, California. He served as Art Director and Illustrator for a U.S. Army newspaper. He attended the Academy of Art, San Francisco, and California State University Chico. As well as illustrating, he is a cartographer for Moon. He is building his own home in his spare time. His art appears on pages 158, and 313.

Sue Strangio Everett was born and raised in Chico, California, where she attended Chico State University, majoring in Fine Art. For the past 12 years she has refined and developed her skills, working primarily as a graphic artist. Sue is also accomplished in pottery design and glazing, silk screening, weaving, etching, stained-glass work, and pen and ink. She drew the illustrations on pages 106, 129, 137, 172, 173, and 460.

Debra Fau is a born artist. She can't help it . . . she's French. Deb lives in Chico where she sings with a rock 'n' roll bond, does batik, tie-dye, and paintings. She keeps the wolf from the door by cocktail waitressing, where she's renowned for carrying the best tray in town. Her drawings appear on pages 8, 174, 322, 353, and 365.

Richard Fields, born in Whittier, California, grew up in an art environment. His father was a film animator. With the encouragement and support of his parents, his talents blossomed and his skills grew to include oil painting, sculpture, and ceramics. Having received an impressive succession of awards throughout his adolescence, he was, at 18, shown at the Laguna Festival of Arts and the Pageant of Masters. His already distinctively styled California landscapes found an appreciative market among Southern California collectors. An amateur botanist and an avid hiker, Richard takes every available opportunity to sketch on locale. He incorporates a mixed media of airbrush, acrylics, colored pencils, India ink, and stencils into his original artwork. His painting appears on the cover.

Louise Foote lives on an experimental urban commune in Chico. She works as an archaeologist, renovates homes, and builds custom furniture. Sometimes, she turns her hand to illustrating, and her work appears on pages 12, 13, 15, 16, 17, 18, 20, 21, 23, 24, 52, 76, 85, 86, 136, 148, 170, 171, 172, 195, 253, 333, 442, 459, 471, 498, 530, 541, 593, 610, 652, 701, 710, 718, and 730.

Diana Lasich Harper has been a contributing artist to several Moon books. After receiving a degree in Art at San Jose State University, California, she moved to Hawaii where she lived for four years. Much of her time there was spent cycling, hiking, and *always* drawing. From Hawaii, Diana moved to Japan where she lived for two years and studied woodblock printing, *sumie,* and kimono painting. Her illustrations appear on pages 11, 43, 70, 89, 90, 93, 105, 118, 128, 131, 151, 153, 155, 157, 203, 244, 258, 305, 362, 541, 542, 547, 552, 614, 650, and 698.

Gordy Ohliger, a free-lance artist and "banjologist" extrordinaire, makes his home in Chico, California. His work appears on page 263.

Keith Perkins is a teacher and artist who has traveled thoughout the Pacific sketching people and places of interest. His work has appeared in numerous magazines and private collections; here it appears on pages 443, 451, 758, 773, and 792.

Bob Race taught Fine Arts at Butte Community College near Chico for 14 years. He now manages the Illustration and Cartography departments at Moon Publications. His drawings appear on pages 3, 22, 48, 163, 181, 220, 259, 298, 306, 334, 345, 357, 399, 411, 428, 467, 472, 490, 493, 518, 555, 591, 611, 636, 651, 674, 684, 691, 702, 711, 723, 780, 811, 825, and 837.

Pathways.

Over one thousand years ago, Polynesians in outrigger canoes crossed the vast ocean with determination, skill and the strong commitment of the people.

Today, Hawaiian Airlines has pathways to the east and west. East to Los Angeles, San Francisco, Seattle, Portland, Las Vegas and Anchorage. West to American Samoa, Western Samoa and the Kingdom of Tonga. And in Hawaii, we still connect these lovely islands just as we've done for the past 60 years. And our deep Polynesian roots make hospitality second nature and every guest first in our heart.

Our spirit is unique. We are Hawaiian.

HAWAiiAN.®
The Colors of Paradise.

U.S. Toll Free 1-800-367-5320, Statewide Toll Free 1-800-882-8811.
Call Hawaiian or your travel agent.

Moon Handbooks—The Ideal Traveling Companions

Open a Moon Handbook and you're opening your eyes and heart to the world. Thoughtful, sensitive, and provocative, Moon Handbooks encourage an intimate understanding of a region, from its rich culture and history to essential practicalities. Fun to read and packed with valuable information on accommodations, dining, recreation, plus indispensable travel tips, detailed maps, charts, illustrations, photos, glossaries, and indexes, Moon Handbooks are ideal traveling companions: informative, entertaining, and highly practical.

TO ORDER BY PHONE: (800) 345-5473 • Monday-Friday • 9 a.m.-5 p.m. PST

The Pacific/Asia Series

BALI HANDBOOK by Bill Dalton
Detailed travel information on the most famous island in the world. 12 color pages, 29 b/w photos, 68 illustrations, 42 maps, 7 charts, glossary, booklist, index. 428 pages. **$12.95**

INDONESIA HANDBOOK by Bill Dalton
This one-volume encyclopedia explores island by island the many facets of this sprawling, kaleidoscopic island nation. 30 b/w photos, 143 illustrations, 250 maps, 17 charts, booklist, extensive Indonesian vocabulary, index. 1,050 pages. **$17.95**

SOUTH KOREA HANDBOOK by Robert Nilsen
Whether you're visiting on business or searching for adventure, *South Korea Handbook* is an invaluable companion. 8 color pages, 78 b/w photos, 93 illustrations, 109 maps, 10 charts, Korean glossary with useful notes on speaking and reading the language, booklist, index. 548 pages. **$14.95**

SOUTHEAST ASIA HANDBOOK by Carl Parkes
Helps the enlightened traveler explore with wide eyes and an open mind to discover the real Southeast Asia. 16 color pages, 75 b/w photos, 11 illustrations, 169 maps, 140 charts, vocabularies and suggested reading, index. 873 pages. **$16.95**

HAWAII HANDBOOK by J.D. Bisignani
Winner of the 1989 Hawaii Visitors Bureau's Best Guide Book Award and the Grand Award for Excellence in Travel Journalism, this guide takes you beyond the glitz and high-priced hype and leads you to a genuine Hawaiian experience. 12 color pages, 86 b/w photos, 132 illustrations, 86 maps, 44 graphs and charts, Hawaiian and pidgin glossaries, appendix, booklist, index. 879 pages.   **$15.95**

KAUAI HANDBOOK by J.D. Bisignani
Kauai Handbook is the perfect antidote to the workaday world. 8 color pages, 36 b/w photos, 48 illustrations, 19 maps, 10 tables and charts, Hawaiian and pidgin glossaries, booklist, index. 236 pages.   **$9.95**

MAUI HANDBOOK: Including Molokai and Lanai by J.D. Bisignani
"No fool-'round" advice on accommodations, eateries, and recreation, plus a comprehensive introduction to island ways, geography, and history. 8 color pages, 60 b/w photos, 72 illustrations, 34 maps, 19 charts, booklist, glossary, index. 350 pages.   **$10.95**

OAHU HANDBOOK by J.D. Bisignani
A handy guide to Honolulu, renowned surfing beaches, and Oahu's countless other diversions. Color and b/w photos, illustrations, 18 maps, charts, booklist, glossary, index. 354 pages. **$11.95**

BIG ISLAND OF HAWAII HANDBOOK by J.D. Bisignani
An entertaining yet informative text packed with insider tips on accommodations, dining, sports and outdoor activities, natural attractions, and must-see sights. Color and b/w photos, illustrations, 20 maps, charts, booklist, glossary, index. 347 pages.   **$11.95**

SOUTH PACIFIC HANDBOOK by David Stanley
The original comprehensive guide to the 16 territories in the South Pacific. 20 color pages, 195 b/w photos, 121 illustrations, 35 charts, 138 maps, booklist, glossary, index. 740 pages. **$15.95**

MICRONESIA HANDBOOK:
Guide to the Caroline, Gilbert, Mariana, and Marshall Islands by David Stanley
Micronesia Handbook guides you on a real Pacific adventure all your own. 8 color pages, 77 b/w photos, 68 illustrations, 69 maps, 18 tables and charts, index. 287 pages.   **$9.95**

FIJI ISLANDS HANDBOOK by David Stanley
The first and still the best source of information on travel around this 322-island archipelago. 8 color pages, 35 b/w photos, 78 illustrations, 26 maps, 3 charts, Fijian glossary, booklist, index. 198 pages.   **$8.95**

TAHITI-POLYNESIA HANDBOOK by David Stanley
All five French-Polynesian archipelagoes are covered in this comprehensive guide by Oceania's best-known travel writer. 12 color pages, 45 b/w photos, 64 illustrations, 33 maps, 7 charts, booklist, glossary, index. 225 pages.   **$9.95**

NEW ZEALAND HANDBOOK by Jane King
Introduces you to the people, places, history, and culture of this extraordinary land. 8 color pages, 99 b/w photos, 146 illustrations, 82 maps, booklist, index. 546 pages. **$14.95**

BLUEPRINT FOR PARADISE: How to Live on a Tropic Island by Ross Norgrove
This one-of-a-kind guide has everything you need to know about moving to and living comfortably on a tropical island. 8 color pages, 40 b/w photos, 3 maps, 14 charts, appendices, index. 212 pages. **$14.95**

The Americas Series

NORTHERN CALIFORNIA HANDBOOK by Kim Weir
An outstanding companion for imaginative travel in the territory north of the Tehachapis. 12 color pages, b/w photos, 69 maps, illustrations, booklist, index. 759 pages. **$16.95**

NEVADA HANDBOOK by Deke Castleman
Nevada Handbook puts the Silver State into perspective and makes it manageable and affordable. 34 b/w photos, 43 illustrations, 37 maps, 17 charts, booklist, index. 301 pages. **$10.95**

NEW MEXICO HANDBOOK by Stephen Metzger
A close-up and complete look at every aspect of this wondrous state. 8 color pages, 85 b/w photos, 63 illustrations, 50 maps, 10 charts, booklist, index. 350 pages. **$11.95**

TEXAS HANDBOOK by Joe Cummings
Seasoned travel writer Joe Cummings brings an insider's perspective to his home state. 12 color pages, b/w photos, maps, illustrations, charts, booklist, index. 483 pages. **$11.95**

ARIZONA TRAVELER'S HANDBOOK by Bill Weir
This meticulously researched guide contains everything necessary to make Arizona accessible and enjoyable. 8 color pages, 194 b/w photos, 74 illustrations, 53 maps, 6 charts, booklist, index. 505 pages. **$13.95**

UTAH HANDBOOK by Bill Weir
Weir gives you all the carefully researched facts and background to make your visit a success. 8 color pages, 102 b/w photos, 61 illustrations, 30 maps, 9 charts, booklist, index. 450 pages. **$11.95**

ALASKA-YUKON HANDBOOK by Deke Castleman, Don Pitcher, and David Stanley
The inside story, with plenty of well-seasoned advice to help you cover more miles on less money. 8 color pages, 26 b/w photos, 92 illustrations, 90 maps, 6 charts, booklist, glossary, index. 384 pages. **$11.95**

WASHINGTON HANDBOOK by Dianne J. Boulerice Lyons
Covers sights, shopping, services, transportation, and outdoor recreation, with complete listings for restaurants and accommodations. 8 color pages, 92 b/w photos, 24 illustrations, 81 maps, 8 charts, booklist, index. 400 pages. **$12.95**

OREGON HANDBOOK by Stuart Warren and Ted Long Ishikawa
Brimming with travel practicalities and insider views on Oregon's history, culture, arts, and activities. Color b/w photos, illustrations, 28 maps, charts, booklist, index. Approx. 400 pages. **$12.95**

BRITISH COLUMBIA HANDBOOK   by Jane King
With an emphasis on outdoor adventures, this guide covers mainland British Columbia, Vancouver Island, the Queen Charlotte Islands, and the Canadian Rockies. 8 color pages, 56 b/w photos, 45 illustrations, 66 maps, 4 charts, booklist, index. 381 pages.   **$11.95**

GUIDE TO CATALINA and California's Channel Islands   by Chicki Mallan
A complete guide to these remarkable islands, from the windy solitude of the Channel Islands National Marine Sanctuary to bustling Avalon. 8 color pages, 105 b/w photos, 65 illustrations, 40 maps, 32 charts, booklist, index. 262 pages.   **$9.95**

YUCATAN HANDBOOK   by Chicki Mallan
All the information you'll need to guide you into every corner of this exotic land. 8 color pages, 154 b/w photos, 55 illustrations, 57 maps, 70 charts, appendix, booklist, Mayan and Spanish glossaries, index. 391 pages.   **$12.95**

CANCUN HANDBOOK and Mexico's Caribbean Coast   by Chicki Mallan
Covers the city's luxury scene as well as more modest attractions, plus many side trips to unspoiled beaches and Mayan ruins. Color and b/w photos, illustrations, over 30 maps, Spanish glossary, booklist, index. 257 pages.   **$9.95**

BELIZE HANDBOOK   by Chicki Mallan
Complete with detailed maps, practical information, and an overview of the area's flamboyant history, culture, and geographical features, *Belize Handbook* is the only comprehensive guide of it's kind to this spectacular region. Color and b/w photos, illustrations, maps, booklist, index. Approx. 225 pages.   **$11.95**

The International Series

EGYPT HANDBOOK   by Kathy Hansen
An invaluable resource for intelligent travel in Egypt. 8 color pages, 20 b/w photos, 150 illustrations, 80 detailed maps and plans to museums and archaeological sites, Arabic glossary, booklist, index. 510 pages.   **$14.95**

PAKISTAN HANDBOOK   by Isobel Shaw
For armchair travelers and trekkers alike, the most detailed and authoritative guide to Pakistan ever published. 28 color pages, 86 maps, appendices, Urdu glossary, booklist, index. 478 pages.   **$15.95**

IMPORTANT ORDERING INFORMATION

TO ORDER BY PHONE: (800) 345-5473 · Monday-Friday · 9 a.m.-5 p.m. PST

PRICES: All prices are subject to change. We always ship the most current edition. We will let you know if there is a price increase on the book you ordered.

SHIPPING & HANDLING OPTIONS:
1) Domestic UPS or USPS 1st class (allow 10 working days for delivery): $3.50 for the 1st item, 50 cents for each additional item.

Exceptions:
· **Moonbelt** shipping is $1.50 for one, 50 cents for each additional belt.
· Add $2.00 for same-day handling.
2) UPS 2nd Day Air or Printed Airmail requires a special quote.
3) International Surface Bookrate (8-12 weeks delivery): $3.00 for the 1st item, $1.00 for each additional item.

FOREIGN ORDERS: All orders which originate outside the U.S.A. must be paid for with either an International Money Order or a check in U.S. currency drawn on a major U.S. bank based in the U.S.A.

TELEPHONE ORDERS: We accept Visa or MasterCard payments. Minimum order is US$15.00. Call in your order: 1 (800) 345-5473. 9 a.m.-5 p.m. Pacific Standard Time.

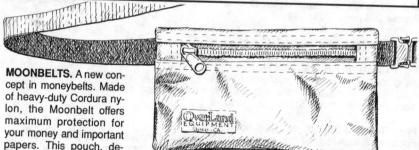

MOONBELTS. A new concept in moneybelts. Made of heavy-duty Cordura nylon, the Moonbelt offers maximum protection for your money and important papers. This pouch, designed for all-weather comfort, slips under your shirt or waistband, rendering it virtually undetectable and inaccessible to pickpockets. Many thoughtful features: 1-inch-wide nylon webbing, heavy-duty zipper, and a 1-inch high-test quick-release buckle. No more fumbling around for the strap or repeated adjustments, this handy plastic buckle opens and closes with a touch, but won't come undone until you want it to. Accommodates traveler's checks, passport, cash, photos. Size 5 x 9 inches. Available in black only. **$8.95**

ORDER FORM

FOR FASTER SERVICE ORDER BY PHONE: (800) 345-5473 · 9 a.m.-5 p.m. PST
(See important ordering information on preceding page)

Name:_____ Date:_____

Street:_____

City:_____

State or Country:_____ Zip Code:_____

Daytime Phone:_____

Quantity	Title	Price

Taxable Total	
Sales Tax (6.25%) for California Residents	
Shipping & Handling	
TOTAL	

Ship to: ☐ address above   ☐ other_____

_____

_____

Make checks payable to:
Moon Publications, Inc., 722 Wall Street, Chico, California 95928, U.S.A.
We Accept Visa and MasterCard
To Order: Call in your Visa or MasterCard number, or send a written order with your Visa or MasterCard number and expiration date clearly written.

Card Number: ☐ **Visa**   ☐ **MasterCard**

☐☐☐☐   ☐☐☐☐   ☐☐☐☐   ☐☐☐☐

expiration date:_____

Exact Name on Card: ☐ same as above

☐ other_____

signature_____

WHERE TO BUY THIS BOOK

Bookstores and Libraries:
Moon Publications handbooks are sold worldwide. Please write Sales Manager Donna Galassi for a list of wholesalers and distributors in your area that stock our travel handbooks.

Travelers:
We would like to have Moon Publications handbooks available throughout the world. Please ask your bookstore to write or call us for ordering information. If your bookstore will not order our guides for you, please write or call for a free catalog.

MOON PUBLICATIONS, INC.
722 WALL STREET
CHICO, CA 95928 U.S.A.
tel: (800) 345-5473
fax: (916) 345-6751